DIETRICH BONHOEFFER

EBERHARD BETHGE

Born in 1909 in Warchau, Eberhard Bethge attended the universities of Königsberg, Berlin, Vienna, Tübingen, and Halle, receiving the Doctor of Divinity degree. From 1935 to 1940 he assisted Dietrich Bonhoeffer at the preacher's seminary in Finkenwalde and, after the Gestapo closed the seminary, in the underground pastorates. In 1953 he became pastor of the German congregation in London. He remained there until 1961, except for one year (1957–1958) spent as visiting lecturer at Harvard Divinity School. In 1962 he was awarded an honorary degree of D.D. at Glasgow University. From 1961 until his retirement in 1975 he was director of the Institute of Continuing Education for Ministers of the Evangelical Church of the Rhineland in Rengsdorf. In 1966 he was Visiting Professor at Chicago Theological Seminary and in 1976 was Fosdick Professor at Union Theological Seminary, New York.

A close friend of Dietrich Bonhoeffer's, and married to his niece, Eberhard Bethge is Bonhoeffer's literary executor as well as his biographer. He edited Bonhoeffer's posthumously published *Ethics* and *Letters and Papers from Prison,* the six volumes of his *Collected Works,* as well as the republished versions of all Bonhoeffer's monographs. Bethge also inspired the publication of the seventeen-volume *Dietrich Bonhoeffer Werke,* which is currently being translated into English as the *Dietrich Bonhoeffer Works English Edition,* published by Fortress Press.

Theologian • Christian • Man for His Times

DIETRICH BONHOEFFER
A BIOGRAPHY

EBERHARD BETHGE

REVISED EDITION

REVISED AND EDITED BY
VICTORIA J. BARNETT

FORTRESS PRESS
MINNEAPOLIS

DIETRICH BONHOEFFER
A Biography

First Fortress Press edition 2000. Translated by Eric Mosbacher, Peter and Betty Ross, Frank Clarke, and William Glen-Doepel under the editorship of Edwin Robertson from the German *Dietrich Bonhoeffer: Eine Biographie,* copyright © 1967 Christian Kaiser Verlag, Munich. This edition revised and edited by Victoria J. Barnett, based on the seventh German edition, copyright © 1989 Christian Kaiser Verlag.

Cover photo: Dietrich Bonhoeffer around Zingsthof, 1935. Reprinted by permission of Christian Kaiser/Gütersloher Verlagshaus.
Cover design: Joe Bonyata

Library of Congress Cataloging-in-Publication Data

Bethge, Eberhard, 1909–
    [Dietrich Bonhoeffer. English]
    Dietrich Bonhoeffer: a biography / Eberhard Bethge ; [translated by Eric Mosbacher ... et al., under the editorship of Edwin Robertson]. — Rev. ed. / rev. and edited by Victoria J. Barnett, 1st Fortress Press ed.
        p.   cm.
    Includes index.
    ISBN 0-8006-2844-6 (alk. paper)
    1.   Bonhoeffer, Dietrich, 1906–1945. 2. Protestants—Germany
Biography. I. Barnett, Victoria. II. Title.
BX4827.B57B43   1999
230'.044'092—dc21
    [B]   99–39507
                                                                CIP

The paper used in this publication meets the minimum requirements for American National Standard for Information Sciences—Permanence of Paper for Printed Library Materials, ANSI Z329.48–1984.

Manufactured in the U.S.A.   AF 1-2844
                                    3   4   5   6   7   8   9   10

CONTENTS

FOREWORD

This new edition of Eberhard Bethge's classic biography of Dietrich Bonhoeffer brings into English for the first time the complete text of the German edition that was first published in 1967. All material that was omitted or abridged in the 1970 English translation has been restored, including the two appendices to the German edition: the moving essay by Christine von Dohnanyi on the background of the Zossen files and the bibliography of Bonhoeffer's readings in prison. The revisions and additions (mainly of new endnotes) of subsequent German editions have also been incorporated into this one.

This new English edition has been enhanced in other ways as well. In addition to citing English translations of Bonhoeffer's books in the notes, it also provides citations to the new German critical edition of his writings, the *Dietrich Bonhoeffer Werke,* now complete in seventeen volumes. Because this critical edition of the complete works contains material not published in the *Gesammelte Schriften* when the biography was first published, it has been possible to add numerous notes that enhance the documentation. The notes now cite the English translations of secondary literature previously cited only by German titles. Finally, and by no means least, Victoria Barnett has compared the entire text of the latest German edition with the previous translation and has made numerous corrections throughout. Because of all these enhancements this classic twentieth-century biography comes back into print with even greater vitality, pertinence, and durability.

Since its first publication in Germany three decades ago, the biography has gone through eight editions. The importance of the book was illustrated by the need for a second edition in the year it was published; at that time it was only possible to correct some printing errors and factual information. The third edition in 1969 was more thoroughly corrected (though again, most of the corrections were matters of form rather than matters of fact), and a great deal of detail was added to the index.

In 1983 the fifth edition was published. By this time the research of a growing number of scholars had begun to supplement Eberhard Bethge's monumental work. Since then, historical research on issues such as the German resistance, the Nazi euthanasia measures, and the role of the Wehrmacht in the murder of the Jews has yielded information not available when the biography was first written. In addition the climate in Germany that Bethge had to address in the original edition has changed. When the biography was written, many Germans still disapproved of the 20 July conspiracy and viewed people like Bonhoeffer as traitors. In discussing Bonhoeffer's role in the conspiracy, Bethge defends him in ways that may seem unnecessary to English-speaking readers but were actually addressed to a German readership still in the process of coming to terms with the past. The 1996 Berlin court decision, confirming a Bavarian court's earlier invalidation of the treason verdict against Bonhoeffer and the other conspirators, is a sign of the changed climate.

How should a biographer respond to this developing state of knowledge and opinion? Should a new, completely revised edition be written, taking account of new knowledge and interpretation? And what if, in preparing the critical edition of Bonhoeffer's complete works, new documents were discovered—as indeed happened? Would this require yet another new edition of the biography? Bethge addressed some of these issues in new prefaces written for the second, third, fifth, and eighth German editions. While welcoming the new studies, Bethge wrote in the preface to the 1983 edition that the biography should "show what its original inspiration was and continued to be." Furthermore, he himself was deeply engaged with other work, especially on the profound issues of Christian-Jewish relations after the Holocaust.

In the eighth edition published in 1994, Bethge noted his ongoing work on Bonhoeffer's relation to the Jews[1] and the recently published letters between Bonhoeffer and his fiancée, Maria von Wedemeyer,[2] an important new source. In response to continuing requests for a new edition, he pointed to the abundance of notes, prefaces, and epilogues in *Dietrich Bonhoeffer Werke*, then approaching completion in German and being translated into English. Modestly he added, "This volume, then, will have to do for a while!"

The phrase on the title page, "Theologian, Christian, Man for His Times," echoes Bethge's original German subtitle, which highlights his interpretation of Bonhoeffer's life. It also includes the author's preface from the first English edition, slightly revised. This second English edition builds on the foundation of the first, which was translated by Eric Mosbacher, Peter and Betty

Ross, Frank Clarke, and William Glen-Doepel, under the editorship of Edwin Robertson; without their labors this edition would not have been possible. Victoria Barnett—a specialist in this period of German church history, and author of *For the Soul of the People: Protestant Protest against Hitler*[3]— has brought to the task of editing, revision, and translation her linguistic expertise, her historical knowledge, and her conviction about the crucial lessons to be learned from this period; she has undertaken the work of this new edition with exemplary devotion as a labor of love. John Godsey generously devoted a great deal of work to the notes, particularly tracking down English translations of volumes previously cited only by their German titles. With equal generosity, Ilse Tödt added citations to the new German *Dietrich Bonhoeffer Werke*. The Religion Division of Lilly Endowment, Inc., under the enlightened leadership of Craig Dykstra, provided the financial support essential to producing this genuinely new edition. Michael West of Fortress Press supervised this work for the publisher with his customary collegiality and good humor.

Now that volumes of the English edition of *Dietrich Bonhoeffer Works* are appearing regularly, this biography is their indispensable companion for studying the life and theology of Dietrich Bonhoeffer. The International Bonhoeffer Society, through its several chapters around the world, its publications, and its national and international conferences, is a rich source of information and assistance. The Burke Library at Union Theological Seminary, New York, contains the Bonhoeffer Archive for the English-speaking world, and maintains a comprehensive collection of dissertations and conference papers in addition to monographs. The Godsey collection at Wesley Theological Seminary in Washington, D.C., is another excellent resource.

This edition of the biography appears in the year of Eberhard Bethge's ninetieth birthday. The publication of this new edition of his major work is a tribute to the outstanding contribution he has made to the church and to the history of our times—not only through this book but also through his decades of work as the editor of Bonhoeffer's writings, as a lecturer and teacher, and as a generous friend and helper to all whose research has built on his own. Bonhoeffer wrote eloquent theology about human community. This was embodied in his leadership in the Confessing church and his work in the resistance movement on behalf of Germany and peace. It was also embodied in friendship. "Finest and rarest blossom, at happy moment springing from the freedom of a lightsome, daring, trusting spirit, is a friend to friend," wrote Bonhoeffer in Tegel Prison in his poem "The Friend." Without Eberhard Bethge, the legacy of Dietrich Bonhoeffer in all likelihood would have gone unnoticed. This biography is a fruit of that friendship, and the biographer has widened the circle and spirit of that friendship around the world.

In the last year of this century we are beginning to assess its achievements and its horrors from a broader perspective than was possible when this biography was first published. In that light, the life and theology of Dietrich Bonhoeffer have a paradigmatic significance for the church that transcends his own lifetime and transcends this century—a witness against humanity's perennial temptation to idolatry and its destruction of life, and a witness to the authentic humanity that is the fruit of a genuine Christianity.

Clifford J. Green   Easter, 1999
Professor of Theology, Hartford Seminary
Executive Director, Dietrich Bonhoeffer Works Project

PREFACE TO THE
FIRST ENGLISH EDITION

Pleasing as it is that this biography is now available in English, twenty-five years ago I would have been astonished if anyone had predicted such widespread interest in Bonhoeffer. What has happened?

A man suffered shipwreck in, with, and because of his country. He saw his church and its claims collapse in ruins. The theological writings he left consisted of barely accessible fragments. In 1945 only a handful of friends and enemies knew who this young man had been; the names of other Christians in Germany were more in the limelight. When his name did emerge from the anonymity of his death, the response from the world of academic theology and the churches was tentative and restrained. Even today, some Germans hesitate to accept him and what he stood for completely.

In a world that moves from one topic to the next with ever greater rapidity, why is there still an interest in this man? Why does this interest continue to grow?

Perhaps the explanation is his unusual combination of thought and action, of his life as martyr and theologian. Perhaps it is the consistency and credibility of his admirable understanding of his cultural and church traditions, and the way in which he accepted the shaking of these foundations, while he lived and conceived a new Christianity for the future. Perhaps part of our sense of his conviction comes from the incompleteness of the man and his answers—because he presents us, not with a finished doctrine, but with an active process of learning. Perhaps it was the strong identity he preserved, even as he wrestled with a complexity of themes, answers, and problems. Perhaps we are fascinated by his utterly unfashionable renunciation of publicity. Perhaps, too, it was the triumph of his humanity over its betrayal by the means he was forced to use. To explain the widespread attention that has been given to his theological contentions, Christian testimony, and actions, we must look along all these lines.

The history of my own contribution to spreading his ideas and telling his life story has many facets; its logic was discernible only in retrospect. I wished to become a minister, and did not aim toward working academically as a systematician or church historian. It was only the course of my own life that led me to work on Bonhoeffer's legacy. In other words, my approach to this subject is not that of a scholar coming from the outside. I am involved, and must try to use this weakness as my strength. The challenge to others is to undertake new and more extensive studies.

Perhaps the process of becoming his biographer began when, at the beginning of the war, Bonhoeffer said in jest that I should carefully note something that he had just said—of course, I have now completely forgotten what it was—so that I might one day have something to write about him. At the time, I did not imagine for one moment that the course of events would really make me his biographer one day.

After his death, as I faced the task of arranging the unfinished manuscript of his *Ethics*, my only thought was that it was a friend's duty to make it available to others. The result was the publication of *Ethics* in 1949. I did not show my collection of letters to the publisher until the early 1950s, and this led to our hesitant publication of parts of them in *Letters and Papers from Prison*. These began to be discussed, first in Germany, then in Britain and America—and finally, after the publication of Robinson's *Honest to God*, in the Catholic world. The early understanding of Bonhoeffer was distorted and exploited by modern theological formulations. This led me to publish inaccessible and previously widely scattered published material from Bonhoeffer in the *Collected Works* (*Gesammelte Schriften*, published in Germany between 1958 and 1974), so that his words in *Letters and Papers from Prison* might be seen in the context of their theological and historical roots. It was my work on these fragments that eventually led to the idea of writing his life.

My qualification for this task derives from my close personal association with him during the last ten years of his life, and the fact that after his death I came into possession of most of his papers. In 1935 I entered the newly founded Confessing church seminary in Zingst, which later moved to Finkenwalde. It was led by Dietrich Bonhoeffer, of whom I knew nothing. I became a member of the smaller community that arose within the seminary, the so-called House of Brethren, and remained a member until the dissolution of the Finkenwalde Community at the end of 1937. Bonhoeffer then made me inspector of studies, a kind of assistant, at one of the two "collective pastorates"—the Confessing church's way of training ordination candidates, which existed in underground form until March 1940.

From the beginning, then, I was associated with Bonhoeffer's training of ministers for the Confessing church. A close friendship resulted, and I accompanied him wherever he lived and worked. In 1940 I followed him to Berlin, where I often stayed at his parents' house, and in 1943 I married Renate Schleicher, the daughter of Bonhoeffer's sister Ursula, who lived next door. Finally, he and I conducted an illegal correspondence that began after Bonhoeffer had survived the first dangerous series of interrogations in Tegel military prison. Eventually, this correspondence led to worldwide discussion. I also saw him several times in Tegel prison, until our contact was finally broken off as a result of my own arrest in October 1944. The Gestapo explored my relation with the Schleicher family, but neglected to investigate my ties to Dietrich Bonhoeffer. Thus I survived.

After his death, the family entrusted me with his unpublished theological work in progress, the surviving parts of his library, and most of his papers. I eventually felt a sense of obligation to make this material available, permitting a sounder interpretation of his life and work. This obligation arose at the point where the significance of his life and work transcended the private sphere and no longer belonged only to those close to him.

Bonhoeffer belonged to an epoch that was drawing to an end—for the church, for Western Christianity and its theology, and for the land of his ancestors as well. He reached beyond his era toward models for the future, helping to create these new models at the cost of his own life. The son of a professor's family that embodied the best traditions of the German bourgeoisie, he made theology his life's work. Within this vocation, he eventually achieved a very personal relationship to the church of Christ. This led him away from nationalistic tendencies and brought him into the ecumenical realm. Finally, he faced the challenges of his political era. With his sacrifice for the sake of his country, a different vision of how to be Christian in the future emerged, and Bonhoeffer was freed to conceive a new theology. This sequence of events, and the inner consistency of this richly talented man's path—his transition from theologian to Christian and, finally, to a man for his times—is precisely what is unique about Bonhoeffer's brief life.

Eberhard Bethge
1970

PORTRAIT

Dietrich Bonhoeffer was a powerful man. He inherited his tall stature from his mother's side, the Hases and the large-limbed Kalckreuths, and his supple strength from the Bonhoeffers. His movements were short and brisk. He didn't like leisurely walks. A successful jumper and sprinter in his schooldays, he still competed with his students when he was a university lecturer. He was impatient with illnesses and tried to shorten their duration through the copious use of medicines. During periods of stress he did not hesitate to take pills in order to sleep.

He bought good material for his clothes and wore suits appropriate to the country and climate in which he lived, although he did not dress to impress others. He liked to eat well and knew the specialities of many different regions. He was annoyed when the mushrooms or berries he had collected himself were badly prepared.

His head was round rather than long, but it did not look out of proportion on his broad shoulders. His short nose emphasized his prominent forehead and mouth. Bonhoeffer's twin sister inherited his father's dark hair and large brown eyes, and Dietrich the blond hair and blue eyes of his mother. His hair became thin early in life, and he wore rimless glasses because of nearsightedness.

He inherited the sensitive mouth and the full, sharply curved lips of his father. Dietrich's smile was very friendly and warm, but it was obvious at times that he enjoyed poking fun. He spoke remarkably quickly and without any dialect. When he preached, however, his speech became heavy, almost hesitant. Although his hands seemed delicately shaped, they were very strong. In conversation he often played with the signet ring bearing the Bonhoeffer crest on his left hand. When he sat down to play the piano he took the ring off and placed it on the left-hand corner of the keyboard.

He smoked many cigarettes when he was engaged in difficult negotiations or concentrated writing. In conversation, he was an attentive listener, asking questions in a manner that gave his partner confidence and led him to say more than he thought he could. Bonhoeffer was incapable of treating anyone in a cursory fashion. He preferred small gatherings to large parties, because he devoted himself entirely to the person he was with. He kept a certain distance from others out of respect for their privacy, and he saw to it that he was treated likewise. This made many people think he was proud. His very manner expressed this distance. When he was angry, his voice grew softer, not louder. The Bonhoeffer family considered anger indolent, not impertinent. They had a very strong sense of what was proper; they also had the quality, often ascribed to the British, of treating the daily routines of life very seriously, whereas the really disturbing matters, where all was at stake, were treated as if they were quite ordinary. The stronger the emotions, the more necessary it was to dress them in insignificant words and gestures.

Dietrich Bonhoeffer was able to work with total concentration. He did whatever work had to be done without hesitation. Yet this ability was accompanied by a willingness to be interrupted, and even a craving for company when playing music. He loved chess, bridge, and guessing games, and demanded the same competitiveness of his fellow players; but he always gave his opponent the benefit of the doubt. Even during the most hectic periods of his life, he never abandoned his recreational breaks. He liked talking to children and took them seriously. He would throw chocolates from his window to his nephews and nieces who were doing their schoolwork in the garden of the house next door.

It was said that Bonhoeffer was a particularly intense child. He remained intense in the way he set about everything: reading, writing, making decisions and giving the reasons for them, helping people or warning them. In short: throughout his brief full life, he dealt with whatever happened and was demanded of him.

ABBREVIATIONS

AB   *Act and Being.* Vol. 2 of Dietrich Bonhoeffer Works. Edited by Wayne Whitson Floyd, Jr. Translated by H. Martin Rumscheidt. Minneapolis: Fortress Press, 1996.

BWP   *Bonhoeffer: Worldly Preaching.* Finkenwalde Homiletics Lecture. Translated by Clyde E. Fant. Nashville: Thomas Nelson, 1995.

CC   *Christ the Center.* Revised translation by Edwin H. Robertson. New York: Harper and Row, 1978.

CD   *The Cost of Discipleship.* Translated by R. H. Fuller, revised by Irmgard Booth. A Touchstone Book. New York: Simon and Schuster, 1995.

CF   *Creation and Fall.* Vol. 3 of Dietrich Bonhoeffer Works. Edited by John W. de Gruchy. Translated by Douglas Stephen Bax. Minneapolis: Fortress Press, 1997.

DBW   *Dietrich Bonhoeffer Werke.* Individual titles in this series are cited by title and volume number.

DBWE   *Dietrich Bonhoeffer Works,* English edition. Individual titles from this series are cited by title and volume number.

E   *Ethics.* Translated by Neville Horton Smith. Rearranged edition. A Touchstone Book. New York: Simon and Schuster, 1995.

FFP   *Fiction from Prison: Gathering up the Past.* Edited by Renate and Eberhard Bethge, with Clifford Green. Translated by Ursula Hoffmann. Philadelphia: Fortress Press, 1981.

GS   *Gesammelte Schriften,* Vols. 1–6. Munich: Kaiser Verlag, 1958–1974.

IBF   *Internationales Bonhoeffer Forum.* Munich: Kaiser Verlag.

IKDB   *I Knew Dietrich Bonhoeffer: Reminiscences by His Friends.* Edited by Wolf-Dieter Zimmermann and Ronald Gregor Smith. Translated by Käthe Gregor Smith. New York: Harper and Row, 1966.

LLC   *Love Letters from Cell 92: The Correspondence between Dietrich Bonhoeffer and Maria von Wedemeyer.* Edited by Ruth-Alice von Bismarck and Ulrich Kabitz. Translated by John Brownjohn. Nashville: Abingdon Press, 1994.

LPP   *Letters and Papers from Prison.* New greatly enlarged edition. Edited by Eberhard Bethge. Translated by R. H. Fuller, John Bowden, et al. A Touchstone Book. New York: Simon and Schuster, 1997.

LT   *Life Together.* Part I of *Life Together/ Prayerbook of the Bible.* Vol. 5 of *Dietrich Bonhoeffer Works.* Edited by Geffrey B. Kelly. Translated by Daniel W. Bloesch. Minneapolis: Fortress Press, 1996.

MW   *Die Mündige Welt.* Vols. 1–5. Edited by Jørgen Glenthoj. Munich: Kaiser Verlag, 1969.

NRS   *No Rusty Swords: Letters, Lectures, and Notes, 1928–1936.* Edited by Edwin H. Robertson. Translated by Edwin H. Robertson and John Bowden. New York: Harper and Row, 1965.

PB   *The Prayerbook of the Bible.* Part II of *Life Together/Prayerbook of the Bible.* Vol. 5 of *Dietrich Bonhoeffer Works.* Edited by Geffrey B. Kelly. Translated by James H. Burtness. Minneapolis: Fortress Press, 1996.

PTB   *Preface to Bonhoeffer: The Man and Two of His Shorter Writings.* Edited and translated by John D. Godsey. Philadelphia: Fortress Press, 1965.

SC   *Sanctorum Communio.* Vol. 1 of *Dietrich Bonhoeffer Works.* Edited by Clifford Green. Translated by Reinhard Krauss and Nancy Lukens. Minneapolis: Fortress Press, 1998.

SPC   *Spiritual Care.* Translated and introduced by Jay C. Rochelle. Philadelphia: Fortress Press, 1985.

TF   *A Testament to Freedom: The Essential Writings of Dietrich Bonhoeffer.* Revised edition. Edited by Geffrey B. Kelly and F. Burton Nelson. New York: HarperCollins, 1995.

TP   *True Patriotism: Letters, Lectures, and Notes, 1939–1945.* Edited by Edwin H. Robertson. Translated by Edwin H. Robertson and John Bowden. New York: Harper and Row, 1973.

WF   *The Way to Freedom: Letters, Lectures and Notes, 1935–1939.* Edited by Edwin H. Robertson. Translated by Edwin H. Robertson and John Bowden. New York: Harper and Row, 1966.

PART ONE

THE LURE
OF THEOLOGY

CHAPTER ONE

CHILDHOOD AND YOUTH: 1906–1923

The twins Dietrich and Sabine were born on 4 February 1906, the sixth and seventh of eight children. Their parents, Karl Bonhoeffer, a professor of psychiatry and neurology, and his wife Paula, née von Hase, lived in Breslau at the time. The family's roots, however, were not in Silesia, but in Swabia, Thuringia, and Prussia.

Of his grandparents, only his Swabian grandmother Julie Bonhoeffer (née Tafel) was alive for a significant period of Dietrich Bonhoeffer's life. Indeed, she was part of the most decisive years of his adult life. The other three grandparents had either died before his birth or during his early childhood. Their ideas and standards, however—from the Thuringian and Prussian world of the Hases and Kalckreuths, and the Württemberg world of the Bonhoeffers—lived on in his parents' home.

Ancestors

Grandmother Clara von Hase, née Countess Kalckreuth. Grandmother von Hase was the first of the four grandparents to die, on 2 December 1903, at the young age of fifty-two. She had great vitality and grace, and was also artistically inclined. She took piano lessons from Clara Schumann and Franz Liszt and loved to sing. Her rich knowledge of songs was passed on to the Bonhoeffer children by Dietrich's mother.

Through this grandmother, Bonhoeffer developed an early sense for music and the fine arts. Clara's father was Count Stanislaus Kalckreuth (1820–1894), who exchanged the military profession of his ancestors for painting and had married a daughter of the Cauer family of sculptors in Kreuznach. Kalckreuth founded and served as director of the Grand Duke's

School of Art in Weimar. His son, Clara's brother Count Leopold Kalckreuth (1855–1928), surpassed his father as a painter. Stanislaus's large Alpine landscapes hang in numerous galleries such as the Munich Pinakothek; Leopold's portraits are primarily in the Hamburg Museum of Art.[1]

In his parents' home and that of his grandparents Hase, Dietrich was surrounded by the paintings of the Kalckreuths and their teachers, friends, and students: Lenbach, Achenbach, Voltz, Schirmer, von Schlicht, and Feddersen. There was no room left on the walls for periods other than that of the late nineteenth century, with its splendid spacious portrayals of nature and its cool portraits. "There is a beauty that is neither classical nor demonic, but simply earthly, though it has its own proper place. . . ."[2] In the room where Dietrich was arrested in 1943 hung a small unfinished Alpine study by his great-grandfather Stanislaus, in brown and glowing rose, and his great-uncle Leopold's ink drawings of a Silesian village pond. In 1931 Bonhoeffer included a spiritual profile of Leopold in his first lecture, as an example of the society that had grown ambivalent at the turn of the century.

The Kalckreuth heritage included the world of Prussia. Clara's marriage to Karl Alfred von Hase in 1872 was celebrated in a double wedding at which her elder sister Anna married Count Hans Yorck von Wartenburg, who lived on the Klein-Oels estate in Silesia. After Anna's death in 1879, he married her younger sister, Helene. Count Yorck, who later became Dietrich's godfather, was the son of the philosopher Paul Yorck, who became known for his correspondence with Wilhelm Dilthey. Clara's and Helene's younger sister Pauline became a lady-in-waiting at the court of Crown Princess Victoria, the cousin of Friedrich III in Potsdam. Dietrich's mother and her parents were active participants in the social scene of the Potsdam court between 1889 and 1894.

The social life in the Bonhoeffer home left its mark in the lively style to which Clara von Hase accustomed Dietrich's mother. The Thuringian branch of the family was amazed at the staff of servants that was necessary when Clara and her daughters came to visit. Her children learned to enhance parties with their effortless performances. The Breslau professor and poet Felix Dahn always depended upon their participation in the performances at his home.

After Clara's early death, her sister Helene, who had no children of her own, took on the grandmother's position at Klein-Oels for the Breslau children. She was a creative artist of a different fashion than the grandmother had been: her needlepoints and necklaces were still treasured three and four generations later. Every Bonhoeffer child was familiar with her games, like the New Year's cards with her illustrations and Uncle Hans Yorck's verses.

Young Dietrich wrote regularly to Klein-Oels. At the age of ten, he reported proudly to his great-aunt Helene: "I'm now playing some Grieg . . . I was at another concert of Nikisch's."[3] Some of the Kalckreuth musicality had been passed on to him; his twin sister inherited more of the artistic talents and enjoyed working with clay.

Aunt Helene's great-nephews, Peter and Paul Yorck from Klein-Oels, encountered the Bonhoeffer children again when the political resistance brought them together during the Second World War.

Grandfather Karl Alfred von Hase. Karl Alfred von Hase, Church Consistory council member and professor of practical theology, was born in Jena in 1842. He survived his wife Clara by ten years. He baptized the twins, and he baptized Dietrich's youngest sister, Susanne, at home in 1909. Dietrich was eight when this grandfather died.

He lived only a few blocks away from the Bonhoeffer home. There, his grandson saw a study filled with his great-grandfather's heirlooms, including the impressive Erlangen Luther editions that would later become his own possession, the engravings from many journeys to Rome, and the olive-wood cross from a stay in Jerusalem.

His grandfather was devoted to cultivating the memory of his famous father, Karl August von Hase, professor of church and dogmatic history in Jena. The figure of this great ancestor influenced Dietrich, although he did not follow the same theological direction. At the same time, the story of his life fascinated Dietrich.

Karl August's renown paved the way for his son's career, but, as the son of a Saxon pastor and orphaned at a young age, he had to build his own life's work from nothing. He confidently told the story of his turbulent youth in his book *Ideals and Errors* (*Ideale und Irrtümer*); Dietrich was given a copy of the seventh edition, published in 1917 for soldiers.

Expelled from Leipzig and Erlangen as a fraternity member, Karl August began his academic career in Tübingen until the authorities tracked him down there as well. He was imprisoned in the Hohenasperg fortress for over a year, from 1824 to 1825. He then settled in Jena, where he taught for sixty years.

The call to the university in Jena came from Goethe, who served as minister under the Duke of Weimar. After Hase returned from his first trip to Italy, he visited Goethe to pay his obligatory respects. On 23 August 1830, he wrote to his wife about how the old gentleman had received him in the room where the renowned bust of Juno Ludovisi stood:

> The conversation remained measured and quiet throughout, in general he
> seemed well-wishing without being personal or warm. The beginning was
> rather ministerial, about what Jena offered me and expected of me. . . .
> (My) inquiry about the Ludovisian Juno, and his reply that it was indeed
> her, finally led us to Italy, and I could tell him of my travels to Italy.[4]

The rosewood cupboard from Goethe's friend Minna Herzlieb, which so
delighted Dietrich Bonhoeffer when he received it as a birthday present in
prison in 1944, came from the Hase household.[5]

In 1831, great-grandfather Karl August married Pauline Härtel, daughter of a Leipzig publisher. The marriage opened new circles to him; these
included the painter Friedrich Preller and the nephew of Richard Volkmann-Leander, author of *Dreams by a French Fireplace* (*Träumereien an
französischen Kaminchen*). In 1870, he was pleased when his three sons
marched into France under the Prussian flag, even though they were not
Prussian.

The great-grandfather was a very successful theological teacher and
writer; his books went through many editions. *Hutterus Redivivus*, a textbook on the history of dogma, was still a respected examination aid during
Dietrich Bonhoeffer's time as a student. The auditorium he set up in his
home was adorned with Christian Rauch's bust of Friedrich Schleiermacher, both in honor of the sculptor, who was a friend, and of Schleiermacher,
with whom Hase felt a bond as one who had overcome theological rationalism. Despite his lively temperament, Hase was not a theological revolutionary like the fervent Ferdinand Christian Baur, with whom he even
fought. While he had deep sensitivity for the historical, particularly within
Catholicism, as a Protestant he wanted to represent "the old, true bond
between freedom and Christianity." Thus, he attacked the orthodox Lutheran thinker, Ernst Hengstenberg:

> The concern has been spread, not without success, that our people will be
> robbed of their religion unless it can be forced back into the antiquated
> form of dogma—a double-edged undertaking against the already awakened reason of the people.[6]

During his ninth trip to Rome in 1870, Hase came into contact with the
opposition group led by Archbishop Hefele at the first Vatican Council,
which opposed the proclamation of the dogma of infallibility. When it
became clear that this resolution could not be prevented, Hase left with the
opposition. Later he was among those who urgently advised the Prussians to
break off their futile battle with the Catholic church.

As an old man, Hase was given a personal peerage by the King of Württemberg, a conciliatory gesture in memory of his imprisonment in the Hohenasperg. At the end of his sixty years as professor in Jena, the Grand Duke of Weimar made him a hereditary peer.

His son, Karl Alfred von Hase, did not possess the successful robustness of his father. As a young pastor, he published a review against Ernest Renan's irritatingly liberal *Life of Jesus*. Later he particularly enjoyed studying the history of the Reformation. He saw himself as one of the "church positivists"; these, however, didn't agree with him when he supported the archliberal pastor Jatho's battle to retain his position in Cologne, where disciplinary proceedings had been instigated against him because of his teachings. Karl Alfred von Hase was interested in the early dialectical theologian Christoph Blumhardt and visited him in Bad Boll.

Following the invasion of France in the years 1870–1871, he became a division chaplain in Hannover and, in 1876, was made senior military chaplain in Königsberg. His daughter Paula was born in Prussia on 30 December 1876. His sermons were praised by Wilhelm I and Friedrich III, and in 1889 Wilhelm II named him chaplain of the Potsdam Court. This situation was difficult from the beginning, since the family preferred Friedrich III, and his sister-in-law, Pauline, was still lady-in-waiting to the widowed Queen Victoria. After two and a half years, Hase asked to be released from his duties. Family accounts offered two reasons. First, Hase had resisted Wilhelm II's insistence on preaching himself; the other reason was that he had dared to contradict the Kaiser when he characterized the proletariat as "a pack of dogs." In the family chronicle that he published, Karl Alfred von Hase loyally did not mention the grounds for his discharge.

In 1894 he moved to Breslau, where he entered the Church Consistory and accepted an honorary professorship. Initially, it was difficult for him to join the theological faculty, which was quite liberal at the time. There was little appreciation for a colleague in practical theology who was also a church official. Such attitudes changed once the openness and thorough erudition of the Hase household became known. In time, their home became a center for friends from many departments, especially because of Clara's abilities. Felix Dahn, a member of the law faculty, composed the *Festspiel* for their silver wedding anniversary. When Clara died, Dahn, a declared atheist, sang her praises in the *Silesian Newspaper* of 4 December 1903: "Even a pagan would be of the opinion that angels still wander the earth." The surgeon Mikulicz, for whom the young Ernst Friedrich Sauerbruch was an assistant, was a visitor to the home, as was the former Prussian culture minister and curator of the university, Count Robert Zedlitz. Zedlitz was also the father of Ruth von Kleist-Retzow, who became such an energetic supporter and ally of Dietrich Bonhoeffer in Pomerania during the 1930s.

At one of these social gatherings, a young medical assistant appeared: Dr. Karl Bonhoeffer. His own account appears in his memoirs:

> At one of the open evenings in the winter of 1896, I met a blond, blue-eyed girl who so captivated me the moment I entered the room by her free natural manner, her open uninhibited gaze, that my impression of this moment when I first saw my future wife remains in my memory as an almost mystical one that determined my life. We quickly became friends that evening, and my way of life, until then confined to the clinic and a few old friends from Tübingen, changed. In the mornings, I joined my boss ice-skating on the canals through Schweidnitzer, where I knew I would meet her, and conducted visits to the houses where we saw each other. . . . Therese Dahn [wife of the poet], however, initially resented my courting her young friend, because she herself was attached to her, and had to see how the regular Latin lessons that she gave her became irregular and the interest in the old languages diminished. She even found it necessary to warn her about the young doctor who had intruded into her circles and, who perhaps, didn't seem to be serious enough to her in that lively milieu. . . . But we soon became good friends, and we celebrated some lovely parties with Felix Dahn and his Therese.[7]

Grandfather Karl Alfred von Hase died on New Year's Day 1914. The Bonhoeffers no longer lived in Breslau, but the progressive stages of his cancer were not hidden from the grandchildren. The reports that their grandfather had continued his work until it was no longer possible left a lasting impression on them.

After his death, Hans von Hase (1873–1958), the elder brother of Bonhoeffer's mother, officiated as family pastor at occasions like weddings and baptisms. The parsonages where he lived, first in Silesia and then in the eastern countryside of Brandenburg, the so-called Mark-Brandenburg, now part of Poland, made the church and its ministry come alive for young Dietrich. Because of the numerous cousins and its farm, the rural parsonage was a paradise for holidays during and after the First World War.

In his book *The Chronicle of Our Home*, Karl Alfred von Hase carefully described the history of the von Hase family. A large portion of it is devoted to his father, Karl August. This commendable work, however, was not always taken entirely seriously by the Bonhoeffers. Family members who displayed a certain pride about their ancestry and history were met with amused derision. When Dietrich Bonhoeffer drafted a novel in his Tegel prison cell in 1943, it included an imaginary uncle who apparently had nothing but the family chronicle in mind; the children could barely conceal their amusement over his unavoidable lectures.[8]

The grandparents' home in Breslau represented a social class that was a pillar of the state in late-nineteenth-century Germany. Its integrity was joined with tolerance. Its ideals of learning were nurtured by the southern cultures and remarkably little by the western ones. The numerous journeys to Italy enriched their knowledge and taste but did little to serve a critical political function. The revolutionary signs of the time in Italy were noted only in passing. Although not blind to certain aberrations within the German monarchical system, they did not criticize the existing social order and led a full life within it. The national ethos was a central value. They saw no discrepancy between this ethos and the lofty humanist standards that they demanded of themselves and their children. In the fate of her sons, Dietrich's mother would be the first to experience the painful break between nationalism and humanism.

Grandfather Friedrich Bonhoeffer. Dietrich Bonhoeffer's life was shaped by another feature, inherited from his Swabian ancestors: an introspective nature and the tendency—a characteristic of the politically active Tafel side of the family—to keep his passions hidden.

The Bonhoeffers had emigrated from Holland (van den Boenhoff from Nimwegen) in 1513 and settled as goldsmiths in Schwäbisch Hall. After the seventeenth century they became pastors, doctors, city council members, and mayors. Their coat of arms, established in the heraldry certificate of 1590, can be seen even today on some of the lovely merchant houses of the town: a lion with a bean vine in his paw, on a blue background. The only jewelry Dietrich Bonhoeffer ever wore was a signet ring with this seal. Among Bonhoeffer's ancestors, Gerd Wunder counts seventy-eight city council members in Schwäbisch Hall, calling this a sign of an "impressively unanimous family mentality."[9] Some of these ancestors gaze down on visitors to the St. Michael Church in Schwäbisch Hall from their baroque epitaphs on the walls. Among them is the remarkable 1794 oil portrait of the "beautiful Bonhoeffer," who received a place among these illustrious ancestors because of her charitable deeds. A copy of the painting hung in Bonhoeffer's parents' home.

Dietrich knew his grandfather Friedrich Ernst Philipp Tobias Bonhoeffer (1828–1907) only from the stories of his father and grandmother. He had left the old ancestral seat in Schwäbisch Hall but remained in Swabia. He served as a high judiciary official for the state of Württemberg in many small Swabian towns. His son Karl, Dietrich's father, was born on 30 March

1868 during his term in Neresheim. Because of this, Karl Bonhoeffer was not a citizen of Schwäbisch Hall, and once expressed regret that he had failed to apply for citizenship later. Friedrich Bonhoeffer ended his career as president of the regional court in Ulm. He then retired in Tübingen, where the king conferred a personal peerage on him. In the year of his father's death, Karl Bonhoeffer wrote in his New Year's diary:

> Of his qualities, I would wish that our children inherit his simplicity and truthfulness. I never heard a cliche from him, he spoke little and was a firm enemy of everything faddish and unnatural.

Free of all ambition, he never did anything to advance his own career. He disliked public appearances, and the obligatory speeches at official functions upset him days in advance. He had a certain restlessness; he didn't like to remain seated during conversations, but preferred walking back and forth—a characteristic of Dietrich's brothers as well. He preferred working at a lectern, as did Dietrich later.

At home he was a comfortable father who never spoke about his work with the family. He loved rigorous long walks. Even at an early age, his sons Karl and Otto hiked nearly twenty-five miles with him, from Tübingen through the Schönbuch region to visit relatives in Stuttgart. He recognized everything that grew along the way. His son Karl later attributed his "A" in botany to his father; and grandson Dietrich was proud of the sure knowledge of wild mushrooms he had inherited. Like his grandfather, he knew the forest by its smells.

Politically, Friedrich Bonhoeffer was conservative, but he disdained the local Württemberg patriotism. In 1862 he already wagered that Germany would be united under Prussian leadership.

In keeping with the Schwäbisch Hall family tradition, he maintained an active connection to the church. His son Karl, however, believed:

> In general I had the impression that attending church didn't lift his spirits, but tended to depress him. Although he didn't make us sons go to church later, he did require that we attend church every Sunday during the school years before we were confirmed. Good Friday was a grim day. During the afternoon walk that was customary that day, it would have been unthinkable and blasphemous, for example, to enter an inn. I think that what repelled him about Swabian democracy was its basically lax or dismissive position toward the church.[10]

Grandmother Julie Bonhoeffer, née Tafel. Friedrich Bonhoeffer's wife Julie was the direct link between a long history and Dietrich Bonhoeffer's life.

Born on 21 August 1842, she could talk about the days of Eduard Mörike and Justinus Kerner. But it was just as characteristic of her that, at the age of ninety-one, she marched past the S.A. (Nazi Storm Troopers) cordons promoting the boycott of Jewish businesses on 1 April 1933, to shop at the Jewish-owned "Kaufhaus des Westens" on Tauentzienstrasse in Berlin.

The marriage of Friedrich Bonhoeffer and Julie Tafel introduced a revolutionary element into the Bonhoeffer ancestry. Here there were fraternity members, passionate republicans and socialists, Freemasons, immigrants, and Swedenborgians. Julie's father Christian Friedrich August Tafel (1798–1856) was one of four famous brothers who, although orphaned early, all made remarkable careers.

Julie's father and his brother Gottlob successfully fought to study law. At one point, as fraternity members and democrats, they were banished from Württemberg. In 1824, as a fellow prisoner in Hohenasperg, Gottlob encountered the theologian Karl August Hase, who recorded the encounter in the memoirs of his youth:

> [The] wild Tafel, who has become one of the first lawyers in Württemberg, very characteristically gave his nickname to distinguish himself from his three brothers, whose nicknames are no less distinguished as the shaggy, the handsome and the pious Tafel, the latter a Swedenborgian and librarian at the University in Tübingen; Tafel didn't make it easy for the interrogating judge, he "told him, very amicably: 'Now, Herr von Prieser, you have betrayed us, you will surely have a fine career because of it.'"[11]

Gottlob Tafel later became a member of the National Congress in 1848 and the *Zoll Parliament* of 1868. Julie Bonhoeffer later remembered how, after 1848, her father's house became a refuge for political refugees and the relatives of those who had been imprisoned. Christian Tafel was a Freemason. At his grave, it was said that his home was the "most hospitable in the town."

Protest against the status quo was characteristic of the two younger brothers as well. Immanuel, the theologian, joined the Swedenborgians and dedicated one of his Swedenborg studies in 1839 to Karl August Hase in Jena. Although the attempt was made to remove him from his pastorate, he never abandoned his convictions. He finally became chief librarian and professor in Tübingen. Bonhoeffer owned many of the Swedenborg volumes from his great-great-uncle's study, although this apparently didn't move him in this direction. The fourth Tafel brother, the linguist Leonhard, left his homeland with his family and made his fortune in America. When Dietrich and his brother Karl Friedrich visited the United States, his descendants in Philadelphia invited them to their home.

The revolutionary zeal of the Tafels had not lessened in Julie's generation. During visits to the Tafels in Stuttgart, Karl Bonhoeffer remembered, there were heated conversations that upset him considerably as a child. In particular he recalled one aunt, who often visited Florence with Isolde Kurz:

> We liked it when she came to visit, even if I sometimes feared that the heated political arguments that arose between her free-spirited, radically democratic views and those of our father, who energetically defended the Reich and the Prussian leadership and expressed his views very temperamentally, might lead to a serious break. This would have pained us deeply, for we were truly fond of our aunt, with her kind vitality, her impetuous personality and the fact that she already took us boys somewhat seriously, even when we disapproved of her black-red-gold convictions, more out of faith in our father's authority than our own judgment.[12]

As a student in Munich in 1890, Karl Bonhoeffer met one of his Tafel cousins, Hermann, a painter and art critic:

> I spent some pleasant evenings with him in some of the pubs. At that time he was influenced totally by his reading of Marx's *Das Kapital*. . . . in him, and in cousin Robert Tafel who was the same age. . . . I encountered two highly idealistic socialists, not partyliners, who bore their membership in a bourgeois family with some shyness and embarrassed discomfort, both of whom, however, through their very superior learning were very instructive for me, and I thought very highly of them as people.[13]

Julie Tafel, too, had inherited the alert critical sensibilities of her ancestors. She actively participated in discussions on women's issues and devoted herself to practical and organizational matters, like establishing a home for older women or vocational centers for girls. Characteristically, she advised her sons Karl and Otto not to enter the civil service or pursue an officer's career, since such professions would "never allow them freedom of movement and would mean a lifelong dependency." As far as he was concerned, Karl Bonhoeffer added:

> This posed no difficulty for me, since I tended toward medicine from the beginning, once I had abandoned the idea of taking my regional examinations and entering a theological or philosophical career, because of my pronounced aversion to talking by myself every Sunday or becoming a teacher.[14]

His grandmother lived in Tübingen until 1924, including Dietrich Bon-hoeffer's first two semesters. She then moved to be near her children in Berlin. Her ninetieth birthday, on 21 August 1932, was a grand summer party for her children, grandchildren, and great-grandchildren in Friedrichs-brunn. Christoph von Dohnanyi, not yet two years of age, recited a verse for his great-grandmother:

> When you were once as small as me
> One rode upon a steed;
> When I am someday old as you
> we'll travel to the moon. . . .

She was still light on her feet. In lively letters, she shared the interests of her grandchildren—and her concerns about the course of political events. At her grave, Dietrich spoke about how the suffering of the Jews had bur-dened her final years.

The rich world of his ancestors set the standards for Dietrich Bonhoef-fer's own life. It gave him a certainty of judgment and manner that cannot be acquired in a single generation. He grew up in a family that believed that the essence of learning lay not in a formal education but in the deeply rooted obligation to be guardians of a great historical heritage and intellectual tra-dition. To Dietrich Bonhoeffer, this meant learning to understand and respect the ideas and experiences of earlier generations. It could also lead him to decisions and actions that conflicted with those of his ancestors—and, precisely in this way, to honor them. Ultimately, it might even mean vol-untarily accepting history's inevitable judgment on the world of his ances-tors—while not allowing this to detract from his delight in its amicable representatives.

Parents' Home in Breslau

The Suburbs. For a Swabian, a city like Breslau was located far from every-thing desirable. Geographically, Karl Bonhoeffer portrayed his acceptance in 1893 of an assistantship to the old master of psychiatry, Carl Wernicke, as a kind of exile. In the years 1947–1948, he wrote in his memoirs:

> Once the horizon opened toward the east after Görlitz, I would have done anything to turn back. . . . This impression didn't become any rosier when I entered the city, with its massive high buildings and chimneys, if I com-pare it with the trip into Stuttgart from Hasenberg.[15]

Nonetheless his work, marriage, and children eventually gave him such roots in the Silesian university town that there were times when he considered it his final place.

During his years of apprenticeship to Wernicke, he specialized in alcoholic psychosis, for which Breslau, with its low standard of living and widespread consumption of *schnapps*, offered a particularly rich field of observation.[16] Wernicke surprised him one day by offering him the chance to do his postdoctoral qualifications. Karl Bonhoeffer took this up so quickly that Wernicke was astonished. In 1898, Bonhoeffer was given a leading position as psychiatrist in the observation ward for mentally disturbed prisoners in Silesia; here, he worked on degenerative psychoses.

On 5 March 1898, at the beginning of his independent career, he married Paula von Hase, who had learned the basics of housekeeping from Aunt Helene in Klein-Oels.

Five years later, Karl Bonhoeffer received his first call to Königsberg, but lectured there only during the winter semester 1903–1904. Heidelberg offered better working conditions; but after spending only the summer semester of 1904 there, he was offered the professorial chair that his teacher Wernicke had held in Breslau. He returned to his wife's hometown that same year. Breslau seemed to offer the greatest range of teaching opportunities and clinical work for his beginning research. Only now was psychiatry becoming a required department in medical schools.

The Bonhoeffer children grew up in a spacious house next to the newly built Breslau mental hospital in Scheitniger Park. The garden was big enough for them to dig caves and set up tents. Next to it was a tennis court where their father played in summer and taught them skating in winter. The house was big enough for a schoolroom with desks, a hobbies room, and another in which—to the servants' alarm—all sorts of pets were kept, such as lizards, snakes, squirrels, and pigeons, as well as collections of beetles and butterflies. Opposite the house was a Catholic cemetery, and from the window the children could watch the funeral cortèges with black-draped horses drawing the hearses. Nearby was a branch of the Oder River.

The children needed only seven minutes to reach their grandfather's house. After the death of their grandmother, their mother's sister, Aunt Elisabeth, ran the household and was an indispensable help at the children's parties.

The rapid growth of the family led the Bonhoeffers to buy a summer home, which they soon found in Wölfelsgrund, a remote, wooded valley in Glatzer Bergland. It was off the beaten track, and almost the only stranger to disturb their privacy there was a bigoted forestry official who made an appearance as *Gelbstiefel* ("Yellow Boots") in the novel Bonhoeffer tried to write in his prison cell at Tegel in 1943.[17] For the older children, the lookout towers and meadows of Wölfelsgrund became the yardstick by which all subsequent holiday places were measured.

Father. Karl Bonhoeffer was not often in the forefront of his children's lives. His study and consulting room were out of bounds to them. Despite the many demands on his time as a university teacher and consulting physician, however, he never missed the family meals. These were rather ceremonial occasions. The children's table manners were strictly supervised, and they were expected to speak only when asked about events of the day. It was generally their mother who decided which situations in their lives should be brought to their father's notice. But during the major holidays of the year he devoted himself to them completely; for instance, he would have himself invited to share in the meals the girls cooked for their dolls in the nursery. When the older children were small he spent the holidays with them in Wölfelsgrund whenever he could. This had become rare by the time of Dietrich's childhood; by then their mother usually took her husband to more distant holiday places.

Despite his retiring nature, their father was a powerful influence. He always spoke quietly, but his eyes gave his words an impressiveness that brooked no contradiction. As his daughter Christine once wrote, a lecture by him might end with the words: "In your place I wouldn't say anything else now, but I advise you to think it over. You can come and talk it over with me again this evening, if you like." But generally, Christine continued, the children realized that this was a good end to the matter and had no desire to reopen it. "He was not the kind of father whose beard one could stroke or whom one could call by a pet name, but when he was needed he was as firm as a rock. And how he always knew what was bothering us is a mystery to me to the present day."

Dietrich's twin sister, Sabine, described her father as follows:

> His rejection of the hollow phrase may have made us at times tongue-tied and uneasy, but as a result we could not abide any cliches, gossip, platitudes or pomposity when we grew up. . . . Sometimes our papa delighted in making us define concepts, or things, and if we managed to do so clearly, without being vague, he was happy. . . . Papa was cautious not to restrict us, if possible not to influence us; he was able to watch and wait for things to grow, and did not want to tie us too closely to himself and others.[18]

In his memoirs Karl Bonhoeffer was really describing himself when he wrote about his relations with his colleagues: "I have always believed that the qualifications for a psychiatrist must include not only a capacity for understanding those who think differently, but the development of a high degree of emotional control."[19] His words evoked those of Proverbs 25:28: "A man without self-control is like a city broken into and left without walls." He taught his children to respect the feelings and opinions of others, to recognize their own limitations and see life in proportion.

By present-day standards the Bonhoeffer household was conducted on an inconceivably lavish scale; but, at the same time, the parents strongly disliked personal boasting or pretension. Money was never discussed in front of the children. The country house in Wölfelsgrund was spacious and airy, but its furnishings were Spartan; later, after they had moved to Berlin, the family's summer home in Friedrichsbrunn was wired for electricity only in autumn 1943. If one of the children dropped a toy on the dirty floor of the railway compartment on the way to the country, their mother was capable of dropping it straight out of the window, but suggestions for improving amenities in the country were ignored. There was never any question of fashionable extravagance, either in dress or in the home.

But nothing was spared in furthering the children's satisfactory and happy development. After the birth of the eighth child, their father wrote in his diary on New Year's Eve in 1909:

> In spite of having eight children, which surprises many people at the present time, we do not have the feeling that it is too many. The house is spacious, the children have developed normally, we parents are not too old, and we try not to spoil them but to give them a happy childhood.

In 1944, after reading the memoirs of his prospective father-in-law Hans von Wedemeyer, Dietrich Bonhoeffer wrote to his fiancée from prison:

> That element of astringency in the father-son relationship is a sign of great strength, and of an inward self-assurance. . . . Most parents today are too spineless. For fear of losing their children, they devalue themselves into their friends and cronies, and end by rendering themselves superfluous to them. I abhor that type of upbringing, which is not an upbringing at all. I believe our families think alike in that respect.[20]

Mother. The household over which Paula Bonhoeffer presided belongs to an earlier era. It had a staff of at least five: a governess for the older children, a nurse for the little ones, a housemaid, a parlormaid, and a cook. Before the

First World War, there was sometimes a French governess; later there was also a receptionist for her husband and a chauffeur. She managed everything, sometimes causing outsiders to suspect that it was she who wore the trousers in the family. But closer knowledge disclosed a happy relationship in which each partner adroitly supplemented the strength of the other. At their golden wedding anniversary it was said that they had not spent a total of one month apart during their fifty years of marriage, even counting single days.

Paula gave the children their first schooling. In her youth, with a spirit of independence that was shocking at the time, she had fought for and obtained permission to take the qualifying examination for women teachers. She gave lessons at home to the older and younger children together, along with the children of some of her husband's professor friends, and at the year's end she was always able to register her pupils successfully for the state examination, where they did very well. Thanks to the excellent start she gave them, they were able to skip entire grades and eventually take the school graduation examinations at a remarkably early age, as Dietrich did.

This home teaching, of course, implied some criticisms of traditional schooling. The Bonhoeffers did not want to hand their children over to others at an early, impressionable age. One of the family sayings was that Germans had their backs broken twice in the course of their lives: first at school, and then during their military service.

Paula Bonhoeffer was a stimulating and indefatigable mother. She managed to make every task interesting and help the children over any obstacles. Without the aid of textbooks, she taught them a large repertoire of poems, songs, and games. As a grandmother, she still performed "Little Red Riding-hood" in the old family puppet theater on her birthday every 30 December.

She had never learned dressmaking, but if one of her daughters' dresses did not fit she took the needle and scissors without hesitation. She designed her children's smocks, generally in the Reutlingen style. Anything ready-made was too "average" for her, and it was inconceivable for her to buy anything ready-made for herself.

She was accustomed to getting her own way both with the children and with adults, and always found some way to do so. When Klaus, the third son, hesitated to jump into the deep end of the swimming pool, she jumped in herself to show him, although she had never learned to swim. When a store salesman tried eloquently to persuade her that a bathtub she was thinking of buying was big enough, she insisted on his proving the point by lying down in it himself.

During the difficult 1930s her letters and telephone calls opened many closed doors. Before anyone else knew what to do, she had undertaken something to help a friend of her son, a pastor who needed protection. Thanks to her intervention, a number of important church matters were brought to a successful conclusion. It was not easy to put her off. She had a disarming manner that helped the hesitant and nervous to "get moving," as she put it.

Despite the obvious influence of her parents, she was nondoctrinaire in church and political matters. She was more interested in people than in nature. In contrast to her husband, she took little notice of the scenery during the long walks in Wölfelsgrund or Friedrichsbrunn, preferring to listen and to talk. When one immediate problem was solved, she became totally absorbed in pondering the next step. Despite all her energy, she never stifled any sign of initiative in others, but encouraged it to develop in its own way.

She was a woman of definite opinions, even in medical matters, to her husband's amusement. She permitted herself to have and express a wealth of feeling, including religious feeling. She sang Beethoven's *Gellert Lieder* with great enthusiasm, and always with her own metrical inaccuracies. But she regarded mistakes as more forgivable than boredom.

Many of her characteristics could be seen later in Dietrich Bonhoeffer.

Brothers and Sisters. The eight Bonhoeffer children were born in the space of ten years. First came the three brothers: Karl-Friedrich (1899–1957), a brilliant physicist who, besides inheriting his father's scientific ability, also adopted his cautious agnosticism; Walter (1899–1918), who became the family expert on the forest and its creatures, distinguished himself early by his linguistic ability, and was killed in the First World War; and Klaus (1901–1945), who became a lawyer, and was believed by his father to be the most difficult but also the most amusing and intelligent of his children.

Then came the two big sisters. Ursula (1902–1983), a girl of unusual beauty, with a ready and sound judgment in making necessary decisions and acting on them, married the lawyer Rüdiger Schleicher (1895–1945). Christine (1903–1965), quickly outpaced her schoolfellows and enjoyed doing so; she would marry Hans von Dohnanyi (1902–1945).

Then came the three "little" ones. Dietrich and Sabine were born in 1906 (Sabine died in 1999). Sabine married a legal scholar, Gerhard Leibholz (1901–1982). The youngest, naturally somewhat spoiled, Susanne (1909–1991), later became the wife of theologian Walter Dress (1904–1979).

The renowned pediatrician A. Czerny tended the development of the newborn twins Dietrich and Sabine. Because of his healthy constitution Dietrich caused his parents little anxiety. The only known serious illness in his childhood was appendicitis, for which he had an operation in 1917, spending several interesting weeks in Professor Hildebrand's nursing home.

As a result, Dietrich played a smaller role in his father's annual New Year's notes than the other children. He got used to being the strongest and most agile of the three youngest children, but he chivalrously helped and protected the two little girls; according to them, he performed this task carefully and selflessly. The Bonhoeffer children played and attended large children's parties with the children of his father's colleagues, Ludloff, Hürthle, and Abegg. In such a large family Dietrich hardly felt the need for outside friends, and indeed he seems to have had no special friendships until his student years. During his early years he played dolls with his sisters; still, his first scribbled Christmas wish list in Breslau began: "Popguns, soldiers!"

As a small boy he once attacked a weaker classmate, whose mother expressed the grave suspicion that perhaps the Bonhoeffer children had been raised to be anti-Semitic. Dietrich's mother replied that her son could not have heard of such a thing in her house. As someone capable of such violence, he was later particularly and carefully concerned about treating those in weaker positions considerately, and instilling self-confidence in them.

For the twins, Breslau was a children's paradise; their formal schooling began only after the family moved in 1912. The energetic and ambitious boy, however, wanted to do everything the elder children could. The final New Year's notes made by the father in Breslau stated: "The twins this year are not yet in school, both however want to be useful around the house and Dietrich is an avid learner. Hopefully this will remain so."

There was no questioning of parental authority in the Bonhoeffer family, yet the children regarded their nursery years as especially happy. Dishonesty and fibbing were severely punished; in comparison, broken windows and torn clothes hardly counted. Talents were encouraged at an early age. The children knew it was not impossible for any of their real wishes to be granted, and when others' wishes came true they were expected to share in the pleasure. What their parents told them to do had to be done without hesitation or argument, and complaining about work or unfair treatment was not tolerated. The children's day followed a disciplined pattern; they always knew where they were, and the routine never struck them as restrictive, for they also knew that their parents arranged happy surprises and outings every now and then.

In later years Dietrich Bonhoeffer sometimes became uneasy about his happy and protected upbringing, for he felt it had sheltered him from some of the darker sides of life and isolated him from those less fortunate in society. In his circle, such people were the recipients of generous gifts, donations, and special invitations. At an early age his sister Ursula was sent for weeks to the home of the family's sick former maid, whose husband was a drinker, to help out in the household. Nevertheless, Dietrich was aware of the sheltered life he lived. As a student, on a walking tour with his youngest sister, he once boldly told her:

> I should like to live an unsheltered life for once. We cannot understand the others. We always have our parents to help us over every difficulty. However far away we may be from them, this gives us such a blatant security.[21]

This sense of uneasiness accompanied him all the way to his cell in Tegel. In a play written in prison, he had a young proletarian reproach another character, a doctor's son, for the security he had enjoyed in life.[22] From his earliest childhood Dietrich Bonhoeffer was accustomed to being privileged, not the underdog.

Admittedly, this was true only up to a point in terms of his position among his siblings. This position had some significance for his development, and probably for his choice of career as well. As the three "little ones," he and his sisters had all the advantages and disadvantages of youngest children. It was natural that the sturdy and gifted boy should sometimes try to rival or even surpass his big brothers and, indeed, in the field of music, he did surpass them. This secret rivalry certainly helped to make theology attractive, since it offered the prospect of achieving something special of his own. The distance between the three groups of children was increased by the war, which confronted the older children with its terrible realities early, while the younger children remained at home.

His exclusion from realms of experience important to his older brothers was a *leitmotiv* in Bonhoeffer's early thought for several years. As a curate in Barcelona, in a lecture delivered to a congregation at the beginning of 1929, he said:

> If I am not mistaken, we can distinguish among four groups of people in today's Germany who have arrived at different ethical ideologies as the result of historical developments. First come those whose period of development and maturation occurred before the beginning of the war. Then there are those who were matured by the war, and then the generation of revolutionary youth whose awakening and development took place in the years from 1918 until, let us say, 1923. Finally, we must not forget those to whom the future will belong, those who know war and revolution only by hearsay. . . . Thus the rapid sequence of events has created four spiritual generations in less than twenty years.[23]

The year 1923 that Bonhoeffer mentions in this passage was that in which he took his school graduation examinations. In a radio talk at the beginning of February 1933, "The Leader and the Individual in the Younger Generation," he reiterated the same theme with only minor modifications:

> There is an invisible but impenetrable line dividing those who were in the war from those, only slightly younger, who grew up and became mature at the time of the collapse. This is felt more strongly by the younger men than by the older ones. . . .
>
> Thus, precisely as a result of this encounter with their older brothers, the younger men were led to become creative; not so much to tolerate and maintain in responsible fashion what already existed, as to create, as a result of radical criticism, their own form of life.[24]

One senses that Bonhoeffer was speaking here of his older brothers and himself. The war experience created a barrier between them. They had faced perils that he knew only by hearsay. Interestingly enough, his consciousness of this barrier disappeared in 1933, as things grew serious for Dietrich Bonhoeffer himself. He never mentioned the *leitmotiv* of a separate generation again. But even in later years his theological and ecclesiastical work betrayed a certain need to explain himself to his skeptical agnostic brother Karl-Friedrich.[25]

Berlin

When Dietrich's father accepted the call to Berlin in 1912, he accepted the leading professorship for psychiatry and neurology in Germany. It included duties that considerably widened his previous range of work: as director of the Society of Neurology, as publisher of the *Monthly for Psychiatry and Neurology* and the "Central Paper for General Neurology and Psychiatry," and other activities as well. He became the center of a circle of colleagues and pupils, many of whom became professors of psychiatry at other German universities. Some of his pupils became friends of the family, such as Krückmann, Kramer, Creutzfeld, Kallmann, Jossmann, Zutt, and Roggenbau, and later Scheller and Dr. Bormann. The political catastrophe of the thirties forced some of them to leave the country; others demonstrated their attachment to the family during the resistance period.[26]

Karl Bonhoeffer's reputation spread from Berlin to the world of academic psychiatry and neurology. He turned the city into a bastion against the invasion of Freudian and Jungian psychoanalysis. His mind was not closed to unorthodox theories, nor did he deny the validity of efforts to investigate unexplored areas of the mind; but he refused to ever have any contact with Freud.

In his biography of Freud, Ernest Jones mentioned only one distant but unhappy link between the two men. Soon after Bonhoeffer began working in Berlin, Freud's contribution to a medical encyclopedia on the problems of hysteria was rejected by Bonhoeffer's closest colleagues.[27] Robert Gaupp, who had been Karl Bonhoeffer's friend since their student days and was professor of psychiatry in Heidelberg, offered the following explanation:

> Perhaps it may seem striking that a man who was a sensitive psychiatrist with a remarkable gift for empathy, and who did outstanding work on the nature of hysterical symptom formation, never took a specific and categorical position, to my knowledge, in the controversy about the theories of Freud, Adler, Jung and other "psychoanalysts." "Psychoanalysis" means the dispassionate "analysis of an individual's mental illness with all the resources of intuitive psychology, accompanied by scrupulous observation." In intuitive psychology and scrupulous observation Bonhoeffer had no superior. But he came from Wernicke's school, which was concerned solely with the brain and permitted no departure from thinking in terms of cerebral pathology. He practiced the psychology of empathy and understanding on the basis of his natural aptitudes and gifts. The theoretical interpretation of what was *behind* that being observed, of what occurred unconsciously and might project itself into consciousness, was foreign to his approach. Intuition was not alien to him, as his entire life's work shows. But he had no urge to advance into the realm of dark, undemonstrable, bold and imaginative interpretation, where so much has to be assumed and so little can be proven. . . .
>
> By nature so astute and critical, Bonhoeffer was cautious and modest toward philosophy, and remained within the boundaries of the empirical world that was accessible to him. There are few research scientists who at the age of eighty, after a scholarly career of more than half a century, have had to retract so little of what they once taught. Bonhoeffer, the research scientist of 1897, could still be compared with the Bonhoeffer of 1948. He adhered to the course carved out by his life experience, cautiously, but with determination.[28]

In Dietrich Bonhoeffer's later work, it cannot be overlooked that psychoanalysis—even when relevant to his own field of pastoral care—either plays no part or is dismissed with contempt. Underlying this, of course, were theological prejudices in the spirit of Karl Barth, but his father's quiet influence on him is undeniable. Though he possessed a copy of Carl Jung's *Modern Man in Search of a Soul* (1931), as well as Edouard Spranger's *Psychologie des Jugendalters*, which he carefully studied, he never really wrestled with Freud, Adler, or Jung. In this area he remained completely within the limits his father had set.

Karl Bonhoeffer was the leading Berlin psychiatrist and neurologist from 1912 until his death in 1948. Only in 1922 did he seriously consider moving to Munich to accept the professorial chair vacated by Kraepelin, the great founder of scientific psychiatry. Sauerbruch, at the time dean in Munich and already acquainted with Bonhoeffer from his time as Mikulicz's assistant in Breslau, urged him to come. But the entire family was so settled in Berlin that Bonhoeffer abandoned the idea.

Thus Dietrich Bonhoeffer, like his brothers and sisters, grew up to be a citizen of Berlin, despite the Swabian, Thuringian, and Silesian influences. His eventful life cannot be considered apart from this background. All the other places that were important to him in the course of his life—Breslau, Tübingen, Barcelona, New York, London, or Finkenwalde—certainly influenced him. The decisive influence, however, was Berlin and its complex diversity: the imperial and republican city that slowly succumbed to Nazism; the liberal and ecclesiastical, the conservative and the cosmopolitan Berlin, with its academic and working-class sectors, its concert halls and museums; the Berlin of street brawls and political plots. "I believe that at the moment this is perhaps intellectually the liveliest city in the world, and we have reached the right age to enjoy it," the much-traveled Klaus Bonhoeffer wrote in 1928 to his friend and brother-in-law Hans von Dohnanyi. Dietrich Bonhoeffer was neither born in Berlin nor did he die there, but it was the scene of all the important turning points in his thought and actions. From the beginning to the end of his career, the ideas that drew recognition and conflict developed here. In Berlin he enjoyed all the privileges of his sphere of life, and it was there that he eventually risked life and limb for their sake.

Brückenallee. The Bonhoeffers moved to their first Berlin home on Brückenallee, near the Bellevue rail station, around Easter 1912, when Dietrich was six. At that time, many professors from the Charité clinic lived in this district north of the zoo. His parents viewed the apartment, with its shapeless "Berlin room" and its tiny garden, as "somewhat dungeon-like" compared to the spaciousness in Breslau. For the children, however, it was all extremely delightful—the paved street for roller-skating, parallel and horizontal bars behind the house, and, above all, the view of Bellevue Castle in the neighboring park.

Until 1916, Babette Kalckreuth née Meyer lived only one street away. She had been the second wife of Dietrich's great-grandfather Stanislaus Count Kalckreuth and came from a Jewish family. His parents esteemed her temperament; they found her house, with its "accentuated simple lifestyle, conspicuously relaxing in contrast to the increasingly hurried, busy and socially lavish life."[29] Until the end of her life, she remained the center of a kind of society that had once set the tone in Berlin in the 1860s and 1870s; she had once moved in the same circle as the Bismarcks. The children occasionally saw Marie von Olfers at her home, who—at the age of ninety—gave them poems and little pictures, General von Wildenbruch, brother of the novelist Ernst von Wildenbruch, and the theologian Count Baudissin. Dietrich had a lovely brass railroad telescope in his room that Aunt Babette Kalckreuth had once received as a gift from the physicist and physiologist Hermann von Helmholtz.

The country house in Wölfelsgrund was sold because it was now too far away. In 1913 the Bonhoeffers bought a former forester's lodge, more accessible from Berlin, located at the edge of the woods in Friedrichsbrunn, in the eastern Harz Mountains. It would have been hard to imagine a more delightful refuge during the war years, and during the Second World War it was an ideal refuge for the family, now enlarged by many grandchildren, and their friends. To Dietrich, Friedrichsbrunn became what Wölfelsgrund had been to his elder brothers. In 1944 he wrote from Tegel prison:

> In my imagination I live a good deal in nature, in the glades near Friedrichsbrunn, or on the slopes from which one can look beyond Treseburg to the Brocken. I lie on my back in the grass, watch the clouds sailing in the breeze across the blue sky, and listen to the rustling of the woods. It's remarkable how greatly these memories of childhood affect one's whole outlook; it would seem to me impossible and unnatural for us to have lived either up in the mountains or by the sea. It is the hills of central Germany, the Harz, the Thuringian forest, the Weser mountains, that to me represent nature, that belong to me and have fashioned me.[30]

With the move to Berlin, the primary change in the life of the twins was the beginning of their formal schooling. Their mother no longer did all the teaching herself; Käthe Horn, the sister of the governess Maria Horn, was the twins' teacher during the first year. In the autumn of 1913 Dietrich, like his brothers, went to the Friedrich Werder Gymnasium. Despite the scientific bent of their father and the older boys, as a matter of course all the children, including Christine, attended schools with a strong humanities curriculum.

Dietrich had shown occasional signs of nervousness and shyness earlier, and was initially quite unhappy on his way to school, but this soon changed. He was put in the eighth form, and found the work child's play. In his 1915 New Year's diary his father wrote: "Dietrich does his work naturally and tidily. He likes fighting, and does a great deal of it."

Soon there was no doubt that Dietrich did not share his elder brothers' scientific inclinations; he preferred thrilling books and made unusual progress in music. Not that his brothers and sisters were unmusical; Klaus later played the cello with great sensitivity, and none of his brothers or sisters ever wanted to miss the family musical evenings. But Dietrich made such musical and technical progress at the piano that for a time both he and his parents thought he might become a professional musician.

He first experienced the attractions of more challenging house musical ensembles at the home of a family friend, a dermatologist named Neisser, whose home was a center of musical life in Breslau. Dietrich was playing Mozart sonatas at the age of ten, and at the age of eleven he wrote his grandmother in Tübingen that he had been deeply affected by a performance of the Ninth Symphony conducted by Nikisch. The time came when he tried composing his own songs. When he was in the fifth form he composed a trio on Schubert's song, "*Gute Ruh*," to perform for his parents with Klaus and Sabine. He wrote a cantata on the sixth verse of Psalm 42, "My soul is cast down within me," on which he liked to preach so much in later years. On Saturday evenings he skillfully accompanied his mother and his sister Ursula, who had a good voice, in songs by Schubert, Schumann, Brahms, and Hugo Wolf. Later he could never be thrown off by unevenness on the part of a singer. He had grown accustomed at an early age to performing without shyness or embarrassment. At age seventeen, he accompanied his sister on the lute while she sang folk songs at family and other parties.

Thus in his boyhood and youth it was music that gave him a special position at school and among his fellow students. His brothers and sisters allowed him this as well. Only when he came home from a school sports meet with the victor's laurel wreath around his shoulders did he have to put up with the taunts of his big brothers.

The War. Dietrich was eight and a half when the First World War broke out. In his memoirs, Karl Bonhoeffer recalled the impressions of those days:

> We did not really believe that there was going to be a war, even though the encirclement by the Triple Entente was perceived with alarm. All the same, I remember getting the uneasy feeling, at a social gathering with some staff officers in the winter of 1913–1914, that the possibility of an early armed clash must be taken into account. But on the whole people comforted themselves with the assurance that the Kaiser, despite his tendency toward magniloquence and his occasional rhetorical *faux pas* about shining armor and that sort of thing, was undoubtedly a lover of peace at heart, and with the superficial hope that international economic interests with their count-

less interconnections would suffice to prevent an armed conflict. . . . One particular memory of those uneasy days that remains in my mind is the evening of the day the British declared war, when we were with the three boys on the Boulevard Unter den Linden. The enthusiasm of the previous days, of the crowds in the streets in front of the castle and the government buildings, had succumbed to a gloomy silence, which made the scene extraordinarily oppressive.[31]

For the younger children the outbreak of war was a time of great excitement. At the end of July they were hurriedly brought home after a month's holiday in glorious weather in Friedrichsbrunn. When one of the girls dashed into the house shouting: "Hurrah, there's a war," her face was slapped. The first German successes filled Dietrich with boyish enthusiasm. When he was nine he wrote his parents from Friedrichsbrunn asking them to send him all the newspaper cuttings with news from the front; he had learned from his big brothers and at school how to stick colored pins into a map showing the advance of the front line.

When food shortages began, his father praised Dietrich's unexpected skill as a "messenger and food scout." He knew the black market prices of all the delicacies, and his familiarity with the lines outside the shops enabled him to direct the servants to the best places. His letters to his grandmother and his parents when they were away were full of information about things like the plums he tracked down somewhere in Halensee, the mushrooms he had dried in Friedrichsbrunn, the goats kept by the family and the difficulty of feeding them on kitchen scraps, and gleaning the harvest on the farm at Uncle Hans von Hase's parsonage. When the holidays came, the nannygoat was taken in the luggage van to Friedrichsbrunn to ensure the children's milk supply. The great treat on his birthday was to have an egg beaten up in sugar all to himself. He spent all his pocket money buying himself a hen. During this time, his generous attitude toward money was already developing. When he discovered one day that his father sent bills to his patients, he burst into tears, because one shouldn't take money from the sick.

Gradually, however, the war began to have a grim impact on the Bonhoeffer family. In 1914 their Uncle Otto Bonhoeffer in Düsseldorf and their mother's sister, Aunt Hanna Countess von der Goltz, received bad news, and the children heard of cousins killed or severely wounded in action. As the war dragged on, the older brothers, who were still in school, approached military age. At the end of 1916 faint hopes clung to the possibility of peace. The New Year's diary reads:

Today we are expecting the reply of the Entente, no doubt a rejection. People view the peace feeler of America, which we have joined, with distrust, because we fear America's interference in peace negotiations because of the close English-American ties. . . . It's hard to form one's own opinion, given the censored press, and what happens politically is so frequently just poorly organized necessity that we are very disturbed. The constant appeal to the trust of [the Kaiser's] subjects, which only allows for retrospective observations, offers nothing very edifying.

In 1917 Karl-Friedrich and Walter were called up. Because of their numerous contacts, the Bonhoeffers could have influenced the course of their sons' military career to some extent, but the boys insisted on enlisting in the infantry, where the need was greatest. They joined the Fifth Regiment of Guards at Spandau, with no intention of becoming officers. With a heavy heart their parents let them do so; they did not want "to try to play Providence."

After a short period of training, they were sent to the front. Karl-Friedrich, who had been about to go to the university, took his physics textbook along in his knapsack. Walter had passed his school graduation examinations with a special distinction in German. On his last evening at home before his unit left for the front, his eleven-year-old brother Dietrich sang a rendition he had composed of "*Nun zu guter Letzt geben wir dir jetzt auf die Wandrung das Geleite*" ("Now, at the last, we say Godspeed on your journey"). "The next day we saw Walter off at the station. When the train started moving, my mother ran alongside calling out to Walter: 'It's only space that separates us,' and for a long time these words moved us deeply."[32]

Walter was wounded in the advance on 23 April 1918. He dictated his last letter in the field hospital three hours before his death on 28 April:

Today I had the second operation, which was less pleasant, because deeper fragments had to be removed. Also, afterwards I had to be given two camphor injections—at intervals, of course—but I hope that is the end of the matter. My technique of not thinking about pain had to serve here too. But there are more interesting things in the world at present than my wound. Mount Kemmel and its possible consequences, and today's news of the taking of Ypres, give us great cause for hope. I dare not think about my poor regiment, so severely did it suffer in the last few days. How are things going with the other officer cadets? I think of you with longing, my dears, every minute of the long days and nights. From so far away, your Walter.

His death seemed to break his mother's spirit. She spent weeks in bed at the home of the Schönes next door. The following Christmas the eldest sister, Ursula, sent the youngest children's wishes to their grandmother in Tübingen; their mother wasn't capable of it. For the next ten years, there were no entries in their father's New Year's diary.

Karl-Friedrich was wounded in the October battles of 1918, but his injuries proved to be slight. Seventeen-year-old Klaus was also called up and, after a brief period of training, served as an orderly at General Headquarters in Spa. Thus he was an eyewitness when Hindenburg, "as rigid as a statue both in countenance and bearing,"[33] left the conference room where he had spoken for the last time with the Kaiser before the latter fled the country.

The death of his brother Walter and his mother's desperate grief left an indelible mark on the child Dietrich Bonhoeffer. At his confirmation three years later, she gave him the Bible that Walter had received at his confirmation in 1914. Bonhoeffer used it throughout his life for his personal meditations and in worship. The figure of his brother and the way in which he died were in Dietrich's mind years later, when he talked to his students about the problem of preaching reverently on Memorial Day, even though he personally had long since turned to thoughts of pacifism.[34]

Wangenheimstrasse. At the time of Walter's death, the family already lived at 14 Wangenheimstrasse in the Grunewald district. In March 1916 they had moved there to a large house, not far from the Halensee rail station, where they remained until 1935. Because of the ever-increasing food shortage they grew vegetables in the garden, but the younger children were also able to use it for playing games they had been unable to play except in the garden at their Uncle Hans von Hase's rectory—an idyllic spot that had lost none of its appeal, as a letter from twelve-year-old Dietrich to his cousin shows:

Dear Hans-Christoph!
I've been waiting all day for a letter from you and nothing comes. Why don't you write? Did you write and the letter didn't arrive? I can't come otherwise. No one says anything anymore about my visiting you, it's always just the girls. So write as often as you can!

I would find it terribly sad if I couldn't come, because then nothing would come of our wonderful plans. And that would really be too bad! . . .

We're building a subterranean cave and passageway. It runs from one side of the arbor to the cave. It's there so that, in case we fight with Klaus again, we can either bring help from the cave or attack the enemy from behind. We're building a wall in front of the cave and a pit, and a very deep hole. Then when someone falls in, we can drag him into the hole. Please say hello to Uncle Hans, Aunt Elisabeth and the cousins. Don't forget to write. Many greetings from your Dietrich.[35]

Grunewald developed into a neighborhood of professors, and a number of Karl Bonhoeffer's friends and colleagues lived there, including the physician His, Planck, Hildebrand, and the anatomist Hertwig, a pupil of Ernst Haeckel.

The historian Hans Delbrück lived only a few doors away, and every Wednesday evening a distinguished company gathered at his house, including Adolf von Harnack, Troeltsch, Meinecke, and Herkner. Theodor Heuss, the future president of the Federal Republic, also put in an occasional appearance, as did Dietrich's future school rector Vilmar, director of the Grunewald Gymnasium. During the war, these circles turned against the too-broad peace goals and unrealistic acquisitiveness of most Germans. They attacked the nationalist colleagues who followed the historian Dietrich Schaefer, Gustav Roethe, Ulrich Wilamowitz, and included Reinhold Seeberg. The Bonhoeffer children were not part of these Wednesday gatherings, but its atmosphere and direction had an effect. Klaus became a close friend of Justus Delbrück, who was his age, and later married his sister Emmi. In 1944, Klaus Bonhoeffer and Delbrück were in the same prison.

Ernst von Harnack also ended up in this prison; he, too, knew the Bonhoeffers from their years on Wangenheimstrasse. The Harnacks lived on the other corner and were related to the Delbrücks. The Schönes lived across from them, in a large estate built by Messel; they were related to Bonhoeffer's mother through the Härtels. An intense relationship developed between grandmother Bonhoeffer and the elderly Helene Schöne. Richard Schöne was general director of the Berlin museums; his circles included Theodore Mommsen and Heinrich von Treitschke. His daughter Johanna sculpted a bust of Walter for the Bonhoeffers. The incentive for Klaus and Dietrich to explore the treasures of Berlin's museums came primarily from this home.

Their new school resulted in new friendships, such as with the von Dohnanyi children. Confirmation classes led to Gerhard Leibholz's joining the group, which at first consisted of Klaus Bonhoeffer, Justus Delbrück, and Hans von Dohnanyi. Dietrich was of course initially too young to join the trio, but it was not long before he was old enough to do so. Notwithstanding his overriding passion for theology, this circle of friends (later related through marriage) kept him in lively contact with other intellectual fields.

Dietrich changed schools only as a sixth-grader, around Easter 1919. The Grunewald Gymnasium for which he left the Friedrich Werder school was somewhat exclusive. Its director, a grandnephew of the controversial Hessian theologian and literary historian A. F. C. Vilmar, taught German and history. Politically a proponent of the People's Party, Vilmar seemed almost leftist compared to Grunewald's conservative church circles and its nationalistic pastor, Hermann Priebe. The Bonhoeffer children particularly esteemed the excellent teacher and Hellenist Dr. Walther Kranz[36] and maintained contact with him up to the time of his persecution by the National Socialists. Dietrich wrote the elective portion of his graduation examination for him.

Revolution. On the morning of 9 November 1918 Karl Bonhoeffer as usual walked from the Lehrter station down the Invalidenstrasse to the Charité clinic. He described the occasion in his memoirs as follows:

> Raggedly marching parties of troops, mingled with civilians carrying posters with the inscription "Don't shoot"; pale, famished-looking creatures covered with sweat, gesticulating excitedly and pleading with the soldiers and grabbing rifles from their hands, in so far as they put up any resistance. On the sidewalk there were other figures who remained aloof from all this and perhaps hurried to their places of work more quickly than usual. No shots were fired. At my clinic the porter, wearing a red rosette, stood facing me on the steps, obviously intending to bar the way to my room, or at any rate to discuss the matter. As I took no further notice of him, but walked past him with the usual greeting and went to my room, he took no further action.[37]

Two months later Dietrich, now nearly thirteen years old, wrote to his grandmother in Tübingen about the fighting between government troops and Spartakists after the latter had made two night attacks on the Halensee station:

> Early today we heard gunfire. There are some more bangs going on now. Karl-Friedrich has at last been discharged from the Charité. He would like to be part of this somehow, but mama and papa do not yet agree. At present, thank heaven, the government troops are getting the better of it. Our holidays have been extended to 17 January. Either because of the unrest or because of the coal shortage.[38]

Karl-Friedrich Bonhoeffer supported the Social Democrat government that came to power as a result of the November revolution. He had become a socialist at the front, and this had already led to conflicts with other branches of the family outside Berlin. His father let him go his own way; still, his politics made him something of an outsider in the Wangenheimstrasse home. Klaus earnestly set about reading Karl Marx's *Das Kapital*, but he and his friends ended up in the German People's Party and the Democratic

Party; Gustav Stresemann and Heinrich Brüning embodied their political hopes. Thus it was Klaus, more than Karl-Friedrich, who represented the family's bourgeois political outlook at that time.

The November revolution and the period that followed coincided with the awakening of Dietrich Bonhoeffer's youthful interest in politics. On 10 February 1919 he predicted to his grandmother in Tübingen that now "Schneidermann is prime minister and Ebert should become provisional president."[39] In 1919 national passions flared up again when the Allied peace terms were published. "What do you think of the peace terms?" he anxiously asked his parents:

> I hardly believe they can be accepted in this form, since then the demonstrations would develop into a general movement. True, one must take into account the possibility that the enemy might say that we should get no food supplies until we accepted them. Giving up the Saar and Upper Silesia would mean complete economic collapse. But getting no food supplies would have the same effect. I hope Ebert will hold a plebiscite, so that he will not have to bear the whole responsibility himself.[40]

The National Assembly faced the dilemma of having to build a new Germany, while the new government it had established faced the prospect of a burden that was still unknown but certainly very heavy, once the amount of war debts and reparations was set. Large sections of the population were only waiting for the new government to fail. Putsches of left-wing and right-wing extremists flared up. But these signs of disintegration strengthened the feeling in some circles that something must be done to establish centers of order. Various renewal movements arose at both the national and international levels. The Youth Movement reappeared on the scene, partly with very ambiguous aims and motivations. Caught up in this wave, thirteen-year-old Dietrich joined the Boy Scouts.

Youth Movement. This was his only active association with the German Youth movement, though it is questionable whether the Scouts should be considered part of it, since the Scout movement was not led by the young but by their elders, often schoolmasters. This had been rejected by the prewar leaders of the Youth movement, the protesters of *Hohen Meissner* (a mass youth festival held in October 1913 in the Hessian mountains), who believed on principle in self-determination by the young. The Bonhoeffers had no contact with this early period of the German Youth movement.

The second, postwar wave of the Youth movement took the form of a "covenanted organization." The German branch of the Scouts, although it was marginal, formally joined this youth federation within the German Youth movement in 1919, and was not immune from its influence and style.

With some of his schoolfellows, Dietrich Bonhoeffer joined the Scouts in the summer of 1919, and at first he rather liked it. "On Sunday mornings we always drill, have mock battles and that sort of thing. It is always very nice."[41] It had not yet occurred to him that Sunday morning was the time to go to church. In the winter he was very useful to the Scouts as a musician. He played Schubert and arranged Haydn trios for their concerts.

But during the course of 1920 he gave them up. There seems to have been no particular reason; he may have decided that the marching and drilling were a waste of time. The general radicalization of the movement may have affected his own unit. His older brothers' and sisters' dislike of war games certainly played a part. In any case, the Scouts did not hold him.

Even later, when a number of Protestant youth groups offered a variety of activities, Bonhoeffer joined none of them; and no one in the family even considered attending the tenth anniversary of the *Hohen Meissner* festival, celebrated on the mountain in 1923 by numerous organizations.

In general, the Bonhoeffer children rejected the Youth movement that had brought so many diverse directions together. In some ways, however, it did have an influence on them. The style of such organizations—the pennants, badges, romanticized camps, and artificial customs—were all objects of derision. They did not tolerate its animosity toward rationalism, its eccentric behaviors and costumes; nor were they drawn to its demonstrative protest against "the petit bourgeoisie and its hypocritical narrowmindedness." Intergenerational problems, a focal complaint of the Youth movement, were not an issue in this family. Their excess energies were constantly diverted into new and attractive challenges, so that this kind of emotion didn't build up and eventually lead to an explosion. With its industriousness, rationality, and warmth, their parents' home immunized the Bonhoeffer children against those aspects of the Youth movement.

At the same time, they did take up some of the fashions of that movement. After the war, they began to "take to the road," wandering through northern and central Germany on foot or bicycle. Their musical repertoire now included songs from the *Zupfgeigenhansl*, a popular 1908 anthology of folk songs. Dietrich played the lute and sang the camping song "On the purest spring morning" and Ricarda Huch's song about the Thirty Years War, "Listen child listen, how the storm wind blows."[42]

Of the Bonhoeffer brothers, Dietrich, as the youngest, was the one most drawn to the Youth movement. His episode in the Boy Scouts was a first attempt to move beyond the sphere of family and school, and to discover his own areas of experience not shared by his brothers and sisters. Many of his classmates did the same, and he did not want to be different from them in everything. In later years he showed a knowledge and appreciation of certain aspects of the Youth movement. "The aim," he said in a lecture to his congregation in Barcelona in 1929, "is to attack a cultural environment that has lost its inner truth, to loosen the shackles of truth. And this ensures the deeply moral nature of the movement, because the consequence otherwise would be complete skepticism."[43] In the years 1930–1931 he even proclaimed his solidarity with a German organization dedicated to international peace—at a time when nationalist slogans and the "goose-stepping ranks" had begun to drown out all else. In America, he spoke almost like the representative of a pacifist community.[44] In his 1933 radio address, he revealed that he was familiar with the other side, too, when he warned against the dangerously falsified concept of leadership.[45]

Despite these influences and his exploration of the Youth movement and its values, it would be too much to say that these values were ever of central importance to him. His interest in theology soon obscured his intermezzo with the Boy Scouts and totally absorbed him.

During his final years in school, there is increasing evidence of his opposition to the right-wing radicalism that was becoming more and more obstreperous. When he left for his last school holiday, he wrote to his parents that on the train he found himself sitting opposite "a man wearing a swastika" and spent the whole time arguing with him. The man "was really quite bigoted and right-wing."[46]

A few days before, on 24 June 1922, Walther Rathenau had been assassinated. Bonhoeffer heard the shots from his classroom on Königsallee. As one of his classmates reports:

> I particularly remember Bonhoeffer on the day of Rathenau's murder. The average age in our class in the Grunewald high school was seventeen, but he and G.S., who ended by committing suicide in exile, were only sixteen. I remember the shots we heard during the lesson, and then, on the playground during the break, we heard what had happened. . . . I still recall my friend Bonhoeffer's passionate indignation, his deep and spontaneous anger. . . . I remember his asking what would become of Germany if its best leaders were killed. I remember it because I was surprised at the time that someone could know so exactly where he stood.[47]

A niece of Rathenau, Ursula Andreae, who, like Bonhoeffer, was interested in theology and later attended Harnack's seminar with him, attended the same class, which included a number of children from prominent, primarily Jewish families, including the daughter of Judge Weigert and Marion Winter, who later became Countess (Peter) Yorck.

The political principles that prevailed in these circles were vividly expressed in a letter Klaus wrote to Hans von Dohnanyi in May 1922:

> I have now got to know them [i.e., his fellow students] politically, but when I think about it I feel sick. . . . A few days ago there was a meeting where Professor Goetz of Leipzig spoke on "The Student in the New Age." He spoke very well indeed, completely free of personal or party [animosities], *but* on the basis of democratic principles. The students bawled at him, stamped their feet, and shouted personal insults. . . . the historian Haller didn't exactly distinguish himself when he tactlessly abused his colleague, giving a vile exhibition of demagogy that made the student mob shout with jubilation. My indignation must have been very plain. In any event, I got involved in an argument with a man sitting behind me, an idiotic former lieutenant wearing a monocle. . . . It is depressing to see the people on whom one relies for the future . . . arguing only with their eyes perpetually turned back to 1870–1871, and even that only in an empty pose. . . . Hans, only think of the trouble we shall have later with these people. If only I were a bit older!

The Decision to Become a Theologian

When we turn to the motives and origins of Bonhoeffer's choice of career, it is hard to find any answer that is not somewhat speculative. Nowhere did Bonhoeffer offer an autobiographical account of his decision. But perhaps this omission itself points to something central: his belief that the roots of one's innermost vocation should remain a secret. Bonhoeffer sensed that the curiosity to make oneself sure of something was self-destructive. So we must accept a certain amount of uncertainty when we search for the decisive factors here.

Christian Life and the Church. The Bonhoeffers were not churchgoers in the sense that they were active members and participated in the life of a congregation. The children were not sent to church, and the family did not attend church even on the major holidays. For religious ceremonies within the family, the parish minister was bypassed in favor of relatives, first Dietrich's grandfather and then his maternal uncle, Hans von Hase. One of the children's favorite games was to have a "home christening." The family, however, had no desire to shirk the bourgeois German church customs, and the children were sent to confirmation class. Their mother tried to make the children take this instruction seriously, which was not easy, given the strange stories the children circulated about the confirmation classes.

The family, including Dietrich's mother, had its own direct relationship with the Bible and the history and traditions of the church, without feeling a need for any ecclesiastical guidance; thus, any direct connection to the institutional church seemed unnecessary. No church dignitary or minister seems to have played a role in the Bonhoeffers' social relationships at that time. Among Dietrich's early friends there were no families with church connections, with the single exception of his cousin Hans-Christoph, with whom he struck up a friendship during the occasional holidays spent at the rectory of his Uncle von Hase. The Berlin-Brandenburg church where Bonhoeffer grew up makes its first appearance in his life during the latter part of his student days. The impulse to become a theologian for the sake of the real church belonged to a later period.

Although the Bonhoeffers could not be described as churchgoers, it would be wrong to describe them as non-Christian. The opposite was true, at the very least for Dietrich's mother. When she was young she had spent months in Herrnhut, and had adopted the ideals of the Moravian Brethren with youthful enthusiasm. After her marriage, however, these things remained below the surface. She would never have tolerated an oppressively devout atmosphere. When Käthe Horn took over the instruction of the twins Dietrich and Sabine, their mother continued their religion lessons herself, telling the children biblical stories from memory and using Schnorr von Carolsfeld's illustrated Bible. Later when Dietrich began teaching religion himself, he simply followed his mother's example. Only much later did he see that the over-beautification of these illustrations ran the risk of implanting dangerous preconceptions about the biblical stories in the childish mind. Maria Horn, the beloved family governess from 1906 to 1923, was an adherent of the Moravian Brethren, but she did not have much religious influence over the children. Because of her attractive and imperturbable personality she was like a member of the family, but it was her personality that was appreciated; expressions of her piety were merely tolerated. As far as the latter were concerned, she certainly would not have done anything without the parents' knowledge and consent. The children knew exactly where they stood with her. Klaus evaded the ban on reading in bed by concealing an exciting book inside the black covers of the Bible, at the sight of which Fräulein Horn silently crept away, leaving the light on.

Domestic religious customs were observed, and were intended to mean something to those who practiced them. One of the children said the grace before meals. Evening prayers were said in a darkened room, to discourage anyone from posing or watching the behavior of others. When they were young the children's prayer was "*Müde bin ich, geh zur Ruh*," and later they said the Lord's Prayer and sang a hymn of their own choice, thus acquiring a store of words and music that remained indelible in their memories. On Christmas Eve their mother read the Christmas story from St. Luke, and New Year's Eve ended with Psalm 90 and Paul Gerhardt's New Year's hymn "*Nun lasst uns gehn und treten*." Their father was always present on these occasions, as usual setting an example of how the feelings of others should be shared and respected, although everyone knew that this was their mother's affair. There was no conflict in this respect, as both parents rejected any kind of exaggerated or forced religion, and doubts and scruples were respected when expressed without offensive cynicism. Their father occasionally said, "I understand nothing of that," in a tone of condescending humor, but he always betrayed a trace of his awareness of the inadequacy of human reason—and thus revealed a somewhat abashed solidarity.

The Christian nature of this household, then, could be sensed more under the surface or behind the scenes. The predominant atmosphere was one of tolerant empiricism. This was encouraged by the friendships and interests of the older brothers, and their father's critical and no-nonsense attitude.

Choice of Profession. Bonhoeffer decided to be a minister and theologian when he was a boy, and he never seems to have wavered in this ambition.

At home he made no bones about it. Even when his brothers and sisters refused to take him seriously, he did not let it disconcert him. When he was about fourteen, for instance, they tried to convince him that he was taking the path of least resistance, and that the church to which he proposed to devote himself was a poor, feeble, boring, petty, and bourgeois institution, but he confidently replied: "In that case I shall reform it!"

His relatives were already taking his ambitions seriously. On his fourteenth birthday his uncle and godfather Hans von Hase wrote him a letter in which he said: "If your path should lead you towards theology . . . ," and went on to give details of what would be involved. Confirmation lessons with Pastor Hermann Priebe at the church in Grunewald followed.[48] Dietrich never referred to these confirmation classes later, except for mentioning once that it was there he had become friends with Hans von Haeften, one of the coconspirators of the 20 July 1944 plot. He sometimes found the lessons interesting, but was bored by the banalities. At the time of his confirmation he had started reading the Bible for himself, and did not hide an exciting novel between the black covers.

Before the final choice was made, his parents wanted to make sure that his true vocation was not music, and they arranged for him to play for the pianist Leonid Kreuzer, a virtuoso of the Vienna school. The outcome was not decisive; like his parents, Dietrich was uncertain. At the beginning of his eighth school year, he casually announced that he had chosen Hebrew as his elective, and the die was cast. He was fifteen years old at the time. In March 1921, when he and Klaus were invited to a party at their friends the Gilberts, he declined because Lent had begun. This made an impression on his friends, who had not previously come across such a reason for refusing an invitation. He now sometimes went to church, occasionally accompanied by his mother.

Once a decision had been made, it was respected in the family. Only many years later did his father reveal what he thought of Dietrich's choice:

> At the time you decided to devote yourself to theology I sometimes thought to myself that a quiet, uneventful minister's life, as I knew it from my Swabian uncles and as Mörike describes it, would really almost be a pity for you. As far as uneventfulness is concerned, I was greatly mistaken. That such a crisis would be possible in the realm of the church seemed out of the question to me, coming from my scientific background.[49]

Inner Motivations. In trying to uncover the inner motivations for Bonhoeffer's choice of career, some possibilities can be excluded from the outset. The impulse did not come from the regional church or local congregation, nor from his confirmation lessons. Nor did it come from hero worship of any great religious personality. It was characteristic that during his life he developed no enthusiasm for outstanding personalities—except, perhaps, in his encounter with Karl Barth, which occurred much later.

At the root of his choice was a basic drive toward independence. This did not exclude his insatiable appetite for all kinds of different knowledge, but the driving force in his life was the need for unchallenged self-realization. The presence of theologians among his forebears made his choice of career not that unusual; while this no doubt played a part, it was hardly a decisive factor. His isolation among his brothers and sisters was probably of far greater importance; it may have nourished his urge to surpass them all. With some exaggeration, it might be said that because he was lonely he became a theologian, and because he became a theologian he was lonely.

The events of the final years of the war had a deep effect on him. His early memories of the Breslau cemetery gained a personal immediacy through the loss of his brother and how his mother had succumbed to her grief. His childish spirit responded with a fervent longing for the life beyond, and a fervent—though unarticulated—wish to convey his unqualified faith in eternity to the others. Two sources document this. The first was a recollection by his twin sister:

> . . . we heard of the deaths of our grown-up cousins and the fathers of our schoolmates. So, after the evening prayers and singing . . . we lay awake a long time and tried to imagine what eternal life and being dead were like. We endeavored every evening to get a little nearer to eternity by concentrating on the word "eternity" and excluding any other thought. It seemed very long and gruesome, and after some time of intense concentration we often felt dizzy. For a long time we clung to this self-imposed exercise. We were very attached to one another and each wanted to be the last to say good night to the other; this went on endlessly and often we struggled out of our sleep to do so. I believed that this ritual saved Dietrich from being "devoured" by Satan. We twins kept all this absolutely secret . . .
>
> Of the hymns we learned, Dietrich especially liked: "Where does the soul find its home, its rest," "Oh, wait, my soul," "Jesus, still lead on," and "Let me go. . . ." Dietrich called them "red" hymns. There were also "black" hymns like "Praise to the Lord" and "Now thank we all our God." This too was a secret language between us. . . . When the lights were extinguished the phosphorescent gleam of our glowing crosses comforted us, though their shape sometimes made us uneasy. When at the age of twelve Dietrich got a room of his own, we arranged that he should drum on the wall at night as a sign that Susi and I should "think of God." These admonitory bangs happened regularly and became a habit, until Dietrich noticed that they sometimes roused us from our sleep; then he stopped them.[50]

The other document is an untitled sheet of paper that must be attributed to 1932, the period of upheaval in his theological and inner life. It is impossible to establish on what occasion or for whom he wrote this fragment about the incursion of vanity into more serious self-contemplation, but it is evidence of his lifelong preoccupation with whether and how he would face up to death.[51] What he wrote was this:

> He liked thinking about death. Even in his boyhood he had enjoyed imagining himself on his deathbed, surrounded by all those who loved him, speaking his last words to them. Secretly he had often thought about what he would say at that moment. To him death was neither grievous nor alien.

He would have liked them all to see and understand that to a believer in God dying was not hard, but a glorious thing. In the evening, when he went to bed overtired, he sometimes thought that it was going to happen. A slight sense of dizziness often alarmed him so much that he furiously bit his tongue, to make sure that he was alive and felt pain. Then in his innocence he cried out to God, asking to be granted a deferment. These experiences confused him to some extent. For obviously he did not want to die, he was a coward; his theatrical ideas disgusted him. And yet in moments of strength he often prayed that God might after all release him, for he was ready to die; it was only his animal nature that again and again made him contemptible in his own eyes, that led him astray from himself.

Then one day he had a grotesque idea. He believed himself to be suffering from the only incurable illness that existed, namely a crazy and irremediable fear of death. The thought that he would really have to die one day had such a grip on him that he faced this inevitable prospect with speechless fear. And there was no one who could free him from this illness, because in reality it was no illness, but the most natural and obvious thing in the world, because it was the most inevitable. He saw himself going from one person to another, pleading and appealing for help. Doctors shook their heads and could do nothing for him. His illness was that he saw reality for what it was, it was incurable. He could tolerate the thought for only a few moments. From that day on he buried inside himself something about which for a long time he did not speak or think again. His favorite subject for discussion and for his imagination had suddenly acquired a bitter taste. He spoke no more about fine, devout death, and forgot about it.[52]

This fragment touches on the early influences on his decision to study theology, although in Kierkegaardian fashion it was written down at a much later stage. But the choice involved its own special temptations.

Another fragment, dating from practically the same period, sadly describes the theologian's despair at the revelation of the diabolical hollowness of his devoutness, after examining its origins, and it declares that the things for which others admire him are those most repugnant to himself. The fragment as written certainly does not belong to his youth, but to the period when he was reflecting on religiosity originating from sin, as he did for his 1932 lecture "Creation and Fall." But every line of the fragment betrays its close connection with the period of his life with which we are now dealing. One can sense the presence of his Greek teacher, Walther Kranz. Dietrich Bonhoeffer became acquainted early with two companions whom he feared, *tristitia* and *accidie*.[53] Even as a boy, despite his reputation for sociability and even-temperedness, he might suddenly withdraw from a lively conversation into solitude. In this piece of writing from 1932, Bonhoeffer seemed to acknowledge how strongly his ambition had influenced his early decision to become a theologian. His eventual discovery that being a Christian consists of liberation from reflecting about one's own beginnings was all the more significant. The 1932 fragment reads:

> One day in the first form, when the master asked him what he wanted to study, he quietly answered "theology," and flushed. The word slipped out so quickly that he did not even stand up; having the teacher's gaze and that of the whole class directed at him personally and not at his work, and being suddenly called upon to speak out like this, gave him such conflicting feelings of vanity and humility that the interruption of ordinary class conduct seemed an appropriate expression of the consternation caused by the question and the answer. The master obviously thought so too, for he rested his gaze on him for only a moment longer than usual, and then quickly and amiably released him. He was nearly as disconcerted as his pupil. "In that case you have more surprises coming," he said, speaking just as quietly.
>
> Actually the question "how long?" had been on his lips, but, as if that would have touched on the secret of his own early study of theology, passionately begun and then quickly abandoned, and also because he felt displeased with himself at having nothing better to say to a boy whom he had known and liked for a long time, he grew embarrassed, cleared his throat, and went back to the Greek text which was the subject of the lesson.
>
> The boy absorbed that brief moment deep into himself. Something extraordinary had happened, and he deeply enjoyed this and, at the same time, felt ashamed. Now they all knew. Now they had to hear it, hear it in silence, now he had told them all, now he was faced with the riddle of his life, now he stood solemnly in the presence of his God, in the presence of his class, now he was the center of attention. . . . Did he look as he had wanted to look, serious and determined? He wondered briefly whether the part in his dark blond hair effectively emphasized the impression of his sincere conviction, and he was filled with an unusual sense of well-being at the thought, though he immediately drove it away by visualizing the greatness of his confession and his task. Nor did it escape him in this moment of complete awareness that his teacher had been somewhat embarrassed by him and, at the same time, had looked at him with pleasure and approval. The moment swelled into endless pleasure, the classroom expanded into the infinite, he stood in the center of the world as the herald and teacher of his knowledge and his ideals, now they all had to listen to him in silence, and the blessing of the Eternal rested on his words and on his parted dark blond head. And again he felt ashamed. For he knew about his pitiful vanity. How often he had tried to master it. But it always crept back, and now it spoiled even the pleasure of this moment. Oh, how well he knew himself at the age of seventeen, he knew all about himself and his weaknesses, and

he also knew that he knew himself well, and in the turmoil of his knowledge his deep vanity again forced its way into his soul and alarmed him.

It had made a tremendous impression on him when he had read in Schiller that man needed only to rid himself of a few small weaknesses to be like the gods. Since then he had been on the watch. It occurred to him that there was no doubt that he would emerge from this struggle as the hero from this struggle, he had just made a solemn vow to do so. Now the path that he had known he must follow since the age of fourteen was clearly marked out for him. But what if he failed, what if the struggle proved vain, what if he was not strong enough to see it through. . . .

The words "You have more surprises coming" suddenly rang in his ears; surprises about what, what could happen, what did this voice mean? What was the meaning of the curious, mistrustful, bored, disappointed, mocking eyes of his classmates? Didn't they think him capable of it, did they not believe in the sincerity of his intentions, did they know something about him that he did not know himself?

Why are you all looking at me like that? Why are you embarrassed, sir, what sort of incomprehensible drivel are you mumbling? Look away from me, for heaven's sake, denounce me as a mendacious, conceited person who does not believe what he says, but don't keep so considerately silent, as if you understood me. Laugh aloud at me, make noise, noise, don't be so abominably dumb—it's intolerable. There is the throng, he stands in the midst of it and speaks, speaks, fervently, passionately, his features. . . . his dark blond hair, his ideal hopes—he corrects himself—a leaden silence lies over the throng, a dreadful, silent mockery. No, it cannot be, he is not the man they take him to be, he really is in earnest. They have no right to scorn me, they are unjust to me, unjust . . . all of you . . . he prays. . . . God, say yourself whether I am in earnest about you, destroy me now if I am lying, or punish them all; they are my enemies, and yours, they do not believe me, I know myself I am not good. But I know it myself—and you, God, know it too. . . . I do not need the others . . . I, I . . . I shall triumph. . . . do you see how I triumph, how they retreat, their consternation. . . . I am with you. . . . I am strong. . . . God, I am with you.

Do you hear me? Or do you not? To whom am I speaking? To myself, to you, or to those others here? Who is it that is speaking? My faith? My vanity. . . . God. . . . I want to study theology. Yes, I have said so, and they all heard it, there is no more retreat. I wish to, I wish to . . . but if . . .

And just as the commotion turns to something new, all he hears is the teacher's voice from a distance—no one else could have spoken in the meantime—: "Aren't you feeling well? You don't look well." He pulls himself together, stands up, and as usual translates the difficult Greek text without error. Somewhat confused but full of pride the teacher looks at the boy.[54]

Last Years at School. Toward the end of his seventh school year, the fourteen-year-old wrote to his parents:

> We have done something terribly funny. Our Greek teacher told us that we would soon have an examination to write. He gave us some vocabulary words for it. We said, we'll be able to get this done. He said, however, that we would never get it and we should only try. But I did find the words in the lexicon and told all the others in class. Our Greek teacher was away for several days, and let the Latin teacher give us the test. Somehow he heard from Justus that we had gotten the words. He told the entire faculty except for the Greek teacher. Thus we all did a good job, and he knows *nothing*. . . .
>
> Our director assigned us some very stupid essays again. . . . One is: what do the trees tell us. Of course he wants dreadful cliches. I'm letting Christel [his older sister, who began her biology studies soon thereafter] write it for me, very scientifically, about the anatomy and physiology of trees. And that's what the trees have to say to me.[55]

Bonhoeffer's youthful decision to become a theologian evidently did not in any way restrict his friendships and interests, as can easily happen to those who choose their career early. "Everyone who knew him at that time was impressed by his radiant nature; his high spirits knew no bounds."[56]

He had always read a great deal. As a boy, he was an active participant in a play Karl-Friedrich wrote based on Hauff's tale "The Cold Heart," and performed it with the aid of his brothers and sisters. Later, with friends, he staged a performance of Hofmannsthal's *The White Fan*. He read his first classics during the holidays in Friedrichsbrunn at the age of thirteen. In the upper forms at school he read the early works of Hermann Hesse. Above all, he discovered Ibsen, whose plays impressed him often in later years.

He had to defend himself against his brother Karl-Friedrich's skepticism, and this spurred him to grapple with epistemology at an early age; he worked hard at philosophy during his last years in school. In a working group in February 1921 he delivered a paper on Plotinus and the Emperor Julian, based on reading Ranke and his great-grandfather Karl August von Hase. In August 1922 he did another paper on the philosophical aspects of Euripides, based on Eduard Meyer's *History of Antiquity*. He read Schleiermacher's *On Religion: Speeches to Its Culture Despisers* while still in school. Through his brothers, he came across Friedrich Naumann's *Letters on Religion*, which he worked through very carefully. He was never able to forget Naumann's sober but deeply felt insight that Christianity could never get past its inherent contradiction: "In practice many are traders with their right hand and benefactors of the poor with their left. . . . All the biddings of the Gospel merely hover like distant, white clouds of aspiration over the real conduct of our time."[57] But Dietrich would not be satisfied with this discrepancy.

After he had read Tönnies's *Community and Society*, his brother Klaus and his friends drew his attention to Max Weber, whose brother Alfred had been a fellow student of Bonhoeffer's father and had introduced him to Max. The family's friendly relations with Alfred Weber never ended.

The available sources offer little evidence of modern theological reading in the period before Bonhoeffer's school graduation examinations. Among his books were the first two volumes of the historian Eduard Meyer's *Birth and Origins of Christianity*, published in 1921. Bonhoeffer already acquired them in 1921 and, although still a schoolboy, wrote his name in them, adding the word "theol." He did a great deal of work in these substantial volumes, but many of the annotations, in which he joined Adolf von Harnack and Heitmüller in criticizing Meyer, may date from his first year at the university. In any case, he went to the university with a considerable knowledge of the historical criticism and religious history of the New Testament. Karl Barth's *The Epistle to the Romans*, published in 1919, had not yet attracted wide attention. The religious instruction in Bonhoeffer's school had barely touched on the other important publications of 1921, Gogarten's *The Religious Decision* and Bultmann's *The History of the Synoptic Tradition*. Harnack's influence set the tone for the religious instruction in Bonhoeffer's school, although Bonhoeffer was not yet discernably attracted to it. Harnack's famous public letters to (or against) Barth in *Christliche Welt* were discussed only after 1923. Gunther Dehn, the socialist pastor in Berlin-Moabit who was close to Barth, was still relatively unknown in Grunewald.[58] Bonhoeffer's connections to Friedrich Siegmund-Schultze's circle in east Berlin, fostered through his father, came much later. There was already a professional relationship between Siegmund-Schultze's social work and Karl Bonhoeffer's neurological clinic. During Anna von Gierke's social pedagogical seminar in 1922, Dietrich's eldest sister had already attended Siegmund-Schultze's lectures, and Klaus worked for a time in the probation service for prisoners; but these were not yet concerns of Dietrich. Only after he discovered the new dialectical theology during his studies did the path open up to people like Gunther Dehn and, through the ecumenical world, to Siegmund-Schultze.

For his graduation examinations, Bonhoeffer's elective paper for Kranz was on the ancient, purely literary topic "Catullus and Horace as Lyric Poets"; it shows no signs of theological reflection.[59] Bonhoeffer's verdict was in Catullus's favor. With the pathos of a sixteen-year-old, he concluded:

"A thinking lyricism is, purely emotionally, an absurdity for me. Reflections have never conquered the world, but emotions have. Even the greatest thoughts must pass away, great sentiments remain eternal."[60] Kranz criticized: "Emotion is sound and smoke, art remains eternal; art, however, can also reflect the character of the eternal. And there is also eternal truth!" Otherwise, he found Bonhoeffer's paper "full of temperament, good ideas and lovely details."[61]

During his last days in school his family noticed how much he was looking forward to the study of theology. If he had any doubts about his calling, he did not mention them. He was attracted by the prospect of grappling with the as yet unexplored subject. He was not yet driven by any love of the church or an articulated theological system of beliefs, and certainly not by a discovery of the Scriptures and their exegesis. His interest in the discipline of theology was still much more philosophical than religious.

Bonhoeffer's path to theology began—despite the Christian foundation of his parents' home—in a "secular" atmosphere. First came the "call," in his youthful vanity, to do something special in life. Then he plunged with intellectual curiosity into theology as a branch of knowledge. Only later did the church enter his field of vision. Unlike theologians who came from families that were active in the church and theology, and discovered the existence of the "world" only later, Bonhoeffer embarked on his journey and eventually discovered the church.

However provisional and ambitious his choice of theology may have been, he made it without any reservations. He did not begin with the notion that he would first explore the broad field of theology and then decide if it offered a satisfactory field of work. His desire to commit himself was always as strong as his desire for knowledge.

The still very vague and ambivalent idea that there was a kind of "call" that had priority over academic study became and remained his objective guiding principle in theological matters. He believed in an indisputable truth that lay beneath all else. His academic background suggested the opposite approach. But from the outset he rejected neutrality, and he instinctively disliked apologetics.

Perhaps, on the eve of going to the university, he wanted to prove his faith to the world of his parents and claim that world for his faith, unarticulated as it still was. He did not articulate this secret intention, but it gave him strength for what was to come.

CHAPTER TWO

STUDENT YEARS: 1923–1927

When he went to the university at the age of seventeen, Bonhoeffer left home for the first time. The world of independent thought and action opened before him; he greedily absorbed what the philosophers and theologians had to offer. His parents wholeheartedly supported his goals.

He remained far more rooted in his home than was customary among his fellow students. He did little without first consulting his parents. Occasionally he felt he should seek out the great teachers of that era, but he always withdrew when they threatened to become too possessive. He returned to Grunewald after his first year away: it was there, not in the world outside, that the beliefs characterizing him as a theologian matured.

Family

During Bonhoeffer's student period, other changes occurred that broadened the family's horizons.

In 1923 Karl-Friedrich became an assistant at the Kaiser Wilhelm Institute of Physical Chemistry. He succeeded in splitting the hydrogen atom. He once explained the complicated problem to Dietrich:

> We [Karl-Friedrich and his friend Harteck] got the idea of experiments that should illustrate that the normal hydrogen. . . . is a mixture, as some theoreticians assert. Isn't that very interesting? If it works, we've succeeded, since there would surely be some people interested in that. But at the moment it's not working, and in the course of the many failed efforts I've already lost half my hair.[1]

The success of his work led to invitations to Harvard, Prague, Zurich, and Charkow in what was then the Soviet Union; at age thirty-one, he was appointed to the chair of physics in Frankfurt. Klaus did his doctorate in jurisprudence in Berlin after studying in Tübingen and Heidelberg. After passing his bar exams, he worked in international law at the League of Nations in Geneva.

Dietrich's eldest sister, Ursula, married Rüdiger Schleicher, a Stuttgart doctor's son, in 1923. It was the first wedding among the Bonhoeffer children. Although it was mid-semester in Tübingen, Dietrich was permitted to come to Berlin—a financial risk, given the inflation at the time—and gave a wedding speech that pleased his critical father. Schleicher was a lawyer and worked as an assessor in the Berlin Reich Transport Ministry. On arriving in Berlin, he had called to pay his respects to Karl Bonhoeffer, who was the Old Master of the Tübingen student association, the Hedgehogs, and had been a fellow student of his father. The entire family soon welcomed him because of his lively philosophical and political interests and his talent as a violinist. Now he would always be connected with it.

At the beginning of 1925 Christine married her former schoolmate, Hans von Dohnanyi, who was two years older. Hans was the son of Ernst von Dohnanyi, the Hungarian composer who occasionally taught at the Berlin Music Academy, and Elsa née Kühnwald, an outstanding pianist. In the Foreign Ministry, Hans von Dohnanyi initially worked on the publication of the Reich government files about the politics of the European cabinets between 1871 and 1914. In 1925 he moved with Christine to Hamburg, where he assisted at the Institute for Foreign Policy at the university until 1929.

Sabine, Dietrich's twin, married Gerhard Leibholz in 1926. Leibholz came from a Jewish home. He did his postdoctoral work in Berlin under Professor Heinrich Triepel, working on the problems of democracy and fascism. In 1929 he was called by the university in Greifswald as professor for public law. Only twenty-eight at the time, he was one of the youngest professors in Germany.

The youngest sister, Susanne, became engaged in 1927 to the theologian Walter Dress. Although he was several semesters ahead of Dietrich in his studies, the two were members of the Hedgehogs and attended the Harnack seminar together. Dress did his postdoctoral work in Berlin in church history and the history of dogma.

In 1923, the family celebrated the marriage of Maria Horn, the children's governess, to Dr. Czeppan, a secondary school teacher for classical languages. Czeppan had tutored Klaus, hiked through Mecklenburg with Dietrich in 1922, introduced the brothers to the secrets of ancient Rome, and was a welcome partner in piano quartets. He passively tolerated the Bonhoeffer children's mockery of his rightist politics.

Fate would bring Dietrich closer to his brothers-in-law than the diversity of their careers might have suggested. Eventually, they became as much a part of his life story as he was of theirs.

This period of engagements, weddings, and baptisms gave his parents the heart to celebrate again. Their parties were renowned among neighbors, students and the colleagues from the Charité. At one masked ball, their father appeared in his own house as a servant without being recognized by his colleagues. At the weddings, Dietrich composed poems in Goethe's *Hexenkuchenstil.*

After the years of hardship, restrictions on travel had been lifted. The Bonhoeffer brothers and sisters explored the Baltic coast and Mecklenburg, the Halligen islands and the heaths, Thuringia and Franken; they visited the art museum in Düsseldorf and the folk art museum in Essen. In 1922, they joined Gerhard von Rad and other friends, leaving Germany for the first time to climb Mount Scesaplana in Austria. When the family gathered each Christmas, the world had grown a little bigger.

Tübingen

It was a family tradition that the children should first attend the University of Tübingen, their father's *alma mater.* Their grandmother still lived there. After returning from the front, Karl-Friedrich had begun studying natural science there in 1919, and Klaus followed him for his first semester of law. During the summer semester of 1922 Sabine enjoyed staying with her grandmother. Christine was in Tübingen studying biology when Dietrich began his theology studies.

His first two terms there coincided with ominous political and economic events: the French occupation of the Ruhr, unrest in Bavaria and Saxony, the declaration of a state of emergency throughout the Reich, and rampant inflation. To save money, Bonhoeffer traveled from Berlin to Tübingen at the end of April 1923 using the cheaper "local" trains, in the fourth-class cars that still existed at that time. The journey took forty-eight hours. When his parents sent him money, it was worth only a fraction of its value by the time it reached Tübingen. At the end of May 1923 he wrote home: "Müller's *History of the Church* now costs 70,000 marks instead of 55,000," and on 27 October he told them that "every meal costs 1,000 million marks."[2] The students then arranged to pay 2,500 million marks for fifty meals in advance.

Dietrich's father had a life insurance policy for 100,000 marks, which had matured just as inflation reached its height. He decided to treat himself to a bottle of wine and some strawberries with the money, but by the time it arrived it was enough to pay for only a pound of strawberries—the reward for a lifetime of paying premiums. Despite this, the Bonhoeffers managed to keep four children at the university. Only the peculiar circumstances prevailing in Berlin made this possible. Foreigners well supplied with foreign exchange swarmed to the German capital and were able to buy property, antiques, and modern art at minimal cost to themselves; they also took advantage of the opportunity to seek advice and treatment from top-ranking psychiatrists. Karl Bonhoeffer acquired priceless dollars or francs this way; he once described how he, his wife, and a colleague spent four days in Jena, paying travel costs, the hotel bill, and all their meals with five dollars.

In the summer of 1923 Dietrich and the other Bonhoeffer children headed south with some emergency pocket money. In October treasury secretary Karl Helfferich's *Rentenmark* reform halted the inflation and stabilized the German currency. Thus a second semester in Tübingen could be added to the turbulent summer semester.

The Igel. Bonhoeffer's university life was not confined to lecture halls. He joined a students' association, the so-called Hedgehogs (*Igel*), to which his father had belonged and which Rudolf Bultmann had joined in 1905. The association's quarters, known to students as the "beer church," were on the hill immediately behind the walls of Twingia Castle, which overlooked a branch of the Neckar surrounding some beautiful green islands. Dietrich was the only one of Karl Bonhoeffer's sons to join the Hedgehogs; he duly became a "Fox," as first-year members were called.

The Hedgehogs group was a Swabian fraternity confined to Tübingen; it was not affiliated with any other organization. It was founded in 1871 and was devoted to the patriotic ideas of the new German Reich. Initially, it deliberately dissociated itself from the behavior of the dueling and color-carrying fraternities. In place of the customary brightly colored cap and breastband, its members wore a hedgehog skin and a breastband striped in shades of gray. With the passage of time and generations, it inevitably became one of many students' associations that adopted disastrous codes of honor; in 1933 it accepted the Aryan clause.

Like his elder brother Otto, Karl Bonhoeffer had joined the Hedgehogs, not one of the more typical fraternities, in 1887. In his memoirs, he looked back critically on the obligatory visits to pubs, and described the results of his Hedgehog days:

> It didn't prevent me from participating in the long night meetings, after the
> official part was over, when future theologians, jurists, philosophers and

doctors argued their points of view. There were hardly any political differences of opinion. All of us were fairly unanimous in our Bismarckian convictions, revered the elderly Kaiser and were outraged by the black-red-gold flags of the greater German Democrats that hung occasionally before the "Kaiser's Inn" during elections or other political events. Without reservation, everyone was happy about the united Germany under Prussia.... The association expressed this by placing particular value on gaining northern German members, to remain free of Swabian provincialism. I believe that this was a certain contribution of this organization. In reality, numerous lifelong friendships developed between members from the south and north. The relatively large number of northern German professors in Tübingen meant that some of their relatives joined the association, which benefited the selection of members and the general intellectual level.[3]

Bonhoeffer's father maintained some of his friendships from the period—with Abegg, a physicist and chemist, and his medical colleague Gaupp; and one of his fraternity brothers who went into the military justice system later helped obtain Christine von Dohnanyi's release from jail in 1943.

Dietrich's elder brothers had not followed their father's example in joining the Hedgehogs. In 1919, after some hesitation, Karl-Friedrich emphatically refused to do so after learning that its members were expected to help suppress the uprisings in Stuttgart and Munich; he objected to the association's members being subjected to nationalist pressure. Karl Vossler, a scholar of the romance languages and friend of Karl Bonhoeffer's, resigned from the Hedgehogs at the same time. Karl-Friedrich later said that he found no difference between it and other nationalist fraternities; his younger brother Klaus was similarly averse to joining.

But in 1923 Dietrich had no political reservations about joining the Hedgehogs. Not until after 1933 did he ostentatiously dissociate himself from the Hedgehogs, along with his brother-in-law Walter Dress, after some of its members exalted the Nazi *Gleichschaltung*, or "synchronization" of society, as a fulfillment of ancient ideals. His resignation is recorded in the March 1936 senior members' bulletin.

During the time of his student membership there were some lively discussions in the fraternity about social questions of the day. A party of his fellow students went on a study trip to the Ruhr. Friedrich Naumann's influence was very marked; Dietrich's brother-in-law Rüdiger Schleicher, like many Swabian Democrats, admired his socially liberal ideas.

The fact that Dietrich was the only one of the brothers to join the Hedgehogs may be related to his position within the family. His elder brothers had ample experience of life with their fellows and contemporaries; for him all that lay ahead. It was an opportunity to move beyond the isolation he had felt among his brothers and sisters and in school, a necessary step in self-discovery.

His fellow students appealed to him: "I basically like the people there very much, so that for the one semester I'm here, I would enjoy going there. . . . [they have] acquired a new piano in the house that I can play at any time. Pressel [Wilhelm Pressel, a friend of Rüdiger Schleicher who later became a leading church official] told me this too. By the way, a fair amount of music is played here."[4] His sponsor was a violinist, Ernst Fritz Schmid, the son of the Tübingen classical languages scholar. Bonhoeffer was used to spending his time wisely, and he fulfilled some of his duties as a "Fox" only with some effort. He hated making the prerequisite visits. He used a required trip to Swabia on behalf of the Student Aid to visit Schwäbisch Hall. He successfully avoided taking any offices in the organization.

His Hedgehog brothers' letters reveal how strongly their youngest member was the center of attention. With his clear sense of direction, Bonhoeffer knew how to help his more hesitant friends make decisions. The way in which he fended off unreasonable demands won him particular respect. Like his mother, he knew about medicines and prescribed them without hesitation. His ability to analyze others' handwriting drew attention and "made people speechless."[5] "I expect you know that I was so successful at it in my student days that it became embarrassing and I gave it up."[6]

Two of his contemporaries in the organization wrote:

> In nearly every field that meant anything to me he was already at home on his own account and stood for something, whether as theologian, musician, philosopher . . . or as a companionable, physically agile and tough young man. . . . He already had a sharp nose for essentials and a determination to get to the bottom of things. He was . . . very natural and receptive to new ideas. . . . He was capable of subtly teasing people and had a great deal of humor. He was not vain, but tolerated criticism.[7]

> In 1923, when Dietrich Bonhoeffer joined the Hedgehogs with me, he was seventeen . . . he was already completely a man of the intellectually active world. . . . I was no match for Dietrich Bonhoeffer's stormy temperament and self-confidence.[8]

For the first time, he had a circle of friends; it consisted mainly of nontheologians. They corresponded for several years, visiting one another and traveling together. But even this group did not give him what he secretly wished for: a circle that would completely fulfill and absorb him. The place where his own strengths were truly drawn upon, where mere hints and subtle gestures were enough to illuminate intentions and questions, where the obligations to be involved and to achieve were embodied—this was still his parents' home and their circle. After 1933 Bonhoeffer never spoke again about his time in the fraternity. For him it had disappeared.

The Black Reichswehr. During the winter term, his second in Tübingen, his membership in the Hedgehogs led to a singular episode. For two weeks he served with the Ulm Rifles Troop as a member of the so-called Black Reichswehr. One amusing story survives: it is said that on the second day Bonhoeffer was ordered to clean out the barracks with a toothbrush as punishment for throwing his washwater out the window; instead, however, he immediately returned to Tübingen. The story tells us something about how hard his contemporaries found it to imagine him subjecting himself to someone else's will. But the story is apocryphal, or concerned someone else—could it have happened to Klaus in 1918? In any case, Dietrich Bonhoeffer voluntarily remained throughout the Ulm exercises at the end of November 1923.

It was an open secret that young men received ongoing military training from the German army. Many students were trained during the semester, with certain days of the week set aside for the purpose. Nationalists were not the only ones to welcome this substitute for the conscription forbidden by the Versailles Treaty. During the crisis of 1923, the centrist and leftist groups also prepared for possible bloody clashes. In a number of provinces like Bavaria, organizations hostile to the constitution accumulated substantial stores of weapons. There was Communist unrest in Saxony, and in Munich the attempted putsch by Ludendorff and Hitler ended in fiasco at the Feldherrnhalle. After the French occupied the Ruhr, there were fears that similar invasions might occur elsewhere, particularly on Germany's eastern borders. Gustav Stresemann, who had entered a coalition with the Social Democrats, was denounced by the right wing because, despite the occupation of the Ruhr, he began negotiating with French prime minister Raymond Poincaré, preaching reconciliation instead of resistance. In the meantime, the Weimar government made hasty military preparations in conjunction with the army command. Even General Reinhardt, commander of the Stuttgart military district, encouraged the military training of students.[9] The Allied Control Commission, on the other hand, made every effort to end the illegal military training.

On 14 November 1923 Bonhoeffer wrote to his parents:

Today I was told that the afternoon military exercises have been canceled, because in Tübingen they would have to be held amidst the danger of spies. Instead, almost all the students' associations, as well as many unaffiliated students, are going to Ulm early tomorrow morning for a fortnight's training. At first I said it was impossible and that I would go some time during the vacation. But, when I was told that after 1 December training was to be supervised by the Entente Control Commission, I reconsidered the matter. I discussed it with a few people who are going—the Hedgehogs and all the other associations are going in full force—and also with (Gerhard) von Rad [the Old Testament scholar, at the time Bonhoeffer's fellow student] and they all said that I should do it as quickly as possible. The fact of the matter is that the Reichswehr, with Reinhardt's personal permission, is training students and others in Ulm and Constance, and actually for a whole fortnight which, stupidly enough, cannot be scheduled during the vacation. One can quit after giving one day's notice, and in serious cases of course it is not compulsory. The purpose is merely to do as much training as possible before the Control Commission begins operating. In view of the one day's notice, and the fact that all the Hedgehogs up to the seventh term are going, and that it will make difficulties if right at the outset one fewer than the number expected turns up, I said I would go for the first few days, that is, until about Tuesday, when I should receive your reply, but would come back if you definitely objected. My initial feeling was that there was plenty of time, after all, and that it would be better not to interrupt the term, but now I think it better to get it over and done with as quickly as possible, so as to have the assurance of being able to help in the event of critical situations. Grandmother . . . also thinks I should go. Jörg Schleicher [Rüdiger Schleicher's brother] is coming too.[10]

A letter quickly followed assuring his mother that "the training of course commits one to nothing else, and in the event of an emergency only citizens of Württemberg will be called on to join this regiment."[11] His parents gave their somewhat anxious consent after Dietrich was already involved.

The fortnight in Ulm gave seventeen-year-old Dietrich a certain satisfaction since he held up well under the training. He wrote home that he found the instructors surprisingly decent and "good-natured." In his free time he sat down with his books. Back in Tübingen, however, he noted that "it was quite wonderful to eat with a knife and fork at a set table again and to sleep in a room of one's own, in one's own bed, and above all to be able to wash in warm water."[12]

As much as this adventure stimulated him, he was greatly concerned by what he had observed politically:

The Reichswehr teams on the whole make a very good impression, but nearly all of them are very reactionary. . . . They are all awaiting the moment when Ludendorff will attempt the [coup] with better, that is, with Reichswehr, support;[13] the very opposite of the people in the house [the Hedgehog dormitory] here, who all want to kill Ludendorff.[14]

Bonhoeffer's Ulm interlude was not based on any secret radical right-wing impulses. By nature and family tradition, he had as little sympathy with this as he had with the numerous flag-waving pastors in the Evangelical church at the time. During fall vacation in 1923, he and his brothers read *Vorwärts*, the leading Berlin Social Democrat newspaper, which Karl-Friedrich had ordered to be sent to them in Friedrichsbrunn. But his letters to his parents show that it was a matter of solidarity for him; he did not wish to cut himself off from the others. He believed he was acting in the service of a state of which he approved, and he was not motivated by a vision of the German people in arms. This military interlude very soon faded from his mind; in Finkelwalde he referred to it once or twice with amusement.

Studies. Except for the Hedgehogs, Bonhoeffer's sole concern was his studies; the church did not yet play a role for him. There is no evidence that he had contact with the German Christian Student Association (DCSV), although Tübingen was a stronghold of the group at the time.[15] During both semesters, he intently attended lectures and seminars. "The lectures in my area this semester are almost all engaging, so that I spend almost the entire day sitting in the theological college."[16]

There is no sign that Bonhoeffer had adopted a specific theological direction in Tübingen. His priority was philosophy. Only with the founding of the magazine *Zwischen den Zeiten* in 1923 did dialectical theology gain a mouthpiece and begin to be discussed. This development had not yet reached Bonhoeffer.

The one teacher in Tübingen who had any lasting influence on him was Adolf Schlatter. "Schlatter interests me most," he wrote.[17] He attended his lectures only during the summer term of 1923, and never met him personally. Among the northern German students, Bonhoeffer was unique in being able to understand Schlatter's dialect at all. He enthusiastically took notes on Schlatter's lecture on the Gospel of John. As he wrote his parents, this concerned the mysteries of the prologue to John, which fascinated the philosophically interested student.

Theologically, Bonhoeffer and Schlatter shared the desire to accept the concrete world as fully as possible; Bonhoeffer was also drawn to Schlatter's distinction allowing room for the good in the New Testament and for responsibility toward the natural, and not merely equating the latter with the night of sin of the Reformation. Bonhoeffer may have forgotten this distinction at times, but even during the *Discipleship* (originally published in English as *The Cost of Discipleship*) period he never failed to draw his students' attention to Schlatter's assessment of the good and the just in the New Testament: that goodness and justice would not be transformed into wickedness and deception.[18] No other writer besides Luther was so fully represented in Bonhoeffer's library in later years, or so frequently consulted.

Schlatter's positive attitude toward National Socialism in 1933 and his obstruction of the Bethel confession of faith aroused bitter indignation in Bonhoeffer. Nonetheless, it did not diminish his high regard for Schlatter's biblical work. Bonhoeffer always acknowledged that Schlatter drew attention to *loci classici* usually left to the Catholics. He hoped to go beyond Schlatter and free these passages from earlier interpretations, and make them binding again for Protestants by linking them to Christology.[19]

In 1943, in his cell in Tegel, Bonhoeffer recalled that Schlatter had told his students that the obligations of a Christian citizen included accepting imprisonment. Bonhoeffer believed this was included "in the Ethics."[20] But Schlatter did not lecture on ethics in 1923 and 1924; in the winter semester that year he lectured on Matthew and Luke. Bonhoeffer may have been recalling some other reading or a statement Schlatter made at one of his open houses. In 1943 Bonhoeffer deliberately included this recollection for the sake of investigative officer Roeder, the censor who read the prison letters. For Bonhoeffer, it was more important that his guard read this calm interpretation of loyalty to the state than that his memory was completely accurate.

Since Bonhoeffer had already learned Hebrew in school, in Tübingen he immediately attended Volz's lectures on the Psalms and—very prematurely—Rudolph's on Old Testament theology. He was gripped by the "passion of the prophets." During the winter term he attended the lectures on the Letter to the Romans by Heitmüller, who had been appointed to Tübingen as one of the leading exegetes of the school. Heitmüller focused on questions of the origin and formation of the text; according to Bonhoeffer's lecture notes, Barth's *Letter to the Romans* was included in the first list of recommended readings, but it was not mentioned in the lectures, even as a foil to put the students on guard. The lectures were less concerned with recognizing basic theological problems extending beyond the epistle itself than with the dissection of an ancient text. This could be learned, and Bonhoeffer took careful and conscientious notes on the lectures. He also attended seventy-one-year-old Karl Müller's lectures on medieval church history, which was good preparation for his forthcoming trip to Rome.

In his second term he could no longer be held back from dogmatics, and registered for Dogmatics II under Karl Heim. Schlatter had been influential in Heim's appointment to Tübingen in 1920 because of the latter's emphasis on incorporating science into his thinking. Bonhoeffer was not drawn in this direction and kept a critical distance, but he showed a good knowledge of Heim's theology.[21]

Since Heim had announced that he was going to concentrate on an introduction to the theology of Schleiermacher and Ritschl, Bonhoeffer took his Schleiermacher along for the summer holidays in Friedrichsbrunn. "I am now busy with Schleiermacher's speeches on religion, which I am finding much more interesting the second time, when I am working through them systematically, because I am attending lectures on them next term," he wrote.[22] His copy, an 1879 critical edition edited by Pünjer, came from the library of his great-grandfather, Karl August von Hase. The number of underlined passages and comments in the margins shows how carefully and critically he read. Opposite the sentence in Schleiermacher's second speech, "but in the infinite everything finite coexists harmoniously, all is one and all is true,"[23] Bonhoeffer wrote: "This does away with individual determinative factors in favor of a general declaration of being. If everything is *true*, the concept of the false is eliminated, and hence that of truth also. In other words, in the infinite all attributes cease to exist, there is only being without determination or any universally valid word."

Bonhoeffer spent much time in Tübingen on the history of religion and philosophy; his expectations of himself were high. He wrote home about "Hauer's history of religion (lectures), which I am eagerly anticipating."[24] Jakob Wilhelm Hauer, the scholar of India and later the unfortunate head of the German Faith movement, stood at the beginning of his influential career. Here, however, Bonhoeffer left no notes; perhaps he dropped this lecture? The only professor whose lectures Bonhoeffer attended during both the summer and winter semesters was the philosopher Karl Groos. Groos had studied the psychological and biological significance of play; Bonhoeffer's father was familiar with his work. In 1923, however, Groos was studying theoretical problems of epistemology. Bonhoeffer was impressed by his lectures on logic four hours every week in the summer semester, and on the history of modern philosophy five hours every week during the winter term. Bonhoeffer also joined Groos's seminar on Kant's *Critique of Pure Reason* and wrote a paper for it. "Today Groos's seminar began and I liked it very much," he wrote.[25] In the summer semester, he also attended Hasse's lecture "Forms in Beethoven's Symphonies" and, in the winter term, Wilbrandt's "Social Politics."

When Reinhold Seeberg met his colleague Karl Bonhoeffer at a Berlin University Senate meeting in 1925, after an initial, somewhat critical encounter with Dietrich, Seeberg expressed his surprise and admiration at the young man's solid philosophical preparation and his extensive knowledge of contemporary philosophy.

That indeed summed up Dietrich's year in Tübingen. It was characterized by his wide range of interest, without a firm commitment to any particular area, and by a persistent exploration of the epistemological field.

Rome

Dietrich Bonhoeffer fell and hurt himself while skating. Alarmed by the news that he had been unconscious for a long time after the fall, his parents visited the convalescent recovering patient in Tübingen. Their visit coincided with his eighteenth birthday, and he expressed a desire to spend a term as a student in Rome. On 5 February 1924 he wrote to his twin sister:

> Just think, it is not impossible that I may spend next term in Rome. . . . I can hardly imagine how splendid that would be. Papa and Mama are going to make inquiries of Axel Harnack [Adolf von Harnack's son, a librarian living in Rome at the time]. . . . Talk them into it, and don't be too jealous. . . . Papa always thinks I should do it later. . . . Talk about it often at home, because that will clinch it.[26]

He went to Rome with Klaus, who had just passed his bar examinations. The brothers crossed the Brenner Pass on 4 April 1924. "Imagination is beginning to turn into reality," he wrote in his diary.[27] Earlier, Karl-Friedrich had hoped to study abroad, but this was not even thinkable in 1919. Dietrich's plans emerged as he tried to think of ways to evade the increasing demands made by the Hedgehogs.

The goal of all his reflections was Rome, not London, New York, or Paris. Rome was the city of the von Hase family. His great-grandfather's experiences were influential: his twenty trips to Rome, his friendships with the Nazarenes on the Pincio, with Bregorovius, Hildebrand, and Thorvaldsen. Like Dietrich, his grandfather had never considered any other destination than Italy. Reproductions of the Roman forum hung on the walls of the classroom in the Grunewald Gymnasium, where Bonhoeffer's teacher Dr. Kranz was an impressive authority on Italy. Another teacher, Dr. Czeppan, was a walking lexicon of ancient Rome. For previous generations, Rome ranked above all other centers of learning. This had changed somewhat for Dietrich Bonhoeffer's generation. War and the Youth movement had led them to discover their homeland more than to venture beyond their own borders. The Bonhoeffer children initially chose destinations like the Cathedral of Doberan, the graves of the Huns in the Wilseder highlands or the pine-covered slopes on Kickelhahn. But they needed little encouragement to reawaken their ancestors' longing for the south in them. As soon as the money for foreign travel became available again, thoughts turned to southern, not western, Europe. Respectable middle-class Germans continued to cut themselves off from the west, which seemed to embody all the misery Germany had suffered under the Treaty of Versailles. Ecumenical ideas and impulses were still unfamiliar. It went beyond their horizons to measure their own political reality by the standards of western democracy, for instance, or to look to the west for theological or ecclesiastical insights. But in studying the origins of their own culture in ancient or Catholic Rome, they could be assured of instant approval and support, at any rate by Dietrich's mother.

At eighteen Bonhoeffer knew far more about ancient Rome than about the contemporary city of the popes. Relations between Catholics and Protestants were still distant and reserved. As a young schoolboy Dietrich was familiar with the art treasures of classical antiquity in the Berlin museums, but it was not until he was in upper school, when he went on a walking tour in the Harz, that it occurred to him to enter a Catholic church in Nordhausen. In a letter to his parents he wrote, almost with alarm, about its magnificence. Not until the summer term in Tübingen did he learn something about Catholic practices, and he readily admitted that his overwhelming impression of the Corpus Christi procession in Rottenburg was one of genuine faith. Thus he traveled south willing to approach Catholicism with as few preconceptions as possible.

A small diary from the journey has survived. Generally he did not keep a diary, but when traveling abroad he sometimes noted down his chief impressions. According to this diary, he conscientiously prepared for the trip and practiced Italian conversation. "By the time the trip began I knew Baedeker by heart."[28]

The diary reveals that Klaus was fascinated by classical antiquity and Mediterranean colorfulness, as well as the sense of adventure, while Dietrich succumbed to the spell of Catholic Rome, and found it difficult to tear himself away from St. Peter's. Unlike other Protestant pilgrims, he was not angered or repelled by the Eternal City; on the contrary, he fell permanently in love with it. In 1944 he wrote from his cell in Tegel it was "one of my favorite parts of the world."[29]

The World of Classical Antiquity and North Africa. The brothers occasionally separated so that each could follow his own interests, but Dietrich missed few of the relics of classical antiquity. Like many visitors to Rome, he was disappointed by his first sight of St. Peter's, but overwhelmed by the Colosseum.

> Antiquity is not dead at all, the saying *"Pan ho megas tethneken"* [The great Pan is dead] is not true, that is completely obvious after only a few moments. The Colosseum is overgrown with luxuriant vegetation, palms, cypresses, pines, weeds and grasses of all sorts; I sat there for nearly an hour. . . . The sight of the Arch of Severus on the Palatine held me in its grip. I went home with the recurrent thought: the great god Pan is not dead.[30]

In the Vatican he had a special objective:

> At the very beginning I was unable to linger in the first galleries, for curiosity made me go straight to the Belvedere. The first sight of the Laocoön was then actually a shock, for it is incredible. I spent a long time there and with Apollo.[31]

Whenever he went to Rome, his first visit was to the Laocoön. From his cell in Tegel he still asked about this "classical man of sorrows."[32]

By coincidence he encountered his old teacher Dr. Kranz on the edge of the crater of Vesuvius, and arranged to revisit the Roman ruins with him. He sat in the Pincio late into the evening—for the sake of reading Kant, which he had included in his luggage.

Naturally, he didn't refuse when Klaus began thirsting for new adventures. The brothers set off for Sicily, where they succumbed to the temptation to see something of Africa. Without informing their parents, they crossed the Mediterranean and spent ten days in Tripoli and in the Libyan desert. After a princely reception by a Bedouin chief on the edge of the Atlas Mountains, complications arose that were not further described, and the brothers were sent packing as "unwelcome guests." The diary is silent about this African episode. Only toward the end of it did Dietrich write home about his first encounter with the Muslim world:

> In Islam everyday life and religion are not kept separate, as they are in the whole of the church, including the Catholic church. With us one goes to

church and when one comes back an entirely different kind of life begins again. . . . Islamic and Jewish piety must naturally be marked religions of law, when the national and ritual elements are so intermingled or actually identical. Only in this way can they achieve such a strict demarcation from other races and religions. . . . It would be very interesting to study Islam longer on its own territory but it is very difficult to gain access to the cultic things. Thus today we entered the Great Mosque for the first time, but were admitted only by permission of the *cadi*.[33]

The trip to Africa ended with the young men's funds at a low point. Back in Sicily, Bonhoeffer wrote in his diary on 10 May 1924: "One should not spend a longer time in Africa without preparation, the shock is too great and increases from day to day, so that one is glad to return to Europe."[34]

The Roman Church. The fascination exercised by Catholic Rome became a permanent influence on Bonhoeffer's thought. It cannot be said that it diminished his critical awareness, but the Roman expression of the universality of the church and its liturgy had a tremendous impact on him, even before his encounter with Karl Barth's theology helped him gain new insights. From this perspective, his own Evangelical church at home struck him as provincial, nationalistic, and narrow-minded. In his letters from Rome and in his diary, when he spoke of his own church background he typically didn't speak of "church" but always of "Protestantism," as was customary in his home. That term had more stature and relevance in the liberal atmosphere that prevailed there. The devotion to the "church" that he encountered in Rome—the sense of the universality of the *ecclesia*—was something new to him.

On their way to Italy the two brothers stopped for one night in Bologna, where they made friends with a young priest who was also bound for Rome. "I spend a great deal of time with our priest from Bologna and let him explain many things to me."[35] He acted as Bonhoeffer's guide to the spectacle of Easter week in Rome and explained the details of the mass to him.

On Palm Sunday he attended his first High Mass in St. Peter's, surrounded by a throng of seminarians, monks, and priests of every skin color. In his diary he wrote down the phrase "universality of the church."[36] That evening he attended vespers in Trinità dei Monti, the beauty of which he still remembered in prison.[37] "I went for a short walk along the Pincio," he wrote in his diary. "It has been a magnificent day; the first in which I gained some real understanding of Catholicism; no romanticism or anything of the sort, but I believe I am beginning to understand the concept of the church."[38]

Next day, the great day of Confession, he spent hours in Santa Maria Maggiore:

> ... all the confessionals occupied and surrounded by worshipers. It is gratifying here to see so many serious faces; none of the things said against Catholicism apply here. Even the children confess with a real ardor that is very moving to see. To many of these people confession is not a "must" but has become a need. Confession does not necessarily lead to scrupulous living, as often as that may occur and always will among the most serious people. Also it is not mere pedagogy, but for primitive people it is the only way to talk to God, while to the religiously more farsighted it is the realization of the idea of the church fulfilling itself in confession and absolution.[39]

On Good Friday he spent four or five more hours in the throng in St. Peter's Square. Then he attended the early church ceremonial of the Feast of the Resurrection. When Klaus had to leave Rome before him, he wrote in his diary: "St. Peter's: Klaus went for the last time; when I tried to put myself in his place I grew quite depressed and I quickly started looking forward to four more marvelous weeks."[40] His stay in the Eternal City ended with a big *Te deum* in St. Peter's on 3 June 1924:

> I had always hoped to have one more splendid experience in St. Peter's . . . Once more at the end I saw what Catholicism is. . . . In the afternoon I walked through the whole city, then I went by way of the Pantheon to throw my coin in the Trevi fountain. . . . I must say that leaving was easier than the thought of it; I parted from most of it without sentimentality. When I looked at St. Peter's for the last time there was a feeling of sadness in my heart, and I quickly got into the tram and went away.[41]

Among all the overwhelming impressions, some critical observations remained. An audience with Pius XI disappointed him. "It was very impersonal and coolly ceremonial. The Pope made a rather indifferent impression. He was lacking in everything papal, in all *grandezza*."[42] Discussions with his mentor from Bologna led him to draw upon the arsenal of his Protestant education:

> After church . . . home with P. A long discussion, conducted with vigor on both sides. He tried to refute Kant, but in the process involuntarily slid into the usual Catholic *circuli vitiosi*. He also accepts the validity of deducing the existence of God from the purposefulness of the world, and, of course, in the process continually confuses logical knowledge with knowledge gained

by faith, hence the vicious circle. He would very much have liked to con-
vert me, and in his way is very genuinely convinced. But the method he
used was the least likely to achieve its purpose—through dialectical tricks
that he was not using as such. The outcome of the discussion was diminished sympathy on my part. Without realizing it, Catholic dogma makes
everything ideal dependent upon Catholicism. There is a great difference
between confession and the dogma of confession, as well as between
"church" and "church" in dogmatics, unfortunately![43]

Yet the experience led him to reflect anew on his own native church,
which until then he had treated only cursorily:

> Unification with Protestantism, however good it might be for both sides,
> at least in part, is out of the question. Catholicism can do without Protes-
> tantism for a long time yet, the people are still very attached to it, and, com-
> pared with the tremendous scale of the ceremonies here, the Protestant
> church often looks like a small sect.[44]

A longer entry in the diary reveals the still vague reflections of the
eighteen-year-old: recollections of discussions at home influenced by
Troeltsch and Max Weber, and the lack of Barthian influence at that point.
Still, it contains ideas that remained dominant in Bonhoeffer's life: the dis-
sociation of the church from its dependence on state privileges; his courage
and determination to sacrifice in order to concentrate in one area; and his
understanding for the concreteness of the Gospel in the act of Confession.
He wrote:

> Perhaps Protestantism should never have aimed at becoming an estab-
> lished church, but should have remained one of the large sects, which
> always have things easier—and perhaps then it would not be in the present
> calamity. An established church believes it possesses an expansive capaci-
> ty that enables it to give something to everyone. That during its formation
> it was able to do so was essentially due to the political turn taken by ques-
> tions that are no longer at issue today; and thus, the more political cir-
> cumstances changed, the more [the church] lost its hold over the people;
> until finally the term Protestantism concealed a great deal that, frankly and
> honestly, was nothing but materialism, with the result that the only thing
> still valued and respected in Protestantism is the potential for free think-
> ing, which for the reformers held an entirely different meaning. Now where
> the official ties between church and state have been dropped, the church is
> confronted by the truth; for too long it has been a refuge for homeless spir-
> its, a shelter for uneducated enlightenment. Had it never become an estab-

lished church, things would be very different: it would still have a significant number of enthusiastic supporters, in view of its size it could hardly
be described as a sect, and it would present an unusual phenomenon of
religious life and serious profound piety; thus it would be the ideal form
of religion that is so sought after today. . . . . It would have become the
church the reformers intended, which it has ceased to be. Perhaps a rem-
edy for the terrible plight of the church lies here; it must begin to limit itself
and make choices in every respect, particularly in the quality of its spiritual educators and what they teach; and in any event it must completely
dissociate itself from the state as soon as possible, perhaps even sacrificing
the right to religious instruction. . . . Is this a possible solution, or not? Or
is the whole game up? Will it shortly return to the bosom of the only saving church, that is, the Roman church, under the semblance of fraternity?
One would like to know.[45]

There is no doubt, then, of Bonhoeffer's open-minded interest in Rome.
While fully conscious of his Protestant roots, he explored it without icono-
clasm or dogmatic prejudice. His educational background and desire to
expand his own horizons led him to seek out the different and detect the
good in it. He did not set out to confirm that his own denomination was
right in all respects; from the beginning, he was positive toward the new. The
result was critical affection and affectionate criticism. It can still be sensed
in the advice he sent from his prison cell in 1944 to his friend who was staying in Rome.[46]

Studies. There was little time for a systematic study of Catholic theology.
April passed with the experiences of Easter week, his travels through the
ancient Roman ruins, and the trip to Sicily; the adventure in north Africa
took up the first half of May. The financial drain of the trip to Tripoli damp-
ened his eagerness for new enterprises. A few short weeks remained in Rome
during which he regularly attended lectures. He wrote home that he managed to follow them very well, having little trouble with the language. "The
lectures are very interesting. Unfortunately there is no course on dogmatics,
but it is very stimulating to have ecclesiastical history dealt with in such a different light."[47] He systematically inspected the early Christian mosaics and
catacombs. "For this reason alone it would be interesting to study here for a
longer time, for the Christian pictures are marvelous sources for understanding dogmatics and religious history."[48]

Unfortunately the diary gives no details about his studies in Rome, nor
does Bonhoeffer even mention where he worked. Was it in the German college, the Gregorian library, or the state university?

His family began to press Dietrich to end his stay in Rome so that he could register in time for the summer semester in Berlin. Filled with the impressions of his two overwhelming months in Rome, he gradually began to look forward to returning to his own books and piano, and to catch up:

> As tempting as it naturally would be to remain here, I do believe that even if I were to do so, I would eventually end up staying more in my room . . . I would like to attend lectures in Berlin that are closely related to these areas, and ultimately, I think, that makes more sense for me—although it is naturally much nicer to have the view directly before me, as it is here. I have observed so much during my weeks here that I would like to study much more in general, and perhaps I would not get around to that here, and so I am looking forward to Berlin again.[49]

On the return journey, the countryside around Siena reminded him of the Württemberg landscape. Florence, Milan, and a brief reunion with his Hedgehog friends in Tübingen could not hold him. He arrived in Berlin at the last possible moment to register for the summer semester—his student I.D. is stamped 16 June 1924.

For a short time it appeared that he might follow the footsteps of his great-grandfather von Hase and devote himself to the early Christian and medieval memorials of the church. But such possibilities were soon forgotten, due to his intellectual curiosity and his theological approach, based upon dogmatics, which was so unconventional in Berlin.

Consequences of His Journey. But the living church that made such an impact on him in Rome permanently influenced his thinking about dogmatics. This was not only true for his dogmatics; on 29 July 1928, as a curate in Barcelona, he preached a sermon on 1 Corinthians 12:25f.:

> There is a word that, when a Catholic hears it, kindles all his feelings of love and bliss; it stirs the depths of his religious sensibility, from dread and awe of the Last Judgment to the sweetness of God's presence; and awakens in him feelings of home, feelings such as those that only a child feels for its mother, of gratitude, reverence and devoted love; the feelings that overcome one when, after a long absence, one returns to one's home, the home of one's childhood.
>
> And there is a word that among Protestants has the sound of something infinitely commonplace, more or less indifferent and superfluous, that does not make their hearts beat faster; which they associate with a sense of boredom, or, at any rate, which does not lend wings to our reli-

gious feelings—and yet our fate is sealed if we cannot acquire a new or perhaps a very old meaning for it. Woe to us if that word does not soon become important to us again, if it does not become a matter of concern in our lives.

Yes, "church" is the word whose sense we have forgotten, and whose glory and greatness we want to examine somewhat today.[50]

He confessed to an acquaintance in Barcelona that Catholic Rome had been a real temptation to him.[51] Wilhelm Dreier, a friend from his Hedgehog days, said that after his visit to Rome he "often defended the value of Catholicism and warned us against spiritual pride."[52]

In 1927, Bonhoeffer organized regular discussion evenings for a group of Grunewald schoolboys; each member had to present a paper for discussion. Among the twenty-two topics, Bonhoeffer reserved only one for himself: the Catholic church. The thought of devoting an evening to the ecumenical movement did not yet occur to him. After discussing the sacraments, the services, and the uniqueness of revelation, he outlined the Protestant position to his pupils. He was still filled by his Rome experiences, but, having encountered Karl Barth, he offered some new accents as well:

> The contributions that the Catholic church has made throughout its history to European culture, to the entire world, can hardly be overestimated. It converted barbaric peoples to Christianity and civilized them, and for a long time was the only guardian of learning and art. Its monasteries took the lead in this. It developed an unparalleled spiritual power, and to the present day we still marvel at how it combines the principle of catholicity with its claim to be the one church of salvation, at its combination of tolerance and intolerance. It constitutes a world in itself. Infinite diversity has converged in it, and this multifaceted picture gives it an irresistible fascination (*complexio oppositorum*). Seldom has any country produced such human diversity as has the Catholic church. With admirable strength it succeeds in preserving unity in all its multiplicity, and in winning the love and reverence of the masses and awakening a strong sense of community.
>
> But it is precisely all this greatness that leads to serious reservations. Has this world really remained the church of Christ? Instead of being a signpost on the way to God, has it not, perhaps, become an obstacle on the road instead? Has it not obstructed the only road to salvation?
>
> But no one has ever obstructed the ways of God. [The church] still has the Bible, and as long as it still has that we can still believe it to be a holy Christian church. For God's word shall not return to him empty (Isaiah 55:11), whether it be preached in our church or in the sister church.

We make the same profession of faith, we pray the same Lord's Prayer, and we share a number of old practices. That creates a bond between us and, so far as we are concerned, we gladly want to live in peace beside this different sister; but we do not want anything to be taken from us that we know to be the word of God. We are not concerned with the terms Catholic or Protestant, but with the word of God.

On the other hand, we shall never try to force the faith of anyone else; God does not want to be served under compulsion, and he has given everyone a conscience. But we can and should pray that our sister church will commune with itself, and know nothing among you except Jesus Christ (1 Corinthians 2:2). Until that comes about we must have patience; and if the "only true church" in a state of mistaken ignorance about our church pronounces an anathema against it, we must put up with it. It does not yet know any better; it does not want to hate the heretic, but his heresy. As long as we let the Word be our sole protection, we can look to the future with confidence.[53]

Rome was the first major experience of his student years, after his study of epistemology in Tübingen in 1923 and prior to his crucial encounter with the theology of Karl Barth in 1925. It is no exaggeration to state that the origins of the theological themes of his early period can be discerned in his Roman experience. While the Barthians and their master, in their early period, concentrated on the theme of revelation and viewed other articles of theology in relation to it, Bonhoeffer's attention was soon completely absorbed by the phenomenon of the church. As we shall see, he based his core theological principles upon this ambiguous but concrete structure. His journey to Rome essentially helped him to articulate the theme of "the church." The motive of concreteness—of not getting lost in metaphysical speculation—was a genuine root of this approach.

Berlin

The Berlin to which Bonhoeffer returned was not the stage of world events or of large political demonstrations. It was a city of great art exhibitions and concerts—and of course Max Reinhardt's great theatrical productions, which Bonhoeffer would not have missed. It was the city where Werner Jaeger, Oncken, Spranger, and Bier taught; and it was the city of the Kaiser Wilhelm Society, where his brother Karl-Friedrich worked under renowned scientists like Laue, Nernst, Einstein, and Planck.

Some of his Hedgehog friends followed him, visiting Siegmund-Schultze's social work community on Fruchtstrasse to study and work under him. Bonhoeffer, however, still took little notice of Siegmund-Schultze and his world. The theological side of Berlin drew him more powerfully than did its church life. The Berlin Christian Student Association remained outside his range of vision as well.

He was a loner. His Tübingen friends were more interested in seeing him than he was in seeing them. It was hard for any group of people to live up to the standards upheld by the home on Wangenheimstrasse. Bonhoeffer himself admitted that newcomers to his home were put under the microscope. With that background, he sometimes gave the impression of being proud and standoffish.

Nor did he try to enter the political student circles, since at the time he wished to associate with neither socialists nor right-wing groups. To the extent he showed any political leanings at all, they tended to reflect the ideas of Friedrich Naumann and Max Weber. In his papers, however, is a detailed essay on the history of the workers' movement from the *Communist Manifesto* to Lenin, which a female friend, a theological colleague, had obtained for him. Its ideas are reflected somewhat in the section on the proletariat in *Sanctorum Communio*.[54] Essentially, his sole focus was the study of theology.

Bonhoeffer was registered at Berlin University from June 1924 to July 1927. In 1925 he briefly considered studying in Scandinavia, since he feared that the demands of Holl, Harnack, or Seeberg might be too much. But he soon abandoned this plan. He began writing his thesis for Seeberg and this held him in its grip; he spent seven semesters (six working ones) in Berlin, in addition to the two semesters in Tübingen. These gave him the qualifications for his theology degree.

At the onset of his studies in Berlin, his impetuous thirst for knowledge still lacked direction. The broad horizon of Berlin's liberal and "positivist" school of theology, embodied by its great teachers, opened before him. At the end of this period, Bonhoeffer had proven himself through his own considerable scholarly achievement, and he had completed an incredible amount of work. The decisive turning point occurred in midyear, when he succumbed to the fascination of dialectical theology; he arrived at this by way of a literary detour. He was eighteen at the time.

The Faculty. Berlin University was just over one hundred years old, but the influence of its theological faculty was worldwide. The influence of Schleiermacher, its founder, was as great as that of Adolf von Harnack, its controversial director in Bonhoeffer's day. When Bonhoeffer began his studies in 1924 the faculty's reputation was considerable. Of its great teachers, only Ernst Troeltsch was no longer there.

In 1924 *Adolf von Harnack*'s authority was no longer disputed; it had long extended beyond the ranks of the theological faculty. Together with Naumann, Harnack had helped draft the sections of the Weimar Constitution that affected the church, education, and training. In 1919 he also helped secure the threatened status of the theological faculties at the state universities.[55] On his seventieth birthday in 1919, he became professor emeritus, but it was not until 1923 that Hans Lietzmann actually succeeded him. After 1924, Harnack continued to lecture, and held a seminar on church history for a selected group. Since he was a neighbor of the Bonhoeffers, Dietrich often accompanied him to the Halensee streetcar station. Harnack held his seminar at home until he finally had to give it up in 1929. Bonhoeffer attended this special seminar for at least three semesters, first as a student and then as a graduate, and it was there that he gained his first laurels. The subject was the origins and early history of the church. Helmut Goes, brother of the poet Albrecht Goes, later described meeting Bonhoeffer at Harnack's home. Bonhoeffer was not only the first to draw his attention to Kierkegaard, but after the seminar occasionally invited Goes home to dance in the evening. The evenings Goes spent at the Bonhoeffers were elegant and stimulating; Dietrich was not only a good dancer, but played the piano and was an accomplished conversationalist. During Harnack's seminar during the winter of 1925–1926, the topic was St. Augustine's *City of God*. As Helmut Goes wrote:

> I had already noticed Dietrich Bonhoeffer at the very first sessions. Not just because he surpassed almost all of us in theological knowledge and ability; that was for me the most impressive thing. But what really drew me to Bonhoeffer was that here was someone who did not merely study and absorb the words and writings of some master, but who thought for himself and already knew what he wanted and also wanted what he knew. I actually had the experience (and to me it was rather alarming and a tremendous novelty) of seeing the young blond student contradict the revered polyhistorian His Excellency von Harnack politely, but on objective theological grounds. Harnack replied, but the student contradicted him again and again. I no longer know the topic of discussion—Karl Barth was mentioned—but I still recall the secret enthusiasm that I felt for this free, critical and independent theological thought.[56]

Another student recalls Bonhoeffer saying: "Harnack never goes beyond the *Epistle of Clement*. If only he would hold a seminar on the Reformation."[57]

At Bonhoeffer's instigation, the seminar group worked together on a study of the concept of *chara* (joy) for the master's seventy-fifth birthday on 7 May 1926.[58] Each member dealt with the use of this concept in one of the

New Testament authors or apostolic fathers: in John, Paul, the Synoptic Gospels, the Epistle to the Hebrews, the Shepherd of Hermas, and the Didache. Bonhoeffer corrected each contribution, making substantial revisions of his own. He wrote the concluding article, entitled "Joy in Primitive Christianity: An Attempted Survey." The basic idea and style reappeared later in Kittel's theological lexicon; it revealed Bonhoeffer's thorough training in the methods of historical criticism. Bonhoeffer thought that Paul had shaped the term "*synchairein*," and referred to the social categories created by this, which so intrigued him in *Sanctorum Communio*. For Paul, "joy" is rooted in mission, "not, as in John, in the religious life of the individual." At the time, Bonhoeffer felt drawn more to Paul than to John. The collective work was given to the seventy-five-year-old Harnack, accompanied by rhymes written by Helmut Goes. Harnack responded kindly to the class's achievement in the next class. In the meantime, Bonhoeffer had succeeded the previous senior of the seminar, Bertha Schulze, who was phenomenally gifted in historical and theological knowledge; thus he became the final senior to serve under Harnack. On Christmas and other occasions, Harnack would write a small dedication to his young neighbor in whatever he had just published. At the conclusion of the seminar, he dedicated his final study of the first letter to Clement, "Introduction to Ancient Church History," to this class. Bonhoeffer thanked him on behalf of all the students.[59] After his graduation, when Bonhoeffer wanted to express gratitude and bid farewell to his teachers, he made some notes on his copy of his thesis. The words he addressed to Harnack stated: "What I have learned and come to understand in your seminar is too closely associated with my whole personality for me to be able ever to forget it."[60]

Karl Holl, the influential interpreter of Luther, was also a friend of Harnack's. Bonhoeffer spent two semesters in 1925 in his seminar on church history. As rector of the university, Holl's workload in 1925 was excessive, and he died a week after his sixtieth birthday in May 1926. Harnack delivered the memorial address. Bonhoeffer thought that Harnack "should have painted a different picture of Holl and concentrated on his strict view of sin."[61]

Bonhoeffer eagerly immersed himself in Holl's interpretation of Luther's doctrine of justification. Holl irrevocably reinforced in him the doctrine of "by grace alone" as the one article by which the church stands and falls. He convinced him that even the devout are not able really to love God. After this, Luther's phrase *cor curvum in se* (heart turned in upon itself) became a key phrase for Bonhoeffer.[62] He continually applied it in epistemology as well, to refute the noetic optimism of idealism and the localization of God in the individual's own mind. But Bonhoeffer became critical quite early of

Holl's interpretation of Luther's faith as a religion of conscience; this seemed to threaten the assurance of faith in *extra me*.[63] Bonhoeffer appreciated Holl's epochal move into the center of Luther's doctrine of justification, as a contrast to a vague cultural Protestantism, although he felt it to be too weakly anchored in Luther's Christology. But Holl had a lasting impact on him.[64] In 1943, in Tegel prison, Bonhoeffer had the three volumes of Holl's collected essays on church history sent to him.[65] As a student, Bonhoeffer had seriously considered studying under Holl; Holl's early death ended such considerations.

Bonhoeffer probably owed his first introduction to Russian or eastern European Christianity to Holl. It was not only the dialectical theologians, with their predilection for Dostoevsky, who fostered the first wave of interest in the East in theological circles. Holl did everything in his power to encourage it; he even learned Russian so that he could read Tolstoy. Bonhoeffer had eagerly read Tolstoy in school, and now he acquired each successive volume of Hans Ehrenberg's *Östliches Christentum*,[66] especially because of the chapter on Berdyayev[67] and Ehrenberg's postscript.[68] He also, of course, plunged into Dostoevsky. On 13 March 1925 he wrote to his parents:

> I have just been reading Dostoevsky's highly interesting speech on Pushkin, where he portrays him as the first man to distinguish between the Russian and the European, as the herald of the Russian ideal: "supranational pan-humanism," as he calls it. Remarkable how a people's typical characteristics should lead them to transcend themselves, in any case as a nation. For Dostoevsky this idea is necessarily and emphatically linked to Christianity, and thus the genuine "catholicism" of original Christianity is re-established.

This discovery of eastern European Christianity led Adolf Deissmann to invite Stefan Zankow to give a series of lectures at Berlin University in 1927, "The Orthodox Christianity of the East," which were later published by the Furche publishing house. Thus, Bonhoeffer was not totally unprepared when he later met Zankow at ecumenical conferences. Holl and the dialectical theologians had roused his interest in the eastern church; yet this did not lead Bonhoeffer to explore Orthodoxy for himself.[69]

Bonhoeffer's favorite subject in Berlin was systematic theology, which was taught by *Reinhold Seeberg*. Bonhoeffer attended his seminar every semester, from summer 1925 until he completed his studies in 1927. Bonhoeffer's decision to write his thesis for Seeberg created a somewhat delicate situation, since relations were cool between Seeberg and Harnack, to whom Bonhoeffer was much closer personally. Although both came from the Baltic region, Seeberg and Harnack differed politically. During the First World War, Seeberg favored the furthest possible expansion of the German borders to include Livonia and Courland, while Harnack regarded such claims as excessive and dangerous.

But Seeberg was the professor in Bonhoeffer's chosen area. Bonhoeffer stayed with this great mediator between the critical historians and the so-called positivists, and learned a great deal from him, although their encounter began with a theological controversy. Seeberg, in turn, took an interest in his polite but stubborn new pupil.

The five volumes of Seeberg's *Textbook of the History of Doctrines* were among the earliest texts Bonhoeffer acquired. He did a great deal of work in them, and they were the source for his knowledge of Augustine, Thomas Aquinas, the scholastics, Melanchthon, and Luther. "In his seminars Seeberg really displayed his mastery of the history of medieval dogmatics."[70] Bonhoeffer's favorite quotations from Luther are underlined in those five volumes.[71] The knowledge of Luther he received from Seeberg and Holl gave Bonhoeffer the critical independence with which he encountered the onslaught of Barth's theology. He became familiar with Seeberg's great models—Schleiermacher, Hegel, and Albrecht Ritschl. He also acquired the difficult jargon of his student years, which is saturated with Seeberg's Hegelian concepts, such as the distinction between "objective" and "absolute spirit." The key to Bonhoeffer's theology during the subsequent five years, the concept of "Christ existing as church-community" (*Christus als Gemeinde existierend*), was forged here as well. Bonhoeffer later abandoned such tedious jargon, but he retained three important elements from Seeberg's thought, shaping each in his own way:[72]

1. It struck him that Seeberg was not content to leave theological tenets in the epistemological field, but emphasized their volitional aspects. To him, "being" also meant "will," and faith was the awareness of the will created by the primary will. This gave wings to Bonhoeffer's antispeculative inclinations.

2. Seeberg conveyed Ritschl's aversion to metaphysics, an aversion that had driven Ritschl along the road to a far-reaching Christocentrism.

3. Seeberg taught Bonhoeffer to take the social aspect of existence seriously. To Seeberg the essential mark of human existence, besides its historical nature, was that people exist in sociality. Bonhoeffer made this aspect an essential part of all theological concepts.

But because Bonhoeffer was already fascinated by Barth when he began his work under Seeberg, his criticism of the master began immediately. He summarily rejected Seeberg's attempt to harmonize the Bible and the modern spirit, Luther and idealism, theology and philosophy. Seeberg attached great importance to the doctrine of the "religious *a priori*":[73]

> The *a priori* in religion is a purely formal primary characteristic of the created spirit or self, enabling and compelling the self to a direct awareness of the absolute spirit. This implies two things: that the created will is concerned with intentionally acquiring awareness of the primary will, and that reason is thereby simultaneously given the capacity to acquire an intuition of the primary will.[74]

Despite his respect for the greatness of the nineteenth century and its church father, Schleiermacher, Bonhoeffer believed that this *a priori* obscured the Reformation. He viewed Seeberg and his friends, with their anthropological and theological optimism, as incapable of understanding the collapse and crisis that had followed the First World War, and thereby incapable of interpreting those events to his generation. For Seeberg and others, this collapse did not give birth to a fundamental reappraisal of ideas; for them, the war had merely been an unhappy episode. For Bonhoeffer, this took the sting out of a burning problem of conscience. He had been wrestling for a long time with the question of what his own "religious a priori" might be, and he reacted energetically against any new attempts to point to a human religious potential, whatever its nature, that led back to self-examination.

In the volume on Luther in Seeberg's history of dogmatics, Seeberg stated: "This enables one to understand the remarkable circumstance that Luther uses religious *experience* as well as the Scriptures as the witness and canon of truth. But it should be experience that establishes the certainty of the truth of the contents of Scripture."[75] Here Bonhoeffer wrote a few words in the margin that underscored his basic theological and personal difference with Seeberg: "No! Scripture is the Lord's and is conveyed via the church: preach!" It was a way of thinking that must have provoked displeasure among the Berlin faculty. Despite this, Bonhoeffer remained loyal to Seeberg. As he wrote to him later:

> So at about the usual time on many Friday evenings I think with longing of your seminar, and I should very much like to be among your listeners and to reflect on the "meaning of history" with you. . . . I think with gratitude of the hours during the past four years which I had the privilege of spending with you.[76]

Bonhoeffer certainly sensed a greater inner strength in Harnack and in Holl, for whom everything was much gloomier and more difficult. But Bonhoeffer never voluntarily surrendered to strong personalities. Karl Barth and George Bell were the only men whose authority he ever truly accepted— although even then he struggled alone to reach the decisions he believed to be right. In Berlin, his choice of Seeberg as mentor reflected this spirit of independence, since Seeberg imposed the fewest restrictions and obligations on him. In addition, his own upbringing and his father's example gave Bonhoeffer a broader perspective, enabling him to respect and learn from those who taught something different from what he believed. Only with the church struggle in 1933 did Bonhoeffer's oppositional stance move from ideas to actively participating in conflict and selecting his personal contacts carefully. At that point, the break with Seeberg became complete.

For two semesters Bonhoeffer attended *Adolf Deissmann*'s seminar on the New Testament; Deissmann's assistant was Georg Bertram. Deissmann was the leading German in the young ecumenical movement, and in Bonhoeffer's student days he played a prominent role in the world conferences "Life and Work" in 1925 in Stockholm and "Faith and Order" in 1927 in Lausanne. These conferences and their subject matter can hardly have escaped Bonhoeffer's notice, but he did not yet recognize that this realm was precisely where exciting innovations were occurring. A student friend's letter to Bonhoeffer certainly reflected his own attitude: "The more one has to do with it [the Stockholm conference], the more dubious it seems. (It would be quite harmless if it sought only to be an international meeting for the cultivation of ethical culture—but it wants to be more! They want to build the kingdom of God!)"[77] It was Deissmann who later helped to open the gates of the ecumenical world to Bonhoeffer and gave him the most flattering recommendations.

Bonhoeffer's first-semester course record shows that he studied theology with Harnack, Gressmann, Holl, and Lietzmann; in the second semester, he attended courses by Sellin, Titius, and Deissmann. He had not yet begun his studies with Seeberg; but he took epistemological theory and a seminar on "Freedom and Necessity" from Heinrich Maier, a representative of the school of critical realism. He also took "History of Logic" from Rieffert and briefly studied psychology and Gestalt theory under the renowned Berlin Gestalt psychologists Wertheimer and Köhler. Only during his third semester did he concentrate entirely on theology. Only once, during the winter semester of 1926–1927, did he take a colloquium on "Philosophy of Culture" from Eduard Spranger. Although Siegmund-Schultze had been an honorary professor on the theological faculty since 1926, Bonhoeffer did not study under him.

Dialectical Theology. After his stay in Rome and before beginning work on his dissertation, around the beginning of the winter of 1924–1925, Bonhoeffer discovered Barth.

During the final weeks of the 1924 Berlin summer semester he had "to neglect the historical and philosophical areas somewhat and take up Hebrew again ... apart from that, every week I meet another theological student and we test each other on church history."[78] His semester break was devoted to philosophy, sociology, and the history of religion. "At the moment I have a very interesting book, Max Weber's *Sociology of Religion.* . . . After Weber I plan to read Troeltsch's *Social Teachings of the Christian Churches* and to finish working through Husserl—and if I have time, to tackle Schleiermacher thoroughly."[79] In letters to friends that autumn he discussed Max Weber, sociological categories like state, people, race, and the characteristics of ethical communities, as well as Kant, Luther, Holl, Husserl, and Hegel's definition of objective spirit. Unfortunately, only his friends' replies survived, not Bonhoeffer's letters themselves.[80]

But in May and June 1925 the tone of these letters suddenly changed. He began discussing Gogarten's *The Religious Decision*[81] with Wilhelm Dreier, and an "entirely new" note crept in. His mother, who sometimes tried to keep up with her son's interests, had read Troeltsch at the beginning of 1925; having completed this in August 1925, she asked Dietrich to send her "the Barth book" during the holidays. This was Barth's first volume of collected lectures, *The Word of God and the Word of Man*, published in German in 1924. Dietrich Bonhoeffer began to promote the book, and in the summer of 1925 he gave a copy to his godfather Hans von Hase, who had been sending him occasional letters of advice.

During the winter of 1924–1925, in fact, Bonhoeffer read more than ever; several attacks of influenza gave him the time. He alternated Ibsen's plays, mainly *Brand* and *Peer Gynt*, with the works of Barth. It may be that in Berlin he came across copies of the new journal *Zwischen den Zeiten* for the first time, and heard that something new had appeared on the horizon. But there were several immediate occasions that brought it to his notice.

Bonhoeffer's papers include several transcripts (copied painstakingly by hand), titled "Karl Barth, dictated notes on 'Instruction in Christian Religion,' 1 and 2." These were the main points of his lectures on dogmatics in the summer of 1924 and winter of 1924–1925, which Barth dictated to his students in Göttingen; they were an abbreviated version of what appeared in his first volume of *Prologomena to Christian Dogmatics* in 1927. Friends passed such transcripts from one university to another. They gave Bonhoeffer his first insight into the structure that would arise from the foundation of Barth's *Epistle to the Romans*. His cousin Hans-Christoph von Hase began studying physics in the summer of 1924 in Göttingen, where Karl Barth was lecturing. He found Barth's lectures so impressive that he soon transferred to the school of theology. Barth was the topic of discussion during the two cousins' travels along Main River that August.

At the beginning of the winter term of 1924–1925, Bonhoeffer joined Harnack's seminar. The early church fathers were examined thoroughly—as were the controversies surrounding the professor. Here, at the very latest, Bonhoeffer must have been drawn into the bitter debate between Barth and Harnack that appeared in *Christliche Welt* in 1923.[82] Each proclaimed a dark future for theology if the field were left to the other one. Neither yielded an inch to the other, and their statements excluded each other:

> Should we theologians [said Barth] not have the courage to let our theology begin with what is, perhaps, the fundamentally skeptical but nonetheless clear memory of the "totally unintelligible," unbelievable and incredible and certainly disturbing testimony that God himself said and did something: something entirely new, outside the correlation of all human words and things, precisely as something new, not just as any word and things alongside other words and things, but this particular word and this particular thing?[83]

Harnack wrote to his friend Martin Rade:

> Our present theology is gratifying (that itself is a great thing) in its seriousness of purpose, and it aims at the heart of the matter. But how weak it is as a science, how narrow and sectarian its horizon . . . how expressionistic is its logical method and how short-sighted its view of history! . . . Ritschl today is scorned, though in my opinion he has a great deal to offer that the Barthians could use; but the sons are even more hostile to their fathers than to their grandfathers.[84]

In 1929 Harnack wrote sadly to the young Bonhoeffer that spiritual life was threatened by the "contempt for scientific theology and the menace posed by unscientific theology." He wrote, "Therefore those who uphold the banner of true science must defend it more steadfastly than ever."[85]

With his discovery of dialectical theology, a new certainty replaced Bonhoeffer's restless wanderings. It was like a liberation; he now began to take real joy in his work. The distinctive task of preaching—the earthly, concrete proof of God's word in the words repeated by human beings—was the starting point for this new theology, and this tore him away from the game of speculation. Initially, this theological experiment was somewhat inelegant. Bonhoeffer scorned apologias and left some inconsistencies unresolved. When he discovered that it was impossible to avoid drawing on philosophy and anthropology, despite the claims of some people, he remained convinced of theology's right to exist independently and in its own right. The derivative themes disappeared; the topic viewed so dubiously by his elders in Bonhoeffer's childhood finally had an independence that made the commitment worthwhile. It was much more than intellectual pleasure that he took in the brilliant rebel and fighter Karl Barth.

Barth forced Bonhoeffer's attention away from those aspects of human nature that had been unmasked so terribly to that generation. He made the religious experience, which Bonhoeffer had long sought with youthful enthusiasm and was the source of such difficulties for him, seem inconsequential. For Barth, the certainty being pursued here was anchored not in people but in the majesty of God, and could not exist as a separate matter apart from God. In contrast to many who found Barth so gloomy, Bonhoeffer ascribed to him true *hilaritas*.[86]

Was it not significant that this new theology was able to convince the young Bonhoeffer? Here was a young man with a thorough philosophical grounding who had familiarized himself with the latest methods of historical criticism. Unlike many young Barthians, he was neither a youthful rebel driven or shattered by the postwar crisis, nor a former pietist rebelling against his upbringing. Here was a well-balanced young man from an upper-middle-class home who had been objectively convinced: a young man who, thanks to the scope of his background and his natural gifts, was able to see things as they were without succumbing to blind enthusiasm.

Thus, despite his gratitude for the essence of this theology, Bonhoeffer retained his right to think critically and independently. But he was criticized as an ally; where he saw weak points, he did not hesitate to offer alternative suggestions. His critique began at a point that characterized his own inner needs: he assumed that Barth's emphasis on the inaccessibility and free majesty of God threatened and dispelled the due emphasis on humanity's concrete, earthly plight. There is a small piece of evidence for this dating from the period of his first acquaintance with Barth's work. Max Strauch's introduction to and defense of Karl Barth's theology had just been published and was widely read.[87] Strauch describes the eschatological dualism, the infinite qualitative difference, between this world and the next: "In contrast to all the visible is the invisible; in contrast to this world the incommensurable next world; in contrast . . . to all reality and transience is the world of the origin and the goal."[88] Bonhoeffer underlined the words "origin" and "goal," and wrote in the margin: "not the faith which is now simply received!" This was the point where he questioned and criticized: he asked whether the free and inaccessible majesty of God is realized in freedom *from* the world, or whether it is not more the case that it enters *into* the world, since the freedom of God has committed itself to the human community.[89]

Bonhoeffer refused to view the contrast between Barth and Harnack merely as the disagreement between neo-scholastic orthodoxy and an evasive liberalism. There is some indication that he feared Barth's developing dogmatics might be a step backward from the *Epistle to the Romans*, and that in discussions with fellow students he criticized and condemned this. An entry in Richard Widmann's diary confirms the concern the students felt at that time. They noted that in the preface to the fifth edition of the *Epistle to the Romans* Barth announced that he would "say and do, one after the other, what must now—if the whole thing is not to be a mirage—be said and done to do justice to the plight and the hope of the church." But in the chapter on Christology, the second half of Barth's lectures on dogmatics, they read: "I would rather err with the fathers of Chalcedon than make my own portrait of Jesus from the New Testament."[90] Bonhoeffer had sent Widmann, a fellow student in Holl's seminar, his copy of Barth's lecture notes. Widmann's 25 February 1926 letter to Bonhoeffer shows how greatly Bonhoeffer feared "reactionary gestures" by his new master—concerns that were restated in the letters from Tegel. Widmann wrote to Bonhoeffer:

> I am still working through the Barth *Dogmatics II*. I'm delighted that some things are said better and more pointedly here than in the *Epistle to the Romans*. It seems to me that the problems are more clearly and carefully outlined and defined (in the *Dogmatics*). Since he is proceeding more systematically here, things find their right place within his train of thought and don't receive more or less emphasis than they should. There is a lot of sensation and journalism in the *Epistle to the Romans*; the *Dogmatics* is more objective. I can't prefer one over the other.
>
> You once mentioned that you deplored Barth's relapse into servitude in these *Dogmatics*—that he takes anxious care (yes, just that) to follow in the footsteps of the dogmaticians of ancient times. I do not regard this reactionary gesture as wrong. The primary purpose, after all, is to establish a link with the past and perhaps not just a link, but reinforcement. Aid, stimulus, fertile ideas—such a dogmatic theology cannot be simply shaken out of one's sleeves, for Barth is cleaning out an Augean stable, and in the process will have reason to be truly grateful to his orthodox assistants. But I certainly also think that what we need just as much is a dogmatics

that manages without these reactionary crutches and looks *forward* for connections. Certainly the *Epistle to the Romans* is much less reactionary in its formulations. In that respect the *Dogmatics* are a step backwards. Perhaps next time, when his *Dogmatics* have fulfilled their "strategic purpose"—this reliance on the ancients is not more than that—Barth will take *two* steps forward.[91]

Benkt-Erik Benktson notes that in 1944 Bonhoeffer described Barth as one who had "*begun* to think" in the direction of nonreligious interpretation, but had "not followed this line of thought to its completion."[92] Where did Barth "begin"? Benktson points to Barth's 1920 lecture "Biblical Questions, Insights, and Prospects" in Aarau, which Bonhoeffer so eagerly read in *Das Wort Gottes und die Theologie* (1924–1925). The similarity in wording to *Letters and Papers from Prison* is astonishing:

> There have been . . . definitely non-religious people who . . . [have felt] the whole weight of the question of the existence of God (p. 73). Biblical piety is not really pietism; it would have to be characterized far more as a well-considered, qualified worldliness . . . [as] worldly objectivity (p. 80). Thinking and speaking derived from totality and directed at totality . . . the worldliness of the biblical line (p. 84). God does not wish to be transcendent, separate from this world. . . . [God] does not wish to be a founder of religious history, but to be the Lord of our lives (p. 85). Biblical history is . . . primarily and above all human history (p. 95).[93]

Perhaps these words were still ringing in Bonhoeffer's ears when he said that Barth had "begun" but "had not finished."

But this direction taken by the early Barth was not what influenced Bonhoeffer now. He adopted Barth's distinction between religion used as human self-justification and faith; he corrected the use of revelation as the point of departure, instead of the church. Bonhoeffer questioned whether the sequence in Barth's thought, in which he moved from revelation toward the church, didn't make the doctrine of salvation too secondary a factor. Bonhoeffer did not want a revelation cut off from its soteriological aspect.

Dissertation

Bonhoeffer began his dissertation one year after his return from Rome. This was not only remarkably early for a nineteen-year-old; it was also rare for someone to take up such an exacting requirement in addition to the normal course of study, without requesting a leave, extension, or some other special status. He did not allow his topic to be decided for him; he chose it himself. His underlying intention became progressively clearer during the various stages of his work—stages during which he disappointed some people's expectations that he take a different focus.

Stages of the Dissertation. Harnack was the first to view Bonhoeffer as a potential doctoral candidate. Bonhoeffer wrote his first essay for Harnack in Berlin in the winter of 1924–1925. He submitted no fewer than fifty-seven pages to the old gentleman, and his success took him aback. Listening to the St. Matthew Passion in his Tegel cell in 1943 evoked memories of his situation in 1925: "I was eighteen, and had just come from Harnack's seminar, in which he had discussed my first essay for the seminar very kindly, and dropped the remark that some day I should write a dissertation in Church History. I was filled with this when I went to the Philharmonic Hall."[94]

The topic of his essay had been "the Judaic element in the first letter from Clement: its existence and relation to the whole." Harnack's evaluation stated:

> Conception and exposition, in view of the completeness and correctness of the viewpoints and the effort given here, very good [Harnack underlined this twice]. If the essay is reworked and polished once more, and the Greco-Roman elements examined more closely [which the topic did not require— the author], this work will represent a genuine advance in the analysis and historical understanding of the Letter. von Harnack 2.2.1925.[95]

The work showed a strict analysis of the text using historical-critical evidence. Bonhoeffer had mastered these tools. When he later chose not to use these means and methods, he knew what he was leaving to the experts.

Admittedly, the attention he received from this success put an additional burden on Bonhoeffer. Should he follow the example of his distinguished forebear and devote himself to church history, or disappoint this eminent and friendly neighbor? His study of Troeltsch had awakened him to the problematic of historicism—but only enough to try what had not yet been done, to prepare himself systematically to tackle the really burning questions.

He wrote his second essay in Holl's seminar, "Luther's Opinions on His Work in the Last Years of His Life, according to His Correspondence of 1540–1546."[96] He handed it in at the beginning of June 1925. As Harnack had done with Bonhoeffer's previous effort, Holl graded it "very good (I)." Again it was a strictly historical exercise, based on the original sources. But the study of the aged Luther's vivid apocalyptic and eschatological visions had a very disturbing effect. The words "*finis, finis, finis instat*" haunted Bonhoeffer and challenged his personal faith. Luther made an enormous impact on him. Should he choose Holl as his mentor?

After these brilliant performances in the historical field, he finally took the plunge into his favorite subject, dogmatics, but the result was near failure. The title of his first essay in the seminar on systematic theology was, "Can a Distinction Be Drawn between a Historical and a Pneumatological Interpretation of the Scriptures, and How Does Dogmatic Theology Regard This?" Underneath appear the words: "Satisfactory. Seeberg. 31.7.1925."[97] In Seeberg's eyes, the whole thing was a disturbing exercise in Barthianism. The margin is filled with his question marks, objections, and "*Neins,*" only rarely interspersed with a "good." But it was this clash that led to the decision about Bonhoeffer's thesis.

The essay began:

> The Christian religion stands or falls by belief in the divine revelation that became historically real, tangible and visible—that is, to those who have eyes to see and ears to hear—and thus in its very essence contains the question that we ask ourselves today about the relationship between history and spirit, or, applied to the Bible, between letter and spirit, scripture and revelation, man's word and God's.[98]

The essay concluded:

> All attempted pneumatological interpretation is prayer, is supplication to the Holy Spirit [here Seeberg with good reason wrote "only?" in the margin] which alone, as it pleases, gives it the hearing and understanding without which the most highly intellectual exegesis is nothing. Textual understanding and interpretation, preaching, that is, the realization of God, is contained in the prayer: *Veni creator spiritus.*[99]

Bonhoeffer began by condemning the skill in which he had just distinguished himself under Harnack and Holl. Textual criticism, he wrote, left nothing behind but "rubble and fragments."[100] The texts are not just historical sources, but agents of revelation, not just specimens of writing, but sacred canon. Proclaiming the significance of that is a task for the future. Bonhoeffer then declared that historical work on the texts must still be done, "for none of us can revert to the pre-critical age."[101] The essay shows how well acquainted he was with the new method of form criticism, but not much of it remained since his discovery of the new perspectives Barth had opened up. He did not explain what he meant by the impossibility of reverting to the precritical age. He believed that textual criticism had little more to say about the scriptural message, and that such criticism was relative. He used Thurneysen's simile for exegesis, visualizing it, as he often did in later years, as crossing an ice bound stream, jumping from one block of ice to another. Revelation is contained in Scripture because God speaks in it; that is undemonstrable—not a conclusion but a premise. Divine revelation enables people to recognize divine revelation, that is, the Holy Spirit. Bonhoeffer adopted Barth's conclusion that things can be known only by their like. "God can be known only through God. Hence it follows that the consistent idea of revelation must be thought of not substantially, but functionally, that is, it is not so much Being as decision, the will of God expressed in scripture."[102] And: "For history, scripture is only a source; for pneumatology, it is testimony."[103]

Today these conclusions seem restrictive; at that time Bonhoeffer and his friends viewed them as a liberation from the inconsistencies of historicism. Seeberg was so stimulated by the spreading "pneumatological exegesis" (later called "theological exegesis"), which had now invaded his own seminar, that he published a paper on it himself soon afterward.[104] In this first essay, Bonhoeffer boldly disputed the doctrine of the "religious *a priori*."

Before the beginning of the 1925 summer vacation, Seeberg spoke to Karl Bonhoeffer at a meeting of the University Senate about his rebellious son, and said that he would like to have a deeper discussion with Dietrich. Dietrich, however, was hiking through the Rhône Valley and along the North Sea coast, and had not yet decided what he should do.

On 25 August 1925 he wrote his father from Lesum near Bremen, where Wilhelm Dreier, his friend from the Hedgehogs, lived:

> I especially wanted to know from you, dear Papa, how I should handle things with Seeberg. Should I somehow refer to your conversation with him? And does he want to speak with me more about my future work or about my essay?[105]

His father replied promptly:

> As far as Seeberg is concerned, his recommendation that you visit him didn't mean a new discussion of your lectures for him, but to talk more in general about the question of systematics or history, and your special inclination for one or the other. If I were you, if you are not yet decided as to whether you want to work under him, I would tell him that you are not yet certain that you will remain in Berlin—that perhaps you should study

one more semester outside of Germany. In any case the visit, I believe, is appropriate so that you can get to know him better.[106]

His mother was distressed by her son's agony about a decision in which his practical and personal sides weren't in harmony. Right after his father's letter she wrote: "I continue to wonder whether you shouldn't write a historical-dogmatic work under Holl. You can do a dissertation on systematics later when Seeberg is gone. Think about it once more."[107]

Bonhoeffer finally decided and on 21 September 1925 wrote to his parents:

> (Seeberg) returned to Berlin . . . and since he was staying only one day, asked me to accompany him to the train station at 7 A.M. In the meantime I had been thinking things over: doing the work for Holl or Harnack would be pointless, since with a dogmatic-historical subject I should meet with no resistance from Seeberg either, so it makes very little difference whether I go to one or the other, as I think that on the whole Seeberg is also well-disposed toward me. So I decided to remain with Seeberg, to whom I have now suggested a subject that is half historical and half systematic; and he is very pleased with it.
>
> It is connected to the theme of the religious community, which I mentioned to you one evening at some point as one that would interest me. It involves doing a great deal of historical work, but there is no harm in that. In any case, Seeberg seems to be pretty interested in the subject himself. He said he had been waiting a long time for someone to work on it; and he was very pleased that I had hit on it by myself. Then he seemed to refer to your conversation with him, Papa, without specifically mentioning it, and said everything would surely go very well; he had already seen that from my work! When I laughed at that, he repeated it. So I have settled this with him and I think that things are fine.
>
> One difficulty remains. In order to begin work at once—which I would like to do—I need several books that, in Seeberg's opinion, I will need throughout—so that I can't get them from the library, where they usually can't be found anyway—and my pocket money isn't sufficient; the most important ones I could get for 25–30 marks, that's Hegel, Spencer,[108] Max Weber. Can I buy them for myself? During the day I work, read and go for many walks. Yesterday grandmother, Suse and I went to "Die Fledermaus."[109]

"Sanctorum Communio." Bonhoeffer began work on his dissertation at the beginning of his sixth term (winter semester 1925–1926) and completed it in eighteen months. It was accepted by the faculty on 1 August 1927. His

concentration and his ability to make the best use of his time must have been extraordinary, for during the same period he also turned in at least seven essays and nine drafts for catechisms and sermons. He also took over a children's religious class and the obligations that went with it. He was no more willing to sacrifice holidays in northern Italy or Friedrichsbrunn than he was to give up playing tennis with new friends such as Helmut Rössler, who also introduced him to the works of Franz Werfel. The Bonhoeffers regarded it as bad form to let it be seen that one had a great deal of work, and it may be true that he dealt too cursorily with his sources. Today, for example, he is criticized for eclecticism and misrepresentation in his treatment of Hegel.[110] But his critics at the university, like Seeberg and Titius, did not accuse him of superficiality.

So now he sat with his topic: the church. For him it was both a puzzle and a longing. Who is it? What is it? Where is it? His subtitle was "A Dogmatic Inquiry into the Sociology of the Church."

> Luther's love for the church and deep dogmatic insight into the significance of its historical nature made it very hard for him to tear himself away from the Church of Rome. We should not allow resentment and dogmatic frivolity to deprive us out of hand of our historical Protestant church.[111] The congregation of the faithful remains our mother.[112]

Was the subject in the air? When Bonhoeffer wrote his friend Widmann about his new work, the latter replied:

> Your thesis may have all sorts of topical consequences: see Althaus and his "living community"; see Barth's speech in Duisburg-Meiderich in the latest number of *Zwischen den Zeiten;*[113] see Kierkegaard's *Attack;* see the latest "movement" in the Youth movement; everything is crying out for "association," "fellowship," "community"; see the Bavarian concordat.[114]

Althaus was working on the same subject; his title was "*Communio Sanctorum:* The Community in Luther's Idea of the Church." He contended that "the renewal of the doctrine of the church that is incumbent upon us today must learn something from the history of the concept of the community on Lutheran soil."[115]

Both are criticized today for a somewhat romanticized concept of community. But, unlike Althaus, Bonhoeffer found himself dealing with too many issues when he tried to reconcile completely divergent disciplines like historicism and sociology on the one hand, and the theology of revelation on the other. His cousin Hans-Christoph von Hase, who was a student in

Marburg and kept him supplied with news of Heidegger and Bultmann, who were working there, wrote to him: "There will not be many who really understand it, the Barthians won't because of the sociology, and the sociologists won't because of Barth."[116]

Bonhoeffer, however, aimed at nothing less than bringing together his divergent heritages: to bring sociology and the critical tradition into harmony with the theology of revelation, that is, to reconcile Troeltsch and Barth. Applying the irreconcilable to the concrete church, he used a phrase from Hegel's *The Absolute Religion*. Hegel's words were "God existing as community";[117] in Bonhoeffer they became "Christ existing as church-community." To Hegel the community was the dwelling place of the Holy Spirit in the form of absolute spirit. To Seeberg it was the dwelling place of the Holy Spirit in the form of absolute will. Bonhoeffer refashioned the whole christologically, believing he had achieved a third standpoint that transcended the Troeltsch-Barth antithesis. Subsequent critics regarded this as more bold than successful.

There was a personal concern in Bonhoeffer's concept that established the word of God in a sociological community of persons. In the living church, salvation acquired its *pro me* in an *extra me,* without the one disappearing in favor of the other.

He found the tools for this ecclesiology in the I-You personalism prevalent in those years. He apparently discovered Grisebach[118] from his reading of Gogarten. He criticized Grisebach for attempting to make the I-You relationship absolute, and tried to prevent it from relapsing into a neo-idealism by incorporating it into his christological ecclesiology. But Seeberg had also introduced him to the idea that people were characterized by sociality and mutuality, and by these means he thought he could describe both the worldly and the transcendent nature of revelation. He was all the more willing to use these tools since he feared that Barth's emphasis on the diastasis of God threatened the "humanly" involved and yet "divinely detached presence of God."[119] Although Ferdinand Ebner is often cited as the source of this personalism, there is no evidence that Bonhoeffer was acquainted with his works at the time.

For Bonhoeffer rigid theological tenets became fluid when their thoroughly social character was revealed. Already he was developing the concept of fellowship (*Mitmenschlichkeit*) that later became so important. This paved the way, theologically and practically, for his rediscovery of the act of confession. Here were the roots of the formula he worked on in Tegel of "being for others." Judging from the quotations, Barth played a minor role in *Sanctorum Communio,* but he was in the background. Bonhoeffer's primary question to Barth now was whether his concept of revelation did not neglect the church. His critics contend that this led Bonhoeffer, in the power of his discovery, to let the difference between Christ and community disappear to the point that the two were identified with one another, and that with his critical function of eschatology he also dispelled the provisional character of the church, losing sight of its "historicity." Regin Prenter, however, has correctly shown that Bonhoeffer never regarded his formula of "Christ existing as church-community" as being true in reverse.[120]

In any case, ecclesiology dominated Bonhoeffer's theology in its early stages, absorbing the Christology. Later the reverse became true. Despite some immature, ambiguous, or mistakenly adopted concepts, this preliminary organization of his ideas served as a barrier against metaphysical speculation and a transcendental evaporation of the idea of God. Although distant, God was the close and concrete encounter with one's fellows. Faith was the bond with the community; to be human was possible through fellowship. Although his theological language would change, Bonhoeffer held fast to these ideas.

The church's cultural significance and its proud place in history were not enough to convince him, despite the respect it inspired in earlier generations and the impact it had on him in Rome. But he was held by the point where revelation manifested itself in preaching, praise, prayer, or service to one another. There, its continuing greatness could be grasped sociologically.

When Bonhoeffer's first systematic attempt was finally published, it was ignored. Only with the publication of the fragmentary *Letters and Papers from Prison* twenty years later was interest in this immature early work first aroused. In 1955 it received a tribute from the man whose unknown, critical ally the young writer had believed himself to be. In his *Church Dogmatics* Barth wrote:

> If there can be any possible vindication of Reinhold Seeberg, it is to be sought in the fact that his school could give rise to this man and this dissertation, which not only awakens respect for the breadth and depth of its insight as we look back to the existing situation, but makes far more instructive and stimulating and genuinely edifying reading today than many of the more famous works which have since been written on the problem of the church.... I openly confess that I have misgivings whether I can even maintain the high level reached by Bonhoeffer, saying no less in my own words and context, and saying it no less forcefully, than did this young man so many years ago.[121]

Seminar Essays

Students were required to show that they had attended all basic required courses. Some of these courses interested Bonhoeffer; in others, he fulfilled the requirement only at the last minute. The areas of study and topics that he examined offer a glimpse of theological academia in that era; they also reveal the roots that nourished his thinking in later years.

Only during his eighth semester did he fulfill the requirement in Old Testament, under Ernst Sellin. It was one time when Bonhoeffer truly began too late. "The Various Answers to the Problem of Suffering in Job" was his final essay as a student.[122] He was apparently in a hurry, since Sellin criticized the lack of any bibliographical references. The "theological" interpretation of the Old Testament, a topic that later became popular, was not an issue at the time. Bonhoeffer employed the entire vocabulary of this topic: "ethical high point," "Christian deepening," "titanic rebellion." Using historical-critical methods, he examined the various sources. He enjoyed tracking down the "writer's achievement," as he had done in his study of Horace and Catullus in secondary school. One of the theses for the defense of his doctorate had to be in Old Testament. His thesis here: "The speeches of God in Job 38–41 are not part of the original plan of the book of Job."[123]

In the summer semester of 1926, he worked on "St. Paul and the Fifteenth Chapter of the Gospel according to St. John" for Deissmann (New Testament).[124] Here he examined Bultmann's newly published religious historical work on the parallels to the parables about the vine and the Mandaean myth about the Tree of Life.[125] He compared the Johannine *"en emoi"* with Paul's concept of the body of Christ, concluding: "The numerous external agreements in particular allow us to recognize the internal discrepancies of the two men that much more clearly."[126] Using Barthian categories, he uncritically tackled the Pauline "in Christ," as "our inclusion in the revelatory exaltation of this human being, in Jesus as Christ, wherein he is established as the *new* person."[127]

Bonhoeffer soon retreated from such attempts to secure the *extra me* in the negation, because here the concreteness of the new person evaporated into Barth's famous "heavenly double,"[128] and the *pro me* disappeared into the *extra me*.

In church history, three months before Holl's death, he wrote the study "Luther's Views of the Holy Spirit, according to the Disputations of 1535–1545."[129] Thirty-two large file sheets of immense work with excerpts remain. They show how technically impractical Bonhoeffer was in working with sources; he couldn't bring himself to set up an index file. Here Bonhoeffer revealed how Holl's interpretation of justification by faith had influenced him. According to Holl, for example, Luther represented an economic doctrine of the Trinity over and against a scholastic-immanent one.[130] Holl made a strong distinction between the scholastic conception of spirit and Luther's conception; the scholastic conception remained bound to a metaphysical Trinitarian systematic. Yet the Spirit does not bring about metaphysical, but moral, discernment; it is revealed in the judicial language of the law and in the Gospels' statement of grace as majestic will.

In systematic theology he wrote four more papers, all of which Seeberg marked "excellent," in contrast to his first early paper:

1. In November 1925, after his earlier encounter with historical and pneumatic interpretation, he had to deal with the classic themes of reason and revelation, philosophy and theology, in his paper "Reason and Revelation in Early Lutheran Dogmatics."[131] Bonhoeffer's point of departure was Luther's *Formula of Concord*, which acknowledged an independent if somewhat weak reason next to the norm set by the Holy Scripture. He then portrayed the development of this starting point under Melanchthon and its influence on Luther's early scholasticism.

2. In January 1926 he submitted a paper entitled "Church and Eschatology, or the Church and the Kingdom of God." It began:

> In theology, it has always been a sign of religious power and genuine seriousness when eschatology became something more than just a somewhat embarrassing and obligatory appendage to dogmatics, as we see so often in 19th century theology, but when it was truly recognized, following the example of the Reformers, as the end and the goal to which everything is related. . . . For the Reformers, a doctrine of justification without eschatology was like a spear without its point. The justified person is *justus nondum in re, sed in spe* [justified not in oneself, but in hope]. . . ."[132]

The definitions of the kingdom of God had been influenced by Ritschl, but Bonhoeffer differed from Ritschl and Seeberg in ruling out the notion of a moral development between the salvation realized in the church and future salvation.

3. In May 1926 he gave another report on the problems of eschatology: "The Teaching of Early Protestant Dogmatics on Life after Death and the Last Things":

> This work states that the old Protestant dogmatic "in general simply took the biblical sayings and elaborated on them in a formalistic fashion." "Difficult problems of scripture like apocatastasis or chiliasm are ignored or

condemned without sufficient investigation in terms of content . . . the eschatological problem in John isn't even touched . . . in the development of eschatology there has been very little sign of a productive systematic energy . . . and yet" . . . "initially, the important things have been retained, the idea of a divided course of history, the purely transcendental concept of the Kingdom of God . . . but what is still more: we cannot overlook that the radical adoption of biblical eschatology included a not insignificant religious and moral force, thus acquiring a kind of seriousness that has not been achieved by the systematically more independent coming generation . . . if we can learn little on this point methodologically from the ancient Protestant fathers, we can learn something from the unbelievable seriousness and awe with which they approached every chapter of dogmatics."[133]

Bonhoeffer's theology is often accused of neglecting the eschatological element. As Martin Honecker writes:

In all Bonhoeffer's writings, the eschatological dimension is noticeably reticent; the body of Christ exists in the world and is not on the path to its future. Beside the unfolding of the historical Christ event and the reference of faith to the current reality of the church, the hope in the coming of the Kingdom of God as the overcoming of the current church dialectic between *peccatorum communio* and *sanctorum communio* withdraws. This abbreviation of the eschatological reservation explains the positive tone in Bonhoeffer's doctrine of the church. Eschatology's critical significance for ecclesiology is that it reminds the church that it did not just originate apostolically in history and affect its present age in general, but, as the wandering people of God, that it hopes for its future as *una sancta ecclesia*.[134]

During his seminar course work, Bonhoeffer confronted the eschatological theme three times. Particularly in the Berlin theological school, this discovery of eschatological tension was new for the understanding of the New Testament and its dialectic between "no longer" and "not yet." During the same period, Althaus's *The Last Things* was published, and each subsequent edition was substantially revised. Bonhoeffer personally found the topic of eschatology very stimulating, although it seems he approached it as part of his routine academic work. Those who came in contact with him were often astonished by the passion with which he treated eschatology as a serious contemporary issue, particularly in his sermons and catechism. It later dominated the entire *Discipleship* period. If it seemed that its importance receded during his final years, this was because of his sure, instinctive opposition to using it as a false refuge in that desperate situation. There he opted to include eschatology within Christology, not vice versa.

4. Finally, in November 1926, he wrote a paper for Seeberg on the Erlangen school of theology, and took as his subject Seeberg's teacher F. H. R. Frank; his title was "Frank's Views of the Spirit and Grace, as Stated in His *System of Christian Certainty* and *System of Christian Truth.*"

Frank came from the Hofmann school. He modified it by applying Schleiermacher's ideas to the subjective experience of spiritual rebirth, and from this developed his "system of Christian truth." Bonhoeffer's critique was sparked by this independent act of the new self, which consents only after the Holy Spirit has brought about justification. Frank and the Erlangen school had vigorously opposed Albrecht Ritschl. Bonhoeffer agreed in part with both Frank and Ritschl. He criticized Frank for not having escaped metaphysics; he also criticized his doctrine of the immanent Trinity (which Seeberg had claimed to detect in Luther). Frank, Bonhoeffer said, taught the "immanence of the Trinity that had been customary in Catholic dogmatics, superseded by Luther, and after his death was re-adopted in the early Protestant scholasticism." Disagreeing with Ritschl, however, he granted that Frank had understood the link between spirit and grace personally and ethically, and "thus at Frank's level of discourse the metaphysical content has been superseded." Bonhoeffer continued to find the Erlangen school stimulating. He acquired the complete works of Frank and Hofmann, and liked to use Frank's four-volume *Theology of the Formula of Concord*[135] when he discovered the "confessions" during the church struggle. At that point Hofmann's hermeneutics also appealed to him.

These documents from his student days reveal which ideas Bonhoeffer was exposed to and which ones remained foreign to him. At the university in Berlin he was confronted with the historical-critical method, early Christianity, Luther and Lutheranism, and the nineteenth century. In comparison, he had little interest in or exposure to the Old Testament, Calvin and his world (which he almost completely ignored), and the great medieval theologians. Yet he discovered the new world of dialectical theology on his own.

Catechetical Writings. Bonhoeffer enthusiastically participated in the practical theological seminars, presenting more papers than were required. He strove to gain more experience in his natural gift for dealing with people, especially children. Dialectical theology taught him new things as well, since its origins were in practical ministry, which it regarded as the crown of the theological existence. Unlike many of his fellow students, he did not regard his work with Friedrich Mahling (professor of practical theology since 1909) as secondary. He wrote his catecheses quickly and with enjoyment. The only thing that bored him was the routine of fixed question-and-answer papers, which he never required of his own students later. He preferred clear, logical, and well-formulated trains of thought over the repetition of set phrases.

The surviving manuscripts show a number of charming characteristics. He had to write his first catecheses on the three would-be disciples (Luke 9:57-52). This was the text with which he began his exciting 1935 lecture to his candidates on "discipleship." But what a difference there is between that later lecture and the catechesis! Here, ten years earlier, he opened with military metaphors.[136] He simplified the first of the three would-be disciples with the phrase "Look before you leap," characterized the second with "All or nothing," and the third with "Up and at 'em." Mahling correctly praised the "vividness with which the children were approached, the rich relationship with real practical life."[137] He was less concerned with the theological content. Bonhoeffer introduced the catecheses with a thoroughly professional critical exegesis.[138]

In his introductory meditation to a catechetical draft on the second article, Bonhoeffer warned against awakening mythical-theological ideas with the term "only begotten Son." True to Harnack, he felt the Apostle's Creed lacked enough references to Jesus' life on earth.

Bonhoeffer's version of the story of the tax collector Zacchaeus (Luke 19:1-9) illustrated his dangerous ability to dramatize biblical stories in his own words. He had a talent for vivid narration, and he had adopted his mother's freedom in adding his own ingredients to the story. Mahling did not stop him from doing this, and Bonhoeffer showed little concern at that point for correctly transposing the text.

In one class on the concept of "honor," he addressed the topic of the duel and war: "The duel as a means of restoring injured honor must be rejected; the same holds for a war that only serves the same purpose."[139]

Curiously, his lowest examination marks were in the area of his greatest natural ability, in his catechesis on Matthew 8:5-13. After receiving the results in Barcelona, he wrote to his parents: "Incidentally you recently . . . gave me a pleasurable afternoon (by sending) the grades from the Consistory."[140] The report stated:

> . . . both didactically and methodologically the catechesis shows considerable shortcomings. . . . The link with similar ideas that are already familiar to the children is meager. . . . The appeal to children's hearts is insufficient. The entire catechesis really just repeats the text. It is often so excessively doctrinaire that the children would be bored. . . . Critique of Luke's text does not belong in the lesson. . . .

This work can only be graded as "passing" by taking into account the undeniable diligence with which the candidate worked on it, and in the expectation that he will make serious efforts to improve himself in the catechetical and psychological realms.[141]

Sermons. His first attempts at homiletics excited Bonhoeffer far more than his catechetical efforts; here, he saw the line between failure and success, between dead sermonizing and the life-giving act. During his fifth semester he preached on the parable of the idle servant (Luke 17:7-10) on 18 October 1925 in the church in Stahnsdorf. He had already corresponded during the summer with his Hedgehogs friend Dreier about the text and the phenomenon of preaching. Dreier envied Bonhoeffer's clarity about the reason and goal for his studies, but Bonhoeffer responded by explaining the discouraging doubts that were part of the path to the pulpit; along that path lurked vanity and the risk of entangling one's own experience with things that were foreign to it.

It was a stiff sermon. It focused on the justification of sinners, relating it to the rejection of morally autonomous people. For this, he was able to use Barth's portrait of this morality as a tower of Babel;[142] and he used it again in his next sermon on Psalm 127:1.[143]

He enjoyed writing a sermon on the Letter of James 1:21-25 ("be doers of the Word") for a youth service he had to hold in July 1926. He obviously felt more sure of himself than he did before the faceless congregation of the usual Sunday morning service. He spoke on the demand for obedience to true authority, to avoid the clutches of the many pseudo-authorities. He concluded with the stirring words:

> Adam, do not hide; the Lord sees behind the entrenchments. Come out, man, from the dugout, there where the air blows free, where the bullets whiz by. There, Brother, there is no one at your back; there you must decide, act! Believe and obey![144]

Mahling found it very fine "in content and form, in its dashing masculine style and heartfelt goodness, pure truthfulness and conscientious seriousness."[145] The introductory exegesis again displayed a detailed historical-critical work; he used the knowledge from his work on the first letter of Clement. He emphatically rejected James as the author and contested Luther's verdict that the epistle was "dry."

In his examination sermon on Luke 9:51-56, the story of the inhospitable Samaritans, he presented his entire hermeneutics to the congregation. He began: "We want to look into this text until the walls of the centuries that separate us from it fall away and we see the eternal core of this story."[146] Then, after he had expounded on this, he continued:

> Now the picture has become clear to us in all its details, the walls of the centuries separating us from this story have fallen away. We face Jesus eye to eye, we see the Samaritans, hear the disciples, and now—are we not startled before this picture? Does this not awaken us? Do our ears remain deaf? Do we not recognize in this picture—our own era? Can't each of us point correctly to the place where we would stand in this picture?[147]

His examiners were not as emphatic as Mahling:

> the writer, who shows the capacity for an enthusiasm for development, will have to discard some things and learn some things before he is able to write a really finished sermon. . . . He is lacking in clarity. . . The writer is advised to study model sermons diligently, Dryander, Conrad, Althaus, etc., and . . . while seizing on whatever the most important point may be . . . to cultivate a simple and noble simplicity. . . .[148]

His father sent Dietrich the letter and reports, signed by general superintendent Otto Dibelius, and added: "We were delighted with the general tenor of the Consistory's verdict. To learn the tone of the official church, you will have to read a great many model sermons. In my case things were quite different; Wernicke told me not to read any psychiatric literature, because it only made one stupid."[149]

First Ties to a Regional Church

At the end of 1925, about the same time Bonhoeffer began work on his dissertation, he began working with a children's Sunday school group. Thus, just as he was embarking on the heavy reading load demanded by *Sanctorum Communio*, he was devoting himself to a group of children who required a considerable amount of his time, for he always prepared his lessons carefully and the children made clamorous demands on him.

Sunday School in Grunewald. Church regulations required candidates for the first theological examination to produce a statement from their superintendent that they had taken an active part in parish work. A Swabian, Max Diestel, was superintendent of the church district that included Grunewald (district Kölln-Land I, today Wilmersdorf); his office was at St. Paul's in Lichterfeld. He took an interest in this young man of half-Swabian ancestry.

In light of the academic load Bonhoeffer was carrying due to his dissertation, he could easily have obtained a statement from Diestel based on minimal church participation. But Bonhoeffer didn't want that.

The Grunewald church was led by the Reverend Hermann Priebe, who had confirmed Bonhoeffer, but forty-year-old Reverend Karl Meumann was in charge of the children's services and religious classes. On Friday evenings, Bonhoeffer prepared the Sunday school classes with the other teachers at Meumann's house. On Sundays he held a catechism class for children, for which he prepared written lessons. After a short time he persuaded his younger sister Susanne to join the circle of helpers and attend the Sunday school. As the children's demands grew, he and Susanne invited them to the Bonhoeffer home for games and took them on outings.

Bonhoeffer preached to the children in his group as much as possible. He made biblical stories as exciting as sagas or as appealing as fairy tales. He went to great trouble to hold the children's attention, which is why he so carefully wrote out in advance what he proposed to tell them. He told them tales such as that about the king in his castle who sent out heralds who never returned; about the devil who stole a pot of red paint and painted the humble mushroom, bestowing upon it the poison of pride; about the old woman caught in a snowstorm outside a locked door (an Advent story); and he gave a dramatic account of the struggle for the people's confidence between the prophets Jeremiah and Hananiah. He had no qualms about taking liberties with the text.

He discovered that when children expect something it is impossible to give only part of oneself to them. He also became aware of the role of psychological and personal factors, and appreciated the risk these could pose to the real purpose of religious instruction. He was disturbed when children began to flock to his group, and became so worried about developing personal ties that he wrote for advice to Richard Widmann, who now led a parish in Württemberg. Bonhoeffer's letter has not survived, but Widmann replied:

> I do not think it dangerous for one to be "successful" with children, provided that they are still children. . . . I would not take children from another group. I believe that for the sake of the cause one must work against one's own personality. Besides, it would certainly give rise to terrible unrest among the children, which would be extremely dangerous.[150]

For Bonhoeffer, this first step in practical church work was much more than the fulfillment of a requirement for taking his examinations. It confronted him with a very personal issue: should practical work be the counterpoint to the theme of his theological existence—or should it be the other way around? After his uncommitted beginnings in Tübingen, it had become plain that there was a gulf between the two realms; but it was also clear that the existence of this gap should not be acknowledged. Thus he spiritedly wrote Widmann that the hardest theological pronouncements of Barth were worthless if they could not be explained thoroughly to the children in Grunewald.

From his village parsonage, Widmann complained about the social gulf that divided him as a theologian from his parishioners:

> The church as it is today is tied to the two social strata of the middle-class bourgeoisie and the farmers—the country people—and this extends as far as dogmatics and ethics. I belong neither to the bourgeoisie nor to the country folk, but to the "intellectual world," which does *not* go to church, which is of necessity nonconfessional. However insignificant that may be for the problem of the "church," to me the sociological limitedness of the church is actually of the greatest importance. I belong to a world that is and can only be different from that of my congregation; for the world to which I speak and from which I speak does not go to church. It would certainly not be the worst thing—though on the other hand it would be objectively insignificant—if I denied my past and out of necessity became reactionary like Barth, because I lacked the confidence to say and do, "blow for blow, what should be said and done" to open the doors of the church to the intellectual world. But I do not want to deny my past.
>
> I have already seen that it is useless to flavor one's preaching with large or small quantities of psychology in order to make oneself intelligible to one's listeners. They still sense this other world and reject [me]. The only alternative for an intellectual minister is to decisively renounce his former world or to leave the ministry, unless he can become a university professor. For preaching is, after all, a dialogue. But a dialogue between an intellectual and a bourgeois or peasant is no longer possible. The two no longer understand each other. As an intellectual priest I am condemned to tragic solitude.
>
> The Barthian psychology of the *Epistle to the Romans* grew from the soil of the modern world, and it is meaningless from the pulpit of the church of the bourgeoisie and the peasantry. Barthian theology has quite definite sociological assumptions that are irrelevant to the present-day church. The Barth who remained in the church became a reactionary. That is how the problem faces us today. For the time being I am waiting and giving myself time to think. What do you say to taking the church seriously as a sociological fact, and drawing the consequences?[151]

Bonhoeffer's reply has not survived, but Widmann's notebook shows that he answered immediately.[152] Widmann's next letter, dated 26 April, indicated Bonhoeffer's vigor in rebutting these clever questions. Bonhoeffer accused his former fellow student of drawing "undialectical conclusions" from Barth. Using the distinction between "ultimate and penultimate" that later became important in his ethics, he reproached Widmann for making the penultimate the decisive criterion, even though "in the last resort it did not matter."[153] Widmann replied by asking: "Do you think that only last things, ultimate things, can force one's decisions?"[154]

Bonhoeffer, of course, was younger and more inexperienced than the correspondent who plied him with these difficult questions. But at a time when he was taking his first step into the real life of the church, it was impossible for him to agree with a friend who was considering the possibility of leaving it. He refused to accept the possibility that the newly discovered gospel might have to stop—and he with it—at the sociological boundaries of the real church. Later in life, Bonhoeffer had to acknowledge that the gulf between the two existed in many different forms, but for the moment, he refused to recognize that it was a decisive factor and could affect his actions. At the age when he was considering whether eventually to take up practical church work instead of the respected, privileged, and uncommitted career of a professor, he did not let himself be frustrated. Widmann's letter did not make him uncertain. If anything, it made him more curious about his ability to put into practice what he had learned.

In Barcelona, he wrote in his diary:

> What affected me most was bidding farewell to church work. On 18 January [1928] we Sunday-school helpers had our last meeting with the Pastor Meumann. He spoke cordially and well, and I answered briefly. Without realizing it, we had grown closer than we thought. Then, on 21 January, we had our last children's service. I spoke on the man sick with palsy, and particularly on the saying: Your sins are forgiven, and tried yet again to reveal the kernel of our gospel to the children. They were attentive and perhaps affected a little . . . Meumann mentioned my name in his general prayer. For some time, the congregational prayer has often sent cold shivers down my spine but when the throng of children with whom I have spent two years prayed for me, the effect was incomparably greater.[155]

The Thursday Group. A lively youth group had developed out of the Sunday school classes. Since April 1927 Bonhoeffer had invited those who had outgrown Sunday school to the Wangenheimstrasse home for a "reading and discussion evening." The program would have done credit to a college; it covered systematic, religious, ethical, denominational, political, and cultural topics. He gave a report on Catholicism, and the young people prepared short introductions to the evening discussions. They attended the opera and concerts together; before taking them to a performance of *Parsifal* Bonhoeffer gave them an introductory talk on the subject.

The group members were very mature for their age; some of them came from Jewish families living in the Grunewald district. They sent him their sentimental, Nietzschean, or atheist attempts at poetry; later some of them wrote to him in Barcelona and New York:

> "You will remember a conversation in which I argued that divine revelation was manifested in art, while you said that this put too low a rating on the idea of God."
>
> "I know no modern lyric poet who will endure except for Rilke. But Carossa's poems, for example, are all good, but not anymore. And his loveliest, simplest and most lyrical were still improved upon by Goethe...."
>
> "I believe that I understand what you wrote about yourself, above all the changes in your philosophy and theology through new perspectives...."
>
> "The third act of *Parsifal* was broadcast a few days ago. I followed with the piano arrangement. Do you still recall taking us to a performance and explaining it to us? I'm still grateful to you for having enabled me, I think with Kundry, to grasp one of the essential aspects of Christianity."
>
> "Examinations for the Reichswehr. Don't imagine I wanted to become an officer, I am hardly that kind of person, but at my father's strong wish I applied to be a medical officer.... Since the prospects for all students are so appallingly slim, one is glad at being *allowed* to work."
>
> "I'm glad I saved up enough money before Easter to be able to buy a collapsible boat, and now I can't talk about anything else."[156]

When Bonhoeffer left for Barcelona, the group gave him a copy of Albert Schweitzer's *On the Edge of the Primeval Forest*. A young student, Goetz Grosch, took over the group; seven years later he became a candidate in Bonhoeffer's Finkenwalde seminary.

In his Barcelona diary Bonhoeffer wrote:

> On 18 January [1928] I held the last meeting of my Thursday group. A newcomer, Peter Rosenbaum, was there, a young man of unusual intelligence and sensitivity—he defended Luther's doctrine of the real presence! The young people had brought questions that we discussed. Finally, I asked what they thought of the fact that Christianity had conquered the world in comparison with many other religions; this led us to the question of the essence of Christianity, and we discussed revelation and religion, and the contrast and connection between them.[157]

Nearly all the members of this group later died in Hitler's war or his concentration camps; Goetz Grosch died in action on the front.

Examinations. Bonhoeffer's student days ended brilliantly with his graduation on 17 December 1927. After his examination by Seeberg, Deissmann,
Mahling, Sellin, and Lietzmann, he publicly defended his theses against
three fellow students: Stupperich, Rössler, and Dress. Nine months earlier,
he had sat opposite his brother-in-law Dress. Bonhoeffer wrote notes on his
copy of his eleven theses.[158] Next to the fourth one, on Bultmann's concept
of potentiality, he wrote: "The cause for the actualization of our potentiality either lies in God alone, in which case the potentiality is superfluous, or
in human beings, which is inconsistent with God's omnipotence."[159] Next to
the eleventh point, in which he rejected the idea of a specifically *Christian*
teaching of history, he wrote:

> A Christian philosophy of history exists, and so do historically edifying
> lessons. The goal of teaching history is to present the most objective por-
> trayal as possible of the great historical figures and the relation between
> them, together with a correct assessment, if possible. We cannot see the
> heart, but the person. We are not judges of the world. Thus basically every-
> thing in history evades a *Christian* evaluation.[160]

Then he wrote down the chief points for his speech of thanks to the faculty, in which he referred especially to Harnack and Seeberg. He received the
rarely awarded *summa cum laude.*

Four weeks later, with his doctoral thesis accepted, he passed the first theological examination of the Consistory of Mark Brandenburg with a grade
of "very good." With that, he entered his regional church's course of training for the ministry. The choice between the ministry and an academic
career lay open to him. His family took it for granted that he would choose
the latter, where few obstacles and only friendly advancement awaited him.
But his problem was not how to enter the academic world, it was how to
escape it. The pulpit appealed to him more than the professor's lectern.

At Christmas 1927 the entire family gathered in the house on Wangenheimstrasse. During that year Karl-Friedrich had qualified as a lecturer, Klaus
had qualified for the Civil Service, and Dietrich had graduated. For the first
time since Walter's death, Karl Bonhoeffer wrote in his New Year journal:

> This Christmas, when we have all our surviving children together with us
> again, allows us to reopen the old book and we shall again report. . . . In the
> spring we held a large masked ball in the house. . . . This evening the Schle-
> ichers and Dohnanyis are with us, and Karl-Friedrich, Klaus and Dietrich.
> Next year Dietrich will be in Barcelona. . . .

CHAPTER THREE

ASSISTANT PASTOR IN BARCELONA: 1928

Bonhoeffer's year as an assistant pastor took him to a completely new environment. He felt he was "starting from the beginning," as he wrote in the diary he now resumed.[1] He had no inner affinity for Spain, as he had felt when he traveled to Italy in 1924, and his new position brought him into contact with a kind of person unfamiliar to him. In Grunewald, he had practically no contact with the type represented by these Germans living abroad: businesspeople with a petit bourgeois outlook. Here there was little sign of the hectic postwar years in Germany and the thirst for novelty and experiment that prevailed in Berlin; the small Protestant community in Barcelona clung to its old patterns and ways of thought. After a fortnight in Barcelona, Bonhoeffer noted in his diary that visits to his parishioners were "very pleasant, except that conversations take a course completely different from what one is used to at home. Since I have been here, I have not had a single conversation in the Berlin-Grunewald style."[2]

Until then, Bonhoeffer had lived in an academic world, where every week he could choose from what the worlds of the theater, music, and literature had to offer. Daily meals had been accompanied by well-informed conversation about political or philosophical matters. Now he was suddenly cut off from all this, and had little time even to keep up correspondence with the world he knew.

Until then, he had been able to devote his time to rigorous theological discussions in the seminars; the latest books came his way almost as a matter of course. Now his time was consumed by local choirs or gymnastic societies, committee meetings, and consultations in the German colony. He devoted the rest of his time to visiting parishioners or preparing for services.

Until then, every plan and every move had been discussed with the other members of his large family. Now he was thrown entirely on his own resources. According to his diary, however, this was the "realization of a wish that had been growing stronger and stronger inside me in recent years and months, namely, to stand entirely on my own feet, outside my previous circle."[3]

He had not relinquished the privileged position into which he was born and that had left its mark on him; this was not yet the step into the unsheltered life he had once wished for, for the sake of solidarity with "the others." For the time being, he was filled with a great curiosity about the vocation of the ministry, and for the first time he had a sense of professionalism:

> It is a very singular experience when one sees work and life really converge—a synthesis that we all sought but hardly found in our student days; when one really lives *one* life and not two, or rather, half of one. It gives value to work and objectivity to the worker, and leads to a recognition of one's own limitations that is to be gained only in concrete living.[4]

For the first time, his personality, time, and talents were devoted to the practical tasks of his church, and for the first time he fell under the authority of one of its average officials. The aristocratic-bourgeois child from Wangenheimstrasse, with his high intellectual standards and demanding tastes, his need for harmony between his bearing and verbal expression, was now plunged into the occasionally pseudoserious and easily satisfied environment of a parish. Far from oppressing him, this conflict between aspiration and realization spurred him on.

Selecting a Post As Vicar

Bonhoeffer was not concerned with ecumenical ideas or ambitions during his year in Barcelona. He still had no more interest in the ecumenical movement than he did as a student.

Bonhoeffer's superintendent at the time, Max Diestel, was very active in the Berlin branch of the World Alliance for Promoting International Friendship through the Churches. Bonhoeffer's library included books from Diestel, including Charles S. Macfarland's *International Christian Movements* and R. H. Wallau's *The Unity of the Church*, both published during the 1920s. Particularly in the passages about the World Alliance, Bonhoeffer made notations in the margins. But it is likely that he planned to read these books in preparation for his trip to the United States.

The only interest Bonhoeffer showed in the ecumenical cause during this period came during his journey home from Barcelona, when he visited his brother Klaus in Geneva.[5] He wanted to learn more at the League of Nations about employment-related issues, which were also very much a part of the World Alliance's work. He even planned to write about this in 1929:

> When I arrived Klaus recommended that I learn more at the League of Nations about the questions concerning the churches and the League; since he had connections to the librarian there, he could help me find material. I was there yesterday for the first time and tried to get an overview, but haven't found anything yet. Today I still have to look through the topics of protection of children, minorities and calendar reform and, if I find something, would prepare an article on it.[6]

Nothing came of this article. Still, Bonhoeffer must have heard of these topics from the World Alliance members who were on the Berlin faculty, such as Deissmann, Richter, and Siegmund-Schultze. But he had not yet taken up these ecumenical efforts as his own cause.

As Bonhoeffer's mentor, Diestel advised the young vicar on his future course of study in the church. Diestel had become acquainted with him at one of the candidates' evenings in his church district, and had conveyed Bonhoeffer's registration for the church examinations to the consistory in the summer of 1927. When Barcelona pastor Fritz Olbricht asked for a vicar, sending the request via High Consistory council member Hans Besig, Diestel recommended Bonhoeffer.

Diestel called at the beginning of November 1927. Bonhoeffer wrote in his diary: "After that telephone conversation I believe I was certain of the matter."[7] He immediately wrote Olbricht in Barcelona and asked a number of questions. Olbricht replied that Bonhoeffer would have much time for his own work, he could play the piano and there was also an opera, and that even in Barcelona one needed winter clothing. He hoped that Bonhoeffer would arrive in time for the church holidays.

But bureaucrats in those days didn't work any faster than they do today. Bonhoeffer still had a great deal of time, during which he received advice against going from Pastor Hermann Priebe, who had confirmed him, and others. They were not entirely wrong when they told him to consider the consequences of leaving the academic breeding ground, breaking his ties to the circles in the Grunewald parish, and they reminded him of Barcelona's insignificance for his practical education. But "without having any persuasive arguments against that—I was at the point where I wanted to do it. I myself find the way such a decision is made problematic . . . but this clarity is not so much intellectual as instinctive, the decision gets made; whether in retrospect it can be justified sufficiently is another question."[8]

He left at the beginning of February 1928; the entire family accompanied him to the station where he caught the night train to Paris. In Paris he was met by a classmate from Grunewald, Peter Olden, who took him to the Louvre, *Rigoletto,* and *Carmen.* He was fascinated by the High Mass at Sacré-Coeur Basilica:

> The people in the church were almost all from Montmartre, prostitutes and their men went to the Mass and submitted to all the ceremonies . . . one saw . . . how close, through their fate and guilt, these heavily burdened people stood to the essence of the Gospel. I've believed for a long time that Tauentzienstrasse in Berlin would be an extremely fruitful field for church work. It is much easier for me to imagine a praying murderer or prostitute than a vain person. Nothing goes more against prayer than vanity.[9]

Paris was cold and wet. When he arrived in Barcelona on 15 February 1928, the almond trees and mimosa were in bloom. He rented a room from three impoverished Spanish ladies. "Dietrich is very comfortable there, though everything is terribly primitive. The only place for everyone to wash is the toilet, which is very like a third-class lavatory on a train, except that it doesn't shake."[10]

The Country

Nineteen twenty-eight was a year of exceptional political calm in Spain. The royalist military dictatorship of General Primo de Rivera was enjoying a pause between the waves of unrest at home and in Morocco. Another three years were to pass before the monarchy was abolished, and five more before the country was plunged into the terrible civil war.

Bonhoeffer was shocked by the extreme social contrasts that he saw, and was surprised that the signs of revolt were not greater. Instead, he noted in his diary, he saw in the cafés "prosperous, rich, petit bourgeois, and truly poor-looking people all mingled together, so that it seems to me that the 'social question' . . . hardly plays any role. The incredible conditions in the Old Town here testify to this."[11]

He took a great liking to Barcelona, with its harbor, the old university, and especially the surrounding countryside, although he found the "Old Town" "even dirtier than Naples."[12] "The Spanish landscape almost seems to be part of history," he wrote to his parents. "The area around Barcelona, which I enjoy more and more, is one of the most beautiful in Spain."[13]

On the other hand, he regretted that he was unable to establish any real contacts with educated Spaniards. When this did occasionally occur, it soon became evident that they were violently anticlerical, as was the case of a professor whom he often saw. Bonhoeffer encountered the same anticlericalism in the course of his search for good modern Spanish literature.

> Barcelona itself is an unusually lively metropolis, caught up in an economic upsurge on the grand scale. . . . there are good concerts, a good though very old-fashioned theater, and only one thing is missing, namely, the intellectual exchange of ideas, which one does not find when one looks for it, even in Spanish academic circles. I believe the Spaniards to be unusually gifted, but so indolent that they simply do not train themselves. In their calm, their patience and their indolence they undoubtedly show strong Oriental characteristics, and in general one never loses the impression—whether in language, dancing or music, and often in the most ordinary actions— of being close to the east. Whether Spain as a whole will one day wake up I dare not say. But a great deal that is unique and traditional is slumbering in these people, and every now and again something breaks through and comes to life. I am at present looking for ancient plays, in which contests between Arab and Christian theologians are still performed in small provincial towns.[14]

He read *Don Quixote* in the original. During the Second World War he acquired a German edition, and the infatuated knight-errant struck him as a key to understanding Christian ethics in the Nazi period and his own situation in Tegel prison.[15]

Bonhoeffer's pleasure in reencountering Catholicism suffered a sharp setback; everything struck him quite differently than it had during his Roman visit:

> There are monks and clerics who really remind one of pictures by El Greco, but the average [priests] have alarmingly uneducated and sensual faces— a remarkable contrast to Rome. I believe that here there is really some justification for the foolish saying that religion is the opium of the people.[16]

> It is almost impossible to make any contact with the clergy, it was only by chance that I made the acquaintance of one priest or another, but as a result, and from their faces, I have no real desire for closer acquaintance.[17]

On the Feast of Corpus Christi, however, he refused to miss any of the bizarre lure of the processions and popular customs.

He liked the people in spite of their strangeness. He tried repeatedly to understand them, although the observations in his diary perhaps reveal more about the observer himself than about the Spaniards.

Spain is a diametrical opposite of Italy, a country that the influence of ancient culture—in pre-Christian times and in the Renaissance—passed by, and which instead has been subject for four hundred years to the domination of western culture. It is a country that at first is totally strange to one of humanist upbringing, and I really lack all clues to understand it; and this applies as much to contemporary as to historical Spain.

But, aside from this strangeness, there is also a certain sympathy or sense of kinship which one does not have toward Italy, and again I can explain this only from the attitude to ancient and humanist culture. In Italy, humanism and the classical period represented the solution of all problems, while in Spain there is a resistance to this which, I think, is also discernible among the Germans to some extent. Common to both Spaniards and Germans, I think, is the fact that neither completely exposed themselves to the impact of humanism, but always held something back.[18]

Spaniards laugh at no one more than at the conceited and the *poseur*. Whenever I discuss German strengths and weaknesses with Spaniards, even the simplest of them very tactfully point out that what we call pose is strange to them. I believe that we have thrown away a great deal of goodwill abroad by this. . . . [The Spaniard] is neither proud in our sense, nor is he temperamental in the way that we think of temperament . . . where one can see master and servant sitting at the same café table, and a well-dressed individual is not abused when he walks through the slums. . . . No one is so humble that he believes himself humbler than anyone else, and no one . . . has such a high opinion of himself that he permits himself to look down on anyone else. This situation appears everywhere, in cafés, in trains, on the street. Of course, there is such a thing here as a closed society, but this is not offensive to social feeling but, on the contrary, seems desirable.

To foreigners, Spaniards are not servile, as Italians often are, but correct, and often actually cool. Among Catalans one often encounters great unpleasantness, which no doubt arises from the political inclination toward France.[19]

Bullfighting. Ten years later, Bonhoeffer's students—amused but unable to connect his enthusiasm for bullfighting to the rest of his personality—often asked him to describe the ritual of the bullfight. It seemed so unexpected in a man who could see nothing in any boxing match. But he described the subtlety of this Spanish exercise in elegance and brute force with obvious expertise. His twin sister wrote to him, "I would not go to a bullfight for anything in the world. In comparison a boxing match must be completely innocuous."[20]

His enchantment with bullfights began when his brother Klaus visited him at Easter 1928. After the Easter sermon Dietrich took him to the arena. Klaus was so impressed that he refused to miss any of the bullfights at the larger arenas during his tour, and got to see the "King's Corridas" in Madrid and Seville. Dietrich described the experience:

> I cannot truly say that I was as horrified by it as many people think they ought to be because of their Central European civilization. It is, after all, a tremendous thing, savage, uninhibited brute force and blind fury attacking and being defeated by disciplined courage, presence of mind and skill. The moment of cruelty plays only a small part, particularly as in these fights the horses' bellies were protected for the first time, so that the dreadful scenes of my first *corrida* were lacking. But it is interesting to note that there was a long struggle before the horses were given this protection. It seems that the majority of spectators simply want to see blood and cruelty.
>
> In general, a tremendous amount of emotion is aroused among the people, and one is sucked into it. I believe it is no accident that the bullfight is ineradicably established in the country of the gloomiest and crudest Catholicism. Here is a remnant of uninhibited passionate living, and perhaps it is the bullfight which, by stirring up the entire soul of the people and producing such an outburst of popular emotion, enables a relatively high standard of morality to prevail in the rest of their lives, because the bullfight kills their passion—with the result that the Sunday *corrida* becomes a necessary appendage to the Sunday mass.[21]

Dietrich even took his parents to a bullfight when they came to see him during the late summer.

Bonhoeffer's minister gave him a great deal of freedom to travel. Occasionally he sent Dietrich to represent him on official visits to Majorca or Madrid. When Klaus came to see him, Olbricht gave him leave, and so the two brothers traveled to Toledo, Córdoba, Seville, Granada, and Algeciras. The North African coast tempted them again, and they attended another caliph's reception, but they decided that Spanish Morocco was more Europeanized than Libya had been. Klaus was again a very stimulating traveling companion.

In Madrid and Toledo Dietrich learned to appreciate the greatness of El Greco, and later he took advantage of every opportunity to see his paintings in New York or London. He very much wanted to take his parents to Granada, but their departure for Spain was postponed repeatedly since in 1928 it seemed likely that his father would become rector of the university. Eventually, however, another physician was appointed; only a few fine autumn days remained for the trip, during which Dietrich showed his parents the shrine of Montserrat and then accompanied them to Arles, Avignon, and Nîmes.

Picasso. With his love for secondhand and antique shops, Bonhoeffer found himself in a profitable milieu, and he surrounded himself later by some of his exquisite finds. Among them were the priceless southern Spanish tapestry with the portrait of Christ that hung above his desk, and a copper brazier that every candidate in Finkenwalde later remembered. It served one final purpose for the prison censor in a letter from Tegel prison. In 1943, Bonhoeffer wrote to his parents: "I read recently about the required registration of copper receptacles. That would include my Spanish brazier, only one would have to note that this is a piece of art from the eighteenth century. Strange, how little these kinds of things matter in such times."[22]

But the most exciting find was when he and Klaus were able to obtain a picture signed "Picasso" for practically nothing:

> I'm including the photograph of a lady . . . the lady that I bought at the flea market in Madrid. A teacher at the German School took the photograph for me so that I could make inquiries about the picture. . . . The picture drew much attention in the German community in Madrid. Opinions as to its value were mixed. But it didn't seem to me that anyone knew what they were talking about.[23]

Klaus was something of an expert on paintings. A Spanish painter in Barcelona "is very enthusiastic about the picture," Dietrich later wrote to his parents.[24] Klaus replied immediately:

> Your message about the Picasso is very interesting indeed. Did the painter compare the picture with the reproduction we saw at Marx's, and does he think it might be a copy of that? . . . If the picture comes to Berlin, we'll soon find out what's behind it. It's just unfortunate that, if it is declared an imitation in Berlin, all the arguments in favor of its authenticity won't help.[25]

The first art dealer in Berlin offered five thousand Reich marks for it. An American agent quadrupled the price. The director of the Folkwang Gallery in Essen also showed interest. In response, the first bidder declared that he had sent a photo of the picture to Picasso in Madrid, "who said that he had often been forged by a friend in Madrid."[26] The arguments went back and forth between Berlin, Hamburg, Essen, and Paris. Klaus postponed the decision again and again. The question of authenticity was never settled. Still, the "Picasso" remained a sensation envied by all his friends. In the spring of 1945, together with Bonhoeffer's other rare finds, it fell victim to the Allied phosphorus bombs.

India. A project that fascinated Bonhoeffer for the next eight years originated during his year in Spain. It deserves a place in his biography because it greatly influenced him, even though nothing came of it. In February 1928 his grandmother wrote: "In your place I should try some time or other to get to know the counterpoint of the world of the east; I am thinking of India, Buddha and his world." This bold suggestion, which was completely in the Tafel tradition, stuck.

In Barcelona, Bonhoeffer toyed with the idea of a voyage to Tenerife, for which his grandmother sent him some money. But before the chance arose he had to return to Berlin to qualify as a lecturer, and he put the money aside for the trip to India he hoped to take some day. In February 1929 he wrote to his grandmother that her present had "brought his eastern plans a whole lot nearer." It was still a vague, generalized thirst for new experience that impelled him to seek contact with a different spiritual world. Possibly, however, he was already drawn to the figure of Gandhi. A fellow student in Tübingen recalls a conversation one night in the winter of 1924–1925 in which they spoke about Gandhi's personality and work.[27]

The Parish

Pastor Olbricht treated his new vicar generously. Bonhoeffer regarded him as a kindly and courteous man, and appreciated the modesty and simplicity with which he carried out his duties. To a considerable degree, Olbricht was at home in the social world that shapes the reality of a congregation abroad. Appreciating that it was right to share these people's lives, Bonhoeffer allowed himself to be carried along by his mentor, in order to meet the demands of this other world. In his diary on 10 March—the last entry he made in Spain—he noted: "My theology is beginning to become humanist; what is the meaning of this? Did Barth ever live abroad?"[28]

The minister's principal reading consisted of "nationalistic literature and newspapers."[29] He called on Dietrich's parents when he returned to Berlin on his annual leave, and Dietrich heralded his visit by describing him as "a man who prefers a good glass of wine and a good cigar to a bad sermon."[30] Olbricht demanded little of his parishioners, and they liked him. He was unsettled by his assistant's energetic efforts to intensify the care of the spiritual needs of the people. In the winter of 1928–1929, when some members of the congregation expressed a desire for extra weekend services, Bonhoeffer wisely declined to avoid possible friction. In his final report he characterized his mentor:

I got along with him well; in light of the fact that I was only staying one year, I allowed much that I would otherwise have opposed. . . . The great popularity of the lectures was disagreeable to him, and the success of the nativity play angered him so that we had a confrontation. Otherwise everything went smoothly. . . . He knew that I stuck up for him everywhere, so that all ended well. During the entire year we never talked about a theological, let alone a religious, question. We essentially remained strangers but we liked one another. He gave me my freedom and for that I was grateful to him.[31]

Despite the freedom and travel he enjoyed, Bonhoeffer's wish to learn church work and make it a priority had not diminished. "I seem to have as much work here as I make for myself," he wrote to his grandmother. "I could be tremendously lazy if I wanted to be, I think, but as it is . . . I shall have plenty to do."[32] He had all kinds of things to do, although initially there were no parish groups or activities besides the worship services and official duties. He made work for himself, and the social obligations that arose from the parish and the larger German colony required a great deal of his time.

Established in 1885, the congregation had no confessional awareness. Although it was called "Evangelical," its origins were presumably Reformed. The church council was called a "presbytery," which led Dietrich's mother, who was brought up in eastern Germany, to ask what the word meant. The presbyters were respectable businesspeople who faithfully paid their dues but did not regularly attend church. "They support the church just as they do sport or the German National Party, but less actively."[33] Of the six thousand Germans in Barcelona, some three hundred belonged to the congregation, and the average attendance at services was about forty. During the summer holidays, when many people sought refuge from the heat by going north, this number was expected to diminish; to his great pleasure, Bonhoeffer succeeded in increasing the average attendance. The consequence was that the minister, who had been in the habit of announcing in advance the name of the preacher each Sunday in his parish newsletters, stopped doing so.

The congregation appeared to be one of the flourishing groups in the expatriate German community; it gave a picture of prosperity and a hectic social life. After his first five days Bonhoeffer wrote to his parents:

I have been received in the most friendly and courteous manner everywhere. . . . Today the director of the German Bank told me that at one of the balls . . . 10,000 *pesetas* had been spent on decorations alone, how many bottles of champagne had been drunk and that he was surprised that at another party only 84 bottles of champagne had been drunk; that at one

ball in a club 3 dancers from the *Moulin Rouge* had been brought in, to the
outrage of everyone, and that Mr. NN had brought them in, who . . . and
the like; that is Kleinstadt with lots of money! But these are always people
who have seen much of the world and who are, I believe, terribly good-
natured. I will have to see how I approach them.[34]

Bonhoeffer showed understanding for these people and their situation:

> . . . the war and in particular the revolutionary period simply bypassed
> these people, but there is also a good side to that, as the current saying goes.
> There is none of the nervousness and strain, the intellectual affectation and
> mannerisms that are so widespread in Germany today . . . in human terms,
> one finds quite admirable character traits here: decency, honesty, simplic-
> ity and a lack of pomposity.[35]

To the amusement of his brothers and sisters, he joined a number of
clubs: the German Club, whose first masked ball he prudently refrained from
attending; the German tennis club, where he played regularly; and the German choral society, where he valiantly played the piano accompaniment to all
the sentimental songs.[36] The Berlin vicar's fashionable round hat was the talk
of the German elementary school children; "perhaps that is the way to introduce oneself here," he commented.[37] He found his skill at music and chess
helpful. "There is only one thing I lack—the ability to play *Skat* [a German
card game]. That is something you have to be good at here; I may learn it
yet."[38] This world amused him, in fact, more than it bored him. There was
only one thing he found it hard to tolerate: the gossip that spread in this kind
of environment. He tried to confront it decisively, "whereby the best thing to
do is to know nothing about it and show not the slightest interest."[39]

But visits to parishioners, which he paid more conscientiously than the
parish was accustomed to, soon revealed other aspects of life in the German
colony. It was a time when the German commercial community in trading
centers had been forced into a difficult economic position. Strong competition from the western countries drove a number of its members into bank-
ruptcy. While Olbricht was away on leave, the twenty-two-year-old Bonhoeffer was faced with his first suicide, a businessman of long-standing
reputation who was a respected member of the congregation. Bonhoeffer
came across cases of bitter poverty and "a great deal of unemployment."[40] In
emergencies he did not hesitate to turn to his parents, not only with requests
for medical advice or prescriptions, but also for interest-free loans. He never
appealed to his father in vain. At Christmas he secured such a loan for his
landladies.

The German general consul Dr. Bobrik and his colleagues were more like the people Bonhoeffer had known in Berlin. Together with them, he devoted himself to the social work of the German welfare society. Every morning he held visiting hours in its office.

[One] has to deal with the strangest persons, with whom one would otherwise scarcely have exchanged a word: bums, vagabonds, criminals on the run, many foreign legionaries, lion and other animal tamers who have run away from the Krone Circus on its Spanish tour, German dancers from the music halls here, German gangster murderers on the run—all of whom tell one their life story in detail. It is often very difficult in these cases to give or to refuse at one's own discretion. As it is impossible to establish any guidelines on principle, the decisive factor has to be one's personal impression; and that can often and easily be mistaken . . . so in the course of time one finds oneself becoming sharper in defending the interests of those who are genuinely in distress and cannot be helped adequately. Twice since I have been here I have seen long-established and prosperous families totally ruined financially, so that they have been unable to go on buying clothes for their children or paying their school fees. . . . Yesterday for the first time I had a man here who behaved so impudently—he claimed that the minister had forged his signature—that I practically shouted at him and threw him out. . . . While taking a hurried departure he cursed and swore, and called out a threat that I have now heard often: "We shall see each other again, just come down to the harbor!" Afterwards I found out at the consulate that he is a well-known swindler who has been hanging about here for a long time, so I was quite pleased that I had dealt with him as I had. On the whole, however, I find that kindness and friendliness is the best way of dealing with these people. . . . When Olbricht does not like someone, he gives him a dressing down and throws him out, and he thinks that is more effective . . . the pleasure of seeing that one has been really helpful is rare, because in most cases the money runs through their fingers as soon as they get it. . . . The real trouble is that we have no employment bureau, and the reason for that is that businesses here are overstaffed already. The German businesses are pulling out. . . . We are continually concerned with Germans going home, though we know that things are no better there.[41]

Facing such situations he wrote to his father: "Dear Papa, can you send me a copy of your book on vagrancy? In view of my present work with such people, I should very much like to read it."[42]

Youth Work. Bonhoeffer was struck by the great contrast between the young people of Berlin and those in the German colony in Barcelona:

They know little or nothing of war, revolution and the painful aftermath of these things, they live well and comfortably, the weather is always fine—how could it be otherwise? The Youth movement period in Germany passed by without a trace here.[43]

When one asks ten-year-olds here what they want to be when they grow up, the answer very often is: "I shall run my father's business." That is so much taken for granted that no other possibility is even considered. The agreeable counterpart to this is that they find nothing more ridiculous than being blasé, and so people do not make themselves out to be what they are not.[44]

Bonhoeffer's first attempt at youth work in the congregation was intended for all age groups. The first thing he did was establish a Sunday school for the children. Here he had the pastor's backing, although there was less support for Bonhoeffer's plans to work with secondary school students.

The Sunday school got off to a bad start. Only one girl responded to the first invitation. The following Sunday, however, there were fifteen children. He wrote in his diary:

[They are] admirably bright and lively. I described to them the fine things there are in children's service, and this caught on. We shall see how things go next time. Since that last lesson I have felt transformed. The slight anxiety that I might not get anywhere with practical work has vanished. I have touched solid ground and shall go further, and I think I already have the children on my side; my next step must be to give religious instruction at the school. But first I must build up the Sunday school, and perhaps that will open a door.[45]

He promptly visited the home of each child who attended. The next time thirty turned up, and attendance never dropped below that number.

The 3 April was a wonderful day. Twice as many children in Sunday school. I told a story about the lost Paradise. The children's ignorance about religious questions is as shocking as it is wonderful and filled with a sense of responsibility. I asked the teachers at the school, and it seems that I have the most difficult children, lazybones, good-for-nothings, early bloomers, etc. I visited some of them this week. Two boys who have a bad reputation at the school turned out to be nice and well-raised at home.[46]

He had his parents send him the illustrated Bible by Schnorr von Carolsfeld, which he knew from his childhood and his mother's lessons. He still had no reservations about its Nazarene style. For the Nativity play (which was something completely new to the parish) he could hardly fend off all the children who wanted to participate. Bonhoeffer himself was moved by the eagerness with which the children participated.[47]

Through his "good-for-nothings" he made contact with the German secondary school. One of the teachers, a Swabian, lived in the same pension as Bonhoeffer. They became friends after discovering their common musical interests. The school had no official connections, however, to the pastor and parish, and offered no religious instruction.

After a short time Bonhoeffer's room was regularly filled with a swarm of schoolboys. He knew how to settle their school problems, help them with their work, and move angry teachers toward a more considerate opinion of their charges. He gave one boy a bicycle and another a tent. His pupils gave him a tremendous Christmas, the first he had spent away from home.

He was less successful in his efforts to arrange regular religious instruction at the secondary school. Here he faced not just opposition from the teachers, but from his colleague; Olbricht could not be won over for an innovation that might leave him with additional duties once Bonhoeffer left. As a result of this failure Bonhoeffer decided to give a series of talks, intended primarily for the older boys, during the winter of 1928–1929; a discussion group developed out of this. He wrote home that "it was shaping up well":

> They are enthusiastic, though very ignorant because of the incredible lack of preparation in school. At present we are discussing the nature of Christianity, and we shall go on to deal with particular problems, first of all that of immortality. The seniors must always read something, which is then reported on and discussed. The young people here of this age and even younger are different from those in Germany. A remarkable mixture of maturity with regard to manners and career questions, and great naïveté in other things. There is little intellectual blaséness or pomposity, nor is intelligence overrated. One has the impression of great honesty and clarity, which may be the result of the Spanish influence.[48]

Preaching. Abroad the range of experience in church work was limited. By the standards of a lively German congregation, Bonhoeffer missed "Bible studies, the young men's association, lecture evenings, religious instruction."[49] But in preaching, which he regarded as the mainspring of his ministry, he missed nothing. Here the twenty-two-year-old assistant was given more to do than church regulations required even of older vicars. In 1928 he had to write and deliver nineteen sermons.

He spent much effort on each one. "Writing sermons still takes up a great deal of my time. I work on them the entire week, devoting some time to them every day."[50] Still, he was always pleased when the minister turned the pulpit over to him: "On the first Sunday of Advent I shall be able to preach again because Olbricht will not be returning until the following week and I am very pleased about that."[51] He wrote Helmut Rössler:

> ... I share your experience. I never know what to do with this precious half hour we are given; I wouldn't have thought I would preach so differently ... and I am grateful. . . . it is a mixture of personal joy, let us say self-esteem, and objective gratitude. But this is indeed what all religions are sentenced to, this mixture of the personal and the objective, which one can perhaps ennoble but never get rid of totally, and as a theologian one suffers under this twofold. But on the other hand, who wouldn't be pleased about a full church, or that people come who haven't come for years, and on the other hand: who analyzes this pleasure to see that it's untainted? . . .
>
> I've noticed that the most powerful sermons were those where I told about the Gospel enticingly, as [I would tell] children a fairy tale about a foreign country. . . .
>
> On Sunday I will be speaking about Matthew 5:8, I have never approached a sermon with such trepidation. But I'm looking forward to Sunday.[52]

He was not satisfied with analyzing the present or presenting a straight-forward scriptural exegesis. He wanted to say something important, and he believed he had something important to say. People were to be confronted and excited, shaken out of their complacency and won over. He approached this goal using his skills and the text boldly and not very accurately. He hardly noticed the excessive demands that his highly specialized theological knowledge made on the businesspeople sitting below his pulpit. Nevertheless, he had a credibility that transcended the elaborate and difficult content of his sermons. Only later did he realize how little the word of God affects the listener independently of the person who speaks it. It uses messengers who are nothing but messengers—and yet it is inevitable that each individual is a specific messenger, and must wish to be so. Although most of the sermons Bonhoeffer preached so passionately to the Barcelona parishioners went far over their heads, he still addressed them as someone who met them during the week with unaccustomed warmth and pastoral concern.

The decisiveness of purpose behind Bonhoeffer's sermons is evident in his choice of texts. He did not stick to the recommended pericopes, but always chose brief phrases. Later in Finkenwalde he did not always hold this to be absolutely correct, but in his own homiletics he held to the rule that the lectionary should, where possible, occasionally have a freely selected text as counterpoint. When following a continuing biblical passage appeared unfruitful, one had that much more freedom to select one's own texts. He refused to be dissuaded from his opinion that a preacher should take interest and joy in what he planned to say from the pulpit on Sunday. It was not that he was scornful of listening to his elders, but he despised the kind of submissiveness that allowed for no joy in the work.

Because of this his Barcelona sermons had great thematic unity. As in the Grunewald Sunday school, he freely dramatized scenes or put himself in the position of the "psalmist." To contemporary tastes, his language borders on the flowery, and he made sweeping assertions. But it did not become jargon. He did not draw on the worldly language of the Kurfürstendamm, newspapers, or tabloids, but from the world of fable and myth, and also, perhaps, on his love of nature. Bonhoeffer did not hesitate to use closely woven images. He picked what suited him from the world of his education—Heraclitus, the giant Antaeus from the world of antiquity, or the nineteenth-century anthropological analyses of Goethe and Nietzsche.[53] In his first and last sermons in Barcelona—and several in between—he quoted St. Augustine on the heart that is unquiet "until it resteth in Thee."[54] In a similar fashion, Barth's Tower of Babel was a recurring example that illustrated the dangers of "religion."[55]

In several ways, these first sermons revealed the full scope of his theological work and perspective.

He reiterated the antithesis between faith and religion throughout. He rediscovered this in every scriptural text:

> What is religion for, except to make life more tolerable to men, occasionally to grant something to the godly that the ungodly do not have? . . . But what a grievous error, what a fearful distortion of the truth. . . .
>
> It is certainly dreadful when one day our life collapses in ruins about us, but there is a reality in the world that is far more dreadful—and actually arises out of religion, out of morality. Renouncing worldly happiness is not the hardest thing that God imposes on us; what is hardest of all to bear, and casts us down utterly, is having to renounce the good and God himself. . . .
>
> Thus it is clear that religion does not give us what the world denies us, that religion is not the creator of earthly happiness; no, with religion, unhappiness, unrest and privation become mighty in the world. The antithesis of everything that happens in the world is the word of grace. . . .
>
> [Thus it is] certain that the cross of Christ destroyed the equation that religion equals happiness. . . .

With that the difference between Christianity and all other religions is clear; here is grace, there happiness; here the cross, there the crown; here God, there the human. . . .[56]

In a similar fashion, his first sermon in Barcelona, in which he systematically proclaimed justification derived solely from faith, in accordance with Romans 11:6 ("But if it is by grace, it is no longer on the basis of works"), came down to this interpretation:

> Both the most grandiose and the frailest of all human attempts to reach the eternal out of the fear and unrest in the human heart is religion. . . . The human race could point proudly to this flowering of its spirit, except for one thing, namely, that God is God and grace is grace. . . . It is not religion that makes us good in the presence of God, but God alone who makes us good. . . . Religion, like morality, is the greatest danger to the understanding of divine grace . . . and yet, so long as grace exists, they remain necessary as a feeble attempt, an illustration, a sacrifice, to which God can say yes or no according to God's will. We have gradually learned to understand that we cannot achieve this through our morality, but that religion, as Luther put it, is also part of human flesh and this is what our text tells us. . . .[57]

For the sake of upholding God's majesty, Bonhoeffer needed to anchor faith correctly by unmasking religion. This was matched by his emphasis on the presence of Christ in the church, as the Thou who imposes restrictions and commandments. Taking as his text 1 Corinthians 12:26, he preached the church as the place where people experienced the grace of sacrifice and prayer for one another and personal confession. He referred to the poverty of the Protestant conception of the church, in comparison with the Catholic one. And he preached the social and ethical transcendence of his theology from *Sanctorum Communio*:

> Jesus is with us in his words . . . in what he wishes and thinks about us . . . Jesus Christ, God himself, addresses us through every human being; the other person, that puzzling, inscrutable Thou, is God's demand upon us, it is God himself who encounters us. . . .[58]

> Christ wanders the earth as long as humans exist, as your neighbor, as one through whom God calls you, speaks to you, makes demands on you. That is the great urgency and the great blessing of the Advent message, that Christ is at the door, lives in the form of the people among us. Will you close or open the door to him?[59]

There are passages in these sermons that point to his insistence on the concrete and the earthly. His need to link the contemporary present with what was to come eschatologically never disappeared. On 23 September 1928, with his parents sitting in his Barcelona congregation, he preached on Romans 12:11 ("Never flag in zeal, be aglow with the Spirit, serve the Lord"). He devoted himself to the concept of time, beginning with the problem of modernity:

> In the whole of world history there is always only one really significant hour—the present. . . . Fashion is what people do with it, which can be either good or despicable. Time is what God does; and to serve not people, but God, means to serve time. Thus the Christian is neither modern nor unmodern, but serves his time. . . .

Then he expressed very concrete solidarity with the political, economic, and moral present, and continued:

> . . . we must learn once more to understand the meaning of human solidarity. . . . God wants to see human beings, not ghosts who shun the world. . . . He made the earth our mother. . . . If you wish for God, hold fast to the world . . . if you want to find eternity, you must serve the times. . . .[60]

This did not prevent him, when he preached on 1 John 17 ("And the world passes away, and the lust of it") on 26 August 1928, from stating that "time and death are the same!" In this sermon he also used the phrase "ultimate and penultimate things."[61]

There were few political references from the Gospel. True, in his farewell sermon in Barcelona he mentioned the efforts for world peace, but only as an occasion to speak of the peace that passed all understanding.

Lectures. Despite his predilection for the pulpit, Bonhoeffer could not resist the appeal of the lecturer's platform. While Pastor Olbricht was on vacation, his vicar made plans for the winter. "I am preparing a series of lectures for the winter, which I propose to give in church," he wrote to his parents.[62]

He planned a series of three evenings, the first on the Old Testament, the second on the New, and the last on ethical questions. He worked carefully on the lectures, writing them out in advance.

On the first evening he began by telling his audience that his underlying theme was that they "should themselves enter into and take part in the struggle and crisis of the modern mind":

> The questions with which we shall deal are profoundly contemporary questions, although their outer dress may seem unfashionable and anti-

quated. Every word is to be spoken out of the present for the present. . . .
We should have so much love for this contemporary world of ours . . . that
we should declare our solidarity with it in its distress as well as in its
hope.[63]

The characteristic feature of the contemporary world, in his view, was
that the ground "or let us say the bourgeois parquet floor" had been pulled
out from beneath its feet; this was reflected in the political, educational,
ethical, and religious uncertainty of the age. Each person had to examine his
or her own foundations. But only a universal process, in which Asia, Europe,
and America took part, could provide the answer. These were ambitious
words, but he believed in them.

1. The subject of his first address, delivered on 13 November 1928, was
"Distress and Hope in the Contemporary Religious Situation: The Tragedy
of the Prophets and Its Lasting Meaning."[64] He wanted to use the prophets
as a signpost, because they had been "such a favorite subject of study" for
him, and because in their time they had marked the collapse of an old and
beginning of a new world. "Walking with God means walking a hard path,
a path on which the heart's blood of the best people flows and has flowed,
as the example of the prophets has amply taught us."[65] But there was little
explicit reference to the present day. Bonhoeffer spent most of his time
introducing his listeners to the world of the prophets. He did this by identifying himself with them to an almost impermissible extent, lingering particularly on Jeremiah, who was already his favorite. Because he was dealing
with God, he tried to avoid any psychological interpretation of "those who
were called" but in the process indulged in plenty of psychologizing himself.

In preparation for these addresses he had his parents send him Bernhard
Duhm's lectures, *The Prophets of Israel*, and he used this translation, though
not without some linguistic revisions of his own. He freely mingled Duhm's
and Barth's theological tenets; he also drew on Stefan Zweig's dramatic treatment of Jeremiah. Bonhoeffer's passion was evident in his description of the
"one called" who suffers because he is in league with God, whose nationalism is destroyed by the universal, who cannot bear to see how the veneer of
cultic acts of worship conceals human "decadence" and cynicism.

2. On the second evening, 11 December 1928, his subject was "Jesus
Christ and the Essence of Christianity." Bonhoeffer's only surviving comment on these talks was what he wrote home: "On Tuesday I gave the second
address, which was even better attended than the first but, I think, was not
as well received."[66] This may well have been true. This time his premises and
solutions were utterly foreign to the bourgeois humanist salespeople of the

parish; his language and train of thought were far more complex. Bonhoeffer's presentation of the historical-critical resolution of the New Testament in its individual sources and embeddedness in parallel religious-historical myths had to confuse them. The dismissal of humanist and idealist "religion" in the name of the free and quite different God of dialectical theology was all too new and provocative.

To us, however, this address is more interesting than the first because it contains nuances and insights that had not been explicitly stated before, which were to make a powerful resurgence in Bonhoeffer's final working period.

(a) The lecture began with a concept that would dominate *Letters and Papers from Prison*: the "provincialism" to which Christ's teaching had succumbed, which Bonhoeffer may have first received from Friedrich Naumann:

> . . . that Christ in practice [has been] eliminated from our lives . . . Christ, instead of being the center of our lives, has become a thing of the church, or of the religiosity of a group of people. To the nineteenth- and twentieth-century mind, religion plays the part of the so-called Sunday room. . . . We do not understand it if we make room for it in merely one province of our spiritual life. . . . The religion of Christ is not the tidbit that follows the bread, but is the bread itself, or it is nothing.[67]

(b) To arrive at the real Jesus, Bonhoeffer began by discussing the phenomenon of the New Testament in its historical setting. He said that the figure of Jesus was embedded in the world of Hellenistic myths and ideas of salvation, and overgrown with themes from fables and legendary reports of miracles. The result was that it is not possible to write a life of Jesus. The New Testament derived solely from worship and proclamation of the *Kyrios*, and had no "interest in the personal or historical" Jesus. Bonhoeffer identified with the scholarship he had heard from Harnack and read in Bultmann.

Yet he found it rash to use the New Testament's embeddedness in its historical environment to deny every characteristic of the Christian message. This was precisely the sin of idealistic philosophy, which did not permit anything new in history, but knew in advance what it would find:

> Yet we allow the New Testament to truly speak and are only listeners, we hear the demand with which this book confronts us in its power, and thus at the heart of the matter we genuinely wrestle with history.[68]

(c) Thus he discovered Jesus, whose remarkable mission was to direct attention away from his own "personality" while simultaneously allowing

God's will to shine through. Bonhoeffer illustrated the demands involved with the aid of Ibsen's *Brand* and Dostoevsky's *Grand Inquisitor*. This finding corresponded with turning attention, shocking though this might be, to children, to social outcasts, to the "fifth estate." Bonhoeffer reconciled the paradox between the absence of prior assumptions and divine injunctions in "Jesus' idea of God. God, who is simply superior to the world . . . totally different . . . demands nothing of people but sheer undemandingness. . . . He wants an empty space in people into which he can move. . . . "[69]

(d) With this he returned to "the way of religion," which he identified with the Tower of Babel. "The germ of hubris is contained in religion and morality . . . thus the Christian message is basically amoral and irreligious, however paradoxical that may sound."[70] Here he went further than he had gone before. Previously, he had made the church dangerously approximate to Christ, almost identifying it with him. Everything had depended on the theological components of the visible church. But now he put greater emphasis on Christology, thus enabling the church to be seen in contrast to Christ:

> With that we have made a basic criticism of the most grandiose of all human attempts to advance toward the divine at all—by way of the church. Concealed in Christianity is a germ hostile to the church. . . . And yet Christianity needs the church. . . . Ethics and religion and church lie in the orientation of the human to God, but Christ speaks only and exclusively of God's orientation to humans.[71]

(e) Bonhoeffer was critical of humanism, the Greek spirit, mysticism, and the cultural salvation of Protestantism, in addition to religion. This must have either affronted or puzzled his audience. Bonhoeffer sensed this:

> By turning against ethics and religion and church as the knowledge of people from God, against humanism and mysticism in their cultural salvation and idolization of creatures, we seem to have robbed humanity of its highest possession. Only in the next session will we be able to illustrate how Christianity uses all this, in turn, in its perfectly limited, relative right.[72]

(f) Only the cross, in which love and death were intertwined, makes this all intelligible. "Thus Jesus' idea of God is summed up in St. Paul's interpretation of the cross; thus the cross becomes the center and the paradoxical emblem of the Christian message." As a path to God, the Christian religion did not differ from other religions. "Christ is not the bringer of a new religion, but the bringer of God."[73] With the exception of the final word—

which is what later enhanced it—this sentence is almost identical to Bon-hoeffer's 1944 statement in *Letters and Papers from Prison*: "Jesus calls us, not to a new religion, but to life."[74] In this 1928 lecture, Bonhoeffer continued: "Thus it is not the Christian religion that is the gift of Christ, but grace and the love of God, which reaches its consummation in the cross."[75]

Bonhoeffer concluded with a phrase that he often used later to charac-terize his decade: with the "thirst" of the twentieth century, expressed in the Youth movement, anthroposophy, and the lust for sensations. Drinking only made this "thirst" burn more, ultimately leading to death, but it could be quenched through the discovery of the cross.

3. The third address, "Basic Questions of a Christian Ethic," was given on 8 February 1929, shortly before Bonhoeffer's departure from Barcelona and after his farewell sermon. "The only thing left is the last lecture the day after tomorrow; then my work is over and I can turn my thoughts entirely to the journey home."[76]

It is the most concrete of the three lectures, although also the most ques-tionable. Many passages must have appealed to his younger listeners. He echoed Nietzsche in speaking of freedom, and attributed his phrase "beyond good and evil" to the "original material of the Christian message, concealed, of course, as it is."[77] He simply denied the continuity of ethical action, because "there are not and cannot be Christian norms and principles of a moral nature."[78] Was it merely naive confidence when he put all his trust in the ethical moment, the "unprecedented situation"?

(a) Ethics, he said, is not a system of general principles of universal application, but is historically bound. Thus, ethics differs according to each nation; in Germany, it cannot be considered in isolation from the experience of war and revolution. Bonhoeffer felt associated with and responsible for these experiences. Yet he did not elaborate on the political aspects of this, but remained within the literary sphere of the times.

> The situation is this, that there is a will toward new ethical forms and exploration of life, and the only thing lacking is the correct point of depar-ture, and our task should be to attempt to show this point of departure.[79]

(b) The commandment to love, he declared, was not specifically Chris-tian; it could be found in Rabbi Hillel or in Seneca.

> The significance of all Jesus' ethical commandments [and of the Sermon on the Mount—the author] is rather to say to [people]: You stand before the face of God, God's grace rules over you; but you are at the disposal of

someone else in the world. . . . The nature of this will of God can only be clear in the moment of action.

. . . when Jesus places people immediately under God, new and afresh at each moment, he restores to humanity the immense gift which it had lost, freedom.[80]

Thus it is not Nietzsche's superman, but Christ, who makes new commandments. But in 1928 the twenty-two-year-old Bonhoeffer still remained loyal to the old earthly principle of the right of the stronger. Without thinking, he placed Tolstoy and conscientious objectors alongside principles and the law. With a certain defiance against a Christian weakness for generalization, he wrote the dreadful phrases:

[The Holy Spirit] does not shine in ideas and principles, but in the necessary decision of the moment. . . . Strength and power and victory also come from God, because God creates youth in peoples and nations, and he loves youth, for God himself is permanently young and strong and victorious . . . God himself will find a way of amply healing the wounds that he inflicts through us, that we inflict for his sake. . . .[81]

(c) This brought him to the subject of war. What he had to say about this—and about the Sermon on the Mount—was quite conventionally Lutheran, although spruced up with the titanic ethics of the immediate moment. Here the later pacifist still proclaimed and defended the relative right of the stronger in the economic competition of the nations and their struggle for life. Better this than a phony rejection of the world! Better this than turning the world over to Nietzsche! It should not be overlooked, however, that here he described war as "sinful and wicked," calling it "dreadful, terrible, murder," and said it defiled the conscience.[82] But he also said: "For what I have, I thank this people, through this people I became what I am."[83] Living in a German community abroad, his own thinking inadvertently resembled the "Volk without room" mentality.

But Bonhoeffer's position cannot be simply left at that. Neither in his sermons nor in his letters did he ever make any such statement again.[84] Such slogans had long since been articles of faith among German nationalists in the Evangelical church, but before they were interpreted anti-Semitically and chauvinistically and became the hallmark of right-wing extremism, they were also used by democrats and members of Stresemann's Volkspartei. Bonhoeffer was not yet speaking his own language here. The idea of the struggle for life as the natural basis of human existence came from Friedrich Naumann, to whom Bonhoeffer explicitly refers in this lecture.[85] The same principle, though justified on different grounds, was also to be found in Max Weber.

It did not take long for Bonhoeffer to discover the self-deception that lay in this unquestioned loyalty to the world. Alliances of a very different kind lay ahead. On 16 March 1929, the Berlin *Tag* reported the resolution of the German nationalists in Magdeburg denouncing Günther Dehn's sober address of 6 September 1928 on the problem of war. This was the beginning of the agitation against "red Dehn," at a time when Bonhoeffer was growing closer to Dehn.[86] His subsequent experiences in America and in the World Alliance for Promoting International Friendship through the Churches helped him see that the strange link he had made between Barth's systematic theology and the conventional Lutheran ethic was at least in need of revision. Ethics had been relatively neglected in his theological work, and here again he had postponed this lecture until the last moment. Perhaps he betrayed some uncertainty when, at the very end, he referred to ethics in a different context, calling it a "demonstration of weak will, arising out of gratitude for what God has done to us," or when he said: "Peoples' action springs from the recognition of the grace of God, towards humankind and towards themselves, and this action hopes for the grace of God, which delivers them from the distress of the time."[87] Finally, he adjusted his balancing act on the ethical moment with an eschatological sigh:

> Only one who has tasted the entire seriousness and depth and misery of the kingdom of the world, the kingdom of the ethical, and longs for release from it, has just one wish, that our world should pass away, and thy kingdom come.[88]

Barely two years later, he felt very uncomfortable at having expressed himself in this way about burning ethical questions and the Sermon on the Mount. The *theologia crucis* and a broader perspective did their work.

Plans for the Future

In November 1928 the presbytery formally invited him to remain in Barcelona but, after briefly considering the matter, he declined. This could not be the church commitment to which he aspired. He was still uncertain about whether to seek the pastorate or an academic appointment. For the time being, he wished to keep both alternatives open, postponing the decision until after he had completed the *Habilitation* (the postdoctoral degree) and had been ordained.

As far as a church appointment was concerned, there was an obstacle that, at the time, he regarded as totally unnecessary: the preacher's seminary. A new church regulation required attendance, and he felt not the slightest inclination to do so. His mother had already spoken somewhat disrespectfully about it in May 1928: "How are you thinking about this matter of the seminary for candidates? How will you get around this. It seems that people become totally confused there; they don't want to give the [residents] a key and don't allow them to participate in any seminars other than what they offer in the way of wisdom. You should have something else ahead of time, like a postdoctoral thesis that you would be working on."

This postdoctoral work provided a way out, and with this in mind Bonhoeffer applied for an assistantship through Seeberg. His parents were able to assist him here, with the help of New Testament scholar Hans Lietzmann; but Seeberg's impending retirement created some difficulties. Bonhoeffer didn't assume that Seeberg's position would be filled by someone who was closer to him theologically. Althaus was mentioned, but Seeberg did not promote this recommendation. The systematic theologian Wilhelm Koepp also appeared to have a chance. Finally Seeberg's successor was named: Wilhelm Lütgert, a scholar of New Testament and systematics. Bonhoeffer wrote, "I think that Seeberg has some influence on him. Lütgert will have even less understanding for my work than Seeberg."[89] This fear proved to be unfounded. Meanwhile his family feared that the situation might lead their son to abandon the path to the professor's lectern. His father wrote to him: "Harnack specifically told me to send you his regards and tell you that you should do your postdoctoral work as soon as possible, that one learns so very much through holding lectures."[90]

He was already actively considering what subject he should choose for his postdoctoral thesis. Whatever time he could spare for theology in Barcelona was devoted initially to preparing his dissertation *Sanctorum Communio* for publication, and he then concentrated on choosing a subject for his postdoctoral thesis.

The prospects for publication of the dissertation were not good. He wrote to Seeberg:

> I am editing and shortening the work, which I should like to send you at the beginning of November, as arranged. I have had to rewrite a great deal and omit long passages. In Brunner's *Mediator,* which, incidentally, I found rather disappointing, I found ideas on original sin and its social significance similar to those that I had developed.[91]

As far as revising my doctoral thesis is concerned, I have more or less finished it. I have not been able to abbreviate or cut as much as I had hoped;
all the same, a fourth or fifth of it has gone. I recently saw an announcement of a book by Althaus to appear this autumn, called *Communio Sanctorum*. [It eventually appeared in spring 1929.] Would you advise me to
wait for its appearance or let my work appear independently of it?[92]

Seeberg was not in favor of awaiting the publication of Althaus's book,
responding: "as far as the publication of your work is concerned, I am afraid
that some time will have to elapse. The publishing house now has a new
owner, and apart from that it works terribly slowly."[93] The result was that
Bonhoeffer's publication was swept into the maelstrom of the great economic crisis.

But he was much more interested in planning his new work than in
abbreviating and polishing the old:

I already have something else in mind, though again it is not historical but
systematic. It is associated with the question of consciousness and conscience in theology, and with some of Luther's comments from the great
commentary on Galatians. . . . In your seminar you once broached the
question of consciousness though this is not to be a psychological but a
theological inquiry.[94]

This is the first reference to what was to take shape a year later as *Act and
Being*. Epistemology still took precedence over ethics. He was fascinated by
the prospect of theologically examining the problem of the form that faith
assumed in the believer's mind when it necessarily developed into religion.
The problem of religious consciousness had confronted him with the phenomenon of the child, as a letter to Helmut Rössler shows, in which he gives
an account of his sermon and Sunday school.[95]

Once more Bonhoeffer had the bit between his teeth and was galloping
away, but Seeberg tried to keep him within the confines of history. Did the
experienced mentor see through the weak side of his pupil? On 19 October
1928, he wrote Bonhoeffer:

Perhaps it would be advisable for you now to find some historical or biblical subject in order to learn to work independently in the approach and
methods of this field. For instance, how about going into the question of
why ethical problems receded so far into the background in twelfth-
century scholasticism, and of how the account in John of Salisbury's *Met-
alogicus* is to be interpreted? But that is only one example, and if you have

anything that appeals to you more, so much the better, of course. But the history of ethics, and even more so that of morality, is a field in which a young man might well establish himself at the present time, perhaps with a view to a systematic and historical treatment of ethics from the Sermon on the Mount to the present day.[96]

But this had no influence; Bonhoeffer was too eager to return to his own work: "Although I basically can't say that things here have become monotonous—it still brings a certain unrest into how I lead my life. I very much long to be able again to read as long and as much as I wish, more than to write—I have done enough writing."[97]

Thus the unread books were repacked in the boxes in which they had come; this time, however, they would find their way to Bonhoeffer's desk. On 17 February 1929 he was home again in snow-covered Grunewald.

Spain did not vanish from his thoughts with the return to academic Berlin. Teachers and young people from Barcelona visited him in Berlin and during holidays in Friedrichsbrunn. Despite his forthcoming examinations and trip to America, he traveled once more to Barcelona in April 1930, for the wedding of Hermann Thumm, his former neighbor at the pension in Barcelona. He enjoyed good coffee and bad cakes on the *Tibidabo*, the mountain above the city from which the Devil is said to have shown Jesus the riches of the world. He attended a performance of *Carmen* with its magnificent Spanish Don José, and once again succumbed to the fascination of the bullfight.

CHAPTER FOUR

ASSISTANT LECTURER
IN BERLIN: 1929–1930

Bonhoeffer quickly sensed the ominous political changes that were taking place in the homeland to which he had returned.

Germany actually faced some alleviation of its international debt burden. The Dawes Plan for the reparations problem was coming to an end; the Young Plan took effect on 17 May 1930. With it, the Reich regained a degree of economic and financial sovereignty. The Rhineland became free again.

But every advance in foreign relations that Stresemann and Curtius achieved was obscured by right-wing propaganda, which denounced these men as defeatist politicians who had accepted the Treaty of Versailles. In the autumn of 1929 the Stahlhelm organization (the largest of the nationalistic veterans' organizations in Germany), the nationalists, and the Nazis—the latter still a small minority, though highly vociferous—organized a "national petition for the drafting of a law against the enslavement of the German people" by the Young Plan. Church circles were among the supporters who helped this coalition secure the 10 percent of the vote necessary to make the Reichstag discuss the petition as if it were a parliamentary bill; once more the churches joined in denouncing the centrist and leftist parties who opposed it as unpatriotic. The Reichstag rejected the petition.

Stresemann died on 3 October 1929, just a few weeks before the Wall Street crash of 29 October 1929. The repercussions of the world economic crisis were grist for the mill of German antidemocratic forces of the right and the left. Radicalized masses went into the streets. It was no coincidence that Dr. Josef Goebbels, the Nazi *Gauleiter* of Berlin, became his party's national propaganda chief that same year. Equally ominous was the Social Democratic Party's withdrawal from the government one year later, marking the breakup of the coalition that had led the government. At the end of

March 1930 Heinrich Brüning became chancellor for the first time, and the period of government by emergency decree began. The only result of this last attempt to rescue the Weimar Republic was its visible wasting away.

The Bonhoeffers expected more of the Brüning government than was in its power to fulfill. "With Brüning as chancellor the general situation seemed to offer a guarantee that both in foreign and economic affairs a period of reconciliation and advancement was at hand."[1] In the Bonhoeffers' immediate circle the deaths of two men who sacrificed old allegiances for the sake of the Weimar Republic epitomized the demise of a great liberal and humanitarian tradition. The historian Hans Delbrück, who was Klaus Bonhoeffer's father-in-law, died in the house next door in the summer of 1929; one year later, Adolf von Harnack died too. Both had been much more active and risked more politically than Karl Bonhoeffer. Years before they had fought together to keep Adolf Stoecker's anti-Semitic activity in check, and successfully blocked his attempt to discuss the Jewish question at the Protestant Social Congress, forcing him to leave the meeting. Likewise, during the 1920s they watched the political course taken by the Protestant church with concern, for royalism and anti-Semitism had not died with the disappearance of the monarch. In 1928 Erik Peterson wrote Harnack: "Spiritually and sociologically the Protestant church corresponds roughly to the mentality and sociological status of the German National People's Party."[2]

The values for which Harnack and Delbrück had stood began to succumb rapidly to the defamation and ridicule of the growing forces of irrational nationalism; these values were viewed as the decadent morality of the "state system," which was now ripe for the final assault. The Christian bourgeoisie did not find much in it to defend; the antiliberal publications such as that of the "Action Group" of Hans Zehrer, Edgar Jung, and Ernst Jünger had that much more impact. The right-wing bourgeoisie's longing for an authoritarian order grew. True, the Christian bourgeoisie did not have much use for the raucous Nazis, but they listened with pleasure to speeches about the "western decadence" that democracy had introduced to Germany, and liked to think that a "rebirth of the German national spirit in a German national community" might yet transform the defeat of 1918 into victory.

Bonhoeffer's brother Klaus and his brothers-in-law, Gerhard Leibholz and Hans von Dohnanyi, identified themselves that much more strongly with the Weimar Republic as they took on more professional responsibilities.

Disinterest. Dietrich Bonhoeffer followed these developments with no less concern, but because his activities were confined to the theological realm he remained much more aloof than his brothers.

But in the lively atmosphere of the Wangenheimstrasse home he could hardly have been unaffected by the political events of the day. He was always a very attentive newspaper reader; in addition to the democratic *Vossische Zeitung* that his parents read, his brothers brought home newspapers of every political persuasion. During the course of this year the Dohnanyis moved from Hamburg to Berlin, and came to live in the Schönes' house across from the Bonhoeffers. Hans von Dohnanyi took the post of personal assistant to the Reich Minister of Justice that had first been offered to Gerhard Leibholz. Through him, the political events and their background grew closer and more vivid.

The year he spent abroad had certainly sharpened Dietrich's view of his own country. Excessively nationalist statements such as those in his Barcelona lectures never crossed his lips again, for he now saw them transformed into nationalistic slogans and interwoven with anti-Semitic agitation. He had nothing to do with the "national opposition" in 1929; nor did he join the right-wing populism. During these months, he established the first close friendship of his life, with a young theologian of Jewish descent, Franz Hildebrandt. These years were also marked by the development of his conditional pacifism—unique at that time in the German church and theological circles. When he attended church in 1929 and 1930—which he did not yet do regularly—he went to Günther Dehn's church in Moabit, and he cannot have been unaware of Dehn's political outlook. His almost Barthian theology increasingly provided him with the tools to resist the theological and ecclesial apostles of nationalism, who were usurping all that was dear to him as a son of the patriotic bourgeoisie.

Nevertheless, he gave no thought to becoming politically active at this time. Years later we can see more clearly the tragedy of these theologians like Bonhoeffer, who tried in their way to set themselves apart from humanist "Westernism." Their "crisis theology" was colored by strong antiliberal sentiment. In addition, the personal backgrounds of many Barthians prevented them from identifying with those forces that were the backbone of the Weimar Republic. Bonhoeffer probably would have affirmed the words of Karl Barth's confession in 1945, "To the German theologians in prisoner-of-war camps":

> I wish to acknowledge to you openly: if I reproach myself for anything when I look back on the years I spent in Germany, it is that, out of sheer concentration on my ecclesial and theological task . . . I failed . . . to give a warning, not just implicitly, but explicitly, not merely privately but also publicly . . . against the tendencies . . . in the church and the world around me.[3]

As early as 1932 Bonhoeffer was ashamed of his "disinterest," calling it "at this time essentially frivolous."[4]

In 1929, however, he took little interest in either right- or left-wing politics, but devoted himself solely to theology. Indeed, after his first practical commitment to church and society in Barcelona, he returned to his studies with greater zeal. He devoted only as much attention as was absolutely necessary even to the requirements for preparation for the ministry. Underlying this attitude was an underestimation of the daily work of the church on the synodal and local levels that was characteristic in Germany. The profound world of academic theology was expected to offer a verdict: reform or salvation. At this point, Bonhoeffer shared the view that scholars possessed the essential and necessary authority to render this verdict.

Still, for all his sense of purpose, he was uncertain about his real goal. This private uncertainty ran like a thread through 1929 and 1930. The sources for this are relatively meager, but there is no mistaking his hesitation about his true vocation. The new subject on which he had chosen to work lay on his desk, and he stalwartly fended off the many distractions that Berlin and his home had to offer. But was this work his real purpose in life? What was it all leading to?

> I shall soon be handing in my postdoctoral thesis . . . and soon I shall be going to Barcelona for a fortnight's visit to my congregation, of which I am very fond, and I feel in general that academic work will not hold me for long. On the other hand, I think it very important to have as thorough an academic grounding as possible . . . Fendt and Dehn are almost the only preachers I can really listen to.[5]

Five years later Bonhoeffer referred critically to this year: "I threw myself into the work . . . the ambition that some people noticed in me made my life difficult."[6] Still, something new was in the making, and it would later lead to a liberating turn. Somewhat later, this became evident in a friend's reply to a letter from Bonhoeffer in America: "I believe that I understood what you wrote about yourself, above all about the revival of your philosophy and theology through new perspectives."[7]

Postdoctoral Work

The theological faculty in Berlin was waiting for its highly promising candidate to complete his postdoctoral thesis. There were various problems, however, that could not be resolved at once. In particular, three questions arose: finding a position for this very young man that would give him status in the university; the obligatory publication of his dissertation *Sanctorum Communio*; and deciding the subject of his postdoctoral thesis.

"Voluntary" Assistant Lecturer. The most important change in the faculty facing Bonhoeffer on his return was that Wilhelm Lütgert had succeeded Reinhold Seeberg. Lütgert had been professor of the New Testament in Halle and also held the chair in systematic theology there, made prominent by Martin Kähler. A specialist in German idealism, Lütgert had trouble tolerating the dialectical theologians' severe conclusions about idealism.

Nonetheless, Seeberg successfully recommended his pupil to his successor. At the beginning of the 1929 summer term, Bonhoeffer became a "voluntary assistant lecturer" in the university seminar in systematic theology, a position that he nominally retained until September 1930.

In this capacity he had to perform duties for the professor, a skill for which he was not especially gifted, such as handing out and securing the return of keys, supervising the seminar library, and recommending new book purchases. He also worked with the other chair in systematic theology (Professor Titius) and kept abreast of his seminar needs: handing out work to the rapidly growing number of students, reading it through, and detecting plagiarisms. Thus in April 1929 he began his new job, not with discussions of Heidegger, but with rearranging the library and introducing the new rules for the seminar. Still, his duties gave him the opportunity to work and access to everything he needed. His talent for finding people to do things for him proved useful. The position also gave him a welcome excuse for extricating himself from obligations that he considered a waste of time, such as his local superintendent's evening meetings for the ordination candidates.

The position of voluntary assistant lecturer was not exactly what Bonhoeffer had looked forward to when he approached Seeberg in 1928. He had hoped that when Seeberg retired, the official assistant's post, occupied by Arnold Stolzenburg, would become vacant. But this came about only after Stolzenburg was given a seminar on social ethics, after Bonhoeffer's return from America.

Lütgert soon learned to appreciate his new assistant lecturer, although he felt that he would be unable to exercise any influence on his development. He once told Hans-Christoph von Hase, who took Bonhoeffer's position after his departure for America: "I really only just took over your cousin (from Seeberg); otherwise I should have wanted to exercise rather more pressure on his philosophy." Lütgert was critical of Heidegger, whom he rejected as a neo-Thomist. When Hase tried to defend his cousin, saying that he was not a Heidegger man, Lütgert merely shook his head thoughtfully.

Publication Difficulties. The publication status of *Sanctorum Communio* was still unsatisfactory. Although two years had passed since its completion, no progress had been made. A cheap method of duplication would have fulfilled the doctoral requirements, but Bonhoeffer wanted publication, insisting that his study and critique of the dialecticians should be accessible to them in book form. In 1926 he had written: "It would be a good thing, for once, to begin the study of dogmatics not with the doctrine of God but with the doctrine of the church."[8] By now Karl Barth had published the first half-volume of his *Christian Dogmatics* without being aware of Bonhoeffer's suggestion, let alone addressing it. Bonhoeffer's nervousness was increased by the fact that he was losing his start, and was about to be overtaken by the publication of Althaus's book with the similar title. Althaus's reputation was already secure, while Bonhoeffer was still looking in vain for a publisher. But the growing economic crisis made publishers more cautious with every month that passed, even when there was a recommendation as impressive as that of Seeberg. What sales could be expected for a printed dissertation?

Finally the Trowitzsch publishing house agreed to accept the work, provided Bonhoeffer met the printing costs of well over one thousand marks. Bonhoeffer was able to guarantee this sum to the publishers with the help of Reichstag delegate Reinhard Mumm from *Christlichen Volksdienst,* who received aid from the Seeberg Foundation and the Prussian Ministry of Culture, and with the support of Harnack, who took care of the remainder through the German Scholarship Emergency Association. In the meantime, however, Althaus's book *Communio Sanctorum* appeared.[9] Bonhoeffer's manuscript was finally delivered to Trowitzsch at the end of March 1930. Some changes to the original version had been made, but, with the exception of a few notations, Bonhoeffer was unable to respond to Althaus's book.[10]

Over three years had elapsed since Bonhoeffer had finished the book. When the first copies were delivered, he was en route to the ship to America. Thus he was unable even to present personal copies to his friends and patrons. The postman delivering the parcel also brought a bill for additional printing costs. His parents paid it.

By this time Bonhoeffer had lost real interest in this work. He had completed *Act and Being* and was concerned with its publication. At the beginning of 1931 Trowitzsch complained vigorously at his lack of interest in *Sanctorum Communio.* He had supplied not one line for publicity purposes and no list of journals that might review the book, and at the price of eighteen marks it was extremely difficult to sell.

Bonhoeffer's beginning as a theological writer was less than successful. His first work met with an insignificant response. The *Theologische Lite-*

raturzeitung published a review by Wobbermin,[11] who misunderstood him, saying that he envisaged establishing common ground in phenomenology for cooperation between theology and general scholarship. Wilhelm Niesel reviewed the book in the literary supplement of the March 1931 *Reformierte Kirchenzeitung* and criticized Bonhoeffer's "sociological tools" as "inappropriate" for the understanding of the "church": "We wished to draw attention to his work only because it contains many very good individual observations, and clearly shows how much a pupil of Seeberg's has learned from Gogarten and Barth."[12] Somewhat bewildered but also impressed, Pastor Wilhelm Schubring reviewed it in the *Protestantenblatt*[13] because he had been struck by Bonhoeffer's address at Harnack's memorial service. He was now surprised to discover a pure systematician in one whom he had assumed to be Harnack's pupil. In 1933 Ernst Wolf referred to the book favorably in an article entitled "The Person and Church in Catholic Thought," in *Zwischen den Zeiten*.[14]

Nonetheless, the book sank unnoticed in the general debate of the time. The dialecticians did not discuss it, as Bonhoeffer had expected, and professors did not use it as a text.

Bonhoeffer neglected it himself, as he did most of his books once they had been published. He disliked ongoing arguments and revised editions; he preferred writing something new. His Finkenwalde candidates, who witnessed the birth pangs of *Discipleship* in 1935, were not even told of the existence of his earlier works. The books were not displayed, and even Bonhoeffer's earliest students in Berlin in the years 1931–1932 did not quote them; he himself seemed to have forgotten them.

The publishing episode of *Sanctorum Communio* showed that, like other German scholars, even the privileged Bonhoeffer paid a price during the desperate world economic crisis. It also illustrated how Bonhoeffer was both conscious of his own achievements and maintained a freedom toward the fruits of his work. When his candidates later recommended a revised edition of *Discipleship* in response to criticisms of the book, Bonhoeffer dismissed the notion with a laugh. "What I wrote, I wrote."

Act and Being. Bonhoeffer's second book, *Act and Being,* was written during the summer and winter of 1929. Once more it dealt with the theme of *Sanctorum Communio*—how revelation becomes concrete—but emphasized it more by addressing the theological discussion of the time. He now posed his critical questions to the Barthians more clearly and decisively than he ever would again. There would soon be too many occasions for defending them rather than calling them into question. True, they took almost as little notice of *Act and Being* as they had of *Sanctorum Communio*. Only later was Bonhoeffer noted and welcomed as an energetic fighter in the church struggle; the earlier theological partner and critic was ignored.

The choice of topic, "Act and Being, Transcendental Philosophy and Ontology in Systematic Theology," was not influenced by either Seeberg or Lütgert. At an early stage Bonhoeffer had written from Barcelona: "I . . . think about a postdoctoral thesis every now and then."[15] The subject of his reflections during those hot summer weeks, the "problem of the child," became the formula for the conclusion and climax of the book: the description of the new being in Christ that unites act and being under the heading of "The Child."[16] Here he forced the hostile brothers together—be they transcendentalists and ontologists, or theologians of act and theologians of being, or Barthians and Lutherans. His understanding of the church was still dominated by his idea of "Christ existing as church-community."

Thus he plunged into systematic theology, ignoring Seeberg's suggestion that he deal with a historical or biblical problem. He wanted to take sides, criticize, press forward into the field where the debate of the late 1920s was raging most fiercely: around the ontologies of Barth and Bultmann, their presuppositions, and the suitability of their methods. In *Christliche Welt* the aged systematic theologian Ferdinand Kattenbusch described the scene with a veteran's humor:

> There is something comic in the fact that practically every one of the theologians whom one sees "pressing into new fields" has his own special philosopher with whom he associates himself. In part one has the impression that the accident of locality has led the "community" to approach the problem in an "ideological" way. . . . Almost all the dialectical theologians hold to their own philosophers and thus *begin* the false way of distinguishing between God and the world, to which they have all hopelessly succumbed, so that they can to some extent *overcome* it.[17]

The phrase "accident of locality" referred to Bultmann and Heidegger in Marburg and Gogarten and Grisebach in Jena. While Kattenbusch's colleague in Leipzig, Horst Stephan, believed that the realm of dogmatics was "dominated by the most intense and multifaceted life since the Reformation era," he also claimed that theology lacked a center and had become bogged down.[18] Kattenbusch believed otherwise:

> (I am) almost envious of our youth. . . . There's only one thing I don't envy them. If they want to enter the discussion the way dialectical theology demands, they have to struggle their way through *stylistic* difficulties that

we older ones didn't have in our day. Particularly where Heidegger is the philosophical helper, even *I* often don't know how to go forward and in many cases can't understand that the *theologians* think they can speak of their issues.[19]

But this was what intrigued Bonhoeffer: to pinpoint the location of this style. His Berlin education had sharpened his eye for how Kant and neo-Kantianism, idealism, and Heidegger's fundamental ontology were determining the questions of theology.

Bonhoeffer now tackled Heidegger more thoroughly. *Being and Time* had appeared in 1927. Hans-Christoph von Hase, who attended Heidegger's lectures in Marburg, had already asked impatiently in Barcelona whether his cousin was finally reading the book. In the index to *Act and Being* Heidegger took second place only to Luther—even before Barth; Husserl, Scheler, Grisebach, and Tillich were also discussed. Bonhoeffer criticized Bultmann for his dependence on Heidegger, claiming that with the introduction of "potentiality," the concept of possibility in Christian decisions, Bultmann destroyed the theological foundation for the preexisting, free act of God—and, with that, certainty was replaced by reflection.[20] He criticized Barth for his formalistic understanding of the freedom of God.[21] Schleiermacher, the founding father of the Berlin school, seemed to have disappeared beyond the horizon;[22] in reality, he remained the opponent behind all the philosophies and theologies being discussed, all the way to Holl. Rudolf Otto, who at the time was viewed abroad as the representative par excellence of modern German theology, was not mentioned at all.[23]

In *Act and Being*, Bonhoeffer was essentially addressing philosophers, whom he found guilty of the original sin of idealism, namely, confinement in the self. The philosophers, however, did not recognize themselves in his schematized version.[24] He also argued with Barth, warning him of the dangers of his transcendental philosophy and trying to make him more "Lutheran." He wanted to persuade him of his own belief in the *finitum capax infiniti*—that, despite everything, God *was* accessible. Both were important to Bonhoeffer: the philosophers he had read and attacked since his school days and Barth, who had convinced him that theology could stand on its own.

Theologically and sociologically, his first book was an argument for the concreteness of revelation in the form of community. The second book argued for the theological and epistemological struggle—basically for the same concreteness. As the classic passage in *Act and Being* stated:

In revelation it is not so much a question of the freedom of God—eternally remaining within the divine self, aseity—on the other side of revelation, as it is of God's coming out of God's own self in revelation. It is a matter of God's *given* Word, the covenant in which God is bound by God's own action. It is a question of the freedom of God, which finds its strongest evidence precisely in that God freely chose to be bound to historical human beings and to be placed at the disposal of human beings. God is free not from human beings but for them. Christ is the word of God's freedom. God *is* present, that is, not in eternal nonobjectivity but—to put it quite provisionally for now—"haveable," graspable in the Word within the church. Here the formal understanding of God's freedom is countered by a substantial one.[25]

To Bonhoeffer, the old *extra calvinisticum* was in error if it ultimately denied the complete entry of God's majesty into this world. Bonhoeffer suspected it at work when he saw Barth establishing the majesty of God by the methods of Kantian transcendentalism. To greatly oversimplify: while the early Barth, desiring to proclaim God's majesty, began by removing him to a remote distance, Bonhoeffer's starting point, inspired by the same desire to proclaim his majesty, brought him into close proximity.

Thus Bonhoeffer's path at the theological-epistemological level of *Act and Being* returned him to ecclesiology, and vice versa. He remained serious about the principal theme of *Sanctorum Communio*, that the church is the essential prerequisite for theology. It is the reality of the church, again conceived of as "Christ existing as church-community," that makes for a fruitful tension between the respective, legitimate interests: between the existentialist theology of "act" on the one hand, as developed theocentrically in Barth and anthropocentrically in Bultmann, and on the other the neoorthodox theology of "being" of the "pure doctrine." This preserved both requirements: of contingency and of the continuity of revelation.

This highly abstract discourse, which the uninitiated are hardly able to follow, concealed a passionate personal involvement. Bonhoeffer's deepest feelings were involved in his insistence on the *extra nos* and *pro nobis* of salvation. His own difficulties sharpened his sensitivity to every loophole in the system through which fatal reflection might invade his own ego and establish its secret domination. Thus he criticized both Barth and Bultmann for introducing into faith a dangerous element of permanent reflection: Barth for making the believing self constantly reflect on its nonself, and Bultmann for referring faith, when it faced its "potentiality," to the point of decision. Bonhoeffer objected passionately that this was precisely what killed faith. Faith must not be guided by itself, but totally directed toward Christ. Reflection was an abstraction from Christ and left one in an ultimate solitude. But faith is the experience of the concrete presence of the Christ who was made flesh, crucified, and resurrected. In all respects, it is dialogical sociality—a sociality that is permanently and already fulfilled, yet permanently fulfilling itself anew, both vertically and horizontally. This was the point to which Bonhoeffer was committed with all his heart.

Act and Being was criticized correctly for its one-sidedness and conceptual oversimplifications. Still, what Bonhoeffer was trying to do was acute and modern for the time. He was grasping for a vital fact that has remained pertinent, despite all changes. Some of his criticisms have been accepted as justified; some of the questions he raised continue to be raised today.

From our biographical point of view, the importance of *Act and Being* was that—taken in conjunction with *Sanctorum Communio*—it contained many of the ideas that were to be applied to the "nonreligious interpretation" in the letters from prison fifteen years later. This fact deprives them of their supposedly fortuitous character; it means that they were better prepared than is generally assumed. The ideas of 1930 that seemed to vanish in the subsequent years suddenly reappeared in 1944. *Act and Being* gave the social and ethical transcendence of one's neighbor (which had already been maintained in *Sanctorum Communio* as against philosophical-metaphysical transcendence) the magnificent formulation "Jesus, the man for others."[26] Here, of course, this applied only to the church. Eventually, Bonhoeffer conceived of this as permanently and essentially freed from all bounds, applied to the world as Christ's own proper dominion.

Bonhoeffer completed the work in February 1930 and duly submitted it for the appraisal of the theological faculty. The formalities took their course, and the *Habilitation* took place on 18 July 1930. On 31 July the university rector, Erhard Schmidt, invited the newly qualified twenty-four-year-old teacher to deliver his inaugural lecture, "The Question of Man in Contemporary Philosophy and Theology." Bonhoeffer used the weapons he had just tried out in *Act and Being* to discuss the anthropology of the period, defending his view of human self-understanding. "God is closer to me than is my existence, inasmuch as it is God who first discloses my existence to me," he said, for "in a reflective theological form of thinking I have no more intimate reference to my existence than to God."[27] He concluded: "Thus not only does every individual theological problem point back to the reality of the church of Christ, but theological thought recognizes itself in its totality as something which belongs alone to the church."[28]

When *Act and Being* was completed, the manuscript of *Sanctorum Communio* had not even reached the printer, but Bonhoeffer had to wait only a year to find a publisher for his second book. Lütgert recommended him to Bertelsmann, who demanded a contribution of only two hundred marks for the printing costs. Althaus gave a recommendation so that it could appear in the series "Contributions to the Advancement of Christian Theology." Bonhoeffer had to wait five months, but when it arrived Althaus's recommendation was very warm. "I consider it to be a very important piece of work, which unquestionably must be printed as soon as possible," Althaus wrote to Bonhoeffer's father on 4 March 1931. His father forwarded the letter to him in America. "It will please you, but not make you presumptuous," he wrote.[29] The book was published in the autumn of 1931 after Dietrich's return from America.

By the time Bonhoeffer sent signed copies to his friends—this time one of the recipients was Günther Dehn—his interests had again moved elsewhere. "In the meantime the project has grown rather disagreeable to me," he wrote on 28 February 1932 to his new friend Erwin Sutz.[30] The "product" had been written in 1929. The period that followed was shaped by his impressions of America, the beginning of his work as a teacher and preacher, and his ecumenical activity.

The critical echo was somewhat greater than it had been for *Sanctorum Communio,* but still relatively small. In 1933 Knittermeyer reviewed it very critically in *Zwischen den Zeiten,* and Eisenhuth did the same in the *Theologische Literaturzeitung.*[31] To his critics, Bonhoeffer's attempt to keep theological epistemology strictly within the doctrine of justification were too philosophically one-sided; he had oversimplified and thus violated the epistemological problem by repeatedly tracing it back to idealism. Even after the appearance of a new edition in 1956, it was observed that one could hardly rely on Bonhoeffer's judgments about Heidegger and Bultmann:

> ... The interpretation of Heidegger in terms of his original ontology completely misjudges the fundamental overcoming of metaphysics that had already occurred in *Being and Time*—a fact that avenges itself in the second and third sections of Bonhoeffer's work. For these two sections remain in the realm of fundamental metaphysical prerequisites, which are sensed but hardly recognized in their scope. . . .[32]

In retrospect, however, one essential fact is clear. At a time when there was a positivist enthusiasm for the church on the one hand, and an energetic critical distance to it on the other, this young voice theologically rediscovered and accepted the empirical church without merely retreating from its critics. Bonhoeffer had established firm ground that could withstand the coming storms:

> The theology of that era, on the brink of the *Kirchenkampf,* was divided between the fronts of the "theology of act" and the "theology of being" and between the theocentric and the anthropocentric approach. The mere fact that Bonhoeffer highlights these approaches is remarkable; more remarkable still is the way in which he strives to abolish the contradictions.
>
> This does not make him a theologian of mediation, although *Act and Being* is a masterpiece of mediating theology. Instead, he senses that the contradictions that exist today are not genuine and ultimate contradictions. Bonhoeffer's astonishing theological freedom during the church struggle where the true fronts were strictly preserved can already be seen here in his capacity to abolish the illusory fronts in a theologically legitimate way.[33]

Family and Friends

The working rhythm of these eighteen months was interrupted by three weddings in the family. Dietrich's organizational talent was drawn on for each of them. One letter from Friedrichsbrunn during a vacation reported: "We are leading an incredibly lazy life up here. . . . We ourselves are always on the go. The unrest in the house makes it difficult to concentrate on a play for the wedding shower."[34] In 1929 his sister Susanne married Walter Dress; in 1930 his brother Karl-Friedrich married Grete von Dohnanyi; and before Dietrich's departure for America, Klaus married Emmi Delbrück, the sister of his friend Justus Delbrück. Dietrich was now the only member of the big family still at home.

Friendships. During these years his friends came from the familiar circles around the Wangenheimstrasse home and theologians from the university. Hans-Christoph von Hase was working on his dissertation[35] and often consulted his cousin on the subject. Walter Dress had qualified as a lecturer with his work on Johannes Gerson;[36] he enjoyed walking with Bonhoeffer in the Grunewald woods, where they explored both theology and botany (in which Dress was an expert). Helmut Rössler already had a parish in Mark Brandenburg, and invited his old friend to visit his village. In Harnack's last private seminar in 1929 Dietrich met Bertha Schulze again; she tirelessly tracked down quotations for his work and helped him in the library. His distant cousin Elisabeth Zinn graduated with a dissertation for Lütgert on the theology of F. C. Oetinger,[37] the eighteenth-century Württemberg theosophist. She and Bonhoeffer exchanged their first books; a quotation from Oetinger that became one of Bonhoeffer's favorites, "embodiment is the end of God's path," came from her.

His friendship with Franz Hildebrandt would have numerous consequences for Bonhoeffer, and would last for the rest of his life. It gave a personal urgency to some of Bonhoeffer's later decisions. Hildebrandt's father was professor of art history at Berlin University; his mother was of Jewish descent. Three years younger than Bonhoeffer, Hildebrandt was working on a thesis on the Lutheran *est*. Bonhoeffer encouraged its completion, and it appeared in 1931 as *EST: The Lutheran Principle*.[38] Titius and, of all people, Wobbermin (who subsequently became a German Christian) published it in their series, *Studies in Systematic Theology*.

The two met for the first time in Seeberg's seminar the day before Bonhoeffer defended his dissertation. They debated the relationship between the Old Testament and the New, and Hildebrandt took the side of Marcion. On Good Friday 1929 they met again by coincidence at a performance of the St. Matthew Passion at the Berlin Choral Academy.

Their friendship was spiced by a lifelong private feud: Hildebrandt attacked Bonhoeffer for his dubious mixture of Hegelian and Barthian categories, and Bonhoeffer counterattacked by criticizing Hildebrandt's dependence on Harnack. But on all practical problems they saw eye-to-eye, and each always knew how the other would act or react. Hildebrandt influenced Bonhoeffer's imminent conversion to a stronger biblicism. He had an extensive memory, and often supplied Bonhoeffer with the decisive quotations from the Bible or from Luther. On 31 July 1930 he presented him with a small book of Luther quotations on the pericopes with the inscription: "To the ancient foe on the occasion of his *Habilitation*." Bonhoeffer liked his dry humor and quick grasp of things. He soon became an agreeable guest in the Wangenheimstrasse home, and his lively musicality made him a welcome replacement at the piano when Dietrich could not attend family concerts. This was Bonhoeffer's first really close friendship, and survived the painful separation when Hildebrandt was forced to emigrate in 1937.

Harnack's Death. In the summer of 1929 Bonhoeffer and his friends attended the final church history seminar taught by eighty-seven-year-old Adolf von Harnack. The farewell ceremony was held at an inn in the Grunewald woods. Bonhoeffer was the speaker: "That you were our teacher for many sessions is a thing of the past; but that we may call ourselves your pupils remains still."[39]

While Bonhoeffer was in the midst of preparing for his examinations and his trip to America, news arrived that the old gentleman had died in Heidelberg on 10 June 1930, as he was about to open the annual meeting of the Kaiser Wilhelm Society. The society held a memorial service in the Goethe Hall of the Harnack House in Berlin on 15 June. Following speeches by Minister of State Friedrich Schmidt-Ott, Professor Hans Lietzmann, Interior Minister Josef Wirth, Culture Minister Adolf Grimme, and Hugo Krüss, director of the state library, Dietrich Bonhoeffer spoke on behalf of Harnack's former students:

> ... it became clear to us through him that truth is born only of freedom. We saw in him the champion of the free expression of a truth once recognized, who formed his free judgment afresh time and time again, and went on to express it clearly despite the fear-ridden restraint of the majority. This made him ... the friend of all young people who spoke their opinions freely, as he asked of them. And if he sometimes expressed concern or warned about recent developments of our scholarship,[40] this was motivated exclusively by his fear that the others' opinion might be in danger of confusing irrelevant issues with the pure search for truth. Because we knew that with him we were in good and solicitous hands, we saw him as the bulwark against all trivialization and stagnation, against all the fossilization of intellectual life.[41]

Bonhoeffer compared favorably with the older and eminent speakers who preceded him, and made a great impression. Many were astonished at the breadth of vision and sympathy he showed for his former teacher, since it was clear that his own path had taken a different direction. Wilhelm Schubring, who published the address in his *Protestantenblatt*, asked Bonhoeffer to criticize the latest attacks on Harnack in his journal, unaware that Bonhoeffer's opinions about Harnack were not only admiring ones.[42]

Bernanos. Throughout his life, Bonhoeffer never limited his reading to theological books; the exploration of contemporary literature was a constant counterpoint. An encounter that had a lasting impact on him stems from this period. His interest in the Catholic world led him to the French novelist Georges Bernanos, whose first novels *Sous le soleil de Satan* (The Star of Satan) and *Der Abtrünnige* (The Apostle) were published in Germany in 1927 and 1929. Bonhoeffer was disconcerted to find his most intimate problems dealt with here—the priest and saint as the chosen target of the tempter, the man barely able to resist the alternative assaults of desperation and pride. Had he not long been familiar with the call to serve God in a special way, and with the longing to know one's own devotion in early years? Was he not already aware of the danger of *accidie* (apathy)? Later Bonhoeffer would be deeply grateful for its absence.[43] Bernanos wrote:

> Futilely, he retreats, step by step, from memory to memory; futilely he peruses his life, word for word. The bill adds up correctly, and still the story makes no more sense. He has become a stranger to his own experience; he no longer recognizes himself. . . . For even given the reach of the average intellect, even given the assumption that someone occasionally got beyond the pictures and fog of illusion to reality, he has not even seized a portion of power, and what could less resemble the recognition of reality than to grasp and hold the feeling of our impotence? . . .[44]
>
> Lord, it is untrue that we cursed you; may he be ruined, the liar, the false witness, your adversary of ridicule and scorn. . . . After me there will be another, and another still, who raises the same scream, over the years, into the arms of the Cross. . . .[45]

The renegade priest is the intellectual skeptic whose "independent thinking is the best weapon against grace"; he writes theological books, "insidious, willful work, glittering, sterile books with a poisoned heart, masterpieces!"[46]

Bonhoeffer's encounter with these early works of Bernanos was the most intimate event that we know of during this period. The question of what he had let himself in for burned more than ever. His discovery of Bernanos was so disturbing that he did something very unusual: he tried to interest his father in what he was reading. His father indeed read the book his son sent him as a somewhat treacherous gift. He replied, in a letter that was both heartfelt and reserved, that the book had gripped him, but

> . . . I am not sure whether I have understood it all; but its real value is that intellectual understanding is less important than the mystical entry into a kind of state of consciousness. Much of the dialogue is such that it is hard to uncover the trains of thought involved between the lines. But, psychologically, the uncertainty whether the experience is supernatural or the dreamlike creation of illusions, the change of affect with its satanic aspects and its human, peasant-like, unintellectual simplicity, is extraordinarily vivid. Is this modern or medieval Catholic mysticism?[47]

Bonhoeffer maintained his interest in Bernanos, adding each of his new books to his library. At his suggestion, many of his seminarians read *The Diary of a Country Priest* when the German translation appeared in 1936.

Berlin Church. During these years the Berlin churches did not see very much of their candidate for the ministry. Superintendent Max Diestel arranged Bonhoeffer's course of study to avoid any bureaucratic disasters. Because of his academic status and his significant postdoctoral work he was exempted from the candidates' seminary.

The dates for the second round of church examinations presented a different problem. The regulations permitted an interval of eighteen months to four years between the first examination and the second. Thus the earliest possible date for Bonhoeffer would have been autumn of 1929, if it had not been so long before he reached the required minimum age for ordination, twenty-five. When his plans to go to America took shape in 1930, everything had to be hurried. He took the second examination before he left, but church officials firmly rejected Diestel's request to ordain Bonhoeffer before his departure for America.

He managed to complete his examination sermon and catechesis before the family left for the holidays. His postdoctoral manuscript *Act and Being* was accepted as his examination thesis, and Bonhoeffer received a "very good" on his oral exams from 5 July to 8 July 1930. His oral catechesis this time was graded "outstanding"; the written form had received only a passing grade. The sermon he delivered was described curiously: "Manner of preaching: simple, natural, dignified; Memorization: very good; Voice: powerful, needs to be louder in the lower registers; Expression: appropriate; Gesticulation: lively."[48]

When the examination results became known, Berlin General Superintendent Otto Dibelius approached Bonhoeffer and told him that he was a man of praxis: "We will keep you in mind for the new student chaplaincy position being established at the technical high school. It can wait until you have returned from America." Ordination had to be postponed until the end of 1931. Given the apprentice year that was still required at the time, Bonhoeffer would become eligible for a full pastorate only in the second half of 1932.

He took little notice of church politics in the years 1929–1930. He joined no group, neither the Christian Socialists (although he had a high opinion of Günther Dehn's sermons and book on Mark) nor the evangelically active Student Christian Movement, which had just published a widely praised anthology, *The Student before God*, with contributions from Althaus, Heim, Köberle, Lilje, Muntschick, and von Thadden. He sought no contacts in the Berlin church hierarchy. *Quousque tandem*, Barth's denunciation of the purple-jacketed *Century of the Church*, and Dibelius's courageous rebuttal, took place only after Bonhoeffer was already in America.[49] Hardly anyone took the occasional incidents of Nazi arrogance in German regional church-

es seriously. In 1929 a minister in Bochum allowed his church to be decorated with swastika flags, while the neighboring Catholic church refused to
allow Nazis in uniform to enter the church. When the board of the
Heiligkreuz parish in Berlin allowed the *Stahlhelm* organization to use its
church for Christmas celebrations, but refused a request from the Reich
Standard Black-Red-Gold, the Berlin Church Consistory expressed disapproval.[50] Bonhoeffer did not yet see any necessity to take a public position
on these issues or give them much thought. The first major success of the
Nazis in the elections of September 1930 created a new situation, but Bonhoeffer had just arrived in New York, and it hardly affected him at first.

American Plans

The idea of spending a year in America as an exchange student arose in the
second half of 1929. Diestel suggested it on ecumenical grounds, but to
Bonhoeffer these considerations were less significant than the prospect of
new fields of study and experience.

The World Alliance for Promoting International Friendship through the
Churches had held its annual conference in 1929 in Kassel; the meeting
received widespread attention when British and German speakers bluntly
addressed the controversial topic of the Versailles Treaty. In 1929 the Berlin
University faculty also held a theological summer session, modeled on the
American format, with presentations by Harnack, Seeberg, Lietzmann,
Sellin, and others. Bonhoeffer took little note of either event. He spent his
summer vacation in Friedrichsbrunn, not realizing how soon he would benefit from these activities.

Initially there was talk of a visit to England, then of a year in America.
Once again, his older brothers had preceded him, since they had already
made their way west. Karl-Friedrich was invited to lecture in America in
1929. For his study of international law, Klaus spent several months in England. Diestel claimed that he had prepared the way for Dietrich to go abroad:
"I advised him, however, that he was still young . . . should look around the
world more first. . . . If it could be arranged somehow, I wanted to send him
to England for several months in the spring, partly because of the language
and partly . . . because the young people who go to America gain a lively look
at the different college system in England and at the academic methods
there."[51] Diestel was aiming for a placement in the United States that could
be arranged by the Academic Exchange Service.

Church Council member August Schreiber promised his help; Deissmann wrote letters of recommendation to America. In addition to men-

tioning Bonhoeffer's outstanding dissertation, the references emphasized his pleasant way of dealing with people.

Still, Bonhoeffer hesitated before submitting his final application. He was suspicious of what awaited him in America. He was not particularly fascinated by the New World. Was he to become a student again and devote a whole year to whatever placement he received? He had heard about American "textbook methods," and he regarded American theology as nonexistent.

He sought information from Johannes Schattenmann, a previous recipient of an American grant, who was not exactly encouraging. Yes, he told Bonhoeffer, one had to go as an ordinary student, subject oneself to the "credit system," and accumulate the required number of credits by attending lectures and seminars and giving reports. Even the American consulate insisted on this before it would grant a visa. To prevent Bonhoeffer from being too disappointed as a result of his German ideas of academic freedom, Schattenmann recommended that he imagine the atmosphere of a German secondary school. In his field of systematic theology, of course, there was nothing to learn. The only place that was worthwhile was Union Theological Seminary in New York, since it offered so much else. But he might well be allotted a place in Hartford or St. Louis. Even in Princeton, seventeenth-century orthodoxy still prevailed. Schattenmann advised him to wait until he could go as a professor.

Bonhoeffer hesitated. He tried to influence his placement through Reinhard Mumm, a pastor and delegate in the Reichstag, even as he told everyone that nothing would come of it. Yet on his birthday Klaus wrote: "I basically predict that you will go; for in the final analysis you do want a year in America; location is of course important, but I don't think it's decisive."[52] By the beginning of May Bonhoeffer's vacillation ended; his placement at Union Theological Seminary was confirmed.

It was his habit to prepare himself thoroughly for enterprises of this kind, not just in the language of the country but in political, theological, and ecclesiastical matters. So far as the latter was concerned, there was not very much that was illuminating. Diestel gave him some literature. Young Willem Visser 't Hooft's *The Background of the Social Gospel* had been published in 1929. There was a book by Hermann Sasse, a minister in the Old Prussian Union Church in Berlin, about theology and church life in America. There was as yet no sign of Bonhoeffer's kind of theology in the United States. True, Emil Brunner, who had been an exchange student from 1919 to 1920, had lectured in America, and his lectures were published in 1929 by Scribner's, under the striking but dubious title *Theology in Crisis*. In 1928 Douglas Horton had published a first translation of Barth, under the more appropriate title *The Word of God and the Word of Man*. The publisher, Pilgrim Press, had insisted that on no account could the word "theology" appear in the title, on the grounds that this would make it impossible to sell. But the title of Brunner's book, unlike that of Horton's, stuck in the American mind, and became the unfortunate slogan in America for Barth's approach.

A notebook in which Bonhoeffer jotted down American idioms also contains some remarkable notes that reveal something about his efforts to prepare himself politically for the trip. It contains arguments on the question of war guilt; and the text of the Versailles Treaty's celebrated Article 231, which attributed war guilt to Germany alone, as well as American and French statements rejecting this. It also includes some dreadful statements made by former Secretary of State Elihu Root (1845–1937), who had written and spoken at mass rallies about the American war aims in 1917:

> The Germans are only half civilized in all that makes for civilization. Germany has the abnormal instincts which characterize her barbarisms and separate her from a civilized people. She has the intolerance, the incapacity to realize the right of existence of others. . . . This war is a war between the civilization of this country and the semicivilization of the past. . . . Most of the Germans have become unclean and will have to walk in the world as marked people, avoided, despised, stoned. . . . We are now in this war to save our country from being overrun by barbarism. We are trying to save infants from being dangled on the bayonet as was done in Belgium.[53]

Should such things ever have been said about the Germans? Bonhoeffer forgot them when he discovered that the wartime mentality had faded among American Christians to a far greater extent than it had in his own country. But in his talks to young Americans, he did not keep silent about the Treaty of Versailles and its effects.[54] In 1929 and 1930 that treaty remained a most painful subject, even in the German circles associated with the World Alliance for Promoting International Friendship through the Churches. At the 1929 World Alliance conference in Kassel, even someone as free of nationalist prejudices as Friedrich Siegmund-Schultze said: "This war educated our German people to peace, this peace educated it to war."[55] Martin Rade, the editor of the *Christliche Welt*, who had no desire to associate himself with the political right, explicitly applauded this statement.

When speaking in New York, Bonhoeffer did not use much of the material he had carefully collected at home. On the contrary, he soon became convinced that the dismantling of old prejudices had gone much further in America than he had previously assumed.

Thus he set out on his first visit to the West. For all his pleasurable expectations, he still felt uncertain about what he wanted. At the time of his departure, he also had hopes of visiting a part of the world not mentioned in his traveling papers—the Far East. This trip marked a turning point in his life, however; it was the beginning of his ties to the English-speaking West. Undertaken hesitantly, with little family precedent for it, it had a more lasting effect on his life than his other youthful travels, and allowed him to make friends who permanently affected him and his outlook.

The day would come when, to his horror, he had to confess to these new western friends that Elihu Root's crude and long-forgotten statements about his country had been confirmed.

CHAPTER FIVE

AMERICA: 1930–1931

> My parents remained with me on board for two hours. . . . So far the days
> have been like being on the Wannsee, totally calm . . . my cabin . . . lies deep
> in the belly of the ship. I have not yet met my traveling companion face to
> face. I have been trying to form a picture of him from the things he leaves
> lying about. The hat, walking stick, and a novel by Seymour have led me
> to the conclusion he is an educated young American. . . . I have already
> eaten two huge meals with a good appetite; I shall go on enjoying the ship
> as long as enjoyment is possible.[1]

Bonhoeffer was sailing into his last year of being footloose and fancy-
free. He had brilliantly fulfilled all the requirements for either an academic
career or a career in the church, but had not yet committed himself to either.
Never before and never again was he able to feel so free. He had achieved
what he had set out to do, and all paths were open to him.

Did he really want to go to America? Even as he prepared for his journey
west, he was planning to return home via the other side of the world. On his
walks in Friedrichsbrunn before he left, he spoke with his brothers and sisters about the possibility of concluding his American year with a visit to
India. His sister Christine encouraged him:

> Perhaps gentle pressure on our parents will do the trick, possibly dressed
> up in the form of a big loan. If you accept a position here immediately
> afterward and promise not to marry soon, you can pay it back. By the way,
> I have a feeling they are sympathetic in the matter, and that in the end it
> will come off.[2]

His traveling companion on the *Columbus* turned out to be Dr. Lucas, a
prosperous American who was president of a college in Lahore. Bonhoeffer
was given expert advice about India, and also received an invitation to
Lucas's home in Lahore. They planned for Bonhoeffer to join him on a trip

to the Indian hills and then to Benares, Allahabad, Agra, and Delhi.[3] When they parted in New York, Bonhoeffer told a fellow scholarship student who was going on to California, "I'll see you when I come through California!" Paul Lehmann, his new friend at the New York seminary, immediately took Bonhoeffer around the docks to find a freighter captain who would take someone cheaply to India. Bonhoeffer asked travel agents for estimates. Klaus wrote a sister-in-law in Manila to say that Dietrich would be traveling through, and gave him the name of an acquaintance in Sumatra.

Further inquiries, however, revealed that returning home via the Pacific would be far more expensive than returning via the Middle East. His initial eagerness subsided; in addition, the new world began to intrigue him. Disappointed, his sister who had worked so energetically at home on his behalf, wrote: "I think it's a shame that you aren't holding firm to your travel plans; the chance certainly won't come again."[4] But his mother consoled him: "I think you will always be able to take a vacation and visit India from here, and you will be better prepared and the timing will be better. But I don't want to talk you into it."[5]

This second attempt to visit Asia was more serious than the first. Some years later a third attempt followed—far more urgent and driven by the new burning questions that had arisen.

The East had also attracted his elder brother Karl-Friedrich. For him, it was mysterious Russia, its people and political direction, whereas Dietrich sought the encounter with the Indian way of dealing with life as a counterpoint to his own philosophy and theology. If he was to see the world of religion so theologically accentuated in contrast to faith, shouldn't he want to examine the subject more closely? And since, in the war question, he had tried to use standard Lutheran teachings to reach a commitment to responsible self-assertion, was it surprising that Gandhi's example so attracted and unsettled him?[6] His natural drive toward action and rational analysis was searching its passive counterpoint of contemplation and the intuition of synthesis. And he was driven by the question of why Christianity had its origins in the East.

But life turned out differently. For years he wanted to broaden his horizon by traveling to the East; instead he did so by going west. This began with his journey to America.

The Country

Bonhoeffer was overwhelmed by New York and the giant concrete buildings between the Hudson and the East River. Lower Manhattan still dominated the skyline. Upper Manhattan did not yet have Rockefeller Center, and the Empire State Building was under construction.

But he soon saw the other side. In 1930 unemployment in America was proportionately much higher than in Germany, and this was causing widespread alarm. Since the Wall Street crash the year before, the Depression had been in full swing. Public opinion was agitated by Prohibition; the "wets" agitated for its abolition and the "dries" for more effective application of the law. "Unfortunately I cannot even raise a glass of wine to your health; it is forbidden by law. This Prohibition in which nobody believes is a dreadful absurdity."[7] There were new concerns about the German lust for another war; these struck Bonhoeffer as very curious. He had not yet taken into account the unusual Nazi gains in the September elections in Germany.[8] A plan for a German-Austrian customs union roused fears of an *Anschluss* and rumors of an impending putsch crossed the Atlantic. Disturbed, Dietrich wrote home. His father's reply was reassuring:

> You say that the news from Germany sounds unpleasant. It certainly is not pleasing, and the perpetual brawls between Communists and Nazis are an indication of the existing tension. But putsches predicted so far in advance generally tend not to happen. Also I think that the Reichswehr is firm under Groener, so that hardly any group will revolt successfully. . . . According to what you write from New York, things there are not that good economically or socially either. In any case, I don't think that any unrest is to be feared between now and your return. . . .[9]
>
> Politically we assume that on the customs union question the Austro-German viewpoint will prevail. Of course it is absurd to talk about war. Aside from everything else, even the Nazis are not so stupid as to believe that we are in a position to go to war.[10]

Whenever he had to give a talk, Bonhoeffer spoke at length about peace aspirations and their proponents in Germany.[11] What he said was hardly an expression of qualified opinion about the state of affairs in Germany, but reflected his own attitude to the peace question, which was still developing.

He quickly came into contact with the busy activity of the New York churches, and soon was hardly able to cope with the invitations that came flooding in. "Now I am constantly and on the most varied occasions having to make speeches and deliver addresses; the day after tomorrow I have to preach in English, and next week I am going to talk about Germany to more than one thousand school children."[12] A Methodist church printed the following invitation:

> Dr. Deitrich Bonhoefier [sic], a professor of the University of Berlin, will speak. From the heart of Germany he will bring to us a message on "WAR." Did you ever wonder what the German people are thinking about war? This is an unusual opportunity to find out. Don't miss it![13]

He was sought as a speaker by student associations ranging from Lutheran to Unitarian. "It is almost incredible that you should want to be in an international association of ninety-seven nations," his father wrote. The organization in question was the Intercollegiate YMCA.

Bonhoeffer was careful, however, not to take things on indiscriminately. The only real commitment he made was to the black neighborhood district of Harlem, not far from Union Theological Seminary. He spent nearly every Sunday and many evenings there. He participated in guided visits to the area, including a "trip to Negro Centres of Life and Culture in Harlem," which began with a flight over the district in which 170,000 African Americans lived per square mile. He collected the publications of the National Association for the Advancement of Colored People, and began to collect gramophone records of spirituals, which he used five years later to introduce his students to this world that was practically unknown at the time. He also read a great deal of African-American literature:

> I have again just finished a quite outstanding novel by a quite young Negro. In contrast to other American writing, which is either cynical or sentimental, I find here a very productive strength and warmth, which continually arouses in one the desire to meet the man himself.[14]

In Reinhold Niebuhr's seminar "Ethical Viewpoints in Modern Literature" he followed the long list of recommended books by African Americans. He wrote an essay on Johnson's *Autobiography of an Ex-Colored Man*. Despite his admiration for American society's capacity for integration and change, he concluded that "according to the whole mood in present Negro literature, it seems to me that the race question is arriving at a turning point. The attempt to overcome the conflict religiously or ethically will turn in a violent political objection."[15] Bonhoeffer erred only about the date; his opinion was unchanged when he found the same situation in 1939.[16]

Albert F. Fisher, an African-American fellow student and friend, helped Bonhoeffer gain a detailed and intimate knowledge of the realities of Harlem life.[17] Nearly every Sunday he accompanied him to Abyssinian Baptist Church at 128 West 138th Street, a bleak, squalid street. He became a regular worker in the Sunday school and the various church clubs, thus gaining entry into people's homes. Fisher also took him to Howard University in Washington, D.C.

Bonhoeffer noted with dismay that the so enviable integration of the white churches into the life of the community was actually an obstacle to the solution of the racial problem. Although greatly impressed by the fervor of the Negro services, he was disturbed by the noticeable and growing estrangement of the younger generation from the faith of their fathers, who had accepted all this discrimination so patiently.[18] He wrote about the problem to his brother Karl-Friedrich, who replied from Frankfurt:

> I am delighted you have the opportunity of studying the Negro question so thoroughly. I had the impression when I was over there that it is really *the* problem, at any rate for people with a conscience and, when I was offered an appointment at Harvard, it was a very basic reason for my disinclination to go to America for good, because I did not want either to take on that legacy myself or to pass it on to my hypothetical children. It seems impossible to see the right way to tackle the problem.

Not suspecting the legacy that would one day affect his own country, Karl-Friedrich continued: "In any case, our Jewish question is a joke by comparison; there won't be many people who claim they are oppressed here. At any rate, not in Frankfurt . . ."[19]

The vast land lured Bonhoeffer beyond the confines of New York. His first trip was to Philadelphia, the cradle of the Quakers and the American Constitution, where relatives of his grandmother Tafel lived. On Thanksgiving Day, Frank Fisher led him around the spacious capital city of Washington; here Bonhoeffer was introduced as a guest from Germany at the annual meeting of the Federal Council of Churches, the predecessor of the present National Council of Churches of Christ in the U.S.A. He was unable to work up any enthusiasm for the ecclesiastical or theological content of the conference.[20] He was impressed, however, by the passage of a widely noted resolution on the question of war guilt, which took the form of a message to Christians in Germany rejecting "the theory of the sole guilt of Germany for the war."[21] This experience encouraged him when he lectured in the United States, and made him react even more bitterly to the 1931 statement by Emmanuel Hirsch and Paul Althaus that accused German supporters of the ecumenical movement of being unpatriotic internationalists.

At Christmas Bonhoeffer and his Swiss friend and fellow student Erwin Sutz accepted an invitation to Cuba. There he visited a sister of Maria and Käthe Horn (his childhood governess), who now taught at a German school in Havana. He visited her class and—after a long interval—preached again. At the Christmas service he painted a gloomy picture to the members of the German colony:

... because it seems strange to celebrate Christmas: with swarms of unemployed right before our eyes, millions of children suffering throughout the world, the starving in China, the oppressed in India and in other unhappy countries.... With all this in mind, who would want to enter the promised land, unsuspecting and unbiased?[22]

He chose an unusual text for his sermon: the story of Moses on Mount Nebo, destined to die without entering the promised land.[23]

At the end of the academic year he went to Mexico with his French friend Jean Lasserre. Catholic culture and memories of Spain attracted him more than the novelties of California. The trip turned into an adventure. He failed to get his driver's license, and later he enjoyed telling how he twice failed to pass the test because he didn't bribe the examiner. Their departure was delayed because Erwin Sutz, who was to join them, first had to sing in the chorus at a performance of Bach's Mass in B minor at Carnegie Hall. Then his parents warned Bonhoeffer not to travel to New Orleans because of the alleged danger of malaria. Finally, on 5 May 1931, Paul Lehmann drove them to Chicago; this was in the days before the turnpikes. At the halfway point in St. Louis, Sutz turned back. The venerable old Oldsmobile, which had been loaned to Bonhoeffer by friends he made during his voyage on the *Columbus,* made it as far as the Mexican border before it died.

Lasserre had friends in Mexico. At the teachers' training college in Victoria he and Bonhoeffer addressed the students on the subject of peace; "for the people of Victoria it was a tremendous event to listen to a German and a Frenchman together!"[24] They spent over a week in Mexico City, visiting pyramids and the sites of ancient sacrifices.

On the return journey they were refused reentry at the United States border. Only after Paul Lehmann and the German ambassador to Mexico sent telegrams could the immigration officials be convinced that the globetrotters would not become a burden on the American labor market, and that the tickets for their return journey to Bremen awaited them in New York. When they finally arrived safely in hot New York on 20 June, just in time to catch the ship home, they had traveled well over 1,200 miles by train through Mexico and nearly 4,000 miles in the decrepit Oldsmobile.

Friends

During the subsequent church struggle, Bonhoeffer abruptly ended some of his student friendships; but those from his period at Union Theological Seminary remained. Four of the friends he made in America between 1930 and 1931—two Americans and two Europeans—played an important part in his life.

One of the Europeans became Bonhoeffer's ally in the uphill task of explaining the theology of old Europe to New World audiences. Erwin Sutz, a Swiss citizen, understood both the source of his friend's discontent and the direction of his arguments. The two friends were also united by their love of the piano, and in New York they recommended one another to places where they could play music together. Together they went to hear Toscanini, whom the spoiled Berlin concertgoer did not feel was that unique. Sutz was astonished and amused by the money Bonhoeffer lavished on keeping in touch with his family through the post office and Western Union; among the far-flung members of this vast clan there were always messages of congratulations or good wishes, worries about illness or other matters. It was Erwin Sutz who finally brought Bonhoeffer and Karl Barth into personal contact with each other. Sutz had studied under Barth and Brunner. Outside the lecture hall the friends discussed Bonhoeffer's criticisms of Barth, which Bonhoeffer completely withheld from his American fellow students. It was not long before Sutz wrote to Barth in Bonn about his new friend. In 1931, before settling down again in Berlin, Bonhoeffer spent a good two weeks in Bonn, for the first time meeting the man who had been most influential in bringing him to the study of theology. Sutz also introduced him to Emil Brunner. During the war Sutz would become Bonhoeffer's vital and reliable contact with the West.

Bonhoeffer initially viewed his other European friend, Jean Lasserre, as much less of a kindred spirit. It was his first encounter with a Christian pacifist of his generation, and Lasserre was a Frenchman; it was much more difficult for a German to shake off all feelings of resentment. Still, unlike his American contemporaries, Lasserre was a European theologian who could not be dismissed as naive or ignorant of the relevant history of dogmatics. In contrast to the undisputed sincerity and earnestness of many young theologians at Union Theological Seminary, Lasserre confronted him with an acceptance of Jesus' peace commandment that he had never encountered before. Not that Bonhoeffer immediately became a convinced pacifist—in fact he never did so—but after meeting Lasserre the question of the concrete reply to the biblical injunction of peace and of the concrete steps to be taken against warlike impulses never left him again. Jean Lasserre's impact on him was deeper than he suspected at the time. He is the object of Bonhoeffer's reference to a "saint" in the letters from Tegel prison written the day after the failure of the 20 July coup;[25] it was also Lasserre who provided the initial impulse for Bonhoeffer's great book *Discipleship*.

In Jean Lasserre he found a man who shared his longing for the concretion of divine grace and his alertness to the danger of intellectually rejecting the proximity of that grace. His friend confronted him with the question of the relationship between God's word and those who uphold it as individuals and citizens of the contemporary world. This soon led Bonhoeffer to a new understanding of the Sermon on the Mount. He also persuaded the reluctant Frenchman to attend ecumenical conferences so that his voice might be heard. Lasserre was present when Bonhoeffer delivered his peace speech in Fanö in 1934. In his New York speeches during 1930–1931, Bonhoeffer stated the biblical arguments for peace and described the embryonic peace movement among the German workers and in the German Youth movement in a way he had not done before.[26] These addresses illustrate Bonhoeffer's awareness of the tiny pacifist movements in Germany. But only now, through his encounter with Lasserre and his first ecumenical confrontation, was Bonhoeffer's academic knowledge of Lutheran ethics transformed into a committed identification with Christ's teachings of peace. The biblical-ecumenical belief in the one body of Christ became his foundation. In the years to come he continued to build upon this structure:

> You have brothers and sisters in our people and in every people; do not forget that. Come what may, let us never more forget that one Christian people is the people of God, that if we are in accord, no nationalism, no hate of races or classes can execute its designs. . . .[27]

Jean Lasserre took the same standpoint in 1953 in his *War and the Gospel*:

> Nothing in the Scriptures gives the Christian authority to tear apart the body of Christ for the State or anything else. Do we believe in the Universal Church, in the communion of saints, or do we believe in the eternal mission of our country? . . . one cannot be Christian *and* nationalist.[28]

In 1930, this was an unfamiliar idea for a German, and those who took it to heart were few indeed.

Bonhoeffer's relationship with the third of these friends, Albert F. (Frank) Fisher, extended beyond the lecture hall to their shared work in Harlem. Fisher was a slender African American with strikingly fine features. It was natural that this friendship was not established with the same ease as was that with Paul Lehmann, and the freedom of this relationship had to be confirmed repeatedly. But Bonhoeffer possessed a convincing talent for extending friendship with no strings attached. When it became clear on one occasion that Fisher was not going to receive the same service in a respectable restaurant as the other customers, the friends ostentatiously walked out. Given the delicate nature of interracial relationships in the United States, the extent to which Bonhoeffer became a welcome guest in the homes of the outcasts of Harlem was astounding. He had a gift for restoring pride and self-confidence to the vulnerable and the sensitive.

> What was so impressive was the way in which he pursued the understanding of the problem to its minutest detail through books and countless visits to Harlem, through participation in Negro youth work, but even more through a remarkable kind of identity with the Negro community, so that he was received there as though he had never been an outsider at all.[29]

The experiences that he owed to Frank Fisher played a significant role when Bonhoeffer talked about America in later years. After he left America they did not meet again. Fisher became a professor in Atlanta, Georgia, and died in 1960.

Finally Paul and Marion Lehmann's house in New York became a kind of American home for Bonhoeffer; he celebrated his twenty-fifth birthday there. With Lehmann he could talk and argue; Lehmann understood the nuances of European culture and theology. Lehmann came from the Evangelical and Reformed Church, but later joined the Presbyterians; he was working on his dissertation at Union Theological Seminary, where he was also a tutor in systematic theology. He could understand why the theological statements of professors and students at the seminary could make Bonhoeffer's hair stand on end.

He found Bonhoeffer very German indeed, not only in his thorough theological training and precise methods of tackling problems, but "he was German in his passion for perfection, whether of manners, or performance, or of all that is connotated by the word *Kultur*. Here, in short, was an aristocracy of the spirit at its best."

But Lehmann also discovered characteristics in Bonhoeffer that did not fit the common picture of Germans at all:

> His aristocracy was unmistakable yet not obtrusive, chiefly, I think owing to his boundless curiosity about every new environment in which he found himself and to his irresistible and unfailing sense of humor. Thus he could suggest without offense that we should not play tennis together since he commanded a certain expertness at the game which I could not claim. . . . This curiosity about the new and different, this unfailing humor . . . always turned the incongruity between human aspiration and human failing away

from human hurt to the enrichment of comradeship ... the capacity to see oneself and the world from a perspective other than one's own. This paradox of birth and nationality in Bonhoeffer has seemed to me increasingly during the years since to have made him an exciting and conspicuous example of the triumph over parochialism of every kind.[30]

Lehmann always hoped that someday Bonhoeffer, as a professor in the United States, would shake up the American "theistic scenery" as it was at the time. In 1939 Lehmann did everything in his power to prevent him from returning from the United States to Germany. He responded patiently to all Bonhoeffer's whims and suggestions; he procured invitations for Bonhoeffer, only to decline them on his behalf. Thus he put himself in a difficult position among his colleagues and college presidents and, when all these efforts proved futile, accepted it with the greatest understanding. He was Bonhoeffer's companion and loyal helper at the most important turning point in his life.

Union Theological Seminary

Despite all these other activities, Bonhoeffer did not neglect the real purpose of his visit to America—studying at Union Theological Seminary in New York. A clear-sighted and astute report he wrote at the time reveals the astonishing extent to which he used this period, both for open-minded critical exploration and to test himself in fields that he had not yet explored.[31]

The seminary was nearly one hundred years old at the time; by American standards this made it an institution steeped in tradition. Originally a Presbyterian college, at the turn of the century it had altered its founding statutes to become an interdenominational seminary, and it had become a focal point for the most progressive liberal minds. In the process it had aroused the mistrust of the fundamentalist churches, many of whose young scholars—often against the wishes of their superiors—nonetheless attended this attractive place of education, which was a "stronghold as notorious as it is distinguished" against political, social, and ecclesiastical conservatism.[32]

Union's reputation was at its height at the time; it already had ecumenical ambitions and was a favorite goal for visitors from Europe. Deissmann had just been there in 1929. It was led by Henry Sloane Coffin, a "church statesman" in the best sense of the word and a great preacher at the Presbyterian church on Madison Avenue. The staff included a number of distinguished men. William Adams Brown, a member of a banking family, a follower of Ritschl, and the leading American ecumenist at the time, was on sabbatical, but Bonhoeffer would soon meet him at ecumenical conferences. Church history was taught by James Moffat from Glasgow. Reinhold Niebuhr had been appointed professor of applied Christianity in 1928. In 1930 John Baillie began his professorship of systematic theology with an inaugural lecture, "The Logic of Religion"; Pitney van Dusen was his assistant professor and John Bennett an instructor. The contemporary style of preaching was taught by two preachers who were in great demand, Harry Emerson Fosdick from Riverside Church and Ralph Sockman from the Madison Avenue Methodist Church. J. W. Bewer, who came from the Rhineland, taught Old Testament literary history; Bonhoeffer did not attend his lectures, but became friends with him and found him a good adviser when he faced his major decision in 1939.[33]

In 1930 Bonhoeffer was granted a Sloane Fellowship. Mrs. William Sloane had established the fellowship in 1920, which initially provided a year's residency for a French student and was then extended to include three "Europeans." Jean Lasserre's predecessors included the French conscientious objector Vernier, of whom Bonhoeffer later told his students, and J. Jézéquel and Charles Monod, who became prominent French ecumenists. Bonhoeffer was preceded by Johannes Schattenmann from Bavaria and Erich Eichele from Württemberg; he was followed by Hans Stroh and his cousin Hans-Christoph von Hase (1933–1934).

College life was entirely new to him, and he did not adapt to it easily. He suffered under the fact that the doors were always open, and he was astonished by the deliberate renunciation of all privacy. But he also discovered the good sides of this, such as the students' constant willingness to discuss anything with anybody, not just among themselves but with their professors. He obtained the necessary credits by attending the required number of lectures and seminars, and he wrote five or six essays that have survived. But he was granted exemption from the examinations, which he considered unnecessary in light of his Berlin degree, although his friends Sutz and Lasserre obtained their S.T.M. (Master of Sacred Theology), the latter summa cum laude. Bonhoeffer never regularly attended morning chapel.

The Barthian. Bonhoeffer found it difficult to suppress his sense of European superiority; he was irritated daily by the American lack of concern for what to him were the genuine problems of theology. He regarded what he heard not as theology, but as long outdated religious philosophy, until it occurred to him that he should study its premises. When the students burst into loud laughter at quotations from Luther's *De servo arbitrio*, which struck them as funny, he lost patience.[34] Nevertheless, he did not express his indignation as

Lütgert had when he said that "the Americans are naive enough to order a theology and philosophy to suit their purpose, just as one orders a car from a factory."[35] In the report to his church on his year in America, Bonhoeffer combined criticism with an overriding concern to emphasize the good side of the phenomenon; as a result, he was able to show his own church and its theology that it might, perhaps, be a little provincial. His advocacy of Barth remained unchanged, but by the end of this period, European theological self-confidence was no longer the only decisive factor.

Although Bonhoeffer's report, based on his experiences, portrayed the theological state of the seminary as hopeless, he had still arrived at the right place at the right time. Horton's translation of Barth and Brunner's lectures had been published. In 1956, John Baillie reported his impressions of Bonhoeffer in America:

> When I had been in America for a little more than ten years [Baillie came to Union Theological Seminary from Canada] a new situation began to declare itself—I think about the winter of 1930–1931. This was when the impact of what I shall call the Barthian movement was first felt on this side of the Atlantic. . . . It was late in reaching America. . . . It so happened that, I think in the year 1933, it was my turn to read a paper at a social meeting of the Faculty of Union Seminary, and I called my paper "A Preface to Barthianism." I was not indeed anything that could be called a Barthian myself, but there were those among my colleagues who could see no significance at all in the movement, and I was bold enough to think that I understood something of what it portended. . . .
>
> Bonhoeffer was my student in this Seminary in 1930–1931 and was then the most convinced disciple of Dr. Barth that had appeared among us up to that time, and withal as stout an opponent of liberalism as had ever come my way.[36]

The seminary records from 1929–1930 contain not a single thesis or dissertation affected by the "theology of crisis." In 1931–1932, however, for the first time there was a thesis reflecting the "new situation": "The theology of Schleiermacher and the challenge of theology of crisis." The avant-garde was at Union Theological Seminary, not at the denominationally linked seminaries.

This new "impact" first became evident in Baillie's seminar, in which van Dusen assisted. Here Bonhoeffer, backed by Paul Lehmann, fought his battles. Baillie, who was a follower of Ritschl's great pupil Harnack, could hardly have imagined Bonhoeffer's high praise of Harnack in his memorial address, and he knew nothing of Bonhoeffer's critical questions to Barth in *Act and Being*. Bonhoeffer suppressed his criticisms so completely that, in the essays he wrote for the seminar, his proselyting zeal led him to mingle his own propositions with those of Barth and actually attribute them to him, no doubt without realizing it.[37] Baillie asked Bonhoeffer to lecture on Barth to his seminar. Bonhoeffer began:

> I confess that I do not see any other possible way for you to get into real contact with his thinking than by forgetting at least for this one hour everything you have learned before.[38]

Baillie was an alert scholar who kept up with developments in his field. He also asked Bonhoeffer for detailed information about Heidegger, and saw to it that Bonhoeffer's essay "Concerning the Christian Idea of God" was published in the *Journal of Religion*.[39]

When Bonhoeffer attempted in 1939 to get a sense of what had happened in the United States in the meantime, he discovered that something new had arisen since his initial visit—precisely through those with whom he had fought, including Reinhold Niebuhr. It still appeared to him, however, to be more a "theology of crisis" than a new passion for the theology of the Word. The name hid the subject.[40]

The 1930–1931 seminary course offerings probably astonished the student from Berlin. There was an almost complete lack of exegesis or dogmatics. To compensate, there was a great deal of ethics, and an abundance of courses devoted to the analysis and explanation of contemporary American philosophy, literature, and society. Future ministers were expected to master these things, not the loci of the creeds or the history of dogmatics. The ability to arrive at a sound judgment on contemporary problems or help shape political opinion was a marginal priority in a German theological faculty, and Bonhoeffer was struck by the fact that the American theology student "knows much more about the things of daily life."[41] Later the curriculum of Union Theological Seminary became more theologically thorough.

The list of courses and lectures Bonhoeffer took for credit during this year included:

> "Religion and Ethics" (Niebuhr); "Religious Aspects of Contemporary Philosophy" (Lyman); "Church and Community: The Cooperation of the Church with Social and Character-Building Agencies" (Webber); "Ethical Interpretations" (Ward and Niebuhr); "Ethical Viewpoints in Modern Literature" (Ward and Niebuhr); "Ethical Issues in the Social Order" (Ward); "Theology I: The Idea of God in His Relations to the World and Man" (Baillie); "Seminar in Philosophical Theology" (Baillie and Lyman); "Brief Sermons" (Fosdick); "The Minister's Work with Individuals" (Coffin).[42]

His teachers were dismayed when Bonhoeffer invariably started his work by dealing with the theology of revelation, the doctrine of justification, and eschatology, instead of arriving properly at the so-called realities. Niebuhr and Baillie in particular took the trouble to make numerous comments on the difficult and demanding essays written by their German guest. Baillie noted the German predilection for impossible associations of ideas such as "revelation in hiddenness." "Is not this a perverse expression?" he wrote.[43] He criticized the gulf that Bonhoeffer drew between thought (in the idealist sense) and reality; that sort of thing inevitably struck him as forced and artificial.

Niebuhr was thirty-eight. Bonhoeffer noted down the beginning of his lecture: "Religion is the experience of the holy, transcendent experience of Goodness, Beauty, Truth, and Holiness." He did not take down very much more. But he liked Niebuhr's free and lively way of explicating the factors on which ethics depended; Niebuhr spoke of the "ethical resources and limitations of religious authoritarianism" and the dubious consequences of religious institutionalism or individualism ("Luther stood for religious individualism, Calvin stood for ethical individualism"). Niebuhr blithely criticized the essays of his seemingly unpolitical student; he was dissatisfied with Bonhoeffer's assertion that "the God of guidance" could be discovered only from the "God of justification," and asked what God's guidance meant *ethically*:

> . . . in making grace as transcendent as you do, I don't see how you can ascribe any ethical significance to it. Obedience to God's will may be a religious experience, but it is not an ethical one until it issues in actions which can be socially valued. Any interpretation of "ethical" other than one which measures an action in terms of consequences and judges actions purely in terms of notions empties the ethical of content and makes it purely formal.[44]

Privately Bonhoeffer was already concerned about the implications of the ethical concreteness of revelation,[45] but he defiantly insisted that the correct premises had to come first, and must remain independent of any premature interest in their ethical effects.

Literature and Contemporary Questions. Although he showed little willingness to listen to opposing arguments in the realm of theology, Bonhoeffer showed unlimited interest in areas where he hoped to gain new knowledge or discover better methods or vantage points. In the second half of his year in America he concentrated on three things: American philosophy, which he decided stood behind everything that struck him as so surprising, new American literature, and sociopolitical studies and excursions. He was soon so overwhelmed by the amount of information and ideas that, as he wrote home, he could hardly cope with the multitude of impressions; all the same, he was enjoying it. "If one really tried tasting New York to the full, it would practically be the death of one."[46]

Eugene Lyman, professor of Philosophy of Religion, gave Bonhoeffer private tutorials that introduced him to the background of the conventional terminology at Union Theological Seminary. Under Lyman's guidance he studied

> almost the complete philosophical works of William James, which I found uncommonly fascinating, then Dewey, Perry, Russell, and finally also J. B. Watson, and the literature of the behaviorist school. The study of Whitehead, Knudson and Santayana was not nearly as illuminating to me as these radically empirical thinkers. In them, particularly in James, I found the key to understanding the modern theological language and ways of thought of the liberal, enlightened American.... Questions such as that of Kantian epistemology are "nonsense," and no problem to them, because they take life no further. It is not truth, but "works" that is "valid," and that is their criterion.[47]

Bonhoeffer planned to conclude his studies in America with a major work on the pragmatic background of American philosophy and theology, and had even asked the Church Federation Office for an extension of his leave. He did not pursue it any further, however, leaving only these comments on the matter in his report.[48]

Reinhold Niebuhr taught the course on modern writers. Bonhoeffer had to write an essay on each book discussed; these essays offer an interesting overview of the writers of that era. Niebuhr dealt with European and American literature, particularly the more recent war literature such as *Letters of Students Killed in Action*, the novels of Erich Remarque and Ludwig Renn, and Englishman R. C. Sheriff's play *Journey's End*, which Bonhoeffer greatly liked, for "it does not belittle idealistic feeling [a matter on which he was highly sensitive], nor does it veil the naked reality."[49] On the whole, however, Bonhoeffer was critical of the literary revival of wartime experiences.

He preferred the Czech Karel Capek to the German expressionist Ernst Toller, whose plays *Mass Man* and *Machine Man* were discussed, and he took the opportunity of using Ibsen's *Brand*, a familiar work that he continued to appreciate in later years, to fight against compromise and its collapse in the face of the *deus caritatis*.[50] He regarded George Bernard Shaw's dry brilliance as regrettably impaired by his cynicism; Shaw had, "as far as I see never taken up any problem of serious ethical or religious importance."[51] Curiously enough, the Shaw work Bonhoeffer misread was *Androcles and the Lion*, which introduced to world literature the Sydenham church in London where Bonhoeffer subsequently worked.[52] Ten years later, perhaps, he would have looked with different eyes on Ferrovius in Shaw's play, who, at the sound of the drum, forgets all his Christian vows and hurries to the arms he had disdained. At the time, however, Bonhoeffer viewed it as mere relativism.

He wrote an essay on the literature of African Americans.[53] He read Ludwig Lewisohn's *Stephen Escott* and *Midchannel*, which opposed Jewish assimilation in the United States. He liked Theodore Dreiser's *Free and Other Stories*, and, although he found longueurs, exaggerations, and indiscretions in Sinclair Lewis's *Elmer Gantry*, Bonhoeffer thought its description of middle-class pietism and misuse of spiritual values was masterly: "Elmer Gantry could serve to many a pastor as the counterpart of the Catholic mirror of confession."[54]

His social and political studies at the seminary consisted of "Church and Community," taught by C. C. Webber and including visits to social and political organizations in New York, and Harry F. Ward's course on contemporary problems, called "Ethical Interpretations."

Webber's course covered labor problems, restriction of profits, civil rights, juvenile crime, and the activity of the churches in these fields. The class visited the National Women's Trade Union League and the Workers' Education Bureau of America, which had emerged from the class-conscious Workers' Educational Association. They discovered which churches had joined this work through their own education committee or even established their own labor school; the churches' slogan was "Knowledge is power—only if it is properly applied." The National Child Labor Committee fought against the use of child labor in the factories. They studied issues such as the appropriate prices for workers and eventual consumer strikes sponsored by the churches, drawing on the experience in England of the Cooperative Movement and the National Consumer League. They spent one day at the American Civil Liberties Union, which fought for freedom of speech, press, and assembly, for the right to strike, and for racial equality. They were preoccupied by a Supreme Court decision that had denied American citizenship to a woman who opposed taking up weapons, and attempted to draw public interest to the case. The Boy Scouts, Big Brother, and Big Sister movements interested them because of their success in fighting delinquency; the students learned that, while there were 1,313 youth "gangs" in Chicago alone, only 7 percent of the members cared for by groups like Big Brothers returned to the gangs.

Bonhoeffer was impressed by the vigor with which churches and other organizations tackled working-class problems, and the selflessness with which Union Theological Seminary students, among others, shared the life of the unemployed.[55] In 1932 this led him to work with his own students in Berlin on behalf of the unemployed, to raise funds, and to create a youth club. Because of this, despite his theological reservations, Bonhoeffer never spoke deprecatingly about the "social gospel."[56]

Harry F. Ward's seminar was even more political. Ward, Professor of Christian Ethics, had a sharp nose, and his thinking was just as sharp. A passionate nonconformist and socialist, he would certainly have been a victim of McCarthyism twenty years later. The students in his seminar had to analyze articles in newspapers and periodicals, forming objective opinions on foreign or domestic political questions. Some of these topics became the subject of lively discussion in Bonhoeffer's correspondence with his parents.

This was the immediate case with the first domestic controversy, the Wickersham Report on Prohibition. The report did not recommend a repeal but a revision of the 1919 Prohibition statute, after it led to increased criminality instead of the expected moral improvement. Bonhoeffer's father asked for his impressions of this experiment; it interested him medically, since he had studied problems of withdrawal in Breslau and during the First World War. Dietrich obtained statistics about deliria from New York neurological clinics.[57] Prohibition was finally repealed in 1933. Bonhoeffer mentioned the study in his *Ethics* during the 1940s, portraying the episode as a decisive experience for the American churches, since they had been a driving force, behind both the original law and then its repeal.[58]

Ward's students also examined the various unemployment insurance systems and the consequences of the Wall Street crash. Learning that 350,000 investors with small savings of up to $400 had been victimized, Bonhoeffer wrote: "The whole story shed a bright light upon a very dark situation . . . of lack of the consciousness of social responsibility. The strong banks are the principal masters of America."[59] In a country without unemployment benefits, he described to the seminar the German policy in which state, employer, and employee all contributed to such insurance. Only a few private firms in America, such as General Electric, had started such insurance programs. Bonhoeffer concluded by looking at Germany's threatened situation due to the burden of reparations:

The situation in the USA is particularly bad, although there is no doubt that, for instance, Germany must break financially if the period lasts for a longer time. A way out of the whole situation can be seen, it seems to me, only in a new regulation of the question of war debt and in a cancellation of those by the USA.

The main evil is poverty and unemployment. It's an achievement of the government that it was able to get through the winter with 5 million unemployed . . . I continue to hope that spring, and an improvement in the labor conditions, will diminish tensions somewhat. When one listens to the large industrialists from the Rhine, they say that wages must drop another 14 percent—they've already dropped 6 percent to make us competitive. At the moment in Cologne English coal is cheaper than that from the Ruhr valley.[60]

Due to the completion of the Tennessee Valley generator, the issue of private or public use of new sources of energy had become the source of dispute between Republicans and Democrats. In 1930 Bonhoeffer calculated in Ward's seminar: "The competitive system in the U.S. makes the price for the consumer considerably higher; the consumer in New York pays five times as much as the consumer in Canada where the government runs the power-works. Roosevelt demands regulation by the government, the big companies oppose."[61]

Bonhoeffer also dealt with the issue of birth control; the Protestants had met with strong criticism from the Catholics. In 1930 the Federal Council of Churches published a report that drew great attention by stating that: "Birth control by means of contraception by married people is valid and moral."[62] The liberal Catholic magazine *Commonweal* responded that the Federal Council's document was the death of the Reformation; protest also arose among some Lutherans. Bonhoeffer concluded with a remark that only he could have made: ". . . it is interesting to see that the issue of conflict between Protestants and Catholics turns out to be an ethical one, since the dogmatic is no longer understood by Protestants."[63]

Ward also required his students to study the areas of tension in the world political realm; India, Russia, Poland, Germany, and Austria stood in the foreground. It was the time of the London Round-Table conference, where the confrontation between Gandhi and Lord Halifax occurred. Bonhoeffer interpreted the effects of the world economic crisis on Russia by explaining that Russia alone had escaped unemployment, but the overall drop in prices had affected its production. Russia in turn raised its exports by dropping its prices, France defended itself with increased tariffs while Italy did not, and this led Russia closer to the anti-French bloc of Italy and Germany.

A different power play could be seen by looking at the Polish problem. To assert the permanence of its western border, Poland set up a system of pacts designed to keep France, Yugoslavia, and Czechoslovakia as allies. Bonhoeffer pointed out that the threatening stance of Poland had led to the exodus of Germans from eastern Prussia, which, in turn, had a negative effect on the problem of unemployment.[64]

In these months France's fears of an alliance against it focused on the negotiations for a customs agreement between Germany and Austria. These had been the subject of the last discussion on foreign policy in the seminar. Bonhoeffer reported what his father had written to him about it, and concluded: "There is no doubt that the whole incident is based upon the intolerable financial situation into which Germany has been brought by the payment of the war reparations. And this aspect of the situation brings the whole issue home to the USA."[65]

When his time in America was up Bonhoeffer had by no means come to terms with the onslaught of information and issues that had bombarded him. Niebuhr and Baillie later recalled that he withdrew into his orthodox European shell:

> He felt that political questions in which our students were so interested were on the whole irrelevant to the life of a Christian. Shortly after his return to Germany he became very much interested in ethical and political issues and for a time considered going to India to study Gandhi's movement. . . . Once very unpolitical, he became a very astute political analyst.[66]

In 1932 Bonhoeffer did not like to be reminded that he had once spoken so antipolitically, for which Helmut Rössler reproached him:

> I hope you will not misunderstand the term "disinterestedness" I used a long time ago—incidentally I can no longer remember it; today it seems to me to be truly frivolous. All it was meant to indicate was the boundaries within which I see these problems, through the fact of the church.[67]

The fact of the matter was that the America he saw on the eve of Roosevelt's New Deal, the activity of churches and students in the economic crisis, and the enthusiasm of the "social gospel," made an ineradicable impression on Bonhoeffer. Although he stood firmly by his fundamental theological principles, he was still strongly motivated by an "insatiable curiosity for every new reality."[68] An existence confined to his desk could no longer satisfy him. Worlds of thought and feeling that had gone unquestioned suddenly seemed one-sided, inadequate, and in need of reappraisal.

As before, the presence of Christ as seen through the eyes of this American theology appeared distorted or inadequately represented to Bonhoeffer. But was it not inadequately represented on the other side of the Atlantic too? How could the two be reconciled? The later Bonhoeffer of *Discipleship* and the church struggle did not forget what he learned in New York. His stay in America reinforced his basic interest in the concrete reality of the word of God. His problem now was how this concreteness was to be developed, not in opposition to the law that he had made his own, but growing out of it. From this point on, the struggle would be to find an answer to this question.

> My stay in America . . . made one thing clear to me: the absolute necessity of working together *and* at the same time the inexplicable conflict that appears to make such unity simply impossible. From the perspective over there, our situation and theology appear so localized, and I just can't understand how, in the entire world, Germany and a few men over there should have grasped what the Gospel is. And yet I don't see a message anywhere else.[69]

The Return Home

Only a few letters of the lively correspondence between Bonhoeffer and his family survive. Some of the letters he received reveal the intense interest with which, despite the distance and all the demands on his time in New York, he followed the news from Berlin, whether political, ecclesiastical, or about events at the university.

After the first turbulent weeks in New York, when he finally saw the implications of the September German elections and read the news about the further growth in unemployment, he realized with concern how hard it was to form an opinion about developments from a distance. For the first time it seemed possible that dangers might loom for his brother-in-law Leibholz, who described how anti-Semitic "Nazis" were making their presence felt among his colleagues at Greifswald University. The drastic economic measures taken by the new government created anxiety that his brothers-in-law might lose their jobs or have their appointments postponed. His brother Klaus wrote to him about the altered political scene:

> Since the elections X has been in a state of exaltation, as he sees the day of vengeance coming for the "sinister men of November." Since your depar-

ture the political situation has changed greatly. The success of Nazism has convinced the widest circles that the democratic regime has failed in the past ten years. The consequences of the world economic crisis are explained in purely domestic terms. People are flirting with fascism. If this radical wave captures the educated classes, I am afraid that it will be all over for this nation of poets and thinkers.[70]

The Social Democrats still governed Prussia, but the *Stahlhelm* was circulating a popular petition for new Prussian elections. The so-called State Party failed to give a new and effective form to the democratic-bourgeois center. But there were also more reassuring messages from home:

> Everything here bodes very pessimistically for the future. Many are afraid that a Nazi government could come and destroy the whole economy and credit. I don't believe it. . . .[71]

> It's not as wild as the newspapers report. People continue to hope that Bruning's government will create a halfway useful budget. If they really manage to reduce the cost of living somewhat, some of the wind will be taken out of the radicals' sails.[72]

> The apparently calm . . . personality of the Reich Chancellor [Bruning], who goes his own way without wavering, is pleasing.[73]

In February 1931, however, a letter from his friend Helmut Rössler in rural Priegnitz gave a detailed picture of the unexpectedly advanced fanaticization of the German population in the countryside.[74] Bonhoeffer was so disturbed by this letter that he discussed it with his American friends.

During the summer of 1931 the tension was only slightly relieved, though more reassuring news came from the family itself. In May Leibholz became a professor at Göttingen University and Dohnanyi was given a post as a public prosecutor in Hamburg, which he held for nine months until he was called in January 1933 by the Reich Minister of Justice. Thus both were promoted at an unusually early age.

Church events played a more incidental role in the New York correspondence. Still, Bonhoeffer wrote Diestel: "I'm attracted more and more by the ministry."[75] Diestel's candidates were reading *Sanctorum Communio*; afterward the superintendent told Bonhoeffer's uncle Hans von Hase: "But your nephew still has to learn German." For their son's sake, Dietrich's parents spent an evening with church superintendents in Lichterfeld. In a letter of 23 February 1931 his mother reported on the evening:

> Recently I was with Dibelius at the Diestels, he spoke of you kindly and asked when you would return, and said that he hoped to win you for the

ministry entirely through your activity as pastor of the students at the technical college. High Consistory Counselor Schreiber also sang your praises.[76]

Official correspondence about the student chaplaincy position began to take its course. Dibelius wrote directly to Bonhoeffer that the general superintendent for that district of Berlin, Emil Karow, awaited him after his return from America. Bonhoeffer's leave of absence for New York officially ended on 1 August 1931. Through Diestel, he tried to get two more months for a project on American philosophy, but the Berlin Consistory showed no understanding for it. Diestel was only able to obtain a leave for the candidate for September 1931 for the impending conference of the World Alliance for Promoting International Friendship through the Churches in Cambridge. Bonhoeffer as yet knew nothing of it.

Bonhoeffer was more affected by events at the university in Berlin than by church matters. In the winter of 1930–1931 professors reacted strongly to the publication of former Reich chancellor Prince Bülow's memoirs, which portrayed a number of prominent Berlin personalities in such a questionable light that professors such as Erich Seeberg, the son of Reinhold Seeberg, began their lectures with critical comments and corrections. The Bonhoeffers were involved because Harnack's reputation was impugned. His mother wrote to Dietrich on 9 November 1930: "Do you know that old Harnack has been so nastily attacked in the Bülow memoirs that have just come out? The family now wants to publish letters from Bülow to Harnack." Bonhoeffer's father wrote an article, "A Psychopathological View of the Recollections of Prince Bülow," which was printed on the front page of the 24 March *Deutsche Allegemeine Zeitung*. In it Bonhoeffer scrupulously examined signs that "seem to indicate that these recollections should not be read as fully authoritative, but in many respects should be regarded as the result of morbid changes due to age." It was an unusual act for a man so averse to putting himself in the public eye.

After this sensation had died down, another far more significant one drew public attention, arising from Günther Dehn's appointments at the universities in Heidelberg and Halle.[77] While Bonhoeffer was still in New York, he heard that Paul Tillich had declined the chair of practical theology in Halle, and that after Minister of Culture Becker appointed Dehn to the position, nationalist socialist student groups staged protest demonstrations. Only later, of course, could Bonhoeffer modestly try to help.

During his absence Berlin University was the scene of excesses against Jewish students. Shouting "death to the Jews!" nationalist students assaulted them in the entrance hall and threw them out of the window into the court-yard. The rector of the university, theologian Adolf Deissmann, hardly knew what to do, because he didn't dare to allow the police to intervene on university grounds. The theological faculty, however, was far more excited by the battle of words between Barth and Dibelius in the university's assembly hall. Barth spoke on 31 January 1931 on the topic "The Plight of the Protestant Church,"[78] and Dibelius responded on 6 February from the same platform with the address "The Responsibility of the Church." The affair was discussed at an evening party at Diestel's, and Dietrich's mother wrote to him: "X, of the Evangelical Church Press, was there and . . . attacked Barth's address in a very uncouth fashion. Dibelius argued with him some and said that Barth was not to be disposed of so simply."[79] Hildebrandt wrote in amusement to his friend that Barth had launched his attack against the German church authorities from Schleiermacher's platform, of all places.

Bonhoeffer was especially interested in the changes in the faculty. That winter Leonhard Fendt succeeded Mahling in practical theology. On 13 March 1931 his mother wrote: "In his inaugural lecture Fendt quoted you very comically,[80] he said: 'Dietrich Bonhoeffer, whom you all know, said . . .'"

In 1930 Arnold Stolzenburg became one of the candidates for the systematics professorship in Breslau, which was then granted to Friedrich Gogarten. Hans-Christoph von Hase wrote his cousin in the spring of 1931 that he had heard from Reinhold Seeberg's office that Stolzenburg would now take over the social ethics institute, and Bonhoeffer had been chosen as his successor in the assistant's position for systematics. This unforeseen position in the systematics department promised financial security to the uncertain life of a university lecturer.

Thus, amid his busy activities in New York, Bonhoeffer's thoughts for the future took a definite direction. A job with both academic and church connections awaited him at home. Concerned about his new academic start, his father advised him to submit his proposed lecture plans for the winter of 1931–1932 to the dean of the faculty in good time—in any event, before he disappeared for Mexico.

There was no longer any place in his plans for a journey to India. "After all this I am really looking forward to Germany again," he wrote.[81]

PART TWO

THE COST OF
BEING A CHRISTIAN

CHAPTER SIX

LECTURER AND PASTOR: 1931–1932

It is not that I am afraid of disappointing   but that sometimes I simply cannot see how I am going to get things right . . . (in) the unprecedented state of our public life in Germany.[1]

How is one to preach such things to these people? Who still believes them? The invisibility destroys us. . . . This absurd, perpetual state of being thrown back upon the invisible God—no one can stand it any longer.[2]

Bonhoeffer's return to Germany in 1931 represented a break in his development that was certainly sharper than the momentous political and ecclesiastical upheaval that followed two years later. The second major phase of his career began now, not in 1933.

The period of learning and roaming had come to an end. He now began to teach on a faculty whose theology he did not share, and to preach in a church whose self-confidence he regarded as unfounded. More aware than before, he now became part of a society that was moving toward political, social, and economic chaos.

In 1928 he had welcomed the beginning of practical work in Barcelona as a "synthesis" of work and life because "it gives the work value and the worker an objectivity."[3] Now he was suddenly overtaken by the loneliness of those who take on public responsibility for the first time. He had kept a deliberate distance between himself and his teachers, but now he felt the absence of a competent mentor, who "would really have become my teacher!—I do not know why that should never happen to me. Or wouldn't I have been able to stand it?"[4]

Bonhoeffer indeed found it difficult to subordinate himself to those who did not measure up to his exacting standards. This made his later submission to the "brothers" in Finkenwalde all the more striking. Even then, however, it was difficult to advise him; he lacked the naïveté to let others make decisions for him. He had an instinctive fear of being surprised by circumstances beyond his control without first having assured himself of an alternative. It was very difficult for him simply to "believe"; indeed, he would have described such "belief" as laziness.

Thus he made the decisions of the following two years without any adviser, while carrying an extremely heavy workload that laid the foundation of *Discipleship* and *Life Together*. In contrast to *Sanctorum Communio* and *Act and Being*, which used the conceptual language of others, Bonhoeffer now used his own words for the contributions he wished to make to theology and the church. The period of Bonhoeffer's life in which these fruits ripened now began.

The questions that Bonhoeffer now posed to his church, its theology, its ethics, and its attitude to Luther were new, an obvious departure from the purely academic sphere. They revolved around the critical questions of the ethical and pastoral authorization to make binding statements. He analyzed the deficient competence of his church, and measured its claims against its credibility; his analysis extended into the ecumenical sphere. Compared to the previous period, his ecclesiology was more concrete, but also more open and more critical of the church. Christology took the center of the field. His sermons at the beginning of this new period had an apprehensive undertone that faded away only in 1933.

In his personal life, something occurred during these months that is hard for us to perceive fully, though its effects are plain. He himself would never have called it a conversion. But a change occurred in him that led to all that was to follow during this phase of his life—*Discipleship*, the Finkenwalde experiment in communal living, his attitude to the ecumenical movement, and the church struggle. It marked the beginning of a phase in his life that continued right up to 1939.

In the next two years, Bonhoeffer—now twenty-five—would work in three different fields:

In the academic sphere, every semester Bonhoeffer gave a number of two-hour lectures and seminars in the theological faculty of Berlin University. Unfortunately, none of the lecture manuscripts, which would have revealed to us the problems in Bonhoeffer's mind and his answers to them, have survived. An approximate reconstruction of his ideas at the time, based upon his students' lecture notes, must suffice.[5]

Pastorally, as a student chaplain Bonhoeffer delivered sermons and talks, and taught a confirmation class in Wedding. His social work for the church included organizing a weekend home in Biesenthal for students and confirmation candidates. He also opened a youth club for the unemployed in Charlottenburg, and tried to obtain a parish position in a working-class area in east Berlin.

In the ecumenical sphere, he became a youth secretary in the World Alliance for Promoting International Friendship through the Churches and in the Ecumenical Council for Practical Christianity (Life and Work); he traveled, spoke and organized.

Under this strenuous schedule, he drew on the support of his parents' home as a matter of course. "In the last few months everything has been in upheaval because of all the things I have been doing, at home as well. . . . I am now greatly looking forward to a quiet summer at home."[6] But there would be no such quiet summer again.

In the late summer of 1931, before taking on these multiple duties, Bonhoeffer conducted a reconnaissance of the three spheres in which he was to work: the university, the church, and the ecumenical movement. He traveled to Bonn to meet Karl Barth, helped write a new catechism, and attended the conference of the World Alliance in Cambridge. The visit to Bonn, arranged by Erwin Sutz, belatedly fulfilled a wish from Bonhoeffer's student days. His work on the catechism was an act of friendship for Franz Hildebrandt, who asked him to help. Superintendent Diestel had paved the way for the trip to Cambridge, which marked the beginning of his ecumenical work.

The church authorities had refused Bonhoeffer an extension of his leave, even though his university and chaplaincy duties could begin only with the new semester in the fall. Because of that, General Superintendent Emil Karow freed him from his residency requirement until October 1931. Thus Bonhoeffer now did half of what he wanted and half of what he had to do.

Bonn

First Meeting with Karl Barth. Once he was home from New York, Bonhoeffer stayed in Berlin only long enough to pay the necessary official calls. He left on 10 July to spend three weeks in Bonn. The trip was so important to him that he had turned down his parents' attractive proposal to take a holiday in Friedrichsbrunn after his return from America. He wanted to spend as much time as possible in Bonn before the end of the semester there. The first meeting between the forty-five-year-old Barth and the twenty-five-year-old Bonhoeffer now took place.

The first report from Bonn—to Erwin Sutz, who had arranged the meeting—was terse: "I am all alone here and waste the rest of the day quite uselessly."[7] A letter to his parents, however, gave his first impressions:

> I have now met Barth and got to know him quite well at a discussion evening at his house.[8] I like him very much indeed, and am also very impressed by his lectures. Everything is so well worked out and has not yet become mechanical to him. I think I shall gain a great deal from the time spent here.[9]

The story told later by Bonhoeffer's students was that in Barth's seminar he had quoted Luther's statement that the curses of the godless sometimes sound better to God's ear than the hallelujahs of the pious. Delighted, Barth asked who had made this contribution to the discussion, and this was the beginning of their personal acquaintance.[10]

On 23 July 1931 Barth invited him to dinner and conversation. Now at last the two were together. The younger man questioned, argued, and posed more questions, and found to his surprise that "Barth was even better than his books":

> There is with him an openness, a readiness for any objection which should hit the mark, and along with this such concentration and impetuous insistence on the point, whether it is made arrogantly or modestly, dogmatically or completely uncertainly, and not only when it serves his own theology.[11]

Like so many of Karl Barth's visitors, Bonhoeffer noted the striking interest Barth ("so hard to pin down in his books") showed in his conversation partner. "I have been impressed even more by discussions with him than by his writings and his lectures. For he is really all there. I have never seen anything like it before."[12]

The result of this encounter was that subsequent relations between the two were characterized by complete frankness and, occasionally, completely frank disagreement. A sporadic correspondence began in which neither concealed anything from the other. The younger man's letters always showed a trace of reverential distance, but the older man respected no barriers.

It was more difficult to gain entry to the inner circle of Barth's disciples in Bonn. Bonhoeffer's position as a "theological illegitimate" among the "genuine initiates" caused him a great deal of amusement. "They have a sharp scent for thoroughbreds here," he wrote. "No Negro passes 'for white'; they even examine his fingernails and the soles of his feet. Up till now they still haven't shown me hospitality as the unknown stranger."[13] Hans Fischer, a friend of Erwin Sutz's, looked after him and provided him with notes of Barth's lectures to read in his spare time. He was also invited to a performance of a play, directed by Helmut Gollwitzer, that Barth had written at the age of fifteen.

His stay in Bonn led to frequent meetings with Barth, which continued until Bonhoeffer left for England in 1933. Through Günther Dehn he made the acquaintance of Gertrud Staewen; Barth was accustomed to staying at her house in Berlin, where a small circle of Barthians used to meet. In April 1932 Bonhoeffer saw Barth with his friend Pestalozzi in Berlin, where Barth delivered his address "Theology and Contemporary Mission."[14] This time there was no rebuttal by Otto Dibelius, but a reply came from Siegfried Knak, the head of the Berlin Missionary Society. Its publication in *Zwischen den Zeiten* conveyed the tone of the heated discussion and the full extent of nationalist animosity against the dialectic thinkers.[15] Bonhoeffer's description of the evening, spent with the members of the Berlin faculty and church leaders, was not particularly respectful:

> ... then, when questions were asked for, nothing happened except a long, painful silence, because no one wanted to make a fool of himself, and then, as the silence began to grow oppressive, Herr Knak started by asking where, in Barth's view, the difference lay between Swiss and Prussian national feeling. With that the level of questions was established. . . .[16]

These were the months in which the "Dehn case" in Halle reached its climax, with demonstrations by right-wing students against Günther Dehn and Minister of Culture Adolf Grimme. Barth and other like-minded people took up Dehn's cause.[17] Through his father, Bonhoeffer tried to interest professors from the other departments in Berlin in the injustice done to Dehn; he provided his father with extensive material on the matter.[18] This suggests that his meetings with Barth in 1932 were already strongly influenced by the unrest about the political future and the future of the church, and did not leave as much time for theological discussion as Bonhoeffer would have liked.

At the beginning of September 1932 he visited Barth on the Bergli in Switzerland, just as Barth had completed the preface to the first volume of *Church Dogmatics*. During this stay, Sutz also introduced him to Brunner.

The following winter, when Titius's chair in Berlin fell vacant, Bonhoeffer used his family connections to propose Barth as a possible successor. But the events of 1933 meant that the appointment went to Wobbermin. Barth's position in Bonn had become difficult because of his membership in the

Social Democratic Party; Bonhoeffer tried to use his connections in the Prussian Ministry of Culture on his behalf. Barth wrote to him:

> In the era of Reich Chancellor Hitler, Wobbermin will certainly fill Schleiermacher's chair in a fashion more true to type than I should have done. I hear that you have come out strongly on my behalf. . . . I should undoubtedly have accepted . . . the world is in bad shape, but we don't want to let our pipe go out under any circumstances, do we?[19]

Barth and Bonhoeffer had become closer than would ever be possible again.

Stages of a Friendship. The relationship between the two men went through four stages:

1. The phase of Bonhoeffer's one-sided knowledge of Barth through the latter's writings, beginning in 1925. As he eagerly and gratefully absorbed Barth's message during 1927 and 1929, Bonhoeffer directed a number of theological-epistemological questions toward Barth, under the principle of *finitum capax infiniti*. Barth did not become familiar with these questions, formulated in *Sanctorum Communio* and *Act and Being*, until after Bonhoeffer's death.

2. The period of the eagerly sought meetings between 1931 and 1933. Bonhoeffer hoped for Barth's support in his concern for the concrete ethical commandments of the church, but did not receive this in the form he had desired.

3. The phase of theological differences, accompanied by a very close alliance in church politics. Bonhoeffer attempted to think through the articles of justification and salvation independently of Barth, but he still longed secretly to claim them. Barth had reservations; only after Bonhoeffer's death did *Discipleship* receive Barth's special praise.

4. The period of indirect new questions, in the letters from prison of 1944. These included, almost incidentally, the ominous term "positivism of revelation," which Barth could not accept and liked least of all in Bonhoeffer's work.

Whatever the implications of Bonhoeffer's criticisms of Barth, throughout these four phases Bonhoeffer viewed these criticisms as coming from within, not without, the Barthian movement. During the bitter period when Barth's former allies deserted him, Bonhoeffer had no desire to be identified with men like Gogarten or Brunner, and he vigorously attacked them. This is evident in the second and third phases of his relationship to Barth.

A Shift of Interest. At their first meeting, as in the years that immediately followed, Bonhoeffer's early critical questions to Barth in 1927 and 1929 appeared to be buried and forgotten. This was not entirely the case, since they did arise in his university lectures, beginning in 1931. Even here, however, they were framed by Bonhoeffer's primary goal of presenting Barth's theological revolution to the Berlin forum in as positive a light as possible. They do not arise at all in the documents about the personal meetings between the two from 1931 to 1933. On Bonhoeffer's side, the topic of discussion had shifted to the realm of ethical questions and the problem of the authoritative proclamation of the commandments through the church of Christ; Bonhoeffer obstinately concentrated on these.

The encounter between the two men in 1931 occurred over a very definite point of interest to both. For all their mutual liking, however, each was at a different phase of his development. One had just arrived at the point of departure for the other—that is, the other was leaving the point that his companion was trying to reach.

Barth's Situation. Barth had no previous knowledge of the man he was meeting in 1931. He had not read *Sanctorum Communio*, and *Act and Being*, with its more significant criticism of him, existed only in proofs. Bonhoeffer was not the type to send people copies of his books before calling on them. Thus Barth knew nothing of Bonhoeffer's subtle transcendental philosophical reservations about his approach and against his description of revelation, so strongly expressed in negations at the time. He knew nothing of Bonhoeffer's ecclesiological suggestions, nor of his antipathy to the *incapax infiniti* (human incapacity for the infinite), nor of his passionate protest against allowing room for reflection in the act of faith, which should seek knowledge only of its content (Christ), and not of itself.[20] Nor could Barth know of Bonhoeffer's concise description of the theological situation in his 1930 inaugural lecture:

> . . . there can be no mention of a possibility for the reality of revelation independent of this revelation itself. Thus the rejection of any fixed *infiniti incapax* [the theological view that the finite is "not capable of the infinite"] follows from the emphasis on the beyond-existence character of revelation.[21]

With the single exception of Knittermeyer's review of *Act and Being* in 1933, the Barthian journal *Zwischen den Zeiten* had not reviewed Bonhoeffer's books or even mentioned them in its list of new publications. This was important because, for the Barthians, Bonhoeffer first appeared on the horizon as the author of *Discipleship*, and it was this that stamped him in their minds. Not knowing his previous theological background, they regarded the newcomer as capable of all sorts of rash theological conclusions—which they wouldn't have believed had they known him more thoroughly.

The first work by Bonhoeffer that Barth read was the critical article on Karl Heim that Bonhoeffer sent him at the end of 1932. The era had already begun in which, increasingly, theological positions entailed existential decisions, not merely intellectual disputes.[22] In this essay, Bonhoeffer's epistemological critique of Barth completely lacked the sharpness of 1929:

> Barth without hesitation concedes that even he is not "protected from the sin" of making "God an object of thought," that even his principles are subject to the danger of being "an ultimate protection against God himself and his intervention in our lives." The very fact that he thinks that he cannot protect himself from this danger, and yet constantly thinks in the face of this danger, is characteristic of his theology; that he knows that the *concretissimum* can be spoken only by the Holy Spirit and that any *concretum* of human speech remains *abstractum*, if the Holy Ghost himself does not say it, fixes the boundary of his theological concerns.[23]

That same year Bonhoeffer's defense of Barth elsewhere was similar: "Because Barth knows that there is no such thing as perfect reason and yet cannot do without it, he can speak 'rationally' more boldly and uninhibitedly than those who want to preserve the ultimate claim of rationality."[24]

Given such literary concessions, Barth had little reason to reply critically to this public defender of his position at the beginning of 1933. Not long afterward *Creation and Fall* was published. It was the first and only book of Bonhoeffer's on which Barth publicly expressed an opinion during the former's lifetime; Barth agreed with its *analogia relationis*.[25]

Barth's real discovery of Bonhoeffer's early works came only years later, when he expressed the highest appreciation for them.[26] But this was preceded by the period during which he had reservations abut the course Bonhoeffer was following in *Discipleship*, and a period of headshaking over Bonhoeffer's "positivism of revelation" and the "nonreligious interpretation."

During the summer of 1931, then, Barth saw a young man from Berlin who came from the school of the dubious Reinhold Seeberg, on top of which he had just returned from America. In short, Bonhoeffer was an unwritten page. The fact that he was so interesting to talk to—his mind was quick, objective, penetrating, well-informed—was all the more surprising. Obviously he was a young man of promise.

Bonhoeffer's Situation. How did things look from Bonhoeffer's perspective? In the summer of 1931 he noted that this conversation partner, whom he had questioned so often in his imagination, "unfortunately" did not lecture on "the encyclopedia"[27] but on "ethics." Barth was not concerned with the theological system within which Bonhoeffer's old questions might have been acute. With that, the entire basis of the discussion shifted, unless Bonhoeffer were to be so presumptuous as to force his host onto his own former field.

Bonhoeffer was well acquainted with Barth's works; moreover, he was aware that changes in Barth's approach would soon become evident. *Anselm*[28] was at the printers, and the first volume of *Church Dogmatics* was nearing completion. In *Church Dogmatics* Barth himself stated that "in this second version I have excluded to the best of my ability anything that might appear to find for theology a foundation, support, or justification in existential philosophy."[29] Bonhoeffer did not regard all his reservations as having been cleared up: "Barth's book about Anselm is a great delight to me. . . . Nothing of course has in fact become any less questionable."[30] Bonhoeffer's earlier questions, however, had lost urgency as other issues moved into the foreground. In addition, Barth had accepted some important criticisms. Bonhoeffer encountered a Barth who had unequivocally accepted the premise of the reality of revelation as a historically given event without extraneous support. He based it more plainly on exegesis, and reconceived everything from the a priori fact of the church. His philosophical assumptions no longer seemed dangerously full of his own ideas.

Thus, to a great extent, Bonhoeffer saw eye-to-eye with him. Shortly after their first meeting in Bonn he said in his first Berlin lecture in the winter of 1931–1932:

> In the whole of modern literature Barth has not been seriously contested. . . . Perhaps in his *Epistle to the Romans* he did not always quite see the danger of this proximity [i.e., to neo-Kantian transcendentalism]. But he begins with concrete revelation; where Natorp and Tillich say "not God," he finds himself forced to say "Jesus Christ."[31]

Bonhoeffer was impressed by Barth's ability "to correct my books where necessary."[32] The Barth he met in person in 1931 was no longer the Barth whom he had so long questioned in absentia. He had changed. But had he changed completely?

For Bonhoeffer the encounter was even more stimulating because he had changed since 1927 and 1929. His stay in the United States had confronted him with ethical questions as never before. Through Jean Lasserre and Frank Fisher, his interest in the essential present form of grace had been renewed and transformed into the problem of acting under the constraint of grace and simple obedience. In posing these questions, however, he saw that his imminent ordination would soon face him with the regular task of proclaiming the message of the church.

Barth had once left the pulpit for the lectern. His questions and answers at the lectern had emerged from his experience as preacher; the preacher, in turn, had needed the systematician. To rescue God's majesty from being squandered from the pulpit, Barth spoke of the wholly Other, the remote and unapproachable God. Thus Barth pondered how to avoid making this an unholy confusing concept in the concrete reality.

Bonhoeffer, however, came from a predominantly academic environment; secretly he had long aspired to the pulpit. He was a systematician searching for the preacher. In direct contrast to Barth, Bonhoeffer concentrated on the terrifying proximity of an actively intervening God to preserve the majesty of God from being cheapened in the pulpit, and sought to proclaim him in the concreteness of grace-filled commandment. The man who faced the master was still in part a systematician, but he was also a preacher pondering the authority and credibility of his proclamation. The old questions were fading into the background.

Bonhoeffer's references to this in his letters are painfully succinct. He reported that in Bonn in 1931 they "very soon came to the problems of ethics."[33] He had alluded to this in *Act and Being*, but paid it no further attention. At that time he had believed that because Barth—the early Barth, of course—had regarded no historical moment as being *capax infiniti*, "so that empirical human activity—be it faith, obedience—is at best reference to God's activity and in its historicity can never be faith and obedience itself."[34] Bonhoeffer refused to be satisfied with this.

In July 1931 Bonhoeffer had apparently spoken of grace and obedience in such absolute terms, or without regard to Barth's eschatological limitation of obedience, that it was impossible to reconcile the two positions or even make them mutually more intelligible.[35] This Barth seemed too cautious to Bonhoeffer, and to Barth this Bonhoeffer seemed too impatient. For the sake of his eschatology, Barth described ethics as being merely "pointers" or "demonstrations," but Bonhoeffer found this an insufficient basis and content for the proclamation of the commandments. He suspected that it was an avoidance mechanism and signified that, in the last resort, grace was not binding. The more deeply Bonhoeffer became involved in the practical work of the church and the ecumenical movement, the more urgently he asked whether the "proclamation of concrete commandments through the church" was possible:

> Basically all this depends on the problem of ethics, that is, the question of the possibility of the proclamation of concrete commandments through the church. . . .
>
> It is the problem of concreteness in our ministry that at present so occupies me. . . .[36]

> If the problem is acute anywhere, it is here. And it seems to me that it is only from there that one can gain an understanding of Barth. I have discussed these things with him several times this year. This was very fruitful.[37]

But was not this insistence on concreteness too much to ask of the church and its preaching? Where was the basis of its authority? The issue of its authority and credibility confronted Bonhoeffer with full force; this was what Bonhoeffer meant. He admitted "that our church today cannot utter a concrete commandment. But the question is whether this lies in its essence—within the inherent limitations of the *eschata*—or represents a decay and loss of substance."[38] Bonhoeffer wrote this to Rössler, but his question was really directed at Karl Barth and the riddle of the church's authority. Because of his concern about false authorities, Barth strengthened the eschatological components of ecclesiology and ethics. Bonhoeffer, however, feared that such eschatological considerations were an elegant alibi, used to bypass the question of the church's real authority to take and to enjoin concrete action. Woe to the church and its authority if Barth's systematically correct warning prevented it from pronouncing the commandments in practice!

> The characteristic of the church's authority (differing from all other authorities) is precisely that it does not begin by possessing authority and acting by reason of it, but possesses authority only through the "arbitrary" pronouncement of God's bidding insofar as it is accepted as such, and with every one of its words puts its whole authority at stake.[39]

Thus Barth was not facing someone who anchored the proclamation of the commandments in the "office" of the church (as Althaus was suspected of doing) or in the "orders of creation" (Brunner was suspected of this) in order to establish its authority or validity, metaphysically or mystically. Barth, however, was ill at ease with Bonhoeffer's directness; he preferred approaching the problem with the "limitations through the *eschata*."

This may have been the point to which Bonhoeffer referred after their meeting in Berlin in April 1932:

> Thus it is now clear to me that Barth himself does not agree with me on this point, but recently he again asked me whether I still thought the same way, and said plainly enough that he too feels at least uncomfortable about it.[40]

All his anxiety in the matter was summed up by a passage from 2 Chronicles 20:12 that Franz Hildebrandt had drawn to his attention: "We do not know what to do, but our eyes are upon thee." Bonhoeffer preached on this text on Exaudi Sunday 1932:[41] "I vented all my desperation."[42] In October 1933, in a letter to Barth from London, he mentioned the passage again.[43]

Amid these concerns about the problem of the church's authority, it occurred to Bonhoeffer that the church might be better served by silence than by the comments and marginal observations about God and the world that it was constantly tempted to make. He took an early interest in a "qualified silence."[44] To his students this was a completely alien point of view, but to him the categories of "authority," "concrete commandment," and "qualified silence" of the church meant the same thing: the risk of preaching.

Some notes from a lecture on the history of twentieth-century systematic theology, delivered during the winter of 1932–1933, concluded:

> The Barthian view of ethics as "demonstration" rules out all concrete ethics and ethical principles. . . . Proclaiming the concrete Christ always means proclaiming him in a concrete situation. What is the scholarly foundation upon which ethics are to be built? Where is the principle of the concreteness of the general command to obedience? This has made the messages of our church so feeble that they end up halfway between general principles and the concrete situation. The predicament of the church is always that of the theological faculties as well, but this is little noticed. Luther was able to write both *De servo arbitrio* and the *Schrift von Zins*. Why are we no longer able to do that? Who shall show us Luther?![45]

At the end of 1932 Bonhoeffer wrote a letter of thanks to Barth, confessing that he was struggling in a theological abyss in which he might perish. But Barth could keep him on the right track:

> Please excuse me if I was a burden to you in August with my perhaps too obstinate and—as you once said—"godless" questions. But at the same time I would like you to know that I know no one who can free me from these

persistent questions as you can. . . . When I am talking with you, I am brought right up against the thing itself, whereas before I was only continually circling round it in the distance. . . . The brief hours we have been together during the year have succeeded in guiding my thoughts, which are always wanting to sink into "godless" questions, and keeping them to the point.[46]

This letter marks the threshold between the second and third phases of the friendship between Barth and Bonhoeffer. Bonhoeffer's questions seemed to have become "godless," with his insistence on concrete proclamation that threatened to rob revelation itself of its majesty, since it promoted and absolutized the authority of concrete proclamation. Barth may have reminded the younger man of their shared foundation—Bonhoeffer later admitted that Barth was right, because he said in prison that his road to *Discipleship* had not been without its perils[47]—but at this point he was not to be diverted from that road. The "tenacious questions" about authority and credibility grew deeper and called for an answer, which Bonhoeffer sought personally in his private life and ecumenically in his church life. Decisions about obedience had to be made, without protection or prejustification, for the sake of the majesty of revelation.

To some extent, the church struggle strengthened the alliance between Barth and Bonhoeffer against secessionists and renegades. Nonetheless, during this third period of their relationship it was not only the geographical distance between them that increased. The warmth of Bonhoeffer's letter of thanks did not conceal the fact that his confidence in his own path was unshaken. He believed he saw things that Barth did not. Barth himself said that the younger man always made him somewhat uneasy, because he was continually surprising him with new perspectives and was able to see things in a different light. Barth's sense of reserve was more significant than the fact that he knew so little in 1931 about this ally who had never been his student.

Bonhoeffer did not show his gratitude and loyalty by repeating what had already been said, but in courageous and critical new statements. The Sermon on the Mount had moved into the foreground of his thought, and he did not yet find anything helpful in Barth:

> . . . the real battle, what it will perhaps later come to, must be simply an endurance with faith and then, then, perhaps, God will again acknowledge God's word to the church. But until that time much must be believed, prayed for and suffered. You know, I believe . . . that the whole thing will be resolved through the Sermon on the Mount. I believe that Barth's theology only postpones this . . . and he certainly made it possible for that to be recognized.[48]

The second phase, between their meeting in Bonn and Bonhoeffer's departure for London, was the high point in the relationship between the two men. It was a happy prelude to the impending church struggle, and it led to a kind of cooperation on the essential questions of the church that would never be broken. Theologically, however, the meeting came too late. For Bonhoeffer, Barth's answers to his questions at this stage did not take him far enough. He provided his own answer in *Discipleship*, but only after his death did Barth express the agreement and approval that Bonhoeffer had longed for.

Still, it is indisputable that there was no contemporary to whom Bonhoeffer opened his heart so completely as he did to Karl Barth. "I have, I think, seldom regretted anything in my theological past so much as the fact that I did not go to him sooner," he wrote Sutz from Bonn in July 1931.[49] Their mutual drive for independence, combined with an intense interest in this colleague who was so different from him, made their encounter one of the most gratifying of Bonhoeffer's life. He expressed this in 1943 when, in his Tegel cell, I brought him Barth's personal greetings from Basel. "Karl's cigar is on the table in front of me, and that is something truly amazing— was he nice? and understanding?"[50]

Catechism

Between his visit to Bonn in July 1931 and the trip to Cambridge in September, Bonhoeffer worked on "a Lutheran catechism," entitled "By Faith Alone."[51] It is a short document, showing the great freedom with which Bonhoeffer devoted himself to a work that lay between systematic theology and praxis. He did not do it as part of any teaching duties; as yet Bonhoeffer knew nothing of the confirmation class in Wedding he would take several months later. Franz Hildebrandt, who was now a practicing clergyman, had suggested he do it, and worked on it together with him.

Hildebrandt had served as vicar under Siegmund-Schultze in east Berlin and completed his training in the small town of Dobrilugk in Brandenburg. He spent a fortnight's holiday in Berlin working with Bonhoeffer on this revolutionary task. During this time Bonhoeffer gave him one of the first copies of *Act and Being*, writing on the flyleaf "And this is to be a catechism?" But teaching was a joy for Bonhoeffer, and his Sunday school work in Harlem had encouraged him to undertake unconventional experiments.

Bonhoeffer was so convinced of the need for new catechisms that he wrote two that have survived: one from 1931 and the other from 1936. They are very different. The first is short and manageable, limited to about forty questions; the second is long and consists of almost 170 questions. Neither is catechetically simple or convincing as a learning tool. Bonhoeffer was not so much interested in teaching as in "attempting to put into words what the Lutheran faith says today. Questions and answers are designed for concentrated reading."[52]

Bonhoeffer's and Hildebrandt's 1931 approach showed Harnack's influence. Instead of the Apostles' Creed, they took as their basis Luther's statement of faith, which Hildebrandt had discovered while working on his dissertation.[53] Bonhoeffer liked it so much that he kept it in his daily prayer and service book for the rest of his life, and occasionally used it instead of the Apostles' creed even in the most orthodox confessional services. Its appeal was Luther's immediate connection between the ontological and functional affirmations with their ethical implications. As a trinitarian profession of faith, Luther's formulation conveyed the fundamental threefold division of the catechism. Thus the creed, the oldest part of the church's catechetical instruction, remained the foundation, but the other relic of the ancient church, the Lord's Prayer, was left out. Luther's arrangement in the *Shorter Catechism* was no longer recognizable; the Ten Commandments no longer appeared as such. The catechism recalled the Barcelona lecture, which portrayed Christians as continually creating their own commandments. Instead everything followed from the first question: "What is the Gospel?" The reply was: The tidings of salvation and of the kingdom and will of God, who speaks today. The catechism ended with the refrain from Luther's statement of faith, which Bonhoeffer continually used as "an antiphon in his sermons, addresses, and letters": "But this is the Christian faith: to know what you should do and what has been given you."[54] The main questions were not followed by imperative "thou shalt" sentences, but by indicative statements of action in the here and now. The whole was imbued with the sovereign tone of a master instead of the forbidding tone of a police officer. Yet the catechism also included modern questions requiring answers:

> How do I know about God? . . . Where is the proof? Does not the story of creation conflict with science? . . . Can a God who is good permit so much wrong in the world? . . . Is the instinct of self-preservation itself a sin? . . . Does one not have to take life in war? . . . How should the Christian behave politically? . . . did Jesus really live? . . . Why are there so many churches? . . . Do I need the church?[55]

The introduction of the subjects of war, peace, or the ecumenical question into the elementary teaching of the church was something entirely new.

Bonhoeffer's conventional defense of war in the Barcelona lectures had vanished. There, he had said: "Love of my people will . . . sanctify war"; never again would he make such a statement.[56] While Bonhoeffer did not yet encourage individuals to refuse to fight in a war—nor did he do so in 1936— he said that the church as a whole should speak:

> . . . therefore the church knows nothing of any sacredness of war. The struggle for existence is carried on here with inhuman means. The church which prays the 'Our Father' asks God only for peace.[57]

He based this bid for peace on the antinationalist principle of the unity of the human family, the argument that he had heard Lasserre use. Bonhoeffer had adopted this ecumenical argument in autumn 1931, as well as the idea of the church's co-responsibility for the course taken in the political struggles among peoples. He never again departed from them.

In 1936, under far more difficult circumstances, Bonhoeffer again wrestled with this part of the catechism. The question was not so much what he personally should do, but to formulate what a church catechism could and should say on this point. In his 1936 draft he first wrote: "Can a Christian go to war?" but crossed this out and wrote instead: "What does God say about war?"[58] He then crossed that out too. After all, this was in 1936, when Bonhoeffer's own tendencies were to reject military service; but he could not yet make a convincing case to the ordination candidates in the Confessing church who were so closely associated with him:

> How should the Christian act in war? There is no plain commandment of God on this point. The church can never bless war or weapons. The Christian can never take part in an unjust war. If a Christian takes to the sword, he will daily pray to God for forgiveness of the sin and pray for peace.[59]

In his second draft of a catechism in 1936 Bonhoeffer returned to the conservative outline. To counter the falsifying modernization of the German Christians, the candidates were to learn to steer their congregations toward the original profession of their church's faith. Thus Bonhoeffer adhered again to Luther's pattern in the *Shorter Catechism*. Under the heading "On Obedience," he began with an interpretation of the Ten Commandments. The Commandments were there "so that we [the community of Christ] may keep them."[60] He no longer used Luther's numbering of the Commandments but the biblical numbering. His affirmations were supported with scriptural quotations, not statements by Luther, as in 1931; he drew upon the Old Testament for the purpose of relating the new "Israel" to the present day. Christ's teaching and passion occupied a central position. The Barmen declaration had become part of the catechism, and the racial question was addressed: "in the congregation there is neither . . . Jew nor German."[61] To include the question of how to live under an unjust government was truly something new in a Lutheran catechism.[62] Oral confession, entirely unmentioned in 1931, was given more space than the passages on baptism and the sacrament together.

In 1936 Bonhoeffer presented this catechism to his students, encouraging them to carry out their own experiments. They asked him for a formulation of what was imperative to say in the parishes about the issue of public confession during those dangerous years; he responded during one of their retreats. After this lecture he did not produce the manuscript again or work on it any further. He viewed this lecture as a proposal, made at a time when the Confessing church was encouraging and organizing a number of attempts to reformulate things.

The 1931 catechism is perhaps the more important of the two. Hildebrandt and Bonhoeffer actually published it,[63] and reprints were distributed in 1933 for discussion at pastors' conferences.[64] But the new challenges of that year led even the authors to lose interest in this enthusiastic, liberal, and central experiment. It had now become necessary to formulate confessions of an entirely different decisiveness.

Apart from its didactic value or lack thereof, the 1936 catechism is interesting because it summarizes what Bonhoeffer viewed at the time as the absolute minimum of what the congregation's message should be. It exists only in a preliminary, fragmentary version, unrevised and uncorrected by others. He jotted it down quickly on rough paper, with the sole aid of his Bible and concordance; it was not a work in which he surrounded himself with the relevant literature and brought that together into a carefully considered whole.

In his own teaching, Bonhoeffer worked freely, without any preconceived ideas, just as when he taught and confirmed the Kleist-Retzow children in 1938.

Cambridge

The most momentous of the three events during the summer between his return from America and the beginning of his career was his participation in the ecumenical conference in Cambridge. His interest in the ecumenical movement was at first incidental, but it took such a hold on him that it became an integral part of his being. He was soon furiously involved in the internal battles about its orientation, and he defended it enthusiastically in public. The emerging world of the Protestant ecumenical movement became a vital part of his theology, his role in the church struggle, and ultimately his political commitment.

The Berlin ecumenists, primarily Superintendent Max Diestel, made him a member of the German youth delegation to the annual conference of the World Alliance for Promoting International Friendship through the Churches, held in Cambridge on 1–5 September 1931. There the executive committee appointed him as one of the three European youth secretaries. At the same time, the world political crisis was converging with the ecumenical movement's own impulses to force new ideas upon the movement.

Ecumenical Berlin. Berlin became a prominent ecumenical center—perhaps *the* center in Germany—at a relatively early stage. The theological faculty of the University of Berlin took the lead. In contrast to Britain, in Germany it was primarily the academics, not church dignitaries, who became the first advocates of the ecumenical idea. This was how Germany's ecumenical representatives were regarded abroad, which had unfortunate consequences during the church struggle, because the professors seldom really represented the church and, as state civil servants, were disastrously linked with the Third Reich.

At the beginning of the 1930s, no other theological faculty in Germany produced as many renowned ecumenical leaders. As in previous summers, Berlin offered an academic summer session in 1931, entitled "Christendom [*sic!*] and the State." At the time the list of Berlin University professors who were active ecumenists was long:

Adolf Deissmann (1866–1937), professor of the New Testament, had been regarded since before World War I as one of *the* German ecumenists. He was a founding member of the World Alliance for Promoting International Friendship through the Churches; a member of the executive committee of Life and Work (established in Stockholm in 1925) and chair of its theological commission; chair of the Commission for Cooperation with the Orthodox Churches; and a member of the Faith and Order movement (established in Lausanne in 1927) and vice-chair of its ongoing council. He was editor, with Bishop Bell, of an ecumenical anthology.

Arthur Titius (1864–1936), professor of systematic theology, served as council member of the World Alliance working committee. He was also a member of the executive committee of Life and Work and its social and publicity commission. He edited *Stockholm*, a trilingual ecumenical newspaper that folded during the economic crisis of 1931, and participated in the Lausanne conference in 1927.

Julius Richter (1862–1940), professor of missions, was a member of the Edinburgh Mission conference in 1910 and its ongoing committee. He participated in the delicate "spiritual peace conference" at Oud Wassenaar in October 1919 and in the Geneva preparatory meetings for Stockholm in 1920, and was a member of the World Alliance working committee and its training and financial committees.

Friedrich Siegmund-Schultze (1885–1969), professor of social pedagogy, was the most valuable founding member of all three branches of the ecumenical movement: the World Alliance, Life and Work (Stockholm), and Faith and Order (Lausanne). He served as international secretary of the World Alliance and its executive and working committees. He founded and published the most influential and significant ecumenical newspaper of the early period, *Die Eiche*, and later the *Ecclesia* anthology.

August Hinderer (1877–1945) was director of the Protestant Press Association and professor for press affairs; chair of the International Christian Press Commission; and a member of the World Alliance and Life and Work, heading the press commissions. He also participated in the Lausanne conference.

Cajus Fabricius (1883–1950), professor of systematic theology, participated in the Lausanne meeting.

Bonhoeffer did not yet have any close ties to these ecumenical leaders. He was becoming closer to Siegmund-Schultze, but this was less due to the latter's ecumenical work (where Bonhoeffer suspected a liberal element) than to his experimental social settlement work in east Berlin. Bonhoeffer learned of this through Franz Hildebrandt, who had spent part of his vicar's training there; Hildebrandt had problems with church authorities who didn't want to count his work with Siegmund-Schultze as part of his education. Hildebrandt wrote to Bonhoeffer in America about this and about his work in the youth clubs of east Berlin, the "worldview courses" for the unemployed, and his encounters with the "freethinker" groups. In his letters to America Hildebrandt characteristically wrote a great deal about what took place in Siegmund-Schultze's center on Fruchtstrasse, but never mentioned ecumenical affairs or *Die Eiche*, which also had its office there.

A remarkable number of the leading ecumenists from the official church also resided in Berlin. (Those outside Berlin included Hermann Maas, Wilhelm Menn, Wilhelm Stählin, Erich Stange, and Wilhelm Zoellner.) One was *Hermann Kapler* (1867–1941), president of the German Evangelical Church Federation. After Söderblum's death in the spring of 1931 he became chair of the Ecumenical Council for Practical Christianity, together with the bishop of Winchester, who died in late 1932 and was succeeded by Bishop George Bell of Chichester. When the preparatory committee for Stockholm decided not to take up any Faith and Order issues, it cited Kapler: "doctrine divides, but service unites." *Otto Dibelius* (1880–1967), general superintendent of Kurmark, participated in the Stockholm and Lausanne conferences; in Lausanne he was one of the speakers. *Hermann Georg Burghart* (1865–1954), vice president of the Protestant High Council, was a council member for Life and Work, and since 1929 chaired the German office of the World Alliance. *Friedrich Albert Spiecker* (1854–1936), director of the Inner Mission, was a layman. Together with Harnack and Siegmund-Schultze, he initiated the British-German friendship attempts before the First World War that led to the founding of the World Alliance. Until 1929 he was chair of the German office of the World Alliance.

August Wilhelm Schreiber (1861–1945), earlier mission director of the North German Mission Society, was now a member of the National Protestant Consistory in the Church Federation. He had participated in the controversial conferences in 1919 in Wassenaar and 1920 in Geneva. He hosted regular ecumenical evenings in his home in Berlin, which led to the joining together of different ecumenical groups into the "Mittelstelle" working committee. In 1933 he returned to the North German Mission Society. *Johannes Hosemann* (1881–1947) was council member of the Church Consistory in the Protestant Church Council and council member for Life and Work. *Theodor Heckel* (1894–1967) of Bavaria was consistory council member in the Berlin Church Federation Office.

Because of his year in America, Bonhoeffer had already had contact with church council member Schreiber, and he had met Otto Dibelius during his examinations in the Berlin church. Other ecumenically interested people from the Berlin church scene included:

Superintendent *Max Diestel* (1872–1919), who had served earlier in a German-speaking parish in England and, since 1931, served as deputy chair of the German World Federation office; Hermann Burghart, the chair, left most of the work to him. Dr. *Carl-Gunther Schweitzer* (1889–1965), director of the Apologetic Central Office in Spandau, was a member of the theologians' commission of the Ecumenical Council for Practical Christianity. Licentiate *Hermann Sasse* (1895–1976), professor of confessional scholarship, was pastor of the Berlin Marienkirche at the time, and worked with Faith and Order. He had written an introduction to the German report on Lausanne and reported regularly in the *Church Yearbook*; he had acute theological insights into ecumenical events. Pastor *Richard Jordan* (1889–) became secretary of the German World Alliance office after Siegmund-Schultze relinquished the office in 1929 to head the International Secretariat.

It was inevitable that once Bonhoeffer became involved in ecumenical activities he would notice Sasse, who had also had a fellowship in America. Both were initially dissatisfied with the ecclesial and theological foundations of ecumenical work. Bonhoeffer was impressed by Sasse's incorruptible political judgment as the Hitler era approached. Unfortunately their paths diverged during the church struggle, after it became clear that Sasse was an uncompromising confessional Lutheran.

The World Alliance. Bonhoeffer's ecumenical career began in the World Alliance, which led to his association with the Council for Practical Christianity (Life and Work). He was never directly associated with the Faith and Order movement.

It was both characteristic and incongruous that he entered the ecumenical movement through the World Alliance for Promoting International Friendship through the Churches, the ecumenical organization most dominated by the spirit of liberal and humanist Anglo-Saxon theology. It was also the freest organization, and not nearly as strongly ecclesiastical as the others. With its emphasis on peace work, it was also the group most committed to something.

Any self-respecting theologian, particularly a Barthian, was bound to have strong reservations about such an organization. Barth himself held out for a long time before finally accepting election to the theological committee of Life and Work in 1932, and his attitude attracted a great deal of attention.

Faith and Order provided a platform for qualified experts in comparative theology. Since the Stockholm conference, Life and Work had been the official domain of the German Evangelical Church Federation. With the World Alliance, the older organization, the situation was different. It was anchored in the various church, semichurch, and nonchurch groups, in contrast to the Life and Work conference in Stockholm and the Faith and Order conference in Lausanne. In the 1931 *Church Yearbook* Sasse wrote: "The World Alliance is the only ecumenical organization which through its national and local groups reaches right down to the congregation," and it had the important task of bringing not just the concept of church peace work, but the ecumenical concept in general, into the parishes. The World Alliance had influential lay members, such as former German Supreme Court president Dr. Simons; its speakers included Weimar foreign minister Julius Curtius. Hans von Haeften, a friend of Bonhoeffer's who had also been confirmed with him, traveled in 1930 to a World Alliance youth camp in

Denmark and spoke there as a young assessor on the topic "International Law and Its Realization."[65]

The high point of the World Alliance's influence on public opinion in Germany came in 1931. At the same time it confronted a threat that eventually proved fatal. Its financial position became critical as a result of the economic crisis. Diestel was compelled to dissolve the secretariat and work from his superintendent's office; traveling abroad became nearly impossible. Most significantly, however, the nationalists began a deliberate campaign of defamation against ecumenical "internationalists," especially the German supporters of the World Alliance. Three years later the German branch of the World Alliance was forced to dissolve. Ecumenical work necessarily passed from the free and fruitful form of activity that had been carried out by numerous groups to the institutional church level of Life and Work and Faith and Order. Only on this basis was it able to survive for a little while longer under the Nazi regime.

The extinction of the driving force and dedication of the World Alliance was a grave loss. The World Alliance itself was forced to retreat from its prophetic call for reconciliation, and seek new outlets within the more cautious church-linked organizations.

For a young German theologian like Bonhoeffer, it was difficult to see the liberal, humanitarian type of theology that prevailed in the World Alliance so freshly and joyfully at work; one of its purposes was actually the promotion of friendship among all religions. Bonhoeffer would hardly have found his way to the World Alliance on his own accord at the time; it was Diestel's persistence that roused his interest in it. Diestel alone, however, could not have kept him there. It was the peace question, and the new wave of defamation in Germany, that assured his loyalty to the organization and reconciled him to its slight theological reputation. He was lured by the opportunities to meet people such as Gandhi's friend C. F. Andrews at its conferences. Bonhoeffer's theology had always made him leery of self-serving church enterprises; there was little chance of this in the World Alliance. Thus, despite his concern at its theological deficiencies, his report from Cambridge was already deeply committed:

> But, notwithstanding all criticism, it is plain that the World Alliance . . . is doing work the urgency of which must set everyone's conscience alight, and so far as we know there is no other way of doing it better or more quickly.[66]

Ethnic-Nationalist Protest. The German delegates' participation in the Cambridge conference was burdened by acute ecclesiastical, political, and economic difficulties. It was a prelude for all the future disagreeable symptoms that went with ecumenical work.

While Bonhoeffer and Lasserre were still in Mexico looking at pyramids and sending peace greetings, an ecumenical scandal occurred in Germany that would preoccupy the religious press for some time.

The German preparatory meeting for the World Alliance conference in Cambridge was held in Hamburg 1–3 June 1931. On the eve of the meeting, not suspecting what the conference would hold for him, Diestel wrote to Bonhoeffer: "Tomorrow morning I leave for the World Alliance meeting in Hamburg, which has given me a lot of trouble . . . I must stand in for Dr. Burghart . . . the *Deutschkirchler* and *Stahlhelm* members are making grand gestures but there's not much behind it."[67] The purpose of the Hamburg meeting was to decide the German positions for Cambridge on three issues: (1) national and international obligations; (2) disarmament; (3) minority questions. Several foreign guests were expected, including Lord Dickinson, the tireless president of the World Alliance, and Bishop Ammundsen from Denmark, who was later such a loyal and informed friend of the Confessing church.

The opening session, however, was disrupted by an article published that morning in the *Hamburger Nachrichten*, entitled "Protestant Church and International Reconciliation," which stated:

> In this situation,[68] in our judgment, there can be no understanding between us Germans and the victorious nations in the world war; we can only show them that as long as they continue the war against us, understanding is impossible. . . . This lends weight to the demand (that we) break through all artificial semblance of cooperation and ruthlessly acknowledge that a Christian and church understanding and cooperation on the questions of rapprochement among the peoples is impossible as long as the others are waging a murderous policy against our people.
>
> Whoever believes that understanding can be better served otherwise, disowns the German destiny and confuses consciences at home and abroad, because this does not honor the truth.
>
> Professor P. Althaus, Erlangen
> Professor E. Hirsch, Göttingen[69]

All the right-wing newspapers in Germany immediately reprinted the statement on their front pages. The target had been hit, and the shot reverberated from all directions until well into the following year.

The German Evangelical Alliance officially backed the Althaus-Hirsch statement. The *Allegemeine Evangelische Lutherische Kirchenzeitung* offered

Hirsch the chance to elaborate on the matter and respond to his critics. Althaus announced that he was not a member of the Nazi Party—Hirsch was not a member either—but that he still supported the movement, which had won over the majority of students, and he again attacked the "superficial jargon about international understanding."[70] In Spandau, the Central Office for Apologetics held courses for pastors about the "national question." Martin Rade energetically refuted the Althaus-Hirsch statement, and Karl Ludwig Schmidt declared it to be theologically, ecclesiastically, politically, and humanly preposterous. Sasse observed that, as theological teachers, Althaus and Hirsch had initiated a political move against the church's work, and thus clearly demonstrated that church questions were subordinate to national ones:

> One can only assume that they have not expressed themselves clearly . . .
> If German Lutheranism withdraws from the task of peace work, then it
> turns this work over to other powers. It condemns itself to unfruitful
> protest that will be greeted enthusiastically in the political world, and the
> ultimate goals of this protest will not be understood.[71]

The Hamburg meeting took up the political problem in its own way. Siegmund-Schultze reported on it in *Die Eiche*.[72] The conference drew up a resolution:

> In deep pain Christians in Germany see how the constant postponement of
> the duty to disarm . . . has allowed a growing sense of broken trust and
> doubts about justice and peace, and that the conviction is growing through-
> out the world that the current situation in Europe can only be preserved or
> changed through violence. . . . (the German World Alliance) welcomes the
> decision that has finally called for a disarmament conference. With great
> concern, however, it sees that the requirements for a successful conference,
> equal rights . . . and with that the goal of a rapid, balanced general disar-
> mament through these preparatory negotiations is not yet assured.
>
> Under these circumstances the German World Alliance welcomes the
> intention of the World Alliance to discuss the disarmament question anew
> in Cambridge, and requests that it emphasize, in an unmistakable way, the
> principles already adopted in Prague and how their importance has
> increased. . . .[73]

The Hamburg conference came to an understanding with its foreign guests that the German delegates at Cambridge would not address the disarmament issue, but would leave it to representatives of other nationalities.

This was the background for Bonhoeffer's letter to Erwin Sutz from Bonn, speaking about his ecumenical debut: "On 15 August I am being sent to England for three weeks, for the Cambridge conference. What are we to say to America about the cooperation of the churches? Anyway, perhaps not such nonsense as Hirsch's recent effort. . . ."[74]

In July 1931, banks, savings institutions, and exchanges were closed for several days, and one emergency decree after another imposed controls on payment transactions and restricted cash withdrawals. Within two weeks the discount rate was raised from 7 to 15 percent. At the end of August all foreign currency holdings exceeding one thousand marks had to be registered with the authorities. Despite the risk of renewed political unrest, pay and pension cuts were introduced, the period of entitlement to unemployment pay was reduced, and economy measures were introduced throughout the country.

These measures included a drastic reduction in the possibilities for travel abroad, and German ecumenical leaders found themselves in a humiliating position. Bonhoeffer was unembarrassed, however, and insisted on sufficient funding for the conferences he was helping to organize. This meant that he had to convince others of the importance of this work; since Bonhoeffer generously spent his own money for the purpose, he expected others to make sacrifices too.

The economic crisis directly affected the Cambridge conference, in connection to the proposed resolution on disarmament. Others joined the Germans in noting the connection between the economic crisis and the payment of war debts. A successful disarmament conference, with the restoration of equal rights to Germany, would contribute to relieving the economic situation. Siegmund-Schulze stressed this point tirelessly in his writings, and the Americans at the Cambridge meeting understood him, since President Hoover had proposed a large-scale remission of debt in the United States' interests. The French showed much less comprehension, and were expected to dispute this in Cambridge.

Bonhoeffer's attention had already been drawn to such problems in New York; now he acquired new knowledge. He wrote to his friend Sutz in Switzerland:

> Come to Berlin, there are no emergency decrees in your country. I have already written to you that I am going to Cambridge. If only I don't have to talk about things I know nothing about yet. Incidentally, I am industriously studying political economy—you cannot completely disclaim responsibility for that—and I am reading some really interesting and simple books on the subject.[75]

He plunged into political economy, not just to have facts with which to back his arguments in Cambridge, but also in light of his forthcoming work as student chaplain at the Berlin Technical University. The necessity of a sober knowledge of economic causes and effects seemed more urgent as he considered how to bring real theological factors to bear on the issue. The lessons he had learned at Union Theological Seminary in New York continued to influence him.

Bonhoeffer's introduction to his new task came in part through writing. Diestel, who had convinced the consistory to give Bonhoeffer leave because he spoke several languages "and could move in the intellectual sphere with enough freedom," wrote to him:

> I've entered you there as youth representative. Pastor Lilje and others are also traveling under this rubric. . . . You might be expected to speak up in the discussion about the "national and international obligations" . . . and, in the spirit of the World Alliance, to say something fundamental and practical about this two-sided obligation from the youth perspective.[76]

Bonhoeffer joined Siegmund-Schultze in Berlin at a preliminary meeting for those going to Cambridge. The difficult relationship between the Germans and the French was addressed, which at the time overshadowed the other problems. Siegmund-Schultze announced that:

> In Cambridge . . . no German will speak on the disarmament question. It is not necessary because all the other representatives of the Christian churches, with the sole exception of the French, will represent the "German thesis," which is not really a specifically German idea, but a human one.[77]

At Cambridge and subsequent World Alliance conferences there was no one with whom Bonhoeffer reached quicker and better understanding than the French; still, for the next two years he too regarded the Franco-German problem as the most burning one. In *Die Eiche* Siegmund-Schultze tried to make up for all the things that had been left undone between Germans and French in previous years by printing the French report that had been presented at Cambridge:

> [The struggle] would certainly have been less hard if the German Evangelical Church's position had not filled the French Reformed church with deep concern and painful bewilderment. After the war mania had disappeared, our churches expected some gesture of regret from the German churches about what had happened and a desire to lead their people along

the path of justice and fellowship. No act of penance was expected from them, only a word of sympathy for our plundered and destroyed churches. But nothing came. The German churches bewailed only the suffering of their own people, whose complete innocence they proclaimed. Hence one can understand the mistrust and suspicion that filled our churches in light of the stance of their sisters in Germany.[78]

The Conference. Bonhoeffer made three stops in England: first at a preliminary student conference in St. Leonard's and Westcliff-on-Sea, then at a youth conference of the World Alliance, and finally the conference in Cambridge. Little is known about the days spent meeting the other delegates in St. Leonard's.

Two factors distinguished the Cambridge conference from previous ones. It was the first time the World Alliance conference was held on the soil of a nation that had played a leading role in the war. Until then it had been impossible to risk this, but the wartime prejudices, at least within the World Alliance, had died away.

In addition, it was the first time that the conference granted full and unrestricted participation to its youth delegates. This came after Bishop Ammundsen, who presided over the conference, announced that the Alliance was in danger of becoming "too respectable." This earned him some criticism, but the experiment was carried out.[79] It was agreed that up to half of each national delegation could consist of youth delegates, who could participate in the deliberations of the main conference as well as in the committee work. The result was a sudden surge of activity by young people in the World Alliance; this carried over into Life and Work, which caused some headaches at the Geneva headquarters.

For Bonhoeffer the youth conference of 29–31 August was a significant event. The youth committee of the World Alliance had existed since the 1928 Prague conference, which had issued the first appeal to the Allies to keep their promises to the defeated powers. But before 1931 the committee had met only once, in Avignon in 1929. Its members included a number of men who later became well known: Dr. E. A. Burroughs, then Bishop of Ripon; Professor Alivisatos; Captain Étienne Bach, a former officer in a French alpine regiment who had become a pacifist; Sir Stafford Cripps, who later served as Labor delegate in the British parliament and as finance minister; Czech theologian Josef Hromádka; Dutch ecumenist Willem Visser 't Hooft; Danish pastor Sparring-Petersen; and Wilhelm Stählin from Münster. The youth conference now demanded a more active role: "Make room for us, give us something to do, give us a good organization."[80] The cooperation of young church members in international tasks was discussed.

The delegates submitted three concrete proposals to the main conference, the third of which was decisive for Bonhoeffer: (1) the enlargement of the youth committee; (2) the appointment of a secretary to work out of Geneva and assist the chairperson, the bishop of Ripon (H. L. Henriod, the Swiss secretary-general of the World Alliance and of Life and Work, was proposed); and (3) the appointment of three international honorary youth secretaries to travel and do coordinating work, with the World Alliance covering their expenses. F. W. Tom Craske, an Englishman, was named to work with the British Empire, the United States, and the Far East; P. C. Toureille from France was to cover France, Latin America, the Balkans, Poland, and Czechoslovakia. Dietrich Bonhoeffer was named to cover Germany, central and northern Europe, Hungary, and Austria. On 4 September these proposals were approved by the management committee and accepted by the World Alliance; the three youth secretaries were also made members of the management committee and of the council itself.

His election to the inner circle of the World Alliance had many consequences for Bonhoeffer. It made him an ex officio member of the councils in Sofia in 1933 and in Fanö in 1934, without the delicate question of German representation at those conferences being affected. The course for the newcomer had been set.

Apart from the official sessions, there was a special Franco-German youth meeting that continued until late at night and revealed the extent to which the aspirations and criticisms of the younger theologians from both countries coincided. French delegate Roger Jézéquel described it in a sketch published 30 September 1931 in *Foi et Vie*:

> [There was] another German there, a young university professor. After ten minutes of discussion we discovered that we shared the same theological position. Suddenly the certainty rose in us that the secret of rapprochement was here, in this religious connection. Security? A revision of the treaties? Pacifist propaganda? Perhaps . . . actually, we are being cornered: compelled to make Christianity a reality, to make the church visible. . . .[81]

The person mistakenly assumed to be "a young university professor" was Bonhoeffer.

Toureille later said that he and Bonhoeffer had made fun of the welcoming poster at Cambridge College: "World Peace depends on World Disarmament and Disarmament depends on you!" One of the main speakers at the general meeting was Sparring-Petersen from Denmark. He gave an impassioned speech against armament and wars that were undertaken with

Christian legitimation. Toureille was selected to respond in the name of the youth conference. Together with Bonhoeffer, he prepared his remarks. "Humanitarian efforts will never make war disappear, the struggle against it must come out of different depths and greater obedience."[82] Here we hear Bonhoeffer's voice in Cambridge.

The British and German press gave detailed reports on the Cambridge meeting; in contrast, the French reported nothing at all. Nonetheless hopes in the disarmament conference had not been abandoned. Bonhoeffer wrote an article for the 12 September 1931 issue of the Königsberg-Hartung paper and a more detailed piece that appeared in *Theologischen Blättern*, which had published the statement by Althaus and Hirsch. He began his report with a clear dig at them, citing an Indian delegate's appeal at the general meeting that the churches in Cambridge should have spoken more directly: ". . . should say in fact what the attitude of the churches would be were another catastrophe to occur . . . that the churches should finally, finally for once say something very concrete."[83] He described the harmony with other "continental" delegates, particularly the French and the Danes; Regin Prenter, later professor in Aarhus, was among the Danish delegates. Bonhoeffer was in agreement with the resolution on disarmament passed by the general conference; he was even more pleased that the "continental" delegates had been able to persuade the youth conference not to issue its own announcement. The report of the youth conference to the general meeting stated:

> . . . the experience of these days allowed us to find something more important than a rally—the consciousness of a personal and collective responsibility, and the readiness to declare our loyalty to this, with God's help.[84]

While Bonhoeffer had grimly fought his conference's lust for passing resolutions for a year and a half, in 1933 he suddenly began to fight its lack of desire to speak out. Both positions were based upon the same reason: first because it was too cheap to witness to the Gospel with a resolution, and then, because it was too cheap not to defend it with a resolution.

The Cambridge World Alliance meeting also served as the occasion for the executive committee of Life and Work to meet. Life and Work also had its youth committee; Dr. Erich Stange, head of the German YMCA, was its deputy chairman. The meeting was noteworthy because it was decided that the Life and Work youth committee should seek ways to work closely with the World Alliance youth committee. At this point, however, leadership remained firmly in the hands of the World Alliance.

The Cambridge conference was the principal reason why 1932 was a very restless year for Bonhoeffer. Organizing ecumenical youth work involved him in an endless succession of meetings. Only the church struggle compelled him to gradually loosen his links with the ecumenical youth secretariat. In 1931–1932, however, such efforts and engagement were by no means associated only with success and popularity for the ecumenical idea. On the contrary, on 4 April 1932, six months after the Cambridge conference, Bonhoeffer reported to a meeting of the youth committee in London:

> The results of the Cambridge conference in Germany are meager, because nationalist professors of theology oppose the work of the World Alliance.[85]

Before they left Cambridge the newly elected youth secretaries discussed and agreed on a program for 1932. Based entirely on their own ideas they aimed for a program that, in addition to practical issues like unemployment, would advance a thorough consideration of basic theological questions. Refusing to be intimidated by the difficult foreign exchange situation, they set their dates and believed the necessary resources would be available.

The youth committee's increased activity and new status did not please everyone at Cambridge. It made the work of the Geneva office of the World Alliance and the Ecumenical Council more complicated. The need for coordination was seen at once by the research department of the Ecumenical Council and its secretary Hans Schönfeld, who was responsible for theological questions. Would the youth secretaries allow themselves to be guided? In fact, complaints soon arose from council and committee members that the youth secretaries were usurping issues and duplicating work already being done out of Geneva.[86]

Thus there were some strains in Bonhoeffer's relations with the Geneva headquarters from the beginning. If he noticed them at all, he did not take them seriously. Behind the scenes, however, they deepened. Eventually they came into the open, and they assumed substantial proportions once the various church groups in Germany divided into deeply hostile camps. In light of these tragic developments, in retrospect it is clear that Bonhoeffer paid insufficient attention to his relations with the Geneva office. Perhaps he persisted too long in believing that everything was in order.

The Transition from Theologian to Christian

Looking back from Tegel prison in 1944, Bonhoeffer wrote that his path in life had been "basically" uninterrupted, though he acknowledged one change:

I don't think I have ever changed very much, except perhaps at the time of my first impressions abroad and under the first conscious influence of father's personality. It was then that I turned from phraseology to reality. . . . Neither of us has really had a break in our lives. Of course, we have deliberately broken with a good deal. . . . I sometimes used to long for something of the kind, but today I think differently about it.[87]

In this passage Bonhoeffer was referring to the juxtaposition in the Letters to Timothy between "I formerly blasphemed" (1 Timothy 1:13) and "I thank God whom I serve with a clear conscience, as did my fathers" (2 Timothy 1:3).

On closer examination, what Bonhoeffer so serenely describes as a "turning away from phraseology" and as "longing for a break" referred to a turning point that occurred at a definite time. It can probably be attributed to the period when he began his university, church, and ecumenical work. In addition to the external signs that his students observed in him, the subsequent researcher can detect some concealed references from Bonhoeffer's own hand that reveal a momentous change.

At this point, we might recall the difficulties that later scholars had in understanding Luther's "evangelical experience," the date and details of which have never been clarified; characteristically, Luther himself never directly spoke about it. Luther's questions were resolved "in the midst of the performance of the daily task," during the period of his first lectures at the university in Wittenberg.[88] Bonhoeffer answered the new demands on his theological existence with steps of practical Christian obedience, in the midst of the daily tasks of his new jobs.

Thus Bonhoeffer said nothing directly during this period to announce such a shift. The seriousness of his decisions was proved precisely by the fact that he no longer made them the subject of observation or spoke of them. He even warned explicitly against expecting or trying to pin down an "experience of vocation": "At the onset of theological studies stands not the experience of the call, but the decisiveness for sober, serious, responsible theological work," he wrote in a leaflet for students in 1933.[89]

Those who met him after 1931 were impressed by his breadth of knowledge, his concentrated energy, analytical and critical acumen, as well as by his personal commitment that engaged his entire personality and his behavior in innumerable ways. What these observers saw was the result of the change in him, not the change itself. Only those who knew him well from earlier days were struck by the difference in him, as Paul Lehmann was, for instance, when he met him again in Berlin in 1933. It seemed to his students that he had always been like that. Bonhoeffer now regularly attended church, although in New York Lehmann had been struck by how freely he behaved in this matter. He also practiced a meditative approach to the Bible that was obviously very different from the exegetical or homiletical use of it. During their retreats in 1932 his students were surprised by this unusual practice, and did not fail to make ironic comments about it. He no longer spoke of oral confession merely theologically, but as an act to be practiced. This was unheard of in the church and academic circles in which he moved. He alluded increasingly to a communal life of obedience and prayer, which could perhaps renew the credibility of the individually isolated and privileged ministry. He viewed all this not as a counter to reformed theology but as based upon it. More and more frequently he quoted the Sermon on the Mount as a statement to be acted upon, not merely used as a mirror. He began taking a stand for Christian pacifism among his students and fellow clergy, although hardly anyone noticed at the time. To his students his piety sometimes appeared too fervent, and was impressive only because it was accompanied by theological rigor and a broad cultural background. One student later recalled a prayer meeting in 1932:

> There, before the church struggle, he said to us near Alexanderplatz, with a simplicity like old Tholuck [Friedrich Tholuck, a systematic theologian] might have used once, that we should not forget that every word of Holy Scripture was a love letter from God directed very personally to us, and he asked us whether we loved Jesus.[90]

But such incidents occurred only in the inner circle of his students. In any case, the world of *disciplina pietatis* was not touched on just incidentally.

When he discovered Barth during his studies in 1925 Bonhoeffer had experienced his first decisive deepening of his thought: he glimpsed and grasped the undeducible self-consciousness of his theological existence. This gave a powerful impetus to his work and ministry. Only once did he state outright what was happening inside him and what he meant, for example, when he wrote to Sutz that "in the meantime he had taken rather a dislike" to *Act and Being*.[91] This was at the beginning of 1936, in a letter to an acquaintance to whom he was close for a time. Looking back on his past life, he wrote:

> I plunged into work in a very unchristian way. An . . . ambition that many noticed in me made my life difficult. . . .

Then something happened, something that has changed and transformed my life to the present day. For the first time I discovered the Bible ... I had often preached, I had seen a great deal of the church, spoken and preached about it—but I had not yet become a Christian. . . .

I know that at that time I turned the doctrine of Jesus Christ into something of personal advantage for myself . . . I pray to God that will never happen again. Also I had never prayed, or prayed only very little. For all my loneliness, I was quite pleased with myself. Then the Bible, and in particular the Sermon on the Mount, freed me from that. Since then everything has changed. I have felt this plainly, and so have other people about me. It was a great liberation. It became clear to me that the life of a servant of Jesus Christ must belong to the church, and step by step it became clearer to me how far that must go.

Then came the crisis of 1933. This strengthened me in it. Also I now found others who shared this purpose with me. The revival of the church and of the ministry became my supreme concern. . . .

I suddenly saw the Christian pacifism that I had recently passionately opposed as self-evident—during the defense of my dissertation, where Gerhard [Jacobi] was also present. And so it went on, step by step. I no longer saw or thought anything else. . . .

My calling is quite clear to me. What God will make of it I do not know . . .

I must follow the path. Perhaps it will not be such a long one. Sometimes we wish that it were so (Philippians 1:23). But it is a fine thing to have realized my calling. . . .

I believe that the nobility of this calling will become plain to us only in the times and events to come. If only we can hold out![92]

With greater reserve but complete honesty, he wrote his brother Karl-Friedrich in January 1935:

It may be that in many things I seem to you rather fanatical and crazy. I myself am sometimes afraid of this. But I know that, if I became "more reasonable," I would have to hang up my entire theology the next day for the sake of honesty. When I first began, I imagined it quite otherwise—perhaps a more academic matter. Now something very different has come of it. I now believe that I know at last that I am at least on the right track—for the first time in my life. And that often makes me very glad . . . I believe I know that inwardly I shall be clear and honest with myself only if I truly begin to take seriously the Sermon on the Mount. That is the only source of power capable of blowing up the whole phantasmagoria [i.e., the Nazi illusion] once and for all. . . .

> I still cannot really believe that you genuinely believe all these ideas to be so completely crazy. There just happen to be things that are worth an uncompromising stand. And it seems to me that peace and social justice, or Christ himself, are such things.[93]

In April 1936 he wrote his brother-in-law Rüdiger Schleicher, who, in contrast to the new "orthodox" Dietrich, liked to consider himself a follower of Harnack and Naumann:

> Is it . . . intelligible to you if I say I am not at any point willing to sacrifice the Bible as this strange word of God, that on the contrary, I ask with all my strength what God is trying to say to us through it? Every other place outside the Bible has become too uncertain for me. I fear that there I will only bump into my own divine *Doppelgänger*. . . .
>
> And I want to say something to you personally: since I learned to read the Bible this way—which has not been long at all—it becomes more wonderful to me with each day. . . .
>
> You wouldn't believe how happy one is to find the way back from the wrong track of some theologies to this elemental thing.[94]

These three are testimonies—one direct and two indirect—to a momentous turning point, stemming from a time when the struggle over whether a theologian could also be a Christian had been fought, and the fruits of that struggle had ripened. But the certainty and joy in the battle had turned into a more drawn-out struggle. On the one hand, he had already written from New York to a young friend in Grunewald of his "new perspectives" that were changing his philosophy and theology. On the other hand, the self-tormented secret sketches about the disclosure of his vocation and his longing for death[95] are from the second half of 1932—the period in which, in his lectures published as *Creation and Fall,* he worked and spoke about the "beginning" that neither can nor should be known.

Bonhoeffer never mentioned the biographical background of this thought to his students. They learned nothing about a conscious moment of a turning point. He had always been repulsed by the pietists' deliberately told stories of their conversions. But this did not mean that he avoided making decisions whose time had come and that held the seeds of the future, including a new responsibility for the world in the final years.

The University

Bonhoeffer's affiliation to the university in Berlin was now determined by two things. The *venia legendi* of 1930 permitted him to hold lectures and seminars. He could choose his topics, how many courses he offered, and their scope. He needed only to register them in time and request the rooms. The other side, of course, was that as an assistant lecturer without a fixed salary, he was dependent upon the scant money of those students who registered for his courses instead of those offered by professors who could give examinations.

Second, thanks to Lütgert's request, Bonhoeffer was taken on as extraordinary assistant in the systematics seminar after Stolzenburg left. This did not give him a civil servant's status, in which he had no interest anyway. But it gave him a firm contract, which ensured him a monthly income of 214 Reich marks—reduced by some of the emergency regulations of those years. When he finally concluded the contract at the beginning of 1932, retroactive to August 1931, and was paid the money due from that point in one sum, he bought a cabin in Biesenthal, built of wood and tar paper. His assistantship included no additional duties; Lütgert gave Bonhoeffer the freedom to unfold.

The Bonhoeffer Circle. Conditions in 1931 were not unfavorable for making a start as an assistant lecturer. Berlin was an active part of the general "boom" in theological studies; some one thousand theology students were studying in the department at that time. The lecture halls and seminar rooms were overcrowded. Even when men such as Romano Guardini attracted crowds from their routine lectures that winter, a beginner still had enough to do as long as he didn't disqualify himself by being too boring. A loyal minority soon emerged, impressed by the strength and exceptional quality of the new lecturer. He apparently fulfilled the needs and longings of students who, confronted by Berlin theology's elegance and meticulousness, as well as the coarse political propaganda, were left without real answers and challenges. Here more was being demanded of them than mere intellect.

"I must say that the students were measurably more interested in theology than the lecturers were," Bonhoeffer wrote Sutz about an open evening to which he had invited both groups.[96]

Even then, the majority of theology students tended toward Hitler's party; more of them read the Nazi *Angriff* than the *Vossische Zeitung*. At the end of 1930 *Christliche Welt* reported of one university that "almost all theology students are National Socialists . . . and some 90 percent of the Protes-

tant theology candidates appear at the college wearing the National Socialists party badge." Even from the preacher's seminaries, the newspaper continues, there were complaints: "Of the candidates of divine learning . . .
more than half are followers of Hitler."[97] This was not yet true in Berlin, but
the political divisions were already playing a role.

During this period a lecturer who stayed independent of the gathering
storm had to attract students who were not drawn to the new magnets.
During his two years in the theological faculty in Berlin Bonhoeffer gradually acquired a respectable audience and a firm core of seminar students. The
all too young man behind the lectern was a small sensation and news about
him began to spread. The boundaries of his firm core of students were set
automatically by the intellectual and personal standards he required. There
were hardly any German Christians among them, although there were several students who initially believed they could politically align themselves
with the Nazi Party.

Through the seminars, open evenings, and excursions, a "Bonhoeffer
circle" of students formed. A number of close colleagues in the church struggle and members of the Finkenwalde community emerged from this group,
including Joachim Kanitz, Albrecht Schönherr, Winfried Maechler, Otto
Dudzus, Jürgen Winterhager, Wolf-Dieter Zimmermann, Herbert Jehle,
Christoph Harhausen, Rudolf Kühn, Reinhard Rütenik, Inge Karding, Helga
Zimmermann, Klaus Block, and Hans-Herbert Kramm. They were instrumental in forming the oppositional group of young theologians in Berlin-
Brandenburg in 1933 and 1934. In 1932 they lugged potatoes, flour, and vegetables on a wheelbarrow to the Stettin train station so that they could spend
the weekend together in the country, first at the Prebelow youth hostel and
then in a cabin in Biesenthal. They talked theology, made hesitant attempts
at spiritual exercises, went for long walks, and listened to Bonhoeffer's collection of Negro spirituals. It was the first time they had spoken about things
like forming fellowship, committing themselves to organized spiritual life,
and the possibilities of serving in social settlement work. But there was still
a long way to go before any of this was put into practice, and everything was
on a free and informal basis. Bonhoeffer did not force anything. These were
the hesitant beginnings of what later took shape in Finkenwalde and in
Bonhoeffer's *Life Together*.

Connections between this group and the German Student Christian
Movement were formed, and Bonhoeffer became known to a wider circle of
students through his chaplaincy. Increasingly he was invited to speak at the
Berlin Student Christian Movement (S.C.M.). At the request of Martin
Fischer, its secretary, he offered a Bible class on texts from Mark and orga-

nized discussions. Jürgen Winterhager's notes from an ecumenical evening held at the S.C.M. show that Bonhoeffer was already talking to his students along the lines of his peace speech at Fanö and of *Discipleship*. His subject was "Christ and Peace," and the point of departure, according to the notes, was the failure of the Geneva disarmament conference.[98] Drawing on Matthew 22:37-38, he proceeded to make four points, with a directness that must have shocked his audience at the time:

> We want to proceed from the central point of the New Testament and hence consider these questions according to the highest and noblest commandment of all. We shall not rip one single word about worldly authority out of the entire context of the New Testament and thus fail to recognize that Christ proclaimed the kingdom of God, against which the whole world, and thus "the powers that be," lives in hostility.
>
> Point 1: Christ does not wish to change things for the sake of our peace and quiet; still less can we do that for ourselves. Discipleship stands entirely on simple faith, and faith is real only in discipleship. The faithful are addressed, but the world is judged through Christ's witness for peace. Faith must be simple, otherwise it breeds reflection, not obedience. There is no such thing as assured peace. The Christian can risk peace only through faith. Thus there is no such thing as direct community among people, there is only access to the enemy by way of prayer to the Lord of all nations.
>
> Point 2: The misunderstood relationship between Law and Gospel, that is, a forgiveness of sin that does not affect the earthly, civil life of people. People are still told they are sinners, but are not called out from their sinful structures. How are we, who go on sinning in the expectation of grace, to go on taking seriously the forgiveness of sins and prayer to God? We make grace cheap and, with the justification of the sinner through the cross, forget the cry of the Lord that never justifies sin. "You shall not kill," "love your enemies," are commandments, requiring simple obedience. Any form of war service, any preparation for war, is forbidden for the Christian. Faith that sees freedom from the law as an arbitrary disposition of the law is a human faith, in defiance of God. Simple obedience knows nothing of good and evil, but follows the call of Christ as something self-evident.
>
> Point 3: Without being at peace ourselves with our brothers and neighbors we cannot preach peace to the nations. When a nation refuses to listen to the peace commandment, Christians are called forth from it to testify. But let us take care that we sinners proclaim peace in a spirit of love and not out of any zeal for security or any political objectives!
>
> Point 4: True peace is in and from God; it is inseparably associated with the Gospel. Hence it is not a reconciliation to religious philosophies of life. Forgiveness is for sinners; but there can be no reconciliation with sin and

false doctrine. The weapons are faith and love, purified by suffering. The pure love, which first seeks God and God's commandments, prefers to see a defenseless brother slain to seeing us and our souls stained with blood. It is impossible for love to direct the sword against a Christian, for that is aiming it at Christ. "Can God have commanded *us* to do such a thing?" is the question of the serpent.

The summary of these notes clearly establishes that *Discipleship* and *Life Together* did not arise from the circumstances of 1933. *Discipleship* emerged from Bonhoeffer's own path, which he had pursued long before the political upheaval of that year. He was already expressing these things to his students with the words that appeared in the later books.

Yet he was not concerned with propagating fanatical slogans, but much more with finding a way to take up the risk of faith and obedience together. In his sermons, lectures, and addresses he would hardly have spoken so plainly had these new ideas not been accompanied by his own concrete steps. In general, he scorned the idea that individuals could undertake to do exceptional things.[99] He spoke more openly at ecumenical meetings abroad, where he encountered colleagues from different traditions who faced similar problems. He responded only indirectly to Wilhelm Stählin's attack on "certain soft pacifist ideas" at the Berlin Center conference in April 1932, but in Ciernohorské Kúpele he spoke openly.[100] The next war must be outlawed, he said,

> not from the fanatical imposition of one commandment—the sixth for instance—but from obedience towards the commandment of God which is directed towards us today, namely that there shall be no more war, because it prevents us from seeing revelation. Nor should we be afraid of the word pacifism today.[101]

The S.C.M. invited Bonhoeffer to address a large audience. Johannes Kühn, its director of studies, invited him to address a meeting in the Hoffbauerstiftung in Potsdam-Herrmanswerder as part of a series with artists and writers during Holy Week in 1932. Bonhoeffer's speech, "Thy Kingdom Come,"[102] showed how the position expressed by his four points was far from being a ghetto of perfectionist personal piety. The entire address was an assault on this world. He took the church to task for its self-satisfied and hypocritical "otherworldliness." The universal earthly implication of Christ's message was more firmly emphasized in this address than ever before in Bonhoeffer's theology.

At the Lectern. It was only natural that uncommitted students were more easily and readily drawn by Bonhoeffer's approach to theology than that of the
more specialized and committed teachers of the subject. His colleagues followed the course taken by this graduate of their own faculty with interest
and a certain suspicion. "My theological pedigree is gradually becoming
suspect here, and they seem to have the feeling that perhaps they have been
nourishing a serpent in their bosom," as Bonhoeffer described his first
impressions of his colleagues to his friend Erwin Sutz.[103] Not only did he
dare to question their theological assumptions; he also appeared to be striving toward a different nature. It soon struck his students that something
about him intrinsically distinguished him from the behavior and ideals of a
professor.

He himself was aware of a certain isolation, but he did not wish to simply get rid of it. After spending one summer day with Karl Barth on the
Bergli, he described Barth's home as a "shelter for the theologically home-
less," to which he "thinks back only with longing in the cold loneliness
here."[104]

Although during his two years at the university Bonhoeffer prepared
new lectures and seminars every semester, he found delivering monologues
a burden. He greatly preferred study groups and seminars, although for his
students, it was the other way around. He disliked repetition and was continually searching for fresh ideas. He still felt far removed from what he
wanted to understand and say, and continued to be skeptical about the
answers he had established. The further he advanced into the unknown, the
more he longed for dialogue and criticism.

It must be assumed that the notes and manuscripts of all his lectures and
seminars perished.[105] Only the lecture course "Creation and Sin" from the
winter of 1932–1933 has survived, because he agreed to print it, at the insistence of his students. Any attempt to learn what Bonhoeffer did during
those two years must be based upon the indirect sources of the scarce and
various notes taken by students. Only from their outlines do we gain an
approximate picture of these theologically influential years for Bonhoeffer.

Bonhoeffer's first course listed in the course of studies was the cautious
topic "The History of Twentieth-Century Systematic Theology." It sounded
neither provocative nor particularly demanding. The course undertook a
solid sketch of his own position on the theological map. Bonhoeffer's assessment that he had arrived at a significant turning point in theological history was the central point of the entire course. This enabled a tight organization of how he presented the material.

Having defined his position, during the following semesters Bonhoeffer ventured into more troubled areas: ecclesiology, ethics, the "theological" exegesis of the scripture, and Christology. These became the logical sequence of topics for the following semesters he was present at the university:

Winter 1931–1932:
  Lecture: "The History of Twentieth-Century Systematic Theology."
  Seminar: "The Concept of Philosophy and Protestant Theology."
Summer 1932:
  Lecture: "The Nature of the Church."[106]
  Seminar: "Is There a Christian Ethic?"[107]
Winter 1932–1933:
  Lecture: "Creation and Fall: Theological Exegesis of Genesis 1–3."
  Lecture: "Recent Theology: Discussion of New Systematic Theology."[108]
  Seminar: "Dogmatics: Problems of a Theological Anthropology."[109]
Summer 1933:
  Lecture: "Christology."[110]
  Seminar: "Dogmatics: Hegel's Philosophy of Religion."
Winter 1933–1934 (listed but not held):
  Lecture: "Faith and the Word."
  Lecture: "Recent Theology."
  Seminar: "Dogmatics."

Winter Semester 1931–1932: Defining His Position. It is particularly unfortunate that no written notes exist from the very first classes of the lecture course "The History of Twentieth-Century Systematic Theology."[111] Bonhoeffer did not begin his systematic exploration epistemologically, but with an overview of the intellectual history of the contemporary world. The key words suggest that he reviewed the lines of his own background with a critical love: the sober, tolerant, bourgeois world of his father; the aristocratic milieu from which his mother came; the empirical art of Leopold von Kalckreuth. It was a world that was disappearing, which he, like his parents, nonetheless loved with every fiber of his being. It was the world he would acknowledge with gratitude from his prison cell in 1944.

The lectures revealed an astonishing interest in Troeltsch and Naumann. For Bonhoeffer these were the two great names from the era before Barth. Bultmann and Heidegger remained on the periphery. Bonhoeffer declared his full support for the turning point that Karl Barth had initiated. Now, however, he was awaiting its consequences and new impulses for the self-understanding of theology and for the ethics of a decisively renewed ecclesiology.

Bultmann and Heidegger were dealt with more in the seminar. Unfortunately, no notes remain; we have only the topic and some notes in Bonhoeffer's handwriting.[112] Otherwise we can only speculate. The topic was the concept of philosophy and Protestant theology. Bonhoeffer's notes concerned Heidegger and Grisebach. It is likely that the seminar session "Act and Being" and his inaugural lecture mentioned, and perhaps even more carefully explored, the relationship between philosophy and theology.

Beyond that, we know only that Bonhoeffer enjoyed this seminar more than the lectures: "The seminar was really good and interesting. I had a couple of quite lively Barth and Gogarten fellows in it."[113]

Summer Semester 1932: The Church as a Source of Theology and Ethics. "The Nature of the Church."[114] Having established his theological standpoint, Bonhoeffer presented his first attempt at a lecture using the topic of his own starting point: the church. He announced two-hour lectures and, despite being a passionate late-sleeper, forced himself to begin teaching at eight o'clock in the morning. The lecture hall began to fill; people had expectations of both critique and concreteness.

What was the nature of that church that, with the "turning point" described in the preceding lectures, brought forth a transformed understanding of itself and a new life? What was the relation between ecclesiology and Christology? Did the latter live from the first, or did it perhaps break it open? In Bonhoeffer's desire for concreteness and his own certainty, a great deal depended on ecclesiology. The statement from *Sanctorum Communio* had long been more than theoretical for him: "It is not only Christ who is both *donum* [gift] and *exemplum* [example] for us human beings, but in the same way also one human being is so for another."[115] Nonetheless, throughout his life Bonhoeffer wrestled with the fact that ecclesiology was burst open by Christology. "I lecture on the nature of the church with a great deal of effort," he wrote Sutz.[116] How can its authority to speak be determined?[117] How, when its "territory" is not a sacred realm but is to be the earth, the entire world?[118] How can its authority be determined "if one thinks about the certainty of the proclamation of salvation and the law? The whole question of the exegesis of *potestas clavium* [power of the keys] belongs here too."[119]

His listeners were captivated because with each chapter the systematic thinker came so surprisingly close to practical theology. The church's recent past appeared to unfold in an intelligible fashion. Subtle theological deductions merged seamlessly with the larger potential consequences for future church policies and practices. Later, in the era of the hefty backlash against this position of a "church" that led the way for all else, it was difficult to imagine how avant-garde these statements about the church as the source of theology and ethics sounded in 1932.

Here, beside the identity (not identification) of Christ and church ("Christ existing as church-community"), Bonhoeffer formulated its counterpart. In a way they would never forget he impressed on his students that this "church" always meant the actual church in a specific place—in this case within the Old Prussian Union. His focus on the church, as unusual as this was, already contained the first attempts at the "church for the world." It was typical of Bonhoeffer that the somewhat alienating phrase "the boundaries of intercession disappear wherever the boundaries of the congregation disappear" continued: "The intercession on behalf of all people brings them into the congregation."[120] The formulations of "arcane discipline" and "worldliness" were introduced. Bonhoeffer's words could not have been more modern: the religious community of Jesus died with its founder, "he is not the founder of the church, but the foundation of the church."[121]

Bonhoeffer addressed the distinctions toward the kingdom of God and the state, as he had examined them in the final sessions of the lectures, more topically in two published pieces that winter, a lecture entitled "Thy Kingdom Come" and a briefer essay "What Is Church?" that he wrote for Söhlmann's *Vormarsch*.[122] Here the resurrection, and the miracle of confession and of fellowship, break through the three powers of death, isolation, and "thirst." These powers are overcome in the church and tamed within the state.

"Is There a Christian Ethic?"[123] To Bonhoeffer the seminar topic for the summer of 1932 appeared even more urgent. His thinking about ethics was what had changed the most since the lecture he had given in Barcelona. He hoped for enlightenment from Barth on this point; and the ecumenical committees required his cooperation on social ethical declarations. A well-grounded position had to be developed in response to the fanatical claims about an "order of creation"; and here he wanted to finally examine the question of obedience more precisely, compared with the commandment of the Sermon on the Mount.

As unsatisfactory as these sketchy words must remain, the topics confirm in any case what is implied in Bonhoeffer's correspondence and the preserved ecumenical contributions from the time. He used the "orders of preservation" in 1932 as a formulation to counter the misused and misunderstood concept of "orders of creation." Contrary to the ethics in Barcelona, eschatology had become the dominant element of the teaching of the Commandments. In its preaching the church was to command concretely. Bon-hoeffer fervently declared this in Ciernohorské Kúpele and in Gland.[124] His sermon on Exaudi Sunday in 1932 supported this.[125] People were not to wait for the authority to do such commanding—practically to give the com-mandment to peace—this authority rested in the venture itself.[126]

Winter Semester 1932–1933: Literary Fronts. "Creation and Fall." The semi-nar in the summer of 1932 had already confronted the first three chapters of Genesis, in the course of discussing the problem of conscience and distin-guishing itself from the nationalist hubbub about the "orders of creation." Bonhoeffer had given a brief interpretation of the story of creation, which he bluntly called a "legend." Now, he devoted half of his two-hour lecture time to the topic "Creation and Sin: A Theological Interpretation of Gene-sis 1–3," and the other half to "recent theology."

Up to then the doctrine of creation had played virtually no role in Bon-hoeffer's writings. In *Act and Being* there is only an incidental reference to it, written in reference to the approaching danger: "There are in theology no ontological categories that are primarily based in creation and divorced from those later concepts."[127] In the meantime, however, the general debate had entered a phase in which theological arguments for the "orders of cre-ation" had almost become paeans or, as in the Dehn case, took the form of threats of excommunication underscored by physical violence against those who resisted them. It was necessary to prepare defenses for the struggles ahead.

Moreover, Bonhoeffer found it stimulating to deal with his old themes of conscience and reflection in combination with his new theme of com-mandment, and to exemplify this in this classical text. As mentioned previ-ously, the question of "origins" in this case had a very personal background; it moved Bonhoeffer in 1940 when he composed his meditation on the 119th Psalm.[128]

He called the work a "theological exposition." His meaning was both modest and ambitious. He did not want to invade the field of professional Old Testament scholars and amend their historical and philological work, but to listen to the text as a systematic thinker, under the premise of the church whose Bible includes the book of Genesis. His method "is its pre-supposition and this presupposition constitutes its method; its method is a continual returning from the text (as determined by all the methods of philological and historical research) to this presupposition. That is the objec-tivity in the method of theological exposition."[129] Since the Barthian "revo-lution," the idea of interpreting the whole of Scripture as the book of the church, as part of hearing the word of *Christus praesens,* had been in the air. Bonhoeffer vigorously drew conclusions from Barth's Christocentric treatment of the Old Testament and the First Article before Barth himself or others had ventured that far.

The lectures made such an impression that Bonhoeffer's students persuaded him to have them published. He had given little thought to making it a proper book, as is shown by the fact that he did not take the trouble to verify the biblical and literary references with footnotes, as he had done in his previous books as a matter of course. Only the title was changed, to avoid confusion with Emanuel Hirsch's *Creation and Sin,* published in 1931, though the remainder of Hirsch's title, ". . . in the natural reality of the human individual," was very different. Thus Bonhoeffer's work was published as *Creation and Fall.*

He wrote a new introduction, however. He had begun the lecture with the words "In these three chapters God speaks to us as we are today, as sinners who are crucified with him."[130] Now he elaborated in more detail on his method of theological interpretation. It was well into 1933 when he wrote his introduction, however, and the brief sentences now assumed a different tone from the earlier one in the lecture hall. What may then have sounded somewhat eschatological had become truly eschatological—particularly in regard to the creation:

> The church of Christ witnesses to the end of all things. It lives from the end, it thinks from the end, it acts from the end, it proclaims its message from the end . . . What must certainly arouse the church to real indignation, however, is that these children of the world that has passed away wish to claim the church, the new, as belonging to them. They want the new, and they know only the old. And in that way they deny Christ, the Lord.[131]

The theological consultants for the Christian Kaiser publishing house were far from enthusiastic about the manuscript. They found its interpretation of the Old Testament too unconventional; it was solely due to publisher Otto Salomon's insistence that it was accepted.

In fact, the little book became Bonhoeffer's first small literary success. "You will be pleased to hear that the *Kreuzzeitung* gave an excellent review of your *Creation and Fall* last week," his mother wrote to him in London.[132] The method, language, and ideas all attracted attention. Wilhelm Vischer's *Christuszeugnis des Alten Testamentes* (The Witness of the Old Testament to Christ) appeared one year later. What were the critics to make of Bonhoeffer's work?

The November 1934 *Kirchliche Anzeiger für Würrtemberg* laconically commented that "Bonhoeffer's theological basic principle might almost be described as the well-known *credo quia absurdum* [I believe because it is absurd]." His incursion into the field of Old Testament scholars was held against him. *Theologischen Blätter* said: "In any event, it is no credit to the Old Testament specialists that nowadays nonspecialists should be the first to attempt and present us with such an exegesis of Genesis 1–3."[133] As in *Sanctorum Communio*, Bonhoeffer had again fallen between two stools. The exegetes regarded the work as systematics, and the systematicians viewed it as exegesis. One group was indignant and the other took no notice.[134]

As mentioned, *Creation and Fall* was the first book of Bonhoeffer's that Barth read.[135] Although he too was critical, he thought that Bonhoeffer's attempt occasionally showed greater fidelity to the biblical text than the parallel passages in Wilhelm Vischer's book.

Bonhoeffer did not abandon the idea of such attempts at "theological interpretation." The content of what he said proved to be more important than the demonstration of any "theological method." Today there is hardly anyone who does not have doubts about this method; but the profundity of his message cannot be ignored, nor can it be denied that it armed the ranks well to detect and resist the enemy of the day. This eschatological interpretation of creation did not represent a retreat from the world. *Creation and Fall* was aimed at the "center of life." Nowhere previously had the idea of the "center," in contrast to the borders and margins of life, played such a role for Bonhoeffer.

It was ethical uneasiness that led Bonhoeffer to devote himself to the topic of these lectures. Ten years later it was again ethical uneasiness that moved him to return to the idea of the "center of life," when he said that God was to be sought in the center and not at the borders of reality.

"Recent Theology: Discussion of New Systematic Theological Literature."[136] In the second course, the influence of Barth's *Anselm* on Bonhoeffer became evident; Bonhoeffer's critical questions to the master moved into the background—although not his questions about the concrete commandment. His intent was that his students learn to navigate the theological map should things become serious. Thus Bonhoeffer gave them a sharply analytical overview of the most recent publications by Heim, Schütz, Barth, Gogarten, Knittermeyer, de Quervain, Stapel, Brunner, and Asmussen. Throughout the discussions, Bonhoeffer's familiar questions run like a red thread as criteria and basic principles: the church as precondition, the battle against the

"order of creation" as a false source of ethics, and the commandment to be concretely proclaimed through the church.

Bonhoeffer rarely inserted comments on current affairs in his lectures—not even in 1933. But this course from the winter of 1932–1933 became increasingly relevant as the political changes grew more turbulent and confusing. In November Bonhoeffer referred to the relation of philosophical tendencies to the ethnic-nationalist movement, referring explicitly to Grisebach and Heidegger. The last week in January 1933 he lectured on Gogarten's *Political Ethics*. Bonhoeffer squeezed in a discussion of revolutionary law as an attack on the Christian conservatives. In February he contrasted Stapel's *The Christian Statesman* with Asmussen's *Altona Confession*. [The Altona confession was one of the first confessions (in Hamburg, in June 1933) issued by the church opposition during the church struggle.] Bonhoeffer concluded the final lecture with the biblical verse he cited most often during 1932: "Judge them, O God our God, for we have no strength to face this great horde which is invading our land" (2 Chronicles 20:12).[137]

"Dogmatics: Problems of a Theological Anthropology."[138] Only fragments of the seminar from winter 1932–1933 can be reconstructed. For the next three semesters the course of studies simply stated "Dogmatics." Wolf-Dieter Zimmermann's notes offer a detailed overview of the material that Bonhoeffer intended to discuss but do not include a title. It is likely that it fits the content of the "problems of a theological anthropology."

Bonhoeffer began by announcing that he would come out against Bultmann and Heidegger; he did not want to begin with a preparatory philosophical course. He recommended that they study Brunner's Berlin lectures on "biblical psychology"; Bonhoeffer was unfamiliar with these when he held his inaugural lecture on anthropology in July 1930.[139] He drew upon his own studies from 1925 to 1932 to shape the program of this seminar: on his papers about the early Luther for the seminar with Holl, on *Act and Being*, right up to his newest theses. Discussion initially revolved around the relation between belief and religiosity, defined in a statement that was evidently very precisely thought out but nonetheless monstrous:

> Belief is that temporal and historical act of religiosity which reveals the intentionality toward Christ established by Christ. . . . belief is veiled by religiosity, just as Christ is veiled in Jesus.[140]

The reflections on the relationship between *habitus* and *esse*, which describe *habitus* as the "penultimate," conclude with extraordinarily practical statements on the "practice" of a Christian character, sense of church, meditation, and pious practices. Here he theologically classified and accounted for his experiments with his pupils in Biesenthal.

So he taught until 1933. Together with the reformers and Karl Barth, he wanted to learn to spell out and teach what "justification," "revelation," and the "word of God" were. In the process, however, his interpretation of all three concepts immediately became something tangible as "peace," "commandment," and "connection to church" (*Kirchlichkeit*). Several years later they would be given a different name, remaining for him what they had been: "justice," "discipleship," and "life together." *Discipleship* came into view with the approach of 1933. This theological teacher forced his students to follow new ways. Were these paths presumptuous or appropriate? What did it mean to add the experiences from Biesenthal to his academic lectures?

Summer Semester 1933: The Question of Foundation. "Christology."[141] Despite the political turbulence of the summer of 1933, it was the high point of Bonhoeffer's academic career, for now he lectured on Christology.

He considered these two-hour lectures more difficult than anything he had done, not because interruptions became more frequent, but because he had to bring together all of his thoughts, statements, and experiments and test their validity and foundation.

Christology, which he had once regarded as having been so remarkably neglected in Holl's seminars on Luther, ultimately lay behind the "turning point" he had acknowledged in his 1931 lecture. It was the magnetic or even the explosive center of "The Nature of the Church" in 1931; and it was to be the basis for ethics and the refutation of the misuse of the "orders of creation" concept. Was it not Christology that must plainly show where and whether the liberal dismantling of the old formulas was justified, and where the new theology of revelation revealed the intentions behind the ancient formulas, and where the convincing authority of one's own churchly or religious ties rested?

The students were expectant. Otto Dudzus reports that almost two hundred attended these demanding lectures throughout this restless summer:

> He looked like a student himself when he mounted the platform. But then what he had to say gripped us all so greatly that we no longer came because of this very young man but because of what he had to say—even though it was dreadfully early in the morning. I have never heard a lecture that impressed me nearly so much as this one.

Bonhoeffer's own notes for this lecture cannot be found either, but the copious notes taken by his students enable a reasonably adequate reconstruction. His outline was new and original at the time. Bonhoeffer's point of departure corresponded to that of previous lectures, decisively beginning with the Christ who is present in the Word, in the sacrament, and in—what we now recognize as the third distinguishing feature of his theology—the church-community. Only then did he discuss the "historical Christ" and critical Christology, in all its vicissitudes, in the history of dogmatics, and its fluctuation between old concepts of substance and more modern dynamic concepts. Only at the end did he attempt to develop a positive Christology, for which he had little time left. But he made suggestions and formulations that he recalled ten years later when he began to revise his theology.

"Dogmatics: Hegel's Philosophy of Religion." The seminar offered in the summer of 1933, announced only as "Dogmatics," was also well attended, which meant that not all the students were able to make the customary presentation. Bonhoeffer gave an introduction into the problem. Then the individual participants gave presentations on segments of Hegel's philosophy of religion, concluded each time by Bonhoeffer's perspective on certain points, as he later did in Finkenwalde at the end of contributions by the candidates there. No notes exist from these. Bonhoeffer's volumes of Hegel remain, however, and here he penciled in numerous notes in the margins. In one of the chapters was a paper on which Bonhoeffer had noted several themes for discussion:

> Goal: overcoming the Enlightenment. Reconciliation of rationality with religion. Acknowledgment of God.
> 1. the question of truth . . . dogma, teaching, the church toward belief.
> 2. the question of reality . . . world, history . . . total abstraction!
> 3. theologically=the question of church, God existing as community . . . salvation. Accusation: intellectualism? No. God at our disposal? Hegel says: God has power over human beings from above. Grace? Sin? Forgiveness? For Hegel all are strongly in the center.
>
> [on the back of the page]:
> But: at some point the dialectic ceases, namely, in the concept of the event itself . . . it happens . . .
> Not: thy will be done! Rather, it happens!
> Leave the devil out of it and then it works out well. Each individual concept (sin, etc.) is in itself viewed correctly, but can never be entirely understood except as something that has occurred.
> Question of truth. Question of reality. Church.
> Overcoming of the intellect through the rational.

But: overcoming the rational through the Holy Spirit, which drives out the devil.

Bonhoeffer's academic career concluded with this work in the summer of 1933. Still uncertain whether he would go to London, he announced two one-hour lecture courses for the winter semester 1933–1934. One was "Faith and Work," in which we might detect the intention of dealing with what later became *Discipleship*: the overdue reexamination and revision of the reformatory approach. The other lecture topic was "Recent Theology." Here Bonhoeffer wanted to deal with the abundance of recent theological statements about the major changes that had occurred. The seminar was listed as "Dogmatics."

Two years later Bonhoeffer once more became aware of his unextinguished *venia legendi* and lectured for several months on "discipleship" until he was prevented by the disciplinary proceedings against him. This renewal of his right to lecture came out of the struggle in which members of the Confessing church used for as long as possible the spheres of work not yet explicitly forbidden to them. This remained a reconnaissance mission; in the meantime the focus of Bonhoeffer's work was on an entirely different point.

When Bonhoeffer reached the high point of his academic life in 1933 and had also achieved a lasting impression among the students, he brought it to an end. His review of Heim's book[142] in the December issue of *Christentum und Wissenschaft* was his last published professional work in which he wrestled with contemporary theology. This kind of disputing with other theologians came to an end. Bonhoeffer had proven that he knew how to maneuver in this distinguished company. He would not enjoy the privileges of an academic position; from now on the lectern and theology no longer fit together. Lütgert's colleague who held the second professorship in systematics in Berlin, the elderly Arthur Titius, expressed regret in 1933: "It is a great pity that our best hope in the faculty is being wasted on the church struggle."

The Church

Ordination. Dietrich Bonhoeffer was ordained on 15 November 1931 by General Superintendent Ernst Vits, Dibelius's colleague for the Neumark and Lausitz districts, in a morning service in the Matthew Church near Potsdam Place. Vits paid five Reich marks "for the defraying of the ordination costs to the warden."[143] He was assisted by church pastor Damerow and High

Church Council member August Schreiber, representative for ecumenical affairs in the Church Federation Office. Only now did the church of Berlin-Brandenburg give its servant the "rights of clerical status," having refused these one year before because he had not yet reached the required age of twenty-five.

At the time no one around Bonhoeffer discussed the laying on of hands as the real assurance of apostolic succession. In addition, the significance that this ceremony of ordination would have for him only a few years later did not exist for him—later he made the occasion and preparations for it an unforgettable experience for his ordination candidates, and by then it meant a great deal when the assurance of commission came from the legal church administration! He did not choose those who ordained him; none of them were especially close to him either spiritually or personally, and later he hardly ever mentioned the occasion. That Sunday was not treated as an unusual one in the family. That afternoon he went to see his friend Franz Hildebrandt, who was now assistant minister to Fendt in Heilsbronnen, and listened to his sermon on the centenary of Hegel's death.

He certainly attached importance to the *rite vocatus* for the proclamation of the Gospel and the celebration of the sacrament, and less importance to the "rights of clerical status" as a privilege. He regarded the latter as threatening, not assuring, the authority and legal power of the ministry. It was during these weeks that he was so troubled by the problem of valid authority: "How is one to preach such things to these people? . . . The invisibility breaks us."[144] Bonhoeffer was ordained during the period when discussion raged about the so-called Harzburg front, the nationalist alliance under whose banner Hitler, Hugenberg, Seldte, and Schacht presented themselves on 11 October 1931 as those who could rescue Germany from chaos. Bonhoeffer saw no hope in such guardians of Christian Germany. He wrote:

> Will our church survive yet another catastrophe, one wonders, will that not really be the end unless we become something completely different? Speak, live completely differently . . . ?[145]

Student Chaplaincy. An ordained university lecturer in the service of the church was not free to seek the pastorate of his choice. Under the regulations of the general synod of 1930, Bonhoeffer was subject to another year's "auxiliary service" at the discretion of the church authorities. Thus, upon his return from Cambridge, another overdue warning was waiting for him. His parents, brothers, and sisters were entertained by its consistorial official language:

> We assign you . . . to take the assistantship as city vicar in Berlin. . . . You are to go by the assigned time to the general superintendent . . . who will oversee your further use in the church assistantship and give you the necessary instructions for your work. You are also to present yourself to the superintendent and pastor and request the necessary instructions for your work. . . . Your compensation consists . . . in compliance with the order by the Reich President of 1 December 1930 for the assurance of Economics and Finance of 183.68 Reich marks per month. . . . The day on which you begin your assistantship is to be announced to us that same day. . . .[146]

The post to which he was appointed was an entirely new one, chaplain to the students of the technical college in Charlottenburg. At that point there were no requirements for this position. According to *Christliche Welt*,[147] in the winter of 1931–1932 there were only twenty Protestant chaplains in all the universities in Germany, as opposed to thirty-seven Catholic ones. The ever alert General Superintendent Otto Dibelius had been advocating the appointment of a chaplain to the technical college since 1930, and his proposal had now been accepted. Emil Karow, the superintendent responsible for the district, instructed Bonhoeffer in his responsibilities:

> Your official duties will consist of serving the students of the Technical College as chaplain and counselor. You will be devoting your energies to a field that has not yet been tilled. It is my wish that you work in harmony with Pastor Bronisch-Holze, whose duties are principally with the university students. The kind of work will be different, since your colleague is also a parish minister who must preach on a regular basis and can use the rooms in his parsonage and the parish hall. He has accumulated experience in this area of work. I request you to get in touch with him and present a plan to me . . . when you are ready to take up your work. . . .[148]

Bonhoeffer's work as student chaplain was unfruitful. He had little success in making his position and plans known. The predecessor of the Berlin Student Christian Movement had only a weak position at the Charlottenburg college. Even under Bonhoeffer's influence, nothing resembling a student group developed. Before it did develop, the years of terror intervened, during which the Student Christian Movement was forcibly dissolved. During those years, a new understanding of church life grew and developed viable forms. Bonhoeffer's work at the technical college preceded the upheaval in which totalitarian pressure led scholars in the humanities to keep their distance from the church, and scientists won a new relationship to it.

Bonhoeffer procured a bulletin board, but it attracted little attention amid the multitude of other notices displayed. He was given a room for two hours each in a barrack in the student quarters, and somewhere or other he found a room for weekly prayers; four of his short homilies have survived.[149] He tried to make contact with the student associations, and at one of them (the Union of German Students) he held an evening on Christianity and technology. With Hanns Lilje, secretary general of the S.C.M. and a colleague from the Cambridge conference, he prepared a series of talks at the technical college in January and February 1932; Lilje spoke on "Technology: The Human Being and God," Stolzenburg on "Occultism and Christianity," and Bonhoeffer on "The Right to Self-Assertion." With this Bonhoeffer wanted to address a prevalent feeling among the students at the time and discuss the spreading Nazi "biological" philosophy. His starting point was the dispensability of the members of the masses—among the academic "proletariat" as well; he concluded by speaking about the right to sacrifice one's own life freely for others, the nation, and humanity. The talk showed how greatly Bonhoeffer was still impressed by Indian ideals; he contrasted the "Indian" answer to the question of life, namely, that suffering is better than living by violence, with the "western" answer. His remarks actually verged on a cautious pacifism. War and machinery were aspects of the western solution, he said, but "the machine has made war impossible, not just through its idea of giving people sovereignty over nature and letting them live like that, but also because of its reality."[150]

Bonhoeffer succeeded in having this series of talks announced in the student journal *Die Technische Hochschule*, but only after they were almost over. The same issue of the journal also carried a short article by Bonhoeffer about the newly established student chaplaincy.[151] It was a conscientious effort to address the students and communicate a sense of the church's presence to them:

> Today the average student is alienated from the church. Everyone knows this. Everyone, including the church, also knows the reasons, both the real ones and the purported ones. The church is pondering this phenomenon more seriously than is generally supposed. How successful it will be is another question, and does not depend only upon the church. In any case, the current situation is that people from the groups with various worldviews have begun to notice what is happening in the church again. The church, however, needs nothing less than spectators and nothing more than coworkers. Thus it is appealing as strongly as possible to the students. Whoever looks at things seriously cannot evade the fact that the shape of the future church and that of future Germans are essentially connected. But

the church does not require students to take a stand and become involved for the sake of something else, but because the church is the church.

But the church is not taking itself seriously, but focusing on what has been its task from the beginning. It believes in all seriousness that, during a period marked by the most profound lack of unity among different worldviews, it may and can take its place at the point where worldviews reach their end and something new and ultimate begins. It will proudly preserve what it has, and not try to extol this as something for sale, possibly under a deceptive name. It knows nothing greater than to help with all its means, if this is what is wanted. This is its message to the students when it assigns a student chaplain to join them.

Whoever still believes today that life can be lived in isolation lives in illusion. Matters have become too difficult for that; no one knows this more than the contemporary Protestant pastor. But the student knows this, too, in a special way. And this recognition connects them. Why shouldn't it be that where people ask together, they wrestle together for an answer?

Bonhoeffer believed here that he could make the church interesting, as a place where something is happening; the church had answers where others were no longer responding. But for him it was also a church—and he only wanted to be identified with it if this were so!—that didn't weakly chase after anything and everything. He tried to attribute to it self-identity and solidarity alike.

Bonhoeffer's sermons as a student chaplain give little indication that his audience consisted of engineers and scientists, and he did not have a pulpit of his own at the technical college. He was included in the preaching schedule of Pastor Bronisch-Holtze, the pastor mentioned in Karow's letter. Bronisch-Holtze, however, had served for some time at Trinity Church in the center of Old Berlin; thus Bonhoeffer's audience consisted primarily of students from the university.

The chaplaincy at the college in Charlottenburg fulfilled Bonhoeffer's statutory obligations from 1931 to 1933. It gave him the pulpit he had wanted, albeit in a different place. A student congregation grew out of the audience from his university lectures and the sermons he held for Bronisch-Holtze. When he needed workers for the youth group in Charlottenburg, two theological candidates but only one student from the technical college came forward. Before he left for London in 1933, he made two serious efforts to obtain a parish position in Berlin. His view of the prospects for the chaplaincy at the technical college were so discouraging that, in light of the new political difficulties, no consideration was given to continuing it. When Bonhoeffer left, no successor was named. On the basis of his final report, Bish-op Karow recommended establishing a teaching post in philosophy at the technical college, to be filled by a theologian. But by 1934 this was no longer even feasible.

The Confirmation Class in Wedding. Amid the demands of his first lectures, ecumenical plans, and the beginning of his ministry, the consistory told Bonhoeffer to take over a confirmation class in the Zion parish in the Berlin district of Wedding. The class was out of control; the minister responsible was at the end of his tether, and in fact died several weeks later. Bonhoeffer wrote Sutz that they had "quite literally harassed [him] to death."[152]

Bonhoeffer gave his own account of the first encounter that autumn with the fifty children who were running wild. The elderly minister and Bonhoeffer slowly walked up the stairs of the school building, which was several stories high. The children looked down on them from over the banisters, making an indescribable din and dropping things on the two men ascending the stairs. When they reached the top, the minister tried to force the throng back into the classroom by shouting and using physical force. He tried to announce that he had brought them a new minister who was going to teach them in the future and that his name was Bonhoeffer, and when they heard the name they started shouting "Bon! Bon! Bon!" louder and louder. The old man left the scene in despair, leaving Bonhoeffer standing silently against the wall with his hands in his pockets. Minutes passed. His failure to react made the noise gradually less enjoyable, and he began speaking quietly, so that only the boys in the front row could catch a few words of what he said. Suddenly all were silent. Bonhoeffer merely remarked that they had put up a remarkable initial performance, and went on to tell them a story about Harlem. If they listened, he told them, he would tell them more next time. Then he told them they could go. After that, he never had reason to complain about their lack of attentiveness.

> This is just about the wildest district in Berlin, with the most difficult social and political conditions. At first the boys behaved as if they were crazy, so that for the first time I had real difficulties with discipline. But what helped the most was that I simply told them stories from the Bible with great emphasis, particularly the eschatological passages. Some of them, by the way, were about Negroes. Now there is absolute quiet, the boys see to that themselves. . . .[153]

The Wedding experience had a deep impact on Bonhoeffer. When it was decided that he should continue with the class until they were confirmed, he reduced his other commitments to the minimum. A student remarked, "Not only could we eight confirmation pupils visit him in his apartment on Oder-bergerstrasse, but even in his parents' home on Wangenheimstrasse. . . ." Thus he lived in the same district as his working-class pupils. When Bonhoeffer wanted to stay with one of them who faced a serious operation, he simply left the other students waiting in the lecture room.[154] "I have devoted almost all the second half of the semester to the candidates."[155] He vividly described to Sutz how he set about teaching them:

> For them it is simply new to be given something besides learning the cat-echism. I have based the entire class on the idea of a worshipping com-munity, and the boys, who hear talk of political organizations every day, see very plainly what it is all about.[156]

He devoted his free evenings to his confirmation candidates. They were allowed to come and see him uninvited, to play chess or take English lessons. Each received a present at Christmas. On weekends he took them on trips to youth hostels. Such exercises in community living were still unknown in ordinary German parishes:

> . . . they also see unbelievably clearly what the limitations are, so that again and again when we are talking about the Holy Spirit in the community, the objection comes: "But surely, it's not like that at all. In all these things, the church is far behind any political youth organization or sports club. We feel at home in the club, but in the church?"[157]

The pleasure he took in teaching and gaining the confidence of difficult delinquent boys was contrasted by the difficulties he experienced in his pas-toral visits to the parents. Bonhoeffer felt he was not up to the task and that his theological training had failed to equip him for it. It took a tremendous amount of effort to ring uninvited at a strange door, and make himself and his purpose known. True, the son of the house gave him something to talk about, but:

> To think of those excruciating hours or minutes when I or the other per-son try to begin a pastoral conversation, and how haltingly and lamely it goes on . . .
> I sometimes try to console myself by thinking that this kind of pastoral work is something that just did not exist in earlier times and is quite unchristian. But perhaps it is really the end of our Christianity that we fail here. We have learned to preach again, at any rate a little, but the care of souls?[158]

Five years later Bonhoeffer knew how to give his ordination candidates in Finkenwalde the courage to carry out such pastoral work. Only five years after that, in the solidarity among those in prison, he discovered the right way to approach and speak to people who were not so very different from those in Wedding.

As the day of confirmation approached, Bonhoeffer distributed a huge bolt of cloth for making confirmation suits. The boys were asked to assist with the sermon by telling him what they expected from it. On the day itself, 13 March 1932, election fever prevailed in the streets. For the first time Hitler was running for the presidency of the Reich (Hindenburg won 49 percent of the votes, Hitler 30 percent, Communist leader Ernst Thälmann 13 percent, and Duesterberg of the reactionary *Stahlhelm* group 7 percent). But the confirmation service proceeded undisturbed. Bonhoeffer preached about Jacob at Jabbok:

> No one shall ever deprive you of the faith that God has prepared for you, too, a day and a sun and a dawn, that he guides us to this sun that is called Jesus Christ, that he wishes us to see the promised land in which justice and peace and love prevail, because Christ prevails.[159]

He rephrased the official confirmation vow so that it contained nothing false or impossible to fulfill. He did the same thing later in the words that he used for confirmation in 1938.[160] He invited them to an evening service two days later to celebrate communion.

A few days afterward he took some of those he had confirmed to Friedrichsbrunn at his own cost. He had asked his parents for the use of the country house for Easter. To the boys from Wedding the 150-mile trip was like a journey to the end of the world.

Bonhoeffer wrote his parents a letter of thanks:

> I am delighted to be able to be up here with the confirmation boys; even though they do not show any special appreciation of the woods and nature, they are enthusiastic about climbing in the Bode valley and playing football on the field. It is often by no means easy to keep these predominantly antisocial boys under control, but the domesticity and inhibitions that simply arise in this situation are a great help. Also I think that afterward you will not notice any aftereffects on the house as a result of these occupants. Apart from a broken windowpane, everything is as it was. . . . Only Frau S. [the housekeeper] is somewhat indignant at the proletarian invasion. Hans-Christoph is here with me, and is a great help. It is only possible to get any work done in the early morning (literally from seven to nine

o'clock) and later in the evening, after they have all gone to bed. On Thursday it will all be over. After such an experience one wonders of course what the value of such an enterprise may have been. But in things of this sort one has to wait and see. . . .[161]

Bonhoeffer's work in Wedding officially ended with the boys' confirmation, but his influence and his concern did not. "The instruction went in such a way that I can hardly tear myself away from it."[162] "I have rented nine acres of land outside Berlin and am putting a little wooden house on it. I intend to spend my weekends there with confirmation candidates and students."[163] The boys from Wedding were allowed to go to Biesenthal whenever they liked. A number of them remained in contact with Bonhoeffer until well into the Second World War; one of them, Richard Rother, was employed by brother Klaus's law firm. He published a brief account about Bonhoeffer's class.[164]

The Youth Club. The Wedding experience was soon supplemented by another: the Charlottenburg youth club. His acquaintance with Harry Ward's work in New York was behind this idea, as well as his contact with Siegmund-Schultze and his social work in east Berlin. Bonhoeffer's contact with Siegmund-Schultze grew out of Hildebrandt's connection to it and Bonhoeffer's own new ecumenical duties.

Some of the supporters of the project were non-Christians or people without formal church ties. Anneliese Schnurmann, a Jewish school friend of Dietrich's sister Susanne, was now a student and wished to use part of her wealth for social and educational purposes. The plans originated in the summer of 1932 at a gathering of family and friends in the room of Dietrich's grandmother Julie Bonhoeffer, who encouraged the project and discussed the first practical steps with them. Bonhoeffer also sought the advice of Hans Brandenburg, at the time an inspector at the Berlin City Mission. Brandenburg led Paul Le Seur's Free Youth Center, where socialist and communist youth groups met. Some of the center's programs included voluntary service work and evening classes for the unemployed. Bonhoeffer had met Brandenburg at the working group of the church-social conference, and at his request had held a Bible study on Genesis 1:1 for the young men's circle in the City Mission. On 23 October 1932 Bonhoeffer turned to him:

A woman I know intends sometime next winter to give 430 Reich marks per month for the establishment of a youth club for the unemployed. It would mean finding a heated room during the day for useful activities, if possible job preparation. It shouldn't be hard to find leaders or students, probably through the Student Activities or "academic self-help." . . . I'd particularly like to talk over the following questions with you. Is there any possibility that rooms somewhere might be available for free? Does one have to apply to municipal offices for this—and which ones? What kinds of activities would you particularly recommend? Would material for workshops eventually be available from some offices? What could be done with 430 Reich marks? It was suggested to this woman that she become part of the "Emergency group for the establishment of homes and kitchens for the unemployed." What do you think of this? Since the youth club is to be interconfessional and not affiliated with any party, we could hardly recommend this association. The woman can guarantee the mentioned amount for six months, beyond that she intends to continue it, but cannot yet offer it with certainty.[165]

In response Brandenburg named several municipal offices. Bonhoeffer and Anneliese Schnurmann went to Anna von Gierke, the daughter of a renowned legal scholar, and the project soon got started. Von Gierke directed a youth home in Charlottenburg and had experience in dealing with the city government and the youth welfare office. She brought them in contact with the two directors of the youth club: E. Astfalk, a teacher at the school for social pedagogy, and Hanna Nacken, a handcrafts teacher.

The youth club opened in autumn 1932 on Schlossstrasse in Charlottenburg. There were successes, but they also had difficulties with troublemakers and drinkers, and there were lively arguments with young Communists.

There has been some trouble at the club. . . . Z., together with A., seems to have made himself very unpopular with the boys. A few days ago, apparently when he was drunk, he gave himself out to be the club leader. I think we shall have to show him the door as soon as possible. Otherwise there will be a real row. Apart from that, things are still going well. But we are thinking of moving. The premises are getting too small. What do you think about that? Two theology students are working there. There is also a student from the technical college who would be glad to earn 25 marks a month and will spend three evenings a week at the club.[166]

The new premises were ready by the end of November; the boys worked hard to help, and they moved in on 1 December. On 8 December Bonhoeffer invited Anneliese Schnurmann to the opening party:

There will be sausages, cakes, cigarettes. The boys worked really splendidly during the last few days, and this is a treat that we must indeed give them. The whole thing will cost 20 marks . . . As for the technical college student, I thought it would be a good idea for him to come three evenings a week, offer shorthand lessons and help in other ways, for which he would receive 15 marks from parish funds and 15 marks from you.[167]

The club flourished for only a brief time. As a result of Hitler's accession to power on 30 January 1933, Anna von Gierke was forced out of her job in Charlottenburg, and Anneliese Schnurmann had to leave Germany. The Communist members of the club were harassed on the streets. When he learned that the club was going to be raided, Bonhoeffer spirited them away to his wooden hut in Biesenthal for a short time. After that, the Communists scattered to different parts of Berlin. After police searched the club hoping to find the card index of members, the organizers had to reconcile themselves to closing it. Concern for the unemployed workers now yielded to concern for another, far more deeply branded group of people: the Jews.

New Plans. His experiences in Harlem, Wedding, and the youth club led Bonhoeffer to seek a ministry in the overcrowded slums of east Berlin. His required yearlong "auxiliary service" ended in the autumn of 1932, and he could now look for a parish. The specialized tasks of a student chaplain no longer interested him. Working in west Berlin where he belonged seemed too easy; working in proletarian east Berlin was much more important.

Through a working group of his students, which after 1932 included Wolf-Dieter Zimmermann, Bonhoeffer began to visit the Zimmermann family home often.[168] His father was superintendent of the church district northeast of Alexanderplatz (Church District Berlin I, which later became part of the Friedrichshain district); Zimmermann invited the young associate professor to speak at a meeting of his pastors. Bonhoeffer talked with him about applying for a pastorate in this difficult church district. He also preached a sermon at St. Bartholomew's Church on Königstor, across from the Berlin Mission Society; the text was Jesus' calming of the storm.[169] Faced with the choice between the university and parish work in east Berlin, Bonhoeffer was prepared to follow a call to the latter:

> At present I am faced with a pretty momentous decision, whether to undertake a ministry in Friedrichshain in east Berlin at Easter. . . . So perhaps when you next come to Berlin you will be able to come and see me at the rectory at Friedrichshain, but perhaps not. . . .[170]

Bonhoeffer, however, had competition: Ernst Pätzold, a superintendent from Havelberg who was fifteen years older, a folksy preacher, and well-loved pastor. When the parish council voted on 28 February 1933, Bonhoeffer was defeated by forty-seven votes to twenty-five.[171]

His first application for a pastorate had failed. He was too young, his preaching too severe, and the demands he made on his congregation too strange. Bonhoeffer never spoke of this defeat later. The failure of his next attempt had a bigger impact on him.

Bonhoeffer, along with Franz Hildebrandt, did not abandon the idea of working in east Berlin. Another position became available, once more in Superintendent Zimmermann's district, at the Lazarus Church, further east in the city between the Frankfurter Allee and the Warsaw Bridge. But the Aryan clause was about to be applied to the church, and this made Hildebrandt's appointment unlikely. Bonhoeffer wrote to Barth:

> I knew that I could not accept the pastorate I longed for in this particular neighborhood without giving up my attitude of unconditional opposition to *this* church, without making myself untrustworthy to my people from the start, and without betraying my solidarity with the Jewish Christian pastors—my closest friend is one of them and is at the moment on the brink. So the alternative remained, lecturer or pastor, and if pastor, at any rate not in Prussia.[172]

Thus the political changes prevented Bonhoeffer's wish for closer contact with the working class. This wish was revived in September 1934, when he visited Jean Lasserre's parish in the coal-mining region of northern France; and ten years later, when he encountered the working class in army uniform in Tegel prison, he recalled Wedding and the youth club. In a play he tried to write in Tegel, one of the characters is a gifted but suspicious working-class man named Heinrich.[173] The play centers on the encounter between this underprivileged, rootless individual and the bourgeois Christoph. Both have been wounded and scarred by the deaths of the war; the theme is Christoph's attempt to overcome Heinrich's mistrust through a sovereign confidence in him.

Bonhoeffer had little time to concern himself seriously with church politics between 1931 and 1933, and perhaps he was still too aloof from this issue. Yet there were ominous developments throughout Germany. In 1931 a wedding was celebrated in Königsberg where the bridegroom wore a brown S.A. shirt and the Horst Wessel song was sung (Horst Wessel, a Nazi killed in a brawl, was considered a Nazi martyr). That same year in Greifswald, legal proceedings for slander were brought against a theology student who had refused an invitation from the Republican Students' Association on the ground that he could not associate with people who had "betrayed their fatherland for money."[174] In 1932 Ernst Röhm, the S.A. chief of staff, appointed chaplains for the S.A. group commandos, and Josef Goebbels was married in a Protestant church with a swastika flag on the altar.[175] And in the Berlin church elections in November 1932, the "German Christians" won 2,282 seats on church councils while their opponents won 2,419. Could these developments be ignored?

Bonhoeffer did not join the public debate on the question of ethnic nationalism in the church, in part because he found the issue distasteful. He did not take Schreiner's half-flirtatious 1931 critique "National Socialism and the Question of God" seriously. He wasn't included in the widely discussed booklet, "The Church and the Third Reich," published by Leopold Klotz Press, with its voices for and against; he did not even refer to it in a lecture. He was concerned with building small groups; he was not interested in publicity or journalism.

Instead, in 1932 he was drawn to a small circle of colleagues that would become the important nucleus of Martin Niemöller's Pastors' Emergency League. This study group of theologically active ministers met at the home of Gerhard Jacobi, pastor of the Kaiser Wilhelm Memorial Church, to discuss matters related to "church and ministry."[176] Jacobi and Pastor Hermann Sasse from the St. Mary's parish led the group. While Bonhoeffer also occasionally attended the working group of the church-social conference, he considered himself a member of Jacobi's circle. There he opposed any rash Christian pacifism, only to acknowledge it later as one possibility of faith. It was here that in April 1933 he presented his first pamphlet attacking the Aryan clause. But his criticism and unusual approach, although it made him a stimulating member of the group, also isolated him to some extent. His own view was that "there are a lot of lively people here, but almost no one with whom one can reasonably discuss theology."[177] "Both of us are people who are somehow on the outskirts of our church," he wrote to Sutz.[178]

Behind everything he did or did not do, the feeling remained that something lay ahead of him, which would have to be discovered and lived through. Every now and then the thought crossed his mind that India had something to offer that he must investigate.

> I can hardly think of it [his stay in America] without feeling tremendously attracted by the idea of going abroad again, this time to the East. I don't know yet when. But it cannot be delayed much longer. There must be other people in the world who know more than we do. And in that case it is simply philistine not to go and learn from them. In all events, those peo-

ple are not the Nazis, nor are they our Communists, as I got to know them better during the past winter. The Germans are hopelessly set upon a fixed direction. One can see and know more than the Americans do, but that is not very much.[179]

When his "auxiliary service" in the church ended in the fall of 1932, the plans for India arose once more in family discussions: "In any case you will be comforted to see from this card that I am not yet in India, but am instead sufficiently occupied here," he wrote Anneliese Schnurmann on 2 December 1932.[180]

Preaching. With his tormented search for a personal commitment, Bon-hoeffer may not strike us as an attractive figure during this period. His sketches of a one-sided church theology may seem immature. He was obvi-ously unsure of what he wanted, and kept withdrawing or pursuing new ideas. Only as a preacher was he fully present; here he devoted himself with-out any reservations or qualifications. Preaching was the great event for him. His severe theologizing and critical love for his church were all for its sake, for preaching proclaimed the message of Christ, the bringer of peace. For Bonhoeffer nothing in his calling competed in importance with preaching.

In Barcelona his preaching had still been accompanied by the pleasure of youthful discovery. In New York he had been shocked to discover that "the sermon is degraded to marginal ecclesiastical observations about events of the day"; it was "the telling of edifying examples . . . eager descriptions of one's own religious experiences, which naturally are not given any objec-tively binding character."[181] But now, in the Berlin of 1931–1932, his preach-ing acquired an urgency in which his own questions and determination came alive. There must be no self-deception, no use of religion as an opiate, for "the living Jesus wishes himself to tell the world from the pulpit that in those he enters, fear vanishes."[182] "Every sermon must be an event," he told Franz Hildebrandt.

> One can't preach the Gospel tangibly enough. A truly evangelical sermon must be like offering a child a fine red apple or offering a thirsty man a cool glass of water and then saying: Do you want it?[183]

In comparison, Barcelona was only a stopping point. There the young preacher had relied completely upon himself and the world of his own expe-riences and belief, neither challenged by nor measured against anyone else. Now, during the months shaken by crises, he stood in the center of Berlin before critical listeners who were in turmoil.

Bonhoeffer searched for models. Hans Fischer had given him Barth's 1931 sermon on Lazarus, and now he preached on this text in a completely different way.[184] He asked Sutz for help:

> I simply can't get beyond this way of preaching in which one tries to say everything, and at the end, always has the dreadful pressure of having completely bypassed the essential issue. . . . I would very much like to hear you preach. Then I would know better what is wrong with my sermons.[185]

He always began working on his monthly sermon very early. Once the idea and the form that it should take were fixed in his mind, he wrote it out word for word in a single draft, and made very few corrections after that. This is why nearly all his sermons could be printed posthumously exactly as they were delivered.

Sermons on specific texts were rarer than they had been in Barcelona, but he still showed independence in his choice of passage; indeed the passage selected was a sort of sermon on the situation itself. Although his fidelity toward the text had increased, there was always one leading message he drew from the text and impressed upon his listeners. On two consecutive Sundays, standing in for Gerhard Jacobi at the Kaiser Wilhelm Memorial Church, he once preached two entirely different sermons on the same brief text from Colossians.[186] He did not yet preach as exclusively Christocentrically as he did later in Finkenwalde, or in such an ardently eschatological way as he did in London.

Though he often took liberties with his text, he avoided modernist tricks that twisted the meaning, and did not comment directly on current political or church events. Nevertheless the reference to events of the day, insofar as we can reconstruct them, are unmistakable. They were that much more powerful and convincing to Bonhoeffer's audience at the time.

His sermon on Thanksgiving Day 1931 was preached against the background of the impending unemployment and hunger of that winter. Bonhoeffer's illustrations went beyond the narrow confines of Germany: "We must be prepared for the fact that this winter seven million people in Germany will find no work, which means hunger for fifteen to twenty million people. Another twelve million or more in England, twenty or more in America. At this very moment sixteen million are starving in China and the position is not much better in India."[187] On Memorial Sunday in 1932, the church's words against the glorification of war heroes clearly reflected the greater context, which included the demonstrations against Günther Dehn in Halle. There had hardly ever been a Memorial Day service as filled with tension. Bonhoeffer said:

We all sense it: there is no disturbance wanted here, there is no disharmony wanted here; [they] want everyone here to go along without exception,
[they] don't want anyone here to see something that the others don't see,
and when this does happen, then the attempt must be made to get rid of
such a person. And so it happens that such visionaries are thrown out of
the assembled company in disgrace, hunted out of the people that they
wished to serve. . . . Seers have never been popular, and thus the church is
not popular either, least of all on such days.[188]

Brüning finally resigned at the beginning of June; Franz von Papen
became Reich chancellor. Many Germans expected the new Christian conservative government to restore stability. But on 12 June 1932 Bonhoeffer
preached incisively in the Kaiser Wilhelm Memorial Church against the
Papen government's misuse of God's name:

We read that a government has proclaimed that a whole nation is to be
saved from collapse—by the Christian worldview. So we, individually and
as a nation, are escaping from an inconceivable final catastrophe. "In the
name of God, amen," is again to be the slogan, religion is again to be cultivated, and the Christian view of life is to be spread. How very meager,
weak and pitiful all this sounds: Do we believe that we will truly let ourselves be taken in by this "In the name of God, amen"? That all our actions
shall be governed by it? That we, rich and poor, Germans and French, will
allow ourselves to be united by the name of God? Or is there not concealed
behind our religious trends our ungovernable urge toward . . . power—in
the name of God to do what *we* want, and in the name of the Christian
worldview to stir up and play off one people against another? . . . Our disobedience is not that we are so irreligious, but that we are very glad to be
religious . . . very relieved when some government proclaims the Christian
worldview . . . so that the more pious we are, the less we let ourselves be told
that God is dangerous, that God will not be mocked.[189]

One week later, again in the Kaiser Wilhelm Memorial Church, he
attacked the church for having given a false twist to the words "seek the
things that are above" from the Epistle to the Colossians: the church, he said,
was turning what was really a stubborn worldly protest into the opium of
false self-satisfaction. He then went on to speak some words whose clair-
voyance, hidden even to himself, would become plain only ten years later:

We should not be surprised if times return for our church, too, when the
blood of martyrs will be called for. But this blood, if we really have the
courage and the fidelity to shed it, will not be so innocent and clear as that

of the first witnesses. On our blood a great guilt would lie: that of the useless servant.[190]

Bonhoeffer understood the emotions of those years well, but saw through them:

> It is not difficult at present to talk of freedom, and to do so in such a way that a German's passions are roused and so completely agitated that he forgets everything else. In present-day Germany there may be many like the ancient Israelites in captivity who, deeply absorbed in themselves, were able to dream of nothing but liberty, and saw great visions of it and grasped for it, until they awakened and the vision faded. . . .[191]

He preached this on 24 July 1932. On 31 July nearly 38 percent of the German electorate voted for Hitler's party.

By the time Bonhoeffer took the pulpit again, after the late summer vacation of 1932, there was another election. Hitler's share of the vote dropped to about 33 percent. Bonhoeffer directed his words less toward the German people as toward the church, which was celebrating the anniversary of the Reformation. His words were more provocative than ever before:

> It should gradually have become clear to us that we are in the twelfth hour of the life of our Protestant church, so that not much more time remains before it is decided whether everything is over or whether a new day is to begin. . . . [The fanfares of the Reformation celebrations are the fanfares for a funeral.] The day of the Reformation celebrations is an evil day. The thousand fanfares that today bear witness to the mortal illness of Germany also proclaim the death of the church in the world. . . . The church of the Reformation . . . does not see that whenever it says "God," God turns against it. *We* sing "A mighty fortress is our God," . . . but *God* says: "I have this against you!"[192] The church that is celebrating the Reformation does not let Luther rest in peace, he must be dragged in to justify all the evil that is taking place in the church. The dead man is propped up in our churches, made to stretch out his hands and point to this church, and repeat with self-confident pathos: Here I stand, I can do no other. . . . It is simply untrue, or it is unpardonable frivolity and pride, when we hide behind this statement. We can do otherwise! . . .[193]

He questioned the point of the churches' protests against secularism and godlessness, against Catholicism, disbelief, and immorality, against all those who took no notice of the protest of that day. "Leave the dead Luther in peace at last and listen to the Gospel!" He ended his sermon to the congregation of the Reformation, who had learned the concept "by faith alone":

> It may sound almost indecent on Reformation day. . . . Do the first things.
> . . . The story of the destruction of Jerusalem by pagans is beginning to have
> a terribly immediate significance for us. However it may come about—it
> would be better for us today to avoid grand statements about our heroic
> deeds in such a catastrophe—God is the Lord![194]

Reich president Hindenburg is said to have attended this service, but this
may be incorrect. In addition to the regular student chaplain's "academic
worship services" occasionally held in the evenings, the less frequent "university services" were held in the morning. Professors of theology preached
at these; Bonhoeffer was not yet among their ranks. Hindenburg would
have attended the university service that Reformation Day, which was also
the opening worship service for the semester. He regularly attended this
service. It was a pompous occasion: the corps, fraternities, and associations
of eastern Germans marched in with flags and full regalia. This service was
certainly more impressive and not as shocking.

Before many weeks passed a new note had crept into Bonhoeffer's sermons. They became more consoling, more confident of victory, and more
defiant. The first sermon after Hitler's accession to power dealt with Gideon,
the champion of God, who attacked and conquered with an absurdly small
force.

Within his own family Bonhoeffer was somewhat obstinate when he
had to assume the role of pastor. His personal reticence was intensified by the
concern that here he was least able to avoid abbreviating the text, even when
that suggested itself. When he could not avoid it he held the ceremonies,
struggling to express the substance of the text while satisfying general
expectations.[195]

Ecumenism

Work at Home. When he returned from Cambridge as a youth secretary of
the ecumenical movement his first task was to acquaint himself more closely with the ecumenical organizations already active in Germany, and to link
up with their activities as quickly as possible. Some groups welcomed him
as a stimulus; others regarded him as an ambitious intruder. What did he
find in the realm of ecumenical youth work in his native land?

The most important group for him was the National Evangelical Youth
Circle for Promoting Ecumenical Friendship, which had been founded and
sponsored by Siegmund-Schultze in 1930. This group included representatives of the major Protestant youth organizations, and those of the free

churches and other independent organizations. Thus Pastor Friedrich Peter, national leader of the eastern German Youth Federation and an early member of the Nazi Party, got into ecumenical work in 1933—the same year he became the "German Christian" bishop of Magdeburg. The working group saw its task as spreading the ecumenical idea throughout the various regions of Germany; after October 1930, it distributed news bulletins. The Baptist leader Herbert Petrick coordinated these various activities and prepared the youth delegation to Cambridge with Siegmund-Schultze.[196]

The German World Alliance office sponsored its own Berlin student group, which was already holding conferences in 1929 and 1930 in the building of the Alliance for Resolute Christianity in Woltersdorf. Superintendent Diestel, Dr. Karl Thieme, Dr. Walter Gutkelch, and others gave talks there.

In Rhineland and Westphalia a working group of young pastors formed at the instigation of General Superintendent Wilhelm Zoellner, primarily to study the issues of Faith and Order. The initiatives of consistory council member Dr. A. W. Schreiber, who invited various interested parties to ecumenical evenings in his home, have already been mentioned.

None of these groups had much influence, but they illustrate the extent to which the new ecumenical movement had roots in pre-Nazi Germany. They show that there were other ecumenical spirits besides the professors named earlier and the church notables whose names appeared in the newspapers.

The Central Office. While Bonhoeffer was still in America various groups had combined to form an umbrella organization called the German Central Office for Ecumenical Youth Work, under the general jurisdiction of Dr. August Schreiber and the Church Federation Office. Their intent was not to add another organization to existing ones, but to devote more attention to their common interests. Professor Wilhelm Stählin of Münster became director of the Central Office and Herbert Petrick from the administrative office of the World Alliance initially served as secretary. The Central Office had three tasks: (1) the joint theological study of ecumenical problems, which necessarily took them beyond the realm of "youth work"—in fact, a number of older and more experienced theologians spoke at the first big conference in April 1932; (2) to promote the ecumenical idea more effectively; and (3) to organize information services, conferences, and international exchanges.

Thus when Bonhoeffer returned from Cambridge an agency already existed that gave him a base from which to work. As an international secretary he soon began to play an important role and replaced Petrick. He was able to use Schreiber's ecumenical office in the Church Federation building.

The chief obstacles were financial and political. Soon after the Cambridge conference H. L. Henriod wrote to his impatient industrious youth secretary that it had been decided in Cambridge that "the youth commission should be active and effective to the maximum with a minimum of means."[197] When Bonhoeffer pointed out that "at present we cannot expect any German participant to be in a position to contribute to his own expenses,"[198] Henriod reassured him that the Geneva budget had been increased.

The political difficulties had to be worked out at home. The 1931 Hirsch-Althaus statement had a particular impact among the youth. As *Christliche Welt* reported on 1 February 1932:

> The national leader of the German Evangelical youth organizations, Dr. Stange, has replied to an invitation to international meetings that the sending of a German delegation is out of the question and that [the Germans] await a clear word of protest against the injustice and rape [i.e., of Germany by the victors of World War I].[199]

Stange's statement was announced even before the Geneva disarmament conference had begun, and the German YMCA explicitly supported him. On 4 April Bonhoeffer reported at the committee meeting in London about the opposition to this and the measures being planned to deal with it:

> . . . the YMCA would not be sending any delegates to international conferences this year. A Central Organization for youth of all religions had been formed [i.e., the Central Office] which cooperated in finding delegates for conferences. Dr. Stählin was President, and Herr Bonhoeffer Secretary. They were producing a list of names of young people who were willing to come to international conferences.[200]

Bonhoeffer found delegates such as Karl G. Steck, Karl Nold, Dietrich von Oppen, and Werner Koch, whom Lilje had recommended. Also among them was Fritz Söhlmann, who later became editor of *Junge Kirche* (at that time called *Vormarsch*), a "monthly Protestant magazine for politics and culture," whose contributors included Eberhard Müller, Ernst zur Nieden, Anna Paulsen, Hermann Sasse, and Hermann Strathmann. Finally, Bonhoeffer could also begin to draw upon a small circle of his students (they comprised the entire German youth delegation to the Fanö meeting). All these people were ready to attend such "international meetings" despite the slanderous attacks on these gatherings.

Conferences in Germany. The Central Office made a good start with a theological conference at the Church Federation Office on 29–30 April 1932. Very much the work of Dietrich Bonhoeffer, it was typically German in the sense that it was exclusively concerned with the theological basis of ecumenical work. As William Temple, then Archbishop of York, wrote rather impatiently to his wife in 1934:

> The Germans can never discuss what to do tomorrow without showing how their view depends on the divine purpose in creation—the existence of which must therefore be first established.[201]

The "divine purpose in creation" was indeed a focal point of the discussion. People's thinking about this "purpose" could have serious consequences, as became evident very quickly in 1933. The conference worked on the two topics that Bonhoeffer regarded as the fundamental questions of ecumenical work: "The Church and the Churches" and "The Church and the Nations," in other words, the confessional question and the peace question, or the continuum of tradition and the current relevance of its tasks. The chief debate focused on the question of the nation and its dignity "according to creation." Although profound divisions within the group were apparent in the final result, and Bonhoeffer noted a "deep bewilderment" that required a continuation of the conference in autumn, he was glad to prepare the continuation. He did so in good conscience, contributed to it vigorously, and finally reported on it at length.[202] The differences that are evident in Bonhoeffer's report already reveal the fronts that would emerge in the church struggle between the German Christians and their church committees, the Lutheran Council, and the moderate and radical wings of the Confessing church.

The two main speakers at the meeting were Zoellner and Stählin. The senior ecumenical experts Deissmann, Diestel, and Knak spoke; the younger generation was represented by Hanns Lilje and Theodor Heckel, at the time the foreign expert in the Church Federation Office and known as a good reformed theologian. Finally, the National Socialist pastor Peter spoke energetically and at some length. Bonhoeffer was the youngest speaker at the conference. He was dissatisfied with the theological arguments that had been presented. With Lilje's support he opposed the older generation, and maintained that ecumenical work was evading the truth if it did not grapple anew with the concept and reality of heresy. He vigorously attacked the idea of "orders of creation" that Wilhelm Stählin introduced. Peter spoke tirelessly about the deployment of "teams ready for the defense" of the state and the *Volk*. He was also the first participant to deliver copies of his excessively long speeches to Bonhoeffer to be printed in the conference proceedings.

Bonhoeffer's report in *Die Eiche* of these discussions was intended to serve as preparation for the second conference, held 9–10 December 1932. The invitation to the meeting, signed by him and Stählin, said: "In connection with our previous discussion, this time both the questions raised will be discussed, that is, the theological place of the *Volk* and the meaning of *confession* in connection with the ecumenical movement."[203] This time the conference was held jointly with the Berlin meeting of the German Ecumenical Study Group, on which the Stockholm, Lausanne, and World Alliance organizations and their subcommittees—to an extent still peaceably—had a vote. A new note emerged in the negotiations about the invitations, since the others now very much wanted to replace Peter. As director of the Central Office, Stählin recommended:

> Recently I had a very good talk at the Student Working committee at the YMCA with Missions Inspector Weichert [from the Berlin Mission] and was deeply impressed by his seriousness and broad perspective. But I could understand the reservations against inviting him, because he is a member of the Reich Office of the Nazi Party. But he really is a very different type than someone like Peter.[204]

Bonhoeffer let Schreiber vote, and Weichert was invited. Later he was among the authors of the more moderate "New Guidelines of the German Christians" of 16 May 1933, which was signed by Ludwig Müller, Karl Fezer, Joachim Hossenfelder, and Ludwig Weichert; these guidelines were characterized by certain populist and missionary tendencies, and were less strident about the "Jewish question." In any case, Weichert withdrew from the German Christians on 31 May 1933.

They decided not to publish a report on the December meeting of the Central Office in *Die Eiche*, since it would not bring "anything essentially new to light,"[205] and they were totally preoccupied with a conference of the Church Federation Office in the spring.

This conference met from 6 to 9 March 1933 in Dassel. Zoellner chaired the meeting; Zänker and Stählin spoke, and Lilje, Sasse, Freytag, Menn, Eger, Marahrens, and Diestel also attended. The topics were similar to those of the Central Office meeting, focusing on "national and international" problems and "Confession and Truth." The 1932–1933 annual report of the World Alliance described the Dassel meeting as the "continuation of a discussion which took place on the 9th of December 1932 at the headquarters of the Church Federation in Berlin on 'Common points of view for German ecumenical work.'"

Two contributions to the discussion from Bonhoeffer, dealing with the confessional problem, have survived.[206] Both are very condensed, and reveal that Bonhoeffer was already the conscious Lutheran he had always wanted to be in the ecumenical movement and that he later proved himself to be in his 1935 statement of principles. He insisted on two things: the necessity of avoiding the danger of confessional relativism, and the necessity of easing the rigidity of confessional absolutism. One of the subjects of the Dassel conference was "Confession and Truth," and he tried to show that the truth of the Word was twofold, representing both the word of God and the confessional word of the Christian church-community.

> Ecumenical dialogue is achieved in the confessional profession of faith and thus, with human modesty, in making one's position known to others. . . . The Lutheran message is this recognition of the church in atonement.[207]

This theological proposition advocated in Dassel would reemerge later, in a more refined form, in Bonhoeffer's battle to gain a place for the Confessing church in the ecumenical movement.[208]

Local Involvement. Bonhoeffer could not completely evade the demands on him made by the local and national branches of the World Alliance; these groups, after all, were his base. They had been instrumental in giving him entry into the ecumenical movement. A busy study program was organized for 1932 in Berlin, and as part of this Bonhoeffer spoke about the social gospel, his impressions of the topic still fresh. He did not rely solely on his own impressions, but devoted a great deal of correspondence to securing a copy of Visser 't Hooft's book on the subject, which was very difficult to obtain. Bonhoeffer's criticism of the social gospel was less violent than was expected. He criticized its shortcomings at conferences abroad, but at home he felt it more important to acknowledge its merits. The kingdom of God "on earth is truly biblical and is the opposite of an otherworldly view of the kingdom!"[209]

At the national level of the World Alliance's activities, the wind was blowing ever more strongly against the ecumenical movement and its "internationalism" and pacifist tendencies. In 1932 the annual conference of the German World Alliance office had to be canceled; the excuse given was the disastrous economic circumstances. In 1933, however, after the invitations to a conference in Herrnhut had already been sent out, they were withdrawn for what were obviously political reasons. For a time the World Alliance lived on in local but very lively groups in the German provinces, but

nationally it came to a standstill in 1932. By 1933, the local groups that
wanted to cling to Bonhoeffer's view of peace on earth as a commandment
of the Gospel and build upon the increasingly crucial foundation of "confession" had to renounce all publicity and go into the catacombs.

The more official church organizations of Life and Work and Faith and
Order had a somewhat stronger position. After the 1932 meetings they
began taking an interest in the young ecumenist who laid such emphasis on
theology. In 1933 Faith and Order invited Bonhoeffer to join the German
preparatory committee of the Lausanne movement, and he was invited to a
meeting that fall.[210] The pioneers of this movement included Wilhelm Zoellner, Martin Dibelius, Hermann Sasse, Georg Wobbermin, Heinz Renkewitz,
and August Lang. Bonhoeffer was immediately asked to lead one of the
working groups that were preparing the 1937 conference to mark the tenth
anniversary of Faith and Order, but his departure for London thwarted this.
His contacts with Faith and Order were revived through Leonard Hodgson,
the secretary-general, in 1935. An important correspondence ensued, but did
not result in cooperation; on the contrary, it uncovered deep and perhaps
tragic differences between the two men.

International Youth Secretary. The emphasis of Bonhoeffer's ecumenical
activities was on relations with churches abroad. Compared to most of his
German colleagues, his combination of overseas experience, a knowledge of
foreign languages unusual among German theologians of his era, and his
theological training put him in a class by himself. For his foreign counter-
parts, particularly those from English-speaking countries, he sometimes
seemed all too German in his devotion to theological analysis, which they
saw as an impractical hindrance. Still, they did not note only his obstinacy
but also his charm, humor, and "good fellowship."

He himself felt as if he were in a magnetic field between powerful alter-
nating attracting and repelling forces. Nowhere else did he find so many
allies for his ongoing call for peacemaking as among these foreigners, but
they showed little understanding of his theological arguments for it.

In October 1931, soon after his return from Cambridge, Bonhoeffer sent
the first letters to organizations within his European area of responsibility in
preparation for the big youth conference planned for 1932. He wanted to get
preparations under way in good time and to have facts and figures on the
unemployment problem, for example, ready for discussion.

His first major goal was the 1932 conference in Gland. In keeping with
a tradition established years before, a number of so-called regional conferences were also planned. The first that Bonhoeffer attended was not in his

area of responsibility. It was in Epsom, London, associated with a routine meeting of the entire Youth Committee there.

Epsom, London. The timing of the meeting was poor for Bonhoeffer. In order to attend the meeting in London on 4 April 1932 he had to leave his Wedding confirmation pupils in Friedrichsbrunn ahead of time. He wanted to be back in Berlin on the 10th, however, so as not to miss the second round of the Reich presidential elections; moreover, Barth was scheduled to be in Berlin that day. Thus Bonhoeffer met his new friends from Cambridge somewhat hurriedly, and he had little positive news to report. The French delegate, P. C. Toureille, was in a more favorable position. The protocol reads: "On the whole the young people [in France—the author] were favourable to internationalism . . . while their parents were not. The opposite was true in Germany." The meeting dealt primarily with the upcoming conference in Gland. Representatives from Life and Work (H. W. Fox, Burlingham, and Steele) were there, since the Gland meeting was to be carried out together with Life and Work.

Epsom was a French-English regional conference; it was organized by Craske and Toureille. Bonhoeffer's report in *Die Eiche* shows that he was a critical guest.[211] He felt that the meeting lacked a foundation of solid theological work, and mainly showed a "fine feeling of international friendship."[212] He was too impatient to be satisfied with the mere exchange of information. Thus, despite his appreciation of the excellent hospitality, in a private letter to Sutz he rather offhandedly dismissed the affair as "a very superfluous meeting."[213]

Westerburg. He took a more favorable view of the Franco-German regional conference that he and Toureille organized in Westerburg in the Westerwald on 12–14 July. The theme was "The Unity of Franco-German Protestantism between Catholicism and Bolshevism." The conference was overshadowed by the revival of old Franco-German tensions, because the unyielding attitude of the French spokespeople had made the Geneva disarmament negotiations hopeless and the German delegation had withdrawn. But the direct confrontation of these differences by young people from both countries was very worthwhile. Papers for discussion had been "long since prepared and in part exchanged."[214] Bonhoeffer introduced the meeting, followed by talks by Karl Nold and a Frenchman. In the evening Fritz Söhlmann and August de Haas, a Reformed minister from Dresden who later became an uncompromising champion of the Confessing church, presented the German viewpoint. Haas told the French what they could expect from National Socialism.

In his report on the ensuing discussion in *Die Eiche*, Bonhoeffer claimed, as he would later do in his 1941 memorandum to the British from Geneva, that "the greatest share of responsibility" for the phenomenon of Nazism in its present form "must be attributed to the policy of foreign countries."[215] The conference proved to be so fruitful that a study group was appointed to prepare for a similar conference in 1933. Later that year Bonhoeffer referred to it in a sermon at the technical college:

> I shall never forget the day on which this text [Daniel 10] first made its impact on me. It was at a meeting of young French and Germans; we had met on the common ground of the church and wished to discuss the things that lay between us, to submit ourselves to the commandment of God in our time under the commandment of "peace on earth." . . . we were all full of fear and dismay about our message . . . and when we were together, somewhat alarmed, a young Frenchman read out these words . . . and when he came to the words [spoken to Daniel] "fear not, peace be with you," we all felt that afterward we could say, "Let my Lord speak, for you have strengthened me."[216]

Ciernohorské Kúpele. Ten days after the Westerburg conference, while the campaign in Berlin for the 31 July elections was in full swing, Bonhoeffer was back on the train. This time he was on his way to Czechoslovakia, representing Diestel, who was ill, and knowing that three weeks later he would have to travel again to more meetings. He made the trip with understandable reluctance, but the result was one of his most important contributions to the ecumenical movement and the peace question.

He was to take part in a youth conference on peace at Ciernohorské in the Carpathians—during the days of the old Austrian empire the place had been known as Bad Schwarzenberg. The initiative for the conference came from the young Czechoslovakian church under Patriarch Prochazka. The ecclesiastical, financial, and political roadblocks had been overcome by Franz M. Hnik, whose efforts as international secretary of the Central Council of the Czechoslovakian Church to make his church part of the ecumenical witness were successful.[217] The conference was attended by I. C. Bacon, director of the Cambridge youth conference; Burlingham, the London World Alliance secretary; H. W. Fox from London; Patriarch Prochazka; Bishop Stejskal; Alois Spisar, a systematic theologian from Prague; Professor Rádl; Dr. Zilka, dean of the Prague Hus faculty; Toureille from Paris; and a Miss Hoffer from Vienna. Among topics like "Present-Day Youth and Its Attitude to Spiritual Ideals" or "Public Opinion and World Peace," the title of Bonhoeffer's address—"On the Theological Basis of the Work of the

World Alliance"—sounded modest and boring. It may indeed have seemed unimportant and tedious to some members of his audience, although they were all given a well-prepared summary in advance.[218]

Bonhoeffer's words went far beyond the scope of the topic of the conference; for many of the delegates the implications of his introductory statement that "there is still no theology of the ecumenical movement" were incalculable.[219] Had the World Alliance ever seen itself in the light in which he presented it? Was it capable of seeing itself in that light? Bonhoeffer himself noted that his reflections isolated him somewhat: "I have just returned . . . from a very mediocre conference, which once more makes me doubt the value of all this ecumenical work." He deplored the lack of discussion of the basic issues involved, and continued self-critically: "[I] tried to assuage my theological conscience, but there are simply too many question marks."[220]

Bonhoeffer's attack was threefold:

1. He criticized the older ecumenists, who shirked the task of establishing a theological foundation for their work. This had made ecumenical committees ad hoc bodies, dependent on changes in the political climate. They comforted themselves by referring to the existence of Faith and Order as an organization in which ecumenical theology was being developed, but that was a mistake. The absence of an ecumenical theology had made the World Alliance practically defenseless against the latest attacks: "Anyone engaged in ecumenical work must suffer the charges of being unconcerned with the Fatherland and unconcerned with the truth, and any attempt at an encounter is quickly cried down."[221]

2. He attacked the nationalism that was aligned with confessionalism, and cited the instance of the *Allgemeine Lutherische Kirchenzeitung*, which had opened its columns to the propaganda of Hirsch and Althaus. Theologically he attacked the concept of the "orders of creation."

3. He criticized the Anglo-Saxon ideals of the kingdom of God and peace, manifested in the tendency of conferences to pass premature resolutions.

The World Alliance's work of trying to reach understanding had no meaning for Bonhoeffer, unless it led to a "great proclamation that brings us together." Meetings that did not search for this "wasted their time in idle talk"; "understanding in the best and truest sense comes only through present preaching and theology."[222] The World Alliance should therefore take up the almost impossible challenge of becoming a "church." Bonhoeffer never wished for anything less than that. This implied that the World Alliance had to go beyond the stage of collecting comparative church statistics and tackle the issue of confession. Yet it could become a "church" only by delivering the message of peace that it had specifically adopted. It should not give reasons for the truth of this message, but deliver it: "The church must . . . resist any attempt at a justification of God's commandment. It delivers it, and that is all."[223] But there would be sharp disharmony, for "the truth is divided. And that must make our word powerless, indeed false"; but that is what would truly promote the efforts of an ecumenical existence.[224]

This is how ambitious Bonhoeffer's view of the ecumenical movement was. Only a few followed him. Later, during the church struggle, the majority regarded it as imprudent to acknowledge these consequences. In 1932 Hermann Sasse was one of the few who persisted in asking the same kinds of questions, and sensed the connection between the confessional problem and the issue of peace.

Siegmund-Schultze was the only one at the time to respond to Bonhoeffer's arguments. He also noted, of course, that the liberal-humanist foundation of the World Alliance was crumbling away. In the last lead article in *Die Eiche* in 1932 he cited the discrediting of internationalism as the "outstanding characteristic" of the ecumenical crisis.[225] He agreed with Bonhoeffer that the World Alliance would perish because of its dependence on the political situation, unless it could channel the overdue work on an ecumenical theology along more certain lines.

Bonhoeffer's own report on the Ciernohorské Kúpele conference was more encouraging.[226] He said that the way to peace must be opened despite everything, and that the "internationalists" must be given the support needed to do this. Two years later, when matters had become much more critical, he met many friends from this conference again in Fanö. Although he arrived late in Ciernohorské Kúpele, he left before the conference ended, in order to vote against Hitler and the German nationalists on 31 July.

Meetings in Geneva. Immediately before Bonhoeffer attended his first meeting of the whole executive committee of the World Alliance, in connection with the Gland conference, the Ecumenical Council of Life and Work met in Geneva (7–14 August 1932). Bonhoeffer was not present at this meeting, so he did not meet all the leading figures in the council.

But the significance of the decisions made at that meeting would become evident only during the turbulent years that followed. It was not only that Karl Barth was elected to the theological committee of Life and Work— Bonhoeffer found this a hopeful sign—nor that there was progress in the consolidation of the youth committees, with Henriod's appointment as general secretary of the World Alliance and of Life and Work. The most significant development was the election (against the rules) of Bishop George Bell of Chichester as president of the Ecumenical Council. After the bishop of

Winchester's death in 1932, before his term as president had expired, Archbishop Hermann Davidson appointed Bell to take his place. At the same time, at Kapler's suggestion, the Geneva office extended the Anglican president's term of office by two years, on the grounds that the reorganization of relations with other ecumenical bodies and the preparations for another world conference (the outcome was the 1937 Oxford conference) required the continuity of an experienced leader like Bell. The significance of this decision would become clear in the years ahead: in 1933 and 1934 the Confessing church had someone in that position who used the full status and prestige of his office on its behalf. Orthodox Archbishop Lukas Germanos served in 1935 and 1936 as regularly elected president, but he was hardly in a position to wage the conflict with Reich bishop Ludwig Müller as Bell had.

Bonhoeffer got to know some of these leaders better in August 1932, not through the Ecumenical Council, but at the meeting of the working committee of the World Alliance (19–22 August 1932), where he also met the head of the committee, Danish Bishop Valdemar Ammundsen. Ammundsen and Bell were the two men on whom Bonhoeffer set great hopes for the future. On this occasion Bonhoeffer also met Gandhi's friend, C. F. Andrews, whom he would hardly have met in Life and Work.

No one envisioned a merger of the World Alliance and the Ecumenical Council. When Bell asked how the splintering of the international Christian organizations was to be prevented, Ammundsen wrote:

> Life and Work is the form with the broadest scope and is the most important. But its organisation is very heavy and its financial position is rather precarious. The World Alliance has a more limited object, but its central organization is more effective, and its financial basis is somewhat better, owing to grants from the Church Peace Foundation. I am afraid that an amalgamation now would only tie the World Alliance down to the heavier body, without helping Life and Work sufficiently.[227]

The two bodies never merged. The World Alliance was dissolved in 1948; its objectives were expressed somewhat differently through the Prague Peace Conference ten years later. Not all the topics discussed during those hot August days at the École Internationale in Geneva were of interest to the new member in an open-necked shirt.

In the wake of the frustration and disappointment caused by the failure of its last meeting, a new position on the disarmament conference was taken.[228] In a sermon at the opening of the disarmament conference in Geneva, William Temple had said:

One clause there is in the existing treaties which offends in principle the Christian conscience and for the deletion of which by proper authority the voice of Christendom must be raised. This is the clause which affixes to one group of belligerents in the Great War the whole guilt for its occurrence. . . . We have to ask not only who dropped the match but who strewed the ground with gunpowder.[229]

The Commission on Minorities had long been a member organization of the World Alliance, and Bishop Ammundsen was its chairman. Under his wing in 1933 Bonhoeffer was able to sound the alarm—as the conference in Sofia would make clear—and make suggestions for combating the Aryan clause.

It was a great surprise to Bonhoeffer and his French cosecretary Toureille when Wilfred Monod, whom the Germans had always regarded as a stubborn French nationalist, presented a memorandum suggesting a reexamination of World Alliance's principles and task precisely along the lines Bonhoeffer had indicated in Ciernohorské Kúpele: through the biblical and dogmatic inquiry into the principles of Christian unity, peace aims, and more clarification of what course should be taken. A debate immediately arose between the veterans, who vigorously opposed plunging into theological questions, and "others, particularly the younger ones," who "all the more vigorously called for an 'ecumenical theology.'"[230] As a result of this debate, the working committee in Sofia asked Bonhoeffer in 1933 to draft proposals in response to Monod's memorandum. This did not go any further, but there is a direct connection between Monod's memorandum and Bonhoeffer's peace speech in Fanö.

C. F. Andrews argued forcefully that east Asia should be included much more in the organization's work, but his proposal that a delegation should be sent there was unsuccessful.

Finally a publications committee was proposed, and Bonhoeffer was suggested as its chairperson. Its object was to publish a newsletter.

The Gland Conference. On 25–31 August, about sixty delegates from all over the world met in Gland, on Lake Geneva, for a joint youth conference of the World Alliance and the Ecumenical Council. Arthur Burroughs, the bishop of Ripon, presided over the meeting, assisted by the three youth secretaries and Mr. Steele from Life and Work.

After long negotiations, it had been agreed that the main theme of the conference should be "the call of Christianity in the present crisis"; the unemployment problem was relegated to second place. Bonhoeffer felt that he had not succeeded in pushing through his ideas. He found the program too concerned with the economic and international crisis and too little with the call of Christianity, which—as we see from his speech in Ciernohorské Kúpele—seemed to him far more appropriate at a Christian gathering. He invited Sutz to the conference, "which is only partially under my leadership. In all events, I already feel I am not responsible for its course. The British have now put their fingers in the pie too much for that . . . though in spite of everything it will perhaps be quite interesting."[231]

Bonhoeffer's student Werner Koch was to step in for Karl Nold; another student, Karl Steck, eventually joined them. Bonhoeffer wrote to Koch:

> Don't be scared off by the program. It has to look this way to please the English. What we do with it is another question. . . . Based on previous experience, I think it is decisively important for us to make a strong case for the theological agenda. . . .[232]

To Bonhoeffer the difficulty lay in the insufficiently discussed and very different understandings of the concept of the kingdom of God that prevailed on the European continent and in the Anglo-Saxon countries.

Toureille, Zernov, and Bonhoeffer gave short opening speeches on the general theme of the conference. Bonhoeffer's speech has not survived; all that remains is a mention of it in the bishop of Ripon's report for the *Yorkshire Post*:

> Opening addresses by the French and German "Youth Secretaries" of the World Alliance quickly struck the keynote of these two national approaches. The Frenchman [Toureille] emphasized that there are no cheap remedies for such conditions as we have to face. The refrain of the German was the Old Testament word: "We know not what we should do, but our eyes are unto Thee," as the expression of a pessimism that verged on passivism. A young Russian [Dr. Zernov from Paris] who followed gave a more constructive picture of an "organic society," in which the creative principle is love.[233]

Thus Bonhoeffer had pursued the thinking in his Exaudi Sunday sermon[234] and his remarks in Ciernohorské Kúpele. He was unable to make a convincing case for his passionate protest at the overhastiness of the British program; the British delegates misunderstood him, thinking that it was an example of German pessimism and passive tendencies. Nonetheless, he drew some support from outside the German delegation. Burroughs quoted the statement of an Indian delegate, Mr. Thacore: "The church has produced Christian activity faster than Christian faith and character."

A broad spectrum of speakers had been won for the conference, including two representatives from the International Labor Organization in Geneva, Tait and van Haan; André Philip, Professor Picard, C. F. Andrews, Lauga-Paris, and Henry Smith Leiper from the Federal Council of Churches in New York.

There were four discussion groups; Bonhoeffer led the German-speaking one. He gave the debate free rein and ample time for a discussion about capitalism, the industrial age, and the situation in India (C. F. Andrews's focus throughout the conference). His group and the French group issued a report that approached Bonhoeffer's intentions:

> ... the church must formulate very precise demands in the name of Jesus, no generalities; judgement has to be pronounced on capitalism and nationalism. . . . We need a new church today for the accomplishment of such divine messages."

But the battle began over a British resolution calling for a public statement: "For we believe that youth will still listen to a message in spite of its outspoken criticism and apparent indifference to the church." Bonhoeffer, however, favored a "qualified silence," and opposed this discarding of religion. His view succeeded. "With that, another proposal or resolution or official message suggested by the Anglo-Saxons was passionately rejected. . . . This very new work should not be so unduly burdened right at the outset. We must learn to wait,"[235] he wrote in his reports.

Bonhoeffer's authority increased measurably in the course of the conference. When Bishop Ammundsen, scheduled to deliver a "summing up message," had to cancel at the last minute, Bonhoeffer was asked to step in. He gave an impressive speech and, this time, did a better job of communicating his thoughts to the English.[236] He replied to the allegation that he was basically pessimistic; he spoke concretely about the burning issues in the world situation, but without diminishing the claims of the church and theology:

> We are not an organization to expedite church action, but we are a definite form of the church itself. . . . The World Alliance is the terrified, anxious church of Christ that has pricked up its ears. . . . and calls upon the Lord.[237]

In the course of the conference a personal concern of his had deepened:

> We are more fond of our own thoughts than of the thoughts of the Bible. We no longer read the Bible seriously; we no longer read it against ourselves, but only for ourselves.[238]

He followed with a call for peace. The Bishop of Ripon listened attentively, and this time reported to the *Yorkshire Post*:

> At a later session the German leader corrected his first pessimistic emphasis by a passionate proclamation of the church, and ended: "Europe has to be conquered a second time by and for Christ. Are we ready?"[239]

But Dr. Burroughs must have changed the wording slightly to a more Crusade-like tone. Bonhoeffer never used the phrase "*for* Christ"; he only said "*by* Christ."

In his article Burroughs revealed that, among the Germans at the conference, "one was a full-fledged Nazi and gave us an impassioned and moving statement of that viewpoint." Among Bonhoeffer's own students there were initially several who identified their hopes for Germany with those of Hitler's party. Bonhoeffer did not reject them out of hand, but preferred to hope that when things became serious he would be able to raise them to a different level; he succeeded. He may have wanted his ecumenical friends in Gland to see a representative of the type that was rising to power in Germany, and also to show the Nazi a different dimension at the international level. The Nazi member's presence in Gland led to the German and French delegates once more spending many hours in discussion together.

Bonhoeffer's strenuous weeks in Switzerland concluded with his climbing Rigi Peak with Sutz, and visiting Brunner and Barth on the Bergli.

Winter 1932–1933. The autumn and winter of 1932 were devoted to planning the ecumenical program for 1933, which was to be similar to that for the previous year, with regional and international conferences and committee meetings. But the new year turned out quite differently.

At the invitation of the Presbyterian church, Bonhoeffer was able to send one of his students, Joachim Kanitz, to America.[240] A planned trip to Austria, however, had to be canceled due to the political changes.

Bonhoeffer's first acquaintance with Bell was literary, as Siegmund-Schultze asked him to translate Bell's *A Brief Sketch of the Church of England*; in the end, however, Bonhoeffer did no more than check the translation, which he handed over to a friend.

The leadership of the publication committee and its *News Letter* created headaches for him. Although he had carefully reported on the conferences for *Die Eiche* and the *Tägliche Rundschau*, he had no journalistic inclinations whatsoever. He may have sensed that, as an acerbic critic, he had been given this job to tie him down somewhat. He sent Henriod written critiques and recommendations for the *News Letter* that were welcomed. But when the first issue of the new edition appeared in March 1933, Bonhoeffer had other things on his mind; he had already resigned from this duty at the memorable meeting of the executive committee of the World Alliance and the administrative committee of Life and Work. This joint meeting of the most important ecumenical leaders convened on 30 January 1933 in, of all places, Berlin.

> Due to the difficult situation in Germany it has proved impossible for the publication committee to carry on any kind of activity. Dr. Bonhoeffer has requested that a different director be appointed.[241]

The situation in January 1933 seemed so precarious to those in Geneva that they were uncertain as to whether they should actually hold the scheduled public programs during the Berlin meeting. Henriod asked Bonhoeffer for his opinion:

> Therefore I would like to have your personal opinion about my visit to Berlin. You doubtlessly know that Siegmund-Schultze has invited me to stay for a week afterward at the end of January. . . . In view of the current political situation and the tense atmosphere, I ask myself whether, in holding this public conference in French, the people from Geneva do not risk running into the greatest difficulties and having rather negative results. . . .

Bonhoeffer, however, was able to reassure him, at least concerning his appearance at the university in Berlin.

At the end of this period it appears that the two opposite poles of Bonhoeffer's thought—the eschatological majesty of revelation and the relevance of the real world—were more firmly and broadly anchored. His knowledge of the real world had grown personally, geographically, and politically. Would these two poles attract or repel each other? Eschatology had undoubtedly gained in intensity, but reality too had become more vivid.

During the final weeks of the year Bonhoeffer emphasized, with more fervor than ever before, the "right of Prometheus, which allows him to be near the kingdom of God, in contrast to the cowardly fugitive into otherworldliness, because he loves the earth, 'the mother of all things' (Ecclesiastes 40:1)."[242] The community of faith consists of the "children of the earth, who refuse to separate themselves from the world and who have no special proposals to offer for its improvement. The people of this community also do not consider themselves superior to the world, but persevere together in the midst of the world, in its depths, in its trivialities and bondages."[243] Such phrases could have been written in the letters from Tegel prison in 1944.

But now this community of faith had to speak and bear witness to the eschatological revelation. A crucial test was imminent:

> The church must be able to say the Word of God, the word of authority, here and now, in the most concrete way possible, from knowledge of the situation, or it will say something else, something different and human, the word of impotence. Thus the church must announce no eternally valid principles, but only commandments that are true today. For what is "always" true is not true "today." To us God is "always" God "today."[244]

That is how Bonhoeffer presents himself to us on the threshold of 1933. A bitter struggle was beginning for the authority and credibility of the earth-bound church. And thus the two poles entered into a new relationship with each other.

CHAPTER SEVEN

BERLIN: 1933

A forest of swastika flags surrounded the altar of Magdeburg Cathedral. The cathedral dean Ernst Martin interpreted the scene from the pulpit with words similar to those used by many other church leaders:

> It has simply become the symbol of German hope. Whoever reviles this symbol is reviling our Germany.... The swastika flags round the altar radiate hope—hope that the day is at last about to dawn.[1]

In the first sermon Bonhoeffer preached in the Trinity Church in Berlin after Hitler's seizure of power. He announced:

> The church has only *one* altar, the altar of the Almighty ... before which all creatures must kneel. . . . Whoever seeks something other than this must keep away; he cannot join us in the house of God.... The church has only *one* pulpit, and from that pulpit, faith in God will be preached, and no other faith, and no other will than the will of God, however well-intentioned.[2]

At noon on 30 January 1933 Hitler took over the leadership of the government from Hindenburg. That evening Dietrich's brother-in-law, Rüdiger Schleicher, returned home and announced: "This means war!" All the Bonhoeffers, including Dietrich, agreed. During the following years, when friends reproached Bonhoeffer for the excessive pessimism of this opinion, he replied that he might have to revise the timing, but there was no question of changing his opinion. Unlike many people of their class, the Bonhoeffers viewed the events of 30 January seriously; they may have underestimated what Hitler was capable of doing, but not his unscrupulousness. Fifteen years later Bonhoeffer's father reviewed the events of that time:

From the start, we regarded the victory of National Socialism in 1933 and Hitler's appointment as Reich Chancellor as a misfortune—the entire family agreed on this. In my own case, I disliked and mistrusted Hitler because of his demagogic propagandistic speeches, his telegram of condolence after the Potempa murder [in 1932, S.A. members in the Silesian village of Potempa beat a young Communist to death], his habit of driving about the country carrying a riding crop, his choice of colleagues—with whose qualities, incidentally, we in Berlin were better acquainted than people elsewhere—and finally because of what I heard from professional colleagues about his psychopathic symptoms.[3]

The political turning point on 30 January 1933 would force Bonhoeffer's life onto a different course. It did not require a reorientation of his personal convictions or theology, but it became increasingly clear that academic discussion must give way to action. It was imperative to relinquish the shelter and privilege of the academic rostrum, as well as the protected "rights and duties of the ministry," if the power of weakness were to be credible.

But this turning point also posed a greater threat to any kind of personal initiative, which was particularly difficult for Bonhoeffer, with his need to make decisions independently. Throughout his life it would be characteristic that, by knowing when to sacrifice himself, he was always able to regain his own freedom; on the path he had to follow, he charted his own unswerving course theologically, ecclesiastically, and historically within the contemporary world.

This turning point meant that the everyday struggle made unprecedented demands on him. It was four years before he was able to finish his next book. Up to now the young lecturer and preacher had not been involved in decisions concerning greater church issues. He had no voice, nor indeed had he desired any. Now, at the age of twenty-seven, he found himself among those whose names had suddenly become prominent. The usual groups were no longer decisive; new people had become involved in the structures of the church. Bonhoeffer's previously private existence acquired a public dimension. It happened so quickly that he found it uncanny: "I often long terribly for a quiet pastorate."[4] Among his reasons for the decision to go to London, "one of the strongest, I believe, was that I simply did not any longer feel up to the questions and demands which came to me."[5]

The changes brought an abrupt and discordant end to friendships that had meant something to Bonhoeffer. He did not antagonize his students— some of whom were Party members—before he could explain the issue to them. But he could not and would not maintain ties to those in church offices who had made their peace—albeit with a sigh—with the Nazi Aryan clause [the legislation that banned "non-Aryans" from certain professions]. So he wrote his farewell letters to them without regard for their professed good reasons and intentions.

His old plans to visit India reawakened. He wanted to learn more about the ethics and practice of passive resistance.

Few original sources remain from his time in Berlin in 1933. There was little time or freedom for letter writing. "If I no longer say anything about conditions here it is because, as you know, there is now no privacy of post."[6]

February: Controlled Chaos

Bonhoeffer's schedule was full during the days of Hitler's rise to power. In addition to his regular lectures at the university and his Bible studies at the German Student Christian Movement, he gave a talk that was broadcast on the Berlin radio. His time was also taken up with visitors and the ecumenical meetings that were convening in Berlin around 30 January.

The Führer Concept. It is not entirely clear how Bonhoeffer came to be at the microphone in the Potsdamerstrasse *Voxhaus* (broadcasting house) on 1 February 1933. The topic, "The Younger Generation's Altered View of the Concept of *Führer*," could have fit in with the perspectives in Fritz Söhlmann's *Vormarsch*. It is possible that Bonhoeffer's talk was arranged by the university; Bonhoeffer's father had given a broadcast not long before, on 17 and 24 January 1933, about mental illness. Wolf-Dieter Zimmermann was probably responsible for suggesting Dietrich Bonhoeffer's name: Zimmermann was a volunteer at the time under Dr. Kurt Böhme, who directed the radio division of the Evangelical Press Union and also worked with Harald Braun and Jochen Klepper (Klepper was a well-known novelist; he committed suicide in 1942 after his Jewish wife and stepdaughter received orders to join a transport of Jews to the East) at Berlin Radio. Bonhoeffer had planned the talk on this controversial subject even before Hitler had become chancellor. Two days after the *Führer's* enthusiastic acclamation by the crowds on Wilhelmsplatz, Bonhoeffer gave his radio talk. The broadcast was cut off before he finished.

Bonhoeffer analyzed the development of the *Führer* concept and the changes it had undergone in the postwar Youth movement. He made no secret of his contempt for the "unnatural narcissism of . . . the youth made vain by old fools."[7] It would be a misinterpretation, however, to see his argument as based upon liberal, democratic ideas. It emerged from a con-

servative notion of order that continued to influence him, despite his thinking that was evolving during the same period about the breaking up of the
"penultimate" (as opposed to the "ultimate") orders.[8] Bonhoeffer's concern
was the correct structure of authority. If recent developments had made the
Führer concept historically and psychologically necessary, its authority—
Bonhoeffer believed—had to be both well founded and circumscribed, lest
it become "a form of collectivism which turns into intensified individualism."[9] Bonhoeffer believed that this had already occurred in the development
of the original concept of leadership within the Youth movement to its
recent political form. His theological insight enabled him to warn his listeners—only two days after the frenzy surrounding Hitler's ascent to
power—that should the leader "surrender to the wishes of his followers, who
would always make him their idol—then the image of the Leader will gradually become the image of the 'misleader.' . . . Leaders or offices which set
themselves up as gods mock God."[10]

Before these last sentences could be broadcast, Bonhoeffer's microphone
had been switched off. Was it merely because he had overrun his time? Can
it be assumed that Goebbels's people had gained complete control of the station in the course of barely two days? Who found the conclusion of this
broadcast so insufferable that he intervened? The script shows that the syl-
lables had been carefully counted and worked out. Whatever the truth of the
matter, it is significant that Bonhoeffer's remarks were cut off at the crucial
point. With his talk deprived of its stinging conclusion, Bonhoeffer was very
upset by the thought that he might actually be suspected of joining in the
general acclaim. He therefore had the script duplicated and sent to his
friends and relations with the explanation that he had been cut off, which
"had distorted the greater picture."[11] Never again did he have to use this
treacherous medium.

He was able to publish the entire script in the conservative *Kreuzzeitung*.
Theodor Heuss, then teaching at the College of Political Science in Berlin,
even asked him to give a longer version as a lecture at the college in the
beginning of March.[12]

The Ecumenical World in Berlin. At the very time the Nazis came to power
Berlin was hosting the leaders of the World Alliance and the Universal Christian Council for Life and Work. There were consecutive meetings of the
executive committee of the World Alliance, the Geneva secretariats, and the
executive committee of Life and Work. On the night of 30 January, Bishop
Ammundsen and Henriod made their way through the cheering and singing
crowds on Wilhelmplatz. Bishop George Bell of Chichester would always

remember how he had spent his fiftieth birthday amid that great sea of flags in Berlin. The March *News Letter* reported:

> The coincidence of the election of Adolf Hitler as Chancellor of the Reich and the meeting of the Executive revealed once more to its leaders the great difficulties of the country of which they were the guests and the frailty of the plans which men make.[13]

Berlin's theological world gave the guests a festive welcome at Harnack House, where Adolph Deissman presided and Martin Dibelius delivered the formal address. Berlin church leaders also held a reception, presided over by Adolph Kapler, at the Church Federation Office. It was the last time German church leaders and theologians met with the ecumenical movement in a relatively free and harmonious atmosphere. From that time on every conference would be burdened by tensions among the German delegates and embarrassed by the uncertainty of not knowing exactly who truly represented the German churches. It was also the last major ecumenical event to be organized by Friedrich Siegmund-Schultze from his office on Fruchtstrasse. Six months later he was forced to leave Germany for Switzerland and was not allowed to return until after the Second World War.

Bonhoeffer met with Henriod on 25 January 1933 for preliminary talks at the university's theological seminar. Henriod was to lecture the Berlin students on "National and Supranational Church Work." He spoke in German, seeking to steer the thinking of his audience beyond their own immediate crises. Several discussions during the meetings were particularly important for Bonhoeffer: those promoting the merging of the youth committees of the World Alliance and Life and Work; the negotiations for a small circle of French and Germans to meet in Basel; and finally the preparations for the World Alliance conference in September in Sofia, Bulgaria—where Bonhoeffer was to play an unexpected role.

The ecumenical sessions in Berlin concluded with the committee meetings of the Universal Council for Life and Work on 3 and 4 February. Visitors departed with the impression that they had witnessed a powerful display of popular enthusiasm. Berlin church leaders wrote them soon afterward that what they had experienced was in fact a revolution brought about with unprecedented discipline. During so brief a visit they could not have discerned the forces of destruction that had been unleashed.

Uncertain Weeks. In his proclamation to the German people published in the 1 February *Völkischer Beobachter,* Hitler promised to place Christianity—

"the basis of our whole morality"—under his "firm protection." What was the significance of this?

In February 1933, the existing political parties had not yet been banned, nor did they intend to dissolve voluntarily. The struggles continued until the 5 March elections. There was constant fighting in the streets. Each party published in its own newspaper lists of those who had died in the bloody demonstrations. In a letter to the *Christliche Welt*, one reader asked whether, in this civil war, there was such a thing as an unbiased casualty list.[14] Was the chaos genuine, or was it being steered?

Out on the streets the S.A. openly attacked politicians such as Adam Stegerwald of the Catholic Center Party. With some effort, unilateral police and emergency decrees (issued by Interior Minister Wilhelm Frick for the Reich and by Hermann Göring for Prussia) systematically transformed this state of disorder into the desired new order. The extraordinary chaos reached its height with the Reichstag fire, which also marked the beginning of Hitler's radical reign of terror and the introduction of his drastic legislation. One week before the elections, the leftist press was outlawed, socialist journalist and subsequent Nobel prize winner (in 1935) Carl von Ossietzky was arrested, and four thousand Communists were taken from their homes.

These events did not immediately affect Bonhoeffer's family. By 3 February, however, Bernhard Rust had been appointed Prussian minister of education. For an academically oriented family it was a danger signal. At a demonstration the evening after his appointment Rust announced: "Monday morning the Bolshevist cultural invasion will come to an end. . . . I shall ask the churches outright whether or not they intend to help us in our fight against Bolshevism." He had moved into the ministry bag and baggage, he said, and had no intention of leaving until he completed his task.[15] Because of his Jewish ancestry, Bonhoeffer's brother-in-law Gerhard Leibholz couldn't take such remarks lightly, although no legal measures had been implemented. This early phase was characterized by brawls that extended to the gates of the churches and universities.

For high-ranking church authorities, February was a period of relative calm, but local churches experienced an invasion of party demonstrations overflowing from the marketplaces. Was this merely a desire for conquest, or did it mark the beginning of a mass movement into the churches? Groups of uniformed S.A. men attended church services. In some cases fights erupted with other political groups outside church doors. This led Pastor Wilhelm Schubring of the Berlin Marien Church to ask Joachim Hossenfelder, the national leader of the German Christians, to suspend such demonstrations outside and inside the churches. The Cathedral in Berlin was

asked to allow the body of a Nazi police official, the victim of a shooting incident, to lie in state; the Cathedral staff refused. In Kassel the local branch of
the National Socialist Party requested permission to hold a special service of
their own on 12 February. Similar incidents occurred throughout the Reich.
Hossenfelder's 1932 directives to the German Christians announced that the
National Socialist Party did not wish "to save the fatherland without the
cooperation of the vital forces of the church." Might this not mean that the
hour of revolution was also the hour of revival—an opportunity not to be
missed but, indeed, to be welcomed with enthusiasm?

The day before the Reichstag fire, it was Dietrich Bonhoeffer's turn to
preach. Taking as its text "The people with you are too many for me" (Judges
7:2), his sermon on Gideon remained imprinted on the minds of his
students:

> Do not desire to be strong, powerful, glorious and respected, but let God
> alone be your strength, your fame and your honor. . . . Gideon, who
> achieved faith in fear and doubt, kneels with us here before the altar of the
> one and only God, and Gideon prays with us: "Our Lord on the cross, be
> thou our one and only Lord. Amen."[16]

March: Hitler's Laws

Out of this controlled chaos, within a short time Hitler had changed the legislature into a tool of his will. In the wave of enthusiasm for the new national era, the German people submitted to one decree after another, one law
after another, in the illusion that they were experiencing a new freedom. In
fact, they were being deprived of numerous rights.

On the night of 27 February, behind an impenetrable police cordon, the
Reichstag was burned to the ground. The following morning Hitler declared
his most ominous emergency decree, the "Reich President's Edict for the
Protection of People and State." To remain in force "until further notice" the
edict remained in effect until 8 May 1945. It abolished virtually all personal rights protected by the constitution. It made the concentration camps possible. In the 5 March election, the majority of Germans accepted de facto the
terms of paragraph 1 of the edict of 28 February 1933:

> Therefore restriction of personal freedom, of the right of free speech, includ-
> ing the freedom of the press, of the right of association and of public assem-
> bly, intervention in the privacy of post, telegraph and telephone, authoriza-
> tion of house searches and the confiscation and restriction of property,
> beyond the hitherto legal limits, will henceforward be admissible.[17]

This gave Hitler the supreme powers he desired. All that remained to be seen was whether he would have the necessary basis to implement them or would fail to exploit them.

Neither the churches nor the universities felt immediately affected by all this. For the most part they saw a new desire for order that they could only applaud. It had been centuries since the Protestant church had been the victim of an omnipotent and ubiquitous police. Why should it be suspicious now?

At this point the Bonhoeffers were not so threatened that they faced possible police visits to their home on Wangenheimstrasse. They were less vulnerable than many active politicians, many of whom slept somewhere else every night during these weeks to avoid the edict's consequences.

Still, the censorship of letters and telephone conversations was disquieting for Dietrich Bonhoeffer, due to his many "internationalist" connections and the outcome of his radio broadcast.[18] Even in his parents' home, they began to avoid discussing political matters openly, particularly because of the household help. At the beginning of April Paul Lehmann and his wife arrived in Berlin from New York to visit his old friend from Union Theological Seminary. It struck Lehmann that Klaus Bonhoeffer would occasionally get up—in the course of conversations that, admittedly, were not wholly innocuous—to see if anyone was listening outside the door.

Before very long the family found itself uncomfortably involved in the affair of the Reichstag fire. Hans von Dohnanyi had been moved temporarily to the Supreme Court (in May 1933 he was reassigned to the Reich Ministry of Justice to work under Franz Gürtner, who had become a minister in Hitler's cabinet) and was named an observer at the trial of Marinus van der Lubbe, who was accused of having started the fire. The trial moved from Berlin to Leipzig, and then back to Berlin. When van der Lubbe went on hunger strike in prison in March, the investigating judge called upon Bonhoeffer's father and his colleague Dr. J. Zutt (later a professor in Frankfurt) for expert psychiatric opinion. For one year the family was oppressed by its involvement in this emotionally complex, and in many ways enigmatic, case.[19] Karl Bonhoeffer and Zutt saw van der Lubbe three times in March 1933 and again in September and October, after his return from Leipzig; during November they saw him four times. Outside Germany the belief had spread immediately that Göring's henchmen had been responsible for burning down the Reichstag and that van der Lubbe was, at most, an unwitting tool. With his reputation for common sense and incorruptibility, the eminent psychiatrist was expected to give the conclusive evidence that had not been forthcoming elsewhere. Karl Bonhoeffer's expert opinion was awaited with eager anticipation, and the disappointment was extreme when his medical and psychiatric findings omitted any mention of guilt or innocence, or of any possibility that van der Lubbe had been incited by others or that drugs had been administered to the prisoner during the period of observation. Indignant letters, and even a scurrilous leaflet, were sent to the Bonhoeffers' home.

In 1933, however, Karl Bonhoeffer still considered it inconceivable to put his name on an expert opinion that dealt with anything besides purely medical matters. Despite its utterly objective professional language, the document betrayed some sympathy for the patient; it appeared in the *Monatschrift für Psychiatrie und Neurologie*.[20] Just as, in this case, his medical ethics led Karl Bonhoeffer to exclude all political considerations, seven years later he was just as resolute in opposing the biological theories advocating the elimination of so-called life unworthy of life [i.e., the Nazi euthanasia measures]. In his memoirs, the doctor mentioned the van der Lubbe case·

> When I was asked to carry out a psychiatric examination of the Reichstag arsonist Lubbe, and to give an expert opinion on the case, I had the opportunity of meeting some of the leading Party members. A large number of them had gathered to attend the proceedings in the Supreme Court at Leipzig. The faces I saw at this gathering were unpleasant. During the hearings, the impassiveness and painstaking objectivity of the President of the Court was a pleasant contrast to the undisciplined manner of the Party members in the witness box. The other defendant, Dimitroff, gave an impression of intellectual superiority, which set Minister President Göring, who had been invited to attend, in an incomprehensible fury. As for Lubbe he was, in human terms, a not unsympathetic young man, a psychopath and a muddle-headed adventurer who, during the proceedings, reacted with a kind of stupefied defiance that he lost only shortly before his execution.[21]

Under Hitler's "Reichstag Fire Edict," bearing Hindenburg's signature, Bonhoeffer's seminary and community house in Finkenwalde was dissolved and sealed four and a half years later by Himmler's deputies. And in one of the concentration camps made possible by this edict, Dietrich Bonhoeffer was murdered, only one month before the edict finally lost its power. Historian Karl Bracher has described the edict as "the fundamental emergency law upon which the National Socialist dictatorship . . . was based," even more important than the Enabling Act of 23 March.[22]

In view of these events, the Reichstag election of 5 March can be regarded only in a limited sense as the last free election in Germany. It was preceded by appeals, half voluntary and half extorted, by public organizations like the Protestant Federation, which hastened to canvass for "the strong national forces" that would "build up a . . . new Germany, in conscious belief in God, out of the wreckage left by the unholy November Revolution of 1918. For fourteen years the *internationally* connected powers of the [Catholic] Centre, Communism and Social Democracy have left their stamp on German politics and the cultural life of our people. . . . Fight . . . so that the national counter-revolutionary movement may come to power by legal means."[23] Under Kapler the German Evangelical Church committee issued a more dignified appeal to take the eighth commandment seriously during the election, and to show devotion to "that which transcends all else—to the whole nation, the whole fatherland."

Before leaving for the Dassel conference, Dietrich Bonhoeffer accompanied Franz Hildebrandt to the polls. Hildebrandt voted for the Christian People's Party, but Bonhoeffer told him that only one party offered any promise of stability and independence—precisely because of its "international" ties—and that was the Catholic Center Party. For a Protestant minister of his background, it was an exceptional step at the time.

The National Socialist Party obtained 44 percent of the vote; thus it still depended on the diminished German National Conservative Party. There was no doubt, however, that the latter would give its assent to Hitler's legislation.

Hitler skillfully captured the imagination of the people in a state ceremony in the Potsdam Garrison Church on 21 March. Before the ceremony Hindenburg and the Protestant members of the Reichstag attended Otto Dibelius's service in the Nikolai Church, while Hitler and Goebbels made their "devotions" beside the graves of the Party dead. The people regarded the ceremony as marking the end of the "bloodless, legal revolution." It is said that a few days before Bonhoeffer had been invited to tea by Dibelius and had remarked that the church's duty was not solely to acclaim.[24] And, in fact, the lavish praise in Dibelius's sermon was followed by the statement: "Political office must not be combined with personal arbitrariness. Once order has been restored, love and justice must once again hold sway."[25]

On the same day, 21 March, the Malicious Practices Act was enacted, and the net of judiciary measures was tightened. It applied to anyone who "with malice aforethought puts forward or spreads an untrue or grossly distorted assertion of a factual nature that is likely to seriously impair the welfare of the Reich or of a province or the reputation of the Reich Government or of a regional government or of the parties or associations behind those governments."[26] Combined with the Emergency Decree of 28 February, the Malicious Practices Act imposed dangerous restrictions on anyone, like Bonhoeffer, who was unwilling to declare loyalty to Germany by affirming Hitler's government.

That danger soon became acute with the increasing anti-Semitic and anti-Communist measures, culminating in the boycott of Jewish firms on 1 April and the first "non-Aryan law" for the "reconstruction of the professional civil service."[27]

On 1 April Bonhoeffer's grandmother, ninety-one years old, calmly walked through the S.A. cordon to shop at the Jewish-owned *Kaufhaus des Westens*, Berlin's leading department store. His parents went to stay with the Leibholz family in Göttingen, to help them in case there were demonstrations. At home Dietrich and Klaus Bonhoeffer discussed with their New York visitor, Paul Lehmann, how to send information about what was really going on to the right circles in America, including Rabbi Stephen Wise, whom Bonhoeffer had met during his 1930–1931 visit.

While Bonhoeffer was thus committing "treason," other church dignitaries were performing services of a quite different nature. Article 10 of a National Socialist directive referring to the boycott procedure of 1 April stated:

> The action committees are further responsible for ensuring that every German with connections outside the country makes use of these, by letter, telegram and telephone, to explain and disseminate the truth—that peace and order reign in Germany, that the German *Volk* desires wholeheartedly to pursue its work in peace and to live at peace with the rest of the world, that their fight against the Jewish conspiracy is only conducted in self-defense . . . National Socialists! On Saturday, at the stroke of 10, Jews will know who they are fighting.[28]

On 30 March, high-ranking officials in the regional and free churches wrote to their ecumenical partners abroad or to their partner churches in England and the United States, requesting them to oppose the propaganda against Germany's new order, and assuring them that everything was being done in an atmosphere of calm discipline. Kapler wrote along these lines to Bell, Germanos, Cadman, and Henriod. Otto Dibelius and Methodist Bishop John Nuelsen broadcast on the German shortwave Overseas Service to America and other countries how peaceful Berlin was and how those who had been arrested were well-treated in prison.[29]

With its enactment the Malicious Practices Act made every foreign contact risky. This later made the Confessing church apprehensive about communications to the ecumenical movement that, under normal circumstances, would have been sent as a matter of course.

The Enabling Act of 23 March was the final blow. Before the concluding session of the Reichstag Hitler ordered a number of deputies arrested under the edict of 28 February, confiscated their mandates, and put the S.A. and S.S. in charge of overseeing the next Reichstag session in the Kroll Opera House. "The Law to Relieve the Emergency of the People and the State"—the Enabling Act—conferred legislative power upon the government, legalized all past and future decrees, and released Hitler from the requirement to conform to constitutional regulations when these got in his way.[30] Legally he had achieved his goal. Six months later, even the collaborationist parties had ceased to exist. Hitler no longer needed to fear legislative restrictions; the only obstacles were what remained of the traditional and politically responsible elements in the law, the administration, the army, and education. These could not be brought into line quite so rapidly or thoroughly.

In his long conciliatory speech on the eve of the Enabling Act, Hitler told the churches: "The National Government sees the two Christian confessions as the most important factors safeguarding our national heritage." He would "concede to them and assure them the influence that is their due"; he saw "in Christianity the unshakable foundations of our people's ethical and moral life."[31] The churches were relieved to hear the word "influence"; they failed to note the qualifying phrase "that is their due." They could hardly have imagined that, only weeks later, the revolution would be knocking at their own doors.

April: The German Christians

The early days of April could have been delightful for Bonhoeffer, since they brought the reunion with Paul Lehmann. Each found the other changed. In 1931 Lehmann, saying good-bye to Dietrich, had presented him with the book *Which Way Religion?* by the archliberal socialist Harry Ward. Now, returning from Bonn where he heard Karl Barth speak, Lehmann gave Dietrich the recently published work by Reinhold Niebuhr, *Moral Man and Immoral Society*, a reformatory critique proclaiming the end of liberalism. Bonhoeffer was impressed by the way Niebuhr uncovered the position of the moral individual in immoral circumstances, but he was less tolerant of its critique of pacifism. In 1940 Bonhoeffer would return to what he regarded as an "abstract" distinction between individual and society in the "American philosopher of religion, Reinhold Niebuhr."[32]

For his part, Lehmann found Dietrich, whom he had known in New York as a young man full of fun and games, "taking life seriously now." Dietrich and Klaus Bonhoeffer predicted that Hitler would not last long, but that as long as he remained in power things would be very dangerous. Dietrich was writing his article on the non-Aryan question at the time.

Lehmann found the home on Wangenheimstrasse extremely old-fashioned. An exquisite piece of furniture stood in every corner, every part of the walls was covered with pictures, the mysterious mechanisms of the household functioned flawlessly, and the quiet orders of Paula Bonhoeffer were hardly noticeable. As best he could, Bonhoeffer guided his visitor around the city, showed him the church in Wedding, and took him to a performance of Richard Strauss's *Electra*.

The Reich Conference. It was not only the Jewish boycott that cast a shadow over Bonhoeffer's time with Paul Lehmann, but also the chauvinistic Reich conference of German Christians on 3–4 April in Berlin. The repercussions of 30 January continued to affect the church, through the pro-National Socialist German Christian Faith movement, which had been organized in 1932. Because of this it was somewhat difficult for Hitler to maintain the official fiction abroad that the revolution was over.

Not a few Protestants envied the Catholics because of their apparent unity in negotiating with the Third Reich—a unity which had enabled them to secure the relatively peaceful terms of the Concordat. Only later did it become clear to Protestants that the Catholics were not as unified as had first appeared.[33] In any case, Protestants were weakened by the fact that National Socialist ideology had infected not only their lay synodal members but a large proportion of the clergy, even those in key positions. They either became instruments of the Party or forfeited their freedom to negotiate, eventually losing every vestige of independence.

The Reich conference of German Christians on 3–4 April triggered radical changes at all levels of the church. Interior Minister Frick and Göring made an appearance. *Gauleiter* (a regional Nazi party leader) Wilhelm Kube, who led the Party's faction in the Prussian parliament, gave the address. The presence of state commissars Leonardo Conti and Hans Hinkel strengthened the official character of the meeting. Some of the proceedings were broadcast. The conference was attended not just by radical, convinced German Christians, but by established theologians as well. Some were eager to transfer the Party tenets of the *Führer* principle and racial conformity to a unified German church. Others, like Professor Karl Fezer of Tübingen and Ludwig Weichert, director of the Berlin Missionary Society, had a less radical interpretation of racial conformity; they were basically inspired by a true missionary zeal. Not surprisingly, the first group was more outspoken at the Reich conference and was responsible for unleashing the subsequent chain

of chaotic action and reaction. People of "alien blood," this group maintained, had no place in the pulpit and should not be allowed to be married
before German Protestant altars. Kube attacked Kapler, despite the latter's
declaration of loyalty on the Day of Potsdam. He also scolded Otto Dibelius
because of the qualifications he had made in his letter of 8 March that
affirmed the Nazi revolution. Kube implied that state commissars might be
appointed in the church, and openly threatened to withdraw state money
from the churches, using the regional parliaments' budget laws.

The slogans of the conference were: *Gleichschaltung* (the alignment of all
sectors with Nazi goals), the *Führer* principle, the Reich church, and racial
conformity. A number of theologians now began to ponder whether a "Reich
church" and "racial conformity" might help the church gain the influence it
desired.

On 16 April Hossenfelder proposed to German Evangelical church president Kapler that a German Christian representative should attend all sessions of the High Church Council, the Church Senate, the consistories, and
the provincial church councils; Kapler refused. On 22 April a state commissar was temporarily appointed to oversee the regional church of Mecklenburg. On 26 April hoping to exploit the state of confusion, Hitler
appointed an unknown military chaplain from Königsberg, Ludwig Müller,
as his "confidential adviser and plenipotentiary in questions concerning the
Protestant church." Müller was an insignificant character who spoke a folk-
loric jargon. But when the church leaders and authorities failed to comply
with the demand to adopt the *Führer* principle and actually began to show
some signs of independent activity, the German Christians reverted somewhat illogically to democratic procedure. On 30 April they asked for new
church elections.

Concerned that they would be bypassed, the existing church administrations began to call for a unified Reich church in place of the twenty-eight
independent regional churches. They hastily set in motion machinery to
create a new constitution for a single Reich church, exchanging proposals
and plans for the reorganization of the German Evangelical church that,
until then, had been so divided. The best known of these proposals was Wilhelm Zoellner's of 13 April. Zoellner wanted to dissolve the Old Prussian
Union Church [the Protestant church encompassing the regions of Berlin,
Brandenburg, Rhineland, and Westphalia] to create a Lutheran and
Reformed Reich church. Theodor Heckel was among those who supported
this proposal.[34] Theologically knowledgeable people had serious hopes that
something positive and valuable would emerge from this transitional state.
Their intense preoccupation with the problem almost led them to believe

they could ignore the German Christians. On 14 April Bonhoeffer wrote to Erwin Sutz:

> We are about to witness a great reorganization of the churches which, to all appearances, will not be a bad thing. It is to be hoped that it will bring about the automatic withdrawal of the German Christians from the churches of both denominations—however regrettable this may be in other respects—and so, *hominum confusione et dei providentia*, we will once again rescue the church. . . .[35]

A letter from Karl Barth to Bonhoeffer on 18 April 1933 illustrates how difficult it was to foresee the future:

> Whether and how I shall be able to adapt spiritually to a Germany that has changed so much is a different question altogether. And this applies particularly to Zoellner's "Evangelical Church of the German Nation." The name speaks for itself! . . . But for the moment I can only wait and see, with as much patience as I can muster. I am really glad to see so many signs that the church is more aware of her responsibilities than she was in 1914.[36]

On their own initiative, the High Church Council and the Church Senate announced plans for a new church constitution. While their declarations said much about the renewal of people and the Reich, they also addressed the proclamation of the pure Gospel. On 25 April a triumvirate was set up, consisting of President Kapler, Bishop Marahrens of Hanover, and Reformed pastor Hermann Hesse of Elberfeld. They had been commissioned by the German Evangelical church committee to draft the new constitution for the Reich church. This independent move, however, was thwarted by Hitler's appointment of Müller and by the German Christians' insistence on elections.

When the triumvirate met in Loccum on 4 May for three weeks of deliberations, they discovered that there were now four of them; an eager Ludwig Müller joined them at the conference table. The discussion could no longer be confined to their common aim, the "Reich church"; the "*Führer* principle" had become an inescapable topic of discussion. The third point, "racial conformity," was not explicitly mentioned. Yet this issue, which had been the province of individual cranks and extremists, now became the subject of serious theological debate. People began to ask whether an issue like the Aryan clause—which personally affected only a dwindling number within the church—should be treated as a scandal when the great opportunity existed to create an influential, evangelizing Reich church. "The Jewish question troubles the church very much and here even the most intelligent people have entirely lost their heads and their Bibles over it," Bonhoeffer wrote.[37]

The Jewish Question. How did Bonhoeffer arrive at this clear assessment so quickly?

At the beginning of April the group of pastors who met under Gerhard Jacobi wanted to discuss the Jewish question, with an introduction by Bonhoeffer; a colleague from Jacobi's church expressed his clear opposition to the choice of this particular topic. Indeed, Leonhard Fendt, one of the most influential members of the group and a man whose sermons Bonhoeffer admired, decided to leave as a result of the discussion. In the Rhineland on 1 April Wilhelm Menn confided to his general superintendent his concern about the church's acclaim for the national revolution at a time when part of the population was exposed to mob violence. The general superintendent's reply was characteristic of the times:

> I can understand why the legitimate resentment (which has built up even among those who are in no way anti-Semitic) at what the Jewish-dominated press, stock exchange, theater, etc. have done to us needs an energetic outlet for once.... Never for a second has the black, red and gold flag [the German flag during the Weimar Republic] had any place either in my heart or in my home. I have always been a man of the extreme right.[38]

The Christian middle class may not have approved of the boycott's methods entirely, but they had few objections against anti-Semitism itself. To resist the Third Reich's intentions toward the church by making an issue of the Aryan clause seemed to the clergy not just distasteful but shortsighted as well, if the church were to be protected and regain its influence. Only in August and September, when the German Christians forced the church to adopt the political Aryan clause, did the clergy begin to show any marked reaction. What happened then, however, fulfilled Bonhoeffer's prediction that one day theology professors and ministers would seek theological justification for a church Aryan clause.

At the time of the political Aryan legislation on 7 April 1933, Bonhoeffer was among the very few who sat down and worked through its possible consequences, from both a political and an ecclesiastical standpoint. Indeed, he may have been the first to see this matter as the crucial problem in the impending struggle.[39] There were other, even earlier, discussions of the concept of race among theologians. On 17 December 1932 Heinz Kloppenburg had published his theses on the topic in the Oldenburg church newspaper.

Heinrich Vogel, pastor in the village of Dobbrikow at the time, argued with the German Christians in the 27 April 1933 *Täglichen Rundschau* and published an early issue entitled "Cross and Swastika." Under his theses, Bonhoeffer wrote "completed on 15.5.33." But he could not publish them until the June issue of *Vormarsch*, which could hardly be assured of a long life if it continued to publish such critiques.

Bonhoeffer's essay on the Jewish question consisted of two initially distinct sections. He apparently worked on the six theses in the second section during late March and early April for the Jacobi circle.[40] These theses dealt with the question of church membership for Christians of Jewish descent, refusing to give the state the right or the power to decide the issue. This section exposed the theological absurdity of a "purely German" church that excluded members on biological grounds. Bonhoeffer's thoughts on the privilege that any "Aryan church" entailed were not as sharply worded as later. He wrote:

> What is at stake is by no means the question whether our German members of congregations can still tolerate church fellowship with the Jews. It is rather the task of Christian preaching to say: here is the church, where Jew and German stand together under the Word of God; here is the proof whether a church is still the church or not.[41]

By August 1933 Bonhoeffer had concluded beyond all doubt that there could be no question of belonging to a church that excluded the Jews. In April the idea of repudiating church membership had still been too abstract for real consideration.

While he was writing the first section of his paper, the boycott of Jewish businesses occurred on 1 April. Through Dohnanyi Bonhoeffer heard of the impending publication of laws affecting non-Aryan civil servants on 7 April. Thus he added an introductory section to the six theses; this became the most stimulating and important part of the paper, even though it contained much conservative thinking.[42] "How does the church judge this state action" that places Jews "because of their ethnic classification under the special law of the state"—Bonhoeffer tacitly questioned the very "criterion of race" and asked, "what should the church do as a result of it?"[43] The subject was the Jewish question as such, not merely the church membership of Christians of Jewish descent. To Bonhoeffer's distress, in the Confessing church's struggle to assert itself this essential question became totally subsumed by the question of church membership. Still, he did not cease to cite the verse from Proverbs: "Open your mouth for the dumb!"[44]

As a good Lutheran theologian, Bonhoeffer struggled in this part of the essay with whether and to what extent the church should intervene in political matters. "It has neither to praise nor to censure the laws of the state."[45] We might ask how that sentence would have sounded to him ten years later; but in 1933 Bonhoeffer's theological language consistently opposed a humanitarian-liberal front. Even then, however, the accent was changing. It even had a distinctly democratic ring, such as when he remarked that "a strong state" needs opposition and argument, and that these "should be fostered by a certain amount of reserved encouragement."[46]

At the time, Bonhoeffer's theological doctrine of the invasion of history by the Christian witness[47] enabled him to write about the state in such subversive terms that it is surprising that the *Vormarsch* issue including Bonhoeffer's remarks escaped Goebbels's sensors. Perhaps the difficult theological argument with which it began was too much for the censor. But it was followed by a perfectly clear exposition of what Bonhoeffer expected of his church in April 1933. He saw three clearly delineated phases of church responsibility:

1. The church must ask the state "whether its action can be justified as legitimate action of the state. . . . It will have to put this question quite clearly today in the matter of the Jewish question."[48] But who was to "pose this question with the utmost clarity"? Who responded to the questions Menn had addressed to his general superintendent? Virtually everyone at the time spoke in terms of the relative right to use force in a revolution; even Martin Rade did this in *Christliche Welt*.[49] The church raised no appreciable objection to the state's actions until its 1936 memorandum to Hitler. And ten years later, when Bonhoeffer acknowledged (in an entirely different context) that there was a "relative right to use force," this was an isolated position within the church.

2. The church's second task, as Bonhoeffer saw it, was to help the victims of the state's actions. "The church has an unconditional obligation towards the victims of any ordering of society, even if they do not belong to the Christian community."[50] It was something that needed to be said. When the persecutions of early April 1933 began to take on considerable proportions in the years that followed, the Grüber office assumed this responsibility on behalf of the Confessing church. (The Grüber office, founded in 1937 and led by Pastor Heinrich Grüber, helped "non-Aryans" on behalf of the Confessing church.)

Bonhoeffer looked for criteria that could determine when the church was confronting these first two responsibilities. His criteria consisted of either "too much" or "too little law and order" when "any one group of political subjects is outlawed." His answer was neither vague nor evasive: "In the Jewish question, the first two possibilities are the obligations the church faces in this hour."[51] This position proved to be such an isolated one that only a few months after his article appeared Bonhoeffer's disappointment at the silence of his church nearly led him to turn away from it. His decision to go to London was related to this disappointment.

3. What, then, was the third task? Here Bonhoeffer pushed the limits of what he believed he was personally capable of. He declared that when the church sees the state unscrupulously wielding too little or too much law and order, the church's position is "not just to bind up the victims beneath the wheel, but to halt the wheel itself."[52] To halt the wheel! Who could assume such a responsibility? Yet Bonhoeffer clearly knew what he was saying. Speaking of the first two tasks, he envisaged the possibility that individual Christians might feel called, "should occasion arise, to accuse the state of offenses against morality."[53] Regarding the third task, he dared only to express the utopian hope: "The necessity for immediate political action by the church, however, must be decided by an Evangelical Council as and when the occasion arises, and hence cannot be casuistically construed beforehand."[54] Characteristically, Bonhoeffer was already aware of the risks, if not the impossibility, of establishing obligatory standards for revolutionary action in advance. It would take years of growing oppression and disillusionment in his own church and in the ecumenical movement before he could take this responsibility himself, instead of transferring it to a "council." The young theologian still shied away from personally deciding on issues that endangered the structure of church and state. In the course of his life, however, various factors led him to this third stage of responsibility and to act alone without the aid of a collective decision. Eventually he became aware of it, and he surrendered his reputation in the church.

The month of April 1933 was indeed disquieting. "It is impossible to say where it will lead us."[55] His brother-in-law Gerhard Leibholz and his friend Franz Hildebrandt were constant reminders of the consequences of the state's and church's treatment of the Jews.

On 11 April Gerhard Leibholz's father died; he had never been baptized. Dietrich's relations wanted him to conduct the funeral service. He was persuaded to consult his general superintendent, however, who strongly advised against conducting a funeral service for a Jew at this particular time. A few months later, on 23 November, Dietrich wrote his brother-in-law:

> I am tormented by the thought . . . that I didn't do as you asked me as a matter of course. To be frank, I can't think what made me behave as I did. How could I have been so much afraid at the time? It must have seemed

equally incomprehensible to all of you, and yet you said nothing. But it
preys on my mind . . . because it's the kind of thing one can never make up
for. So all I can do is to ask you to forgive my weakness then. I know now
for certain that I ought to have behaved differently. . . .[56]

Thus it was primarily the Jewish question, personally and theologically,
that made Bonhoeffer reluctant from the very beginning to engage in any
discussion of *Weltanschauung* with the National Socialists. This was also
the reason for his lack of interest in evangelizing the German people; he left
the fervent evangelization of the S.A. to the more moderate German Christians and their tracts. His energies were wholly consumed in the fight against
the Aryan clause. He believed that only if everything were staked upon this
one point would the Gospel worthy of proclamation be revealed.

It was entirely consistent with his theology and character that Bonhoeffer's
first statement in the church struggle was provoked precisely by the issue that
his church superiors, and even some friends, viewed as a secondary problem.

Dismissals. During these weeks the universities faced their first serious crises.
The Law for the Reconstruction of the Civil Service affected not just the so-
called non-Aryan academic teachers, but professors with left-wing sympa-
thies. On 1 April National Socialist action committees at the universities were
instructed to enact resolutions that restricted Jewish participation in academic disciplines, particularly medicine and law. All this was to prepare the
ground (and give Minister of Education Bernhard Rust a pretext) for the law
of 7 April.

Rust had already suspended Emil Fuchs, a religious socialist and professor of theology in Kiel, in March. This was followed by campaigns against
Paul Tillich in Frankfurt, Günther Dehn in Halle, and Karl Ludwig Schmidt
in Bonn, which eventually ended in their dismissal or exile.

Now all eyes were directed toward Bonn: what would happen to Karl
Barth, who was a card-holding member of the Social Democratic Party? In
Berlin Bonhoeffer met Georg Merz, who told him that Barth was in danger.
Bonhoeffer immediately tried to rally friends and colleagues to publicly
support Barth, and asked ecumenical friends to put outside pressure on the
Ministry of Cultural Affairs. It was said at the time that he used his contacts
inside the Ministry to "avert a disastrous mistake."[57] But Barth soon wrote
him that work for the present "was going on as usual," although he had
informed Rust that he would not resign from the Social Democratic Party
and had reminded him of his advocacy on behalf of Günther Dehn.[58]

Bonhoeffer correctly believed it might still be possible to oppose the enemy. Outcries about measures taken against respected individuals was still of some avail. When, for example, philosopher Eduard Spranger protested the measures by applying for his own leave of absence at the beginning of the new term, officials took great pains to move him to withdraw his request. The departure of individuals such as Werner Jäger, Wilhelm Röpke, or Paul Hindemith was unwelcome to the Nazi state, since it damaged its reputation abroad.

Hindenburg also intervened in the spate of dismissals that followed the 7 April legislation, securing the exemption of non-Aryan war veterans from the law. It was possible to postpone the dismissal of Bonhoeffer's brother-in-law, Leibholz, who was not suspended from his job until March 1935.

But isolated actions could not change the general developments. Never in its history had Berlin University lost so much academic ability. Six months later, when Bonhoeffer became pastor in London, he took up the difficult task of helping the emigrants from this first wave of job dismissals find new livelihoods.[59]

Ecumenism. After such tremendous upheavals, it was not surprising that all kinds of visitors converged upon Berlin during this month to make their own assessment of the new situation.

Bishop Bell of Chichester, chairman of the Universal Council for Life and Work, had received Kapler's official letter of 30 March.[60] Its assurances were contradicted by the disquieting news from Berlin that he read daily in *The Times*. He initiated the first of a long series of actions for the German church. Immobilized during April by a tonsillectomy, Bell sent Henriod from Geneva to Berlin to obtain firsthand information. Henriod was accompanied by Schönfeld and Ehrenström. Bonhoeffer met with Henriod; only the notes taken before and after the visit give any information on their discussion.

Before their arrival Bonhoeffer asked Ehrenström to convey a message to Henriod:

> It would be of the utmost importance for me to speak with him immediately after his arrival. . . . I believe that the matter is also rather important to Henriod. . . . With deepest wishes for a peaceful Easter in these turbulent days.[61]

Bonhoeffer probably hoped to inform Henriod about the Jewish question and Barth's situation before Henriod made his official visits; through

Dohnanyi, Bonhoeffer was better informed than most. Bonhoeffer feared his colleagues and superiors might give Bell's envoy too optimistic a picture. They might try to reassure him and ask him not to upset the situation from the outside during this critical early stage, with the added argument, perhaps, that what was at stake was the construction of a strong bulwark of order against the atheist East. Bonhoeffer's own views were totally different.

In his diary Henriod wrote of his April visit to Berlin: "It is astonishing in Germany to discover that foreigners are expected to be grateful that Germany has raised a bulwark against Bolshevism." The annual report of Life and Work, in fact, contained the information that the leaders of the German church

> . . . explained to them the difficulties which the church was facing, and the steps they were taking to deal with them, and had requested their fellow Christians to have patience and not to press them for action which might be premature.[62]

Even Theodor Heckel shared Bonhoeffer's pessimistic analysis at that point. Henriod wrote in his diary: "19 April, breakfast with Heckel, who is very skeptical about the situation."

The annual report of the World Alliance also demonstrated what Bonhoeffer saw as the excessive caution shown in Berlin:

> It became increasingly clear in the course of these discussions that, in passing judgement upon the conditions in Germany, there is one thing above all that foreign countries must not overlook; in Germany they are experiencing, not a change of Government, not a reorganization, but a real revolution. It is owing to this fact that so little that is definite, so little that is final and conclusive can be said in regard to ecclesiastical conditions and likewise to the work of the Alliance.[63]

Bonhoeffer believed that at this point it was the National Socialists who were most anxious to say as little as possible. This was reason enough to speak out.

At this meeting in Berlin with the representatives from Geneva, Bonhoeffer canceled his plans to participate in the English-French conference in the north of France and the meeting of the youth commission in Luneray on 22 April 1933, although the merger of the World Alliance and Life and Work youth commissions was planned for the Luneray meeting—and despite the fact that Henriod had strongly urged him on 7 March: "It is essential that you be present at the commission." Bonhoeffer asked Siegmund-Schultze's advice: "Do you find it advisable to travel at this time? Moreover: should the Foreign Office be asked at this point to state its position?" The Jewish question, the problems at the universities, or ecumenical alliances—where was his presence most required? It would be the first of many ecumenical cancelations.

May: The Young Reformation Movement

The Beginning of the Semester. In the house on Wangenheimstrasse preparations were being made for the beginning of the semester. The new cultural policies now began to affect the universities. Karl Bonhoeffer recalled those early weeks of the summer term at Berlin University with shame:

> Of the official ceremonies at the university, the only one I attended was the address by Rust, the Minister for Cultural Affairs. Unfortunately neither I nor any of the other professors had the courage on this occasion to get up and walk out in protest against the Minister's insulting position toward the professors.[64]
>
> Young and hitherto wholly unknown medical trainees came, as representatives of the Party, to suggest to the heads of hospitals that they immediately dismiss the Jewish doctors. Some allowed themselves to be persuaded. Any suggestion that such matters came under the jurisdiction of the Ministry and not of the Party were met with threats. The Dean tried to persuade faculty members to join the Party collectively. His attempt was foiled by individual refusals. Nor did the Ministry at first make any move to meet the demand for the dismissal of Jewish assistants. But doctors in individual hospitals were constantly spied upon to discover their attitude towards the Party. . . . So far as my own hospital was concerned, I can say that most doctors withstood the pressure. But the hospital was a thorn in the flesh of the *Dozentenführung* [the leadership of the university teachers]. I managed to avoid putting up a portrait of Hitler until I left in 1938, and in this my hospital was unique among those of the Charité. My successor made up for this by placing an oversized bust in the entrance hall.[65]

Initially the circumstances among the theological faculty were somewhat better. But, although they were training future servants of the church, the professors here were also civil servants and subject to the Aryan clause. Several weeks would pass before the activity of the German Christians became evident among the students.

As in every other university town in Germany, the new cultural "will to live" was celebrated on 10 May with a book burning that took place on the

Opernplatz. In front of the university, beneath the monument to the Humboldt brethren, students threw hundreds of books into the blazing bonfire, shouting the names of the banned authors as they did so: Albert Einstein and Thomas Mann, Sigmund Freud and Walther Rathenau, Stefan Zweig, Erich Maria Remarque, and Theodor Heuss. Goebbels concluded this anti-intellectual celebration with Ulrich von Hutten's cry: "Oh century, oh scholarship, it is a joy to be alive!"

But should not some theologians' names also have been numbered among the "decadent" writers? The new church journal, *Evangelium im Dritten Reich*, in its issue of 7 May, suggested that the faculties were reacting too sluggishly.

> *Gleichschaltung* of the theological faculties. . . . In Kiel, Marburg and Bonn, to name only a few, former Democrats and even Marxists occupy the desks where they ply their long-defunct liberalism. According to reliable reports, when a chair fell vacant in Berlin, the faculty suggested names that would grace a museum. . . . We demand that chairs now vacant, or that become so in the next few years, be filled by theologians with our own way of thinking, until the time comes when only German Christians are working in German faculties.[66]

After Titius's retirement, his vacant chair at Berlin University was given to Georg Wobbermin, who proceeded to do all that the Third Reich expected of him. There was no immediate public rift in the faculty, however. Being "politically unacceptable," Siegmund-Schultze's dismissal during the summer was tolerated. As a junior lecturer, Bonhoeffer was not really involved in departmental politics. The only influence he could exert was through mediators, of whom there were very few. He did his best to concentrate on the most difficult of his lectures, on Christology.

Early Opposition. The German Christians' advances during April did more than cause the church leadership to defend the church's independence tactically and with constitutional means; it led theologically oriented circles throughout the country to become active. In their early, informal gatherings they looked for appropriate slogans to express and safeguard the character of the church against the new challenges. These responses ranged from defenses of the besieged church leadership to reluctant criticism of the oppressed church administrations. At the end of April, on behalf of the Sydow Brotherhood, Georg Schulz published a manifesto, "Discerning the Spirits." In May eleven Westphalian pastors, including Ludwig Steil [Steil was later imprisoned and died in Dachau], issued a declaration similar to Bonhoeffer's, rejecting the exclusion of Christians of Jewish descent from the church as heretical and schismatic. This was also the message of Heinrich Vogel's "Eight Articles of Evangelical Doctrine."

The opposition that emerged at the beginning of May from the Young Reformation movement, which consisted of a number of different groups, was milder. They wanted an unabridged Reformed theology, but they also wanted to influence church politics—indeed, they found it imperative. The Café am Knie in Berlin-Charlottenburg was the meeting place of Gerhard Jacobi, Walter Künneth, H. M. Schreiner-Rostock, and Hanns Lilje. Each represented several groups with varying tendencies. A manifesto appeared on 9 May with a list of impressive names; it was imposing enough to cause a considerable stir in Germany. But those in the know realized that the hopes this aroused rested on too many unresolved theological and ecclesiastical contradictions, embodied by these very names. It was a peaceful compilation of the signatures of many who would soon be only too anxious to part company: Dannenbaum, Doerne, Eduard and Theodor Ellwein, Gogarten, Görnandt, Heckel, Heim, Jacobi, Kochheim, Krukenberg, Künneth, Lehmann, Lilje, Lütgert, Müller, Müller-Schwefe, Nitzsche, Paulsen, Riethmüller, K. B. Ritter, Schreiner, Schulz, Stählin, Tiling, Verschuer, von Wedemeyer, Wendland, Zinn. The title stated: "A Call to Convene"; the signers stood behind the four (not three!) [namely, Church President Kapler, Bishop Marahrens, Pastor Hermann Hesse—and Ludwig Müller] men who were working in Loccum on the new constitution. There was much "joyful affirmation" for the new German state; the signers demanded influence and called energetically for a renewal of the church "from the essence of the church" (only this phrase was in bold print); and they didn't forget to reject the exclusion of non-Aryans, under point 7. The desire to be Reformed culminated in strongly antiliberal tendencies, which led to rather remarkable similarities with the German Christians.

The Berlin members of the group distributed the manifesto with an appendix that was distinctly sharper in tone and had a "confessionally conscious" ring about it.[67] This leaflet bore the names of thirty-seven people in Berlin who would later move into the forefront of the church struggle. Martin Niemöller's name appeared here for the first time. Here, too—but not in the manifesto mentioned above—were the signatures of Hermann Sasse and Bonhoeffer. The Berlin appendix was a sign of independence; it passed on the "rallying cry" as "guiding principles which we regard as a suitable working program for the restructuring of our church." It concluded with powerful terms like "abuse" and "leading astray."

The compromising tone of the Reformed manifesto can hardly have escaped Bonhoeffer. Gertrud Staewen wrote Barth a letter full of misgivings about the Young Reformation members, "among whom Bonhoeffer, to my distress, regards himself." But in all likelihood Bonhoeffer wanted to be involved because he was uncertain whether the movement would uphold its demand for independence in church affairs and the rejection of the Aryan clause, or whether the dangerous elements of the "Church of the German Nation" would win the day.

The fronts were still remarkably malleable. To many Young Reformation members it was a pleasant surprise to discover that their antiliberalism and rejection of parliamentary procedure were shared by the east Prussian branch of the German Christians, who also shared their strong revulsion for the old church and a desire for a new one. During the second half of May, the groups parted ways when the question arose of the future Reich church leadership, as laid down in the Loccum constitution.

During Ascension week the German Christians nominated Ludwig Müller as their candidate, since they maintained that only a man who enjoyed Hitler's trust could now become Reich bishop. On 27 May, however, the regional church leaders, who had agreed to the Loccum constitution in Eisenach, elected Friedrich von Bodelschwingh as Reich bishop by a small majority (although Bishops Schöffel, Wurm, and Rendtorff voted for Müller). The Young Reformation members immediately threw their support behind Bodelschwingh. The German Christians enlisted the help of the media and Party offices in an attempt to overturn Bodelschwingh's election. This controversy brought the Young Reformers into the limelight sooner than they would have liked. They did not realize that the time was somewhat favorable, since Hitler hoped for a calmer public mood after his important appeasement speech of 17 May.

Sermons. On 28 May 1933, from his pulpit in Klein-Machnow, Franz Hildebrandt announced that those who raised their voices against Bodelschwingh should be ashamed to the very depths of their souls. Bonhoeffer, who was preaching for Jacobi the same Sunday at Kaiser Wilhelm Memorial Church, made the same point, but less blatantly. He preached—once more selecting the text himself—on the golden calf. His meaning was clear:

> What is the use of the church, if [it is] only left to wait? No, our church ought to have something. We want to see something in our church. . . . The concern expressed here is really not as bad as all that. . . . The priest is not driven out, he is told: "Do your duty!" "Preserve religion for the people, give them worship services." . . . [Aaron] looks to his office, to his conse-

cration, he looks to the people. He understands their impatience, their thirst for action, and their pious raging only too well—and he yields. . . .

The human race is ready for any sacrifice in which it may celebrate itself and worship its own work. . . . No, the church of Aaron does not stint, it is not mean, it is lavish with its God. . . .

Yet . . . there he stands among them, the unexpected prophet . . . I am the Lord your God![68]

June: The State Commissar

Basel. In the week after Whitsunday, four Frenchmen and four Germans met on 7–9 June at the home of Pastor Iselin in Basel. Lord Dickinson and Henriod were also there, on behalf of the World Alliance. Bonhoeffer, Toureille, and Henriod were optimistic when they arranged the discussions during the previous winter. Wilfred Monod and Siegmund-Schultze had long desired this sort of consultation, unattended by any kind of publicity.

When the meeting finally took place, however, circumstances were very different from what had been anticipated. Controversial matters such as Versailles, disarmament, and equality of status still remained unresolved. Both parties were conscious of the tragic omissions of past years. But whereas on the German side the question of allegiance or nonallegiance to the new German state remained unclarified, the old mistrust had been rekindled among the French, who found some of the church's statements disturbing. The 1933–1934 annual report of the World Alliance states: "The French delegates expressed the keen uneasiness which some aspects of the aforesaid revolution and the orientation of the German Evangelical Church cause them."[69]

No minutes of the three-day discussions exist. Not even the names of all those who attended has been established. The participation of Siegmund-Schultze and Pastor Richard Jordan from Germany, and Toureille from France, has been vouched for. Of Bonhoeffer we can be sure only that he helped plan the entire meeting, that he had planned to stay with Sutz in Switzerland that week, and that he was not at the university in Berlin that week. A postcard Toureille sent to Theodor de Félice on 10 June 1933 stated: "Yesterday in Basel! . . . That the older ones are so energetic in defending their governments' policies drives the younger ones very much to argue with them."[70] It is easy to imagine Bonhoeffer in the midst of these different factions from both nations.

In his report for the World Alliance in 1932–1933, Henriod noted:

Since the conference took place at a time when the National Socialist revolution was still in flux and some fundamental changes in the structure of the church were being made, the conference proved to be of great value in the exchange of questions and news and for the explicit and repeated declaration of agreement with the goals of the World Alliance.

The meeting was overshadowed by the anxiety that Siegmund-Schultze's days in Germany might now be numbered. His social work and voluntary service association in Berlin had already been dissolved. He had recently devoted himself to helping non-Aryan officials and academics who were being forced to emigrate. On 24 June 1933, three weeks after the Basel meeting, Hitler ordered his expulsion from Germany. As far as church politics was concerned, there was still some hope during these early June days that Bodelschwingh's election might stabilize the situation.

Bodelschwingh. The German Christians lost a great deal of sympathy in Germany with their attacks on someone as patently sincere and moderate as the director of Bethel (the renowned community for the disabled in Bielefeld, Westphalia), almost as soon as he had been elected Reich bishop. On the evening after the election Ludwig Müller blatantly expressed his sentiments in a radio broadcast that, in more normal times, would have disqualified him for good. Having been defeated on 27 May, Müller announced to his compatriots: "The church governments have not listened to the call of the hour. . . . The solution they have proposed to us in the question of the Reich bishop has nothing to do with the faith, hope and love now stirring among the hitherto apathetic millions. . . ."[71]

Almost reluctantly, Bodelschwingh came to Berlin and his rooms in the Church Federation Office. He brought a Westphalian pastor, Gerhard Stratenwerth, as his assistant and also assigned special duties to Martin Niemöller, who originally came from Westphalia and was now pastor in Dahlem. From then on, Niemöller was constantly involved in the church troubles. He appeared from time to time in the Jacobi circle where church politics increasingly became the topic of discussion as things grew more turbulent; it was here that Bonhoeffer met Niemöller.

With each day, the German Christian campaign against the "undesirable" Reich bishop intensified. They prevented Hitler from receiving him, obtained readily forthcoming expert legal opinions on procedural errors in the Eisenach election, and organized demonstrations of "seething popular emotion" throughout the country. The wave of concocted anti-Bodelschwingh and pro-Müller agitation eventually reached the universities, leading to Bonhoeffer's first public appearance in the church troubles.

The clash for which the German Christians had been waiting came soon. Toward the end of the month, the minister for cultural affairs discovered that the church had violated its regulations in the matter of Kapler's succession, and used this as an excuse to appoint a state commissar. This development was to take a more serious turn than Hitler wanted at the time.

Stormy Meetings. In June the German Christians succeeded in setting up a "German Christian Students' Fighting League" at nearly every university. Partly with the support of other student groups, they organized meetings that passed resolutions in favor of Ludwig Müller, and used nationalistic terror to put their plans into action.

Junge Kirche, recently established by Hans Lilje and Fritz Söhlmann as the publication of the Young Reformation movement, reported that 200 of the 300 people attending a students' meeting in Breslau had already left when a resolution supporting Müller was proposed.

The arguments at the university in Berlin began during the dramatic week that would end with the appointment of a state commissar for the church. Two large meetings took place: one of the German Christians on Monday, 19 June, and the other on Thursday, 22 June, organized by the university chaplains and the opposition. The second meeting was carefully prepared as a discussion of the conflicting points of view, but, after the German Christians suddenly scheduled their own meeting first, it was uncertain whether the opposition meeting would take place at all. Bonhoeffer took a back seat at the German Christian meeting and left the talking to his students in the audience. At the opposition meeting he took a public stand as one of the speakers.

The activities and statements of those days are understandable only if it is remembered that at that point the opposition's sole battle was against Müller's demands and the terrorizing of the church. They did not want their national loyalty to be questioned or found guilty of being "reactionary"— nor did anyone with political objections to Hitler wish to have that kind of opposition noted, and be prosecuted for it.

Bonhoeffer and his circle hastily concocted a plan of action for the German Christian meeting on Monday. They agreed that the signal to walk out would be given when the resolution in favor of Müller reached the floor. It was a dangerous gesture, since it could be branded as reactionary and unpatriotic, and lead to the expulsion of the speakers and a banning of any kind of assembly by the opposition. That, in turn, could jeopardize the meeting of 22 June.

For that reason, Bonhoeffer and the university chaplain Bronisch-Holtze tried to reach Secretary of State Hans-Heinrich Lammers at the Reich chancellery on Saturday, 17 June. Lammers arranged a preliminary meeting between them and Ministerial Counselor Richard Wienstein early Monday.[72] Bonhoeffer and Bronisch-Holtze pointed out to him that the students' meeting on Monday would likely be browbeaten into conformity and that this would present a false picture, since in reality most of the students, including those organized by the National Socialists, supported Bodelschwingh and not Müller. Wienstein noted these objections, but referred his visitors to the Ministry for Cultural Affairs.

At one o'clock that afternoon hundreds of students assembled in the university's large auditorium. According to the *Tägliche Rundschau* report, the meeting had been organized by the German Student Association, which had very little to do with the church. But such a misuse of terms was not unusual in those overzealous times. Four months later in Bradford Bonhoeffer reported that the German Christian Student Movement had organized the meeting, but this was erroneous since at the time that organization was strongly divided about its eventual *Gleichschaltung*. It was anticipated that the student organization would spontaneously vote to join the German Christian Faith movement at the 19 June meeting. But, as the 20 June *Tägliche Rundschau* reported, "upon the announcement of the resolution supporting Chaplain Müller's candidacy for bishop, nine-tenths of the audience left the auditorium." Immediately afterward the opposition held its own meeting in the courtyard beside Hegel's statue; men who were recognized as Party and S.A. members were present. While rejecting the proceedings in the auditorium, the opposition affirmed their allegiance to the state; according to the *Tägliche Rundschau*, "at a rally that followed they submitted themselves to Adolf Hitler's leadership."[73]

These two demonstrations had aroused considerable tension because so much of what happened was unplanned. Afterward Bonhoeffer and Bronisch-Holtze went to the Ministry of Education and the Arts, accompanied by two student supporters of Bodelschwingh in S.A. uniforms. As Bonhoeffer subsequently related in Bradford, they did not succeed in speaking to Minister Rust, but were received by a Counselor Gerullis, whom they told what had happened.[74] As a precaution, however, that same day Bonhoeffer also sent a short account of the proceedings to Wienstein at the Reich chancellery, who gave it to Lammers.[75] Concluding his description of the students' actions opposing Müller, Bonhoeffer wrote: ". . . immediately afterward there was a brief demonstration . . . during which one student gave a *Heil* for the Reich chancellor, the rest following suit."[76]

Three days later, on 22 June, the more serious meeting took place in the university's new assembly hall. Though lively, it was more dignified and academic than the Monday meeting, and there were no interruptions.

This time, with the backing of the university chaplain's office, a working committee of Protestant students called the meeting. This group had been founded and named in 1930 by Bronisch-Holtze as a loosely knit association of Protestant students; it included both fraternity members and nonmembers. This "Working Committee" was able to bypass the German Christian group as well as the German Christian Student Movement. The topic was "The Struggle for the Church." Those speaking for the German Christians were Emanuel Hirsch, Luther scholar Ernst Vogelsang (a colleague of Ludwig Müller's), and Professor Caius Fabricius; Berlin professors Adolf Deissmann, Ernst Sellin, and Wilhelm Lütgert spoke for the Catholic Center Party, as did F. K. Schumann from Halle; Bonhoeffer spoke on behalf of the Young Reformation members. There were heated exchanges between professors and individual students before a university audience said to have numbered two thousand.

Hirsch and his friends insisted that there should be no attempt to dissociate the church from the new state, and that the great missionary opportunities that had arisen should be used. Schumann appealed to both sides, incurring vehement reproaches from Bonhoeffer after the meeting. The minutes of the meeting stated:

> Lic. Bonhoeffer discussed the meaning of the struggle. If God had involved the church in struggle, it was to humble it. There was therefore no place in this dispute for self-justification. Anyone who simply made accusations without also accusing himself had failed to understand the meaning of the struggle. (The strength of the church rests in her ability to enter into repentance.)
>
> Once again the contrast in Romans 14 between the strong in faith and the weak in faith became apparent. Someone strong in faith did not expel others; the weak in faith was the person who barred people from the community. Today the weak in faith had introduced a racial law. The strength of the others would now consist in being open to the cause of the weak. But they must beware, for it was precisely the weak who were the active ones, the reformers. (The substance of the church is at stake in the tension between the strong and the weak.)
>
> A faith movement should not underrate the Confession (in a refutation of Fabricius's remarks about the Jewish question). The first Council was convened when this happened in early Christian times.
>
> Today, too, there was a need for a council. Its decisions should be binding. (Everyone must be legitimated in light of the Confession.) The last

possibility open to Protestantism was schism. Now the Confession was at stake. There were two points of doctrine to be decided: the doctrine of the church and the doctrine of Creation. While the struggle in the church was a great gift, the greatest gift of all was peace.[77]

Junge Kirche reported on the meeting:

> The greatest impact on the meeting were the words of Licentiate Bonhoeffer when he pointed to the possibilities and limitations of a struggle within the church. This struggle could only be conducted in the collective knowledge of the forgiveness of sins and in the spirit of "judge not." [Bonhoeffer directed this toward his colleagues, not the Aryan clause.] Those who were weak in faith, who wanted to set up a law like the Aryan clause before the doorway to the church, had to be borne by those who were strong in faith, as stated in Romans 14. If the law established by the weak really became the law of the church, then the decision could be given only to a Protestant council, which—aside from the prophetic and Reformation authority of the revelation of God to each individual—would be the decisive authority to decide all questions that affected the substance of the church. This Protestant council would then have to decide about the unity and schism of the church. The church should thank God for the hour of its confession, but should also always know that God's highest gift to God's church was peace.[78]

Three points emerged clearly from this report:

1. Bonhoeffer's serious conviction that the struggle was taking place within a still undivided church.

2. During the preceding weeks theologians had consulted the Bible to see if it presented any opportunity of permitting acceptance of the Aryan clause. Increasingly the argument was being made that, for the sake of the weak in faith, it might actually be possible to eliminate the offense of racial nonconformity in certain members of the community by establishing new groups. Bonhoeffer unmasked this argument as a trick of the "weak" who had not yet succeeded in making their wish become the heretical law of the "strong."

3. A triumph by the "weak" would inevitably lead to schism. Here Bonhoeffer introduced his idea of a conciliar decision. To most in the audience the idea must have seemed archaic, and Schumann emphatically rejected any idea of "schism." But this was the point in Bonhoeffer's speech, more than any other that was talked about. "I'm told that in your speech you suggested convening a 'Council,'" Gertrud Staewen wrote in a postcard.[79] Bonhoeffer displayed a faith in the concreteness of the church that astounded his

audience. Schumann immediately warned against any "idolization" of the church. And how should a council be created that was willing and able to make decisions? But Bonhoeffer was aiming high: his own church and the ecumenical churches must be brought to have greater faith in themselves and in their concrete assembly. Was this not a repudiation of Protestantism's sacred possessions, tolerance, and liberalism?

In fact, Bonhoeffer, though thoroughly shaped by a liberal tradition, was growing antiliberal. His instincts were certain that now, in 1933, respectable political and theological liberalism was digging its own grave because it was leaving the decisions to the tyrant, out of superciliousness or merely a weak laissez-faire attitude. He saw that the time for compromise was disappearing quickly, and that the time for a clear yes or no was coming. In his writings of 1932 and 1933 Bonhoeffer proposed to his own church and to the ecumenical movement that they should rediscover "council," "heresy," "confession," and "doctrinal decision"—and this at a time when skepticism was paralyzing those with more experience. His elders looked upon the younger man as a mere visionary.

But these were not idle dreams. What Bonhoeffer had in mind would be realized one year later, to his intense joy: the Barmen and Dahlem synods— as a "council"—confessed and arrived at doctrinal decisions, defined the heretic, and called upon the church, in obedience to the Gospel, to separate itself from heresy. But it soon became apparent that Bonhoeffer believed in synods more deeply and literally than most of those who attended them. At home and in the ecumenical movement, he eventually lost the battle against synod delegates and their image of themselves as "fathers of the council."

Personally Bonhoeffer's commitment was made possible by his own decisiveness; theologically it was fostered through his faith in the Holy Spirit. He may also have believed that once decisions had been made, only by adhering to them could the valuable tradition of liberalism be preserved throughout a period of tyranny. It was a sign of true liberalism when Bonhoeffer confronted the dictates with counter-dictates, instead of exhausting himself with the responses of a ravaged old liberal.

Two days after the debate at Berlin University the position had drastically changed. Here, again, Bonhoeffer had very definite ideas that were too much for his colleagues and which they regarded as illusory.

August Jäger. On Thursday, 22 June, Kapler resigned as president of the Evangelical Church Federation (at the Reich level) and of the High Church Council (in Prussia). His successor in the Church Council, although only provisionally appointed by the Church Senate, was Rhineland General

Superintendent Ernst Stoltenhoff. Although Stoltenhoff's attitude toward
the new state was one of impeccable conformity, the minister for Religious
Affairs saw this as a favorable opportunity for intervention. He decreed that
there had been an infringement of the 1931 state agreement that provided
for the Prussian government (now with Göring at the helm) to have a say
in the appointment, and declared a state of emergency in Prussia. On Saturday, 24 June (Saturday was a favorite day for revolutionary action), he
nominated the Wiesbaden magistrate August Jäger as state commissar of
Prussia, "to put an end to strife within the church." This action, in fact,
marked the real beginning of that battle. Without delay Jäger appointed
state commissars for each of the church provinces in Old Prussia and for
the larger church associations. The commissars, some of them in S.A. uniform, immediately took over the consistorial presidents' offices. In a broadcast on 27 June Jäger declared that resistance was "treason against the
people and the state" and would be suppressed "as revolt and rebellion
against the state's authority." The police chiefs were instructed to prevent
any sabotage of these orders; all representative church bodies were declared
dissolved, the employees of the Evangelical High Church Council were
suspended, and the general superintendent was relieved of his office. Dr.
Friedrich Werner, a lawyer who would subsequently play a significant role,
appointed Jäger president of the High Church Council, Joachim Hossenfelder (leader of the German Christians) as spiritual vice president, and
Ludwig Müller head of the Church of the Old Prussian Union and of the
Church Federation Office. On 28 June Müller ordered the S.A. to occupy
the Church Federation Office.

It was a tremendous shock, and the resulting chaos was indescribable.
Nothing of the kind had ever happened before. Bodelschwingh immediately resigned as Reich bishop on 24 June, in protest against the installation of
a state commissar. Otto Dibelius also protested—and his position was greeted throughout the country with jubilation—"I cannot allow any state commissar to relieve me of these deepest responsibilities of my office."[80]

The situation reached a dramatic climax on Sunday, 2 July. As the
supreme spiritual authority in Old Prussia, Hossenfelder ordered services of
praise and thanksgiving for which the churches were to be decorated with
flags, and ordered the following message to be read from the pulpit:

> All those who are concerned for the safe structure of our church in the
> great revolution of these times, must . . . feel deeply thankful that the state
> should have assumed, in addition to all its tremendous tasks, the great load
> and burden of reorganizing the church.[81]

At ten o'clock Ludwig Müller conducted a service in the cathedral, and Hossenfelder presided at the service in the Kaiser Wilhelm Memorial Church; both men read this proclamation.

The suspended general superintendents had suggested a service of atonement and prayer on 2 July; the Young Reformation members did everything possible to spread word of this throughout Berlin. In Steglitz Pastor Grossmann was arrested by an S.A. commando—the first arrest in the church struggle. That evening Jacobi conducted a service of atonement in the Kaiser Wilhelm Memorial Church; he began by announcing Grossmann's arrest, and called for prayers of intercession. In Dahlem, the three pastors of the Jesus Christus Church (Fritz Müller, Eberhard Röhricht, and Martin Niemöller) appeared together before the congregation. As they spoke the words of the second article of the creed, the congregation spontaneously joined in; such a thing had never happened before. From then on the practice continued until it was ultimately accepted throughout the entire German church.

The unrest in the churches assumed the proportions of an avalanche. Protest delegations and teachers traveled to Berlin and converged on the Reich chancellery. Bonhoeffer composed a "Declaration of the Ministers of Greater Berlin" that was concluded on 6 July and sent, with 106 signatures, to the Reich chancellor.[82] Bodelschwingh gained a hearing with Hindenburg, who conveyed his protest to Hitler. Hitler, who was in the midst of a campaign to reassure the foreign community and was also concerned with gaining more support in the Catholic church, promised Hindenburg that he would soon placate the Protestant church. Interior Minister Wilhelm Frick was told to speed up the work of producing a new constitution for a Reich church, in cooperation with the twenty-eight regional church authorities. The state commissars were withdrawn and the suspensions of the general superintendents and church councillors revoked. On 14 July Hitler proclaimed that work on the constitution was complete. Soon afterward, on 23 July, he made the surprise announcement of general church elections. Everything seemed to fit in with Hitler's speech of 6 July, in which he announced the end of the revolution, and with the Concordat, which the Holy See concluded with the Third Reich on 20 July.

The battle had been short but hard. Now it remained to be seen if victory had really been won.

Interdict. The struggle had suddenly turned not just against one part of the church, but against the state and its political measures. Bonhoeffer and his students had been energetically involved in a dramatic conflict that lasted barely three weeks. Not only had the students provided an indispensable news service for those who had been suspended, but they also formulated and disseminated their own protests. One such declaration, which had the character of a short confession, clearly indicated Bonhoeffer's influence. It stated the truth in three theses, from the perspective of the Bible and the Reformation: renewal could only come through a return to pure proclamation, race was irrelevant to church membership, and church vocations could be filled only according to spiritual considerations. The entire essay was written in the first person plural—"we see," "we want," "we believe"—and concluded with concrete and real demands: "We reject . . . we demand . . . no intervention, no Hossenfelder . . ."[83]

The demonstrations on behalf of the general superintendents, protest delegations, and services of atonement went off with encouraging smoothness. At the beginning of July Barth arrived on the scene. But Bonhoeffer was still not satisfied; he was alarmed by the sluggish reactions of the pastors. He felt that the clergy should have displayed greater vigor and efficacy against the state's actions, and in a way that would have made it clear to everyone that this issue confronted the entire church, not just its top leaders.

Bonhoeffer and Hildebrandt believed that the clergy and general superintendents should proclaim what amounted to an interdict. This would mean that the clergy would carry out a boycott against conducting funeral services, as long as government by the state commissars lasted. Their efforts to gain acceptance for the idea were in vain; few people showed any understanding for the ideas of these two young men. They either reacted indignantly over such political intransigence or failed to recognize the potential of these tactics. Yet the idea was not as illusory as people thought; in 1941 the Norwegian clergy did not hesitate to boycott their duties in this way, thus securing a permanent victory.

During this period the two friends contemplated for the first time the possibility of leaving the Protestant church; Martin Niemöller also considered such a move.[84] On 18 June, one week before the seizure of power by Jäger, Hossenfelder, and Müller, Hildebrandt had been ordained. Now his worried friends asked what this ordination meant in a church that had accommodated itself to Nazism and was issuing decrees on "racial conformity" that would legally exclude the newly ordained man from the ministry. They argued that this organization should not be called a "church" and that words alone would not suffice. Sooner than might have been expected they seemed to have reached the point of a possible *status confessionis*, which the students had only nervously hinted at during their demonstration.

To Bonhoeffer and Hildebrandt the struggle seemed too much like a reactionary attempt to recapture former positions; indeed, this would soon be the outcome. What they sought, however, was the rebirth of a regenerated church. "I am afraid . . . that the erosion will be gradual and continuous since there is now insufficient strength for united action. . . . Then back we go to the small groups."[85] By "united action," Bonhoeffer meant an interdict.

While the two friends impatiently thought about these things, a message came from Bonn that clarified the situation: Karl Barth's document *Theological Existence Today*. In a very short time thirty thousand copies had been distributed throughout the country.

July: Church Elections

To a large extent the 1933 church elections were rigged, and there was little doubt that the German Christians would win; still the Young Reformation members had to play their part and do the best they could. Bonhoeffer threw himself into the desperate campaign without reservation.

> The ecclesial political events have kept me fully occupied. Now a decision is hanging directly over us, a decision, I believe, of the utmost importance for church politics. I have little doubt that the German Christians will emerge victorious and that, because of this, the outlines of the new church will very quickly be revealed. Consequently, it will be questionable whether we can continue as a church.[86]

Election Prospects. The Reich government's decree ordering church elections, issued on short notice, was of dubious legality. It clearly favored the German Christians, who had the help of Party organizations and the media at their disposal. With hardly a week between the announcement and the actual elections, the opposition had little hope of success. Although discredited and unorganized, the church opposition remained the only sector capable of reminding the state of the need for justice, impartiality, and dignity in the elections. There was no longer enough time for such an opposition to establish itself by reinstating the general superintendents and the members of the High Church Council, let alone become an effective force.

The state appointed Secretary of State Hans Pfundtner "plenipotentiary of the Reich interior minister for the supervision of the impartial implementation of the church elections," and declared that the elections were free and that any attempt to influence them by coercive means was inadmissible; but who was going to investigate or expose the innumerable local cases of coercion? *Tägliche Rundschau*, the only daily paper that published reports favorable to the opposition, had been banned. S.A. commandos broke up local opposition election rallies. Intimidation was the order of the day in the form of threats of dismissal or financial sanctions against anyone who, by opposing the German Christians, was revealed as a traitor to the National Socialist state. Hitler himself wrote pointedly to Ludwig Müller on 19 July: "I wish . . . to thank you and the German Christians, and to assure you of my special and lasting confidence."[87] It was almost a miracle that the Young Reformation members were able to draw up any list of candidates in many places as an alternative to the German Christians.

The traditional parties in church elections, the Positive Union and the Liberals, seemed to have totally disappeared. Both liberal and orthodox individuals suddenly found themselves side by side with the German Christians or else with the Young Reformation members; some, surprised to find themselves in such company, felt ashamed of their new allies. Everyone, however, hastened to affirm that the past had been overcome and that they were throwing all their energies into ensuring the success of Hitler's state. Even the Young Reformation members surpassed themselves in their efforts not to become politically suspect. *Junge Kirche* declared:

> Grateful and determined, we stand behind Hindenburg and Hitler as the leaders of our state, for by their intervention they have now paved the way to freedom for the church. . . . There is no place for reaction either within the church or in her politics. . . . Our attitude to the state is one of obedience and love. In this election we are concerned *only* with the church.[88]

The other side, of course, immediately spotted the different wording. They would never have spoken of "leaders" in the plural, mentioning Hindenburg as one of them, nor would they have mentioned both names in that sequence. Their turn of phrase was somewhat different—and this was not only true of the polemical German Christian leader Joachim Hossenfelder. Even a churchman as trusted and influential as Erich Stange could bring himself to say:

> It is inexcusable that the church today should remain aloof from a state that patently and explicitly seeks to redress that [earlier] fall from grace [he meant that during the nineteenth century the German state had maintained a (supposedly) false neutrality toward the church], instead of welcoming this state with open arms.[89]

Student director Hans Schomerus even recommended the dissolution of the church as an independent organization, so that a "Reich standard of

Christian education" might be formed on a denominational basis, under a state-appointed archbishop who would serve as "supreme head of Reich Christian education."[90]

Despite so many zealous assurances of loyalty to the Third Reich, the electorate understood the difference between the German Christian slogan, ("Build the new Church of Christ in the new State of Adolf Hitler") and that of the Young Reformation movement ("Gospel and Church").

The Gestapo. Bonhoeffer rarely permitted any of these tumultuous events to interfere with his Christology lectures, but he canceled his lecture for the week of the elections. He and his students worked feverishly night and day on election preparations. His parents put their home and his father's car and chauffeur at his disposal. During the weekend of 15–16 July Bonhoeffer and his students wrote and duplicated leaflets.[91]

On the evening of Monday, 17 July, the Gestapo entered the offices of the Young Reformation movement in Dahlem and confiscated the leaflets and lists of candidates, rendering their laborious preparations in vain.[92] The German Christians had succeeded in obtaining a legal injunction against the title the Young Reformation movement had selected for their party program, "List of the Evangelical Church."

In response to this shock, on the afternoon of 18 July Bonhoeffer and Jacobi drove to the Gestapo offices on Prinz Albrecht Strasse that would later become so notorious. The Gestapo was not yet pursuing Bonhoeffer and Jacobi; for the time being it was they who were on the tracks of the Gestapo.

Jacobi later said that the Gestapo headquarters showed every evidence of its recent move. He himself was wearing, as was then customary, the two Iron Crosses he had won in the First World War. They would like to have taken with them (but at the last moment decided to leave behind) a real, flesh-and-blood, uniformed S.A. member who was also a member of the Young Reformation movement. With obstinate insistence Bonhoeffer and Jacobi finally succeeded in seeing Rudolf Diels, head of the Gestapo. They reminded him and another official that the state had promised a free and secret election, but that the previous day's events were a clear case of electoral obstruction and interference. Diels yielded on the condition that they drop the title, "List of the Evangelical Church,"[93] and consented to Jacobi's suggestion that the words "Gospel and Church" be used instead. Some of the confiscated leaflets were returned. Diels made both men responsible for the strict observance of the agreement; if any leaflets appeared with the old or similar slogans or if they libeled the German Christians, Bonhoeffer and Jacobi would be liable to arrest.

This visit took place five days before the election. That same afternoon the two men distributed a letter asking Young Reformation members to honor their agreement with Diels, but also urging that irregularities in electoral procedure should be reported promptly and without hesitation.[94] *Junge Kirche* printed a revised edition of its most recent issue (17 July, Number 4), and new leaflets were distributed by the "Reich leadership" of the Young Reformation movement.

The two pastors' first visit to Gestapo headquarters led to rumors that became increasingly dramatic by the time they reached friends abroad. When the events of September revived the rumors, Siegmund-Schultze wrote to Bonhoeffer from Switzerland: "Some very important people in the ecumenical movement have heard wild rumors alleging, for instance, that you are to be sent to a concentration camp and that it is not yet certain that you will be able to avoid this."[95] Bonhoeffer replied: "I have not actually been in a concentration camp, although, on the occasion of the church election, the highest police official raised the prospect that I and my colleague might be sent there."[96]

On the eve of the election, during an interval in the Wagner Festival in Bayreuth, Hitler made a radio broadcast to the German people. He expected, he said, that in support of all he had achieved that the people on Sunday would elect those forces "that are exemplified by the German Christians who stand firmly upon the foundation of the Nationalist Socialist State."[97]

The election results were overwhelming. Seventy percent of the vote, in some places even more, enabled the German Christians to move into key positions in the church. Their exultation knew no bounds.

On 23 July Bonhoeffer preached in the Trinity Church about the rock against which the gates of hell shall not prevail:

> Nothing shall be made easy for us. We are confronted by a decision that will not be taken from us—it means a decision, it means a parting of the ways. . . . Come . . . all you who are abandoned and left alone, we will go back to the Holy Scriptures, we will go and look for the church together. . . . It may be that from a human point of view great times for the church are actually times of demolition. . . . Let the church remain the church! . . . confess, confess, confess.[98]

Defeat. The day after the election, "in loyal recognition of the altered situation," General Superintendent Otto Dibelius and a number of High Church Council members asked to be released from office.[99] During the fever of the election week church authorities had gone to considerable length to show "objective" restraint and neutrality. Now the more moderate German Christians were entrusted with the administration of the German Evangelical Church until the national synod, which Ludwig Müller had called for the end of September. These provisional administrators were Professor Karl Fezer (Tübingen), Bishop Schöffel (Hamburg), Professor F. K. Schumann (Halle), and President Koopman. In the Old Prussian Union Church, Müller was made president of the High Church Council with the title of bishop. In keeping with the leadership principle, he was also invested with supreme powers enabling him to exercise the authority of the High Church Council independently. Thus the "leadership principle" and "racial conformity" were already being enforced, although legally such matters could be formulated and approved only by synods. While there could be no doubt of the majorities that would prevail in the synods, there were still some grounds for hope in the unresolved tensions between the moderate, evangelistic German Christians and their more extreme colleagues.

The day after the elections, the Young Reformation members rapidly took stock of their defeat, and announced their withdrawal from church politics as a result. The origins of that movement made church politics secondary anyway; they had entered the world of tactics only reluctantly. Now that responsibility lay entirely with the newly elected authorities, the energies of the Young Reformation movement were to be devoted to evangelistic work.

This declaration set the tone for the future, and marked the beginning of a new period. Now it was a question of forcing the German Christians to decide what they would preach from the pulpit: what, in 1933, was indispensable for a church of the Reformation? In other words, the Young Reformation members intended to confront the German Christians with a relevant and painstakingly worked-out confession.[100]

The events of the 23 July election had decided the question of power in the church, but not the question of truth. An appreciable divergence between power and truth was to be expected. The point might soon be reached where a minority, however small, could no longer remain silent, and the future seemed to hold a struggle of a new kind that would be fought on new ground. Who, until now, had been concerned with both the center and the boundaries of the confession? Only three years earlier, at a general synod of the Old Prussian Union Church, during deliberations about a way of life for the church, one passage had been deleted on the grounds that it contained a "confession of faith" and "it cannot conceivably be the task of the General Synod to vote on a confession of faith."[101]

At the meeting of the Young Reformation movement on 24–25 July Martin Niemöller played a pivotal role in moving them toward their decision to formulate a binding confession. This decision was an attempt to synthesize what had been only sporadic and individual attempts to formulate new confessions. The practical work began immediately, and a deadline was set. Bonhoeffer (the youngest of those discussing the question) and Hermann Sasse were instructed to go on a retreat in Bethel during August to write a first draft. At Bodelschwingh's behest—and this meant on behalf of the entire German church—Georg Merz, Wilhelm Vischer, and eventually others were to join them. Bodelschwingh would sign the resulting document, which would then be presented to theological authorities throughout the entire German Evangelical Church. Gerhard Stratenwerth joined Bonhoeffer and Sasse as secretary.

Bonhoeffer took a leave of absence for the month of August to go to Bethel. On 26 July his general superintendent wrote him: "I'm delighted that you get a period of rest. During the past weeks we have all suffered as much from psychological tension as from physical strain."[102] Karow did not yet know the ulterior motive behind this request for leave.

London. Bonhoeffer took a circuitous route to Bethel. He left for London on 27 July. On 30 July he preached to two German-speaking congregations, the Reformed congregation of St. Paul's in the East End, and the United congregation in Sydenham. He was also able to inspect the pastorate in Sydenham. This did not resolve his "inner tension" or lessen his uncertainty about what course he should take: if anything, it added to his problems.

Small wonder, then, that Bonhoeffer canceled all his commitments that summer that were related to the regional and international ecumenical youth conferences. During the week of the elections, he had already canceled his participation at the French counterpart to the Westerburg conference, which he originally planned to attend en route to London. He sacrificed the second Gland conference for the work in Bethel, sending Fritz Söhlmann to represent him, although the bishop of Ripon had urged him to attend:

> I most particularly hope that you will be there, with a Delegation from Germany. If this falls through, the Conference will be robbed of a great part of its value at the present time.[103]

In mid-July, during the last weeks of the state commissariat, Theodor Heckel in the Church Federation Office conveyed an invitation to the Sydenham pastorate to Bonhoeffer; he accepted it during the hectic week of the election.[104] Heckel had met Bonhoeffer frequently since the April 1932 conference at the Church Federation Office, most recently in the spring with the Young Reformation members. Heckel's office oversaw the German parishes abroad, and the two London parishes had asked him to help them find a successor to Pastor Singer. Bonhoeffer was attracted by the possibility of finally extricating himself from the internal and external problems facing the church, particularly since recent developments had also led Franz Hildebrandt to consider the possibility of a ministry abroad.

> My personal future may well take a decisive turn rather soon. It has been proposed to me that I go to London as a German pastor with a special commission for ecumenical work. I have been thinking about it very much and I believe, of course, that, given all the possibilities that one must take into consideration for the church, closer contacts with the English churches might eventually be of very great importance.[105]

Tempting though the offer was, Bonhoeffer still could not make up his mind. In his search for the right decision, he tormented those around him almost as much as he tormented himself. Asked for advice about whether Bonhoeffer should go to London, the bishop of Ripon wrote him:

> As to the move suggested to you, it is only you who knows how far you would be accepting a narrower sphere of influence by leaving the Student world of Berlin, or on the contrary giving yourself freer scope for development and wider experience. What you say about the disinclination in Germany at present for the goods the World Alliance seeks to supply, is perhaps a sufficient reason for coming to England, where you might be available as an interpreter of Germany at a time when such interpreters are badly needed. . . .[106]

Hermann Sasse tried to persuade him to go: "I saw in him one of Germany's best theologians, and did not want to see him go under in the petty war against the Gestapo and Rosenberg."[107] The London parish urged Bonhoeffer to come; Heckel had warmly recommended him as one whom "I personally like very much, and who has proved himself well here in the most diverse situations."[108] The pressure grew after his trial sermon, yet Bonhoeffer did not agree at once. Only after the events in Bethel and the developments connected with the Berlin provincial synod took a disappointing turn did he finally decide on London. His general superintendent wrote to him in resignation:

> I am deeply distressed by the fact that theologians of your kind should believe that there is no more room for them in the German church. Your

relations already established with other countries through your ecumenical work will have been a positive influence on your decision. Thus in your case the line of development is at least apparent. . . . [Your activity abroad] will give you the opportunity of rendering more valuable services to the Protestant church and to the German heritage, perhaps, than would be possible here. . . .[109]

August: The Bethel Confession

Upon his return from London Bonhoeffer went to Bethel where he met Hildebrandt, who had arrived there from Hengelo in Holland. Whereas all doors in London had been open to Bonhoeffer, Hildebrandt had met with little success. Bonhoeffer promised his friend that he would invite him to London, if the decisions made by the impending synods made a move imperative.

Friedrich von Bodelschwingh welcomed the newly appointed confessional experts and showed them through the Bethel community's institutions. Bonhoeffer had never been to Bethel before. Shaken by the experience, he wrote to his grandmother who, after playing a lively part in the events of the previous weeks, was on holiday in Friedrichsbrunn:

> It is said of the Buddha that he was converted by an encounter with a man who was gravely ill. It is sheer madness, as some believe today, that the sick can or ought to be legally eliminated. It is virtually the same as building a Tower of Babel, and is bound to avenge itself.[110]

During his visit Bonhoeffer also had the chance to meet some of the teachers at the school of theology in Bethel, such as Edmund Schlink, Robert Frick, Wilhelm Vischer, and Georg Merz.

Intention. In Berlin the German Christians' growing power was demonstrated by Göring's appointment of Ludwig Müller as a Prussian state counselor on 4 August. In Bethel, Sasse and Bonhoeffer began work on the document that was to confront those same German Christians with the question of truth. The time seemed ripe for such a move. Throughout the country people were working on drafts for confessions.

In May a group in the Rhineland connected to Barth, Goeters, Niesel, and de Quervain had already published a "Theological Declaration on the Form of the Church." In Westphalia numerous groups had worked since June on similar projects. Their colleagues from the district synod in Tecklenburg submitted the so-called Tecklenburg Confession to the Westphalian provincial synod in August. In southern Germany, the "Riederauer Theses" were written under Hermann Sasse's direction and published by Theodor Ellwein and Christian Stoll.[111] On 14 July, the day the new church constitution was announced, Walter Künneth, Martin Niemöller, and Hans Lilje published a declaration for the Young Reformation members that used the term "heresy"—still somewhat unusual. They stated:

> It is not enough to speak of the inviolability of the confessions; the issue is acknowledging of the present validity of the confessions, and taking it seriously as the standard for proclamation.[112]

Niemöller addressed the new situation even more pointedly on 2 August, at a meeting of the inner circle of the Young Reformation members where he presented the decisions of 24–25 July in his own sixteen theses:

> Is there theologically a fundamental difference between the teachings of the Reformation and those proclaimed by the German Christians? We fear: Yes!—They say: No!—This lack of clarity must be cleared up through a confession for our time. If this doesn't come from the other side—and there's no sign of it coming soon—then it has to come from us; and it has to come in such a way that the others must say Yes or No to it. . . .[113]

This question of confession was now being dealt with outside the circles of theological experts. At the end of August the Young Reformation members encouraged people to discuss the confessions in the parishes:

> . . . this does not just mean the confessions of the Reformation, but particularly the more recent confessions, such as the "Confession of Altona Pastors" or the "Attempt at a Lutheran Catechism" by Bonhoeffer and Hildebrandt.[114]

> It will not be much longer before a confession is produced by our circle as well, which will offer the most suitable foundation for such teaching in the parish.[115]

The groundwork had been laid, the atmosphere was expectant, and Bonhoeffer and Sasse had a clear assignment when they began their work in Bethel. Their intent was to produce something usable and widely accepted by the time the national synod met at the beginning of September. They set to work on 15 August.

The first stage of work was, Sasse tells us, "a phase of happy collaboration." In Bonhoeffer's letter to his grandmother on 20 August, delight was tempered by skepticism:

Our work here gives us much pleasure but also much trouble. We want to try to make the German Christians declare their intentions. Whether we shall succeed I rather doubt. For even now if they officially make concessions in their formulations, the pressure they are placed under is so powerful that sooner or later all promises are bound to be broken. It is becoming increasingly clear to me that what we're going to get is a big, popular, national church whose nature cannot any longer be reconciled with Christianity and that we must be prepared to enter upon entirely new paths which we will have to tread. The question really is: Germanism or Christianity? The sooner the conflict comes out into the open, the better. Nothing is more dangerous than concealing this.[116]

Hans Ehrenberg, who was also working on a confession, sent Hans Fischer on a visit to Bethel to convey his ideas. Regarding his own role, Bonhoeffer said that he "truly worked with passion."[117]

With theological conscientiousness, the group in Bethel tried to make its teachings relevant for the times. In an address to German pastors in Bradford, Yorkshire, Bonhoeffer described the nature of the work that had defined Confessing statements from trinitarian doctrine to eschatology.[118] They had made a number of reformulations: in the doctrine of justification, to unmask Ludwig Müller's trite reduction of Christianity to trust in God and being good fellows; in the doctrine of the cross, so as to pillory the reinterpretation of the cross as a symbol of the Nazi slogan "public interest before self-interest" by Friedrich Wieneke, the German Christian chaplain to the Prussian court; and finally, in the doctrine of the Holy Spirit, from a christological standpoint, with renewed emphasis on the *filioque*, so as to guard against the dangerous emphasis that Hirsch, Althaus, and Fezer put on the revelation in the creation, and to refute its consequences in Stapel's independent notion of the law of race. To Bonhoeffer's delight, Wilhelm Vischer produced the first draft of the section on the Jewish question.

The work was concluded in a spirit less happy than that in which it had begun. This may have been because the Bethel confession was hampered from the start by its authors' anxiety not to omit anything, or perhaps because it took too Lutheran a turn. Whatever the case, its reception by the experts was unexpectedly disappointing. The path that led from individual and local confessional attempts to the Bethel undertaking, and finally to the more effective Barmen confession, was to be longer and more painful than Bonhoeffer and Sasse imagined at the time.

Reactions. Around 25 August the authors of the first draft handed in their work. Now, in Bonhoeffer's view, a period of compromise began, during which their text was watered down to such an extent that he ultimately refused to work on the final edition.

He even objected to the list of some twenty experts to be consulted. On 26 August Bodelschwingh sent the confession out for opinions and signatures.[119] The recipients included Niemöller, Künneth, Lilje, Jacobi, Ehrenberg, Asmussen, Barth, Schlatter, and Heim. Bonhoeffer immediately sensed that Heim and Schlatter would never approve the entire text. Indeed, Schlatter's sarcastic rejection was not slow in coming: if there had to be any confession, he maintained, it should be directed toward Bonn—that is, against Karl Barth. In his Bradford speech Bonhoeffer spoke of the "strange course taken by Bodelschwingh" that "thwarted" the progress of this attempt at a confession.[120]

They were unable to keep to their deadline. In light of the impending synods, the experts had been given far too much time to respond. In Berlin Bonhoeffer himself collected the corrections suggested by Künneth, Niemöller, and Jacobi, but to no avail.

Moreover, he felt that the most important parts of the confession had been watered down. This was particularly true of Vischer's section on the Jewish question. The section on the state included laudatory additions about "joyful collaboration" with the state's aims. A statement about sharing responsibility for the country's guilt had been changed to express the church's part "in the glory and guilt of her people."

Finally, in the ensuing debate about signing the document, new reservations arose on the confessional side; even Sasse and Merz refused to sign if their names had to appear alongside those of Reformed representatives.

Merz eventually informed Niemöller that Bonhoeffer—who had left for London some time before—"has declared himself wholly dissatisfied with the new version and [is] opposed to its publication in its present form."[121] When Bodelschwingh finally realized that his team of older and younger theologians could no longer be kept together he tired of the whole business. But at the insistence of Karl Lücking, Gerhard Stratenwerth, and Georg Merz, Niemöller eventually brought out the revised form of the Bethel confession.[122]

This version went through several editions, but it lacked the impact it had initially promised. Apparently the time was not yet ripe for what Bonhoeffer had in mind. When he gave Barth his reasons for going to London he added, "Another symptom for me was that there was an almost total lack of understanding for the Bethel Confession."[123]

Alarm in Berlin. Bonhoeffer made the final decision to go to London while in Bethel. Dean Erich Seeberg gave him a leave of absence from the university, adding kindly that in the discussions about filling Titius's vacant post Bonhoeffer's name "had been mentioned with great respect."[124] But for the time being, his eagerness to get away was tempered by the events of late summer in Berlin. Indeed, Bonhoeffer eventually postponed his starting date in London until mid-October. Once more he was totally preoccupied by the inevitable aftermath of the German Christians' overwhelming victory in the summer elections.

He returned by way of Friedrichsbrunn; it had been eighteen months since he had walked through its woods. Meanwhile, on 24 August, Jacobi and a small minority of supporters had waged a futile battle at the Berlin provincial synod. Jacobi tried to win a majority at the meeting for a proposal, along the lines of the Young Reformation movement, that the synod develop guidelines for the church's proclamation at the current time. The proposal was given to the Provincial Church Council, which meant the same as rejection.[125] Things became worse: Jacobi and his supporters were unable to prevent the synod from adopting the state's Aryan legislation to apply to the church's civil servants in Berlin. This was a storm warning for the approaching general synod. Bonhoeffer's place was in Berlin. He had already decided what this would mean for him personally—schism. But what would it mean for his colleagues?

September: The Aryan Clause

The crisis reached its climax and turning point in September. This was not the work of the national synod at the end of August; it was brought about at the beginning of September by the Prussian general synod, known as the "brown synod." [This was because many of the church delegates appeared in their brown S.A. uniforms.] The Young Reformation movement was no longer on the front lines; it had been replaced by the Pastors' Emergency League, which was to become the most important next step in the formation of the Confessing church.

Pamphlet. During August it was still unclear what resolutions the synods would pass on "racial conformity" within the church. Would a milder or a stricter form of the Aryan clause be enacted? Would they decide on the radical exclusion of Christians of Jewish descent from congregations, or less drastic legislation on fitness for the ministry—and apply that only to those still unordained, and not to those already in the ministry?

Bonhoeffer drafted a pamphlet predicting the consequences of each decision.[126] He probably wrote it during the first days of August, between

Bethel and London.[127] Titled "The Aryan Clause in the Church," it reached the synodal delegates and congregations in good time, and had some effect.[128] Siegfried Knak, the director of the Berlin Mission, wrote to Professor Julius Richter: "Others within the group [the Gospel and Church group], of course, repudiated any differentiation between Jews and Germans within the church. A short private memorandum by Bonhoeffer helped to confirm many in this opinion."[129] A few weeks later the Church Federation Office decided that Bonhoeffer "could not be sent abroad in light of such positions."[130]

The style of the pamphlet, like that of Hildebrandt's election leaflets, was sharp and succinct: "The German Christians say—We answer!" As compared with the April theses on the Jewish question, it addressed the new issues that had arisen in the meantime: the argument that the "ethnic national order" came from God; the argument stressing the evangelistic opportunities among millions of fellow citizens that would be created by the exclusion of a few hundred Christians of Jewish descent; the *adiaphora*, and the "weak in faith" to whom Paul had yielded.

Bonhoeffer considered three possibilities and spelled out their consequences:

1. Non-Aryans would be excluded from the Reich church and gathered into special congregations: this would necessitate an immediate departure from such a church. To do this would be "my final act of solidarity with my church, which I can serve only with the entire truth and all its consequences."[131] This was not, however, the conclusion of the 1933 synods.

2. The state's Civil Service Law would be applied to church officials: this would necessitate resigning from the ministry. At this point we find Bonhoeffer's characteristic argument about "fatal privilege." The clergy "must see that the only service they can still in all truthfulness render their church is to lay down the ministry that has become a privilege."[132] This became a crucial issue in Berlin on 24 August, and at the general synod of 5–6 September.

3. The Reich church constitution of 14 July 1933, by its silence on the legislation already in force for the universities (including the theological faculties), had already ruled out any possibility of a new generation of pastors of Jewish descent. No one had said a word in protest. Bonhoeffer and Hildebrandt must have felt they were crying in the wilderness. In his pamphlet, therefore, Bonhoeffer envisioned the possibility that the church might have to find means to prepare Christians of Jewish descent for the ministry outside the realm of the existing universities. "Should it fail to do so, then it must accept responsibility for the whole of the Aryan clause."[133]

Although his position was primarily concerned with the internal affairs of the church, with this final point Bonhoeffer had again raised the problem of the church's silence on the Jewish question as such. It was a lone stand. He had gone much too far for his colleagues; even among the Young Reformation members there were good colleagues who had studied under Werner Elert and Paul Althaus—two theologians who would soon put their signatures on the ominous Erlangen opinion, which stated that "The church must therefore demand that its Christians of Jewish descent stay away from the ministry."[134]

Even Martin Niemöller found it difficult to take a position on the Aryan clause. This indecision was evident—although Niemöller was never one to keep silent whenever something needed to be said—in his "Propositions on the Aryan Question in the Church," which he published after repeated requests on 2 November 1933.[135] He did not disguise the fact that he would greatly have preferred to consider the Aryan clause as *adiaphoron*. A comparison of the statements by Bonhoeffer and Niemöller reveals their different emphases, despite the similarity of their actions at this time. Niemöller acknowledged the possibility of reconciling the exclusion of Christians of Jewish descent from church office, using 1 Corinthians 8 and its concept of the "weaker brethren."[136] Bonhoeffer, on the other hand, asked "whether such a bone of contention [namely, "Jewish Christians" in the ministry] must not be demanded of the congregation, for the very sake of the church. ... Those who remain unaffected by this, and hence privileged, will wish to align themselves with their less privileged brethren, rather than make use of privileges within the church."[137]

The Brown Synod. On the final day of the Nuremberg "victory of faith" Party rally, the Old Prussian general synod met in the upper chamber in Berlin for a two-day session. Martin Niemöller took the minutes of this ominous synod.

The dwindling minority of Young Reformation members was led by Westphalian church president Karl Koch. When they arrived at the scene of action on 5 September a paramilitary spectacle met their eyes. The majority of delegates had appeared in brown uniform. Dr. Friedrich Werner was elected president of the synod; German Christian Reich leader Joachim Hossenfelder and August Jäger were elected his deputies.

From the start the synod was more like a demonstration than the usual deliberative assembly. When Jacobi tried to motion, as he had attempted two weeks before, "that guidelines must be worked out for the church's proclamation to our people, and the church's confession obligates today's pastors to follow such guidelines,"[138] the presidium summarily refused to give him permission to speak. Committee work on the important new legislation was not permitted. Everything was passed with a minimum of delay. The Bishops' Law replaced the general superintendents in Old Prussia with ten bishops under the jurisdiction of Reich bishop Ludwig Müller; Bonhoeffer's general superintendent Emil Karow accepted an appointment as bishop of Berlin. The Church Law on the Legal Position of Clergy and Church Officials ordered that clergy could only come from the ranks of those who stood in "unconditional support for the National Socialist State and the German Protestant Church"—and were also of Aryan descent.

The general superintendents present voted against dismissing non-Aryans or those married to non-Aryans who were already in office, yet they voted that such persons should not be eligible for employment in the future. Pomeranian General Superintendent Kalmus spoke for his colleagues when he said: "We understand and appreciate the measures taken by the state and recognize that the Protestant church must also be vigilant in the preservation of the German race."[139] Karow was delighted that at least those who had already been ordained could remain in office.

When Koch finally expressed the opposition's objection to this law he was literally shouted down. He and his supporters then left the hall. Thus no member of the minority was still present when the Prussian representatives to the Wittenberg national synod were elected, and not one of the Prussian Young Reformation members was nominated as a delegate. A few of them turned up in Wittenberg, but only to create a disturbance by handing out leaflets in the streets.

Schism. The work on the Bethel confession, Jacobi's motions at the synods, and the possibility of discussions with moderate German Christians—suddenly all this seemed unimportant.

On the evening of 6 September, when the general synod was over, a few stalwarts met with the opposition at Jacobi's house; the following day they reassembled at Niemöller's. Bonhoeffer and Hildebrandt made an impassioned plea for widespread resignations from office. They believed that, with the Aryan clause, the other side had brought about a schism of the realm to which they all belonged. All that remained was to recognize that fact. In Bonhoeffer's opinion, the exceptions that had been made (which would have applied to Hildebrandt) only obscured the issue. The best service that could be rendered to the other side was to take their schismatic decision in earnest.

But neither at Jacobi's home on Achenbachstrasse nor at Niemöller's on Cecilienallee[140] did Bonhoeffer and Hildebrandt win support for their view. It was too difficult for even this group to link the step toward a church schism with the anti-Semitic problem, since there were only eleven pastors in Prussia who would be affected by the Aryan clause. Siegfried Knak rejected the Aryan clause not because it would bar Christians of Jewish descent from the ministry in the future, but only because of its unchristian retroactive effect on those who had already been ordained.[141] Under Knak's leadership, the circle decided to postpone any schismatic action until the national synod. Bonhoeffer and Hildebrandt insisted that an immediate exodus would not only be more theologically consistent but more strategically successful than a delay. Hildebrandt declared that for the time being he would refuse to preach in any German church. Bonhoeffer announced his intent to win allies for his views in academic circles and in the ecumenical movement.

As far as the impending national synod was concerned, the group proposed to issue a collective statement from the dissenting clergy, so that the bishops of the "intact" churches in the south of Germany could offer more effective opposition. Bonhoeffer was invited to play a leading role in writing the statement.

On 5 September Bonhoeffer sent a telegram to Henriod, hoping it would reach him before the ecumenical conferences in the Balkans:

> General Assembly finished. All General superintendents dismissed. Only Teutonic Christians admitted to national synod. Aryan clause now in action, please work out memorandum against this and inform press at once. Separation at hand. Further information in Sofia.[142]

Next he wrote to Sasse, now a professor in Erlangen, and to Barth in Bonn, asking them for their opinions. While Sasse shared Bonhoeffer's view of the gravity of the decision, he, too, advised postponement until the national synod. He recommended placing as much responsibility as possible in Wittenberg on Lutheran Bishop Hans Meiser.[143] Unfortunately, the hope that Meiser would precipitate a decision in the national synod was to prove illusory.

Bonhoeffer's question to Barth was:

> Several of us are now very drawn to the idea of the Free Church.... I know ... that you will counsel us to wait until we are thrown out. In fact, there are people who have already been thrown out. .... How do things stand with the solidarity among the clergy?[144]

Barth replied immediately on 11 September from Bergli: "I, too, am of the opinion that there is a *status confessionis* here." But to Barth this meant that this church government had to be told openly and directly: in this respect you are no longer the church of Christ! This protest should be followed by others until silence was imposed and the protesters were expelled: "If there is to be schism, it must come from the other side." Bonhoeffer was surprised that even Barth recommended waiting until "there is a clash over an even more central point." The older man advised the younger one to allow the decision to take effect, "to let the facts, as it were, speak for themselves."

> We shall certainly have no cause later to regret a highly active and polemical delay. . . . This battle will be won by those who save their ammunition at the beginning, but who know how to employ it ruthlessly and with unerring aim. One day, believe me, one day all this Hossenfelder business will dissolve, and leave a very foul stink behind it.[145]

Indeed, within three months Hossenfelder had played himself out—unlike the church that supported him. What point, though, could be more "central" than the Aryan clause? This time Barth had disappointed Bonhoeffer, and more especially Hildebrandt. The delaying tactics of their other friends did not bear much resemblance to Barth's "highly active and polemical delay"—quite the contrary. The essential question that affected Hildebrandt was not answered directly, but in a more reserved manner.

The Birth of the Pastors' Emergency League. The long-term consequence of the events of 6–7 September was an association of pastors which, against all expectations, rapidly gained support throughout the country. This was a show of solidarity with non-Aryan colleagues. The brown synod led directly to the establishment of the Pastors' Emergency League.

The League, with its celebrated four points of commitment, grew out of a protest to the church government, drafted and signed by Bonhoeffer and Niemöller. It was then sent by special messenger to Bodelschwingh on 7 September for transmission to the new leaders of the church. The text stated:

> 1. According to the confession of our church, the church's teaching office is bound only to the authorized vocation. The Aryan clause of the new Church Civil Service Law has given rise to a legal situation that directly contradicts this fundamental principle of the confession. This proclaims a situation that is unjust according to the confession as church law, and violates the confession.

> 2. There can be no doubt that the ordained ministers affected by the Civil Service Law, insofar as they have not been deprived by formal procedure of the rights of the clerical profession, should continue to exercise in full the right freely to proclaim the Word and freely to administer the sacra-

ments in the Evangelical Church of the Old Prussian Union, which is based upon the confessions of the Reformation.

3. Anyone who assents to such a breach of the confession excludes himself from the communion of the church. We therefore demand the repeal of this law which separates the Evangelical Church of the Old Prussian Union from the Christian church.[146]

This brought an immediate invitation on 8 September from Bodelschwingh to some of the pastors; Bodelschwingh added, however, that he had reservations about the first sentence of the third paragraph. He regarded the threat of exclusion as impossible to implement. But on 11 September Bodelschwingh sent a protest to Ludwig Müller that largely incorporated the Emergency League statement. He watered down the second sentence of paragraph one:

> In the Aryan clause of the new Church Civil Service Law, the clauses on the exclusion of clergy from their ministries (para. 3, section 2) are at the very least contrary to the basic confession of our church.

In this way he left open the discussion about future ordination of non-Aryans. He reduced the severity of the third paragraph to a tentative request:

> I would earnestly request the immediate withdrawal of those clauses in this law that would separate the Protestant Church of the Old Prussian Union from its confessional foundation.[147]

The three points drawn up by Bonhoeffer and Niemöller on 7 September needed only the addition of the promise to aid those affected by the new law or by forcible measures; this would complete the four points of the Pastors' Emergency League pledge. On 12 September Niemöller called upon the German clergy to protest and to commit themselves: (1) to a new allegiance to the scriptures and confessions, (2) to resist infringement of these, (3) to give financial help to those affected by the law or by violence, and (4) to reject the Aryan clause. He sent the document via trusted Young Reformation members to pastors "for the sake of the many lonely ones, for the sake of our church and for the sake of those who are threatened by the decisions of the Prussian general synod which infringe the confession."[148]

After this pledge an appeal "to the German national synod" was distributed.[149] The main substance of this appeal was based upon the Bonhoeffer-Niemöller declaration of 7 September. On 9 September Bonhoeffer wrote to Barth on behalf of the Young Reformation movement pastors in Berlin:

We have in the first place drawn up a declaration in which we wish to inform the church authorities that, with the Aryan clause, the Evangelical Church of the Old Prussian Union has cut itself off from the church of Christ.[150]

The response exceeded all expectations. It was not long before the first twenty-two signatories of the appeal distributed the protest in Wittenberg in the name of two thousand pastors. By the end of the year membership in the Pastors' Emergency League had risen to six thousand. On 20 October it convened a Council of Brethren, becoming a distinct organization. Elected by the Emergency League members, this council included Superintendent Hugo Hahn of Dresden, Pastor Gerhard Jacobi of Berlin, Pastor Eberhard Klügel of Hanover, Pastor Karl Lücking of Dortmund, Superintendent Ludolf Müller of Heiligenstadt, Pastor Georg Schulz of Barmen, and Pastor D. Ludwig Heitmann of Hamburg. Until the end of the Nazi period, the Council of Brethren administered and distributed voluntary contributions to their persecuted colleagues. The day would come when Bonhoeffer himself would be among the persecuted.

The new phase of church resistance was now ushered in by a team more homogeneous than the original band of Young Reformation members in May. Those early militants could hardly have been expected to take the Aryan clause as their sole point of departure; that would have led to an immediate disintegration of the ranks.

Sofia. The World Alliance conference in Sofia, Bulgaria, from 15 to 30 September, was the only scheduled ecumenical conference Bonhoeffer attended during those hectic days of 1933. For him the moment was opportune.

As usual the World Alliance and the Life and Work conferences took place in close conjunction. Although Bonhoeffer took no part in the Life and Work conference in Novi Sad, it is of interest because of the subtle differences that distinguished it from the Sofia meeting, and also because of its consequences for Bonhoeffer.

Bonhoeffer had been the chief German protagonist in Sofia; in Novi Sad it was Theodor Heckel. Heckel had failed to draw any consequences from the brown synod for his own official position, nor had he been involved with the Young Reformation members' deliberations of 6–7 September. As the German Evangelical Church's official for foreign affairs, he would soon become Bonhoeffer's superior. Novi Sad and Sofia revealed the extent to which the two men's paths had diverged. Heckel now pursued a completely different course in his attempt to bring the pitching ship of the German church, with its congregations abroad, safely into harbor. While he never joined the German Christians, he jeopardized his reputation throughout the Nazi period and, as far as Bonhoeffer and his friends at home and abroad were concerned, irretrievably lost it. In Bonhoeffer's eyes Heckel's course amounted to surrender; Bonhoeffer viewed his policies as a betrayal of the church and the ecumenical movement. Even among Bonhoeffer's friends, including Niemöller, appreciation for the new state was not unknown; but in Heckel this appreciation was combined with actual decisions that angered Bonhoeffer.

The executive committee of Life and Work met in Novi Sad from 9 to 12 September under the leadership of the bishop of Chichester. The German Evangelical Church was represented by Heckel, August Schreiber, Hans Wahl, and August Hinderer, director of the Protestant Press Association. Because Kapler's resignation had taken effect, Heckel moved more into the limelight. After Bishop Bell's account of the initial steps he had taken during the church conflict in the spring, Heckel gave his report. The minutes recorded the following:

> [Heckel] painted a bold picture of the vast changes and preliminary reconstruction in Nation, State and Church, and sought to clarify the great questions and tasks which hereby assume particular importance for the whole work of the churches in the ecumenical field.[151]

Right after the general synod and before the national synod, it was indeed a delicate task for a church representative to interpret the German domestic scene before an audience of foreigners in a foreign country. The ensuing conflict was inevitable.

Wilfred Monod did not let Heckel's version stand uncontradicted. He expressed regret that the Germans had silently ignored certain points that would have been of particular interest to this Christian assembly, such as the recent resolutions passed by the brown synod and the general discrimination against Christians of Jewish descent. After a heated debate the conference passed two resolutions; and, for the first time at an ecumenical conference, the German delegation put its dissent on record. The first resolution, instigated by Bishop Bell, was a declaration:

> . . . grave anxieties were expressed by the representatives of different churches in Europe and America in particular with regard to the severe action taken against persons of Jewish origin, and the serious restrictions placed upon freedom of thought and expression in Germany. . . .

The other resolution was that Bell should undertake the task of writing a letter to the current German church government. This resolution led to the now famous correspondence between Bell and Ludwig Müller, beginning with Bell's letter to Müller of 23 October and culminating in Bell's 1934 Ascension Day message to the member churches of the ecumenical movement. Dietrich Bonhoeffer was to become Bell's chief adviser in this correspondence. Thus Heckel was unable to control the church opposition's influence on people like Bell, whom they continued to keep informed. Bell always remained aware of the existence of another leadership. This state of affairs had begun with Bonhoeffer's telegram to Henriod after the events of 6 September. Yet the ecumenical movement was not unanimous in these matters; those in Geneva did not remain Bonhoeffer's ideal partners, and in the course of time, they established far closer relations to Heckel's office. Even in the ecumenical movement, only a minority ultimately showed any understanding for Bonhoeffer's point of view. But for the time being he continued to enjoy the support of influential leaders such as Bishops Bell and Ammundsen.

Some of the delegates who came to Sofia from Novi Sad had already been forewarned; one of these was Norwegian bishop Ove Ammundsen, who was to preside over the World Alliance conference. The only Germans present were seventy-one-year-old Julius Richter and twenty-seven-year-old Bonhoeffer. Siegmund-Schultze, ill in Switzerland, was anxious lest the conference should show too much hostility toward conditions in Germany and thus prove fatal to his World Alliance work; in fact, his journal, *Die Eiche*, did cease publication in 1933.

Due to the devaluation of the dollar, the circle of those attending had been reduced to thirty people: the eleven members of the executive board and selected members of the working committee. Bonhoeffer was among them, because he had already been invited as one of the speakers at the 1934 meeting in Fanö, which was being planned in Budapest. Henriod had already told him this on 1 June, urging him to attend; at the same time he mentioned that the Dutch and French delegates wanted to deal with the issue of racial minorities in Sofia, as Bonhoeffer had hoped for.

Next on the agenda, after questions of disarmament and problems concerning the merger of the two youth commissions, was the forthcoming major conference (in Budapest or Fanö). Monod, who had resigned from the presidency of the French branch of the World Alliance, entrusted his 1932 theological memorandum on the peace question to French ecumenist J. Jézéquel. Out of this debate arose the program for the 1934 international conference:

The suggestion was made that Professor Monod should be asked to formulate more precisely the *catechism of peace* for the Budapest meeting, that this should be sent to two or three persons . . . that they should formulate together the memorandum for Budapest; and thirdly, that one member of the Youth Commission should be asked to sit with these members . . . It was ultimately agreed that Dr. Monod should be asked to prepare his memorandum, that Dr. Bonhoeffer should be responsible for another and Professor Zankow for another and the Bishop of Ripon for another.[152]

The next ecumenical meeting Monod could attend was in 1935; there he came into conflict with Heckel. In Fanö he was represented by A. Bouvier. Archdeacon G. Marten replaced the bishop of Ripon, who had died unexpectedly. It was a sign of Bonhoeffer's growing reputation that after only two years of ecumenical involvement he was asked to hold the "catechism of peace" in Fanö.

For the next and most burning question of the day, "racial minorities," Bonhoeffer had laid the groundwork outside the plenary sessions. The previous evening Ammundsen, William Adams Brown, Atkinson, Toureille, Henriod, and Bonhoeffer had met in Bouvier's hotel room. In his diary Henriod wrote:

> In Sofia, Bonhoeffer was able to inform us in a private group . . . about the real situation in Germany and of the brutal and intransigent attitude of the German Christians. We are instructed to tell his friends:
>   1. that they can count on our sympathy and understanding abroad.
>   2. that in principle it would be necessary for a delegation to decide whether the churches are able to recognize the new German church.
>   We closed with prayer together. Bonhoeffer was very moved.[153]

Bonhoeffer himself described that evening in a letter to Siegmund-Schultze:

> On this occasion I spoke very frankly about the Jewish question, the Aryan clause in the church, and the general synod, and about the question of the future of the minority as well, and met with a great deal of understanding. . . . Incidentally, during this little meeting we decided on a plan to send a delegation to the German church government, and this is still under discussion here in London.[154]

Thus, despite all the discouraging experiences, Bonhoeffer continued to work along the lines of his earlier proposals of 6–7 September, and now suggested that the ecumenical movement should withhold recognition of the new church government and send a delegation. He kept to this plan, for on 6 November he wrote to Siegmund-Schultze that the idea of a delegation "is still under discussion here in London. . . . A few days ago I met with all the ecumenical people."[155] Bonhoeffer did not achieve what he had hoped, but he believed that the world organization, so impotent in other respects, held the trump card in this particular instance. This view was corroborated by the extreme sensitivity in Berlin to reactions from abroad. Both Ammundsen and U.S. ecumenical leader William Adams Brown, and later the bishop of Chichester, seemed inclined to favor the suggestion. From that point on, one of Heckel's more disagreeable tasks was to ward off "outside interference," on the grounds that the ecumenical movement was going beyond its area of competence. Heckel gradually won ecumenical allies for this viewpoint; indeed, Bonhoeffer took too much for granted. He was not the kind of person to cautiously respect the competence of the informal ecumenical organizations; he tended more to spur the movement on by challenging it with the tasks that lay ahead, and to mold it through his demands.

The next issue on the agenda of the Sofia plenary sessions was the Jewish question. Previously so opposed to resolutions, Bonhoeffer became energetically involved. Henriod wrote in his diary:

> 20 September. A resolution on racial minorities proposed by Atkinson, an amendment to the text proposed by Bonhoeffer which was accepted.

Thus the Sofia conference produced a resolution that was more outspoken than that from Novi Sad:

> We especially deplore the fact that the State measures against the Jews in Germany have had such an effect on public opinion that in some circles the Jewish race is considered a race of inferior status. We protest against the resolution of the Prussian General Synod and other Synods which apply the Aryan clause of the State to the Church, putting serious disabilities upon ministers and church officers who by chance of birth are non-Aryan, which we believe to be a denial of the explicit teaching and spirit of the Gospel of Jesus Christ. . . .[156]

This judgment about "a denial of the explicit teaching and spirit of the Gospel" brought the theology of the World Alliance extraordinarily close to the theology of the German confessionalists. Yet it also took many of those present to the limits of what they could accept. When the debate on the Jewish question began in the plenary session, Julius Richter, who knew nothing of the previous evening's discussion,[157] insisted on going with Bonhoeffer to the German Embassy in Sofia to assure them that the German government as such was not being attacked. Later Richter wrote to Siegmund-Schultze:

> Bishop Ammundsen was moved almost to tears by the proceedings in the plenary session.... Perhaps the finest and deepest religious experience was the occasion when Bonhoeffer conducted morning prayers.[158]

In Novi Sad Heckel's tactic had been to conceal issues and prevent any clear positions from being taken. In Sofia Bonhoeffer's objective was to bring issues into the open and encourage the gathering to make a clear statement.

Despite the serious situation, Bonhoeffer and Toureille did not miss the opportunity to explore the Bulgarian markets and purchase Eastern antiques.

The Aftermath of Sofia. Even Siegmund-Schultze, in exile in Switzerland, had some misgivings when he heard the news from Sofia and the resolution that had been passed there. He wrote Bonhoeffer that the resolution would have far-reaching consequences for the World Alliance's position in Germany.[159] In what was to be the final issue of *Die Eiche*, he wrote about these events, being careful not to create any difficulties for Richter and Bonhoeffer, who were now back in Germany.[160] However, the account also revealed that an attempt had been made before the Sofia meeting to prevent any public statement from being made, in order not to imperil what still survived. According to this, the presidium and secretariat had agreed before Sofia that the conference, as a limited executive session, should not be empowered to pass resolutions. But Bonhoeffer's influence, along with the pressing circumstances, had overridden this arrangement. Thus Bonhoeffer, in his letter to Siegmund-Schultze on 6 November, emphasized that the private evening meeting at the hotel had taken place "at Henriod's request"— at the request, that is, of the secretary of the World Alliance.[161]

Understandably, the report in *Die Eiche* was not altogether free of deliberate embellishment:

> During the Sofia conference, however, the executive committee overrode this agreement, and passed a resolution on the racial question that addressed the position of the German church. The representatives of the churches of the great powers declared that it would mean the end of the World Alliance's work if one of its bodies, meeting this year, were to fail to declare itself on this question of such import to the whole of Christianity.

Thus the German representatives who took part in the session were unable to prevent the passing of a resolution. They took good care, however, that this resolution contained no criticism of the government of their country and applied only to those church measures that are controversial in Germany itself. It would not be fair were we in Germany to suppress this resolution. . . .

The text of the resolution then follows. On 6 November Bonhoeffer wrote to Siegmund-Schultze from London in an attempt to allay his misgivings:

In fact I regard the resolution as it stands as both good and defensible, and objectively would not feel able to alter its wording. . . . I doubt whether the German Christians will seriously attack the Sofia resolution, since there is a certain amount of embarrassment within their own ranks about the Aryan clause. I don't know by what means the resolution was officially conveyed to the church government, but I do know that they received a copy. I really don't think we need be afraid of publicizing it as much as we can. *Junge Kirche*, too, ought to publish the text.[162]

There were no immediate political repercussions for Bonhoeffer from the events in Sofia, but there was some reaction from the church. The church government, of course, knew exactly what had taken place. "There's been a fearful row at the Church Ministry about my mission; apparently it almost toppled Theodor [Heckel]," Bonhoeffer wrote to Siegmund-Schultze.[163]

After the events of Novi Sad and Sofia, Heckel felt obliged to send his own account with comments to all pastors abroad. Bonhoeffer, by then in London, was automatically sent a copy of the document, which explained:

The German delegation frustrated all attempts at a detailed statement of opinion by the executive committee [in Novi Sad]. . . . during the course of difficult deliberations, so that the enclosed comparatively meaningless resolution was passed. . . .

The pastors serving abroad were to help avert the threat of deteriorating relationships with other churches by correcting false ideas and placing the development within a wider context:

The need for a theological counterattack and for theological attacks on the untenable theology, the *Weltanschauung*, and the ideology upon which the attacks from abroad are so largely based, has already been shown. In general, circles abroad are surprisingly well-informed about details, yet are not in a position to judge the general development within the German church correctly. . . . The German Christians, however, must be credited with having taken responsibility for building something new with exceptional vigor. . . . Next to these broad outlines of development, individual developments are of little importance. Especially with regard to the Aryan clause in the church, there are very considerable difficulties. . . . [More recently, the report goes on to say, the questionable regulations affecting the regional churches had been suspended under the law of 16 November.] It must be noted, however, that this does not finally solve the Aryan problem for the German Evangelical Church. There is a real possibility that similar regulations, albeit somewhat milder, will be included in the planned guidelines for the German Evangelical Church. We are of the opinion that there are very strong elements among the National Socialists that would not understand the church's rejection of the Aryan clause, which would hinder or jeopardize the work of the church among the German people. . . . It is not now the business of other countries to judge but to get to know the facts. Above all, public demonstrations, particularly by church circles abroad, must be avoided in the future, since in the current international situation these would appear to be primarily political demonstrations. Special discretion in voicing such opinions should be exercised particularly in former enemy countries. For in the eyes of the German people these countries have to a considerable extent forfeited the moral right to pass judgment on conditions in Germany . . . Signed Heckel.[164]

Heckel had maneuvered himself into a position that credited the German Christians with valuable services and defended the Aryan clause on the basis of the evangelistic possibilities it offered among the German people. As a result, he forfeited a great deal of confidence among Bonhoeffer's colleagues, the German pastors serving in England. This attitude changed in the following years, due to the foreign congregations' financial dependency on Berlin.

The National Synod. Bonhoeffer returned from Sofia in time for the national synod in Wittenberg. Various things had happened during his absence.

After the devastating international repercussions of the brown synod, the Foreign Ministry intervened on political grounds. It forbade discussion of the Aryan clause in Wittenberg and hence its enactment by the national synod. Indeed, the Ministry sent an observer to Wittenberg on 27 September, as Bonhoeffer was aware at the time.

The Emergency League's manifesto, "To the National Synod," had been signed by two thousand people. Various church councils had requested expert opinions on the Aryan clause from faculties and individual academics. Support for the opposition came from the Marburg expert opinion,

written by its theological faculty and signed by church historian Hans von
Soden; another report, equally lucid and authoritative, came from twenty-
two New Testament professors, and later another from Bultmann. Yet even
the scholarly community did not produce unequivocal results. The Erlangen
faculty issued a report that did not reject the Aryan clause outright, signed
by Althaus and Elert. Georg Wobbermin explicitly opposed the Marburg theologians and described the opinion of the twenty-two New Testament scholars as "premature and misleading." The law passed by the brown synod, he
believed, was "proper and justified." Exceptions should not be allowed, "since
with that the church would endanger the unity of German culture, which it
is so imperative to secure at the present time, above all in the Protestant
church."[165] Two years later, when Bonhoeffer became involved in an argument with Professor Leonard Hodgson, the secretary of Faith and Order,
Hodgson turned to Wobbermin, of all people, for support.

Nevertheless, an impressive wave of protest preceded the Wittenberg
meeting. Early on that beautiful autumn morning, Bonhoeffer was driven to
Wittenberg by his father's chauffeur. He took Gertrud Staewen and Franz
Hildebrandt with him; the back of the car was filled with parcels containing
the pamphlet "To the National Synod." In Wittenberg "the first theological
teaching platoon of the Augustusburg Leadership College in Saxony, complete with field-gray uniforms and knapsacks, formed an honor guard
beneath the windows of the future Reich bishop.[166] Bishop Wurm of
Stuttgart preached the inaugural sermon. Bonhoeffer witnessed the ceremony from a corner in the castle church. Ludwig Müller gave a report that
included the term "racial conformity" but did not give an opinion on the law
passed by the general synod on 5 September, nor did he mention either the
expert opinions from the faculties or the two thousand signatures. In
response Bonhoeffer and Hildebrandt sent a telegram during the lunch
break to Müller demanding that he address these things during the afternoon, but to no effect. They and their friends then distributed the leaflets in
the streets and nailed them to trees. The church paper *Evangelium im Dritten Reich* reported:

> Meanwhile the town is full of rumors. Impossible though it may seem, it
> is true: the enemies are making their presence felt. Appeals without any
> printer's name, minutes, communiqués, details, etc., are being circulated.
> But with unerring certainty and calm, our leaders will take steps...

The afternoon was not particularly peaceful, however. The election of the
Reich bishop and the staffing of the Church Ministry aroused heated argu-

ment. Lutheran bishops such as Meiser, Wurm, and Schöffel quarreled with Hossenfelder, because they felt that appointments to the Ministry should be proportionate to the numbers in each denomination. But Ludwig Müller was unanimously elected. Over Luther's tomb in the church of Wittenberg Castle Hossenfelder declaimed: "I greet thee, my Reich Bishop!"[167] Hildebrandt whispered to Bonhoeffer that now he believed Luther really would turn over in his grave in the castle church.

Both regarded the outcome of Wittenberg as disastrous—precisely because nothing unpredictable had happened. The much-needed protest by the still intact regional churches outside the Old Prussian Union Church, especially those in southern Germany, had failed to occur. While nothing immediately heretical had been decided, the most crucial issue had been bypassed. Practically speaking, the performance in Wittenberg had confirmed the brown synod and the decisions of that synod remained in effect. In fact, the close association of the new "Spiritual Ministry" of the German Protestant church (its members were Hossenfelder, Werner, Weber, and Schöffel) with the Old Prussian church—Bavarian Bishop Meiser tried to protest this—only increased the authority and power of the German Christians. There had been no mention of repealing "the law that violated the confession of the regional churches." For the sake of preserving their own intact regional churches, the Lutheran bishops had remained silent. The Spiritual Ministry's soothing words afterward about a peaceful implementation of administrative power meant nothing.

Bonhoeffer and Hildebrandt now reconsidered the need for a free church. On Sunday, 1 October, they went to the Old Lutherans on Nassauische Strasse in Berlin-Wilmersdorf to assess the possibilities. Though the facade was swathed in a flowing swastika flag, they were warmly welcomed; they were told, however, that they must bring their congregations with them.[168] This was naturally no solution. The idea of a "free church" remained a burning issue until the Barmen synod altered the situation.

The victories in Wittenberg marked the apogee of German Christian power. Novelist Ricarda Huch had resigned from the Prussian Academy of the Arts to protest against the abusive expulsion of Thomas Mann, Fritz von Unruh, and Franz Werfel. In contrast, the new Reich bishop and Theodor Heckel were nominated "honorary senators" of the Academy of Sciences. Magdeburg Cathedral, "the only former arch-episcopal cathedral . . . in Protestant hands," was chosen for Müller's consecration. It was supposed that there would now be peace. But neither his consecration nor peace was that easy.

Departure. Since his decision in August to go to London, so much had happened that Bonhoeffer could hardly expect his departure to remain unchallenged. At the beginning of October Heckel informed him that, all things considered, he could not be allowed to go so easily. Bonhoeffer replied that he would retract nothing, nor would he sign any promise not to engage in ecumenical activity. He insisted on speaking to the Reich bishop himself. He told Müller that he had no intention of representing the German Christian cause abroad, and would speak, as before, for the ecumenical movement. When Bonhoeffer suggested that they should prohibit his departure altogether, they asked him to explain that he had changed his mind because of church obligations. Bonhoeffer stood his ground, causing Heckel to complain: "What complicated people you all are!"[169] The following day the Reich bishop informed Bonhoeffer that he could leave. The German Christians were trying to smooth the waters in the weeks after the Wittenberg victory.

> No doubt what finally persuaded them to ask me to go to London was the fear that the congregations here would break away. I then arranged that my conversation with the Reich bishop and my opinions be put in the records so that I could have an absolutely free hand and did not need in any way to see myself as the emissary of a German Christian church—quite the opposite, in fact.[170]

In his declaration made for the records, Bonhoeffer did not neglect to squelch the dangerous rumors about "foreign propaganda" by affirming his loyalty to his country. [171] But he did not say "National Socialist state"; he said "Germany." He was also careful to mention his family origins and connections, among them one cousin in particular who was a state counselor and trustee. It would have been foolish to ignore the tendency, even in the church struggle, that viewed every contact with other countries as tantamount to collaboration in the "atrocity campaign of the foreign press" (as the Malicious Practices Act illustrated). At the notorious meeting between Chancellor Hitler and the church leaders in January 1934, Göring created a considerable stir with a list of foreign reports on German church affairs, charging that this seriously interfered with the general reconstruction of Germany.

In a genial misinterpretation of the situation, Julius Richter remarked to Siegmund-Schultze that since Bonhoeffer differed in almost every respect on church matters from Ludwig Müller, the Reich bishop had again given an "astonishing sign of understanding" in sending Bonhoeffer to England, even entrusting him with the task of "looking after the new church government's ecumenical interests."

Jørgen Glenthoj cites a letter written by Birger Forell, the Swedish pastor in Berlin, to his archbishop on 6 October; it gives a lively account of what happened. According to this letter, Bonhoeffer was not to be allowed to go abroad because he had signed the Wittenberg leaflet, "since this implied an attack on the unity of the church."

> B. was summoned by the Reich bishop and asked if he still stood by his signature. He affirmed this, with a reference to *Augustana*, Chapter 7, but when he proceeded to recite the whole of this chapter in Latin, M. got a bit hot under the collar and suggested postponing the conversation until later . . . [Forell further reported that the Foreign Ministry had intimated that] when filling appointments . . . that include the duty of representing the church, there should be some consideration that the person appointed is trusted abroad.[172]

Bonhoeffer was loath to leave his students. As a small parting gift he gave them his fine essay "What Must the Student of Theology Do Today?"[173] It was significant that he forbade them "from speaking contemptuously of theological learning" at a time when he was leaving the academic realm, and that he urged them to "test the spirits in the church" at a time when the appointed representatives of theological scholarship were not doing this. The students should realize, he wrote, that the theologian "does not live by superior knowledge or by self-righteousness, but by forgiveness alone." It is interesting, considering his statements in 1944, to see how in 1933 Bonhoeffer warned the theologians that "the worldliness which he likes to assume may yet serve him very ill, and it is really quite impossible to see how unmitigated worldliness can be regarded as the decisive criterion of the good theologian."[174] We may be certain that the man who discovered the "worldliness" of the Gospel in 1944 would not have retracted his 1933 admonition for the sake of a worldliness understood in nondialectical terms.

This essay was written either at the beginning of August, during the short time in Berlin between the London and Bethel visits, or during October, just before his departure for England. During the interval at the beginning of August, he had once more invited his seminar to go hiking in the Mark of Brandenburg. In the autumn he went out to Prebelow with a group of students closest to him. They celebrated with bread rolls and cocoa. Bonhoeffer's farewell, as recorded by Winfried Maechler, was that "We must now endure in silence, and set the firebrand of truth to all four corners of the proud German Christian palace, so that one day the whole structure may collapse."[175]

It may have been on this occasion, or perhaps during the outing with the seminary at the beginning of August, that Bonhoeffer debated his "Theses on Youth Work in the Church."[176] In August 1933 Baldur von Schirach decreed that no one could belong both to the Hitler Youth and to denominational youth clubs. The prohibition affected a great many young people and congregations, and gave rise to considerable uncertainty. In this essay Bonhoeffer called upon the congregations to see themselves in proper perspective, and to avoid the godless idolization of youth.[177]

On 14 October 1933—two days before Bonhoeffer's departure for London—Hitler announced that Germany had left the League of Nations. This was the chancellor's reply to the rejection of his demand for "equality of status," and it was welcomed in jubilation by everyone, including the church opposition. In the name of the Pastors' Emergency League, Niemöller immediately sent a telegram to the *Führer* expressing gratitude and swearing loyal allegiance.

This view was not shared by Bonhoeffer and Hildebrandt. Julius Rieger, who was able to meet his future colleague in the "Pilsen" restaurant near the Berlin Zoo, noted in his diary a remark of Bonhoeffer's which at the time seemed to him exaggerated: "This has brought the danger of war very much closer."[178]

Bonhoeffer and Hildebrandt went to Dahlem to hear Pastor Röhricht preach the sermon "God Is Faithful" (the text was 1 Corinthians 1:9). Then they said good-bye, and Bonhoeffer assured his friend that he hoped to see him soon in London. They planned to share Bonhoeffer's salary between them.

A few days later Franz Hildebrandt turned down the offer of a post in the Pastors' Emergency League. He wrote to Niemöller, saying he was leaving shortly to join Bonhoeffer in London, and concluded:

I find it impossible to understand how you can joyfully welcome the political move in Geneva when you yourselves refuse to adopt an unequivocal attitude toward a church which persistently denies us equality of status. . . . As one who is comparatively young and to some extent suspect, I don't want to harm your cause by repeating in public what has been my constant refrain within our own circle ever since the end of June. Anyway, what does "public" mean here now? It is my role to remain silent and this, I hope, you will forgive your old friend, Hildebrandt.[179]

CHAPTER EIGHT

LONDON: 1933–1935

The conflicts of the past six months had taken Bonhoeffer far beyond his previous sphere of influence. They had also revealed how greatly his views differed from those of his fellow fighters. In nearly all his suggestions he stood alone.

His notion of an interdict at the beginning of July had seemed quite impracticable to his colleagues. In September his ideas about a free church had come to nothing. When the church adopted an Aryan clause, the schism Bonhoeffer hoped for among the clergy never materialized. More influential groups watered down the Bethel confession. In September his friends postponed any kind of mass resignations from the ministry indefinitely. Even like-minded theologians such as Karl Barth and Hermann Sasse decided to wait for even "worse" heresies than the "racial conformity" of the Civil Service Law. Experienced comrades-in-arms feared the resolutions and delegations from abroad that they should have welcomed. Unlike Bonhoeffer, the leaders of the church opposition applauded Hitler's withdrawal from the League of Nations. Even the perceptive circle of pastors who met at Gerhard Jacobi's home on Achenbachstrasse in Berlin failed to understand Bonhoeffer's secret yearnings for India and his interest in Gandhi's methods of resistance. No one shared his pacifist leanings toward pacifism.

Had Bonhoeffer lost confidence? He wrote to Barth:

I feel that in some way I don't understand, I find myself in radical opposition to all my friends; I became increasingly isolated with my views of things, even though I was and remain personally close to these people. All this has frightened me and shaken my confidence so that I began to fear that dogmatism might be leading me astray—since there seemed no particular reason why my own view in these matters should be any better, any more right, than the views of many really capable pastors whom I sincere-

ly respect—and so I thought it was about time to go into the wilderness for
a spell. . . . It seems to me that at the moment it is more dangerous for me
to make a gesture than to retreat into silence.[1]

Friends who were close to Bonhoeffer during that late summer of 1933
recall that he continued to be tormented by doubts about the proper course
of action, even after he had decided to go to London. The decision in favor
of a distant parish in a foreign country was not an easy one, but it led to one
of the liveliest exchanges of letters between Bonhoeffer and Barth.[2] Bonhoeffer's letters betrayed how closely his confidential search for advice was tied
to his need for independence.

At the time there was no one he was more willing to listen to than Barth;
but he only wrote Barth once there was no longer any chance of canceling
his London plans. In the first letter, he remarked that he could not understand why he had not simply let Barth make the decision for him. Barth did
not mince words in his reply: "Under no circumstances should you now play
Elijah under the juniper tree or Jonah under the gourd, and in fact you
ought to return to your post by the next ship."[3] Bonhoeffer was so impressed
by Barth's letter that he sent it to his parents. His father replied:

> It is striking testimony to a fiery spirit. I don't venture to comment on the
> matter itself. I only think that it is also valuable to be able to look at things
> from the outside whence, perhaps, some influence can be brought to bear,
> and particularly to save oneself until the right moment.[4]

"The right moment"—his father was expressing something that both
unsettled and guided Bonhoeffer in his decision. He did not want (nor
would he have allowed) anyone else to tell him how or when he should act.
He asked himself whether his moment had really come with the Young
Reformation movement, the Pastors' Emergency League, or Karl Barth. He
left Germany because the experiences of the summer had only added to his
uncertainty. He had also realized something else:

> . . . although I am working with all my might for the church opposition, it
> is perfectly clear to me that *this* opposition is only a very temporary tran-
> sition to an opposition of a very different kind, and that very few of those
> engaged in this preliminary skirmish will be part of the next struggle. And
> I believe that the whole of Christendom should pray with us that it will be
> a "resistance unto death," and that the people will be found to suffer it. Sim-
> ply suffering—that is what will be needed then—not parries, blows or
> thrusts such as may still be possible or admissible in the preliminary fight;
> the real struggle that perhaps lies ahead must simply be to suffer faithful-

ly, and then, then perhaps God will once more confess his church with his Word. . . .[5]

The characteristics of a new political ethic cannot yet be discerned in Bonhoeffer's vision of "an opposition of a very different kind." This commitment was still shaped entirely by the concept of "discipleship." Discipleship—not political resistance (and its conceptions of the future)—was what lent seriousness and depth to the initial skirmish with its "blows and thrusts." In his clear distinction between the political struggle and the church struggle, Bonhoeffer differed little from his theological friends in Berlin at this point. When it came to actively finding political alternatives to Hitler's state, or at least being vigilant on behalf of the democratic constitution, he looked to those most suited for these tasks by virtue of their career and position within the state. Unlike most of the opposition, he was not bothered by the fact that the church opposition represented a manifestly political factor. He even went farther, in his desire to study nonviolent resistance under Gandhi as an appropriate form of struggle for Christians against the National Socialist claim to power.

Thus Bonhoeffer left Berlin partly because of doubts about the course he should take and partly to keep his thoughts and actions from being constricted into a narrow ecclesiastical dimension. What he wanted was a period of seeking and testing in a small, quiet congregation.

This attempt at evasion, however, was completely unsuccessful: "one is close enough to want to take part in everything, and too far away for active participation. And during the past weeks this has made things exceptionally difficult for me."[6] Even in the small London parishes Bonhoeffer was unable to win even a week's respite from the turbulence in Berlin. Protest letters went back and forth; friends and official couriers arrived to ask what his position was. Every few weeks he traveled between London and Berlin, although he did not particularly like crossing the English Channel or flying. The telephone bill in Forest Hill was so astronomical that, as Franz Hildebrandt and Julius Rieger later recalled, the local post office reduced the amount owed by the foreign pastor to a reasonable sum.

Thus the eighteen months he spent in London were dominated by the church struggle and its effects on the ecumenical movement. The latter took up a great deal of Bonhoeffer's time. He did not neglect his parish duties, but, to a great extent, they became part of the battle itself. During this period he devoted much time to reflecting on the Sermon on the Mount and on "discipleship."

From this point on, Bonhoeffer displayed two different sides. One was of a man who was prepared to risk far more for the sake of the church than most of his friends, and who took the decisions of the German church opposition—from which the Confessing church would soon evolve—more seriously than did most of his fellow activists. He behaved as though the ideas of tomorrow were the realities of today; when the inevitable setbacks came, he was prepared to renew the attack. The other side was of a man who sometimes seemed reserved, almost a stranger to these struggles. He could become irritated by the constraints of his confession; he was driven by visions of an entirely different realization of the Gospel.

√ Parish Minister

On 17 October 1933 Bonhoeffer moved into the German parsonage in the South London suburb of Forest Hill. The house stood on a slope extending south of the well-kept grounds of Horniman Park; it overlooked a sea of houses and, far on the horizon, Kent and Surrey. North of the park was a view of the city, Parliament, St. Paul's Cathedral, and the harbor, and in the distance the hills of Hampstead and Finsbury Park.

The huge Victorian parsonage was surrounded by a garden and many trees. Most of the rooms in the house were used by a private German school. Bonhoeffer lived in two grand rooms that faced northeast. Neither the windows nor the ill-fitting doors shut completely and, despite Bonhoeffer's sturdy constitution, he was frequently ill with influenza and colds due to the drafts and the fog. He fought a losing battle against an invasion of mice. He did his best to make both rooms inhabitable with furniture imported from home, including, of course, the Bechstein piano.

He shared these rooms for nearly three months with Franz Hildebrandt. The physicist and pacifist Herbert Jehle occasionally visited from Cambridge, and Wolf-Dieter Zimmermann and Jürgen Winterhager, two of his students from Berlin, came for several weeks. Even relatives accustomed to better quarters—like his brothers-in-law, Dohnanyi and Dress, and their wives—stayed there.

The parish's youth and music groups met there—to rehearse a nativity play, play trios and quartets, or sometimes to listen to his large collection of gramophone records. Enthusiastic about the quality of English choirs, Bonhoeffer bought an English recording of Bach's Mass in B Minor. Through music he made friends with the Whitburns, relatives of Hans Lokies, director of the Berlin Gossner Mission; they taught him English carols. Despite his meager salary, he was invariably a generous host.

Ministry. Bonhoeffer now had a regular pastorate for the first time. He could not entirely enjoy the "rights of the clerical profession"—indeed, he would never do so because the conditions under which he worked never became normal. The London parish correctly followed the German church regulations and elected Bonhoeffer on 12 November. This election, however, needed to be ratified by Theodor Heckel's Foreign Office, according to the agreements between the London congregations and the German Evangelical Church Federation. Bonhoeffer deliberately postponed sending the application for ratification; eventually, after the controversy surrounding Ludwig Müller at the beginning of 1934, he allowed the correspondence to lapse. He wanted to avoid recognition of the Reich church government.[7] This naturally jeopardized his pension rights and retirement insurance.

Bonhoeffer was responsible for two of the six German congregations in London. Their independence and clear structure made them similar to free churches. In earlier times each had paid its own pastor and organist, and financed the maintenance of its buildings. After the First World War, lack of funds led some of them, including St. Paul's and Sydenham, to merge and share a pastor. They continued to maintain a relatively independent attitude toward the church authorities in Germany.

Bonhoeffer's parish in Sydenham owned a church in South London that had been founded by Elias Schrenk, the Swabian missionary and evangelist, in 1875. The congregation consisted mainly of prosperous merchants, but included German diplomats who had lived in that part of London before the First World War. Before 1914, while serving as Legation Counselor in London, Baron von Neurath had belonged to this parish. During Bonhoeffer's ministry there, the chancellor of the German Embassy, Theodor Lang, lived there. Lang admired Bonhoeffer and passed important political information on to him, and was also helpful in aiding German refugees. Theologically, Sydenham was a congregation of the United Church. Some thirty to forty people attended Bonhoeffer's services.

St. Paul's, the other parish, belonged to the Reformed church. Its history went back more than two hundred years. During the eighteenth century, the church had stood where the north pier of Waterloo Bridge stands today. In Bonhoeffer's time the church was in the East End. During the war it was destroyed in an air raid; where it once stood, Petticoat Lane market in Whitechapel attracts visitors on Sunday mornings today. Over fifty parishioners would come to hear Bonhoeffer's sermons and stay afterward to socialize. They came from families of tradespeople—butchers, bakers, and tailors—that had emigrated mostly from Württemberg; most spoke only English. During the First World War they had endured a good deal of hostility, and some had been forced to close their businesses. But now they listened readily to Bonhoeffer's plea to help German emigrants. Bonhoeffer could also depend on the church warden, Gottlob Henne, who helped German refugees make a new start even after the Second World War.

Bonhoeffer did not care much for parish meetings and minute taking on routine matters. He introduced several innovations, including a children's Sunday school, youth clubs, and performances of Nativity and passion plays. He approved the collections for Dr. Goebbels's Winter Aid Fund that had been adopted in German churches; at the same time he insisted that collections also be taken for German refugees in England. With his parish council, Bonhoeffer successfully blocked a German Embassy proposal to collaborate with the German parishes in setting up a "German House" in London.

His main concern was for the first wave of refugees from Germany: ". . . in London I spent most of my time with these people and I felt it was a great privilege to do so."[8] Members of the Epstein and Cromwell families met at his house; Bonhoeffer confirmed the son of former Minister Treviranus; Münster theology professor Otto Piper came to him. Bonhoeffer introduced his cousin's husband Hans Wedell, a lawyer who later entered the ministry, to Bishop George Bell; Wedell eventually worked on supporting "non-Aryan" youth. Bonhoeffer and Bell tried together to combat the narrow restrictions on working papers for immigrants. "Besides my parish work, I have countless . . . visitors, most of them Jews, who know me from somewhere and want something of me."[9]

Bonhoeffer's congregations were apt to find him too demanding. He immediately tried to introduce the revised hymnbook for churches abroad, and he scheduled services on Christmas Eve and New Year's Day that his faithful working families could not attend because they did not coincide with English holidays. His parishioners found the severe standards of his sermons particularly hard to accept. They were accustomed to the mild, folksy, pious sermons of his predecessor. Bonhoeffer's sermons, by comparison, seemed too oppressive and emphatic. Indeed, some responded by staying away.

For the first time he had to give a sermon every Sunday, which he found difficult. Each sermon was written out in full; he often mailed copies to acquaintances in Germany. Sixteen of the sermons preached in London have survived.[10] Unfortunately, they do not include those in which he dealt with the Sermon on the Mount.

> Please write and tell me some time how you preach about the Sermon on the Mount. I am working on this now—trying to keep it extremely simple

and straightforward, but it always comes back to *keeping* the commandment and not evading it. Discipleship to Christ—I'd like to know what that
is—it is not exhausted in our concept of faith.[11]

Otherwise, the theme of "discipleship" appeared only in an article that he
wrote for the London parish newsletter at the beginning of 1934. There he
did an exegesis of the three disciples; it later appeared in his Finkenwalde lecture on discipleship and opened his book on discipleship.[12]

He also tried to enter into the world of his parishioners, using images in
his sermons with which they could identify. In November 1933 they were
shaken by a great mining disaster in Wales.[13] In his sermon he used familiar
images, such as a chess partner in the game of life.[14] Once he coolly translated the scriptural text into a familiar expression, "We are each masters of
our destiny."[15] He left a lasting impression with his sermons in the fall of
1934 about the passage on love in 1 Corinthians 13.[16]

There is no doubt that the church struggle was constantly in the background, yet there were few references to it in his sermons. His own impassioned commitment was most evident in a sermon delivered in January
1934; given at a time when Bonhoeffer was pessimistic about what would
happen, it was almost a personal confession. His model was Jeremiah, the
prophet who, though mocked by God, was caught up in his mission. Following the Röhm putsch and the accompanying massacres of 30 June 1934,
Bonhoeffer gave an undisguised sermon of atonement.

The London sermons were predominantly marked by a strong eschatological fervor; he sought to awaken a longing for the kingdom of heaven.
While preparing his Memorial Day sermon in 1933, he wrote to his brother-in-law:

> Memorial Day is particularly moving this time, because after all that has
> happened during the past months, one feels such a tremendous longing for
> real peace, in which all the misery and injustice, the lying and cowardice
> will come to an end.[17]

Colleagues. Bonhoeffer's arrival in England meant that the German pastors
already there acquired a first-class source of information about events that
had been difficult to assess from afar. Like most expatriate Germans, they
had welcomed the spring's developments as a German renewal, and had
combated the unfavorable public reactions in England. The church troubles
of the past months had considerably upset their picture of the new Germany.
They continued to distinguish between Hitler's "good policy" and the

"excesses" of his more objectionable henchmen in church affairs. A letter, written on New Year's Eve in 1933 by a pastor who had joined the National Socialist Party, offers a picture of what well-meaning clergy abroad were thinking at the time:

> I spent two years at the front, where I fought and bled for my fatherland. With my own eyes I saw many of my best friends give their lives in service to their fatherland. . . . In my youthful enthusiasm I regarded their death as a sacred legacy . . . we had to fight on so that their death for Germany should not have been in vain or even be forgotten. But what had become of Germany? A land of injustice and corruption, subject to the whims of black and red rulers alike. As a pastor it was not my business to take part in politics, let alone party politics. . . . Then the National Socialist Party came into power, a party that didn't want to be a party, with a program that had a moral and religious basis. That's why I became a member of the movement. Another reason . . . was the realization that the lower ranks of the Party hierarchy were not permeated with the same deep morality and religion as the *Führer* and his ideas, that many of them believed they could simply change the color of their hearts from red to brown, and that unscrupulous agitators—I regard the "German Christians" as such—would use the movement to gain influence. The result could be that the proclamation of the Gospel would be hindered, thus destroying the only possible foundation for the reconstruction of the fatherland. . . . For this reason it seems to me absolutely necessary to participate for the sake of the Church of Christ and for the sake of the national community in which God has placed us. That this is best done as a Party member is self-evident. . . .
>
> And I believe that the opportunity to participate in this way exists. The Party is trying to bring our youth work in line, like the sorry example of the Reich Bishop. This might be possible in Germany but those of us abroad cannot go along. . . . Today I present my ideas to the *Obergruppenleiter* [Nazi group leader] who will listen to me because I am a Party member. Under no circumstances will I allow any deviation from the clear line we must follow in our work. . . .

Although disturbed by Bonhoeffer's commitment to the church opposition and his poor opinion of the National Socialist Party, even the writer of this letter succumbed to Bonhoeffer's persuasion and joined the struggle for the German church.

During 1933 the Party courted the London pastors rather emphatically. In Lancaster Gate, the local Nazi organization organized regular evening discussion groups, to which the pastors and their congregations were invited and plied with beer. The Party regarded the pastors as potential contacts and mediators between the registered passport-holding Germans and the unregistered ethnic Germans. During the summer the Nazis also sent contingents of Party members to the lectures organized by the churches.

In July 1933 German Christian leader Joachim Hossenfelder contacted St. George's Church, offering to come and lecture there. The pastor and his council sidetracked the proposal by saying that the date was unsuitable. In late autumn, invited by Frank Buchman and supported by Bishop A. C. Headlam of Gloucester, Hossenfelder proposed another visit, but the fronts in the church struggle were already clearly demarcated. Pastor Julius Rieger and his congregation successfully evaded the compromise a Hossenfelder demonstration would have involved.

The North London congregations were led by two older colleagues: Pastor Fritz Wehrhan, the eldest of the German pastors in London, and Gustav Schönberger, who was an active Nazi Party member. Both supported the church opposition and the Confessing church as long as Bonhoeffer was in London. The young clergyman Dr. Rieger worked in the East End. He became a close friend of Bonhoeffer and Hildebrandt; later, after Bonhoeffer's return to Germany, he was the contact for Bishop Bell whenever information on events in Germany was urgently required.[18] Rieger also assumed responsibility for helping emigrants; St. George's Church eventually became the church's refugee center. One refugee was Franz Hildebrandt, who had to flee suddenly in 1937. Outside London there were about five other German pastors elsewhere in Great Britain.

Bonhoeffer stood out in this group from the beginning, distinguished by his youth, theological expertise, and his intimate knowledge of ecclesiastical and political circles in Berlin. All but one colleague immediately acknowledged his authority and, until his departure, adhered to the decisions of the Confessing church, even when they did not share all of Bonhoeffer's political views.

The German pastors in London met at frequent and regular intervals. Those from the whole of Great Britain convened at an annual conference and at the Association of the German Evangelical Congregations of Great Britain and Ireland. This association was chaired by a London banker, Baron Bruno Schröder, who supported a number of German charitable foundations in London and showed a lively interest in church affairs; he sided with Bonhoeffer in the church troubles. Wehrhan served as secretary of this association.

The pastors also belonged to the Foreign Pastoral Society, which included ministers from all countries. These gatherings listened eagerly to what Bonhoeffer had to say on the German situation, especially after the Fanö meeting. The society's records show that he was a speaker on 4 December 1933, and 14 May and 1 October 1934. Several members of Bonhoeffer's congregation at St. Paul's held responsibilities in the YMCA, and he offered his services there too,[19] although he was not altogether happy about the organization's German branch.

It was undoubtedly due to Bonhoeffer's presence in London that, of all the German congregations abroad, only those in England made any attempt to intervene in the church struggle at home. Since such congregations were the focal point for Germans living abroad, it was difficult to move them toward active opposition. In London Bonhoeffer also had some difficulty in overcoming occasional manifestations of "national discipline." The understandable opinion that it was better to maintain a discreet silence outside Germany was shared even by certain Confessing church circles, in their anxiety not to appear in a false light politically. This was compounded by a reluctance to get involved with the distant "church dispute," the term that Party and state authorities preferred to the term "church struggle." They astutely counted on the widespread aversion to involvement in ecclesiastical or theological disputes, figuring that even a good pious Christian would rather keep away from "church disputes."

Bonhoeffer had little time for such considerations. He continued to be successful in getting his colleagues, parish councils, and Baron Schröder to agree with his viewpoint.

First Attack against the Reich Church Government, Winter 1933–1934

Two factors that received wide publicity during Bonhoeffer's early period in England helped increase his influence in ecumenical and German circles in London.

First the English press, from *The Times* down to local newspapers, had published detailed accounts of the Wittenberg manifesto, "To the National Synod," signed by two thousand pastors. Bonhoeffer's name stood at the top of the list of the twenty-two initial signatories.

The second event was the November Sports Palace demonstration; the resulting scandal shattered the German Christian movement and its church government. Everyone was eager to learn the details of what had happened, why it had happened, and what the likely consequences would be. Bonhoeffer, with his insider's knowledge, could not have been in a better situation to demonstrate convincingly the justice of his cause.

The Sports Palace Demonstration. As planned, Franz Hildebrandt arrived in London on 11 November. Shortly after he concluded his account of recent events in Berlin, sensational news arrived that seemed to overshadow all that had gone before. On 13 November the German Christians had staged a massive demonstration in the Berlin Sports Palace, attended by the "spiritual ministers" of the new Reich church government. Its main feature was a speech by Berlin Nazi Party leader, Dr. Reinhard Krause. Now that leading church positions had been taken over by "men of the movement," declared Krause, there must be further dismissals and the immediate implementation of the Aryan clause. Above all he called for "liberation from the Old Testament with its Jewish money morality and from these stories of cattle dealers and pimps." The Church Affairs officials and bishops present allowed this speech to pass without protest. The following morning the German press—where not all criticism had yet been suppressed—carried detailed reports. Indignation spread even within the ranks of German Christians, who had never dreamed such a thing could happen. The opposition began to hope that the weakness of the Church Affairs officials would lead to the reorganization of the church government. The Emergency League believed it might be possible to compel the Reich bishop either to follow a new course or resign.

Bonhoeffer was not unduly surprised by the events at the Sports Palace. He used the controversy to spread the word about what was really happening. He had no illusions about the steadfastness of those in Berlin who responded only to Krause's crude style. Once the difference between the two sides in the church struggle became more pronounced, he knew, they would not hold out for very long.

Concern for His Berlin Friends. The state of uncertainty in Berlin affected both the German Christians and the Emergency League. Far away in London it made Bonhoeffer and Hildebrandt nervous. The news that reached them was not always clear, and it was difficult to relieve their skepticism about the attitudes of those on their own side. Every morning they read the excellent reports in *The Times;* nearly every evening they carried on anguished telephone conversations with Jacobi, Niemöller, or with Bonhoeffer's mother, who was as involved as they were.

In the wake of the Sports Palace rally, everything enacted by the brown synod and the Wittenberg synod seemed to be in jeopardy. On 16 November Ludwig Müller was forced to rescind the Aryan clause. The Emergency League issued a proclamation about the Sports Palace demonstration, to be read from the pulpits. These were confiscated and, for the first time, Emergency League pastors were suspended. Then Interior Minister Wilhelm Frick announced that Hitler would not intervene in the church dispute and had no intention of using police measures. At the end of November Hossenfelder's Church Ministry Council was forced to resign, and Ludwig Müller had to cancel his installation as Reich bishop, scheduled in the Berlin Cathedral on 3 December.

Was a victorious mood justified? In Berlin the regional church bishops were preparing to fight with the Reich bishop for a new church government. What did this mean for the opposition?

On 30 November Bonhoeffer and Hildebrandt learned that several German bishops—those who had elected Müller without protest in Wittenberg—were negotiating with him. Niemöller saw no way he could responsibly intervene. The friends immediately wrote Niemöller in Dahlem:

> . . . more than anything we would have liked to telephone you again, from our side to embrace you in fellowship, with all the force of our youth, and to implore you not to hand over the control of the ship, at this decisive moment, to those who will certainly steer it back into uncharted seas and who will not give back the helm until it is too late. . . . False modesty and timidity brought about our downfall once before, last June.[20]

They then developed an emergency plan for Niemöller to follow: the synods named in the summer of 1933 were to be dissolved; members of those synods who wanted to participate in the new synods had to go through a disciplinary review. The Emergency League should bar new members to prevent infiltration by the defeated German Christians. In the new church leadership, Hermann Sasse should represent the Lutherans and Barth the Reformed church. In their telephone conversation, Niemöller had told them it was not a question of individual personalities and jobs, but of the church and its doctrine. Their response was that this was precisely why Niemöller and his friends should not exercise false restraint.

Having sent the letter, Bonhoeffer and Hildebrandt began to draft forms of repentance for German Christians who wanted to resume their functions in the synods or the church administration under the new conditions.

Almost immediately, however, the disquieting rumor reached Bonhoeffer that his allies, Niemöller and Jacobi, disagreed about the situation and the necessary strategy. Bonhoeffer and Hildebrandt had just persuaded the German pastors in England to join the Pastors' Emergency League. On 4 December they dispatched an urgent telegram to Niemöller:

> Dismayed to hear of breach in Council of Brethren. Jacobi's exclusion from negotiations would force us to resign immediately and prevent the

German pastors in England from joining. . . . Stop shameful fence sitting.
Why evade responsibility? Brotherly greetings from Londoners.[21]

By the time the message reached Berlin the situation had changed. The
reputation of the Reich bishop had suffered, but he had not lost much
power. Faced with massive opposition, he flouted the recommendations of
the regional church leaders and independently convened a new Spiritual
Ministry (which was also dissolved by the end of that year).

Niemöller wrote his friends in London that it had been necessary to
oppose the Reich bishop's attempt to split the opposition by naming certain
individuals to the new leadership councils; those who served on these councils were a besieged minority and had to work under impossible regulations.
He assured them, however, that "united action would be taken regarding the
Lutheran bishops."[22]

Behind this assurance, Bonhoeffer and Hildebrandt sensed the danger
that those who had to contend with the Lutheran bishops might be reluctant
to confront the National Socialist regime with a clear church position on the
Aryan clause:

> This is the time when we must be radical upon all points, and that includes
> the Aryan clause, without any fear of the disagreeable consequences for
> ourselves. If we are untrue to ourselves here, then we will discredit the
> whole of last summer's struggle. Please, please, do everything you can to
> keep things clear, courageous and untainted.[23]

Although deeply concerned that the events in Berlin had so clearly
revealed the opposition's weaknesses, Bonhoeffer was also pleased at the
unexpected turn of events:

> In recent weeks as the authoritarian church government has collapsed, I
> cannot help feeling rather ashamed. Not that I believe that the line we have
> been following was wrong—on the contrary, it has been proved right; but
> that we could be so incredibly shortsighted, viewing things as hard cer-
> tainties that, when the moment came, collapsed into nothingness.[24]

But he feared that the old church would simply return, and that the
newly begun struggle for the confession and the sovereignty of the church
might be ended prematurely. In his thinking and actions, he had already
arrived at a point that the rest of the opposition only reached months later,
after new upheavals. Five months were to elapse before Barmen, and during
that time the forces upon which he was counting began to muster them-

selves. On 3–4 January, at Barth's instigation, a "free, reformed synod" convened in the Rhineland.[25] At a church conference on 14 January in Berlin, the Berlin-Brandenburg Emergency League of pastors and laity prepared the way for a free synod. This was scheduled for 27 January 1934, but was canceled when events took a different turn. The return of the old church began to seem increasingly unlikely. These conditions transformed the opposition into what came to be known as the "Confessing church" during the days of the Barmen synod.

The crisis among the German Christians and the Emergency League after the Sports Palace scandal had personal repercussions for the two friends. With their constant interference, Bonhoeffer and Hildebrandt had drawn so much attention to themselves that Niemöller now asked Hildebrandt to take over the affairs of the Pastors' Emergency League. Niemöller was encountering difficulties because his previous colleague and onetime fellow naval officer, Captain Schulze, was leaving. Since the prospects were improving that the "opposition" might develop into the "Confessing church," Hildebrandt responded to Niemöller's call for help. He left Bonhoeffer in London on 22 January. Two weeks later he was already preaching from the Dahlem pulpit, from which Niemöller, in the meantime, had been banned.

Bradford. The annual conference of the German pastors living in England met in Bradford in Yorkshire from 27 to 30 November, coinciding with the period in which the German Christian movement collapsed.

As usual, the pastors worked on theological issues; Bonhoeffer set the central agenda. "Licentiate Bonhoeffer explained the tasks of the ministry as, within the framework of an evangelically understood sermon, working out very concrete commandments on the basis of the scriptures, and that can be presented to the congregation as commandments that are valid today."[26] Bonhoeffer was asked to hold the main lecture, on the "concept of church" at the next conference. His colleagues also heard short talks about the small parish in the grim mill town of Bradford; Bonhoeffer spoke about his experiences in Berlin. The real emphasis of the gathering had shifted to the difficult discussions about what position to take on the events in Berlin. Bonhoeffer now had the opportunity to present his views for the first time to all his colleagues.

The discussion and formulation of a position was necessary because the pastors in England had been invited to send a delegation to the formal consecration of the Reich bishop at Berlin Cathedral on 3 December. Those in Bradford did not yet know that the invitation would be canceled. What they did know, however, was that during the past few days several pastors in Germany had been suspended from office.

Bonhoeffer found it unacceptable for the conference to send a delegation to Berlin at that point. He was unable to convince everyone, however, and so he insisted that the delegation take a document that stated clearly how difficult it was for pastors abroad to feel any kind of confidence in Ludwig Müller's administration. The discussion revolved around this document.

Bonhoeffer described in detail what had happened since the summer, including the September synods and the suspension of Pomeranian pastor Gerhard Wilde, who had proclaimed in his church on 19 November:

> Before God and this Christian congregation I accuse the Reich bishop, Hossenfelder, Peter and the other German Christians of having violated the honor of the church by their principles and of having enacted church laws that are contrary to the spirit and the teaching of Christ.[27]

The pastors finally agreed upon a statement, "To the Reich Church Government."[28] In heavy theological language, it acknowledged that on 14 November the Reich bishop "had spoken strongly in favor of the purity of doctrine," but unequivocally warned that "the close tie between the German Evangelical diaspora in England and the mother church will be broken" if members of the church administration continued to infringe upon the unity of the Old and New Testaments or the Reformation doctrine of justification.

Bonhoeffer's notes recommended even more direct language:

> . . . we still don't understand that the Reich bishop is still the sponsor of the German Christian movement [Ludwig Müller did not resign as Reich bishop until mid-December], whose Reich leaders silently watched while the church's confession was attacked unbearably in the form of mockery of the Bible and the cross of Christ; and they found it right that Dr. Krause's successor in the movement should be the very person [Pastor Tausch of Berlin] whose behavior at [the Sports Palace] expressed only approval.[29]

When the pastors learned that Müller's consecration had been postponed they mailed the declaration to the Reich church government. A copy was sent to the Emergency League. The London pastors suggested to Baron Schröder that he should send a similar document to Berlin in the name of the Association of Congregations. This was a more sharply worded version of the Bradford text, declaring that "the statutes . . . give us the full liberty to resign from the Church Federation should we so desire."[30]

Those in Berlin recognized the twofold threat. On 20 December Theodor Heckel sent a soothing reply:

> The events which have since occurred[31] testify to the earnest desire, not only to uphold the full authority of [the] Bible and confession as the inviolable foundations of the church, but to bring peace to the church itself.... The responsible church authority is fully aware of the special nature and situation of the German Evangelical congregations in Great Britain.... It therefore derives considerable pleasure and satisfaction from the evidence in this declaration of their complete unanimity in confessing to the fundamentals of the Evangelical church.[32]

But it was too late for appeasement. Heckel's reply sounded implausible to those in London, since recent events had not only confirmed but exceeded their earlier fears. On the day Heckel's letter was sent, the Reich bishop arbitrarily signed an agreement incorporating the Evangelical Youth into the Hitler Youth. The second Spiritual Ministry, established at the beginning of December, had dissolved after one member (Hans Lauerer) never began serving and the other two members resigned, Weber on 22 December and Beyer after New Year's. Instead of the attempts to smooth the waters that had been promised, Müller enacted the notorious "muzzling decree" on 4 January 1934, entirely on his own responsibility and without consulting the Spiritual Ministry or regional church leaders. The decree despotically prohibited any discussion of the church struggle (*Kirchenkampf*) in church buildings or by church publications, and threatened to dismiss anyone who disregarded the ban. As if that were not enough, he reenacted the Aryan clause, which had been suspended on 16 November.

Given these circumstances, the London pastors now viewed the Bradford declaration as little more than a mild admonition. The Reich bishop was making it exceptionally difficult for Heckel, who had oversight of the parishes abroad, to make the pacification and "inviolability" of the church sound plausible to those in London.

Telegrams. Bonhoeffer and his colleagues soon knew only too well what was happening in the Reich church government, the Pastors' Emergency League, and, occasionally, even at the Reich chancellery on Wilhelmstrasse. They used the threat to withdraw their congregations from the German Evangelical Church as leverage, and decided to hinder each new step by the church government and relieve the burden on their colleagues in the Emergency League. They sent a series of telegrams,[33] eventually driving Heckel to visit London to stop that source of constant disturbance:

1. When Ludwig Müller independently began negotiations merging the Evangelical Youth with the Hitler Youth, the pastors sent a cable on 19 December to Bishops Marahrens and Meiser with a somewhat strange text:

> Expect Lutheran bishops to preserve Gospel for Christian youth and honor of German Evangelical Church. Congregations here extremely perturbed. German pastors in London. Wehrhan.[34]

The amalgamation of the two organizations was supposed to extend even to the London parishes. At the beginning of the year a Party official arrived for the purpose of incorporating the church youth into the Hitler Youth. On British soil the intention was easily thwarted.

2. After the appearance of the "muzzling decree" (entitled "The Decree for the Restoration of Orderly Conditions in the German Evangelical Church"), which was an attempt to protect the church government and its policies against criticism by threatening immediate punishment against those who failed to comply, they sent a telegram directly to the Reich church government:

> Following today's *Times* report extremely worried about relations of churches here with home church. Request elucidation facts. German pastors in London 6 January.[35]

3. On the day this telegram was sent the text of the Emergency League proclamation arrived in London, urging pastors not to obey the "muzzling decree" of 4 January. It was the first proclamation of a *status confessionis*. Most pastors did not read the proclamation from their pulpits until 14 January. Some did so on 7 January, the day the London pastors also cabled the Reich church government:

> For the sake of the Gospel and our conscience we associate ourselves with Emergency League proclamation and withdraw our confidence from Reich Bishop Müller. German pastors in London. Wehrhan.[36]

In fact, they wanted to send the telegram in the name of all the German pastors in the country, but there were complications. Bonhoeffer's draft telegram bluntly declared: ". . . and no longer recognize the Reich bishop," instead of "withdraw our confidence." His version was stronger than the Emergency League's phrase "loss of confidence"—too strong, indeed, for his colleagues—and so he yielded. Pastor Schreiner in Liverpool refused to sign the text of this telegram. Rather than become involved in a prolonged discussion, Bonhoeffer and Hildebrandt decided to go ahead; they felt that a rapid and strong reaction was more important than unanimity reached only at the expense of a delay.

4. The pastors' message was followed by another cable from Baron Schröder, chairman of the Association of Congregations, to Müller on 9 January:

> ... rooted in the biblical Gospel our congregations, much as they love their home church, cannot tolerate it when the church's foundation is shaken and when pastors are persecuted by the church government for obeying their consciences in fighting for this foundation. I fear fateful consequences in the form of a secession of overseas German parishes from their home church which would deeply sadden me, on behalf of the past community of faith.[37]

Schröder was an independent Englishman whose telegram provided authoritative support for the pastors' protest.

Bonhoeffer thought that there might be rapid changes favoring the opposition, and energetically fostered similar hopes in those around him. In a New Year's letter to Henriod he wrote:

> Since we met last, things have changed very rapidly. The process of cleansing has gone on faster than anyone of us would have thought. And it is very satisfactory to me to see that the aims of the opposition become more and more radical and to the point. Müller must be done away with and with him all his bishops, and what seems most important of all—the new court theologians (you find their names in the new periodical *Deutsche Theologie*) must all undergo an "*Irrlehreverfahren*" [heresy trial], "*Lehrzuchtverfahren*" [doctrinal examination]; for they are the real source from which the poison goes out.... I personally do not believe that with the settlement of the struggle with the German Christians the dangerous time for the church is over. On the contrary, it is only the beginning of much more serious and dangerous fights in the near future. But—anyway—the fronts become clear and that is all we want.
>
> The youth commission meeting Febr. 15th will probably have to deal already with more or less clear conditions in Germany....[38]

Bonhoeffer was not mistaken about the increasing gravity of the situation, but his prognosis of imminent changes proved overly optimistic. He underestimated the half measures that would impede so much that was attempted in the ensuing weeks.

The Londoners had received no reply to their first four telegrams. In Berlin one event rapidly succeeded another. Proclamation Sunday, on 7 January, ushered in one of the most turbulent weeks in the church struggle.

The opposition had planned a protest service for Monday, 8 January in the Berlin Cathedral. Müller obtained a police prohibition. In response a large crowd gathered before the cathedral and began singing "A Mighty Fortress Is Our God." Some of the regional church leaders let it be known that they would not enforce Müller's decree of 4 January. They decided to confer in Berlin on 13 January, and the possibility of secession from the Reich church was mentioned. Seventy-two professors and university lecturers published a protest against the Reich bishop. In response the culture minister forbade professors of theology, as civil servants of the Third Reich, to associate themselves with manifestos concerning the church government or join oppositional organizations like the Emergency League. On 11 January Reich President Paul von Hindenburg personally summoned Müller, hoping to influence him. On 12 January, Bodelschwingh and Finance Minister Graf Schwerin von Krosigk, a member of the Dahlem congregation, visited Hindenburg. Meanwhile all the factions were preparing for a reception Hitler had originally scheduled for 17 January. On 13 January all the church leaders who were not German Christians convened and decided to postpone the threatened secession; they even made a "truce" with the Reich bishop until after the reception with Hitler. For his part, the Reich bishop promised to renew efforts to pacify the churches. The same day, Saturday, 13 January, the church leaders, including Bishops Wurm and Meiser, broadcast a radio message to their clergy asking them not to read the Emergency League proclamation from the pulpit on 14 January. The reception with Hitler was postponed twice, however, and did not take place until 25 January. This not only prolonged the already unendurable tension, but intensified the uncertainties and intrigues behind the scenes.[39]

Influence on Chancellery Reception. Bonhoeffer was now telephoning Berlin almost daily. His mother proved to be extremely well informed, since she was actively supporting his friends in the Emergency League and able to establish important contacts for them. It was still uncertain whether Hitler would get rid of the Reich bishop; everyone expected the decision to be announced at the chancellery reception. It appeared that Hindenburg and Frick advocated Müller's dismissal, whereas Göring and Rust sought an opportunity to weaken the opposition. On 17 January Bonhoeffer received a letter from his mother:

Müller's audience with the Reich Chancellor has been postponed from today until tomorrow. At the moment all we can think about is how to make him realize before the meeting that the bishops' truce is not in fact a peace. I may have found a way of doing this, with Uncle Rudi's [General von der Goltz, Paula Bonhoeffer's brother-in-law] help; we hope that our man in Dahlem [Niemöller] may get an audience with [Hindenburg]. So now we can only wait and see, but our man in Dahlem is stout-hearted and abounds in confidence.[40]

Meanwhile the London pastors had stopped sending telegrams to the Reich church government; they were now writing the state authorities directly. On 15 January they sent a letter to Hindenburg:

We implore you, Mr. President, to avert the terrible danger that threatens the unity of the church and the Third Reich now, in the eleventh hour. As long as Reich Bishop Müller remains in office, the danger of secession remains imminent.[41]

Copies of the letter were sent to Hitler, Foreign Minister von Neurath, Interior Minister Frick, Finance Minister Schwerin-Krosigk, and the Reich bishop.

In addition Bonhoeffer persuaded the bishop of Chichester to approach Hindenhurg as the presiding member of the German Evangelical Church.[42] In his capacity as chairman of the Universal Christian Council for Life and Work, Bell wrote a letter—which Bonhoeffer translated into German—to Hindenburg; he also sent a curt inquiry to the Reich bishop to whom he had already officially voiced his misgivings after the Novi Sad meeting.[43]

The London petitions drew considerable attention in Berlin.[44] On 17 January von Neurath replied from the State Department:

I too have followed with considerable concern what has been happening in Germany's Evangelical church. . . . I have tried wherever possible to influence the course of the disputes in the Evangelical church. . . . However, I would strongly advise the German Evangelical churches in Great Britain to postpone for the time being the drafting of their proposed resolutions.[45]

Secretary of State Meissner confirmed that Hindenburg had received the letter on 19 January "with the comment that the Reich president is devoting particular attention to the events in the Evangelical church."[46] On the previous day Hindenburg had, in fact, forwarded the London document to Hitler, with the observation that he viewed the worsening situation "with strong misgivings, in particular its repercussions on the German Evangelical churches abroad, and would be very grateful if the Reich chancellor could . . . give the petition his closest attention." This letter was put before Hitler, but he and Göring had other ideas about handling the "repercussions abroad." They turned this argument not against Müller, but against those in the opposition who were allegedly disseminating atrocity propaganda. Even Heckel warned the London pastors soon thereafter against interfering from outside; those in London rebutted the warning as discriminatory and threatening.

Hitler's reception for the leading protagonists, from Ludwig Müller and the bishops to Martin Niemöller, finally took place on 25 January. It took an extremely dramatic turn and failed to result in Müller's dismissal, thus disappointing the more extravagant hopes of the opposition. The blame for this was laid on a telephone conversation of Niemöller's in which he had spoken disparagingly of Hindenburg's influence on Hitler. Göring, who had tapped Niemöller's line, opened the meeting by reading the text of the conversation to the assembled guests.[47]

Publicly, the outcome of the reception seemed to be the regional church leaders' complete submission to the Reich bishop, who emerged stronger from the meeting than before. On 27 January the church leaders, including Wurm, Meiser, and Marahrens, issued an astonishing declaration "under the impression of the great hour when the heads of the German Evangelical Church met the Reich chancellor":

> The assembled leaders of the church stand entirely behind the Reich bishop and declare themselves willing to enforce his policies and decrees in the sense he desires, to hinder church-political opposition to the Reich bishop, and to consolidate his authority by all available constitutional means. . . .[48]

Only now did Heckel respond to the disturbing petitions and telegrams from London. In a general letter to all pastors abroad containing the church leaders' declaration of 27 January, Heckel commented:

> In particular I would impress upon the clergy abroad the necessity for the greatest possible discretion in regard to church politics. Just as the front-line soldier is not in a position to assess the overall plan but must carry out the duties that immediately concern him, so I expect the clergy abroad to distinguish between their own particular task and the task of the church authorities in shaping the German Evangelical Church at home. . . .[49]

But for the London pastors, who had succeeded in making so deep an impression on so many people, mere generalities would not be enough. Heckel informed Bonhoeffer and his colleagues, as well as Baron Schröder and the bishop of Chichester, that he intended to visit England.

Bonhoeffer viewed the chancellery reception as a severe reversal. Before he had written to Geneva: "with any luck this will clarify matters."[50] Now he wrote to de Félice: "My best regards; may your work prosper at this disastrous time."[51] Despite this reversal, his faith in the cause never wavered.

On 21 January, when the outcome was still undecided and tension was at its height, he chose as his sermon text Jeremiah 20:7: "O Lord, thou hast deceived me . . ." His depiction of the refractory yet obedient Jeremiah became a kind of personal confession to the congregation:

> The noose is drawn tighter and more painfully, reminding Jeremiah that he is a prisoner. He is a prisoner and he has to follow. His path is prescribed. It is the path of the man whom God will not let go, who will never be rid of God. . . .
>
> He was upbraided as a disturber of the peace, an enemy of the people, just like all those, throughout the ages until the present day, who have been possessed and seized by God, for whom God had become too strong . . . how gladly would he have shouted peace and *Heil* with the rest. . . .
>
> The triumphal procession of truth and justice, the triumphal procession of God and his Scriptures through the world, drags in the wake of the chariot of victory a train of prisoners in chains. May he at the last bind us to his triumphal carriage so that, although in bonds and oppressed, we may participate in his victory![52]

Heckel's Visit. It has sometimes been said that British public opinion showed more sympathy for the travails of the church in Germany in January 1934 than toward the first refugees in the spring of 1933. If Ludwig Müller were to consolidate his victory of 25 January, something had to be done to mollify or dissipate the unfavorable reactions in the foreign press. From Heckel's perspective, it was essential to prevent the pastors in London from abusing their freedom by making contacts with ecumenical circles and with the world press. Eventually, of course, they must find their way back to allegiance to the Reich bishop and his church government.

Heckel informed the pastors, Baron Schröder, and the bishop of Chichester that he would be in London on 8–9 February. He regarded the mission as so important that he took with him theologian Friedrich-Wilhelm Krummacher and jurist Hans Wahl from the Church Federation Office. Church developments since 25 January seemed ominous indeed to the pastors in

London, as they awaited the arrival of the delegation from Berlin, nor were they reassured by what they learned from telephone conversations and letters from home, and read in the daily press.

The most portentous news for those in London was of Niemöller's suspension from office on 26 January, and the fact that so far he had observed the prohibition. A *Morning Post* reporter had visited the Dahlem church on Sunday, 4 February, fully expecting to find a member of the "other side" officiating. From his dramatic report we learn that a slim, dark-haired man entered the pulpit, his first words betraying the surprising fact that "another Niemöller" was preaching. It was Franz Hildebrandt.

Before the arrival of the delegation the pastors in London also learned that the Reich bishop, in the name of "unified leadership," had taken charge of the Church Senate and the Old Prussian Union church. On 3 February the Prussian church administration had assumed the power to remove clergy "in the interests of the church," thus infringing on one of the most cherished of the pastors' rights. At the beginning of February more than fifty pastors were suspended. In view of all this, Heckel could hardly expect a conciliatory atmosphere in London.

So ominous was this news that Bonhoeffer and his colleagues felt impelled to make meticulous preparations for the unwelcome visitation. Together, on 5 February, they drafted a six-point memorandum:

1. It is questionable whether decrees enacted by the Reich Bishop of the Reich Church Government are binding upon the churches abroad, since the transfer of authority from the German Evangelical Church Federation, or original party to the agreement, to the new German Evangelical Church was effected on 11.6.1933 without the prior assent of the other free party to the agreement (churches abroad). Until further clarification of this question, no decree is binding.

2. Compulsory measures taken by the German Evangelical Church must first be rescinded (only last month the Reich Bishop requested police intervention to assist him in his duties).

3. There can be no confidence so long as a Reich Bishop remains in power who has been the patron of the German Christians and who, after introducing the Aryan clause into the church, first rescinds and then reintroduces it.

4. The incorporation of the [Evangelical] Youth into the Hitler Youth is dangerous, and the Reich Bishop's authority in this matter is questionable.

5. There can be no question of confidence where the highest minister in the church can insult his clergy with vulgar abuse in the press.

6. We would support Baron Schröder's proposal that the Reich Bishop should give a written guarantee that the conditions enabling churches abroad to remain within the home church will be upheld, and that the compulsory measures will be rescinded, this to be effective retroactively.[53]

The atmosphere was already stormy when discussions began on 8 February between the Berlin delegation and seven of the German pastors in England. The pastors were critical of Heckel's decision to visit Schröder first. Heckel, in turn, demanded an explanation of the Bradford declaration on the Reich bishop's consecration, and criticized the group's choice of recipients for copies of their 15 January letter to Hindenburg.[54]

According to the minutes, Heckel then outlined a "General Plan" of the future tasks of the German church, drafted on 31 January by the church chancellery.[55] It comprised a reorganization of German Protestantism parallel to the state's efforts at centralization elsewhere; administrative centralization of youth work, the home mission, and evangelical social organizations; and finally, a theological survey of topical problems, especially that of the relationship between law and the Gospel. This plan had been agreed to by the bishops and church leaders. In an allusion to the chancellery reception, Heckel added, "I would not venture to say whether agreement in such cases is wholly spontaneous or whether it is influenced entirely by specific circumstances." Church-political partisanship, he went on, was incompatible with the continued independence of the congregations abroad and would also invalidate the 1924 Diaspora Law.

Hitler believed that Protestantism had achieved unity too late and that, given the current crisis, it was likely to disintegrate within five months if the squabbles among its leaders deteriorated into a chronic dispute. For that reason there must be unity and orderly conditions. "I have been empowered to inform you that there is no cause for further concern in the matter of the Aryan clause." Heckel then described what had happened after the Sports Palace demonstration as a total failure either to change the climate of opinion or to get Niemöller into the Church Ministry. The opposition, he said, had presented the Reich bishop with an ultimatum which he had to reject, because he could not tie himself down to any one set of proposals. Yet Müller had remained open to suggestions. His agreement with Baldur von Schirach on merging the Evangelical Youth Associations with the Hitler Youth had been sanctioned by church leaders; Hitler had described it as the Christmas present that pleased him most. The fact remained that Müller was the man most highly esteemed by the Party, and in this respect nothing had changed after the chancellery reception. Heckel then described the reception, his words written down in the notes taken by the London pastors on 8 February 1934:

> Reception with Hitler. Niemöller's telephone conversation: "Now Hitler is with the old man. Extreme unction. Buttered up. When he enters the parlor, he will receive a memo, and the old gentleman will say: "This is how you march." We have set everything up wonderfully. Then Göring intervenes in the meeting. Hitler: "This is totally outrageous. Rebellion. I will not allow my leadership to be exploded. I will use every means available to me against this rebellion." Niemöller: "But we are all enthusiastic about the Third Reich." Hitler: "I built the Third Reich, you just worry about your sermons." Hitler asks about objections against the Reich bishop. The church leaders are silent. Hitler: "It is deeply painful to me that the Evangelical church isn't moving ahead faster. I am much closer to it than to the Catholic church." A pledge of loyalty to the *Führer* follows. Niemöller has a talk with Göring. The outcome was a complete failure for the opposition.[56]

Heckel turned next to the disciplinary actions taken against the clergy and reported on the incriminating evidence against opposition pastors. Foreign influence, he said, especially by an "English and a Swedish bishop"—obviously meaning Bell and Ammundsen—was dangerous. It should not be forgotten that to oppose Ludwig Müller was tantamount to opposing the state. The second phase of church development was now over, he said. It was time to look at the situation realistically and for the best theological minds to apply themselves to confessional work in the German Evangelical Church. Should Niemöller not conform, he added, there might be a "terrible ending." Finally Heckel sought to allay their fears by saying that Müller's emergency decrees would only be applied in extreme cases; no one had been dismissed, but only suspended, from office.

When the meeting was thrown open for discussion, Bonhoeffer was the first to speak. The London minutes record him as asking why discussion was almost always confined to strategic and church-political concerns, and seldom dealt with questions of principle relating to the Old Testament, the confessions, or freedom of speech. Could Müller, he said, really be regarded as a responsible representative of the church in view of his lamentable failure to solve the problem of youth work, his use of dictatorial force, and his inability to make up his mind over the Aryan clause? Bonhoeffer then suggested that the most urgent church-political task was secession from such a church, rather than an attempt to achieve unified organization whatever the circumstances.

Heckel replied that the Old Testament presented an unresolved task. As for freedom of speech, he said, they must concede that, despite Rust's decree, it was still possible to publish things like *Junge Kirche* and Künneth's *Nation vor Gott*. The proposal for the eventual repeal of the Aryan clause had not come from the Lutheran bishops, but from the German Christian bishops. "Relations with the Reich preclude open discussion of the clause" which, by the common assent of the bishops, would not be dealt with. The situation was this: first, the Aryan clause was not applicable to the Reich church but only to individual regional churches; second, it applied only to the ministry; third, it would not be systematically applied abroad; and fourth, there was no cause for disquiet about the future. The Reich bishop's dictatorial emergency decree (the "Decree to Establish Unified Leadership in the Evangelical Church of the Old Prussian Union" of 2 January 1934) had been essential for the authorities to continue working; in the Church Senate alone, for instance, there had been five "parties." The Reich bishop, according to Heckel, had not really wanted the Aryan clause; the incorporation of the Evangelical Youth into the Hitler Youth had occurred without any friction; the Reich bishop's language was simply the "soldier's slang" of today; Bishop Glondys of Siebenbürg had praised Müller's strategic foresight. And, Heckel concluded, the work overseas was very close to the Reich bishop's heart. Dr. Wahl added that the German Evangelical Church was the lawful successor to the Church Federation.

At the end of the day Heckel's real objective emerged. The vote of no confidence in the Reich bishop, expressed by the telegrams and the letter of 15 January from London, was symptomatic of undesirable radicalism. He wanted to return to Berlin with a declaration of loyalty from his colleagues, in which each of the German pastors would affirm his "regard for the whole."

Before the next day's meeting further widened the gap, Heckel, Krummacher, and Wahl spent two hours with Bishop Bell at the Athenaeum Club [one of the elite private clubs on the Pall Mall]. Here, too, things did not go as smoothly as Heckel had hoped. In preparation he had consulted Schönfeld, who had advised him to stick to questions of principle and not be drawn into a discussion of "concrete" matters; in other words, he should try to make plain that, ecclesiastically and theologically, Lutheranism sought to sever itself from the theology of the West, which had been shaped by political liberalism.[57] But the conversation quickly became more concrete. Heckel suggested that Bell not concern himself with German problems, since the question of heresy was not being debated. He asked Bell to consider refraining from all public comment for a period of six months—virtually until the time of the Fanö conference. Bell refused.

The German press, reporting on the visit to the Athenaeum, noted that the discussion had led to improved relations between the ecumenical movement and the German Evangelical Church; their relation could now be regarded as unclouded. Bishop Bell heatedly refuted this in a letter to *The Times* on 10 March, in which he said that in fact he had put questions before the delegation that had not been dealt with. Nor could he modify the protest expressed in his letter of 18 January to the Reich bishop; unfortunately, new difficulties had arisen in the meantime.[58] Obviously the delegation from the Church Federation Office was in something of a dilemma with regard to both Berlin and London.

Following this conversation with Bell, the second session with the pastors was no more successful and came to an abrupt end. The argument revolved round which document should be signed—the declaration put forward by the pastors or Heckel's proposed declaration of loyalty.

The dispute was overshadowed by the ominous suggestion that the pastors had unwittingly or even consciously submitted to "foreign influence." It was not a coincidence that the church leaders, after meeting with Hitler, had included the following sentences in their declaration—one which Heckel had been quick to convey to the pastors abroad:

> [The church leaders] most strongly condemn any intrigue involving criticism of the state, people, or movement, which are intended to imperil the Third Reich. They particularly condemn using the foreign press to present the false view that the controversy within the church is a struggle against the state.[59]

The pastors drew Heckel's attention to the fact that the account he had given them on the previous day largely tallied with the regular reports carried in *The Times*; hence there could be no question of the London clergy having been driven into opposition by false press reports.

When the London pastors offered their declaration along the lines of their previous memorandum Heckel rejected it. The German Evangelical Church had no intention of meddling in the affairs of the churches abroad, and the latter, he said, should refrain from meddling in the affairs of the German Evangelical Church.

Bonhoeffer objected at once that "meddling" was not the issue. The preeminent theological concern was a credible and religiously acceptable connection to the German church, from which clergy abroad could not withdraw. Now, however, the group of pastors began to waver. The colleague in Liverpool, Pastor Karl Schreiner, declared that he was satisfied with Heckel's explanations and wished to disassociate himself from the earlier declarations of his London colleagues, since the latter were in opposition on principle. Heckel then read a draft of his declaration he had drafted:

> Due to the steps undertaken in January of this year by the parish organizations of the German Evangelical congregations in England and the German Evangelical pastors in London, on 8 February 1934 I gave a detailed report to the meeting of German Evangelical clergy in England about the general church situation. On this occasion, with the understanding that my remarks would not be used publicly, I explained that with respect to the Aryan clause—aside from the fact that there had been no normative Reich church regulation as yet—there was no longer any cause for anxiety. Insofar as the German Evangelical churches in England showed concern about alterations to the Bible, I denied that the German Evangelical Church had any such intentions. As far as the existing ties to the German Evangelical parishes in England, I presented the legal situation that the new constitution of the German Evangelical Church had not introduced any changes in the legal foundation of the overseas diaspora law. Under the assurance that the German Evangelical clergy are prepared to recognize the authority of the GEC, I declared my willingness to recommend to the Reich bishop a written declaration that, within the framework of the relationship that has existed up to now, expresses the guaranteed autonomy that preserves the current confessional status of the German Evangelical congregations in England.
>
> During the session of 9 February 1934 this declaration was unanimously agreed to by all the German Evangelical pastors in England.[60]

Heckel now asked the pastors to sign this declaration for the record. Schönberger exclaimed: "I find all this reassurance far from reassuring!"[61] Bonhoeffer pointed out that the declaration included only what Heckel held to be important, while it ignored practically all the critical points they had raised. There was no need, he said, to assure the independence of the churches abroad, since that had never been questioned, and it was not their motive in attacking the present church government.

Heckel expressed deep regret over the course the talks had taken. Since he could not "go home empty-handed," he suggested that each pastor receive a copy of his draft so that they could study its wording carefully. He ominously added that obedience was in their own interest, lest they find themselves among the ranks of the "Prague emigrants"—the common term used for refugee journalists and left-wing politicians. Nationalists and those in the churches viewed it as an especially disparaging term. When Heckel began to cite examples of treasonous activities, Bonhoeffer, Rieger, and Steiniger got up and left the room in protest.

Schönberger and Wehrhan tried to find a loophole that would allow further consideration of Heckel's declaration. Heckel left his draft with the remaining pastors, expressing hope that they might eventually sign it. The conference concluded without any final agreement having been reached.

Bonhoeffer's ties to the Reich church were strained to the utmost, but not yet severed permanently; his relations with Heckel, however, had reached a low point. After an early interest in one another, they now viewed each other as antagonists in the ecumenical realm. Because of their considerable gifts, they saw each other as dangerous, but also—not without regret—at risk. Nevertheless, each man was committed to his cause and his group. There was no going back, and certainly no chance of reconciliation.

Aftermath. The London meetings with Heckel and his delegation immediately led to difficulties, primarily in the respective interpretations of the discussions. Bonhoeffer felt the first repercussions the following weekend, when the leaders of his parish in Sydenham rebelled. On the evening of 9 February they had been invited to the German Embassy for a reception with the three visitors from Berlin. There they had a long conversation with Heckel, who succeeded in winning them over to his viewpoint. Suddenly they saw the conflict not as a "church struggle," but as a regrettable "church dispute." Now they confronted Bonhoeffer who, like Rieger, had refused an invitation to the reception: How could he have involved the overseas parishes so dangerously in internal German disputes? Why should a parish in England ally itself with a movement like the Confessing front in Germany? The discussion with his council members continued late into the night. They finally authorized Bonhoeffer to give a detailed report after the next church service, explaining to the congregation what had happened, his proposed actions, and the reason behind them. After his report the congregation voted unanimously to support their pastor.

It was more difficult to find consensus on an accurate version of the meeting on 9 February. Before his departure Heckel had seen Baron Schröder; the two men assured each other that they should do everything possible to promote peace, keep politics out of the church, and hold the congregations together.[62]

When Heckel proposed leaving his declaration behind for their consideration, the pastors feared that this might be used against them. In the minutes they recorded that the declaration had not been unanimously approved, that objections had been raised, and that no vote had been taken. They added: "Discussion of the declaration was severely hindered because the impression was given that the pastors might face political defamation." The rumor spread among them that the State Department might revoke their passports.

A letter from Heckel to Schröder on 8 May confirmed their suspicion that the Berlin delegation would give too rosy an account of the conference:

> During our last conversation in London in February we agreed that to finally resolve the situation caused by your telegram to the Reich bishop and that of the London pastors to the Reich church government, you would present to the committee of the Association of Congregations the declaration I gave to the London pastors, a declaration which received their unanimous assent. Might I perhaps inquire whether the committee has met and what conclusions were reached?[63]

Schröder replied on 25 May:

> My deepest thanks for your letter of 8 May which I found on my return here. In light of the still very unsettled church situation in Germany, the parishes here are not in a position to make any reply at present. I hope that the time may soon come when unity will be restored in the Evangelical church in Germany, and we shall then have to reconsider the question of the churches here. To avoid any misunderstanding I would point out that there was no unanimous assent to the declaration of 9 February.[64]

Heckel's attempts to pacify the churches became increasingly difficult. In May Jäger, the Reich-appointed legal administrator of the churches, ordered the first major compulsory incorporation of the regional churches into the centralized German Evangelical Church. This was the act that eventually led to the Ulm and Barmen confessions.

As a result of the 9 February meeting, the church government made a final effort to extract a declaration from Bonhoeffer. This attempt was connected to Bonhoeffer's ecumenical activity in London, which greatly disturbed Heckel's office.

George K. A. Bell, Bishop of Chichester

The Sports Palace demonstration and its aftermath helped Bonhoeffer by bringing him into contact with British circles that welcomed a reliable informant. "I have been talking to English churchpeople and to some very interesting politicians [about] all sorts of plans."[65] Yet unless Bonhoeffer intended to emigrate, these conversations and plans could not fail to have dangerous consequences.

English Contacts. Two other Germans arrived in London in October 1933, three days before Bonhoeffer: Joachim Hossenfelder, German Christian Bishop of Berlin, and Professor Karl Fezer of Tübingen, author of the German Christian principles. They were an ill-matched pair, tactically and theologically. They had come to England to win the support of prominent ecumenical leaders for the consecration of the Reich bishop, scheduled to take place in Berlin Cathedral on 3 December 1933. The invitation to England had not come from one of the Anglican bishops, as they so much desired, but from Frank Buchman's Oxford movement. Their trip gave them a platform in London and Oxford, from which to make soothing statements about the German church and, according to the *Deutsche Allgemeine Zeitung* of 21 October, to convey "greetings from church members in Germany in the German language."

The London papers reacted coolly to these "greetings." Instead they carried detailed reports from Berlin about the dubious pronouncements of the visitors' boss, Ludwig Müller, who had been demanding the ruthless implementation of the Aryan clause, regardless of public opinion in other countries. There was some anxiety in ecumenical circles that Hossenfelder and Fezer might gain a hearing. But Bonhoeffer reported to Siegmund-Schultze:

> . . . Hossenfelder had no discussion at all with [the archbishop of] Canterbury. [The bishop of] Chichester told me about this in detail the day before yesterday. Canterbury refused because he wished to avoid any misunderstanding or misrepresentation about such a reception—which he apparently regarded as not improbable. Hossenfelder saw the Bishop of Gloucester,[66] who was evidently rather taken with him. Chichester told me in confidence about a misunderstanding that this discussion concerned the eventual participation by English bishops in the installation of the Reich bishop, but this was clarified afterward in a letter. Hossenfelder was invited to London by the Oxford movement, about which he was very enthusiastic. Apparently the reception was nothing much. He wanted to give a speech in the hall of a German parish whose trustees included some eminent Jews, but this was prevented.[67] Instead, after a dinner given by Hoesch [the German ambassador] to which parsons and church elders had been invited, he gave a speech that was extremely inept and made little impression. The newspapers printed almost nothing about Hossenfelder's visit but the fact that he had attended the Oxford movement and that, to the best of my knowledge, was only 4 or 6 lines in 2 newspapers. His obvious intention of ingratiating himself with the English church has just as obviously failed.[68]

Unlike the Reich bishop's two envoys, Bonhoeffer had gained access to a number of ecumenical leaders within a fortnight of his arrival in London.

From 2 to 4 November the executive board of the World Alliance was meeting in London, as was the Universal Council for Life and Work, chaired by Bishop George Bell of Chichester. On this occasion Bonhoeffer met Bishop Burroughs of Ripon and Bishop Tom Craske, with whom he was well acquainted from his work with the Youth Commission. Siegmund-Schultze recommended that he contact H. W. Fox, the English general secretary of the British World Alliance. During the meetings Bishop Bell invited Bonhoeffer to lunch for the first time at his club, the Athenaeum, in Pall Mall. "A few days ago I was together with all the ecumenical people here," Bonhoeffer wrote to Siegmund-Schultze on 6 November.

The Bishop of Chichester. Bonhoeffer had first seen the bishop of Chichester, George K. A. Bell (1883–1958), at the Geneva meetings in the summer of 1932, but Bonhoeffer had encountered him previously in literary form, while overseeing the translation of Bell's *A Brief Sketch of the Church of England.*[69] For the bishop, however, Bonhoeffer had been only one of the many committee members of the World Alliance, and had little connection with his own immediate sphere of responsibility. Now this changed radically.

Bonhoeffer carried an introduction from Professor Adolf Deissmann, Bell's old friend from the 1925 Stockholm days; but it was a letter from H. L. Henriod on 3 October 1933 that really aroused the bishop's interest:

> I want to report briefly to you, also on that occasion [i.e., the Sofia meeting], a conversation some of us had with Bonhoeffer, who is *Privatdozent* at the University of Berlin, and one of the most promising young men in Germany, who spoke freely to us and made a deep impression on all of us at Sofia. . . . He promised to write me again from Germany without signature but with a sign on which we had agreed, so that I can forward to you this information. He is one of those who are prepared to accept any sufferings but cannot in conscience remain in the New Church, as finally elaborated at Wittenberg.[70]

After the meeting at the Athenaeum, the bishop recommended the young German to other friends. A few days later he wrote to Canon Peter Green of Manchester, a well-known representative of the evangelicals in the Church of England, and a friend of William Temple:

> If you want to get really first hand information of the situation in the German church I would recommend your seeing Herr Dietrich Bonhoeffer. He has just come over from Berlin as German Pastor. He was one of those who

signed the manifesto of the two thousand Protestant Pastors. He is a pupil of Deissmann and was introduced by Deissmann to me as one of the best younger theologians. He is under 30, unmarried, and speaks English perfectly. He is extraordinarily critical of the present rulers of the German church. But of course one must be careful not to embarrass him. . . .[71]

He went on to say that Bonhoeffer had told him that Hossenfelder was not a "slum pastor" with a great gift for missionizing, as Frank Buchman and the bishop of Gloucester had portrayed him. On the contrary, Hossenfelder had served in a very small parish in Berlin, which had been one of the only two parishes in Berlin that had not voted for the German Christians in the church elections of 23 July 1933.

Bell soon recommended the young German to interested politicians such as Lord Lothian; but Bonhoeffer himself felt that this placed him in a questionable position.

Despite the surprisingly rapid rapport established between Bell and Bonhoeffer, during those early November days they did not come to any agreement about a possible ecumenical initiative. As in Sofia, Bonhoeffer did not confine himself to purveying information. He continued to advocate his idea of a delegation that, he wrote, "has been pursued further during these days in London."[72] Those attending the London meeting discussed the suitability and proper timing of this plan, but decided to postpone it for the time being. As they had agreed upon in Novi Sad, Bell had written to Müller on 23 October; now he wished to wait for a reaction to his letter and give the Reich bishop a chance. The representatives from Geneva had not thought much of Bonhoeffer's idea of a delegation from the beginning. What Schönfeld probably had in mind at this juncture was not a delegation that would intervene with the Reich bishop, but a representative ecumenical delegation as Müller had requested. In any case, Bell wrote Swedish archbishop Eidem on 11 November that everyone had agreed that a delegation was not advisable at the present, but might become necessary should a fresh emergency arise. Bonhoeffer viewed the deferment of his plan not as a rejection, but as a consideration that would "be pursued." It was a view to which he clung tenaciously during the weeks that followed, although his plan was never put into effect.

A few months later a delegation did come into being, but it bore little resemblance to what Bonhoeffer had intended. In conjunction with Schönfeld, the Swedish Embassy chaplain in Berlin, Birger Forell, began to urge Eidem and Bell to intervene personally with Hitler. Bell, in agreement with Bonhoeffer, refused to consider this suggestion. He did not want to risk making Hitler the *deus ex machina* who would settle the turmoil in the churches; this would make Hitler the highest authority in spiritual matters.[73] Eventually, in May 1934, Eidem went on his own to see Hitler, who treated him outrageously. The visit had no tangible results.

Like Bell, Bonhoeffer did not expect any good to come of such an intervention with Hitler in 1934. When his Swiss friend Erwin Sutz made a similar proposal, he refuted it outright with theological arguments:

> At the present time, I believe that any discussion between Hitler and Barth would be quite hopeless and, indeed, no longer sanctioned. Hitler has shown himself quite clearly for what he is, and the church ought to know with whom it has to reckon. Likewise, Isaiah did not go to Sennacherib. We have often—too often—attempted to make Hitler aware of what is going on. It may be that we haven't gone about it in the right way, but then Barth won't go about it correctly either. Hitler ought to and cannot hear; he is obdurate and, as such, ought to compel *us* to hear—the question is thus turned completely around. The Oxford Movement was naïve enough to try to convert Hitler—a laughable failure to understand what is really happening—it is we who ought to be converted, not Hitler. . . .
>
> What sort of person is Brandt [Hitler's personal physician; Sutz had met him on a tour of glaciers in Switzerland and hoped the contact would be useful]? I cannot understand how a man can remain in Hitler's entourage unless he is either a Nathan or an accomplice in the events of 30 June and 25 July, of the lie of 19 August [reference is to the Röhm purge, the assassination of Austrian Chancellor Dollfuss, and the plebiscite approving the merging of the offices of Reich president and Reich chancellor under the title of *Führer*]—and guilty of the next war! Please forgive me, but these things seem to me terribly serious, and to trifle about them is to me now quite unbearable.[74]

A great deal had happened by the time Bonhoeffer wrote this letter. He and Bell had grown very close. Bell understood why Bonhoeffer had to keep political and theological judgments both separate and yet closely connected. After their first meeting in the Athenaeum the events unleashed by the Sports Palace demonstration on 13 November led to a lively correspondence between the two men. This led to Bonhoeffer's visit to the bishop in Chichester, where he bombarded Bell with pleas and suggestions.

Bonhoeffer's letter of 16 November shows that in the aftermath of the Sports Palace demonstration he did not share the widespread hopes in a renewed church, but rather envisioned that the opposition would ultimately secede from the legal church body of the German Evangelical Church.[75] Such a step, however, would mean an eventually clandestine opposition, which would lead to intensified police surveillance and lend plausibility to the accusations of political unreliability. For that reason it was important that the ecumenical movement should announce clearly and early enough which church it regarded as the true Evangelical church in Germany. This was a matter that directly concerned Bell as chairman of the Universal Council, and he should therefore demand a decision from the Reich bishop.

Bonhoeffer wrote this letter on his own initiative; this was evident in the way he already thought in terms of two separate stages. He wrote from the actual situation facing his friends in Berlin: in the awareness that it might be possible to detach Müller from his German Christian advisers, in which case a letter from the bishop would help. But he also wrote from the perspective of a future stage and a much later decision—that of separation. It was a step his Berlin friends were not at all prepared to take in 1933, but to Bonhoeffer it already seemed inevitable. In this way he emphasized those aspects of a situation that would move events forward most quickly; he used them to actively influence the future course of events. This was not without risk, for when no one followed his lead he was isolated.

Bell replied immediately, but with some reserve.[76] He was still waiting for Müller's reaction to the letter of 23 October, particularly since Schönfeld had visited the Reich bishop and received permission to announce an early reply and perhaps even an invitation for an ecumenical delegation to visit Berlin. Ever since the Sofia meeting, the possibility had loomed that ecumenical plans to send an investigating delegation could be usurped if the Reich bishop issued an official invitation first; it was a plan too clever to have been conceived by Müller himself. But Schönfeld had conveyed the Reich bishop's message to Bell before the Sports Palace scandal. Afterward the time for a move like an official invitation to the ecumenical movement had passed.

When news arrived of the first suspensions following the Emergency League proclamation Bonhoeffer immediately urged that the Ecumenical Council should initiate a campaign to help the families of the victims.[77] Unlike many of his friends, he was not worried about the risk of compromising the cause by enlisting foreign aid. But nothing came of Bonhoeffer's suggestion. Only much later, when non-Aryan pastors were forced to leave Germany, did the diocese of Chichester initiate a major relief plan.

On 21–22 November 1933 Bonhoeffer visited Bell for the first time in his fine old chambers in Chichester. The visit resulted in fruitful discussions and introduced an element of personal and theological sympathy into a relationship that had been based on church politics. This led to more frequent and close consultations, sometimes continuing from one day to the next.

Bonhoeffer and Bell agreed on their mutual interests, but only friendship could have rendered the demands they made upon each other tolerable.

As chairman of the Universal Council, Bell was already receiving information through his council secretaries in Geneva, Henriod and Schönfeld. His information was complemented and confirmed by frequent letters he requested from Cragg, the British Embassy chaplain in Berlin. Bell also valued highly the cool precise judgment shown by Pastor Koechlin in Basel, who later headed the Swiss Church Federation.

In Bonhoeffer, Bell now had a source of information and advice that came not from some outside observer, but from someone who was intimately involved. He tolerated and, to some extent, even encouraged his new partner's theological intransigence and passionate pursuit of a certain conception of things. There can be no doubt that Bell also felt a certain anxiety lest the German church opposition and its young representative, Bonhoeffer, lack the necessary levelheadedness and advocate a theology that was too one-sided. He was obviously relieved when in the autumn of 1934 he finally visited Westphalian church president Karl Koch at Bonhoeffer's behest, and was able to see for himself that the man who represented the allegedly radical sector of the German church was in fact a phlegmatic Westphalian and a natural conservative. But Bell's concern was also tempered by his astute realization that, in critical situations, levelheadedness could be used as an excuse for a lack of decisiveness. Whether Bonhoeffer came as the emissary of the Confessing church leaders or, more frequently, of his own accord, the bishop never doubted either his judgment or the information he supplied, but relied constantly upon both. Bell possessed the rare gift of being able to accept advice, which he avidly sought, and yet preserve his own independent objectivity.

Bell bad been motivated by practical considerations in seeking out Bonhoeffer as a partner. Bonhoeffer also had a concrete interest in establishing contact with the president of the Ecumenical Council. The bishop had been chairman in Novi Sad and was to preside in Fanö. Bonhoeffer found that no one else had so quickly grasped the unprecedented nature of the situation in the German church and ecumenical Christianity. Nearly everyone in the ecumenical movement was outraged by what was happening in Germany and was doing something to help the refugees. But Bonhoeffer demonstrated that this was not enough; it was necessary to decide between two ecclesiastical bodies. By what standards should one group be recognized and the other rejected, when no such criteria had been foreseen in the statutes of the ecumenical federations and, moreover, when the theological friends and foes from earlier years could be found in both camps? Bonhoeffer saw that the problem of a confessionally bound church within a federally organized, judicially powerless ecumenical movement was becoming acute. He did not hesitate to confront Bell as the responsible authority. Here, to his astonishment, he encountered understanding.

There is no doubt that the decisions he expected of Bell were difficult to implement in an organization as loose-knit as Life and Work, even for such a powerful director. Yet he hoped—as perhaps the bishop did—that the ecumenical movement, as it came to understand itself better, would grow to accept this new challenge. Bonhoeffer believed that the most recent church events had called in to question the ecumenical movement's very right to exist, more because of its excessive neutrality and failure to act than because of blatant partisanship. Bell also seemed ready to renew the movement by taking a bolder course. There were enough formal reasons to avoid making such decisions, as indeed had been suggested to Bell. Instead, between conferences he so adroitly used the freedom of his executive powers that no one—in Fanö, for example—could accuse him of abusing the authority of his office. When given a choice between doing too little or going too far, he proceeded to the limits of the latter. Bonhoeffer knew this and encouraged it, and Bell never begrudged him his demands.

Their practical relationship was enriched by their personal interest in one another. Bell was a high church diocesan bishop, highly disciplined and widely educated. As a young man he had won a coveted Oxford poetry award, and as dean of Canterbury he had initiated the Festival of Music and Drama, securing the participation of T. S. Eliot, Christopher Fry, and Dorothy Sayers. While fulfilling his added ecumenical responsibilities, he also wrote a 1,400-page biography of Archbishop R. Davidson, which placed him among the foremost English biographers. After the 1925 Stockholm conference Nathan Söderblom wrote Davidson: "This Bell never rings for nothing."

Bell liked the well-bred young German, who never got so carried away that he forgot his good manners, who was a good listener and who knew that repeating something in excitement only detracts from its original impact. Their mutual affection was expressed in mutual trust. Later, after Hildebrandt had joined them, Bell referred to them as "my two boys." He and Bonhoeffer shared the same birthday, 4 February. Every year they exchanged greetings and, when this was no longer possible, the bishop wrote to Bonhoeffer's twin sister, who had emigrated to England. When the end came, it was to Bell that Bonhoeffer's last recorded words were addressed.[78]

In his foreword to *Discipleship* in 1948, Bell wrote:

I knew him in London in the early days of the evil regime: and from him, more than from any other German, I learned the true character of the conflict, in an intimate friendship. I have no doubt that he did fine work with his German congregation: but he taught many besides his fellow countrymen while a pastor in England. He was crystal clear in his convictions; and young as he was, and humble-minded as he was, he saw the truth, and spoke it with a complete absence of fear.[79]

Dangers. Bonhoeffer's close ties to the bishop did not go unnoticed by the authorities in Berlin. His situation became increasingly imperiled: through rumors about his contacts with the press, through an article in *The Round Table,* through Bell's letter to Hindenburg, and finally because of a reception at Lambeth Palace:

1. Around Christmas it was rumored in Berlin that Dietrich Bonhoeffer was involved with *The Times*'s embarrassingly accurate accounts of church troubles. Unlike many of his allies in the struggle, Bonhoeffer was undistressed about the international press reports; later he even helped supply accurate information.[80] But at this point journalists were still able to obtain information themselves, and it seemed foolish to him to risk prosecution under the Malicious Practices Act. He therefore deemed it necessary to indignantly deny any such contact with the press. At the beginning of January he called Spiritual Ministry council member Professor Hermann Beyer, whom he (incorrectly) believed was still in office, to help him fight the rumors.[81] In addition, he allowed Rieger to tell the Berlin authorities that such rumors generated unrest in the London congregations and reduced their trust in the church government.

2. *The Round Table* was one of the most respectable English monthlies, so distinguished that it didn't print the names of authors, assuming that its readers knew who they were. Lord Lothian, subsequently ambassador in Washington, was closely connected with it. Early in 1934, Lothian decided that the March issue should include an analysis of the crisis in German Protestantism. He approached Bell, who passed the request on to Bonhoeffer: "I have an important proposal with regard to a long article in a very important periodical to put before you."[82] On 2 January, Bell wrote the editors about Bonhoeffer:

He knows the personnel of the German church at Berlin extremely well and is a follower of Karl Barth. He is also in almost daily touch with the situation in Berlin. Further he is one of the earliest members of the Pastors' Emergency League, now swollen to 6,000 members, and his name is actually the first of the twenty or so signatures of the famous manifesto

which pioneers of the Pastors' Emergency League presented to the Prussian Synod [the national synod] in September. I do not think you could get
anyone to write an article of the kind you want with more authority, and
you can be very certain of his ability. . . . he is coming to stay with me again
shortly.[83]

During the same days, Müller's "muzzling decree" was enacted, and Bonhoeffer declined to write the article. Bell undertook the work himself, on the
condition that Bonhoeffer would read it through.[84] But Lord Lothian still
wished to meet him. They met on St. James Street, 16 January, at a most crucial moment in church politics.[85] Inexplicably the Church Federation Office
soon learned that Bonhoeffer was helping Bell with an article for *The Round
Table.*

3. Bell's intervention with Müller and Hindenburg during the January
upheavals in Berlin created more of a stir in the Church Federation Office
than either of the two other matters described above. On 8 December 1933,
the Reich bishop responded to Bell's letter of 23 October, promising the president of the Ecumenical Council that the church situation would be pacified.
The insincerity of those promises now became evident. This moved Bell to
an unprecedented burst of activity, beginning with a letter to *The Times* on
17 January—the date initially scheduled for the reception with Hitler—
intended to draw attention in Berlin to Müller's breach of faith. Secondly, at
Bonhoeffer's behest, he wrote two more letters, one to Müller and one to
Hindenburg. Bonhoeffer urged him to tell the Reich bishop that he was no
longer fit to be associated with the ecumenical movement.[86] The bishop
did not go so far, but his tone was sharper than before, and he also wrote to
Hindenburg.[87] During these critical days, Bell and Bonhoeffer reconsidered
sending a delegation to Berlin, particularly after Niemöller's suspension.
Nothing came of this, but their considerations are reflected in a letter Bonhoeffer's mother wrote to him in London:

> Later I am going again to Gerhard [Jacobi] to speak with him about
> whether he thinks it's a good idea for you to come here with George [Bell].
> Franz [Hildebrandt] was much in favor of it. I thought it would be better
> if he came either later or perhaps ahead of time;[88] I will write to you with
> what Gerhard thinks. . . . Yesterday Hildebrandt preached at the *Chris-
> tuskirche*, standing in very well for Niemöller.[89]

When Heckel and his companions arrived in London, they found the
bishop surprisingly well informed and little inclined to be mollified by any
exchange of mutual assurances. When the Life and Work executive com-

mittee met in Chichester on 26–29 January 1934, Bell had taken the precaution of having them approve his most recent letter to Müller, written on 18 January.

Berlin now had proof enough of Bonhoeffer's disturbing influence and attempted once again to suppress it. The occasion for this arose shortly after Heckel's return from London.

4. Heckel's office learned—oddly enough, before even Bonhoeffer himself knew about it—that the archbishop of Canterbury wished to speak to the German pastor. The gates of Lambeth Palace had remained closed to Hossenfelder and Fezer, and Heckel's delegation had gotten no further than the Athenaeum club. Could it really be true that Bonhoeffer was to be received?

The delay in Bonhoeffer's receiving this information was due to one of his frequent visits to Germany. Shortly after the London meeting with Heckel he went to Hannover to attend the Pastors' Emergency League meeting on 13 February. There they discussed whether the opposition should continue to fight for the true church within the German Evangelical Church under Müller, or proceed toward a schism, a move for which the first free synods were paving the way.[90] Bonhoeffer left Hannover, disappointed that the conference had confined itself to theoretical discussions and warnings about the dangers of separation. When he arrived home in Berlin he went to bed with the flu.

Meanwhile, on 19 February there had been a routine reception at Lambeth Palace for foreign clergy working in London. Archbishop of Canterbury Cosmo Lang, who knew about Bonhoeffer and events in Germany through Bell, inquired about Bonhoeffer and said he would like to see him when he returned to England. By the following day this little item of news had reached Heckel's office in Berlin.

Heckel's office then learned that the chairman of Life and Work was planning a confidential discussion on the church situation in Germany. A German delegation was to be invited[91] and Bonhoeffer was to be involved. Heckel now decided to trap him.

Summoned to Berlin. Dr. Krummacher, a distant relative of the Bonhoeffers, called the Bonhoeffer home from his office at the church chancellery on Jebenstrasse, only to learn that his cousin Dietrich had returned to London. Heckel called him there and ordered him to return at once by air.[92] Bonhoeffer flew back to Berlin on 5 March and remained there until the 10th. The journey was his last act of obedience toward those who were still nominally his superiors.

The discussion took a serious turn. It concerned questions of jurisdiction within the ecumenical realm and Bonhoeffer's interests there. He also raised concerns about his personal safety.

The question of jurisdiction had grown more acute since 21 February, when the Reich bishop had set up the Church Foreign Office with Heckel, now a bishop, at its head. He was to combine oversight of the Evangelical Germans abroad with the work of "nurturing relations between the German Evangelical Church and its church friends abroad under one administrative unit."[93] Thus Heckel was now responsible to the state authorities for improving the attitudes overseas toward church affairs in Germany. It was not long before any ecumenical activity that had not received his sanction was apt to be condemned as "participation in foreign intervention in German internal affairs." The Reich bishop went so far as to accuse pastors who gave information about German church matters to foreigners of "high treason."

Heckel now asked whether Bonhoeffer intended to continue his opposition to the existing authorities, thus moving toward a lack of nationalistic discipline. He further suggested that Bonhoeffer's job in London and the respect he enjoyed there might prove dangerous, which would be regrettable in light of the pastor's youth and talents.

In the interests of both sides, Heckel demanded, Bonhoeffer "should refrain from now on from all ecumenical activity."[94] He presented Bonhoeffer with a written declaration to that effect and asked him to sign it. Bonhoeffer refused, but promised to think matters over, after which he would write. After much reflection, in a letter dated 18 March, he stated that he would not sign the document.[95] He had nothing to add to his October declaration to the Reich bishop and intended to continue his "purely ecclesiastical, theological, ecumenical work." He could reassure Heckel that he had no plans to participate in the Paris conference; he had heard no more about being received by the archbishop and had concluded "that nothing would come of it, at least for the present."[96]

The letter had just been mailed when Bonhoeffer received an invitation through H. W. Fox to go to Lambeth Palace on Monday, 26 March. Rieger described the conversation there in his diary:

> Lang knew that the prospect of this interview had created difficulties for Bonhoeffer in Berlin [with Heckel]. Lang asked for an account of this and wanted to know about a great many other things. Recognition of the existing church is out of the question for Lang. This would mean, for example, that Lang would refuse to receive Heckel. The conversation lasted three-

quarters of an hour. At the end the archbishop expressed the wish to see Bonhoeffer again soon.[97]

Bonhoeffer did not allow the Church Foreign Office to decide what was meant by "purely ecclesiastical, theological, ecumenical work." To Sutz he wrote: "They'd give anything to get me away from here and, if only for that reason, I am digging my heels in."[98]

Preparation for Barmen. It was wholly unrealistic to suppose that anything could stop or silence Bonhoeffer in the spring of 1934. His "purely ecclesiastical, theological" frame of mind wouldn't allow it, nor would the developments in Germany, which were moving irrevocably toward the crucial events in Barmen and the birth of the Confessing church that would become the center of the entire church struggle. Bonhoeffer's collaboration with Bishop Bell now entered its most vital phase. For the first time, however, his relations with the ecumenical secretariats in Geneva were becoming strained.

With his increased confidence in Hitler's support, the Reich bishop was doing everything possible to promote a schism within the church. In March he appointed as his "chief of staff" the young, energetic Dr. Heinrich Oberheid, who had been promoted from curate to bishop in his native Rhineland because he was a National Socialist. Oberheid was given executive powers. When the police dissolved the Westphalian synod, Oberheid suspended regional church president Karl Koch from office. The Reich bishop closed down all the preachers' seminaries in Old Prussia. On 12 April he nominated Dr. August Jäger, who had won notoriety as state commissar during the summer of 1933, to the post of "legal administrator" (*Rechtswalter*) of the entire German Evangelical Church. The church struggle had reached a new climax, which unleashed a series of chaotic attempts in Berlin to centralize and take over the individual regional churches.

The opposition had fallen virtually silent since its reception with Hitler; now it began to find its voice again. By summoning Bonhoeffer to Berlin, Heckel unintentionally gave him a chance to participate in the first "free synod" of the Berlin-Brandenburg churches, which met on 7 March 1934. The Westphalian synod, following its dissolution by the police, had reconstituted itself as a "Confessing synod," and there were plans to inaugurate a free general synod for all of Germany on 18 April. But because of the confusion caused by the attempts at centralization, on 22 April there was a rally in Ulm of the "Confessing front," attended by interested clergy and laity from all over the country. The first national Confessing synod convened in

Barmen on 29 May; here all the teachings of the German Christians were condemned as heretical. With that the threat of separation from the German Evangelical Church became imminent.

The closer they drew to this decision, the more urgent the warnings against it naturally became, both inside Germany and from the ecumenical movement. In March the dispassionate and politically incorruptible pastor Wilhelm Menn wrote Schönfeld in Geneva, declaring that separation would be disastrous for the Confessing congregations. Once the Confessing church had become a "free church," anyone who sought or maintained relations with it would be exposing themselves to suspicion of treason. It would, he thought, mean the end of the opposition if it succeeded in winning the support of the ecumenical movement.

As early as November, Bonhoeffer had recognized the dangers of separation, but he drew quite different conclusions.[99] He used every opportunity to urge the ecumenical offices to recognize that separation was imminent and necessary, and that they should help bring it about. But there were now signs that he could not impose his views upon those in Geneva. Heckel's newly consolidated office was making its presence felt, at least to the extent that no steps were being taken in Geneva that might prejudice the issue one way or the other.

During this period, Schönfeld and Henriod developed a plan in Geneva for an ecumenical observer to be sent to Berlin. This observer could be close to the opposition but at the same time maintain ties to the Reich church. Bell and Koechlin rejected the plan as inopportune. Henriod and Bell were preparing a meeting in Paris of selected members of the Reich church government, the opposition, and ecumenical leaders. The meeting was to take place on 16–17 April, following the scheduled ecumenical study conference on "Church and State." Bonhoeffer had been asked to speak at this conference, but had canceled after his trip to meet Heckel, citing his parish responsibilities (he was to give a lecture at an English conference of clergy during the Paris meeting).[100] Thus he was not on the list of those invited to the internal debate in Paris.

This is evident from correspondence with Henriod, although Bonhoeffer's initial letter of 14 March 1934 has never been found. It can be assumed that Bonhoeffer reported to Henriod on his talk with Heckel, and asked for Henriod's understanding for his hesitation to meet with Heckel's deputies. When Bonhoeffer wrote on 3 April to ask whether he should come to Paris Henriod made a note of Schönfeld's reply to Bonhoeffer: "He would be very useful but we should not press if it makes the situation too difficult for him."[101] Schönfeld telegraphed him not to come, perhaps somewhat too readily. But the main accent in Bonhoeffer's letter—as shown by Henriod's reply of 16 March—was his plea that the ecumenical offices acknowledge how soon they would have to decisively choose between the unequal partners in Germany.[102] On 16 March Henriod wrote Bishop Bell, citing Bonhoeffer's letter of 14 March: "I know of many very leading men whose names I may not mention in this letter who expect almost everything from a definite step from the side of the ecumenical movement. It might soon be too late."

On 16 March Henriod replied to Bonhoeffer that the ecumenical world lacked the qualification for such an ultimate step, suggesting that they might have gone further if "best friends" in Germany had not themselves cautioned against a demonstrative break with the Reich church government. In his reply on 7 April 1934 Bonhoeffer eloquently expressed his impatience with those who were apprehensive, inside Germany and elsewhere:

> My Dear Henriod ... I would very much have liked to discuss the situation with you again, since the slowness of ecumenical procedure is beginning to look to me like irresponsibility. A decision must be made at some point, and it's no good waiting indefinitely for a sign from heaven that will solve the difficulty without further trouble. Even the ecumenical movement has to make up its mind and is therefore subject to error, like everything human. But to procrastinate and prevaricate simply because you're afraid of erring, when others—I mean our brethren in Germany—must make infinitely difficult decisions every day, seems to me almost to run counter to love. To delay or fail to make decisions may be more sinful than to make wrong decisions out of faith and love. "Allow me to go before . . . ," says the Gospel—how often we use this as an excuse!—and in this particular case, it really is now or never. "Too late" means "never." Should the ecumenical movement fail to realize this, and if there are none who are "violent to take heaven by force" (Matt. 11:12), then the ecumenical movement is no longer church, but a useless association that holds nice speeches. "If ye believe not, do not stay," but to believe means to decide. And can there still be any doubt as to the nature of that decision? For Germany today it is the Confession, as it is the Confession for the ecumenical movement. We must shake off our fear of this word—the cause of Christ is at stake, and are we to be found sleeping?
>
> I am writing to you because your last letter seemed to be hinting at much the same thing. And if all the "wise," the elders and the powerful, are unwilling to act with us and are held back by all kinds of considerations— then it is you who must attack, you who must advance. Don't let yourself be stopped or misled; after all, if we're really honest with ourselves, we do know in this case what is right and what is wrong. Someone has got to show the way, fearlessly and unflinchingly—why not you? For there's much

more at stake than just people or organizational difficulties—Christ is looking down at us and asking whether there is anyone who still confesses him. I think I am right in believing that you and I think alike in such matters. Very sincerely yours, Dietrich Bonhoeffer.[103]

The intentions of writer and recipient appeared so similar as to be almost indistinguishable. There was a kind of brotherly directness in the way each demanded extraordinary steps of the other. This mutual confidence seemed to be justified by the way they had worked together ever since the Berlin conference during Hitler's seizure of power and later in their discussions in Sofia. Yet the more imminent the real demands of a schism became, the shakier this consensus proved to be. It suddenly became clear that each man understood the situation very differently. From his administrative office Henriod saw the power of his organization's statutes and found himself constrained by procedural questions. In contrast, Bonhoeffer asked how this organization could justify its very existence. The ecumenical secretary maintained ties with the Reich church, while Bonhoeffer endeavored to prevent any kind of infiltration of the ecumenical movement by German Christians or neutral representatives of the Reich church. It was only the beginning of what would become Bonhoeffer's campaign to persuade the ecumenical movement in the months that followed. He was convinced that the ecumenical movement would forego a significant experience if it failed to come to a decision. At the same time—he hinted as much to his friends in Berlin—he had no illusions about the difficulties in store should those in Geneva and in the Ecumenical Council decide to give them their definitive support.

Pastoral Letter. During these months his partner in these efforts was not so much the Geneva secretaries as the president of the whole ecumenical movement, Bishop Bell. In the weeks that followed they worked together to produce a letter from the bishop to all members of the World Council on the occasion of Ascension Day 1934. This "pastoral letter" carefully laid down the lines for the Fano conference.

Bonhoeffer's letters to Bell contain suggestions for an "ultimatum" that Bell was to send to the Berlin church government as soon as he received the information that the Barmen synod was about to convene. In November 1933 Bonhoeffer asked for nothing more than "a strong demand from the side of the ecumenic churches."[104] In January he requested "a most drastic disapproval of Müller's policy. . . . A definite disqualification of Müller by the ecumenical movement."[105] But in March, on the same day as his letter to Henriod, he wrote: "I beg to ask you once more to consider the possibility of an ecumenical delegation and *ultimatum*."[106] Bonhoeffer insisted that in taking such a step the bishop would not lay himself open to the charge of "intervention," and that the common cause of European Christianity was at stake: "Please do not remain silent now!"

Upon hearing the alarming news of August Jäger's return he wrote on 15 April that the moment had come "to take a definitive attitude, perhaps in the way of an ultimatum or in expressing publicly the sympathy with the oppositional pastors."[107] He urged the bishop, as president of the ecumenical council, to warn all member churches against independently recognizing the existing church government in Germany. He knew that this government, in its renewed attempt to consolidate the German Evangelical Church, would certainly try to gain recognition—as it had already successfully done in the case of Bishop Headlam of Gloucester. For this reason Bell must "send a letter to all other churches connected with the ecumenical movement warning them . . ."[108]

Bell was unable to envisage exactly what this ultimatum might be, but he agreed to write a letter warning all member churches.

On 27 April Bell and Bonhoeffer met at the Athenaeum to discuss this letter. Five days before the Confessing front in Ulm had for the first time publicly declared itself "the lawful Evangelical church in Germany before the whole of Christendom."[109] Having heard that Hitler had angrily responded that he intended to retain Müller, Bonhoeffer proposed that Bell should include in the letter a strong expression of solidarity for those in danger.

With characteristic modesty Bell sent Bonhoeffer a draft on 2 May, requesting amendments, deletions or additions.[110] Bonhoeffer advised him to avoid saying anything in his letter that left the choice between the two groups in Germany open. He had no inhibitions about steering the bishop toward the ultimatum he had in mind, and recommended that the Fanö conference should plan not only to speak out but to act. This was the only thing that the Reich bishop's people feared.[111]

On 10 May the ecumenical chairman's pastoral letter was distributed: "A message regarding the German Evangelical Church to the representatives of the churches on the Universal Council for Life and Work from the bishop of Chichester."[112] The letter did not contain everything Bonhoeffer would have wished, nor was it an "ultimatum" in the exact sense of the word. Yet at this crucial juncture between the controversies in the German churches and the Barmen synod, the letter did spell out the essential grievances unequivocally: the *Führer* principle, a violent regime, disciplinary measures, and racial discrimination "without precedent in the history of the Church . . . incompatible with the Christian principle."[113]

No one else would have gone so far, except perhaps Norwegian Bishop Ammundsen, who was not as prominent as Bell. Bonhoeffer thanked the bishop effusively:

> In its conciseness it strikes at the chief points and leaves no escape for mis-interpretation . . . your letter which is a living document of ecumenic and mutual responsibility. I hope, it will help others to speak out as clearly as you did.[114]

Bell received no answer to his pastoral letter from the Reich bishop or from Bishop Heckel. Ludwig Müller alluded to it briefly in a coarse speech early that summer, declaring that the Christian faith in Germany was not in a state of emergency. Bell's authority had gained in stature, however, for in November Hitler's special envoy Joachim von Ribbentrop actually visited him in Chichester.

Fortified by Bell's display of ecumenical solidarity, the opposition met in Barmen two weeks after Ascension Day. Bonhoeffer's contribution to the Barmen synod was his initiative and assistance in promoting the pastoral let-ter. He did not attend this most important event of the whole church strug-gle and there is no evidence that any thought was given to him playing a part in it. He participated only in the preliminary meetings such as the one in Hannover.

In Barmen, under the chairmanship of President Koch, free and legal representatives from every regional church proclaimed a confession to the fundamental truths of the Gospel in opposition to the "false doctrines" of the German Christian church government, thus breaking with the teachings and practices of the "brown church." In the famous Barmen declaration, based upon a draft by Karl Barth, they rejected

> . . . the false teaching that the church can and must recognize other events, powers, images and truths as divine revelation alongside the one word of God, as a source of its preaching. . .
> . . . the false teaching that the church can turn over the form of its mes-sage and ordinances at will or according to some dominant ideological and political convictions . . . or that the church can or may, apart from this min-istry, set up special leaders [Führer] with sovereign powers.[115]

After Barmen the opposition was no longer an "opposition" that still acknowledged the authority of the Reich church, but understood itself as the one "Confessing church" in Germany. Bonhoeffer was relieved by this justi-fication of his views. The Barmen synod had proclaimed and enacted the criterion for his own words and actions. Like those who attended Barmen, he had used the term "opposition" but had always understood this, both as an issue and in its demands, as the Confessing church. There had been little understanding or assent for this viewpoint. Now almost everyone spoke of the Confessing church, but in reality continued to understand it as a synonym for "opposition." Bonhoeffer did not want to see this. Bell, on the other hand, sympathized with Bonhoeffer's analysis and conception, and grasped its inherent consequences.

To a large extent the ecumenical leaders' concern was shaped by practical political considerations. When the church struggle became a tedious contest for the sake of confession, their interest flagged; whenever there was any sensational news of police action in Germany it flared up again. Given his political views, Bonhoeffer could have easily won ecumenical sympathy. Instead he began a campaign against "heresy" and became markedly isolated. He had been able to prepare very few people (one of them was Bell) for this crisis; in the eyes of the rest he merely seemed to tend toward a complicated orthodoxy.

Bonhoeffer was in a peculiar position. Despite his wholehearted involvement, his colleagues in the Confessing church viewed him as an outsider because of his constant concern with the Sermon on the Mount. Yet among his ecumenical friends, to whom the Sermon on the Mount was of prime importance, he was isolated because of his insistence on the confession and the repudiation of heresy. He believed that the confessionally based opposition could be saved from sterility by the Sermon on the Mount, while that segment of the opposition with its roots in the Sermon could be rescued from mere enthusiasm by the confession.

Fanö

During the summer of 1934 Bonhoeffer was completely preoccupied with the preparations and disputes that preceded the Fanö conference. Yet the central significance of these months was in the political events that culminated in a decisive increase in Hitler's power. The deliberations before and during Fanö were overshadowed by this threatening background: the Schacht crisis, the Röhm putsch, the Dollfuss murder, and Hindenburg's death, followed by the merger of the two highest state offices into the single office of "*Führer* and Reich chancellor."

Political Pressure. In early summer, there were some hopes of a crisis within the cabinet and among the Party leadership; people began to ask whether the

1933 forecast that Hitler would "play himself out" was about to be fulfilled. In May, Bonhoeffer learned from his brother-in-law Hans von Dohnanyi of certain tensions that might make things difficult for Hitler. Schacht, president of the Reichsbank, was thinking of resigning. On 30 June news arrived of the suppression of the Röhm putsch. In his defense to the Reichstag, Hitler said there had been seventy-seven deaths. This did not tally with the figures Bonhoeffer got from his brother-in-law, as we learn from Rieger's diary: "Bonhoeffer has heard from the Ministry of Justice that 207 people were shot on 30 June and 1 July."[116] During July there was news of attempted coups by the Austrian National Socialists, and on 25 July the Austrian chancellor, Dollfuss, was assassinated in Vienna. Italian troops were deployed along the Tyrolean border. On 2 August Hindenburg died. Although the expectations that Hindenburg would be a moderating influence had hardly been justified, many people had put their confidence in him. Now Hitler combined the two highest offices in the country in his own person and was confirmed by plebiscite on 19 August 1934 in his new capacity as "*Führer* and Reich chancellor of the German people."

During this period of extreme political tension, the factions within the church found themselves in a strange position. The difficulties for the opposition were growing. On 9 July Interior Minister Frick issued a decree "for the protection of the national community" that prohibited all discussion of church disputes in the press and in public assemblies. The church press, which had remained relatively independent, was brought under control on 7 July by a "Church Law for the Evangelical Press." On 9 August the national synod ratified the legality of Ludwig Müller's measures and laws. In gratitude for Germany's rescue from the dangers of revolution and for the creation of the new office of *Führer*, the synod resolved that pastors should swear an "oath of service," although they had already taken an oath of allegiance to the state on their ordination: "I swear before God . . . that I . . . will be true and obedient to the *Führer* of the German people and state, Adolf Hitler, and I pledge myself to every sacrifice and every service on behalf of the German people such as befits an Evangelical German. . . ."[117] Heckel and his followers, who were busy preparing for the Fanö conference, were party to this resolution. Because of Frick's prohibition, no one could publicly challenge or criticize the decision.

But there were also many within the Confessing church who stressed their allegiance in worship services on 8 July 1934. Innumerable sermons and prayers gave thanks to the *Führer* for having saved the nation from the most dire peril. Even the parish newsletter of the German congregations in London carried an enthusiastic article that praised Hitler for rescuing not just Germany, but the entire world. Yet it was becoming increasingly difficult to maintain the Confessing church's thesis that its ranks consisted of the "better National Socialists." In a letter to Erwin Sutz at the end of April 1934 Bonhoeffer vented his feelings on the subject:

> Naive visionaries like Niemöller still believe themselves to be the true national socialists—and perhaps it is a benevolent providence that has fostered their illusion, and this might even be in the interests of the church struggle. . . .[118]

On 8 July 1934 Bonhoeffer preached a sermon to his London congregation that was subsequently circulated among his students. They sensed the contrast between his determined call to repentance, wholly directed toward the congregation, and the widespread emotionalism of the enthusiastic or tormented sermons of thanksgiving that had followed the bloodbath. For his text, Bonhoeffer had taken the ancient report of a murder, the pericope of the tower of Siloam, and the murder of the Galileans in the temple, in Luke 13:1-5:

> Perhaps this text shocks you; perhaps you think it is much too current and therefore dangerous for a service. We in the church really want to finally get free of the world of newspapers and sensational reports. . . .[119]

With almost impermissible directness, Bonhoeffer juxtaposed the great tension he and his listeners felt about the bloody outcome in Berlin with Jesus' call to repent:

> Unless you repent you will all likewise perish. . . . Now things are getting dangerous. We are no longer spectators, observers or judges to what is happening. We are being addressed, we are affected. It has happened for us, God is speaking in us, it is we who are meant . . . it is my world in which this is happening . . . those affected are my brothers in sin, in hatred, in evil, in lack of love, my brothers in guilt.[120]

He concluded:

> If we return home from church with this recognition and want to be serious, then we alone have overcome the world of the newspapers, the world of horror and the world of judges. Lord, lead your people toward repentance and begin with us. Amen.[121]

It would seem later that Bonhoeffer's words to the congregation on 8 July had only said part of what needed to be said. Bonhoeffer later spoke quite differently, drawing other conclusions from events that went beyond a call to repentance. At the time, however, his words appeared truthful. To understand this sermon, the passage from an earlier letter should be recalled: "*We should be converted, not Hitler.*"[122] The form of this "conversion" would still undergo many changes.

Division of Labor. The Barmen synod and the increasing gravity of the political situation had a decisive influence on Bonhoeffer's preparations for Fanö. He had already received two assignments: a lecture and the organization of the youth conference. Now he acquired a third task which threatened, at times, to undermine the other two—to fight so that the newly constituted Confessing church could participate in Fanö.

It was in his capacity as youth secretary that he prepared the youth conference, which was to be jointly sponsored by the World Alliance and Life and Work. The events of 1933 had forced Bonhoeffer to drastically reduce the attention he devoted to the Youth Commission. At the commission meeting in Paris from 31 January to 1 February 1934 he had asked that one of his former students, Dr. Jürgen Winterhager, be recognized as his assistant and representative for the preparatory work. Bonhoeffer still remained more active in the preparations than he had wanted; in particular, the leadership duties in Fanö remained entirely in his hands.

Bonhoeffer intended to bring the anti-heresy Barmen declaration into the youth programs without any compromise. He became energetically involved in discussions in Germany and Geneva about the composition of the German delegation to the youth conference. He was prepared only to recognize participants with no connections to the Reich church government; this meant limiting the circle of delegates to his former students in Berlin. He recommended several consultants from this group: Otto Dudzus, Inge Karding, Jürgen Winterhager, and Winfried Maechler.[123] When he feared that separate negotiations between Geneva and organizations like the YMCA would appoint participants whose stance toward the Reich church government and the Foreign Office was ambivalent, he responded immediately:

> Before I can give my consent to Mr. Jaensch for the desired invitation to Mr. Müller, the theological and church political position of Mr. Müller, who is completely unknown to us, must be clarified somehow.[124]

> Dr. Wendland was not invited by me or by Winterhager to the youth conference, since he was or still is (?) a member of the German Christians. The

ten members of our German youth delegation all stand on the foundation of the Confessing church.[125]

His threat was unmistakable:

> Incidentally, I have already written Herr Schönfeld that participation by our German delegation in Fanö will essentially depend on whether representatives of the present Reich Church Government are to take part in the conference. In any case the members of our delegation are agreed that they will stay away from those Fanö meetings that are attended by representatives of the church government. It would be a good thing if this alternative is generally and clearly realized. And I hope that you, too, will help us to get the ecumenical movement to state openly, before it is too late, which of the two churches in Germany it is prepared to recognize.[126]

Those preparing to go to Fanö were so alarmed by the steady deterioration of the political climate after the deaths of Röhm, Dollfuss, and Hindenburg that they asked for extra consideration in planning the youth program. On 12 August Bonhoeffer wrote to de Félice:

> In view of the extreme seriousness of the situation we are most anxious that you should not schedule a "social evening" or any other form of lighthearted entertainment. Some of the members of the German youth delegation will have been involved in very difficult church-political circumstances, and do not know what lies in store for them and all other confessing Protestants after their return from Fanö and in the weeks to come.[127]

Winterhager visited Bonhoeffer in London twice, staying for weeks to make the necessary plans and to assist Bonhoeffer in his pastorate.

Bonhoeffer had been assigned his second task, a plenary lecture, at the meeting in Sofia. This diverted him somewhat from the problem of the divided German delegation; still, he was more willing to abandon the honor of holding one of the main speeches than to submit to Geneva's interpretation of the requirements for inviting delegates to Fanö. Once he decided to go to Fanö, his theories created some headaches for those in Geneva. This revealed not just the separate directions Bonhoeffer and his Geneva colleagues were taking, but highlighted their theological differences, particularly between Bonhoeffer and Schönfeld. As he wrote de Félice on 12 August:

> You will have heard from Schönfeld or Miss Marcks that I would like to hold my talk in Fanö, but have altered the contents to fit the current situ-

ation. While I am a delegate from the Evangelical Confessing Church (of Germany), I will hold my lecture as Youth Secretary.[128]

At times his worries about the youth conference and his lecture were completely overshadowed by his passion for the third task: advocating the participation of the Confessing church born in Barmen. He was directly involved in the first two assignments, but he made them conditional upon ecumenical recognition of the Barmen declaration. More than either of his other duties, this third task brought him into conflict with people and the general circumstances.

The Crisis about Participation. Immediately after the Barmen synod (29–31 May 1934), the Geneva office sent Bonhoeffer the preparatory material, directives, and questions for Fanö. Schönfeld asked him to send suggestions and ideas on the theme "The Church and the World of Nations," on which Bonhoeffer was to speak.[129] The question immediately arose as to whether he could carry out his assigned duties as if nothing had happened in the meantime. Whom was he likely to encounter from the Reich church at the Fanö meetings? Could he share a table with them? Didn't a modicum of self-respect require the ecumenical movement to recognize the Barmen synod's claim that, as the true German Evangelical church, it had stated what must be confessed or rejected by the present Christian faith? Didn't this necessarily have consequences?

Before replying to Schönfeld's letter, Bonhoeffer went to Berlin on 19 June to discuss the matter with Karl Koch, head of the Confessing synod, and Martin Niemöller. All three agreed that no member of the Confessing church could participate in Fanö unless one of them was invited explicitly as a representative of the Confessing church. Bonhoeffer proposed that they should confront Geneva with the alternative either of inviting such a representative or of forfeiting his participation altogether. Should such an invitation not be forthcoming, it would be better to let the Church Foreign Office appear alone at the ecumenical gathering. The silence of those absent would speak for itself, and there would be influential spokespeople from other churches. Bonhoeffer also attended a meeting of the Berlin branch of the World Alliance, where they considered keeping the German World Alliance delegates away from Fanö if Heckel alone represented the Reich church.

Bonhoeffer returned to London entrusted with the task of clearing up the question of invitations. He began by writing to Geneva and then initiated a joint action with the bishop of Chichester.

Encouraged by Koch and Niemöller, he wrote immediately to Schönfeld. There is no record of his letter (when a German invasion threatened in 1940, the Geneva office reportedly destroyed some files that could have incriminated German colleagues). But Henriod's reply (Schönfeld was on vacation) gives some indication of Bonhoeffer's arguments.[130] Bonhoeffer apparently described the situation following Barmen and the political tension, and asked about the formation of the Fanö committees and the invitation to the Confessing synod. In the case of an exclusive invitation to the Reich church, he would announce his own withdrawal.

Henriod replied on 7 July, going to considerable pains to express sympathy for the awkward quandary in which the men of the Confessing church found themselves. He saw no possibility, however, of canceling the invitation to the Church Foreign Office as the representative of the Evangelical church in Fanö. Nor could he envisage any possibility of issuing a further invitation to the Confessing synod. He handed the initiative back to them: first the Confessing synod must explicitly declare itself to be a second church, next to the Reich church, and inform Geneva officially of this step.

Through other channels Bonhoeffer heard that his refusal to give the plenary speech had already been accepted. In response to this premature reaction he wrote, "I am glad you have found so quickly a substitute for me for Fanö," and returned the preparatory material to Geneva.[131]

He strenuously denied the misconception that the Confessing church was a separate, free church alongside the Reich church—an assumption that would have been welcomed by many.[132] At the Ulm and Barmen synods, the opposition had made it perfectly clear that, unlike the other churches, it was grounded both theologically and legally in the constitution of the German Evangelical Church. Hence the Confessing synod could never declare that it had founded another church or ask to be recognized as a separate institution by the ecumenical movement. The responsibility for the problems with Fanö did not lie with the Confessing synod's Council of Brethren, but with the organization in Geneva.

The general secretary of the Ecumenical Federation regarded himself as bound by his statutes, which made no allowance for the Germans' notion. Bonhoeffer saw that his church's claim and struggle could not be postponed, and found it hard to believe that the statutes were so completely inflexible. In 1934 he fought solely for an invitation to the Confessing church alongside the Reich church. In 1935, after the Dahlem synod, he argued for a choice between one or the other.

With Bishop Bell's help, the second attempt to solve the invitation problem was somewhat more successful. Since existing circumstances barred the

Confessing synod from Fanö, Bonhoeffer asked the bishop to consider the possibility of issuing an invitation himself. At this late stage Bell searched for a way to do so within his area of competence. He even took the trouble to study legal expert opinions—such as that from Reich court counselor Dr. Wilhelm Flor—to establish the legitimacy of the Confessing church's claims. Bell had to be careful to avoid charges of irregularity or an abuse of authority. The Church Foreign Office was conspicuously nursing its ecumenical connections, as Bonhoeffer had predicted when he and Bell were preparing the Ascension Day message. Now it was fighting for recognition of the unimpaired legality of the Reich church. The archbishop of Canterbury had received a letter from a previously unknown "Central Authority for Ecumenical Matters," signed by German Christian Professor Caius Fabricius, requesting an explanation for the assertion that "the German Evangelical Church is in danger to cease to be fully Christian."[133] Bell asked Bonhoeffer to draw up a list of arguments and write an account of Fabricius's position and background for the archbishop.

Bell also turned for advice to the man with whom he shared the responsibility for the Fanö meeting: Bishop Ammundsen, chairman of the World Alliance. Like Henriod, Bell was aware that, according to the statutes, every country determined who it would send as delegates. But he also knew that there could be no negotiations between Koch and Heckel about a German delegation at this point, and he based his argument upon that fact. In writing this to Ammundsen, he insinuated that he was very anxious to see the Confessing church represented in Fanö.[134] On 11 July Ammundsen gave a reserved but encouraging reply. His letter shows that even Bonhoeffer's well-wishers were sometimes confused by the stormy course of events. He wrote:

> As to the question raised in your letter I think:—
>
> 1. that it would be premature to take any step involving a formal recognition from our side of the German Free Synods; the position of these Synods inside Germany is not yet clear enough, and it would be wrong for the Presidency to do anything which would prejudicate the opinion of the Ecumenical Council.
>
> 2. that it would be most helpful to us to have such representatives and that we are only true to our convictions when we let them feel our sympathy and fellowship.
>
> The conclusion of this is that, in virtue of the power, which an Executive and in emergency cases the President is always regarded as possessing to invite people helpful to clear up the problems, you should invite Präses Koch to send say two representatives to our meeting in no official capacity

but so to say as experts for giving us information and adding to our discussions. It then must be for our German friends themselves to decide
whether it will be wise to accept the invitation or not. Sincerely yours . . .
In fact I think it is a good suggestion to invite such people, only that we do
not precipitate matters.

On 12 July Bonhoeffer impatiently asked Bell about the invitation, which
was sent to Koch on 18 July. Bell sent a warm letter requesting the presence
in Fanö of Koch and, if possible, Bodelschwingh, showing utmost understanding for the difficulties involved, since the invitation might put its recipients in a politically awkward position.[135]

The Church Foreign Office in Berlin learned of the invitation from the
people in Geneva. It immediately tried to stop the Confessing church's entry
into the official ecumenical proceedings. Heckel sent Dr. van der Vaart Smit,
a mysterious Dutchman, to Berlin, Geneva and Oeynhausen (where he visited Koch). Smit hoped to visit Chichester, but Bell sent a message, via Koch,
refusing to meet him. The Berlin Council of Brethren asked Bonhoeffer to
advise the Geneva office that it would be better for Mr. Smit not to have any
assignment to the Council of Brethren. Koch was unwilling to relinquish this
invitation.

Did this mean that Bonhoeffer could now go to Fanö? The matter was
still not quite clear. The stipulation that he, Koch, and Niemöller had made
on 19 June had been met; there was nothing further that Bell could do. But
the invitation and the circumstances under which it had been made showed
that there was still no widespread appreciation for the Confessing church's
claim in Barmen that it was the legitimate German Evangelical church.
Because of Bell's Ascension Day message, the issue of domestic German
affairs was likely to come up in Fanö; in that event, the two separate German
factions would take opposing positions—in the tense political atmosphere
following Röhm's assassination and Hindenburg's death.

Bonhoeffer hesitated; Koch, too, was in some doubt. On 30 July Siegmund-Schultze arrived in London to urge Bonhoeffer to go, and Ammundsen wrote to say how much he counted on seeing him in Fanö.[136] Bonhoeffer finally made up his mind, only to hear the disappointing news that Koch
and Bodelschwingh would not attend because of the political situation.

On 1 August Bonhoeffer left on vacation, which he devoted to preparing
for the conference. Some two weeks later he went to Esbjerg, opposite the
island of Fanö. En route he met an old friend with whom he had been confirmed, Hans Bernd von Haeften, who was now a government counsel in
Copenhagen. Hildebrandt visited him in Esbjerg and brought the latest

news from Berlin and the Council of Brethren; Hildebrandt returned to London to relieve Winterhager. The youth conference began on 22 August and the main Fanö conference two days later.

The Resolution. In *A History of the Ecumenical Movement*, Rouse and Neill write:

> The biennial meeting of the Council at Fanö . . . stands out as perhaps the most critical and decisive meeting in its history. Here the Council solemnly resolved to throw its weight on the side of the Confessing Church in Germany against the so-called "German Christians" and by implication against the Nazi régime.[137]

It could not have been assumed that the conference would arrive at a resolution. There were many, inside and outside Germany, who believed that a statement on the German question at that point was inopportune and wrong. Whereas nationalists like Wilhelm Stapel protested against the "international, western, liberal, democratic" character of the conference, there were also those in the Confessing church who feared the unsettling effect of a statement from abroad, given the tense political situation.[138] "I am more afraid of many of our own supporters than I am of the German Christians," Bonhoeffer wrote to Ammundsen.[139] Many outside Germany were dubious as well. They were confused to find people of "Christian character" on both fronts in the German church struggle, and wished to avoid any firm stand or "intervention."

It was clear, however, that the Universal Christian Council for Life and Work had to take a position for or against the Ascension Day pastoral letter from its chairman, Bishop Bell. It remained to be seen whether this would lead to a joint resolution with the World Alliance.

Wherever he could, Bonhoeffer began to seek support for a strongly worded resolution. He could be certain of Bell, and found other good allies as well. On 8 August he turned to Ammundsen:

> It's possible that our side may be terribly cautious for fear of seeming unpatriotic—not that fear is the motive, but rather a false sense of honor. Many people, even those who have been doing ecumenical work for quite some time, still seem incapable of realizing or believing that we really are here together purely as *Christians*. They are horribly suspicious and it prevents them from being completely frank. If only, honorable Bishop, you could manage to break the ice so that people became more trusting and completely open with each other! And it is particularly here, *in our attitude*

towards the State, that we must speak out with absolute sincerity for the sake of Jesus Christ and the ecumenical cause. It must be made quite clear—terrible though this is—that an immediate decision confronts us: National Socialist *or* Christian, and that we must advance beyond where we stood a year ago (I know you said so at the time!) [in Sofia]. However hard and difficult it may be for us all, we have got to face it and go through with it, without trying to be diplomatic, but speaking frankly and as Christians. And we shall discover the way by praying together. I just wanted to say that.

In my opinion a resolution ought to be taken—no good can come of evasion . . . The only thing that can help us now is *complete truth* and *complete truthfulness*. I know that many of my German friends think otherwise. But I do beg you to consider this thought.[140]

After Hildebrandt arrived with the news that the national synod and the Council of Brethren would not send anyone to Fanö, Bonhoeffer wrote Ammundsen again on 18 August:

In view of the most recent events, it now seems to me imperative that not only "Life and Work," but also the World Alliance, should put forward a resolution, perhaps indeed the same resolution. I know there are strong feelings against this, but I shall do everything I can to counteract them . . . I would like . . . you to advise me what I ought to do about this and, what is much more important, to help me do it. I would so very much appreciate your assistance![141]

Ammundsen arranged a meeting with the Reich Council of Brethren in Hamburg to discuss its decision not to send delegates to Fanö. He recognized the risk of political defamation that faced them in Germany should their presence compel them to speak on the proposed resolution; and he promised that, should occasion arise, he would speak for them in their absence. Bonhoeffer's attendance was no longer in question—indeed, it was viewed as desirable, since he was based in England, for him to attend Fanö in the dual role of conference speaker and delegate of the Confessing church. Bonhoeffer disagreed with his colleagues' refusal to attend: "I am eager to see how things will turn out. I'm the only one of us here, which I think is a bad mistake."[142]

The conference discussed the German churches' situation on the opening day, Saturday, 25 August. The meeting began with a declaration by the German World Alliance members, who attended independently of the Reich church delegation and of the confessing synod:

The peculiar situation in the political and ecclesiastical development in Germany induces the members of the German delegation of the World Alliance to request you, Mr. Chairman, to make the following statement *before* the commencement of the proceedings: The German Delegation of the World Alliance does not wish to take any part in a public discussion on the internal affairs of the German Church.[143]

Bonhoeffer's name was not on the list of those who spoke on the resolution; there was no longer any need to mention it.

The conference appointed a committee to draft the resolution. Its composition satisfied Bonhoeffer, since it consisted of Bell, Ammundsen, Marc Boegner (later cochairman of Life and Work), Professor Brun of Norway, Professor Keller of Switzerland, Dr. Leiper of the United States, who took a lively interest in the church struggle, and, finally, Henriod. There was an animated plenary discussion but, after an incident with the press, further discussions of this subject were held in closed meetings. On Wednesday, 29 August, church council member Walter Birnbaum, a special envoy sent by the Reich bishop and Prussian church commissioner Jäger, arrived in a special aircraft and asked to address the meeting. This was an affront to Heckel, who, as Bonhoeffer later told Rieger, had brushed aside the Jewish question and other issues on the grounds that "this was not his province." Birnbaum was given fifteen minutes to speak in which, according to Rieger's diary, he "related some absurd rigmarole about his personal experiences of people who became Christians because [they were] National Socialists."[144]

The resolution was passed on 30 August.[145] It confirmed Bell's message and the course he was following, and listed the most recent grievances: the autocratic government, the use of force, the oath of service, the ban on free discussion. It spoke unequivocally on behalf of those not present:

The Council [Life and Work] desires to assure its brethren in the Confessional Synod of the German Evangelical Church of its prayers and heartfelt sympathy in their witness to the principles of the Gospel, and of its resolve to maintain close fellowship with them.[146]

That same day the assembly, using its right of co-option, ostentatiously elected Dietrich Bonhoeffer and absent leader of the Confessing synod President Karl Koch "consultative and co-opted members" of the Universal Christian Council for Life and Work.

Caught between this assembly and his supervisors at home, Bishop Heckel was in an uncomfortable position. He responded by doing three things. First he succeeded in introducing a small clause into the resolution that seemed inconsequential; it held the door to ecumenical involvement open for the Reich church, however, thus preventing the Confessing church from ever fully achieving its aim. The clause stated that the Council wished "to remain in friendly contact with all groups in the German Evangelical Church."[147] With that the meeting's stand on behalf of the Confessing church, although meaningful in Fanö, had no effect on the future.

Second, Heckel recorded a protest in the minutes on behalf of his delegation.[148] In it he denied the alleged abuses or interpreted them differently, accused the council of exceeding its competence, and objected to the "one-sided emphasis on a particular group in Germany." The German delegation repudiated "the allegation that in the German Reich the free proclamation of the spoken and written Gospel is imperiled. . . . On the contrary, it holds that the prevalent conditions in Germany today provide a more favorable opportunity for proclaiming the Gospel than ever before. . . ."[149] Referring directly to the election of Bonhoeffer and Koch, Heckel recorded his objection to "the biased attitude towards the internal affairs of the German Evangelical Church."[150]

The only statements to receive wide public attention, however, were those in the resolution rejecting the use of force, and the decision to support the Confessing church. The bishop of Chichester wrote an excellent report on Fanö for *The Times*[151] that portrayed the meeting's recognition of the Confessing church as the key event. The official Reich church publications substantiated this viewpoint by complaining for weeks about "foreign interference." There were strange undertones even in the reports carried by the *Junge Kirche*, which, hampered by Frick's decree of 9 July, could no longer provide full and accurate information; it expressed approval for the first part of Heckel's protest and opposed foreign intervention in internal German affairs.[152] *Junge Kirche* also reiterated, for its own protection, that the Confessing church was not represented in Fanö.[153] It did not mention Bonhoeffer's presence, although he gave one of the principal addresses, nor did it mention his election to the council. Hence even some prominent early postwar histories failed to note this election.[154]

Nonetheless, the members of the Councils of Brethren in Germany and their ecumenical friends initially viewed Fanö as a major breakthrough. Bonhoeffer warmly thanked Bell and Ammundsen for all they had accomplished.[155] One year later, in his long ecumenical essay, he maintained that Fanö had represented an incomparable step forward for Christianity.[156]

In fact, in Fanö the ecumenical movement went as far as it would ever go in its commitment toward the Confessing church. At the time, Bonhoeffer believed this was only the beginning; this is why he raised no objection to the dubious clause about "friendly contact" with all German groups. He thought the Confessing church would first have to learn to take itself seriously. Everything seemed to have gone smoothly; it had proved possible to initiate ecumenical discussions on the concept and reality of "heresy." Leading people had agreed to contribute in this area. Only later was Bonhoeffer forced to see that Fanö did not represent a first step, but a short-lived climax. He did not yet take seriously the divergent forces within the "Confessing front" itself; he would not allow himself to feel skepticism about possible weaknesses within its ranks.

Lecture: The Universal Church and the World of Nations. To Bonhoeffer the resolution seemed of infinitely greater import than his own contributions, a lecture and a sermon; yet posterity has shown more interest in his Fanö speech than in the dramatic resolutions of the conference.

The chairman and speakers for the specialized discussions at Fanö were selected on alternate days by Life and Work and the World Alliance. The first day was devoted to the theme of "The Church and the State Today"; the second, on which Bonhoeffer spoke, to "The Universal Church and the World of Nations." The questions to be addressed included whether the church was empowered to take sides in international disputes, the lengths to which it might go and the means it ought to employ in the solution of such problems. To elucidate this, Bonhoeffer had based his lecture on the debate over Wilfred Monod's "Peace Catechism" in Sofia. Not only did a "peace catechism" interest him personally, but it would highlight the urgency of the recent events in Europe.

The theses for the lecture were to have reached Geneva by July for general distribution. But because of the temporary cancellation of his plans to attend, Bonhoeffer did not begin to draft his lecture until early August—at a time when political storm warnings were out. Italian troops had been deployed on the Austrian border and disarmament talks had broken down; this was soon followed by the outbreak of the Abyssinian War and the failure to apply sanctions. Bonhoeffer did not regard these occurrences as the birth pangs of a new age but as sinister confirmation of his prediction that Hitler meant war.

When his succinct text finally arrived in Geneva, it aroused displeasure in the ecumenical research department responsible for the preparation of the specialized discussions in Fanö.[157] The topics for the sessions had already been decided at an April meeting in Paris that Bonhoeffer did not attend. Schönfeld wrote Wilhelm Menn, "I must confess that I am rather upset by

Herr Bonhoeffer's material and its narrow concern with the problem of war."[158] He wrote critically to Bonhoeffer:

> I have just seen your theses for discussion in Denmark; might I ask you to arrange to deal rather more comprehensively with the theme "The Church and the World of Nations," or "Internationalism and the Ecumenical Movement" in your introductory words than you have done in your theses.[159]

The way in which Bonhoeffer had altered his lecture to "fit the present circumstances" revealed not just his own high-handed methods, but the fact that he and Schönfeld were thinking in two wholly different theological dimensions.[160] Schönfeld felt that the German speaker should help his ecumenical audience grasp the concept and right of the term "*Volk*," the church's responsibility for what is intrinsic to a nation and the orders of creation and preservation. Schönfeld had organized a group within his own department to study the question of "the order of creation and the natural law."[161] A December 1933 letter from Schönfeld to Krummacher, a theological adviser in Heckel's Church Foreign Office, strikingly reveals his attitude. *The Times* had printed a strong indictment by the archbishop of Canterbury concerning Jewish refugees; Krummacher had consulted Schönfeld about the best way to protest against this. Schönfeld advised against a protest, suggesting instead that those in Berlin should press "for a fundamental theological rethinking of the racial problem." He added: "This is an area in which, more than in any other, these people [the British] have much to learn!"[162]

Far from complying with Schönfeld's wishes, Bonhoeffer spoke of the war threatening the nations, as Monod had done. As a German Lutheran theologian, perhaps his words were too christological for his western liberal audience, yet what he said coincided enough with their own views for them to recognize its essentially pacifist premises.

The questions he posed—the World Alliance's mandate for peace work—were similar to those raised at the 1932 meeting in Ciernohorské Kúpele; they were based more upon christological ecclesiology than upon humanitarianism: the working community of the World Alliance was to be transformed into the community of the church by hearkening to the divine message of peace, which it freely imposed. Compared with 1932, he showed a new forthrightness that ruled out any exception from this command and its realization. It was a foretaste of the intellectual climate of *Discipleship*; his terminology was highly provocative. Never before had he declared that there could be no justification for war, even a defensive war.

He had ignored Schönfeld's appeal to treat the assigned topic "in more detail." Bonhoeffer altered nothing; the theses were delivered in exactly the form in which they had been drafted at the beginning of August. There were translations in three languages for the preliminary speakers' conference on 24 August and for the conference day, 28 August. The manuscript of his actual lecture is still missing. From the minutes of the 28 August discussion, which were edited in Geneva, we learn only that:

> The discussion dealt with the attitude of the churches to concrete international conflicts, and especially to the war problem, which was seen, however, as being only one problem in the whole struggle for the creation of international order. The Churches were recognized as having a unique contribution to make towards the achievement of genuine cooperation between the states and nations.[163]

The working committee resolved that the subgroups of the World Alliance should work out a common position on the new wave of rearmament and the flourishing arms industry.[164]

Richard Crossman, later an official in the British Labor government, went to hear Bonhoeffer on Bell's advice. He was highly critical of the lecture and the discussion that followed it; but he was, of course, unfamiliar with the theological premise. An editorial in *The Church in Action News Letter* commented:

> Unfortunately the discussions on the 2nd day did not seem to attain the same level of earnestness and of clarity as those of the first. Stirring statements were made on pacifism, and these never failed to arouse feelings of approval and applause. But feelings are fickle guides; the pressing problem of peace needs the deduction of hard, clear-cut thinking and of decision and will. Mr. Crossman sought to compel the conference to face the full cost of radical pacifism. . . .
>
> The resolution of the Youth Conference put in a needed plea for the right of conscientious objectors in peace as in war. Dr. Bonhoeffer made the important point that there is no path to peace by way of security; behind the quest for security there lies the same distrust and defensiveness which is the root cause of war.[165]

The Sermon on Peace. The document entitled "The Universal Church and the World of Nations" which has become known as Bonhoeffer's Fanö "peace speech," was the homily Bonhoeffer delivered during the morning worship that day, according to Otto Dudzus and others who were present.[166]

The text of his sermon was Psalm 85:9. He had often discussed this psalm with Hildebrandt and preached on it in his parish.[167] An English participant to the youth conference wrote in her notes that day: "morning, striking speech by Bonhoeffer!"

This homily, densely written, is the most unequivocal and emphatic of his statements on peace that we possess. While it bears the stamp of those ominous weeks, its impact has lasted far beyond Hitler's time. In this sermon delivered in a worship service, Bonhoeffer was able to ignore considerations that would have arisen within a debate. He was not concerned here with the helpless exchange of open-ended questions, but with the direct demand that certain decisions be risked.

He had elected on his own authority, at the age of twenty-eight, to appear before this assembly; he was as capable as anyone else of analyzing the world situation; he could have sought and given advice; he concluded, however, that he could rely on no other authority than that found in the commandment for peace itself. Thus he passionately exhorted this carefully convened assembly to justify its right to exist by imposing the Gospel of peace in its fullest extent. He used the word "council," which must have shocked some of his listeners. But he wanted to lead them beyond the idea that they were merely an advisory or opinion-forming body. A council proclaims, commits, and resolves, and in the process commits and resolves itself. As in the lecture of 1932, in the 1933 Christology lectures and the address to the student meeting, and again in the 1935 ecumenical essay, his concern was with the concrete and committed nature of this community, now gathered in the name of Christ.[168] He believed that the command of a council carried more weight than that of an individual or an individual church. The individual church ". . . is suffocated by the power of hate."[169] The very fact that this council had met was an act of peace that would lend authority to its words.

Even in this peace sermon, Bonhoeffer cannot be placed unequivocally among the supporters of a fundamental and general pacifism; but never before had he stated so decisively that, for the disciple, the renunciation of force meant the renunciation of defense.[170] Christians "may not use weapons against one another because they know that in so doing they are aiming those weapons at Christ himself."[171] This was the strongest argument on which his "Christian pacifism" was based.

It should be noted that these statements bear the characteristics of a sermon; they are not a chapter on nonviolent resistance in an ethics text exploring and defining the nature of valid behavior. The call of proclamation ignores reservations and qualifications. Peace was not being discussed; like the assembly gathered together in Christ, it was being addressed as a present reality and, hence, as a commandment.

The audience in Fanö on 28 August 1934 was probably the most eminent congregation before whom Bonhoeffer had ever preached. He had seldom preached to large numbers of people, nor did this really appeal to him. He preferred a small, easily defined congregation that could move with him as he developed his train of thought. Dudzus recalled:

> From the first moment the assembly was breathless with tension. Many may have felt that they would never forget what they had just heard. . . . Bonhoeffer had charged so far ahead that the conference could not follow him. Did that surprise anybody? But on the other hand: could anybody have a good conscience about it?[172]

The Youth Conference. Even the Fanö youth conference earned a special mention in Rouse and Neill's book:

> A conference held at the same time by the Ecumenical Youth Commission went even further than its elders in bluntly urging the churches "to dissociate themselves from every church that does not affirm this universalism of the Word of God, on the ground that it is not Christian."[173]

More than fifty people attended the youth conference. Bonhoeffer encountered Jean Lasserre and Marcel Sturm, the old friends he had made in America. The political developments in Germany had made many afraid of traveling to Fanö, and the German delegation consisted almost exclusively of Bonhoeffer's Berlin students: Dudzus, Karding, Winterhager, Maechler, Willi Brandenburg, Hilde Enterlein (who later married Albrecht Schönherr), Rudi Kühn, Ernst Tillich, and Herbert Jehle. Nearly all of these individuals later became ordination candidates at his preachers' seminary in Finkenwalde. Hence this group was not representative of German students in general. They were already disenchanted with nationalism in Germany and were seriously considering the question of conscientious objection. They cannot have been particularly surprised by Bonhoeffer's reply when,

> on the beach a Swede asked, "What would you do, sir, if war broke out?" Reflectively, he allowed the sand to trickle through his fingers, then turned calmly toward the questioner and replied: "I pray that God will give me the strength not to take up arms."[174]

Bonhoeffer opened the conference with a service and led the session on the first day. The group discussions were concerned primarily with the universal (which at this time meant antinationalist) nature of the church and the question of conscientious objection. The fact that ten German students could play a leading role in the discussion of these dangerous themes, without serious consequences, indicates that the National Socialist authorities still possessed only a rudimentary intelligence network that must have been engaged elsewhere.

The youth conference debated two resolutions.[175] Controversy arose over the first when it was suggested that the superiority of God's commandment over all claims by the state might, for instance, give the foreign press the inherent right to criticize incidents inside Germany. In his notes Bonhoeffer wrote that violations of the divine commandments were "increasingly and rightly incurring general opprobrium in a number of different countries." He hoped that the Fanö conference would support this kind of "right," yet when the resolution was voted on many opposed it, including some of his students.

The second resolution expressed the church's independence from national aims in even more radical terms, and rejected support for "any war whatsoever." This latter phrase was opposed by the Polish and Hungarian delegates, who proposed substituting the words "aggressive war." The French and English delegates joined Bonhoeffer in opposing this. Only after a dramatic break in the discussion and a time of communal meditation and prayer did the conference finally agree to retain the words "any war whatsoever." One of the participants took notes on Bonhoeffer's warning to the group at the beginning of the communal meditation:

> Remember prayers of the first day. Situation of conference here is full of difficulty and challenge. We have been in danger of causing the conference to become merely a big show and to disguise under the outward form of resolutions, the main manifestation of our dependence. But we are one Church in spite of differences of opinions. Human attitudes will not build the Church, but the common listening to God. No doubt in this that we are one Church. Must remember that disruption is one of our main temptations. But the building of the Church is seen in the common longing for the voice of God, and in cherishing this certainty of the Church.
>
> The remark that we are divided is not as a reproach but as witness to the profound problematics of the Church. There is suffering in the divided Church. We welcome the Hungarian speaker and are in sympathy with him and his people. We Germans understand the Hungarian feelings better than any other nation because of the similarity of our sufferings.—The

fellowship of suffering. If we disagree with those whom we love we suffer. It is the expression of the divisions of the Church which we love and we long to heal these divisions. Strong expression is a good thing to show the real facts. But having said them we then join in common prayer and penitence and worship.[176]

On the same day that Bonhoeffer gave his sermon and lecture before the main conference, Jean Lasserre presented "the resolutions that it had adopted on conscientious objection and on the universal nature of the church" on behalf of the youth conference.[177]

In the years that followed the German participants in the Fanö youth conference were to show considerable enterprise. They held several "Fanö fellowship reunions" at the Swedish church in Berlin, under Birger Forell's patronage, inviting friends and leaders of the Confessing church.[178] At the January 1935 Youth Commission meeting Bonhoeffer reported:

> The German Fanö group has been doing a great deal of propagandistic work in the respective universities. A very encouraging step forward could be taken in Tübingen and in Heidelberg. Some of the speeches delivered at Fanö were mimeographed and spread among the students. There seems to be—mostly perhaps under the influence of the steadily growing military spirit—a readiness to take seriously the Christian message of peace. In Berlin a group of students of various nationalities met under the auspices of the youth commission in the house of the Swedish pastor Forell and had a very satisfactory meeting.[179]

Aftereffects: Würzburg and Bruay. Bonhoeffer took a roundabout route from Fanö back to his parishes in London. After a brief stay with his twin sister in Göttingen, he was invited by President Koch to attend a session of the Reich Council of Brethren in Würzburg on 3 September.[180] He informed the assembly that the failure to send delegates to Fanö had led to disappointment and some confusion; people had asked why the Confessing church was remaining a "group" within the German Evangelical Church. By emphasizing this and similar points, Bonhoeffer pressed once more for the consequences that were finally drawn by the Dahlem Confessing synod, when the Confessing church declared itself the only legal church in Germany. Bonhoeffer also referred to the weak point of the Fanö declaration (about maintaining "contacts with all groups"). This, he declared, was the inevitable result of the Confessing church's failure to make its position absolutely clear. Still, he urged the Council of Brethren to express its gratitude for the declaration, particularly to Bell. Finally he suggested that the situation required the Confessing church to appoint a representative whose sole concern would be ecumenical affairs—a recommendation he made repeatedly, but in vain.

The minutes of the Würzburg session showed two areas of concern. The first was the Reich bishop's consecration in Berlin Cathedral on 23 September and the possibility that representatives from churches abroad might attend. After Fanö, Bonhoeffer asserted, any attempts to win ecumenical guests for the occasion would fail. This proved to be correct; of all the prelates who honored Ludwig Müller that day, Heckel was the only one who was not a German Christian. On the second point of concern—the possibility of a Lutheran breakaway—Bonhoeffer asked whether the "Lutheran confessionalists were relatively insignificant and would not necessarily mean a breach in the Confessing front."[181]

From Würzburg Bonhoeffer went to Bruay in the Artois, where Jean Lasserre was working as a pastor among the poorest factory workers. In a last-minute decision, the heads of the Youth Commission in Fanö had scheduled an Anglo-French-German regional meeting. This time it took a somewhat unconventional turn when the group ventured out to preach in the streets.

> Dietrich spoke one or two names . . . I remember his speeches were very direct. . . . He gave me the feeling that he was quite at ease in such a work to which he probably was not accustomed. . . . He really spoke the Gospel to the people in the street.[182]

Back in London Bonhoeffer preached on 16 September, taking as his text Matthew 11:28-30, speaking of those "who labor and are heavy-laden." He described the profound impressions the French mining towns had made upon him. But this renewed confrontation with social questions was soon totally forgotten in the new struggles for the church.

Second Attack against the Reich Church Government, Winter 1934–1935

By the autumn of 1934 Bonhoeffer's energies shifted once more to the disputes with the Reich church government. In the winter of 1933–1934 the disputes had revolved around whether to withdraw confidence from that government. In this new phase an actual breach of relations loomed in the transfer of allegiance by the German congregations abroad to the new emergency church government of the Confessing church.

October Storms in Berlin. The logical conclusion of the May Barmen declaration on the German Christian heresy was the formation of an emergency church government by the Dahlem Confessing synod in October. This was made possible by Ludwig Müller's heavy-handed measures, which briefly unified the divided opposition once more.

The consecration of the Reich bishop finally took place on 23 September in the Berlin Cathedral—without ecumenical representatives. Hildebrandt sent Bonhoeffer a postcard containing only the chapter and verse of that Sunday's text, Luke 4:11: "For every one who exalts himself ..." Indeed, humiliation was not long in coming.

Müller's church commissioner, August Jäger, now dared to attempt a compulsory centralization of the southern German regional churches. Barely two weeks after Müller's consecration Jäger placed the insubordinate Bishop Wurm of Württemberg under house arrest. Six days later, on 12 October, he meted out the same treatment to Bishop Meiser of Bavaria. This led to spontaneous demonstrations supporting the bishops in the streets of Munich and Stuttgart. Once again the church struggle had made world headlines.

In response the Reich Council of Brethren unanimously agreed to convene the Reich Confessing synod at the end of the month. In accordance with the general terms of the Barmen declaration, the synod was to instruct the congregations that they no longer owed obedience to the Reich church government that had violated the constitution, but must pledge themselves to whatever church emergency organizations the synod should appoint.

In the midst of all this, Hildebrandt arrived in London on 11 October with instructions that Bonhoeffer was to inform Bishop Bell, as chairman of Life and Work, of what had happened and ask him to attend the synod.[183] Bell was not free at the time, and asked Swiss church president Alphons Koechin to undertake this mission on behalf of the council. When Hildebrandt arrived in Düsseldorf on his way home, Joachim Beckmann informed him that the date of the synod had been moved up because of the events in Bavaria, it would convene on 19–20 October. Koechlin arranged to be present in Dahlem on those days. As before, Bonhoeffer did not participate in the synod.

On 20 October 1934 there was surprising unanimity in Dahlem for the resolutions enacting an emergency organization and accusing Müller of violating the constitution. Along with the nationwide protest against the Reich bishop, this led to new activity in the Reich chancellery. From his brother-in-law Bonhoeffer learned that Hitler had summoned Justice Minister Franz Gürtner to discuss the legal aspect of recent events in the church.

The outcome was an order revoking the August 1934 legislation authorized by the national synod for the centralization of the German Evangelical Church. Suddenly hopes revived that the chancellery on Wilhelmstrasse seriously intended to change its tune. When these hopes were only partially fulfilled the ensuing disappointment led to disintegration. On 26 October August Jäger resigned. The southern German bishops were released and received by Hitler on 30 October. They returned in triumph to their dioceses, where they restored the previous status quo. Hitler declared his lack of interest in the Reich church; indeed, he declared that professions of loyalty to the Third Reich and its *Führer* could not be identified with partisan support for one of the factions in the church.

But what was to be done now about the "destroyed" church regions, such as Old Prussia? What did this mean for the emergency church law passed unanimously by the Dahlem synod? In no sense had Ludwig Müller been forced to retreat. Bell asked Bonhoeffer what was likely to happen should Hitler really allow the conflict to find a satisfactory conclusion. In the hope of fostering such a solution, the bishop accompanied the archbishop of Canterbury to the German Embassy, where Archbishop Lang saw Ambassador von Hoesch and Bell visited First Secretary von Bismarck. The Foreign Ministry in Berlin authorized the embassy to tell the two men that changes were imminent, but Bonhoeffer, who had been kept informed by Dohnanyi, gave the bishop his own analysis of the precarious situation, which was soon proved correct.[184] Hitler, he said, would probably postpone any decision, including the possible recognition of the Dahlem emergency organizations, at least until after the Saar plebiscite.[185]

Did Hitler know too much about the "opposition"? A few weeks of indecision had revealed to everyone the cracks in the front that had appeared so united on 19 and 20 October in Dahlem. There was growing criticism in the Confessing church of the Dahlem resolution, and increasing anxiety at the group's own courage. Beyond a small gesture imposing some restraint upon Ludwig Müller, the Reich government had little reason to placate the opposition that had been provoked so turbulently in October.

Resolution to Secede. This, of course, did not keep Bonhoeffer from supporting and practicing the Dahlem resolutions, which had declared:

> We call upon the Christian congregations, their pastors and elders, to ignore any instructions received from the former Reich church government and its authorities and to refrain from cooperating with those who wish to continue to obey that same church government. We call upon

them to adhere to the directions of the Confessional synod of the German Evangelical Church and its recognized bodies.[186]

Bonhoeffer had been longing to hear this kind of plain language for a year. He could not wait to see whether and to what extent the emergency church government would be able to assert itself and win recognition. It was essential to show immediate recognition of the step that had been taken and to enforce the new order. This should be done promptly and unequivocally, so that the Confessing synod and its organs would be confirmed in the path they were taking. This would inspire others to follow suit, and leave the central church offices on Jebensstrasse little time or opportunity to adopt countermeasures.

On 5 November 1934 the elders of nearly all the German Evangelical congregations in England met in London in Christ Church. Bonhoeffer even canceled a meeting with Bell to help prepare for the meeting, which was chaired by Pastor Wehrhan. Bonhoeffer spoke about the German church situation; Rieger spoke about the church struggle's effects on opinion abroad. The forty-four church officials from nine congregations resolved that:

> The elders assembled here in Christ Church declare that they intrinsically hold the same position as the Confessing church, and that they will immediately initiate the necessary negotiations with the church authorities [Church Foreign Office of the Reich church government and the Confessing church] arising from this . . . London, 5 November 1934. The Church Vestries.[187]

The resolution was a tremendous achievement for Bonhoeffer and Rieger, since the prevailing mood had seemed to be against it. On 3 November Wehrhan had written to Baron Schröder: "In my opinion we ought to wait until we see how things are shaping at home." On the morning of 5 November the Baron replied: "I quite agree that the situation of the German Evangelical Church is still far too nebulous for us to come to any decision now." This may account for the inclusion of the word "intrinsically," which would later become such a point of contention. Heckel and his followers regarded it as a qualification that actually contradicted an organizational break with the Reich church. His opponents insisted that they had intended to express their total agreement with the Confessing church as constituted in Dahlem. Bonhoeffer wrote to inform Bell that the step toward union with the Confessing church had now been definitely taken: "I am very happy about it."[188]

Copies of the resolution were sent to three separate destinations with cover letters. On 10 November Wehrhan and Schröder sent it to Heckel's Foreign Office, with a letter from the Association of Congregations stating:

> The German Evangelical congregations in Great Britain have heard with great pleasure that, as a result of the Führer's declarations, the conscious profession of loyalty to the Third Reich and its Führer is not identical with membership in any one church group. These congregations have been based, some of them for centuries, upon the Bible and the Confession, and therefore consider the Confessional church to be the rightful successor of the German Evangelical Church Federation which they joined in 1928 so as to preserve their connections with the church at home. The representatives of the German Evangelical congregations who met on 5 November in the German Evangelical Christ Church have therefore unanimously resolved to inform the Church Foreign Office in Berlin of the foregoing, and at the same time to enter into negotiations with the Confessional church in Oeynhausen. . . . [189]

On 13 November the resolution was sent to the Confessing synod in Oeynhausen, addressed to President Koch, with the request that he should receive Bonhoeffer and Pastor Schönberger for the purpose of negotiating the union. The letter also recommended that an authority similar to the Foreign Office be established.[190]

Finally, the pastors in London composed a letter to send to other German pastors abroad, in the name of the ministers' association in Great Britain.[191] It contained their resolutions and expressed the hope that this was only a prelude to official action by the Confessing synod. They asked their fellow clergy to take a position on the London actions as soon as possible, so that negotiations could be conducted with the Confessing synod upon "as broad a basis" as possible.

Initial Reactions. Before this letter reached the Church Foreign Office, Heckel had been informed privately about the 5 November gathering. He immediately grasped that this posed a far more serious threat than the crisis in February, and understood that it could jeopardize his hard-won position. Early in the morning of 13 November he called the German Embassy in London. The notes of this telephone call were sent from London to the Reich chancellery, where they were brought to Hitler's attention:

> Bishop Heckel rang up Prince Bismarck early this morning and told him that he had been informed that the German Evangelical churches, in close collaboration with Baron Schröder, had unanimously resolved to join the

German Confessional Church. Because he believed this could be followed by unfavorable international repercussions, Heckel asked Bismarck to contact Baron Schröder, so that he could at least delay this step, which he characterized as premature, since the internal German church questions had not yet been clarified. . . .

Bismarck replied that (the) embassy . . . would be unable to intervene without instructions from the Ministry of Foreign Affairs, as Bishop Heckel had asked on his own initiative. . . .

I would request . . . guidance on this point. Hoesch.[192]

Heckel then summoned the German pastor in Liverpool, K. H. Schreiner, a fellow Bavarian whom he knew personally.

By this time Heckel assumed that the Reich bishop would be forced to resign, like church commissioner Jäger. The larger regional churches were calling for Müller's dismissal, the theological faculties were requesting his removal with resolutions signed by the overwhelming majority of their professors, and even moderate German Christians were expressing their dissatisfaction with the Reich bishop. Heckel was drawn into the controversy himself. On 14 November, in a confidential letter to the pastors abroad, he suggested:

> The former church commissioner's resignation from office was an unmistakable symptom of crisis; it was in no way a solution. . . .
>
> I would beg you, my brethren in the ministry, to believe me if I say no more than . . . that I have, during the recent days and weeks, held frank and open discussions with the Reich bishop about the need for a genuine church decision. With the consent of all my colleagues I made several specific recommendations.[193]

Needless to say, Heckel had no intention of helping consolidate the Confessing synod's emergency church government. His letter assured the pastors that he intended to "preserve the independence of German overseas church work against the demands of the various church factions and opinions." "The church's work abroad, like the Church Foreign Office, should be above all differences."[194] Rumors even spread that Heckel, not content with joining the attacks on the beleaguered Reich bishop, was actually on the verge of joining the Confessing church. This rumor also reached London, leading Wehrhan to write Koch on 13 November on behalf of the London pastors that, while they would welcome such a move, they could not accept Heckel in any leadership capacity after their experience with him in February.

Heckel and Pastor Schreiner in Liverpool now agreed that the section of the London resolution that addressed the unacceptability of the Reich bishop should be allowed to stand; but that the other section, concerning union with the Confessing synod, should be postponed and eventually dropped altogether. In other words, the London delegation to church president Koch should be canceled. Pastor Schreiner and others called at the Reich chancellery in Berlin to submit the protest of the German congregations in England against Ludwig Müller.[195] The withdrawal of congregations from the Reich church that had begun in London would spread, he argued, unless Müller resigned. On 16 November, Schreiner also wrote Baron Schröder and Pastor Rieger about his talks in Berlin, including those "with leading members of the Confessing front." These members had assured him that relations between the congregations abroad and the Church Foreign Office should not be upset; "the evidence has only intensified my fears that this step [secession from the Reich church] could be premature." In his letter to Rieger, Schreiner also polemically attacked Bonhoeffer, whose account of things he described as inaccurate and too pessimistic. He followed this by repeating a favorite expression of the "neutral" church leaders: "we don't have to play at being confessing heroes." The 5 November resolution, he continued, was a good weapon and could do no harm "*if* it has no further repercussions."

Schreiner had described Bonhoeffer's reports as "inaccurate." Bonhoeffer, of course, deliberately emphasized those aspects of the situation that could be used to move things forward; he was not interested in focusing on the objections and versions of events that came from the neutral center. Everything depended on which voices in the broad "Confessing front" were listened to; Schreiner therefore implored his colleagues in London to proceed no further. After consulting Baron Schröder, however, they refused to postpone their own plans or to negotiate with Schreiner upon his return.

Yet Schreiner's visit had provided Heckel with proof that the front in England was not wholly united and given him detailed knowledge that helped him plan future policy. On 16 November Heckel wrote his first official reply to the senders of the 5 November London resolution. He expressed regret that such a momentous decision should have been based on "insufficient information" and made without prior verbal consultations. He contested the Confessing church's legal status as a church on the grounds that it had not yet been publicly and legally recognized as such by the state. The former Church Federation's rightful successor in the agreement with the overseas congregations could only be the German Evangelical Church, which had been validated by the legislation signed by the *Führer* on 14 July 1933. The Association of German Evangelical Congregations in England was not empowered to speak for the congregations in the question of secession; this required a notice in writing from each individual church council. In fact, this was a procedural matter that had been overlooked in England; and, from what he had gathered during Schreiner's visit, Heckel could be fairly certain that such decisions would not be made with the same unanimity as the general resolution on 5 November.

Heckel was also able to diminish the impact of the letter sent by the London pastors to their colleagues elsewhere in Europe. He conferred with Helmut Rössler, pastor of the German congregation in Heerlen, Holland. On 16 November Rössler sent a message to the West European Pastors' Convention, which included the German clergy in Holland, Belgium, Luxembourg, and France, urging them to refrain from further support for the Confessing church. Rössler wrote:

> The Confessing synod, citing the Reich Ministry of Justice, proclaims a state of emergency according to which the legislation enacted by Müller's church government has been invalidated since the implementation of the new church constitution. In complete disregard of the existing church government, the synod proposes a fundamental legal reconstruction on the basis of the church constitution of 11 July 1933. Conversely, Hitler, speaking for the state, has declared his profound disappointment about the course of the church dispute, and his neutrality and impartiality toward the church struggle as such. Although the Confessing synod will be considerably relieved by this declaration, it can hardly hope, in light of the statement made last week by Interior Minister Frick, to be accorded corporate rights by the state.
>
> This is a matter for serious anxiety, for if the Third Reich should dissociate itself altogether from church affairs, the church struggle might well end with a drift toward the establishment of free churches, as in America. With that, the alliance that has existed since Luther's day between the Evangelical church and the German state would cease to be, and the destined community of the German Evangelical Church and the Third Reich would be annulled. Whether we in Germany would then find ourselves with one or more free churches in place of the federation represented by the present German Evangelical Church is of minor importance, compared with the certain prospect that state subsidies for all church bodies and activities—the evangelical theological faculties, confessional schools and work among the German communities abroad—would be in jeopardy. It would therefore seem obvious that a complete victory for the confessional front would mean the end of the existence of the *Volkskirche* and the beginning of a trend toward free churches—indeed, would even mean, perhaps a permanent schism within German Protestantism. . . .

Here Rössler inserted an apologia for the Church Foreign Office:

> ... it has introduced integrity into church administration. As a consequence, until now those of us abroad have largely escaped, thanks be to God, the internal arguments within the church. ...
>
> I can well imagine that many colleagues feel themselves to be spiritual members of the Confessing church and don't understand why they should not simply give in to it. But as things are now, this would be stabbing the Church Foreign Office in the back at a time when it is struggling, with full awareness of its responsibility for German Protestantism throughout the world, to find a solution for the entire church that does not necessitate the complete disintegration of what now exists. ...
>
> In this situation, individual actions by congregations abroad would do more harm than good, quite aside from the fact that congregations abroad that intervene in internal German church disputes can easily be accused of treason, which is difficult to refute. ... This would achieve the very opposite of what we must fight for today—a unified, German Evangelical National Church for the Third Reich and for Evangelical German culture throughout the world. ...[196]

In 1935 Bonhoeffer informed church president Koch that there had been a few victories for the Confessing church in Southwest Africa, but he had no others to report.[197] The Confessing synod had no power to act. By November it had gambled away the strong position it had attained by the end of October. Rössler had correctly observed, "If one is to believe what one hears, the Confessing synod is torn by profound differences of opinion about the situation in general and the course to be pursued, and this impairs its powers of decision."[198] The letter from the Association of Pastors in England had only a slight effect, especially since the German congregations in other countries were financially much more dependent on the church offices on Jebensstrasse. The initiative and decisions necessary to make secession a viable proposition would have required infinitely larger resources than those available to the congregations abroad.

On 15 November Koch wrote on behalf of the Confessing synod to thank the London pastors, and asked Bonhoeffer and Schönberger to come for negotiations on the church union. The journey was apparently postponed by the painful controversy about the formation of the emergency church administration (the Provisional Church Administration, ultimately founded on 22 November under Bishop Marahrens). A letter from Bonhoeffer's mother to the Leibholzes suggested Bonhoeffer's intention of achieving his goal quickly, and described the developments in Berlin:

> In the coming week we're expecting Dietrich, who is coming here with two pastors [from London] to announce to the Interior Ministry that their parishes have joined the Confessing church. . . . Things are very much in flux, but there are still numerous difficulties because of the moderate German Christians, etc., and the lack of uncompromising Bavarians, on the one side, and people like Dietrich on the other.

On 25 November, the evening of Memorial Sunday, after singing with his St. Paul's choir in a performance of Brahms's *Requiem*, Bonhoeffer finally left with Wehrhan and Schönberger. Before going to Berlin they stopped in Oeynhausen, where they held discussions with church president Koch of the Confessing synod and church counsel Breit of the Provisional Church Administration, probably on 28 November. Only fragmentary notes remain of this meeting, in which Pastor Hans Asmussen apparently took part on behalf of the Council of Brethren; the protocol includes an explanation of the situation in England and proposals for a plan to abolish the Church Foreign Office and set up temporary offices in England to oversee church work abroad.[199] There are no notes about what they had hoped to achieve and what agreements were made. Perhaps the Provisional Church Administration and the Council of Brethren were unable to make any definite statements, but could only acknowledge the intentions of those in London to join the Confessing church, and compile their recommendations about a future structure for overseas ministries. On 30 November Asmussen described the situation in a letter to Dr. Hans Beyer in Danzig:

> Up to now our procedure has been to concern ourselves with the Protestant Germans abroad only when they approached us. Our primary connections with the Germans abroad has been with those in Anglo-Saxon countries; with those in the East we have had virtually no connections. I hope this will improve once [Hans] Iwand has arrived in Riga. The best thing for you to do would be to get in touch with Pastor D. Bonhoeffer . . . whose main concern, however, is also the Anglo-Saxon regions.

On arriving in Berlin, Bonhoeffer went to the Ministry of Foreign Affairs where he saw Hans-Bernd von Haeften who had returned from Copenhagen. Haeften introduced him to Adolf Freudenberg, a counselor in the Cultural Department of the German Foreign Ministry. Forced to emigrate in 1937, Freudenberg became an ordained minister and worked in Geneva for the Ecumenical Council.[200] The readiness to prepare and eventually protect the overseas ministries of the Confessing church testifies to the optimism of those involved, though these future plans never materialized. The files of the London parishes and the Association of Congregations show that exchanges between London and the Berlin offices on Jebenstrasse were lively and prompt; by comparison, the correspondence with the Confessing synod and the Provisional Church Administration was meager, and soon almost nonexistent. All the initiative and drive behind this communication came entirely from London—in other words, from Bonhoeffer. The visit to Berlin was not decisive for him; he and his parishes had already crossed the Rubicon.

The relative lack of material on the relations between the Confessing church and the congregations abroad can be ascribed partly to a shortage of people and money; Bonhoeffer later attempted several times to change this. The main reason, however, was the internal dilemma of the Provisional Church Administration, whose leaders included people who found the Dahlem resolutions too extreme; one of these was its own chairman, Bishop Marahrens, who explicitly spoke of the "confessional movement" instead of the "Confessing church." Marahrens had been selected in the belief that this would make the Reich government more inclined to recognize the Provisional Church Administration. When this failed to materialize, every consequence of the Dahlem resolutions was prevented. Finally the Provisional Church Administration was hesitant to venture into the dangerous zone of foreign relations by its fear of becoming politically suspect.

As a result the Confessing church never had an office responsible for overseas congregations, although Bonhoeffer urged this on several occasions.[201] When Müller's administration was subsequently replaced by general superintendent Zoellner and the church committees, there was no institutionalized body to maintain relations between the Provisional Church Administration and the congregations abroad. The initiative taken in November 1934 by those in London was no longer operative. It was astonishing, then, that a minority among the English congregations remained loyal to the Confessing church. The motives behind the 5 November resolution on seceding had been strong enough to shape their further course independently. This soon became evident in their persistence in fighting Heckel's counterattacks.

Confrontation. While the London deputation was still in Berlin, Schröder wrote Heckel:

> I greatly regret that, in your opinion, the congregations and myself have erred in sending you our decision without first consulting you. Previous experience led us to conclude that discussions such as took place earlier

this year would prove unfruitful. This step was decided upon after long and careful consideration and no discussion could have influenced our decision.[202]

On 28 November Heckel, having received no answer to his letter of 16 November, learned that the three pastors were holding discussions in Berlin. He threatened to draw the attention of each pastor and parish to their "false conception of the law"; he figured that the undecided among them would waver.[203]

Meanwhile the Reich bishop, who seemed to have survived the difficult period of public demands for his resignation, declared in the official journal of the German Evangelical Church on 27 November: "I forbid all pastors and church officials to subordinate themselves to the unconstitutional 'Provisional Church Government.'"[204]

But those in London did not intend to listen to Heckel, much less to Ludwig Müller. Heckel struck back, writing Baron Schröder and all the parishes on 10 December.[205] He repeated the objections from his first letter of 16 November, indicating that he knew "from reliable sources" what was afoot in London and Berlin:

> I am sorry to say that two representatives of the London congregations ... spent some time in Berlin without deeming it necessary to so much as try to discuss matters with the Church Foreign Office. I am aware of the proposals which they made in official quarters in Berlin concerning the reorganization of church work abroad, proposals which the said persons are in no way legally qualified to make and which, indeed, represent a plan that is wholly impracticable, both on church and national grounds.[206]
>
> From what I hear, the proposed plans were rejected by the offices to which they were submitted. The extent to which the two gentlemen's procedure was authorized by the congregations in England is not altogether clear to this office.[207]

Heckel's main target was the 5 November resolution and the way it had been handled. While the tenor of the resolution had been determined by the word "intrinsically" and it had provided for negotiations with the Church Foreign Office, he said, the resolution would not be valid until every single congregation had sent its own declaration. By doing so, however, the congregations would jeopardize their pastors' rights to return to parishes in Germany and their pensions. He concluded: "To the best of my knowledge, the action of the Association of Congregations does not have the approval of the Liverpool, Bradford, South Shields and Newcastle congregations."[208]

Those in London had two responses. First they repudiated Heckel's aspersions on their national loyalties, implied by his warning on 16 November against "opposition to the constitution sanctioned by the Reich Chancellor" and more recently against plans that were impracticable "on national grounds."[209] They announced they would take "serious measures against any repetition of this kind of allusion."[210] They also refuted his attempt to drive a wedge between pastors, congregations, and the Association of Congregations.

Second they brought in Edouard Crüsemann, a lawyer and member of the Sydenham congregation, to take the measures necessary to render their decision to secede from the German Evangelical Church watertight, in terms of the existing contracts with the congregations.[211] Baron Schröder wrote to the office on Jebenstrasse:

> ... with reference to your communications of 28.11. and 10.12. of this year, it is axiomatic that, insofar as individual congregations here intend to secede from the German Evangelical Church, this requires an explicit resolution by the parish council concerned.[212]

On 4 January 1935, with London engulfed in almost impenetrable fog, Bonhoeffer held an extraordinary meeting of his church council members. They unanimously approved a resolution stating:

> The councils of St. Paul's and Sydenham here assembled unanimously declare that they refuse to recognize the present Reich church government now administered by Reich Bishop L. Müller. The congregations of St. Paul's and Sydenham can no longer tolerate a church government whose aims and methods are contrary to the most elementary principles of the Protestant faith. The councils declare further that the Reich church government's unevangelical behavior during the past eighteen months has severely impaired the reputation of the German nation abroad. The councils emphasize that they are prepared to recognize the Reich church constitution as laid down by the Reich law of 15 July 1933 as a legal basis for union, and feel themselves bound, now as hitherto, to a German Evangelical Church having such a basis.[213]

Without Bonhoeffer's strong backing, the congregations in Britain might not have overcome their misgivings in the face of Berlin's threats of financial and legal sanctions—the consequences of which were not foreseeable at that point. At the same time these congregations had also been influenced by the free church environment in England, and had developed a need for independence that now helped them.

But here, too, no one wanted to be accused of lacking patriotic or political conviction. It was agreed that, "out of consideration for the political situation," the resolution should not be sent to Berlin until after the Saar plebiscite on 13 January 1935.[214]

Inconclusive Results. This resolution was to be the last such step; shortly thereafter Bonhoeffer left London. The legalistic details of the London church struggle could no longer hold his interest. Two years after this resolution the Church Foreign Office—still under Heckel's administration—contacted Bonhoeffer's former parishes of Sydenham and St. Paul's through his successor, Pastor Boeckheler. Devotedly loyal to their former pastor, the parishioners were still collecting money for his preachers' seminary in Finkenwalde. Now they were informed by Dr. Krummacher in the Church Foreign Office that their secession had not been put on record. In other words, the final legal step had been omitted, which meant that finalized ties to the Confessing church had never been legally ratified.

Julius Rieger's St. George's parish became increasingly embroiled in difficulties with the office on Jebenstrasse. When the church celebrated its 175th anniversary, Rieger invited Confessing church leader Karl Koch, not Bishop Heckel. In response, a grant that had been promised by the Church Foreign Office to build an organ was withdrawn; only much later, after strong intervention, was the money forthcoming. St. George's Church was Franz Hildebrandt's first place of refuge after he was forced to flee. Bonhoeffer had hoped that Hildebrandt could take over his position in Forest Hill. But at the beginning of 1935 the creation of the Confessing church was still gaining momentum; Hildebrandt could not bring himself to abandon his work in Dahlem. After Niemöller's arrest in 1937, however, Hildebrandt had to leave immediately. St. George's took him in. Until the very end of the Nazi era, Rieger's church was the first point of refuge for numerous refugees. This contributed in no small measure to Rieger's difficulties with the Church Foreign Office.

No sooner had Bonhoeffer disappeared from the London scene than the majority of German congregations in England began to see the church struggle in a different light. During this new era of General Superintendent Zoellner's church committees, most fell under the spell of a new slogan, "the preservation of the *Volkskirche*." The files of the English Pastors' conference reveal that the phrase "Bible and Confession" was decisive during Bonhoeffer's period there. After 1936, however, concern for the *Volkskirche* prevailed. Pastor Schönberger ceased to play any role in the cause, devoting himself to work on behalf of the National Socialist Party in London. Pastor Wehrhan visited Zoellner in 1936 as the self-appointed spokesman of *Volkskirche* interests. The minutes of the pastors' conference of June 1936 record the isolated remark of a participant: "You will, I hope, not think too ill of me if, having been subjected for years to Bonhoeffer's influence, voluntarily or involuntarily . . . we stand more on the side of the Confessing church!"[215]

Plans

The decisions taken by the Dahlem Confessing synod established the direction that Bonhoeffer would follow during the next five years. They led to the creation of the Confessing church's preachers' seminaries, and Bonhoeffer was summoned home by the Old Prussian Council of Brethren to take charge of one of them. For this he finally abandoned his plan to go to India.

India. Bonhoeffer gave up his long-standing idea of going to India only reluctantly and with a heavy heart. This was the third time he had seriously considered it, and never before had he come so close to realizing his desire. His friends among the clergy and theologians found this incomprehensible, since he was such an example of wholehearted engagement in the church struggle. They failed to realize that Bonhoeffer's spiritual ardor concealed a certain skepticism combined with a thirst for knowledge:

> . . . since I am becoming more convinced each day that Christianity is approaching its end in the West—at least in its previous form and its previous interpretation—I should like to go to the Far Fast before returning to Germany.

He had written this to his brother, Karl-Friedrich, after barely three months in London.[216] In April 1934 he wrote to Erwin Sutz:

> How long I shall remain a pastor, and how long in this church, I don't know. Possibly not very long. This winter I'd like to go to India.[217]

From the time of his arrival in London he missed no opportunity to further his plan; even a major crisis, such as that of Fanö, could not dissuade him. On 22 May he wrote to his grandmother:

Before I finally commit myself to anything, however, I'm thinking again of going to India. I've given a good deal of thought lately to Indian questions and believe that there's quite a lot to be learned there. Sometimes it even seems to me that there's more Christianity in their "paganism" than in our entire Reich Church. Of course, Christianity did come from the East originally. But it has been so westernized and so permeated by civilized thought that, as we can now see, it is almost lost to us. Unfortunately I have little confidence left in the church opposition. I don't at all like the way they're going about things, and really dread the time when they assume responsibility and we may be compelled yet again to witness a dreadful compromising of Christianity. Practically I'm not yet sure how the Indian plan is going to work out. There's a possibility—but please don't mention this to students and so on—that I might go to Rabindranath Tagore's university. But I'd much rather go directly to Gandhi, and already have some very good introductions from his close friends. I might be able to stay there for six months or more as a guest. If this is ever arranged and I can manage it financially, I shall go in the winter.[218]

People in Berlin regarded Bonhoeffer's Indian scheme as thoroughly eccentric. Word of it reached Karl Barth. In an October 1936 letter to Bonhoeffer, about other things, he said:

> Do you remember that business of "the next ship but one"? And yet the only thing I have heard about you in ages is the strange news that you intend to go to India so as to learn some kind of spiritual technique from Gandhi or some other holy man and that you expect great things of its application in the west![219]

Jacobi did everything in his power to dissuade him from these ideas and to induce him to take up the post at the preachers' seminary without further delay. Even Hildebrandt begrudged him the time that would have been required for this trip.

Disregarding all this, he worked for months to increase his Far Eastern connections. His acquaintance with C. F. Andrews of the World Alliance opened many doors to him. In the summer of 1934 Mira Bai, formerly an admiral's daughter named Madeline Slade, returned to England; she had been a close associate of Gandhi since 1925 and was a disciple in his ashram. In order to share fully in the Mahatma's fight for freedom, she had transformed herself into an Indian, learned to weave and raise cattle, and had given up everything she owned. Like Gandhi, she had patiently spent time in prison. Bonhoeffer read accounts about her and heard her speak. He studied the writings of Jack Winslow, an expert on Asian spiritual exercises, and sought out English pacifists who were in sympathy with Gandhi. One of these gave him Beverley Nichols's book *Cry Havoc!* It was Gandhi's way of life that inspired part of Bonhoeffer's sermon on peace at Fanö. "Must we be put to shame by non-Christian people in the East? Shall we desert the individuals who are risking their lives for this message?"[220]

Reinhold Niebuhr relates that Bonhoeffer corresponded with him from London about his projected Indian journey.[221] Bonhoeffer spent some evenings with Theodor Lang, first secretary at the German Embassy, who had spent some time in Singapore and was able to give advice about living conditions in the East. He also gave Bonhoeffer his tropical suits, which Frau Lang altered to fit him. Rieger sometimes joined in these deliberations.[222] Herbert Jehle, a physicist and mathematician in Cambridge, was a supportive ally in these preparations; he completely shared Bonhoeffer's interest in the Sermon on the Mount and his pacifist ideas. Bonhoeffer even went to the Wellcome Tropical Medicine Institute in London, where he underwent tests to see if he was fit for the tropics.

In the late summer of 1934 Fanö temporarily distracted him from his projected trip. Later there was renewed pressure on him to take on the preachers' seminary. It was difficult for Bonhoeffer to evade this request. In fact, he was willing to do it; but repeatedly he postponed taking the position, largely because of the proposed journey to India. Finally the Confessing synod agreed to wait until the spring of 1935 so he could begin making definite plans.

He now wished to obtain a personal introduction to Gandhi, and as soon as Bishop Bell returned from the Continent to Chichester that October, Bonhoeffer asked him if he could help. Bell wrote to Gandhi:

> A friend of mine, a young man, at present German Pastor in London, Pastor Bonhoeffer, 23 Manor Mount, London S.E.23, is most anxious that I should give him an introduction to you. I can most heartily commend him. He expects to be in India for the first two or three months of 1935. He is intimately identified with the Church Opposition Movement in Germany. He is a very good theologian, a most earnest man, and is probably to have charge of the training of Ordination candidates for the Ministry in the future Confessional Church of Germany. He wants to study community life as well as methods of training. It would be a very great kindness if you could let him come to you.[223]

Soon after this, Herbert Jehle tells us, a friendly letter of invitation arrived from Gandhi. Gandhi invited Bonhoeffer and his friend to live in the Mahatma's ashram and to accompany him on some of his journeys.[224]

The invitation, however, arrived just as the events preceding the secession of the London congregations from the Reich church were reaching their climax. Bonhoeffer could not possibly have abandoned his colleagues and his congregations at that moment. By the time the quarrel with the Church Foreign Office had begun to die down, the seminary was preparing to open; no time remained for the journey. For a long time Bonhoeffer had been trying to avoid having to choose between India and the seminary, seeing the first as a necessary preparation for the second. Now, faced with a clear alternative, he chose Pomerania, where he would have to form his own ashram—the seminary—without prior experience in the Far East.

In 1928 the desire for a wider experience of the world had led to his first Indian plans. In 1931 his skepticism about the western form of Christianity became an additional factor. And in 1934 Bonhoeffer was motivated by the desire to witness Gandhi's exemplification of the Sermon on the Mount—in the spiritual exercises aimed toward a certain goal, and the Indian ways of resistance against tyrannical power. At that point it was still unthinkable to Bonhoeffer to join a conspiracy against Hitler; he sought a prototype for passive resistance that could induce changes without violence. His quest concealed his private fear that the church struggle might become an end in itself, remaining satisfied with reiterated confessions and ceaseless activity. He sought a means of fighting Hitler that went beyond the aims and methods of the church struggle while remaining legitimate from a Christian standpoint. While he supported the church struggle with all his might, at a deeper level he was looking for a different form of commitment that would be legitimate. This was one of the reasons for Bonhoeffer's third attempt to go to India.

Preachers' Seminary. His pastorate, the church struggle, the ecumenical movement, and his Indian plans consumed all of Bonhoeffer's time and energy. Yet he was still aware of what, since his university days, he had seen not only as his greatest pleasure but his vocation—teaching and writing theology. When he heard of Barth's struggle to retain his professorial chair at Bonn, he began to wonder where he belonged:

> I have just read about Barth's dismissal in *The Times*. I can hardly believe it's true. But if it is, perhaps I ought to come home, so that there's at least someone at the universities who's prepared to say these things.[225]

The initial impetus to return to teaching came from his own university—although the form this took was not altogether reassuring. On 9 May Dean

Erich Seeberg of the Berlin faculty wrote: "But I have not given up hope that conditions within the church will become settled enough for you to feel inwardly able to return."[226] The reason for this friendly letter was a new regulation concerning leave. Minister for Cultural Affairs Bernhard Rust had decreed that leave of absence for university teachers was to be subject to a new ministerial decision, as of the summer of 1934. Thus Bonhoeffer's name crossed Rust's desk again at a time when his reputation had not improved there. His family was so well connected academically, however, that they were able to muster support for an extension of his leave from the university. But the incident made him ponder what his final decision ought to be—either "this, the university, or something entirely different . . ."[227]

> [I assume] that I shall then have to decide definitely whether or not I shall return to an academic career. I'm not so tremendously interested in it any more, and I don't think my interest will increase much by this winter. It's just that I'm concerned about the students. But perhaps other ways will be open to me.[228]

Those "other ways" would lead to an independent theological chair in the Confessing church. This began with the March 1934 Reich bishop order to shut down the Old Prussian preachers' seminaries. Moreover, theological students were no longer able to take examinations unless they could prove "Aryan" descent. As a result, the Confessing church was forced to take the responsibility for theological training, colleges, seminaries, and examination officials into its own hands. In March, after the Reformed seminary in Elberfeld simply ignored the Reich bishop's order to close down, the Confessing church found itself obliged to take over the support of the seminary. In autumn of 1934 the Confessing church established the first of its own preachers' seminaries when it reopened the institution in Bielefeld-Sieker.

Bonhoeffer was approached on 4 June about possibly participating in this new work, but nothing definite was settled. According to Rieger's diary, Jacobi and Hildebrandt telephoned Bonhoeffer in London: "The Emergency Committee is looking for a school director for pastors, vicars and students. Bonhoeffer has been asked whether he wants to take such an office."[229] A fortnight later, while he was in Berlin to discuss the Fanö invitation with Koch and Niemöller, he spoke about the project with friends and allowed them to mention that he would be willing to accept the post at the next meeting of the Council of Brethren. The 4 July session of the Old Prussian Council was concerned with the preachers' seminary. Jacobi recommended Bonhoeffer as a possible director, but encountered some opposition. Bonhoeffer's political church recommendations from 1933 were still too vivid in many minds; he was not regarded as flexible or discreet enough for a teaching post in the church. His influence upon theological students was known, but there was some doubt as to whether he would really follow the Reformed line. Jacobi finally prevailed over the objectors, however, and Niemöller closed the session with the statement: "It is agreed that Bonhoeffer may take up the post of director of the Berlin-Brandenburg preachers' seminary on 1 January 1935."[230]

Although greatly tempted by the idea of practicing theology under the aegis of the Confessing church, Bonhoeffer still did not abandon his Indian plans. There was no doubt he realized that an early return to Germany under the conditions that prevailed would alter the course of his life. He was still uncertain when Hildebrandt arrived from Denmark with a message from Koch stating that Koch wanted Bonhoeffer to stay in London, at least during the coming winter, to maintain ties to the ecumenical movement. Bonhoeffer wrote to his grandmother: "This would mean turning down the seminary—it seems to me—and that is rather painful for me."[231] Yet a letter of 11 September to Erwin Sutz (which contained a passage about Hitler's obduracy and about complicity in the next war) revealed that he was completely undecided, although his comments on the place of theology in the new Germany were unambiguous:

> I am hopelessly torn between staying here, going to India and returning to Germany to take charge of a preachers' seminary shortly to be opened there. I no longer believe in the university, and never really have believed in it—to your irritation. The entire education of the younger generation of theologians belongs today in church cloister-like schools, in which pure doctrine, the Sermon on the Mount and worship are taken seriously—as they never are (and in present circumstances couldn't be) at the university. It is also high time we broke with our theologically based restraint towards the state's actions—which is, after all, only fear. "Speak out for those who cannot speak"—who in the church today realizes that this is the very least that the Bible requires of us? And then there's the matter of military service and war, etc. etc. . . .[232]

When Hildebrandt returned to Berlin in mid-September after substituting for Bonhoeffer in London, he brought a message from Bonhoeffer accepting the post of director of the seminary, on the condition that he would not have to begin until the spring of 1935.

When he asked Bell for an introduction to Gandhi, he had also requested recommendations to Anglican seminaries and communities. He wanted to gain an impression of other traditions before beginning his own attempt at communal life. In October the bishop wrote on his behalf to Father Talbot of the Community of the Resurrection in Mirfield, to Father Tribe of the Society of the Sacred Mission in Kelham, to Father O'Brien of the Society of St. John the Evangelist in Cowley, to Canon Tomlin of St. Augustine's College, Canterbury, and to the Reverend J. R. S. Taylor of Wycliffe Hall, Oxford, which was a Low Church center. The others were all High Church.

> He is very anxious to have some acquaintance with our methods in England, both with regard to training for the ministry and with regard to community life. He expects to leave England at the end of December.[233]

The "end of December" was in fact the time he hoped to leave for India. Bonhoeffer did eventually visit nearly all the places named above, although not until March 1935 and then more briefly than he had hoped, due to church politics. He went to Mirfield, where he joined in the horary prayers in which Psalm 119 was recited every day of the week; this psalm became the biblical passage most frequently quoted by Bonhoeffer. Together with Rieger he went to Kelham, but he also visited seminaries belonging to other denominations.[234] He noted the way in which a candidate's personal life during the period of study was influenced by the church in general and his home parish, for example, among Presbyterians, Congregationalists, or Baptists. He often spoke of the impression the Methodist college in Richmond had made on him, where he had been introduced by a German exchange student, Rudolf Weckerling. In the entrance hall there were boards with long lists of names, each followed by the date of ordination and the date of death, often in the same year: for decades the candidates from the college had rapidly succeeded one another in the fatal climate of the mission posts. Bonhoeffer also visited the Quakers at their center in Selly Oak near Birmingham. "I liked it very much there."[235]

During the winter he visited Berlin in connection with the delegation that was to negotiate the union of the congregations with the Confessing synod. He then stayed on in early December, to go house hunting in the province of Brandenburg with his friends, including Jacobi, Albertz, and Hildebrandt. It was essential, he thought, that the work should be done in a place remote from the distractions of Berlin, but he had not decided exactly where this should be.

The closer this new task approached, the more it became a focal point for everything that had preoccupied Bonhoeffer in recent years: a theology of the Sermon on the Mount, a community in service and spiritual exercises, a witness to passive resistance and ecumenical openness. The optimism about his future project induced by this train of thought is reflected in the memorandum he addressed to the session of the Ecumenical Youth Commission in Paris on 29 January 1935, which he could not attend. His main premise was the concept that his Berlin students had pursued since the Fanö meeting:

> ... it is also there that a group of young Christians are seriously considering the possibility of starting a small Christian community in the form of a settlement or any other form on the basis of the Sermon on the Mount. It is felt that only by a clear and uncompromising stand can Christianity be a vital force for our people. It is also felt that the developments of the church dispute in Germany are tending more and more toward a sort of conservative Christianity which of course would go very well with the rather conservative spirit which is steadily growing under the present Reichswehr and Industry regime. This group would also make a definite stand for peace by conscientious objection. ...
>
> Finally, would you be willing to help me to find some young students or pastors for the Seminary which I am supposed to start in the near future on behalf of the Confessional synod. I should like to have the ecumenic aspect of it made clear from the beginning. We are now thinking if we could combine the idea of a Christian community mentioned above with the new Seminary. At any rate the support from the ecumenic movements would be most valuable for the carrying out of plans. I know of similar ideas in England among some student groups. ... [236]

De Félice quoted excerpts from this memorandum in the newsletter he sent out from Geneva at the end of February 1935 to the ecumenical youth groups. Two years later Bonhoeffer made one more attempt to incorporate the Confessing church seminaries in an ecumenical exchange program. [237]

Quasi-Political Activity. During Bonhoeffer's final weeks in England he and Bell called upon each another in matters that went beyond the scope of the church struggle.

The Saar plebiscite was due to take place in January 1935. Bonhoeffer, realizing that the incorporation of that area into the Reich would bring a fresh wave of refugees, organized a receiving office for refugee children in his parish. This was no simple matter, given the general patriotic fervor for the plebiscite. Bonhoeffer asked a lawyer who had emigrated to prepare a memorandum exposing Britain's disgraceful attitude toward the refugees. On the one hand, it contained England's solemn declaration before the council of the League of Nations that it was proud to provide asylum for the exiles; on the other, it illustrated the impasse in which the exiles had been placed by the law, which denied them the right to work. He first passed this memorandum to Bell, who replied immediately without, however, being able to offer any solution to the problem.[238] Only in 1938 did Bell receive a seat in the House of Lords, where he then became a frequent participant in the debates. Bonhoeffer estimated the number of refugees from the Saar at approximately eight thousand—a mere trickle compared with what came later, when the bishop initiated the British churches' major aid association for refugees. Hildebrandt reports that Bell even considered relinquishing his diocese in order to become the bishop of refugees. In practice, he already was. When the war broke out, he and his wife visited the German refugees interned on the Isle of Man. Both Jews and Christians would say to Hildebrandt: "I am in trouble; will you write to the bishop of Chichester?"

Another plan—which proved fruitless—was connected with the Anglo-German rapprochement in the winter of 1934–1935.[239] Bell had hoped to be able to exploit this for his own ends, but the leaders of the Confessing church did not know what to make of his proposal, if they understood it at all.

In 1934 Hitler was anxious to improve his relations with Britain, while the British government, in turn, seemed ready to acknowledge the status quo. Trade agreements were negotiated between the two countries, and in March 1935 Anthony Eden and Lord Simon saw Hitler in Berlin. The talks culminated in the Anglo-German naval treaty of 18 June 1935. Among the advocates of equal rights for Germany, its bad domestic behavior notwithstanding, were people such as the archbishop of Canterbury, Cosmo Lang. *Junge Kirche* found it helpful to publish a selection of pro-German remarks made by English church people.[240]

In accordance with Hitler's policy, his special envoy Joachim von Ribbentrop called on Bishop Bell in Chichester on 6 November 1934 and was treated to a detailed inventory of complaints about the coercive acts against the church in Germany. In 1935 Ribbentrop met the bishop again, this time at the Athenaeum Club, and promised that when Bell next visited Berlin he should meet Hitler's deputy Rudolf Hess and newly appointed Minister of Church Affairs Hans Kerrl. These meetings did in fact take place in September of the same year. The second encounter between Ribbentrop and Bell received far more publicity than the earlier one, since it coincided with the first release of Protestant pastors who had been taken to concentration camps, including Peter Brunner.

Bell was not the kind of person to let such a favorable political opportunity pass. With several friends he planned a meeting between leading public figures in Britain and eminent members of the Confessing church to discuss what contribution the churches might make to improve relations between the two countries. He had even found people who were prepared to financially support such a plan. It seemed to the bishop that the Confessing church could only benefit from the political respectability it would acquire. He discussed this with Bonhoeffer, who tried to win church president Koch on the idea:

> Do you still think of the plan of an official British delegation to the Confessional Church on behalf of world peace? The more I think of this idea, the more it strikes me as most important and helpful.[241]

Unfortunately, however, this project came at a time when Koch had an entirely different kind of delegation in mind. In Old Prussia the Council of Brethren was preparing a major declaration against the idolatry of "Blood, Race, and *Volkstum*." They were also planning a new Confessing synod of the entire German church in Augsburg, which was initially scheduled for April but convened in June. The council, and Koch in particular, would have liked an ecumenical delegation to be present on both occasions, a project that was incompatible with the London plan. Bell's idea was greeted only with misunderstanding by Franz Hildebrandt:

> Bonhoeffer has just written me, very worried about the following: in response to Chichester's offer to send a delegation to discuss the peace issue—that is, the problems of the World Alliance in Fanö—your reply sounded as though you were expecting a discussion of disputed *church* questions, which is *not* what they were thinking of over there. So Chichester doesn't quite know what to do; because he thinks his plan would be in our interest and has interested all sorts of people in it (e.g., Dr. Oldham). Bonhoeffer promised him that you'll be writing again when you will clear up what was perhaps only a linguistic misunderstanding and will state your intentions about the peace delegation. . . .[242]

But the plan proved to be impossible, although Bell and the archbishop of Canterbury had already held discussions with von Hoesch and von Bismarck at the German Embassy.[243]

This did not rule out the possibility that Bell might comply with Koch's wish to attend the synods. When Bonhoeffer said good-bye to him on 15 April 1935, Bell asked him to take a message to Koch "assuring him of my sympathy and my desire to help in case of need."[244]

Return. Bonhoeffer arranged his move from the ministry to the seminary so that he could return to a parish if necessary—a precaution he never failed to take, as long as circumstances allowed. In 1933, after he had begun his ministry in London, the Foreign Department of the German Evangelical Church had suggested that he resign his post as lecturer at Berlin University. This led Bonhoeffer to obtain a resolution from the church wardens of Sydenham and St. Paul's stating that he should not resign from his teaching post, since the times demanded that no post should be left voluntarily but only under compulsion. Now, on 11 February 1935, he asked the parish council to record that he was leaving London on a leave of absence, initially for six months, and that Pastor Boeckheler from Hull would take over his duties during that time. He exercised similar caution in 1939, when he again proposed to strike out in a new direction; only after that did he burn all his bridges behind him.

This remarkably consistent procedure when changing jobs was not due only to a simple desire for security. In that case, he would have showed more concern for the rights to which he was entitled as a member of the clergy, but he was very casual about such privileges. It was probably due more to his need for freedom; he disliked being utterly dependent on one employer, even the Council of Brethren. Throughout his career he was careful and creative in keeping his options open.

Bonhoeffer preached his farewell sermon on 10 March 1935. Collections were being taken in all the churches for the Third Reich's Winter Aid, but Bonhoeffer explicitly recommended that the second collection taken during the service go to assist German refugees in England. Afterward he began his tour of the cloisters and colleges, going to Scotland to visit John Baillie, his former teacher at Union Theological Seminary in New York.

Bonhoeffer's return to Germany coincided almost exactly with Karl Barth's departure from Bonn, which had become inevitable. In September 1934 Bonhoeffer had asked Sutz: "Is Barth remaining in Switzerland?"[245] Barth's refusal to take the unconditional oath incumbent on all civil servants had brought him into conflict with the National Socialist state—a battle that he had fought alone, without the support of the Confessing church. Thus at a time when Bonhoeffer was preparing himself for his return Barth moved back to Basel. Both men had devoted considerable effort, inside and outside Germany, to uphold and emphasize the clear distinction between the church struggle and political resistance to the Nazi regime. In the fifth volume of *Theological Existence Today*, Barth wrote:

> Above all I would like to point out that to interpret the church opposition in Germany as actual resistance to the current state government is to mis-

understand its character. . . . I am not a National Socialist. But that has nothing at all to do with the battle I am waging in these pages. . . .[246]

That passage was written at the end of 1933. Could this position still be held unchanged? In May 1934, when Bonhoeffer thanked Bell for his Ascension Day message, he said: "this letter will help the opposition to see that this whole conflict is not only within the Church, but strikes at the very roots of National Socialism."[247] In July, after Frick's decree banned all public debate about the church struggle, he wrote: "I hope that the pastors will this time dare to come up against the State"[248] At the time Bonhoeffer did not expect the church to provide a new political conception, either in opposition to Hitler or for the period that would follow his overthrow. Yet he felt that the church could justify its existence only if it spoke out against tyranny and on behalf of its victims. Would this happen in Germany?

On 17 April Bonhoeffer reported to his new supervisor, Wilhelm Niesel, who headed the department for the preachers' seminaries in the Old Prussian Council of Brethren. Now, under intense pressure, they finally had to find a building to house the seminary. Hildebrandt and Bonhoeffer drove through Brandenburg from one estate to the next, but none of the quarters offered seemed suitable. Bonhoeffer then went to church president Koch, who had a new message to convey to Bell. When Bonhoeffer returned to Berlin during Easter vacation, the first candidates began to arrive at Niesel's office. They had been waiting since March to be summoned to the new seminary. They were about to be temporarily accommodated in Burckhardt House (a church building in Berlin that housed social and educational offices) when on 25 April they were offered the use of the Rhineland Bible School in Zingst on the Baltic Sea until the beginning of the summer season. It was still bitterly cold, but there was little doubt that it would be deserted. On 26 April the candidates and their director, who was their own age, made their way to the cabins among the dunes on the Baltic coast.

CHAPTER NINE

PREACHERS' SEMINARY: 1935

"The summer of 1935 . . . has been the fullest time of my life, both professionally and personally," Bonhoeffer wrote in a letter to the members of his first course at the seminary.[1] He had finally begun a work about which he had no reservations. In preceding years he had been haunted by the thought that he had not yet found his true task in life; now his new calling gave him the opportunity he had longed for.

The small intimate circle of students enabled him to devote all his energies to his new theological theme of discipleship, and his new task was begun under the oversight of the church. Bonhoeffer had reflected about communal life for four years; now he could put his ideas into practice. His theological enthusiasm was unfolding in a setting marked by a practical piety.

Once he had taken pleasure in avoiding a preachers' seminary; now it became the place where, for a few years, his doubt and restlessness gave way to the satisfaction of meaningful activity. His search for other realms and values ceased. He enjoyed confirming young theologians in their calling within this besieged church, and sharing all his wealth and talents with them. Those students who were meeting him for the first time remarked on the surprising and intense readiness of their seminary director to make himself available to them.

The Seminaries

Aside from a few special institutes, the preachers' seminaries were a late (and, to many, undesirable) innovation within the regional churches' theological training programs. Traditionally theological education—as opposed to "training"—was in the hands of the state-appointed professors at the universities. Academic theological study and research were seen as constituting an education in themselves. Theological "training" was not considered independently worthwhile, and therefore was often neglected. By the twentieth century the churches had recognized the need to acquire some influence over young ordinands before they entered the ministry, but the establishment of separate church seminaries that could hold their own against the academic world and, most importantly, be recognized as valid, proved difficult. The traditional academic curriculum still set the standard, leading the seminaries to offer courses already covered by the universities, where the students had enjoyed not just greater freedom but probably a higher level of instruction.

Older reputable seminaries such as Loccum, Wittenberg, or the Berlin Cathedral Seminary had been established as elite institutes for those with the best university examinations. They provided a sinecure for brilliant students to devote themselves to theological research; in some ways they resembled a college of fellows such as All Souls at Oxford. They were no doubt useful institutions, yet their very existence confirmed the inadequacy of the church's own conception of theological training. At the turn of the century the number of seminaries increased and attendance at one of them became compulsory, although this did not occur in the Old Prussian Union Church until 1928. During the two years between the first and second examinations, six to twelve months were allocated to this part of the training. Ordinands such as Bonhoeffer and Hildebrandt regarded even this as a waste of time.

Now, however, a fundamental change had occurred, and the stepchild became the darling of the church. The severe crises within the university faculties and the regional churches forced the Confessing church to set up new preachers' seminaries. What followed was almost miraculous. Protected by their relative obscurity, the new seminaries were able to turn themselves into remarkable power centers of theology. They were able to carry on their work unhampered and with fewer interruptions than the church *Hochschulen*. (The church *Hochschulen*, or colleges, did not prepare candidates for ordination like the seminaries, but competed with the university theological faculties by offering course work up to the first theological examinations.) These colleges had come into existence at the same time as the seminaries, but because they had been established in open opposition to the state university faculties, they achieved immediate notoriety. They were banned from the very day of their inauguration, 1 November 1935, and immediately forced underground.

The seminaries, although they owed their immediate existence to the struggle of the churches of the Old Prussian Union, remained outside the fray for some time. Only after two and a half years of intensive work did the police come to seal their doors. Even while they flourished, however, the state was already taking measures that would relegate them to hopeless "illegality." It was not very long before the activities of Bonhoeffer, his superiors and his ordinands at the seminary were in direct contravention of state laws.

The State's Church Policies. In terms of institutional development, the Confessing church reached its pinnacle in 1935. It still appeared that the church opposition might succeed, particularly in its Dahlem resolutions. The Councils of Brethren continued to hope that the state and regional churches would eventually recognize the Dahlem decisions that had established the emergency church bodies. The German Christians' fiasco was evident to everyone; Ludwig Müller's power seemed to be on the wane.

At the same time, 1935 included the early phase of legislation that would ultimately bring about the destruction, internally and externally, of the newly created Confessing church. Three laws were passed, the first signed by Göring and the other two by Hitler. In their tone they portrayed the state as a patient arbitrator that sought to restore order among the squabbling pastors:

1. In March 1935 the Prussian state government set up *finance departments* as a "legal aid" to the churches of the Old Prussian Union. Their alleged purpose was to protect the congregations' property and charities. In fact, however, their ultimate goal was to bring all congregational and regional church offices under state jurisdiction.

2. In June 1935 the Reich government created a *Legislative Authority* for the administration of legal matters in the German Evangelical Church. The Confessing church had been successful in its appeals before the regular courts; the Legislative Authority was to stop this. The activities of this body represented a powerful state encroachment upon the independence of church law.

3. In July 1935 Hitler established the Ministry of Church Affairs under the leadership of Hanns Kerrl. This initially aroused vague hopes that the era of Ludwig Müller would end and allow a new beginning. But in September 1935 the means by which Kerrl intended to direct the church appeared: the *Law for the Protection of the German Evangelical Church.* The repercussions of its seventeen clauses were eventually far greater than those of the other decrees, for it led to the disintegration of the Confessing church by creating irreparable schisms within its ranks.

Thus the year in which Bonhoeffer's seminary was founded was also one of fundamental changes in the course of the church struggle. The previous resistance against the German Christians and their methods now seemed simple by comparison. That resistance had never lost a certain vigor and joy, and it had given the old concept of heresy a new lease on life. Now, however, the issue was whether to directly oppose the state and disobey its laws. Had previous interpretations of Romans 13 prepared people for this? Was their insistence on the distinction between internal church resistance and political resistance now coming home to roost? The National Socialist regime had been somewhat clumsy in using the German Christians to attack the church. Things now became far more dangerous and insidious, for the regime had discovered its opponent's weak spot. The Evangelical church was not accustomed to opposing state legislation, but after 1935 it became increasingly clear that even at this level it would have to resist.

At the beginning, however, the seminaries in the Old Prussian Confessing church felt little anxiety. Emerging from the period of the protest movement against Ludwig Müller, they began with fresh energy. The seminaries had not been officially ordered into being; the ordination candidates, clergy, and presbyteries had themselves urged the "official" Councils of Brethren to open their own seminaries. The young ministers saw such seminaries as proof that the Councils of Brethren took them and their demands seriously, and were prepared to take risks. The students viewed the early primitive conditions in the seminaries as a privilege and believed that an eventual clash with the official church or state authorities would be unavoidable. Thus the formation of the seminaries was marked by the enthusiasm of the "young brethren."

The Old Prussian Seminaries. The Old Prussian Council of Brethren established and maintained five preachers' seminaries. The first was the Reformed seminary in Elberfeld, opened under the Council of Brethren in 1934 and directed by Pastor Hermann Hesse. This was followed in November 1934 by the opening of a seminary in Bielefeld-Sieker under Professor Otto Schmitz. The others opened in 1935: one in Bloestau, East Prussia, under Professor Hans J. Iwand; another in Naumburg, Silesia, under Pastor Dr. Gerhard Gloege; and the third in Pomerania under Bonhoeffer. This third seminary had originally been planned in the Rhineland, and for a while the ordinands had expected to be summoned to Düsseldorf.

All five directors were a good choice. They aroused the interest of young theologians, were respected for their scholarship, and had demonstrated their spirit of determination. The placement of ordinands was decided primarily by their home districts, although each seminary was to include representatives from as many of the Old Prussian Union provinces as possible.

When Bonhoeffer's seminary opened in the summer semester, approximately one hundred ordinands were attending the five seminaries under the oversight of the Old Prussian Council of Brethren. The responsible official in the Council of Brethren was Wilhelm Niesel, who had been a classmate of Bonhoeffer's elder brother at the Gymnasium in Friedrichswerder. Niesel was responsible for equipping, financing, and coordinating the seminaries and for assigning the ordinands.

The members of the Old Prussian Union Council of Brethren took on a great responsibility in opening these five seminaries. After the Dahlem synod declared an emergency law for the church, the majority of ordinands in the churches of the Old Prussian Union had put themselves under the jurisdiction of the Council of Brethren who, they hoped, would train, ordain, and assign them to congregations. They expected challenges, but they also expected the Council of Brethren to provide for them.

But the opening of the five seminaries also marked the period in the church struggle in which the profound estrangement between the "intact" Lutheran churches and the "destroyed" churches of Old Prussia became evident. [The three regional churches (Bavaria, Hannover, and Württemberg) were still unified under their Lutheran bishops; the "destroyed" churches were those in which the German Christians had gain enough power to disrupt the existing order. In the "destroyed" churches, after the Dahlem synod, the Confessing church set up emergency church administrations parallel to the official church hierarchies.] The financial and legal problems faced by the "young brethren" who were being trained and placed according to the Dahlem resolutions were not issues in the intact churches, which continued to provide for their candidates as before. The Councils of Brethren in the "destroyed" churches had to find means where none existed, and to develop completely new forms in an illegal situation. Their candidates had to be supported by voluntary donations. This fine achievement by the Councils of Brethren, however, only isolated them from the other regional churches.

Step by step, the intact churches such as those of Bavaria and Württemberg disassociated themselves from the common resolutions passed in Dahlem—the proclamation of disobedience toward the Reich church government and the declaration of emergency church law. For the intact churches, this had no consequences for their institutional structure. Even if the Councils of Brethren had considered such a retreat, however, they could not have reversed the consequences of the Dahlem resolutions for their churches. They remained responsible for the group of young theologians who had followed the call of Dahlem and all it implied.

After the Barmen synod the Lutheran Council was formed parallel to the government of the Confessing church, thus establishing an advisory body unhampered by the pressures of emergency law. It became one more reason for mutual embittered disclaimers. The members of the Old Prussian Council of Brethren denied the Lutherans the right to use the name "Confessing church," emphasizing that they were only a "confessional movement" or "confessional front." The Lutherans, in turn, castigated their opponents as "Dahlemites"—a name which became a label for "radical fanatic" and was directed especially toward those responsible for the seminaries.

Zingst and Finkenwalde

Although Bonhoeffer had a clear, far-reaching vision of the structure and curriculum of the new institution, its beginning was extremely improvised and inadequate.

As director of the institution, he was employed by the Old Prussian Council of Brethren and remained so until the end of his life, although later he was technically on leave. His stipend was 360 marks a month. His status subsequently protected him from many of the dilemmas faced by the pastors who were employed by the regional church consistory; in 1938, for example, he was not required to swear the oath of loyalty to Hitler.

The Council of Brethren appointed a young pastor from the Rhineland, Wilhelm Rott, as his assistant. Rott was a Barthian influenced by the Reformed tradition of the Rhineland; some regarded his appointment as a sensible step that would counterbalance Bonhoeffer's influence on the ordinands. Unaware of such intentions, Rott was able to make his own mark; he was an independent and responsible element in the seminary's communal life and theological dialogue. This was not easy, for a number of the ordinands were former students of Bonhoeffer's from Berlin and had been members of the Fanö delegation; from the beginning they strengthened the director and his own particular customs. Rott good-naturedly adhered to the principle that "of course things could be done another way."[2] He and Bonhoeffer were far too magnanimous to let themselves be played off against each other. Bonhoeffer used some of Rott's ideas, and Rott introduced him to the works of the Reformed theologian Hermann Kohlbrugge and Pastor Paul Geyser, whose books Bonhoeffer acquired and used.

The majority of students came from Berlin-Brandenburg. Some of them had heard Bonhoeffer's lectures on "Creation and Sin" and Christology, or participated in the seminar on Hegel. They were familiar with the Prebelow and Biesenthal experiments in meditation, and had joined Bonhoeffer in the student forum against Emanuel Hirsch. One of them was Joachim Kanitz, whom the Council of Brethren had summoned from his vacation and ordered to the new seminary because the local police in his parish were waiting to interrogate and perhaps arrest him. Haunted by the thought that he had fled to the peace of the seminary, Kanitz let Bonhoeffer convince him that he could accept the Council of Brethren's decision in good conscience.

Three groups of seminarians came from Pomerania, East Prussia, and the province of Saxony (including author Eberhard Bethge). These students knew nothing about Bonhoeffer, and their provincial outlook colored their anticipation of what lay before them. For the four ordinands from the province of Saxony, Bonhoeffer's seminary was their second attempt to study at a preacher's seminary. At the time of the Dahlem synod they had been called to the Wittenberg seminary, where they had supported the synodal mandate refusing to obey Ludwig Müller's church government. In response the Reich bishop had telegraphed an order for their expulsion from the seminary.

Zingst. A few days elapsed before all twenty-three candidates arrived and had moved into the Zingsthof cabins. The place turned out to be an ideal refuge. A timber-framed house, surrounded by smaller buildings with low thatched roofs, stood only a hundred yards from the beach and the dunes; the whole complex extended as far as the heath. No other farmhouse was visible and the village of Zingst lay a mile or more to the west. In good weather it was possible from the dunes to see Hiddensee to the east and beyond it the island of Rügen. The members of the seminary would have been only too glad to spend the entire summer in Zingst. Whenever the May sun shone warmly enough, the classes adjourned to a hollow among the dunes where they would hold a discussion or perhaps sing a setting for four voices by Josquin des Prés. But on 14 June they had to move out, and the seminary's early days were disrupted by the need to find a fixed abode. Between the time they left Zingst and began again in their permanent home, they spent ten days in youth hostels in Greifswald while an advance group prepared the new quarters.[3]

Finkenwalde. Of all the houses that had been considered, from Lake Constance to the Ziethen Castle near Neuruppin, the final choice was the former estate of the von Katte family, in the small country town of Finkenwalde. Finkenwalde was the first station on the main railway line from Stettin to the east. To the north and west were the waters of the Oder estuary; to the south the land rose toward green beech forests. The estate had been spoiled by the inroads of commercial businesses. The back part of the grounds had been turned into a gravel pit, and the roomy house, which had been used for a private school, had been enlarged by a poorly constructed gymnasium which did, however, offer useful extra rooms. The private school had fallen victim to the National Socialists' disfavor toward such establishments, and a new tenant was wanted for the building. Unattractive as much of it was, its many rooms were perfect for the seminary's needs. As head of the Old Prussian Confessing synod, Westphalian church president Karl Koch rented the house. In Berlin Hermann Ehlers (and later Friedrich Justus Perels) took care of the contractual and tax formalities.

By the time Bonhoeffer gave his first lecture in the almost empty house on 26 June, the advance group had already mailed letters to the Confessing congregations containing the "Ordinands' Humble Request," a poem by Winfried Maechler:

> We want to move everything
> to Finkenwalde near Stettin.
> There stands an empty old estate
> for which we do not have to wait.
> It is in utter disrepair
> with few beds and cupboards there
> standing in the house's hall.
> Therefore it would please us all
> and has become our greatest goal
> to make this great house once more whole.
> Please offer us a little aid;
> we hope that these lines may persuade.
> For in this world, you know, the church
> for every penny needs to search.
> We ask of you just two more things
> Please send all help without any strings
> And hear, dear people, our glad refrain
> that we have not written this in vain . . .[4]

The letter evoked a tremendous response, from both congregations and individual patrons. The church struggle was still at the stage where people wanted to express their sentiments in tangible ways, and the opposition was supported occasionally by wealthy patrons. Martin Niemöller's parish in Dahlem, Günther Harder's congregation in Fehrbellin, Superintendent Onnasch's district in Köslin, and the district of Stolp furnished entire rooms, as did Herr Griebel, the owner of a shipping company in Stettin. As almost no other German preachers' seminary in Germany before or since, Finkenwalde became a living cause for congregations. Letters of thanks followed immediately:

> Dear Herr Councilman Griebel
> Our gratitude is much too feeble
> For your generous thought
> In sending money that we sought.

But additional pleas for money were sent as well:

> . . . how useful is the nicest home
> if there, reading a lengthy tome,
> the student sitting in his room
> has no food to consume?
> This poem, then, is admonition
> Even theologians need nutrition!

The gifts continued over the years. When the harvest thanksgiving was celebrated, boxes of fruit and an enormous joint of meat arrived from the Kleist estates. One March day in 1937 the telephone rang: "This is the freight yard. A live pig has just arrived for Pastor Bonhoeffer." The slaughtering and processing of the animal presented something of a problem, since in those days a special permit was required; somehow that permit was obtained.

Bonhoeffer and many of the ordinands also helped furnish and decorate the house. Two Bechstein grand pianos immediately found a place in the music room and were in constant use. The covers for the chairs were all handmade by Ewald von Kleist-Schmenzin's mother. The sculptor Wilhelm Gross helped the students transform the gymnasium into a chapel using whitewash, packing cases, and coarse cotton, and Gross himself carved the heavy wooden cover of the altar Bible. On the end wall in shining gold letters stood the central phrase "HAPAX," from the Epistle to the Hebrews (9:26-28), "once and for all." The Greek word succinctly expressed the first Christocentric principle confessed in Barmen against the German Christians' false doctrine of revelation in contemporary history. Every week a different series of drawings and etchings from Rembrandt's Bible illustrations was hung in the entrance hall; these came from a large Dutch edition owned by Bonhoeffer. His collection of gramophone records, remarkable for those days, was at everyone's disposal; the rooms often rang with then little-known Negro spirituals such as "Swing Low, Sweet Chariot."

The creation of a working library out of nothing proved more difficult. Its foundation was Bonhoeffer's fine collection of reference books, commentaries, and histories of dogma from Berlin. He also placed the Erlangen edition of Luther, which he had inherited from his great-grandfather von Hase, in the library. His generosity with his most valuable possessions for the benefit of all was a tremendous inspiration. When the police dissolved the seminary two and a half years later, Bonhoeffer's collection of books was scattered; he was never again able to reassemble them all in one place.

Curriculum and Work Methods. The early days were marked by improvisation, transition, a lack of books, and the church struggle. All this might have easily impeded the successful training and work of the first Finkenwalde course. Two factors prevented these distracting influences from gaining the upper hand: the daily routine Bonhoeffer established, and the inspiration offered by his own way of working.

The day began and ended with two long services. In the morning the service was followed by a half-hour meditation, an exercise that was maintained even during the seminary's move, when their only furniture consisted of packing cases and youth hostel bunks. The services did not take place in church but around the ordinary dinner table. They invariably began with a choral psalm and a hymn selected for that day. This was followed by a lesson from the Old Testament, a set verse from a hymn (sung daily for several weeks), a New Testament lesson, a period of extempore prayer, and the recital of the Lord's Prayer. Each service concluded with another set verse from a hymn. Readings from the Psalms and the Scripture took the form of a *lectio continua*, if possible without any omissions, resembling Anglican evensong. Bonhoeffer believed this sequence of readings and prayers was the most natural and suitable form of worship for theologians. Only on Saturdays did he include a sermon, which was usually very direct. The ordinands discovered that he liked to choose hymns such as Tersteegen's "*Kommt, Kinder, lasst uns gehen*," Michael Weisse's "*O ihr alle, die ihr euch im Herrn vereiniget*," and Christian Friedrich Richter's evocative poem, "*Sie wandeln auf Erden und leben im Himmel*."

Bonhoeffer did not look kindly on attempts to evade this daily routine. To avoid the dangers arising from too much proximity during the restless weeks of the move, he asked the ordinands to observe only one rule—never to speak about another ordinand in that person's absence or to tell that person about it afterward when such a thing did happen. The participants learned almost as much from the failure to observe this simple rule, and from the renewed resolution to keep it, as they did from the sermons and exegeses. Bonhoeffer was able to impose this discipline on the seminary because he also left sufficient room for pleasure and outspoken discussions.

Sometimes in fine weather he might suddenly cancel a class and go with his students to the woods or the coast. On Sundays he didn't permit any class work to be done, but organized all kinds of games. When he discovered the inadequacy of his students' literary background he gave them readings from Keller, Stifter, and—very deliberately—Droste-Hülshoff's *Judenbuche* (Jewish Books). When he wanted to introduce the practice of reading aloud during meals, however, there was protest against such a monkish custom. Still, some books were read in this way—C. B. Büchsel's *Erinnerungen aus dem Leben eines Landgeistlichen* (Memoirs from the Life of a Country Pastor) and Agnes von Zahn-Harnack's biography of her father, Adolf von Harnack. But Bonhoeffer's proposal to substitute a light lunch for the heavy German dinner and have the principal meal in the evening met with insurmountable opposition.

His love of making music was truly impressive, whether he was persuaded to perform for the others or was inspired to explore musical areas hitherto unknown to him. His romantic heritage was strongly evident in his playing of Chopin, Brahms, and excerpts from the delightfully stylish *Rosenkavalier*. But he never turned down a request to join in playing one of Bach's concertos for two pianos. While in Finkenwalde he was introduced to what for him was the new world of Schütz, Schein, and Scheidt, and he loved to sing one of the voices in Schütz's duets *Eins bitte ich vom Herren* and *Meister, wir haben die ganze Nacht gearbeitet*.

All this was clearly part of the practice of communal living and the personal training of future preachers; it occurred more through indirect suggestions than explicit words. In England Bonhoeffer had been struck by the pledge given by Baptist students before entering seminary, in which they affirmed their intention to become a preacher and undertook to conduct themselves accordingly. On their second day in Zingst, the students received their first lesson in this. A request arrived from the kitchen for help with the washing up, but there were no immediate volunteers. Without saying a word Bonhoeffer rose from the table, disappeared into the kitchen, and refused to let in the others who hurried to follow him. Afterward he rejoined the students on the beach but made no comment. And in Finkenwalde many a student was to discover with shame that someone else had made his bed in the big dormitory.

Bonhoeffer's work habits were especially remarkable. He accomplished in two or three hours what to someone else would have seemed a normal day's work. Even during the most turbulent periods of his life he never gave up his leisure time. His desk was far from being a model of tidiness; it was not nearly big enough and had only two small pigeonholes. But he wouldn't

have known what to do with more room, for he had no use for card index-
es and colored pencils. He had an excellent memory and relied upon it. He
was also a very fast reader, and his only notes were an occasional line or question mark written in the margin with a blunt pencil. For teaching or discussion, however, he did take notes from his readings.

While he was in Finkenwalde exegetical literature was a priority. However debatable his "theological exegesis" of that time appears today, he did not
fail to keep up with contemporary scholarship or the relatively new method
of Kittel's *Dictionary of the New Testament*. In fact, he was careful to keep up
with current theological knowledge. In addition to his exegetical readings, he
concerned himself primarily with the Reformation fathers and with confessional writings. He showed little interest in church history. While he could
absorb an enormous amount, he seldom reproduced what he read undigest-
ed. His own questions and conclusions led him to sift it and brilliantly use it
for his own purposes. He had confidence in his ability to recognize what was
essential, yet he could listen objectively to the specialist's arguments. When
these proved valid, he would approach his subject from this new angle.

He never worked during the night and seldom in the evenings. When he
had to preach or lecture, he needed only a few hours of complete seclusion
to write a completed text. At first sight his manuscripts appear as untidy as
his writing desk, but they actually contain full texts with no gaps or omissions. Even when Bonhoeffer was not considering publication, his manuscripts could have been sent to the press virtually as they were written. He
was among those who write down what they have already thought out, not
one of those whose thoughts are taken further by the process of writing. This
does not mean that he made no preliminary notes; many such notes still
exist, but they are in a state of disorder that is far from pedantic. He only sat
down to write when he knew what his goal was going to be. This contributed
to the taut style in his books. He refused to revise them after they had been
printed; if he went over a work again it was only as a preliminary to something else. It was as though he already realized that his days were numbered
and too few.

Bonhoeffer's pace, and his ability to interrupt work for play without
ever falling behind, occasionally made him unfair toward others who were
toiling night and day to prepare for some examination. But he could also
make them discover resources within themselves that they had never previously suspected.

Discussion Evenings. One evening a week was devoted to the discussion of
current issues; the politics of the day supplied more than enough subject

matter. Despite its seclusion, the seminary community could not withdraw from the political situation.

The new law affecting military service went into effect on 1 May 1935.[5] In a ceremony at Tempelhof Field in Berlin in the midst of an unseasonable blizzard, Hitler proclaimed Germany's rebirth as a military power. The ordinands in Zingst listened with excitement to his speech on the radio, wondering when it would be their turn to put on the uniform. Most of them looked forward to it, unaware of their director's feelings on the subject. The number of conscientious objectors in the Evangelical church at that time could have been counted on the fingers of one hand. Even within the Confessing church the Lutheran view of military service was uncontested. Hitler's new move to "remove the shame of Versailles" met with general approval. Even those ordinands who had been among the seven hundred arrested in March 1935 after a celebrated Sunday proclamation ("Against Idolatry") viewed the revival of the "military ethos" as a matter of course, and some of them volunteered for military service soon thereafter. "All we can feel toward the state is an unhappy love that does not ask to be requited or recognized . . . but if all goes well, 1 November will see me in uniform. . . ."[6] At the time there was even a widespread desire in the Confessing church to provide as many commissioned reservists from its own ranks as possible, and the church's sympathizers in the state bureaucracy agreed with this. To some degree it showed a genuine desire to participate, but there was also a calculated desire to prove that the church opposition was truly patriotic, reliable, and honorable, despite its detractors in the Party and the German Christians. The status of officer still enjoyed undiminished respect.

A casual question raised by Bonhoeffer during Hitler's speech suddenly showed the unsuspecting students that his views on the subject were quite different from their own. This triggered a heated argument; as a result the evening discussions had to begin with the subject of pacifism. The majority of the students completely rejected his suggestion that conscientious objection was something a Christian should consider, and cheerfully endorsed the decision reached by their ethical theologians and church leaders. When Bonhoeffer's friend, the scientist Herbert Jehle, came to the seminary on a visit, they accused him of theological naïveté because of his pacifism. Gradually, however, the climate of these discussions changed as the ordinands came to realize that their director was not in the least fanatical about the matter. The most he required of them, if he could not gain their sympathy for this possible mode of Christian behavior, was to respect anyone who adopted it in the belief that he was complying with Christ's commandment. Far from seeking to impose a universal doctrine of non-violence, he merely sought personally to believe and obey Jesus' difficult command.

Word spread through church circles, however, that Bonhoeffer's opinion on this issue differed from that of most people. This led to the appearance in Finkenwalde of Dr. Hermann Stöhr of Stettin, secretary of the German Fellowship of Reconciliation, who also worked on behalf of the World Alliance for Promoting International Friendship through the Churches. His pacifism was more strongly rooted in the principle of total disarmament than was Bonhoeffer's, but this did not bother Bonhoeffer, who defended Stöhr. The two never worked closely together, however, because Bonhoeffer found Stöhr indifferent to questions involving the Confessing church, and believed that Stöhr should not be in charge of arrangements for ecumenical visitors. Bonhoeffer refused to support Stöhr's ecumenical work in Stettin.[7] He was all the more distressed in 1939 when Stöhr was prosecuted by the military authorities and, despite all the attempts to save him, was executed as a conscientious objector.[8]

The news of Karl Barth's expulsion from Germany led to heated discussion about the question of the loyalty oath. In vain, Barth had declared his willingness to take the civil service oath if he could add the phrase, "insofar as I can responsibly do so as a Christian." As the Reich Confessing synod in Augsburg (4–6 June 1935) approached, the question as to whether the Confessing church would take up the cause of the "political" Barth became more urgent. Would it call him to a teaching position at one of the church seminaries or keep its distance and show relief at Barth's departure? Anticipating what would happen, Bonhoeffer had vigorously taken a position even before he left London. In a letter to president Koch on 1 December 1934 he had written:

> Should the church government [i.e., the emergency bodies formed by the national synod of Dahlem] fail to make any gesture of sympathy or solidarity with Barth's cause, this would most seriously jeopardize the interest that the ecumenical movement has shown till now in the Confessing church. People would get the impression that the Confessing church has departed from its original and true course, and will be alienated by such a stance. I know that the eyes of the entire Protestant world are at the moment focused upon the decision of the new church government and I feel it my responsibility to let you know this.[9]

In the weeks preceding the Augsburg national synod, there were numerous intrigues within the "Confessing front" designed to prevent Karl Barth from attending the synod and thus compromising it. Even some of the candidates at the seminary argued about whether Barth's fight against the oath really constituted a Christian question with which the church should concern itself, or whether it was "merely" political and hence not a matter for the church at all—as many confessional people maintained. Bonhoeffer could persuade his students more on this issue than on the question of pacifism. When Barth finally accepted an appointment in Basel on 25 June, he wrote a farewell letter to Pastor Hermann Hesse; a copy was sent to Bonhoeffer. The ordinands duplicated the letter and sent it to all their friends, not in the hope of reversing what had happened, but because its final passage expressed something that had troubled both Barth and Bonhoeffer for some time: the fact that the Confessing church "has as yet shown no sympathy for the millions who are suffering injustice. It has not once spoken out on the most simple matters of public integrity. And if and when it does speak, it is always on its own behalf."[10]

Spiritual Center. Soon the entire Evangelical church was buzzing with rumors about the terrible heresies in Finkenwalde—Catholic practices, enthusiastic pacifist activities, and radical fanaticism. But Finkenwalde attracted more than it repelled, drawing visitors who knew that they would hear questions discussed there which had too long remained unasked. Bonhoeffer found it crucial that the housemother, Erna Struwe, and the candidates display generous hospitality; indeed, that had been one of the reasons for choosing Finkenwalde with its many rooms.

1. One visitor who came while they were still far away in Zingst was, as a candidate wrote, "a provincial councilman who had been dismissed, and whose wife sang Bach and Frank very well." It was Theodor Steltzer. Bonhoeffer liked his political attitudes better than his Berneuchen convictions. (The Berneuchen movement sought to revive old church liturgies and introduce a Protestant mass.) Other guests included the sculptor Wilhelm Gross, Walter Dress, Hans von Dohnanyi, and parliamentary president Hermann Ehlers. Representatives from the other preachers' seminaries also visited Finkenwalde to see if there was any truth to the rumors.

2. Students from Greifswald, finding their own faculty deficient in following the clear lines laid down by the Dahlem synod, asked the seminary to arrange informal study sessions that would stimulate and support them, both theologically and in church politics. The Finkenwalde group undertook this work in Greifswald, a step which the university faculty there viewed as an infringement of its territory. Relations were already considerably strained when Bonhoeffer wrote to the council of the Old Prussian Union, asking to be assigned to work regularly among the Greifswald students:

> In cooperation with, but at the same time as a supplement to the work of
> the professors, who as teachers of the church have to play the chief part in
> this work, the (Finkenwalde) community will . . . prevent the drifting back
> to the consistory, by regular work among the young theologians of Greif-
> swald. . . . Finally they are to try to help in the advancement of a fraterni-
> ty of students in Greifswald, which has had so promising a beginning.[11]

The first meeting in Finkenwalde with this student group was led by
Gerhard Krause; Bonhoeffer lectured for the first time on his interpretation
of the Psalms.[12] This had become necessary for the entire seminar because
its daily and detailed reading of the Psalms—unusual within the German
Evangelical tradition—had raised a number of questions.

3. Led by Günter Gesch and Gerhard Krause, the Pomeranian Brotherhood of younger Confessing preachers and ministers liked to hold its conferences in Finkenwalde. During their first conference Bonhoeffer gave a
three-day Bible study on King David that provoked fervent disagreement
from the Old Testament scholars.[13] He spoke regularly at these conferences;
as time went on he increasingly emphasized the need to observe the decisions and resolutions made in Barmen and Dahlem.

4. Neighboring parishes also liked to hold their pastoral conferences in
the seminary until around 1936, when they began to view the Finkenwalde
group's forthright positions as so disruptive that they moved their meetings
elsewhere. These parish meetings were replaced by voluntary working associations of pastors, who wished to hold discussions and pursue the course
they had begun under Bonhoeffer's guidance.

5. In 1934 "Brotherhoods" of young Confessing theologians formed in
every church province; in 1935 these merged to form the "Reich Brotherhood
of Young Theologians." Westphalian pastor Hans Thimme planned a meeting of representatives from all the regional churches that would reflect on the
internal rules of the Brotherhoods and the disintegration of these groups,
which was already felt in 1935. Bonhoeffer met Thimme at a provincial conference in Hauteroda, Saxony, and offered Finkenwalde as a site for the meeting. Thimme replied that they would "all welcome being able to talk about
brotherhood in a place where brotherhood is alive."[14] Bonhoeffer responded
to the legitimate spiritual expectation: "There is certainly no place that you
could gratify so much with your meeting there as with us . . . the area around
the seminary is a lovely forest and water, with a boat!"[15] This meeting was
postponed for the end of the year due to scheduling problems. By that time
the church committees that had been established had created such confusion
and dissent within the Reich Brotherhood that the plan failed.

Still, the Finkenwalde experiment aroused much interest. It had obviously revealed a weak point in German Protestantism. An emissary from the Bielefeld seminary expressed his thanks in the visitors' book for "the opportunity of seeing the work and the—so very different—way of life of the brotherhood."

Pomerania. Locating the preachers' seminary in Finkenwalde planted Bonhoeffer in an unfamiliar milieu for the urbanite who had lived in the academic Grunewald neighborhood. He discovered a confident and deeply rooted church life, often supported by the independent nobility of the estates, and he was pleasantly surprised to find that some elements of the Pomeranian revivalist movement still survived. Sometimes, however, when necessary decisions had to be reached in church politics, he found the slow pace of the rural province irritating. He made enduring friendships in Pomerania; these connections would bring out Bonhoeffer's inherent conservatism during the course of the common political struggle. Here, too, he met his future fiancée.

Up to that point Bonhoeffer knew little about the Pomeranian church. It had not entered his range of vision during the struggles of 1933–1934. The initial location in Zingst was a coincidence due solely to the remoteness of the area. In Zingst he had met a neutral Pomeranian pastor who had little sympathy for the issues that were moving his new temporary wards. Still, he allowed Bonhoeffer to preach the first sermon on Exaudi Sunday, on Psalm 42.[16] The candidates augmented the church choir.

By the time the seminary opened in Zingst, Pomerania had long since concluded a successful campaign against its inept German Christian bishop, Karl Thom, who had assumed the title "bishop of Cammin." A provincial Confessing church Council of Brethren had been established under the leadership of Reinhold von Thadden. It was difficult to carry out the measures based on the Barmen and Dahlem resolutions because the people of Pomerania had always prided themselves on their "Lutheranism." Even under the leadership of "Dahlemite" Pomeranians, there was almost universal acceptance for the viewpoint Althaus and Elert had represented in the Erlangen statement. Their criticism that the Barmen theses had erred in its Barthian rejection of "original revelation" in creation and history met with widespread agreement; this made Bonhoeffer seem isolated and radical.

Thus he immediately found himself among the small minority that did not share the widespread satisfaction over the outcome of the Augsburg Confessing synod (2–4 June 1935). Although the synod apparently succeeded in consolidating the entire Confessing church, and had passed a useful resolution on the question of training, Bonhoeffer distrusted its unanimity. He did not see the Barth affair as trivial, but as symptomatic; and he found the Augsburg synod guilty of four omissions.[17] First, it had failed to say anything positive about the freedom of the church; second, it had not mentioned the lie contained in paragraph 24 of the National Socialist Party program (on "positive Christianity"); third, it had remained silent on the Jewish question (he was informed in advance about the preparation of the Nuremberg Laws by his brother-in-law, Hans von Dohnanyi); and fourth, nothing had been said about the military oath Christians could not take without qualification, after the rejection of Barth's interpretation of the civil service oath. It seemed all too obvious to Bonhoeffer that the readiness to hold firm to the Dahlem resolutions was waning, and the fear of showing any opposition toward the state was growing. He was all the more relieved when Martin Niemöller called for renewed determination, and circulated his manifesto "To Our Brethren in the Ministry" for signatures.[18] The manifesto appeared on 30 July 1935 and contained the names of Pomeranians such as Johannes Bartelt, Eberhard Baumann, and Heinrich Rendtorff. The latter's signature carried special weight, for in 1933 he had supported the other side. Bonhoeffer wrote to Niemöller:

> I am delighted that you have again given the signal for the attack. . . . I think the time has come to form an Emergency League within the Emergency League, and we shall have to find a very different interpretation of Matt. 22: 21 ["Render unto Caesar the things that are Caesar's, and to God the things that are God's"] from the one that prevails now. I hope we have now got to the stage of speaking out and deciding, and if no one else speaks out, I shall certainly give voice to this important matter. I really believe that you've chosen the right moment, and for this I am most thankful. The whole seminary, myself included, sends you warmest regards. . . .[19]

The relationship to the state, whose decrees for law and order had only made things more confused, had reached a point where Bonhoeffer now foresaw a parting of the ways. It was no longer the Reich bishop's decrees but the state's laws that would have to be combated.

Hence it is not surprising that the first encounters between Bonhoeffer's seminary and other centers in Pomerania were mixed. Their different approaches were underscored by the ordinands' nonchalance and their extreme youthfulness. During the ten-day interval between Zingst and Finkenwalde, Bonhoeffer and his seminarians spent some time in Greifswald, a visit that did not restore harmony in any way; from there they moved on to Stettin to attend the third Pomeranian Confessing synod.

1. The visit to Greifswald had been planned to introduce the students to the theological faculty, and to enable them to do some missionary work in the town. The city church superintendent, K. von Scheven, made the cathedral available for them. Von Scheven was still a member of the Pomeranian Confessing synod, although six months later he became head of the Pomeranian church committee (the neutral official governing body). Rudolf Hermann, the leading theologian on the faculty in Greifswald, had participated in the Barmen and Dahlem synods. Now, however, he did not hide his fear that the Dahlem decisions and their consequences could lead to a bad spirit of new educational legalism. Professor H. W. Beyer, the "Spiritual Minister" in the winter of 1933, taught church history, and was aware of the role Bonhoeffer had played in Sofia and Wittenberg. Otto Haendler, who lectured on practical theology, found little favor among the Finkenwalde group due to his Berneuchen tendencies. Bonhoeffer had a long visit with Rudolf Hermann, and the candidates spent an evening with him in an open debate.

The days spent in Greifswald resembled a preliminary skirmish that set the course for future disputes more than an amicable visit among allies. When, at one of the student gatherings, a member of the seminary shouted, "We're here to get something done!" he may have coined a slogan for Finkenwalde; but his remarks evoked more disapproval than sympathy from the faculty.

2. The Greifswald visit was immediately followed by the third Pomeranian Confessing synod, which convened in H. Rendtorff's Wartburg church in Stettin from 20 to 22 June. The latest developments had been the Reich Ministry of Church Affairs' establishment of Legislative Offices and finance departments in the churches; the ramifications of this were still confusing and unpredictable. Joachim Beckmann from Düsseldorf gave the keynote address. The synod passed a statement by the young theologians that soberly declared:

> Whereas in most of the Reich the overwhelming majority of the new theological generation is in the ranks of the Confessing church, most of the younger theologians in Pomerania have avoided a clear decision up to now. This is due to the apparent peace within the churches of our province and the relatively small evidence of German Christian heresy. . . .[20]

The appearance of the Finkenwalde seminary was one of the highlights of the synod. When church president Koch announced the decision to buy the house at Finkenwalde "eight of the church districts present spontaneously offered each to furnish a room" (synod report).

The synod brought Bonhoeffer into contact with the Pomeranian Council of Brethren for the first time. He met Eberhard Baumann, the Reformed pastor in Stettin, and Stefanie von Mackensen, wife of the vice president of Pomerania and the tireless manager of the Council of Brethren's office; he particularly enjoyed working with both of them. From that point on the council's office on Pölitzer Strasse was frequently visited by impatient Finkenwalde candidates who were either protesting some move by the Council of Brethren or offering their services to one of the Confessing congregations.

Contacts with local churches proved less fruitful to Bonhoeffer than his encounters with the landed aristocracy of Pomerania. These had begun with the Finkenwalde letters asking for contributions. Bonhoeffer made new friends when he had to call on the local patron in his attempt to find a parish position for one of his students. Depending on one's viewpoint, the system of patronage on these landed estates was not purely an anachronistic nuisance; it proved to be an enormous support for the Councils of Brethren when they were able to benefit from the patron's independent right to name the local pastor. There were some patrons who thought nothing of going over the heads of the church consistorial authorities. As president of the Confessing synod, Reinhold von Thadden helped Bonhoeffer make the contacts he needed.

In this way Bonhoeffer made the acquaintance of families with whom he maintained close ties even after Finkenwalde was closed—the Kleist-Retzows of Kieckow, Ewald von Kleist of Schmenzin, the Bismarcks of Lasbeck, and finally the Wedemeyers of Pätzig. Frau von Wedemeyer and Frau von Bismarck were sisters of von Kleist-Retzow of Kieckow. Their widowed mother, Ruth von Kleist-Retzow, had retired to the estate of Klein-Krössin near Kieckow, but still possessed a flat in Stettin during the time the seminary was in Finkenwalde; this enabled her grandchildren from Kieckow, Lasbeck, and Pätzig to attend school in the provincial capital. She became a resolute champion of the seminary's needs, and when, in the autumn of 1935, regular services began to be held in Finkenwalde's emergency chapel she made a habit of driving out to attend them with some of her grandchildren.

Ruth von Kleist-Retzow, a daughter of Count Zedlitz of Breslau, was a remarkable woman. Throughout her life she was sympathetic toward movements that brought fresh life to the church, and even in her old age she read every new book written by Karl Barth. She had a good sense for quality and substance, and never hesitated to say exactly what she thought, which often led her to speak with refreshing forthrightness of this or that cleric's insidious lack of backbone, or perhaps his cloying tone. Bonhoeffer's arrival in the Stettin area introduced a new spiritual stimulus into her life, and she promoted his interests with every means at her disposal. With feminine candor she would remind patrons of their duties and would persist until they had really done something to help. She was thrilled by the progress of Bonhoeffer's book *Discipleship*, and was insatiable in her thirst for answers. Initially Bonhoeffer was almost alarmed by her torrent of questions and wished that his ordinands might share something of her ardor. As time went on he began to spend more of his holidays at Klein-Krössin or with Hans-Jürgen von Kleist-Retzow at Kieckow. Between 1935 and 1937 the Kleist-Retzow grandchildren frequently attended services in Finkenwalde, afterward enjoying games of table tennis in the garden with the ordinands. In 1938 their grandmother—perhaps with the ulterior motive of attending some of the classes herself—was able to persuade Bonhoeffer to prepare three of the children for confirmation. The dissolution of Finkenwalde interrupted this plan and occasionally Albrecht Schönherr had to stand in for Bonhoeffer; Bonhoeffer, however, was able to conduct the final class at Kieckow, where he also confirmed his pupils.[21] Among those who sometimes attended services in Finkenwalde were Frau von Kleist's granddaughters, Ruth-Alice and Maria von Wedemeyer, as well as Ruth's fiancé Klaus von Bismarck. Years later, after two of the boys he had confirmed had already been killed in active duty, Bonhoeffer encountered Maria von Wedermeyer again in Klein-Krössin. By the time their engagement was announced Bonhoeffer was in Tegel prison. Ruth von Kleist-Retzow sent him the biography of her father-in-law, Hans von Kleist-Retzow (1814–1892), once president of the Rhineland and Bismarck's pugnacious opponent.[22] On the flyleaf she wrote:

> To my dear Dietrich, to whom I owe some of the most important insights of my life. I am happy to send you this book on the day when you have definitely become a member of our family. The man who is its subject has left a tangible blessing behind him, and one in which you are now included. Klein-Krössin (Kieckow), 24 June 1943.

In these great houses of Pomerania, Bonhoeffer encountered a society which, while somewhat familiar to him, was also strange in many ways. There were few close ties at that time between the academic circles in Grunewald and the farming, political, and military circles of the landed aristocracy. For the Junkers of Pomerania, Bonhoeffer, as someone who did not seek to conceal his pacifist tendencies, was an unusual friend. The close rapport that quickly grew between Bonhoeffer and the Kleists had both personal and historical grounds. The hospitality, manners, and style of life Bonhoeffer encountered in Pomerania were very similar to that in his own home. The main difference was in how feelings and inclinations were expressed. The Kleists were emotional and direct; the Bonhoeffers were restrained, and only the practiced eye could detect the strong feelings behind their ordinary, terse, matter-of-fact gestures. What really broke down their mutual reserve, however, was that both sides, when confronted by the demands of their era, were prepared to risk their inherited privileges, in politics or in the church. The dividing line that ran through the academic world of Grunewald and that of the Junkers was the question of the meaning and readiness to become engaged for what was right. In this way the minorities in these two worlds discovered each other.

The Province of Saxony. The period in Finkenwalde provided Bonhoeffer with another friendship that fell outside his direct area of responsibility. Bonhoeffer's ordinands from Saxony had persuaded him to attend the conference of their fellowship in Hauteroda at the end of August 1935, after a last-minute cancellation by Hans Asmussen. The Confessing church in Magdeburg knew nothing at all about the young theologian and had strong misgivings about this "stand-in." He was to introduce the subject "The Contemporary Interpretation of New Testament Texts."[23] Bonhoeffer's appearance there was very successful; as a result he continued to help in Saxony as long as circumstances allowed him to do so.

This was where he met Wolfgang Staemmler, the mentor of the young Confessing theologians in the province of Saxony. In Staemmler he found a man with a rare facility for meeting him on his own ground, someone who also possessed biblical insight and was willing to translate what he heard into concrete action. Staemmler had a disarming, almost childlike directness; he demanded much of his charges and had no patience for self-pity when the church of Christ was at stake. Bonhoeffer was similar, if perhaps somewhat more reserved and aristocratic. From the very first the two men agreed that it was their responsibility to demand sacrifice and self-denial of the young theologians. It was a determination that was remarkably scarce among the leaders of the Confessing church.

After this first encounter Bonhoeffer never turned down a request from Staemmler's province. One factor was certainly that the heartfelt echo he found in Staemmler came from a region renowned for its lack of religiosity. Bonhoeffer also met with sympathy here for his plans for a community; the questions people posed about his experience in meditation were not inquisitory but full of expectation.[24] Staemmler entrusted one of his candidates to Bonhoeffer as the community was about to be founded. This didn't prevent arguments between the two men about what kind of activity in the vacant pastorate was right or wrong.

The Syllabus

Bonhoeffer's seminary syllabus did not appear particularly unusual. Homiletics and catechetical studies, pastoral care and liturgical studies, lectures on church, ministry, and community—these were part of any German preachers' seminary. Only one theme distinguished Bonhoeffer's seminary from the rest for the first two and a half years: the series of lectures on discipleship. After only a few hours newcomers realized that this was the heart of everything, and they realized they were witnessing a theological event that would stimulate every area of their professional life.

Wilhelm Rott was responsible for the catechetical section and the work on the Heidelberg Catechism. Little attention was paid to liturgical studies, although the seminary experimented with liturgy and tried out Asmussen's suggestions for liturgical singing.[25] From his previous studies of the Psalter, Bonhoeffer had retained a real interest in liturgical problems, but this area had fallen victim to the tone of the times. The indifference of most liturgists toward church politics, particularly those in the Berneuchen movement, made them suspect to the Confessing church and they were often judged harshly. "Only he who cries out for the Jews can sing the Gregorian chant," Bonhoeffer once remarked to his ordinands in this connection.[26] Thus there was no special "teaching" of liturgy at Finkenwalde, although Bonhoeffer conveyed an instinctive sense for the content of worship. He could spend entire homiletics classes on the inner reasons for right speech and action in worship, and he made very explicit statements about congregational devotions and about singing and reading in "communal life."[27] This was not the result of thorough liturgical research, however; it emerged from a genuine theology and the practice of prayer.

Homiletics. Bonhoeffer sometimes entrusted the discussion of sermons to his assistant, but the actual teaching of homiletics he always reserved for himself.

It initially seemed strange to his students that their sermons, however hesitant and inadequate, were treated in all seriousness as the expression of the true and living voice of Christ. Nothing, insisted Bonhoeffer, is more concrete than the real voice of Christ speaking in the sermon. He adhered strictly to this principle with regard to any sermon preached in the worship service. It was to be listened to in all humility, not analyzed. The only sermons he allowed to be discussed were those that were read aloud, never those that had been delivered before a congregation. On rare occasions he might say a word in private about a sermon that had been preached. Once, when Erich Klapproth read a sermon aloud during the class, he had no sooner finished than Bonhoeffer dismissed the class because he felt that at that moment a critical analysis would be inopportune. He devoted attention to problems of method and form, of course, but nothing was as chastening as Bonhoeffer's own method of listening to sermons. He himself demonstrated daily what he required in the way of expression, taste, and imagination. Thus homiletics began with the most difficult lesson of all—one's own listening to sermons.

Earlier Bonhoeffer had searched desperately to make the act of proclamation concrete and to explore the realm of preaching. Later he would ask whether our generation understood at all the essential and concrete message of the Gospel, in the words passed down to us. In Finkenwalde, however, it all came down to certainty: the Gospel of mercy is concrete and imperious without any additions or omissions. Of course this certain word is embedded in the existence of those who speak it, and this may be credible or unreliable. But prayer and meditation can do something for credibility. Thus there is a special chapter in the lectures on homiletics concerning the pastor and the Bible, divided into three parts: the scripture from the pulpit, the scripture on the desk, and the scripture on the kneeling bench.[28]

In 1932 he had said that a good sermon should be like a lovely red apple which is held out to a child with the question "Would you like it?" Now he continued this train of thought: "Thus we must be able to speak about our faith so that hands will be stretched out toward us faster than we can fill them."[29] But whereas he had then used the conditional "should," he did not do so now. He no longer yearned for a truly evangelical sermon or intimidated his ordinands by setting his sights impossibly high. On the contrary, their confidence grew with every lecture because of his insistence that the preacher already has the red apple and gives it out. Therefore, he said: "Do not try to make the Bible relevant. Its relevance is axiomatic. . . . Do not defend God's Word, but testify to it. . . . Trust to the Word. It is a ship loaded to the very limits of its capacity!"[30]

Bonhoeffer had difficulty persuading his ordinands that there was more to preaching than the reasonable but useless pattern of an explication followed by an application. In the very first class discussion arose after an ordinand who had been taught by Karl Heim passionately advocated the need for concrete "application." Bonhoeffer allowed two of the students to address the topic and then, as was his method, posed his own theses for discussion: God alone is concrete . . . the concrete situation is the substance within which the Word of God speaks; it is the object, not the subject, of concretion.[31]

Bonhoeffer's understanding of the sermon was based on his Lutheran Christology. In the first seminary course in 1935 he still saw the sermon as grounded in ecclesiology: the sermon has its "causality and its finality" in the church.[32] The church preaches nothing but the church. Preaching exists because the church exists—and people preach in order that the church shall exist.[33] In the second Finkenwalde course, without revoking that argument, he omitted this lecture and replaced it with one about the roots of the sermon being grounded in the incarnation: The word of the sermon is Christ accepting and bearing human nature. It is not a new incarnation, but the Incarnate One who bears the sins of the world. The word of the sermon seeks nothing more than to accept human beings. The word of the Bible assumes form as a sermon; thus it goes out to the congregation in order to bear it. The preacher must permit this autonomous outgoing of the Word toward the congregation to occur and not hinder it.[34] Luther's hypostatization of the "Word" was taken up by Bonhoeffer as *sacramentum verbi* in such a way that to other confessions and denominations it seemed strange and difficult to realize.[35]

Nevertheless, Bonhoeffer's homiletics lectures were extremely practical and full of useful advice: write your sermon in daylight; do not write it all at once; "in Christ" there is no room for conditional clauses; the first minutes on the pulpit are the most favorable, so do not waste them with generalities but confront the congregation straight off with the core of the matter; extemporaneous preaching can be done by anyone who really knows the Bible.[36] These were homiletical lessons that few ordinands elsewhere had the opportunity of hearing, whether in Berlin, Halle, or Greifswald. There were few students who did not return to their preaching and their congregations changed and happier. And there were few who did not grow in confidence and determination to do things and demand things of others, or who were not convinced that the freshness of their sermons depended on their view of Scripture as an end in itself and their belief in what it offered. It was both the strength and the weakness of these homiletics that were so precisely what was called for during the 1930s.

Bonhoeffer fought against regaining the pulpit's distinctive independence by confusing it with the academic lectern. He respected the value of the academy and recognized its responsibility to serve as a corrective to the sermon—but it never made the pulpit superfluous. His own sermons from those years were startling in their directness; they made things clear and they made demands. He did not look for the assistance of new communication media or the refinements of interpretation. At that time he knew just what he wanted—and he wanted what he knew.

Ministry and Church. The series of lectures on "The Ministry and the Church" did not offer a positivistic study of churches of that age, but dealt with the most burning questions of the time.[37] Each dogmatic article was removed from its context of past controversies and became a contemporary existential argument against the German Christian solutions of ecclesio-logical problems. In the second half of the semester the lectures followed the ecclesio-theological tendency of that era by turning to the study and inter-pretation of the confessions.[38] These were largely unfamiliar to the ordinands of 1935, nor had they formed a part of Bonhoeffer's own studies in Berlin.

Thus during the 1935 summer term Bonhoeffer began by considering a few of the general problems that were central to the controversy of that time, going on to demonstrate that the decisions against the German Christians and their neutral henchmen were grounded in the confessional writings. Today it is difficult to convey the excitement of those classes.

1. The lectures on "The Ministry and the Church" began with a discussion of constitutional and legal problems. Two years of struggle had familiarized the ordinands with the German Christians' remarkable thesis that constitutional questions did not affect the essence of the church. They based their intervention within the church upon this respectable premise, put forward by legal scholar Rudolf Sohm. This meant that the ordinands had to learn to deduce an opposite view from their understanding of the visible church. On the issue of the church's legal authority Bonhoeffer taught that this could not be possessed externally, but only internally in the form of church discipline over its own members. Externally all the church could do was confess and suffer. In 1934 and 1935 it was quite common for Confessing ministers to bring actions against new church governments before the civil courts; the ministers were still winning such cases. This used to delight the ordinands; Bonhoeffer was more skeptical and attached little value to the lawsuits beyond their capacity to create "a better-informed republic from a badly informed republic."

2. The lecture on church schism and reunification—the substance of the confession—proved equally exciting and topical.[39] While still in Zingst,

Bonhoeffer had already been developing the theses upon which he based his articles on the ecumenical movement[40] and on church relations.[41] Here he investigated the process by which the differences in opinion intensified to become "schismatic differences," leading to a *status confessionis*, as well as the reverse process by which schismatic differences diminish until they are nothing more than differences between schools of opinion,[42] a process which must have become evident to everyone in the common confession affirmed by Lutheran and Reformed Protestants in Barmen. He found evidence to support this distinction in the Apology of the Augsburg Confession Article VII, according to which the early church fathers "sometimes divided up the ground for straw or hay, but for all that did not seek to destroy the ground." Thus Bonhoeffer maintained that the church must leave room for bad theologies, and that the better ones must not be allowed to expel the worse. This brought him back to the Smalcald Articles that he discussed in greater detail. In this context he noted the particular ecumenical openness of the Lutheran confession because it saw and recognized as the very essence of its teaching the insistence on atonement. This excluded all possibility of its clinging to orthodoxy, for to do so would be to teach the very opposite of what was implied in its essence. It seems strange that for so many years ecumenical discussion ignored this viewpoint, while the confessional problem was becoming ever more explosive. It did not make use of the distinction Bonhoeffer believed could preserve both the seriousness of the confession and the possibility of ecumenical progress. Bonhoeffer won his conceptual recommendations from the oppressive situation of the times and the newly awakened desire to grasp the process of the Reformation confessions.

3. In his lecture on the relationship between the ministry and the congregation he touched on the question of apostolic succession; this appears to be the only time he ever did so.[43] Despite his time in England and his ecumenical experience, he had never considered this article very important in the interchurch disputes among continental European Protestants. The Anglicans had not arrived at the point of expressing this loudly in a conditional sense. Bonhoeffer only mentioned apostolic succession incidentally, as one understanding of the ministry that assures its priority over the congregation, based upon the same premise that Christ created the ministry and the latter created the congregation—as opposed to the thesis that the congregation appoints the ministry. Bonhoeffer criticized this on the ground that it postulated history, in the sense of uninterrupted continuity, as the mediator of the means and effectiveness of grace and, at the same time, turned the true proposition "no congregation without a ministry" into the false proposition "the ministry creates the congregation." Bonhoeffer's own

view was that grace derived only from "conformity to the Scripture" and not from the succession within the ministry. The Anglican doctrine and practice of apostolic succession was also not mentioned in the section of Barth's *Dogmatics* that dealt with the problem of succession.[44]

4. Bonhoeffer, however, did not hold the congregationalist doctrine that deduced from the true proposition that the ministry exists for the congregation the false proposition that it exists through the congregation. His thesis stood between the Roman, Orthodox, and Anglican viewpoint on the one hand and the congregationalist on the other: the ministry comes neither before nor after, neither above nor beneath the congregation, but within and together with it. One is not the subject of the other—the subject of both is the Holy Spirit—nor is one the object of the other, for that would mean that the office of ministry was at the mercy of the communal spirit or, alternatively, that the congregation was deprived of its right to judge doctrine. By this means Bonhoeffer sought to prevent any contradiction between the ministry and the priesthood of all believers.

5. A discussion of the three classical grounds for defrocking a priest—doctrine, conduct, and gifts—was of immediate relevant concern, both because of the Dahlem declaration and its implications for Ludwig Müller, and because of the impending expulsion of the non-Aryan clergy.[45] Bonhoeffer declared expulsion on grounds of false doctrine to be the *duty* of the congregation and expulsion on grounds of conduct to be the *right* of the congregation. What grounds, however, applied in the case of "gifts"? Here it became difficult. Bonhoeffer posed the dilemma of that era to his seminar: "Can the Aryan clause be justified on the basis of the requirement that a pastor must qualify as a suitable holder of office, not only by doctrine and conduct, but also by having the necessary gifts?"[46] Bonhoeffer had already stated his views on this burning question publicly and clearly in 1933. The argument he now put forward in the closed circle of his ordinands ran as follows: Where gifts are concerned the minister is not suspended for the sake of the Gospel, as in the case of false doctrine, nor because of public offense, as in the case of conduct but, if at all, only "for the sake of the congregation's weakness." Where this is the case it should not be described as "removal from office." The argument based on the weakness of the congregation can apply only to the individual, isolated case where perhaps resignation from the ministry, but not defrocking, might be considered. In other words, exclusion from the ministry should never occur on principle, for then the congregation's shortcomings, its weakness, would become the essential criterion. As a result, where gifts are concerned, there could be no question of the duty or the right of the church leadership to remove someone from the ministry. At

the very most, others in the community might *request* the person concerned to consider resignation. This would completely rule out any procedure of suspension. Bonhoeffer thus responded negatively to the question, while still theoretically leaving the way open for the remote eventuality of a congregation being unable, in regard to the Aryan clause, to achieve complete clarity in its testimony and its faith. Bonhoeffer obviously did not feel in a position to concede such a borderline case, and he directed his criticism and warning toward the congregation that portrayed its weakness as a strength.

Confessional Writings. After July 1935 the seminary's work focused almost entirely on the confessional writings, which were discussed as passionately in that era as the hermeneutical question would be later. With each passing semester Bonhoeffer devoted more time to classes on the confessions than to any other subject. The students tested the authenticity of the commitments made in the Reformation churches' declarations in light of the concepts of ministry, church, state, *adiaphora,* and scriptural doctrine.

1. Bonhoeffer enjoyed spending time on the Smalcald Articles. In discussing the question of church schism, he emphasized that the reformers had confined themselves exclusively here to the Article of Justification as the grounds for disagreement, and he emphasized the exemplary unity that existed with Catholics in the other articles, such as those concerning the doctrine of the Trinity or of Christology. The ordinands were impressed when Bonhoeffer, a consistent and unwavering proponent of Barmen and Dahlem, drew their attention to this point and advised them to remain moderate here. Their theological education had led them to see a different spirit at work, rooted in the old schism, that could be detected in each of the articles. Now, however, they were being instructed by someone with a keen awareness of the different spirit behind all the present-day pronouncements; he taught them that there was a great distinction between the church's theologies and the decisions it made. Each was deserving of a different kind of respect; there were, he held, as many theologies as there were spirits. They might or they might not be convincing and must remain open to discussion. Once decisions had been reached, however, they must be obeyed. The church could not wait for theological unanimity, but must decide and demand respect for its decisions.

His ecumenical experience may have given the Protestant Bonhoeffer some special insight here; perhaps, too, he had a feeling for what the British called "policy"—a word for which there is no exact equivalent in Germany, because it is relatively seldom found there. Within the German tradition, theology (above all, one's own!) takes precedence; the church's decisions are relegated to second place and enjoy little respect—simply because German theologians have learned to scrutinize them for false or bad theology. As a theologian, Bonhoeffer tried to be cautious here. This is one of the keys to his attitude and arguments about the synod decisions of Barmen and Dahlem. When his students came out with the cliché that liberal Christians ended with the German Christians and orthodox or positive Christians moved toward the Confessing church because this was the logical outcome of their theologies, he objected not only that this was factually untrue but that the components of the decision being made did not revolve around theology. As a Lutheran, he condemned the 1937 Halle synod's decision on the common celebration of the Eucharist as bad and poorly reasoned theology, yet he gratefully welcomed the decision as such: "Much as I approve of the result, I cannot but deplore its theological premise."[47]

He had a keen sense for theological inconsistency, but distrusted even this ability, since it so often gave people a pretext to evade decisions or made them incapable of sticking with decisions that had already been made. The demand for solutions that appeared theologically clear and well-thought-out might suggest a sense of responsibility; in reality this was nothing but evasion, the indefinite procrastination of what ought to be done. In this Bonhoeffer discerned an inability to be a church. On the one hand, this inability was leading to the progressive fragmentation of the church, while on the other it increased the readiness to accept a unity that had been imposed with tyrannical means.

2. After a heated discussion on the articles on the state in the Augsburg Confession and its Apology, Bonhoeffer concluded by telling the class: "The whole business is extremely problematic."[48] The abstract and diverse nature of the terminology betrayed a certain awkwardness and vacillation between concepts of function ("authority") and concepts of being ("state"). The relationship between the actual positiveness of order and its obligatory law remained unsatisfactorily vague; none of the solutions were sufficient. Bonhoeffer presented not only Luther's "unresolved and contradictory answers," but the answers of Thomas Münzer, the Scottish Calvinists, and the visionaries Melchior Hoffman and Sebastian Franck—without bluntly dismissing them. And he discussed the attempts to distinguish between the right to resist in one's private and official capacities.[49]

Unfortunately, we have no written record of these classes. The notes that exist show only that those taking them became most confused at this point. The students were filled with what they were hearing in the other lecture, "Discipleship," and its message that someone attacked for the sake of faith did not fight back. Although his ordinands did not know it at the time,

Bonhoeffer was much troubled by another aspect of this issue: many of his closest friends and relatives held responsible posts in the legislature and the government, and faced the alternative of either fulfilling their official duties or resisting the regime. The Nuremberg Laws were being prepared; every time he met Hans von Dohnanyi in Berlin Bonhoeffer received an update on the developments. Hence it was not always easy for his students to follow his train of thought when he criticized the familiar Protestant Lutheran solutions and cast doubt on their traditional rejection of the right to revolutionary resistance.

3. In his final lectures of this series Bonhoeffer dealt exclusively with Luther's *Formula of Concord*. He discussed the articles on free will, predestination, the doctrine of original sin, good works, Law and Gospel, *tertius usus legis,* and justification. The *Formula of Concord* had not been part of his own studies, nor that of his ordinands during their university studies. When Bonhoeffer was a student interest had centered mainly on the "genuine" Luther and the premises of Troeltsch; now it had become necessary to listen to the central voices within the church in an era of its most passionate disputes. Every page of the *Formula of Concord* in Bonhoeffer's copy of the confessional writings is covered with underlined passages, exclamation marks, and question marks. During the later courses at Finkenwalde it became the predominant theme in this series of lectures. His notes from the entire seminary period contain no fewer than eighty-one themes and questions on this subject that he assigned the ordinands to work on. He loved the *Formula of Concord* and enjoyed exploring its tendency, through traditional philosophical formulas, to express saving truth and the comforting meaning to be found in the confessional teaching about the "true distinctions."

The more deeply the world of the confessional writings impressed Bonhoeffer, the more freely he moved into the realm of ecclesiological, ethical, and confessional questions. He longed for a more thorough interpretation and examination of the positions. In 1936 he wrote Karl Barth:

> I think it would be very important for the present situation if some of the questions of substance which divide Lutherans and Reformed could be brought into the open and discussed. . . . The overall view is lacking and still more the time in which to acquire it. There is the need of a worthy successor to Schneckenburger's book. . . .[50]

In 1940 Edmund Schlink's *Theology of the Lutheran Confessions* finally appeared. Bonhoeffer welcomed it and recommended it everywhere. But his own time and attention were already directed toward other matters.

"*Discipleship.*" The two series of lectures would have been enough to give Bonhoeffer the reputation of an industrious seminary director. They dealt with the required subjects that were expected. The number of classes and the time needed for their preparation were enough to keep him fully occupied. But the reason Finkenwalde was "the fullest time" of his life was that he was finally able to work on the theme of his own choice.[51] Within the constraints of his course schedule, he was able to give shape and form to the subject whose fascination for him had been growing ever since the early 1930s. *Discipleship* (originally published in English as *The Cost of Discipleship*) would become Finkenwalde's own badge of distinction. For the newcomers the first classes in Zingst were a breathtaking surprise. They suddenly realized that they were not there simply to learn new techniques of preaching and instruction, but would be initiated into something that would radically change the prerequisites for those activities.

Bonhoeffer did not begin in Zingst with the phrase found in the opening pages of the book, "grace sold on the market like cheap wares."[52] Instead he began by investigating the nature of "the call," which alone constitutes the relationship between Jesus and Peter. Nor in the summer of 1935 did he go into the detailed analysis of Luther's deed and its perversion by his undialectical imitators.[53] Bonhoeffer dealt with the situation of the call and explored it in the story of the tax collector Levi and the three disciples in Luke 9. In his first lecture the central concept of the book, "Only the believer is obedient—only the obedient believe," was not yet so deeply developed. He proceeded immediately to the story of the rich young man.[54] The interlude that is so important in the book, about the initial steps toward belief, was also absent at the beginning, but was included in later courses along with the analysis of the rich young man as the basis and point of departure for Bonhoeffer's lectures on pastoral care.[55] The third chapter of the published book, "Single-Minded Obedience," was only written after the first lectures, in the course of work on the book. Yet the chapter "Discipleship and the Cross" was a cornerstone of the work from the beginning. As in the book, the lecture on "Discipleship and the Individual" proceeded to a discussion of the Sermon on the Mount, which Bonhoeffer completed at the end of the first course on 14 October 1935. He concluded the lectures with a postscript (which does not appear in the same form in the book):

> The Sermon on the Mount is not a statement to be treated in a cavalier fashion—by saying that this or that isn't right or that here we find an

inconsistency. Its validity depends on its being obeyed. This is not a statement that we can freely choose to take or leave. It is a compelling, lordly statement.[56]

Thus Bonhoeffer did not appear at the preachers' seminary with a manuscript ready for publication; but entire sections of his lectures went straight into the book. He continued to make alterations and deletions and to insert whole new chapters until the last page of the manuscript was delivered. The essence of the exegetical sections had been written well before the Finkenwalde period, but the final version of the important systematic theories was completed at the same time as the book itself.[57] "The Messengers"—the section now found between "Sermon on the Mount" and "The Church of Jesus Christ"—was inserted later.

It has been noted that this third part of the book, "The Messengers," is not as compact and finished as the first two sections.[58] Actually, it is an abridged and rearranged version of Bonhoeffer's main series of lectures on the New Testament, which he delivered to all the Finkenwalde groups but the first. He had intended from the beginning, however, to use this material for *Discipleship.* The book clearly owes its conclusive style and momentum to his preoccupation with the Sermon on the Mount that had begun long before 1935. Bonhoeffer's reconsideration and reexamination of its implications with respect to the Pauline writings was a new step.

The second part of *Discipleship* stemmed from the Finkenwalde lectures on "The Visible Church" (winter 1935–1936), "The New Life in Paul" (summer 1936), "Concrete Ethics in Paul" (winter 1936–1937), and "Discipline and Formation of Congregations in the New Testament"(summer 1937). The original manuscript for *Discipleship* has been lost. After the first group's fascination with the topic, the community house in Finkenwalde attempted to share the content of the subsequent lectures in the Finkenwalde newsletter (*Rundbrief*) with those who had moved on; they did not get as far with this as they had hoped.[59] But the concern that Bonhoeffer would not reach his goal with this work diminished with each semester.

Bonhoeffer concluded the book shortly before the police closed down the seminary. On 26 August 1937 what was to be the last regular newsletter from Finkenwalde to the brethren announced: "And now for some good news. Despite all our many other activities, the book we have been waiting for has now been completed and is being typed up...."[60]

The book appeared in Advent 1937. The first copies were sent to the members of the newly dissolved community, with the inscription:

> 1 Advent 1937. In gratitude for two and a half years of loyal community in Finkenwalde. May our path become ever more the path of joyous discipleship. *Jesu juva!*[61]

After Bonhoeffer secretly resumed his work, he wrote a newsletter to all Finkenwaldians:

> When it appeared, I dedicated it in spirit to you all. I would have done so on the title page had I not feared to lay the responsibility for my theology and my ideas on your shoulders. Our community is founded upon something else. I would have liked each one of you to receive the book as a Christmas present, but finances would not allow it. In any case, you all know what's in it.[62]

Needless to say, the ordinands would have been only too glad to accept "the responsibility." But this was typical of Bonhoeffer's modesty; the more certain he was of his subject, the less confident he felt about it. One copy found its way to a prison cell, inscribed: "To Martin Niemöller in Advent, 1937, in brotherly gratitude! A book he could have written better than its author."[63] Another copy was sent to Franz Hildebrandt, who had emigrated to London and was working on the topic of "Gospel and Humanity." From his perspective, it seemed that Bonhoeffer's preoccupation with the commandment and the law was in danger of becoming somewhat one-sided. Responding to Hildebrandt's thanks and criticism, Bonhoeffer wrote:

> I am delighted both by your approval and your criticism of my book. I'm perfectly willing to admit that Asmussen's commentary on Galatians does not agree with my interpretation of Matt. 5:17ff. But it's a *very* different matter where Luther's commentary on Galatians is concerned.
>   Watch, you antinomian, that you don't end up establishing a law of humanitarianism! I am very eager for your work and I follow it with approval and criticism as you do mine.[64]

In light of his full teaching load, frequent travels, and the growing number of arrests of his pupils and friends, the completion of the book was a tremendous achievement. Up to the very last Bonhoeffer continued to devote his Sundays and evenings to the ordinands, and to write articles, Bible studies, and lectures. Yet had he not completed the work before Finkenwalde was dissolved, it is unlikely that this would ever have been possible, since after that he did not even have a study to work in.

The study of the New Testament in the collective vicars' courses from 1937 to 1940 (this was the underground form of educating ordinands after the Gestapo closed Finkenwalde, when Bonhoeffer continued to travel and teach for the Confessing church) occurred in the form of working groups of seminarians who studied the terminology. After a presentation by one of them, Bonhoeffer offered his own theses (only the first two volumes of Kittel's *Dictionary of the New Testament* had appeared). Among Bonhoeffer's papers are numerous fragmentary notes on classifications of biblical material and systematic principles, including sin, the good, work, change and growth, *dokimos*, peace, *hodos*, the Holy Spirit, angels, the wrath of God, the law, death, temptation, *pistis*, gratitude, *Eucharistia, egkrateia, diakonia, nikan*, catalogue of vices, *tapeinophrosyne*, false doctrine. In his discussion of all these topics he drew upon parts of *Discipleship*. His newsletters to the Finkenwalde brethren give an idea of this work, since on two occasions he shared the conclusions that had been drawn about "*chara*" and "patience."[65]

Discipleship found a wide readership fairly quickly. Their attention was drawn by the book's discussion of the ancient theme of "sanctification" that was now to be wrested from the conventicles and won back for the church. The book's success, however, was not yet evident from any reviews but only from its sales. Bonhoeffer realized it had gone beyond the small world of specialists when he was working on his *Ethics* at the Benedictine monastery in Ettal in 1940, where the monks read aloud passages from *Discipleship* at Christmastime.[66] Until 1945 there was no significant critical reaction to Bonhoeffer's view of discipleship. Early reviews spoke highly of his use of language—a rather unusual standard to apply to a new book on theology. There was one opinion which would have meant far more to Bonhoeffer than all the rest—that of Karl Barth—but it was not to appear until many years later. While still in the midst of writing his book, Bonhoeffer had written to Barth:

> Basically, I have been conducting a silent argument with you the entire time . . . there is such a very great deal I would like to ask you and could learn from you.[67]

Barth replied without having seen exactly what Bonhoeffer was doing. He saw "not without concern" that Bonhoeffer was wrestling "with the inexhaustible theme of justification and sanctification." He continued, "I shall have to watch carefully to see which way the wind blows before I can tell you whether I think your ideas are feasible or not."[68]

Twenty years later, he wrote in *Church Dogmatics*:

> Easily the best that has been written on this subject is to be found in *The Cost of Discipleship* by Dietrich Bonhoeffer. . . . We do not refer to all the parts . . . but to the opening sections. . . . In these the matter is handled with such depth and precision that I am almost tempted simply to reproduce them in an extended quotation. For I cannot hope to say anything better on the subject than what is said here. . . . In following my own course, I am happy that on this occasion I can lean as heavily as I do upon another.[69]

The Thesis of the Book. 1. Basically what Bonhoeffer was seeking to do in this book was to reaffirm the elusive concept of "faith" in all its implications. Ultimately his tireless search since the time of *Sanctorum Communio* for the concrete social nature of the Body of Christ was bound to make him reexamine the Reformers' general condemnation of faith as a "*habitus.*" Did this rejection really mean that any interest in its dimension of existence was rooted by definition in evil? This is what Bonhoeffer himself had been taught and passed on to others. Yet Bonhoeffer had always been inclined to add a third note, that of the earthly community, to the two classic ecclesial notes, word and sacrament:

> Church is not a community of souls, as is maintained today. Nor is church merely the proclamation of the Gospel. In other words, church is not merely pulpit, but church is the real body of Christ on earth.[70]

He then tried to grasp the Reformed articles of faith, justification, and sanctification within the single concept of discipleship. Yet with his key formula, "only the believer is obedient, and only those who are obedient believe," he did not mean to question the complete validity of Luther's *sola fide* and *sola gratia*, but to reassert their validity by restoring to them their concreteness here on earth.[71] He emphatically and explicitly denied that this represented a betrayal or distortion in any way. Justification is an uncontested prerequisite that needs no amplification. On the contrary, the aim was to go beyond mere words, and rediscover and restore its preciousness. Discipleship is an interpretation of justification in which justification applies to the sinner, rather than to the sin:

> Justification is the new creation of the new person, and sanctification is the preservation and protection of that person until the day of Jesus Christ.[72]

Yet, in contrast to the Reformation era, Bonhoeffer was entering new ground and an altered intellectual climate in his emphasis on the concreteness of faith in his interpretation of earthly discipleship, and his location of the disciple within the boundaries of historical and local decisions, fraught as they were with visible inconsistencies. When he attempted to support his thesis with quotations from confessional writings, he could find little more than allusions.[73] Like Kierkegaard, Bonhoeffer had always believed that "today Luther would say the opposite of what he said then" in order to state the same essential message.[74] Once, faith had meant leaving the cloister. Now, faith might mean a reopening of the cloister; and faith could also mean entering the world of politics.

2. Bonhoeffer's conception of faith as discipleship was strengthened rather than weakened by his early discovery of the social nature of each individual Christian doctrine:

> It is impossible to become a new person as a solitary individual. . . . The new person is not the individual believer who has been justified and sanctified, but the church, the Body of Christ, Christ himself.[75]

It is true that the emphasis in *Discipleship* is on the fact that social organization occurs through the self-giving of the individual; similarly, in the individual sphere the social realm becomes concrete within. Jesus calls individuals so they can no longer disappear into the crowd. Discipleship opposes mass credos and "world movements" because it is personal commitment. The church is based upon individual disciples, not upon the flock. At the same time individual discipleship and "individualism" are mutually exclusive. When, in his letters from prison, Bonhoeffer described "religion" as "individualism" among other things, this was not in contradiction to his emphasis on the individual in *Discipleship*.

3. He drew a sharp distinction between discipleship and an ideal. The call of Jesus cannot be turned into a program or an ideology; indeed, that would mean a failure of discipleship. Ideals and programs lead to a craving for casuistic realization; this was the very opposite of the step into discipleship, for discipleship means breaking away from casuistic and legalistic programs. To be called, to go, and to follow—this is a true Christology. To be called and not to follow, but instead to work out a program for use in this or that situation—this is a false Christology. It leaves Christ out in the cold as an occasional aid toward salvation. But the call creates a new and full existence; it creates a new point of reference, and hence breaks away from legalism. It does not create constitutions and decrees, but brings human beings into relation with each other. In this context there is an impressive passage on the "weakness" of the Word:

> The Word is weaker than any ideology, and this means that with only the
> gospel at their command the witnesses are weaker than the propagandists
> of an opinion. But although they are weak, they are ready to suffer with the
> Word, and so are free from that morbid restlessness which is so character-
> istic of fanaticism.[76]

The Word of Christ must not be mistaken for triumphant, all-pervasive
conviction. It can also respect the impossible, taking into account the barriers it encounters; it respects the individual—all the more so when that individual disagrees. The idea, on the other hand, invades the individual, and
nothing is impossible for any "program." But the Word Incarnate is content
to be despised and rejected.

God's freedom confines itself within the limits of a weak human community of individuals. This had already been the view of the Bonhoeffer who
wrote *Act and Being*, whereas "the weak Christ, the weak Word" addressed
here presages the Christology of the final year of his life. The belief in the
power of weakness was one of Bonhoeffer's most basic insights, which he
would hold throughout his theological life.

4. The interpretation of the weak Word touches on the most profound
idea ever expressed by Bonhoeffer: discipleship as participation in Christ's
suffering for others, as communion with the Crucified One. A wealth of personal experience is apparent here between the lines. Yet Bonhoeffer managed
to avoid both the painful, self-pitying mood found in many hymns and the
glorification of mysticism. The element of "representation" within discipleship prevents it from becoming introverted and an end in itself. Disciples are
the kind of people who take upon themselves what others would like to
shake off. On the last page of the book, Bonhoeffer writes, "Christ's life on
earth is not finished yet, for he continues to live in the lives of his followers."[77] Thus the premise of *Christus praesens* from *Sanctorum Communio* was
developed further. This viewpoint was expressed in the Bible study on temptation[78] that Bonhoeffer held during a critical situation in 1938, and during
the last year of his life it remained a decisive part of his notion of "religionless Christianity."

5. There is a particularly interesting passage in which Bonhoeffer writes
of the "first step" prior to, or toward, faith.[79] This foreshadows the later distinction drawn in *Ethics* between the "ultimate" and the "penultimate": the
ultimate and the penultimate are correlatives that determine, qualify, and
validate one another.[80] Even in *Discipleship*, where he resolutely devotes
attention to the ultimate, his desire for concreteness keeps him close to the
penultimate. It cannot be overlooked that the "first step" is of little sig-

nificance in the "penultimate"; it is merely a transitional stage without the autonomy that is later attributed to it. Later Bonhoeffer wrote:

> One cannot and must not speak the last word before the last but one. . . .
> In *Discipleship* I just hinted at this, but did not follow it up; I must do so later.[81]

Discipleship's Place in Bonhoeffer's Theological Development. As the author of *Discipleship*, Bonhoeffer made a deep impression on the consciousness of the Protestant church. It continued to characterize him until the publication of his letters from prison offered another picture of him. This led to the thesis that Bonhoeffer had gone through a constrained period brought about by the church struggle—a thesis particularly favored by Hanfried Müller.[82]

It is indeed striking that the scope and variety of themes Bonhoeffer tackled in 1932 dwindled after 1933, and reemerged only during the final years of his life. This raises questions about the nature and depth of the change marked by *Discipleship*. When did this change actually occur, where was its temporal emphasis, and where were its consequences accidental? Was it a kind of intellectual mishap that interrupted a promising development for an entire decade, to resume only in 1943 for two brief and difficult years? Didn't Bonhoeffer himself recognize the limitations of *Discipleship*, although he refused to disown one word of it?[83] And what role did the events of 1933 play?

The answer is self-evident: both the theme and the underlying thesis of *Discipleship* were already fully evolved before 1933, but the book owes its single-minded, exclusive claims to that year. It may be recalled that in Barcelona in 1928 Bonhoeffer's reading of the Sermon on the Mount was still the conventional Lutheran harmless understanding of it. A literal interpretation would turn it into a law, and that law had been abolished through Christ.[84] During his time in America he began to be less sure of this interpretation, and in his university seminar of 1932 he had dealt with the relationship between faith, commandment, and obedience along the lines of *Discipleship*, even using the same terminology;[85] compared with their fellow students, the ordinands from Berlin who came to Zingst were already familiar with some of this. The preaching of a noncommittal message of grace and the triviality of ecumenical statements on peace posed new questions after 1931 that were related to purely personal crises and decisions. Indeed, in departing from the concrete, earthly image of the body of Christ in *Sanctorum Communio* and from the actuality of revelation in *Act and Being*, he had already committed himself to the subject of *Discipleship*. The theological relevance of the "child,"[86] the twin concepts "simplicity and discord,"[87] intuition as opposed to reflection—all these helped to form his concept of faith at an early stage: "Belief is never directed toward itself, but only toward Christ."[88] These trains of thought provided crucial insights for his book. Obedience *is* action, he said in a 1932 lecture, and the idea of "cheap grace" was formulated in a lecture to a branch of the German S.C.M.[89]

Bonhoeffer does not appear to have written anything explicitly on the New Testament passages about the call or the Sermon on the Mount until he became a pastor in London after the stormy summer of 1933. In a lecture in Zingst in May 1935, he dealt at some length with the three disciples in Luke 9: the disciple who offered himself, the disciple who was called, and the disciple who turned back. He had also written a reflection on this in a 1934 New Year's Day article for the parish newsletter.[90] In April 1934 he wrote to Erwin Sutz:

> Please write and tell me some time what you say when you preach about the Sermon on the Mount. I am working on this now—trying to keep it extremely simple and straightforward, but it always comes back to keeping the commandment and not evading it. Discipleship of Christ—I'd like to know what that is—it is not exhausted in our concept of faith. I am setting to work on something I might describe as an exercise—this is a first step.[91]

In summary, not only did the direction and basic questions underlying *Discipleship* already exist in 1932 in a complete form, but the answers had also been formulated. The events of 1933 interrupted Bonhoeffer's plans to work them through. He began to make notes during 1934 in London; the book itself came into being between 1935 and 1937.[92] Thus it owes its origin, not to the single-mindedness induced by the events of 1933, but to the independent theological foundations Bonhoeffer himself had laid. His train of thought was not an aberration, created by the circumstances of that time, that allows us to bypass it in order to proceed as quickly and as directly as possible to the Bonhoeffer of the final years. On the contrary, it was here that Bonhoeffer first developed his original view of faith and Christology—material that cannot be overlooked.

Yet 1933 was not without significance for *Discipleship*. There can be no doubt that it made Bonhoeffer more sure of his subject, and enabled him to devote himself to it with focused intensity. This contributed both to the limitation and to the greatness of his exposition; in this light the book might be seen as one of the strongest answers to the events of 1933.

Realizing that he was dealing not just with his own personal theme, but with that of his entire church, Bonhoeffer abandoned topics that had greatly interested him to that point. Thus he proceeded no further with a doctrine of Christ's lordship over the world, a project he had just begun in 1932; and there was to be no more of the constructive reflections on the state that had just appeared in *Thy Kingdom Come.*[93] Nor is the category of "the orders of preservation" discernible after 1933. He abandoned work on it at the very time when other Lutherans, such as Walter Künneth, were adopting it as the foundation for their own concept of the two kingdoms. He lost all interest in further discussion of the topics Brunner and Gogarten were raising during that period. The more loudly the periodicals and Sunday newspapers clamored for a new "theology of creation," the more disparaging Bonhoeffer's silence became. It was not that he claimed to be more capable here than Gogarten, Althaus, Elert, and Hirsch, who had all produced imposing works on this complex aspect of Christian theology, but he felt that the time to focus on the issue had already passed. To show any interest, however genuine and earnest, in this particular subject at this particular time would come dangerously close to making an offering on the altar of Hitler. In his theories of 1932 Bonhoeffer had suggested that the time for considering a "theology of order" was over; the time for a "breakthough theology" had come.[94] In other words, the emphasis now had to be on eschatology, not the theology of creation. To pursue the theology of creation at that point was anything but concrete. The time for a theology of creation might return, but only after they had withstood the time for the theology of the *eschaton.*

The role of the "world" had indeed changed for Bonhoeffer since 1933. This explains why those who look back from the "worldly" Bonhoeffer of *Letters and Papers from Prison* tend to regard *Discipleship* as a detour from his path. The Bonhoeffer of that era viewed the world as a dangerous jungle that had to be traversed: the world has not disappeared; its dominion is very evident. Yet it would be a mistake to interpret this as Bonhoeffer's attempt to escape from the world. The ghetto of *Discipleship* is not the peaceful backwater of the pietists, nor is it the otherworldliness of the visionaries, neither of whom are particularly loyal to the world. *Discipleship* is a call to battle, it is concentration and hence restriction, so that the entire earth may be reconquered by the infinite message. To use Bonhoeffer's later terminology, when the penultimate, in its lust for glory and its thirst for adulation and sacrifice, thrust itself forward—and even in the church those who bowed before it were legion—Bonhoeffer turned toward the ultimate, for the sake of the penultimate. He usurped a theme that had been the exclusive possession of the pietists, at a time when its ghetto-like character was more inescapable than ever before. But now this was as it should be: in 1933 the ghetto of Jesus had become *the* theme of the church.

Thus Bonhoeffer's theological development showed an intrinsic consistency and continuity. Its tendency to concentrate on the issues and narrow them down was determined by a deep inner need, not by the requirements of methodology. In 1927 Bonhoeffer had sought the concrete entity of the body of Christ in the church in the form of a sociological structure (*Sanctorum Communio*). In 1929 he reformulated the question, asking whether the earthly continuity of revelation, in its free contingency, could be conceived in terms of the concrete church (*Act and Being*). In 1932 he examined the relationship of the body of Christ to the world by inquiring into the actual obedience to God's commandments. In 1933 his exposé of the structure of Christology was based upon the implications of all his previous thinking. And now, by interpreting belief in Christ as discipleship, he raised this Christology from its academic deathbed.

At first the ordinands at Finkenwalde were overwhelmed by Bonhoeffer's theology of discipleship. Some of them protested courageously against the reversal of the hallowed order which put faith before obedience, a reversal which made these terms an interchangeable dialectic. But the longer the National Socialist regime remained in power, the more the ordinands—and many others with them—became familiar with the Bonhoeffer of *Discipleship*. An increasing number of sermons spoke of the eschatological otherness of the disciples, but this gradually led to something else: Bonhoeffer's dynamic ghetto began to resemble a ghetto that was cut off and had grown sterile. With familiarity, the costly otherness of grace once again grew "cheap."

Perhaps Bonhoeffer sensed that eventually he would have to embark in a new direction. This soon became patently imperative, ethically, politically, and theologically as well. As he completed work on *Discipleship*, Bonhoeffer contemplated making a start on hermeneutics: "There seems to be a very large gap here."[95] Yet there would be no time for this. In 1944, in the midst of new considerations, he looked back at *Discipleship* and wrote: "Today I can see the dangers of that book, although I still stand by what I wrote."[96]

The House of Brethren

In 1935 Finkenwalde provided Bonhoeffer with the opportunity, not only of writing the first chapters of *Discipleship*, but to finally see the realization of a community: the creation of a "house of brethren" in the preachers' seminary. *Discipleship* and this community house are closely related. Anyone with an ear for the language of the book must have realized at once that it meant a departure from the academic sphere. Its subject matter did not allow neutral objectivity. Indeed, one Greifswald professor was not altogether wrong when he wrote to the Council of Brethren in Stettin: "I know that Bonhoeffer simply overwhelms the young men by his religious ardor—one might even say passion."[97]

Bonhoeffer believed that the circumstances of the time and his own theological principles now demanded the creation for Protestants of something which, for centuries, they could only find under Roman Catholic auspices. There had been some precedents in the Protestant brotherhood movements of recent decades. After the First World War there had been not only official conferences for the clergy, but also free associations such as the Sydow Brotherhood or the St. Michael's Brethren within the Berneuchen movement. In contrast to these free experiments that entailed a certain degree of commitment, 1934 saw the sudden and seemingly fortuitous emergence, throughout the Confessing church, of new fellowships of young pastors who wanted to stay within the church and develop new forms of ministry that would be ecclesiastically legitimate. They deliberately subordinated themselves to the government of the Councils of Brethren, from whom they requested spiritual leadership. Later Bonhoeffer was to use this movement to support his own proposal that "the beginning of associations of fellowship reveal[s] the need for a more defined form."[98] So far, however, these fellowships had not attempted any form of *convivium*, and it had certainly never occurred to them to abandon the traditional form of parish ministry in order to revive the classical vows.

But Bonhoeffer had contemplated the communal life for many years. He had the idea of a compact, committed community from the time he began to think about discipleship. His 1930 book review of Parpert's *Das Mönchtum und die evangelische Kirche* (*The Monastic Order and the Evangelical Church*) betrayed his academic passion for clear theological and sociological terms, but not for the phenomenon of the community as such.[99] By the time of the Prebelow and Biesenthal retreats in 1932, however, he had thought this completely through; for the first time Bonhoeffer included periods of "quiet" and "meditation" in the daily routine, although he was the only one who knew what to make of them.[100] While he vacillated in London between his plans for India and a possible return to the university, he wrote Jürgen Winterhager: "It appears incomparably more important to me that our plans for a settlement become more concrete."[101] In 1932 these "plans for a settlement" were still closely tied to ideas of social work. After 1933 they took a new direction. He wrote to his brother Karl-Friedrich, who was far removed from such thoughts but whom Dietrich hoped to convince, in light of the new political circumstances:

> I think I am right in saying that I would only achieve true inner clarity and sincerity by really starting to take the Sermon on the Mount seriously. This is the only source of strength that can blow all this stuff and nonsense sky-high, in a fireworks display that will leave nothing behind but one or two charred remains. The restoration of the church will surely come from a new kind of monasticism, which will have nothing in common with the old but a life of uncompromising adherence to the Sermon on the Mount in imitation of Christ. I believe the time has come to rally people together for this.[102]

To Sutz he described his first attempts to write on the subject of "discipleship" not as exegeses but, typically, as "spiritual exercises."[103] He wished training to take place in "cloistered church seminaries where the pure doctrine, the Sermon on the Mount and divine worship are taken seriously...."[104] This was one of the reasons for his study of Anglican communities.

Thus Bonhoeffer arrived in Zingst with the very definite ideas he had expressed to de Félice on 29 January 1935.[105] The majority of the young theologians he encountered in Zingst had no idea of this, and it would be a while before they heard of it. Yet they were meeting Bonhoeffer at a time when it was evident that, at the very least, some changes in the ministry would be necessary and would involve sacrifices. Contrary to the general earlier reluctance to try new things, the seminaries appeared to be a good place for such an attempt.

Bonhoeffer did not yet intend to express his ideas for a community house openly. Only toward the end of July did he mention it to one or two people. But he was able to build upon the prerequisites that already existed in the communal life of the seminary.

Meditation. The daily schedule Bonhoeffer established in Zingst included a half-hour silent meditation every morning after breakfast, before the theological work was to begin. He proposed that each week meditation should revolve around a few scriptural verses that everyone would have agreed upon beforehand. These verses were not to be connected to the current theological work, sermon texts, or the church year, but were to be free of any ulterior goal. He did not expand any further on the subject, leaving it completely up to the ordinands to carry out what for them was an utterly novel proposal. His suggestions were always made in such a way that those addressed felt obliged to comply; in this case, however, the resentment, perplexity, and general discontent were so intense that they eventually had to come out. This did not happen immediately, since the ordinands felt entitled to spend the half hour as they saw fit. On the other hand, their director's evident ability to concentrate upon this exercise put them to shame.

But the meditative routine collapsed immediately when Bonhoeffer was summoned on 12 May by telephone to Berlin (following the Gestapo's first raid on the Dahlem office of the Council of Brethren). From Berlin he was sent by church president Koch to see Bishop Bell in England, and thus was gone for nearly a fortnight.[106] In his absence Wilhelm Rott, who could not incorporate Bonhoeffer's concept of meditation any more than the ordinands, was unable to maintain a disciplined adherence to this part of the schedule. Yet when Bonhoeffer returned, bringing not only the latest news but cheese, eels, and a large ham for the community, the students were ready for another try to put his proposal into practice.

Finally an evening was set aside for discussion of the unpopular meditation. Because this discussion was held some time after the practice had been introduced, it could not be confined to theoretical aspects or to theological preliminaries. Everyone spoke from personal experiences of trial and error. Bonhoeffer was willing to listen to anything, but made it clear from the beginning that the arrangement would continue and would not be decided by the wish of the majority. Some people said that they went to sleep, others that they spent the half hour working on sermons, since they had absolutely no idea what else to do; others admitted that half an hour's recollection was too much for them and their minds wandered, so they read commentaries instead. The more advanced meditators complained that some students had been smoking pipes during meditation, but this met with Bonhoeffer's approval. The worship services were then criticized on the grounds that the lessons and prayers were unendurably long. Other seminaries were already regarding Zingst as a joke—a place, they said, where the ordinands had to meditate while they brushed their teeth and were forced to submit to an unevangelical legalism.

Bonhoeffer did his best to advise them and show them that the enterprise was a vital personal exercise, as prescribed by "Introduction to Daily Meditation"[107] or *Life Together*.[108] They agreed on one innovation; once a week they would gather for communal meditation during which, in much the same way as at Quaker meetings, they might speak—provided they stuck to Scripture—or remain silent, as they wished. This practice proved helpful, since what others had said could be reflected upon during solitary meditation. As time went on fewer and fewer of the students tried to get out of the exercise. Some continued to practice it long after leaving Finkenwalde; at the very least, they had learned that the Scripture was more than just a tool of their trade. Until the time of Bonhoeffer's arrest the newsletter sent to all Finkenwaldians contained weekly texts for meditation and occasional encouragement that they continue this salutary practice.

There are a number of reasons why Bonhoeffer found others who joined him here, and why he was able to allay the suspicion that meditation only induced a hothouse atmosphere that was narrow, esoteric, and impractical. In the first place, the exercise was more than offset by the daily study of practical theology. The ordinands learned to distinguish between an intellectual exercise and the care of souls. The periods of concentration were also offset by times of relaxation and entertainment that Bonhoeffer, with his wit and imagination, was able to organize so well. He even regarded the inability to enjoy leisure time as a gap in a student's education. Aside from all this, Bonhoeffer made it absolutely clear that this schedule in no way represented a withdrawal from decisions in church politics, but was a way of preparing to meet them.

Finally, the strongest incentive to the hesitant students was Bonhoeffer's own manner of prayer. During seminary worship he spoke almost all the prayers himself. His prayers were long and usually extemporaneous; occasionally he also used liturgical prayers. He would begin with detailed thanks for the gift of faith, for the seminary's communal life, for the sun and the sea. Next he would ask for daily and mutual tolerance within the fellowship. Much time was devoted to prayer for the Confessing church, its leaders and synods, for those in prison, those who had fallen by the wayside, and for enemies. There was a confession of those sins peculiar to the theologians and clergy, and intercession for them. He devoted much time and trouble to the preparation of these prayers and their inner structure. His language was devoted wholly to the issue at hand and free of all self-portrayal. He put his will, understanding, and heart into these prayers; yet he also believed that the language of prayer should be modeled and in harmony with that of the Psalms.

He was convinced that prayer could be taught and learned, yet neither the university faculties nor seminaries included prayer in their curricula. Bonhoeffer's daily example, however, gradually began to bear fruit. He deliberately insisted on the observance of the imposed schedule, and could also offer very simple and practical advice on prayer:

[The need to pray] has not been met . . . even by the Confessing Church. . . . The charge that these [i.e., periods of meditation and prayer] are legalistic I find totally incorrect. How can it possibly be legalistic for a Christian to learn what prayer is, and to spend a fair amount of time learning it? Recently a leading member of the Confessing Church told me: "We haven't the time for meditation now; the ordinands must learn to preach and to catechize." This either shows a total lack of understanding of young theologians today, or else a blasphemous ignorance of how preaching and teaching come about. The kind of questions that young theologians seriously put to us today are: How can I learn to pray? How can I learn to read the Bible? Either we can help them to do this, or we can't help them at all. None of this can be taken for granted.[109]

Confession. The first Eucharist at the seminary in Zingst was on the sixth Sunday after Easter. For a whole week before, Bonhoeffer reflected on this in his prayers at the evening and morning service. He canceled all work on the day before communion. He made it known early that a prerequisite for the celebration of communion was mutual reconciliation and had intimated— to the surprise of most of the ordinands—that they might confess privately to one of the others or else to him personally. Hardly anyone could bring himself to do this and the atmosphere was somewhat embarrassed and resentful, since that kind of thing was not usually done in the Protestant church. The last service on Saturday took place in an atmosphere of seriousness and gloom, in strong contrast to the joyous communion that was celebrated on Sunday morning. Bonhoeffer suspended all work for the rest of the day, suggesting instead that they should go for a walk. The evening was devoted to reading aloud and to general recreation.

Only gradually did the community become accustomed to this monthly practice of communion. As the summer wore on, one or another of the ordinands began to go to private confession; who did so, or how often, was never generally discussed. Yet everyone had an indefinable feeling that things had changed, although the atmosphere did not in any way become inquisitorial. Then one day Bonhoeffer himself asked one of the brothers—one who was quite inexperienced in such matters—to hear his confession.

Bonhoeffer did not lay down any liturgical form for this procedure. Just as services were held around the dinner table and not in the chapel, private confession in Finkenwalde was conducted without vestments or formal ceremony. Bonhoeffer gave excellent instruction on the subject of confession and its elements. He advised pastors to preach an annual sermon on the blessing of private confession, which enabled people to unburden their consciences to one another instead of God. The absolution that was offered in God's name carried more conviction than the absolution after general confession, fraught as this was with the danger of self-deception and self-forgiveness. His advice was that there should not be too much insistence on the trustworthiness of the confessor, but rather that the person confessing should be humble and trust that, in the other person, Christ was present and listening. The meaning of Bonhoeffer's sermon on forgiveness was clear:

> My dear brothers, anyone who has ever had the experience of being wrest-ed away from grave sin and then forgiven by God, anyone to whom God in such an hour has sent someone to whom we can tell our sins, whoever is familiar with the sinner's resistance to that help because he does not real-ly want to be helped, and has nevertheless found himself absolved from his sin by his brother in the name and at the behest of God—he will lose all desire to judge and to apportion blame. He will only ask to share in his brother's burden, and to serve, to help, to forgive, without measure, with-out conditions, without end.[110]

The New Proposal. Before the August holidays for the first group of ordi-nands had begun, Bonhoeffer began to speak about a "house of brethren." His intention was that a group of ordinands should remain in the spacious house in Finkenwalde, where they would continue to work with him when the new group of ordinands arrived in late autumn. Toward the end of July the first discussion was held with those who wished to stay on; Bonhoeffer suggested that they take time during the holidays to think the matter over and discuss it with their superiors in the church. When the holidays ended at the beginning of September, Bonhoeffer drew up an official proposal with them for a community house, to be sent to the Council of Brethren of the Old Prussian Union, asking the council to give the young ministers leave and the necessary accommodation for the purpose. The name "Evangelical House of Brethren" in the proposal of 6 September 1935 was new.[111] The comment that the plans had been under consideration "for several years" referred to the discussions with the Berlin students that had been going on since the Prebelow and Biesenthal retreats.[112] Bonhoeffer offered the fol-lowing grounds to support the proposal:

1. The content and manner of preaching can be sustained with greater objectivity and steadfastness by a community than by an isolated individual. The principal objective, therefore, is not contemplative introversion, but proclamation.

2. The reply to the question that was being asked everywhere about the nature of the Christian life cannot be given abstractly, but only by a concrete experiment in communal living and communal awareness of Christ's com-mandments. Thus the second objective is the theological question of discipleship.

3. The renunciation of traditional privileges requires a group of ministers who are always available and who, in community, will find that concentration is necessary for service outside. In other words, the church struggle demands a new form of ministry.

4. The community would create a spiritual refuge for pastors working on their own who, from time to time, could retreat there and renew their strength for further service.

The communal life envisaged in the proposal was to take the form of a daily order of prayer, mutual exhortation, free personal confession, common theological work, and a very simple communal life. The brethren would pledge themselves to answer every emergency call from the church and, should they wish to leave the community, they would be free to do so. Admission would be by common consent of the community.

Bonhoeffer further pointed out that, for him, a group of this kind was a personal necessity if he was to assure the seminary's ongoing work and standards. In 1936, when he was trying to persuade Staemmler to allow a member of the community from Saxony to stay there, he wrote:

> There are two things the brothers have to learn during their short time in
> the seminary—first, how to lead a communal life in daily and strict obe-
> dience to the will of Christ Jesus, in the exercise of the humblest and high-
> est service one Christian can perform for another; they must learn to rec-
> ognize the strength and liberation to be found in service to one another
> and communal life in a Christian community. This is something they are
> going to need.
>
> Secondly, they have to learn to serve the truth alone in the study of
> the Bible and its interpretation in their sermons and teaching. I person-
> ally am responsible for this second duty, but the first I cannot shoulder
> by myself.
>
> For this there must be a core group of brothers who, without fuss,
> involve the others in their communal life. That is what the House of
> Brethren is.[113]

The proposal for the House of Brethren was signed by Bonhoeffer and the postulants on 6 September 1935.[114] In light of the fact that parishes urgently needed young theologians, Bonhoeffer was not at all sure the proposal would be favorably received. Indeed, it met with some reluctance, and a certain amount of criticism would always remain. Bonhoeffer's reputation, however, was such that the Council of Brethren hesitated to turn down the proposal altogether.

Six candidates were granted permission to remain in Finkenwalde, where they stayed during the holidays and during the second and subsequent terms for ordinands. Three came from the Berlin-Brandenburg church: Joachim Kanitz, who was entrusted with the care of the Reformed congregation in Pasewalk and several confessional congregations in Stettin, as well as giving tutorials in the seminary; Winfried Maechler, who took over the Confessing congregation and the emergency church in Finkenwalde itself; and Albrecht Schönherr, who was responsible for correspondence, newsletters, substitutes, and tutorials. From the East Prussian church there was Horst Lekzsas (who was killed in the war), who did the difficult work with the Greifswald students, and Friedrich Onnasch (who also died in the war), who came from Pomerania and worked in the nearby town of Podejuch as an assistant for the church superintendent, a Confessing church sympathizer. The sixth was this author; I was put in charge of the financial accounts and also conducted a tutorial.

All these young men were also preparing for their second examination at the university. It was not long before Maechler, Kanitz, and Schönherr were called to serve regular congregations and got married. Inevitably, there was much coming and going at the House of Brethren; some of the more transitory members of the community included Willi Brandenburg (killed in active duty) and Richard Grunow from the province of Brandenburg, Karl-Ferdinand Müller from Pomerania, Horst Thurmann from the Rhineland, Otto Lerche (killed in active duty) from Saxony, and Paul Wälde (killed in active duty) from Hesse.

Room and board were covered by pooling the very unequal stipends of the ministers and assistant preachers, who were paid (or not, as the case might be) by their respective Councils of Brethren. The highest contribution came out of Bonhoeffer's own pocket. The House of Brethren followed the seminary's routine as closely as possible and convened alone only for a short period of discussion and prayer in Bonhoeffer's room at noon, while the ordinands had singing instruction.

The proposal for the House of Brethren and the way of life followed there showed the very beginnings of classical monastic vows, but these were never explicitly taken, nor were they envisioned for the immediate future. (This was a step the Anglican community at Mirfield, founded at the end of the nineteenth century, postponed for thirty years.)

The rumor that Bonhoeffer insisted on celibacy was soon refuted by the marriages of the first three members from Brandenburg. But although the community was unaware of it, Bonhoeffer had broken off with a young woman to whom he had been close during the 1920s and resumed the relationship with at the beginning of the church struggle. One reason was his belief that during those years, while he was experimenting with a communal life, he did not want to commit himself to marriage. Indeed, the fact that Bonhoeffer had no commitment to a family and could make do with only one and a half rooms was an invaluable asset during the development of the seminary and the House of Brethren.[115] For him, the plans he had so long nurtured permitted no other alternative. He dedicated himself entirely to the house of brethren.

In the autumn of 1937 when the Gestapo closed down Finkenwalde Seminary, it also brought an end to the House of Brethren after an existence of only two short years. The new, clandestine seminary form taken by the "collective vicars' courses" precluded any continuation of the House of Brethren's communal life. Bonhoeffer's dearest wish, the goal of which was not "the seclusion of a monastery, but a place of the deepest inward concentration for service outside," was never to get beyond the first, rudimentary stage.[116]

Life Together. The premature dissolution of the community, however, led to the publication in 1939 of a little booklet entitled *Life Together* (Munich, 1939).[117] This was the most widely read of all Bonhoeffer's books during his lifetime. It would never have been written had the police not intervened, for Bonhoeffer was reluctant to publicize his experiment too soon, or to have to justify something in detail when it was barely past the stage of trial and error. When in 1936 Finkenwalde and the House of Brethren had become a topic of general interest, he left the group to cope with the inquiries that started pouring in; a request from Staemmler resulted in the production of "Introduction to Daily Meditation."[118] Bonhoeffer began to write a small sketch for the members of the house itself, but never finished it.[119] But once Finkenwalde had ceased to exist, he wanted to record what had been done there. Thus the experiments that had been devised especially for Finkenwalde as a theological community were given a new and more generally applicable form.

The publication of *Life Together* caused quite a sensation, for this was something entirely new in Protestant Germany. Although short-lived, Finkenwalde had revealed a weak spot within Protestantism and, moreover, had sought practical solutions where others felt helpless. It seemed as though something had been restored to the church which had long been confined to conventicles or sects, and had been sought by group movements or brotherhoods such as those of St. Michael's and Sydow. Here were the outlines of a living Protestant community, not revived in opposition to or outside the churches of the Reformation (as had happened in Herrnhut), but within the church itself, undertaken and upheld out of a renewed understanding of the church. In the midst of the great crisis and weakness besieging the privileged ministry of the *Volkskirche*, Finkenwalde offered an alternative with its new forms of service, for Bonhoeffer always drew a sharp distinction between the office of the pastor as preacher—an office that could not be relinquished—and the office of the parish minister, which need not be preserved at all costs.[120]

During the nineteenth century German Protestantism had gone so far as to develop monastic training for deacons and deaconesses, but it had never established free communities such as those in England. When, in the twentieth century, Bonhoeffer finally attempted this, it was in exceptional circumstances, even though the project had been conceived before 1933. It would have been interesting to know how his ideas would have evolved under more normal conditions; what we do know, however, is that his experiment began to prove its worth once the crisis in the privileged *Volkskirche* became evident. Similar experiments and reflections could be discerned in the Bonhoeffer of the final years: in his thinking about the arcane discipline in which Christians surrender their privileges, pray, study, and act in ways that are not for everyone, nor intended to make the headlines.

While word spread about Finkenwalde and the House of Brethren, they were visited by members of the Oxford movement [an organization founded in 1921 in England that advocated strict morality in public and private life] who thought that Bonhoeffer seemed a likely ally. In this they were mistaken. The man who had advocated "the first step" in *Discipleship* found the Oxford movement's demand for "change" very disturbing. He believed that they had replaced the witness of the Gospel with the witness of personal change.[121] He was incensed by people who allowed themselves to be led full circle into reflecting upon their own beginnings, and he reacted strongly against any interpretation of *Discipleship* or *Life Together* as teachings aimed at conversion. He believed that the Oxford movement and its supporters lacked the strength of the preaching of the cross, and he criticized their indifference to the "Confession" and their "unsteadiness"[122] that paralyzed them with regard to church politics:

> The Oxford Movement has been naïve enough to try to convert Hitler—a ridiculous failure to understand what is going on. . . .[123]

> But here the affair's beginning to look very dubious indeed. Uncommitted church members are rushing . . . full of interest, to look at and dally with this live, unpolitical phenomenon.[124]

Other things had to be repudiated, however, in addition to the Oxford movement. While working on his lectures on Zinzendorf's hymns in 1936, his love of these did not prevent him from writing:

> By the time I'd finished, I felt really depressed. What a musty cellarful of piety.... And all this in hymns! Yes, such are people—pious people! I have a horror of the consequences of this *finitum capax infiniti*! We must have the pure and genuine air of the Word around us. And yet we are incapable of getting away from ourselves. But for goodness' sake let's turn our eyes away from ourselves![125]

But there was another area in which he felt it even more essential to define his limits. To the head of the Berneuchen movement in Pomerania, Dr. Friedrich Schauer, he wrote:

> It would seem to you that the Holy Spirit is not only the reality committed to the true, consistent Word of God by which, in knowledge and life, we are inescapably bound, but is also the formative principle of a Christian ideal of life.... The Confessing church would sacrifice the promise that has been given it should any power other than obedience to the truth wrought by the Holy Spirit be brought in to infuse new life into the church.[126]

Some members of the Berneuchen movement were members of the Pomeranian Council of Brethren; it might have been expected that they would be anxious to foster relations with Finkenwalde because they, too, were concerned with the renewal of the ministry and of the laity in the church. Yet their relations with Finkenwalde became acrimonious to the point of a final break, and in due course they left the Council of Brethren altogether.[127] Yet Finkenwalde established warm relations with Dr. Baumann, the Reformed member of the Pomeranian Council, despite his innate mistrust of pious conventicles and his undisguised theological reservations toward Bonhoeffer as a Lutheran. Nevertheless, Baumann sent young ministers in whose spiritual development he took a special interest to spend a few weeks in Finkenwalde, where they could participate in the life there for several weeks, even if for some reason they could not become members of the seminary.

When Bonhoeffer was working in Ettal at the end of 1940 he encountered the monastic wisdom of the Benedictines as one who was no stranger to it himself.[128] Biographically the time of community life was over, but this was not so in practice. In 1943 and 1944, when he was compelled to lead a cruelly lonely existence, the exercises he had practiced in Finkenwalde proved an invaluable solace, and made him frank and open-minded toward his agnostic fellow sufferers.

The Ecumenical World

Bonhoeffer's work in Finkenwalde meant his withdrawal from the round of ecumenical conferences. His involvement in the ecumenical movement had reached its peak in 1934; during the following year he allowed his duties to lapse almost entirely. Only when the leaders of the Confessing church needed him or church president Koch sought his intervention would he leave the seminary to manage without him. He now expressed his ecumenical convictions mostly through the cancellations that he more or less explained. On the other hand, in his writings and his disagreements with leading ecumenical representatives, Bonhoeffer's views of the ecumenical question in 1935 were expressed with a cogency unmatched before or afterward.

Unavoidable Journeys. Now that he was again living in Germany, it was difficult for Bonhoeffer to escape the problems of the Confessing church's representation at future ecumenical conferences, problems which had grown much more acute since the Dahlem synod. He attended two conferences of ecumenical experts from the Confessing church and disagreed with several experienced men, and this precipitated the crisis in his relations with Geneva.

Hannover. In preparation for the 1937 Oxford conference, a conference was scheduled for 13–14 May 1935 in Hannover.[129] Among those expected was Dr. J. H. Oldham, who was responsible for preparing the themes for Oxford and was cooperating closely with the Research Department in Geneva. From Hannover he would be going to a meeting of the executive committee of Life and Work in Paris, where he was to give Bell the news from Germany. Bonhoeffer was summoned to the Hannover meeting by telegram.

He arrived at a time when matters were beginning to look very serious for the church: Peter Brunner and two other pastors from Hesse had been interned in the Dachau concentration camp for more than a month and the Councils of Brethren had ordered weekly services of intercession on their behalf. On 11 May the council's office in Dahlem was searched by the Gestapo for the first time. With this in the background, Bonhoeffer made two things very clear to the meeting: first, that the ecumenical representatives from abroad must no longer expect to persuade the Reich church (i.e.,

Bishop Heckel in the Foreign Office) and the Confessing church to work together in preparation for Oxford; second, that the Confessing church, in conformity with Barmen and Dahlem, must insist that the Research Department take a clearer stand on the claims made by these two synods. The preparations for Oxford could only emanate from a theology supported by a real church; Geneva, he said, was evading the decision as to which was the real church in Germany.

Six weeks later, at a meeting in Berlin, the first item on the agenda was a paper from Schönfeld defending Geneva's attitude. This led to a heated discussion. Menn, Wendland, and, to some extent, Lilje defended the Research Department. In reply to Bonhoeffer's allegations, Schönfeld had written that in Geneva the entire preparatory work for the Oxford meeting sprang from the very "soil of the church," but that "if what is demanded here is a theology that declares itself to be absolute, then it will hardly be possible to deal with this within the framework of our ecumenical research."[130] Despite the assurances of Geneva's sympathy for the Confessing church, Bonhoeffer insisted that the Geneva officials were dealing with the other side on terms of parity. Geneva was advancing "theological problems" which, he pointed out, "Heckel is using to confuse the decision. What is demanded is an ecclesiastical decision, not a theological dialogue with the German Christians."[131] The official minutes of the meeting were summed up:

> A message transmitted by Dr. Schönfeld (Geneva), under the heading "An Unspoken Last Word," was submitted (by Dr. Lilje) to those present. . . . Discussion of the message: This concerns the attitude of the Ecumenical Research Department in Geneva toward the Confessing church. While some deplored the absence of any clear decision in favor of the Confessing church and complained about parity of treatment with the German Christians, others called attention to the Department's confessional and ecclesiastical work and its considerable commitments. Views differ. . . .[132]

In Hannover Bonhoeffer once more urged the establishment of an ecumenical office in the Confessing church and summarized his proposals in a memorandum, but again without result.[133] It was decided, however, to form a "Provisional Church Administration Ecumenical Advisory Board." This advisory board failed to survive the collapse of the first Provisional Church Administration in 1936. In the second Provisional Church Administration, ecumenical affairs were overseen by Dr. Hans Böhm, with whom Bonhoeffer would form a close relationship; but by then the major battles had been fought and lost. Böhm retained this post for the remainder of the Confessing church's existence. Bonhoeffer was still relatively optimistic at that point, as a letter he wrote to president Koch indicates: "It seems to me more than ever that things depend upon how this work is handled."[134]

Berlin. On 27 June the Provisional Church Administration Ecumenical Advisory Board, chaired by president Koch, met for the first time in Berlin to discuss their position on the impending summer conference. Bonhoeffer had just declined an invitation to participate in a Faith and Order conference in Hindsgavl on equal terms with German delegates from the other faction. At the meeting he now complained that, "Lausanne says nothing about the German church question."[135] The minutes show how the advisory board viewed the steadily deteriorating situation:

> The Confessing church may well have the right to demand that the Provisional Church Government be the one lawful representative of the German Evangelical Church. On the other hand, there is some doubt about whether the ecumenical movement is ready for this, or whether it might not attempt to treat the two Evangelical church governments in Germany on equal terms. A literal interpretation of the constitution of "Life and Work" would require this, unless the ecumenical movement has the courage to refuse recognition to the Reich church as a church. It is also thought that the fundamental position of the Confessing church does not allow it to negotiate with the Foreign Office of the Reich church on terms of parity.
>
> Conclusion: the general feeling is that an invitation to an ecumenical conference should be declined if representatives of Bishop Heckel are there.[136]

Given the general uncertainty, it was clear to Bonhoeffer after this meeting that he would have to speak out in public, so that both the Confessing church and the ecumenical movement recognized that this was their hour of crisis. The result was his important essay, "The Confessing Church and the Ecumenical Movement."[137]

London. During his first summer in Finkenwalde, Bonhoeffer was sent twice by president Koch to see Bishop Bell.

Having learned at the Paris meeting of the misgivings about his proposed visit to Düsseldorf with Bishop Ammundsen, Bell did not want to imperil the Council of Brethren still further by his presence. An additional factor may have been the Gestapo search of the council office in Dahlem. But Koch had some new requests to make of Bell in connection with the major assembly of representatives of the "destroyed" regional churches, scheduled for 22–23 May in Gohlfeld. This event was being kept strictly secret as a precaution against police interference, who by then were accustomed to breaking up all assemblies. Koch hoped that the chairman of Life and Work would send a message to Gohlfeld and also, if at all possible, attend the upcoming Reich synod of the Confessing church in Augsburg.

Koch therefore asked Bonhoeffer, on his way home from Hannover, to turn around and proceed to London, where he reported to the bishop of Chichester on 18 May. The two men arranged that, should the situation suddenly deteriorate, Bell and Koechlin would come to Berlin to confer with their friends in the Confessing church, "say at the Grand Hotel am Knie."[138]

In view of his long absence from Zingst, Bonhoeffer wrote in his memorandum for Koch: "A traveling secretary for the church whose job would be to keep both sides regularly informed. Very important!"[139]

The second visit to England on Koch's behalf took place during the first two weeks of August. Bonhoeffer used this chance to permanently end his leave of absence status from the London parishes, thus opening the way for his successor, Licentiate Boeckheler.

There were two reasons why the bishop of Chichester needed to be thoroughly briefed: first, the Provisional Church Administration had decided not to attend the 1935 Chamby conference because Heckel would be there; second, Bell was coming to Germany after Chamby as a follow-up to his June talk with Ribbentrop at the Athenaeum Club, where Ribbentrop had promised to introduce him to Rudolf Hess and Hanns Kerrl, the newly appointed Minister for Church Affairs. Prior to these meetings Bell wanted the Council of Brethren's comments on the "finance departments" that the state had set up for the church.

Bonhoeffer went to Bell with Niemöller's 30 July manifesto "To Our Brethren in the Ministry"[140] in his pocket. The manifesto had been signed by forty-nine prominent people from all parts of Germany. Bell referred to it in Chamby when he emphasized that the Ecumenical Council "could not ignore the growth in compactness within the Evangelical Confessional Church" in opposition to the state's "pacification measures."[141] Bell now asked that arrangements be made for his visit to Germany.

After Chamby Bell met with Koch, Asmussen, and Lilje on 12 September. By the time he saw Hitler's deputy Hess and Minister for Church Affairs Kerrl, the Nuremberg Laws had been enacted. At their meeting on 20 September Hess mollified Bell by saying that the clear legislation would in fact make the treatment of the Jews more consistent and therefore better. With great optimism Kerrl assured the bishop on 28 September that his laws for "the protection of the German Evangelical Church" would bring peace back to the church, and that he was negotiating with reliable people, including members of the Confessing church.

Cancellations. Bonhoeffer's official duties would have required him to help prepare and lead the 1935 ecumenical youth conference in Chamby. As "co-opted member" he could also participate in the 1935 meetings of the World Alliance (12–18 August) and the Ecumenical Council in Chamby (18–22 August) without being affected by the issue of equal representation by the two German factions. Both he and Koch had received direct invitations.[142]

Youth Conference. Still powerfully influenced by the Fanö meeting, Bonhoeffer was initially interested in the youth conference. In his memorandum to de Félice on 29 January 1935 he made some very definite proposals for topics that had emerged from the Fanö youth conference:

> The question which it has not yet succeeded to find an answer to is whether in case of war a service in a sanitary group would be Christianly justifiable. ... I am in favor of an international youth conference and I should be glad if the question of conscientious objection would be one of the subjects under discussion. I feel that one of the weaknesses of our cause is the lack of a common and definite attitude in the very crucial question. We should march on whatever the older people think and do. . . .
>
>   One of the special topics I should like to propose for the youth conference is: the use of coercion, its right and its limitations. Before this fundamental question is given an answer to, the theoretical basis of pacifism is very weak.[143]

Indeed, the theme of conscientious objection came up briefly at the 1935 Chamby youth conference: "The presentation by Pasteur Toureille of recent experiences of Christian conscientious objectors in France made a deep impression."[144] Meanwhile the main discussions focused on the topic "Freedom and Authority."

Shortly after writing this memorandum, Bonhoeffer decided against making a serious commitment to the Youth Commission and arranged for Jürgen Winterhager to represent him. He had lost hope that these major conferences would reach any real solution to the essential questions about a decision on heresy and the issue of obedience to the commandment to peace. He was also fully aware of the Geneva secretariat's increasing hostility toward him. He was not sorry, then, when his mission to England at the beginning of August prevented his attendance at the youth conference.

The World Alliance and the Geneva headquarters had also begun to consider a reorganization of the ecumenical youth secretariat. To those in Geneva, the Fanö youth meetings had seemed a little frightening, highly explosive, and much too close to the deliberations of the main conference. This led to some proposed changes, and Henriod, in his progress report, explained: "[It] had met with various objections and difficulties which made it desirable that the youth conference in the future should be held separately."[145]

The executive committee of Life and Work envisaged a full-time youth secretary based in Geneva—a plan for which the World Alliance promised financial support.[146] An American, Edwin Espy, was appointed to the post in the autumn and began his duties at the beginning of 1936. There was never any intention to dispose of the services of the honorary youth secretaries, since Espy's main task was to prepare for a world youth conference, which eventually took place in 1939 in Amsterdam. Nevertheless, it was hoped that the Geneva office would more closely supervise the youth work. Espy had been acquainted with Bonhoeffer at Union Theological Seminary in 1930–1931, although they had not known each other well. In accordance with the wishes of the Geneva staff, he recommended that Bonhoeffer assemble a delegation for the upcoming 1936 youth conference of representatives, not just from the Confessing church, but from other groups as well.[147] Bonhoeffer apparently did not respond to this unreasonable demand. In June 1936 Espy met Bonhoeffer in Berlin for the first time. In his report to Henriod he spoke only of "Bonhoeffer's outright rejection of Gerstenmaier, and his readiness to admit members of the free churches and the Lutheran Council, but no delegates from the Reich church, to the youth delegation."[148]

Before Espy's visit to Berlin, Schönfeld sent an effusive letter recommending him to the Church Office for Foreign Affairs. Introducing the youth secretary and Henriod to Eugen Gerstenmaier, the responsible official in the Berlin office, Schönfeld wrote:

> Perhaps you have already heard a lot of alarming things about the work of this ecumenical youth commission, and I might say that my feelings would be the same as yours had not the status of this work changed fundamentally now that we have found the right man for it. . . . If we had not found such a solution, we in the Research Department would have done all we could to put a stop to the work in the form it has taken in the past. . . .
>
> You may be certain that Mr. Espy's work is in complete accord with the methods of the Research Department and with the problems and tasks we have set for ourselves here. . . . I am telling you all this so that you will understand that a fundamental change has begun here as well. Personally

I have long found it inexcusable that this part of the work should be determined exclusively—or almost exclusively—by a man like Bonhoeffer. But
it is most desirable, particularly when this is about to be changed, that people should be available who will support Mr. Espy in his work. In case
Monsieur Henriod has already spoken with you about matters, may I
request a favorable hearing from you; you may be convinced that this will
be worth it. . . .[149]

Thus the exchanges taking place between the Geneva secretariat and
Heckel's office were now far more lively than the correspondence between
the secretariat and the Councils of Brethren.

Chamby 1935. The agenda of the 1935 conference in Chamby included an
endorsement of the Fanö resolution and preliminary arrangements for the
1937 Oxford conference. Bonhoeffer and the Provisional Church Administration of the Confessing church, however, found themselves unable to
accept the invitation to Chamby, since representatives of the Reich church
led by Heckel would be present.

In the summer of 1934 the battle in Fanö had centered on the question
of whether the Barmen "opposition" should be invited together with the
Reich church. That battle had been won. The resolution passed, and, despite
the fact that the Confessing church did not attend the conference, this represented its greatest success. Now, in 1935, it was no longer a question of
being invited along with the other delegation, but as the sole representation
of the German Evangelical Church. This was consistent with the Dahlem
synod's statement in October 1934 (i.e., after Fanö), which placed the Reich
church government outside the Church of Christ in Germany and established the emergency offices of the Confessing church. The situation now
became genuinely tragic. On the one hand, the Geneva headquarters and its
committees felt that to recognize the Dahlem decision and act accordingly
would be going too far, while the Confessing church believed that if it withdrew its claim it would be abandoning its own case.

In this impasse it must have come as a relief to outside observers and to
those ecumenists who were incapable of seeing the true situation that they
were able to deal with German church bodies which did not insist on an
immediate decision. One such group was the Lutheran Council, the new
body of the "intact" Lutheran churches, which had existed since 1934 and
became a fully established assembly in March 1936. Many of its members
were respected theologians, and this led some outside observers to question
the necessity of the radical decision taken in Dahlem. The confusion was

intensified by the fact that the theologians in the Church Foreign Office, particularly Heckel, readily and confidently drew on these Lutherans' theological categories. The Confessing church Councils of Brethren found themselves falling behind in the contest to enter the ecumenical sphere, so much so that confusion even began to spread within their own ranks. They either made their case halfheartedly or without understanding the circumstances in the ecumenical realm. Even today, the actual course of events remains so obscure that scholars tend either to bypass this part of the history in silence or to approach it purely emotionally.

The 1935 Chamby conference was presided over by Orthodox Archbishop Germanos, who had now succeeded Bell. On the German side, Bishop Heckel had the field to himself. His Church Foreign Office had survived the end of the era of Ludwig Müller and August Jäger successfully; thus he was in a decidedly more favorable situation than he had been in Fanö. Heckel gave an optimistic and comforting picture of developments in the German church, referring especially to the state's "legal aid" in the form of finance departments, the Legislative Authority, and the newly established Ministry of Church Affairs.[150] On the subject of the Jewish question he even gave the assurance that "it was being dealt with much more openly in Germany than a year ago, and that plans that had been put in hand by the Reich church were on the way to fulfillment." Only a few days before the announcement of the Nuremberg Laws, Heckel was presenting the same arguments that Bishop Bell subsequently heard from Rudolf Hess.

Bishop Bell spoke out on behalf of those who were absent and referred to the rejection by the Councils of Brethren of the ostensibly reassuring finance departments. His speech endorsed "the resolution adopted by the council at Fanö to maintain close fellowship with the Confessional Synod" and "to inform the leaders . . . of the Committee's strong desire for their attendance at all future meetings, and to make it plain that the help of the leaders of the Confessional Church Government and of those whom they represented was indispensable to the Ecumenical Movement. . . ."[151] The wary Heckel pointed out that this "implied that the reference in the Fanö minutes to a desire to remain in friendly relations with *all* Christian brethren in Germany, still held good. The ecclesiastical officers of the Foreign Department of the German Evangelical Church claimed to represent the whole Church in a legal and equitable manner. . . ."[152]

The third invitation that Bonhoeffer refused that year was of a new and very flattering kind; it came from Faith and Order. The related correspondence gives an important background to his significant essay on the ecumenical movement.

Canon Leonard Hodgson. On 17 June 1935 Bonhoeffer received an invitation from Faith and Order through its secretary, Canon Leonard Hodgson, asking him to take part in the summer session of the Continuation Committee in Hindsgavl.[153] The proposal to include Bonhoeffer came from a Swedish churchman, Dr. Brilioth, after a desire to have young blood at the meeting had been expressed. Brilioth gave Hodgson the names of three potential German participants, all of them people who had already made their mark: New Testament scholar Hans Lietzmann, Paul Althaus, and Bonhoeffer. Replying to an inquiry from Hodgson, Deissmann wrote: "It would, of course, be a very good thing if our young lecturer, Pastor Dietrich Bonhoeffer, were to take part. He is now twenty-nine and one of the most eminent representatives of the younger generation here."[154]

Bonhoeffer's refusal of the invitation was not due to schedule conflicts, too many other duties, or even his old critique of Faith and Order.[155] He turned it down because Hodgson had failed to give an assurance that the Reich church—that is, Heckel and Krummacher—would not be appearing on equal terms with himself. Hodgson had written Bonhoeffer:

> . . . we cannot, as a Movement, exclude the representatives of any Church which "accepts our Lord Jesus Christ as God and Saviour" . . . we cannot arrogate to ourselves the right to discriminate between them.[156]

This was straightforward and was only to be expected. But Bonhoeffer had hoped for something else. In a long letter he pointed out that the Reich church had betrayed Jesus Christ as God and Savior; in contrast, his church had declared its commitment on this point, and thus could not spare the ecumenical movement from drawing the necessary conclusions.[157] He went on to say that he was well aware that, to anyone removed from the arena, all this must sound very pharisaical and appear as the opposite of the necessary humility. Bonhoeffer fully recognized that he was not making things easy for his British correspondent, far removed from the scene of the crisis, who had learned to appreciate the complexity of a crisis and to become mistrustful whenever an attempt was made to reduce everything to one common denominator. How could Hodgson accept and endorse the dictum "The Confessional Church has therefore declared, that the Reich church Government has dissociated itself from the Church of Christ"?[158] It was neither accepted nor endorsed. But Bonhoeffer did not relent, although he was fully aware that by taking this course, he risked excluding himself:

> [We know] that we are fighting for Christianity not only with regard to the Church in Germany but in the whole world. . . . If now the ecumenical

movement, and in particular the Faith and Order Movement were complying with that decisive question and taking the challenge seriously in
obedience towards Jesus Christ and His Word, an inward regeneration
and a new unification might well be bestowed upon all Christendom. . . .
On the other hand, if the ecumenical movement were to leave this question out of sight, it might bring in its own verdict and lose the power of
speaking and acting in the name of Jesus Christ. . . .[159]

Bonhoeffer requested and was given Koch's approval for his decision and the
reasons behind it.[160]

Once again the two virtually irreconcilable elements within the ecumenical movement had clashed—elements which remain both disruptive
and productive up to the present day. Unlike Hodgson, Bonhoeffer was not
the general secretary of an organization restricted by the rules, and he
believed that he was not just addressing a general secretary and his organization. For his part, Hodgson had not been a member of the Barmen and
Dahlem synods but was a cautious and skeptical church historian. More than
ever, Bonhoeffer believed in the church within the ecumenical movement
and acted on that belief. Hodgson continued to believe that the ecumenical
movement was only a platform for the churches:

> . . . it is necessary for us to guarantee to every church, when we invite it to
> send representatives, that it will not find itself in any way compromised by
> action taken by the conference at which it is represented. . . .[161]

While Bishop Bell recognized that one had to compromise for the sake
of the cause of Christ, from his perspective Hodgson was incapable of this.
Yet he acknowledged:

> It may be the duty of the Life and Work Movement to run the risk of
> this—of that I cannot express any opinion. But for Faith and Order to do
> so would be to be false to its own vocation.[162]

A careful study of the relations between Faith and Order and the disputing parties in Germany during those years confirms that it maintained
much better and closer contacts with the opponents of the Confessing
church than did Life and Work and, more especially, the World Alliance. Dr.
A. C. Headlam, for example, who was bishop of Gloucester and a leading
member of Faith and Order, was also the German Christians' spokesman in
England for a number of years. When Bonhoeffer read Hodgson's warmhearted and careful reply to his letter, he probably thought it curious that the

sole opposing witness on behalf of the claims of the Reich church was, of all people, Professor Wobbermin—who had so unequivocally defended the Aryan clause.[163]

Hodgson thought that Faith and Order could provide a platform for the disputing parties without prejudice to their own cause, but there could be no neutrality anywhere for the struggling church in Germany at the time. Thus Faith and Order continued to adhere to its correct but narrow concept of giving everyone a platform, and declined the challenge in an unequivocal but friendly manner. The Confessing church refused to cede its uncomfortable and absolute claim, and so excluded itself from the conferences. In view of all this, Bonhoeffer hoped that the well-considered challenge contained in his article might help shed fresh light on the question. But it evoked no response.

Nearly four years later the correspondence with Hodgson resumed, but the outcome was no different.[164]

The Essay. Bonhoeffer's article, "The Confessing Church and the Ecumenical Movement," written in late June and early July 1935, appeared in the seventh issue of *Evangelische Theologie* that year.[165] It was organized programmatically, concluding not in reflection but with categorical statements about "commandment and obedience." Every word was weighed; Bonhoeffer sought and demanded something of both sides—the ecumenists as well as the leaders of the Confessing church. He ascertained a certain shortsightedness on both sides that prevented them from recognizing the utterly new situation, full of possibilities for the future of the church of Christ, that had been created by the confrontation between the ecumenical world and the Confessing church.

He began with an intriguing analysis of the events of the two preceding years in the ecumenical movement: ". . . never before has the Protestant ecumenical movement been so much in evidence on the occasion of a church dispute. . . ."[166] He castigated his own colleagues for their fear of ecumenical connections that resulted from "the ostracism of the political concept of internationalism in church circles."[167] Today it is difficult to grasp how little ecumenical interest existed at the time. As a result of Fanö, Bonhoeffer said, "many leading churchmen saw the reality of the ecumenical movement for the first time."[168] The movement had "committed itself to stand as godparent for the Confessing church."[169] This surprised Bonhoeffer at the time, since to the nationally conscious Confessing Christians the ecumenical world seemed irritating and unserious theologically, while the humanist and liberal ecumenists viewed the Confessing church as theologically carried away and hysterical.

The essay has two sections. In the first, Bonhoeffer examined the questions the Confessing church's existence posed for the ecumenical movement. In the second, he explored which questions the Confessing church had to confront through the existence of ecumenism.

The Confessing church posed the question of confession. With that, it shut itself off "against any invasion by the political, social and humanitarian. The Confession fills its entire room."[170] All too clearly, he recognized how "unprecedented" the Confessing church's demand was that, in recognition of its decision, the ecumenical movement had to accept that its dialogue with the Reich church government had been broken because the Confessing church had broken it off. But if the Confessing church were to abandon this demand, it would mean "that the German church struggle was already decided against her, and with it the struggle for Christianity."[171] To Bonhoeffer, the confession at stake here did not serve a primarily juristic or legal function, nor was it a kind of security that one faction possessed. Its character was exclusive and divisive, but its content was totally one of the confession of sins and hymns of praise, and this made it much more than a kind of formalism. This point was explicitly expressed at the end of the essay, but cannot be forgotten throughout the rest of it.

The first question the Confessing church posed to the ecumenical movement was: Is the ecumenical movement a church? This question had preoccupied Bonhoeffer since the beginning of his work with the movement, leading him to suffer and, at times, making him incomprehensible to his audience. For Bonhoeffer, this cardinal question was linked to another: Where was the authority "by which the ecumenical movement speaks and acts?"[172] Like any other supporter of the movement, Bonhoeffer knew that it was not a church and said so. But what, then, was the movement's point of departure if it did not claim to be a church and did not seek to become a church? This question never left Bonhoeffer, and he never stopped raising it. He acknowledged that it was a question that had long been successfully evaded: "But now this question has been raised by the Confessing church and demands a clear answer."[173]

Explicitly praising the achievements of the Ecumenical Research Department in Geneva, Bonhoeffer then examined the recent years in which the "spirit of theological inquiry" had so auspiciously dissolved and broken through the uninformed optimism of the past. From the Cambridge meeting to Gland, Bonhoeffer had energetically promoted this development. But this stage was now over. To persist any longer in "theological dialogue" was a dangerous, indeed diabolical, camouflage that only served to create a respectable facade behind which overdue decisions on theological as well as church matters were neglected or even prevented. Referring to Schönfeld and his Research Department, he said:

> With the question of the Confessing church we have already gone beyond the stage, necessary in itself, of theological conversation.[174]

The insistence on "defining" the church now became the refusal to "be" the church. For Hodgson's benefit, Bonhoeffer wrote:

> There is still one way out for the ecumenical movement and that is to accept this question courageously in the form in which it has been received and in obedience to leave everything else to the Lord of the church. Who knows that it is not precisely by way of this disruptive task that the ecumenical movement will emerge from the struggle strengthened and with greater authority?[175]

Here Bonhoeffer showed that he recognized the difficulties that threatened to lead to a difficult crisis. Still, "with the Fanö conference, the ecumenical world has entered a new epoch."[176] He then posed the delicate question as to how ecumenism could be a church—that is, how it could take a confessional position that would be legitimate within the church. But this goal could not be attained by seeking a confessionally pure combination such as "World Lutheranism"; instead, he played the act of contemporary confession off against the handed-down confessional stands.

The second section reversed the question: can the Confessing church be called into question by the ecumenical movement?[177] Bonhoeffer replied that this was the case in three ways:

First, the mere existence of the ecumenical movement did not prove anything, but only suggested it. The ecumenical movement had existed prior to and independently of the Confessing church. More profoundly, this meant:

> Should the Confessing church become so isolated in its confessional claims that its confession leaves no further room for ecumenical ideas, the question would then arise in all seriousness whether the Confessing church herself was still the Church of Christ.[178]

That would be an "orthodoxy in unlimited self-glorification all on its own."[179] In Bonhoeffer's view the limits of the confessional claim were acknowledged by the very participation of the Confessing church in the ecumenical movement.

Second, the Confessing church, together with other churches, recognized the sacrament of Baptism, thereby placing "the grace of God above the doctrine of the church," not to make light of the schism, but in order to become aware of its full oppressiveness.[180]

Third, and this was of particular concern to Bonhoeffer, the confession of a Lutheran church was essentially a confession of atonement "because this church receives its life from outside, not from within, and therefore in every word it utters exists on the basis of ecumenism. This makes ecumenical work its innermost necessity."[181] Thus the Confessing church takes part in the ecumenical movement not as a group or as a movement, nor even as an opposition group that must be taken seriously within the German Evangelical Church, but "as the church." This was what had not yet happened in the ecumenical movement, but Bonhoeffer had hopes that it would happen soon. In reality, it never did happen.

Underlying the confessional problem, which threatened to become agonizingly absolutized, Bonhoeffer addressed his earlier question about the authoritative command to both sides. He concluded the essay by asking whether an ecumenical council would "speak a word of judgment about war, race hatred and social exploitation; whether, through such true ecumenical unity among Protestant Christians of all nations, war itself will one day become impossible . . . what is demanded is not the realization of our own aims but obedience."[182] Only in light of this conclusion is the correctness of his reasoning to this point established. The ecumenical movement would not be legitimated by its confessional legality, but through an internal validity that would create or renew the legitimacy of the ecumenical movement as church.

The confessional problem remained in the foreground for Bonhoeffer for some time. The issues of schism and heresy were becoming more existential. This led him one year later to write another paper that would provoke the most violent reactions. Intended for internal German consumption, his wording was more provocative than ever. Bonhoeffer received a hearing, but his views were largely dismissed. Both essays should be considered together.

At the time, the ecumenical movement remained unaware of this article tucked away in a German theological periodical. The headquarters in Geneva continued to negotiate with the leaders of the Confessing church without wrestling with the issues Bonhoeffer raised or taking the Confessing church's claims seriously. The Geneva office continued to negotiate with the Reich church as well, failing to face its leaders' acceptance and tolerance of the National Socialists' "national evolution" based on blood, race, and soil. Could such a thing be overlooked in 1935? Could the ecumenical world accept this way of talking as a mere tactical ploy by the Reich church so that it could continue to exist? Such attitudes at the ecumenical level met with Bonhoeffer's sharpest disapproval.

Rouse and Neill's *A History of the Ecumenical Movement* does not mention the 1935 essay and its dramatic history. Yet the issue that troubled Bonhoeffer increasingly became a part of the history of the ecumenical movement.[183]

The Steglitz Resolutions

The Mission Tour. Before the beginning of the final term of that first year in Finkenwalde, Bonhoeffer and a group of ordinands set out on a bicycle tour that took them through the Pomeranian church districts of Naugard and Daber, eventually ending on the shores of the Baltic, where they spent a few days relaxing. The idea of visiting isolated Confessing pastors and holding evangelization evenings in their parishes sprang from a mutual need. The August 1935 expedition was the beginning of the mission work that the Finkenwalde seminary later did more systematically.

Old Prussian Confessing Synod. The seminary's visit to Berlin-Steglitz from 23 to 26 September 1935 was prompted by an urgent telephone call from Niemöller's parsonage in Dahlem; the response showed Bonhoeffer's capacity for making lightning-quick decisions in an emergency. At the meeting of the Steglitz Confessing synod the seminary operated simply as a pressure group in the gallery. The students began the day in class in Finkenwalde. The morning was taken up with "discipleship"—possessions and concern[184]—and the discussion of confessional writings. By that evening they all attended the opening service in Berlin-Steglitz where Rendtorff preached on confession and denial. The following morning, after an address on "discipleship" by Hans Iwand, the tense proceedings began.

The state's interference through the finance department, the Legislative Authority, the Ministry for Church Affairs, and the protection laws (which had just been announced on 24 September) primarily affected the churches of the Old Prussian Union. Uncertainty spread rapidly in that region. Some saw these new "legal aid measures" as the work of levelheaded, sensible people, and found them harmless compared with the German Christian attacks of 1933; others immediately recognized them as a far more effective stranglehold on the church's freedom. The work of Kerrl's new Ministry for Church Affairs began under the motto of pacification so that the "church

may again be the church." Would it not be better to play for time and negotiate rather than simply say no? The Councils of Brethren could no longer
assume the sole responsibility for a negative answer, one that might involve
considerable sacrifices; they needed the support of a synod resolution. But
the synod that convened on the morning of 24 September was no longer an
assembly united in its resolve to say no.

It was the only instance in the history of the church struggle where a representative of the state appeared at a Confessing synod and was given permission to speak. On behalf of Minister Kerrl, Dr. Julius Stahn attempted to
make the meaning and intentions of the new "finance departments" more
palatable.[185] Heckling from the Finkenwaldians in the gallery highlighted
this disagreeable situation, particularly during and immediately after Dr.
Stahn's speech.

The end result of the Steglitz synod upheld the independence of spiritual
decisions. While it could not stop the directives from the state's legal and
financial organs, it reserved the right to reconsider them from time to time—
whatever this might ultimately mean in practice. It continued to demand
control over the use of church property and the money received from collections. Indeed, after a heated discussion, it forbade members of the Confessing church from cooperating with the agencies of the finance departments in the Old Prussian Union.

But these decisions aroused somewhat ambivalent feelings. The discussions revealed weak points in the oppositional front; the rift between those
who supported and those who rejected the finance departments could not
be delayed long. Some delegates to the Steglitz synod soon became members of the church committees that Kerrl established in the provinces, and
the previously well-respected church superintendent Wilhelm Zoellner
assumed the oversight of these committees. Eventually the break within the
ranks of the Confessing church reached the very doors of the preachers'
seminary.

But the real reason behind the Finkenwalde seminarians' journey to
Berlin was neither Stahn's presence nor the signals that the synod might ratify the finance departments. The impetus had been provided by Franz Hildebrandt, who had called from Dahlem with the alarming news that the Confessing synod committee was considering a resolution on Jewish baptism,
which included a clause apparently approving the recently enacted Nuremberg Laws.

These laws, which had been announced by Hitler on 15 September at the
Nuremberg Party rally to thunderous applause, introduced a second, "more
ordered" phase of Jewish persecution. The "Reich Citizens' Law" distin-

guished Reich citizens "of German or related blood" from a second class of "nationals" who were without political rights. The "Blood Protection Law" forbade so-called mixed marriages and the employment of female "Aryans" under the age of forty-five in allegedly Jewish households. Dohnanyi had informed Bonhoeffer about the various stages in the preparation of these rigid laws and about the strategies to modify them or find suitable compromises that would allow a more flexible interpretation.

Now, within the realm of the church, the Steglitz synod wished to reaffirm its outright rejection of the Aryan clause with respect to baptism; but some people also envisioned making a qualification in which the church explicitly conceded the state's right to legislate the Jewish question in the political sphere. Ten days after the proclamation of the Nuremberg Laws, this could only be seen as condoning these laws. Hildebrandt told Niemöller that he would resign his post in the Pastors' Emergency League and would feel compelled to leave the Confessing church if the Steglitz resolutions, instead of condemning the new laws, went so far as to endorse them.

On receiving Hildebrandt's telephone call, Bonhoeffer reacted instantly. In June 1935 he had already accused the Augsburg synod of saying nothing about the Jewish question (not only the question of the baptism of Jews). He did, of course, hope for a statement that the baptism of Jews and its role in forming Christian community could not be restricted or hampered. But to his mind such a pronouncement on Jewish baptism would be an embarrassment if it was not accompanied by a clear statement condemning the general persecution of the Jews. Here Bonhoeffer was not alone. That summer, after the Augsburg synod, Superintendent Martin Albertz in Spandau had asked Marga Meusel, a church social worker, to write a detailed memorandum on "The Situation of German Non-Aryans." Meusel went beyond the problems of the Jewish Christians to explore the physical and legal persecution of the Jews in general. In a spirit similar to Bonhoeffer's, she wrote:

> Where is Abel your brother? In our case, too, in the case of the Confessing church, there can be no answer other than that given by Cain.... And if the church, afraid for its own destruction, can do nothing in many instances, why is it not at least aware of its guilt? Why does it not pray for those who are afflicted by this undeserved suffering and persecution? Why are there no services of intercession as there were for the imprisoned pastors? The church makes it bitterly difficult for anyone to defend it.... The fact that there can be people in the Confessing church who dare assume that they are entitled, even called, to preach God's justice and mercy to the Jews in the present historical situation when their present sufferings are our crime, is a fact that must fill us with icy fear. Since when has the evil-

doer had the right to pass off his evil deed as the will of God? Let us take care that we do not conceal the horror of our sins in the sanctuary of God's will. Otherwise it could well be that we too will receive the punishment of those who desecrated the temple, that we too must hear the curse of him who made the scourge and drove them out.

Meusel finished the memorandum in mid-September 1935, shortly before the Nuremberg Laws were announced. On 8 May 1936 she added a postscript regarding the consequences of the Nuremberg Laws and the experiences of non-Aryan Christian children. Bonhoeffer sent a copy of the memorandum to his friend Julius Rieger in London.[186]

Not being a delegate to the Steglitz synod, Bonhoeffer himself was unable to speak, but he stood by his friends such as Albertz. The synod did not adopt the favorable resolution on the Nuremberg Laws that had been initially considered and had aroused such misgivings; it made a declaration that defended the mission to the Jews and Jewish baptism.[187] Given the actual situation of Jews in Germany, this was embarrassing; but within the National Socialist state even this statement was a kind of protest. It stated the church's position and avoided any kind of acclamation for the state. The synod then referred what it saw as the disagreeable discussion on the Jewish question to the Council of Brethren for further action:

> The present public treatment of the Jewish question is to a large extent connected to a denial of the Gospel and the Christian church. In light of the confusion [sic!] this has provoked for our congregations, the Reich Council of Brethren intends, at the earliest opportunity and guided by the Bible and the confession, to assume responsibility for finding answers to the specific issues that have been raised.

The "assumption of responsibility" became reality in 1936 with the famous Confessing church memorandum to Hitler, which, at least, affirms that for Christians the commandment to love one's neighbor must still prevail over the officially inspired hatred of the Jews.

Bonhoeffer was depressed when he returned to Finkenwalde and discussed Romans 9–11 with his ordinands.[188] He had expected more from his Confessing colleagues in the Old Prussian church than he had from the Augsburg Reich synod, and Steglitz could hardly have been convened at a more dramatic moment—ten days after Nuremberg. Bonhoeffer often mentioned Steglitz as a vital opportunity that had been wasted. He believed that Steglitz had allowed the issues of financial autonomy and state recognition to be foisted upon it as its primary theme, instead of breaking new ground and becoming "a voice for the voiceless." It had fallen short by confining its remarks to the issue of the baptism of Jews and dilatorily handing the other questions over to the Reich Council of Brethren.

With its Pyrrhic victory at Steglitz, he maintained, the Old Prussian Confessing church had consented to a fatal reversal of priorities, and he feared that the same thing might happen in ecumenical discussions. The church was trying to derive its inner legitimacy from the struggle for its legal status, instead of regaining its legal status through its legitimacy. Bonhoeffer was convinced that its legitimacy could not be safeguarded by constitution and law, but only through its witness on behalf of those who were voiceless. Hence he saw Steglitz less as a victory than as a defeat.

There were also personal reasons for his shame about the weakness of his church. In the home on Wangenheimstrasse, his family was discussing how the Leibholzes, the in-laws of his twin sister's, could order their affairs. The thought that they might have to emigrate to an uncertain future was almost unbearable; their sense of helplessness grew as developments could no longer be controlled. In her last letter to Dietrich, his ninety-three-year-old grandmother wrote of her concern about her granddaughter Gertrud Wedell, whose husband had been forced to give up his legal practice in Düsseldorf some time before:

> Now this fifty-four-year-old man is traveling around the world looking for work so that he can finish raising his children. . . . A family's life destroyed! . . . Everything is affected, down to the smallest details. Can you actively advise or help us here? . . . I hope you can give some energetic thought to this and perhaps know some way out. . . .[189]

Hardly a month after the Steglitz synod, the Reich church committee set up by Minister Kerrl made its first public appearance. One of its misleading aspects was its leader, the respected Lutheran clergyman and general superintendent Wilhelm Zoellner. Some of the delegates to the Steglitz synod believed that he would be able to save and preserve the *Volkskirche*—their primary objective—and that he would also guarantee their confessional status and create peace within the churches. For this reason they put themselves at his disposal. Yet Zoellner's first major call for cooperation with the church committees, on 19 October 1935, contained the words: "We accept the National Socialist development of our people on the foundation of blood, race, and soil. . . ."

The End of the First Finkenwalde Course. The seminary was still filled with optimism and a fighting spirit. No one even considered accepting the tempting offers from the official church consistories to return to their fold. The first course at the Finkenwalde seminary celebrated its conclusion on the evening of 16 October 1935, before Zoellner had issued his general summons to rally around Kerrl's church committees.

The ordinands returned to their home churches. Although they were soon ordained, they remained "illegal." Hardly any of them could expect to be given an ordinary pastorate with a house and garden. In Pomerania anyone wanting this had to attend the preachers' seminary in Kückenmühle on the far bank of the Oder River, which had been set up by the consistory's church committee. Wherever possible the neutral or German Christian consistories barred anyone who had been trained or ordained under the Councils of Brethren from a regular and salaried ministry. If the occasion arose these Confessing candidates could hope for an appointment in their province from one of the independent patrons who had the right to fill a pastorate; the salary for these positions could only come from the limited resources of the provincial Council of Brethren. Or they might expect to be accepted as an assistant preacher by a superintendent who was not intimidated; but this meant working without official recognition in a kind of permanent apprenticeship. Or the newly formed Confessing congregations in the towns might, when a vacancy allowed, call one of the young theologians and fight for use of the church and church buildings. Other ordinands, in association with the provincial Councils of Brethren, traveled and tried to form emergency congregations in private homes—an operation that grew increasingly dangerous.

This was what lay in store for those now leaving Finkenwalde. Whatever course they followed Bonhoeffer promised to support them with letters, visits, and informal study conferences.

First, however, he spent a brief holiday with his parents. In October 1935 they had moved from his boyhood home in Grunewald to a new house near Heerstrasse in Charlottenburg. Surrounded by tall pines, the house at 43 Marienburger Allee had been built to their own design. The attic room facing west became Dietrich's own; from his window he could look over to 42 Marienburger Allee, the house belonging to the Schleichers, which had been built at the same time. It was in this room that Dietrich was arrested in 1943. One year later his brother Klaus would be arrested in the music room of the neighboring home.

Friedrich Bonhoeffer

Julie Bonhoeffer

Karl Alfred von Hase

Clara von Hase

*Bonhoeffer and his
siblings, 1908*

In Wölfelsgrund, 1911

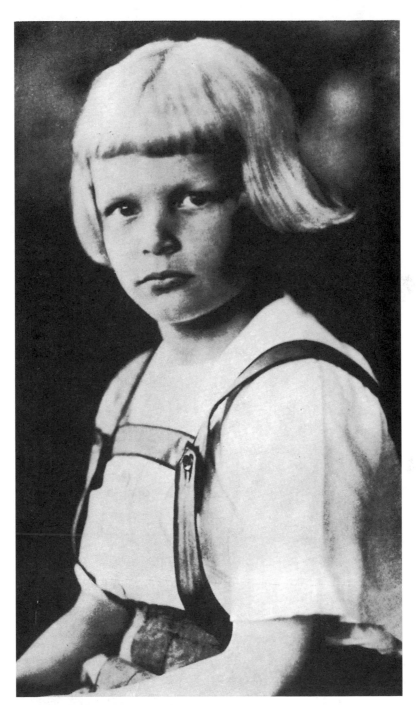

Dietrich, aged 9, 1915

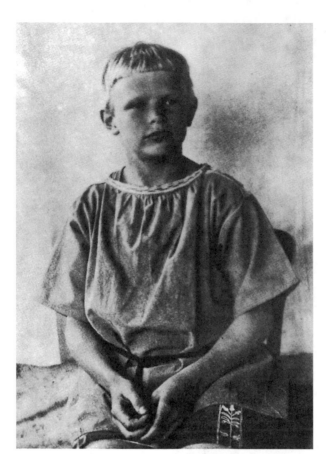

Dietrich
(probably 1917)

Dietrich at Grunewald Gymnasium, 1920/21 (2nd row, 2nd from right)

Dietrich as a student in Tübingen

Parlor of the Bonhoeffer home on Wangenheimstrasse

Karl von Hase

Adolf von Harnack

Reinhold Seeberg

Karl Barth

Bonhoeffer with professor and fellow students at Union Theological Seminary, New York, 1930/31 (2nd row, 2nd from right)

Bonhoeffer with confirmation students, 1932

Bonhoeffer with his students, 1932

World Alliance Meeting in Geneva, 1932 (Bonhoeffer in last row, 2nd from right)

Boycott of Jewish businesses in Berlin, 1933

Reich Bishop Ludwig Müller at National Synod in Wittenberg, September 1933

Delegates on the beach at Fanö conference, 1934

Bishop George Bell with Franz Hildebrandt

Preacher's Seminary in Finkenwalde

Arrival of Bonhoeffer and Finkenwalde group, Stockholm, 1936 (Bonhoeffer in front row, 3rd from left)

Bonhoeffer's parents' home on Marienburger Allee, Berlin

Confessing church intercession list, July 1939

```
120.    "    Bröning- Klingenthal
121.    "    Bohert- Gelenau
122.
    2.Ausreiseverbote:
1.  Pfarrer Müller- Bln.-Dahlem
2.  Sup. Lic. Albertz-Bln.-Spandau
3.  Pfarrer Dr. Böhm- Bln.-Schlendorf
4.  Pastor Lic. Wiesel- Bln.- Lichterfelde
5.  Vikar Fritz Dartz- Bln.-Adlershof
6.    "    Hans Gaehner- Bln.-Friedenau
7.    "    Schmökel- Bln.-Lichterfelde
8.    "    Racke- Berlin
9.  Pfarrer Rackwitz-Bln.-Neukölln
    3. Aufenthaltsverbote:
Berlin:
1.  Gen. sup. D. Dibelius-Berlin: für Österreich
Brandenburg:
2.  Vikar Deutsch- Babelsberg: für Berlin
Schlesien:
3.  Pfarrer Hornig- Breslau:    für Berlin und Prov. Brandenb
4.  Pastor Reichert- Kreuzberg:   "    "    "    "    "    burg
5.  Vikar Pichert- Bunzlau:     "    "    "    "    "
6.    "    Grundke- Breslau:    "    "    "    "    "
Pommern:
7.  Pastor Lic. Bonhoeffer:     "    "    "    "    "
8.    "    "    de Boer- Stolp:  "    "    "    "    "
Ostpreussen:
9.  Vikar Gers- Treuburg:       "    "    "    "    "
10.   "    Klatt- Gumbinnen:     "    "    "    "    "
```

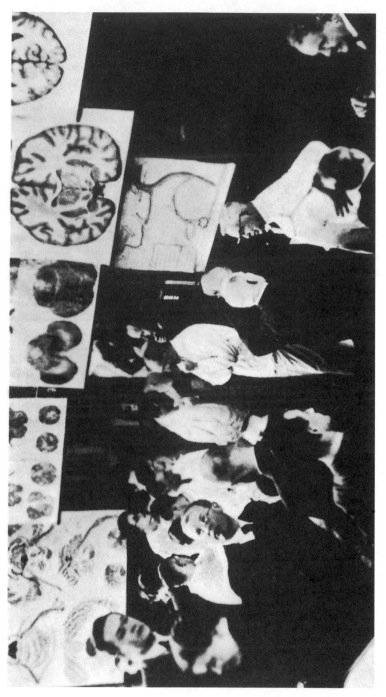

Karl Bonhoeffer's final lecture in Berlin, 1938 (Dietrich 2nd from left, looking up; Karl Bonhoeffer 3rd from right)

Final collective pastorate group in Sigurdshof, 1939/40 (Bonhoeffer 2nd from left)

Bonhoeffer and Ruth von Kleist in Kieckow, 1940

Bonhoeffer (on left) and Eberhard Bethge (on right) in Ettal, 1940

Bonhoeffer's address list during the war

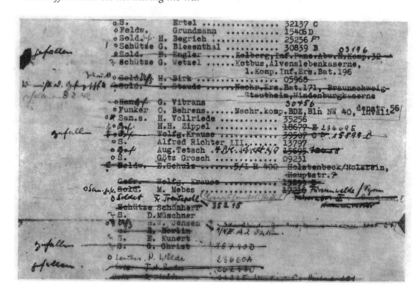

*Maria von
Wedemeyer, 1942*

*The Bonhoeffer family
at Karl Bonhoeffer's
75th birthday, 1943
(Dietrich on far left;
Friedrich Justus Perels
far right; Klaus Bon-
hoeffer front row, 4th
from right; Rüdiger
Schleicher front row,
6th from right)*

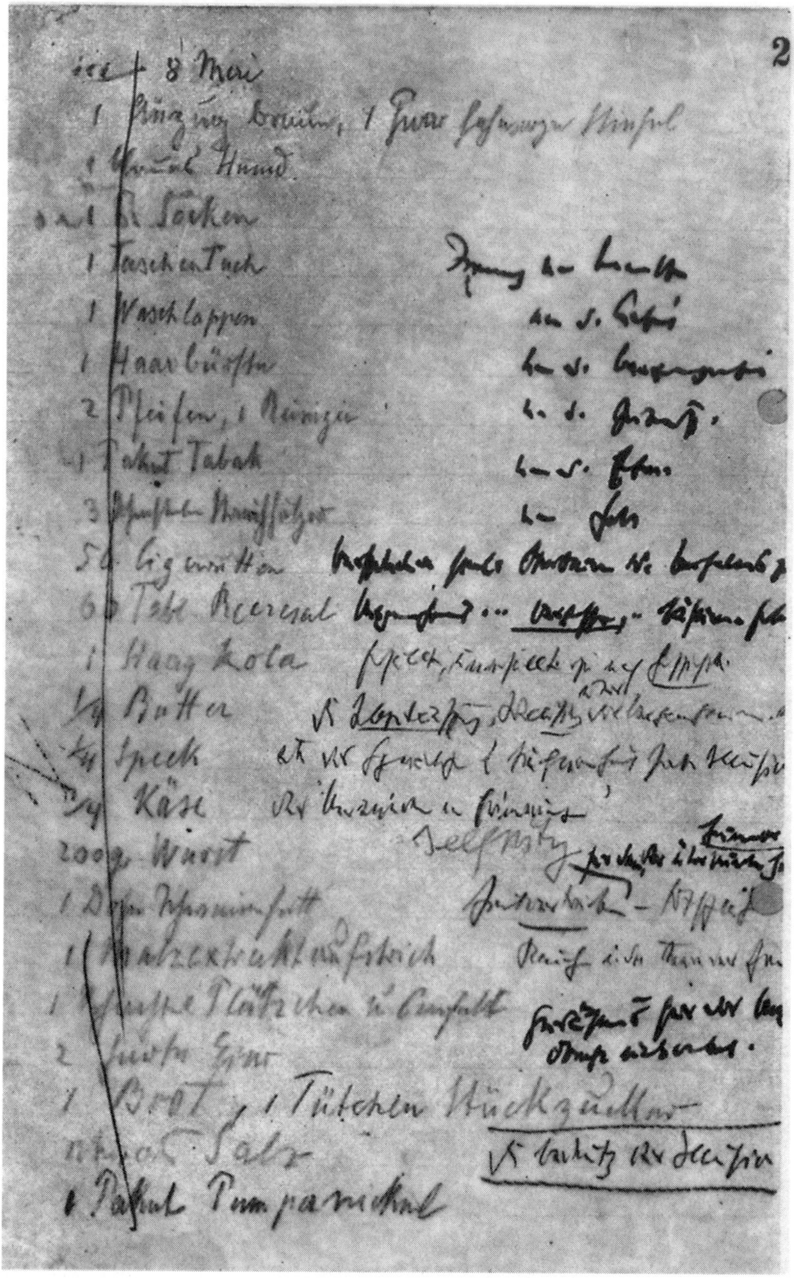

Bonhoeffer's notes in Tegel

Hans von Dohnanyi

Bonhoeffer (3rd from left) with
fellow prisoners and guard in
Tegel, 1944

Klaus Bonhoefer

Rüdiger Schleicher

Bonhoeffer's parents, 1945

CHAPTER TEN

FINKENWALDE: 1936–1937

During its brief existence from 1935 to 1937, the Finkenwalde seminary played a role in the three major stages of the German church struggle—the eras of Ludwig Müller (1933–1935), Wilhelm Zoellner (1935–1937), and Friedrich Werner (1937–1945).

When the seminary opened Reich bishop Ludwig Müller was still nominally in power. There was still some hope that the leadership of the church might be transferred from the Reich bishop to the Confessing church; the church struggle was not yet in its death throes.

Finkenwalde's most flourishing period was overshadowed by the agonizing controversy over Zoellner's attempts to govern the churches with what was considered a false mandate. This widely respected churchman, who was well versed in theological matters, accepted the mandate from Reich Minister of Church Affairs Hanns Kerrl. The classic *notae ecclesiae*, the Word and the Sacrament, had paled in significance beside the issue of state recognition of the church, which threatened to assume paramount importance in the church. The church struggle became a tedious tug-of-war between Zoellner's church committees, the Councils of Brethren, the Lutheran Council, and the still-active German Christians. It became extraordinarily difficult to clarify to those outside Germany exactly what was at stake. Only the most dramatic highlights—and there was no lack of these—occasionally reached the public. Zoellner eventually had the courage to hand back the state's mandate. He was forced to see that his attempts to establish a spiritual authority had been ludicrous, because his mandate from the state made him intolerably dependent upon it.

After Finkenwalde was closed in 1937 Dr. Friedrich Werner, a lawyer and president of the Office of Church Affairs, finance department, and Evangelical High Church Council, established a church government that threatened to stifle all traces of spiritual independence. This obsequious church lawyer ruthlessly connived to isolate what still remained of the Confessing church. The church struggle became more than a genuine "struggle of the churches"; it turned into an unequal contest with Himmler's police.

The deterioration of relations between the ecumenical movement and the Confessing church became increasingly evident during the second and third phases of the church struggle. In 1935 the secretariats in Geneva were unable to answer the Confessing church's crucial question: whether or not the ecumenical movement was a church. During 1936 men such as Henry Louis Henriod and Wilhelm Menn expressed misgivings that the Confessing church—particularly Bonhoeffer and Asmussen—was unable to view ecumenical work from any other perspective than that of the church struggle. In 1937 the Geneva office's dilemma about which German delegation to invite to the Oxford conference was resolved because the Confessing church withdrew and because the Nazi state withheld the passports of the German delegates.

During the second phase marked by Zoellner's leadership of the church committees, Bonhoeffer acquired a notorious reputation in the church. Up to that point, he was relatively little known; his books *Discipleship* and *Life Together* had not yet appeared. But in 1936 everybody was talking of his ominous statement, "He who separates himself from the Confessing church separates himself from salvation,"[1] a modern rendition of the early church dogma *extra ecclesiam nulla salus*. This destroyed Bonhoeffer's good reputation as a theologian, and with his Old Testament Bible studies in *Junge Kirche* he also laid himself open to severe criticism. He was accused of being incorrigibly radical, of drawing overly rash theological conclusions, of abusing exegesis, and of reviving legalism and monasticism.

Yet there were still many ordinands who asked their provincial Councils of Brethren to send them to the seminary at Finkenwalde if at all possible. Once there, they found Bonhoeffer little troubled by the attacks on him. He continued to raise even more incisive questions about the church's spiritual legitimacy in the Third Reich. Sometimes the ordinands were at a loss as to how to interpret their director's provocative proposals, particularly when they came under attack themselves. Nevertheless, from its establishment until the day its doors were sealed Finkenwalde constituted one of the focal points of the Confessing church—a church to which Barmen and Dahlem had given birth.

The Fifth Implementation Decree

The second Finkenwalde course began in mid-November 1935, a particularly dark time for church politics. All the portents indicated a fatal attack on the institutions of the Confessing church. Bonhoeffer, who had resumed his university lectures at the beginning of the winter term, traveled frequently to Berlin; there he met regularly with Hildebrandt and Niemöller. He always returned with the latest alarming news.

As a result, those in Finkenwalde took a well-informed interest in the meetings that were being planned between Reich Minister Kerrl and each of the main church factions. These meetings were awaited with some anxiety, for they would determine Kerrl's final decision about the measures he planned for dealing with the church opposition. These meetings took place on 27 November 1935, in the following order:

1. Kerrl first received Zoellner and his colleagues, the members of the Reich church committee who later formed the provincial church committees. Some of them had been members of the Confessing church. At this first meeting, after he was asked to remove the infamous German Christian church provost Otto Eckert and other bishops, Kerrl abruptly left the room instead of replying.

2. His second interview was with the First Provisional Church Administration, led by Marahrens. Kerrl informed them that he intended to dissolve the Councils of Brethren within a few days, but would prefer them to dissolve themselves.

3. The third interview was the most significant one for the Finkenwaldians, since it concerned the Old Prussian Council of Brethren, the body with direct jurisdiction over them. Westphalian church president Karl Koch was represented by Pastor Fritz Müller of Dahlem, a firm but quiet man. Kerrl made a nervous speech: "I shall no longer tolerate any attempts by the Councils of Brethren to intervene in the internal affairs of the church. The church committees, through those serving on them, guarantee that the Confessing church's vital interests are looked after. . . . I do not wish to hear anything more about heresy. . . . I have set time limits. I shall wait until the end of this week. . . ." Fritz Müller replied, but after several minutes Kerrl interrupted: "Why talk so much? As far as I'm concerned it's quite pointless." Müller answered: "I note that the Reich Minister considers what we have to say pointless. Then we will end the negotiations."[2]

Thus the meetings of 27 November presaged a dark future. Two days later a newsletter went out to former members of Finkenwalde, preparing them for the possibility of extensive restrictions:

We are writing to let you know that you will not be left on your own in the days to come. After recent events we must now reckon seriously with the possibility of the Confessing church being banned—camouflaged perhaps as the closing down of our Church Administration. Now, as always, our Church Administration stands firmly behind Barmen and Dahlem. . . . Even a forbidden Church Administration will remain irrevocably ours. . . . No directive that invalidates or goes against our Church Administration may be complied with, unless at the explicit instructions from the church leadership. . . .[3]

In referring to the determination of "our Church Administration," this advice contained a premise which, although it might hold true for the Old Prussian Council of Brethren, no longer applied to the other provincial churches. In Hannover, for example, Heinz Brunotte thought they should adopt an impartial attitude toward the Reich Church Committee: "What in fact is left; is there really anything more than a small circle in Old Prussia which has come to a dead end as a result of Niemöller's tactics?"[4] Bavaria, Hessen-Nassau, and Saxony came out in support of the church committees. On behalf of the First Provisional Church Administration of the Confessing church, Marahrens expressed his readiness to cooperate with the Reich church committee, thereby sealing the Provisional Administration's fate and conceding a major victory to Wilhelm Zoellner.

2 December. In the late afternoon of Monday, 2 December (there were no Monday morning newspapers in Germany at the time, nor did everyone listen to the radio in Finkenwalde), one of the students returned from Stettin excitedly brandishing an evening paper, which contained the "Fifth Decree for the Implementation of the Law for the Protection of the German Evangelical Church." He immediately took it to Bonhoeffer's room. Did this decree mean the total proscription of the Confessing church? Not altogether; but the content was clear enough: "no powers of ecclesiastical government or administration [are] to be vested in associations or groups within the church," and it had been signed by a Reich minister. Not only were the filling of positions and church proclamations, and the raising of funds through collections and subscriptions, prohibited, but the decree explicitly forbade all examinations and ordinations as well. Had things really come to such a pass that a National Socialist minister was to decide spiritual questions of church order, examinations, and ordination? There could be no doubt that the preachers' seminaries fell under the powers of ecclesiastical government and administration vested in a "group"—in this case, the Old Prussian Council of Brethren.

Finkenwalde, which Ludwig Müller had already declared illegal within the church, was now confirmed as such by the state. The question arose whether the ordinands could be asked to stay on at the seminary; sooner or later it was inevitable that the church committees would reorganize the training, examinations, and ordination of candidates in accordance with the new law. The other question was how the work could be carried on, since the ban on church activities extended to the newsletters from the Councils of Brethren; this would increase the isolation of ordinands and assistant preachers. This detailed and direct intervention in the church's internal activities and organization was unprecedented in the church struggle; the first four decrees had been confined to creating national and regional church committees. Such were the results of Kerrl's interviews on 27 November.

That Monday evening Bonhoeffer summoned everyone to explain the situation created by the Fifth Decree. He was anxious that each person be free to make up his own mind, and he therefore soberly evaluated the consequences of carrying on. He explained why he had decided to continue with the work, and assured them that everyone who remained would be fully provided for. How the Councils of Brethren would reply, and what they would say to those under their care, was their own affair; but they did badly need the independent cooperation of those on whose behalf they continued to exercise their "powers."

Bonhoeffer's frankness made a deep impression. The evening ended with mutual assurances that the daily routine of the course would stay unchanged; each member pledged to yield to nothing but force. The following day Bonhoeffer wrote to Martin Niemöller:

> Despite the seriousness of the situation we are very happy and confident. For the rest we act in accordance with Matthias Claudius's wonderful hymn . . .
>
> I pray that God may grant
>   The little that I want;
> For if he doth the sparrows feed,
>   Will he not fill my daily need?[5]

In a letter to friends on 8 December the author was somewhat less composed:

> Everything we do here is now illegal and contrary to the law of the state. First there were the bans on newspapers and newsletters, and now copies run off on duplicating machines are forbidden. . . . The church committees are merely a screen to mask the destruction of the church.

But the students were energized by the fact that something was really being demanded of them; in the past they had often lacked a clear lead. This was now provided by Bonhoeffer and by Staemmler, who asked those in his charge to stand firm. He gained a hearing with his sober demand:

> The time has now come for you to make your decision. . . . We can give no guarantee that you will find employment, that you will receive a stipend, or that you will be recognized by any state office. We neither want nor are entitled to conceal this from you. It is likely that your path from now on will be very hard. . . .[6]

Curiously, some time elapsed before the first consequences of the Fifth Decree became evident; only gradually did its restrictive provisions begin to take effect.

The entire German confessional movement was torn bitterly about whether to make concessions or resist. The Finkenwalde seminary and its director did everything in their power to recall any ministers and students who were uncertain or confused, and present them with the case for disobedience to Kerrl's decrees. Worried, they followed the negotiations between the Rhineland and Westphalian Councils of Brethren and the church committees, which were trying to convince them to drop their claim to leadership. They were relieved when Joachim Beckmann and Karl Koch returned from this tightrope walk to the path approved by those in Finkenwalde.

The seminary gave time and money to distribute the pamphlet *The State Church Is Here*, written by Otto Dibelius and edited by Martin Niemöller as a protest against the Fifth Decree. Throughout a wide area the students descended on bookshops to buy up stocks of the pamphlet, and when the police began to hunt for the pamphlet they placed their orders by telephone. There was feverish activity in Finkenwalde as consignments were packed and then mailed to widely separated addresses. Although the police searched parsonages for copies of the pamphlets, it did not occur to them to search Finkenwalde. Hermann Ehlers, who visited the seminary, reported that there were one hundred thousand copies of the pamphlet, and hence it would be absurd for the police to hope to confiscate them all.[7]

Strife in Stettin-Bredow. In Pomerania the struggle came to a head on 27 December 1935 with the appointment of a provincial church committee, led by Greifswald Superintendent Karl von Scheven. The bewilderment that followed even spread to the Council of Brethren. It was felt necessary to obtain a general picture to find out who could still be counted on, whether it would be possible to continue, and what position to take at the Reich Confessing synod planned for 17–22 February 1936 in Oeynhausen. For this reason the Pomeranian clergy were invited to Stettin-Bredow on 10 January. Some two hundred came and spent the entire day arguing; the whole seminary attended.

Bonhoeffer spoke; he tried to express his uncompromising opinion as pastorally as possible. He began with the unfortunate circumstance that respectable people had been misled into accepting a false vocation:

> The false vocation necessarily included the decision to keep silent about the false doctrine of the German Christians for the sake of political peace. Already, the concern for the survival of the Reich church has virtually replaced concern for the undisguised word of truth. Instead of going forward, we are standing still and asking who we really are—a church, a movement or a group? Whoever looks on the Confessing church as a movement or as the upholder of a cause is lost; all he sees is a wretched crowd of obstinate, despondent people barely worthy of the name "movement"; he sees, in fact, nothing more than an undisciplined crowd without obedience, a nonchurch in fact. But he must not see us like that! By standing still we destroy the church which can exist only by going forward. The way ahead is marked by the beacons of the synods: Barmen as a tower against the subversion of church doctrine and Dahlem as one against the subversion of the ecclesiastical order. Barmen holds the sword forged by the Word. Without Dahlem, however, Barmen would be like a weapon carelessly left in the hands of a foreign power's general staff. A third synod [Oeynhausen] must now provide protection against the subversion of the church by the world which, in the shape of the National Socialist state, is intervening through its finance departments, Legislative Authority and committees, and is now tearing apart the church of those who confess. Here we cannot and must not give in one single time![8]

Bonhoeffer's speech elicited some applause, which was not the case after a respected pastor spoke expressing the opposing point of view. Despite the Council of Brethren's plea to avoid emotional statements in an already overheated atmosphere, there were a number of embarrassing outbursts. Both sides at the meeting were fighting for their future. As a result the speeches made by two of Finkenwalde's ordinands after Bonhoeffer's remarks left much to be desired in the way of moderation.

At the end of this difficult day three-quarters of those present surprisingly expressed willingness to recognize the Council of Brethren's governance in church affairs. The remaining quarter of the "apostates" did not lack power, however, for they aligned themselves with Greifswald and its theological faculty.

The Bredow meeting led to a painful exchange of letters with the Stettin pastor, Dr. Friedrich Schauer. He was a Berneuchen member who had been one of the dissenting minority in the brown synod in 1933 and had led the Pomeranian Young Reformation members; now, although still a member of the Council of Brethren, he sympathized with the Greifswald group. He accused the Finkenwalde group of a "lack of discipline."[9] Bonhoeffer replied at some length, saying that he could "not get very worked up" about the outbursts of temperament for which the Finkenwaldians had, in this case, only been partly responsible:

> But it is much harder to make good the damage when, in her testimony of Christ, the church strays from the path of faith and truth. . . . I do not need to tell you that I agree with you that every lack of discipline damages the credibility of the truth we proclaim. But the proper testimony to Christ lies not in the act of discipline, but in the assurance of hope for the future.
>
> I do not enter such meetings as would a Quaker who must await the directions of the Holy Spirit on principle, but rather as one who arrives on a battlefield where God's Word is in conflict with all manner of human opinions . . . what takes place here is not the presentation of a fragment of Christian life made real, but a battle for the truth.[10]

Bonhoeffer defended one of his ordinands, Winfried Krause, who had made a speech accusing Marahrens of betraying the church:

> Moreover he did not say that Marahrens was a "traitor" but that he had betrayed the church. There is a specific difference. It is a judgment about an objective decision and action, not about an individual. There can be no dispute about the theological justice of this statement. And my only factual objection to it would be that Marahrens could not possibly have betrayed the Confessing church since he had never belonged to it.[11]

This was a harsh and stubborn verdict. Bonhoeffer felt that the situation left no room for any kind of compromise. This was even more the case since, with Marahrens's support, the church committee had established a preachers' seminary on the other side of the Oder in Kückenmühle, in an attempt to challenge Finkenwalde's inherent right to exist and cut off its access to students. Bonhoeffer's words were harsh because, from his standpoint, any exchange between the two sides was now plainly impossible.

Proclamation from the Pulpit. The Sunday after the Bredow meeting, the Old Prussian Council of Brethren had scheduled an important proclamation about the position to be taken toward the church committees. Given the strict police observation, more and more people were wondering who would (or would not) read the statement from the pulpit. Pastors who read the statement now would be formally disobeying a state order; there could be no doubt that the authorities would carefully note the names of those who continued to support the Councils of Brethren. Yet to remain silent would damage the cause more than ever.

Finkenwalde scheduled a Confessing service in its emergency church for 12 January 1936, inviting people from the neighboring areas and from Stettin. Bonhoeffer preached, choosing a pointed text from the passages in Ezra and Nehemiah about the building of the wall:

> Only God himself can render judgment over his people. . . . It would be a rebellion against God's judgment when someone of his own accord, uncalled and unasked, went about rebuilding the church—even if this happens with the most pious intent, the purest doctrine, the greatest pastoral love for the people. . . . The church's renewal comes from its awakening by the spirit of God, never through restoration, never through highhanded desire to undo God's judgment. Only by going through his judgment, not bypassing it, will God return to his congregation.[12]

Ezra and Nehemiah had rejected the opposition's offer to help with the restoration of the wall (Ezra 4:3). For Bonhoeffer and his audience it was as if the centuries between the biblical passage and their own situation had been washed away:

> It is always wiser to win over the more difficult opponent first. Concessions must be made, often extensive ones; the church's enemies must join in offering their help to restore it: let us take this work up equally, men of political power and men of the church, let us build together![13]

The outline of his sermon has been lost, but in April 1936 Bonhoeffer elaborated on this text for a Bible study that was published in *Junge Kirche*.[14] This provoked an energetic rebuttal from those in Greifswald, who accused Bonhoeffer of misusing the Old Testament. Yet his questionable use of the text went to the heart of the questions that faced his church at the time. The sermon followed the reading of the Council of Brethren's proclamation:

> Complying with the Minister's request and handing over the leadership of the church to the state's church committees is not an option . . . we have to make it quite clear to ourselves that we shall not arbitrarily abandon the

claims of the Confessing church, even if this should lead us along a fresh path of suffering. . . .[15]

Many evaded the issues that the reading of the proclamation raised, saying that nothing should be ruled out before a new Reich synod had decided the matter. In fact, those who read this proclamation from the pulpit needed courage and determination—each of them had to take this step alone, on their own responsibility, and often in hostile circumstances. Bonhoeffer set an important example on this day. Almost all of Finkenwalde's former members acted as he did:

> I am glad that you read out the proclamation, for otherwise you would have been plagued by a bad conscience later on. Ehlers confirmed yesterday that about 80 percent read it in Berlin-Brandenburg . . . those on the Council of Brethren think that the state is taking the proclamation lying down (1) because of the Winter Olympics and (2) because it does not wish to disturb the Confessing church's self-disintegration. . . .[16]

But for the Finkenwalde group this was still not enough. After the service, the congregation was invited to a meeting where, having met for three months, it constituted itself as a Confessing congregation and elected a parish Council of Brethren. Those present, including Ruth von Kleist-Retzow, signed the Confessing church's card of personal commitment—at the very moment when such things had been forbidden. The Finkenwalde Confessing congregation that was founded that day maintained its independence until well into the war, long after the seminary had been disbanded.

Divisions among Themselves. During this period the community in Finkenwalde had shown vigor and spirit, but it also underwent some painful experiences. After the Christmas vacation one of the quietest and most serious students approached Bonhoeffer and told him that, after discussing it with Superintendent von Scheven, he had decided to follow the lead of the Pomeranian church committee.[17] Hardly anything could have hit Bonhoeffer harder in those weeks: a brother, with whom he was linked in daily prayer for the church, was now turning away. There were long talks, but the day came when his departure could no longer be prevented, and it weighed heavily upon the community.[18] It was the first time that the tragic rift in the Confessing church had invaded Bonhoeffer's own domain in Finkenwalde; this meant a humiliating reversal for the house and its community. Because of this the seminary assembled at the Bredow meeting, not as a self-confident group but as one aware of a potential weakness. They were still determined, however, that everything possible must be done to keep the dam from bursting.

In the period that followed almost every Finkenwalde course lost a member who went to the committees or, as they said, "went over to the consistory." Compared to the general trend in the German churches, this represented an extremely small percentage of students. Nothing, however, took a greater toll on Bonhoeffer than the impending departure of someone from his circle. Suddenly all efforts to prevent it seemed vain. "Nothing we have been able to say has done any good."[19]

It now seemed that the theological criticism made by the Lutherans in Erlangen had prevailed over Barmen's claim of scriptural justification for its synod declaration. Confronted with the lure of consistorial legality, the students' determination to endure the hardships of illegality began to wane. Ministry in the *Volkskirche* seemed more sensible than in the limited emergency congregations. The members of the state-appointed church committees, who were pious men and theologically educated, appeared so much more reasonable than the tough, uncompromising men of Dahlem. The truth of love had turned against the love of truth.

Bonhoeffer attempted to describe the situation to Pastor Schauer, who was concerned about the "fanaticism" of the Finkenwaldians. As bitter as the rift was, Bonhoeffer insisted that they could not budge one centimeter from the decisions of Barmen and Dahlem. This rift had become evident in the fact that they could no longer join in a common confession of guilt; they commended each other to the grace of God, that it might prevail over both factions. Bonhoeffer's letter to Schauer was a preliminary to his essay "The Community of the Church."[20]

Counterforces. There were two reasons for the unusual delay in the implementation of drastic measures against the institutions of the Confessing church, and the surprising freedom of movement and protest that its members continued to enjoy. First was the purely technical problem of destroying an organization the size of the Confessing church with bureaucratic and police measures. Furthermore, the ministry and the Reich church authorities harbored the hope, not entirely unfounded, that their best ally would be the internal erosion and disintegration of the groups supporting Barmen and Dahlem.

The state still refrained from using police and penal measures to enforce its Security law and the Fifth Implementation Decree. The members of the church were fighting each other enough. In addition, with the approach of the Olympic Games, it was in the regime's interest to avoid even the slightest sign of church persecution while large numbers of foreigners were visiting the country. Police measures at that point would have seemed inconsistent with the enforcement of Kerrl's new order by a churchman such as Zoellner. Of course, the powerful apparatus of the National Socialist press and the corresponding rallies held by the officially recognized church authorities aided the attacks on the "disturbers of the peace" from the Old Prussian Confessing church until the time came when the police joined in. No action was taken to stop the seditious pulpit proclamation against the Fifth Implementation Decree, although the names of those who read it were carefully recorded for use at a later date.

From the viewpoint of the church committees, it seemed that they could confidently let matters take their own course. Zoellner was correct that "the Lutheran regional churches, such as those of Bavaria, Württemberg and Hannover—not to mention others—have won a relation toward us that is much more favorable than is the case among the Prussian Councils of Brethren under their united [theologically] leadership."[21] But the mood was not only turning in Zoellner's favor in the Lutheran churches, but in the churches of the Old Prussian Union as well. Members of the Prussian Union church had discovered their Lutheran heart and, with it, some critical reservations toward the Barmen and Dahlem resolutions. They now viewed these resolutions, which had once been the Confessing church's "claim," as commendable "suggestions" that might even be included in Zoellner's attempts at pacification. Theodor Kuessner, until then the Confessing church's leader in East Prussia, wrote his colleagues on 25 November:

> The East Prussian Confessional Synod is preparing to give up its governing authority to the East Prussian Provincial Church Committee. You may be assured that the Council of Brethren will liquidate all the legal matters, especially all questions concerning the new generation of theologians, with the greatest care.

To a pronounced Lutheran theologian such as Bonhoeffer, this form of Lutheranism had become the most dangerous enemy of all, for he believed that it provided ideological justification for those who were confused or had grown weary. "For me, the greatest anxiety is the Lutheran Council."[22] Curiously enough, Bonhoeffer's position was viewed as "too far Reformed." Yet he believed that this attitude represented the correct interpretation of Lutheran confessional writings, and that the other view was false because it held that the safeguarding of an established Lutheran confessional tradition was possible, although its real desire was to rescue the traditional *Volkskirche* at too high a cost.

Many viewed Zoellner's work as a valiant and promising attempt to repair the damage that had been done to the *Volkskirche* and its order in 1933; having done that, he would then seek to clarify the theological questions. And they viewed Bonhoeffer and his friends as "radicals" who were incapable of understanding the justification for these calm and clever tactics.

But there were those who, like Bonhoeffer, had become ministers not in order to rescue what still survived; their only hope for a mission of truth in the Germany of that era rested in a church without privileges. This made their harsh judgments more comprehensible:

> Where there is no sense of vocation, then no good can be expected, for even should "successes" be achieved, these might well be the successes of Satan. The rite of vocation belongs only to the Councils of Brethren of the synods of the Confessing church.[23]

In Bonhoeffer's eyes, those who followed the lead of the Fifth Decree and pressed for the reconstruction of the *Volkskirche* disqualified themselves; they were ignoring the authority of the Councils of Brethren established in Barmen and Dahlem. Moreover, they were acknowledging the state's authority to appoint spiritual leaders. They had thereby consented to the curtailment of the testimony of truth.

The end of 1935 and early 1936 was a strenuous time for Bonhoeffer. The Finkenwalde group required his attention and he also held weekly lectures in Berlin. All the members of the House of Brethren remained in Finkenwalde for Christmas Eve. Those who had completed the first Finkenwalde course were scattered in isolated parishes throughout Brandenburg, Pomerania, and Saxony and were awaiting Bonhoeffer's visit; they did not wait in vain. Assemblies and brotherhoods in these provinces looked to him for support in their discussions with ministers who had begun to falter. At home the Nuremberg Laws threatened the family's peace.

After Christmas Bonhoeffer's grandmother contracted pneumonia; there were daily telephone calls between Berlin and Finkenwalde.[24] On 15 January 1936 Dietrich gave the homily at her funeral service, taking his text from Psalm 90, the psalm always read at home on New Year's Eve.[25] After he finished one cousin who was present, a high government official, refused to shake his hand. His grandmother had been the oldest member of the family; she was ninety-three when she died. Bonhoeffer said of her:

The uncompromising nature of law and justice, the free word of a free
man, the obligation to stand by a promise once it is made, clarity and
sobriety of speech, uprightness and simplicity in public and private life—
on these she set her whole heart. . . . She could not bear to see these aims
held in contempt or see the violation of another's rights. Thus her last years
were clouded by the great sorrow she endured on account of the fate of the
Jews among our people, a fate she bore and suffered in sympathy with
them. She was the product of another time, of another spiritual world—
and that world goes down with her to the grave.[26]

The second half of the term was a bad time for Bonhoeffer. There were
days when he was overcome by what he later called his *"accidie, tristitia*, with
all its menacing consequences."[27] These depressions were not occasioned by
feelings of deprivation or by vain desires. They tended to beset him precisely when he realized how strongly others believed in the success of his path
and placed great faith in his leadership. They were less the doubts of weakness than of weariness brought about through his own talents. His own
power to control and influence others shocked him. He would be overwhelmed by self-contempt and a sense of inadequacy so strong that it threatened to rob his happiest and most successful undertakings of all meaning.
His intellect had gained an evil ascendancy over faith. Then, in private confession, he would seek and find a renewed innocence and sense of vocation.

Eventually he came down with a severe attack of influenza, which nearly prevented what was to be a splendid ending to the second term in Finkenwalde—the visit to Sweden.

The Journey to Sweden

Birthday Wish. At the beginning of February 1936, on Bonhoeffer's thirtieth
birthday, the members of the seminary gathered around the open fire in the
hall in front of the copper brazier Bonhoeffer had brought from Spain. After
he had been prevailed upon to talk yet again about Barcelona, Mexico, and
London, one of those present suggested that now it was the students' turn to
express a birthday wish. They asked Bonhoeffer, through his ecumenical
connections, to help them organize a visit to Sweden before the end of the
term. He agreed to arrange it for 1 March, saying that he would use his
influence as a secretary of the Ecumenical Youth Commission—a post he
still held. Dr. Eugen Rose assumed responsibility for all the preparations and
immediately set about learning some basic Swedish.

In fact, it was somewhat rude not only to ask for an invitation but to do
so without having given the Swedish church proper notice. The seminary

would be wholly dependent on Swedish hospitality, since German nationals at that time were only permitted to take the equivalent of about one pound sterling in foreign exchange out of the country. But a Confessing seminary could only contrive to cross the border by making preparations so quickly that there was no time for the interested agencies in the Reich church and the state to become aware of the plans and take the necessary steps to frustrate them. The aftermath of this journey would show that Bonhoeffer had been correct on this point; and at this point they still suspected that the seminary would be less vulnerable if the ecumenical world had shown open interest in this institution of the Confessing church.

At the advice of Chaplain Birger Forell at the Swedish Embassy in Berlin, on 11 February Bonhoeffer requested an invitation from Nils Karlström, whom he had met in Geneva and Gland, and who was now the secretary of the Ecumenical Committee in Uppsala.[28] Karlström immediately began to solve the urgent scheduling and financial questions and sent a representative, Astrid Fjellmo, to Finkenwalde to discuss the itinerary and nuances of the invitation. The letter of invitation played a greater role later, when state and church authorities in Germany began to look at the trip. On 22 February this invitation, signed by Karlström on behalf of the Ecumenical Committee of the Swedish church, arrived in Finkenwalde:

> I would be honored to invite the preachers' seminary for a study trip to Sweden from 1 to 10 March. . . . It would be a pleasure for us to host the members of the seminary during this time. . . .[29]

The Old Prussian Council of Brethren was the first "authority" that was informed and asked; it was only too glad to allow this ecumenical contact. The most urgent matter was the passports and exit visas for the twenty-six candidates who were making the trip. The average German citizen at that time didn't even have a passport. Amazingly the candidates received their passports and permissions in the various home provinces without any difficulties.

Their joy over the proposed journey was only clouded by the Oeynhausen synod (17–22 February), which proved unable to make a clear break with the church committees. But the Provisional Administration had been reconstituted after Marahrens's withdrawal, and now included Superintendent Albertz, who was spiritual director of the Brandenburg ordinands. Thus the seminarians felt some confidence that their complaints would be heard. On the eve of their departure, they sent a protest against the Oeynhausen resolutions to the Provisional Administration, which included the following statement:

According to the Oeynhausen Synod, a man has a home in the Confessing Church even if he cooperates with the committees or pays attention to them, although the Councils of Brethren have up to now urgently advised against this. How do we younger clergy stand towards those who allow themselves to be tested or set in office by the committees? Is it only a matter of conscience or the Word of God that separates us from them?[30]

The party sailed from the port of Stettin after Bonhoeffer warned them urgently to be discreet in Sweden, and strictly pledged them to refrain from sensational stories of resistance and similar matters when speaking to the press. The report of the trip that was later published in *Junge Kirche* was somewhat overdramatic: "Slowly the steamship moved through the ice. The triumphal procession of the Confessing church begins." Bonhoeffer had joined an undertaking that would bring him all kinds of worries—and not only because the newspapers in Stockholm wrote about the "persecuted" church visitors.

The Journey. Copenhagen was the first stop on the journey that Karlström had prepared so admirably and on such short notice.[31] Bonhoeffer saw Bishop Ammundsen and Dr. Görnandt. The ordinands used every opportunity to find out whether German Lutherans, should they decide to cooperate with the state church committees in Germany, might be justified in pleading the satisfactory functioning of the Lutheran state churches in Scandinavia. Almost everywhere they got the unfavorable answer they had hoped to hear; indeed the Swedish verdict on the Oeynhausen synod was distinctly harsh. Schönherr's newsletter report on the journey related:

> [There was] a splendid evening with Professors Nörregaard and Torm. We were amazed to discover how clearly they saw our situation and understood our attitude; above all to discover how clearly these Lutheran professors rejected the attitude of our Lutheran bishops. This was something we found again and again . . . it is to our great benefit that among these Lutheran churches our attitude is not condemned as non-Lutheran but meets with approval. . . . On Monday we spent several hours among the professors in Lund. . . . Professor Nygren is here, who among the foreigners is most familiar with the current church conditions. . . . We were in the heart of the Swedish church in Uppsala; the reception with Archbishop Eidem was particularly impressive, as was the visit to the widow of Archbishop Söderblom and the service at his grave [Eidem and Mrs. Söderblom hosted members of the preachers' seminary] . . . Stockholm was the last stop and completely different. . . . Sigtuna was a certain tran-

sition. . . . A lecture by Björquist profoundly summarized the position that
dominates in the Swedish church: the *Volkskirche* as the perfect example
and crown of a completely Christian culture; the high school in Sigtuna
is working on regaining this. A conception that makes a Thomist impression on many. Here, too, [there is] once more predominately an unqualified religiosity. . . .[32]

Despite Karl Barth's *Church Dogmatics*, it was still rare for German theologians to discover that theology was constituted by the church, not the
church by theology. Bonhoeffer met Pastor Sparring-Petersen, whom he
knew from Cambridge in 1931, and had conversations with Archbishop Brilioth, mission scholar Knut Westman, Bishop Runestam, and Pastor Paul
Sandegren. The meeting between Bonhoeffer and Bishop Björquist was
somewhat disappointing for both; their basic assumptions were too different
at the time. Bonhoeffer could hardly bear it that a man like Björquist should
listen to German theologians who did not support Barmen and Dahlem.

Bonhoeffer gave a number of lectures, not only on church politics, but
on the Christology of discipleship, like those he delivered at Finkenwalde.
His question-and-answer method was almost as strange and unusual for
Swedish audiences as it had been to his students. The direction he took in his
lectures is indicated in Gerhard Lohmann's report on the visit:

> How does a Christian show himself to be Christian? Is Christian existence
> no more than a purified bourgeois existence, or is it necessary in the life of
> a Christian, as a friend of God, that he becomes an enemy of the world?

And elsewhere:

> It is no longer possible, as it was in the past, to lead a bourgeois life and a
> Christian life at the same time. Rather, three things are demanded of Chris-
> tian youth today: confessing Christ and with this the renunciation of all
> other gods in this world; discipleship of Christ in simple and modest obe-
> dience to his Word; communion in the community of Christ which is the
> church.

When the German guests left Uppsala their Swedish host said, "Even if
we do not agree on all theological questions, we have one thing in common:
the one Christian belief. And we Swedes have noticed one thing, that your
hearts burn."

On board the ship, the Finkenwalde group sent letters of thanks to Sweden and invited their hosts to visit Finkenwalde and the Confessing church.

Lohmann wrote a detailed report; an excerpt was published in *Junge Kirche*.[33] Such a trip at that time was so unusual that extra copies were distributed, to let as many as possible in the Confessing church know that people outside Germany's borders were in solidarity with them and supported their activities.

Interaction between the Foreign Ministry and the Church Foreign Office. The boldness of this journey is clearer in retrospect. Heckel's Church Foreign Office, the Reich Foreign Ministry, and the Reich Ministry for Education attempted to sabotage this enterprise by the Confessing church, but they also sought to damage Bonhoeffer personally.

Bonhoeffer apparently brought this down upon his own head. Wishing to observe correct procedure, he had written shortly before his departure not only to his superiors at the Old Prussian Council of Brethren, but to the Foreign Ministry as well. On 25 February he wrote from Finkenwalde:

> I hereby send the information that our preachers' seminary through the ecumenical committee in Sweden . . . has received . . . an invitation to a study trip in Sweden. . . . I have accepted this invitation and would be grateful if the German representatives in Sweden, where I will present myself, could be informed. His excellency Kriege has been informed of our plans and is kind enough to give more information as necessary. . . .[34]

Privy Councillor Johannes Kriege, known by the Bonhoeffer family and in the Dahlem parish, had been director of the Justice Department in the Foreign Ministry and participated in the peace conference in the Hague. He was well respected in the Foreign Ministry, but no longer had an active role there. His undisputed prominence did not help Bonhoeffer. Instead, the responsible official in the Foreign Ministry, Fritz von Twardowski, who later became a friend of Eugen Gerstenmaier, immediately sent inquiries to Heckel at the Church Foreign Office. The information he received from Heckel led him to warn the German Embassy in Stockholm on 29 February:

> The Reich and Prussian Ministries for Church Affairs, and the Church Foreign Office, warn against Pastor Bonhoeffer because his influence is not conducive to German interests. Government and church departments have the strongest objections to his visit which has just now become known. I respectfully ask to report about his appearances and the Swedish press reports. . . .[35]

Upon arriving in Stockholm, Bonhoeffer paid the announced visit to the German consulate, where he met the German ambassador himself, Prince

Victor zu Wied. Unaware of the background events, Eugen Rose wrote: "The Prince received him with marked coolness beneath a life-sized portrait of Hitler."

After the trip Bonhoeffer, in his efforts to behave correctly toward the Foreign Ministry, asked the two who had helped with the journey, Eugen Rose and Werner Koch, to send an official report to the ministry. They did this on 7 April, emphasizing the official church nature of the trip, its national usefulness, and the correct behavior of all participants with regard to state political issues.[36] This report was passed on to Heckel with the query "whether and with what success the Reich church committee [i.e., Zoellner] had protested to the leaders of the Swedish church over the invitation."[37] Heckel had already done everything in his power that was required by the state. He recalled his initial actions against the trip and his warning at the end of February "that this tour, which was only made known at the last minute, was to be treated with the utmost suspicion as far as church politics were concerned. The Foreign Ministry also informed the German Embassy in Stockholm to the same effect."[38]

As a result of his first contact with the Foreign Ministry and the subsequent Swedish press reports about the Finkenwaldians' visit, Heckel became involved again several days later. On 3 March the newspapers reported the arrival of the seminary in Stockholm on the front page; the next day they reported on their reception by Archbishop Eidem in Uppsala. Two days later all the major Swedish and Danish newspapers published photos and reports of the meetings in the Swedish capital. On 6 March Heckel, Krummacher, and Wahl drafted a letter on behalf of Zoellner to Archbishop Eidem, asking whether the Swedish church, through its invitation, had perhaps officially "taken sides against the responsible church administration of the German Evangelical Church" on behalf of the "'Confessional' church which in a particularly sharp form has rejected the leadership of the German Evangelical Church and the Evangelical Church of the Old Prussian Union." Despite Heckel's notation that it was "very urgent," Zoellner didn't see the draft of this letter until 13 March, and it was mailed to Eidem on 14 March. Copies of the letter were also sent to the Foreign Ministry and the Reich Ministry of Church Affairs.[39]

After drafting this letter Heckel sent another warning about Bonhoeffer to the Prussian church committee on 7 March:

> Lecturer and Pastor Bonhoeffer, director of a confessional seminary in Finkenwalde near Stettin, has received an invitation from the Ecumenical Committee of the Swedish church to visit Sweden with the confessional

seminary. The ramifications of this action for foreign policy are being dealt with by the appropriate authorities. I feel impelled, however, to draw the attention of the provincial church committee to the fact that the incident has brought Bonhoeffer very much into the public eye. Since he can be accused of being a pacifist and an enemy of the state, it might well be advisable for the provincial church committee to disassociate itself from him and take steps to ensure that he will no longer train German theologians.[40]

As the bishop in charge of foreign affairs, Heckel had once again been surprised by Bonhoeffer's activities in the ecumenical sphere; this naturally made his situation with his political and ecclesiastical superiors a disagreeable one. He must have felt it as a setback for his efforts to centralize and monopolize German ecumenical relations. Also present in his mind was the knowledge that Bonhoeffer and his friends had been accusing both him and his officials of aiding and abetting heresy since 1933. So he now struck back with weapons that could hardly have been more deadly. In 1936 no form of denunciation was more fatal than the description "a pacifist and an enemy of the state," especially when this was used officially and in writing, along with the insistence that Bonhoeffer no longer be permitted to train "German theologians." In the eyes of the National Socialist officials, to be described as a "heretic" by someone like Bonhoeffer could only work to Heckel's advantage. By shifting the conflict to such a highly political level, however, Heckel was placing Bonhoeffer at the mercy of the National Socialist state.

Eidem's Dilemma. On 14 March Archbishop Eidem received both Bonhoeffer's warm letter of thanks and a letter from Zoellner which seemed to offer a way out: "I assume that . . . the invitation is to be regarded as a private matter." In his reply to Zoellner on 18 March Eidem wrote that he would prepare a report on the background of the invitation, but could assure him that the Ecumenical Committee had wished to help the Finkenwaldians. The invitation had been a personal one, and did not represent an official position of the Swedish church; "the young German colleagues were very nice and stayed away from church politics."

After seeing Karlström's report, however, Eidem was compelled to inform Zoellner on 13 May that the invitation had been "in fact semi-official." Two weeks prior to this cheerless correction the Finkenwalde report on the trip had been published in *Junge Kirche*. It understandably emphasized that Finkenwalde had received an "official invitation from the Swedish

Ecumenical Council, conveyed by D. Erling Eidem's private secretary with the archbishop's approval."[41] In light of his correspondence with Zoellner, the archbishop was disgruntled by the publication of the Finkenwalde report.

On 13 May Bonhoeffer, completely ignorant of these events, wrote to Eidem from Finkenwalde, saying how much he looked forward to the archbishop's visit to Germany—the journey had been mentioned in Uppsala on 4 March: "the colleagues from our church leadership would also like to meet you here. What days can you make available for us?"[42] Eidem sent an evasive reply on 20 May, saying that in Stettin he would only be able to visit the Swedish Seamen's Church; he added that the article in *Junge Kirche* had emphasized the official nature of the invitation too strongly. The last thing he had wanted was to see their trip to Sweden in a church-political light; they had only wanted to be friendly.[43]

Bonhoeffer wrote back that he regretted not having read the *Junge Kirche* report before it had been printed; still, he hoped that the archbishop could visit them the next time. The Finkenwalde group still knew nothing of this background when they wrote in their newsletter:

> Unfortunately, a letter arrived today from Archbishop Eidem stating that he has unexpectedly been compelled to curtail his visit; he will only be able to spend a few days in Germany and hence cannot fit in anything extra.[44]

When Eidem visited the Seaman's Church in Stettin, Bonhoeffer was with his seminarians on an evangelization trip in rural Pomerania. At the same time, he left a written greeting for the archbishop in Stettin. But Eidem found it impossible to single out Finkenwalde for a visit after all that had happened.

The experience with Bonhoeffer's seminary made the Swedes cautious toward future visitors from Germany. In September 1936 the Berlin Cathedral ordinands went to Sweden with Zoellner's and Heckel's blessing as a model church committee seminary, in deliberate contrast to Bonhoeffer's party. Their director, Dr. W. Schütz, contacted the archbishop: "we are under the auspices of the Regional church committee. I myself am a member of the Confessing church and my candidates stand theologically behind the Bible and confession, although most of them are uncommitted in church politics."[45] For appearances it was necessary to emphasize their membership in the Confessing church; on another level it was wiser to be "uncommitted theologically"—that is, not under the direction of a Council of Brethren. Nonetheless, Eidem did not receive them, conveying his regrets to the visitors.

Later the Finkenwalde candidate Eugen Rose became secretary of the Ecumenical Office of the Confessing Provisional Church Administration in Berlin. In 1937 he asked Archbishop Eidem to send a delegation of young Swedish theologians and suggested a general exchange of candidates; once more, however, the reply from Uppsala was friendly but reserved. Bonhoeffer, too, was turned down in 1937 when he tried to obtain an invitation to Sweden for Berlin youth minister Eugene Weschke and mentioned his desire to invite a group from Sweden. In his letter, Bonhoeffer added: "Might we still have the great pleasure of a visit from you?"[46] In his reply Eidem mentioned that he would read the confession of sin in German at the opening worship of the upcoming Oxford ecumenical conference in St. Paul's Cathedral in London; it was already clear that no German delegates would be allowed to attend the meeting.

After Eidem's more or less satisfactory answer to Zoellner in May 1936, Heckel was able to inform the state authorities that the Swedish archbishop had acted in good faith and had expressed his indignation that the members of Finkenwalde should have given the visit so official a character. Hence "the responsibility for bringing this into the realm of church politics must be ascribed to the German participants, not the Swedish church."[47]

Heckel was exaggerating when he maintained that Eidem had "clearly and consistently emphasized that the affair must not be treated officially," since the archbishop had invited the twenty-six candidates to a reception at his home, where he had made some very pointed remarks, and he had raised no objection to this being fully reported in the press. Furthermore, the Swedish committee had arranged a welcoming reception for the seminary in Stockholm, which was attended by the king's brother, Prince Bernadotte, and a visit to the private art gallery of a second brother, Prince Eugen.

It was impossible to prevent the seminary's Swedish visit from being drawn into the struggle, even if the Confessing church had wanted to do so, which was far from being the case. For its part, the official Reich church was eager to safeguard its rights of sole representation. It had to comply with the demands of a powerful state; by attacking the rebels it could protect itself from its superiors. Each side had already made irreconcilable decisions about the church's role in the Third Reich.

Uninhibited by the presence of Heckel and his minions, at the 1936 Life and Work conference in Chamby Bonhoeffer announced that the Swedish trip had been part of his work as youth secretary of the World Alliance; his remarks were entered in the minutes and the annual report of the World Alliance.[48]

Bonhoeffer's Right to Teach Is Revoked. The most drastic consequence of the visit to Sweden was the termination of Bonhoeffer's duties as a lecturer at Berlin University by the Reich Ministry of Education. Was this perhaps the result of the Church Foreign Office's call for measures ensuring "that he will no longer train German theologians"? The visit to Sweden gave the ministry a welcome opportunity to make a long deferred move. Bonhoeffer had anticipated it, but did not submit without a struggle. He did everything in his power to stave off the end of his academic career.

Upon his return from London in 1935, he had notified the university authorities that the sabbatical leave he had begun in 1933 was over. During the 1935–1936 winter term he announced and held a series of lectures on "discipleship," and also reported that he was taking over the preachers' seminary. In fact, on 29 November 1935 the Reich Ministry of Education, in agreement with the Reich Minister of Church Affairs (which at the time of Bonhoeffer's notification did not yet exist), made a preliminary decision that he could not direct the Finkenwalde seminary and at the same time pursue his university activities.[49] This document lay in the faculty's files for many months and was treated in a dilatory fashion until Bonhoeffer finally had to declare that he would not abandon the seminary.

From Sweden he mailed in the long political questionnaire that was required of all active lecturers, including his father and eldest brother. He attested that he had not belonged to communist or socialist associations, that he was not a member of a Freemasons' lodge, and that neither his parents nor grandparents were Jewish. He also provided the required "Aryan certificate"; curiously enough, his cousin Leibholz, whose own inability to produce this document had cost him his post, advised him to do so. Positions and views had shifted since 1933. The Confessing church no longer recommended that those affected by the new laws should resign of their own accord from official posts, but that they should wait until dismissed. It may have been during this period that Bonhoeffer's thoughts first turned to the possibility of political action. In any case, he thought it worth the effort to hold on to his university post, even if this meant producing an Aryan certificate. He viewed this not as a timid compromise but as a necessity. He must not be forced away from his students and removed from yet one more position in public life.

But it was too late. Upon returning home he discovered that he had unwittingly contravened an order issued by the Reich Minister of Education in June 1935 concerning the authorization of journeys abroad taken by university lecturers.[50] On 18 April he attempted to rectify the situation by requesting a further leave of absence from his teaching post. The application was unsuccessful. On 5 August 1936 he received a written notice that his right to teach had been permanently rescinded. The reason given was that he continued to direct a seminary that had been banned under the terms of the Fifth Decree and that, although the visit to Sweden had been "at the invitation of the Ecumenical Committee" there, he had not obtained permission from the Ministry of Education to travel.[51]

Bonhoeffer gave his final lecture at Berlin University on 14 February 1936, at the same time his thirty-four-year-old brother-in-law, Gerhard Leibholz, was forced to retire. His father reached retirement age on 1 April 1936, although he continued to hold his position for another two years. Thus the family's ties to the university were becoming more tenuous.

The second Finkenwalde course had begun under the new compulsory orders of Minister Kerrl, and it ended with the experience of freedom in Sweden. Within the realm of church politics, too, prospects seemed to be improving. After a period of turbulence in the Confessing church the forces were regrouping.

The Oeynhausen synod was followed on 12 March by the formation of the Second Provisional Administration of the Confessing church, which succeeded the Provisional Church Administration. Consisting of Pastor Fritz Müller from Dahlem, Pastor Otto Fricke from Frankfurt, Berlin superintendent Martin Albertz, Berlin church provost Hans Böhm, and superintendent Bernhard Forck, it was not as large or extensive as the first administration under Marahrens had been. On the other hand, this group was far more determined to uphold the Barmen and Dahlem resolutions against Kerrl's prohibitions.

By contrast, the Lutherans' independent tendencies had been strengthened by long-standing tradition and by their theological criticism of Barmen and their aloofness from the consequences of Dahlem. This led to the final formation of the Lutheran Council on 18 March. Its members were the Lutheran bishops of the intact churches, Marahrens, Meiser, and Wurm; church councilman Thomas Breit; Hanns Lilje; and Bishops Hugo Hahn and Niklot Beste. Lilje was appointed secretary, with an office in Berlin. The Lutheran Council did not wish to break away from the Confessing church's Reich Council of Brethren, but intended to pursue its own policy so far as the "Dahlemites" were concerned. As a result, its member churches were free to establish positive ties to the church committee—the organization with which the "Dahlemites" were locked in such bitter strife. Thus the conflict between the Provisional Administration and the Lutheran Council could not be long in coming. The open break in relations was created by a lengthy memorandum to Hitler prepared by the Reich Council of Brethren.

While the seminary was in Sweden, Hitler had created a political sensation by marching into the Rhineland; the Allies failed to take any measures against this military reoccupation. He celebrated the victory on 29 March with a plebiscite intended to show the world the support he enjoyed from 99 percent of the population. At the time of the plebiscite the seminary was on holiday. Bonhoeffer was glad he had been able to avoid handing in his ballot paper at home; instead his "no" was recorded in a village somewhere in Saxony. During his holiday travels in Saxony he and Staemmler ordained several candidates in the town of Stendal. It was a daring thing to do after Kerrl's decree, but one in which the parish actively participated. Then he toured the old town of Hildesheim and enjoyed the spring weather in Friedrichsbrunn.

The Essay on Church-Community

During the 1936 summer term Bonhoeffer earned a reputation that caused many to disassociate themselves theologically from the group of which he was a member. On the other hand, he now aroused the interest of some people more than ever. The reason for this was a paper in *Evangelische Theologie* and a Bible study in *Junge Kirche*. Both pieces had been written originally for his students in Finkenwalde.

Retreats with Former Candidates. A "retreat" in 1936 did not mean a retreat from work. Anyone who didn't attend probably did not want to have his behavior and his position discussed, and whoever was unable to attend knew that he was missing essential help in staying the course. If possible, Bonhoeffer began with each new group of seminarians by holding a joint retreat with those who had just finished, in the hope of influencing the spirit of the new candidates from the onset:

> I probably don't need to remind you that we committed ourselves to this meeting when we left one another. . . . whoever thinks he doesn't need to attend, please write me immediately so I can convince him that he does have to come.[52]

At the meeting of the educational offices of the Confessing church Bonhoeffer had appointed himself to do this work, and he led five such retreats in those years. Fairly complete copies of the works he wrote for discussion during these retreats have been preserved. Only a few sections were published during his lifetime; they caused a furor even before people knew of *Discipleship*. He treated several themes:

April 1936 (first candidates' course): "The Rebuilding of Jerusalem according to Ezra and Nehemiah" (Bible study); "The Question of the Church-
Community" (lecture).[53]

October 1936 (second course): "Timothy, the Servant in the House of
God" (Bible study); "Teaching Plan for Confirmation Students" (lecture).[54]

April 1937 (first course): "Timothy" (Bible study); review of Hermann
Sasse's book *What Does It Mean to Be Lutheran?*; "The Power of the Keys
and Community Discipline in the New Testament" (lecture).[55]

June 1937 (third course): "The Power of the Keys and Community Discipline in the New Testament"; "The Confessional Question in Light of the
Halle Resolutions."[56]

June 1938 in Zingst (courses 1–5): "Temptation" (Bible study).[57]

As this syllabus shows, the studies had been conceived to meet the
demands of the moment; indeed, that was their main purpose. This is not
only true of the piece on "the church-community"; it shows the oppressive
and concrete circumstances behind the study of "temptation" and the justification for the study of Ezra and Nehemiah. Bonhoeffer's intellectual and
academic interest was dominated entirely by his desire in that moment to
convey something that could alter people and their decisions. This sharpens
the attention on particular aspects (and against others) in the scripture and
the confessions.

Inspiration for the Article. When the 1935 summer course reassembled in
April 1936 for a refresher conference at Finkenwalde, they confronted a very
different situation from what they had known in 1935. In 1935 there were no
committees and no Fifth Decree; the Oeynhausen synod had not yet met. In
view of the many pressing questions, Bonhoeffer thought it advisable to
give the students a report and an overview, so that they could assess the
recent developments theologically and with regard to the internal affairs of
the church. Who was still in the church with them? What criteria should set
the standards here? What was the significance of the separation from those
who had previously been good friends? What consequences could be expected and what conclusions should be drawn? Should the decision about
whether to preserve or abandon fellowship be based objectively on the decisions made in Barmen and Dahlem, or should they be contingent on the
willingness of those in positions of authority? Should they continue to recognize the Old Prussian Council of Brethren as their church leadership
because of that church's excellence, its numbers, or its confession? The good
reputations of many of the members on the church committees was bewil-
dering. How much weight should be given the distinctions made in Oeynhausen, and how much to the inconclusive advice it had proffered?

Bonhoeffer hoped to cut through this tangle of problems and perspectives and reassure his students. As he saw it, he was not saying anything new. For the last six months the Finkenwalde newsletters had been dealing with the *rite vocatus*[58] and the danger that a false sense of vocation might lead people to succumb to heresy in silence.[59] If the question of *rite vocatus* had finally been passed over and the corresponding reality had been created within the Confessing church, then the question of community inevitably had to be answered together with those who saw vocation differently. This should have been clarified by the Oeynhausen synod, but it had not been. Hence the seminary's complaint on the eve of its visit to Sweden: "The statement for which we have waited in vain is a ruling on the question of church recognition and should have formed the basis of church discipline."[60] By allowing the provincial Councils of Brethren to decide whether or not to cooperate with the committees, the synod had opened the door to all kinds of divisions and alliances; thus it showed "the highest measure of unfraternal and uncharitable conduct."[61]

Bonhoeffer thought this excessive concern about the boundaries of the church, and the attention it was drawing, was dangerous. For this reason he devoted the main portion of his essay to the principle that the church did not determine its own boundaries. But he also held that it had become necessary to acknowledge another fact: namely, that the church was now encountering boundaries "drawn against her from outside."[62] To what extent did these have to be recognized? Bonhoeffer had already vividly described to Stettin Pastor Schauer how oppressively this boundary was felt when one of the members decided to leave. In a letter to Schauer on 25 January 1936 he commented that the decision on where to draw the line could hardly be expected of individuals. The synod alone must decide:

> I am, of course, of the opinion that anyone who in any way subordinates himself to the Committees is not in the same church with us. What is valid here is not the word of the individual, but the word of the synods or Councils of Brethren for which many are waiting. Up to now the lack of clarity on this point strikes me as both ominous and symptomatic.... My concern in all that is said and done in the church is solely with the primacy, the unique dignity and truth of God's Word. There is no greater service of love than to place someone in the light of the truth of this Word, even when it gives pain. God's Word discerns the spirits. This implies no spirit of judgment but only the humble and truly awed understanding of the ways which God himself desires to go with his Word in his church. The boundaries of this Word are our boundaries as well.[63]

Bonhoeffer's paper was written because the Oeynhausen synod had failed. He could not, of course, compensate for what the synod had left undone; but, under the relevant and controversial title "On the Question of the Church Community," he could offer these questions as incisively as possible:

> The intention of these brief remarks cannot be to anticipate the church's decision. But they must serve to remind the church leadership that it must make this decision. By doing this step by step, it will be doing the strange work so as to carry out its true work correctly. The dissolution of community is the last offer of community.[64]

Publication. The participants of the retreats immediately agreed that this controversial lecture should be published as soon as possible. Ernst Wolf published it in the June 1936 issue of *Evangelische Theologie.* One sentence in the third section of the paper—"Whoever knowingly separates himself from the Confessing church in Germany separates himself from salvation"[65]—spread like wildfire throughout the German churches. In the hundreds of discussions and meetings about it, it was repeated simplistically: "Anyone without a Red Card won't go to heaven!" (Members of the Confessing church signed a red card that listed their commitments; in a few provinces, it was green.) On 1 July the sentence appeared in bold type in the *Information Service of the Evangelical Church of the Old Prussian Union,* published by the church committee Information Service, an agency headed by General Superintendent Eger. It was followed by the comment:

> No, this sentence is not some sort of malicious invention or imputation by which the "enemies of Christ" seek to harm the cause of the Confessing church; it was set down in black and white by a man of the Confessing church, Lic. Bonhoeffer. . . . Poor Evangelical church, in which it is possible to achieve notoriety by such trifling conceits.[66]

It seemed that the case had never been stated so confidently and provocatively. Was it really necessary to read it in its entire context? New Testament Professor Hans Lietzmann wrote Archbishop Eidem:

> . . . and recently Lic. Bonhoeffer, a highly gifted but now altogether fanatical teacher, declared *extra ecclesiam nulla salus,* that is, whoever cooperates with the Reich church committee stands outside the Church of Salvation.[67]

The Lutheran clergy in Pomerania demanded a theological debate, noting that "some people don't want to take up any more collections."[68]

By mid-July the issue of *Evangelische Theologie* was sold out. "I had hoped to send each of you a separate copy of "The Church Community" but it was no longer obtainable."[69] The uproar took Bonhoeffer somewhat by surprise. He maintained that he had suggested the same demand in his 1935 ecumenical essay, when he wrote: "But if the Confessing church were to abandon this demand, the German church struggle would already have been decided against it, and with it the struggle for Christianity as well."[70] This had created no stir at the time. But now the thesis of this offensive sentence created turmoil among a church population that had grown nervous and was under pressure to justify itself in public. Bonhoeffer wrote to Barth: "They are getting terribly excited about it. And really I thought I was simply writing something obvious."[71] In a letter to Sutz he noted:

> By the way, my paper has made me the most reviled man of our persuasion.[72] Recently some "Lutheran" association even proposed that I should be removed from my teaching post in the Confessing Church. The Rhinelanders are standing by me splendidly. . . . Things are approaching the stage when the beast before which the idol worshippers bow down will bear the caricature of Luther's features. "They are adorning the graves of the prophets. . . ."[73]

Some of the church councils and leaders, in fact, did ask the Councils of Brethren to disassociate themselves entirely from Bonhoeffer.

Wherever the members of Finkenwalde went, they were hard put to defend their mentor's theses. They themselves had to learn not to focus on this one passage, but to see the primary emphasis of the paper in its first section, which refuted the legalistic view that the church had to set and draw its own boundaries. They had to grasp that they could not keep quiet about Bonhoeffer's use of the word "knowingly" in his controversial sentence. Only gradually did many begin to see that such a statement should never be adopted by the church as a rigid device for counting heads, or as a "prerequisite for pious speculation over who was saved and who was lost."[74] Bonhoeffer patiently answered every timid question.[75]

The Lutherans now applied many labels to Bonhoeffer: "legalism," "fanaticism," and "Romanism." On 9 July Pastor Duensing of Hannover accused him in *Um Glauben und Kirche* of a "legalistic interpretation of the Protestant concept of church," and elaborated on this in a letter to Helmut Gollwitzer on 20 August:

> Has not another revelation now been placed alongside Holy Scripture as the sole rule and guiding principle, thus throwing the door wide open to

fanaticism? Or again, the question might be asked: Is not this claim on the part of the "Confessing church" an exact repetition of the claim raised by the pope?

The extent of the rift can be gauged from the criticism that came from Walter Künneth and from an article written by Hermann Sasse, Bonhoeffer's staunch ally in 1933 in Bethel:

> This Confessing church shaped according to the wishes of Barth and Asmussen, as distinct from the confessional movement upheld by the Lutheran churches, is a sect, the worst sect in fact ever to have set foot on the soil of German Protestantism. Anyone who doubts this should read the papers by Bonhoeffer and Gollwitzer in the June issue of *Evangelische Theologie*. Founded on the miracle of Barmen, held together by Barth's *Theologumenon* on the worthlessness of the remnants of natural theology to which Calvin and Luther adhered, beaten down by the harsh experience of the church struggle, there stands the alleged church.[76]

Georg Merz wrote Gollwitzer saying that he could only interpret Bonhoeffer's sentence "as the ecstatic effusion of a hitherto levelheaded man, contradicting everything that was essential to Luther."[77] Finally there was an exchange of correspondence at the highest levels of the church. On 17 July the Lutheran Council sent the following inquiry to the Provisional Administration:

> What attitude does the Provisional Administration plan to adopt regarding the declarations made in the following passages? . . .[78] We should like to have a clear position on these passages, since they are not a matter of one enthusiastic individual's false doctrine but represent views which are widely shared and which, on occasion, have consequences in a definite course of action.

The Provisional Administration replied on 28 July 1936:

> The important question discussed by Bonhoeffer in his article . . . derives from the ecumenical sphere; he seeks to introduce a theological debate on the question of the ecclesiastical community. Bonhoeffer's article cannot be dismissed by taking a passage at random and out of context. The questions he has raised, just like the countertheses of Hermann Sasse in his book *Union und Bekenntnis* [Union and Confession], must become part of theological work and need a conclusive statement from a Confessional synod.

In the Rhineland General Superintendent Stoltenhoff demanded information from the Rhineland Council of the Confessing synod on 1 August: "I am inquiring from the council whether Dr. Bonhoeffer's sentence . . . is approved or not. To me it is nothing more than an atrocious piece of false doctrine." The Rhineland Council replied on 23 September. After an allusion to the general context of Bonhoeffer's sentence, the letter continued:

> Bonhoeffer's statements are based on the thesis that the call "Here is the Church" is synonymous with the call "Here is the Gospel." The Rhineland Council sees in this thesis a legitimate interpretation of the Reformation concept of the church. . . .
>
> In 1934, anyone who persistently repudiates the call "Here is the Church, here is the Gospel" raised by the Confessing church and who knowingly breaks with the Confessing church, has broken with the Gospel as it is preached. . . .
>
> The Rhineland Council of Brethren cannot decide here and now whether a future synod of the Confessing church might see itself compelled, in accordance with Bonhoeffer's recommendation, to determine the boundaries of the church-community over against those who practice and support the anticonfessional church government of the committees,[79] just as these boundaries once had to be drawn against the German Christian church officials. Only the Confessional synods themselves can decide this. But, together with the entire Confessing church, the Rhineland Council has the task, even today in 1936, to witness to everyone concerned: "Here is the church, here is the Gospel."
>
> . . . Thus you must agree with us when we can find no heretical church concept in the controversial sentence "Whoever knowingly . . ." after we have placed this phrase in the light of Bonhoeffer's entire remarks. Signed, President Paul Humburg.[80]

Even before Bonhoeffer had been accused of "false doctrine," a term now lightly and generally bandied about, he had drafted an expert opinion for the Pomeranian Council on "False Doctrine in the Confessing Church?" in June:

> The Confessing church is allegedly to be defeated with its own weapons. . . . The rejection of the committees as the lawful church leadership and the grounds for this rejection are said to be false doctrine. Thus, what is now proclaimed in the name of "Lutheranism" does an ill service to true Lutheranism. These accusations are accompanied by the pseudo-scholarly assertion that the Confessing church has long been infiltrated by an alien "Reformed" doctrine. But Lutheran pastors and communities are concerned with freeing themselves from servitude to Reformed "legalism"

which ultimately means accepting the oversight of the committees or alternatively, the Lutheran Council.[81]

Ernst Wolf now asked Gollwitzer to write an article for *Evangelische Theologie* to refute the subtle and obvious misinterpretations, and to give Bonhoeffer the floor again. Gollwitzer had already tried to do this somewhat in individual letters. He did not conceal his own view that a number of Bonhoeffer's formulations demanded some review, notably his identification of the word of the synod with the Word of God.[82] In fact, Bonhoeffer, replying in an article entitled "Questions" to Gollwitzer's "Comments and Reservations," did not defend this passage but adopted the term "testimony."[83] On the other hand, Gollwitzer made it clear how blind the critics were to their own "legalism," "fanaticism," and "Romanism."

Bonhoeffer's latest contribution was wholly characteristic. His confidence in the cause was evidently quite unshaken, for he did not lose himself in justifying his earlier theses, but continued the discussion with combative new questions and his criticism of the Oeynhausen synod's shortcomings. He gave little satisfaction to those readers eagerly awaiting a sharp clash with Gollwitzer, Künneth, and Sasse over the confessional question. He was not essentially interested in who was proven right, since he too had undoubtedly been responsible for misunderstandings. He was even prepared to agree with serious critics on occasion. To him more important things were at stake.

The resumption of the controversy in the October issue of *Evangelische Theologie* did not lead to any change. All kinds of accusations against Bonhoeffer's essay were still the fashion. On both sides existing preconceptions proved stronger than the arguments as, to an even greater extent, did membership in one or another influential organization. Nevertheless, Gollwitzer continued to speak on Bonhoeffer's behalf. He wrote Wilhelm Pressel, a councillor on the High Church Council:

> You have . . . accused Bonhoeffer of fanaticism. It is unfortunate that nowhere did you define this word that is currently so popular. The "equating of things" you attack is in no sense the enthusiastic equation of the organized congregation with the church of the saints but the Lutheran identification of the church, visibly gathering around the true confession, with the true church of Christ. Your attack is upon the Lutheran fathers no less than upon Bonhoeffer. You will surely not wish seriously to maintain that this fanatical equation among our Prussian brethren represents an "acute danger." . . . The real dangers of an [enthusiastic] evasion of word and sacrament today seem to me to lie in the theology of the order of cre-

ation propounded by many alleged Lutheran theologians who, I notice, have yet to be disavowed by the Lutheran Council. . . .[84]

Bonhoeffer himself had described the alternative clearly:

Either the Barmen Declaration is a true confession of the Lord Jesus Christ which has been brought about through the Holy Spirit, in which case it can make or divide a church—or it is an unofficial expression of the opinion of a number of theologians, in which case the Confessing Church has been on the wrong track for a long time.[85]

His emphatic and self-confident style sprang from an intense concern for steadfastness in the prevailing state of instability. As a watchman speaking to the need of the times, his main anxiety was for the word and the true church, and he was as little concerned with confessional dogmatism as with a conservative insistence upon the position of the church. The price of dogmatism was too high, and what remained of the church was not worth defending. But he was prepared to risk his reputation in order to preserve or rebuild the place where the voice for the voiceless might make itself heard. At the time he was all the more willing to do this because the Provisional Administration had prepared a memorandum addressed to Hitler—undoubtedly a dangerous step, but one that justified its existence.

But Bonhoeffer also feared that the confessors of old would now break their word. At the grave of his grandmother he had praised the "free words of free men, the commitment to a word once given."[86] He found it almost intolerable that the words spoken in Barmen and Dahlem should have been abandoned so quickly and universally:

We are not vagabonds who obey one government one day and another the next. We have no grounds for suddenly breaking faith with one church government when another is presented to us from outside.[87]

That the origins and motives of the Barmen declaration should suddenly have become more crucial than the declaration itself was, in his view, an ominous confusion of theology with church decisions. He continued to hold this viewpoint when he had to draw a distinction between his negative verdict on the Oeynhausen synod and the resolution actually passed there. When he attended the Chamby meeting in 1936 he accepted the practical consequences of the synod's lack of determination, probably in the hope that there might yet be another decision.

His third concern was for a new community of the faithful; this closed his mind to the worthy attempts to save the *Volkskirche*. Those who saw Zoellner's attempt as the last chance of preserving the *Volkskirche* had to accept that even pious and conservative men such as Zoellner and Eger undertook this task by paying humiliating tributes to the National Socialist "national evolution." Bonhoeffer could never have brought himself to pay such tributes, even if he had wished to save the *Volkskirche*.

In his polemics of 1936, in contrast to other years, it is striking that Bonhoeffer did not assail the essential elements, word and sacrament, of the *notae ecclesiae*. By now state recognition had virtually acquired the rank of *nota ecclesiae*, or the determining factor was the patently "Christian personalities" who comprised the church committees. So he now adhered carefully to the reliable doctrine that only the true administration of the sacrament and correct teaching of the word were necessary to be the church of God. When accused of being influenced by Reformed teachings, however, he could be more Lutheran than the Lutherans—for instance, by quoting the statements made by the Lutheran bishops in 1934 and 1935 in his essay "False Doctrine in the Confessing Church?"[88]

Perhaps Bonhoeffer's error was that he underestimated the staying power of the *Volkskirche*. Or was he so intransigent because he recognized its tenacity only too well? In any case, it was not where his heart was.

Ezra and Nehemiah. The April 1936 retreat from which this offending essay had emerged also destroyed Bonhoeffer's reputation as an interpreter of the Old Testament. His exegesis on "The Reconstruction of Jerusalem according to Ezra and Nehemiah"[89] was affected by the fact that his professional status as an Old Testament scholar, of course, was weaker. Both the essay and the exegesis, however, sprang from the same impulses; both sought to clarify and strengthen the minds of those who had become confused. This makes them absorbing reading, even if the principles of exegetical scholarship applied by Bonhoeffer are not entirely defensible.

At the beginning of 1936 a similar Bible study on King David had already appeared in *Junge Kirche*.[90] This aroused little scholarly interest but there was a political reaction in the National Socialist paper, *Durchbruch*, from journalist Friedrich Imholz: "there is much that might be called innocuous, when compared with such exponents of an oriental religious doctrine that has the impudence, even now in the year 1936, to represent the world-enemy Judah as the 'eternal people,' the 'true nobility,' 'the people of God.'"[91]

The controversial Confessing pulpit proclamation of 12 January 1936 had led Bonhoeffer to consider doing a Bible study on Ezra and Nehemiah, and his confessional sermon the day after the Bredow meeting also influenced the tone of the longer exegesis he did on 21 April. Thus, although the actual events of 1936 may have influenced the Old Testament chapters he read and the verses he selected, as a scholar he sought to exclude contemporary events as far as possible, in order to achieve greater proximity to these literary documents of the late canonical Jewish period. Bonhoeffer did not draw attention to the distance in time to that era; he eliminated it altogether. His Bible study was more of a sermon than a critical examination of the text. It was also sent to *Junge Kirche* as a topical comment.

Junge Kirche, under the editorial team of Hanns Lilje and Fritz Söhlmann, was a platform for carrying out the debates of the time. Bonhoeffer's Bible study now served both as a target and as ammunition in the skirmishes between Lutherans, the supporters of the church committees, and the "Dahlemites," the purpose of which was to capture this periodical as a publicity weapon. On 3 July Söhlmann wrote to Bonhoeffer:

> ... the Bible study gives me particular pleasure. If it were up to me alone I would bring it out at once. I do not anticipate any difficulties from Dr. Lilje. Now the publishers are pushing him so hard that it seems highly probable he will at last resign his co-editorship, which he has been hesitating to do. . . . But I must expect difficulties from the publishers. Generally I don't allow myself to be influenced. But an article by [Hans] Ehrenberg has just gone through to the accompaniment of terrific arguments. . . . Because of this I have written to the publishers today telling them that I am considering printing your Bible study in one of the next issues. . . .[92]

Bonhoeffer certainly intended his contribution to embrace both the contemporary struggle in church politics and the question of Old Testament textual exegesis. The exegetical question had become particularly controversial since the appearance of Wilhelm Vischer's *The Witness of the Old Testament to Christ* in 1934. With its christological elimination of the historical distance to the text, Vischer's book had divided theologians between outraged specialists and enthusiastic followers of Barth. Since *Creation and Fall* Bonhoeffer had been a member of the second group; in his "theological" exegesis he, too, sought to preach Christ in the Old Testament.

As soon as the 18 July issue of *Junge Kirche* appeared, Friedrich Baumgärtel, the Greifswald Old Testament scholar, sent a letter of protest to Eberhard Baumann, the theological expert of the Stettin Council of Brethren. He also began working on a pointed refutation the preface of which had been completed by 4 August.[93] Baumgärtel's critique found wide acceptance, for

example, in the Westphalian church paper: "Baumgärtel's demand for clarification is patently necessary. Bonhoeffer's 'Bible study' cannot remain
uncontested."[94] An exhaustive correspondence began between Baumgärtel
and Eberhard Baumann.[95] After Baumann assured him that the articles
published in *Junge Kirche* were not the official pronouncements of the Confessing church and were open to discussion, Baumgärtel wrote:

> I know that young pastors and ordinands feel inwardly distressed about the
> Old Testament since they find themselves defenseless against Bonhoeffer's
> onslaught. I have written this booklet for the sake of these weak ones, all
> the more readily because I realize how difficult it is for students at the
> moment to meet academically and really get to the roots of a problem. I
> simply had to help them. My anxiety is not lessened by your writing to me
> that Bonhoeffer's pronouncements are not to be seen as the pronounce-
> ments of the Confessing church. How can a man hold such a decisive
> position as a teacher of theology when the Confessing church must ex-
> plicitly disassociate itself from his theological statements?[96]

Baumgärtel was able to prove the opposite of what Bonhoeffer, who had
ignored the context of the verses he had selected, had written: that, contrary
to Bonhoeffer's thesis, at the time of Israel's return from Babylon the reconstruction of the "church" of Ezra and Nehemiah had been undertaken with
considerable "state assistance" and under the protection of the state
commissars.

At the time Bonhoeffer did not respond any further to these attacks
from the experts. There is no doubt that he had been too hasty in compiling the material for his message. Perhaps he also sensed the weakness of his
exegetical method, for not long afterward he thought of drafting an article
on "hermeneutics." Although he never carried out this plan, there is a noticeable change in his treatment of Old Testament texts in his letters from Tegel
prison.[97]

Bonhoeffer did not let himself be deterred from applying his subjective
contemporary experience to an eclectic examination of texts. He could even
inspire his students with highly questionable theses—for example, the idea
that one contestable exegesis does not necessarily result in a false sermon,
and conversely that the correct use of exegetical material does not guarantee that a sermon will be true. He would not admit that the wealth of a text
is exhausted in its literal meaning. Without this element of risk in the transition from exegesis to sermon, Bonhoeffer's sermons on Judas, the Psalms
of Vengeance, and his experiment with Psalm 119 would never have come
into being.

His Bible study on Ezra, therefore, is at once false and correct. It does not stand up to an examination of its biblical-historical context, but its message remains valid: that the church does not escape judgment and can find its truth not in restoration, however well intentioned, but only in the independent renewal of its faith.

Greifswald. There was an acrimonious background to the theological criticism of Bonhoeffer's exegetical work that emerged from the Greifswald faculty, although Baumgärtel went to great pains to assert that his polemic concerned only theology and exegesis, and was entirely unconnected to questions of church politics. The differences with the Greifswald faculty that had begun with the seminary's passing visit in 1935 had grown into a deep rift after the formation of the Pomeranian church committee. Lacking the support of the university professors and, in fact, forced to oppose them, the Finkenwalde seminary was now working in Greifswald with those students who did not wish to leave the Councils of Brethren. When the members of Finkenwalde actually set up a seminary in Greifswald, the professors were conspicuous by their absence from the dedication service.

Yet the work in Greifswald was not solely the brainchild of Finkenwalde. The Confessing church as a whole was compelled to look after the students in the theological faculties, for the church colleges (*Hochschulen*) had been banned and forced into illegality. Furthermore, the universities were becoming increasingly nazified; it was almost impossible for a state-appointed lecturer to keep his students informed about events in the church struggle, or, for instance, to go into any detail about the Confessing church's memorandum to Hitler. What is more, the overwhelming majority of lecturers (in Greifswald, the entire faculty) were advocating the cause of the church committees and the abandonment of all demands put forward by the Confessing church.

> Thus the new theological generation is in great danger of having no contact at all with a decisive confessional theology. At this moment the preachers' seminaries of the Confessing church are the only places where the Confessing church can, with complete independence, show the way to a clear confessional attitude in life and doctrine.[98]

Hence the Provisional Administration set up its own boards for theological students, including one in Greifswald at the beginning of the 1936 summer term. After consulting with the Pomeranian and Old Prussian Councils of Brethren, Finkenwalde House of Brethren member Horst Lekszas and then Albrecht Schönherr took up this work among the Greifswald students. Toward the end of the semester the Pomeranian Council of Brethren even held "substitute lectures" by Ernst Wolf, Eberhard Baumann, Heinrich Rendtorff, and Bonhoeffer.[99]

That summer, after he had been forced to stop lecturing in Berlin, Bonhoeffer went to Greifswald nearly every week. Lekszas and student leader Günther Schultz tried to find parish halls for the lecture programs, encountering difficulties since many Greifswald professors were members of the parish councils. In addition to Bonhoeffer Martin Niemöller, Otto Dibelius, Hans Asmussen, Reinhold von Thadden, Heinrich Rendtorff, and cultural minister Edo Osterloh came to Greifswald. The indefatigable Countess Behr of Behrenhof offered the group her estate. At the end of the semester Schultz announced that "the professors unanimously rejected the theological student office," but that those in Finkenwalde believed that Lekszas "did achieve his aim that the students did not simply go along with the church committee course in Greifswald."[100]

At the beginning of the 1936 winter term the work gained a firmer foothold after Schönherr was able to adapt an old fraternity house to use as a seminary, modeled along the lines of Finkenwalde. Whenever he could find a church Bonhoeffer preached; on such occasions congregations of five hundred were not unusual. The conflict attracted sympathy on all sides. Bonhoeffer wrote:

> It is a hard struggle in which he [Schönherr] is opposed by the entire faculty, but harder still for the small band of students who have taken it upon themselves to break with the faculty whose members once meant a great deal to them. Now, in fact, it is as if they had been turned out, solely because they stand firmly behind the Council of Brethren. . . . The fronts unfortunately seem to be hardening a little so that it is no longer possible to count on a hearing. In fact the Confessing church is being torn asunder here in the name of the Confessing church, a circumstance which in truth cannot remain tolerable for long. Everything goes to show that clarification is necessary. . . . Unfortunately the situation in Greifswald is fairly typical of the province as a whole.[101]

There were repeated attempts at fresh discussions; these were all unsuccessful. In 1936 it was virtually impossible to remain united when one colleague belonged to a theological faculty and another to a confessional seminary. On the Stettin Council of Brethren, Eberhard Baumann shared Baumgärtel's criticism of Bonhoeffer's exegetical methods. In their correspondence over the interpretation of Ezra and Nehemiah, however, the situation in Greifswald constantly intervened. Despite his wise caution, on this point Baumann was closer to Bonhoeffer. In his last letter to Baumgärtel, Baumann wrote:

> The students' confidence is based not only on what the teaching staff *say*, on the *thoughts* they express in the exercise of their teaching responsibility, but also on the position those same lecturers take on the church's decisions. When the younger generation, averse to all forms of schism, suspects a lack of logical consistency between thought and action, confidence is likely to evaporate. From the students' perspective, this would seem to be the crux of the matter. And this is the source of all the distress which deeply affects both sides.
>
> The foregoing problem completely dwarfs the dread question of how long teachers of Protestant theology, in their capacity as civil servants, will be able in the universities to teach both in the sense and in the service of the Protestant church to which they belong; of how long here the freedom to teach and to research, such freedom as still remains will exist in the universities of the Third Reich. These lines can only be written with pain.[102]

The Memorandum to Hitler

The stubborn dispute over the *rite vocatus* of a spiritual church leadership, in which Bonhoeffer felt himself increasingly involved, consumed more of his time and energy than he would have liked. In his view, the church's justification depended on whether the church and its properly called leadership still had something to say.

Now it indeed had something to say. Bonhoeffer passionately followed the evolution of the memorandum to the Reich chancellor; he believed this document presented these disputes in their true perspective for the first time. After his disappointment over the Steglitz synod, he saw a ray of hope in spring 1936, when the new Provisional Church Administration joined the Reich Council of Brethren in preparing a documentation of the state's legal encroachments. Whereas the important proclamations of 1935 and earlier had been concerned essentially with warding off political encroachments within the church itself or had warned against the new paganism, the Confessing church was now finally raising its voice for the "voiceless in the land" against the alarming developments outside the church sphere. This was to be aimed first, not to the general public, but to Hitler alone, so that he might have the opportunity of responding to the facts.

Each charge was accompanied by numerous comments. Because of Hitler's mentality, an effort was made to present the truth in such a way that the door was left open for discussion. The charges and questions were compiled in seven main sections: (1) Was the de-Christianization of the people official government policy? (2) What was the actual or ostensible meaning of the Party formula "positive Christianity"? (3) The recent "pacification work" muzzled the churches. (4) In breach of existing agreements, young people, schools, universities, and the press were forcibly being de-Christianized under the slogan "deconfessionalization." (5) The new ideology was imposing an anti-Semitism that necessarily committed people to a *hatred of the Jews*, which parents had to combat in the education of their children. (6) The church saw reason for anxiety in the popular materialistic morality, the exalting of the loyalty oath, manipulation of the Reichstag elections, concentration camps that mocked a constitutional state, and the activities, unhampered by legal scrutiny, of the Gestapo. (7) Spying and eavesdropping exert an unhealthy influence.[103] The church was still speaking largely on its own behalf, but it was the first and, indeed, the last time it would go so far in matters that concerned every German.

General confusion still reigned in discussions about even the far too mildly worded clause on anti-Semitism. This is evident from a notice within Confessing church circles. Next to an excellent analysis of the church from the perspective of Dahlem, the March 1936 newspaper of the Rhineland Confessing synod printed the following note under "News in Brief":

> 40 to 60 percent of leading posts serving the Bolshevist cause are filled by *Jews* [emphasized in the original]; in important fields such as foreign politics, overseas trade, etc., the proportion of Jews in leading posts is as high as 95 percent.[104]

The memorandum to Hitler was written after the appointment of the new Provisional Administration on 12 March 1936. Three committees worked on it. The second committee, which compiled the individual preliminary drafts, included Franz Hildebrandt, who frequently conferred with Bonhoeffer on problems connected with the form and content of the project. Hildebrandt also played an important role in the final editing of the whole. The memorandum was signed by members of the Provisional Administration and several representatives from the Reich Council of Brethren: Fritz Müller, Martin Albertz, Hans Böhm, Bernhard Forck, Otto Frick, Hans Asmussen, Karl Lücking, Friedrich Middendorf, Martin Niemöller, and Reinhold von Thadden. On 4 June 1936 Wilhelm Jannasch personally handed in the original of the memorandum to the Reich chancellery. Officially there were only two other copies. One was given for protection to Birger Forell, who was to keep it in his Swedish parsonage in Berlin; the other was kept by the director of the provincial court and chief of the Provisional Administration office, Dr. Friedrich Weissler.

Among those in the know there was considerable tension over Hitler's possible reaction. Things turned out otherwise than expected, in a way that would also involve Bonhoeffer.

Premature Publication. Hitler neither acknowledged the memo nor replied to it. Six weeks had passed when, on 17 July, the London *Morning Post* published a report about a memorandum that had challenged Hitler. On 23 July the entire memorandum appeared verbatim in the Swiss *Basler Nachrichten.* Suddenly the entire world could read a text of which not even its authors and signers themselves possessed a copy. The situation was most embarrassing for those who had sent the document, particularly since they still were awaiting a reasonably proper reply from Hitler. Now the Provisional Administration had to try to prove its genuine loyalty and seriousness. It had already written to the regional church governments and Councils of Brethren on 20 July: "Publication occurred without the knowledge or assistance of the Provisional Administration"—which, on the face of it, was correct. They even visited the presidential chancellery of the Reich chancellor and called for the unmasking of the perpetrator, since there were suspicions that someone from the state had attempted to discredit the Confessing church. They also provided the Gestapo with a copy of a foreign newspaper and requested them to search for the culprits—a unique case of cooperation between the Gestapo and the Confessing church.

Although the memorandum's publication created a deep impression within the ecumenical movement, the only thing it did in Germany was further increase the estrangement between "Dahlemites" and Lutherans. After its publication abroad, the Lutheran Council publicly disassociated itself from the memorandum; Nazi regional director Holtz described the authors as "guilty of high treason."[105] When the memorandum was suggested as the basis for a pulpit proclamation, the representatives of the regional church es affiliated with the Lutheran Council absented themselves from the 30 July session of the Reich Council of Brethren, depriving the meeting of the quorum necessary for action. Doubly distressing was the fact that this disassociation coincided with Kerrl's prohibition of the use by the Provisional Administration of the word "administration" and his instructions to all authorities to sever their connections with it. At the time Bonhoeffer wrote to former members of Finkenwalde:

Dear Brothers, we can all tell that things have once more started moving in our church. We do not know where they will go. The most serious anxiety of all is the Lutheran Council. We are faced with the announcement of a Lutheran Reich church. Then we shall have the Confessing church for which many yearn. And the incomprehensible thing is that we shall not be able to participate. Then our conscience will be racked with fear and anguish . . . may God build a wall around us so that we can keep together.[106]

And in a letter to Eberhard Bethge he wrote:

. . . the unrest in church politics! "The heart is a stubborn and despondent thing." Stubbornness and despondency—these can only be overcome in prayer.[107]

The signers of the memorandum had meant to present Hitler with a sincere plea and an admonition. This made it all the more easy to brand them as the tools of foreign propaganda. For a time they were in genuine ignorance of what could have happened, but Bonhoeffer soon knew.[108] Two of his students, Werner Koch and Ernst Tillich, had been instrumental in the memorandum's publication.

Ernst Tillich had at one time belonged to the Berlin student group that traveled out to Prebelow and Biesenthal with Bonhoeffer in 1932.[109] He had also been one of the youth delegates to Fanö, but had lost touch with these earlier connections. Werner Koch, a vicar from the Rhineland, had been suggested to Bonhoeffer by Hanns Lilje in 1932 as a possible member of the youth delegation to the Gland conference. He then joined the second course at Finkenwalde in the winter of 1935–1936 and had been helpful during the Swedish visit in handling the press. He was a fluent and gifted writer; this, along with the fact that he had studied abroad, earned him the recommendation of Karl Barth, which led to his contributing of articles and information to a number of important foreign periodicals. Bonhoeffer, who had rejected any kind of cooperation with foreign journalists during his stay in England, wrote Koch a letter of recommendation to Bishop Ammundsen at the beginning of the second course:

Since I . . . have observed that very few here or abroad have the right view of things (after the recent intensification of the church situation) I would like to recommend the work of our young pastor from the Confessing church. For several months Herr Werner Koch has provided various church and nonchurch offices abroad with scarce firsthand information and explanatory articles.[110]

Since Koch's journalistic activity was a source of some disquiet to those members of the Councils of Brethren who knew of it, steps were taken to make his contacts with Berlin more difficult by transferring him to a seminary in Barmen. Once there, he successfully continued his activities as a correspondent with the help of his friend Ernst Tillich in Berlin. Both Koch and Tillich had long been in contact with Dr. Weissler.

Many years later, on 12 July 1948, Werner Koch gave an account of how the memorandum came to be published:

> [Ernst Tillich] was the one who borrowed the Hitler memorandum for one night from Weissler and who, during the course of that night, secretly copied out the whole text word for word. It was Weissler's tacit and my explicit intention that Tillich should do no more than issue a brief communiqué to the foreign press on the existence and the essential contents of the memorandum. When Hitler continued to maintain an obstinate silence about the document, however, and when the Confessing church, despite its earlier proclamation to the contrary, appeared to acquiesce in this silence, Tillich felt himself bound to give full weight to the memorandum by publishing the complete text.

During the second half of July Bonhoeffer was in Berlin, and it was not long after the appearance of the report in the *Morning Post* that he learned the details of what had happened. On 21 July he wrote Eberhard Bethge: "Of course you will not pass on the matter of which I told you yesterday after my telephone conversation with Hildebrandt, particularly concerning its last bit of bad news. That could only make things worse...."[111] How long, however, could silence protect the actors from being revealed?

Ernst Tillich and Friedrich Weissler were both arrested on 6 October, Werner Koch on 13 November. During interrogation by the Gestapo, Koch was able to remain silent about his most recent contacts with Bonhoeffer, although these details were discovered. In the Gestapo archives in Düsseldorf there is a note: "Apparently Koch has passed on his valuable connections to Herr Tillich. A Mr. Jöde, a writer and friend of Bonhoeffer, apparently also plays a key role in these circles."[112] Mr. "Jöde" probably meant Herbert Jehle, who had meanwhile emigrated to the west.

On 13 February 1937 the three men were moved from the jail on Alexanderplatz in Berlin to Sachsenhausen concentration camp. As a Jew, Weissler was separated from the other two; he died six days later as a result of the maltreatment he suffered there. Ernst Tillich was released in 1939. Werner Koch regained his freedom on 2 December 1938 after a harsh spell in a penal company. No one in Finkenwalde considered disavowing him.

Declaration from the Pulpit. While the memorandum was being prepared, consideration turned to what message should be given to the congregations in case Hitler failed to reply. This was to provide unmistakable evidence that the church had not completely lost its voice about the flagrant injustice, although in June 1936 the state had become even more powerful through Heinrich Himmler's consolidation of all the police forces in the Reich. Once again the Gestapo visited the Berlin office of the Provisional Administration. Could parish ministers be expected, by making a proclamation from their pulpits, to incriminate themselves in something that bore the stigma of having been published abroad? Despite the approaching Olympics, there was no lack of intimidation by Party speakers and the Party press. In a Berlin bookshop Bonhoeffer came across a card bearing these lines of doggerel:

> After the end of the Olympiade
> We'll beat the CC [Confessing church] to marmalade,
> Then we'll chuck out the Jew,
> The CC will end too.[113]

On the other hand, it was obvious that the influx of foreign visitors had forced the state to be cautious. Too many martyrs could only damage Zoellner's success; so far there had been little interference in 1936. Bonhoeffer believed that the prospects for the pulpit proclamation were good and was in favor of it:

> Opinions vary tremendously. For my part I don't think that anything violent will happen. You do know about my English friend. The day before yesterday he wrote something that was very good and useful.[114]

Finally it was decided on 3 August that the proclamation, a modified version of the memorandum, should be read on 23 August. It was also issued as a pamphlet, with around one million copies being printed. Thus, in a year during which everything seemed to have gone right for Hitler—from the occupation of the Rhineland, the Rome-Berlin axis, Franco's recognition, and the anti-Comintern pact with Japan to the splendid Olympic Games— the church was venturing open criticism, which could be portrayed to most Germans as outrageous grumbling at the new Germany and its *Führer* whose foreign policy had been crowned with such success.

The decision to publish the proclamation soon became known. The Lutheran regional churches, which had failed to send representatives to the decisive sessions of the Reich Council of Brethren, stayed completely out of it. Reich Minister Kerrl instructed the church committee to discipline anyone who read the proclamation; the committee then sent telegrams to its superintendents asking them to warn their clergy.

Now the Provisional Administration urged that, come what may, Bonhoeffer must attend the summer Life and Work conference in Chamby. He had not planned to attend, but had promised to work at a retreat for candidates in Saxony. Now he received the "order of the Provisional Church Administration to go to Geneva with Koch and Dibelius from 20 to 25, to the ecumenical council. Important."[115] Shortly thereafter he wrote:

> At the moment, I can only say this, we should try to remain in Switzerland beyond the time of the conference. This can be very important. . . . It might be that we must stay another ten days.[116] . . . Please don't speak to anyone about this. . . . It's just a matter of having someone there at this time. It's connected to the memorandum. . . .[117]

In the event that the state took drastic action against the authors of the statement and those who read it from their pulpits, the Provisional Administration wanted to have a spokesperson in the ecumenical movement—someone who knew the history of the memorandum and could help with possible measures from the outside, perhaps in the form of a delegation.

Sunday, 23 August arrived. A number of courageous men read the proclamation from the pulpit, including the majority of the Finkenwalde pastors, in their isolated villages. After the service conducted by Gerhard Vibrans, a former ordinand from the first Finkenwalde course, the local schoolmaster came up to him and, hailing the village policeman who happened to be passing, demanded: "Arrest this traitor!" The policeman replied: "Can't. No orders."[118] Indeed, this was the case—there were no orders. The Gestapo had been instructed to avoid violent intervention. All that was done was to register the names of those who had read out the proclamation. There was also a press campaign against the "fellows without a fatherland." Nevertheless the state authorities realized that they had gone as far as possible with the Zoellner experiment. If they were to proceed further, some other means would eventually have to be found.

On the morning after the Sunday proclamation the Swiss newspapers published detailed reports, which were examined as anxiously by the other ecumenical delegates in Chamby as they were by the Germans. Some of the delegates already knew what had happened, for Henriod had been in Berlin and had managed to bring out a copy of the memorandum at the beginning of June.[119] Now they congratulated the four members of the Confessing church on what had been done.[120]

The Berlin Olympic Games. Part of the extravagance and display during the Berlin Olympics was intended to demonstrate to visitors from abroad that the Reich capital was eminently Christian in character. Frank Buchman, the founder of the Moral Rearmament movement, was received by high Party officials including, it is believed, Heinrich Himmler himself. In a 25 August interview with the *New York World Telegram*, Buchman said: "I thank Heaven for a man like Adolf Hitler, who built a front line of defense against the anti-Christ of Communism."

The Reich church erected an enormous tent near the stadium for religious services. For a time it was thought that pastors from the Confessing church, including Bonhoeffer, might participate. A series of scholarly theological lectures by professors from the university was held in Holy Trinity Church. Nor was the Berlin Council of Brethren idle. It announced a program of lectures on the theme "The Way of the German Evangelical Church in the Present Day" at St. Paul's Church, with Jacobi, Asmussen, Dibelius, Niemöller, Iwand, and Bonhoeffer as speakers. But once again Bonhoeffer disapproved of the way in which an auspicious occasion was being exploited:

> I would far rather call everything off. I was particularly annoyed when we were asked to send a photograph because they wanted to bring out a propaganda booklet with our pictures in it. This I find both ludicrous and degrading, and in any case I shall send nothing. I think the time for this has passed. I shall write and tell them so.[121]

Behind the seductive pomp and the universal jubilation over Hitler's successes Bonhoeffer saw only renewed signs of the war he had predicted earlier: "On the whole things certainly seem to be getting more and more critical. We must keep very calm and pray much more."[122]

The propaganda booklet appeared, only to be immediately confiscated. Nevertheless, every meeting was packed. The magazine *Christliche Welt*, at that time hostile to the Confessing church, reported that the church committees' lectures in Holy Trinity Church, though highly satisfactory from a scholarly point of view, were being poorly attended while those of the Confessing church, whose theological content was controversial in the extreme, were attracting crowds of listeners: "a huge, very reverently attentive congregation. Such a state of affairs must arouse the gravest misgivings over the future of the Evangelical church."[123]

On 5 August Bonhoeffer spoke at St. Paul's Church and at the overflow meeting in the Church of the Twelve Apostles. It was the last occasion in his life when he stood before such a multitude of people:

Not a bad evening yesterday. The church packed; people were sitting on the altar steps and standing everywhere. I wish I could have preached instead of giving a lecture. . . . A large group of Berlin friends, pastors, etc., gathered at Rabenau's. I had to talk about Finkenwalde until midnight. I didn't get home until 2 a.m.[124]

Bonhoeffer's subject was "The Inner Life of the German Evangelical Church." Using typical hymn verses by Luther, Paul Gerhardt, Zinzendorf, Gellert, and Spitta, he described Protestant modes of prayer and concluded by showing how the spirit of the Reformation was again manifesting itself in prayer in the Confessing church.[125]

The reporter from *Christliche Welt* wrote: "When we consider that this man is a pupil of Harnack's, we can only feel deeply saddened when confronted by such a 'view of history.'"[126]

"Service to Others"

The phrase "intensive preparation for service to others" that Bonhoeffer used in his proposal for a community house was more than an empty phrase.[127] The seminary's 1936 summer course was characterized by concern for issues that transcended personal life and studies. Supported by the House of Brethren, Bonhoeffer identified the seminary with the cause of persecuted colleagues. Together with the entire community, he also embarked on an important mission to the people of Pomerania, a mission imprinted by Bonhoeffer's own style and which would become a Finkenwalde institution.[128]

The formulation he made eight years later, which postulated an indissoluble relation between the *arcanum* of the Christian (understood as compassion) and the new interpretation of the Gospel, had its roots in Finkenwalde even though the "interpretation" was still expressed in conventional terms. But one was already implicit in the other, and everyone concerned sensed that this was right.

Identification with the Persecuted. Despite Zoellner's tactics and the Olympics, there were terrorist incidents in 1936 which, by their very isolation, made a deeper impression than did the much more widespread wave of arrests in 1937. Bonhoeffer mentioned the name of each victim without fail during prayers, devotions, and meditation. Everyone in Finkenwalde learned to concern himself like a brother with at least one of these cases, and eventually to regard such incidents as nothing out of the ordinary.

1. At the very beginning of the third course Willy Süssbach, a young pastor of Jewish origin, was attacked by an S.A. group in the province of Brandenburg and badly beaten up. Bonhoeffer immediately brought him to Finkenwalde so that he could recover from his injuries and shock. He later helped him to emigrate.

2. A few days later Pastor Johannes Pecina and Willi Brandenburg, the minister sent by the Council of Brethren to replace him, were arrested in Seelow, a small town near Frankfurt on the Oder River. Pecina had refused to be turned out of his church and parsonage by a rival nominated by the consistory, and had failed to comply with a state order to leave the province. Adolf Preuss from the first Finkenwalde course then took over. Bonhoeffer traveled to Frankfurt and unsuccessfully tried to enter the prison. A lively correspondence subsequently arose between the prisoners and the seminary.[129] One of Bonhoeffer's favorite hymns at this time was Tersteegen's *"Kommt, Kinder, lasst uns gehen"* with its lines, "Each sets his face with steadfastness toward Jerusalem" and "Where the weaker brother falleth, the stronger grasps his hand." Bonhoeffer included a personal message in his newsletter to former Finkenwaldians:

> I think that we should all prepare ourselves through physical and spiritual discipline for the day when we shall be put to the test. My thoughts are almost continually with our imprisoned brethren. They have much to tell us. Everything now depends upon our daily loyalty.[130]

Pecina and Brandenburg had already become part of Finkenwalde long before their release at the end of August 1936, when they arrived there to recuperate from the months of detention.[131] Willi Brandenburg then joined the fourth course and eventually became a member of the House of Brethren, where he participated in many of Finkenwalde's popular missions. He was killed on the Russian front.[132]

3. In Helbra, a mining town in the province of Saxony, the large Confessing congregation was locked in a bitter struggle with a German Christian church council backed by the state and the consistory. Since the Council of Brethren urgently needed help, the House of Brethren sent the author.[133] Although this did not result in any serious confrontation with the police, it did lead to some acrimonious correspondence between Bonhoeffer and Staemmler, whom he esteemed so highly, about the correct priorities for the House of Brethren.[134] The Councils of Brethren were getting into the habit of drawing on the House of Brethren whenever the need arose. Yet the whole purpose of the House of Brethren would be lost if its members were kept to

occupy permanent appointments. Accordingly, Bonhoeffer insisted in the Helbra case that the term of replacement should not exceed the period already agreed upon.[135]

4. In the summer of 1936 Wolfgang Büsing, a member of the second course, was forced to emigrate because his wife was "non-Aryan." Herbert Jehle, an old friend from Berlin and London days, was also seriously considering leaving the country, since he had found no support within the church for his unwavering pacifism. Both men had been frequent visitors to the seminary. Bonhoeffer used his London connections to help Büsing and advised Jehle to leave as well.[136] He often thought that it might be sensible if he and his family were to emigrate, but at the time any more serious consideration of the matter was out of the question.

5. Finally, after Werner Koch's arrest and imprisonment in a concentration camp, Bonhoeffer and the seminary added his name to Finkenwalde's intercession list. In the rest of the Confessing church, the Councils of Brethren were afraid to put Koch on the list of those who were named openly. Bonhoeffer missed no opportunity to send him news. At Christmas 1936 he conveyed greetings to Koch in the Alexanderplatz prison from "Brother Glocke, one of the most trustworthy men. I look forward to seeing him before long."[137] Koch, who was familiar with the ecumenical movement, knew that "Glocke" meant Bishop Bell of Chichester. Bonhoeffer took responsibility for Koch's fiancée, whom he entrusted to the care of Ruth von Kleist-Retzow. "In these times," he said, "you belong to us more than ever." When Koch was finally released Bonhoeffer congratulated him:

> Our joy is indescribable. What we have hoped and prayed for from day to day has come true. To me it still seems like a dream. And now you are reunited with your splendid fiancée whom we all admire. It must seem as though you've been given a new life. Now there's only one thing I look forward to and that is to see you again as soon as possible, so as to make quite sure that you are back among us. . . . There's a great deal to tell but it all seems trivial compared with the joy of your release. At the moment I can't think of anything more to say. You yourself know better than I do what is most important. . . .[138]

The picture would be incomplete, however, if there were no mention of Bonhoeffer's infectious joie de vivre at the very time when things were growing more dangerous: his delight in games, music, and the summer in the country. For the sheer pleasure of it, he paid the airfare to Berlin for two of his ordinands out of his own pocket, thereby fulfilling their dearest wish, for they had never been in an aircraft before. Far from falling silent, the grand piano resounded more often than ever before. Bonhoeffer got out his tennis racket, and gave people tickets to the Olympics. In hot summer weather, classes were canceled on short notice so that everyone could spend a few days on the beach at Misdroy.

But if he suspected that anybody confused relaxation with a lapse from order and moderation, he could be harsh to the point of injustice. Once, when he had been deeply upset by one such incident, he wrote:

> The five stood against me and against themselves. . . . I was overwhelmed. The only thing I could do was to pray against it inwardly without ceasing.[139]

The Finkenwalde Mission. The "evangelical mission," as it was called at the time, did not enjoy the best of reputations. A number of its official representatives were maintaining a middle, neutral course in the church struggle, which they called the "church dispute," and regarded as likely to harm and obstruct evangelism. Many of them expected something of the Oxford movement, while others supported the German Christians because they offered "possibilities for evangelism."

In 1936 they were embarrassed by the Reich bishop, in an evangelistic publication entitled *Deutsche Gottesworte* (German Words of God). In the foreword he wrote: "For you, my comrades in the Third Reich, I have not translated the Sermon on the Mount but Germanicized it. . . . Your Reich Bishop." The blessing of the meek he interpreted as: "Happy is he who always observes good comradeship. He will get on well in the world"; and the cross: "Take pains to maintain a noble, calm attitude, even to one who insults or persecutes you."[140] This caused Bonhoeffer to ask where faith and the church were to be found in all this.

The criticism of the Confessing church in evangelical mission circles was justified insofar as there was a real danger that the "Dahlemites" might waste increasing time and energy on complicated legal disputes. Yet for the Confessing church and especially for Bonhoeffer the church struggle could not be seriously separated from "evangelization." On the contrary, Bonhoeffer believed that the only people entitled to evangelize were those who were not concerned about maintaining a respectable closeness between the Gospel and the "German awakening." If Finkenwalde was to undertake independent missionary work, it had to be on the condition that such work would promote a clearer revelation of the Gospel: The missionary sermon must be the entire Word in all circumstances. It must not be doled out. The whole Word is its sole strength.[141] Bonhoeffer's homiletics concluded with a comment on mission work in which he hints at its true essence: the promise holds true that God's Word will always create a church-community for itself, but not that the entire German people will be converted.[142] From his earliest days right up to the end, he never tried to popularize the message through artifice, nor did he do so now in this missionary undertaking.

In June 1936 the entire seminary made its way to Belgard, a group of parishes in eastern Pomerania where four of the Finkenwalde brothers were serving six parishes. Bonhoeffer stayed with the Kleist-Retzows in Kieckow; every evening he visited one of the parishes. The House of Brethren had already tried out this working method in a parish in the western Pomeranian region of Uckermark, and now prepared its work in Belgard with the entire seminary. Each four-man team spent the whole week in one village. During the day they split up to visit houses, and attend children's classes and Bible discussions. For four days these activities were followed by an evening meeting in the church, where each of them spent ten minutes on the pulpit dealing with one particular aspect of the theme they had prepared. As a result the evening service never lasted longer than an hour. The number of villagers attending was far larger than they had dared to expect.

Wherever they happened to be, the four brothers followed the same pattern of morning devotions and meditation that was practiced in Finkenwalde. In Bonhoeffer's proposal for a House of Brethren he had declared that the content and actual practice of preaching needed mutual help and fellowship.[143] This phrase now become a practical experience for the whole seminary. In the conclusion to his homiletics on mission preaching Bonhoeffer stated:

> There is promise in bearing the burden of temptation in proclamation with brothers who are united in prayer, confession and forgiveness. This fellowship is necessary in order to call the core members of a particular congregation to their responsibility as examples, because these are the people who in turn must take over the follow-up work. . . .
>
> A fellowship of common witness concerning the Savior helps to correct the psychological emphasis through a spiritual one. Excessive enthusiasm on the part of any of the witnesses soon becomes obvious.[144]

Dead Congregations. In considering these activities, one important aspect was whether the people had not "already heard and rejected the Word."[145] Bonhoeffer was concerned with whether a pastor's parochial work shouldn't give way to a more sensible deployment of forces that would give preaching more clarity and dignity. The House of Brethren itself was a contribution, and helped eradicate the customary division of energies among pastors.

One of the first Finkenwalde candidates, Gerhard Vibrans, was sent by his Council of Brethren to a totally moribund parish. There he wrote Bonhoeffer:

> My parish of six hundred souls at Schweinitz is a very poor one, on average only one or two people go to church there every Sunday . . . every Sunday, wearing my vestments, I make a pilgrimage through the whole village primarily to bring home to the people that it is Sunday. . . . The people try to comfort me by saying that I will get my salary even though no one goes to church. On Trinity Sunday nobody was there apart from the woman sexton. . . . From the point of view of church politics things are quite dead. They don't know who or what a Reich bishop is. . . .[146]

In response Bonhoeffer wrote some letters. The first was to the Council of Brethren to say that their energies must be used more effectively. In another letter he offered Vibrans some practical suggestions:

> If one village will not listen we go to another. There are limits. Now, to begin with, of course you must carry on. . . . Your loyal observance of our advice almost puts me to shame. Don't take it too literally or one day you might get fed up with it.[147]

Bonhoeffer traveled to the village at the earliest opportunity and preached.

> Twelve people in the best congregations, still less in others. . . . I have advised Brother Vibrans in a while to write a letter to his whole congregation telling them that this is possibly the last offer of the Gospel to them and that there are other communities whose hunger for the Word cannot be satisfied because there are too few workers.[148]

This particular case remained without practical consequences or solutions until after the outbreak of war. The entrenched parochialism of ministry in the *Volkskirche* resisted every revolutionary attack. As a result, the attempts during the church struggle to create a genuine church of congregations were thwarted, although here and there they proved very effective. While Bonhoeffer realized this, he also thought it might be necessary to leave positions that were not worth the trouble and expense, and he had the courage of his convictions. He had always felt that preaching included responsibility for the image of the church and its ministry. Thus the view he would express in 1944 was already becoming evident: namely, that the time was past when the church could proclaim its cause by words alone.[149]

The experience gained during the mission to Belgard led to the extension of this missionary enterprise; it continued until Finkenwalde closed. By then, thirty-six parishes in Pomerania, Saxony, and Brandenburg had been visited in this way. The 1936–1937 winter course visited the Greifenberg district under far more difficult circumstances than those encountered by the Belgard party, while the 1937 summer course traveled to the Anklam district in western Pomerania. Preliminary experiments were carried out by the House of Brethren in urban districts such as Guben and Köslin.

As time went by, the number of incidents multiplied, for news of the mission's success had spread. Occasionally the lectern in the church would be confiscated. On a later occasion a Nazi district group leader in the border area forced the local people, under threat of punishment, to evict the members of the House of Brethren who were staying with them. On that day, however, more people attended church than ever. But there were negative experiences as well. In one village in the Altmark some of the peasants visited by the mission remained aggressive and unapproachable. The seminarians found it impossible to establish contact with people who were openly hostile and others who had been intimidated. In another locality fifteen of forty-four confirmation candidates attended the first class and only three came to the next one—because the Old Testament prophets had been mentioned and these prophets were Jews. In 1937 some of the collections were confiscated. In addition, the seminarians' names were regularly taken by the police although no mission was ever fully banned until 1937. After the breakup of the House of Brethren, when helpers could no longer be provided, neighboring Finkenwaldians joined together on occasion to carry out a communal mission on the well-tried pattern:

> In October we had a mission week in R. Kühn's parish. Kühn, Lerche, Veckenstedt and I were there. It gave us all great pleasure. The blessing of such a thing is, perhaps, most evident in oneself and one's subsequent work in one's own parish. I have never preached so gladly as after that week.[150]

Fund-raising Campaigns. The first large-scale mission to Belgard in June 1936 was linked to another plan. The Prussian Council of Brethren had made it known that the premises in Finkenwalde could not be kept up for financial reasons and that another accommodation must be found. Understandably, Bonhoeffer was not in favor of a move; they began to consider founding an association of friends of Finkenwalde to supplement the fund-raising efforts being conducted by the brethren in their home provinces.[151]

Hans-Jürgen von Kleist-Retzow was prepared to give the necessary aid to start the enterprise. On Saturday, the last day of the Belgard mission, friends and patrons of parishes in the district were invited to an afternoon meeting in the manor house at Kieckow. Bonhoeffer gave a report on the state of the church struggle, and succeeded in interesting the group in an association of friends to support Finkenwalde. Not long afterward, food and money began to arrive at the seminary. Once more thoughts of a move were relegated to the distant future.

It was on this occasion that Bonhoeffer got to know Ewald von Kleist-Schmenzin; the two quickly achieved a close rapport. Whenever he spent a holiday in Kieckow Bonhoeffer would be driven over to Schmenzin. There he also met Dr. Fabian von Schlabrendorff, who often discussed politics with Ewald von Kleist. Schlabrendorff married one of Ruth von Kleist-Retzow's grandchildren, a daughter of Herbert von Bismarck of Lasbeck. In the winter of 1944–1945 he was among the last friends near Bonhoeffer in the detention cells at police headquarters, while, in the prison on Lehrter Strasse, Ewald von Kleist, like Klaus Bonhoeffer and his brother-in-law Rüdiger Schleicher, was confined in a cell on the landing reserved for prisoners condemned to death.

Chamby, 1936

Contrary to his earlier plans, Bonhoeffer, accompanied by Bethge, traveled south on 18 August 1936 to participate in the ecumenical conference in Chamby, the last Life and Work meeting prior to the big world conference in Oxford. His interest in ecumenical church politics had not grown since 1935. He had not yielded to the urging of others that spring when he attended the ecumenical youth commission meeting in La Borcarderie (28–30 March 1936); time in Friedrichsbrunn, a meeting with Staemmler, and the German S.C.M. conference in Dassel had a higher priority. Now, however, Bonhoeffer had to go. Rather hastily he found a substitute for the last weeks of the Finkenwalde semester. Günther Dehn and Wilhelm Vischer stepped in for him—Vischer particularly because of the controversy raging over Bonhoeffer's exegesis of Ezra and Nehemiah.

The background of the 1936 Chamby meeting, the sessions themselves, and the interpretation they received afterward were no less complex than those of Chamby 1935. Zoellner's Reich church committee insisted that it alone represented the German churches. The Geneva office may well have been relieved to find that Heckel was no longer the mouthpiece of the Reich bishop but was now working with more serious church leaders; for those in Berlin, however, this only increased the confusion. The 1936 Chamby meeting was the first and last conference attended by official delegates from the Confessing church. Nevertheless, they do not appear in the minutes of the conference.

The Battle over the Invitations to Chamby. At a meeting of the Provisional Administration's advisory board on 20 May there was discussion about attendance at the Oxford meeting. The minutes indicate that Bonhoeffer stood by his earlier opinion, but that the board was equally convinced of the hopelessness of the situation:

> Bonhoeffer pointed out that it was no longer admissible that the leading personalities of the Confessing church should be treated as private individuals by the ecumenical movement. The ecumenical movement should be asked whether it intended to recognize the Confessing church as the only lawful church. This was the best service that could be rendered to Life and Work for it would save it from the danger of doing theology in an uncommitted fashion.
>
> To this the objection was raised that such a procedure would be practically futile since, given the current organization of the Ecumenical Council, it would spend years on the issue of recognition. There was unanimous agreement, however, that the ecumenical movement could not avoid this question.[152]

There was dissent both within the Reich Council of Brethren and in the Provisional Administration, and some expressed willingness to hold discussions with Zoellner on the subject of the Oxford meeting. President Koch agreed to speak to Zoellner about the German role in the literary preparations for the Conference of World Churches.

Yet on 16 June 1936 the Provisional Administration informed Geneva, through Albertz, of its earlier standpoint and warned against Zoellner's claims:

> According to the resolution of the Oeynhausen synod, the church is prohibited from recognizing the state-appointed church committees, even temporarily, as the leaders and representatives of the church. For this reason we ask that you refuse to recognize any such demand that the head of the Reich church committee, Dr. Zoellner, might convey to the ecumenical council. . . . We also request the Ecumenical Council to invite the Provisional Administration [to the Life and Work conference], as the authorized executive body of the German Evangelical Church. . . .[153]

Henriod sent a detailed reply to this letter on 19 June, in accordance with the instructions already issued by Bell and after consulting with the Ecumenical Council's administrative committee in Paris on 19 June. Confining himself to general categories such as "sections," "parties," and "personalities," he replied that: (1) The decisions about representatives to the 1937 Oxford meeting had to be settled within the German church itself. (2) The ecumenical council's administrative committee reserved the right to approve the German nominees in order to ensure equal participation by the "parties." Henriod added that this did not mean that they intended to decide on a spiritual matter—which showed how difficult it was in this situation to avoid such a dilemma. (3) In the specific case of Chamby, the national "sections" would nominate the important "personalities"; the council would then co-opt additional members to this group to ensure that the various "parties" of the German Evangelical Church should make "a broad and valuable contribution to the life and thought of the ecumenical movement." This would be arranged by Bishop Bell. (4) The Fanö decisions still set the standard insofar as it had established that the ecumenical council, "as a body without ecclesiastical authority[154] . . . [must] refrain from taking sides in questions which concern the constitution of any one church and [must] remain in friendly contact with all groups of the German Evangelical Church. Since its members do not feel either competent or entitled to pass judgement on questions of spiritual authority in any specific country, they think it important to reassert their adherence to the principles of Fanö." Should the discussions of German joint representation in Chamby be unsuccessful, "the Bishop of Chichester must be notified so that he can take steps, notwithstanding, to ensure the presence in Chamby of personalities who share in our work."[155] The fateful insertion that had made the 1934 Fanö declaration acceptable to Heckel (that the council should maintain friendly ties to all factions within the German church) now carried more weight than the main clause to which it had been appended.

Nor did Bell himself see any possibility of breaking with Zoellner's Reich church committee. It was evident from the reports on the situation he received from Koechlin that even within the Confessing church some circles were warning against a breach with the church committee. On 8 June Bell had received a copy of the memorandum to Hitler which Henriod had smuggled out to Geneva. Bell wrote to him on 13 June:

> . . . that it is absolutely vital to maintain the position we adopted at Fanö and not to deviate from those resolutions; 2. that we should not break with Dr. Zoellner and those whom he represents or leads . . . on one thing I am

clear and that is that we must not weaken in our connection with the
Confessional Church. . . .

Since dictating above, I have read the Confessional Church's address to
Hitler—a fine document—our support of the Confessional Church is all
the more necessary.[156]

Henriod carried out these instructions, but in such a way that, for those
in the Provisional Administration who received his letter, his impartiality
was more evident than was Bell's anxiety that the Confessing church should
attend Chamby at all costs. In the other direction, however, even Henriod's
letter appeared to show an inadmissible degree of attention toward the Confessing church. For when Zoellner realized that the Provisional Administration had insisted on being represented in Chamby, he let it be known that he
would not come if his delegation from the German Evangelical Church was
made questionable by the simultaneous appearance of a delegation from the
Confessing church. Lilje yielded to Zoellner on the basis of Bell's instructions
and Henriod's disclosures of 19 June.

After Chamby Bell described the situation in a letter to Eidem:

Dr. Zoellner, before coming to Chamby had been very much upset because
I had sent an invitation to President Koch, inviting representatives of the
Confessional Church to our Council Meeting—asking that in addition to
President Koch and Dr. Bonhoeffer [who were co-opted at Fanö] a couple
of other Confessional representatives might come. Dr. Zoellner was at first
inclined to take the line that this would make it impossible for the Reich
Church Committee to have anything further to do with the Universal
Christian Council. As a result however of telephone and other communications, he was pacified, and not only did the original German official delegation arrive, but they arrived headed by Zoellner.[157]

Thus the invitation Bell sent to the Provisional Administration contained the description "representatives of the Confessional church," in contrast to Henriod's wording, which had spoken of including "personalities."
In Chamby the members of the Provisional Administration wished to be
regarded as nothing else than a "delegation of the Confessing church." No
sooner had the conference ended than a fresh dispute broke out over this
invitation.

Bonhoeffer, who had in fact been a co-opted member since Fanö, was
asked by Henriod before the conference to come to Chamby as an interpreter. He refused, adding pointedly that he was "of course" coming "as a
member of the delegation of the Confessing church." At the conference, the

members of the Provisional Administration were indeed treated as the delegation of the Confessing church, a factor that augmented their moral weight perceptibly on 23 August, when the pulpit proclamation based on the memorandum to Hitler was made.

But the rules of the Geneva office do not appear to have permitted any mention of the delegation in the minutes. The wording of the minutes describes two delegates of the Confessing church as "co-opted members" and two as "invited to the meeting (with the right to speak)."[158] In fact, there is not a single protocol of the ecumenical movement that states that the Confessing church either took part in, or was a member of, any ecumenical conference during the thirties. Either it was not possible to make the journey (Fanö), or there was no desire to attend (Chamby, 1935), or there was no procedure for officially recording the church's presence, as in the case of the 1936 Chamby meeting.

For the Provisional Administration, but more especially for Bonhoeffer, appearing as a delegation alongside that of the Reich church committee deviated from the requisite line they had drawn. During the negotiations following Zoellner's protest, the possibility had been raised that they could join in a united representation under Zoellner's leadership. But the Provisional Administration had replied that this was out of the question and that the invitation to the two separate delegations must stand, since "Zoellner cannot represent *us.*"

Bonhoeffer complied with the Provisional Administration's instructions to travel to Chamby. He felt he should not withdraw from the dangerous situation that had arisen after the publication of the memorandum and the proclamation. Of all the Confessing church delegates, he was the only one who was fluent in English, and he had the widest acquaintance and was well acquainted personally with Bell and Ammundsen, both of whom trusted him implicitly. Bonhoeffer also drew a distinction between his personal opinion, about which he had left no doubt, and the decisions taken, or rather not taken, by his church during and after Oeynhausen. In 1935 there had as yet been no church committee; now it existed and Bonhoeffer's church was still of two minds about it. Bonhoeffer accepted his share of the responsibility for this ambivalence in the ecumenical field. His own view remained unchanged and he intended to express it in unmistakable terms should the occasion arise.

When Fritz Müller visited Finkenwalde on 12 August to let Bonhoeffer know exactly what was happening, he reported that Niemöller and Asmussen were considering going to Chamby. Bonhoeffer thought this was too much of an attempt to win the goodwill of the ecumenical movement:

Firstly, no one will be able to understand why you are there as well as the official representatives. I can almost hear the conjectures on the part of our well-wishers there. You versus Koch,[159] or something of the sort. . . . Secondly—and this seems to me the main point—we must at all costs avoid giving the impression that we are in any way running after our foreign friends. If anything, it would be better the other way round. We should not make them feel that they are absolutely essential to us. This detracts some from our halo, and that's not altogether without importance! Basically they are all so interested in our cause that they will come to us should we wish it. You are, indeed, regarded there as an official person in the truest sense. You must therefore either go in an official capacity, or not at all. Lastly, the whole thing is an internal committee meeting and too much importance should not be attached to it. Next year [Oxford] is quite a different matter.[160]

Niemöller and Asmussen did not go.

The Conference. When the conference opened on Friday, 21 August three German delegations took their seats at the table, the Confessing church being represented by president Karl Koch, Otto Dibelius, Hans Böhm, and Bonhoeffer; the Lutheran Council by Hanns Lilje; and the Reich church committee by Wilhelm Zoellner, Friedrich Brunstäd, Hans Wahl, and Theodor Heckel. Heckel was accompanied by Eugen Gerstenmaier, who appears in the minutes under "Guests or Friends." Besides these there were Erich Stange, who attended as the secretary of the German section, and Adolf Deissmann and Martin Dibelius on behalf of the Standing Theological Commission.

The Reich church group around Heckel (of which Hans Schönfeld was effectively a member) and the group from the Confessing church kept scrupulously apart and did not speak to one another during the conference. On the other hand, Bell's efforts led to some contact between Koch, Dibelius, and Zoellner. Despite all the measures the Reich church had taken against the Confessing church's proclamation, Zoellner was open to discussing the subject, for he was planning his own memorandum on de-Christianization. Bell's integrity and patience eventually brought the hostile colleagues together so they could discuss the situation resulting from the pulpit proclamation in Germany and, more especially, plans for a possible joint representation at the 1937 Oxford conference.

Bishop Bell later wrote a detailed letter to Eidem in Uppsala so that other ecumenical friends could help with some satisfactory arrangement for the 1937 conference. Since Eidem had his own contacts with the Church Foreign Office, he needed to know what had happened in Chamby and what possibilities had opened up as a result. Bell hinted:

> Bishop Heckel might come for private conversations on the German Church question. But we felt that not very much would be likely to come from conversations with Bishop Heckel. But Bishop Ammundsen will tell you when you see him I think of a little bit of new light of a more hopeful kind which did actually appear at Chamby under the aegis of our Life and Work meetings.[161]

Bonhoeffer stayed out of the official discussions at the plenary sessions; but he had much to do behind the scenes. On the very first day he and Koch conferred at length with Bell, reviewing the whole situation. Bell was glad to learn that his letter to *The Times* regarding Kerrl's ban on all relations with the Provisional Administration and on its use of this title had been accurate. He got their permission to hold conversations with Zoellner.

Zoellner made a fair impression on Bell; even Bell commented that at first Zoellner "really did all the talking." This impression was reinforced at the plenary conference when Zoellner, as Bell wrote Eidem, made a "very important speech about the duty and witness of the Christian Church" whereas Heckel and Brunstäd, in their speeches at the preceding meeting on "Church and Community," "had appeared to leave out some of the most distinctively Christian factors which Zoellner emphasized in a striking way."

After Zoellner's fine speech, the Confessing church delegates approached Bell late the same night with the request that he point out to Zoellner how close his speech was "in essence" to the proclamation of 23 August. Bell was to ask Zoellner whether, when he returned to Germany, he would be prepared to act in accordance with what he had said. Zoellner explained to Bell the following day that he felt very close to the Confessing church on this point. It should be noted, however, that the proclamation (in contrast to the memorandum to Hitler) had completely subordinated the complaints about anti-Semitism and concentration camps to those about the de-Christianization of the people. While Zoellner was approachable about this latter point, he was much less so on the former—as were many in the Confessing church.

On Tuesday, 25 August Bell arranged a first meeting between Zoellner, Koch, and Dibelius. Besides discussions on a future joint synod, the possibility of church elections, and the necessary conditions for them, they agreed to negotiate the feasibility of a joint delegation to Oxford, although no immediate decision about its leadership was contemplated. The meeting was obviously a relief to Zoellner. Bishop Ammundsen said later that at the end of the conference Zoellner took leave of Böhm with a handshake and the words "Until we meet again in a concentration camp."[162] Concluding his report to Eidem, Bell wrote: "It is of course the first step, if they can only be led to take it, which will make so great a difference. And one must hope and pray."

The official discussions resulting from this relaxation of tension had one further effect that was discreditably exploited after the conference. Some of those taking part in the conference, including Henry Leiper, Joseph Oldham, and Marc Boegner, had moved for a fresh discussion and resolution on the Jewish question. Koch and Dibelius, on the other hand, expressed doubt whether, in view of the memorandum and the proclamation in Germany, a pronouncement from Chamby in the presence of the members of the Confessing church was either appropriate or in the interests of the brethren at home. During a further discussion between Bell, Zoellner, Koch, and Dibelius it was agreed that on this occasion they should jointly advise against the proposal. Accordingly, in submitting the motion to the final plenary session, Bell spoke:

> . . . of the great reluctance with which he personally and the Administrative Committee generally had been led to the conclusion that it was not possible to adopt a resolution adequate to the situation and with due justice both to the necessities of the case and to the rights of members of the Council specially concerned.[163]

Bonhoeffer did not speak during this debate, either, although he had reservations about the above procedure, particularly since Dibelius and Zoellner spoke in support of Bell's opposing motion at the plenary session. In his remarks, Zoellner expressed everything that Bonhoeffer, since 1933, had held to be false:

> I cannot here describe to what depths Germany has been taken, essentially as a result of decades of activities that seemed open and aboveboard yet behind which German Jewry was the driving force. . . . These forces, against whom no power could prevail, were the pacemakers and leaders in the struggle to uphold bolshevism in Germany. . . .
>
> For my part I should raise no objection if sometime there were to be an opportunity of discussing here the racial problem in an exhaustive, thoroughly prepared debate. . . .
>
> In our country we are fighting an honorable battle so that the Evangelical church, founded on the Gospel as interpreted by the Reformation, can have its place even in an authoritarian state. . . . Do not destroy, with

an overly hasty resolution, the chances possessed by the Evangelical church in Germany to achieve validity and to succeed within the limits of the Gospel. . . .[164]

The Chamby minutes contain no record of the text of this speech nor of any reaction to its tone; the sponsors of the resolution, such as Leiper and Boegner, would hardly have been convinced by it. The minutes mention only briefly the "great disquiet over those who in various parts of the world must suffer because of their faith, nationality, or race" and record the fact that the motion was referred to the Administrative Committee for further action.[165] The resolution was passed, although the motives that led to this unanimous decision were highly contradictory.

While at this time Bonhoeffer was satisfied with the memorandum and the proclamation at home, he felt some resignation when he looked at the Ecumenical Council in 1936; he no longer saw it as the authorized body, the "council." A few days later he described his resignation and lack of enthusiasm for Chamby in a letter to Henriod:

> One day if I have time, I should like to write and tell you what I too would have to say about wholly fundamental things related to present ecumenical activities. It wasn't without reason that I kept silent at Chamby. But more of that later.[166]

He had carried out the duties demanded of him by the Provisional Administration, had shared in the halfhearted resolutions, and, as compared with two years before, expected little or nothing from the ecumenical movement. He did not want to disturb the now easier relationship with Zoellner.

Holidays in Italy. After the end of the Chamby conference on 25 August 1936 Bonhoeffer traveled south. The alarming reports expected from home following the Sunday of the proclamation had not materialized. A small bank account he had kept since his time abroad helped support him for a few days and so, leaving everything behind him and accompanied by Bethge, he traveled by way of the Simplon Pass to Rome. Once again entranced by St. Peter's, he sought to reveal the beauty of the magnificent building to his companion. A less agreeable impression during these late summer days was created by the entrances to the towns and villages, which were plastered with strident, martial posters claiming victory in the Abyssinian war: a foretaste of what Bonhoeffer saw coming at home. Dwindling funds necessitated a return north, but not before they had called on Erwin Sutz in Wiesendangen near Zurich and visited Karl Ludwig Schmidt in Basel. Having missed Karl Barth, Bonhoeffer wrote him about progress on *Discipleship* and received a skeptical reply.[167] He returned to Finkenwalde via Berlin on 13 September, just in time to nurse a seriously ill seminarian back to health with paternal efficiency. And he was finally able to find time to resume work on *Discipleship*.

War of the Reporters. The rapprochement in Chamby between Zoellner and Koch was of short duration. Zoellner had other preoccupations; administratively ecumenical affairs were the responsibility of the Church Foreign Office. It was therefore Heckel who sent an official report on 28 September to all church governments, to be forwarded to their clergy.[168] Three of the points in this report were of particular interest: the summary of what Heckel and Brunstäd had stood for in Chamby; the version offered of how the resolution on racial discrimination came to be abandoned; and the lists of participants.

1. The report stated that, in close concert with the views of the Geneva Research Department, it had been possible to make clear that "an ecumenical collaborator, one conscious of his responsibilities to the church," cannot "disregard the national situation in his own country and in his church." The German delegates had managed to have the term "*Volk*," previously deleted, restored to the German version of Oxford's theme of "*Kirche, Volk und Staat*" ("Church, Community, and State"), an achievement made possible with arguments based "on a detailed knowledge of the numerous learned works submitted to them by the Research Department in Geneva." They had warned against the use "in ecumenical discussions of certain catchwords such as 'the totalitarian state' without profound reflection and a genuine knowledge of the political reality."[169]

Through Brunstäd and Heckel, Schönfeld was now better able to determine the direction he had vainly hoped Bonhoeffer would follow in Fanö. Schönfeld had already expressed his own opinion when he stated that this was "a field in which, more than in any other, these people have much to learn."[170]

In Heckel's office, Schönfeld's friend Eugen Gerstenmaier was compiling articles for the Oxford conference from a number of eminent theologians unconnected with the Confessing church, including Brunstäd and Schreiner, his teachers at Rostock. These papers appeared in a book edited by Gerstenmaier and published in 1937 under the title *Kirche, Volk und Staat: Stimmen aus der deutschen evangelischen Kirche zur Oxforder Weltkirchen-*

konferenz (Church, Volk, State: Voices from the German Evangelical Church for the World Church Conference in Oxford).[171]

In most of the contributions the terminology and thinking differed considerably from that of Bonhoeffer and his friends. For his part, Bonhoeffer contributed theses on the theme of "War and Peace" as preparatory material for the Provisional Administration under Hans Böhm.[172] It need hardly be said that Heckel and his friends did not welcome this topic, and indeed thought it dangerous.

2. Heckel described the abandonment of the resolution on Jewish persecution in the following manner:

> When they were confronted at the last minute with a portentous resolution in which it was proposed to deal with German domestic political questions, it was . . . significant that General Superintendent Dr. Dibelius and General Superintendent Zoellner maintained emphatically that it was not the concern of those present to revert to earlier methods by placing Germany as it were in the dock.[173]

In one sense this account afforded protection from inquisitive ministries for those Germans, including Dibelius, who had taken part in the Chamby discussions. On the other hand, it concealed the true nature of the proceedings from the German clergy, to whom the report was addressed.

3. Heckel listed the representatives with some interesting deviations; he reported that "in accordance with the constitution of the Ecumenical Council, an official representative body of the German Evangelical Church" had been in attendance, and had consisted of Zoellner, Heckel, Brunstäd, Deissmann, Lilje, and Wahl. In addition, "German members of the Council . . . who had already long exercised official functions" such as Martin Dibelius, Stange, Koch, and Bonhoeffer, had attended as "advisory members." Next, and this provoked an immediate outcry from the Provisional Administration, there appeared the entry "Guests . . . O. Dibelius and Böhm." Heckel concluded with the pointed remark: "The German Evangelical Church was thus represented by only *one* official delegation, composed in the most diverse way possible, of persons with specialized knowledge."

Not surprisingly, the Provisional Administration issued a disclaimer in the wake of this widely publicized account. On 13 November Böhm recounted the distressing story of the events that had led to the Provisional Administration's invitation: "So it came about that despite the limitations inherent in the structure of the Ecumenical Council, the Provisional Administration of the German Evangelical Church . . . received a special invitation to the Chamby conference . . . from Bishop Bell of Chichester." Böhm then spoke of Zoellner's impressive contribution in Chamby and the resulting rapprochement, continuing:

> At this point it must be said that Dr. Zoellner did the Evangelical church the worst imaginable service when he delegated the preparatory work for the upcoming Oxford conference to Dr. Heckel. . . . Now, as in the past, the Provisional Administration of the German Evangelical Church, as the legitimate representative of the German Evangelical Church, will carry out its work on the common tasks of the world church independently of the bodies of the Reich church committee.[174]

With that, prospects for joint preparation of the Oxford meeting once more became remote.

Meeting of the Youth Commission in London. By 16 February 1937, when Bonhoeffer and Böhm flew together to London for several group meetings in connection with the Oxford conference, the situation had grown even more complicated.

Zoellner had resigned under dramatic circumstances. The day before Bonhoeffer's departure Hitler had made a surprise announcement ordering church elections. Numerous questions arose: To what extent would the Minister for Church Affairs exercise sole power? How much influence would the Church Foreign Office have, and how would it be used? Could Böhm and Bonhoeffer afford to be associated at this point with the Reich church and those officials at the consistory offices on Jebensstrasse who had survived Zoellner's fall? Was the vague agreement they had made in Chamby with Zoellner (but not with Heckel) still valid? Certainly not for Bonhoeffer, who had been skeptical even then. In fact there were strong clashes at the London meeting over Bonhoeffer's joint responsibility for the youth delegation to Oxford.

Despite his intention of resigning as youth secretary, Bonhoeffer once again found himself involved in his former ecumenical work. After Chamby, when he again had to stay away from the ecumenical youth conference,[175] he wrote to Henriod on 19 September:

> I realize that things cannot go on this way. It is highly unsatisfactory for you as well as for me. We must make a change for the sake of the cause. I must resign my post . . . I should like to ask you to leave everything as it is until after Oxford. I have certain reasons for this. I shall do all in my power to carry out the necessary work. But afterward, that will be that.[176]

The "certain reasons" were that he was no longer willing to send his deputy, Jürgen Winterhager. Winterhager was now pursuing a course that would end with his legalization in 1938 under the consistory. Bonhoeffer sought to replace him with Udo Smidt, a pastor in Wesermünde and secretary of the Schoolchildren's Bible Circles, but this could not be arranged in time for the London meeting.

The minutes of the 19 February 1937 meeting, which Henriod, Schönfeld, and Espy also attended, record Bonhoeffer as saying that in his view "the differences between the churches [were] so great that he would be unwilling to secure a German youth delegation in which the Reich Church would be represented."[177] The Geneva secretaries thought he should nominate three representatives, from the Reich church, the Lutheran Council, and the Confessing church, and they reminded him of the agreement in Chamby about a joint delegation. They continued to consider Heckel a party to these discussions; as far as Bonhoeffer was concerned, this had never been the case. Moreover, Zoellner, who *had* been a party to the Chamby agreement, had announced publicly that he would no longer consider holding any responsibility in the Reich church. Those present eventually relented by asking Bonhoeffer whether he would at least nominate the other two representatives and agree to direct negotiations between Henriod and the Reich church to choose the third. Even then Bonhoeffer did not express unqualified approval, but "agreed to discuss the proposal with his colleagues in Germany, and to report his decision at an early date." Having received an answer, Hunter, Espy, and Henriod were then to "act as they find best in light of developments in Germany."[178]

The Break with Geneva and the Barrier to Oxford. Immediately after the meeting Bonhoeffer sought out Bishop Bell, to discuss the nature of the Chamby discussions and their possible interpretation. Bell agreed that it was unnecessary to ensure three German delegations with equal rights—three groups or none, as Henriod put it[179]—if Zoellner's withdrawal signified the withdrawal of the Reich church committee as well. For his own part, Henriod could not simply ignore his relations with the Church Foreign Office or exclude the Reich church it represented.[180] Bonhoeffer wrote to him: "It was never mentioned that if one German group failed to attend, this would preclude the attendance of another."[181] On 24 March Bonhoeffer again sought to clarify matters:

> Your goal was to have one of Dr. Heckel's delegates at Oxford. My goal was to prevent this. I should mention that I am fully aware that your only con-

cern was to be fair and to have a complete representation of the German churches at Oxford. But my view is that such an arrangement, although it may appear just in a formal sense, is in fact unjust and spiritually indefensible for reasons which need not be discussed here. . . . Do you insist, come what may, on having one of Heckel's delegates at the youth conference in Oxford? . . . How can your decision to nominate the German youth delegates personally in association with the church governments be reconciled with the statutes of the Youth Commission and the functions of the youth secretary? . . . To what extent does this differ from autocracy against which I would be compelled to protest most emphatically in matters affecting the church? I am afraid that this is where we come into sharp conflict. . . .[182]

In his notes of a meeting on 13 April in Dahlem Constantin von Dietze remarked:

> Bonhoeffer. For the Youth Conference Geneva is demanding, at all costs, a church representative named by Heckel . . . Henriod is demanding Bonhoeffer's withdrawal from the Youth Secretariat. Basically not blaming Henriod but the general situation in the ecumenical movement, right up to the archbishop of Canterbury: fundamental lack of understanding for the Confessing church. . . . Probably Henriod himself will seek a representative of Heckel, then Bonhoeffer will refuse to participate. . . .[183]

Finally, on 17 April, Henriod asked Bonhoeffer to nominate at least the delegate from the Confessing church, while the others would be selected from lists that had been received in Geneva. It was also suggested that he should address any further letters to Espy.[184] With this the fruitless correspondence between Henriod and Bonhoeffer ended; it ended his personal ties to the secretaries in Geneva as well. In fact, there was nothing left to argue about, since the Minister for Church Affairs refused to issue passports to anyone except the Methodist bishop—thereby preventing any delegation from the German churches from traveling.

Kerrl had been advised in this matter by members of church and theological circles. Church historian Peter Meinhold, for example, produced a report on an ecumenical seminar in Geneva, concluding with the proposal:

> For all journeys abroad, an office should be set up in association with the liaison staff of the National Socialist Party or the Reich Ministry of Education from which permission to travel abroad would have to be sought by theologians, clergy and students. This office would be empowered to deny exit if the participation of an individual appeared to be contrary to interests of German policy.[185]

Another church historian, Professor Ernst Benz, referred to Meinhold's report in a letter dated 27 November 1936;[186] citing the Thuringian German Christians, Benz recommended that any kind of participation at the Oxford conference and the "attendance of a German delegation or delegation at ecumenical conferences" should be forbidden altogether. The only possible objection might be that "the views of the German Evangelical Church would be represented solely by a group of German émigrés and that an anti-National Socialist resolution could be passed . . . unopposed." According to a file entry of 6 January 1937 by consistory counsel Erich Ruppel, Benz was in contact with the Ministry for Church Affairs and had been asked by Heckel "to cooperate in the scholarly preparations for the ecumenical conferences and to [join] the section preparing work on the theme 'Church and State.'"[187]

The attendance of Böhm and Bonhoeffer at the London Youth Commission meetings of 16–24 February 1937 was the last time prominent figures in the Confessing church appeared at a regular ecumenical meeting. Bonhoeffer requested that Udo Smidt replace him as youth secretary. It marked the end of the unhappy chapter of official relations and disputes over invitations between the "Dahlemite"-oriented Confessing church and the organized ecumenical movement in Geneva. From now on, Heckel's Church Foreign Office had complete control of the field. He exploited this position and sent his representatives as frequently and for as long as possible.

Thus the Confessing church was not represented at the 1938 Utrecht meeting, where the formation of an ecumenical Provisional Committee was discussed and Dr. Willem Visser 't Hooft was invited to become the new general secretary in the Geneva office. Nor was the Confessing church present at the important youth conference in Amsterdam. Some members of the ecumenical movement grew accustomed to seeing only emissaries from the Church Foreign Office at their meetings and conferences.[188]

But the Confessing church, and Bonhoeffer himself, did not simply disappear from the sight and mind of the ecumenical movement. Different channels, most of them private, arranged relief work and meetings, particularly after the plight of Confessing church members began to assume new dimensions. The secretariats of the ecumenical associations would not really have been suited to these tasks.

As was his custom, Bonhoeffer also pursued his own plans during the February 1937 visit to London. He paid a second visit to Bell and introduced him to Hans Böhm, thus providing the Provisional Administration's ecumenical adviser with a contact that was urgently needed; the other great friend of the Councils of Brethren, Bishop Ammundsen, had died in Denmark in October, an event Bonhoeffer felt as a personal loss.[189] Bonhoeffer mainly discussed Zoellner's resignation and Hitler's orders for elections with Bell. The bishop then informed his friends in England and the London *Times* that the announced elections were a "delusion," since the only real help the state could give the churches was to stop intervening in the preparations for the elections and in the elections themselves: "let the state cease from intervention in the inner life of the church."[190] Bonhoeffer also reported about the colleagues in concentration camps, Dr. Weissler, Ernst Tillich, Werner Koch, and the Silesian lawyer Bunke, who had been arrested at a Confessing meeting in Glogau and was now in protective custody.

Bonhoeffer also tried once more to introduce a candidate exchange between the ecumenical world and the preachers' seminary. He extended an invitation to the next semester in Finkenwalde and drafted a memorandum on the topic.[191] Through the former Finkenwalde student Eugen Rose, who now worked in the ecumenical department of the Provisional Administration in Berlin, he arranged for the Old Prussian Council of Brethren and the other seminary directors to work with him on the plan. But the project and the preparations in Finkenwalde for a trip to England were abandoned after the wave of arrests in 1937.[192]

The Last Year in Finkenwalde

During the last two courses at Finkenwalde there was no sign that everything would end so soon. Never had the seminary's theological studies been so intensive as during the 1936–1937 winter term, while the following summer term was marked primarily by the great wave of arrests that included so many friends and colleagues. Although Bonhoeffer's travel schedule was extensive—he probably never traveled as much as he did in 1936—his home base was the preachers' seminary, and his holidays were spent at the House of Brethren, although he naturally saw his relatives in Berlin in between. Of course, the classes and liturgical life were not insulated from the bad news on the church political front, but Finkenwalde never became a breeding ground of rumor that lived from one real or fictitious news item to the next. Meditation and evening prayer continued to determine the routine. The closer disaster loomed, the fewer restrictions existed upon the community's recreational life. In the 1936 annual report Bonhoeffer wrote:

> We all know the distress, the inner contradiction, the sloth which seek to hold us back.... We still have enough time and warning. When one person disappears, that is a visible or invisible weakening of everyone else in the fellowship of prayer. Let us not despise what God has given to us.[193]

The Family. During his time with the House of Brethren Bonhoeffer deliberately tried to shift the emphasis of his private life to Finkenwalde and away from the close ties with his relatives in Berlin. But as Hitler's power spread, the different branches of the family drew closer together around the two houses on Marienburger Allee, which acquired new significance as a rendezvous for the exchange of political views and information.

Karl-Friedrich had moved from Frankfurt in 1934 when he was appointed to the chair of physical chemistry at Leipzig, the place "which, since Ostwald, may be described as the birthplace of this science."[194] He abandoned his earlier field of research into nuclear hydrogen, parahydrogen, and heavy hydrogen in favor of electrochemistry and the kinetics of electrode processes, in order to clarify the question of biological processes and basic electrophysical principles in nervous stimulation. He made this change so that he could avoid having to cooperate in the development of nuclear armaments. Since he now made frequent trips to Berlin, he saw Dietrich more often.

Klaus had become the legal representative of Lufthansa. Dr. Otto John joined him as an assistant in 1937; both men quickly realized that they saw eye-to-eye on political matters. Klaus moved from Bendlerstrasse to the Eichkamp neighborhood; he could reach his parents' home in ten minutes. In 1937 the Dohnanyis moved from Eichkamp to Kürlinder Allee, a street that ran parallel to Marienburger Allee; they used to see Dietrich at his parents' home and also visited him in Finkenwalde. Gerhard Leibholz, by then forcibly retired, wondered halfheartedly whether he should try to find a teaching job abroad. In 1936 and 1937 those in the Marienburger Allee homes still hoped to postpone or even avoid this separation. After Niemöller's arrest, Walter Dress took over a pastorate in Dahlem.[195]

At the sixtieth birthday of Bonhoeffer's mother the grandchildren gave a performance of Haydn's "Toy" symphony. Dietrich had to join in the arduous rehearsals that were held next door at the Schleichers'. He then came down with an attack of influenza that kept him at home with his parents until January 1937, longer than he had expected. During his illness he renewed his acquaintance with the writings of Georges Bernanos. The German edition of *The Diary of a Country Priest* had been published in 1936. From then on Bonhoeffer never tired of recommending the book to his Finkenwaldians, since he thought it of fundamental importance on the subject of pastoral counseling.[196] It had been a long time since a work of contemporary literature had made such a deep impression on him:

> You must surely know Bernanos's books? When the priests speak in them, their words carry weight. The reason is that they are not the products of

some sort of linguistic reflection or observation but simply of daily, personal contact with the crucified Jesus Christ. This is the depth from which a word must come if it is to carry weight.[197]

In 1937 the Charité celebrated his father's twenty-fifth anniversary as director of the psychiatric clinic. Dr. Bonhoeffer gave an improvised review of his academic career. Although retired, in compliance with the law of 1 April 1936, he agreed to the request that he remain in his post. It was not until the summer of 1938 that he gave his valedictory speech, to an audience that included his colleagues and his three sons. A great period for the clinic had come to an end, making way for a new approach personified by Professor de Crinis, who was a member of the S.S. Ten years later, in a study dedicated to Karl Bonhoeffer, Professor J. Zutt described his working methods:

Whoever . . . is familiar with the life of such a large clinic will be surprised that Bonhoeffer arrived every morning at 8:30 and left at 1:30 P.M. The remainder of the day belonged to his private work, his practice and the family. It might be asked how it was possible to do the kind of work described above in the short period of five hours, and to do it in such a way that the major empirical needs were met and that each assistant had the feeling of being constantly accompanied, so that the work of each person culminated in discussions about this work with Bonhoeffer. And all this happened without any formal organization. The conference and meeting of the colleagues were the scheduled events of the day. Everything else was not formally set, including the visits to the patients.

This achievement can only be grasped and explained from the entirety of the inner sense of order that Bonhoeffer brought to the tasks of his life. His punctuality was just an external expression of this inner sense of order. His ever-patient openness for every situation, his sovereign general mastery of psychiatric and neurological knowledge, his extraordinary ability to make clinical distinctions, tied to his phenomenal memory, his strong certainty of judgment coupled with cautious reserve—all made him able to see through any concrete situation on the sickbed, and explain it so thoroughly that his colleagues felt enlightened and excited at the same time. And the entire process was completely lacking in hurriedness or public virtuosity. Everything was always careful and natural, in the best sense: a collective questioning, listening, looking, examining and considering that made everyone present participate—not just to accept an opinion, but to think with him. Little would be said, but whatever was said was never superficial. . . .

His openness for the essence of things led him in his work to concentrate on the essential and, as a result, to a collectively unusual achievement

in a short time. . . . All superficial chatter disappeared in Bonhoeffer's presence. He detested poorly founded speculation and theoretical extravagance, exaggerated or false pathos and pretentious faddish wording. . . .
There was no one from whom one could better learn that silence, too, is an
important form of speech. . . . Rhetorically, his lectures were not inviting.
But whoever took notes had a completed text. . . . He was "the privy councillor" to everyone and was addressed in the third person. This was not an
empty form of address.[198]

Some of these observations about Bonhoeffer could have been said of his
sons as well. There were no noticeable signs of aging in the Bonhoeffer parents. In the fall of 1936 they both passed their driving test. As Karl Bonhoeffer wrote in his New Year's diary: "Both of us passed what is probably our
last exam, if not with distinction, at least properly."

Changes. In the winter of 1936–1937 tax complications arose between the
various offices responsible for Finkenwalde—the Provisional Administration
in Oeynhausen, the council of the Old Prussian Union in Berlin-Dahlem,
and the Pomeranian office in Stettin. In addition, a potential buyer had
appeared for the valuable Finkenwalde property. To settle these matters
Friedrich Justus Perels, the legal adviser to the Old Prussian Council who
occasionally helped the Pomeranian Council of Brethren, arrived at the
seminary. A friendship with Bonhoeffer grew out of his official contacts
that lasted until Dietrich's death. Levelheaded and objective, Perels was
endowed with the native Berlin dry wit, and his resourceful ability to cope
with disagreeable bureaucracies delighted Bonhoeffer. Perels understood
Bonhoeffer's interests and was able to thwart the threats against the House
of Brethren. He soon became a familiar guest at Finkenwalde. They held similar attitudes on church politics. The two men were a complete contrast, both
physically and in their way of expressing themselves, but they appealed to
one another because each came quickly and without pomposity to the point.
When it later became necessary to reach mutual understanding about more
delicate matters, they needed few words to communicate. Bonhoeffer introduced his new acquaintance to his brother-in-law, Hans von Dohnanyi, and
to his brother Klaus. By April 1943 Perels had become a member of the
innermost circle of conspirators; he was a frequent visitor to the family and
was later helpful in covering up Bonhoeffer's and Dohnanyi's traces when
both men were in prison. At the same time Perels was at constant risk himself, especially because one of his grandparents was Jewish.

Wilhelm Rott's term as director of studies ended with the fourth course. One of Finkenwalde's pioneers, he left for a more important post but remained an active friend. He now took over Department IV of the Provisional Administration (responsible for the schools and the Reformed churches) under Superintendent Albertz. There were now two Finkenwaldians in the Berlin headquarters: Rott and Eugen Rose, whom Bonhoeffer had sent to Hans Böhm. During the turbulent years that followed Bonhoeffer rarely visited Berlin without discussing church-political measures with Rott. This became even more important after Hildebrandt was forced to leave the country in 1937; this meant that, after their many years together, Bonhoeffer lost his best-informed and most like-minded friend. At the same time, in Rott and Perels he had acquired two excellent informants and supporters at church headquarters. During the war Bonhoeffer pulled every string he could to obtain an exemption for Rott from military service; at times Rott had to run the Provisional Administration single-handedly in the absence of its other leaders through arrests, police restrictions on entering Berlin, or conscription.

The new director of studies at Finkenwalde was the imperturbable Fritz Onnasch. Bonhoeffer thus acquired a colleague for the House of Brethren who had grown up with its style and routine from the start. Onnasch's father, no less steadfast, was the superintendent of Köslin in Pomerania; his friendship with the seminary was to prove particularly valuable after its dissolution.

Disputations. The fourth course in the winter of 1936–1937 was distinguished by an insatiable theological hunger; its members included Erich Klapproth and Gerhard Ebeling from Berlin, and Gerhard Krause from Pomerania. The last section of Bonhoeffer's lecture on discipleship was "Law, Commandment, and Exhortation in Paul"; this was joined into their daily prayers with his christological interpretation of the Old Testament and his customary incorporation of Psalm 119 and other psalms in praise of the law. This might have been thought quite sufficient to make the question of the law the unofficial theme for the term. As if this were not enough, accusations that law and legalism held sway in the Confessing church were made through pamphlets and in discussions at pastoral assemblies; and at the end of 1935 Karl Barth's booklet *Gospel and Law* was published which, to the discomfiture of Lutherans, gave the Gospel precedence over law.

Because of this, the fourth course held a debate lasting several days on the question "How do we preach the law?" It was preceded by weeks of preparation during which various groups investigated the term in the context of the Old and New Testaments and confessional writings. The proceedings were conducted by Gerhard Ebeling, who also put forward his own concept consisting of forty-one theses under the four headings: I. Law: Christ, II. Law: Scripture, III. Law: The World, and IV. Law: Church. In his fifth thesis he moved in the direction of Karl Barth:

> The Law of God's Word is so encompassed by the revelation of God in Jesus Christ that, apart from this revelation, it is impossible to give a satisfactory definition of the term "Law."[199]

The actual substance of the debate was less concerned with contemporary controversies than with an objective inquiry into biblical findings, combined with an attempt to tackle the problem systematically. One of Ebeling's theses (III: 15) included a concept expressed by Bonhoeffer in *Ethics*:

> In the strict sense, the ecclesiastical preaching of law is directed only at those to whom the ecclesiastical preaching of the Gospel is addressed.[200]

This also encompassed thesis IV: 3:

> The church cannot itself decide to preach law or the Gospel here or there, or to disseminate law and the Gospel on imperative or indicative; rather, it can only preach the fact of salvation in its full revelation through explication of the Holy Scripture, and in this leave the laying out into law and Gospel up to Christ himself, as the subject of the Word.[201]

Bonhoeffer contributed a list of questions to the disputation, from the enigmatic question "Is law revelation and what does this mean?" to the more direct (but rarely directly stated) question "Does the church simply have to act on behalf of the human?" According to the notes, in his reply Bonhoeffer must have said something about the "honor of God over the *entire* creation."[202]

In his 1936 annual report Bonhoeffer wrote that in theological work "with the current course . . . a certain high point has been reached":

> While I am writing this report a two-and-a-half-day long disputation is going on, from morning to evening, on the "Preaching of the Law." For some weeks a chosen group of brothers has been working during all its free time to prepare this disputation.[203]

The question of the law was also dealt with in other fellowships of the Confessing church. At the end of August 1937 Bonhoeffer spoke on this at the fellowship of young theologians in Stecklenberg in Saxony, together with Julius Schniewind and Johannes Hamel.[204] This circle of listeners was already familiar with the newly published *Discipleship*.

After spending the winter months in Finkenwalde, Ebeling was faced with the problem of his doctorate. Because of the fresh wave of arrests in 1937 and the difficult position of the illegal theologian, he had reservations about withdrawing to enjoy a year of quiet study; and the Berlin-Brandenburg Council of Brethren was most reluctant to release anybody. But Bonhoeffer thought differently, and would not permit judgments in terms of desertion or loyalty. This kind of thinking dominated the Confessing church at the time, and anyone who withdrew to an academic retreat was suspect. Hence only a small and dwindling number of young theologians in the Confessing church continued their academic education, a fact that made itself felt particularly after the war. Meanwhile Bonhoeffer urged the reluctant Council of Brethren to grant Ebeling leave. He argued that if the Confessing church were no longer in a position to pull someone out of the fight for the purpose of academic study or to give them special tasks, it would all be over for the church. For all his criticism of theological training at the universities, Bonhoeffer never abandoned the criterion of realistic responsibility or his vision of the nature of contemporary theology. Ebeling left for Zurich to write his doctoral thesis under Fritz Blanke.[205] On returning to the church struggle, he became the illegal pastor of the church in Berlin-Hermsdorf supported by the Council of Brethren.

Bonhoeffer not only took an active role in getting Ebeling's leave for academic work, but influenced his choice of theme: hermeneutics. Another Finkenwalde student, Gerhard Krause, began his doctoral work under Rudolf Hermann in Greifswald with similar intentions. While Ebeling explored Luther's hermeneutics in light of the Gospel, Krause took the topic "Studies of Luther's Exegesis of the Lesser Prophets." Assisted by Ebeling, he was able to complete his doctoral work only after a very long period as a Russian prisoner of war.

Before the course that included Ebeling and Krause had really started, Bonhoeffer wrote to Erwin Sutz:

> I hope now . . . to finish my book, and it would then give me the greatest pleasure to return to hermeneutics. There seems to be quite a large gap here.[206]

The term "hermeneutics" was little used at the time; few theologians had heard of it. But Bonhoeffer had just acquired a copy of *Interpreting the*

Bible by J. C. K. Hofmann, first published in German in 1880. He must have felt some misgivings that his own theological activities had not been sufficiently thought through. In 1925 in Berlin, the stronghold of historical-critical research under Seeberg, he had tackled the problem of historical and "pneumatic" interpretation, following the direction taken by Karl Barth. He had then made an ally of Wilhelm Vischer, who visited Finkenwalde at the beginning of March 1937 and was himself the target of angry criticism by Old Testament exegetes. This was due primarily to the sudden and unprecedented revival of the use of scripture as a weapon in the course of the church struggle. Furthermore, Bonhoeffer rejected the notion that there had been no correct exegesis in the days before scholarly research; this was why he took a particular interest in the inquiries into Luther's foundation and premise that Ebeling and Krause were making. Hence it is understandable that Bonhoeffer would gladly have devoted more time to the detail and background of the historic and systematic methods of interpretation of the Word—to what he saw as "quite a large gap."

Characteristically, however, he abandoned this plan, despite his awareness of that "gap"—perhaps because circumstances no longer allowed him the time for it. The substantive questions of his *Ethics* seemed more urgent; at the time he viewed these questions as his life's work. Methodology belonged to another time and another existence.

The winter course's disputation on the preaching of the law was followed that summer by a similar debate, although with a more immediate theme. Problems of church discipline were becoming more significant for the confessional communities. The disintegration of the Confessing church, the number of people who left the church at the instigation of the Party, the ridicule directed at the ministers in the villages, and at the same time the demand for their services—after the introduction of the "Red Card" all this called for a reappraisal. The theologians who had grown up in the *Volkskirche* were unprepared for all this. Some lacked a clear conscience; few dared to risk as much as Pastor Paul Schneider in Dickenschied, who disciplined those parish members who were in the Nazi Party. (Schneider was murdered in Buchenwald in 1938.) People either sought guidance and advice from the Councils of Brethren or complained of their inability to help. After Whitsuntide 1937 Bonhoeffer invited some of the most resolute pastors from Pomerania, Saxony, and Brandenburg to Finkenwalde for a discussion on the law and possibilities of church discipline; here he gave his lecture "The Power of the Keys and Church Discipline in the New Testament."[207]

Church discipline presupposes not only an intact teaching ministry but also a right ordering of the offices in the church-community. The ordering of the church-community must help towards the proper use of the keys and all the actions of the congregation which stem from that. . . . It is inconceivable for the New Testament that people should be appointed to offices in the church from outside the church-community.[208]

The impotence of the ministry within the reality of the *Volkskirche* placed an agonizing burden on the discussion. Everyone present had sought to impose church discipline in some form, either by making confirmation contingent upon obedience or reading aloud the names of those who had left the church, thereby incurring the wrath of secular and church authorities. The goal must be a congregation that would eventually be mature enough to practice these things as a matter of congregational discipline rather than of civic responsibility, and to interpret them in a way that revealed the Gospel in a clearer light.

The Confessional Question. During the final Finkenwalde term the entire confessional question was dealt with more seriously, provoked by Sasse's newly published book *Was heisst lutherisch?* (What is Lutheranism?),[209] as well as the May 1937 Halle synod of the Old Prussian Union, which examined the disagreement between Lutherans and Reformed about the Eucharist—not to mention the ongoing problems with the Lutheran Council.

Ever since meeting him in Berlin before the church struggle began, Bonhoeffer had read everything Sasse published with particular attention. Even when Sasse's work aroused sharp disagreement and dismayed criticism in him, Bonhoeffer invariably found something that impressed him. He discussed the book with the ordinands and during the informal study conferences. By then Bonhoeffer's earlier delight at discovering that Sasse's resistance and views sprang not from ecclesiastical conservatism, but from a new relationship to the confession, had naturally given way to profound disagreement over Sasse's assessment of the function and dignity of historical confessions. Sasse had come to see Bonhoeffer as a "zealot" because Bonhoeffer credited the living experience of communal, present confessing with so much power to change things that he reduced the points that divided churches to mere differences in outlook among different schools of thought. Bonhoeffer, on the other hand, viewed Sasse as a formalistic confessionalist who, when there was "dissent on only one score," regarded the antithesis as "wholly torn asunder" and who for this reason "went further than Luther."[210]

In fact, many theologians thought it strange at the time that Bonhoeffer questioned individual points of Lutheranism that were held to be inviolable, yet at the same time chose to base his Christology, for example, on Luther. He asked whether "we Lutherans" were not preoccupied with too narrow a concept of "law" and, as a corollary, of "Gospel," and again whether "law" in Scripture was not attested in at least two ways, although it was customarily restricted to one. He also asked whether it was sufficient to regard the whole of biblical testimony as being comprised in the forgiveness of sins.

These were contemporary questions, but Bonhoeffer would raise them even more urgently in 1944 during his time in Tegel. He believed that the controversy between Lutherans and Reformed was wholly unresolved, although it would be worth trying to put it right. In a letter on the subject to Karl Barth he wrote:

> I think it would be very important for the present situation if some of the questions of substance that divide Lutherans and Reformed could be brought into the open and discussed. But as far as I know there is no one in Germany who could do it, as Sasse's arguments are always completely formal and so too all the statements of our opponents. No one knows enough.[211]

Bonhoeffer's confessional candor and his testing of what was held to be inviolable for possible weaknesses did not, however, make him a Unionist who united the Lutheran and Reformed principles. He noted how the union he had so welcomed at Barmen was treated by theologians, synods, and church governments: decision (which he thought indispensable) and the reasons for it (for which he demanded theological exactitude) were held apart. On the subject of the Halle synod he wrote to his candidates:

> However much I agree with the result, I am equally troubled by the theological reasoning behind it. This, I should say, is simply the Reformed thesis which holds that the confessional dispute over Eucharist centers solely around the *modus praesentiae* rather than the real presence, without explaining this further. This leads to conflict with the Formula of Concord and a total failure to absorb its message. It seems to me that this greatly undermines a synodal decision.[212]

His views on Holy Communion were so decidedly Lutheran that he became embroiled in further controversy in 1940 when Eberhard Baumann, the Reformed member on the Stettin Council of Brethren, attacked him for his remarks on Holy Communion in the pastors' newsletter.[213] What Bonhoeffer had in mind was a renewed and really comprehensive airing of differences—in the invigorating and healthy atmosphere of theological controversy—after which the necessary decisions could be made. He did not want one of these things without the other.

When he heard that Finkenwalde's candidates were preparing for their ordination on the basis of various confessional writings, and made their confessional selection known to the congregation during the ordination proceedings, Bonhoeffer remarked: "This hardly seems the right way to solve the confessional problem."[214] This was not perfectionism, but the need to avoid deceiving himself and his generation. He did not expect for these questions to be solved in all cases, only that people should be clear what they were doing when they made a decision. In November 1940, in connection with the Catholic question, he returned once more to the subject of Halle:

> How have we Lutherans got along with the Reformed churches? Really quite untheologically (the theological formulation of Halle is really more a statement of fact than a theological solution, which it certainly is not!). We have managed to work together on the basis of two things: the "guidance"of God (Union, Confessing Church) and the recognition of what is given objectively in the sacraments: Christ is more important than our thoughts of him and his presence. Both are theologically questionable foundations for unity, and yet the church decided in faith for eucharistic—i.e., inter-church—communion. It decided to recognize the union as the guiding hand of God, and it decided to subordinate its ideas or doctrine about Christ to the objectivity of the presence of Christ (in the Reformed Eucharist, too). But it did not bring about a theological union (except at Halle). . . . It seems to me that churches have united, not primarily theologically, but through decisions of faith, in the sense that I have mentioned. That's a very dangerous statement, isn't it! One can do anything with it! But in the Confessing Church have we not in fact done just that?[215]

There would still be half measures and limitations, for better or worse. But they had to be recognized and defined as such, and it must then be established why they persist. The Bonhoeffer of the Union church was not prepared to leave the Lutheran interpretation of the Gospel to his Lutheran contemporaries.

But the dyed-in-the-wool Reformed church colleagues were suspicious of Bonhoeffer's combination of Lutheranism and his interest in revising the Reformed heritage. In a letter from Finkenwalde to his spiritual mentor, the Reformed pastor Hermann Hesse in Elberfeld, Horst Thurmann asked to be released to enter the House of Brethren: "Furthermore, many theological pronouncements are in need of correction and one particular development on Bonhoeffer's part needs 'supervision.'"[216]

Crisis in Pomerania. Neither classes, nor disputations, nor the completion of *Discipleship* could save Bonhoeffer from getting entangled in the struggles that occurred in Pomerania during the last year in Finkenwalde. He even faced new tasks, since some people hoped that his theological influence might benefit those who remained loyal.

Some months after the pastors' meeting in Bredow in January 1936 the split widened between the supporters of the Councils of Brethren and the church committees. During May and June the Confessing church of the Old Prussian Union had started a far-reaching visitation throughout the regions between the Rhine and the Pregel, in an attempt to induce greater spiritual resoluteness.

The crisis then intensified in Pomerania, somewhat later than it had elsewhere. There had been a period of uncertainty in Bielefeld (Westphalia) and Düsseldorf (Rhineland) after president Koch's and Joachim Beckmann's negotiations with the church committees in those regions. Once this was over and all prospects for agreement had failed, however, the situation in Stettin seriously disintegrated. At the beginning of August 1936 Bonhoeffer wrote:

> In the Reich the crisis seems to have been overcome. President Koch has regained his senses ... not long ago Koch began to stand upright again! The nadir seems to have been passed.[217]

From Pomerania, however, Baumann reported:

> At the moment the position in our provincial church is extremely serious. The Confessing church is on the verge of complete collapse, or else of the majority moving to establish relations to the committees.[218]

Matters then reached the stage when Bonhoeffer was compelled to write:

> The news today: Schauer and Faisst have left the Council of Brethren! Treat this as confidential for the present. The Confessing church [is said to be] pharisaically legalistic. This is a blow. But Pomerania always lags behind a bit.[219]

Friedrich Schauer and Hans Faisst were two of the most respected members of the Pomeranian Council of Brethren; one had been a pioneer in the

Confessing church, the other was a highly esteemed superintendent, and both were tirelessly concerned about renewing the ministry.

The Pomeranian Council of Brethren now faced the alternative of either renewing its claim to legitimacy in a fundamental way or losing it altogether. Such a renewal could no longer be achieved by calling a full Confessing synod such as the one in June 1935. As a solution Reinhold von Thadden called for a "general assembly" of the Confessing church in mid-October 1936 in Stettin. He proposed an airing of all points of view before deciding whether the Council of Brethren should be regenerated or dissolved in favor of the committees. Thadden faced a complicated situation in which feelings ran high. Niemöller and Asmussen came hurrying from Berlin. Superintendent Otto Riehl from Brandenburg, who earlier had been an advocate of the Confessing church, spoke on behalf of the church committees. He portrayed the consequences should the Council of Brethren persist in its claims to leadership:

> . . . no longer a body corporate in the eyes of the public law, no more state assistance, no more service among the general public, no more pastoral counseling in the armed forces, no more religious instruction in schools, the congregations thrown back on their own financial resources—what then will become of the church? A heap of rubble! The question is "do you want that?" If the answer is no, then you must follow the course taken by the committees and avoid any offense that might compromise your activities: then, despite all your unfulfilled desires, you must make use of the great opportunity that the state is offering the church.[220]

Riehl described Superintendent Albertz and the two arrested pastors Johannes Pecina and Willi Brandenburg as "needlessly and futilely fanaticized," and held Albertz responsible for their arrests. The Finkenwalde contingent could be subdued only with difficulty, since Willi Brandenburg sat among them. When Riehl used Bonhoeffer's paper on church-community to illustrate the theological-legal threat to the Confessing church, as usual quoting the phrase "those without a Red Card won't go to heaven," Bonhoeffer jumped to his feet and cried: "Bonhoeffer here. You're misquoting!" Referring to the Eighth Commandment, Bonhoeffer protested the caricature of his statements and their use out of context. He was attacked again later in the debate because he had attempted in his "False Doctrine in the Confessing Church"[221] in the June newsletter to justify the Council of Brethren's position in accordance with the Barmen and Dahlem decision. It was now said that this represented a "sin against reality." Reality proved that God had "struck off the arm" of the Confessing church. This was the sense in which supporters of the church committee claimed a "conformity with Christ," as opposed to Bonhoeffer's conformity to Scripture.

The general assembly decided that everyone should send in a written declaration saying whether or not the Council of Brethren should continue to administer the church government. The result was better than had been expected: 181 of those attending the assembly voted that the administration should continue, 58 voted to transfer it to the provincial church committee.

Still, the crumbling of the ranks could not be stopped. Increasingly the numbers of those supporting the committees grew, in part because Zoellner's efforts were most successful only a short time before his fall. On 20 November 1936 the regional church committees and the Lutheran Council issued a joint statement about their future cooperation. The vice president of the church committee of Hannover, Dr. Paul Fleisch, described this as "conditional collaboration," but Zoellner justifiably recorded it as his greatest success. Inevitably, the joint declaration contained the passage: "With the Reich church committee we stand behind the *Führer* in the German people's struggle for existence against bolshevism." It was signed by Marahrens, Wurm, Meiser, and, on behalf of Prussia, General Superintendent Johannes Eger.[222]

Only those who were still wholly resolute saw a ray of light on 16 December 1936, when the Confessing synod of the Old Prussian Union dared to challenge the legally entrenched principle of requiring six semesters of theological studies at a state faculty; the synod claimed that the stance of many faculties could not be supported.[223] The "Dahlemites" were once more demanding disobedience against existing laws. Yet this only increased the temptation among the "illegal" candidates to acquire legitimation through training, examination, and ordination under the authority of the committees or the consistories, which would open the way to a regular ministry, official recognition, and a salary. A report from the Rhineland in October 1936 estimated that two hundred assistant ministers and vicars had placed themselves under the consistory, while two hundred remained with the Council of Brethren. Even one of the Finkenwalde candidates wrote Bonhoeffer that he was unable to "elude the reasons offered by Faisst and Schauer." The Finkenwalde newsletter commented:

> We are painfully afflicted by the fact that Brother X should have taken this step without having first sought a discussion either with us or with Brother Bonhoeffer . . . only our own inquiry confirmed that he had indeed taken this step. As recently as the summer term, Brother X had added his signature to the declaration made by our brotherhood, "Do you wish to con-

summate it in the flesh?"[224] We commend him and ourselves to our Lord and his grace. Dear brothers, we must make a firm promise that whenever temptation becomes too strong because of the way things are going in the Confessing church, we should turn either to a brother who stands firmly by the Council of Brethren, or to Finkenwalde. We owe this to our brotherhood.[225]

Zoellner's Resignation and Werner's Rise. During the winter Zoellner used declarations and other measures to oppose the more extreme German Christians and the small provincial churches under their control. On 4 February 1937, as he was about to preach in the German Christian stronghold of Lübeck, the Gestapo prevented Zoellner from entering the pulpit. He was a man of sufficient character to tender his resignation from the Reich church committee on 12 February.

Thus the Zoellner era ended, although many regional and provincial church committees remained in office during the months to come and Heckel's Church Foreign Office continued to function without any adverse effects. It was difficult to forecast what would happen next, for the state's actions were highly inconsistent. To begin with, Kerrl, in an angry speech on 13 February before what remained of the committees, spoke of the precedence of the National Socialist state over the church: "the church's proclamation must fall into the correct relationship with National Socialism."[226] He announced that, as Minister for Church Affairs, he would take personal charge of the church committee.

Then, on 15 February 1937, Hitler made a surprise announcement ordering church elections through which "the church, in full freedom, may now provide itself with a new constitution and thereby a new order as determined by her members." Minister Kerrl was to prepare for the election of a general synod.[227] The situation immediately eased from Berlin to Geneva, as new hopes for better times for the church arose; things grew more difficult for the skeptics. A confusing abundance of position papers, proposed agreements, and speculation emerged from the various camps, from the Confessing church in Dahlem to the German Christians in Thuringia. As the negotiations in London had revealed, Bonhoeffer was still among the unpersuaded skeptics; and, in fact, the election never took place. It was formally canceled in November 1937. It seemed as though the era of Ludwig Müller and that of Zoellner was to be followed by an era of anonymity.

The day arrived, however, when this third phase of the church struggle became identified with a name. On 20 March 1937 Kerrl appointed Dr. Friedrich Werner "to revise current activities," under Decree Number 13—

yet another instrument ostensibly designed for the "protection of the German Evangelical Church." This paralyzed every religious decision of those church committees that still existed. The last committee was dissolved in summer 1937. In September 1937 Kerrl appointed Werner director of the three most important coordinating offices: German Evangelical Church chancellery, the High Church Council of the Old Prussian Union church, and the financial departments. One of his personal assistants was the infamous German Christian Dr. Albert Freitag. The cornerstone was provided by Decree Number 17, which on 10 December 1937 established that the leadership of the German Evangelical Church would come under the head of the church committee, namely, Dr. Werner.

There was no longer a bishop, general superintendent, spiritual council, or synod who had control of the church. All these functions had effectively been assumed by Dr. Werner, a lawyer with no interest in theology. Behind the scenes, he was actually helped and guided by Dr. Hermann Muhs, the state secretary in the Ministry for Church Affairs. Muhs, the former district president in Hildesheim, had left the church four weeks before his appointment to the Ministry of Church Affairs in the autumn of 1936. Having lost no time in rejoining—questions of church discipline were, indeed, of negligible significance—he was now in charge of the affairs of the Ministry, a task he carried out with growing enthusiasm, particularly after Kerrl's death in 1941 when existing policy was continued without a break. The association of Muhs and Werner was to last until 1945.

In the individual Prussian provinces the real power was now in the hands of the finance departments; the consistories could act only according to their instructions. Presiding over the individual consistories were legally trained senior officials, who conveyed Werner's orders and proclamations to the superintendents and pastors. Referenda, bell ringing in celebration of Hitler's victories, even prayers, were all prescribed in this way.

The first two periods of the church struggle had not been without a certain grandeur. The Reich bishop's era had been marked by the liberating emergence of the Confessing church, and even Müller's supporters had been inspired to some degree by an amateurish enthusiasm. There was a tragic aspect to some of the confusion during the Zoellner period; for, while the true objectives of the Confessing church had almost vanished from sight, men who had once been united in brotherhood and who had a deep and real concern for the preservation of the *Volkskirche* were now enemies. It was also, of course, a time of great illusions.

The third period allowed few illusions. Dr. Werner's time in office was the most cynical of all. As the true nature of his leadership became evident in the summer of 1937, even the "Dahlemites" and the adherents of the Lutheran Council, who were bitterly at odds, came together. In March 1937 the entire Reich Council of Brethren convened again for the first time; at the beginning of July the Provisional Administration and the Lutheran Council joined forces for a while on the "Kassel Council." But by then the great wave of arrests of 1937 had begun; its aim was to subdue the remaining intransigent remnants of the Confessing church.

The End of Finkenwalde

During the first weeks of Finkenwalde's 1937 summer course little occurred to give cause for anxiety, since the election decree offered some protection. On Pentecost, the Council of Brethren's intercessory list contained only about a dozen names of church members who had either been expelled or prohibited from speaking. A few months later, however, lists with over a hundred names of people arrested or otherwise disciplined had become customary. By the end of 1937, 804 members of the Confessing church had been imprisoned briefly or longer.

The Net Tightens. The principal method used to subdue the church of the Council of Brethren consisted of tightening the net of intricate regulations imposed by the Ministry of Church Affairs, in cooperation with other ministries, particularly the Ministry of the Interior. These regulations applied primarily to the regions of the so-called destroyed churches—that is, the Confessing church of the Old Prussian Union. The majority of Lutheran churches were relatively unaffected.[228] The intercessory list of 13 October 1937 names seventy-three pastors, all of whom, except for Pastor Karl Steinbauer from Bavaria, were from "destroyed" church districts. As this indicates, the methods used were not so much aimed at banning the Confessing church directly, but gradually liquidating it through intimidation and the suppression of individual activities.

For example, it was forbidden to hold services and church gatherings on "secular" or emergency church premises. This measure was aimed at places where a separate Confessing congregation had formed and appointed a so-called illegal pastor to serve an emergency pastorate, next to a parish operating under either a neutral or German Christian administration. This affected many of those who had trained in Finkenwalde. Initially they were ordered to report for questioning at the local police station, where they were likely to be detained for one or two nights. Despite this prohibition, they continued to carry out their duties and deliberately provoked the authorities.

On 18 February 1937 the Ministry of the Interior had forbidden clergy from reading from the pulpit the names of those who had left the church, thus interfering with the ecclesiastical practice of issuing proclamations. In response to some denunciations, the police sought to end the reading of intercessory prayer lists. In response, in June the Old Prussian Council of Brethren instructed its clergy to ignore these restrictions, which affected their pastoral activities. When, as a result, some council members were arrested on 23 July in the church near the Friedrichswerder market in Berlin, the council confirmed its resolution.

At the end of May the passports of Niemöller and Albertz, the delegates to Oxford, were revoked. Shortly thereafter those lecturers who had continued to pursue their activities illegally at the theological college in Berlin were ordered to stop teaching. University students who had attended their lectures were expelled; one was Bernhard Schöne, son of the Bonhoeffer family's friend, surgeon Georg Schöne.

On 9 June the Ministry of the Interior declared that collections taken during Confessing church services were a punishable offense. Anyone who allegedly infringed against state collection regulations through taking up a collection other than that ordered by the state-legitimated church authority would be liable to arrest. Every Sunday every Confessing pastor in the "destroyed" church regions was bedeviled by this prohibition, which threatened seriously to impair the continued existence of the Confessing church and its institutions, which were completely dependent on the voluntary gifts of its members.

Finally, on 30 July, the Propaganda Ministry announced that all duplicated communication was subject to the Editorial Law. This jeopardized communication between the Councils of Brethren and their pastors; it also served as a warning to the Finkenwaldians to exercise caution with their newsletters. They took care of this by writing "Personal Letter" at the top of every copy, while Bonhoeffer signed each one himself—a method which ensured their freedom from interference until war broke out, and even after that point.

Because of all this, church activities came to a virtual standstill. Hardly a day passed without either the administration or the pastors of the Confessing church contravening one of the laws or falling into some form of trap. It had become impossible to serve the Confessing church while remaining within the law.

The early measures affecting pastors were confined to a summons to the police station where, in interrogations of varying degrees of thoroughness, note was taken of an individual's degree of intransigence. Gestapo action was primarily directed against those in positions of responsibility. The council's offices were searched on frequent occasions. Wilhelm Niesel, Gerhard Jacobi, Hermann Ehlers, and Wilhelm von Arnim-Lützlow were arrested because of the council's instructions to pastors to disregard the prohibition on proclamations, and brought before a summary court. Reinhold von Thadden was arrested and accused on several charges, one being that he had encouraged illegal studies. On 16 June 1937 in Dickenschied Paul Schneider was arrested for the first time after he announced church disciplinary measures against Party members. On 23 June the Gestapo burst into a meeting of the Reich Council of Brethren in the Friedrichswerder Church in Berlin, arresting Beckmann, Böhm, Iwand, Lücking, Bishop Ludolf Müller, Perels, von Rabenau, and Rendtorff. On 1 July the Gestapo sealed the Provisional Administration's offices and arrested Martin Niemöller.

1 July 1937. Bonhoeffer traveled to Berlin on 16 June after hearing of Niesel's arrest that day. He conferred with Hildebrandt and the Council of Brethren members he could reach; they all agreed that no one must cede any ground. Rieger happened to be in Berlin on a visit from London, so Bonhoeffer was able to provide him with authentic information for Bishop Bell. He also discussed the situation with Birger Forell, with whom Nils Karlström was then staying.

After the alarming news of the events in the Friedrichs-Werder Church reached Finkenwalde and the trial of Niesel, Jacobi, Ehlers, and Arnim-Lützlow had been set for 2 July, Bonhoeffer and Eberhard Bethge returned to Berlin without delay, planning to discuss the situation with Niemöller and Hildebrandt in Dahlem. Unsuspecting, they entered the parsonage at Cecilienallee 61 on the morning of Thursday, 1 July to be confronted by Hildebrandt and Eugen Rose with the news that Niemöller had just been taken away by the Gestapo. Nobody imagined at the time that he would not see his house again for eight years. A hasty consultation between Niemöller's wife, Bonhoeffer, Hildebrandt, Rose, and Bethge was broken short when, through the windows, they saw the arrival of a procession of the unmistakable black Mercedes Gestapo cars. Attempting to escape through a back door, they ran into the arms of a Gestapo official named Höhle, already familiar to Confessing Christians in Berlin. He led them back to the room, where each of them was searched under the supervision of Gestapo official von Scheven, the leader of the operation, and then placed under house arrest. Thus they became involuntary witnesses to a seven-hour search in which every corner of Niemöller's study was painstakingly examined; it eventually led to the discovery, behind a picture, of a safe containing thirty thousand marks that belonged to the Pastors' Emergency League. Everyone was astounded at the meticulous tidiness of Niemöller's desk, which contained neatly written verbatim copies of his sermons; it was something no one had expected of this spirited man. Unaware of what had happened, Assessor Vogel, the brother of the systematic theologian Heinrich Vogel, appeared at the front door; he, too, was placed under house arrest. Although all incoming telephone calls were taken by the Gestapo, Bonhoeffer's parents must have gotten wind of the operation in some way, for their car kept passing the house during the afternoon, with his mother peering anxiously out of the window. When the search ended that evening, those under house arrest were permitted to return home after their particulars had been taken. It was Bonhoeffer's second encounter with the Gestapo; compared with his first confrontation in July 1933, it was clear that they now faced a well-trained team.

Eugen Rose sent a message to Bishop Bell, via Karl Barth in Constance, telling him of the sealing of the Provisional Administration's office and the confiscation of funds. He asked Bell to exercise caution with the press, and to refrain from sending letters to the Provisional Administration for the time being. He also hinted that it would be of service to the administration and those under arrest if somebody were to come to Berlin. "You will learn further details from Rieger."[229] On 3 July Bell had written to *The Times*: "This is a critical hour. It is not only a case of the fate of individual pastors, it is a case of the attitude of the German State to Christianity." On Bell's behalf the dean of Chichester, Arthur Duncan-Jones, left for Berlin to intervene with the Reich chancellery and Ministry of Justice.

No attempt was made to prevent Bonhoeffer's return to Finkenwalde on 5 July. He sent a delegation from the seminary to Dahlem, where an important service of intercession was planned for 8 August. This developed into an open street demonstration because the police had cordoned off the church. The protest march by the excluded congregation was one of the very few instances of spontaneous "revolt" against National Socialism during the thirties. That evening, after vain attempts to disperse the crowd, the police made a large number of arrests. About 250 of the demonstrators, including some ordinands from Finkenwalde, were taken in trucks to the prison in Alexanderplatz where they were temporarily detained.

Bonhoeffer's thoughts constantly returned to Niemöller's arrest. Every birthday and Christmas he sent a thoughtfully worded greeting to Frau Niemöller. In his short letters to Bell from Switzerland during the war there was always be some news of how "Martin" was getting on, for instance on 12 July 1941: "Martin is sound in health and faith and many of my friends are with him now."[230] In Bonhoeffer's 1939 American diary he wrote:

I must learn again how fortunate I have been until now always to have been in the company of the brothers. And for the past two years Niemöller has been alone. Inconceivable. What faith, what discipline and what a clear act of God![231]

The most drastic consequence of Niemöller's arrest for Bonhoeffer was the departure of Franz Hildebrandt. Following the arrest, Hildebrandt had conducted the 12 and 18 July worship services in Dahlem and, as instructed by the Council of Brethren, had read the intercessory lists and taken the Confessional collections. He was then taken away by the Gestapo; the following day *The Times* reported his arrest. Bonhoeffer and other friends thought Hildebrandt's situation highly precarious since he was a "non-Aryan" and therefore likely to be mistreated. Intensive efforts by the Bonhoeffers and others were successful in securing his release after four weeks. Fortunately, the Gestapo had not found his passport and it was still valid, so that the Bonhoeffers were able to arrange his journey to England. Now, finally, he was an emigrant. Rieger took him on as an assistant preacher at St. George's Church.

For Bonhoeffer this was a grievous separation after nine years of the closest communication. On the other hand, in Hildebrandt important ecumenical colleagues were acquiring someone with a useful knowledge of the church struggle and one who shared Bonhoeffer's views. And they still took comfort in the hope that his return home to a new political climate might not be long delayed.

Prisoners from Finkenwalde. Bonhoeffer expected his widely dispersed Finkenwaldians to disobey any prohibitions that affected their village or emergency church congregations. But this demanded increased support from the House of Brethren. In his newsletter on 24 June he wrote:

During these days of trial for our Confessing church we often think of you all and pray more intensely for you, particularly for those who are very much on their own. It is now, especially, that we should rejoice in our community and remain loyal to one another in daily intercession. During the period of meditation please keep in mind the names of all the brethren who were with you here so that none is excluded from our common prayer. In addition, let us especially remember those who have separated themselves from us. These are times when we learn again to pray the first petitions of the Lord's Prayer: Hallowed be thy name; Thy kingdom come; Thy will be done. By these we learn to forget ourselves and our personal condition and to hold them as of little account. How can we remain steadfast as long as we remain so important to ourselves? And nowhere, indeed, could we be better sustained than in the cause of our church, which is the main concern.[232]

In July 1937 the wave of persecution began to engulf former Finkenwaldians. Letters told of interrogations, house searches, confiscations, and arrests. Among the first to be affected was Erich Klapproth in Berlin. Bonhoeffer now had to deal with the parents of the "illegals" for whom the consequences of their sons' disobedience to church and state had gone too far. One mother wrote her son in Finkenwalde, after visiting one of his friends in prison:

> I find it awful and am sad that it is so. Must it truly be this way? "Evangelical Pastor" is written in large letters above the cell door. Every day they are allowed half an hour in the fresh air. Bernhard Riemer was admirable and said that things were really not too bad. But I can't believe him because he somehow looks different and he is suffering. . . . When you see your dearest relatives inside the place, you ask yourself again and again: must it really be so? Isn't there any other way? I am afraid for you. The reality is hard. May God point the way clearly for you. . . . I don't know why it is, but despite your explanations which at the time seem quite clear to me, I always return to a different point of view.

Riemer's mother saw it otherwise:

> I haven't yet come round to "Father forgive them." . . . He was content and sent his greetings to everyone and said you must not worry on his account. Annemarie [his wife] is brave and not one to be sorry for herself. On Sunday Heider [the neighboring pastor] was arrested and taken away immediately after church, so there are no longer any services in Völpke. Heider had already counted on this and in his last sermon again said clearly what needed to be said. . . . Heider gave instructions that if no one was available on Sunday, the bells should not be rung, nor should a service be held, nor should there be a reading. . . .

Bonhoeffer now began to write detailed letters to relatives whenever a Finkenwaldian was arrested:

> It is often difficult for us to grasp God's way with his church. But we may attain peace in the certainty that your son is suffering for the sake of the Lord and that the church of Jesus intercedes for him in prayer. The Lord confers great honor on his servants when he brings them suffering. . . . G.,

however, will pray that you place everything in God's hands and that you will give thanks for everything that God may visit on you and on his church.[233]

He arranged with Frau von Kleist-Retzow that she should invite the young wives of the arrested men to her country home in Klein-Krössin.

While the wave of arrests was at its height the Confessing church of the Old Prussian Union held a Confessing synod in Lippstadt from 23 to 27 August 1937. There were fears that at the forthcoming Party rally in Nuremberg the entire Confessing church would be banned. In this atmosphere the Lippstadt synod unanimously demanded a firm stand on every point of contention: For the sake of the Gospel we must assert our right to our own teaching office in the church, we must hold fast to what remains of church discipline by naming those who have left us, we must name individually in intercession those who have been disciplined or arrested, we may not yield one step in the matter of offertories.[234] Of all the synods during the German church struggle, Lippstadt was the one most overshadowed by the arrests, yet it was also the most unequivocal of them all. To Bonhoeffer it came as particularly welcome backing for his actions.

By Christmas 1937 his assistant director of studies, Fritz Onnasch, had also been arrested. Bonhoeffer summed up:

> This time the annual balance sheet pretty well speaks for itself. Twenty-seven of your circle have been in prison, in many cases for several months. Some are there still and have spent the entire Advent in prison. Of the others, there cannot be anyone who has not had some sort of experience either in his work or in his private life of the increasingly impatient attacks by the anti-Christian forces.[235]

Bonhoeffer organized a visiting service; the House of Brethren circulated the names and addresses of those who had been arrested. He was deeply moved by some of the visits he made himself, for example, to Fritz Onnasch, Willi Rott, and others. He was concerned that those arrested might not know how to pass the time when shut up in a cell. "Horrid if nothing occurs to you," he remarked to Rott in Moabit.[236]

Sealing the Doors. Remarkably, however, during the summer of 1937 the seminary was still removed from the immediate line of fire. The emergency church in Finkenwalde, with its proclamations and collections every Sunday, had either escaped attention or been deliberately overlooked. This was not that unusual at the time. There was still no known ministerial prohibition that explicitly mentioned the preachers' seminaries, and even the far from inconspicuous evangelical missions had not been banned entirely.

Bonhoeffer, therefore, carried on the work as before. He finished his *Discipleship* manuscript as planned, spent a few sunny July days on the Baltic with the fifth student group, and then, on 8 September 1937, concluded the term with the customary farewell party. From a distance he followed foreign newspaper accounts of the ecumenical world conferences in Oxford and Edinburgh. He became convinced that the Confessing church's absence and Niemöller's imprisonment spoke more eloquently than a full delegation could have done.

Accompanied by Bethge, Bonhoeffer went on holiday to the Königssee and Grainau, but because of bad weather he returned north to visit his relatives in Göttingen. There, on 28 September 1937, he received a surprise telephone call from Stettin. The Gestapo had arrived at the almost empty house in Finkenwalde; Fritz Onnasch and the housekeeper, Frau Struwe, had been forced to accept the closing down of the house and had moved out after the doors were sealed. Not until the next day did the newspapers publish the order "issued by the S.S. National Leader and Chief of the German Police" to close the seminary. Mysteriously, this document, dated 29 August 1937, had just been made public:

> The position of the bodies of the so-called Confessing church, as exemplified by their long-standing practice of using their own organizations to train and examine young theologians in defiance of the institutions set up by the state, implies a deliberate contravention of the Fifth Decree for the Implementation of the Law for the Protection of the German Evangelical Church of 2 December 1935 and is likely to endanger the state's authority and welfare. By agreement with the Reich and Prussian Minister for Science, Education and Popular Training and the Reich and Prussian Minister for Church Affairs, I hereby direct that in accordance with Article 1 of the Reich President's Decree for the Protection of People and State of 28 February 1933 the ad hoc academic institutions, study communities and the teaching, students' and examination boards set up by the so-called Confessing church be dissolved and all theological courses and study conferences under its administration forbidden.[237]

The other Confessional seminaries were closed soon afterward. There was much sympathy everywhere with these last centers of church resistance. On 29 September 1937 the Confessing congregation in Neuruppin put out a leaflet:

We have been informed that the preachers' seminary in Finkenwalde has been sealed by the Gestapo. Since the welfare of the seminary and particularly the fortunes of its ordinands—Seydel and Klapproth were among their number—have been the object of our sympathy through our prayers and offerings, it is now our duty to commend the brethren to God's protection in their hour of need. . . . The Council of Brethren.[238]

Should this blow be taken lying down? Must the work that Bonhoeffer held most dear be ended this way? Must the House of Brethren become a thing of the past? Could anything be done? These questions occupied Bonhoeffer's mind as he traveled from Göttingen to Berlin. On arriving he could barely make his way to the house on Marienburger Allee because of the crowds and barricades: the streetcar station on Heerstrasse, only five minutes away from his parents' home, had been prepared for the lavish reception ordered by Hitler for Mussolini's state visit to Berlin.

Now Bonhoeffer and his colleagues went into action. They circulated a petition stating that the preachers' seminaries could not be affected by the order since they had not been named in it, nor had they taught "in defiance of the institutions set up by the state." Perels sent a memorandum to the state police in Stettin suggesting that perhaps they had gone too far in what was an isolated, local case. Other seminaries were still in existence. Albrecht Schönherr, who had become the pastor in Brüssow, the village on the Mackensen estate, persuaded the elderly Field Marshal von Mackensen to write a personal letter to the minister. On 26 October the Lutheran Council and the Provisional Administration even issued a joint protest against Himmler's order; once again, the signatures of Bishop Marahrens, Thomas Breit, and Pastor Fritz Müller from Dahlem appeared together.

It became evident by mid-November 1937 that neither legal representations, nor petitions, nor personal letters would be successful in forcing a review of the decision. The notice terminating the lease of the Finkenwalde house was effective as of 1 December 1937. The Confessional parish in Finkenwalde was able to hold its gatherings for another two years.

Now the weeks in Berlin were filled with new considerations. While events such as the resignation of economic minister Hjalmar Schacht on 26 November 1937 gave Bonhoeffer some vague political hopes, thoughts about a new career or even some political activity were still far off. He still felt committed to his office as an educational director for the Confessing church; it was simply that new forms for this had to be discovered. Aside from being forbidden to teach at the university, Bonhoeffer had no other personal restrictions.

Besides the many discussions, however, Berlin had much else to offer and Bonhoeffer did not fail to take full advantage of it. They celebrated Wilhelm Rott's release from prison by attending *Don Giovanni* at the State Opera. At the end of October 1937 there was the festival of German church music in Berlin. Bonhoeffer maintained that this had brought together the most gifted composers who, as part of the process of inner emigration, had turned to church music. On New Year's Eve 1937 Karl Bonhoeffer wrote: "So far as we are concerned the [Gestapo's] intervention had its good side because we had Dietrich and his friend Bethge with us for a number of weeks."

CHAPTER ELEVEN

THE COLLECTIVE PASTORATES: 1938–1940

Bonhoeffer spent the last days of September 1938 alone with Bethge in the Leibholz home in Göttingen; he had helped his twin sister Sabine and her family to emigrate. Now he worked in Gerhard Leibholz's study on his little book *Life Together*. But the times were anything but tranquil; the Sudeten crisis was intensifying and the English and German radio news grew more ominous every day. Was war coming? Would the coup being prepared be in time to forestall Hitler? Suddenly it was time to stop writing; they hurried to Berlin.

When he returned to Göttingen, Bethge wrote several friends:

> We are quite exhausted after the frantic strain, and many people are still in no condition to enjoy any peace of mind [i.e., through the Munich agreement]. In this threatening situation we went to Berlin to get more precise information, through endless lines of confiscated cars and trucks, to discuss our own position with the leaders of the Confessing church as pastors in the event of war, and possibly to force the Evangelical church Council to recognize us so that we could put in a claim. Indeed, if it came to the worst, the entire administration of the Confessing church might be put out of action. . . . We introduced this argument with all possible force. Everyone was overburdened; it was a good thing we could help to get things moving . . . but hopefully now all this is no longer necessary. . . . In fact, after twenty-four hours we wanted to return here. But then events happened so quickly that we had to postpone our departure from hour to hour.[1]

The overwhelming events not only included the surprising departure of Chamberlain, Daladier, and Mussolini for Munich. Some insiders had expected General von Witzleben to instigate a coup after Hitler ordered the action against Czechoslovakia; this had now been prevented by the different turn of events. In addition, Albertz and Böhm recommended a special prayer liturgy in the name of the Provisional Church Administration, which contained a prayer of repentance for averting "God's judgment." And menacing reactions came from the S.S. "Black Corps" and the Minister for Church Affairs.

Life Together and war, Confessing church and a coup, the ministry and emigration—all these things converged to shape the period of Bonhoeffer's life that was now beginning and would bring him to his most momentous decision.

Neither Bonhoeffer nor those in his charge realized at first that the new form of training ordinands—shifting the work from the Finkenwalde seminary to a collective pastorate—meant considerable changes for Bonhoeffer personally. The educational activities in the villages of eastern Pomerania were designed to be a direct continuation of the previous work. His teaching lost little of its former freshness. And yet, imperceptibly, his path had been set in a different direction. Each of the following years was a significant turning point:

In 1938 he was heavily engaged in ecclesiastical, political, and family affairs, but he still tried with undiminished strength to keep up his former way of life.

In 1939 he tried hard, with the help of English and American friends, to continue his theological existence; with that in view he went to England and America.

In 1940, after he had returned from America, he was ready for the tasks that would bring more ambiguity, even duplicity, into his life. Those same tasks, however, empowered his theology with a new freedom.

The issues that dominated the next two and a half years were the collective pastorate, the disappointments of the church struggle, the political maelstrom, the fate of the family, the attempt to "flee" westward, and his return to Germany in the first winter of the war.

The Backwoods of Pomerania

In November 1937 Field Marshal von Mackensen's intervention on behalf of Finkenwalde was summarily rejected, and the Stettin superintendent of police bluntly rebuffed the petition Perels had prepared for the Council of Brethren. The church authorities in Berlin were uncertain how to respond. Niesel, Perels, and Bonhoeffer considered whether the training of candidates shouldn't simply be resumed—openly, in the old form of a seminary—in a new location. Wasn't this the right time for the Confessing church to claim publicly its right to run its own system of instruction? That was Hans Iwand's opinion; with the backing of Superintendent Fritz Heuner, he tried to reopen his East Prussian seminary in its old form in Dortmund. But the entire group was arrested and later expelled from Dortmund; and the police now dissolved the seminaries in Elberfeld and Bielefeld as well. Only Gerhard Gloege's seminary in Naumburg-on-Queis remained until March 1938. If they really wanted to keep training ministers, their insistence on working as they always had was becoming more questionable. Bonhoeffer hesitated: "Either we remain in Stettin, even in a different form, or we go right away from Pomerania, as I should not be loath to do in view of the wretched Council of Brethren."[2]

Finally, the importance of the work itself won out over trying to make a point, and they agreed to use the model of "collective pastorates." Similar arrangements already existed among minority church groups such as the West German Reformed Church. Their reasoning was based upon the observation that apprenticeships under clergymen in legal ministries had not yet been challenged, even in cases where these clergy were known as uncompromising supporters of the Confessing church. Ordinands could be placed together as "apprentice vicars" in those church districts where enough superintendents and pastors were prepared to let these "apprenticeships" be used for continuing education. Each ordinand simply had to register individually with the local police that he was working under the parish pastor, and perform occasional parish duties. They could try to bring the ordinands together in a few places for ongoing training and have them live most of the time in the same location.

Thus Bonhoeffer's ordinands lived in two vicarages in eastern Pomerania almost as they had lived in Finkenwalde, only in smaller numbers and under more primitive conditions. Both collective pastorates included from seven to ten ordinands for each course. None of them could claim to be enrolled in a preaching seminary; they had to assert that their position was that of an apprentice vicar in a parish whose name they hardly knew. This arrangement worked smoothly until strict military conscription brought all the ordinands of the Confessing church into the army. In March 1940 the police came on the scene to shut down the secluded retreat. In those two and a half years Bonhoeffer's collective pastorate added five more courses in eastern Pomerania to the five in Finkenwalde. The seminaries in Elberfeld (under the direction of Hermann Hesse) and Frankfurt-am-Main (supervised by Walter Kreck and Karl Gerhard Steck) also continued until that date.

Köslin and Schlawe. An offer made by two neighboring superintendents turned the scales in favor of the seclusion of eastern Pomerania; they accepted the risk of the collective pastorate and immediately began to work on the details. During the confusion of the period of the church committees, both superintendents had been able to keep an appreciable number of their pastors in the newly formed Confessing church. They were accustomed to using every possibility they still had to govern their own local church affairs. They now managed to house the two groups of ordinands or apprentice vicars unostentatiously in remote parishes.

One of them was candidate Fritz Onnasch's father, the superintendent of Köslin. The capital of the district, Köslin had some thirty thousand inhabitants and was about a hundred miles northeast of Stettin. As in many northeast German towns, a massive St. Mary's Church stood in the town center. The town's five Confessing pastors and a few in the villages were able to accept up to ten vicars or seminary candidates; all the candidates lived together in Superintendent Onnasch's spacious vicarage on Elisenstrasse. There was room in the house for classes, as well as a room for Bonhoeffer when he stayed in Köslin; Bonhoeffer, however, did not register with the police there as a resident. Fritz Onnasch led the group as inspector of studies. His father had installed him in the vacant post of assistant preacher in his parish, thus saving the Old Prussian Council of Brethren one salary. The collective pastorate in Köslin shared in the life of the local capital in eastern Pomerania, and the active Confessing congregation took the young men to its heart. There was regular contact with the well-known doctor August Knorr. The work in Köslin ended in the autumn of 1939 when the number of candidates dwindled because of the war.

The other superintendent, Eduard Block, lived in the small town of Schlawe, twenty-five miles further to the east toward Stolp; its population was barely ten thousand. Two old town gates and the solid St. Mary's Church overlooked the rows of houses around the cobbled market square. Both Bonhoeffer and Bethge had positions here as assistant ministers; Bethge was inspector of studies. When Bonhoeffer registered with the police he gave the address of Superintendent Block on Koppelstrasse as his place of residence. In 1939 he received communications at that address from the military recruitment office, and in 1940 the local Gestapo headquarters contacted him there.

Although there was seldom any need for it, Block always kept a bed ready for Bonhoeffer. He also took care of official inquiries and telephone calls, skillfully thwarted police inquiries, or ensured that if Bonhoeffer was wanted he was there at the right time. Using a code, Block sent shrewdly worded messages on postcards. He was not easily rattled, and Bonhoeffer valued his way of doing things as much as he valued his wife's cooking.

The ordinands moved even further east, into the rambling, wind-battered parsonage in Gross-Schlönwitz, at the boundary of the church district. The tiny parish was a few miles south of Reich Highway 2, which ran from Köslin to Stolp. The ordinands could only live there if they had adequate transportation, and so they began to work toward the previously unheard-of purchase of an additional car and a motorcycle. Bonhoeffer taught regularly in Schlawe during the second half of the week and stayed on weekends. He was always concerned that the Köslin ordinands get some relaxation elsewhere, perhaps by taking a lengthy break on the Baltic. Whatever the weather, he covered the forty miles between his two places of work twice a week, besides having to travel frequently to Berlin on personal or church political matters.

A year and a half later, when the young pastor in charge of the parish in Gross-Schlönwitz married and needed the vicarage, the group in Schlawe moved (in April 1939) to nearby Sigurdshof, an empty farmstead that the landowner, von Kleist of Wendisch-Tychow, had put at the superintendent's disposal. The small house was two miles south of the village on the estate, and it was more secluded than anywhere they had lived up to that point. Four tiny windows looked out the front onto a little-used courtyard, under an overhanging roof and through luxurious climbing plants. In the back the idyllic Wipper River flowed by. There was a water pump beneath the nearest trees, where a vast forest began that merged with the Varzin woods of the Bismarck estate to the south. There was no electricity, and the housekeeper Erna Struwe, who had remained loyal since Finkenwalde days, had to solve problems that were unrelated to the wartime economy that had set in. Anyone who did not find even this situation quiet enough could withdraw to a hunting lodge farther away in the forest. In the summer they could use the count's fishing skiff on the pond and the tennis court at the Tychow manor house. In the winter of 1939–1940 Bonhoeffer and his ordinands went skiing and skating. Difficulties in obtaining supplies alternated with times of special pleasure:

> We are anxious about our coal; and besides that, we have no paraffin, so we have to use candles. We all stay in one room, and someone plays or reads aloud.[3]

> I arrived here yesterday. . . . Yesterday afternoon I could not stop myself from joining the skiers in the snow-covered wood. It was really lovely, and so peaceful that everything else seemed like an apparition. Generally speak-

ing, I really feel more and more that life in the country, especially in times like these, has much more human dignity than in towns. All the manifestations of the masses simply fall away. I think the contrast between Berlin and this secluded farmstead is particularly striking now.[4]

We are now fairly snowed in and cut off. The postal van can't get through, and we can get nothing except now and then by sled. . . . Minus 28 degrees. . . . Under the circumstances the work goes well. The forester has let us have two loads of wood and two hundred kilograms of coal, and that will do for a few weeks. Of course, the food supply is rather difficult too, but we still have enough. If I had my way, I think I should like to leave town for good.[5]

The black ice here is indescribable after a good deal of flooding. Up to within ten yards of the house the meadows have turned into a magnificent skating rink. But that is catastrophic for the fields, and for the wildlife too. . . . We again have enough fuel for a week.[6]

For two days we have been deep in snow with almost uninterrupted snowstorms. Now the thaw will have to start all over again. From an agricultural point of view things are really very bad. People had been so pleased about the few days' thaw, and now they are quite depressed.[7]

When the thaw finally set in on 15 March they went on holiday. Three days later, the Gestapo ordered Frau Struwe to shut the place down, just as they had done in Finkenwalde.

Work and meditation, worship, homiletics, and examining the underlying concepts of the New Testament—all this was carried on in the small undistracted circle of the collective pastorates almost more intensively than in the spacious house in Finkenwalde. Elsewhere in the country those in the Confessing church knew that Bonhoeffer was carrying on his work. They did not ask where and how, but rumors still circulated about the "legalism" and "monasticism" of Bonhoeffer's seminaries; these arose especially from the new divisions within the church and the stubborn battles about what course the Confessing church should take. After the course, a Berlin ordinand who was later killed in the war wrote to Bonhoeffer:

I did not go to Schlönwitz eagerly or hopefully. . . . I looked toward this period of physical and mental constriction with a shudder. I thought of it as a necessary evil that one had to bear with a good grace and go through for the sake of self-discipline. . . . It all turned out differently from the way I had feared. Instead of the stuffy atmosphere of theological cant, I found a world that embraced a great deal of what I love and need: straightforward theological work in a friendly community, where no unpleasant notice was taken of one's limitations, but where the work was made a pleasure; brotherhood under the Word irrespective of the person, and with it all, open-mindedness and love for everything that still makes this fallen creation lovable—music, literature, sport and the beauty of the earth—a grand way of life. . . . When I look back today, I have a clear picture before me: the brothers sitting down to their afternoon coffee and their bread and jam. The chief has come back after being away rather a long time. . . . Now we get the latest news, and the world breaks into the peacefulness and simplicity of life on a Pomeranian estate. . . . Does it dull the objectivity of your theological view, when I write that it was the peripheral things that increased my delight in what is central?[8]

A Changed Style. 1. The collective pastorate did not get the support from the House of Brethren that the Finkenwalde seminary had. This was more noticeable from the outside. In both collective pastorates Bonhoeffer was assisted by inspectors of studies who had been familiar with the methods and goals of daily community life since 1935; in addition, the groups were rarely as small as those in the House of Brethren. Outside the community, however, a number of undertakings that had been made possible by the House of Brethren, such as the evangelical mission, failed to survive.

This cessation of all help made contact with the former Finkenwalde students very difficult. Initially they were not even told Bonhoeffer's addresses or that of his collective pastorates, or anything about the organization of the new work. Bonhoeffer wrote every newsletter himself. Because of press restrictions these had to be marked "personal letter"; thus there are more newsletters in Bonhoeffer's own handwriting from the period of the collective pastorates than from the previous years.

The increased distances made frequent visits to the candidates impossible, and so Bonhoeffer proposed that they should send him their sermons and that he would return them with his suggestions. A number of them availed themselves gratefully of the offer.

Bonhoeffer managed to arrange one more retreat for all his former students. At the end of July 1938, a time of extremely passionate debates within the Confessing church, he gathered forty five young pastors in Zingst, the original meeting place. The tenacious campaign of the consistories to legalize the illegal ordinands had just begun—an attempt to break the ranks of those who still stood firm, partly with threats and partly with enticements. The struggle over the pastors' oath of allegiance to Hitler was almost lost. During those days in Zingst Bonhoeffer conducted a biblical study on "temptation." Those present committed themselves to the "pastoral service that we owe to our fellows who have left us for the consistory. It is intended that each of them shall be visited by two ordinands in the near future."[9]

We owe not only *Temptation* and *Life Together* to the end of the House of Brethren, but also the collection of Finkenwalde newsletters, which provide a colorful picture of the life of the illegal pastors in the Confessing church during this long troubled period.

2. From this time on, Bonhoeffer's way of life was unsettled. Up to his death he never again had a permanent residence. His small writing desk stood for a year and a half in Gross-Schlönwitz and for another year in Sigurdshof; but he never used it for more than three days a week, and his books and manuscripts were never again together in one place. The university lectures and the rough draft of *Discipleship* stayed in the cartons that a loyal member of the Finkenwalde community stored in his attic in Altdamm. Some of Bonhoeffer's tasteful furniture went to the collective pastorates, some to Berlin with a number of his books. During the war his possessions were again dispersed, when he transferred valuable books, furniture, and diaries from his time in Spain to the estate of his fiancée's parents in Neumark, where they were lost in 1945.

Thus Bonhoeffer taught, reflected, and wrote after 1937 with no settled place to work and without his book collection, which was such a valuable reference and had always been at hand until then. Only for the work on ethics during the war did he try once more in Berlin to collect any considerable number of relevant books. He hardly ever spoke of the handicap caused by the lack of a fixed address. He could rely on his memory, which generally provided what he needed.

Increasingly, however—more than he actually admitted—he longed for settled work, and sometimes he would heave a deep sigh over his gypsy-like existence. Although he never acknowledged it, the flight in 1939 to the United States was partly a result of this yearning to settle down. He expressed the unattainable wish for a few quiet months to work in a letter to Erwin Sutz in September 1938, when he wrote: "It is a pity that you did not get me to Zurich for a year as a substitute for Brunner! That would not have been bad at all."[10] He told friends abroad what he would not say in Gross-Schlönwitz and Köslin, especially when they told him of their professional progress out there:

> The only strange thing is this existence in which there can be no anxieties, because each day is a gift. If one forgets that, one sometimes gets rather restive, and would prefer to choose a more settled existence with all the "rights" that normally go with one's "rank" and age. But this would mean abandoning the work, and it will not do at the moment.[11]

Lasserre has married. That course is not yet open to people like ourselves; life is too nomadic. But we have a great deal of pleasure in our work instead.[12]

My work goes on normally. Only one sometimes gets a bit fed up with the nomadic life, and would like to be more settled and domesticated. . . . But it will not do just now, and I am glad to be allowed to work here.[13]

Thus the former university lecturer and seminary director clearly felt the drawbacks of his new status as an assistant minister.

3. Of course, the discontinuance of the House of Brethren and his unsettled life made those people who offered him a home even more significant.

Since Finkenwalde had been closed down, Bonhoeffer had grown to enjoy the holiday home that Hans-Jürgen von Kleist-Retzow in Kieckow and his mother in nearby Klein-Krössin made available. The elderly woman had been deeply affected when the "Finkenwalde people" had to move to a place more than 120 miles from Stettin, particularly since she and friends in Stettin had begun to study the recently published *Discipleship* and always had some question about it.

Bonhoeffer began to send people from his own circle who were feeling worn out to the Kleist estates fairly often. Werner Koch's fiancée found rest and friendship there after his arrest, and after his release Koch himself was immediately invited to Klein-Krössin. After an operation, another ordinand was well cared for in a good hospital at Bonhoeffer's expense, and then was able to recuperate at the Kleist home.[14] Their hospitality was unlimited; anyone whom Bonhoeffer recommended was accepted at once.

Above all, however, his parents' home became a renewed center of his attention. Its importance as a meeting place and a source of political information grew after some of the resistance circles in the conspiracy had begun to form. On the other hand, the Bonhoeffers' anxieties intensified after the police action in Finkenwalde. They said little about this kind of thing, but Karl-Friedrich, the eldest son, felt it advisable to warn his younger brother not to do anything to attract unnecessary attention, as this would only increase the anxiety of their parents, who were already disturbed about the fate of the Leibholzes. Bonhoeffer wrote to his brother:

I am sorry if mother is worried and causing others to worry as well. Indeed, there is really no reason for this. The fact that I may be affected just as hundreds of people have already been affected by Himmler's edict really must no longer be permitted to upset us. We cannot hold out on the church question without making sacrifices. You, in fact, risked a lot in the war. Why shouldn't we do likewise for the church? And why should someone want to dissuade us? Certainly none of us is eager to go to prison. However, if it does come to that, then we shall do so—hopefully, anyway—with joy since it is such a worthy cause. We start again at the beginning of next week.[15]

In 1943, when Bonhoeffer was finally arrested under quite different circumstances, his parents made no reproaches.

Despite the greater distances, Bonhoeffer visited his parents' home more frequently and for longer periods than he had from Finkenwalde. When he returned to Köslin or Gross-Schlönwitz, eagerly awaited, he brought the latest news to his ordinands. But if the conversation began to move toward topics that might affect him and his future course of action, he could no longer take the ordinands into his confidence. The newcomers hardly noticed that a slight reserve crept in at this point. But some of the older Finkenwalde students could already sense that, in the changed times, Bonhoeffer was beginning to turn his attention toward other spheres with which they were less familiar.

The Low Point of the Church Struggle

In 1938 the greatest weaknesses of the Confessing church became evident.

Dr. Werner's most startling accomplishments were his promise of the pastors' oath of loyalty on Hitler's birthday in 1938, and the Godesberg declaration in 1939. The loyalty oath issue drove the Confessing church into a state of paralysis that lasted a long time; because of the controversy there was little or no reaction from the Confessing church to Barth's letter to Professor Hromádka in Prague, to the pressing question of the 1938 prayer liturgy, or to the November 1938 pogrom—the so-called *Kristallnacht*. Only their indignation over the Godesberg declaration united the disordered ranks once more. These matters, which were not usually published in the daily papers, were constantly accompanied by the far less spectacular question of the legal status of the illegal pastors. But the legalization issue became the central challenge to the Councils of Brethren and their claim to leadership during the final part of the German church struggle. It demanded Bonhoeffer's attention more than the other matters, called "Werner's trump cards."

In fact, at the beginning of 1938 the church's situation seemed to have eased somewhat. The numbers of those arrested fell rapidly and did not seem likely to increase again. During the heavy-handed police measures of 1937 a respectable portion of the clergy had stood its ground. In response the Nazi state seemed willing to avoid a public commotion, at the least. But it developed new methods, which proved even more effective.

Paralyzed Communications. The "intercession lists" (*Fürbittenlisten*) remained lengthy, but the lists of those arrested were shorter. Instead people grew accustomed to a range of new expressions for "restraints": prohibitions against public speaking, expulsions, banishments, residential prohibitions, travel restrictions, restrictions on official ministerial functions. Each of these measures was deliberately ordered to make communication among the leading men of the Confessing church impossible, without their being arrested. It was largely successful. A September 1938 intercession list, for instance, showed only ten arrests, including those sent to concentration camps; but to make up for that there were 93 ministerial prohibitions and 97 residential and travel prohibitions and expulsions. Another list on 30 August 1939, on the eve of the war, lists 121 ministerial prohibitions; 150 residential and travel prohibitions, expulsions, and banishments; 44 prohibitions against public speaking; and only 11 arrests, besides 3 internments in concentration camps.

An "expulsion" forbade a person to stay in the place where he normally worked and lived (as, for example, in the case of Pastor Paul Schneider in Dickenschied), but allowed him to live anywhere else in Germany. A "banishment" was a police order directing an arrested person to live in a place distant from his home, as when Dortmund church superintendent Karl Lücking and, later, Superintendent Onnasch were banished to the Grenzmark region near Poland. A "residential prohibition" kept important people from attending any meetings in Berlin; this, together with the "travel restriction," prevented them from seeing people from Berlin such as Niesel, Albertz, Böhm, and Fritz Müller. "Prohibitions on official duties" prevented Confessing church pastors from entering certain church buildings to which they had rightful access. Through this ingenious system, the state made consultations (for example, about the oath of allegiance) among church leaders from the different regions very difficult. All this contributed greatly to the widespread perplexity about what to do next.

Exiled from Berlin. In January 1938 Bonhoeffer's name was added to the intercession list; he had been banned from staying in Berlin. But his first trip from the collective pastorates had taken him to the capital city.

On 11 January 1938 the chief instructors and chairmen of the ordinands' brotherhoods in the Old Prussian Confessing church met under Niesel's leadership in the parish hall in Dahlem. A column of Gestapo officers appeared, thinking they would be able to disrupt a secret lecture of the banned church seminary. The thirty men at the meeting were taken to the Gestapo offices on Alexanderplatz. After an interrogation lasting seven hours, those who lived in Berlin received a prohibition on traveling. The Gestapo prohibited those from the provinces from entering Berlin, and put each of them on the train for his particular destination. The police put Bonhoeffer and Fritz Onnasch, who had attended the meeting as leaders of the Pomeranian ordinands' brotherhood, onto a train for Stettin.

Expecting the building to be searched, the ordinands in Köslin and Gross-Schlönwitz cleared all the documents related to the Council of Brethren out of the desks and cupboards. They naturally feared that the collective pastorates' work that had just been begun would now be subjected to a most unwelcome investigation.

But the Gestapo action in Berlin had obviously not been directed at Bonhoeffer personally, nor did it mean that his work as the "assistant minister of Schlawe" would be halted. At the same time, this new encounter with the Gestapo was far from welcome. At the very time when political crises were brewing in Berlin, it was fatal to be cut off from his information center on Marienburger Allee by the restriction on entering Berlin. Schacht's retirement and the beginning of the General Fritsch crisis had aroused new hopes. For that reason Bonhoeffer's father intervened with the Gestapo against his son's exclusion from Berlin. His prestige brought success; the authorities conceded that the prohibition applied only to work-related matters. The son was free to visit his family in Berlin. At the beginning of February, Dietrich and his parents met at Ruth von Kleist-Retzow's home in Stettin to discuss the matter. He then returned with his parents to Berlin, where meanwhile Hans von Dohnanyi had become involved with the Fritsch crisis and Martin Niemöller's trial was beginning. Bonhoeffer lodged a formal complaint with the police, giving his own account of the meeting on 11 January and asking for the prohibition to be rescinded entirely, but received no reply.[16]

Thus the prohibition on entering Berlin for Bonhoeffer was never rescinded, but his father was able to modify its effects. Bonhoeffer went to Berlin more frequently than before, but did not appear at conferences. He went to the homes of Niesel, Böhm, or Perels to deal with matters of work or church politics, or he received his friends at his parents' home. He preferred personal messengers to telephone conversations.

Bonhoeffer had a fundamental dislike for unconsidered risks, whether in matters small or great. Otto Dudzus once told of Bonhoeffer's annoyance after his students ran across the lines at the Danish border station, instead of using the bridge.[17] However untidy his desk was, there were never any compromising slips of paper or memoranda to be found there. He could become quite angry when things were not thought out beforehand. He calculated every possible sequence of events carefully and in good time. His capacity for imagination sometimes caused him more distress than his friends thought necessary.

The Loyalty Oath. That April Bonhoeffer's holiday journey took him through a Thuringian countryside decorated with flags. On the occasion of the Austrian *Anschluss* the cross on the Wartburg had been replaced during Holy Week by an immense floodlit swastika. Bishop Sasse of Thuringia had already required his pastors to take an oath of allegiance to Hitler on 15 March, and he telegraphed Hitler:

> My *Führer,* I report: in a great historic hour all the pastors of the Thuringian Evangelical Church, obeying an inner command, have with joyful hearts taken an oath of loyalty to *Führer* and Reich. . . . One God— one obedience in the faith. Hail, my *Führer!*[18]

Mecklenburg, Saxony, and other regional churches followed the same "inner command."

Bonhoeffer soon turned back and sought rest in the Friedrichsbrunn house. From there he wrote to Frau Niemöller, whose husband had been taken to the Sachsenhausen concentration camp after being acquitted by the court: "God has so directed it that a special blessing goes out from your house to the parish and to the whole church."[19] Meanwhile Dr. Werner in Berlin was preparing the evangelical pastors' "spontaneous" birthday present for Hitler.

As director of the evangelical consistory, Friedrich Werner would use legal, financial, and administrative measures to bring the pastors into line with the Third Reich. Beyond that, however, he set out to tie people to Hitler intellectually and emotionally, and to complete the "Aryanization" of church doctrine. He now turned to administrative measures to implement what had been attempted more spontaneously in 1933. In 1934 the Reich bishop would have been only too pleased to present Hitler with an oath of loyalty at the national synod, but the attempt had failed at that time. Now, drawing on the wave of enthusiasm for the Austrian *Anschluss,* Werner issued an order in the *Legal Gazette* of 20 April 1938 that all pastors in active office were to take the oath of allegiance to the *Führer.* The order, and the explanation of the oath that went with it, attested to Werner's cynical thoughtlessness. But the action was a great success for Werner, as it plunged the Confessing church into its most shameful affair.

In that moment of general enthusiasm anyone who pointed out that he had already taken an oath of allegiance at his ordination, and had voted "yes" in the plebiscite on 10 April, was already betraying a caution that made him suspicious to the Nazis. The text of Werner's ordinance in the *Legal Gazette* was strongly worded:

> In the recognition that only those may hold office in the church who are unswervingly loyal to the *Führer,* the people and the Reich, it is hereby decreed:
>
> Anyone who is called to a spiritual office is to affirm his loyal duty with the following oath: "I swear that I will be faithful and obedient to Adolf Hitler, the *Führer* of the German Reich and people, that I will conscientiously observe the laws and carry out the duties of my office, so help me God." . . . Anyone who was called before this decree came into force . . . is to take the oath of allegiance retroactively. . . .
>
> Anyone who refuses to take the oath of allegiance is to be dismissed. 20 April 1938. Dr. Werner.

That announcement in the *Legal Gazette* also contained a forceful "address of the Evangelical High Church Council regarding the oath of allegiance," which stated that the oath was "more than a mere confirmation of the duty enjoined on Christians by the New Testament to be subject to the authorities." "It means the most intimate solidarity with the Third Reich . . . and with the man who has created that community and embodies it." The oath of allegiance "means personal commitment to the *Führer* under the solemn summons of God." Indeed, the person who takes the oath testified "that he is prepared to fulfill in its entirety the commission that he accepted at his ordination, in the steadfast consciousness of his obligation toward *Führer*, people and Reich."[20]

This oath expressed more than most pastors could declare with a clear conscience at that point, for it made a farce of their ordination vows. Among the "Dahlemites," the first reaction in the Confessing church was widespread refusal. Bonhoeffer felt that the oath was quite impossible; but, like the illegal pastors who were supported only by the Confessing church, the peculiar terms of his employment meant that he had no official status as a pastor within the church. Thus he was in the fortunate position of not being on the list of those required to take the oath by Werner's office.

With pastors caught between the dilemma of not feeling able to act against their consciences and yet still wishing to preserve national proprieties, the Confessing church entered into negotiations for its pastors who were under the jurisdiction of the consistory—that is, for most of the older clergy. Permission was given to take the oath, provided that four conditions were fulfilled: (1) There must be a clear demand by the state, since the

Church of Christ does not introduce oaths; (2) The statement by the High Church Council interpreting the oath must be withdrawn; (3) The authority demanding the oath must accept an interpretation given by pastors who are advised by the Confessing church; and (4) The ordination vows must be publicly recognized, thereby rendering the loyalty oath to the *Führer* the explicit introduction of a civil service law into the church.

When the Confessing synod of the Old Prussian Union discussed these conditions on 11–13 June many pastors in that church had already taken the oath: 60 percent in the Rhineland, 70 percent in Brandenburg, 78 percent in Saxony, 80 percent in Pomerania, 82 percent in Silesia, and 89 percent in the Grenzmark. The remaining pastors, who supported the "Dahlemite" view, viewed the moment when those four conditions might be considered fulfilled with very mixed feelings. This eventually did become the case, although not unambiguously and not, in fact, at Werner's instigation. A second session of the Confessing synod of the Old Prussian Union on 31 July 1938 gave pastors permission to take the oath, by deciding—over the heads of the minority—the criteria by which those four conditions could be considered fulfilled. No one felt entirely at ease during the agonizing deliberations about such discretionary judgments, but the responsible people in the Confessing church no longer wished to take responsibility for refusing the oath.

The pastors' meetings during those weeks were almost unendurable. Bonhoeffer went with his candidates from one meeting to another, but his arguments did not prevail. They were viewed as coming from someone who was not affected. Ultimately there were only a few people who obstinately held their ground, such as K. H. Reimer, the pastor in Naseband, Ewald von Kleist's parish. Guilty consciences burdened the discussions between minority and majority, and spoiled the relationship between the members of the Stettin Council of Brethren, who were in favor of the oath, and the pastors who still refused. There were venomous accusations.

Then, after the overwhelming majority of the pastors had taken the oath, a letter from Martin Bormann (leader of the Nazi office in Munich) to his district leaders was published in the middle of August: "The churches have issued this regulation of their own accord." The oath, Bormann stated, had no significance outside the church. The Party and state were to make no distinction "whether a clergyman has taken an oath of loyalty to the *Führer* or not." An oath was significant "only if the individual took it on the *Führer*'s orders by the Party or by the state."[21]

It was a crushing blow. "When I think of the troubled consciences of individual pastors, until they finally took the oath with a violated conscience, my heart almost stops beating. . . . Reimer is said to have handed in his resignation with some pretty straight language," Frau von Kleist-Retzow lamented to Bonhoeffer after learning how things stood with the Council of Brethren in Stettin.[22]

After the church had consented to the oath on 31 July 1938, Karl Barth had written a bitter letter to Berlin. If no one would say "no" anymore, he said, he would have to say it from abroad:

> I am most deeply shocked by that decision and the arguments used to support it, after I have read and reread them. . . . Was this defeat possible, permissible or necessary? Was there and is there really no one among you at all who can lead you back to the simplicity of the straight and narrow way? . . . No one who beseeches you not to jeopardize the future credibility of the Confessing church in this dreadful way?[23]

There were indeed such people, but they could hardly get a hearing, either technically or, more importantly, spiritually.

At the very time that Barth's letter reached Berlin, a letter from Bonhoeffer arrived as well. Although he had been a solid advocate of the synod's authority, the Old Prussian Confessing synod's treatment of the oath issue had plunged him into a crisis that had never occurred before and never occurred again. He wrote:

> It is a hard step for a Confessing pastor to be compelled to oppose the decision of an Old Prussian Confessing synod, particularly when he is able to look back with nothing but great thankfulness and respect to the service that synod has rendered up to now.[24]

Bonhoeffer denounced the procedure by which the synod had overruled the minority on such a question and had accused the wrong side of being "unclear." With this, he believed, the synod was risking its demand for a spirit of sacrifice among the young "illegal" pastors. How could one demand clarity from the young clergy, if a synod accepted the absence of clarity between Dr. Werner and the pastors, reaching its decision on the oath on this basis? Bonhoeffer had already opposed the very idea of bargaining about the conditions under which the oath could be taken. But now the synod's authority "to speak again to the young brethren" had been lost.[25]

For Bonhoeffer the events connected with the oath were far more than an episode. The mere demand for the oath, however grotesque and blameworthy it was, did not upset him too much, since everyone knew where it came from. But the synod's decision was like a gash in his own flesh that would heal only with difficulty. And it had been inflicted, not by the separated Lutherans, but by his own people:

Shall we learn from this? Will the Confessing church be willing to confess publicly its guilt and the rupture within its ranks? Will it find the room it now needs for prayer, forgiveness and a fresh start? Will it be able in that way to honor the truth, to revive again the disunited brethren's consciences which are simply anxious to reach the truth, and recommit them to God's Word? . . . Does it see how it has endangered its word through its latest meeting? Today these are open questions.[26]

Bonhoeffer was ashamed of the Confessing church, the way one feels shame for a scandal in one's own family. This Confessing synod had approved the oath to the *Führer* when it already knew of the impending order that non-Aryans must have a large "J" stamped on their identity cards—an omen of worse things to come, and the thing that finally moved his twin sister's family to flee. And the threat of war against Czechoslovakia was growing. The possibility of a gap between Bonhoeffer and the Confessing church was becoming real.

Essen III. Bonhoeffer's isolation grew, as did that of the few in Old Prussia who thought as he did. Since the hopes for the 1937 church election and the heavier pressure being exerted by Kerrl, many people were again pursuing the ideal of a "broadly based front." But Bonhoeffer feared that this would only weaken the chances of speaking out clearly on the burning questions in the struggle.

Throughout 1938, repeated attempts were made to bring the church leaders from Munich and Düsseldorf, Stuttgart and Bielefeld, Hannover and Berlin around the same table. Lutheran church leaders and the Provisional Administration had already joined in the "Kassel Council," and had issued a joint pulpit declaration against Alfred Rosenberg (the Nazi propagandist who attacked the churches and called for a "positive" Aryanized Christianity) on the 1937 anniversary of the Reformation, and had even protested together against the Himmler decree. Now Bonhoeffer saw with uneasiness how the Confessing Christians traveled around—when they could still travel!—and drew up one plan after another to bring everyone together: "Dahlemites" with the neutrals, Lutherans with members of the Church of the Prussian Union.

In April 1938 they began to work with concrete goals in mind. Iwand, Karl Koch, and Held from the one side, Meiser and Wurm from the other, along with one of the neutrals such as Hermann Burghart, met under Koch's chairmanship. They sought first to reach a common understanding of "Barmen"; second, to work out transitional regulations to establish peace with the German Evangelical Church; and third, to work out regulations for the appointment of a church government for the Church of the Old Prussian Union. The draft plans were called "Essen I" (report on Barmen), "Essen II" (German Evangelical Church regulations), and "Essen III" (Old Prussian Union administration).

As a pastor within the Old Prussian Union church, Bonhoeffer was directly affected by "Essen III." The draft, with a cover letter from Koch and Fritz Müller to the pastors, was dated 23 August 1938, but it did not reach Bonhoeffer until he was traveling with the Leibholzes from Göttingen as they prepared to leave Germany. After that he took a position on the document. He wanted to destroy the hope, which was emerging from the widespread need for pacification, that this draft designed to promote unity and order would gain the consent of all the factions:

> The denial of everything that God revealed to the synods of Barmen and Dahlem has been made obvious here. (Barmen and Dahlem cannot be ignored for tactical reasons. . . . What is to happen with the "illegal" pastors?) Please do not say that for all kinds of reasons it is most ill-advised to put up any opposition at this particular time. In this situation none of us knows what is ill-advised and what is not. But that it is not advisable to act against God's clear direction, against the acknowledged truth, and against one's conscience, that is certain. You yourself know what confusion the sixth synod caused in the Confessing church.[27] After that defeat we really had expected a different and more spiritual word from our church leaders. What we are being advised now is the self-sacrifice of the Confessing church. Here we can no longer follow.[28]

Ruth von Kleist-Retzow's verdict was: "The Essen draft seems to me nothing but plain unvarnished unbelief, all I have to do is look at the potpourri of signatures."[29] It was a caustic remark, given the difficulty of trying to bring old comrades-in-arms together again; but Bonhoeffer essentially shared her opinion.

It may be that Bonhoeffer did not take the question of unity and the broadest possible "Confessing front" seriously enough at that point. But since he didn't expect anything else, he did not suffer so much from the Evangelical church's lack of unity as a whole. What really worried him was whether there would be a voice on behalf of acknowledged truth. He viewed the understandable demand for appeasement as evil counsel. How should a newly formed assembly of people who had previously maintained cautious silence about the Nazi pretensions suddenly bring itself to speak clearly with one voice? Bonhoeffer did not expect a clearer voice from the Essen negotiations, but a muffled one, even a completely silent one. His apprehensions were confirmed on 9 November 1938, the day of the anti-Jewish pogroms, when everyone was silent.

The church historian Gerhard Niemöller has described how far the isolation of the "Dahlemites" had already gone at the Essen negotiations; some people refused to be seen with them.[30] Being branded as a man of radical temperament did not worry Bonhoeffer. What others considered Dahlem radicalism he viewed as the unsightly remnants of a witness that would later be a cause of shame. Only those who ignored the truly burning questions of the Christian church in the Nazi state could accuse others of "Dahlemitism" and "self-martyrdom." In 1938 "Dahlemitism" was too costly for anyone to indulge in it simply out of temperament or political leanings. Despite his adherence to its original course, Bonhoeffer did not overestimate the merits of the "Dahlemite" sector of the Confessing church. In 1943 he would be prepared to forget any difficulties between the Confessing church and the "Confessional movement" when Bishop Wurm, a man whom he had once distrusted as coming from the Confessional movement, raised his voice against the state's injustice and tried to promote unity at the same time. But in 1938 Bonhoeffer preferred to remain isolated rather than be disloyal to the pathetic group which at least made the occasional attempt at a prophetic ministry, and was prepared to support an activist group of young theologians.

Hromádka and the Prayer Liturgy. Only a few weeks after the Essen III meeting an event occurred that gave marked impetus to the desire for a broadly based and peaceful middle ground that would exclude the radical "Dahlemites" of the left and the Thuringian "German Christians" of the right. It also painfully exposed the nationalism within the Confessing church. In fact, there were two events that were widely viewed as related, but which those involved were most anxious to keep separate.

In late September 1938 Martin Albertz and Hans Böhm produced a prayer liturgy for the Provisional Administration of the Confessing church. As Hitler's armored units paraded through Berlin on 27 September, Albertz and Böhm displayed what at that time was an uncommonly daring confession of guilt, summoning the congregations to pray that the imminent threat of war might be averted. It was a spiritual step that does not seem extraordinary or surprising today; given the tradition set in 1914, however, it was an unusually sober and daring move in 1938.

At the same time, a letter from Karl Barth in Basel to his colleague in Prague, Professor Josef Hromádka, became public. It encouraged the Czechoslovakian people to vigorous military resistance:

> Every Czech soldier who fights and suffers will be doing so for us too, and
> I say this without reservation—he will also be doing it for the church of
> Jesus, which in the atmosphere of Hitler and Mussolini must become the
> victim of either ridicule or extermination.[31]

This was too much. The combination of the Albertz-Böhm statement and
the Barth-Hromádka letter appeared indefensible to many in the church.
Who could protect whom?

The S.S. newspaper *Das Schwarze Korps*, together with Church Affairs
Minister Kerrl, accused Albertz, Böhm, and the Provisional Administration
of "treasonable action in clerical garb." The men of the Provisional Administration, however, accused Barth of heretically mixing politics and religion,
and they backed away from these dangerous friends. With some difficulty the
issue of political resistance had been kept under the surface during the discussions about the loyalty oath. Now it was suddenly in the open. Even the
"Dahlemites" in the Confessing church were unprepared. The frightened
Provisional Administration, under attack from the right wing from the S.S.
to the Lutherans, tried to pass the responsibility to the left. In a letter to all
provincial church governing bodies the administration assured: We have
nothing to do with this democratically ideologized political theology directed from Switzerland against our fatherland; there is no connection between
Barth and the special prayer liturgy or its spirit.[32]

But it was no use. In one blow the Kassel Council and the Essen meetings had become irrelevant. Many friends of the Confessing church were
caught helplessly between the two fronts. At the beginning of November the
German news agency announced:

> By unanimous resolve all Christians, including Bishops Marahrens, Meiser,
> Wurm and Kühlewein, have categorically assured the Reich Minister for
> Church Affairs that they disapprove of the letter on religious and patriotic
> grounds, and most strongly condemn the position expressed therein, and
> that they sever themselves from the persons responsible for that declaration.
>
> The Reich Minister for Church Affairs has taken disciplinary mea-
> sures by stopping the salaries of the members of the so-called Provisional
> Administration of the German Evangelical Church, who may be dismissed
> from their offices. This measure has also been applied to those responsible
> for the so-called Councils of Brethren, and who have thereby supported the
> so-called Provisional Administration in this matter.

After the war, Bishop Wurm had the moral courage to refer publicly to
this hour of new triumph for the Minister of Church Affairs as one in which
"the power of darkness was greater than the power of light."[33]

The "Kristallnacht." In the midst of the Confessing church's desperate state, the events of 9 November occurred, with countless acts of terror against the Jewish population. It confronted a group of Christians who were out of step and bereft of speech. That Wednesday night, as the synagogue in Köslin was burning, Bonhoeffer had gone straight to Gross-Schlönwitz on the other side of the forest, as he usually did for the second half of the week. Only later did he learn about what had happened throughout the country.[34] He then sent Bethge to Göttingen to check on the Leibholz's house. It was still undamaged.

In the Bible that Bonhoeffer used for prayer and meditation he underlined the verse in Psalm 74, "they burned all the meeting places of God in the land," and wrote beside it "9.11.38." He also underlined the next verse, adding an exclamation mark: "We do not see our signs; there is no longer any prophet, and there is none among us who knows how long." In the newsletter sent to the Finkenwaldians a few days later he wrote: "I have lately been thinking a great deal about Psalm 74, Zach. 2:8 and Rom. 9:4f. and 11:11-15. That leads us to very earnest prayer."[35] He urged the Finkenwaldians to look up the passages and heed the words: "He who touches you touches the apple of his eye" (Zachariah 2:8.) It was later speculated that this was when he said the words that so impressed his students: "Only he who cries out for the Jews may sing Gregorian chants"; but in fact he had said this earlier, in 1935.[36]

It was during this difficult year that Bonhoeffer began to distance himself from the rearguard actions of the Confessing church's defeated remnants.

Legalization

The consequences of the collapse of the Confessing church fell most heavily upon the young illegal pastors. In the Old Prussian Union the difference between Confessing pastors who could work legally as pastors and the illegals who were excluded from official posts (those who had been ordained under the Dahlem emergency law) became increasing pronounced. This affected only a limited number of people whose fate could hardly attract much public notice inside or outside the German borders. But Bonhoeffer lived and thought more for these people than for anything else; to him they represented everything that Barmen and Dahlem had promised. The conflicts over their status and their steadfastness affected him more than the other, more visible events of those days. It was his own people who were involved here.

The Situation. During Werner's period in office, the Confessing church and its administrative bodies were not yet prohibited as such. But anyone who tried to make the system work or to comply with it became tangled in a net of multiple regulations. One could be prosecuted under the Malicious Practices Act, the clause affecting the pulpits, the ban on collections, the Himmler decree, or the Press Law. Confessing pastors simply could no longer perform their duties legally. They operated in open protest, or in the vague hope—sometimes justified—that their disobedience might be overlooked.

In 1938 the *Volkskirche* still had buildings, names, customs, and perhaps even sermons as before; otherwise there was little similarity to the provincial churches of earlier decades. From Berlin Werner and his finance departments exercised strict control over the church authorities, who could no longer disagree with them even when laws were violated.

In the provincial consistories, the work was carried out by the old experienced officials whose attitudes had not changed—but they had no power to make decisions. On the other hand, there were also officials whose anti-church actions and statements were well known. The old system of collegially run consistories had been abolished, in accordance with the "leadership principle," to the advantage of the juridical president. Those consistorial advisers who were favorably disposed toward the Confessing church no longer had the right to object.

At the beginning of 1939 parish pastors lost their traditional independence; now the authorities could remove or transfer them from their positions at any time "for official reasons." Congregations also lost the right to administer their own money from church taxes and collections. Some places already had finance commissars at the congregational level, where local church committees had been disbanded because they had opposed some regulation or had refused to fire a disobedient pastor or withhold his salary.

Should the young illegal pastors let themselves be forced or recruited back into these churches? The legal ministry in the provincial churches still offered a number of attractive privileges—the parsonage alone was one—and more peaceful possibilities of work than those offered by the Confessing church. Clearly Werner could make life hard for the illegal pastors: he could close down their buildings, evict them, block their salaries, and take legal measures against church committees who supported them. And indeed he did so. Should older pastors with official positions dare to accept the young illegals, shield them with their own legality, and give them half the work? Things became genuinely difficult.

Until this point the illegal pastors had been the group within the Confessing church least under attack, relatively speaking. Now the presidents of the consistories began to woo them systematically. Since the end of 1937 the consistories had repeatedly enticed or pressured them—whichever approach seemed more effective—with new "final" dates for entering the official ministry. Each candidate was asked to apply individually and to submit the examination papers and reports that were in the possession of the Councils of Brethren. They also had to be checked and interviewed by the consistories, and, finally, give a written acknowledgment of the consistories' authority.

The Alternative. The choice between the Councils of Brethren and the consistory became agonizing. The illegals had gallantly endured the period of arrests in 1937, but now there was hardly any chance for them to work independently. The questions they had answered previously with confidence now became dubious.

Everything centered on the alternative: preacher or parish minister. Could an office of "preacher" exist without the parish? For those pastors installed in their ministries before the outbreak of the church struggle, the ministry did offer a certain freedom of movement. Perhaps this status could be accepted with insignificant compromise; after all, for centuries the state had held certain rights of supervision, which had always been tolerated in return for the status of being a legally recognized public body. And there were the congregations! Given the existing lack of pastors, every opportunity ought to be seized to fill the vacancies, so that church members were not left untended. Viewed from this perspective, the danger was that clinging to the position taken in Dahlem would be mere obstinacy. Even if it were lawfully conferred by the Confessing church, what could the preaching ministry still mean, if those who held it were excluded from the structures of the *Volkskirche* and if it abandoned what existed?

The alternative was to question the link between Barmen and Dahlem, and its justification. Many people now began to wonder whether one could accept the consistorial legalization and yet retain the Barmen declaration, which, after all, was more important than Dahlem. To put it differently: to abandon the Dahlem resolutions meant the rejection of training, examination, and ordination by the Councils of Brethren, but it did not acknowledge the theological justification of the "German Christians" and their claim to authority.

This alternative led to widespread uncertainty and weariness; a process of theological reorientation began in many minds. Some leading members of the Councils of Brethren were frightened, given their responsibilities for the congregations and the human and financial consequences of their obligation toward the illegal pastors. Many illegals had already had disillusioning experiences (or were disappointed now) with certain members of the Councils of Brethren, whose treatment of the loyalty oath and the prayer liturgy controversies had not been especially creditable. They also saw that even the "neutral" pastors produced respectable Reformation theology.

In 1938 and 1939 Bonhoeffer's briefcase was filled with letters, laments, and calls for help from his Finkenwalde students:

> I am worried about what to do if the Confessing church is really at the end of its road, at any rate here in Pomerania. Should I look for a different job? Or should I declare that I will go over to the consistory, against my better judgment and my understanding of the church, because otherwise I shall not be able to follow my calling?[37]

> We long for full responsibility in our ministry. This, in my opinion, is the real reason for all the sidelong glances at the consistory. After all, while it is more or less true that we have enough work and that we do it gladly, the ministry of the Word demands more from us! I mean the ministry of the Word in contrast to the word of the synods, where it is said that the "brothers in office" are to share their ministry and house with us. That is just where the difficulty is: we may be able to share the house, but the ministry is simply indivisible, because there is only one responsibility for it.[38]

> One of the congregation said to me lately: "Will the young pastors stand firm?" I answered: "If the congregation stands firm, yes. . . . According to reports, about forty brethren have stood firm, even in Westphalia.[39]

> I cannot see that it is theologically right to continue on the way followed so far, nor can I answer for it any longer, either for myself or for others. And so I am writing to you now; I have been glad to hear your advice up to now, and I should not like to be without it in the future. My question is: Will the community of brethren which has united me with the Finkenwaldians be able to survive—no doubt with the frankness that is particularly needed at present—or not? It certainly is not breaking up and shall not break up on my account. But shall you, and all those who in fact accuse us of destroying the church and of other faults, still be willing to have us in your heart and in your midst?[40]

Bonhoeffer did not want to yield to the outside or internal pressures on any point. On visits and at conferences, through lectures, newsletters, and personal letters, he tried to make his theological and pastoral position clear:

> We think that we are acting particularly responsibly if every other week we look again at the question of whether the path we are on is the right one. It is particularly striking that such a "responsible reappraisal" always begins

the moment serious difficulties appear. We then speak as though we no longer had "a proper joy and certainty" about our path, or, even worse, as though God and God's Word were no longer as clearly present with us as they used to be. In all this, we are ultimately trying to evade what the New Testament calls "patience" and "testing." Paul, in any case, did not begin to reflect whether his way was the right one when opposition and suffering threatened.... We still cannot imagine that God today really doesn't want anything new from us, but simply wants to test us in the old way.[41]

He permitted no defeatism in his company. Yet during this period he admitted to his brother Karl-Friedrich:

It has been to some extent quite depressing in recent weeks to see how many people use all kinds of reasons and pretexts to look for quietness and safety ... in such times there is always a great deal to do, with visits, lectures etc. I am quite sure that what matters most of all for the church is that we hold out now, even if it means great sacrifices. The greatest sacrifices now are small compared with what we would lose by wrongly backing down. I do not know of anything worth our wholehearted commitment today if not this cause. The main point is not how many are involved in it, but only that there are at least some.[42]

Stages of Development. 1. For Bonhoeffer this tiring struggle had already become acute in the winter of 1937–1938, when the Pomeranian consistory demanded that illegal pastors apply personally and in writing for legalized status. It set a deadline, which was extended three times during the following year, and required candidates to take a new examination and offer documented proof of ordination. In January 1938, at a meeting in Stettin of those who were affected, forty-six ordinands and young pastors roundly rejected the consistory's demands, under the chairmanship of Fritz Onnasch. Bonhoeffer had sent each of them a pastoral letter in which he spoke very plainly of obedience and disobedience, saying that the church struggle had to be endured and carried on "as gospel" and not "as law."[43] He tried to refer to the positive gifts of Barmen and Dahlem as a support and not a burden. He viewed the weariness over the struggle as a consequence of the creeping disobedience toward what had previously been accepted. What other people now described as a "new situation" he bluntly called a "smoke screen."

2. Anxiety increased again on 26 February 1938, when Werner issued an "order concerning the reception of unofficially examined theologians into the service of the provincial churches."[44] Could this order possibly be interpreted to mean that legalization was not necessarily bound to the acknowl-

edgment of a certain spiritual leadership? On 5 April the regulations implementing this order caused some disappointment, for they did not permit the consistorial requirements to be regarded simply as a "legal aid" to help everyone into the pastorate to which he was entitled. On the contrary, they required unreserved acknowledgment of the entire consistorial leadership.

Despite this, there was widespread discussion about whether the term "legal aid" was open to interpretation, or whether it might not be achieved through individual negotiations. Perhaps the Councils of Brethren, with their undoubted spiritual resources, could retain the right to exercise an "inner guidance." Provincial churches and the individual groups within them began to drive the best bargains they could for themselves. The Old Prussian Council of Brethren tried to steer things as much as it could. Contending that the church's ministry must recognize the state's right to exercise some supervision, it advocated submitting all examination documents to the consistories, although this was not to imply a recognition of the consistories as the church leadership. Unfortunately, the provincial Councils of Brethren and groups proceeded separately, and the provincial consistories varied in their willingness to make concessions. Under the guidance of church president Koch, Westphalia went the farthest in making special agreements; four-fifths of its illegal pastors voted to compromise, and only one-fifth advocated standing firm.[45]

Bonhoeffer reacted sharply:

> In the first place, anyone who looks solely after himself is deluded as to the community of the church. . . .
>
> Secondly, whoever urges us now to seek a solution for our difficulties at all costs is giving bad advice. . . .
>
> Thirdly, to whoever wants to make us fainthearted and diffident by telling us that we should at least save what we have, that we have been battered, questioned and locked up quite enough, we must reply that we make no promises to ourselves on the basis of those resources. What God intends to batter we are quite willing to see battered. We have nothing to salvage. We have not attached our hearts to organizations and institutions, not even to our own. The works that depend on those so-called church resources are just as godless as any others, and are bound to rob us of the prize of victory. But we trust confidently that God will salvage his Word, and us with it, in his miraculous way. That is the only possession on which we intend to take our stand.[46]

3. In Pomerania everything now seemed to be in a state of indecision. The consistory issued a final deadline for legalization: 30 September. On 1 September Bonhoeffer and Fritz Onnasch struggled for almost twenty-four hours with those who were still wavering and who asked: Hadn't the Con-

fessing church already failed and surrendered on the loyalty oath question? Wasn't the Confessing church's influence so small that it ought to disband? How could they continue and finance themselves for any length of time?[47] After the meeting the entire group turned in their papers to the consistory, in accordance with the Old Prussian Council of Brethren's proposal.

In response, the Pomeranian Council of Brethren invited all the pastors still loyal to it to an extraordinary convention in October. Council members Reinhold von Thadden, Eberhard Baumann, Werner de Boor, and Johannes Bartelt described the problems. Bonhoeffer gave the principal address.

Von Thadden outlined a depressing and unvarnished picture. Years ago 318 of the 600 Pomeranian clergy in office had signed a commitment to the Confessing church; of those 318, only 60 pastors still held to the Council of Brethren. There were 57 young illegal theologians; only 17 of them held regular pastorates, 22 were in positions that were not legal, and 15 could not be placed at all. The Council of Brethren had to raise 9,000 Reich marks a month, 6,000 of which was earmarked for the illegal pastors. At that moment, however, they were only bringing in 4,500 Reich marks.

After that introduction, Bonhoeffer gave a theological lecture to rouse the consciences of those who were ready to compromise.[48] He was concerned about the issue of the certainty of the Barmen and Dahlem declarations. "What had happened since then" could not be given priority over this issue:

> The Bible does not know the pathos and problems of the question, "Which way?" ... Our way ... is not important, problematic, tragic, in itself ... [but we want] to see the path before we take it. .... The Scripture does not demonstrate a course of action, but is evidence of God's truth. Scriptural evidence does not free us from believing, but leads us right into the wager of faith and obedience to God's Word.[49]

To those who had hurried on their own to the consistory he suggested:

> It is almost too obvious to be worth mentioning that we do not leave a brother in distress, that we stand by a brother who is attacked for the sake of the Gospel, even if by chance we ourselves are not attacked, that we side with one another in danger, battle and suffering. Every question, even if it is put unconditionally, already makes this situation problematic and can only lead to evasion.[50]

He rejected the temptation to get rid of the unpleasant dispute over the spiritual authority of the consistories:

> Do not let us persuade ourselves that over there, in the ranks of the con-
> sistory, we will be free for all the practical questions! There we have sur-
> rendered all internal authority, because we have not remained in the
> truth.[51]

The text of this address was duplicated for further discussion. It played
a part in the Epiphany synod of 1939, and in many groups and provinces it
was studied, attacked, and analyzed in written critiques.

4. The disintegration in the ranks did not yet seem final. It grew more
evident with each day that a nucleus of theologians remained who were
unpersuaded by arguments or pressure. A drastic change was in the making.
Except in Westphalia, the leaders of all the brotherhoods of illegal pastors
issued a call to their members to stand firm on 6 January 1939:

> Is a church-community built up when such authorities [the consistories
> aligned with Dr. Werner] frequently test future servants of the Word on
> matters of flesh and blood [i.e., require an Aryan certificate] but are nei-
> ther willing nor able to test the spirits?

Then came the clear message from the Old Prussian synod of 28 January
1939 in Nikolassee:

> We warn those colleagues who are considering accepting the measures of
> the national church authorities relating to the office of preacher. Otherwise
> they incur guilt by losing the comfort of ordination, by supporting a false
> system of church government, and by bypassing the administrative bod-
> ies of the Confessing church, they help themselves by abandoning their
> brethren and confusing the congregations.[52]

In condensed form it used Bonhoeffer's arguments. After the terrible year of
1938 he felt that the synod was a liberation after a long period of waiting:

> The new beginning that was recently granted us through God's goodness
> against all expectation has freed us from a constricting pressure . . . with
> our cheerless, resigned and refractory nature we had no longer deserved
> this [liberation].[53]

Only a few weeks later the notorious Godesberg declaration was issued.
It amounted to an official legitimization of the extreme "German Christian"
position. Bonhoeffer wrote his colleagues:

Since I last wrote, much has become clearer. . . . In the decisive weeks it has again been shown that at a certain point the possibilities of discussion are over. We were nearly destroyed by the arguments going back and forth. From that we have been delivered.[54]

5. After the Epiphany synod, the consistories in most provinces sent a summons to a "reexamination," to the illegals as a response to the papers that had been sent in. In plain language, that simply meant an examination. Moreover, whatever the objections and discussions, the ordinands must be "prepared duly to obey the laws of church and state, particularly with regard to collection and proclamations."[55]

But it now appeared that the winter's efforts were bearing some fruit. The great majority of those summoned to reexamination refused to comply with the demand for legalization:

Together with the other brethren, I must refuse to participate in an affair in which the authorities employ all their resources against the scruples, often stated in detail, of consciences bound firmly to Scripture and creed. . . . I greatly regret that, even now, the consistory does not offer to help us exercise our rightful ministry in the provincial church with the clear and easy conscience necessary for that office with all its duties and rights.[56]

Staemmler reported that in Saxony "everyone, with hardly any exception, wanted to continue on the path of the Confessing church." In fact, the Council of Brethren had just ordained ministers, in the presence of many theological students from Halle—where Julius Schniewind and Ernst Wolf were still teaching! Everyone had received an assignment and had plenty to do.[57]

Even in Westphalia the expected landslide did not occur. One illegal pastor, who had attended the collective pastorate in Gross-Schlönwitz, wrote Bonhoeffer:

I should like to tell you that I received the "Thoughts about our way" on 30 January.[58] This, together with the declarations of this week [at the Epiphany synod], has contributed toward my now seeing the whole business quite differently. . . . Think especially of me in these days, and of the many, many brethren in Westphalia![59]

6. In Bonhoeffer's immediate neighborhood in Pomerania, however, the disintegration in the ranks could not be stopped. The respected members of the Council of Brethren had recommended reexamination for too long, and

the professors in Greifswald had repeatedly attacked the theology of Bonhoeffer's 1936 essay on the question of church-community, and raised questions about its basis in Reformation theology. There were obviously some conciliatory gentlemen in the Stettin consistory, while among the illegal pastors there were competent spokesmen who could make a plausible case for their willingness to be reexamined. They suggested that the fact of a regrettable "split" be accepted. It was possible to acknowledge the existence of a group supporting "Way A" (those who refused legalization on principle, led by Fritz Onnasch) and another "Way B" (the legalizers, under Gerhard Krause), and still support one another in a brotherhood that continued to exist despite everything. That led to difficult arguments, in which Bonhoeffer became deeply involved.

Gerhard Sass movingly expressed his dissatisfaction with the Epiphany synod's decision in a newsletter that his colleague Werner de Boor recommended sending to their divided comrades in Pomerania. Sass argued that the synod's basic views—its appeal to the correct sense of vocation and the correct church regime—remained theologically unresolved. The *Volkskirche* was still the practical route to the congregations, and the consistories sent legitimate preachers—even if they were "in captivity" to the congregations:

> The battle on the front for who shall govern the church is long since decided—the Confessing church has lost. But the front of the church struggle is much broader, and the decisive point is no longer the church government. But the synod wants to continue to fight for that position, and thus ties down the forces that are so necessary in other places, and abandons them to the enemy. . . . Way A means charging repeatedly, with diminishing forces and reasons, against a locked door.[60]

For the sake of the community, which was so much more important, those who supported Way B should now be "led to the consistory by their spiritual leaders, that is, the Council of Brethren."[61]

Bonhoeffer found a commentary by Zinzendorf on Jeremiah 15:19-21, and the ordinands made sure it was circulated:

> Do you hear that, you servants of the Lord? You may be suspended, removed, you may lose your income, be turned out of house and home, but you will again become preachers—that is the word of promise! And if you are dismissed from a dozen posts and again get a fresh one, then you are a preacher in thirteen parishes, for in all the previous ones our innocence, our cross, and our faith preach more powerfully than if we were there.[62]

The correspondence between Bonhoeffer and Gerhard Krause openly discussed the difficulties, theological and personal, of Way A and Way B. Only a portion of this exchange remains, written by Krause, but that fragment is enough to show what the issue and the arguments were:

As far as possible, I followed your advice to remain silent until the church had spoken. . . . Meanwhile the Confessing church has itself gone beyond those sketchy ideas [at the Epiphany synod]. I have been listened to in many places, but the Confessing church would not and, I suppose, could not bring itself at all to do so. I suppose the ideas of "B" would have had to be presented more substantively and with more readiness to shoulder responsibility than was actually the case. We did not think of our proposals as a good private solution for us, but as a help for the entire Confessing church. Where they are now rejected, the conflict between the Confessing church and myself remains. . . .

In preparation for the Prussian synod I have reread fairly long sections of your *Discipleship*, because I wanted to keep open the possibility of reversing my opinion. But you are quite right when you write of the "bottomless pit of theological dissent" between us. It exists, though I cannot yet formulate it. . . . In [your] doctrine of justification, and much more so in the doctrine of the church (especially in the "questions"), I sense errors that I have only seen elsewhere in Catholic theology.

Perhaps the ethical contrast is even more important than the theological one. . . . It is the practical question: how are Christians to behave toward a tyrannical government, where do disavowal and necessary resistance begin? Christians today decide this quite differently in their lives. Unfortunately, they often turn it into a far-reaching doctrinal contrast, and give it a momentum that divides the church. . . .

So the question remains open about what caused me now to change the decision that was indeed made in faith.

1. One may refer here to the above-mentioned theological contrast, which impressed me more deeply from day to day. It is also relevant that the situation has changed through the fact that many former "German Christians" are today authorized preachers, that the church government and the consistory today is less heretical than tyrannical, that our political situation is becoming increasingly plain, and that in my own case the stormy periods have been followed by times of reflection.

2. Added to this was the decisive factor of the "certainty of the others," from whom the Confessing church had separated. The existence of orthodox "neutrals" shook me, and I could not understand the need to break with them.

3. Finally I was stopped by the realization that this path would force me to give up the officially instituted church, because my work was possible

only within the circles of Confessing church congregations—yet I know that I am called to serve in the church, for the admonition and edification of the congregations, not simply to serve in Confessing church circles alone.

4. Finally, I could not help seeing that the way to the consistory would not necessarily have to be a denial and an "action-without-faith." That has been confirmed by my personal discussions in recent weeks. . . . To be sure, the men there are "bound" and little qualified theologically to guide a church. But the legalization they demand includes nothing that I should have to reject as "against the faith" or "against the truth." If that is so, it means that the protest against the consistory loses for me that necessity that it would need to have if it meant my renouncing the ministry, the official church, the fellowship with many like-minded colleagues etc., and [that I must] endure all sorrows. . . .

It is for the Confessing church to decide whether I remain in it; whether I remain in the Finkenwalde brotherhood is my question to you.[63]

The discussion was not always as clearly or carefully argued. How could it be when uncertainty began to spread inside the Council of Brethren itself?

At present everything is going backwards. Almost the entire Council of Brethren shares the sentiments of the Westphalians. . . . Gerhard Krause, Rendtorff, and von Thadden all favor reexamination. . . . So we wrote a letter which should make it clear that we others do not intend to be ignored, and that the "resignation in Pomerania" is not so widespread.[64]

In mid-February the pastors of East Pomerania convened in Köslin, where fifty clergy and laity, including Dr. Knorr, approved Way A. Bonhoeffer spoke. Onnasch reported: "Strangely enough, the laity were more radical than the radicals among the clergy, and are firmly in favor of letting the Confessing church collapse before cooperating with the B-people."[65] This was followed at the end of February by the West Pomeranian pastors' meeting (also called the Kirchentag). Rendtorff and Gerhard Krause spoke for Way B, Gerhard Gehlhoff, Baumann, and Bonhoeffer for Way A. Krause challenged the statement that "the Confessing church is the church of Jesus Christ,"[66] and proposed that those who had been legalized should continue to be recognized as members of the Confessing church. Baumann warned against any arrangement with the wrong church government. Bonhoeffer attacked Rendtorff's exegesis of John 17 and Matthew 9 and 28, which referred to the field ripe for harvest into which the young pastors were now to be sent with all available resources. Bonhoeffer retorted that these very passages meant that one could not preach on the strength of one's own impulse; scripture did not teach self-offering, but the power of the commission that was given. A consistory councillor, Boeters, summoned the obstinate people to come into line, so that the spiritual capital of the Confessing church could become effective throughout the church as a whole, like that of other free brotherhoods: "Yes, we rejoice if the Confessing church is like the spiritual movements of Berneuchen and Sydow."[67]

One week later the young pastors in Stettin voted. Eleven decided for legalization through the consistory, twenty-eight for standing by the Council of Brethren unconditionally, and six abstained from voting. They finally adopted the resolution "that we all wish to try to remain together, despite the different ways, though Way A is generally preferred."[68] The attempt to remain together immediately came under great pressure. Some radicals of Way A declined to pursue the idea of unity, as though what the others did was of no consequence. On the other hand, those who supported Way B proved to be very active. De Boor and Gerhard Krause drew up a theological expert opinion against Bonhoeffer, "which greatly upset the radical brothers who supported Way A."[69]

The specific problems in Pomerania were never resolved, but they ended when Bonhoeffer went to England and America, and men like Gerhard Krause were called up for military service and thus pulled away from further developments. The war created a new situation. Bonhoeffer had no misgivings about including Krause and his friends in the circle of the Finkenwalde brethren. Once they were on the front, he even intensified his correspondence with them, without any further mention of Way A and Way B.

There is no doubt that the struggle over legalization in the Old Prussian Union made heavy demands on Bonhoeffer, both because of who was involved and because of the duration of the debate. One outcome was that Werner's offensive against the young candidates either slackened or achieved its aims through greater willingness to compromise. Still, it was impossible to shut one's eyes to the fact that deep rifts had been made in the Confessional front. It became more common in the Confessing church to take individual steps without discussion. The Councils of Brethren did not prevent such steps, or else they became accustomed to decisions and recommendations which were not unanimous. The Old Prussian Council of Brethren's authority had weakened appreciably. Some of the young theologians looked for employment in an "intact" Lutheran provincial church, or grew interested in a theology that allowed some freedom from turmoil.

Like Wilhelm Niesel, Bonhoeffer did not yield an inch, nor did he show his disappointment. The realm of energetic disputes with the Pomeranian theologians was no longer so exclusively the place where he lived and thought. It was inevitable that he would find it absurd to let Dr. Werner and the consistories dictate the conditions for the ministry in a provincial church, in light of the steps he had taken in 1933 and 1935 to get away from the embarrassing privileges of the *Volkskirche*. He had not expressed concerns about the Christian witness in the Nazi state in order to be appointed to an official post.

The Lure of the Political Realm

Toward the end of this period, in snowbound Sigurdshof, Bonhoeffer began to write down something he had pondered for years—a meditation on Psalm 119, that text of interwoven sayings, with neither beginning nor end, on the theme of the commandment.[70] Here, in the last place he taught theology and lived a spiritual life in community, he wrote about verse 19 ("I am a sojourner on earth; hide not thy commandments from me!") in the face of the approaching political challenges:

> The earth that nourishes me has a right to my work and my strength. It is not fitting that I should despise the earth on which I have my life; I owe it faithfulness and gratitude. I must not dream away my earthly life with thoughts of heaven and thereby evade my lot—that I must be a sojourner and a stranger—and with it God's call into this world of strangers. There is a very godless homesickness for the other world, and it will certainly not produce any homecoming. I am to be a sojourner, with everything that entails. I should not close my heart indifferently to earth's problems, sorrows and joys; and I am to wait patiently for the redemption of the divine promise—really wait, and not rob myself of it in advance by wishing and dreaming.[71]

For years Bonhoeffer had meditated on the Christian's "sojourning," and had practiced it personally, ecclesiastically, and ecumenically. Now he began to look at the qualifying phrase "on earth." How was this to be understood?

Hellmut Traub tells of a very characteristic meeting in Stettin in 1938, where a theological circle discussed Romans 13. He was disappointed at the first meeting to find Bonhoeffer so unhelpfully silent on the subject of political resistance, while he, Gollwitzer, and others spoke impatiently and passionately about it. Afterward he took Bonhoeffer aside:

> He assured me emphatically that he had understood me perfectly. "But then you must be quite logical, quite different, you must proceed in quite

a different way." . . . It became clear to me that what I had taken for "hesitation" belonged to an entirely different category. . . .[72]

At that time Bonhoeffer was already so involved in knowledge of the details of underground political activity that he no longer wanted to remain in the noncommittal realm between discussion and practical steps. So he said nothing, because he knew better what was really being discussed and what it might cost; perhaps, too, because he suspected that new steps of that kind could not be justified programmatically in advance.

Nor—for similar reasons—do we find in Bonhoeffer's writings a single line commenting on Karl Barth's essay "The Christian Community and the Civil Community," which caused such a stir. Barth's attack on the usual sterile differentiation between the two realms appeared in 1938; Bonhoeffer no doubt knew about it and later even moved toward Barth's position.[73] But he was already too involved with those who were taking action; moreover, this problem in German theology seemed to him too new and comprehensive to be settled briefly and incidentally with no systematic presentation. In a postwar essay honoring Bonhoeffer, Reinhold Niebuhr, who in 1930–1931 had been unable to find a political streak in Bonhoeffer, recalled an incident from the spring of 1939:

> I still remember a discussion of theological and political matters I had with him in London in 1939 when he assured me that Barth was right in becoming more political;[74] but he criticized Barth for defining his position in a little pamphlet. "If," he declared in rather typical German fashion, "one states an original position in many big volumes, one ought to define the change in one's position in an equally impressive volume and not in a little pamphlet."[75]

As a German theologian and a Lutheran, the step into political action, over which Bonhoeffer still hesitated, meant entering new and untraveled country. It was certainly a momentous step to move from silent opposition to open ideological protest and direct warning, as some individual bishops and the Confessing church, in its memorandum to Hitler, had done. But the step toward politically accountable plans for a coup and the future to follow was a different and more difficult one; and this was what Bonhoeffer was concerned about. For a long time he merely knew and approved of what was going on, until his knowledge and approval led to cooperation. This was preceded by far-reaching experiences, positive and negative, which emerged from the ecclesiastical, political, and personal experiences of 1938 and 1939.

Dietrich Bonhoeffer's participation in the German political resistance movement can be divided into five periods. The first is from the Fritsch crisis at the beginning of 1938 to the Munich agreement on 30 September of that year; the second goes until the beginning of the offensive in France on 10 May 1940. In both of these periods Bonhoeffer knew and approved of what was going on. The third period extends from the campaign in France to his arrest on 5 April 1943, the day on which the resistance work in the Military Intelligence Office was crippled; during this third period Bonhoeffer actively participated in the resistance operations. The fourth is from then to 20 July 1944; during this time he tried to cover up his actions. The fifth period was marked by the struggle for survival.

The first period was one in which the movement toward political activity was beginning, but had not yet brought any changes in his occupation or any new theological departures. His decisions and those of the people close to him did not yet affect his position with respect to the church; they mainly concerned either his family (his sister had to emigrate) or himself personally (he wanted to avoid military conscription). Yet these decisions were already affecting his political involvements as a whole.

Becoming an Accessory. To be an accessory or to be informed was dangerous in the Third Reich. In Judge Roland Freisler's court in 1944 it meant a death sentence. Under Hitler the initial curiosity of many people about what was happening gradually changed to an instinctive reluctance to know what was going on. This reluctance was fostered by the regime. Any knowledge of the actual situation, especially after the outbreak of war, exposed one to danger. But Bonhoeffer took considerable pains to have access to exclusive information; he felt that knowledge of what was happening was part of his indispensable responsibility for the future.

He insisted on supplementing his knowledge by reading *The Times* and the *Basler Nachrichten* as long as it was possible. Nor was he inclined to stop listening to foreign radio. This rekindled his very underdeveloped interest in technical matters. Once the location of the collective pastorates had been decided in November 1937, he assured himself that radio reception would be possible in eastern Pomerania. When it turned out that there was no electricity in Sigurdshof, he got an engineer to supply him with a portable battery set, something rare at the time. For him, information was the first necessity to assert one's independence; he would not delegate his judgment to anyone else or allow Hitler's sudden actions to take him by surprise. The hardest thing for him to bear was to be the victim of some unforeseen occurrence. He wanted to maintain a certain sovereignty, even when he was taken to prison, and he did so in 1943.

Of course, he was also too anxious to hear details of when and where "the beams were creaking." This was the expression used by those who were waiting for Hitler to fail—in the Röhm affair, after Hindenburg's death, over the occupation of the Rhineland, or after Schacht's resignation. The prognosis of well-informed people could serve them as a responsibly handled weapon—such as the warning by the Bonhoeffer family and friends after 1933: "Hitler means war." Of course, every prognosis needed to be strengthened by fresh information and knowledge of the facts. Even for his sermon in Fanö Bonhoeffer needed a good deal of information and concise prognosis.

His political knowledge had the twofold effect of irrevocably separating him from some people and bringing him closer to others. It separated him from many of his colleagues in the church on a central matter; but it brought him into the company of people who neither shared nor pursued his theological and ecclesiastical ideas, and whose motives were not always his. But he drew closer to them, and did not try to make their motives his own. For instance, Ewald von Kleist's notion of Christianity was certainly similar to that of Harnack, but that did not particularly worry Bonhoeffer. Bonhoeffer did not travel to Schmenzin from Klein-Krössin in order to change Ewald's mind—although Frau von Kleist-Retzow would have been delighted to hear him try.

Hans von Dohnanyi. For a pastor, Bonhoeffer had unusual connections. His father was on familiar terms with Ferdinand Sauerbruch, who was often able to bring along fresh news from the Party hierarchy. His mother cultivated the relationship with her cousin Paul von Hase (who was executed after the attempted 20 July coup), who became military commander of Berlin in 1940. Klaus had connections with the lawyer Josef Wirmer, the industrialist Walter Bauer, and the businessman Nikolaus van Halem (arrested before the coup), and with Otto John and Prince Louis Ferdinand, both bitter opponents of the regime who had important contacts at home and abroad. Klaus and Dietrich often met for a musical evening with Ernst von Harnack, a Social Democrat and former government president of Merseburg. Rüdiger Schleicher got on well with Dr. Karl Sack, the head of the army's legal department. Dietrich Bonhoeffer renewed his youthful acquaintance with Hans-Bernd von Haeften in the Foreign Ministry.

No one, however, was closer to him during those critical years than his brother-in-law Hans von Dohnanyi, who gave Bonhoeffer information, advice, and, later, certain assignments. Dohnanyi turned to Bonhoeffer both for ethical certainty and enlightened conversation. After being employed after 1929 as personal information officer to justice ministers Koch-Weser, Bredt, and Joel, Dohnanyi was assigned to Reich Minister of Justice Franz Gürtner in May 1933. Dohnanyi never had anything to do with the Party and did not join any of its organizations, including the National Socialist Legal Union (*Rechtswahrerbund*) led by Hans Frank. In the early period the Ministry of Justice still offered some political freedom of movement; the struggle to preserve a legal system was not equally hopeless everywhere. Because of his position, Dohnanyi was able to give his brother-in-law in the church struggle useful and timely hints or warnings. As Christine von Dohnanyi later said, he always had "the full backing of Gürtner, a tragic figure in the truest sense of that word, who was destined to dig the grave of German law." When in 1935 Dohnanyi was offered a lectureship on criminal and procedural law at the University of Leipzig, he declined the offer at Gürtner's request.

In those years Dohnanyi had a constant close-up view of the Nazis' evil deeds. He began to document their crimes in a "chronicle of shame"; General Beck later attached great importance to this journal because it could refute, if necessary, any new *Dolchstoss* ("stab in the back") legends such as those that had spread through Germany in the wake of the First World War. Dohnanyi's journal would play a fatal role later, after certain sections of it could not be destroyed in time.[76]

Dohnanyi was able to remain behind the scenes for a long time, until the first conspiracy that was sparked by the Fritsch crisis, when the ground threatened to become too hot for him. At that time Martin Bormann wrote from the Party chancellery to Gürtner, complaining that Gürtner allowed someone like Dohnanyi, with no connection with National Socialism, to be in such proximity to him. Dohnanyi had been denounced by a Party clique in the ministry that included Roland Freisler. With Gürtner's help, Dohnanyi then became a supreme court judge in Leipzig in September 1938. Dietrich Bonhoeffer feared that his supply of information would now be badly interrupted; but after the failure of the attempted coup Dohnanyi regarded the change as a fortunate removal from the dangerous ground of Berlin. At the beginning of November Dohnanyi's family moved from Kurländer Allee in Charlottenburg to Leipzig.

But Dohnanyi had agreed to give a weekly lecture in Berlin, where he still met regularly with resistance members Major General Hans Oster, Carl Goerdeler, and diplomat Ulrich von Hassell. At one of those meetings, after Hitler on 21 October ordered the armed forces to prepare to occupy the rest of Czechoslovakia, Wilhelm Canaris, the head of Military Intelligence, sent a message via Oster that in case of war he wanted to appoint Dohnanyi to his staff at once. That was the outcome of the meetings between Oster and Dohnanyi over the Fritsch affair.

On 25 August 1939 Dohnanyi became a "special leader" (*Sonderführer*) on Admiral Canaris's staff. In Oster's central department he attended to policy issues, but in a certain sense he acted as a private secretary to Canaris. This meant that he was settled in the center of information—and the conspiracy. After August 1939 he always stayed, as he had during his weekly journeys to Berlin from Leipzig, with Bonhoeffer's parents on Marienburger Allee; this greatly facilitated the contacts with his brother-in-law Dietrich.

Dohnanyi combined a cool intelligence with an ever quick and effective readiness to help, even if at times he was almost too reticent. His close friends sometimes found him boyishly high-spirited, but he also had a surprising straightforward piety. His extraordinary abilities led to his being given tasks and positions so early in life that it aroused envy among some colleagues, creating some precarious situations.

He was attracted to the Bonhoeffers by the large family and its unfailing high standards. He had been friends with Christine, whom he married, in school, as well as with Klaus Bonhoeffer, Gerhard Leibholz, and Justus Delbrück. These friendships slackened during the church struggle and in subsequent years, when he and Dietrich became closer. Perhaps he was annoyed by Klaus Bonhoeffer's slight difficulty in making decisions. As a lawyer, Klaus constantly had new ideas and visions of the possibilities in any given situation; Hans von Dohnanyi found this more a hindrance than a help. But he felt that in Dietrich, even Dietrich the theologian, he found a stronger sense of reality; and, in fact, Dietrich possessed an unusual capacity to help other people arrive at decisions.

Thus Dohnanyi confided in no one more during this period than in Dietrich Bonhoeffer. Almost everyone else commented on Dohnanyi's abrupt and reserved manner, but Dietrich Bonhoeffer met his brother-in-law as often as possible when he was in Berlin. Dohnanyi introduced him at a relatively early point to the inner circle of conspirators, and asked Bonhoeffer one evening what he thought about the New Testament passage "all who take the sword will perish by the sword" (Matthew 26:52). Bonhoeffer replied that this held true for their circle as well. They would have to accept that they were subject to that judgment, but there was now a need for such people who would take the responsibility for deciding its validity for themselves.

Sources. The first two periods of revolutionary activity provide few written sources or memoranda to show that Bonhoeffer knew of the plans to overthrow the regime and was in close touch with the conspirators. There are two pieces of circumstantial evidence, however.

In Bonhoeffer's 1938 and 1939 diaries, all the pages connected to critical days have been torn out. The pages for 10–20 February 1938 are missing; this was the period in which there was some hope that Fritsch's protest against his defamation would set something in motion. In 1939 the pages for January, the end of April, and the beginning of May, and for August and September have been removed; during all these times he was in Berlin. Those pages contained Berlin addresses and telephone numbers that were not in Bonhoeffer's diaries from previous years, and initials and numbers of the Zehlendorf and Grunewald district, but especially from Tirpitzufer Allee, where the Military Intelligence Office had its headquarters. He did not want the Gestapo to be able to question him about such entries, should his notebooks fall into their hands during a house search provoked by church affairs.

The other piece of evidence was the increasing use of code words in correspondence with relatives and friends—names of people and places whose significance today has been partly forgotten, and which therefore make some passages in Bonhoeffer's letters obscure. For example, "Uncle Rudi" plays a very important part. There actually was such a person: he was Count Rüdiger von der Goltz, a retired general and brother-in-law of Frau Bonhoeffer who lived near the home on Marienburger Allee. His name became the code word for Hitler's preparations for war: "I hear that we are to expect no change in our work in the near future. I wonder whether that has anything to do with Uncle Rudi."[77] This meant that in view of the military mobilization, no steps would be taken against the illegal pastors.

The Fritsch Crisis. The first intentional conspiracy in which Dohnanyi took part was preceded by every possible attempt to make contact with people close to Hitler or who held key positions in the army. Through this Dohnanyi had early knowledge of Hitler's preparations for war; from Captain Wiedemann he learned of Hitler's war speech to the commanders in chief of the three branches of the armed forces on 5 November 1937 in the Reich chancellery.[78]

Wiedemann had been Hitler's company commander in the First World War and had been adjutant in the Reich chancellery since 1935. As Gürtner's assistant, Dohnanyi got to know him and soon gained his confidence, thereby learning important information about what was happening in the Reich chancellery and in Hitler's headquarters on the Obersalzberg. According to Wiedemann, on 5 November 1937 Hitler had said: "Every generation needs its own war, and I shall take care that this generation gets its war." After

Dohnanyi expressed outrage Wiedemann said: "I admit that nothing but the revolver is any use here, but who is to do it? I cannot murder someone who has made me his confidant."[79] This important connection was broken after Wiedemann fell into Hitler's disfavor and was appointed general consul in San Francisco in January 1939. Frau Bonhoeffer wrote Dietrich: "Hans is coming tomorrow. He will be very sorry that his friend is being moved; last time, too, he was quite depressed. . . . What is happening to Uncle Rudi is very worrying."[80]

After General Werner von Fritsch and War Minister Werner Blomberg raised political and military objections to Hitler's remarks on 5 November 1937, both were both removed at the end of January by infamous methods. On 4 February a small circle was informed that Blomberg and Fritsch had been dismissed; Fritsch had been accused of indulging in homosexual acts. The witness and evidence had been prepared by S.S. Deputy Director Reinhard Heydrich. Hitler now took over the supreme command of the armed forces, and Field Marshal Walter von Brauchitsch succeeded Fritsch as commander in chief of the army. Hitler ordered Gürtner to investigate the case of Fritsch: "You will know for yourself which end of the rope to pull." With the same words Gürtner handed the documents over to Dohnanyi for him to deal with the matter, and, of course, Dohnanyi understood which end of the rope had to be pulled.[81] He was freed from all other duties for a certain time, so that he could work on the defamation of Fritsch.

Through this he became acquainted more closely with Dr. Karl Sack of the army judiciary and Colonel Oster, the head of central Military Intelligence Office. Those meetings led to the first clearly defined resistance group with specific aims; General Ludwig Beck was also a member. Their initial assumption was that the army could not submit to Hitler's defamatory encroachments, and that Fritsch must challenge Himmler; this would launch a coup. Dohnanyi drafted a written challenge by Fritsch to Himmler, but Fritsch hesitated. Then Hitler marched into Austria on 12 March 1938. In light of the triumph in Vienna, the military protagonists who had planned to oppose Hitler felt that the moment had passed. Nothing happened. Walter Schellenberg, the S.S. brigade commander and later head of the secret service, later wrote in his memoirs that Heydrich did, in fact, fear that the army would march against him.[82]

Even though this first attempt at a coup had been unsuccessful, it led to some important conclusions: any opposition serious about stopping Hitler had to ensure that it held the instruments of power; only this could restrain him. Efforts in the economic or legislative sphere, or international opinion, were of secondary importance compared with the task of keeping or gaining influence in the army. If the scattered "resistances" were to become a constructive conspiracy of "resistance," this would have to become a military plot. This much had been clearly proved in February 1938. Given their own backgrounds and convictions, this was a recognition that Dohnanyi and Bonhoeffer had to reach on their own.

This radical change in Bonhoeffer's outlook was connected to another change. Until then he had eagerly looked for people who could summon the courage to say "no" in public, and were willing to accept dismissal from their posts as a consequence. Now a period began when it was of the utmost importance that people of character remained at the controls at all costs, and did not let themselves be pushed out. This meant that things which had been issues of character were now mere bagatelles—greeting with the Hitler salute, for instance. Even if it meant giving up a "clean slate," they had to try to get into key positions. The use of camouflage became a moral duty. The uncompromising Bonhoeffer was no longer offended when Oster and Dohnanyi kept in touch with such shady people as Himmler's chief of staff, the S.S. supreme group commander Karl Wolff, the Berlin police president Count Helldorf, or the director of the Reich criminal investigation office Arthur Nebe. If there was to be conspiracy, then they had to enter the lion's den and gain a foothold there. This was a consequence that had to be accepted, after the disempowerment of every profession in the country had been tolerated for years, hopes for evolutionary change had remained unfulfilled, war was now deliberately risked, other countries were ravished, and the Jewish question was intensifying in an unthinkable manner. Bonhoeffer never tried to dissuade Dohnanyi from his course of action. The situation had been clear to him since the spring of 1938: someone had to take on this disreputable task. And if the pastor Bonhoeffer was not yet called to be one of those directly involved, it could at least be his business to set their consciences at rest.

The Sudeten Crisis. In the summer of 1938 the conspiracy was given new cause for action, in connection with the Sudeten crisis. On 28 May Hitler presented the heads of the army, state, and Party the plan to eliminate Czechoslovakia. One blow quickly followed another: on 22 June the order for compulsory civilian service came; on 13 July the law requiring the population to help in national defense was enacted; on 17 August came the formation of the armed S.S. as an independent auxiliary to the existing armed forces. The same day it was announced that at the beginning of the next year the Jews' freedom of movement would be restricted by adding the names "Israel" and "Sarah" in their passports.

On 18 August an unusual thing happened: Beck, the chief of the general staff, handed in his resignation. He had tried to move the generals to uniformly oppose the plans Hitler had announced on 28 May. On 16 July he had handed Brauchitsch a memorandum preparing a diplomatic protest to be given to Hitler. It contained a passage that deserves always to be remembered:

> The final decisions for the nation's existence are at stake here; history will charge those leaders [of the various Wehrmacht divisions] with bloodshed if they do not act in accordance with their professional and political knowledge and conscience. Their obedience as soldiers must have a limit where their knowledge, their conscience and their responsibility forbid the execution of a command.
>
> It shows a lack of stature and a failure to understand his task, if in such times a soldier in the highest position sees his duties and tasks only within the limited context of his military orders, without being conscious that his highest responsibility is to the people as a whole.
>
> Exceptional times demand exceptional actions![83]

But Brauchitsch refused to join Beck's plans. Meanwhile, at the Berghof on 10 August, Hitler succeeded in arousing the younger generals' enthusiasm for his warlike ideas. In this situation Beck declined to share any responsibility for starting a world war, and retired. The nation did not learn of this crisis till 1 October.

Meanwhile the nation had become both participant and victim of Hitler's dramatic tricks: the threats at the Party rally that the country would intervene on behalf of the Sudeten Germans, the demands that continued to increase when Chamberlain made his two appeasement visits to Germany, the mobilization that was called off when Mussolini intervened at the last moment, and the days in Munich, on 29 and 30 September, when the representatives of the great European powers met on Hitler's ground.

The world, and with it the Germans, breathed again, as if something wonderful had happened. The German-speaking church of St. George in London wrote to Chamberlain:

> The German Lutheran Church of St. George in London, assembled today for divine service, thinks of you in warm solidarity. . . . It therefore welcomes gratefully everything that you, Prime Minister, have done to preserve peace. . . . Its church building is the oldest German landmark in Great Britain. It has directly experienced what a world war means. It will do its utmost, through confessing the name of Jesus Christ, to serve the

cause of peace between our two countries, and it remembers in its intercession your statesmanlike work which is directed to the same end.[84]

Hildebrandt and Rieger could not know that Bonhoeffer's impression of
these events at home was entirely different. Once more his hopes for a coup
had been destroyed. Psychologically everything was more favorable, and the
action itself was better prepared than in the spring; this was the moment, if
at all, when there would have been some understanding for the generals'
intervention against a Hitler who had gone beyond all bounds. Franz Halder,
Beck's successor, would have been ready to launch the coup as soon as Hitler
gave orders to attack Czechoslovakia. General von Witzleben, the military
commander of the Berlin-Brandenburg district, would have marched on the
Reich chancellery; he was somewhat popular at the time.

The hour of action had been palpably at hand. It had been thwarted by
the Munich agreement. The day on which the world breathed freely again
was for the conspirators the "day of misfortune."[85] The internal and external
conditions for a revolution changed so completely after 30 September that
the underground movement did not recover from this setback for a long
time. Hitler had success on his side, and he used it, not just through propaganda promoting the correctness of his policy, but also by reducing the
power of the general staff. In the future they would no longer share responsibility for the decisions of the commander in chief, but only draft the plans
in a subordinate capacity. Hitler now called any divergent views "defeatism."
Witzleben, previously the commanding general of the third army division,
was moved from this key position in Berlin to the western fortifications. It
was two years before his successor, Paul von Hase, was given a command post
close to the Reich chancellery.[86] For a long time the civilians opposed to the
regime, like Dohnanyi, and the few stalwart officers without battalions, like
Oster, lost the close connections to the indecisive military. They were viewed
as pessimists who had made incorrect forecasts about the behavior of the
western powers. The shock lasted so long that the conspirators were unable
to prepare for a new coup—when Hitler's army marched into Prague on 15
March 1939, or at the beginning of the Polish campaign in September that
same year—as they had done in September 1938. The civilians in the resistance did make some efforts, but there was no response from the army commanders. When at last in the winter of 1939–1940 the possibility of a coup
d'état again became real, conditions had become much more complicated.

During the planning period in the summer of 1938 some of the conspirators still thought that a spontaneous popular uprising was possible if
Hitler were prevented by force from starting a new war. Dohnanyi was more

pessimistic, and advocated a tougher course that included Hitler's removal. In August 1938, when Ewald von Kleist of Schmenzin visited Churchill and discussed ways of getting a new German government, Churchill was reported to say: "You can have everything, but first bring us Hitler's head."[87] But at that time people did not go so far as to think that an assassination was either possible or necessary. They were more inclined to favor Hitler's arrest and public arraignment; the possibility was discussed of having him certified as mentally ill, on the strength of a psychiatric report that Karl Bonhoeffer was to draw up. In 1938 the conspirators could still appeal to the generals' expert knowledge and strengthen their conviction that their resistance against Hitler had to be regarded as more than a "plot." Initially Beck had not thought in terms of a plot and conspiracy, but had believed that common sense and freedom could be regained by presenting the professional point of view directly—that a resolute memorandum could clear everything up. This was already dubious by the end of September, and by 1939 it was a complete illusion. In the next phase of the resistance it was clear, even to those who had hesitated, that Hitler could not be eliminated except through a conspiracy and its consequences.

The Leibholz Family's Emigration. The two attempted coups in 1939 raised the Bonhoeffers' hopes that their family would evade the consequences of the anti-Aryan legislation, and Dietrich hoped to be relieved of the dilemma a military draft would present. In the hope that there would be a successful coup, they all tried for a long time in the web of laws and regulations to find gaps through which the Göttingen relatives could slip to find some basis for life in their homeland.

In the early years no one in the family ventured to think about what a permanent separation would mean. Emigration presented practical difficulties. A lawyer hardly stood as good a chance in an English-speaking foreign country as did, perhaps, a scientist; money and possessions could not legally be taken across the border. Wouldn't they be better off if they remained at home, within the greater family circle?

It was only after the threat of immediate war in 1938, and the information (from Hans von Dohnanyi) of the coming regulation about Jewish names, that the decision to emigrate was made and put into action. Everyone was now convinced that even Gerhard Leibholz could no longer be protected under wartime conditions. In the meantime a fifth regulation was appended to the Nuremberg Laws that excluded "non-Aryans" from the last professions still open to them. The S.S. newspaper *Das Schwarze Korps* wrote that if war broke out the fate of the Jews would be "total annihilation."[88]

Could this be believed? Were there still possibilities of avoiding it, or should they put their hopes in the success of the coup preparations? Dietrich's twin sister Sabine wrote to him on 26 August 1938:

> In the last few weeks he [Gerhard] has been unable to maintain his old equanimity. After all, one's nerves become somewhat frayed in time. It is difficult to think out to the end all the decisions that have to be made and that makes one feel on edge. . . . So now I have to be more than ever up to the mark, and it is not always an easy matter to keep in one's head such various things as questions of existence and urgent things that have to be provided for, as well as the children's needs and wishes in large and small matters. . . . We should so much have liked to see you before we leave.[89]

Dietrich Bonhoeffer left with the Leibholzes after the BBC in London announced the first steps toward mobilization in Great Britain—the significance of this was overestimated—and they feared that the borders might close. He accompanied them part of the way on 9 September, so that they could cross the border near Basel before midnight.[90]

This meant emigration. Toward authorities and officials, however—and even to themselves—they maintained the fiction of a "journey." The coup might still come, and perhaps there would again be a few quieter months that would allow them to live in Göttingen again, as before the September crisis. But on 5 October all non-Aryans' passports that were not stamped with a "J" were declared invalid. The Bonhoeffer parents telegraphed the Leibholz family: "Your coming now unsuitable."

Wherever he could, Dietrich Bonhoeffer tried to prepare the way for his relatives in London, first by writing to Bishop Bell and Sir Walter Moberley in Oxford, whom he had come to know in Chamby in 1936. He used the contacts in his old congregations:

> Many thanks for your greeting from my former congregation. I am glad you have been well received and have already had your first invitations. Once you are settled a bit, you will like it much better than just at first. For instance, the badly heated rooms are an English affliction that cannot be escaped anywhere. . . . I hope you will have a good time with really fine weather. That helps very much to cheer you up when you are in London![91]

He soon decided to go to London himself. In preparation he sent more letters than ever before to his old congregations during Christmas 1938. On 1 February he wrote his twin sister a birthday letter with new hopes:

Now, everything has changed. It occurred to me recently that perhaps there really are laws governing the special case of twins—I don't think they always hold true for us—but certain twins often have the same experiences of life, even when they are not living near each other. I must say that seems to be true to a certain extent, in any case when we compare ourselves with the other members of the family. Our recent experiences have at least been different from what we had imagined, although they were not the same in each case. In this respect perhaps we can understand our paths through life particularly well at present. It is really one and the same thing that has so decisively determined our life and given it the unexpected course. However that may be, we shall at least think of each other a great deal on the 4th, and we shall expect less of all the good wishes than from our really standing up for one another. I am already very much looking forward to our meeting each other again.[92]

Leibholz finally received a scholarship from the provisional World Council of Churches to go to Magdalen College, Oxford; his activities there included giving political tutorials and lectures at Oxford. He was introduced to Bishop Bell at a fortunate time, since Bell had been a member of the British House of Lords since July 1938—a fact that gave his remarks on political matters added importance, just when war was looming. With respect to the events in Germany, it turned out well that Bonhoeffer the theological adviser was now followed by Leibholz the political expert. During and after the war, Bishop Bell made full use of his analyses and interpretations.[93]

The Call to Military Duty. The political developments of 1938 brought the personal decision about military service closer to home. In 1934 and 1935, Bonhoeffer's answer to the question had been fairly clear due to his Christian discipleship. Now the problem was substantially more complicated. In 1938 the threatened summons to the armed forces was the event about which he spoke least, for who in his church would understand the problems involved? Perhaps if political developments had been more peaceful, he would have been quietly relieved of the need for a decision, because a few years later he would have been too old to be enlisted. But now the preparations for war had begun to move alarmingly fast.

Feeling that he ought to avoid the limelight as far as possible, he gave up plans for a holiday in Italy: "Our intent to avoid reminding the recruiting offices of us finally kept us away from any plans that involved [crossing] the German borders."[94]

On 3 November 1938 Bonhoeffer, like everyone else, had to record his place of residence with the police registration authorities in the "Military Registration Record." It was not yet conscription, but he was now obliged to report any change of address and longer holiday journeys, and to apply for special permission in case of foreign travel. His mother wrote him from Berlin on 23 January 1939:

> On our advertising placards there was a notice calling on the 1906 and 1907 classes to register. . . . Anyone who has not been called up on or before 15 February has to report. I often wonder whether and how that will affect your journey. We have been with Karl-Friedrich in Leipzig on his for-tieth birthday. In the evening we had a very happy time with Heisenberg and his wife.[95]

For his brother's fortieth birthday Bonhoeffer wrote to him: "In some ways I envy you for having reached this age," referring to the fact that he was now ineligible for military duty.

But in the military district of Schlawe in January, things were not mov-ing as fast as in Berlin. The local recruiting station was under the charge of a Major von Kleist; Bonhoeffer's friends in the von Kleist family, as well as Superintendent Block, were able to influence him on Dietrich's behalf. The potential difficulties with a journey to England were easily bypassed, and Bonhoeffer was given official permission to go abroad in March. But a shack-le was now attached that could not be shaken off.

After his journey to England, Bonhoeffer immediately applied for per-mission to go to America for a year. Instead, in mid-May he received orders to report for call-up on 22 May. This was precisely the summons Bonhoef-fer had hoped to forestall and which had made his application so urgent. On 13 April he wrote his parents: "I may have to go to Niebuhr as early as June. If only it comes off!" On 1 May Niebuhr wrote to Leiper: "Today I received word from Bonhoeffer saying that time was short. If he is to make necessary arrangements, he ought to have a cable as well as a confirming letter." On 5 May he wrote his parents: "My leave of absence has not yet come through . . . everything is still uncertain." On 11 May Niebuhr wrote Paul Lehmann: Bonhoeffer is "anxious to come to America to evade for the time being a call to the colors. . . . There will be some difficulty in getting him out and if he fails he will land in prison."[96]

In distress, he called on his father to help:

> That in itself has nothing to do with my application for leave. The people in the mayor's office work through the conscriptions simply according to

the lists. For all that, the question of granting the leave is now urgent. As I am not going to Schlawe at all in the next five days, and (after consultation here) I do not want to go there personally unless it is absolutely necessary, I want to ask you, Father, whether you might not be able to inquire of Major von Kleist by letter, or, perhaps more effectively, by telephone, how the matter stands. I have just gone away for the time being, and am waiting urgently for news, as I want to leave as soon as possible. The application for leave was sent off on 23 April, and contained a request for leave from 1 May 1939 to 1 May 1940. The recommendations were in the form of private letters to v. K., and may not have been sent on to the other authorities. . . . I should be very grateful to you if you could find some way or other of pushing the matter forward.[97]

The intervention succeeded just in time; the local recruiting station did, in fact, withdraw Bonhoeffer's orders to report to duty, and was willing to grant formal consent for one year. On 2 June 1939 Bonhoeffer was able to leave Berlin for the west. His personal decision, and the danger to which it would have exposed his church, seemed to have been postponed for at least a year.

Otherwise he would have had to decide on 22 May whether he would allow himself to be posted to an army unit or would appear as a conscientious objector before a court-martial. Hermann Stöhr of the Fellowship of Reconciliation in Stettin had already decided to apply for conscientious objection. (Stöhr was arrested and shot as a result.) One year later Superintendent Block, Major von Kleist, and even his father could no longer help Bonhoeffer. Having tried to avoid the issue, Bonhoeffer saw his responsibilities in a new light, and found help elsewhere.

England: March and April 1939

Flight. At first, Bonhoeffer spoke only playfully of staying abroad, as in his question to Sutz about standing in for Brunner who held a professorship in Zurich,[98] and in his renewed contact with Paul Lehmann: "It would be best if you just invited me for one term; that would not be at all bad!"[99] But then came his sister's letters, which could not quite conceal the difficulties of life abroad. He immediately asked Rieger and Boeckheler, his successor in Sydenham, to invite him to the two London congregations over Christmas and New Year's. Meanwhile, however, it appeared that the Bonhoeffer parents could see their emigrant children in Holland during the holidays, and so the invitations were postponed until March. Bonhoeffer then learned that Reinhold Niebuhr was to be in Britain during that time for the Gifford

Lectures, and he wrote to him that he must meet him. If the English didn't know what to do, Niebuhr would surely help him.

The practical preparations for traveling west were triggered by his sister's letters and made more urgent by his imminent call to the military. When he was ready he discussed his journey with the ecumenical delegate of the Provisional Administration, Hans Böhm, and was given some official duties to carry out abroad. On his previous trips abroad he had either been invited to a conference or sent by the Council of Brethren, traveling within the ecumenical world primarily for official reasons and only secondarily for his own affairs. Now the position was reversed, and it was the official assignments that took second place, although this did not mean they were unimportant.

On church matters, the numerous disappointments had added up: the loyalty oath controversy, the efforts to achieve unity, the legalization of the young pastors, and the reactions to the prayer liturgy and the "*Kristallnacht.*" Politically he was disturbed by the failure of the attempt to overthrow Hitler, the preparations for war, and the supposed exclusion of Dohnanyi from the Berlin circle. Personally the restlessness of life in the collective pastorate, imminent conscription, and his emigrant sister's fate all took their toll.

So it is not surprising that a number of urgent questions arose in connection with his future: Must he really wear himself out over church and national affairs in Germany? For what, really, were his life's ambitions to be sacrificed? Couldn't he pursue theology, the thing most important to him, in more conducive surroundings? Would not the universal church and its theology benefit more if he could develop his gifts freely elsewhere? Might there not be a call waiting for him outside, and wasn't it necessary to leave in order to hear this clearly? Moreover, didn't his own church view a refusal of military service as a destructive and isolated course?

Finally, Bonhoeffer had a growing sense that if he remained in Germany, he would be drawn more deeply into the conspiracy against Hitler. Was it right for him as a pastor and theologian to go beyond the role of accessory, to actively participate in such a conspiracy? Wouldn't it be better to avoid this dilemma? Everything suggested that it might be easier for him to arrive at a definite conclusion on these matters outside Germany.

Only in retrospect can Bonhoeffer's 1939 travels be described as a "flight." He did not use that term, either to his friends—who among them was familiar with the whole tangle of motives and should have told him that this step was an evasion?—or to his relatives, although they would have been delighted if he had fled and stayed abroad. Bonhoeffer himself was by no means entirely clear about the crucial reasons for those journeys.

During his time in England, he came closest to the real facts of the case in a letter that was something like a confession to Bishop Bell. Even here, however, he described only a part of the whole:

> I am thinking of leaving Germany sometime. The main reason is the compulsory military service to which the men of my age [born 1906] will be called up this year. It seems to me conscientiously impossible to join in a war under the present circumstances. On the other hand the Confessional Church as such has not taken any definite attitude in this respect and probably cannot take it as things are. So I should cause a tremendous damage to my brethren if I would make a stand on this point which would be regarded by the regime as typical of the hostility of our Church towards the State. Perhaps the worst thing of all is the military oath which I should have to swear. So I am rather puzzled in this situation, and perhaps even more because I feel, it is really only on Christian grounds that I find it difficult to do military service under the present conditions, *and yet there are only very few friends who would approve of my attitude* [Bonhoeffer's italics]. In spite of much reading and thinking concerning this matter I have not yet made up my mind what I should do under different circumstances. But actually as things are I should have to do violence to my Christian conviction, if I would take up arms "here and now."[100]

Thus Bonhoeffer sought a solution that would not make the Confessing church suffer for his own individual decision based upon his conscience. His decision to leave for a certain period might well please his colleagues, who were still smarting from their experience with Barth's letter to Hromádka. This was the case he made to the Council of Brethren, whom he asked for a leave of absence, and it was what he told Niebuhr: "The *Bruderrat* [Council of Brethren] of the Confessional church would like to have him evade the issue."[101]

Several weeks later Bonhoeffer used a very different emphasis in describing the matter to Henry Smith Leiper. This was in June, when he was already thinking of going back to Germany:

> At first they [the Council of Brethren] were very reluctant to let me go at all, since they are in need of teachers. It was only when I expressed my hopes that I could be of some use to them by establishing contacts with American theologians and churchmen . . . that they gave me leave. So from the point of view of the Confessional Church my trip to America was meant to be an ecumenic link between our isolated Church in Germany and our friends over here. . . . My personal question and difficulty with regard to military service etc. came in only as a second consideration. Of

course, my colleagues were glad, that I would be able to postpone my decision for at least one year.[102]

This letter certainly gave a correct account of the Council of Brethren's real
views.

Thus for some time Bonhoeffer himself vacillated between which priorities really shaped his decision, testing the strength of each motive. It was
only during his stay in America, on this second journey, that it became evident to him why he had gone. He confided the true facts of the matter to his
diary; while he did not use the word "flight," the meaning was obvious.
Years later, in his letters from prison, he was clear that his return from abroad
had truly signified something other than a return home from a normally
planned mission, writing serenely: "I have not for a moment regretted coming back in 1939."[103]

Bishop Bell's Advice. On 10 March 1939 Bonhoeffer and I took the night train
for Ostend, Belgium. Bonhoeffer was unable to sleep until the train had
passed the German border controls. He already knew that Hitler's attack on
Prague was imminent, and what would his military leave of absence be
worth then?

When he reached London he arranged at once to visit the bishop of
Chichester. This time, in contrast to former visits, he wanted to approach
him about his personal affairs. This incident had no parallel in Bonhoeffer's
life. In 1931 he had regretted never having met the "mentor" whose advice
he might have felt to be valid. Now he sought out the man who stood in
another world, but could listen to him calmly and yet realize the force of the
alternatives: Confessing church and family, pacifism and theology, political
conspiracy and ecumenism. Within his family he could expect no close
commitment to church theology, and among his friends on the Council of
Brethren no freedom toward the political realm. Bell understood both. In
recent years, Bonhoeffer had grown accustomed to discussing things critically with members of the House of Brethren and had found both commitment and relief there in personal confession. For years he had suffered no
lack of friendship with people of his own age or younger. Yet none of this was
sufficient any longer. Now he confided in the older man who, as he knew,
understood how to pray and how to demand what was necessary. He wanted to hear his advice—possibly even his yes or no. Yet later Bonhoeffer carried out his great decision entirely alone.

Everything we know about the conversation between the two men comes
from Bonhoeffer's initial letter and Bell's comments in a later lecture.[104] In

his letter Bonhoeffer told the bishop that he was planning to leave Germany and to go on a mission "somewhere where service is really wanted," and yet where at the same time he could—perhaps as an ecumenical secretary?—serve the Confessing church. Bell probably eased Bonhoeffer's conscience about temporarily leaving Germany. Bonhoeffer, who naturally discussed with him the ticklish problems of the relationship between the Confessing church and the ecumenical movement and found him sympathetic, was very pleased about the renewed contact:

> Before returning to Germany I just wish to thank you once again for the great help you gave me in our talk at Chichester. I do not know what will be the outcome of it all, but it means much to me to realize that you see the great conscientious difficulties with which we are faced.[105]

On 3 April Bonhoeffer went with Leibholz and Rieger to Bexhill in Sussex, where Reinhold Niebuhr was on holiday.[106] There was plenty to talk about, theologically and personally, from the time between 1931 and 1939, for since Paul Lehmann had given Bonhoeffer Niebuhr's *Moral Man and Immoral Society* in 1933, Bonhoeffer had seen little else from this direction. Niebuhr was most helpful, and immediately obtained an invitation for Bonhoeffer to visit his friends Henry Smith Leiper at the Federal Council of Churches in New York and Paul Lehmann at Elmhurst College. This set the course for deliberations as to how Bonhoeffer was to escape from his dilemma in Germany, and discussion of other matters was cut short.

Official Tasks. Although the immediate occasion of the journey to England was Bonhoeffer's personal affairs, most of his time there was spent on official matters concerning the Confessing church.

At a conference of German pastors in Rieger's Church of St. George, Bonhoeffer gave the principal lecture, "Law and Gospel in Pastoral Counseling." Some of the London colleagues who had stood together with him in 1934 were not there, since they now had other views. Bonhoeffer had an affectionate reunion with others, including Franz Hildebrandt and Wolfgang Büsing, Hans Kramm, and the retired legation counselor Adolf Freudenberg, who had emigrated and become a theologian. Meanwhile Bishop Bell had brought over many non-Aryan pastors from the German Evangelical Church—the number of families had now reached forty. After the November pogrom he had already taken care to have the necessary funds ready for them in advance, and he had promised the British government to be responsible for them. Bonhoeffer joined them at a reception for the committee for non-Aryan Christians (founded by Bell) in Bloomsbury House, hosted by Barbara Murray and Helen Roberts. The atmosphere of the gathering was greatly affected by the action "taking Bohemia and Moravia into the protection of the German Reich," as Hitler called his occupation of Prague on 15 March. What new refugee problems would this create, and what helplessness would it reveal among the Allies? There was bewilderment, especially among the older members of the German congregations, that foreign minister Konstantin von Neurath, formerly an active member of the Sydenham congregation, was now to be "*Reichsprotektor*" in the *Hradschin*.

In accordance with his mission from the Berlin Provisional Administration, Bonhoeffer spent much time fostering the ecumenical contacts about which he had spoken to Böhm before leaving Berlin. He was to explore the possibilities for making the ecumenical associations more aware of the Confessing church's interests, discuss proposals for this, and possibly bring in one of the colleagues who had emigrated, such as Hildebrandt. Since the failure of the preliminary negotiations for Oxford in 1937—really since the Chamby meeting in 1936—precious time had elapsed, during which the Confessing church had continued to be excluded from conferences and sessions. In the meantime, however, the provisional World Council of Churches had been formed, and important personnel decisions had been settled. The attendance of associated organizations' representatives, such as Max Diestel of the World Alliance in Larvik, and certain professors at the theologians' commissions, or Hanns Lilje who represented the Lutheran Council, had not been arranged by the governing body of the Confessing church. In May 1938 the Utrecht conference had laid the basis of the Provisional Committee of the World Council of Churches without any official German representation. Schönfeld and Siegmund-Schultze had been present, and Bishop Marahrens should have officially represented the German Evangelical Church, but had not taken part. In view of the difficult situation of the church in Germany, no other invitations had been sent there. There had been a similar state of affairs at the second session of the Provisional Committee at St. Germain in January 1939, where Schönfeld's research department had held a two-day session of the committee to which Gerstenmaier and Menn had been invited. Although the Church Foreign Office could not simply appear everywhere as it liked, its people could at least act and present their points of view as "visitors" here and there, without being bothered by the claims of the Council of Brethren or the Provisional Administration. Canon Hodgson negotiated with Heckel and Krummacher about filling the German places on the Faith and Order research committee, and in 1938 Schönfeld asked Gerstenmaier whether, if need be, he (Schönfeld) should represent the German Evangelical Church. Such letters from Geneva asking for representatives were not received by Böhm at the Provisional Church Administration. After the Utrecht meeting, Willem Visser 't Hooft, not H. L. Henriod, had been working in Geneva as general secretary. This hampered Heckel's attempts to get his office for the German Evangelical Church to the conference table with Schönfeld's help. But for the Confessing church the change was not of much consequence at first.

In this situation Bonhoeffer now took action, first with Bell, Canon Hodgson, and Visser 't Hooft. His conversation with Bell was soon settled. Hodgson visited Bonhoeffer by arrangement, Visser 't Hooft he met by chance. Thus, on the one hand, the tiresome problems reappeared; on the other hand, new and hopeful perspectives became evident.

The Second Attempt with Canon Hodgson. On 29 March Bonhoeffer went to Oxford with the Leibholz family. While Hans Herbert Kramm showed the family the university, and Gerhard Leibholz met the political economist Arthur Beveridge, Dietrich paid a long visit to Canon Leonard Hodgson, the general secretary of Faith and Order. Bonhoeffer's introductory letter and Hodgson's memorandum of the following day give a detailed picture of their second attempt to make their viewpoints clear to one another.[107]

Bonhoeffer proposed that the Confessing church should be permanently represented outside Germany. In his letter to Bell he had described the inadequacy of the Geneva representation even more bluntly.[108] He stressed to Canon Hodgson that the matter had to be dealt with very quickly, since the political situation might soon mean that this was the last attempt. No doubt the "representative" he had in mind was Franz Hildebrandt, who had not yet found a permanent post in England, had the advantage of being free from difficulties over passport and foreign currency, and was very well informed about the German church.

Bonhoeffer's proposals did not fall on fruitful soil. As in 1935, they came to grief over legalistic regulations, which Hodgson carefully and patiently enumerated. In contrast to 1935, Bonhoeffer now raised no claims to exclusiveness, but made what sounded more like a call for help. Canon Hodgson offered to invite the provisional leaders of the Confessing church to the summer conference in Clarens as "visitors," and to give them as friendly a welcome as that given to the Reich church. Bonhoeffer found this impartial gesture hard to stomach. In fact, it was very one-sided, since Heckel and his representatives could be certain of their passports and foreign currency, whereas foreign travel would always be a more difficult problem for representatives of the Provisional Administration. It became clear that Hodgson knew this quite well.

Hodgson's memorandum shows with depressing plainness how tragically the situation of the German church had developed, and how helpless the ecumenical reaction toward this had been. This unfortunate church now received another blow; the ecumenical organizations were not capable of easing their well-organized restrictions. Hodgson was again being asked to do far too much:

> We are advised that "at the present time there is no such Church (i.e., a body having full confidence of the whole church, and able to nominate representatives in its name), and that we must not attempt to treat the different groups within that Church independently as if they were separate churches.[109]

Practically, this embarrassingly correct attempt not to spoil relations with either side shut the Confessing church out. Bonhoeffer had to tell the Provisional Administration that the appointment of a permanent Confessing church representative to Faith and Order was out of the question. At the most, they could send a "visitor" to conferences and meetings, for which Faith and Order was prepared to provide the foreign currency. This actually meant that the delegates to the conferences would be appointed as before, and that their information would continue to be one-sided.

Consequences. Canon Hodgson reported on his conversation with Bonhoeffer to his superior and the Geneva headquarters (among others). It did not escape Schönfeld how Bonhoeffer, after a period of silence, had once more crossed his path. This was the last acute crisis between the two before a radical change developed during the course of the war and Schönfeld took an interest in Bonhoeffer. Schönfeld's view of things is revealed by his letter of 24 February 1939 to Wilhelm Bachmann, who was a young colleague of Heckel and was staying in Cambridge for a time.[110] Schönfeld urged him to use every opportunity in personal conversations to point out the efforts Gerstenmaier and the other gentlemen in the Church Foreign Office, including Bishop Heckel, were making on behalf of ecumenical work. Bachmann was to keep in mind that assertions to the contrary were widespread, partly because of inadequate information about the actual accomplishments of the department.

A few weeks later Schönfeld's friends abroad found such advocacy on behalf of the Church Foreign Office far more difficult, after Heckel openly defended the German Christians' Godesberg declaration against ecumenical protests from throughout the world. The close association between Schönfeld's Geneva office and the Church Foreign Office was what Bonhoeffer had in mind when he wrote to Bell:

> I am afraid we shall very soon be cut off entirely from our brethren abroad. . . . Frankly and with all due respect, the German representatives in Geneva simply cannot represent the cause of the Confessional Church. So there is a real vacancy. . . .[111]

The information that Hodgson passed on to Archbishop of York William Temple, who chaired his commission, increased the difficulties. Unlike Bell, William Temple apparently never had a close relationship to the Confessing church. He did not meet Dietrich Bonhoeffer, nor did Bonhoeffer manage to look him up in March 1939. Bonhoeffer may have failed to note the shift in power within the ecumenical movement after the Oxford and Edinburgh meetings and Temple's greatly enhanced prestige. Since Utrecht, Temple had been chairman of the Provisional Committee for the World Council, with Mott, Germanos, and Boegner as vice chairmen. Until then Temple had been more closely associated with Faith and Order, and so had never really been confronted with Bonhoeffer's ideas and wishes.

Since Temple had very little to do with the German church struggle before the Second World War, his judgments were sometimes strange. This was now the case. By return post, he approved Hodgson's memorandum about the negotiations with Bonhoeffer—"Your statement is entirely exact"; but he added: "I am becoming more than ever eager to raise the question of putting Heckel into the Provisional Committee."[112] This went too far even for Hodgson, who was better informed; he replied that he could quite well understand Temple's opinion, but wished for "some other method" than bringing Heckel into the Provisional Committee of the World Council. He then gave new and interesting glimpses of his conversation with Bonhoeffer:

> It was quite clear to me in my conversation with Bonhoeffer last week that any action on our part which gave any kind of official status to Wahl, Heckel, Krummacher or any of that group, would be regarded as a partisan move unless equivalent status were given simultaneously to Boehm or one of his colleagues. I told him something of our discussion last year and of the argument that the appointment of Heckel would be made possible by the attendance at meetings of Marahrens as well, and quite clearly he did not regard Marahrens as being sufficiently "Confessionalist" to balance Heckel. He felt that on the essential decisive issues they were both on the

wrong side. If we had two places open and could put on both Heckel and a Confessionalist it would be another matter. As it is I fear that the proposal to put on Heckel only may both internally divide our ranks and externally produce an impression of partisanship. . . . Might it not be possible for the Provisional Committee to issue such an invitation (invited to sit with the Prov. Com. like Dusen, Henriod, Keller) both to Heckel and a Confessionalist leader? Even if only Heckel could get the passport and wherewithal to attend, the Committee would nevertheless have maintained its impartiality. . . .[113]

Temple stated more precisely how he had come up with his proposal, but did not insist on it:

I am certainly not going to press this matter against your judgement, but Paton, who was lately here, told me that he thought Visser 't Hooft now agrees with Schönfeld that all the groups in Germany do accept Heckel as their channel of communication with the outside world. It was because of this that I raised the question again. . . .[114]

Paton's information may have been based on the lengthy negotiations that emanated from the Kassel Council that aimed for a unified representation of German church circles, Lutherans, and members of the Confessing church. These negotiations had suffered new setbacks and finally collapsed in 1938; Bonhoeffer did not think much of them. The correspondence revealed how neutral Temple and Hodgson from Faith and Order remained about the issue of who was to represent the German Evangelical Church on the Provisional Committee. They still viewed Marahrens as Heckel's counterpart or even a representative of the Confessing church. Only a few weeks later Temple signed a protest, which had been initiated by Visser 't Hooft, against the Godesberg declaration. Temple had to see how Heckel had severely compromised himself as a "channel of communication," and that Marahrens had also signed a somewhat watered-down Godesberg declaration.

The Godesberg Declaration. On 4 April 1939, immediately after Bonhoeffer's Oxford conversation and the correspondence between the secretary and chairman, the official journal of the German Evangelical Church published the Godesberg declaration signed by Dr. Werner. In part, it stated:

[National Socialism continues] the work of Martin Luther on the ideological and political side [and thus helps], in its religious aspect, the recovery of a true understanding of the Christian faith. . . . The Christian faith is the unbridgeable religious opposite to Judaism. . . . Supra-national and international church structure of a Roman Catholic or world-Protestant character is a political degeneration of Christianity. A fruitful development of genuine Christian faith is possible only within the given orders of creation.[115]

These statements, with their bias toward a nationalistic church, appeared in the official journal with the announcement of the establishment of an "Institute for Investigating and Eliminating Jewish Influence on the Church Life of the German People."

In response, the Provisional Committee of the World Council of Churches issued to its member churches a manifesto signed by Temple, Boegner, Paton, and Visser 't Hooft. In 1961 Visser 't Hooft told the author that this manifesto had been initiated by him, drafted by Barth, and corrected by Temple. It included the following:

> The national structure of the Christian church is not a necessary element of its life. . . . Recognition of spiritual unity . . . without regard to race, nation, or sex, belongs, however, to the nature of the church. The Gospel of Jesus Christ is the fulfillment of the Jewish hope. . . . The Christian church . . . rejoices in the maintenance of community with those of the Jewish race who have accepted the Gospel. . . . The church [has] to proclaim his [Christ's] lordship over all spheres of life, including politics and ideology.[116]

On 6 May the Church Foreign Office sent a telegram signed by Heckel to the Provisional Committee in Geneva:

> Expect immediate withdrawal of manifesto to churches, which far exceeds authority, is based upon a false judgement of actual general situation of Church in Germany and represents an intolerable interference in Germany's internal affairs. German Evangelical Church.

Was this the "channel of communication with the outside world" accepted by all groups in Germany?

Visser 't Hooft. Whereas Bonhoeffer's prearranged meeting with Visser 't Hooft in Oxford proved to be hesitant and reserved, their other informal meeting at Paddington station, arranged almost on the spot, was more promising.

Bonhoeffer had never met Visser 't Hooft, although he had been familiar with his essay on the social gospel since 1930, and the two had often been around each other at neighboring conferences. At any rate, Bonhoeffer knew that this man, as Bonhoeffer himself did, heartily rejected German creation theology. Now Visser 't Hooft had moved into a key position, if not *the* key position, of the ecumenical movement. In May 1938 Temple had been able to prevail that the general secretary of the provisional World Council should be, not the experienced Henriod, but the young Dutchman; William Paton and Henry Leiper served as cosecretaries.

This change meant an increasingly marked change of atmosphere at the Geneva headquarters. Visser 't Hooft had a complete mastery of German and was acquainted with German theological literature. His Barthian theological background and his extensive visits to Germany made it possible for him to judge the forces in the church struggle from a fresh point of view. This became evident to everyone when he energetically promoted the provisional World Council's protest manifesto against the Godesberg declaration.

Bonhoeffer was in London when he heard that the new general secretary was coming to the country. "Would you kindly tell Visser 't Hooft that I am very anxious to see him during his stay in London?"[117] he wrote Bell. He was so certain that he and Visser 't Hooft would see eye-to-eye that he also wanted to discuss his own affairs with him. So he met him at Paddington a few days after his visit to Canon Hodgson.

The long conversation with a man six years his senior relieved Bonhoeffer of his fears that the Confessing church had already been dismissed in Geneva. Two years after that first meeting the confidence that emerged from this encounter assumed an even greater significance. Even now, however, Bonhoeffer discussed not only the question of his church's representation in Geneva, but matters of war and peace, and of theological and political ethics. Directly after the war Visser 't Hooft wrote of the meeting:

> We had heard a great deal about each other, but it was surprising how quickly we were able to get beyond the first stage of merely feeling our way, into the deeper realm of real conversation—that, in fact, he was soon treating me as an old friend. . . . We walked up and down the platform for a long time. He described the situation of his church and country. He spoke in a way that was remarkably free from illusions, and sometimes almost clairvoyantly, about the coming war, which would start soon, probably in the summer. It would drive the Confessing church into even greater distress. . . . Had not the time now come to refuse to serve a government that was heading straight for war and breaking all the commandments? But what consequences would this position have for the Confessing church? I remember his acute questions better than his answers; but I think I learned more from his questions than he did from my answers. In the impenetra-

ble world between "Munich" and "Warsaw," in which hardly anyone ventured to formulate the actual problems clearly, this questioning voice was
a liberation.[118]

The reason why Visser 't Hooft remembered the questions better than the
answers may be that Bonhoeffer had just begun to seek answers for his questions. And he tried these out on several people before he began to give his
own original answers.

The balance of ecumenical forces was changing considerably, but certain
old laws remained in effect. In Utrecht in 1938, Life and Work had handed
over its responsibilities to the provisional World Council and its general
secretaries. As secretary of the provisional World Council, Visser 't Hooft
became responsible at the same time for Life and Work as long as it still existed. After the formation of the provisional World Council was approved,
however, Faith and Order retained its independent organization and executive, with Canon Hodgson remaining its general secretary. Among the successful campaigners for that independence was the aged Bishop Headlam of
Gloucester, who during the great wave of arrests in 1937 had written to
Dorothy Buxton that it was nonsense to speak of a persecution of Christians
in Germany.

Thus Bonhoeffer saw the new general secretary of Life and Work continue what Bell and Ammundsen had already begun, namely, to support
spiritually—with whatever interruptions—the Confessing church "which
was felt to represent the whole Church of Christ in its battle for the purity
and truth of the Christian message," in Visser 't Hooft's words.[119]

On the other hand, he saw how the usual strict impartiality of Faith and
Order benefited the Reich church's representatives. It had again become
clear that, in view of German conditions, no one could avoid taking sides,
however anxious he might be to do so. Even reserving judgment meant giving support to one side against the other.

After his visits to Bell and his meeting with Visser 't Hooft, Bonhoeffer
had more confidence that the excluded Confessing church would continue
to be heard in the ecumenical world. When he met Visser 't Hooft for the
second time—two years later in Geneva—it was as if they had been close
friends for a long time.

Departure. Bonhoeffer stayed longer in London than he had planned, more
than five weeks, although he soon finished what he had intended to do. The
reason was that he thought war might break out at any moment. He was
impressed by the complete change of public opinion in London after Hitler's

abrupt breach of the Munich agreement on 15 March; everyone approved of the British government's answer in the form of a guarantee for Poland.

Bonhoeffer wondered whether he ought not to let himself be caught by the war while he was near his sister in England. "The main question that is rather holding me back is whether I should still expect Uncle Rudi here," he wrote to his parents on 13 April.[120] But they reassured him, saying that it was not yet time for the arrival of "Uncle Rudi." While he was in London, he saw the film *Queen Victoria* with Adolf Wohlbrück. When he saw the ongoing history of the country that was now threatened, he confessed, he could not hold back tears of anger.

He returned to Berlin on 18 April. As he was coming home Hitler was holding a booming birthday parade in front of the technical college in Charlottenburg. In the official journal of the German Evangelical Church, above Dr. Werner's signature, the words appeared:

> [We celebrate] with jubilation our *Führer*'s fiftieth birthday. In him God has given the German people a real miracle worker. . . . Let our thanks be the resolute and inflexible will not to disappoint . . . our *Führer* and the great historic hour.[121]

Even *Junge Kirche*, which had formerly been so brave, wrote:

> It has today become evident to everyone without exception that the figure of the *Führer*, powerfully fighting his way through old worlds, seeing with his mind's eye what is new and compelling its realization, is named on those few pages of world history that are reserved for the initiators of a new epoch. . . . The figure of the *Führer* has brought a new obligation for the church too.[122]

America: June and July 1939

Only a month and a half after coming home from England, Bonhoeffer left Germany again. May was filled with efforts to forestall the military authorities' order to report to the recruitment office, and to convince the Old Prussian Union Council of Brethren, which had no desire to give up one of its few theological teachers who held uncompromisingly to Barmen and Dahlem, that it would be right and proper for him to go to America. But the Council of Brethren had never liked to refuse Bonhoeffer's wishes. This time there were three reasons for thinking the journey would be advisable: first, because it might do something to mitigate the ecumenical isolation of the Confessing church; second, because of Bonhoeffer's old maxim that a church was in a bad state if it could no longer grant people leave for carrying out special missions, as he had arranged for Gerhard Ebeling; and third, there was the hope of once again avoiding a decision to refuse military service if he were called up.

A Difficult Departure. Bonhoeffer and his friends had reason for relief when the journey began at the Tempelhof airfield on 2 June. Everything had turned out well; he would see the Leibholz family in London, and then, with his brother Karl-Friedrich, who had been invited to lecture in Chicago, he would begin the journey across the Atlantic on board the *Bremen*. In addition, May had brought no worsening of the international political situation.

But the departure was becoming more difficult than he wanted to admit. For the first time Bonhoeffer handed me a written will, and the state of his church duties in Germany was not as he would have wished to leave them. No substitute had been found to take over the directorship of the collective pastorate. For the unknown person who would take his place in Sigurdshof he left a note on the table: "To my successor. He will find here: 1. one of the finest tasks in the Confessing Church. . . ." To requests about the subjects of instruction he added: "He is asked . . . to go out walking with the brothers as much as possible, or to be with them in some other way."[123]

It was not till weeks later that Hellmut Traub, one of Karl Barth's former students, began shuttling between teaching in Köslin and in Sigurdshof. Unfortunately, Bonhoeffer did not get news of this for some weeks, and he was still worrying about it in New York when his mind should have been free to think of other things.

In addition, the church struggle had intensified just about the time he was leaving. On 1 June Werner halted the subsidies for pastors' salaries in parishes where pastors still did not collect and turn in the collections according to his official plan, but followed the Confessing church's collection schedule. On 2 June he placed Martin Niemöller, who was in a concentration camp, on the retired list. While the small minority within the Confessing church was thus being further deprived of its rights, the majority was making efforts to accommodate itself to the new language. On 31 May the church leaders' conference endorsed a declaration addressed to Kerrl and signed by Marahrens, Wurm, Meiser, and others, stating the conditions under which they would agree to the Godesberg declaration. The statement maintained that the Evangelical church directed its members "to join fully and devotedly in the *Führer*'s national political constructive work. . . . In the national sphere of life there must be a serious and responsible racial policy of maintaining the purity of our nation."[124] Thus Bonhoeffer was plagued, from the very beginning of the journey, by the thought of the people who were left behind:

> My thoughts alternate between you and the future. . . . Greetings to all the brethren; you will now be having evening prayers!
>
> So far I am still surprised that everything has turned out like this. I am already looking forward to your coming to see me![125]

Aboard the ship he wrote, referring to the daily lectionary for 8 June ("Judge rightly"):

> First of all I beg this of you, the brothers who are still at home. I do not want to be spared in your thoughts.
>
> Great programs always simply lead us to where we are; but we ought to be found only where he [God] is. We can no longer, in fact, be anywhere else than where he is. Whether it is you working over there, or I working in America, we are all only where he is. He takes us with him. Or have I, after all, avoided the place where he is? The place where he is for me? No, God says, you are my servant.

And on the day before he landed in New York he wrote:

> If only the doubts about my own course had been overcome.[126]

As he had done on long journeys in previous years, he kept a diary with short notes about that day's scriptural reading.[127] It offers distressing insight into his inner conflicts about which path he should follow.

An Uneasy Arrival. Instead of ending this inner uncertainty, Bonhoeffer's arrival in New York intensified his agonized misgivings. There is no doubt that he was received with nothing but generosity, affection, and helpfulness. Leiper, the executive secretary of the Federal Council of Churches, remembered him from Gland, Sofia, and Fanö, where he had always taken Bonhoeffer's and Monod's side. Leiper looked forward to his coming: "I know him well and am keen about him. I shall certainly be glad to do anything I can to help him," he had replied to Niebuhr.[128] And to Samuel Cavert he wrote:

> Knowing Bonhoeffer very well, I was struck with the peculiar fitness of the man for just the thing we had been discussing and immediately called up Dr. Paul Tillich who had been appointed with me as a committee to find a man. Tillich was even more enthusiastic about Bonhoeffer than I and stated his conviction that he was exactly the right person for this delicate and difficult task. . . . His skill and aptitude in pastoral work are exceptional.[129]

But the short notice of the invitation to America and the necessary caution that had to be observed when writing by post led to misunderstandings on both sides and mistakes about the basic requirements. Bonhoeffer's own unacknowledged uncertainty made him want too much: he wanted to leave Germany, but he did not want to burn all his bridges. How were the New York friends to understand this, after Niebuhr had wired them that Bonhoeffer was in danger and must be rescued?

Only gradually did Bonhoeffer realize that the proposals intended to help him had come from four different organizations whose proposed projects were, in part, hardly compatible with his ideas.

The first proposal, to put Bonhoeffer to work for the summer conferences of the Student Christian Movement from June onward, soon fell through. The second proposal came from Union Theological Seminary, whose president, Dr. Coffin, invited him to lecture during the traditional summer sessions in July and August. That invitation had been the first to reach Bonhoeffer, and made it possible to receive a deferment from the army recruitment office. It also shaped his initial picture of the future he imagined, that would "give me an opportunity of seeing a good deal of the theological schools."[130] He began to prepare for the task.

Third, Paul Lehmann had promised to arrange for him to give courses of lectures at various colleges and universities. Lehmann undertook this in June, and had already received promising responses, but by that time Bonhoeffer was already preparing to return home.

The fourth proposal became the crucial one; it envisaged that the Federal Council should employ Bonhoeffer to work with the refugees in New York and employ him at denominational conferences and summer camps. In agreement with van Dusen and Samuel McCrea Cavert, Leiper planned a sphere of activity that would have engaged Bonhoeffer for three years. That plan reached Bonhoeffer just before he left Berlin, but it was not clearly worded and seemed merely to ratify the second proposal: "Important Combination Post Theological Lectureship and Church Work at Summer Conferences and Universities."[131] What this really meant—refugee work—could not, of course, be openly telegraphed to Berlin.

Only after his arrival did Bonhoeffer learn that he was to be entrusted with the care of emigrants in New York, on behalf of the "American Committee for Christian German Refugees in the City of New York." But to accept such a post would have ruled out any return to Germany. Thus on 13 June, after his first meeting with Leiper, he wrote in his diary:

> My starting-point for everything is that I intend to go back in one year at the latest. Surprise. But it is quite clear to me that I must go back.[132]

In the days that followed, without advice or news from Germany, he struggled with his conscience in the guest room at Union Theological Seminary (the so-called prophets' chamber), during his stay in President Coffin's country house, and as he walked the streets of New York. On the evening of 13 June, at Coffin's house in the opulent countryside near Lakeville, he wrote:

> With all this, only Germany is missing, the brothers. The first lonely hours are difficult. I do not understand why I am here, whether it was a sensible thing to do, whether the results will be worth while. . . . I have now been almost two weeks without knowing what is going on there. It is almost unbearable. . . .

On 14 June:

> Prayers. I was almost overcome by the short prayer—the whole family knelt down—in which we thought of the German brothers.

On 15 June:

> Since yesterday evening I haven't been able to stop thinking about Germany. I would not have thought it possible that at my age, after so many years abroad, one could get so dreadfully homesick. . . . This inactivity, or rather activity in unimportant things, is quite intolerable when one thinks of the brothers and of how precious time is. The whole burden of self-reproach because of a wrong decision comes back again and almost overwhelms me.[133]

That same day he wrote Dr. Leiper a long letter, giving in advance his points of view for the definitive conversation they were to have on 20 June about his future. The way back, he said, must remain open. "I must not for the sake of loyalty to the Confessional church accept a post which on principle would make my return to Germany impossible." He asked whether the work could not at least be organized under a name that would omit the "refugees" in the title; secondly, he said, he had come to get acquainted with theological training centers, and he wanted to keep time for this. In addition, the job in question ought to be filled by a genuine refugee; he (Bonhoeffer) would not on any account stand in the way of any such person who did not have the same opportunities for work that he did.[134]

Such considerations suggested that Bonhoeffer was no longer indifferent about whether war broke out while he was abroad, as he had felt only two months before in England. On 16 June he noted: "Disquieting political news from Japan. If it becomes unsettled now, I am definitely going back to Germany. I cannot stay outside by myself. This is quite clear. My whole life is over there."[135]

20 June. Then came 20 June 1939, the day that decided Bonhoeffer's future. He had suspected it would. The previous evening he walked aimlessly around Times Square. Then he wrote:

> Without news from Germany the whole day, from post to post; waiting in vain. It is no use getting angry.... I want to know what is happening to the work over there, whether all is well or whether I am needed. I want to have some sign from over there before the decisive meeting tomorrow. Perhaps it is a good thing that it has not come.[136]

The next day he went to see Henry Leiper at the Federal Council of Churches. Leiper had already cleared the first thousand dollars for the new work, but Bonhoeffer declined. Leiper felt he had been let down. In the evening Bonhoeffer wrote in his diary:

> Visited Leiper. The decision has been made. I have refused. They were clearly disappointed, and rather upset. It probably means more for me than I can see at the moment. God alone knows what. It is remarkable how I am never quite clear about the motives for any of my decisions. Is that a sign of confusion, of inner dishonesty, or is it a sign that we are guided without our knowing, or is it both? ... Today's scripture reading speaks dreadfully harshly of God's incorruptible judgement. He certainly sees how much personal feeling, how much anxiety, there is in today's decision, however brave it may seem. The reasons that one gives for an action to others and to one's self are certainly inadequate. One can give a reason for everything. In the last resort one acts from a level which remains hidden from us. So we can only ask God to judge us and forgive us.... At the end of the day I can only ask God to give a merciful judgement on today and all its decisions. It is now in his hands.[137]

Bonhoeffer had made the great decision of his life entirely alone. Paul Lehmann, who with his warmth and wisdom was the person in America who meant the most to Bonhoeffer, was not in New York. His friends at home were too busy; they did not write in time, and did not even know what was at stake for him.

Although Bonhoeffer had made up his mind, he was assailed by new objections in the days that followed. Only now could he tell what had been behind one wish or another:

> Of course I still keep having second thoughts about my decision. One could have also given quite different reasons: first, I am here (and perhaps the misunderstanding [i.e., with Leiper] itself was a form of being guided?); they say that it was like an answer to a prayer when my coming was announced; they would like to have *me*; they cannot understand why

I refuse; it upsets all their plans for the future; I have no news from home and perhaps everything there is going well without me, etc. Or one could ask: have I simply acted out of a longing for Germany and the work there? And is this almost incomprehensible homesickness, which has hardly ever affected me before, an accompanying sign from above to make refusal easier for me? Or, isn't it irresponsible with so many other people involved, simply to say No to one's own future and to that of many others? Will I regret it? I may not—that is certain. Despite everything, there is first of all the promise, then the joy of working at home, and lastly of the person whose job I would be taking. The reading is again so harsh: "He will sit as a refiner and purifier of silver" (Mal. 3: 3). And it is necessary. I am at my wits' end: but [God] knows, and in the end all doings and actions will be clear and pure.

On 22 June he wrote: "I am most sorry for Sabine about my decision."[138] He told his parents about the new situation at once:

[Discussions have] shown that just about everything has changed. I was invited to stay as long as I wanted, but I have declined. . . . So I think I shall return in the autumn. Nothing else is possible, if I am to reconcile the wishes from here and over there. And after all, that is quite right. I do not know whether I should have stood the atmosphere here for long; it is all terribly sensational and full of hatred and horribly pharisaic. Personally I have found the friendliest reception everywhere from my former friends, but that is really not enough. Now I am working hard on my lecture courses, and that is giving me a great deal of pleasure.[139]

What had really caused him to decide on 20 June 1939 to return to Germany was not always clear in the letters and conversations of those days. It was simply his readiness to recognize that he was and would have to remain a German, fully accepting of guilt and responsibility. In his diary, Germany now entered the picture beside the church, as it hardly ever had before. On 22 June he wrote:

To be here during a catastrophe is simply unthinkable, unless things are so ordained. But to be guilty of it myself, and to have to reproach myself that I left unnecessarily, is certainly devastating. We cannot separate ourselves from our destiny, least of all out here. . . .

It is so strange how strongly these particular thoughts move me in these days, and *how difficult it is for any thoughts of the Una sancta to make headway*.[140]

Direct access to the *Una sancta*, which in his flight from Germany he had longed for and sought, was now barred. On the contrary, he had to relinquish the *Una sancta* in order to share his nation's destiny and guilt in those evil days. Only in that way would he be able to find access once more to a universal church.

Perhaps he put his case most clearly in a letter to Reinhold Niebuhr, to whom he particularly owed an explanation of his startling decision:

> I have made a mistake in coming to America. I must live through this difficult period of our national history with the Christian people of Germany. I will have no right to participate in the reconstruction of Christian life in Germany after the war if I do not share the trials of this time with my people. . . . Christians in Germany will face the terrible alternative of either willing the defeat of their nation in order that Christian civilization may survive, or willing the victory of their nation and thereby destroying our civilization. I know which of these alternatives I must choose; but I cannot make that choice in security.[141]

When the summer school at Union Seminary began, Professor John McNeill, the specialist on Calvin, occupied the "prophets' chamber." He was surprised by the amount of illegible sheets of paper left by his unknown predecessor, and at the quantities of cigarettes he had smoked. McNeill thought he must be either a very hard worker or very disorderly. Only later did he realize who had lived there before him and had made the most difficult of all his decisions in that room.

Travel Plans. No sooner had the decision to return home been taken than worries arose about leaving on time.

The problem of paying for the return journey created no difficulty between Bonhoeffer and his hosts, since the cost was paid out of his brother-in-law Gerhard Leibholz's account, which had not yet been blocked. But there remained the obligation of delivering the lectures at the summer school. So on 23 June Bonhoeffer fixed the date of departure for 12 August, just after the end of the course. On 24 June came the long and anxiously awaited post from eastern Pomerania; now "it is completely clear to me that I must go back to the work."[142] On 26 June the daily scripture from 2 Timothy 4:21 read: "Do your best to come before winter."

> That has followed me throughout the day. It is as if we were soldiers on leave who then return to action despite everything that awaits them. We cannot get away from it. Not as if we were essential, as if we were needed (by God?!), but simply because that is where our life is, and because we leave our life behind, we destroy it, if we are not back there. It is not a mat-

ter of piety, but of something more vital. But God acts not just through pious feelings but through these vital ones. "Do your best to come before winter"—it is not a misuse of scripture if I apply that to myself. If God gives me grace to do it.[143]

The news grew more alarming with each day. In Danzig Goebbels had made a speech with threats that could hardly be surpassed. Then Bonhoeffer heard from Chicago that his brother Karl-Friedrich was also going home and had declined the offer of a professorship. With that, he decided to leave on 8 July.

> 28 June: I cannot imagine that it is God's will for me to remain here without anything particular to do in case of war. I must travel at the first possible opportunity. . . .
>
> 30 June: As in the present situation I would in any case have gone in four weeks at the latest, with things as they are I have decided to go on the eighth with Karl-Friedrich. If war breaks out I do not want to be here, and it is impossible to get any objective news about the situation. That was a great decision.
>
> 1 July: I could not get away all day from thinking about the situation in Germany and in the church.[144]

The next day he wrote anxiously to his parents: Can you "please write Uncle Rudi's birthday to Sabine for me in good time, so that I can, if necessary, send my personal congratulations?"[145] This time he did not want to be caught in England if war broke out.

Meanwhile there was one person who, in gloomy foreboding, would all too gladly have changed Bonhoeffer's mind—Paul Lehmann. Bonhoeffer himself wrote: "It would be good to stay another four weeks. But the price is too high."[146]

Paul Lehmann. In spite of the long silence, the old friendship had continued with undiminished cordiality. When Bonhoeffer decided to leave on 8 July he wrote in his diary: "This morning there is another letter from Paul, who was so optimistic about my staying here."[147]

Lehmann had written:

> I do know that it is unthinkable that you should return before America shall have had the fullest opportunity to be enriched by your contribution to its theological hour of destiny. At least I like to think of it in this way. The tragic political occasion for these disturbed times may have one great and

positive overtone in the widening of the American theological understanding by the cross fertilization with the continental tradition. So that
you must see this also as a responsibility as well as the German need for
teachers.—And besides, Marion and I need very badly to see you again.
Surely you would not deprive us of the hope that we have carried with us
since the day when we left the café on Unter den Linden. With your anticipated permission I have already taken steps to bring this about.[148]

Lehmann had written from Elmhurst College to some thirty or forty colleges, not without stressing Niebuhr's interest in Bonhoeffer; the first positive answers were already coming in. When Bonhoeffer saw the letter, he
noticed that it contained a sentence which was hardly diplomatic; the résumé
mentioned that Bonhoeffer had continued to teach secretly in Pomerania
after the seminary had been closed by the authorities. Bonhoeffer drew
Lehmann's attention to this: "If such a document were to get into the hands
of any German authority, the work that is going on meanwhile would be
over,"[149] and he asked him to inform the colleges that it was all a misunderstanding, and that Bonhoeffer had already gone back to Germany. Lehmann
at once accepted responsibility for this mistake and for the likelihood that
those who received his second letter would shake their heads over such
inefficiency:

> Word has just come that the circumstances of Mr. Bonhoeffer's visit to the
> United States have been entirely misunderstood and that the contemplat-
> ed opportunity of inviting him cannot materialize owing to his return to
> Germany. The committee[150] appreciates the courtesy of your interest in its
> effort and regrets very much the error of its earlier communication.[151]

It is distressing to imagine what would have happened if Paul Lehmann
had been able to meet Bonhoeffer when he arrived on 12 June on the New
York pier. Now it was too late: "I cannot tell you how deeply it troubles both
Marion and me. I write now, believe me, with great heaviness of spirit."[152]
There was only just enough time to hurry to New York and take his friend
to the pier.

> 6 July: At half past two I meet Paul Lehmann in my room; he has come
> from Columbus, Ohio, to see me again. A great pleasure. From now on we
> shall have the rest of the time together.
>   7 July: The last day. Paul is still trying to keep me back. It will not do
> now. . . . I go on board with Paul. Good-bye at half past eleven. . . .[153]

"*Protestantism Without Reformation*." His decision not only turned his thoughts to the journey home, but inspired new concentration to write and observe. When he left, Bonhoeffer wrote: "I have perhaps learned more during this month than in the whole year nine years ago."[154] The "month" that he had worked had hardly been a fortnight.

In 1939 Bonhoeffer saw things with different eyes than he had in 1930. His American friends seemed changed to him and more open. A number of university lecturers arrived on 1 July for the beginning of the summer course. Bonhoeffer did not see Reinhold Niebuhr, who was staying in Glasgow, but he saw his brother Richard.[155] In the course of a few days he read an amazing amount of material. He analyzed the series of articles, "How My Mind Has Changed," published every ten years by the *Christian Century*.[156] In 1939 it contained a feisty retrospective by Barth for the first time. Bonhoeffer thought that the Americans had partly reached the position he had fought for—in vain, he had thought—ten years before. He wrote down on a slip of paper: "Barthianism in small doses; here, as everywhere, amazing ignorance." As in 1931, he had much criticism of America's religious propensities; his critique was even blunter since the church struggle and *Discipleship*:

> The Anglo-Saxons may be more religious than we are, but they are certainly not more Christian if they put up with sermons like these.[157]

In Riverside Church he heard a sermon on 18 June on the philosopher James's phrase "accepting a horizon." That evening, feeling desperately in need of direction instead of brilliant analysis, he went to the Broadway Presbyterian Church, and found what he was seeking from the arch-fundamentalist Dr. McComb. McComb preached on "our likeness with Christ," not suspecting the decision taking shape in the mind of one worshiper. A few days later Bonhoeffer discussed the two sermons with friends. He did not know that fundamentalists were totally opposed to any church union, and was told that they really could not be regarded as more reliable than the people at Riverside, despite their biblicism. Bonhoeffer knew as much from his experience with pietist groups in Germany. On one essay in *Christian Century* by a fundamentalist, who saw the root of all evil in the existence of "modernists" and "unionists," Bonhoeffer commented: "That does not get at Satan."

The real reason Bonhoeffer thought he was more perceptive during this short stay in America in 1939 than he had been in 1930 was his own experience of existential insecurity. This time the refugee and person turning back home could appreciate the nation of refugees. In 1930 he had reacted to

Christian America with European theological arrogance. In 1939 he respected, with clearsighted love, America's special history as the nation of refugees who have escaped the ultimate conflict and regard tolerance as sacred.

After a few days' study he began to formulate the essay that lay in his desk until after the war: "Protestantism Without Reformation."[158] He wrote most of it at Union Seminary and in London, and the rest during the days of mobilization in Berlin. It did not concern him that there was no longer any possibility of having it published; he wanted to organize and write down his observations.

The essay represents a modification of Bonhoeffer's earlier ecumenical reflections. He still anchored his ecclesiology Christocentrically and not in positivism, but he had a more differentiated view of the historical reality of denomination. He did not rashly confine his judgment to one theological systematic, but took sociological factors into account. His analytical observations and power to think systematically did not exclude but inform each other.

The heart of the essay consists of parts II and III on the "Christian's Refuge" and "Freedom."[159] Both themes were new compared with the America report of 1931 and his 1935 essay on the ecumenical movement. In the most recent phase of the church struggle, in the discussion on whether Gestapo orders of expulsion should be accepted or refused, the alternative between "holding out and fleeing in times of persecution" had been posed very clearly.[160] Paul Schneider's answer to this dilemma set a magnificent example, but others responded differently. (After repeatedly criticizing the Nazis in his sermons, Schneider was arrested and murdered in Buchenwald in 1938.) In *Discipleship* Bonhoeffer had written about the weakness of the Word, stating his opinion that flight might be legitimate for the disciples.[161] Now he had put flight to the test existentially, and he discovered that it was a key to a new understanding of the American "denomination." In "denomination"—that indefinite self-characterization of the churches that consciously lags behind the European concept of the Church—he found a certain dialectic of humility and demand. This theological phenomenology was filled by Bonhoeffer's latest experiences:

> Perseverance to the end can be necessary; flight may be permissible, even necessary. The flight of Christians in persecution does not of itself signify apostasy and disgrace; for God does not call everyone to martyrdom. Not to flee, but to disavow one's faith, is sin; that is to say that there can be a situation where flight is equivalent to renunciation, just as on the other hand flight itself can be a part of martyrdom. . . . The Christian refugee claimed

for himself the right to forgo the ultimate suffering, in order to be able to serve God in quietness and peace. Now, in the place of refuge, there is no more justification for a continuation of the struggle. . . . His longing for a decision for truth against its distortion remains, and must remain, unfulfilled. In the last resort, it is faithfulness to its own church history that is expressed in this peculiar relativism of the question of truth in the thought and deeds of American Christianity.[162]

On the American pride in the freedom that had been institutionalized by the churches he was far more critical, based upon his rich experience in Germany:

The essential freedom of the church is not a gift of the world to the church, but the freedom of the Word of God itself to gain a hearing. . . . But where thanks for institutional freedom is rendered through sacrificing the freedom of preaching, the church is in chains, even if it believes itself to be free.[163]

As in 1931, Bonhoeffer missed Christology:

In American theology, Christianity is still essentially religion and ethics. But because of this, the person and work of Jesus Christ for theology must sink into the background and in the long run remain misunderstood.[164]

He felt obligated to indicate that a substantial distance remained between him and American Christians, even when their mutual understanding for each other's history had grown.

Bonhoeffer also revived his ecumenical passion by critically expressing what disturbed him, since part of ecumenical community is the characterizing of contrasts. Dawdling on the noncommittal conversational level would not have been a positive response, and he could not have remained silent on the question: "What is God doing to and with his church in America? What is he doing through it to us, and through us to it?"[165]

Because of this he believed that the ecumenical partners should pay careful attention to each other's questions. In Europe the churches of the Reformation wanted to be questioned on the basis of their confession in the act of splitting off; but the American denominations—"Protestantism without Reformation"—which had inherited the consequences of this schism but were no longer conscious of the schismatic act itself, did not want to be judged on the basis of a committed confessional statement and its theology.

With this essay Bonhoeffer turned his very personal American experience into a cornerstone of ecumenical awareness that held true in general.

The Journey Home. The ship glided out of the New York harbor on the warm summer night of 7 July; Dietrich and Karl-Friedrich Bonhoeffer were returning to Europe to face war.

> The journey is over. I am glad to have been over there, and glad to be on my way home again . . . at least I have acquired some important insight for all future personal decisions. Probably this visit will have a great effect on me.
>
> Since I have been on the ship my inner uncertainty about the future has ceased. I can think of my shortened time in America without reproaches. Reading: "It is good for me that I was afflicted, that I might learn thy statutes" (Psalm 119:71). One of my favorite passages from my favorite psalm.[166]

Bonhoeffer stayed ten days with his sister in London and met Hildebrandt, but communicated with Bishop Bell only by letter:

> My passport expires next spring; it is therefore uncertain when I shall be in this country again. . . . We shall never forget you during the coming events.[167]

In the meantime Niebuhr had suggested another project to John Baillie, his colleague at Union Seminary from 1930, and Bonhoeffer received an invitation to deliver the Edinburgh "Croall Lectures" the following winter. While still in London, Bonhoeffer accepted; from Berlin on 24 August he sent Baillie the topic: "The Death in the Christian Message."[168] A few days later the war began. In this disastrous moment he returned to a theme from his youthful days. Just after the First World War, when he was fourteen, he had obtained a reproduction of the lithograph *Vom Tode* from an exhibition of Max Klinger's work. He later remarked, almost incidentally, that he expected an early death.[169] Now, at the beginning of the Second World War, he wrote a letter to the Finkenwalde students about the death that belongs to us and the death that does not belong to us, about a "death from without" and a "death from within": "We may pray that death from without does not come to us till we have been made ready for it through this inner death; for our death is really only the gateway to the perfect love of God."[170] Bonhoeffer was already beginning to take a literary interest in the theme of death, for example, in the works of Joachim Wach (which August Knorr gave him in Köslin), Fritz Dehn, and Georges Barbarin.[171]

One afternoon during his last few days in London, Bonhoeffer was sitting at the piano, teaching his sister's children some English nursery rhymes. Rieger came in, took him aside, and told him that on 19 July Paul Schneider had been tortured to death in Buchenwald. This was the pure martyrdom Bonhoeffer had visualized in his London sermon on Jeremiah in 1934, and was now closed to him. On 25 July 1939 his relatives went with him to the station. On his journey home he visited Pastor Hermann Hesse in Elberfeld and Hans Iwand in Dortmund, to discuss with them the continuation of the seminary. On 27 July he was back in Berlin.

The War

The Old Work Continues. Bonhoeffer's unexpectedly short absence did not permit his friends and those on the Councils of Brethren to know what had happened meanwhile in his life. No one knew of his correspondence with Leiper and Niebuhr, let alone its content; everyone was preoccupied with what was happening in church and state. At first there was no striking change in Bonhoeffer himself; he returned to the collective pastorates in eastern Pomerania as a matter of course, to finish the term despite the general preparations for war.

To celebrate his return, each group of ordinands spent a week that summer on the Baltic coast, little affected by the daily *Luftwaffe* squadron maneuvers and the eastward movement of tanks and troops along Highway 2. Bonhoeffer brought along one of Paul Lehmann's students, George Kalbfleisch, who had attended the Amsterdam youth conference.

But after a messenger came from his parents with the news that "Uncle Rudi" was doing so badly that there was now no hope and Ribbentrop arrived in Moscow on 23 August to sign the nonaggression pact, Bonhoeffer broke off the Sigurdshof and Köslin summer courses. They were much too close to the front. On 26 August Bonhoeffer and the author arrived at his parents' home on Marienburger Allee, where he spent the last days of peace and the first days of war, up to mid-October.

On 20 June in New York, Bonhoeffer had probably imagined that the impact of the beginning of the war would be different from what it turned out to be. Everything seemed much less complicated. There was no crisis within the population, no intensification of hopes for a coup, no onslaught by the Allied Powers, not even an enlistment order or a halt to the secret training of seminarians. On 3 September Bonhoeffer and his brother Klaus were in Eichkamp discussing the situation—against Hitler's and Ribbentrop's calculations, Great Britain had declared war after all. Suddenly the sirens wailed through the town. Bonhoeffer jumped on his bicycle and reached his parents in five minutes, but no bomb fell, no plane was to be seen, no shot was to be heard; nothing happened.

Nor was there any great display of emotion in those early September days. Dietrich's father, Karl Bonhoeffer, wrote in his memoirs:

> The mood with which we entered the war in 1939 was basically different from that of 1914. Then, there was a fairly general consensus that this was a defensive war in a righteous cause; the attitude of the Social Democratic Party in the Reichstag was characteristic. Hardly anyone who knew the Kaiser doubted that his outlook was that of a peace lover who feared war. True, there was widespread recognition and regret at his provocative enlargement of the fleet and his unfortunate penchant for making speeches in which he brandished the sword rather theatrically, and Great Britain's growing prosperity was disliked and regarded as upsetting the balance of power; but it is probably true that the German government did not actively want an armed conflict. In 1939 the people had no doubt that this was a war of aggression, prepared for and organized by Hitler, for which there was no kind of sympathy among most of the population.[172]

Karl Bonhoeffer's view of the events of 1914 may now be questionable, but his account conveyed the widespread belief of the time.

In some Christian circles, on 1 September 1939, the dominant emotion was a grim acceptance of the catastrophe as a necessary judgment. Bonhoeffer expressed this in the first Finkenwalde newsletter of the war, where he lamented the death of Theodor Maass, the first former seminarian to be killed in action:

> I don't know whether we shall have as difficult a time now with the question of theodicy as we did in the last war. . . . Christians probably know more today about the Biblical verdict upon the world and history, so they may be confirmed in their faith, rather than sorely tried, by present events.[173]

In contrast to the situation in September 1938, there was nothing to raise the hopes for a coup. At Hitler's *Berghof* on 22 August the commanders offered no opposition, although some of them, even the National Socialist General von Reichenau, had doubts.[174] Admonitory memos from Canaris or General Thomas, head of the Department of Economic Defense, did not get past Commander in Chief Wilhelm Keitel. With respect to the National Socialist leaders, who were counting on a blitzkrieg, the generals' position was weaker than ever. At that point the civilians in the resistance could not make any headway with the generals with whom they had contact. The only reply they received was that the situation was different from that of 1938, that Hitler had success on his side, and that now, above all, the commitment the military leaders had made with their oath could not be disregarded. Only after the war had brought the most bitter experiences were these military leaders prepared to consider new revolutionary plots, but that time was still a long way off. Although Bonhoeffer thought the beginning of the war would bring about the final catastrophe for Hitler, he had no idea how far away the end would be.

The outbreak of war brought some changes for the church's situation. After 1 September 1939 the church struggle became less important and received less publicity. To give his new church administration a more impressive facade, Dr. Werner convened a Confidential Spiritual Council on 29 August. It consisted of three men: Bishop Marahrens, Dr. Friedrich Hymmen, vice president of the central consistory in Berlin, and Bishop Walther Schultz of Mecklenburg, an extreme "German Christian" who allowed the Eucharist to be celebrated in his church as a cult of blood and the soil. No one took this Confidential Spiritual Council very seriously. On 2 September it issued a public proclamation, which said of the Evangelical church: "It has supplied the weapons of steel with the invincible forces out of God's Word. . . ."[175]

The Confessing church's situation eased somewhat. Some consistories, such as that in Saxony, now allowed illegal pastors to pursue their calling— unless they had already been inducted into the army—and made it possible to pay them out of official funds, although they explicitly stated that this did not imply any recognition of their eligibility. Still, in September 1939, 360 Confessing church pastors suffered some form of police restrictions; fourteen were arrested, and only a few were granted amnesty. Indeed, after the war broke out there were widespread fears that the war economy would have severe consequences for inmates of the concentration camps, and that the authorities would make short work of some of them.

Niemöller Volunteers for the Military. In the first few days of the war, such fears were also felt for Martin Niemöller. Dr. Werner had just rescinded his official rights as a member of the clergy. Bonhoeffer was consulted about how and whether to protect Niemöller. Without hesitation, Bonhoeffer supported the advice that the former submarine captain should volunteer for the navy; perhaps such a message from Niemöller's cell might cause Heydrich's newly created Reich Central Security Office to review its former decisions. In any case, Bonhoeffer found military enlistment a potentially useful instrument for rescuing important people. He also already considered it advisable to have reliable men at headquarters and in key military positions, in the event of an attempt to overthrow the regime. It was difficult, of course, for this to be understood abroad. Through his friend Arnold

Ehrhardt, the patristics scholar in England, Karl Barth issued a solemn and definite denial of rumors that Niemöller had volunteered.[176] And yet it was so. It would never have entered Bonhoeffer's head that he could have betrayed the opposition to Hitler through this advice, and that he and Niemöller had gone over to the other side, as some people interpreted the incident after 1945. In 1939 it was common for loyal Confessing pastors who were reserve officers to volunteer (some did this too quickly for Bonhoeffer's liking!) so as to find a way out of a dangerous situation. In its painfully ambivalent patriotism, the diary of novelist Jochen Klepper, a Christian married to a non-Aryan, reflects the thoughts and emotions of many of those tied to the Confessing church, during those early days of war.

Despite their close friendship and the battles they had fought together, Bonhoeffer's theological thinking and his actions were not always the same as Niemöller's. During the 1930s Niemöller did not share Bonhoeffer's pacifism; and, as he later acknowledged, he would not have associated himself with Bonhoeffer's engagement in the conspiracy, if he had been free. He was more inclined to distinguish between service in the church and service to one's country, and this was an idea that had become suspect to Bonhoeffer.

But it would never have occurred to Bonhoeffer that Niemöller's volunteering would shake the confidence of someone such as Bishop Bell. One now had to take responsibility for doing things that might seem ambiguous, as Bell himself did without reservation. This was illustrated by his letters, an expression of continued fellowship, to the three men who to him represented the German church at that moment—Hans Böhm, Martin Niemöller, and Dietrich Bonhoeffer. Bell had heard that Rieger's family would be repatriated and go home (although that did not happen), and asked Rieger's wife to convey the letters at the very moment when Niemöller was writing his offer to navy admiral Erich Raeder. Bell wrote Bonhoeffer:

> My dear Dietrich, You know how deeply I feel for you and yours in this melancholy time. May God comfort and guide you. I think often of our talk in the summer. May He keep you. Let us pray together often by reading the Beatitudes; *Pax Dei quae superat omnia nos custodiat*. Your affectionate George.[177]

No Military Chaplaincy. While the summons to the army offered a respite for some Confessing pastors whose position was precarious, it also meant that they were suddenly cut off from their work. No official church authority submitted claims for their exemption. More than any other sector in the country, the Confessing church was immediately affected by the loss of its colleagues. Almost all its young pastors went to the front, and eventually most of them were killed in action. But there were a few men in the army and in the administration who recognized the problem, and they used the possibilities open to them, as long as possible, to keep individual pastors out of the army.

Bonhoeffer could assume that his friends in Schlawe would try to keep him from being drafted as long as possible, but he did not want things to reach that point. The idea occurred to him to seek an appointment as chaplain with the troops and in a military hospital. The proper line of approach was through the consistories, which negotiated with the armed forces regarding chaplains; Bonhoeffer would not consider this.

His mother got her cousin, the military governor, to invite her and Chief Chaplain Dohrmann to explore suitable ways and means. In September 1939 Bonhoeffer, acting on Dohrmann's advice, applied for employment as army chaplain.[178] The answer did not come until mid-February 1940, and it was negative. The reason given was that, according to a regulation from the army high command, only people with a record of active duty could become chaplains; all other applications were to be refused. Bonhoeffer wrote home:

> The other side of the matter is that all the pastors who have already served or are army officers are of course conscripted to fight, and so there is nothing else left for chaplains! Besides, the conscription of Confessing pastors, the application for exemption by the consistory people, and the occupation of Confessing church posts by the consistory's people, in the absence of Confessing pastors, is leading more clearly to a destruction of the congregations that still exist.[179]

The Last Semester. When the campaign in Poland was over, and conditions in the interior of the country had been somewhat stabilized, discussions between Niesel, Perels, and Bonhoeffer led to the Old Prussian Council of Brethren's decision to continue the collective pastorate in Sigurdshof, despite the war. Surprisingly there were still a few ordinands who had passed their examinations with the Confessing church and awaited their final training. Their quarters in eastern Pomerania were now again outside the area of military activity. In the middle of October eight ordinands were called to Sigurdshof from Berlin, Pomerania, Westphalia, and the Rhineland. They began their work with Bonhoeffer in primitive conditions, and relied on their own ingenuity to solve the problems of obtaining coal, paraffin, petrol, and food. They succeeded, both threatened and protected by one of the most severe winters. Only one ordinand was taken away from the course by the recruiting officials.

Freed from the reflections of the previous winter, Bonhoeffer once again devoted himself with extraordinary concentration to his theological work. Now he was finally able to make some progress with his meditation on Psalm 119. At the university he had learned that this was the most boring of the psalms; now he regarded its interpretation as the climax of his theological life. For years he had tried to penetrate the mystery of its verses. On 18 January 1938 he had written to Franz Hildebrandt:

> Now I want to try for the third time; Julius [Rieger] might get me, with the help of Cromwell [an emigrant in Bonhoeffer's London parish], *The Way of Holiness* by Father Benson, Oxford. I need it for the exposition of Psalm 119. Many thanks for your trouble.[180]

In Sigurdshof he got as far as verse 21.[181]

That winter he began to work together with Joachim Beckmann and Georg Eichholz on their volumes of sermons and meditations.[182] Eichholz's attempt was one of the first results of the renewal of preaching in the church struggle, and the precursor of the postwar *Göttingen Sermon Meditations*. Although Bonhoeffer was prepared to cooperate, he was initially critical and wrote to Eichholz:

> I had admitted openly all along that I had misgivings about your undertaking. What are sermon meditations? I have never quite understood and that hasn't changed. They seem to be partly exegesis and partly sermon drafts.[183] With regard to this, I feel that exegesis can be found elsewhere, and that there are enough and better collections of sermons on the gospels that we have often produced. Theological observations (see Vogel) or very general marginal notes on the text (see Asmussen) can be found better elsewhere. I include myself in this judgment. . . .
>
> I still have doubts about the whole thing. On the other hand, I must say that, judging by what I hear from the young theologians, they are very grateful for the work; and that applies not only to the less self-reliant people, but to the others as well. So a gap—it may often be simply the gap in the library—is no doubt being filled, and that fully justifies the effort being made. . . .
>
> I should certainly think it is much more necessary to deal with the Old Testament readings than with the Epistles [Bonhoeffer was to work on the Epistles after the Old Testament]. I ought to tell you, too, that this is the wish of several young colleagues. Could you not still change that? There is really a lack of help here. . . .
>
> Do invite all the colleagues to get together![184]

> I am quite ready to cooperate further, especially since my last few months' work in East Prussia convinced me that particularly the very isolated colleagues found the meditations a real help in their preaching. I repeat my request that you soon go over to the Old Testament texts! There is a great deal of theological, exegetical, and homiletical helplessness here.[185]

> Although I agree with you that a treatment of the Old Testament pericopes is far from easy, I would infer from that very fact that it is precisely this that should be tackled. At the moment we expect of any pastor on Sundays that he will preach on those texts, while frankly we assume that in practice he will not do so. In my opinion, help is more urgently needed here than anywhere else.[186]

Inevitably, the Pomeranian Council of Brethren inquired about its old critical colleague. Bonhoeffer committed himself to write a regular theological supplement for the monthly newsletter to the Pomeranian clergy, although this brought him into another disagreement, this time with Eberhard Baumann of the Reformed church about an article on the Eucharist.[187] Even the theological commission of the Pomeranian Council of Brethren came back to life. "The theological commission very active with Bonhoeffer!" Frau Ohnesorge wrote in her diary after the Council of Brethren's session on 8 January 1940.

Bonhoeffer sometimes found it hard not to be able to spend all his time in Berlin. Renewed preparations for a coup had begun, and Dohnanyi was one of the main people involved. But he was always happy again to escape from the hectic atmosphere of Berlin, and return once more to theology and the "life together" in the seclusion of the forest.

Hesitancy toward Ecumenical Movement. Insofar as his professional work left him time for Berlin in the first winter of the war, Bonhoeffer was occupied with political matters, only a little with the church struggle, and not at all with what was happening in the ecumenical sphere. Yet many things were changing in that arena.

In the western and northern European countries various church people were feverishly busy, even in the winter of 1939–1940, trying to save the "peace." In September 1939 Bishop Berggrav went to see British foreign secretary Lord Halifax; in December he visited Bishop Bell; and in January 1940 he saw Göring in Karinhall, visited Lord Halifax again, and finally, before Hitler invaded Norway, went to Berlin again. The provisional World Council of Churches, meeting in Apeldoorn, Holland, in January 1940, tried to draft an appeal for peace; but the leaders of the British and Scandinavian churches could not agree whether the emphasis should be on peace at all costs or on the conditions for peace.[188]

The Confessing church, really Hans Böhm for its Provisional Administration, was excluded from those proceedings. Neither did Berggrav cultivate relations with Böhm's office when he went to Berlin, but with the Church Foreign Office instead. Bonhoeffer took no notice of those efforts, not because he had been isolated by the tragic previous history of ecumenical relationships, but because he had no interest now in any peace feelers whose goal was to maintain or even affirm the Hitler regime. But in the first few months of the war there were numerous ecumenical attempts to restore peace by whatever means necessary; only secondarily did they reflect on whether and how Hitler could be gotten rid of. Bonhoeffer distrusted this. For him the only correct course was to eliminate Hitler and then negotiate peace.

Nor did Bonhoeffer see any need to reconsider his attitude toward Schönfeld and the Geneva Research Department. It was not until two years later that friendly contacts were reestablished between the two. Now, however, it was still too early for any such rapprochement; the old antagonism had not abated. For Bonhoeffer Schönfeld was still simply the man at the Church Foreign Office; indeed, since the beginning of the war, Schönfeld was more dependent than ever on Heckel's office. Since a drastic financial retrenchment in 1938 he had been living in Geneva on the foreign currency that Heckel managed to secure for him in Berlin; this was possible only as long as the political results abroad were demonstrated to the Foreign Office. This in turn made Schönfeld's position in Geneva suspicious to those who shared the theological and political views of Karl Barth. Schönfeld's difficult situation almost overtaxed his strength. He had to produce reports that showed the German State Department how well suited his church office in Geneva was for observing Allied propaganda, while convincing the skeptics that he belonged to the resistance.

Of course, it did not occur to Bonhoeffer to change his relationship to the Church Foreign Office, which was sending representatives abroad to search for contacts. While Bonhoeffer was on his way back from America, Heckel commissioned Eugen Gerstenmaier to attend an ecumenical study session at Archbishop Temple's See at Bishopsthorpe near York, in which J. Baillie, R. Niebuhr, A. Nygren, J. Oldham, N. Soe, Lyman, Green, Schönfeld, and Ehrenström took part. In October Gerstenmaier, Ehrenström, and Schönfeld went to the three Scandinavian countries; Gerstenmaier had to make a report on this, showing the German Foreign Ministry how the contacts with the neutral Lutheran churches served the German cause and promoted "the active debate with the Western ideologies."[189] In April 1940 the

Church Foreign Office, together with the Geneva Research Department, held an ecumenical working session in Berlin on the theme "The Church's Responsibility for the International Order." The roots of all subsequent ecumenical relief work were in that conference, and Bonhoeffer himself took an interest in such matters not long afterward. But in April 1940 his views on the nature of "international order" hardly coincided with those of the Church Foreign Office. Although he was in Berlin at the time, he did not see any of the delegates at the conference.

But the two hostile sides—the representatives of the Church Foreign Office and Bonhoeffer—began with increasing frequency to work with the same friends. For its travels and plans, the Church Foreign Office was dependent on good relations with the appropriate departments in the German Foreign Ministry, which gave it "indispensable" status and foreign currency, and delivered its reports. This is where Gerstenmaier came into contact with the men who took him into the Kreisau circle in 1942. For his part, Bonhoeffer that winter renewed his association with Hans-Bernd von Haeften in the Foreign Ministry and saw Adam von Trott before the latter left for his journey to America. Bonhoeffer's brothers and sisters, particularly Karl-Friedrich, had known von Trott well for a long time.

But the difficulty of any approach to the Church Foreign Office was illustrated by the case of Friedrich Siegmund-Schultze. He already had connections with the resistance groups led by Beck and Goerdeler, and he had contacts with England,[190] and, of course, Bonhoeffer visited him later on his Swiss journeys. But the Church Foreign Office found it necessary to prevent this emigrant from traveling to Sweden when he was invited to lecture there in the spring of 1940. In a letter to the Foreign Ministry Heckel's office stated:

> His [Siegmund-Schultze's] negative attitude . . . must be expected to stand in the way of any meaningful German work in Scandinavia. I therefore think, in agreement with Swedish circles that are anxious for a planned strengthening of Swedish-German relations,[191] to express the confidential wish that, without drawing attention to it, you should take steps to prevent Professor S. Schultze's journey to Sweden.[192]

Thus in the first year of the war Bonhoeffer did not try to get into touch with either foreign churchmen or ecumenically active Germans. Of course, ecumenical conferences and synods had to advocate peace at all costs before the war broke out in full fury in May 1940. Bonhoeffer, however, had already taken his stand on the one condition for peace that could not be discussed in any church body inside Germany—the removal of Hitler.

New Hopes for a Coup.[193] During the first winter of the war there were two phases of activity among the German conspirators. Dohnanyi was one of the driving forces. Bonhoeffer played only a small role; he did not yet have any special commission to carry out, or any field of action for which he was responsible within the group. But he became more and more involved, and was sometimes present when tactics and principles were discussed. For the conspirators the opinion of an expert in Protestant and ecumenical questions, although not decisively important, was worth hearing.

Two events renewed hopes among the conspirators that a coup might succeed:

1. On 27 September 1939, the day Warsaw surrendered, Hitler ordered preparations for the invasion of Holland and Belgium. Wouldn't the generals now face the alternative—either to stay with Hitler from a threatened to an actual world war, or go against Hitler from a threatened world war to a respectable peace? Could it be assumed that if the German resisters acquiesced in the invasion the Allies would still make a distinction between Hitler and Germany? Everything depended on the timing of the western offensive. The decisive stroke, the removal of Hitler, had to be successfully carried out before then.

2. Information about S.S. atrocities in Poland began to circulate. Of course, the ordinary citizen assumed that the appalling stories were foreign propaganda; at first he could not, and then he would not, believe them. At that time it was already difficult to stay informed, and to repeat among friends and acquaintances what was being done in Poland in the German name.

Canaris, together with General Blaskowitz, the military commander in Poland, gave the other generals accounts of the S.S. atrocities. Could the army tolerate these cruelties against civilians and Jews, which were contrary to international law? Could they permit their authority to be restricted by the S.S. units and the Gestapo? Blaskowitz protested:

> What the foreign radio stations have broadcast up to now is only a tiny fraction of what has actually happened. . . . The only possibility of fending off this pestilence lies in bringing the guilty parties and their followers under military command and military justice with all possible speed.[194]

Hitler responded by recalling Blaskowitz from his post.

In the winter of 1939–1940 the two preparatory phases for a coup were determined by the dates set for the western offensive: first the November date, which was repeatedly postponed and then canceled, and then the April date. Bonhoeffer was in Berlin during the critical stages in October and March. There were rumors that Halder and Brauchitsch intended to resist Hitler's aggressive plans, and that they were even considering resigning.

The First Phase. Beck urged Dohnanyi to update his record of Hitler's evil deeds, including details about the Gleiwitz radio station reports on the invasion of Poland and the atrocities in the occupied areas. The idea was to arrest Hitler and use such material to open the eyes of the public to the true nature of the regime. Through Count Helldorf, Dohnanyi obtained security reports and S.S. films of the massacres in Poland, incorporated them in his "chronicle of shame," and circulated the material among generals who were inclined to be sympathetic. He also helped establish contacts with trade unionists. There was even a meeting between Beck and Interior Minister Wilhelm Leuschner, and the possibility of a general strike was considered.

The most important thing, however, was the attempt to negotiate tolerable peace terms as a precaution, thereby undermining the generals' objection that the Allies would exploit a coup as evidence of weakness. This was the most dangerous and most uncertain task. After the Polish campaign Dohnanyi and Oster got in touch with the Munich lawyer Dr. Josef Müller, who was on friendly terms with the Vatican. Beck commissioned Müller to establish contacts with the British government through his Vatican ties. The pope gave his word to the Allied countries that the resistance efforts were serious and came from circles belonging to the "other Germany." As a fundamental condition of the negotiations, it was agreed that the Allied assurances should hold good only if there were a successful revolt *before* an offensive in the west. In October the British government sent an initial response indicating its readiness to enter into serious peace negotiations on these terms.

The western offensive was planned to begin on 12 November. On 4 November General Thomas, on Beck's behalf, delivered a memorandum for Brauchitsch to Chief of Staff General Halder; it had been prepared by Dohnanyi, Oster, and Gisevius. Halder seemed to be cooperative, but Brauchitsch, whose authority to give the command to start the coup was essential, refused. There were signs that Hitler had heard rumors of the coup plans. Halder destroyed documents. The conspirators were slowed down by the mysterious attempt on Hitler's life in the Munich *Bürgerbräukeller,* and Schellenberg's arrest of the Englishmen Richard Stevens and Payne Best at Venlo in Holland, until it was established that nothing had been leaked. Nor, apparently, did the incidents in Munich and Venlo have anything to do with those planning the conspiracy. They resumed their race against the date for the offensive, which was postponed repeatedly in November. Since Brauchitsch rejected any kind of active resistance, however, the question of a possible authoritative order to go ahead was made extremely difficult. With the offensive finally postponed and winter approaching, there was less activity among the conspirators for some weeks.[195]

The Second Phase. Meanwhile Josef Müller continued his conversations in Rome. Canaris had "installed" him in the German Military Intelligence and assigned him to its Munich office. This removed his journeys from Gestapo oversight, and any objections or checks from that quarter. After January 1940 he went often to the Dohnanyi home in Berlin, and there he got to know Dietrich Bonhoeffer. Although they were quite different in temperament and appearance, and belonged to different religious institutions (Müller was Catholic), they took a liking to each other that often brought them together, altogether apart from their common political activities. Bonhoeffer was referring to those first meetings when he wrote optimistically in a letter to his brother Karl-Friedrich: "Well, the time of uncertainty will not last much longer now."[196] For one night at the end of January, Josef Müller dictated Christine von Dohnanyi's final report onto a tape.[197]

Müller's name as negotiator was denoted by an "X," and so that document was given the name "X-report." The negotiations through the Vatican had shown that Great Britain was prepared to agree to an armistice before an attack in the west and *after* Hitler's removal. The basis for subsequent peace talks would be an intact Germany within its 1937 borders.

In February the final work on this project was unfortunately delayed. One reason was American special envoy Sumner Welles's audience with Hitler, which held things up after Hitler suddenly appeared capable of negotiating with the west, although the resistance circles had maintained that there was no chance of this.

From his collective pastorate in the snow and ice, Bonhoeffer had just returned to Berlin where Dohnanyi, Oster, Hassell, and Beck were discussing how the "X-report" was to be implemented. Hassell's diary entry on 19 March stated:

> I first found him [Beck] alone, and discussed the situation with him. Then came O. [Oster] and D. [Dohnanyi]; they read me some very interesting papers about conversations between a Roman Catholic confidential agent and the pope, who had thereupon got into touch through Osborne [British envoy at the Vatican] with Halifax. According to this the pope went surprisingly far in expressing sympathy with German interests. Halifax, who

spoke expressly for the British government, is essentially more cautious in his way of putting things, and touches on such things as "decentralization in Germany" and "plebiscite in Austria." On the whole, the wish for a respectable peace is clearly there and the pope strongly emphasized to the confidential agent that such things as "decentralization" and "plebiscite in Austria" would be no obstacle whatever to peace if agreement existed on other matters. Of course, the prerequisite for everything is a change of regime and a recognition of Christian morality. The object of the discussion with me was: 1. to hear my view of the international situation; 2. to ask me to approach Halder on the matter, because there was no promise of success from other intermediaries.[198]

Dohnanyi now worked the "X-report" into a memorandum that summarized the arguments for quick action, dealt with possible objections such as the stab-in-the-back legend and the oath of allegiance, and drew attention in detail to S.S. atrocities and to the increasing destruction of the army's independence by the S.S. troops. Bonhoeffer joined the very small group that met in Dohnanyi's house to consider the memorandum. Unfortunately, General Thomas did not take the memorandum to Halder until 4 April; Halder showed it to Brauchitsch the next day. Both of them were busy with the final details of the imminent invasion of Scandinavia and the west, and could hardly give much time and thought to the study of a detailed document. On the other hand, shouldn't Brauchitsch have been more willing to listen, since the entire burden of responsibility might soon be laid on him? Halder reported on Brauchitsch's reaction:

> He handed me back the paper and said: "You ought not to have submitted that to me! What is happening here is absolute treason." . . . Then he demanded I should have the man who had delivered the paper to me arrested. I then replied: "If anyone is to be arrested, arrest me!"[199]

Thus the commander in chief of the army—the most important instrument for carrying out their plans—was not available for the purpose. The avalanche began to move. The chance passed that a still undefeated Germany might negotiate terms with the Allied Powers. The opposition's credibility was at stake. They feared that the West would regard Josef Müller's negotiations as a sham, just as the meetings in Venlo between Heydrich's confidant Schellenberg with Stevens and Best had been. Didn't the opposition now have to rescue what could be saved, through showing that it did not identify itself with the approaching violation of neutrality? In April Josef Müller returned to Rome to break the news that the possibility of a coup had fallen through, and that the feared offensive was to be expected. "We must be able to establish contacts again some day; and for that the people must know whom they are dealing with, that there is a decent Germany that is capable of negotiating."[200]

Colonel Oster. During those days of despair, with each hour that passed there was less hope of ending the wrongs that were being committed in Germany's name, and of preventing fresh atrocities. One of the people Bonhoeffer met during those weeks was Hans Oster, with whom he went to his death five years later. He knew from Dohnanyi that Oster was about to inform the Dutch of the date of the coming attack, and thereby stop Hitler's successes, which were bringing disaster on Germany.[201]

Bonhoeffer regarded Oster's action on the eve of the western offensive as a step taken on his own final responsibility. It seemed appropriate to him in a situation into which a presumptuous German had maneuvered his country, and in which all those who were capable of acting suffered from paralysis of the conscience. The patriot had to perform what in normal times is the action of a scoundrel. "Treason" had become true patriotism, and what was normally "patriotism" had become treason. An officer saw the diabolical reversal of all values, and acted entirely alone to prevent new outrages in other countries, such as those he had experienced in Poland—and the pastor approved of what he did. He was willing to incur the odium of having his name mentioned only cautiously after the war, of risking everything, even his good name.

For people and nations who have never found themselves in the unhappy state of divided loyalty, it is difficult in retrospect to empathize with this borderline situation where the most conscientious person was the one who had to accept disgrace. To measure the situation of that era by the yardstick of our own principles or deliberately overlook its peculiar characteristics is to distort it and fail to see the realities of those months. Germany's name could no longer be rescued through ordinary but blind respectability. Throughout the world, "treason" is normally viewed as a horrible sentiment, characterized by speculation for personal advantage and the intent to injure one's own country. The opposite was true of Oster, Dohnanyi, and Bonhoeffer.

Bonhoeffer soon began to write *Ethics*, which includes the passage: "What is worse than doing evil is being evil. It is worse for a liar to tell the truth than for a lover of truth to lie."[202] And in 1942, in the reflections called "After Ten Years," a Christmas gift to Oster and Dohnanyi, he wrote:

Are we still of any use? We have been silent witnesses of evil deeds; we have been drenched by many storms; we have learned the arts of equivocation and pretense; experience has made us suspicious of others and kept us from being truthful and open; intolerable conflicts have worn us down and even made us cynical. Are we still of any use? . . . Will our inward power of resistance be strong enough, and our honesty with ourselves remorseless enough, for us to find our way back to simplicity and straightforwardness?[203]

Christian and Man for His Times

In the spring of 1940 little could be observed about Bonhoeffer that distinguished him from other uncompromising Confessing pastors. His theology and language still resembled what could be read in *Discipleship* and *Life Together*. The sermons and newsletter of those months comforted and admonished as before.

It was only later that friends discovered turns of speech, in expositions such as his meditation on Psalm 119, that pointed to what was to come. Afterward they recalled conversations such as the one on his thirty-third birthday on 4 February 1939 around the tiled stove of the vicarage in eastern Pomerania, when he said that it might be worthwhile, even for a pastor, to risk one's life for political freedom.[204] It subsequently became clear that Bonhoeffer had always, in fact, left the door open a crack for such a step. This was not so astounding, given the conversations in his home and his family's attitude toward the Nazi crimes from the very beginning. Even in *Discipleship* there was the sentence: "It is important that Jesus gives his blessing not merely to suffering incurred directly for the confession of his name, but to suffering in any just cause."[205] There were also his comments at the Steglitz synod, and later his reference to the *humanum* in the disputation on the law. But all this was nothing more than an opening, barely noticeable; it was not yet an open door through which he had already passed.

Yet during this period, the way was being prepared for a change that became evident in a new way of life and action, and gave new impetus to his theology. The beginning of that period was still marked by his rigid adherence to the kind of pastoral training he regarded as necessary for a professional minister. At the end there was a readiness for underground activity and a desire to rethink ethical questions. The "borderline situation" that Bonhoeffer once mentioned in Tegel was approaching, with the particular opportunities it offered for knowledge.[206]

The first change, around 1931–1932, was when Bonhoeffer the theologian consciously grasped the fact that he was a Christian. At the beginning of 1939 Bonhoeffer the theologian and Christian was entering fully into his contemporary world, his place, and his time—into a world his bourgeois class had helped to bring about rather than prevent. He accepted the burden of that collective responsibility, and began to identify himself with those who were prepared to acknowledge their guilt and to begin shaping something new for the future—instead of merely protesting on ideological grounds, as the church had done up to that point. In 1939 the theologian and Christian became a man for his times.

Theologian, Christian, man for his times—those three identities, which may at first sight seem to be a matter of course, do not often go together in history. Each of the steps Bonhoeffer took from one role to the other changed the dimensions of the course of his life.

Both steps, in 1932 and 1939, occurred quietly. Bonhoeffer never spoke of them directly or even publicly. On the contrary, he thought his life had gone on continuously with no breaks.[207] But his friends became aware, if not of these changes in direction, at least of their visible results.

In 1932 he found his calling, in 1939 his destiny. In 1932 he found the unmistakable language in which he wrote his original contribution to theological history: the finished books, *Discipleship* and *Life Together*. His development after 1939 was also expressed in two books: *Ethics* and *Letters and Papers from Prison*. But one of these is a fragment, and the other is a book of posthumously selected letters; indeed, they have been largely responsible for his growing reputation. He once referred jokingly to the change by calling *Life Together* his "swan song."[208]

In 1932 Bonhoeffer moved into the community of Christians which was confined to the group within the church that protested publicly with him. Nineteen thirty-nine led him into an even more restricted circle of kindred spirits. From that time on the members of Finkenwalde felt there was something incognito about his existence that they mustn't question. For the new companions, on the other hand, his Christian existence seldom emerged openly. Whether among his old friends or new ones, he instinctively hid the other side of his being. Anyone who had anything to do with him sensed that there was more there than could be seen; but no one had the impression of any inner conflict. Everything was in order.

The year 1932 had placed Bonhoeffer in a world where things were comparatively clear-cut, where it was a matter of confessing and denying—in his case, of confessing the one church for the whole world and denying its betrayal to nationalist particularism. At the end of this road stood the fate of people like Paul Schneider. In 1939 he entered the difficult world of assessing what was expedient—of success and failure, tactics and camouflage. The certainty of his calling in 1932 now became an acceptance of the uncertain, the incomplete, and the provisional. The new turning point demanded an entirely different sacrifice: the sacrifice of his Christian reputation.

The year 1932 had opened up the ecumenical movement to Bonhoeffer, and he became its passionate advocate as Germany increasingly isolated itself. In 1939, when he could have saved himself within that ecumenical movement, he shut himself out from it. He narrowed his path to the separate and deadly fate of Germany.

After 1939 the old priorities could be fulfilled only by exchanging them. To want to be only a Christian, a timeless disciple—that now became a costly privilege. To become engaged for his times, where he stood, was far more open to misinterpretation, less glorious, more confined. Yet this alone was what it now meant to be a Christian.

The possibility of "life together" ended forever in the spring of 1940 and, eventually, the theology of discipleship needed revision. Its context had been shattered. Ecclesiology as a priority receded. The earthly, bourgeois, and national future demanded responsibility. The traces of this turning point provide a less coherent picture than those of his first turning point in 1932, but they touch other depths.

PART THREE

SHARING GERMANY'S DESTINY

CHAPTER TWELVE

TRAVELS: 1940–1943

It was 17 June 1940, in the village of Memel. That morning Bonhoeffer had been talking to Dr. Werner Wiesner at a poorly attended pastors' meeting; in the evening there was to be a Confessing church service. That afternoon he was sitting with me in an open-air café just opposite the town, on the peninsula. We had come by ferry, past submarine tenders and minesweepers. The previous day Stalin had delivered an ultimatum to the Baltic states, but the world's attention was centered on Hitler's victory in France.

While we were enjoying the sun, suddenly the fanfare boomed out of the café's loudspeaker, signaling a special announcement: the message that France had surrendered. The people around the tables could hardly contain themselves; they jumped up, and some even climbed on the chairs. With outstretched arms they sang "*Deutschland, Deutschland über alles*" and the Horst Wessel song. We had stood up, too. Bonhoeffer raised his arm in the regulation Hitler salute, while I stood there dazed. "Raise your arm! Are you crazy?" he whispered to me, and later: "We shall have to run risks for very different things now, but not for that salute!"

A Double Life. It was then that Bonhoeffer's double life began: the involvement as a pastor in the political underground movement, which, he wrote in 1943, "may prevent me from taking up my ministry again later on."[1] That passage in a letter from Tegel was not an expression of secret uncertainty about the way that was beginning; on the contrary, he meant that he was acting out of an inner necessity for which his church as yet had no formulas. By normal standards everything had been turned upside down.

That evening Bonhoeffer preached, as far as I remember, without reference to the day's events. One would not have preached like that twenty-five years previously, at any rate in a German Protestant church. The victory in France had just brought about what the circles to which Bonhoeffer belonged had dreamed of in 1914, and now he was standing there shocked, separated from the jubilant people. His contemporaries and students were helping win battles that were smashing a world to pieces, while he was holding Bible classes in remote spots and taking no part in strengthening the patriotic morale of people at the front or at home. The crowd jumped onto the chairs and forgot, in the jubilant tumult, both the means and the end of the victory. He felt only shame at the success of the crime.

Such sentiments were shared by his family and by a number of Confessing church members. On 17 June, however, other hopes had been dashed for him, of which few people knew. The expectation that the first military difficulties would topple the hated regime had proven false, and all dreams of its removal had vanished. The victory in France sealed an immense miscalculation by Bonhoeffer's informants and friends in the resistance movement. The professionals—General Ludwig Beck, Georg Thomas, Carl Goerdeler, and Admiral Walter Canaris—were wrong, and Hitler the amateur was right. Hitler's estimate of the enemy and of his own methods had been confirmed before the entire world; the estimates of the others were branded as defeatism. They now struggled to regain their bearings. "Behind everything that we see stands the specter of other events with which we will have to wrestle, even in our dreams," Bonhoeffer wrote his parents from Königsberg on 21 June.[2] In comparison with the First World War, the military situation seemed to be fundamentally changed; anyone who had not forgotten the stalemate of 1914 was bound to be overwhelmed by this lightning victory in the west. What did it mean?

A few members of the Old Prussian Council of Brethren, like Kurt Scharf, Wilhelm Niesel, and Wilhelm Jannasch, later especially recalled a session at the beginning of July with Viktor Hasse in Nowawes (today called Babelsberg; it was a remote site they often used for meetings). They say that Bonhoeffer appeared there and surprised his friends by indicating that he, like everyone else, was capitulating before Hitler's incredible success as before a divine judgment, and recommended a new attitude toward the National Socialist state.[3] Younger representatives of the Provisional Church Administration like Pastor Wilhelm Rott and Dr. Herbert Werner were at the same session. Even then they understood Bonhoeffer's statement differently:

> I think they were all very surprised, as I was, at what he said. If I remember rightly, it was noted in silence. It was a kind of analysis of the situation after the regrettably successful campaign in France. . . . Whether in implicit or explicit reference to the elderly Frau von Kleist-Retzow's fallen grand-

son, Bonhoeffer reminded us that the death in action of young men from families firmly opposed to the regime implied a commitment to the hard facts of the new situation created by Hitler. The belief of many of our circle that the clash of weapons would bring catastrophe upon the regime had been shattered. We would have to adjust ourselves to Hitler's rule, at any rate for a long time. Then on the way home I talked with Brother Werner about the meeting and about Bonhoeffer's speech. We discussed the possibility that it might be taken as an inner capitulation to the new facts, and as a recognition of the "new reality." I myself rejected any such possibility then and there. It was clear to me that Bonhoeffer, who was always a good psychologist, described the situation (I admit, for those listening, perhaps unguardedly) so insistently only so that we could witness properly, in this new situation, the old testimony that was required of us. The friend to whom I was talking then agrees with me today, too, that it would be absurd to infer from that speech that Bonhoeffer had changed sides; and this is confirmed by his obvious attitude both before and after the session. . . . It would be beyond me to imagine how anyone could turn what was said in Babelsberg into a sudden enthusiasm for National Socialism and a confession of loyalty to Hitler.[4]

In addition, we have the diary of a woman who took part in a session of the Pomeranian Council of Brethren in Stettin immediately after Nowawes. Her entry on 11 July 1940 stated:

> Dr. Bonhoeffer on the situation: Fundamental change in the nation has taken place; historical "Yes" given to National Socialism; widespread change of opinion; collapse of liberal democratic world; conspicuous success for Party. This puts church in a very difficult position; many people ask, "Is it worthwhile. . . ?" Many pastors, now officers in the army, ask, "Shall I go back to such a meager ministry?" Important (among other things) to bring ourselves to speak of the glory of the Gospel, and of the glory of the ministry![5]

Bonhoeffer's remarks to people who had responsible positions in the church went along those lines. To other people at that time he said quite different things. According to that diary he was speaking of a "historical yes," but not of an ethical or even theological yes, which he regarded as quite a different matter. The historical circumstances were recognized and acknowledged, without succumbing to the ideology of the victor. The audience recollected that Bonhoeffer had revised his outlook. They were correct, but some obviously did not understand the manner of the "revision."

There can be no talk of Bonhoeffer's surrender to the facts, not even for a moment; something quite different was going on in his mind. He wanted to grasp the significance of the fact that the success of this unjust regime would ensure its existence for a much longer time than all his friends in the church and political resistance movement had assumed. In that context the contrast between the hopes that were still cherished and the consolidation of the regime was much sharper for Bonhoeffer than for his less well informed audiences.

Further, he wanted to impress on himself and others that after 17 June there could no longer be a simple return to things as they had been before then. The relationship to neighboring countries, the social structure, the political status quo—everything from now on would be irrevocably influenced by Hitler's action, and would remain so. The goal of eliminating Hitler could no longer be a restoration of the past. The road to something new would be infinitely more lengthy and costly; the form that the goal would take was unknown.

Only a few weeks after that session Bonhoeffer wrote down clearly what he felt all this amounted to. At the time he was working on the earlier sections of his *Ethics*. In September 1940 he produced the chapter on "success":

> The successful man presents us with accomplished facts which can never again be reversed. What he destroys cannot be restored. What he constructs will acquire at least a prescriptive right in the next generation. No indictment can make good the guilt which the successful man has left behind him. The indictment falls silent with the passage of time, but the success remains and determines the course of history. The judges of history play a sad role in comparison with its protagonists. History rides roughshod over their heads. . . .
>
> If one is engaged in fruitless and pharisaical criticism of what is past, one can oneself never find one's way to the present, to action and to success, and precisely in this one sees yet another proof of the wickedness of the successful man. . . .
>
> Jesus is certainly no apologist for the successful men in history, but neither does he lead the insurrection of shipwrecked existences against their successful rivals. He is not concerned with success or failure but with the willing acceptance of God's judgement.[6]

That was a bit of pragmatism Bonhoeffer thought it necessary to learn. For him this had nothing to do with "appeasement," although he was often misunderstood on this point. He was anxious lest the regime's opponents, who had just suffered a defeat, allow themselves to be deflected by the course of history or try to hold fast to what was over and done with. With his fellow theologians in the Confessing church in mind, his efforts to find the right way do not indicate any desire for the easy way out by concentrating on the "last things."

His remarks in Nowawes were made at the precise moment Bonhoeffer's double life for the church and a different Germany actually began. Now, for the first time, things became truly serious. What his colleagues experienced in the council session was part of a process of reorientation. Obviously the political background and personal factors that were decisive for Bonhoeffer could not be discussed in a Council of Brethren meeting.

The three years that followed were very unsettled. They were shaped by his work for the Confessing church, work on his *Ethics*, and the various tasks he performed for the conspiracy. Bonhoeffer traveled between eastern Pomerania, Berlin, Bavaria, and to the countries on Germany's northern and southern borders. In those three years he managed to remain a civilian, although in the end he was sent to a military prison as a member of Military Intelligence.

He had two places of residence, which had to be reported in accordance with police regulations, although he did not actually live at either one. Until the late autumn of 1940 he still had a room at Superintendent Block's home in Schlawe. Then, until his arrest, he sometimes stayed in Munich with his aunt, Countess Christine Kalckreuth, a well-known graphic artist and daughter of the painter Leopold von Kalckreuth. But the true center of his life was once more his parents' home in Berlin. In October 1940 he arranged in his attic there all of his books that he could collect from Finkenwalde, Köslin, and Sigurdshof. He also found room for the clavichord he had owned since his visit to the Kassel Music Festival in 1938.[7] Apart from his parents' home, there were three places he could sometimes go for quiet, the Benedictine monastery at Ettal in the south and the two Kleist estates of Kieckow and Klein-Krössin in the north. From eastern Pomerania he wrote: "It is strange, and really disgraceful, that staying in Berlin always takes away from me, so to speak, the spiritual air of life."[8] Otherwise he often had to struggle for a place in the blacked-out passenger trains. Sometimes his two Military Intelligence posts in Berlin and Munich gave him the enviable privilege of traveling in the comfortable trains reserved for the services.

During those three years his life alternated between extreme tension and occasional luxurious relaxation, between involvement in conspiracy and absorption in theology. At the end of that period he became engaged to Maria von Wedemeyer, the clearest sign that he did not intend to be pushed back into an apocalyptically determined opposition.

The course of events during this period can be only approximately reconstructed. The months of the western offensive, April and May 1940, were spent in Berlin. From June to August he went to East Prussia three times on church business. In September and October he was in Klein-Krössin. From November 1940 to February 1941 he lived in the Ettal monastery. From 24 February to 24 March 1941 he undertook the first journey to Switzerland. He returned to Friedrichsbrunn at Easter; from May to August he commuted between Klein-Krössin, Berlin, and occasionally Munich. His second journey to Switzerland was from 28 August to 26 September 1941. In late October and during November he had pneumonia and stayed at his parents' home; December he spent convalescing in Kieckow. From January to April 1942 he was mainly in Berlin, spending Easter in Kieckow. From 10 to 18 April 1942 he went to Norway, and from 12 to 23 May 1942 to Switzerland for the third time. From 30 May to 2 June 1942 he was in Sweden. In June he visited Klein-Krössin, Munich, and Freiburg, leaving several times for Berlin in between these trips. From 26 June to 10 July he was in Italy. During the autumn and winter of 1942–1943 he left Berlin only for short spells in Munich, Klein-Krössin, Freiburg, Magdeburg, and Pätzig—his prospective mother-in-law's estate.

SECTION ONE: THE CHURCH

The Confessing Church during the War

The double life Bonhoeffer was leading had not reduced his solidarity with the fate of the Confessing church. Despite his new obligations toward the military authorities, his official relationship to this church remained intact; and although he had sharply criticized the Confessing synods, his conviction that the Barmen and Dahlem resolutions were still valid had not changed. To the very end, there was no other church he would rather have supported or where he would have liked to find his home. The Confessing church remained his church, even when it could no longer look after him or identify with his cause.

In 1940 Bonhoeffer's close ties to the central Council of Brethren in Berlin resumed, since he was staying more often and longer with his parents, and his future occupation was uncertain. They naturally had to be cautious because of the official restrictions on his movements and activities in church work and meetings. He later used his special political and military connections as far as he legitimately could to get military deferments for some clergy, so that the remaining authorities of the Confessing church could continue their work. This was one of the charges against him after his arrest in 1943.

The Church in 1940. In 1940 the church struggle did not sharpen percepti-bly. After the military campaign in France ended Hitler even told the Reich provincial governors and presidents, through the Ministry of the Interior, that he wished them "to avoid all measures that might impair the relation-ship of the state and party to the church, unless such measures were absolutely necessary."[9] And, in fact, the church's intercession lists during 1940 were shorter.

But there were interventions that could hardly be tolerated in silence. In April and May 1940 the consistory took disciplinary action against Martin Albertz and Hans Böhm because of the prayer liturgy in the autumn of 1938, revoking their rights as pastors. Erich Klapproth, one of the former Finkenwalde students and the spokesman of the illegals in Berlin-Brandenburg, informed Bonhoeffer of the protest he sent from the front:

> To the Disciplinary Board of the Brandenburg Consistory. . . . Belgium, 30.5.1940. . . .
>
> As a frontline soldier who must risk his life every day and is therefore used to speaking frankly, I must tell you to your faces, gentlemen, what anger and disgust I feel at your conduct. Men whose merits and patriotism cannot be seriously doubted are being hunted down at a time when most of their friends are engaged in the defense of the fatherland and are there-fore in no position to protest effectively. . . . Like countless frontline sol-diers, I am entirely on the side of the condemned pastors in this matter. With the "judgment" that you, sirs, have now delivered from the security of your green baize table, you have also insulted me in an impudent man-ner. You may as well be clear that with your decision you have wantonly injured the morale of countless soldiers. I do not regard *your* regime, gen-tlemen, as worth defending in any way. . . . However helpless it may be, the Confessing church is more confident and sure than you in your unspiritual position of power . . . according to the evidence of Scripture and of the liv-ing church, [Albertz and Böhm] have a right to their spiritual status and their vocation to serve the Word; where do you get *your* right from? I fear you are desperately poor. After incidents like this, I do not know whether you call upon God in earnest or are able to offer serious intercession. But this much is certain: the prayers that are prayed out here, between death and destruction, are earnest, and will be fulfilled. And those prayers are *for* the people whom you have condemned, and against you and your evil deeds. Erich Klapproth, soldier.

In the course of that year the Old Prussian Council of Brethren lost most of its ability to work. Pastor Fritz Müller of Dahlem was on the front. Niesel, arrested for the eighth time and then expelled from Berlin, had to find something in Silesia. Despite this the necessary meetings were held, using substitutes. With those members who had been expelled, they met outside the town boundaries, as in Nowawes. This increased the importance of Friedrich Justus Perels, who was familiar with the bureaucratic procedures and kept up the connections on all sides. Wolfgang Staemmler from Saxony took over the chairmanship of the Old Prussian Council of Brethren, but he was gone after November 1940, when he was sentenced to a year in prison after expressing himself too boldly. He was in office, however, just at the time when some important decisions that affected Bonhoeffer were made.

Kerrl issued a decree forbidding "civil church agencies" from mailing religious literature, including duplicated letters sent to the members of the armed forces on the front.[10] This affected the work of every parish pastor. Bonhoeffer, too, had to think about how he could write to the Finkenwalde students in active duty without making himself liable for prosecution.

The church was most concerned, however, by the thirteen points announced in March by the provincial governor Arthur Greiser.[11] These gave the church in the newly formed district of Warthegau the status of an association, which meant it ceased to be a body with public statutory rights. Everyone saw this as a model for a privately financed and autonomous church in the Reich after the war had been won; this even made the neutral faction and the Church Foreign Office uneasy.[12]

People spoke only in whispers about the euthanasia measures being carried out in remote locations made inaccessible through the war. In the summer of 1940, on behalf of Fritz von Bodelschwingh of the Bethel institutions and Pastor Paul Braune of the Lobethal institution, Bonhoeffer spoke with his father about giving them authoritative medical documents that they could use as grounds for refusing to hand their patients over. Only after August 1941 were these euthanasia measures stopped on Hitler's orders.

The first rumors about the deportation of Jews came from Stettin in 1940. In February the Nazi district leader had deported a group of Stettin Jews in freight cars to Poland. It was not yet known whether this marked the beginning of a larger operation or was an isolated case. Pastor Heinrich Grüber, who had established an office in Berlin for helping non-Aryans, protested. This led to a warning, and his arrest and internment in a concentration camp months later.

In response to these events Bishop Wurm protested to Nazi authorities in July 1940 about euthanasia, and in 1941 about the treatment of the Jews.[13]

This led to a new relationship between the Württemburg bishop and the "Dahlemites" in the Confessing church.

Wurm, of course, had known about the "radical" Bonhoeffer for some time, but had never had any personal contact with him. This now came about through Bonhoeffer's mediation between his father and Bodelschwingh, who was in close contact with Wurm over the euthanasia issue.[14] A correspondence began between Wurm and Bonhoeffer, in which the bishop asked him what his attitude was toward his notorious earlier remarks.[15] Wurm's serious illness, and Bonhoeffer's pneumonia and subsequent travels, prevented this initial contact from proceeding much further. In 1942 they were in touch again with respect to the Freiburg group conversations. In 1942–1943, after Wurm proposed a comprehensive thirteen-point plan for unifying the hostile church factions, Bonhoeffer critically scrutinized them to see if they might contradict the decisions of Barmen and Dahlem. But he did not find Wurm's proposals to be the kind of cautious tiptoeing that the attempts of the Kassel Council and the Essen I–III memoranda had been. On the contrary, Bonhoeffer felt that Wurm was openly stating the duty of a Confessing church in the Nazi state. Before he could write down the opinions he had expressed in conversation on Wurm's thirteen propositions, however, he was arrested.

The Church in 1941. In the second year of the war the church press and publications had to close down because of paper rationing; this probably spared the church a good many printed statements of "which it would probably later have been ashamed."[16]

In May 1941 the entire examination committee of the Old Prussian Council of Brethren was arrested; two days before Christmas they were sentenced after a major trial:

> In Berlin things have again been quite unsettled lately. Among others, Albertz, Dehn, Asmussen, Böhm, Vogel, Harder, and a few women have been arrested because of examinations. It is almost incomprehensible why the congregations should be so provoked and harassed just now. But it can only serve the cause.[17]

The severe sentences handed down to the twenty-three men and women on the committee indirectly affected the illegal pastors on active duty.[18]

When the "final solution" of the Jewish question began in the autumn of 1941, there were only a few brave isolated actions. What still remained of the Confessing church was totally preoccupied with questions concerning its own existence. In a synod session, the Old Prussian Council of Brethren appointed a committee to consider the current understanding of the Commandment "Thou shalt not kill"; but there was no large-scale protest anywhere. After the night deportations from Berlin began Bonhoeffer and Perels began work at once on a memorandum documenting the deportations, but this was already connected to his activity in the resistance.

In the autumn of 1941 Bonhoeffer and Perels also wrote a memorandum to the army, drawing attention to the fact that the state's antichurch measures were adversely affecting the military efforts. It was a record of everything during the two years of war that had impeded the church's public work, including the events in Warthegau, those related to the press and the euthanasia measures, the arrests, and the prohibition of pastoral work even in church hospitals:

> The hope of Protestant Christians that measures hostile to the church might be discontinued, at least for the duration of the war, has been bitterly disappointed. . . . We ask the army to take the following steps: 1. discontinue, for the duration of the war, all measures hostile to the church; 2. rescind arrests, expulsions and prohibitions of speech that have been put into effect for reasons connected with the church or church politics; 3. offer the church help and protection for its responsible work at home for the duration of the war.[19]

Bonhoeffer could not be very confident of the likelihood that this would influence the military authorities, but it was at least an attempt. He tirelessly used his connections to keep the Confessing church from withering away through the indiscriminate conscription of pastors into the army or for compulsory labor, and he had some success. At the beginning of 1940 he had put Confessing church pastor Kurt Scharf and Wilhelm Niesel in touch with Helmuth Groscurth, the liaison officer of the Army Intelligence Corps, to check the unlimited conscription of illegal pastors. Through intermediaries he even tried to influence Minister for Church Affairs Kerrl; Dohnanyi spoke with Canaris and Friedrich Olbricht, the head of the general army office, about urging Kerrl to offer Confessing pastors the same treatment and exemptions available to others. Through Dohnanyi he convinced Minister of Justice Franz Gürtner to point out to Kerrl that Confessing pastors had proven their patriotic loyalty. "The Gürtner-Kerrl conversation seems to have gone successfully," Bonhoeffer wrote on 8 December 1940.[20] It was to be continued with further documentary evidence that Perels was preparing. On a long walk in icy cold weather in Ettal Bonhoeffer was able to speak personally with Gürtner about the matter. Gürtner gave optimistic hints:

Gürtner came at midday yesterday. We spent the whole day together, and talked over a good many things. He is quite optimistic as to the [Kerrl] business, only it is questionable what K. himself is still able to do. The matter needs to be hurried on somewhat, for the conscription [of pastors] for work is increasing.[21]

One month later, however, Gürtner was carried to his grave. The matter could not be revived at that ministerial level; on the contrary, the Russian offensive increased the number of those called up. According to Erich Klapproth, in the summer of 1941 out of 300 young Rhineland Confessing pastors 270 were on active military duty, and 132 out of the 154 Confessing pastors in Brandenburg. More than 80 of the 150 Finkenwalde students were killed in action.

Although the efforts to regulate the conscription of theologians failed, an astonishing number of exemptions were possible on the individual level. No net was so tightly woven that the recruiting offices could keep all the people they caught. Various superintendents and individual officials in the consistories or High Church Council who were favorably inclined could obtain exemptions for one person or another. The help of Dohnanyi and Oster was the most effective. They managed to have Bonhoeffer declared officially indispensable so that, although he had been drafted, he was able to remain in his civilian occupation; over the years they were able to help other friends as well. Because of these efforts they had considerable difficulty after their arrests defending themselves against the charge that they had helped men to evade military service. With their help Bonhoeffer obtained exemptions or deferments for a number of people who were at risk (including myself; I worked for the Gossner Mission), such as Wilhelm Niesel, Wilhelm Jannasch, and Ernst Wolf, as well as Friedrich Justus Perels and Wilhelm Rott, whose Provisional Church Administration was one of the few Confessing church departments that was still functioning.[22]

The only person whose officially indispensable status committed him directly to the Military Intelligence Office or its resistance circle was Bonhoeffer himself. The others were free of any such ties. With a clear conscience they felt they had been helped by "Mr. X" to serve their church, and that is exactly what was intended. Bonhoeffer's only concern was that there were so few people he could approach for help. Too much of the burden fell on his brother-in-law and his friends in the Military Intelligence Office. When they succeeded again in freeing someone for church work Bonhoeffer wrote:

We find that the moral of this story consists in the fact that we know too
few people and the circle is too small. I had a long talk with Wolfgang
before his illness [the reference is to Staemmler's arrest on 16 November
1940] on this very point, and he wanted to begin something like this. Now
he probably won't be able to get around to it.[23]

After the arrest of Dohnanyi and his friends in the military high command in 1943, they were accused of taking imprudent risks in trying to
protect the churches. Yet these things occurred during the long life-and-
death struggle of the Confessing church, at a time when it seemed reasonable to hope that everything would change soon and that the overthrow of
Hitler was imminent. They undertook these steps out of their sense of
responsibility that competent younger people had to be preserved, at all
costs, for this turning point. Unless they were willing to consign the aftermath to chaos, everyone who worked for the conspiracy had to think about
the survival of at least a few people who would assume the new responsibility afterward. It is to Canaris's lasting credit that he did not act from a limited perspective, but assumed these risks and used the possibilities of his dual
position to serve good ends.

Continued Legalization. In the second year of the war the argument about
the bravery of the many young Confessing church pastors on active duty
lost more of its impact. The unpleasant temptation of legalization reappeared. The church consistories increased the pressure and enticement
on candidates. The prosecution of the examination committee of the Council of Brethren in Berlin seemed to pull the ground from under the feet of
the illegal pastors, since a court had now invalidated all the examinations
by the Confessing church. In addition, a new labor conscription act affecting people unfit for active duty threatened to remove the last possibility of
working for the Confessing church from those who were still at home.
Bonhoeffer had his hands full, giving advice to his illegal Finkenwalde
pastors.

In November 1940 the Reich Minister of Labor decreed that "Evangelical theological ordinands, ministers, assistant preachers, etc., who have been
trained in the prohibited substitute colleges of the Confessing Party or illegally ordained, and who are exercising a disturbing influence among the
population by their slanderous activities" were to be "directed immediately
into a suitable occupation."[24] The decree was proof that there was still a
steadfast, hard core of people who would not yield to pressure; it primarily
affected those physically ineligible for military duty and the women

theologians of the Confessing church. Suddenly and unintentionally, the Confessing church had its "worker-priests." The woman minister Inge Koch, the appointed representative of the illegal pastors in Saxony, was assigned to work in the Leuna factories.[25] She wrote:

> It is strange what temptations suddenly raise their heads in front of the few of us here, how we learn that all available forces are used up in the mobilization of labor, how tired and empty we become, until we don't know how we can prepare a Bible lesson or preach a sermon.[26]

The Magdeburg consistory told Johannes Hamel, who was also ordered to work in a factory, that he could be exempted if he would "1. take up all the consistory's collections, 2. read out all the announcements of the official church, and 3. stop praying for imprisoned and prohibited people by name from the pulpit."[27]

Bonhoeffer did not yield here either; he did not advise anyone to submit to legalization. In contrast to former years, however, he sent newsletters to illegal and legalized pastors alike, and answered personal letters from those who had been legalized without going into differences of opinion. Thus, to some extent, he accepted Way B.

Their new existence at the front and in the factory made some Christians more obstinate. Others became more uneasy. How could they not want to know that their congregation, their official position, and their family at home were secure? And how could they maintain the subtle distinctions of former times? Willi Brandenburg wrote from the eastern front:

> You have heard that, after struggling for years, I have seen my way to undergoing the legalizing process with the consistory. I know, too, that you consider that I am on the wrong track. I felt inhibited from telling you personally about it, as I ought to have done; but that was not because I felt objectively uncertain about it—I still think I acted correctly—but because I have caused some grief and stress to you and my colleagues with this step. . . .[28]

Another, who remained at home, praised his legalized position:

> I should never have thought it possible for legalization to make one's work so much easier! And I find this easing of work most welcome. . . . I have been told that the theological work of the Confessing church is fully recognized, and that it alone can be thanked for preserving the substance of the church.[29]

Bonhoeffer's advice was at least to wait and see:

> Who can fail to see that with this war we have been granted an interval
> which we really cannot bridge with our thoughts? So we should wait
> patiently.[30]

One of those at the front bluntly refused after his consistory wrote him that
he could have the office of pastor with all its privileges if, when he was on
leave, he submitted to a simplified examination. But he wrote Bonhoeffer:

> But I keep on having doubts whether we young pastors of the Confessing
> church are taking a course that is right and necessary. After all, there are
> indications that after the war, and to some extent even now, we shall be
> deprived of every possibility of a ministry. Hasn't the Confessing church
> laid too heavy a burden on our shoulders? . . . Don't those of us who were
> examined by the Confessing church resemble the shock troops cut off
> from the main unit, who are gradually becoming casualties? . . . That we are
> just treated as unemployed and assigned work as such? Is this path we are
> following still necessary? . . . I no longer feel certain. . . . Please advise me!
> You once wrote: Wait and see; the war will bring changes that we cannot
> yet foresee. . . . We may then be relegated to a completely illegal status as
> Confessing church pastors. . . . Who else am I to ask? As far as I can see, the
> Council of Brethren has withdrawn. So, Brother Bonhoeffer, give me the
> answer that I am waiting for and shall listen to. . . .[31]

On one such letter Bonhoeffer made some notes for his reply: "1. Never
act out of uncertainty; 2. Never act alone; 3. Never be hasty or allow yourself to be pushed. God can open what is locked up." He gave this answer in
a newsletter; it was his last statement on legalization.[32] In it, he stuck to the
rule "that our present military situation is unfavorable for undertaking a far-
reaching change of direction for the church. . . . Any decision that places the
colleagues at home in a more favorable position than those at the front is
more questionable than ever."[33] For the first time, he admitted that after the
trial of the examination committee it might be possible for some to seek new
paths, without thereby acknowledging the consistories as the spiritual leadership. Risking the loss of a ministry within the *Volkskirche*, however, might
bear fruit in the future:

> Readiness to leave the ordained ministry, even to refrain from any exercis-
> ing of spiritual office and to serve Christ in another calling rather than to
> subject oneself to a false spiritual leadership (for this is what it is) remains
> a legitimate evangelical position. . . .

Readiness to enter the ministry without allegiance to any church government (for a recognition of the false church government is impossible), while "preserving one's personal theological convictions" in order to serve Christ as a pastor, can under the present circumstances no longer be rejected *in principle* as a Christian possibility; but it is fraught with heavy dangers for the church and the individual. This must be recognized.[34]

It was still not Bonhoeffer's goal to patch things up; given that option he would prefer no ministry in that church at all. If the trial of the examination committee had finally ended all the possibilities of training and an introduction to the ministry, he still did not see this as a reason for surrender. They needed to look for some other form of service that would make it possible to deliver a credible message; then they could finally discard their old protective shell. Bonhoeffer was still appealing to the free decision of the individual; this final statement on legalization was intended to leave his students' consciences whole and free, without hurting any of those who decided differently.

What if his loyalty to what he had once professed—even this letter from 1942 contained an urgent reminder of the Dahlem synod decision![35]—was hopelessly overtaken by the historical developments? Things were looking this way. Bonhoeffer did not try to visualize the whole thing to the end. But there was never a time, even during the bleakest moment of the war, when he wanted to follow the movement toward that all-approving makeshift consistorial church he had once left.

At the end of 1942 the legalization problem flared up again in several provinces, without causing any essential changes.[36] Then it died out in the total war.

After the war the consistories hastened to grant those who were still illegal their full, unconditional qualifications, seniority, and privileges of the ministry. Hardly anyone thought to ask about the new concept of ministry that had been behind that bitter and wearying struggle, and what it might have meant.

Professional Problems

After the dissolution of the collective pastorates in March 1940 Bonhoeffer's professional situation did not initially appear to be a problem. The Council of Brethren took its time deciding on a new task for him, and it suited him quite well to wait during April and May. Things did not become critical till the autumn of 1940. Until then there were plenty of possibilities open to him, as no official restrictions hampered him outside of Berlin. He could still preach, and he liked to do so.

A few months after he had been prohibited from speaking in public, he heard that an aunt who was suffering from cancer, Countess von der Goltz, had only a few months to live. At that time he wrote to me: "What should I do, if I knew that it would be all over in four to six months' time? . . . I think I should still try to teach theology as I used to, and to *preach often*."[37] When Frau von Kleist-Retzow urged him to give a daily exegesis to a circle of worshipers in her household he was very gratified, and if one of his friends asked him for assistance with a sermon he was always ready to help with a suggested outline. When he was forbidden to preach in public after the autumn of 1940 it was a blow to him.

Inspector. Given the difficulties of communication between the different provincial churches, visitations were a necessary element in the life of the Confessing church. Bonhoeffer seemed admirably suited for giving information and theological guidance, and for substituting as preacher for those who were serving as soldiers. He undertook three such journeys for the East Prussian Council of Brethren, and those journeys led to fundamental complications for his professional status.

First East Prussian Journey. Bonhoeffer delayed his first official journey eastward because of the dramatic developments on the western front. It was not until the day after Dunkirk—he was very anxious for his relatives in England as he followed the BBC's news of the debacle on the coast—that he left with me to visit the church districts around Tilsit and Memel after a pastors' meeting in Schlawe. He found parishes where services were led by a farmer who was an elder in the church, pastors' wives who took over all the religious instruction in their districts, and places where he was not allowed to enter the church because intercession by name for imprisoned Confessing Christians was prohibited. In Tilsit he found fuller churches than he was used to in the "Reich." He visited old colleagues from the House of Brethren like Horst Lekszas in Königsberg or Richard Grunow with his group of students in Danzig. He got to know Willy Kramp, whose novel *The Fisherman of Lissau* was causing something of a stir; on his way back from Köslin he renewed his contact with the versatile Dr. Knorr and his lay group, and returned home with proposals for teaching the laity. There were no incidents during this first journey. France's surrender was exciting enough. It was not until the second journey that his situation became difficult.

Second East Prussian Journey. In Königsberg Bonhoeffer was fully occupied for several days with pastors who were having a conference. He conducted the Bible study, lectured on "Preaching Today," "Baptismal Grace and Discipline," "Protestant Oral Confession," and "The Problem of Death," his theme for the Croall Lectures.[38] He also led discussions on "The Church's Prophetic Ministry" and "Church and Ministry." It was a full meeting. He also met with the East Prussian fellowship leaders from the "Dahlemite" wing of the Confessing church, and with groups of soldier-theologians.

The weekend of 13–14 July he went out to Bloestau, where Hans Iwand had previously worked. Invitations on duplicated handbills had been circulated announcing a meeting of Confessing students. This was foolish. Bonhoeffer was to speak on the situation and conduct a Bible study on the text about the rich young ruler. Just as he had finished the Sunday morning service and sat chatting with a few students, a fairly large group of police appeared on the orders of the Gestapo, and the conference members were told to disperse. The reason given for the order was a decree issued in June that prohibited meetings of Christian youth and "confessional organizations" of adults. The Gestapo chief took no further interest in what had been going on, implying that he had expected a much bigger meeting. After personal details had been noted everyone dispersed in relief that no one had been interrogated or even arrested. Bonhoeffer could not shake the feeling that there was more behind this than simply the breaking up of a conference in Bloestau. The Gestapo did not approve of speakers from other parts of the country, and even less of speakers with his record.

For the time being he continued his journey eastward, visiting parishes in Stallupönen, Trakehnen, and Eydtkuhnen. The general mood there was depressed; Soviet troops had appeared across from Eydtkuhnen on the former Lithuanian frontier. While the Germans in the Reich were distracted by the events in France, Stalin had issued an ultimatum and occupied the Baltic territory that Ribbentrop had conceded to be within his sphere of influence. This action had caused great anxiety in East Prussia. "I made myself go around on what is now the Russian border just at the time when things were happening. I preached in villages a mile or so away and found the most surprising changes."[39] Bonhoeffer now broke off his journey and canceled the short holiday he had planned in Klein Krössin, returning to Berlin to discuss things with his brother-in-law Hans von Dohnanyi.

That was in early August 1940. After consulting Canaris and Oster, Dohnanyi assured Bonhoeffer that if the Gestapo interfered the Military Intelligence Office would be quite willing to state its interest in his journeys along the border, on the grounds that they would provide information. As a precautionary measure for his next journey to East Prussia, he would be given a commission that would offer him adequate protection. Eydtkuhnen had been near a potential area of combat since, at the end of July, Hitler had begun preparations for an offensive against the Soviet Union. So Canaris or Oster had a good case for trying to get information about the situation in this region, and could very well ask a Confessing pastor to report on it. Dohnanyi believed that this would avert any Gestapo measures and also avoid the problem of being drafted by the army. Most importantly—and this, of course, was the central point of the discussions—it freed Bonhoeffer for the work of the conspiracy in Oster's and Dohnanyi's circle. When Oster, Gisevius, Dohnanyi, Bonhoeffer, and I met in the house on Marienburger Allee one afternoon in August, these arrangements were still only provisional. Bonhoeffer's finalized connection to Military Intelligence came about as a result of the next Gestapo measures.

Third East Prussian Journey. On 25 August Bonhoeffer went to Königsberg for the third time, once more as an inspector on behalf of the Old Prussian Council of Brethren. He called not only on the Council of Brethren, but also on the officer of the Königsberg Military Intelligence Office, who was to protect him if anything unforeseen happened. This time he insisted that his visits on behalf of the Council of Brethren should not be advertised by handbills, so as not to draw the Gestapo's attention unnecessarily. He also stopped keeping his usual diary of his visits to the townships and people, and of the meetings arranged. He came back to Eydtkuhnen. Feeling that he had come to a turning point, he wrote: "I think with gratitude of the years that have gone, and with confidence of those that are to come."[40] Then he received an urgent telephone call from Superintendent Block, telling him to go at once to his official residence at 9 Koppelstrasse, Schlawe.

New Police Restrictions on Bonhoeffer. On 4 September 1940 an official authorized by the state police in Köslin told him that an order had been issued by the Reich Central Security Office, prohibiting him from making any public speeches throughout the Reich on the grounds of "subversive activity." He was also ordered from that time on to report his movements to the police regularly, at his place of residence. That was an unpleasant combination of restraints. Bonhoeffer was given nothing in writing, and he could only note down the reference number of the order: Reich Central Security Office IV A 4b 776/40.[41]

The prohibition on public speaking might not matter too much; but the obligation to report was a deadly blow which, like his expulsion from Berlin, had to be avoided at all costs. First he wrote a protest to the Reich Central Security Office to put the matter on record. He emphasized the defamatory nature of the reasons for the prohibition and the patriotic reputation of his forebears: "It is out of the question . . . for me to identify myself with circles that are rightly tainted by such reproaches [of subversive activity]." He included a list, which under other circumstances he would have found ridiculous, of his forebears: the families Kalckreuth, Hase, Cauer, von der Goltz, and the honorable city councilmen of Schwäbisch Hall.[42] The protest remained unanswered.

Before any decision was made about plans for his future occupation, Bonhoeffer went to Klein-Krössin, where he worked hard for four weeks on the first chapters of *Ethics*. In the evenings he listened closely to the BBC's reports of the battle of Britain. "While there is a violent autumnal storm outside stripping the trees of their leaves . . . I am sitting here working quietly."[43]

The Solution. Bonhoeffer's professional situation now truly become complicated. What chance was there of further work for the church? How could the offer of the Military Intelligence be carried out effectively?

Any teaching activity was out of the question; his inspections of parishes and church districts on behalf of the church was forbidden, as was the exercise of his ministry in Berlin. What could the Old Prussian Council of Brethren do with its pastor-at-large? It was understandable that some of the council members now wanted to send him to a small parish in some remote district. Wouldn't this be the best way to grant his wish for theological work? The small town of Bismarck in Altmark was mentioned.

Perels spoke against this in the Old Prussian council. He could not, of course, reveal his full knowledge of Bonhoeffer's wishes. He pleaded that Bonhoeffer be given a position that left him free for academic work, because he was writing *Ethics* and was "needed militarily" in Berlin anyway—this was the wording used at the time. I went to Jena to discuss Bonhoeffer's future confidentially with the chairman of the council, Wolfgang Staemmler, and especially to eliminate Altmark from the discussions. The decision of the next council session corresponded to Bonhoeffer's own desires.

On 15 November, en route to Munich, he visited Staemmler (it was the day before Staemmler's arrest), reporting afterward to his parents:

> St. told me that they attach importance to my doing scholarly work now; with regard to a parish position he was pessimistic; they would rather have me free to be at their disposal. I told him that I should like soon to get out of my nomadic existence. Anyway, as far as they are concerned I am free till next spring. . . . But first I must wait and see how the military affair

goes; I cannot decide anything before then. But it is at least a relief to know that I am not doing my academic work on my own account, but on other people's orders.[44]

He wrote to me:

So they have decided that I shall continue to head the Confessing Church training office and that they will keep me at their disposal, but that in the meantime I can do academic work, as there is a great deal of interest in it. ... So for the time being I am free, with the satisfaction of knowing that this is what they want. What should I do now?[45]

It was not difficult to have Bonhoeffer declared indispensable for Military Intelligence. This went through, and he was told in Oster's headquarters what he duly repeated in later interrogations: "Military intelligence works with everyone, with Communists and with Jews; why not also with people of the Confessing church?"[46] But the latest order from the Reich Central Security Office created difficulties even for the Office of Military Intelligence with regard to Bonhoeffer's work for them. Therefore they found it advisable to keep him as far away as possible from the Pomeranian state police office that had begun to watch him, and to avoid provoking the Gestapo by placing him too obviously in the Berlin Military Intelligence Office.

Oster and Dohnanyi arrived at the idea of putting Bonhoeffer on the staff of the Munich Military Intelligence Office. A number of reliable people worked there, especially since Dr. Josef Müller had joined the staff in the autumn of 1939. In October 1940, while on an official trip to Italy, Dohnanyi discussed Bonhoeffer's future activity with his Munich colleagues. This was the basic reason why Bonhoeffer during that time spent four weeks in Klein-Krössin doing theological work; in November Bonhoeffer had to present himself at the Munich office. He first had to register at the town hall as a resident of Munich, although he did not intend actually to live there. His aunt Countess Kalckreuth kindly took it upon herself to make him a resident of Munich by giving him nominal accommodation in her home. It was only after he had formally registered with a Munich address that the local Military Intelligence Office could apply to the recruiting office there for Bonhoeffer to retain his civilian status. This was granted on 14 January. Meanwhile, of course, the police had stayed on his trail since he had left Schlawe, since the Munich Military Intelligence Office and the Gestapo could only work out the orders for Bonhoeffer to report on a regular basis after Bonhoeffer's "indispensable" status had been clarified. The orders for him to report were in fact suspended for the duration of Bonhoeffer's service in the Military Intelligence. In the meantime Countess Kalckreuth had received an alarming telephone call for the absent Bonhoeffer: "This is the secret state police. There is a Herr Bonhoeffer living at your house. He is to come here at once!" With some trouble and anxiety she reached her nephew at the Ettal monastery, and learned that there was good news waiting for him: the requirement that he report regularly to the police was canceled for the time being. On 31 January the lengthy operation was successfully finished.

Two things remained unsettled—the problem of his livelihood and where he would actually live. Strictly speaking, Bonhoeffer still had a right to his salary from the Old Prussian Council of Brethren. His leave of absence was a partial one for the purpose of theological work. Anyone who wanted to know was to be told that he was freed for work with the high command of the Wehrmacht; such military requirements were not unusual in war. But of course the Confessing church found itself in strained financial circumstances, and the Pastors' Emergency League had too many problems trying to support those pastors who had been disciplined. To ease the burden on the church Bonhoeffer began regularly to receive money that the Leibholzes gave him from their German account, despite existing difficulties. His inadequate talents for the essentials of bookkeeping caused considerable difficulty for the financial experts of the Council of Brethren in their dealings with the tax authorities, and occasionally led to his having to answer further inquiries. But this arrangement gave him a feeling of independence, now that he was devoting so much time to other matters that he could not speak about and for which he would not make his church liable. From now on he saved the Council of Brethren between one-third and one-half of his salary. It must be added that Bonhoeffer neither expected nor received any remuneration for his activity in the Military Intelligence— as did other agents.

To resolve the question of his future residence, he visited his theological colleague Gerhard von Rad on his way through Jena on 15 November. Von Rad, who had been a friend of Bonhoeffer's brothers and sisters in their younger days, offered his home on the Chiemsee. In a letter to von Rad Bonhoeffer said: "I should be glad if this plan materialized."[47] But Josef Müller found a more attractive solution—the monastery in Ettal. Müller introduced his new Protestant friend to the abbot and commended him to the care of Father Johannes. The latter looked after everything necessary, was aware of the underlying circumstances—and said nothing. Thus Bonhoeffer remained a civilian, and could continue his theological work in the church's service. He wrote accurately to his Finkenwalde students about the "academic work in the library of the Ettal monastery."[48] He had free time, which was a luxury in those years.

And yet he was now—a grotesque situation for the man of *Discipleship* and the ecumenical movement—a confidential agent ("*V-Mann*") in Germany's war machine. Secret services all over the world use "confidential agents." To the enemy they are "agents"; one cannot be quite sure where the camouflage begins and where it ends. But here the camouflage went one stage further than usual (or was the notorious designation "confidential agent" appropriate in this case?). Those who commissioned Bonhoeffer wanted him and his unusual foreign connections to serve their political aims for Germany; he no longer wanted to withdraw from those who were risking their own lives to achieve those aims. He was no longer connected to the seminary or any congregation. The means to the goal had to be examined according to what was most feasible, now that the only remaining path open was that of "conspiracy."

Bonhoeffer did not deceive himself about the strangely ambiguous position in which he would find himself if he put his ecumenical connections at the disposal of the resistance group in the Military Intelligence while, at the same time, he was ostensibly putting them at the disposal of the German military secret service. Later, under interrogation, he cleverly argued that his sacrifice in betraying his ecumenical connections proved his loyalty to the Reich. He went this way alone, and took sole responsibility for it, but he also knew that he could and must put a severe burden on the trust that his ecumenical friends had in him. He never disclosed the exact state of affairs to any of his friends in the church, with a few absolutely necessary exceptions such as Perels. Because of their unlimited trust in Bonhoeffer, they respected that, too.

It was February 1941 before he was assigned to make his first journey for the Military Intelligence Office. Until then he continued to write *Ethics*, got to know Roman Catholic life from the inside, and corresponded busily with his Finkenwalde students.

The Finkenwalde Students. The chance he had been given to continue as a civilian liberated him to continue the work he had felt called to for the last ten years: to stand by the young theologians even under the prevailing conditions of war, and to work on his theology. The new double life did not make him feel divided; on the contrary, one side of his work supported the other and continually justified it anew. He took pains to keep abreast of the changing field post numbers of those who were called up, and he included in his correspondence the wives and parents of those who had been killed in action. At Christmas 1940 he sent personal letters, enclosing a copy of Altdorfer's *Holy Family in the Ruined House,* to more than a hundred Confessing colleagues; Kerrl's regulation prevented him from duplicating.

Bonhoeffer strongly empathized with the insecure and lonely situation of the Finkenwaldians who now were soldiers. He, too, had been placed in a lonely situation, and saw how privileged and protected the "life together" in Finkenwalde had been. He now understood how to describe the gift of meditation vividly to his former students,[49] but a new note became more prominent in the letters. It did not impose any unrealistic laws on the theologians for their existence in Hitler's war, but set their consciences free:

> But where we then come up so clearly against the limits of our service, we shouldn't be worried to death by scruples. . . . I don't know now whether it is quite right to keep writing to you and telling you that even at the front you are and must be "in the ministry." . . . One of you writes in some distress that he can only be a soldier among soldiers, and that in so doing he is trying to remain a Christian, but that he has no strength for more than this. I would like to reassure him and all who feel the same. I cannot see any unfaithfulness towards one's ministry in this. . . . The great difference between your existence and ours . . . may well be that we can put ourselves in a place which in a certain sense we have chosen for ourselves, through our profession, whereas you now share the life of millions of people who have never been free in this sense because of the conditions governing their life and work. . . . We should not let ourselves be made slaves. God knows your present life and finds his way to you even in the most tense and tedious days, if you can no longer find your way to him.[50]

Bonhoeffer felt even more ashamed when he got answers from those on active service who had once expressed dislike for his regulations in Finkenwalde:

> I have meditated when I found time, and when that failed, I have learned texts by heart. In that way they have often opened out at an unexpected depth. One has to live with the texts, and then they unfold. I am very grateful now for your having kept us to it.[51]

> You know that I am one of your very grateful pupils; the psalms that I first began to understand in Finkenwalde accompany me through the valley of the shadow of these weeks.[52]

Bonhoeffer sent quantities of reading matter that he paid for himself. In fact, he was already beginning to collect theological literature when he could for the time his colleagues returned to their profession.

He was confronted just as plainly with the other side of life at the front, the involvement of these illegal Confessing pastors in Hitler's ruthless warfare. This only drove Bonhoeffer into the conspiracy with more bitter determination. A letter from Erich Klapproth came in the middle of February 1942, shortly before his death:

> Our clothes have been sticking to our bodies—we reckon it is minus 45 degrees [Celsius] outside, but we keep them on even in the overheated farmhouse—since the beginning of the year. For days at a stretch we cannot even wash our hands, but go from the dead bodies to a meal and from there back to the rifle. All one's energy has to be summoned up to fight against the danger of freezing, to be on the move even when one is dead tired. Sometimes, when we are away from the mess hall for a long time, we invade the farmhouse after the fighting and slaughter geese, hens and sheep, get filled and overfilled with sides of bacon, honey and the nice Russian potatoes. . . . We often dream of being relieved, but we are now reduced already to 40 instead of 150, still more we dream of Germany—I dream of the "calm and quiet life in all godliness and integrity." But we do not any of us know whether we shall be allowed to go home again.

And he heard this, too, not only from the composed reports on the desks of the Military Intelligence, but from a former student of whom he had a high opinion, who was later killed in action:

> In the middle of January, a unit of our detachment had to shoot fifty prisoners in one day, because we were on the march and could not take them with us. In districts where there are partisans, women and children who are suspected of supplying partisans with provisions have to be killed by shooting them in the back of the neck. Those people have to be got rid of like that, because otherwise it is a question of German soldiers' lives. . . . We have had to burn down villages in the last three weeks out of military necessity. . . .[53]

A few of the Finkenwalde students became officers; others received military decorations. Some were taken prisoner and later sent to forced labor camps; others were condemned to death by Soviet courts martial. Most were killed in action.

> Death has now reaped a rich harvest of our Finkenwalde brotherhood. . . . It would be easier for us to give them up if we could say that they died for Christ.[54]

Bonhoeffer grieved for every one of them, and wrote letters such as the one he wrote on the death of Gerhard Vibrans:

I think the pain and feeling of emptiness that his death leaves in me could scarcely be different if he had been my own brother. . . . The closer we came to each other, the humbler I felt. . . . I shall be grateful to him all my life for two things: for the way he observed Sunday, and for teaching me Claudius's hymn "*Ich danke Gott und freue mich.*"[55]

To the whole group he wrote:

God no doubt means to tear especially large gaps in the ranks of our young pastors, and thereby lay a special burden on us.[56]

In 1943, when the cell door shut behind Bonhoeffer in Tegel, he had written to the relatives of a fallen brother on twenty-five occasions. He did not live to know that the final number of dead Finkenwalde students was more than three times that number.

Bonhoeffer's association with the Finkenwalde seminarians was the fulfillment of his calling. It remained a joy to him, even after he now began to take a different path. But after 1940 he no longer involved the Finkenwalde students in his decisions and the risks he took.

Theology

Bonhoeffer lived a remarkable life during the war. For weeks at a time he worked in the peaceful surroundings of the Kieckow fields or the snow-covered slopes of Ettal. In terms of time alone, he had more periods of time for steady work than he had during the Finkenwalde years. And in Berlin not every meeting for quartet playing served conspiratorial ends; as in his youth Dietrich Bonhoeffer accompanied his brother-in-law Rüdiger Schleicher in the violin sonatas of Mozart, Beethoven, and Brahms. A person who knew nothing of his involvement in the conspiracy might find his way of life in those weeks difficult to understand. Even those who knew about it, such as Frau von Kleist-Retzow, sometimes had their own thoughts. After two of her Kieckow grandsons fell in Russia within three days (one of them, Hans-Friedrich von Kleist-Retzow, had been confirmed by Bonhoeffer), she wrote to me:

I've become aware of belonging to these frightful events in a new way. . . . One does not want to be somehow shut out from all the inexorable fate and guilt that has come upon us. And that, if I may say so, is what makes me uncertain for the first time about the course that you and Dietrich are taking at this time. Are we not all part of this intricate business, and shouldn't we put our spiritual energies into action there, where things are being fought out—without considering everything? Wouldn't we continue our course more sure of its goal if we did not avoid this last contact?[57]

Immediately afterward, however, she again supplied Bonhoeffer with notepaper that had become scarce: "I still have 500 sheets of typing paper and 200 sheets of foolscap. . . . Shall I send the parcel to Berlin?"[58]

Bonhoeffer understood her well. He himself had often tried, when he was young, to find his place in the common destiny. Even in Hitler's war he took the same attitude when his nephew did not want to differ from his classmates:

> Now that it's happened, now that it's no longer a matter of possibilities, reflections, free decisions, but of an actual fact, in the face of which there are no more considerations and options, suddenly many things look very different. So the first thing that I would like to tell you is that I am really very glad on your account that the time of uncertainty and waiting is over, and that you can now have the inner tranquility of being where your contemporaries are. It was probably that which chiefly bothered you, and it will probably be that too which will give you inner help in different situations. Not to want to be separate from the fate and need of others, to wish to have their companionship, is something quite different from simply wishing to go with the crowd. One probably should be on one's guard against "wanting to experience" the war and its horrors, for who, among those who desire that in a light-hearted moment, knows how he will stand in the hour of crisis? But to be called, to participate in fellowship with others, to contribute one's own share and to help bear things up—that, I think, is fairly firm ground to stand on and to live through difficult times.[59]

The only time he was really worried about his way of life was for several weeks in the autumn of 1940, when his situation was still so unclear. My own church employment had already been settled, and he wrote to me: "In any case you are now leading . . . a life that, seen as a whole, is more productive than mine."[60]

Bonhoeffer had not returned from America to separate himself from other people's needs and destiny—on the contrary. That did not mean letting himself be sacrificed prematurely, deliberately, and passively to that destiny. He was prepared to make his full contribution, but as long and as far as possible through his own personal decision.

What surprised him now was the extent to which clarity about his political decision gave him more freedom for theological work. At times he could concentrate on it completely, once he had fought his way through the matters relating to the Military Intelligence. But in the intervals of purely theological work he never allowed his political friends to feel that he was withdrawing from them and avoiding the consequences of the conspiracy.

The content of Bonhoeffer's new way of life inevitably moved him to work even more on ethical problems, and strengthened the sense that his life's work was to be a theological ethic. He acquired the ability to alternate frequently between writing and traveling without sacrificing concentration. The one task had to do with the other, and so he could break off in the middle of his work when he was told that a visa had arrived, and could continue reflecting on his theme at once after he had carried out his task.

Of course, his way of working, which had always allowed him a few hours of quiet in the day for carrying on his projects, proved valuable here, too. He was not dependent on a particular desk and a filing cabinet that was difficult to move about.

Expert Opinion on Baptism. The Old Prussian Council of Brethren occasionally made use of the theologian whom they had given leave, and asked for his expert opinion on current questions. In 1942 he was asked to formulate a detailed opinion on baptism.[61]

The disintegration of the *Volkskirche*, the beginning of the Confessing church, and in particular its new efforts to deal with church discipline had unleashed a discussion on baptism even before the appearance of Karl Barth's *The Teaching of the Church Regarding Baptism*,[62] a work that vigorously attacked infant baptism, and which, in fact, Bonhoeffer had never seen. In 1941 a pamphlet by the Silesian Confessing pastor A. Hitzer, criticizing the practice of infant baptism, caused something of a stir.

Hitzer went further than Barth. He produced passages from the New Testament and extracts from the confessions showing that belief was a precondition of baptism; and he passionately called upon the Confessing church to pull itself together and make a decision at least to allow "believer's baptism" for adults. The Old Prussian Council of Brethren took the call seriously and commissioned a few theologians, including Bonhoeffer, to give detailed advice on Hitzer's effort.

Bonhoeffer worked out his statement of the case as well as he could, given the limited time available and the absence of a library. Perhaps he did not take Hitzer seriously enough. If he had seen Barth's pamphlet on baptism that appeared later, we should probably possess a more detailed statement of Bonhoeffer's views, which would have given us some insight into the changing ideas of the two men regarding the Sacrament of Baptism.

Bonhoeffer took exception to Hitzer's concept of belief as subjective and individualistic. In refuting it, he defended the right to baptize infants. He preferred to regard this as a praise of God's grace and a means of keeping open the boundary between those inside and those outside the congregation. But he did not by any means consider advocating compulsory infant baptism; it was out of the question for the church to discipline those pastors and church members who refused on conscientious grounds to have their children baptized: "'In both cases [i.e., church members and pastors] the church will regard it as a practical indication of the seriousness of baptismal grace."[63] He even reversed the inquiry about "the freedom to baptize adults," arguing that what should really be demanded is "the freedom to baptize infants." The situation of the *Volkskirche* meant that the church was no longer very familiar with adult baptism, so that what should be a matter of course had become a rare exception. Bonhoeffer thought that Hitzer was wrong in basing the church's renewal on the "believer's baptism" of adults; renewal could come only through correct baptismal discipline. But he agreed with Hitzer that the existing custom was hardly acceptable and was, to a great extent, a mockery of the sacrament.[64]

Bonhoeffer's position here was much as it had been in *Sanctorum Communio*.[65] There, too, he had set a limit on infant baptism "where the church can no longer seriously consider 'carrying' the child."[66] What had then only been hinted at was now clearly expressed. Although this opinion makes Bonhoeffer look very conservative by comparison with Hitzer and Barth, his attitude would appear far too revolutionary in today's German churches.

When we realize how Bonhoeffer's *Discipleship* was read in those years, as a plea for conversion and a faithful core of believers, it must be stressed that in this expert opinion on baptism he was clearly arguing against faith and baptism as one's own work. However, "Cheap grace is . . . baptism without church discipline,"[67] and baptism is baptism into Jesus' death[68] and into membership in the church-community in all the concrete relationships of life.[69]

It was a relief when he wrote to his godchild's father, who was on active duty in 1944, that infant baptism was certainly not a law in the New Testament. When "regarded purely as a demonstration, infant baptism loses its justification."[70]

Primus Usus Legis. During the war the Old Prussian Union held its Confessing synods outside its territory—for example, in Hamburg or Leipzig—so that people who were hindered by expulsion orders or residential restrictions could participate in the sessions, which were arranged unobtrusively. The tenth Old Prussian Confessing synod was held in Hamburg in November 1941; it appointed a committee to report on "the meaning of the signs of the time." The Rhineland Confessing pastor Joachim Beckmann was chairman, and Hans Iwand, Peter Brunner, Lothar Kreyssig, Ernst Wilm, and Bonhoeffer were members of the committee. At the end of 1941 they issued a detailed statement, prepared mainly by Beckmann, on the signs of the de-Christianizing of Germany.[71] Its main line of approach was similar to that of Bonhoeffer's memorandum to the Wehrmacht.[72] At the time of the synod Bonhoeffer was in bed with pneumonia in Berlin, and did not take part in any of the committee's sessions. Perels, who was present for part of the meeting, may have had Bonhoeffer's draft of that memorandum.

Meanwhile the first news began to circulate about the deportations of the Jews in Berlin and elsewhere. The pastors, who were under no illusions about those criminal measures, were troubled about what they now ought to preach. Without any direct order from the synod, the Council of Brethren appointed a committee to prepare a synod declaration on the Commandment "Thou shalt not kill." Bonhoeffer took part in this.

Under the chairmanship of pastor Günther Harder, the working group met for the first time in Magdeburg on 10 August 1942; it included Count Peter Yorck, Niesel, Oskar Hammelsbeck, Peter Brunner, and Bonhoeffer. Theologically the question for Bonhoeffer was what had been discussed in Finkenwalde: "How do we preach the law?" At the second session he gave a critical presentation of the doctrine of *primus usus legis* in the confessions as a doctrine of external discipline among the people. This session met in Magdeburg on 15 March 1943, only a few days before Bonhoeffer's arrest, just after Schlabrendorff's attempted coup had failed. Yorck, Harder, Perels, Niesel, and Bonhoeffer worked an entire day on Bonhoeffer's presentation.[73] At the final Old Prussian Confessing synod in Breslau on 16–17 October 1943, after Bonhoeffer had been in prison for six months, the committee produced a message on the Fifth Commandment, denouncing the solution of the Jewish question by the "elimination" and "liquidation" of the Jews. It was called "Recommendations for Pastors and Elders about the Fifth Commandment," and confined itself to the question of preaching; it was not intended as a public announcement from the pulpit.[74] In the message for the day of repentance in 1943 the statement was to be read from the pulpits: ". . . Woe to us and our nation if it is held to be justified to kill men because they are regarded as unworthy to live, or because they belong to another race. . . ."[75]

Did the audience in Magdeburg on 15 March 1943 listening to Bonhoeffer's dry exploration of the issue realize that a new theological emphasis was taking shape in his thought? Here he firmly opposed the division between those who hear the gospel and those who hear the law into believers and unbelievers. Without explicitly discussing Barth's pamphlet "Gospel and Law," Bonhoeffer declined to fix the sequence of gospel and law, either in the distinction between them or in their relationship to each other:

> God desires the external order not only because the gospel exists but also in order that it may exist. . . . Both sequences are, therefore, theologically justified and necessary: gospel and law as well as law and gospel. In the confessions the second sequence predominates. But in both sequences the gospel is the "actual" kingdom of God.[76]

As the confessional writings would have it, and as he himself held in *Sanctorum Communio*, he no longer wanted to view the kingdom of Christ as related simply and solely to the church.[77] The *primus usus legis* belongs to the confession of Christ by the Christian who accepts his responsibility to the world:

> But even the congregation in the catacombs will never be deprived of the universality of its mission. . . . It will learn that the world is in disorder and that the kingdom of Christ is not of this world, but precisely in this it will be reminded of its mission towards the world. . . . Apocalyptic proclamation may well be a flight from the *primus usus*.
> . . . [the *primus usus*] is not concerned with the Christianization of worldly institutions or with their incorporation in the church, but with their genuine worldliness, their "naturalness" in obedience to God's word.[78]

On that basis he pleaded for the "necessary collaboration between Christians and non-Christians in the clarification of certain questions of fact and in the furthering of certain concrete tasks."[79] On this point, therefore, Bonhoeffer clearly rejected a one-sided eschatological preaching, and asserted a "genuine worldliness" as opposed to a Christianizing and churchifying of the worldly order of things.[80] This emphasis also characterized the final phase of his *Ethics*.

Against Theological Isolation. In February 1940 the "Society for Protestant Theology" was formed at Ernst Wolf's initiative. There had been a disquieting and growing isolation, practical and spiritual, of the remaining Confessing groups. Wolf's group offered a new opportunity for all the provincial churches and what was left of the theological faculties to meet together.

Six years earlier in London Bonhoeffer had congratulated Wolf on his flair and enterprise in founding the monthly periodical *Evangelische Theologie*:

> I shall be glad to help, if you can use me; and my wish to you for this great undertaking is that it may help toward the elucidation of what is obscure and the discovery of hitherto untrodden ways.[81]

Now Bonhoeffer promoted this new development: "You will join the Society of Protestant Theology, won't you? At least, if you have any regard for yourself!"[82] He was rarely able to attend its meetings, of course, especially when they were held in Berlin, and he was prevented by the expulsion order from coming. But he hoped that the society would offer a platform from which theological thought could break away from the narrowing circle of the Confessing church's standard theology. It did so more quickly than expected. The meetings soon produced vigorous arguments.

Rudolf Bultmann. At the society's Whitsuntide meeting on 1 June 1941 Rudolf Bultmann gave his famous lecture "The New Testament and Mythology." Ernst Fuchs, who took the minutes of the meeting, announced the paper as an essay in *Beiträgen zur Evangelischen Theologie*.[83] In a communication sent to all members Fuchs also reported on the initial discussion of the issue, in which Peter Brunner, Edmund Schlink, Friedrich Delekat, Ernst Bizer, Gerhard Krüger, Ernst Wolf, Hermann Diem, Günther Bornkamm, Ernst Fuchs, Erich Foerster, and Richard Widmann had taken part.[84] Bonhoeffer did not participate, but received Fuchs's minutes and Bultmann's essay at the end of 1941. When former students who were on leave visited him in 1942 he urgently recommended this essay, as well as Bultmann's commentary on John, which had also appeared in 1941. He described those works as "the most important event among the latest theological publications."

Bonhoeffer did not take part in those Berlin meetings either, but he received the minutes and personal reports of the proceedings. His response was angry when he learned that the Berlin pastors' meeting had spoken in terms that suggested judgment on a heretic. He wrote to Ernst Wolf:

> I am delighted with Bultmann's new booklet. I am continually impressed by the intellectual honesty of his work. I was told that the [pastors'] meeting almost sent a protest to you against Bultmann's theology! And that from the Berliners of all people! I should like to know whether any one of those people has worked through the commentary on John. The arrogance that flourishes here ... is a real scandal for the Confessing church.[85]

During 1942 the society's Berlin-Brandenburg section met several times to discuss the question of demythologing raised by Bultmann. On 17 June Hammelsbeck opened the fifth meeting by reading a letter from Hans Asmussen, who refused "the invitation because of 'serious misgivings' about the society in general, and in order to remain 'unequivocal' in his rejection of Bultmann's lecture."[86] In addition to Hammelsbeck and Günther Harder, Martin Fischer and Volkmar Herntrich, Hans Lokies and Siegfried Knak, young Gerhard Ebeling also spoke:

> Dr. Ebeling regards the double approach as problematic, that is, to proceed in the same way, both on the basis of our modern understanding of our existence and on the basis of a New Testament view. Against this, some say that the mythical view of life is closer to faith than the modern view, and others say, as Bultmann does, that the modern view is closer to faith. It would be particularly beneficial to pose the comparative question about demythologizing in Luther, for example, after the Torgau sermon about Christ's descent into hell![87]

Winfried Krause, a Finkenwalde student writing from a military hospital in Marburg, asked Bonhoeffer what he had to say about Bultmann's thesis which so excited the theologians of the Confessing church. Bonhoeffer answered:

> . . . I am one of those who welcomed this treatise, not because I agree with it; I regret the double approach in it (the argument from John 1:14 and from the radio ought not to be mixed up; I consider that the second, too, is an argument, only the separation would have to be plainer); so up to this point I may perhaps still be a pupil of Harnack. To put it crudely: B. [Bultmann] has let the cat out of the bag, not only for himself, but for a great many people (the Liberal cat out of the Confessional bag), and for that I am glad. He has ventured to say what many people inwardly repress (I include myself) without having overcome it. In that way he has rendered a service in intellectual integrity and honesty. The dogmatic pharisaism that many Christians are now calling up against it I regard as fatal. The questions now have to be answered plainly. I should like to talk to B. about it, and I would willingly expose myself to the draft of fresh air that he brings. But then the window must be shut again, or the susceptible people will catch cold too easily. . . . When you see B., please give him my regards, and tell him that I should be glad to see him, and how I look at things. . . .[88]

It cannot be denied that Bonhoeffer came down early and vigorously on Bultmann's side in this brief opinion, expressed incidentally. This supports Gerhard Krause's criticism of those during the 1950s who sought to claim

Bonhoeffer as being for Barth and against Bultmann.[89] In any case, Bonhoeffer welcomed the fact that the questions had been squarely put; he perceived that Bultmann's message was a liberation for himself as well. This did not mean that he wanted to adopt Bultmann's view fully as his own. He believed that the hermeneutical question, which he had once regarded as urgent, was still by no means answered.

Bonhoeffer was more and more inclined to have misgivings when he saw how the Confessing church's necessary concentration on the Bible led to a dangerous hostility to philosophy. The Confessing church was being pushed away from the sources of culture and science, so that questions that had been acute were wrongly regarded as settled. Eight years before he had spoken out fervently against theology at the university,[90] and had favored its transfer to "cloistered church seminaries." But this was just a vote against theological faculties that had grown sterile and servile, and in favor of recovering a free horizon. He was now capable of seeing that the horizon within his own circles might become narrow in a new and different kind of way, "a real scandal for the Confessing church."[91]

Thus he welcomed Bultmann's effort. But although he found that the questions Bultmann had raised were important, there was no time to work more intensively on the problem being posed. Other questions, such as those in his *Ethics*, had to take precedence. Otherwise Bonhoeffer probably would have found it possible to participate in one of his colleagues' debates during 1942.

Theodor Litt. The need to break through the narrowing horizon had become strong even before these first Bultmann debates. In the winter of 1938–1939 Bonhoeffer obtained two booklets by the philosopher and pedagogue Theodor Litt: *The German Spirit and Christianity* and *Protestant Sense of History*. He found a surprising correspondence with his own thoughts in those works, and was moved to enter into conversations with Litt. Litt's concern was the relationship of the Christian faith to the world. Bonhoeffer wrote and told him how keen he felt the question of the Christian's commission or refusal to work within the world. It was a long time since he had posed this question so pointedly;[92] but he was on the threshold between *Discipleship* and *Ethics*. Bonhoeffer felt compelled to supply, by pointing to Christ's incarnation, the foundation that was absent in Litt's affirmation of this world; but he wrote above all because Litt's "loyalty to the earth" pleased him so much, and because he wanted it to be possible to accept with a good theological conscience that "the present earth can be taken seriously in its dignity, its glory, and its curse."[93]

Oskar Hammelsbeck. Bonhoeffer's new relationship to Oskar Hammelsbeck was part of this period of outer and inner realignments. Hammelsbeck had been a pupil of the philosopher Karl Jaspers. In the Weimar period he had devoted himself to adult education and worked together with the socialist Adolf Reichwein,[94] and had then left the secular sphere for the church. As Bonhoeffer had done in his young days, Hammelsbeck discovered the church not in its privileged form of *Volkskirche*, but as it had been shaped by the Barmen and Dahlem synods during the church struggle. Late in life he had decided that the rest of his life's work should be for that church. Now he had come to Berlin from the Saarland, and was doing catechetical training work in the Old Prussian Confessing church. In his new service within the church Hammelsbeck was anxious to retain the secular sphere of life that had once been his own, and not simply to leave it to its own devices. Here he found a partner in Bonhoeffer, who had once tried to leave his former sphere of life behind him both internally and outwardly, but who was now engaged in reuniting secular existence and the church.

Bonhoeffer had occasionally met Hammelsbeck since 1937 at a meeting of the directors of the Confessing church's educational institutions. In 1939 Hammelsbeck had assisted in the collective pastorate when Bonhoeffer had gone to the United States; only after that did their professional contacts develop into personal meetings. Politics and philosophy were the main topics of discussion in Bonhoeffer's attic in Berlin. Hammelsbeck also wanted to introduce Bonhoeffer to Jochen Klepper, but before he could do so Klepper and his family had committed suicide.[95]

Hammelsbeck summarized their useful exchange of ideas in an autobiographical sketch in connection with a 1941 entry in his diary:

> The question whether my way into the church-community can be directed back into the world, this question that moves me about the Christian's responsibility to the world, the question "Church for the World," was exactly what Dietrich Bonhoeffer was asking, and so the conversations with him were the most important also for me during this period. . . .
>
> What had been common ground for a fruitful encounter in other conversations,[96] namely, the question of education and the consciousness of social and cultural responsibility, existed more than ever in a happy exchange of ideas with Bonhoeffer. For me it was especially thrilling and a great gain, because I found my timid theological ventures received, understood and confirmed as further questions in his mastery of systematic exegesis, and then critically changed and helped further. . . . He took a special interest in my preliminary work on the *Festschrift* for Karl Jaspers's sixtieth birthday in February 1943. . . . My own contribution on "Philosophy

as a Theological Problem" was once more to become the subject of a special exchange of views, when all those hopes were dashed by Bonhoeffer's arrest.[97]

Dietrich Bonhoeffer also took me into his confidence about his active participation in the resistance movement. We agreed that he should not tell me the names of any of the conspirators, so that I would be ignorant in case I were interrogated. I worked out a cultural-political memorandum, of which only three copies existed. . . . To ease my mind, Bonhoeffer sent me a message from prison, through Perels, that both had been destroyed by coconspirators. . . .[98]

We endured the time in the strange schizophrenia of happy gratitude for the parish experience and of suffering because of the church's guilt, in a strange mixture of power and weakness.[99]

The meeting was fruitful for Bonhoeffer's further reflection. An entry in Hammelsbeck's diary on 24 January 1941 sounded like Bonhoeffer's later terminology:

We can make no progress here [in serving Christ in the world] until we radically grasp the idea of our "godless" existence in the world. This means until we refuse to entertain any illusion of being able to act "with God" from day to day in the world. That illusion repeatedly misleads us into abandoning justification and grace, into an artificial piety, into making a legalized ethic, into losing our freedom in a kind of reverse servitude. . . .[100]

Shortly before Bonhoeffer was arrested, he received a postcard from Hammelsbeck dated 4 February 1943, on which there was only a quotation from Luther: "A Christian is a strange bird; would to God that most of us were good pagans who keep the natural law—to say nothing of the Christian law."[101]

Ethics. Since 1939, Bonhoeffer had been accumulating works on theological and philosophical ethics whenever he could get anything of the kind, new or secondhand, from a bookshop. His books included the four volumes of the *History of Ethics* by O. Dittrich (1926), five volumes of the *Theological Ethics* by Richard Rothe (2d edition, 1867), Hofmann's *Ethics*, the works of Oettingen, Harless, and Otto Piper, as well as Roman Catholic moral theologies and the Ethics of Scheler and Nikolai Hartmann. Other authors he consulted were Hermann Nohl (*Die sittlichen Grunderfahrungen*), Karl Jaspers (*Man in the Modern Age* and his *Nietzsche*), Bauch, Wittmann, Noack, and Prell. In 1940 he read Kamlah's *Christentum und Selbstbehaup-*

tung. He also went to the historians. He found Reinhold Schneider's books stimulating, and he discovered the idea of "historical healing" in the work of Jacques Maritain. He was impressed by F. W. von Oertzen's *Die Junker* (1939), Heuss's *Friedrich Naumann*, Trevelyan's *History of England*, Alfred von Martin's *Nietzsche und Burckhardt* and *Die Religion in Jakob Burck-hardts Leben und Denken*. He thought he learned more from *Don Quixote* than from many books on ethics. He reread Balzac and *Simplizissimus*, and began to read the German-speaking writers of the nineteenth century: Gott-fried Keller, Stifter, Fontane, all of whom enriched him so much in prison. He was taken by Montaigne's wisdom, but Bernanos receded somewhat into the background; to make up for that he discovered Ernest Hello in 1938–1939.

The list is certainly not complete, nor can we be sure that it is complete-ly reliable; but the books show his literary inclinations and capacity for absorption. There was not very much existentialist literature in his attic; he preferred writers with historical and humanistic ideas. Although he read a great deal, he rarely compiled lists of references or presented discussions with other authors. He confined himself to a general outline, in order to formu-late his own drafts free from the material he had been reading. In *Ethics*, in contrast to *Discipleship*, he worked entirely on his own; there was no longer any preparation, as had previously been the case, through exchanging ideas in seminars or lectures. Hardly anyone offered corrections, modifications, or argued with him. Seldom did he read a few pages to one of his friends, and even these sessions were cut short all too soon and for a long period. He never heard a real response to *Ethics*.

Bonhoeffer himself thought that the problem was more complicated than in *Discipleship*. For years, among the theologians influenced by Barth it was considered presumptuous to formulate an ethic; Brunner's and Go-garten's attempts in 1932 were subjected to severe criticism. The impulse to make new ethical outlines that emerged after 1945 was not yet perceptible. Thus Bonhoeffer's new undertaking was not modern. He thought Dilschnei-der's attempt brave but unsuccessful; he wanted to overcome Dilschneider's Christianization of the worldly order of things in the name of a "personal ethos."[102]

Bonhoeffer often asserted that ethics was his life's task. When he wrote *Discipleship*, he felt certain he was dealing with a theme that no one else was tackling and was awaiting him; this was even more the case with *Ethics*. "I sometimes feel as if my life were more or less over, and as if all I had to do now were to finish my *Ethics*."[103] In 1932–1933 he had dropped the ethical theme that had held him since Barcelona, and no longer participated in the discussion of the orders of creation and of preservation. The question that stirred him at the time was how the church could preach the concrete commandment, and he had pursued the question of Christ's lordship, not only over the church, but over the world. But then he had focused for years on the smaller realm of rules of life for those people who wanted to put into practice the lordship of Christ in the church. Now the issue he had put aside in 1933 returned forcefully. He began to test or change his concepts from 1932.

He developed anew the idea of "reality," applied in *Act and Being* and stressed in his lecture in Czechoslovakia; it now appeared firmly anchored in Christology. Reality is always the acceptance of the world by the one who has become human. Here Bonhoeffer sought to avoid the positivist and idealistic understanding of reality; he regarded both as abstractions.

He wanted to bypass the rocks of an actualistic situation ethic and yet retain its validity. He wanted to surmount the abstractness of a normative ethic and still accept its interest in continuity. Thus, once again, his work sought to mediate between two opposing positions.

A new side emerged in his concept of the "world." In *Discipleship* he had declined to pay the "world" the tribute of glorification. But the concentration on the glorification of Christ in an earthly discipleship called for the "continuous process of establishing the message across from unoccupied spheres of existence."[104] In the middle of the catastrophe of 1939–1940, the "world" came under judgment and grace into a field of vision that included both humanity's historical responsibility and its grateful acceptance of its creative possibilities. For a long time the church had claimed Bonhoeffer's attention, and the world, with its insistence upon creation and history, had— with good reason—remained unheeded. Now it received new attention as the sphere of the *regnum Christi*.

In 1932 Bonhoeffer had still tried to establish, as a counterpart to the concept of the *regnum Christi*, the critical formula of "order of preservation" as opposed to the dangerous "order of creation," which he viewed as linked to an impermissible revaluation of the world. Now he was at the point of grasping the human relation to the world as the sphere of the *regnum Christi* with the less static idea of "mandate": *only* "mandate," so that the *one* claim of Christ could be preserved in each gift and duty of the world; but *precisely* "mandate," so that those who bear the responsibility may have full independence while history is allowed to take its course. The christological basis of the mandate held the balance between the worldly and the eschatological element.

As a book, *Ethics* was never finished; what we have are only fragments arranged posthumously. That means we have no "ethics" from Bonhoeffer such as he would have thought ripe for publication. What we have is the record of his process of reasoning on that subject, which breaks off at a certain point.[105]

"The more exclusively we acknowledge and confess Christ as our Lord, the more fully the wide range of his dominion will be disclosed to us."[106] The exclusiveness of Christ's lordship—that is the message of *Discipleship*, the wide range of his lordship—that is the new emphasis of *Ethics*. The exclusiveness, unless it is misunderstood to mean a self-constructed ghetto, presses on to freedoms, permissions, responsibilities, discoveries, and to legitimate secularization.

At Klein-Krössin in September 1940 he began with the immediacy of the present and the aspects of the western world. Bonhoeffer had met Colonel Oster; Hitler had pulled off his grandiose victories—and Bonhoeffer wrote the astounding confession of the church's guilt.[107] Europe's new master had put himself beyond good and evil, and whoever thought in terms of conventional ethics would have nothing to set against him.

Theologically Bonhoeffer now found his theological location in the incarnation. The keyword is the Christocentric "conformity" ("*Gleichgestaltung*"). Christ, by shaping himself in conformity with the temporal nature of this world, draws it into conformity with himself. Thus for Bonhoeffer the scenery of the western world became the determining field for ethical reflection. There is no question that Bonhoeffer's concept here dangerously approaches a clericalization of the world. Nonetheless, the church is regarded as a part of the reconciled world and this, in any case, provides a much more positive relation between the church and the world than existed in *Discipleship*. There the world was merely the location of faith's first step; now, in *Ethics*, Christ's lordship creates historical responsibilities. Thus, for the first time, the Enlightenment could be appraised positively. In those September days of 1940 the relation between the church and the world had assumed, in *Ethics*, the character of a surprisingly mutual discovery of each other.[108]

Bonhoeffer stayed at the Ettal monastery at the end of 1940 and the early part of 1941, the longest working period of those war years. He began with justification; from there he achieved his new and fruitful distinction between the ultimate and the penultimate, to which he repeatedly returned while he was in prison.[109] That distinction had existed for a long time in his theology without his being aware of it. The last word of justification [the Ultimate] includes the beginning and the end, and, while limiting the penultimate, puts it into force. It prepares the way for the end, but has its time and place before it—yet receives from it its complete and far-reaching autonomy. Christ, representing the structure of the ultimate and the penultimate, "neither renders the human reality independent nor destroys it, but he allows it to remain as that which is before the last, as a penultimate which demands to be taken seriously in its own way, and yet not to be taken seriously, a penultimate which has become the outer covering of the ultimate."[110] The cross is the ultimate, and is the judgment and the pardoning of the penultimate. Christian life is "neither a destruction nor a sanctioning of the penultimate . . . [it] is participation in the encounter of Christ with the world."[111]

Thus Bonhoeffer opened the way for a rediscovery (so rare on Protestant soil) of a theology of the "natural," but one derived, not from the *analogia entis* as in Roman Catholic theology or from natural law, but from the doctrine of justification and Christology. Previously this area had always either been left to the Roman Catholics or derived from the article of creation, with dubious results. He joyfully formulated that article while he was in Ettal:

> I'm now beginning with the section on "natural life." You are right, it is dangerous material, but all the more attractive for that very reason.[112]

In the middle of this period of the tyranny of the unnatural, Bonhoeffer, on the strength of his Christology, placed reason and what is natural into their own right, so that beyond any moralizing "life is not only a means to an end but is also an end in itself."[113] Unlike Kant, he began not with life's duties but with its rights. "God gives before He demands."[114] The first journey to Switzerland on Military Intelligence business ended this happy period of work on *Ethics*; but its concept of the ultimate and the penultimate remained effective.

Then came the chapters with the strongest political imprint; these were drafted at the height of the conspiratorial actions in 1941 and 1942, during breaks in Krössin, Friedrichsbrunn, and occasionally his parents' home in Berlin. The terms "appropriateness" and "taking on guilt" indicated a new and sober tone:

> Ideologies vent their fury on human beings and then leave them as a bad dream leaves the waking dreamer. The memory of them is bitter. They have not made the person stronger or more mature, but only poorer and more mistrustful.[115]

He now critiqued the spatial line of thought that seemed to him helpful in *Discipleship*, and presumed the unity of reality:

> It is from *the* reality, whose name is Jesus Christ, that all factual reality
> derives its ultimate foundation and its ultimate annulment, its justification
> and its ultimate contradiction, its ultimate affirmation and its ultimate
> negation.[116]

During this time Bonhoeffer reread *Don Quixote,* the story of an honorable knight who isolates himself from reality in his fight for his principles. In
1932 Bonhoeffer thought of reality as the field for preaching; in 1935 he saw
it simply as a transitory stopping point. Now, for the first time, it became a
necessary partner for action to take shape. There is no longer any reality
without God in Christ, and there is no longer a God in Christ without reality. Christ is not absolute reality, like a norm from outside; and reality is not
simply material that is to have programs or ideals forced on it. Christ neither
abolishes reality nor makes it "Christian." Reality is no longer devalued (as by
idealists), or revalued and enhanced (as by positivists). "To be in Christ"
means to share in the world. Good, therefore, is not an abstraction but a
process, movement, constantly accepting the world and people and taking
part in their life. Thus ethics is helping people "to learn to live with,"[117] it is
the Christlike in the midst of the human. Christ does not establish foreign
rule: the "commandment of Jesus Christ sets creation free for the fulfillment
of the law which is its own."[118] Christ leads, not beyond, but right into the
reality of everyday life. Christian life is not an end in itself, but puts one in a
position to live as a person before God, not as superhumans, but "to exist for
others."[119] The unity of worldly reality that exists in Christ is not a synthet-
ic one, as the Roman Catholic conception would have it, nor is it reached by
standing apart, as the zealots do. It is real, not in some cosmically magical way
but in a dynamic validity, and thus it is real, through the mediation of Christ.

Bonhoeffer had now reached the place where his letters from prison, with
their surprisingly simple formulations, entered in. He concluded with the
formulation of "worldliness":

> The cross of atonement is the liberation for life before God in the midst of
> the godless world; it is the liberation for life in genuine worldliness.[120]

This page of his manuscript was on his desk in the Marienburger Allee when
Bonhoeffer was arrested there in April 1943. Beside it the notes for the chapter "The 'Ethical' and the 'Christian' as a Theme" lay strewn about, and on
one of them was the heading "Existing for the World."[121]

In the essay he wrote for his fellow conspirators at Christmas 1942, "After
Ten Years," he said:

We are not Christ, but if we want to be Christians, we must have some share in Christ's large-heartedness by acting with responsibility and in freedom when the hour of danger comes, and by showing a real sympathy that springs, not from fear, but from the liberating and redeeming love of Christ for all who suffer. Mere waiting and looking on is not Christian behavior. The Christian is called to sympathy and action, not in the first place by one's own sufferings, but by the sufferings of one's brethren, for whose sake Christ suffered.[122]

Thus in his three years' work on *Ethics* Bonhoeffer began with the idea of the scope of Christ's lordship from the conformity with Christ. He then brought the world as the penultimate under justification; and finally he reasoned from Christ's incarnation to his historical responsibility. Each line of approach deepened each of the two aspects—a more resolute Christocentrism and a more realistic openness to the world.

Behind the results of his work the contours of the surroundings in which he was living at that time are evident: the politically conservative world of Kieckow and Klein-Krössin, including Ewald von Kleist's disgust at the vulgarization of the environment, and the Roman Catholic atmosphere of Ettal. He was influenced in his writing not only by his study of the relevant books but also by his own role in recent history, by the impression of the ruling and contending powers, and by the influence of friends and acquaintances.

The goal of the chapters he was writing at the time was not simply to argue logically but to free people for action. At the same time, anyone who searches *Ethics* for a direct justification and detailed instructions for a coup will be disappointed. It is a question of liberation and awakening responsibility, not of offering safeguards in advance to serve as justification for timid souls when the time came for action. Historical action, insofar as it can be called this, is not justified in advance. The broader view that was Bonhoeffer's concern in *Ethics*, and which he had never heard discussed until then, was successful only by rigorously bringing together the christological approach and the concrete structure of his world.

In June 1942, in the midst of his work on *Ethics* and his journeys for the conspiracy, he once spoke of being possibly on the verge of new insights. Dimensions were unfolding that, until then, had remained veiled from him; he began to grasp where some approaches that he had already perceived were really heading. Bonhoeffer had returned from meeting Bishop Bell in Sweden and was on a military train en route to Munich when he wrote:

My recent activity, which has been predominately in the worldly sphere, gives me plenty to think about. I am amazed that I live, and can live, for days without the Bible; I should feel it to be auto-suggestion, not obedience, if I were to force myself to read it. I understand that such auto-suggestion might be, and is, a great help, but I would be afraid in this way of falsifying a genuine experience and ultimately not getting genuine help. When I open the Bible again, it is new and wonderful as never before, and I should like just to preach. I know that I only need to open my own books to hear what can be said against all this. And I do not want to justify myself, for I realize that "spiritually" I have had much richer times. But I feel how my resistance against everything "religious" grows. Often it amounts to an instinctive revulsion, which is certainly not good. I am not religious by nature. But I have to think continually of God and Christ; authenticity, life, freedom, and compassion mean a great deal to me. It is just their religious manifestations which are so unattractive. Do you understand? These ideas and insights are not new at all, but as I think I shall now be able to see my way through them, I am letting things take their course and not resisting them. That is how I understand my present activity in the secular sphere.[123]

SECTION TWO: THE CONSPIRACY

In 1945 Bishop Bell, in the first publication about his meeting with Bonhoeffer in Sweden in 1942, gave an account of a scene from the summer of 1940:

> We know of the despair which seized all those who were engaged in subversive activities in July and August 1940. We know of a meeting held at that time where it was proposed that further action should be postponed, so as to avoid giving Hitler the character of a martyr if he should be killed. Bonhoeffer's rejoinder was decisive: "If we claim to be Christians, there is no room for expediency. Hitler is the Anti-Christ. Therefore we must go on with our work and eliminate him whether he be successful or not."[124]

The account contains both accurate and unlikely parts, and among the latter Bonhoeffer's description of Hitler as the antichrist should be included. But that quotation from Bell led to its citation in many speeches and books.[125]

Bell's report was based on notes in his diary, which he was accustomed to making very accurately and usually directly after the event. The above account might well be related to Bonhoeffer's report in Sweden on his first meetings with Oster, Gisevius, and Dohnanyi in his parents' home. But the expression about Hitler being the antichrist does not occur anywhere else in

Bonhoeffer's writings. Even the passage in the memorandum for William Paton,[126] about the small "band . . . that recognized just here [i.e., in Hitler as "the accomplisher of historical justice"] Satan in the guise of an angel of light," differs from language which Bonhoeffer's theological conscience can scarcely have allowed him to use. I remember clearly how we once came to talk about it. We eagerly waited for his reply and really expected something from the Bible in answer to our question, when he said: "No, he is not the antichrist; Hitler is not big enough for that; the antichrist uses him, but he is not as stupid as that man!"

It is also likely that Bishop Bell's account of despondency and determination is too simplistic and stylized. Bonhoeffer's depression at the reverses during the summer of 1940 was evident not only at the Council of Brethren meeting in Nowawes; even at the end of the year, on 28 December 1940, he wrote to his mother on her birthday:

> Last year . . . as we approached the new year, I suppose we all thought that this year we should be decisively further and see more clearly. Now it is dubious, at least, whether this hope has been realized. . . . It almost seems to me that we shall have to resign ourselves to this for a long time, to live more on the past and the present, and that means to live more from thankfulness than from any view of the future.[127]

Bishop Bell's description, however, correctly indicated that Bonhoeffer joined the conspiracy at the lowest ebb of its fortunes, and associated his fate irrevocably with that of Oster and Dohnanyi. So if that rather crude theological expression could have encouraged his friends, Bonhoeffer might perhaps have used it in conversation. But he would hardly have been in a position to put it down in writing.

This brings us to the third stage of the German resistance movement, that is, the period between the western offensive in 1940, and the attempted assassination by Schlabrendorff in March 1943 and Bonhoeffer's arrest on 5 April 1943. It includes Bonhoeffer's actual complicity in the plot against Hitler. The whole period is overshadowed by a dilemma from which clear-sighted people constantly had to try to escape: anyone who continued to work for Hitler's overthrow after the tremendous success in France evoked a new stab-in-the-back legend—as Bishop Bell correctly noted. On the other hand, the risk of waiting until the tables had been turned was that the members of the conspiracy would become a liquidation squad for the victorious powers. Under this burden the decision to go ahead had to be made and a new approach toward the regime's overthrow sought, after the sector of the conspirators that controlled the weapons—the army high command—had dropped out after the beginning of April 1940.

This period of active resistance had three phases. Each began in a hopeless situation, where a new starting point was discovered and hopes of a coup revived, before once again ending in disappointment. Bonhoeffer's participation and involvement in the conspiracy progressively increased in each of these phases.

The first stage began with France's surrender on 17 June 1940 and ended with Hitler's so-called commissar order for the Russian campaign in June 1941. During that period Bonhoeffer was working to restore the relations that had been broken off since Müller's journeys to Rome and to exchange information.

The second stage began with the invasion of the Soviet Union and ended with the winter crisis, culminating in Brauchitsch's dismissal on 19 December 1941. During this period the purpose of Bonhoeffer's journeys was to explore and eventually influence the peace aims of Christian circles in the Allied countries.

In the third stage the organizational plan was modified with regard to who would give the final order to begin the revolt. It ended after the unsuccessful coup attempt in March 1943 with the smashing of Oster's resistance center. In this phase Bonhoeffer traveled to carry preliminary information about the planned coup to his foreign contacts.

Thus the course of Bonhoeffer's life was now much more tied to victory and defeat at the front, the prognoses of politicians, and the adventurous conspiracies of soldiers, than with details of the church struggle and its church council sessions. To his friends in the Confessing church he was loyal. To those in the conspiracy he was tense and watchful, waiting to carry out the revolt together.

The First Stage: Information, Spring 1941

Staying in Munich had its attractions; it opened to Bonhoeffer the resistance circle of Bavarian Roman Catholics who had gathered around the Military Intelligence Office there. Josef Müller took his new friend with him wherever he wanted this northern Protestant opposition figure to meet his fellow conspirators. The hospitality in Ettal, where he was given the key to a room in the monastery set aside for total silence and study (he lived in the monastery's guest quarters), opened theological, liturgical, pastoral, and religio-political insights and experiences to him.[128] There were also men who came to meet with Father Johannes who were politically important to him.

At Christmas 1940 they sat up for half the night together: the abbots of Metten and Ettal; Fathers Leiber, Zeiger, and Schönhöfer from the Vatican; Consul Wilhelm Schmidhuber and Captain Ickradt; Josef Müller; Dohnanyi; and Bonhoeffer. Bonhoeffer often drove over to the Metten monastery in the Bavarian forest, whose abbot, Hofmeister, cooperated closely with Josef Müller. Schmidhuber, who represented the Portuguese consulate in Munich and was also a member of Military Intelligence, became Bonhoeffer's mentor, together with Captain Ickradt. In Munich Josef Müller also introduced Bonhoeffer to Prelate Johannes Neuhäusler. Bonhoeffer conferred with him several times, before the prelate disappeared in a concentration camp in February 1941.[129]

The "Ten Commandments." Bonhoeffer depended on these good counselors and friends in Munich, for he had to learn to move about in the delicate routine of a provincial Military Intelligence Office that, in reality, was making him available to the central office in Berlin. The Military Intelligence was not staffed solely by resistance people; anything likely to arouse suspicion could not be too conspicuous. The arrangement by which Bonhoeffer's commissions and visits were assigned from Berlin worked because Colonel Oster, as head of the central office in Berlin, could also intervene and direct matters locally.

With his information from East Prussia in 1940 and the newly awaited information from abroad—the grounds on which Admiral Canaris based his decision to employ the pastor officially—Bonhoeffer entered the danger zone between the rival secret services: the Military Intelligence Office, which of all Himmler's organizations was the only secret intelligence organization able to maintain some independence, and the Reich Central Security Office directed by Reinhard Heydrich, who would not allow any areas controlled by state offices to be withheld from him.

This insistence on being the only person responsible for the political intelligence had already forced Heydrich into difficult negotiations with Canaris. Their vehement arguments had finally led to the "Ten Commandments," a written statement that precisely delineated the respective realms of the political and the military branches of the secret service. Since then, Heydrich had worked from as narrow an interpretation of that agreement as possible: Canaris was to inquire into nothing but military matters, whereas all political information was the exclusive domain of the Reich Central Security Office on Prinz-Albrecht-Strasse. But as before, Canaris did not want to be told where the dividing line should run. Asserting his right to be informed wherever military politics were involved, he developed any further foreign or domestic sources of information he felt were needed. This continued even after the "Ten Commandments" was replaced by an agreement, even less favorable to the Military Intelligence Office, that Canaris and Heydrich signed in Prague in May 1942, only a few days before Heydrich's assassination.

By their very nature, Bonhoeffer's commissions for the Military Intelligence fell either on or beyond this embattled dividing line. Canaris protected him, not because of any kindheartedness toward a pastor, but because he was unwilling to yield to the other side's attempts to restrict his authority. But it was also clear that Bonhoeffer, like the other secret agents, had to help preserve the fiction of the agreement, if the conspiratorial activity were to be continued within the Military Intelligence Office. He could not jeopardize his hard-fought-for civilian status. The 1943 interrogations of Bonhoeffer focused for a long time on whether he and some of his friends had been exempted legitimately from military service. This meant that his friends in Munich and Berlin had to edit his reports that contained official material so that their secret political content appeared relevant in military terms. It would become evident that, where necessary, Admiral Canaris later accepted and concealed everything of this nature on his own responsibility.

First Swiss Journey. On 24 February 1941 Bonhoeffer left Munich for Switzerland on his first commission abroad. The political situation was finally showing signs that gave the opposition hope of new alliances and new prospects. The invasion of England had not occurred, Churchill seemed to be unyielding, Roosevelt had been reelected, and Italy had suffered a disastrous setback in its invasion of Greece. Meanwhile the armed S.S. continued to expand; this made it easier for the conspirators to approach those generals who were inclined to be critical. After a conversation Hassell, Oster, and Dohnanyi had with General von Falkenhausen, the military commander in Belgium, Falkenhausen and General von Rabenau again went to Brauchitsch, but were unable to induce him to make any move at all. The conspiracy was not looking for a center—this already existed in the person of General Ludwig Beck, at least for Oster's circle—but the difficult question remained of who in the military center had the power to give and enforce the crucial order launching the coup. As he left for his trip Bonhoeffer's hopes for an overthrow had been revived, even though they were not very concrete.

In view of these new factors, the main idea that Oster and Dohnanyi had in sending Bonhoeffer was to resume cautious communication with the other side. There were naturally other channels, for instance, through Hassell and Josef Müller; but they did not want to neglect any possible contact that the other side might think trustworthy. Not much was expected as yet. On the contrary, it seemed likely that the difficulties in making foreign contacts had increased proportionally with the bitter passions aroused by the Nazis' western offensive and with the thought, incredible for those in Germany at the time, that the Allies were calculating their first chances of victory. Bonhoeffer's tasks for that journey were: first, to restore communication with the churches; second, if possible, to give signs of new resistance activity; and third, to explore ideas about peace aims.

Bonhoeffer's previous history made it particularly likely that his name would inspire confidence, through his contacts in Geneva, among ecumenical intermediaries and representatives on both sides of the English Channel. In Geneva Hans Schönfeld had no ties at that point to the Beck-Oster-Dohnanyi circle; and Schönfeld had not been recommended by Oster's confidential agent in Switzerland, vice-consul Hans Bernd Gisevius in Zurich. Because of his old ties to the Confessing church, especially to Niemöller and Asmussen, Gisevius was familiar with the past struggles and the resulting reservations against Schönfeld; both Bonhoeffer and Gisevius tended to warn against using Schönfeld as an intermediary with the British. Gisevius certainly had doubts about the political aspect of Bonhoeffer's mission as well, because he viewed the politically inexperienced pastor as acting in his (Gisevius's) own sphere. Still, Bonhoeffer's name was irreplaceable for some of the important people on the other side.

Bonhoeffer's departure was preceded by annoying delays. In Germany the journey, passport, and necessary foreign currency had been authorized by the Munich Military Intelligence Office promptly and without incident. But authorities in Bern would not grant the visa to enter Switzerland. The Berlin central *Abwehr* office had to get Schmidhuber to use his connections in Switzerland. Finally he managed to get the visa for Bonhoeffer, but there was another delay at the border.

The Swiss border police asked Bonhoeffer for a guarantor. He immediately named Karl Barth. Barth later recounted his mixed feelings and uncertainty as he vouched for Bonhoeffer over the telephone. Wasn't it strange that someone like Bonhoeffer, a Confessing pastor who had been banned by the Gestapo, was crossing the Swiss border with valid papers in the middle of the war? How did he come to do that? Could it be that even Bonhoeffer had changed his mind, after all the German victories? Barth asked him to come; the visit took place on Bonhoeffer's return trip from Zurich to Geneva. Bonhoeffer was only too glad to seize the chance of seeing Barth again. He had a confidential and exhaustive conversation with him, and told him the whole truth.[130]

Bonhoeffer spent four weeks in Switzerland, primarily in Zurich and Geneva. First he used the opportunity to send letters freely to England. He wrote to his sister Sabine:

> You cannot imagine my joy to be able to write to you directly after this period of silence and after all you had to pass through during the last year.[131]

That same day, he sent a greeting to the bishop of Chichester:

> My thoughts have been with you and with our fellow Christians in your country almost every day. . . . I need not assure you that we shall do everything to maintain that fellowship in faith and prayer. . . . When will we meet again? God knows and we have to wait. But I cannot help hoping and praying that it will not last too long. . . .[132]

Bonhoeffer stayed a fairly long time in Zurich. He went out to Rapperswil to see Erwin Sutz, who since the beginning of the war had been conveying news regularly between Bonhoeffer in Berlin and the Leibholzes, who had moved to Oxford. Sutz remembered how, to his surprise, Bonhoeffer said very definitely: "You can rely on it, we shall overthrow Hitler!"

Bonhoeffer also looked up his old mentor Siegmund-Schultze, with whom Goerdeler was cooperating. Siegmund-Schultze had his own lines of communication with London, reaching as far as Neville Chamberlain; but since Churchill had taken over the government Siegmund-Schultze had grown skeptical about the attempts at negotiation, especially since they had never been accompanied by any concrete report about a plot.[133] This weak aspect of the conspiracy became clearer even to its most sympathetic supporters, as one new plan followed another.

In the second week of March Bonhoeffer reached his main objective, Geneva. There he met Adolf Freudenberg, who had moved there from London and had worked for the provisional World Council of Churches since the autumn of 1940, organizing relief for refugees. Bonhoeffer asked about the camp at Gurs in the south of France, where one of Perels's uncles and Herbert Jehle were said to be interned. He met Professor Courvoisier, who was organizing ecumenical relief efforts for prisoners of war. In the office of the World Council of Churches he caught up on two years of ecumenical church history and what he could find in publications from London and New York. His intimations about the political opposition in Germany encountered a good deal of doubt.[134] But there was one person who listened to him openly and readily—Willem Visser 't Hooft. This was the man whom

Bonhoeffer had principally wanted to see, and he gave his German visitor a great deal of time for consultation.[135]

At this first meeting during the war, no messages or memoranda were exchanged—only Bonhoeffer's reports that the opposition still existed. Visser 't Hooft immediately wrote a personal report to Bishop Bell about the surprising fact that people in Germany reacted to the events "exactly as you and I" would have reacted, and he sent western ecumenical leaders, through his cosecretary William Paton, a detailed account of the situation. In a personal letter to Bishop Bell, he wrote:

> Bonhoeffer was a week with us and spent most of his time extracting ecumenical information from persons and documents. It is touching to see how hungry people like him are for news about their brothers in other countries, and it is good to know that he can take back so much which will encourage his friends at home.
>
> On the other hand, we learned a lot from him. The picture which he gave is pretty black in respect to the exterior circumstances for the community [the Confessing church] which he represents. The pressure is greater than ever. But fortunately he could also tell of many signs that their fundamental position has not changed at all and that they are as eager as ever for fellowship. Many of them have really the same reaction to all that has happened and is happening as you or as I have. And this is remarkable after such a long period of isolation. I hope to send soon through Bill [Paton] some fuller notes on all that we learned through him about the situation.[136]

During those months rumors had circulated that, in the concentration camp, Martin Niemöller had converted to the Roman Catholic Church. Visser 't Hooft passed on Bonhoeffer's assurance that this was not so. Before leaving Germany Bonhoeffer had actually inquired about whether the rumor was true from Frau Niemöller and from the bishop's seat in Berlin. I had myself told him on the telephone what Catholic Bishop Count von Galen had said to Frau Niemöller: "He should stay where he is."

Visser 't Hooft's detailed report, which Paton ("Bill") took to England, contained news about the church-state conflict, a conflict that the war had by no means silenced. It also enumerated the arrests and labor conscription of pastors, the thirteen points for the *Warthegau*, the euthanasia measures, the prohibitions against sending periodicals to the front, and so on; but it also assured him that the Confessing church was continuing to ordain clergy. Visser 't Hooft sympathetically portrayed the attitude toward the political dilemma which, in contrast to other politically minded people, Bonhoeffer increasingly talked about:

Inside the Confessing Church there is a certain difference of conviction with regard to the stand which the Church should take. There is, on the other hand, a group which believes that the Church should stick to what is called "the inner line," and concentrate exclusively on the building up of its own spiritual life. This tendency is often combined with a strongly apocalyptic note. There is, however, another group which believes that the Church has also a prophetic and ethical function in relation to the world and that it must prepare for the moment when it can again fulfill that function.

With regard to the attitude to the war, it is generally recognized among believing Christians that a victory of their government will have the most fateful consequences for the Church in their own country as well as in other countries. On the other hand, they consider that a defeat of their country would probably mean its end as a nation. Thus many have come to believe that whatever the outcome of it all will be, it will be an evil thing for them. One hears, however, also voices which say that after all the suffering which their country has brought upon others they almost hope for an opportunity to pay the price by suffering themselves.[137]

Bonhoeffer returned to Germany on 24 March 1941, leaving word in Geneva that he would be back soon. The old foundation of confidence with his ecumenical friends had been restored; for the moment, that was enough. Visser 't Hooft was left with little doubt about the strength of purpose among those of Bonhoeffer's circle; and he had been given a reliable glimpse of the obstacles that stood in their way.

Forbidden to Publish. On his way to report in Berlin Bonhoeffer interrupted his journey on 25 March to see Ernst Wolf in Halle, since he needed his advice about a new complication. On returning to Munich he had found two communications from the Reich Writers' Guild (*Reichsschrifttumskammer*) dated 17 and 19 March 1941. The first letter stated that, as a writer, Bonhoeffer had neglected to apply for membership to the writer's guild and had to pay a disciplinary fine. The second announced that his application for admission to the guild had been denied, since he had been prohibited from speaking in public due to "subversive activities." He was now "prohibited from all activity as a writer."[138]

As it turned out, Bonhoeffer had not been especially singled out. He had been discovered in a general survey by the Reich Writer's Guild that had finally extended to church publishers and theologians after the autumn of 1940. Bonhoeffer had already heard of it, but he had also heard that earlier decisions provided for specialist writers (*Fachwissenschaftler*) to be excused from membership, although only through special application. Bonhoeffer had submitted such an application in November 1940. This was the answer.

On the strength of this distinction between authors and specialists he protested: "I don't even have the right to enroll in the Reich Writers' Guild."[139] He then pointed to the negligence through which the penalty had been imposed, since his works had been incorrectly classified. The fine was rescinded, but both membership and exemption from membership were refused:

> This refusal has the effect of an official occupational prohibition of literary activity.... Only those theologians who occupy chairs at state colleges are exempted. Moreover, because of their predominantly dogmatic commitments, I cannot readily recognize clergymen as specialists in this sense.[140]

Of all the obstacles that had so far been placed in Bonhoeffer's way, the prohibition against writing made the smallest impression on him. One of his needs in life was certainly enough leisure and concentration for writing, but for some time he had been among those who couldn't publish everything they wrote. Despite that, he used every available day for his *Ethics*, and he wanted to do so in the future. His employers in the Military Intelligence Office were uninterested in this interference; it was obviously a routine measure. For one administrative department in the Reich to act against another was too common an experience for a fuss to be made about it every time. But it is true that when he was interrogated later the prohibition against writing did not work in Bonhoeffer's favor.

Optimism. The first Swiss journey was followed by a period of tense expectation; because of this Bonhoeffer had no desire to go and live in remote Ettal again at that point. Aside from spending Easter in Friedrichsbrunn and a few weeks that summer in Klein-Krössin, he spent the whole time in Berlin. There were signs of Hitler's coming attack on the Soviet Union. What would be the consequences? Berlin was full of rumors.

Among the Allies the feeling was spreading that the time had come to strike back. On 11 March 1941 Great Britain and America agreed on the Lend-Lease Act, which initiated the flow of war material across the Atlantic. A few weeks later the British landed in Greece, forcing Hitler to divert some of his forces to the Balkans. On 12 July the Soviet Union and Great Britain concluded a mutual assistance pact, which naturally made the resistance's attempts to contact the West more precarious, since each party to the treaty could now enter negotiations only with the other's agreement. On 14 August Roosevelt and Churchill signed the Atlantic Charter, which did not draw much notice in Germany as Rommel in North Africa and the German armies in Russia stormed ahead; but its impact was all the stronger outside: "The meeting . . . was a thrilling episode and the eight points of the Atlantic Charter can hardly fail to affect opinion throughout the world."[141]

In the Reich Hitler's "commissar order" gave the opposition new leverage for appealing to the honor and patriotism of the military commanders. Hitler had summoned them on 30 March and briefed them on the planned attack on Russia. It was necessary, he asserted, "to smash the governing machinery of the Russian empire." Civil and military commissars who fell into German hands were to be summarily liquidated by the troops without legal proceedings. Until then, criminal measures had been confined to the S.S. and its special units. Now, for the first time, the regular German Wehrmacht was expected to give and carry out orders that were clearly criminal. Once Hitler had left the room after his declaration on 30 March several generals began to press Brauchitsch vehemently. Halder urged him to resign because of the order. Finally Brauchitsch said, in answer to all arguments about international law, that Hitler had made his decision and would never reverse it. The "commissar order" was issued to the troops concerned and signed by Keitel. After it was appended by a provision that German soldiers who committed offenses against Russian civilians should in practice be freed from the liability of court-martial, Brauchitsch did indeed try to counter this outrage with a "supplementary order on discipline," but the stain of the regulations remained on the army. "With that submission to Hitler's orders Brauchitsch is sacrificing the honor of the German army."[142]

The effect of the orders was mixed. They drove some officers more than ever into Hitler's arms; others were perplexed and more inclined to have grave misgivings and consider revolt. In the Military Intelligence Office Oster and Dohnanyi vigorously took initiative by working on a memorandum to demonstrate the military and political lunacy of the order.[143] In other places such as the staffs of individual army detachments, resentment was openly or secretly expressed.[144]

This made the conditions for preparing a revolt more favorable. There were remarkable incidents and examples of people who now changed their minds. Rudolf Hess, "the *Führer's* representative," flew to Great Britain with the idea of starting talks to end the war on terms favorable to Nazi Germany before the catastrophe. The eyes of some former collaborators were opened. On 13 July 1941 Ulrich von Hassell wrote in his diary:

> Bishop Heckel, who formerly joined very complaisantly in all the attempts
> to build a bridge between the Protestant church and Nazism, was with me
> lately, and now shows complete recognition of the Party's undoubted will
> to smash the churches. . . .[145]

For weeks the optimism of the circle to which Bonhoeffer belonged concentrated on the possibility that the commanders could and must resist being put on the same footing as the murder squads of the S.S. As late as 16 June, only six days before the invasion of Russia, the matter was discussed with Beck.[146] Then the offensive began, and its initial successes left no room for any further thought of unified action.

Yet Bonhoeffer's optimism did not suffer anything like the setback it had at the beginning of the French campaign. Everything was different. The conspirators among the opposition began to cultivate a cautious and responsible optimism. While skeptics had come to admire Hitler's complete absence of restraint and saw his "fanatical will for the new order" as achieving the impossible, the conspirators did not let themselves be deluded about his terrible acceleration toward self-destruction. They believed they had to urge themselves and others to continue working to bring the terror to an even earlier end. Admittedly this work had become more complicated, since at the onset of the Russian campaign Hitler moved into *Wolfsschanze*, his headquarters retreat in East Prussia. Now it was even harder to get to him because of the numerous prohibited areas.

The conspirators worked energetically with the documentary material its members obtained through friends in important positions such as in the high military command or the Military Intelligence. Facts can always be differently interpreted and are soon superseded; much depends on how they are handled. Goerdeler's much-discussed optimism and his way of dealing with the facts played a real role in how the opposition proceeded. He was not alone in his optimism. Some set a deadline for Hitler's failures; when these proved to be incorrect they were immediately replaced by new deadlines. Numerical data were drawn up, showing his enterprises to be utopian, and when the conclusions proved to be false the data were revised. Some of the evenings spent at the Schleichers' or at Klaus Bonhoeffer's home were much occupied by such predictions, to which everyone contributed—Klaus Bonhoeffer and Otto John, Justus Delbrück and Baron Guttenberg, Rüdiger Schleicher and Dietrich Bonhoeffer himself. Hans von Dohnanyi was always a little more skeptical about all this, but Dietrich Bonhoeffer defended the inner stance that allowed for such forecasts. He viewed this not as blindness or seductive fantasy, but as a necessary weapon in the unequal struggle, dismissing the accusations being made even then against Goerdeler's new forecasts after every failure. Their tired bourgeois skepticism had to be countered with confidence, and this confidence needed strengthening. For Bonhoeffer this was part of the daily work of resistance, which did not surrender to the "facts," but tried to create new facts.

In the essay for his friends at Christmas 1942 he wrote a specific passage about "optimism," a paragraph which at first sight was unexpected, coming from a Lutheran theologian and pupil of Karl Barth:

> The essence of optimism is not its view of the present, but the fact that it is the inspiration of life and hope when others give in; it enables a man to hold his head high when everything seems to be going wrong; it gives him strength to sustain reverses and yet to claim the future for himself instead of abandoning it to his opponent. . . . The optimism that is will for the future should never be despised, even if it is proved wrong a hundred times.[147]

One person whom Bonhoeffer had in mind when he wrote such passages was Carl Goerdeler. He understood him, and felt a kinship with him on this point. Bonhoeffer concisely termed this a responsibility for life's "health and vitality, and the sick man has no business to impugn it."[148] People like Guttenberg and Oster shared this attitude and, because of it, there were not a few of the conspirators who were glad of the pastor's support.

The Second Stage: Peace Aims, Autumn 1941

The Second Swiss Journey. After the war Visser 't Hooft described how Bonhoeffer greeted him on the second visit in September 1941:

> The general impression was still that the German army had met little effective resistance and that Hitler might succeed in the East as he had succeeded in the West. So I was taken aback when he opened the conversation by saying: "So this is the beginning of the end." He saw my startled expression and added: "The old man will never get out of this."[149]

At the end of the visit Bonhoeffer wrote to Bishop Bell from Zurich:

> Personally I am rather optimistic in hope for better days to be not too far off and I do not abandon the hope that in the coming year we may meet again. What a strange day that will be.[150]

This optimism was nourished by the opposition's most recent activity in Berlin; it was certainly not based on anything Bonhoeffer and his friends could expect from the Allies.

As Bonhoeffer crossed the border on his way to Basel on 29 August 1941 the Military Intelligence Office also sent General Thomas, head of the army supplies department, to inquire about and possibly activate the readiness for revolt among some of the commanders on the eastern front. Thomas not only kept the group around Beck, Goerdeler, Oster, and Dohnanyi informed of the status of raw materials, he also tirelessly undertook missions that could be carried out unnoticed in the course of his official duties.

Parallel to the conspiracy there were constant efforts at peace contacts. These peace feelers were not a condition for the coup, as has often been asserted, but they could play an important part. It would have been irresponsible if the conspirators had not made every possible effort to make contact with the Allies. In 1941, it is true, the favorable conditions for negotiation that had existed at the time of the X-report (1939–1940) had passed; a negotiated peace was no longer possible. But the conspirators had to explore the background and perhaps even the dissent that lay behind the war and peace aims of the Atlantic Charter, which had placed Germany under special regulations. The question was whether they could still influence the other side's thinking about the future, and whether the Allies were conscious of the mistakes and consequences of the Treaty of Versailles, so that they would consider how the danger of chaos in central Europe could be averted, which was in their own interest as well.

Compared with his first journey, Bonhoeffer was able this time to get a much more vivid impression of the discussion on the other side, particularly in responsible Christian circles. Officially, of course, the Atlantic Charter had ended the discussion for the time being. It identified Germany in general with Hitler, and that was something the German opposition could not allow to be accepted without protest. Were there circles over there who realized the full consequences of such identification, and if so could they be strengthened? Was the discussion still going on?

Bonhoeffer did not confine himself this time to reporting his presence and to a mere exchange of information, as he had on his first visit. He entered actively into the discussion among leading western Christians of peace aims.

Bell's Penguin Book. Bishop Bell did not tire of shifting the discussion of his country's peace aims away from the realm of propaganda to a more objective level, although this made him very unpopular. From the beginning of the war he had been in constant touch with Bonhoeffer's brother-in-law Gerhard Leibholz in Oxford, asking for his advice and comments when Bell wanted to make a public statement, so as to get as accurate an idea as possible of the German point of view. Bell's speeches, most of which were delivered in the House of Lords, were published in the volume *The Church and Humanity*. The outlook expressed in these speeches generally agreed with that in Gerhard Leibholz's English publications during the war.[151]

Bonhoeffer got hold of Bell's 1940 Penguin book *Christianity and World Order*. Its tone was so familiar to him that it could easily have led him to misjudge the response in the England of 1940. He wrote to the bishop from Zurich: "I have had the great pleasure and satisfaction to read your newest book and I am sharing your hope for a strong stand of the churches after the war."[152]

In that book, which was published for mass circulation, the bishop spoke of Great Britain's and France's share of guilt for the rise of Hitler, but also that "the war is not just the protest of the injured German people against the victors of 1918":[153]

> I have no doubt in my own mind that the results of a victory by Hitler would be so disastrous, morally and spiritually, that Christians ought to do their utmost to defeat him.[154]

But the bishop firmly refused to call the war "Christian" or "holy" or a "crusade." They should take care "not to let slip any genuine chance of a negotiated peace which observes the principles of Order and justice. . . ."[155]

Here Bonhoeffer read a reply to everything for which, at the risk of his life, he had been striving:

> Links should be strengthened between the Churches in warring countries on both sides in any way that is possible through the help of the Churches in neutral countries . . .[156]

It was an outstretched hand from the other side:

> It cannot be wrong for Christians in one belligerent country to seek such opportunities as may be open, to discover through neutral channels, in every way possible, from fellow-Christians in another belligerent country, what terms of peace would be likely to create a lasting peace and not lead to a further poisoning of international relationships . . .[157]

What naive lack of concern when, on the strength of those sentences in the newspapers, groups of readers in England publicly demanded that the bishop should say "whether any steps had actually been taken on the lines of my suggestion."[158]

The most important chapter in the book was the eighth, "Christianity and Peace Aims," which treated Germany's participation in a new order, on the condition of its complete renunciation of National Socialism, as a sensible, wise, and Christian measure.[159] It reflected the bishop's repeated demand for the distinction that he later painfully made in all his speeches after the Sigtuna meeting of 1942: "Germany and National Socialism are *not* the same thing."[160] Using quotations from Visser 't Hooft, the bishop justified this statement in detail and urged that the distinction must be recognized if there were to be a tolerable future.

From Siegmund-Schultze, whom he visited again in Zurich, Bonhoeffer learned how little that attitude conformed to official Allied policy. Siegmund-Schultze had had depressing experiences. The British Embassy in Berne had refused to accept a document with peace proposals that he had submitted as Goerdeler's intermediary; the reason given was that the embassy was forbidden by London "to receive any suggestions whatever for peace."[161] Siegmund-Schultze then tried to make headway with the help of Archbishop Temple and Bishop Bell. Bell wrote Gerhard Leibholz about this on 27 August 1941:

> I have been asked by Siegmund-Schultze a few weeks ago whether I could put him on to any statement in British official circles which was at all in line with the sentiment expressed in my Penguin and particularly the contents of my Chapter VIII.

It was blatantly clear that Churchill did not want any discussions about peace. His speeches and those of Anthony Eden left little doubt that even an opposition government in Germany would have to surrender unconditionally. They were even less willing to say something different when they saw little or nothing happening in Germany that gave a signal of any decisive change.

Demonstration at the Stoll Theater. Because it seemed that official circles could still think only in terms of victory and unconditional surrender, the discussion among influential Christians in Great Britain about responsible peace aims and about what was to happen afterward became more active. This led to collective demonstrations by the different denominations.

In *The Times* of 21 December 1940 a letter appeared that attracted a good deal of notice, signed by the archbishops of Canterbury and York, Cardinal

Hinsley, and the moderator of the Free Church Council. The letter concerned the pope's famous five peace points of Christmas 1940—the equal right to live and independence for all nations, reduction of armaments, the formation of an international commission to revise the Treaty of Versailles, and respect for the needs of national minorities. It then added five more points, according to which a future economic world order (this was the influence of Archbishop of Canterbury Temple) should be tested:

> 1. The crying inequality in the standard of life and possessions must be abolished.
>
> 2. Every child, of whatever race or color, is to have the same opportunities for education.
>
> 3. The family is to be protected as a social unit.
>
> 4. The consciousness of divine vocation is to be restored to human work.
>
> 5. The natural treasures of the earth are to be safeguarded, with due regard to future generations, as God's gifts to all humankind.

During 1941 the pope's five points and this letter to *The Times* were raised in every British church statement on peace, and gave the discussion a public importance that the skeptics who thought purely about issues of power simply could not ignore. The discussion can be followed quite well in the issues of the *News Letter* of those months. Important stages were Temple's Malvern conference in January 1941, with the theme "Christianity and the Social Order," and a large demonstration on 10 May 1941 in the Stoll Theater, led by Cardinal Hinsley. Bishop Bell spoke:

> The year 1941, says Hitler, will become the historic year of the New Order in Europe. . . . *We* proclaim, no "Order" at all. *We* speak only of "victory" and "survival" and "liberation" of the vanquished nations. Our official spokesmen have never yet uttered any statement of British aims which envisages a situation after victory which could be immediately seen by enemies and neutrals alike to be better than that with which the war began, and out of which the war arose. . . .
>
> I am sure that there are very many in Germany, silenced now by the Gestapo and the machine-gun, who long for deliverance from a godless Nazi rule, and for the coming of Christian Order in which they and we can take our part. Is no trumpet call to come from England, to awaken them from despair? . . . It is right that this meeting, fully representative of Christian opinion throughout the country, should urge the British Government to make them [the ten points mentioned in the letter to *The Times*] the basis of any future statement of war and peace aims.[162]

Bell concluded with an appeal to Christians of other countries, especially to those in Germany, to make the ten points the common basis of a just and honorable peace.

A Highly Political Book Review. From Visser 't Hooft in Geneva Bonhoeffer received another book that had reached Geneva from London, where it had been published by the S.C.M. Press: William Paton's *The Church and the New Order*. It extended the discussion that was taking place in the circles led by Archbishop Temple, Joseph Oldham, Arnold Toynbee, Sir Alfred Zimmern, A. D. K. Owen, and Henry van Dusen in America. On reading the book, Bonhoeffer and Visser 't Hooft decided to convey to these circles the view of a German who spoke from the perspective of the resistance itself. Early in September Bonhoeffer wrote a memorandum that followed the sequence of the topics in Paton's book.[163] Visser 't Hooft prepared the English version and made it known through Archdeacon Hugh Martin in London.

Bonhoeffer enjoyed taking theological positions, but in this literary review he really wanted something quite different. It upset him to read the academic observation by the English general secretary of the provisional World Council of Churches:

> It may be urged as conceivable that the totalitarian system might collapse from internal causes, but there seems little hope that the anti-totalitarian forces which exist can become effective except after a major reverse.[164]

Paton looked to the future: "The conquest of so much of Europe by the German National Socialists has smashed much of the old order beyond repair.[165] In his opinion, there needed to be a considerable interval between the armistice and the conclusion of peace, so that the right people on each side could find their way to each other. This would be possible, for

> I suppose that few who have known the Confessional Church leaders would doubt that there are no Germans with whom fellowship in the post-war talks will be so quickly resumed. . . .[166]

Bonhoeffer found it depressing that any prerequisite for planning the future, like that which Paton set out in his book, was completely absent in his own church. Ten years earlier he would barely have been able to endure the secular Anglo-Saxon tone of the resolutions. Now, in contrast to most of his friends at home, he was preoccupied with that very secular future which might soon have to be shaped.

In his second point ("Why peace aims?") Bonhoeffer went directly to the conditions for the coming coup: the Allied propaganda that insisted on the unilateral disarming of Germany was an unfavorable influence on preparations for a coup. Bonhoeffer expressed surprise that BBC broadcasts mentioned nothing "about the churches' great discussion of the new order," since what little had been heard about this by important political opposition circles in Berlin had made a deep impression (of course, it had been heard in Berlin through him). Perhaps Bonhoeffer did not sufficiently realize how little this church discussion mattered to the British government (i.e., Churchill), which viewed it as a pernicious distraction from its efforts to achieve a victory that was still so far off. But for the conspirators and for Bonhoeffer, such sensible planning for the future meant a good deal. Could its political value be raised from outside? He stated the question positively in Visser 't Hooft's English version:

> A positive statement of peace aims may have a very strong influence in strengthening the hands of this group. It is clear that recent events [the commissar order] have created a psychological situation in which they have an opportunity such as they have not had since 1933. There is, therefore, reason to give very great prominence to this aspect of the whole question. . . . We understand that the disarmament of Germany will have to be demanded. But it should certainly not be mentioned as the main peace aim, as is being done too often.[167]

Here was the message Bonhoeffer wanted to convey to the other side at all costs—the announcement of the coming revolt, in the hope that its recipients could influence the Allies to suspend military action during the revolt.

Bonhoeffer then attempted to discourage expectations that the revolt would make it possible for the "other Germany" to immediately establish a government that would be democratic in the western sense. The government that would emerge from a military coup "might be formed suddenly. A great deal would depend on whether we could then count on the immediate support of the Allies."[168] That is what the German draft said. The English text stated:

> . . . the question must be faced whether a German government which makes a complete break with Hitler and all he stands for, can hope to get such terms of peace that it has some chance to survive. . . . It is clear that the answering of this question is a matter of urgency, since the attitude of opposition groups in Germany depends upon the answer given. . . .[169]

The documents by Bonhoeffer and Visser 't Hooft are in the form of a theological-ethical discussion of a book by an English churchman. But it was obvious that Bonhoeffer was anxious to provide information about the conspiracy for practical reasons. Visser 't Hooft understood this very well. In his cover letter of 12 September he wrote to Hugh Martin:

> These comments on your book have been written by me in close collaboration with a friend who came to us and who is a good friend of George Bell. I hope you will circulate them to all who are interested and also send a copy to Pit van Dusen. You must accept my word for it that all that we say about the next steps and *the urgency of the situation is not based upon wishful thinking on our part*, but on actual developments in discussion with responsible persons in the country concerned. That is also why I hope that *some* of these considerations will be *brought before responsible* people in Britain.[170]

Careful examination shows that this message was intended both for British government circles and for the German organizers of the revolt. Indeed, it was with this practical aspect in mind (not in the hope of a theological reply) that Visser 't Hooft added: "We should, of course, appreciate some answer to this statement, and, if possible, in the near future."[171] Bonhoeffer indulged in the delusive hope he might receive a response to his political ideas if he waited in Switzerland. He did not leave until 26 September.

Paton Does Not Understand. But the scope and aim of the letter from Visser 't Hooft and Bonhoeffer were hardly understood in London. At the time their names were probably not significant enough in Great Britain; the recipients of the letter did not feel compelled to approach the political leaders and argue that these communications were authoritative enough to be taken seriously. The message was noted, but no specific answer was given. For that to happen a much more goal-oriented action was necessary. It was not until 1942, after his conversations in Sigtuna, that Bishop Bell confronted the British government and extracted an answer. But by then the "unconditional surrender" demanded at Casablanca was much closer. The reply to Bell was as negative as possible.

Visser 't Hooft and Bonhoeffer received some echo to their exploratory effort, but the answer only proved that the letter had not been as convincing as they had hoped. The "Peace Aims Group" in London received copies of the memorandum from Geneva. Henry Pitney van Dusen, who came to England in October 1941, participated; he was a member of a parallel group in the United States, the "Just and Durable Peace Commission of the Federal Council of Churches." On 9 October 1941 Paton did, in fact, send Visser 't Hooft a hopeful answer:

> Let me say with what immense interest and gratitude I studied the critique of the book which you sent. I am having it copied and sent to a few people and shall be able, I hope, to send you some considerable reply.

But the "considerable reply" never came. A more detailed examination produced no action, but only doubts "as to whether there really can be a sufficiently strong party on the lines described to be able really to affect the situation, which I share and have shared with *very important people.*"[172] Conversations had taken place with influential people, but they had broken off because they could not believe that there was, as Bonhoeffer had said, a German opposition that could be taken seriously. The outcome was discouraging.

Bell did not share Paton's opinion, but he knew all too well how widespread it was. This was why, in Sigtuna in 1942, he had put a considerable damper on his German visitors' hopes of a positive British answer. He now gave the September 1941 Geneva memorandum to Leibholz, who pointed out the important political points in his brother-in-law's discussion of the book. Bell wrote to Leibholz:

> I entirely agree with your view on the comments from Geneva on Dr. Paton's book. I am also entirely with you in what you say endorsing the comments, and have written to Paton strongly in that sense myself.[173]

He answered Visser 't Hooft separately on 5 November:

> I read your comments on Paton's book with the greatest interest, and find myself very much in accord with your cautionary remarks about Germany itself.[174]

The London "Peace Aims Group" received a new impulse to look at the independent movements in Germany in May 1942, when Visser 't Hooft brought a memorandum from Adam von Trott to London, and Bell, with some emotion, recounted his experiences in Sigtuna. This revived interest in the views that Bonhoeffer had expressed in his "book review."

Karl Barth later told me that Bonhoeffer at that time was too naive in thinking that the German borders of 1939 could remain intact after an overthrow.[175] I am sure that Bonhoeffer no longer believed this to be possible. It may be that he was repeating here the opinion of some of the people around

Beck. For some in the opposition, Bonhoeffer himself went too far in his willingness that Germany would have to accept sanctions on moral grounds; some resistance members called him "unpolitical" for that reason. In his review of Paton's book he wrote clearly enough that the Allies might expect "safeguards" against a return of Nazism and "far-reaching military measures against Germany."[176] His concern now was not with negotiations about the borders, but the ecumenical movement's readiness to help improve the chances of a successful revolt. Beck, Oster, and Dohnanyi had sent him out for talks with his ecumenical associates in the hope that this would prove to be a political tool. More competent friends, such as Ulrich von Hassell and Josef Müller, had been commissioned to discuss practical questions of foreign policy. Bonhoeffer may have miscalculated the possibility he would be listened to and could exercise some influence; after all, he could furnish no proofs of the existence of an effective political faction. His justification consisted of a series of actions, like those undertaken by Bishop Bell, that tried to compel the British government to make certain declarations that might encourage a revolutionary government in Germany. The realism of such actions is less disputed today than it was then.

Visits to Friends. On that second visit to Switzerland Bonhoeffer saw old friends and new ones. Otto Salomon, who had convinced Christian Kaiser publishers to publish *Creation and Fall*, invited Bonhoeffer to stay with him in Zurich.[177] He went with him to see Erwin Sutz in Rapperswil, to congratulate his friend on his marriage—a visit that gave him some anticipatory thoughts:

> Now, in the midst of demolition, we want to build up; in the midst of life by the day and by the hour, we want a future; in the midst of banishment from the earth, a bit of room; in the midst of the general misery, a bit of happiness. And what overwhelms us is that God says Yes to this strange desire, that God acquiesces in our will, though the reverse should normally be true. So marriage becomes something quite new, mighty, grand, for us who want to be Christians in Germany.[178]

When he wrote those positive words about marriage, at least a year would pass before his decision to become engaged.

He called on Barth the morning of 31 August and the afternoon of 19 September.[179] He visited Alphons Koechlin, president of the Federation of Swiss Churches, whose help he would soon want urgently for a Jewish group. He saw Karl Ludwig Schmidt, who introduced him to Eberhard Vischer, the father of the Old Testament scholar Wilhelm Vischer. The fact that Eberhard Vischer had some association with the English chargé d'affaires was bound to interest Bonhoeffer, but so far no details have come to light about any attempt to contact him; it was probably unsuccessful. Bonhoeffer gladly accepted an invitation to relax in Adolf Freudenberg's summer house on Lake Champaix in Valais.[180]

Bonhoeffer did not visit Zurich until the second half of his four weeks in freedom. It was probably during the first half when he had a conversation that Visser 't Hooft reported immediately after the war, which produced an unforgettable remark.[181] One evening with Courvoisier, d'Espine, and others Visser 't Hooft asked: "What do you really pray for in the present situation?" Bonhoeffer is said to have answered: "If you want to know, I pray for the defeat of my country, for I think that is the only possibility of paying for all the suffering that my country has caused in the world."

This was a statement people did not like to hear repeated in postwar Germany, but its essential content can hardly be denied, whatever the actual wording may have been. More than anything, it proved how absurd and extraordinary the situation was under Hitler, when the true patriot had to speak unpatriotically to show his patriotism. It is a reaction that defies normal feelings in normal times; it may be a good thing that it has been passed on without defense or explanation, so that one confronts it directly and relives the incredible sentiments in those days. It is abundantly true that the best people of that era lived with the constant thought that they had to wish for Germany's defeat to end the injustice.

Before Bonhoeffer returned to Germany he reported to Bell that Niemöller had been moved from Sachsenhausen to Dachau, where he shared a cell with two Roman Catholic brethren, but that "there is no reason to worry about his physical and spiritual state of health."[182]

He left Switzerland on 26 September. He did not let himself be influenced by Siegmund-Schultze's disheartening experiences with the Allies, but believed he had made some progress in his contact with London through Visser 't Hooft and Paton. He could not have known of Paton's disillusioning answer at the time. He was strongly influenced by the confident hope that decisive action in Germany would soon change the circumstances for talks, and he was pleased by the cooperation he had encountered in Geneva. He saw no reason to abandon the optimism he had expressed before the journey:

> I shall be thinking . . . of horizons we enlarged together, which are connected with those journeys, of hopes and tasks for Europe, of the task of

the church in the future and all this in the hope that you and I, and a great many others who are of one mind, will all be able to work together one day for this future. . . . One cannot imagine how the year will go. But I am very confident.[183]

And so he took leave of his sister in a letter from Switzerland:

It has been an extremely satisfactory time with my friends here. I am going home to work with new strength and hope.[184]

The Deportation of the Jews. But when Bonhoeffer arrived back in Berlin disturbing news awaited him. On 1 September, during his absence, the decree about the yellow star had been issued: as of 19 September all Jews had to wear the sign sewn on to their clothing. On his way back he saw the star for the first time. The private reinterpretation of it as a badge of honor did not help. Then, between 5 and 12 October, the first notifications arrived among Jewish families in Berlin that their rooms in "Aryan houses" were "scheduled for evacuation." During the night of 16 October those people who had been notified were taken from their homes and gathered in the Levetzowstrasse synagogue for deportation.

So the action in Stettin had not been an exception, but a preliminary test. The previous stories that had been heard from Poland or from the occupied areas of Russia could now be witnessed firsthand, as next-door neighbors were picked up and people were transported out of the Siemens factories.

Soon a sixty-eight-year-old friend of the Bonhoeffer family was notified that her home was to be evacuated and that she was to go to Theresienstadt. Everyone tried zealously to stand by her, but could do nothing more than help her pack what the severely restricted rules for luggage would allow her to take. During their 1944 interrogations the Bonhoeffers and Schleichers were reproached that their homes on Marienburger Allee had been visited by people wearing the star.

That first day Dietrich Bonhoeffer collected all the facts he could confirm, to pass them on to sympathizers in the army command. Perels helped him get information from elsewhere in the Reich. By 18 October 1941 they had completed a report describing what was happening in Berlin, and mentioning similar proceedings in Cologne, Düsseldorf, and Elberfeld. On 20 October a more detailed report was concluded, and warned that further deportations were expected on the nights of 23 and 28 October:

As the families that are now affected know already what these official communications mean, the despair is unprecedented. The understandable results are severe attacks of illness in the case of people with weak hearts, gall-bladder trouble, etc., and there is also the danger of suicide and other rash acts such as futile flight, and so on.[185]

Perels and Bonhoeffer gave the reports to Dohnanyi to pass on to Oster and Beck, in the hope that the military would either agree to intervene or accelerate its preparations for revolt.

H. G. Adler later described these papers as the first documentary evidence known to him of any action by the German conspiracy movement in connection with the deportation policy.[186] Besides the drafts of the two reports, another report exists, dating from the same period, about the so-called people of mixed blood. The reports by Perels and Bonhoeffer show the signs of haste; they were not the product of careful work by a commission, for such a thing would not have been possible.

In late October Bonhoeffer's information work and attempts to persuade were brought to an end for several weeks—months, in fact—by a severe and prolonged attack of pneumonia. As it happened, Berlin at the time was free from night attacks by the British bomber squadrons. Bonhoeffer could use the rest; but at that very time the Jews were wishing that bombs would come down on all the post offices and police stations in Berlin.

The churches' isolated actions for the Jews were hardly noticed by the public. In Breslau the woman minister Katharina Staritz published a statement on behalf of those who had to wear the yellow star, and was arrested immediately. In parishes where special intercessory prayers were offered, everyone knew what the issue was when Staritz's name was mentioned. In the Confessing church fellow workers and members helped some individuals disappear illegally by cleverly contrived subterfuge, through forged papers, rationing cards, and shelter—as did, for example, Pastor Karl-Heinrich Reimer in Naseband and Gertrud Staewen in Dahlem. In the winter of 1942–1943 Bishop Wurm included the Jews in his list of protests against infringements of rights and acts of violence, and Bishops von Galen and von Preysing did the same on the Roman Catholic side. The Breslau Confessing synod's message on the Fifth Commandment has already been mentioned. It did not occur to anyone to be proud of those small acts of bravery; everyone knew how inadequate all this was compared to what was actually happening, even though there were still only vague suspicions about the numbers of victims and the methods being used. But, as the Breslau synod's message shows, the public was soon well acquainted with words like "eliminate" and "liquidate."

For those who were already deeply involved in undercover work to gain leverage in the government machinery, the deportation was an incentive to hurry. They could no longer expose themselves by uttering belated public proclamations (like pastors from the pulpit). They said nothing. But with each day that passed without action, the torment of their dilemma grew.

"*Operation 7.*" Now, however, as the months went on, Bonhoeffer got involved in a bold action initiated by the Military Intelligence Office (the *Abwehr*) on behalf of several Jews; it would play a serious role in the 1943 interrogations. Canaris gave instructions to save a group of about twelve or fifteen Jews by getting them to Switzerland on the pretext that they were being used by the *Abwehr*. The enterprise was called "Operation 7," since initially only seven people were concerned. Canaris was anxious to save a few friends (Conzen and Rennefeld and their dependents), and Dohnanyi wanted to help the lawyers Dr. Fliess and Dr. Arnold to get out of the country. The "Operation 7" action involved Dohnanyi in an extraordinary amount of work, camouflage, and subterfuge that lasted for well over a year, until its successful conclusion in the late summer of 1942. Six months later, however, the issue was revived with fateful consequences for its initiators.

Shortly after Bonhoeffer returned from his second Swiss journey, Wilhelm Rott visited him to discuss what could be done to save Charlotte Friedenthal, a colleague of his for years in the Provisional Administration of the Confessing church, who now had to wear the yellow star. Dohnanyi brought her into the fictitious body of Military Intelligence agents. Dr. Arnold became the group's go-between and spokesman. In 1946 he wrote a report of the rescue, describing his surprise and his initial refusal when Dohnanyi told him that he wanted to take them out of Germany as *Abwehr* agents, after Admiral Canaris had so decided. First Dohnanyi had been able to have Arnold's name taken off the deportation list. "The deep empathy of that much younger man was quite unfeigned and unmistakable," Arnold wrote. But when told how the escape was to be managed, Arnold replied:

> Neither my friend Dr. Fliess nor I would ever be willing to take part in helping that firm's business.
>
> His answer showed that, for the first time since Herr Dohnanyi and I had been in contact with each other, I had completely misunderstood him. He now told me quite frankly that he did not expect either me or any of the others selected to undertake any action on behalf of the Third Reich, and that his chief Admiral Canaris, his office partner Colonel Oster, and his colleagues Count Moltke, Delbrück, and Count von Guttenberg thought as he did.[187]

There were immense difficulties, both on the German and the Swiss side. For Jews to be employed by the Military Intelligence Office it was not only necessary to get them freed by finance offices, labor offices, and foreign currency offices, where things could be painfully delayed by the passive resistance of minor officials, there also had to be direct negotiations with the Reich Central Security Office. For the long duration of the whole process, Dohnanyi gave each of them a letter of safe conduct from the Military Intelligence Office that did not always give them the desired protection. Occasionally a member of the group was put on the deportation list, and had to be removed from the list with difficulty. Only Canaris's personal intervention with the notorious S.S. group leader Heinrich Müller managed to get them past the last dangerous delays. In the Military Intelligence Office itself, where a whole group of officers were routinely involved with such "agent affairs," there were both friends and foes. Only a very small number of people suspected what the aim of the whole business really was.

But there were difficulties on the Swiss side as well, for Switzerland was hardly willing to take in Jews. Since at the time the members of the Provisional Church Administration were all in Moabit prison, awaiting prosecution because of the illegal examinations, Wilhelm Rott, after consulting the sick Bonhoeffer, sent a petition with Perels's help to Koechlin, the president of the Federation of Swiss Churches:

> On behalf of the arrested head of the Provisional Administration of the German Evangelical Church, Superintendent Albertz, I beg to send to you as president of the Federation of Swiss Churches and the churches themselves a request as sincere as it is urgent.
>
> It is a question of the extreme distress in which many of our non-Aryan Christian brothers and sisters have been for some weeks.... Since about the middle of October, they have begun to transport to the east non-Aryans from Berlin and other towns. The whole matter confronts the Christian churches with questions and needs in the face of which we are almost entirely helpless.
>
> We know that your hands, too, are almost tied. Taking the immediately threatened non-Aryan Christians into Switzerland seems impossible in view of the attitude of the police toward foreigners, and for other reasons; this was confirmed lately by Professor Courvoisier in Geneva.... What we now ask you is whether, by urgent representations and official action by the Swiss churches, the door might possibly be opened for just a few, or at least for one solitary case for which we specially plead....[188]

An account of Friedenthal's situation followed; Inge Jacobsen and Dr. Emil Zweig were also included in the request:

It would be of great importance and might lessen the danger if those concerned could soon have word (by telegram) that their immigration into (or transit through) Switzerland is arranged.... But we ask God, the Father of the forsaken, to show us a way out of all this dire distress.[189]

Rott took this letter personally to Consul Schmidhuber in Munich, as well as a second letter from Bonhoeffer to Karl Barth, who arranged with Koechlin in Switzerland for the necessary guarantees for the group being helped by Military Intelligence. Since an entry visa did not allow them to work and earn money in Switzerland, Dohnanyi had to arrange for the foreign currency needed to support the "Operation 7" group.

Friedenthal was then ordered to go to the Gestapo office on Alexanderplatz to receive the completed passport. But with her star she was not allowed to use any transportation from Dahlem; it was decided that she should go with a rolled-up coat to the Alexanderplatz, so that she would appear there with a star as ordered. After a long wait, she was at last told: "Jewess Friedenthal, come along!" But how was she to go on now to the Swiss consulate, where the visa had to be stamped? With a star or without it? And how was she to travel? She was told: "Without a star!" An hour before she left Dahlem Dohnanyi came to her for the last time: "With the star after all!" The star, which had already been taken off, had to be sewn on again in a hurry. On the train the carefully rolled-up coat served as a cushion to sit on, since no one wearing the star could travel in the same compartment as Aryans. It was only after the last German station in Weil that Charlotte Friedenthal put her coat on again—to the horror of her fellow passengers in the compartment. At the border station the officials took all her papers from her, but after a few anxious minutes they returned and handed everything back to her. Finally the train came into Basel. She was still quite dazed, and Gisevius had to tell her, pointing to her coat: "You don't wear the star here!" This was at the beginning of September 1942. The successful journey was reported to Berlin, and four weeks later the rest of those rescued reached Basel, where Koechlin at once saw to their immediate needs.

There is no doubt that the Reich Central Security officials were very suspicious about the whole affair, and it is likely that they felt Canaris had caught them napping and tricked them. In 1943 the matter was reinvestigated during the interrogations of Bonhoeffer and Dohnanyi. An official was sent to Switzerland to look into the financial aspect and ascertain whether (and if so, how) Dohnanyi and his friends had enriched themselves from it. Of course, nothing of the kind was found, but the authorities remained suspicious. They probably could not imagine that any other factors had played a decisive role in such a risky venture.

The Fall of Brauchitsch. In the autumn of 1941 Germany's name seemed to be indelibly branded with the "final solution of the Jewish question." The opposition could hardly hope for an honorable peace. During these months the activity of the opposition increased to an unprecedented degree. New participants joined, and those who had grown hesitant became more responsive. Hassell's diary reveals that Hans von Dohnanyi hurried from one discussion to another.[190] This revival was a hopeful sign, but it revealed new problems.

Dietrich Bonhoeffer was meeting more frequently with his brother Klaus, who with his Lufthansa colleague Dr. Otto John was working on his own contacts: Joseph Wirmer and Jacob Kaiser, Wilhelm Leuschner and Ernst von Harnack. Otto John had known Prince Louis Ferdinand since 1937 and brought him into this group; he also put Dohnanyi in contact with people in the labor unions, including Hermann Maas. Dohnanyi was interested only in people whom he absolutely needed, since he believed that too many contacts entailed additional risks.

The existence of a group of younger people who were later known as the "Kreisau circle" now became evident. This intelligent group expressed some serious criticism of the leading men in the active resistance movement. They charged that Goerdeler's plans were full of reactionary elements, and they naturally rejected the monarchist ideas that had recently emerged. Count Helmuth Moltke (adviser on international law to the high military command and assigned to the Military Intelligence), Count Peter Yorck (senior government councillor, and later in the military economics office), and Adam von Trott (after the summer of 1940 legation councillor in the cultural political department of the Foreign Ministry) contacted Hassell, since they expected that he might show some sympathy for their criticism. During the winter of 1941–1942, however, the tension between the Kreisau circle and the other resistance groups was held in check, to the extent that they all recognized Ludwig Beck's leadership of the political opposition.

Dohnanyi devoted only as much time as was necessary to these smoldering discussions. Because of his immediate concerns he stayed away from circles whose conversations, though certainly not unimportant, were more theoretical. He did, however, have personal and official ties to Moltke, who was part of the Military Intelligence, and with Trott and Yorck through Baron Guttenberg and Hassell. Nor did Dietrich Bonhoeffer seize the opportunity to develop closer ties to the Kreisau group, although he had enough grounds, intellectually and personally, to have done so. One reason was that he was already too deeply involved elsewhere in practical preparations for the revolt. Another was that by the time the Kreisau group became more active Bonhoeffer already faced the possibility of being arrested. In addition, the composition of the group made him cautious.

In October 1941 Oster and Dohnanyi were offered new and interesting starting points when Schlabrendorff appeared one day from the army unit at the heart of the eastern front. On behalf of Major General Henning von Tresckow, he asked whether new practical steps to end the Hitler regime could be taken together with the Berlin office. Tresckow and Schlabrendorff believed that the S.S. standby troops in the countryside and Hitler's interference with the operations on the front had made some officers more inclined to join in a coup. A vital connection now began to form between the resistance center in Berlin and a group that was prepared to act and able to activate the regular army units. A firm and substantive offer had been made.

The expectations for early action rose further after Brauchitsch became unusually approachable. With the approach of winter, the operations in the east were no longer proceeding according to expectations, and Hitler was interfering drastically in their conduct. Brauchitsch sent for Generals Falkenhausen and Thomas, and promised that he would no longer stand in the way of Hitler's removal.[191]

In the midst of these tense preparations, on 19 December 1941 the news came like a bombshell that Hitler had dismissed Brauchitsch and made himself commander in chief of the army. Hassell wrote with despair in his diary: "The work of many months has been ruined."[192] The commander with whom they had striven for so long, finally with some chance of success, was gone. This meant that the army high command, now directly under Hitler's command, was ruled out as the place for setting off the revolt.

Bonhoeffer was convalescing with the Kleist-Retzow family in Kieckow at the time. A friend with whom he had spoken about the new expectations wrote to him: "You can imagine how my heart stood still when we read today of Brauchitsch's resignation."[193] Drastic changes of organization now had to be thought out and carried through. But from that time new ideas began to develop, which, after many variations, were actually carried out on 20 July 1944. The planned sequence of events was: first the assassination, and then the issuing of the order from Berlin under Ludwig Beck's direction of the high command. In other words, the coup d'état had to begin with the killing of Hitler. Given the backgrounds and the nature of the conspirators, it cost a great deal to bring themselves to this logical conclusion, and they never felt entirely at ease about it. This may have had something to do with Bonhoeffer's remark in Sakrow, where the Dohnanyis had been living since September 1941 in a house on the Havel River, that if it fell to him to carry out the deed, he was prepared to do so, but that he must first resign, formally and officially, from his church. The church could not shield him, and he had no wish to claim its protection. It was a theoretical statement, of course, since Bonhoeffer knew nothing about guns or explosives.

The Third Stage: Information on the Coup, 1942

Brauchitsch's loss was a shock, but the result was only delay, not an actual loss of determination. On his way back from Oslo Bonhoeffer wrote from Stockholm to his relatives in England:

> I went to see friends of mine up there [in Oslo] . . . and in spite of all difficulties, I had a very satisfactory time. . . . I am traveling a good deal besides I am writing a book. . . . When I wrote to you last,[194] I thought Uncle Rudi [Bonhoeffer's code word for war] would not live much longer, but in January and February he recovered a little [through von Brauchitsch's removal, the disciplinary proceedings against Hoepner, and von Witzleben's illness and dismissal], though I am quite convinced only for a very short time. He is so weak that I and my people do not believe that he can live longer than a few more months. . . .[195]

The plans for action changed and became more detailed. The further they progressed, the greater the need grew to plan Germany's reconstruction after the revolt, and to strive for political assurances from abroad that, for all the skepticism, Germany would not be attacked at its moment of weakness in the middle of the war.

During 1942 Bonhoeffer participated in both efforts. The first was helped by statements prepared for the Beck group about the future ordering of church-state relations, and the second by additional journeys abroad. As a result this third period of Bonhoeffer's activity in the conspiracy was the most unsettled. Expectations were taking more definite shape, and toward the end his work became a race between assassination and arrest. His urgent private affairs ranged from making a will to his decision to become engaged.

Norwegian Journey.[196] When Bonhoeffer embarked on a new journey in the spring of 1942, both he and Dohnanyi had received their first warnings. The lawyer Dr. Carl Langbehn[197] and Captain Ludwig Gehre, one of Oster's colleagues, told Dohnanyi in mid-February that the Gestapo was tapping his telephone and intercepting his correspondence. Langbehn believed that Heydrich and Bormann were behind it; Gehre mentioned a man by the name of Sommer from the Reich Central Security Office.

Before he left Bonhoeffer drew up a written will, for his new mission overlapped rather directly with the Reich Security Office's own sphere of interest. Making a joke, he handed me the sheet of paper for safe custody, to avoid giving anyone in his family cause for anxiety. The journey was to Norway from 10 to 18 April; its purpose was not "contact with the enemy" but to strengthen the people around Bishop Berggrav, who were regarded as allies, at a crucial time in their opposition to the Nazis.

The Norwegian church struggle had flared up on 1 February 1942, when Quisling became prime minister. That same day Quisling forbade Provost Fjellbu of Trondheim Cathedral from holding a worship service. This immediately linked the Norwegian church struggle with the patriotic resistance. After Fjellbu was removed from office on 20 February the Norwegian bishops gave up all offices connected to state church duties. In March, after a decree establishing a parallel group to the Hitler Youth for the young Norwegians, more than one thousand teachers resigned. On 5 April, Easter Sunday, all the pastors laid down their offices. Berggrav, who had initiated and inspired the pastors' resistance, was placed under house arrest on Maundy Thursday; on Easter Monday interrogations and house searches began, and on 8 April he was imprisoned. Because of his journeys to Great Britain in 1940, it was expected that he would be prosecuted before the "People's Court" on 13 April and charged with sedition and associating with the enemy. But nothing happened. Instead, on 16 April Berggrav was moved from prison to a mountain chalet near Asker, where he spent three lonely years under house arrest.

Berlin had intervened. The former Pomeranian district president Theodor Steltzer was in Norway, serving as transport officer on the staff of Wehrmacht commander von Falkenhorst, with other good friends from the St. Michael's Brotherhood such as Pastor Friedrich Schauer and Herbert Krimm. In 1935 Steltzer had visited Bonhoeffer in Zingst; now he belonged, with Moltke and Yorck, to the Kreisau circle. He had agreed with Moltke that a telegram should be sent to Berlin at once if Berggrav were arrested. That was done, and the Berlin *Abwehr* office quickly sent two emissaries to object that Germany's military position would be seriously jeopardized if the National Socialist church policy upset the whole population of Norway by removing Berggrav. Reich commissar Terboven in Oslo received a telegram ordering him to intervene, and, in fact, on 15 April a telegram from Bormann arrived ordering Berggrav's release.[198]

The two emissaries were Moltke and Bonhoeffer. Officially they were sent to observe the Norwegian church struggle as a possible danger to the German occupation troops; secretly their intention was to advise the Norwegian

Lutherans not to deviate one step from their course. Fifteen years later Berggrav told Steltzer:

> Alex Johnson thinks the intention was to declare their concern . . . whether the newly revived Norwegian church struggle was damaging the Nazis. . . .
>   Bonhoeffer seems to have made a deep impression. . . . Johnson sketches Bonhoeffer's line: here in Norway it would be seen how impossible the Nazis were. Bonhoeffer insisted on bitter resistance—even as far as martyrdom.[199]

The journey was arranged on short notice and carried out very quickly; Bonhoeffer was really getting ready for another journey to Switzerland, and hoped to go to Sweden later. Busy with his *Ethics*, he spent a few quiet days in Kieckow and Klein-Krössin, awaiting the preparations for the Swiss journey. Then, on the Wednesday after Easter, Dohnanyi called him back to Berlin, and two days later he was on the way to Oslo with Moltke. In the three days there they could not visit Berggrav in prison; they could only send him a message. But they did meet for detailed talks with his colleagues A. Johnson, Pastor C. B. Svendsen, Professor H. Ording, and H. Sørensen, a painter and a friend of Berggrav. On the day that Berggrav was exiled to the forest chalet near Asker and thus seemed to have been rescued, Moltke and Bonhoeffer left on their return journey.[200]

Of course, Bonhoeffer was extremely interested in the Norwegian church struggle, because here he saw that they had suddenly accomplished what he had proposed, without response, in 1933: a pastors' strike, the laying down of church offices, and church resignations. His advice was authoritative; based on his own experience, he warned the Norwegians not to give in now.

Without foreseeing how soon he would be in Sweden again, he took advantage of the return journey to write his relatives in Oxford from Stockholm, where he stayed from 16 to 17 April.[201] He also renewed his acquaintance with Archbishop Eidem, writing to him that he had seen Ehrenström fairly often in Geneva, and that he agreed with his judgment of the situation and the problems that resulted from it.[202] He was sorry, he said, that Birger Forell was now being recalled from Berlin, but those two would prepare a journey to Sweden for him. But it was not possible for Eidem to understand the background of the letter. When Bishop Bell asked him several weeks later whether he could tell him where Bonhoeffer was and how he was getting on, Eidem said that Bonhoeffer had probably been through Sweden recently on his way to Norway as a soldier.[203]

Moltke and Bonhoeffer returned to Berlin from Copenhagen, and returned to the *Abwehr* office on Tirpitzufer to report. There I picked Bonhoeffer up. His few days with Helmuth von Moltke had made quite an impression on him. Moltke was a year younger, and had founded the Kreisau group. I cannot remember in detail what Bonhoeffer told me about their conversations. We did not yet realize the group's special potential; in fact, it was not yet called the "Kreisau" group. It was four weeks before their first meeting on Moltke's Kreisau estate, which was concerned with questions of cultural and church politics, using Steltzer and the provincial Jesuit Father Rösch as experts. I remember, however, that Bonhoeffer remarked to me how stimulating the journey had been, "but we are not of the same opinion." They were united in the depth of their Christian convictions and in their judgment of Germany's desperate position, and they certainly agreed about putting their hopes in someone like Ludwig Beck. But Moltke "rejected . . . for his own part the violent removal of Hitler."[204] And Bonhoeffer, who knew that the judgment of God cannot be halted, was already pleading the need for assassination. I cannot remember whether Moltke asked Bonhoeffer on that occasion to attend the meeting in Kreisau; it is quite likely. In any case, the date of the upcoming Swiss journey did not allow him to take part in it. Neither time nor circumstances permitted the two to meet again as intensively as they did on the Norwegian journey. It was impossible to participate in many circles of the conspiracy at the same time. The dangers involved demanded exclusivity.

The Third Swiss Journey.[205] Three weeks later Bonhoeffer wrote to Oxford again—oddly enough, at the very time Canaris and Heydrich were at the castle in Prague signing the agreement that circumscribed Canaris's information service:

> Uncle Rudy has recovered a little bit [Bonhoeffer is referring to the new German offensive against the Volga and the Caucasus, and Rommel's attack on El Alamein], but he is terribly nervous and full of anxieties with regard of his personal future . . . his illness is so grave that I believe he will not do much longer.[206]

Bonhoeffer was on his third Swiss journey; the visit was cut short.

The dates are not unimportant, as they throw some light on Bonhoeffer's and Schönfeld's twofold commission for their journey to Sweden. Bonhoeffer probably arrived in Switzerland on 11 May, and he was certainly in Zurich on the 12th. After the 13th he turned up in Geneva. On 23 May he wrote to Bell in England from Zurich, as if he had no idea of their forth-coming meeting in Stockholm.

When Bonhoeffer arrived in Geneva on 14 May he was disappointed not to meet Visser 't Hooft, who had already left at the end of April to go via Spain to England. Among other things, he took with him Trott's memorandum and saw Sir Stafford Cripps, who showed the memorandum to Churchill.[207] Visser 't Hooft now personally presented Bonhoeffer's points of September 1941 before the assembled "Peace Aims Group," which included Zimmern, Lindsay, and Toynbee, and had been convened by Paton. Bonhoeffer's argu-ments were weakened politically by the fact that another six months had passed without any sign of upheaval in Germany.[208] At best, Bonhoeffer in Geneva could cherish expectations about this and rely on Visser 't Hooft to present a strong case to the circle. Bonhoeffer knew little about Trott's enter-prise through Visser 't Hooft; Trott belonged to the resistance group in the Foreign Ministry and the Kreisau group. At that time it was impossible to coordinate all the contacts abroad to the last detail. Opportunities arose unexpectedly, and the achievement of goals was never certain.

Presumably Bonhoeffer did not meet Schönfeld and Ehrenström again in Geneva;[209] that could not have happened before 14 May. But on 26 May Schönfeld and Bonhoeffer had both been in Stockholm several days, having gone there not directly from Geneva but from Germany, where Schönfeld had seen Gerstenmaier in Berlin. Indeed, Bishop Bell later asserted that nei-ther of his two visitors knew anything of the other's intended journey. When Bonhoeffer arrived back in Berlin from Switzerland—on Monday the 27th at the earliest, if not on the 28th—Schönfeld was meeting for the first time with Bishop Bell in Stockholm.

Thus in Geneva Bonhoeffer did not meet the people whom he was most anxious to see. A pleasant evening with the Freudenbergs brought him together with Frau Visser 't Hooft; Professor Jacques Courvoisier, the church historian and chairman of the ecumenical prisoners-of-war commission; Professor Henri d'Espine, later president of the Federation of Swiss Churches; Alexander von Weymarn of the Ecumenical Press Service; Pro-fessor Lenard; Pastor Charles Brütsch; the preacher Johannes Schneider; Roland de Pury; and Pastor Witt who was engaged in relief work for Jews.

It was here Bonhoeffer heard that Bell was in Sweden, or at least en route there. On 1 May a telegram from Bell had arrived in Geneva, telling Visser 't Hooft (who had already left): "Visiting Sweden for three weeks com-mencing May 11." Bonhoeffer must have been disappointed not to have heard of this sooner, since he was busy preparing a visit to Sweden with Forell, who was in Berlin. But it then occurred to him that he might break off the Swiss journey and suggest to his friends in Berlin the daring idea of going for a quick meeting with the bishop. He returned to Zurich, saw Koechlin—this was necessary because of "Operation 7"—and on 23 May wrote from Zurich to Bell in England, giving no indication that he knew that he was in Sweden, or what plans were brewing. A meeting with the prominent Englishman was "top secret." Above all, he did not consult with anyone in Berlin:

> Let me please thank you for your kind letter which I received only now.... Mrs. Martin [Niemöller] has been ill for a few weeks, so we have no news about her husband. But last time I heard from him he was said to be well physically and mentally. Since I know that Wednesday is your special day for intercessions I will meet you in prayers and my friends when I tell them will do the same. Thank you so much for letting me know that. It means so much to us. As far as I can see the day is not so far when we might meet again not only in spirit. What a comfort to know that you will be there in that moment! May God give us strength for the days that will come....[210]

Swedish Journey: The Commission. In Geneva Bonhoeffer learned that Bell's visit to Sweden was to end officially on 2 June 1942.[211] His trip there was proposed, discussed, settled, and made technically possible in three days in Berlin. It had to be made in consultation with Beck, since Oster and Dohnanyi now took no decisive step without his approval.

The commission was basically the same as in September 1941, but the aims were stated more precisely. In the event of a coup led by certain persons whose names would be disclosed, Bonhoeffer was to give assurances that its underlying position was peaceful, "however these men may first have had to disguise themselves to the people, before everything can be truly resolved," and—this was addressed particularly to the British government—"to ask the military commands not to use that moment to attack, but to give the new government time to restore healthy conditions."[212]

Bonhoeffer boarded the Berlin-Stockholm flight on Saturday 30 May, a day that was much too stormy for him, since he tended toward air- and sea-sickness. In his parents' home there was the greatest secrecy about his haste and the errand itself. This had not been the case before his journeys to Switzerland, when he had spoken about possible contacts with the relatives in Oxford. This time Canaris's office supplied him with a courier pass from the Foreign Ministry:

> Courier Pass No. 474. The bearer of this, Herr Bonhoeffer, is traveling on 30 May 1942 with official documents and luggage of the Foreign Ministry

to Stockholm. It is requested that the person named be afforded all possible facilities and in case of need all necessary protection and support.

The pass was not issued until early on 30 May.[213]

The Riddle of the Two Messengers. Obviously at least two groups in the resistance movement had the idea of using Bishop Bell's presence in neutral Sweden to obtain foreign safeguards for the coup. Who was responsible for this step, and who decided it? Who authorized the mission? Why did these groups not consult each other in advance? This puzzle is unresolved even today; only a few points of view can be suggested.

Bishop Bell said several times that the two emissaries, Schönfeld and Bonhoeffer, visited him independently of each other and not knowing of each other's plans, although their intentions were almost identical. He offered this fact to his government as one of the proofs that their concerns were authentic. Within the German resistance movement's work, however, this duplication made less sense. It seems fairly certain that Schönfeld neither knew nor could have known that Bonhoeffer was coming. The reverse is not quite so certain, although Bishop Bell assumed it to be so.[214] It is likely that Bonhoeffer heard about Schönfeld's and Ehrenström's journey in Geneva; but his own journey was not conceived and finalized in Berlin until Schönfeld was already in Sweden. Schönfeld had no personal contacts at the time with Oster and Dohnanyi, nor, of course, with Beck; and his Kreisau friends had reservations about Goerdeler. Schönfeld's friend and adviser Eugen Gerstenmaier, and his colleagues in the Church Foreign Office, associated with the opposition members in the Foreign Ministry: von Trott, finance minister Johannes Popitz, and increasingly with Hassell, whom the so-called boys trusted despite his close ties to Beck and Goerdeler.

These circles in Berlin may have already discussed approaching the British government with a request for its cooperation early in May, and they may have encouraged Schönfeld to use his journey to meet with Bishop Bell for this purpose. Schönfeld saw Trott in Geneva in April and felt that he had a link with him through Gerstenmaier. He did not need special passports or visas, since as part of his trip he would be visiting neutral countries on behalf of the Geneva organizations, and he was covered by the Church Foreign Office and the German Foreign Ministry. Beck may have known of Schönfeld's journey in advance, possibly through Hassell; it is just as likely, however, that he did not know of it before Bonhoeffer left. Schönfeld's journey to Sweden did not guarantee that he was certain to meet Bell; he was not traveling, as was Bonhoeffer, solely for that purpose.

Even if Oster, Dohnanyi, and Beck knew of Schönfeld's attempt to meet Bell, it was still reasonable to send Bonhoeffer. Under the influence of Bonhoeffer and Gisevius, the Military Intelligence Office believed at the time that Schönfeld's reputation was not that reliable (as it became later), and that Bonhoeffer had Bell's personal confidence to a degree that no one else had. Bonhoeffer and his superiors had been working along these lines continuously since 1938; for them Schönfeld and his friends were newcomers to conspiracy. They were certainly an addition, but still no substitute for the old hands in personal prestige, and they had not quite shaken off their past record in church politics. For Beck, Oster, and Dohnanyi the appropriate ecumenical emissary to the English bishop was Bonhoeffer, not Schönfeld.

It is fairly certain that Bonhoeffer knew of Schönfeld's journey, but he may not have been clear about whether Schönfeld would really meet Bell. I think I recall Bonhoeffer's expressing surprise, when he came home, at having met them together. We can understand that surprise, if we remember the talks between Bell and Bonhoeffer in the spring of 1939 about the very unsatisfactory representation of the Confessing church in Geneva.

Sources. Bell's notes, made at various times, serve as excellent sources from the British perspective about Bonhoeffer's two days in Sigtuna and Stockholm. Bell's final version from 1957 showed a few slight alterations that seemed to him advisable at a distance of twelve years.

Bell wrote down his experiences in five different stages. The sources are arranged chronologically: (1) Bell's first letter to Anthony Eden, of 18 June 1942, in which he indicated what had happened and asked for an audience;[215] (2) the memorandum of what had happened in Stockholm, with the inclusion of Schönfeld's notes, all of which Bell submitted to Eden on 30 June;[216] (3) the relevant correspondence between Eden and Bell in July and August 1942;[217] (4) the first comprehensive account of the event, based on his diaries, given in *The Contemporary Review* of October 1945, in which the distance between Schönfeld and his circle and Bonhoeffer's is still quite evident, and in which he mentioned the Confessional church, whereas he later wrote "Evangelical Church;"[218] (5) the second complete account, more specific in many details, in his Göttingen lecture of May 1957; here Bell acknowledged the serious risks Schönfeld had taken.[219]

It cannot be expected that similarly detailed authentic records or reports of the meetings in Sweden will come to light on the German side to give an equally exhaustive picture.[220] As far as the Military Intelligence was concerned, the matter was kept so strictly secret that even Josef Müller, who was interested in the Stockholm talks because of his British contacts via the Vat-

ican, could not induce Dohnanyi to give him a report. At the time Müller
finally asked me to get him a report from Bonhoeffer himself; and so in that
way he notified the Vatican of what had happened.

Bell's reports do not mention whether he hoped to make contact with
Bonhoeffer even before he left for Sweden. On 6 May he wrote Gerhard Leibholz: "I wish I could see Dietrich there. But I shall certainly hear his news." He
even tried, with Eidem's help, to find out Bonhoeffer's movements:

> I had heard of his passing through Sweden on his way to Norway . . . but
> Archbishop Eidem thought he had gone through as a soldier and I could
> not find any way of communicating with him in any case. But he heard that
> I was in Stockholm and so arrived.[221]

Meeting with the Bishop. On Sunday 31 May 1942 Bonhoeffer heard in
Stockholm that the bishop was in Sigtuna. Bonhoeffer then set off for Manfred Björquist's renowned evangelical college and academy there. When he
made his unexpected appearance in the bishop's room—a memorable
moment for both of them after being separated since 1939—Schönfeld had
already covered most of the preliminaries. Bonhoeffer, in his first private
conversation with Bell, had the important duty of confirming what Schönfeld had said. In addition, he handed over a list of names of those in the conspiracy and their significance, and then stressed what Visser 't Hooft had
already emphasized in September 1941: "'A rising led by them should be
taken very seriously."[222] This message now had a different urgency than
those in 1941, since they were conveyed personally and much more directly to the recipients.

The names mentioned—Beck, Hammerstein, Goerdeler, Leuschner,
Kaiser, and, somewhat cautiously, Schacht (the "seismograph of contemporary events," as Bonhoeffer called him)[223]—reveal some of the constellations
within the resistance leadership at that time. Hassell is not mentioned.
Among the generals taking part were Field Marshals Günther von Kluge and
Fedor von Bock. Through Oster, Kleist-Schmenzin, and Schlabrendorff,
Bonhoeffer knew that these two men, or their units on the front, were to initiate the coup. The slightly hesitant mention of Witzleben reflected the fact
that he had actually withdrawn for a time from the front rank of the conspirators. He was not only disappointed but, at the time, ill and without a
division.

After Bonhoeffer's private talk with Bell, they discussed more general
matters together with Schönfeld and some Swedish friends. Despite Bell's
warning not to hope for encouragement from London, they agreed on var-

ious codes and ways of conveying information about the nature of possible further negotiations between London and the resistance movement on neutral ground. Sigtuna was initially mentioned as one possible location. This was changed at the second meeting the following day in Stockholm, as Björquist had reconsidered the matter and believed that the participation of his colleague Johansson would be incompatible with Sweden's neutrality. One factor may have been that ever since his journey to Sweden in 1936, Bonhoeffer had always seemed a bit sinister to Björquist, who was unwilling now to put himself at Bonhoeffer's mercy in such unfamiliar terrain as a conspiracy.

Bell's first report in 1945 still reflected his impression that Schönfeld and Bonhoeffer, although they had a common commission and concern, represented two different temperaments and two distinguishable lines of approach. (I share Hans Rothfels's view that Schönfeld's memorandum came from the Kreisau circle, not from that of Goerdeler and Beck.)[224] Schönfeld negotiated, Bonhoeffer informed. Schönfeld sought a common basis, Bonhoeffer presumed it. Schönfeld threatened, with German strength, in order to get cooperation on the decisive day; Bonhoeffer asked. Schönfeld warned, Bonhoeffer spoke of repentance. Schönfeld was strategic; Bonhoeffer was concerned for the fundamentals. Without doubt Schönfeld was the more political emissary here—but in that moment, on behalf of that cause, Bonhoeffer was the better and more effective diplomat.[225]

Bell's account contains things that could come only from Schönfeld, and others that only Bonhoeffer could have said. Finally, there were some things that, although they were not central, appealed particularly to the bishop because they fit in to his struggle in England. As Rothfels correctly observes, the emphasis on the "truly socialistic lines" of the conspiracy could only have come from Schönfeld, with his Kreisau connections; since, at the time, Bonhoeffer thought more about the renewal of conservative possibilities. The claim that the churches' opposition in Germany had been successful could only have come from the Church Foreign Office; it was just as unthinkable coming from Bonhoeffer's mouth as was the mention of Superintendent Blau in Posen. The summary by historian Gerhard Ritter (in his book on Goerdeler), "The enduring strength of faith and self-affirmation that is more and more impressive in reports from the Christian churches in Germany gave their words the right background,"[226] did not fit Bonhoeffer, whose view of that "self-affirmation" was far more critical. He certainly would never have expressed this viewpoint to Bell. The colonies did not interest Bonhoeffer, and he would never have said that a British victory was very unlikely. The mention of a possible coup by the S.S. can be attributed to either of them, since Popitz and Dohnanyi (through Langbehn) at times seriously considered using this, although they finally decided against it. The question of the British attitude toward a possible restoration of the monarchy, with Prince Louis Ferdinand, was probably raised by Bonhoeffer, who knew about such considerations through his brother Klaus.

Ritter believes that the Beck circle could not possibly have told Schönfeld and Bonhoeffer to ask for a public declaration by the Allied governments. "It would be *best* [author's italics] for that declaration [of willingness to negotiate with an opposition government] to be made publicly."[227] This shows a shift, if not confusion, between agreements for serious negotiations and wishes expressed for western propaganda. According to the reports, a detailed code and secret methods had been expressly considered for the negotiations, but not any public declarations. Ideas of a public statement emerged only in the concluding parts of Schönfeld's or Bell's reports, not in the substance of the talks themselves.[228] But what Schönfeld wrote down at the bishop's request, perhaps not very fortunately, in the hurry of the Stockholm meeting,[229] was essentially the same as what Bonhoeffer had previously asked for in his comments on Paton's book: a reasonable statement and advocacy of British peace aims through the press and radio.[230] This was also the point that Bell himself had been trying to make in London since 1941, and which he never tired of stressing in his opposition to Vansittartism. Bell noted Stalin's politically clever public declaration distinguishing between Hitler and the German people, while London maintained an obstinate silence on the subject.[231]

On 2 June Bonhoeffer was already back in Berlin. He had to keep up the appearance of being a courier, coming and going again quickly as a courier does. He still found time to write the Leibholzes in Oxford again:

> What an indescribable joy to have heard from you through George! It still seems to me like a miracle. . . . You will have heard, of course, as we have here in Sweden, that all persons of non-Aryan descent who are outside of Germany have been in general expatriated. As far as I can tell the future of your fatherland that is a good thing for you and will make your return only easier on that day for which we are all longing. . . . My heart is full of thanks for these last days. George is one of the very great personalities I have met in my life.[232]

He said farewell to the bishop:

> This spirit of fellowship and of Christian brotherliness will carry me through the darkest hours, and even if things go worse than we hope and

expect, the light of these few days will never extinguish in my heart. . . . I shall think of you on Wednesday. Please pray for us.[233]

Bell's Struggle for Negotiation. In his later publications Bishop Bell was too modest in describing his efforts to gain a hearing for the unexpected concerns of the German conspirators.[234] In fact, he never became resigned to accepting any refusal. On 11 July 1942, Leibholz wrote a letter to Erwin Sutz for the Bonhoeffer family:

> I have seen George recently. . . . His most recent journey impressed him very much, and I very much hope that his efforts will be rewarded by some appreciable success, although, unfortunately, many of his friends and ours do not possess his breadth of judgment, and will have difficulty freeing themselves from erroneous prejudices.[235]

Passionately but in vain, Bell had called earlier for rational, formulated peace aims and the proclamation of a future European order in which Germany, freed from National Socialism, would have its place without being subjected to the mistakes of the Treaty of Versailles. Loyal to his own government, he knew the situation all too well when he warned the two men in Sweden against exaggerated hopes. But he was not prepared to accept Churchill's attitude passively; his experience in Sigtuna was too strong a corroboration of his own efforts. So he did two things: he persisted in following up his secret commission from Sweden to the government, and he appealed once more to the British public for reasonable peace aims.

1. The Cabinet's Refusal. Bell knew of Visser 't Hooft's visit to London and the delivery of Trott's memorandum, which he must have regarded as very welcome assistance from a third party. He reported on 18 June to Foreign Secretary Anthony Eden with a short account of his meeting in Sweden and a reference to Trott's memorandum; Bell was received in person on 30 June.[236] Bell was very pleased that Eden "was much interested" but was unable to dissipate the foreign secretary's feeling that the German pastors might unwittingly have been used, or misused, by the Nazis as "peace feelers." Eden promised a careful study of the documents that had been handed to him and a prompt answer. On 10 July Bell wrote to Leibholz:

> I have heard nothing from Mr. Eden since my interview with him on 30th June. I hope that he is giving careful consideration to the matters I laid before him. I hope indeed that other members of the cabinet may also have been informed of what I told him. . . . I realize that one has to act fairly quickly.

On 13 July Bishop Bell saw his friend Sir Stafford Cripps, who was also a member of the cabinet. Cripps reported that he had seen Visser 't Hooft and told him that Trott should be given a word of encouragement for his memorandum. He promised to tell Eden of his support for Bell's commissions and wishes.[237] But on 17 July the reply from Eden was completely negative:

> Without casting any reflection on the bona fides of your informants, I am satisfied that it would not be in the national interest for any reply whatever to be sent to them. I realize that this decision may cause you some disappointment, but in view of the delicacy of the issues involved I feel that I must ask you to accept it.[238]

The official checks made by the government between 30 June and 17 July had not cast any doubt on the reliability of the two German emissaries, but "delicacy" had to be considered. With the British-Soviet treaty of alliance of 26 May 1942, Churchill's government was trying to soothe Soviet annoyance at the absence of a second front in the west; that treaty expressly confirmed the Atlantic Charter, which put Germany under special law. The two partners, the Soviet Union and Britain, had thus undertaken "not to enter into any negotiations either with the Hitler government or with any other German government that does not clearly renounce all aggressive intentions and not to conclude an armistice or peace treaty without mutual agreement."[239] London carefully avoided anything that might resemble a lack of loyalty to the alliance.

On 30 July Bell took his material to the American ambassador John Gilbert Winant, at Leibholz's urging.[240] Bell wrote:

> He was clearly attentive, and I thought more alive to the importance of my conversations and their provenance than the two English statesmen.

Winant promised to inform Washington, but no answer came. At about the same time the American journalist Louis Lochner, who had returned from Germany in June 1942, also had disappointing experiences with the American government. He tried to pass his information about the resistance circles in Berlin—all of them were people with whom Dietrich Bonhoeffer was in touch, including Josef Wirmer, an intimate friend of Klaus Bonhoeffer—to Roosevelt, and to convince him of the seriousness of the German opposition. Roosevelt did not receive him; in fact, Lochner's written request for authorization to reply to the opposition in Berlin met with a flat refusal, because it was "highly embarrassing."[241] Even the mere recognition of opposition elements fell outside the official Allied policy; it was no wonder, then, that no answer came from Winant either.

Bell could do nothing but send a telegram of refusal to Visser 't Hooft in Geneva on 23 July, not without a gentle attempt to portray the situation as not entirely bleak: "Interest undoubted, but deeply regret no reply possible. Bell."[242] He had pondered every word of the telegram. But for all his loyalty, Bell was unwilling to be satisfied with this; he was too convinced that the decision was not a wise one. Twice more he wrote to Eden, attempting to express, in his own way, his convictions to the contrary. He pressed Eden at least to make it clear publicly that, contrary to the general assumption, Vansittart's policy was not that of the British government:

> If there are men in Germany also ready to wage war against the monstrous tyranny of the Nazis from within, is it right to discourage or ignore them? Can we afford to reject their aid in achieving our end?[243]

As Bell admitted, the weak side of his case was that there still seemed to be no visible sign of resistance inside Germany; he could only assert that the movement existed.

Were the Berlin resistance group and Bonhoeffer completely wrong in their appraisal of the strength of the opposition? Was the British cabinet's opinion really as clear-cut all along as it later seemed, when the opinion of so influential a man as Cripps obviously differed from that of his prime minister and foreign secretary?

2. A Public Campaign. Bell now tried harder than ever, with every possible means, to exert public pressure on his government, although he made little mention of this in his postwar accounts.

As soon as he was back from Sweden he wrote a report for Joe Oldham's *Christian News Letter* in which, while avoiding any reference to his exciting experiences, he again cautioned that after Hitler's fall the most important task would still remain: to establish a new order in Europe.[244] The background of his remark is clear to us today:

> Hitler's system is doomed, and the crash may come *more suddenly and sooner than some expect*. . . . The collapse of Hitler will leave a vacuum in Europe. Unless the problem of how that vacuum can be rightly filled is squarely and immediately faced, the last state of Europe may be worse than the first . . . but the problem of securing immediate order has to be prepared for and faced *now* by the Allied Powers. Unless our statesmen tackle it now, the victory of which we are certain will be turned into ashes. . . .[245]

On 15 October 1942, in the House of Bishops of the Canterbury Convocation of the Church of England, he said:

> I could wish that the British government would make it very much clearer than they have yet done that this is a war between rival philosophies of life, in which the United Nations welcome all the help they can receive from the anti-Nazis everywhere—in Germany as well as outside—and would assure the anti-Nazis in Germany that they would treat a Germany which effectively repudiated Hitler and Hitlerism in a very different way from the Germany in which Hitler continued to rule.[246]

In November Bell discovered, through a recently published book,[247] that in July 1942 the BBC had broadcast to Germany a program with questions and answers, questions such as the following being answered entirely on the lines of Bell's views: "Does Hitler's defeat mean Germany's destruction? . . . Does England expect that the German people will take part in the destruction of the Hitler regime?"[248] Bell now made that broadcast and the book's publication the occasion for submitting a parliamentary question in the House of Lords "to see whether they are a correct representation of the policy of His Majesty's Government"[249] so that he could have a basis for his challenge in a speech. But he came up against difficulties. The leader of the House of Lords, Lord Cranborne, asked Bell to postpone the question until he had talked over the delicate matter. In that conversation the bishop was able to get his question on the list for the House of Lords session on 9 December. But shortly before that date he was asked once more to postpone the question, so as to give time for a talk with Eden.

> There is great reluctance to give any publicity to these Questions and Answers [from the BBC program] in this country. This makes me very anxious. The answers seem to me to give a far clearer and more satisfactory description of what our war aims should be than any we have yet heard.[250]

Bell met Eden on 15 December, and listened to the government's urgent wish not to connect a parliamentary question in the House of Lords with the BBC broadcast, which had not been intended for the British public. When Bell refused to yield and cleverly proposed to Eden, as a way out, that he should connect his question about the distinction between Hitlerism and Germany with Stalin's speech of 6 November 1942, which had sharply distinguished between Germany and Hitler, Eden finally consented. Now, however, the parliamentary question and speech were not possible till after the parliamentary recess. When it was scheduled for 27 January 1943, the Foreign Office again asked for a postponement, this time until 10 February. In the meantime Bell gave a speech against Vansittart on 11 February, independently of the parliamentary question, in which he argued against the identification of all the cruelties of Hitler and his people with Germany as a whole.[251]

It was not till 10 March 1943, after consultation with Leibholz, who suggested a few improvements, that Bell finally posed his question to parliament:

> Hitler knows that his only hope of appeasing the opposition is to persuade them that they as well as he are threatened by destruction by the Allies, that the Allies make no distinction between Nazis and other Germans, and regard all Germans as black. . . . I can only hope that I have given some evidence of the reality of an opposition in Germany, and of the necessity for encouragement and assistance if it is to carry out its own principles and to be of value to the cause. I also hope that I may have given some ground for believing that on drawing this distinction, and making as crystal clear as possible the choice between Fascism and freedom, between tyranny and democracy, the future of Europe depends. . . .[252]

The government spokesman replied:

> I now say in plain terms, on behalf of His Majesty's Government that we agree with Premier Stalin, first that the Hitlerite State should be destroyed and secondly, that the whole German people is not, as Goebbels has been trying to persuade them, thereby doomed to destruction.[253]

That afternoon, Bell had the impression that the sympathy of the House was on his side:

> The clearness of the answer on the precise point which I raised was a real satisfaction. . . . I am in touch with the Ministry of Information about the possibilities of getting a few copies of Hansard [the parliamentary report] over to Sweden.[254]

Three days after Bell's speech in London Hitler's plane left Smolensk for East Prussia, carrying the time bomb which Schlabrendorff and Tresckow in Kluge's headquarters had smuggled on board. Dohnanyi, Bonhoeffer, and their friends waited anxiously in Berlin for news that the plane had crashed. The coup d'état was so far prepared that it would have been set in motion from Olbricht's office if the attempted assassination had succeeded. But the bomb did not explode. One can well imagine how Bell would have taken the news of the coup so soon after his predictions, and how it would have changed his position all at once.

Instead, he received word on 7 April that Bonhoeffer had been arrested.

3. Anxiety for the German Friends. The bishop must have wondered constantly what effect his negative telegram had on his German friends, and what he could do to encourage them in spite of it. For a long time he waited in vain for a direct reaction from Bonhoeffer. In his anxiety he asked Leibholz whether his telegraphic answer to Geneva had actually reached Bonhoeffer. A letter that Bell at last received from Bonhoeffer in September was dated 28 August 1942; Dohnanyi had taken it to Switzerland, where he wanted, among other things, to see about the London answer. Bonhoeffer's letter betrayed no reaction to the "no reply possible."[255]

Those in Geneva knew about it, however, and sent word through a personal messenger, Tracy Strong, secretary of the YMCA, to the bishop, who passed it on to Leibholz:

> I also hear from an American [YMCA secretary] who was over from Geneva . . . that his colleagues in Geneva—in touch with Dietrich—were disappointed that nothing had come of the proposals, and they thought nothing further was likely while Russia was in the foreground.[256]

Bell now used every possible means, through Sweden and Switzerland, through visitors and letters, of letting his friends know that things in England were not entirely unfavorable to them, despite everything. In November Swedish Bishop Yngve Brilioth went from Sweden to Chichester, and Bell gave him a detailed report. Bell wrote to Johansson, suggesting he and Ehrenström see to it that Brilioth made contact with his German informants. He sent the speech he had made at the Canterbury Convocation, and recommended that he read Eden's remarks of 21 May 1942, which contained a glimmer of hope. He mentioned the BBC broadcast with its questions and answers, and told him of the upcoming debate in the House of Lords.[257]

Brilioth did, in fact, meet Schönfeld and Gerstenmaier in Sweden in December 1942 to report to them, and he told Bell about it on 12 January 1943:

> After my return I had—about a month ago—a most interesting visit from two Germans well known to you. They wanted to hear of my impressions,

above all what might be the attitude of England to a Germany that had changed its government and its policy. I don't think that what I had to tell was very reassuring to them. I tried to make them understand how difficult it is for people in England to form a true estimate of the strength and the reliability of an opposition of which so far they knew little. But I also said that public opinion in England probably would be much surprised if something really happened in Germany—although they could hardly hope for much encouragement before some decisive steps were taken. This makes the situation so very complicated. Yet it is much to be wished in my opinion that some sort of encouragement could be given. On the other hand it is very difficult to make them understand that public opinion in England cannot easily exonerate the German people from all responsibility for the acts of its Government—although as we know, there is very little possibility for the German people to influence the policy of its Government—also because they are largely ignorant of much that has happened.[258]

Bell erroneously assumed from this letter that the "two Germans well known to you" were Schönfeld and Bonhoeffer. But this time it was Gerstenmaier who had visited Sweden with Schönfeld.[259] The nature of the talks revealed in Brilioth's letter had an accent that did not suggest the contrast Bonhoeffer would have presented, and Bonhoeffer had no opportunity to go abroad during the winter of 1942–1943.

Bell also tried to communicate with Bonhoeffer through Sutz in Switzerland, although he was afraid that after the Germans' occupation of southern France this thread of communication might snap as well:

I do not know how much reaches Switzerland about the policy very often connected with the name of Lord Vansittart. While it is true that there are quite a number of private individuals who agree with him in this country, such personal opinions are opposed to this country's official policy towards the German people. I know that Mr. Eden attaches a great deal of importance to a speech which he made on 21 May, in which he distinguishes between the Nazis and the Germans. . . .[260]

At the end of March 1943, Bell received an anxious telegram from Siegmund-Schultze in Switzerland, concerning the churches' heavy responsibility in the Allied countries in light of the intensification of the war, caused by the Casablanca declaration's call for unconditional surrender on 24 January 1943. Bell discussed it with the British undersecretary of state in the Foreign Office, and replied to Siegmund-Schultze on 7 April 1943:

Official declaration most deliberate and positive yet made on differentiation between Nazi regime and German people—stop—declaration also reaffirmed refusal negotiate with Hitler or any Nazi representatives stop but should Hitler and Nazis be overthrown within Germany am personally convinced whole situation transformed—stop—deeply appreciate your communion of spirit and your emphasis on Church's reconciling function—stop.

Bell sent a report to Leibholz, commenting on his conversation with the undersecretary of state:

I impressed upon him the importance of recognizing the existence of sound forces in the army and of trying to find phrases when talking about disarmament which would make it plain that the whole army was not brought under complete condemnation; I pointed out that it would only be with the help of armed forces that any overthrow from within could take place. He saw and appreciated this point.[261]

That last telegram to Siegmund-Schultze came after Bonhoeffer had already spent several days in a Tegel prison cell, and revealed once more how closely Bishop Bell's thoughts agreed with those of the conspirators in Germany. Because this was in marked contrast to the officially promulgated opinion in Great Britain, he could hardly get a hearing at the time. But the German resistance movement had a unique advocate and ally in Bishop Bell. This ally had no great influence in Great Britain, and the conspiracy's placing too much hope on him was a political mistake—but only in terms of everyday politics, not from the long-term perspective. On 15 June 1959 the well-known English military writer Liddell Hart wrote in the *Daily Telegraph*:

For the wisdom and foresight of George Bell's wartime speeches in the House of Lords, although they met much disagreement at the time, have now come to be widely recognized—and especially by military historians of the war. Hardly anyone would now question the truth of his repeated warnings about the folly of the Allies' unconditional surrender policy. . . . While the horizon of technical strategy is confined to immediate success in a campaign, grand strategy looks beyond the war to the subsequent state of peace—and thus tends to coincide with morality. In this way George Bell, standing for the principles of his creed, came to achieve a far clearer grasp of grand strategy than did the statesmen. The present situation of the West would be better if more attention had been paid to his temporarily unpalatable warnings and guidance.

The Journey to Italy. On 26 June 1942 Bonhoeffer began his fourth journey abroad that year, traveling with Hans von Dohnanyi to Italy. They spent a few days in Venice, where Schmidhuber joined them from Munich. Dohnanyi was on good terms with the German consul in Florence, who had ties to Italian resistance groups. In Rome they hoped to find an answer from London awaiting them. Bonhoeffer met Josef Müller's friends, Fathers Leiber, Schönhöfer,[262] and Prelate Kaas; and in the Vatican he spoke to Dr. Zeiger, the head of the Collegium Germanicum, whose help he used to send an uncensored letter from the Vatican to his sister in Oxford:

> I had a most enjoyable time with George. You will certainly have had a letter from him too. I am still optimistic enough to believe that it will not last long till we meet again.[263]

But when they left Italy on 10 July they still had no news from London.

At the end of August Dohnanyi went to Switzerland without Bonhoeffer, his main purpose being to make the final arrangements for "Operation 7." There he received Bell's disappointing telegram to Visser 't Hooft. Dohnanyi had not had expected the British government to be very forthcoming, but this meant that he had one less argument to use in winning the cooperation of some of the generals.

Bonhoeffer had interrupted the work on his *Ethics* in Klein-Krössin, to say good-bye to Dohnanyi before his journey to Switzerland. Dohnanyi took with him Bonhoeffer's letter of 28 August to Bell. The letter disturbed the bishop, because it did not mention his telegram, and it had an undertone of slight fatigue:

> Things are going as I expected them to go. But the length of time is, of course, sometimes a little enervating. Still I am hopeful that the day might not be too far when the bad dream will be over and we shall meet again. The task before us will then be greater than ever before. But I hope we shall be prepared for it. I should be glad to hear from you soon.[264]

It was the last handwritten greeting the bishop and the relatives in Oxford received from Dietrich Bonhoeffer from free territory. Things continued to be "a little enervating," because Hitler's new successes in Russia and Africa made the conspirators' activities more difficult and the ever lengthening time needed to prepare the coup increased the risks for the resistance circles.

From Switzerland Dohnanyi also wrote to the Leibholzes in Oxford:

> What is going on in the invisible sphere you will have to guess; if you proceed from certain unshakable assumptions, the solution of the riddle is not

difficult.... Our solidarity as brothers and sisters, and with our parents, is as firm as ever; we stand by each other; and so we can be sure of overcoming the difficulties of these violent times.[265]

Structures for the Future: Cooperation. In 1942 the number of branches within the resistance movement continued to grow; its planners were active as never before. Individuals and entire study circles began to reflect about various fields of public life. Bonhoeffer himself did not outline or advocate any special form a future government should take.

In July 1942 Otto John and Goerdeler visited Prince Louis Ferdinand in Cadinen. At Klaus Bonhoeffer's house there were discussions with Jakob Kaiser and Josef Wirmer about whether the prince should give the signal for revolt. The difficulties among the Hohenzollerns themselves soon put an end to any such plans; but in Sigtuna Bonhoeffer had correctly told Bell that the resistance was considering a Hohenzollern because of the royal family's popularity, stability, and potential authority to issue the order. The Bonhoeffer brothers assented to these considerations mainly on pragmatic grounds, not royalist motives. Bonhoeffer did not seek the restoration of the monarchy through a revolt; but if a monarchical beginning could offer advantages when the revolt was launched, it should be considered a possibility. The sympathy the wartime death of the crown prince's eldest son aroused among the people had led Hitler to withdraw the other members of the Hohenzollern family from the front; this was worth considering, in light of the popular support needed for an overthrow.

Bonhoeffer's cooperation in planning the program to immediately follow the coup was confined to working with Perels on future church-state relations.[266] Goerdeler's draft of a constitution raised questions about this issue, in particular about a new organization of the disrupted churches after the coup. Within the Beck group Dohnanyi was entrusted with the coordination of the measures that would immediately follow the coup.

Reorganizing the Churches. A rough outline by Bonhoeffer and some penciled notes by Perels are what remain of the proposals on the immediate measures to be taken for the churches.[267]

Bonhoeffer's notes make clear which of the Confessing church's forces should carry out the reorganization, so that a "Confessing leadership" would be restored, and neither the special interests of the provincial churches nor traditional "Confessional hindrances" would threaten the new German Evangelical Church. "The reactionary circles of the former general superintendents and of the bureaucracy of church authorities must not be in a position to regain control." In the proposals for individual measures that were to restore legal status and confessional freedom, it was considered possible for some German Christians to coexist as a free religious association. "The Church Foreign Office, which has lost the confidence of foreign churches and of most Germans abroad, will be reorganized with regard to its personnel, in agreement with the council of the German Evangelical Church." The theological faculties, which had been "to a great extent destroyed and robbed of their academic prestige since 1933," would be re-formed with the churches' cooperation. There would, of course, no longer be a Ministry for Church Affairs. Efforts should be made to settle financial questions, because they "persistently plague" the relationship between state and church; Bonhoeffer was considering the possibility of a church independent of the state.

Perels's draft was concentrated on certain paragraphs that corresponded to Bonhoeffer's ideas. It offers a clue as to the date, since in the proposals about future personnel it mentioned Fritz Müller of Dahlem, whose unexplained death occurred in the East on 20 September 1942. The draft contained a regulation concerning the "competence of the Reich in church affairs," a law about "the freedom of Christian belief," orders of implementation, a law on "freedom of belief in the German Evangelical Church," and a list of names for official positions.

It is not impossible to know how the final version of the Beck group's proposals for the reorganization of the churches looked. A copy fell into the hands of the military counsel for the court, Manfred Roeder, when Bonhoeffer was arrested. The title of that draft, "Ending the Church Struggle," enabled Bonhoeffer to conceal the document's real background during his interrogation.

In preparing the measures that would follow the coup, Bonhoeffer also drafted a pulpit proclamation for the church and a message to the clergy.[268] The declaration contained a strong confession of guilt and a call for the liberation of consciences after so much unfaithfulness and disunity. Significantly Bonhoeffer did not see any contradiction in pondering and being satisfied with the church's "mandate" while in the midst of the conspiracy. On the contrary, the break he had made liberated him for the necessary spiritual tasks.

Work on Future Institutions. All kinds of ideas were emerging from those at the heart of the conspiracy for memoranda about the future shape of society. In the summer of 1942, for example, Goerdeler asked Hans Asmussen for a written report of the church's views on economic questions.[269] Bonhoeffer developed his own initiative, based upon his ecumenical contacts, which grew into a position paper (*Denkschrift*) that has been preserved; he was helped by friends and experts in particular subjects.

Bonhoeffer was impressed by the publications of British Christian groups that he read in Switzerland in 1941, and by Bell's description in 1942 of the ideas his friends were entertaining for the period between Hitler's fall and the establishment of a new order. Even more, it frightened him when he realized how much his ecumenical friends expected from the Confessing church, and how little it was doing to ponder and prepare for society's future needs.

In England prominent laity and clergy were at work: the group around Oldham's *Christian News Letter,* the "Peace Aims Group," Temple's "Malvern conference," and the "P.E.P." ("Political and Economic Planning Group"). In his book Paton took it for granted that, as soon as hostilities were suspended, talks would begin with the leaders of the Confessing church. The "*dictated* peace of Versailles"[270] would have to be avoided, by general consent, as a blunder "of the first order"; "there are no Germans with whom fellowship in the post-war tasks will be so quickly resumed"[271] as with the Confessing Christians. In his book Bell referred to the need for Christians behind both fronts to strive to influence the peace terms, at a time when reason was being suppressed by the bitterness and passions of a long war:

> Preparation should be made now for the calling of a conference of Christian leaders, Protestant and Catholic, from amongst the belligerent and neutral countries to meet together as soon as possible after the Armistice ... both the clergy and the laity from the belligerent and neutral countries ... should meet before the negotiation of the final treaty.[272]

But on the German side all the prerequisites for taking up this line of thought and getting ready for any kind of partnership were absent. Anyone who planned, discussed, or wrote down ideas for the future risked being accused of subversive activities. But not only that: the Lutheran theological tradition went against it. Paul Althaus wrote quite characteristically in 1940:

> Christianity has no political program, nor does it have the right to exercise control or censorship over political life in the name of Jesus and the Gospel. . . . In reality, politics follows its own laws and necessities.[273]

In his discussion outline of Paton's book in Geneva in September 1941 Bonhoeffer issued a brief preliminary warning to his British partners:

> The absolute uncertainty of human existence leads . . . Christians almost everywhere to renounce entirely all thought for the future, and this in

turn results in a strong apocalyptic attitude. When the day of judgement is felt to be at hand, the awareness of the historical future is easily lost.[274]

Bonhoeffer occasionally discussed these concerns with Hammelsbeck. Both were uneasy about the eschatological theology that was becoming sterile and about the Confessing church's growing lack of contact. Bonhoeffer also talked about this with Perels, with the idea of organizing practical work on these problems. He spoke with Hans Böhm, the ecumenical representative of the Provisional Administration, and with Otto Dibelius.[275] His persistence finally led to a discussion in the Provisional Administration of the Confessing church.

The Freiburg Memorandum. In the Provisional Administration meeting they remembered the distinguished experts in the Freiburg circle who were at the disposal of the Confessing church. This group had met in Freiburg for some time to deal with issues of political ethics. The group included the economists Walter Eucken, Constantin von Dietze, and Adolf Lampe, the historian Gerhard Ritter, and the legal scholar and philosopher Erik Wolf. Bonhoeffer contacted them at the behest of the Provisional Administration (and secretly for ecumenical circles, specifically for Bell in Sigtuna). Von Dietze wrote in his diary: "Bonhoeffer came one afternoon to me, and I went with him to Erik Wolf."[276] The official charge against von Dietze on 20 April 1945 portrayed what happened:

> [Bonhoeffer came] with the suggestion to work together on developing recommendations that should be presented after the end of the war at an ecumenical conference that was being planned. . . . Von Dietze promised to work with Bonhoeffer and, in agreement with him, invited the Freiburg professors Ritter, Erik Wolf, Lampe and Eucken . . . to work with them. At the end of October or beginning of November 1942 he then shared the names of his Freiburg colleagues whom he had won for [this work] at a discussion in Berlin where, in addition to Bonhoeffer, general superintendent Dibelius, Pastors Asmussen and Böhm, Assessor Perels and probably . . . [the industrialist Walter] Bauer participated, and agreed with the Berlin friends that the next meeting should take place in Freiburg. Goerdeler "as someone with political experience and knowledge" was to be brought in. . . .[277]

Bonhoeffer did not attend this November meeting in Freiburg. But they discussed "the Freiburg memorandum often in Berlin . . . a consultation about the draft of the memorandum that had already been worked on took place at the beginning of 1943 in the Bonhoeffer home; and I met with

Bonhoeffer at Dibelius's home once, and another time with him and Walter Bauer in a restaurant."[278]

Bonhoeffer's notes for the November discussion in Freiburg were probably made at the preliminary discussion in Berlin at the beginning of November. Besides the date ("Tuesday, 17 November, meeting in Freiburg") he entered the following headings:

> Economic questions: Eucken, von Dietze, Bauer, Karrenberg.
> Law of the State inside decalogue God and State outside Europe . . . Asmussen, Ritter, Luther.
> God and justice: fundamental and human rights . . . [v. Simson] Böhm-Jena natural law, Mensing, criminal law, State-Church.
> The Jews.
> Education.
> The Church's proclamation to the world. The Word of God and counsel. The basis of right. Existence of the Church in the world. Perels.

These notes suggest that Bonhoeffer conceived the manuscripts "State and Church"[279] and "On the Possibility of the Word of the Church to the World" for the Freiburg plans.[280] The Freiburg memorandum was finished in January 1943. It took more or less exhaustive positions on the future legal system, church policy, education, social and economic policy, foreign policy, and future peace. In July 1945, Gerhard Ritter duplicated the salvaged memorandum, with an introductory account of its origin, under the heading: "Political Ordering of the Community: An Attempted Self-Reflection of the Christian Conscience in the Political Troubles of Our Time." Ritter confirmed that the work was a German reply or preparation for a reply to Paton's and Bell's suggestions.

Perels's contribution on legal questions arrived too late to be included; it was found by the Gestapo, and led to his being tortured in 1944. Most of those who worked on the memorandum were arrested; all except Goerdeler, Perels, and Bonhoeffer escaped with their lives. The memorandum did have some effect; it was used as one of the preparatory works for the Amsterdam conference that founded the World Council of Churches in 1948, since it had successfully combined theological principles with practical details.

In the course of his collaboration on the memorandum, Bonhoeffer did not contact the members of the Kreisau group, nor did he attempt to work out an agreement with them.[281] Apart from the fact that the Kreisau circle's work reached its climax somewhat later than that of the Freiburg group, Bonhoeffer believed that the conclusions related to the period after a coup belonged in the ecumenical forum that had emerged out of the direct responsibility of the Confessing church. Despite his demand that the Confessing church, which was dangerously narrow, should open up and expand its horizons, Bonhoeffer still found it difficult to cooperate with church people who had not made the sacrifices that characterized the provisional leaders and the Councils of Brethren. And the Confessing church, to the extent that it stood by Barmen and Dahlem, could not regard the Protestant churchmen in the Kreisau group, such as Schönfeld, Gerstenmaier, Harald Poelchau, or even Steltzer, as its own people. It was somewhat tragic that the Kreisau and Freiburg groups did not seek out and complement each other at the time. Bonhoeffer did not live to see what doors opened in that direction.

The Assassination That Did Not Take Place. The period of Bonhoeffer's important journeys had ended. The autumn and winter of 1942–1943 became a relentless race against time. The need to deliver the blow grew more urgent, as Germany's military and political state was getting visibly worse. At the same time, the Reich Central Security Office was preparing its blow to Canaris's office. The Gestapo thought that by prosecuting Dohnanyi and his friends it could deal the Military Intelligence Office a deadly blow; it did not yet know that in reality it was disturbing, if not paralyzing, a center of conspiracy. In the winter of 1942–1943, the center worked so effectively that it had completed its preparations and seemed to be on the verge of success.

The Military-Political Situation. The German public did not yet see that the turning point in Hitler's military situation was approaching. To some the extension of the fighting may have seemed inauspicious, but during that autumn Hitler achieved his greatest conquests. He pushed as far as the Volga and the Caucasus, and almost to the Nile. Vichy France was occupied, and it was an anxious time for those in Geneva, who feared they might be cut off from the world.

Only a few people saw the reverse side. In September, when Halder was still trying to keep Hitler from advancing on Stalingrad, Hitler dismissed him and replaced him with General Zeitzler; this upset the plans for a coup once again. On 24 September Bonhoeffer wrote to his parents who were on holiday:

> Stalingrad seems to be a fearful struggle. It is very depressing for everyone, and gets on one's nerves.[282]

On 23 October General Montgomery attacked at El Alamein, and after twelve days' fighting he succeeded in breaking through toward the west. On

8 November the Allies landed in Morocco and at Algiers, and advanced toward Tunisia. From 19 November the Soviets attacked in Stalingrad and surrounded twenty-two German divisions. Hitler telegraphed to General Paulus: "Surrender inconceivable." Before Christmas 1942 posters appeared in German shop windows: "Think only of victory, and afterward of presents." On 24 January 1943, in Casablanca, Churchill and Roosevelt announced the policy of "unconditional surrender." On 31 January the survivors of the Stalingrad cauldron trudged away into captivity.

On 22 January 1943, referring to the generals who were responsible, Hassell wrote in his diary:

> If the Josefs had the ambition to delay their intervention until it was quite clear that the lance corporal is leading us into the abyss, that dream has come true. The worst of it is that we were right in thinking beforehand that it would then be too late, and that any new regime would be a liquidation commission.[283]

For the first time in the war Stalingrad produced a perceptible shock in Germany. This was followed, in the middle of February, by the distribution of the "white rose" pamphlets and the appearance before the People's Court of the Scholls and their friends from the University of Munich. To most people it was a signal that seemed tragically meaningless.[284]

Attempted Putsch in March 1943. At the time when the Munich students went to their deaths, the conspirators felt they were closer to their goal than ever before. The plans for the assassination received the finishing touches. It was simply a case of waiting for the moment of their execution.

Under Beck's guidance, the working relationship between Oster-Dohnanyi and Tresckow-Schlabrendorff in the central army unit in the east had developed steadily since the summer. Tresckow and Schlabrendorff had succeeded in having increasing numbers of like-minded officers appointed under their commanders, von Bock and later von Kluge. The plan was to assassinate Hitler on his anticipated visit to the front held by the central army unit. When Halder was dropped from the army high command in Berlin, the planning focused on that central point on the eastern front for unleashing the coup. With passes provided by Oster, Goerdeler traveled to Smolensk to help the plans along, visiting Kluge and Tresckow. Tresckow tried hard and persistently to get his chief to cooperate. In his letters to me Bonhoeffer referred in code to the progress in that part of the preparations: "Hans-Christoph and his wife are improving gradually but steadily."[285] "Hans-Christoph" was his cousin in the east, and was ill.

In Berlin the responsibility for the steps to be taken after the beginning of
the revolt rested with General Olbricht, who as chief of the general staff had
authority over the Central Information Office of the Wehrmacht and the
provincial commanders. He could prepare and issue the crucial orders for the
measures to be taken after the assassination. He was an old friend of Oster,
and he had also helped obtain military exemptions for Confessing pastors.[286]
Bonhoeffer wrote about how things were going with Olbricht on 29 November 1942, using Josef Müller's name to represent the internal situation:

> Sepp is again in very good form and cheerful, and hopes to have finished
> his work in four weeks at the most.[287]

Again, the estimated time was too short by at least half.

In February 1943 Schlabrendorff made a last journey to Berlin. Hitler
was expected to visit the central army unit on Saturday 13 March. Dohnanyi
now hurried to his friends in Smolensk to make the final arrangements. But
this was not all: in his suitcase there was a special English explosive (available to the *Abwehr*) for Tresckow and Schlabrendorff. With no inkling of
what was in the suitcase, I drove Dohnanyi, in the car specially permitted to
doctors that belonged to Bonhoeffer's father, to the night train that was to
take him to East Prussia. There he took the plane to meet Canaris. While
Canaris called his intelligence officers of the central army unit to a meeting,
Dohnanyi, Tresckow, and Schlabrendorff settled the code for the intended
notification.

The carefully arranged revolutionary plot began for the first time to take
its irrevocable course.[288] When Hitler entered his plane for the return flight,
after visiting Kluge's headquarters at Smolensk, there was a small parcel
containing the fused time bombs on board. But he landed safely in East
Prussia; the ignition had failed. In his memoirs Schlabrendorff has related
how he managed to save the critical situation undetected.

The preparations for revolt were not abandoned. Without hesitation the
conspirators turned their attention to the new opportunity on 21 March, at
the occasion of the national ceremony of "Heroes' Remembrance Day." They
obtained the timetable for Hitler's tour of the arsenal, in which the central
army unit's trophies were to be inspected. Major von Gersdorff, a Military
Intelligence Officer from the unit, was determined to carry two bombs in his
coat pocket, thus delivering the blow at the cost of his own life.

That Sunday afternoon the family with all the grandchildren was in the
Schleicher home, practicing the birthday cantata for the seventy-fifth birthday of Bonhoeffer's father.[289] Dietrich Bonhoeffer was at the piano, Klaus

played the cello, Rüdiger Schleicher the violin, and Hans von Dohnanyi was in the choir. At the front door Dohnanyi's car was ready to leave; the others had no idea how anxiously Dohnanyi kept looking at the clock, waiting for the decisive telephone call. Ursula Schleicher observed how excited her sister Christine von Dohnanyi was; there had certainly often been tense moments due to the Gestapo observation of her husband. But now she whispered to her sister: "It must start any moment!" But minute after minute went by, and the telephone did not ring.

What had happened? Hitler had finished his inspection in the arsenal after ten minutes, instead of staying for half an hour as expected; so Gersdorff had not been able either to get into the prearranged position close to him, or to ignite the fuse in time.

Two weeks later Bonhoeffer, Dohnanyi and his wife, and Josef Müller were arrested; Oster was banned from the Military Intelligence Office on Tirpitzufer Allee. Moreover, Beck dropped out for several months, as he had to undergo an operation performed by Sauerbruch; Hammerstein died. Suddenly everyone involved realized how serious a break had been caused by the failure of the attempted coup of March 1943.

At the end of March Schlabrendorff, Justus Delbrück, Gehre, and Klaus Bonhoeffer were certainly correct in celebrating with Otto John their unexpected good fortune: nothing had been discovered and no part of the coup organization destroyed. In fact the most promising period of the German resistance was over. Costly work had been done in vain, fresh crimes and suffering mounted. What Stauffenberg was to say shortly before 20 July 1944 was already true: the overthrow can no longer change anything in the hopeless political and military situation.

At the time, the Gestapo itself did not know what it had accomplished with the arrests on 5 April—the smashing of the conspiracy's center of activity. It was many months before everything was covered up and a new organizing center was created for the work needed for the coup.

With the arrest, Bonhoeffer was eliminated from the active conspiracy; from now on his efforts were devoted to putting the bloodhounds off the scent. The conspiracy continued, undiscovered. In his prison cell Bonhoeffer was kept adequately informed through coded messages, and remained full of hope until 20 July 1944.

The Arrest

The tension during the preparations for the March 1943 putsch had been made worse for Dohnanyi and Bonhoeffer through their involvement in an unfortunate affair inside the Munich Military Intelligence Office. One day in October 1942 Dohnanyi received a warning from Group Commander Nebe of the Reich Central Security Office, who for a long time had secretly collaborated with the resistance: he and Bonhoeffer had been named and incriminated in the proceedings against Consul Schmidhuber. A storm was brewing over the entire Military Intelligence. The warning to Dohnanyi at the beginning of 1942 that his telephone and post were under surveillance had been of a general nature. But the new warning was connected to an attempt by the Reich Central Security Office to exploit specific irregularities in the *Abwehr* in order to destroy it.

Since the beginning of September 1942 Bonhoeffer had been preparing new journeys; he was to visit ecumenical friends in the Balkans and Switzerland. On 10 September the Munich Military Intelligence Office had applied for him to be given new visas "for repeated journeys to and from Hungary, Bulgaria, Greece, Croatia, and Italy for a period of three months." The granting of the visas was delayed by new passport regulations. On 2 October he went to Munich to get the visas and begin the journeys; he told his parents that he might be away for six weeks.

Then the crisis in the Munich Military Intelligence came to a head. Instead of visiting the Balkans, Bonhoeffer had to return to Berlin in mid-October and wait for matters to be "clarified." What had happened? The customs-search office in Prague had uncovered a currency irregularity by a man who alleged that he had been acting for the consul Schmidhuber and in his interest. Thereupon Schmidhuber and Captain Ickradt of the Munich Military Intelligence Office were interrogated; among other things, they were questioned about the currency transactions for the Jews of "Operation 7." Their answers were incriminating. Josef Müller was also interrogated. In late October Schmidhuber was arrested and imprisoned for months in the Gestapo prison on Prinz-Albrecht-Strasse. This gave cause for alarm; in his two years of work with the group he had learned a great deal about "Operation 7," Bonhoeffer's exemption from military duty, and the ties abroad.

It was now unavoidable that the investigations should be directed to the activities of the main Military Intelligence Office in Berlin. But it was not simply a matter of course that the Gestapo appeared in the Tirpitzufer office and began to make inquiries there. The courts still recognized that the affairs of Military Intelligence were subject to certain special rules as to secrecy. It was largely at Canaris's discretion, as far as he had the power, to decide what steps should be taken by his Military Intelligence Office as being necessary for the services and how far to cover them up. But the final decision about whether the Military Intelligence's actions might be investigated by security officials lay with Wilhelm Keitel, who had to give his consent as chief of the Wehrmacht high command. If he gave permission for the disclosure of the Military Intelligence's activities in particular matters, that could put an end to the organization's independence, or at least give the Reich Central Security Office the chance it so desperately wanted to turn the spotlight on to Canaris's office.

For months the question was who could make or prevent a decision in the matter. Where did an individual's currency offenses begin to be a matter for prosecution? How far was the Military Intelligence justified in claiming secrecy for its affairs? Numerous parties had an interest in the affair. The Reich Central Security Office hoped that an individual's lapse would enable it to expose Canaris's office as a whole. But the Luftwaffe, headed by Göring, was also taking notice. It had previously been embarrassed by the "scandal" of the "*Rote Kapelle*" (a Communist resistance cell) that had occurred inside the Luftwaffe, and was only waiting for a scandal that would implicate the army. There was no lack of people in the Military Intelligence itself who would feel satisfaction if Dohnanyi encountered difficulties; they viewed him as a young civilian who had pushed his way to the top too quickly. One of Dohnanyi's colleagues and opponents from the Military Intelligence legal department played a role in Schmidhuber's arrest; and later the chief investigator, Judge Advocate Roeder, could count on willing support from some people within the Military Intelligence Office on Tirpitzufer Allee.

There was no doubt that Canaris was prepared to use the Military Intelligence to cover up Dohnanyi's and Bonhoeffer's steps. But their names had been given in the Gestapo office on Prinz-Albrecht-Strasse. Keitel's approval was sought for their possible arrest and for more comprehensive investigations.

Precautions. In that situation, all possible actions had to be scrutinized as to their soundness in relation to Military Intelligence, and safeguarded from unwelcome disclosure.

First, Dohnanyi went to Switzerland. After being mentioned in the Schmidhuber interrogations, the Jews who had been saved in "Operation 7" were not safe there from possible visits by an emissary of the head Reich Central Security Office. Dohnanyi looked up the German military attaché and met Dr. Arnold in Bern to ensure that the documents for all financial matters related to the group were in order. He urged the utmost discretion in answering any inquiries, and returned home on 29 November. The accounts in the office on Tirpitzufer had been checked, and the reliability of the group in Switzerland confirmed as far as humanly possible.

The question of Bonhoeffer's military exemption was critical, and it became more so once the theaters of war extended and the casualties increased. The documents had to show precisely why someone like Bonhoeffer had been declared indispensable for the military organization of the *Abwehr*. Dohnanyi and Bonhoeffer talked it over and composed a long letter, postdated 4 November 1940 in Munich, in which Bonhoeffer wrote his brother-in-law that the Military Intelligence might be interested in his information on ecumenical matters. They carefully obtained the necessary notepaper, the "M-K paper," which had actually been used in 1939 and 1940. The draft stated:

> Dear Hans, When we were discussing ecumenical matters recently, you asked me whether I would not be prepared, if need be, to make available my knowledge of foreign countries and my connections with people in public life in Europe and overseas, to assist in the acquisition of reliable information about foreign countries. I have been thinking the matter over.
>
> In the context of the problems you are interested in, the special feature of the ecumenical work is, of course, the fact that leading political personalities in various countries are interested in the movement, in which all the larger churches of the world, except the Church of Rome, have joined together. So it really might not be difficult to learn the views and judgments of these personalities by way of such ecumenical relationships. Beyond that, I think it is quite within the realm of possibility that one might establish fresh contacts that could perhaps be of use in dealing with specialized questions. . . .[290]

He then pointed out how many laymen could be contacted in that way, suggesting a long list of names, including Cripps, Lord Lothian (who was still alive in 1940), Crossman, Noel-Buxton, and Moberley:

> I am in Munich for a while, and of course I would be willing to be at your disposal in any way that suits you, possibly from here, or wherever you think best. I do not think it would be difficult, even under existing circumstances, to take up the great majority of the connections—perhaps in a neutral country—and use them in the German interest.[291]

This apparent handing over of ecumenical church contacts to Hitler's leadership of the war was necessary in 1942, to camouflage the group planning the coup while it was in its most promising stage. Aid to Jews, feelers to the enemy, journeys—everything had to look like an obvious activity of the Military Intelligence in Canaris's office, so that it could be protected from possible outside investigation, on the grounds of high secrecy.

The military exemptions of other pastors by Oster's office remained a dangerous loose end. We hastened to have a few supporting documents prepared by other pastors who had been exempted. I myself, on the strength of my activity with the India-based Gossner missionary society, wrote reports that implied the military importance of this area; in fact, a journey to the International Missionary Council in Switzerland was arranged for me. While this did not take place until July 1943, I could then convey information to Visser 't Hooft and Barth about what had happened to Dohnanyi and Bonhoeffer in the meantime.[292]

It was crucial that not the slightest trace of suspicion be aroused. On the contrary, the traveling agent now had to really be a traveling agent. This is why, as the affair grew more and more protracted, more journeys for Bonhoeffer were envisaged, and at the end of January 1943 plans for trips to the Balkans and Switzerland were revived. Since the date for the coup was so close, he did not want to be away just then if avoidable. But he left for Munich expecting to make a short trip to Switzerland (which never materialized). Josef Müller was just leaving Munich for Rome—out of similar considerations, but also in connection with the imminent coup attempt. But the latest news from group commander Nebe was again unfavorable, and so Bonhoeffer returned to Berlin on 12 February, on the grounds that he had been "urgently warned against it yesterday."[293] They did not want to risk Bonhoeffer's arrest at the border as someone being sought by the police.

On 13 March 1943—the day of the attempted assassination by Tresckow and Schlabrendorff—a new order arrived from the Munich recruiting station for Bonhoeffer to report for military service. After Stalingrad all the German state offices had been scrutinized for physically fit men who had been exempted because their jobs were indispensable. Bonhoeffer was told to report to the Seidlstrasse recruitment station in Munich with all his papers on 22 March. Yet it was crucial at that moment that his exemption not be lifted; Oster therefore used his authority one last time by releasing Bonhoeffer from the obligation to report. At the same time, Oster worked harder than ever with Dohnanyi—it was the week between Schlabrendorff's and Gersdorff's attempted assassinations of Hitler—to send Bonhoeffer on another journey. In this connection the documents contained a note for Beck, which would play a disastrous role when Dohnanyi was arrested. It was arranged that Bonhoeffer should visit the Balkans, Italy, and Switzerland during the first half of April.

Thus for more than six months they lived between good and bad news from the Gestapo office on Prinz-Albrecht-Strasse and Field Marshal Keitel's office, between bold plans and detailed arrangements in case of arrest.

The Last Week. Torn between disappointment and relief, the entire family celebrated Professor Karl Bonhoeffer's seventy-fifth birthday on 31 March 1943. The children and grandchildren performed Walcha's cantata "*Lobe den Herren*" for the grandfather. A telegram of congratulations from the Oxford relatives was forwarded by Erwin Sutz from Switzerland. Klaus made a speech proposing the toast, and thanked his father for an upbringing marked by understanding and truth. With the well-wishers from the Charité someone also came bearing greetings from Hitler:

> In the name of the German people I bestow on Professor Emeritus Bonhoeffer the Goethe medal for art and science, instituted by the President Hindenburg. The *Führer* Adolf Hitler.

Only a few days later the chief of the Wehrmacht's legal department, Dr. Lehmann, who was favorably inclined toward Dohnanyi, reassured Admiral Canaris that nothing unpleasant would be happening in the next few days. He was anxious for the matter to be taken out of the Gestapo's hands, if it could not be quashed altogether. Canaris passed that information on to Dohnanyi and Bonhoeffer as late as Sunday, 4 April.[294]

At noon on Monday, 5 April, in the house on Marienburger Allee, Bonhoeffer tried to call his sister Christine von Dohnanyi at her house in Sakrow. His call was answered by an unknown man's voice. He thought at once: the house is being searched! Without disturbing his parents, he went next door to his sister Ursula Schleicher to consult her. She quickly prepared a good meal for him. He then went to his room in the attic to check the contents of his desk once more, and then waited next door with the Schleichers and me. About four o'clock his father came across: "There are two men wanting to speak to you upstairs in your room!" Shortly afterward, Judge Advocate Roeder and the Gestapo official Sonderegger drove off with him.

It was the third arrest Roeder and Sonderegger personally made that day, and the fifth that was made on their orders. The others were Dohnanyi, Josef Müller, and their wives.

Dohnanyi's Arrest. Had Keitel now consented to getting rid of Canaris and his office? In any case, the military court was now taking its first measures in the presence of an official from the Reich Central Security Office, and the hearings later conducted by Roeder were regularly attended by Gestapo members.

On Monday morning Roeder had informed Canaris of the investigation that was to take place at once in his office. Then, with Sonderegger, he searched Dohnanyi's office in the presence of Canaris and Oster. In many works dealing with the resistance, the account given about the events of that Monday morning is from Hans Bernd Gisevius's version after 1945 in his book *To the Bitter End*, which sides with Oster against Dohnanyi, with whom Gisevius's relationship had grown difficult.[295] The account given here is from Christine von Dohnanyi's written account of 1945. At the time, there was still no public account of the proceedings, so that what she wrote could hardly be dictated by polemical considerations.

The affair concerned some of Dohnanyi's notes that were intended for Beck. One note said that Bonhoeffer would go with Josef Müller on 9 April to Rome, where Müller was to explain the failure of the attempted assassination in March. The note, which was on a kind of "card" found in the Military Intelligence, bore an "O," with which Beck, whose code name was "Eye of a Needle" (*Nadelöhr*) and used this as his initial, had consented to the commission. Christine von Dohnanyi reported that Bonhoeffer was to see Dr. Zeiger, the rector of the *Collegium Germanicum* in Rome, to discuss Protestant proposals and wishes regarding the pope's peace message.

These questions had been put down in the document referred to, a slip of paper. It was understood all along by the people concerned that drafts of that kind, if they fell into the wrong hands, were to be called "coded words" (*Sprachregelung*) by everyone concerned—that is, material that is not to be taken literally as written, but as simply indicating the direction in which the other party is to take his soundings, and is therefore the so-called playing card of the Military Intelligence. . . . A talk with Beck was arranged for the afternoon of the day of his arrest. At this talk some points in those proposals were to be discussed, so that Bonhoeffer, whose arrest was not considered likely, could start the journey as soon as possible. . . .

When Roeder now searched my husband's safe, there was nothing my husband could do except put the slip of paper before the admiral in Roeder's presence and ask that he might still be allowed to finish that urgent business. But now an unfortunate misunderstanding led Oster to think that my husband had put down the paper, whose contents he knew quite well, so that Oster could let it disappear quickly. Then my husband, as he told me later, whispered to Oster: "Send my wife a slip." He meant that I was to be warned. Obviously, Oster only heard the word "slip." His loyalty as a comrade was stronger than his caution and when he thought for a moment that he was not being watched, he took the slip to hide it in the back pocket of his coat.

Sonderegger of the Gestapo noticed this move, which worsened the situation, both for Oster and for the whole business. Oster was told to go home where he would be under house arrest, and was not allowed to enter the High Military Command again, or to have any further contact with the members of the Military Intelligence. . . .

The first interrogations essentially concerned that slip of paper. It represented irrefutable proof of highly treasonable activity for those being charged, unless they could make it appear to be official material. At the moment of his arrest my husband had tried to take that line by making the slips a matter of open discussion. Oster had misunderstood him, and the situation now became critical because Oster suddenly denied ever having known its contents—an incredible assertion in view of the fact that he had tried to conceal it. He tried to prove this by the kind of initialing that was on it, and denied that he had himself written the initial, an "O," under it. Only my husband's urgent request to acknowledge the slip as official, in the general interest, which he conveyed to me in a secret note, . . . induced Oster—who had certainly acted with the best intentions and, as he himself said, had been advised in the matter by Gisevius—to acknowledge he had initialed it. After Canaris, under interrogation, had also acknowledged the slip as being part of official activity, the main danger was eliminated, and Roeder now simply took the usual course of looking for any formal infringements in the official channels and in the production of the slip.

After Frau von Dohnanyi had been released at the beginning of May from the women's prison on Kaiserdamm in Charlottenburg, and had secretly contacted her husband, Oster, and others, the dangerous affair of the slips of paper was so successfully maneuvered out of the danger zone that it played no further part in the whole business of the prosecution. It did not arise at all during Bonhoeffer's interrogations.

The Engagement

In the race between overthrow and arrest, Bonhoeffer wrote the short essay "After Ten Years" at Christmas 1942. He gave it to his parents, Dohnanyi, and Oster, and left me a copy which was preserved in a hiding place under the roof of his parents' house. In it he wrote:

> There remains for us only the very narrow way, often extremely difficult to find, of living every day as if it were our last, and yet living in faith and responsibility as though there were to be a great future. . . . It may be that the day of judgement will dawn tomorrow; and in that case, we shall gladly stop working for a better future. But not before.[296]

Bonhoeffer's resistance against a false apocalyptic interpretation of that era is most clearly evident in the story of his betrothal. During that winter he was so charmed by the naturalness and grace of an eighteen-year-old young woman that he began to see her as his future life partner. She gave him the freedom to take a step that he had not been able to take ten years earlier.

To Bonhoeffer, Maria von Wedemeyer embodied what he had learned to treasure in the von Kleist family in Kieckow and Klein-Krössin—alert wisdom, freshness, nobility, and a poise that made her more than equal to deal with life's gifts as well as its burdens. She was the third of the seven children of Hans and Ruth von Wedemeyer, and thus was a granddaughter of the elderly Ruth von Kleist-Retzow and an older sister of Bonhoeffer's former confirmation candidate Max von Wedemeyer. Her father, a landowner in Pätzig in the Neumark, some sixty miles northeast of Berlin, was a man of wide-ranging interests who was upright and responsive. He was an enthusiastic and successful manager of his farm and lands, had created the finest hunting grounds in the region, and devoted himself with equal vigor to renewal movements for the Evangelical church. He was one of the founders of the Berneuchen brotherhood, whose annual working sessions had taken place in Pätzig since the death of the Berneuchen landowner von Viebahn. Deeply concerned about the rise of National Socialism, he agreed to help his former comrade-in-arms Franz von Papen in the formation of a new cabinet. But after Hitler had seized power, when he saw how hopeless and compromising any attempt at cooperation would be, he withdrew with determination. He immediately felt the consequences of political animosity toward him. Suffering from the inner conflict between the conspiracy (his cousin Fabian von Schlabrendorff used to visit Pätzig) and his own military tradition, Hans von Wedemeyer died an officer on the eastern front in August 1942. Bonhoeffer wrote his widow on 25 August 1942:

> It was about seven years ago that your husband sat in my room in Finkenwalde, to discuss the instruction that Max was then to have as a confirmation candidate. I have never forgotten that meeting. It stayed with me throughout the entire time of instruction. I knew that Max had already received the most important education in his parents' home, and would continue to do so. It was also clear to me what it means today for a boy to have a godly father who lives a full and busy life. When, as the years went by, I got to know nearly all your children, I was often impressed by seeing what a great blessing it is to have a truly Christian father. It is really one and the same impression that I have felt so deeply in meeting your family and relatives, your mother and your brothers and sisters. The blessing is not purely spiritual, but something that goes deep down to affect one's earthly life. Under the true blessing, life becomes sound, firm, confident, active, just because it is lived from the source of life, of strength, joy, and action.

The picture of your husband that I have before my eyes today is of one who lived from such a blessing and handed it on in ultimate responsibility; I am grateful for it, and I should like to tell you so, esteemed lady, in these difficult days. When someone hands on to his own people, and to many others, the blessing that he himself received, he has indeed fulfilled the most important duty in life, for he has himself become happy in God, and has made others happy in God. But the blessing in which he lived remains upon him as the light of God's countenance.

The spirit in which he lived will be the spirit in which you and your children are now together. The same earnestness with which he spoke to me then about his son's Christian upbringing will now inspire you to help your children to a Christian mourning for their father; the same love that was given to him for the Word and Sacrament will unite you with each other and with the community in heaven; the same spirit of sacrifice and obedience to the will of God will cause you to accept in quietness and thankfulness what God has sent you. How God can be praised by such Christian mourning of a whole family for the father who has been called home to God! My thoughts go out specially to Max. How he must miss his father now. And I am quite sure that he can never forget or lose what he has received from his father, and that he is safe as his father was and is.

God help you, esteemed lady, through his Word and Sacrament, to be comforted and to comfort others. With kind regards to you and all your people, yours respectfully and sincerely, Dietrich Bonhoeffer.[297]

As a child Maria had sometimes visited her grandmother in Stettin, and had once been to Finkenwalde with her cousins. Now Bonhoeffer saw her again as a young lady when he spent a few days in Klein-Krössin between his journeys to Sweden and Italy. He remarked afterward that the reencounter preoccupied him more than he initially liked to admit. But on the way to Rome he said in a letter to me:

I have *not* written to Maria. As things stand it is impossible now. If no further meeting is possible, the delightful thought of a few highly intense minutes will no doubt melt once again in the realm of unfulfilled fantasies that is already adequately populated in any case. On the other hand, I do not see how a meeting could be contrived that she would find unobtrusive and inoffensive. One cannot expect that of Frau von Kleist either, in any case not as an idea of mine, for I am really not at all clear and decided about it as yet.[298]

Not long after her father's death, Bonhoeffer saw Maria von Wedemeyer again several times in Klein-Krössin and in Berlin. Now he was no longer in doubt. But her mother was not ignorant of how things stood, and was naturally anxious for her daughter, who was still quite young. Could the girl really gauge what it meant to marry a man whose political commitment and many involvements she certainly could not assess? Maria's mother invited Bonhoeffer to talk things over with her.

On 24 November 1942 he went to see Frau von Wedemeyer in Pätzig, simply telling his relatives that he had to go to Pomerania again. The conversation concluded with Maria's mother proposing that they remain apart for a year. He was rather at a loss, and wrote to me on 27 November:

> I think I could get my way if I wanted to; I can argue better than the others, and could probably talk her round; but that would not be natural to me, it seems to me wrong . . . and like exploiting other people's weakness. Frau von Wedemeyer is stronger through the loss of her husband—that is, in her very weakness—than if I had had to deal with him too. I must not allow her to feel defenseless; that would be mean, but it makes my situation more difficult.[299]

Bonhoeffer rebelled. The next day he wrote: "everywhere the same out-of-date ideas from past times"[300] and shortly afterward: "I have also been wondering whether you will just—without my knowing—very nicely and gently and skillfully . . . if you will write to Frau von Wedemeyer as a friend. But this could be later, too, perhaps that would be even better."[301]

But no such letter was needed, for on 17 January 1943 Dietrich Bonhoeffer and Maria von Wedemeyer became engaged. He told his parents at the beginning of February. At the request of Maria's mother and her guardian, Hans-Jürgen von Kleist-Retzow, Bonhoeffer promised a fairly long interval before the public announcement of their engagement and before their marriage.

His arrest thwarted all their arrangements, and at that point the families decided that the news should be made public. A strange engagement began. Bonhoeffer wrote from his cell in Tegel on 4 June 1943:

> I can hardly tell you how very much my mother-in-law's letter moved me. That I must cause her such added grief after all the anguish of the past year has haunted me since the first day of my arrest, and now she has actually made this distress that has come on us the occasion to shorten the period of waiting, and through that has made me very happy.[302]

The "Borderline Case"

> You must know that I have not for a moment regretted coming back in 1939—nor any of the consequences, either. I knew quite well what I was doing, and I acted with a clear conscience. I have no wish to cross out of my life anything that has happened since.[303]

> I became certain that it was my duty to endure this borderline situation with all its problems.[304]

The end of his resistance activities as a free man suggests a few thoughts summarizing Bonhoeffer's role as "conspirator." The unusual consequences of these actions for a Lutheran pastor and theologian will become even more evident in the following account of his interrogations, and may shock the susceptibilities of anyone whose standards are those of traditional ethics and normal times. What went on in those interrogations, however, was only a continuation of all that he had thought about and decided long before.

Today, in more ordered times, some people are reluctant to call Bonhoeffer a "conspirator," and to give such central importance to a term that was once viewed as degrading. The more removed we are from the events, the more we hesitate to use the term. But all the attempts to downplay it ignore the extraordinary reality that Bonhoeffer faced.

Stages of Resistance. Bonhoeffer undoubtedly was among the small and vanishing group of church people who took the step to active political underground involvement—that is, to "conspiracy." Besides the numerous people from the middle class and the nobility, the military, and the socialists, the list of the victims of 20 July 1944[305] contains the names of three Roman Catholic churchmen: Father Alfred Delp, Prelate Otto Müller, and Chaplain Hermann Wehrle; on the Protestant side we must add Bonhoeffer and the Confessing church's legal adviser, Friedrich Justus Perels.[306]

Bonhoeffer's entry into the conspiracy therefore placed him in a "borderline situation." It helped that in 1940 he was not tied to a parish ministry, as were most of his colleagues. Perhaps his life would have taken a different course if Bonhoeffer had been the pastor of a parish that year. As it was, however, the call to a "conspiracy" against Hitler came to him under peculiar circumstances. He faced that call after he had gone through several stages of resistance to the Third Reich, and had initially hesitated at some of the points where the struggle intensified. Each new stage of his resistance made him perceptibly more isolated.

I have tried elsewhere[307] to distinguish five different stages of resistance in the National Socialist period, and to describe what it meant to be in opposition at each stage. First, there was simple passive resistance. Then came the openly ideological stance that characterized the churches and men like Bishop von Galen, Martin Niemöller, and Bishop Wurm, although they did not conceive of a new political future and work toward it. Third, there was the stage of being informed accessories to the preparations for the coup; some church officials such as Asmussen,[308] Dibelius, Grüber, or Hanns Lilje belong in this category. Then came the fourth stage of active preparations for the post-revolt period; its most distinguished representative was Moltke, but Theodor Steltzer, Harald Poelchau, and Oskar Hammelsbeck were part of this as well. Finally there was the last stage: active conspiracy. For members of the Evangelical Lutheran tradition this was most difficult, since their tradition allowed for nothing of this kind. In this final stage the church offered no protection and no prior justification for something that fell outside all normal contingencies.

Of the Protestant church officials, only four took that final step— Bonhoeffer and his friend Perels, and Gerstenmaier and his friend Schönfeld. Each of them entered the ambiguous world of active political conspiracy under different circumstances, with different presuppositions, and at different points.

The course of events did not allow Bonhoeffer and Perels to join forces with Gerstenmaier and Schönfeld. Gerstenmaier had begun working for Bishop Heckel at the very time (in 1936) when Heckel's differences with Bonhoeffer were at their height. Thus Bonhoeffer always saw Gerstenmaier as being associated with the Church Foreign Office that had collaborated theologically, ecclesiastically, and politically with the Third Reich. Gerstenmaier remained a consistory councillor for that office, even during the conspiracy, although after 1941 Klaus Bonhoeffer encountered him more often in resistance circles. For his part, Gerstenmaier viewed Dietrich Bonhoeffer as a Barthian who belonged to the "Dahlemite" wing of the orthodox and impractical Confessing people. The theological interests of the two men had always been in contrast to one another; they belonged to two different groups, each of which had at different points played a leading part in political resistance.

The strained relationship between Gerstenmaier's friend Hans Schönfeld and Bonhoeffer has already been mentioned. The early years of the war brought about a certain change. From the time he realized how exceptionally well informed Bonhoeffer was politically, Schönfeld had taken an interest in him; and Bonhoeffer had relied on Schönfeld, who had been able to help him keep in touch with his Oxford relatives. Schönfeld visited Bonhoeffer's parents' home for the first time in the winter of 1940–1941, while

Bonhoeffer was staying in Ettal; and later, when Schönfeld went with Courvoisier to help prisoners of war, he and Courvoisier visited Justus Delbrück,
Otto John, and the Bonhoeffer brothers in Berlin.[309]

The Nature of Resistance. The transitions from the first to the fourth stage of
the resistance were almost insignificant compared with the final transition
to the fifth and last stage. In open protest everything was unequivocal—
thoughts, actions, and personal integrity. But in the fifth stage this was no
longer possible. Bonhoeffer and Gerstenmaier took upon themselves the
odium of leading a double life, and they had to face the consequences.

By profession Bonhoeffer was the academic theological adviser to the
Confessing church, but he had also become an undercover man of the Military Intelligence. Gerstenmaier continued to serve in the Church Foreign
Office and as an "academic consultant in the information department of the
German Foreign Ministry." Bonhoeffer had been drawn into the Military
Intelligence circle through his family relationship to Dohnanyi. Through his
work for the Church Foreign Office Gerstenmaier had official contacts with
the Foreign Ministry, which sponsored his "journeys abroad in the interest
of the Reich." With its help he kept Schönfeld in his post at Geneva, cooperated with people like von Twardowski, and made friends there with Trott,
Werner von Haeften, and Hassell; they brought him into the Kreisau group.
The Military Intelligence Office and Foreign Ministry obtained the much-
needed military exemptions for Bonhoeffer and Gerstenmaier, as well as
their passports during the war. They filed their official agents' reports for
those offices while secretly passing on the information needed by the conspirators. Everyone had to assume that those offices contained numerous fervent Nazis and might even have alarming connections to the Reich Central
Security Office. Thus they constantly had to play a double role in their
church and their secular offices.

Any responsible resistance under the conditions that existed under Hitler
had to take the form of a conspiracy. A spontaneous uprising did not occur
and could not be expected to occur. The spontaneous actions of individuals might be brave, but took no responsibility for the future; and there was
not the homogeneous group necessary for a revolution with the eruptive
force to lead to new social structures.

Bonhoeffer did not commit himself either to the desperate action of an
individual, or to the turmoil of a rebellion, or to the ideology of a revolution.

> [He joined] a planned "conspiracy" that answered for the past and was
> answerable for the future. This meant a conspiracy that could not

announce its existence in advance with premature jolts, but acted only once the prospects for success were good domestically and abroad—a conspiracy that would carry camouflage and disguise to extreme limits, so that one would lie better than the master liar. This meant that nearly all the conspirators who survived would have had to count on an act of indemnity; the files in their offices, in which they had to strive to reach top positions, naturally contain documents that vouch for their indispensable usefulness for Hitler's war machine. The things that might be necessary were not only party badges and the Hitler salute; one might also have to remain in incriminating command posts, in the army, in the Military Intelligence, in the Foreign Ministry, even in the S.S. The price had to be paid. "We must stay, to preserve us from worse things"; that guilty remark from the early years of the Nazi period now became the order of the day for those who assumed responsibility.[310]

This resistance of "conspiracy" could not be undertaken until late. It was only after all the ways of legal opposition were barred and those called upon to bear responsibility in the various branches of public life had ceased to speak out that the moment for a conspiracy came. And it was only when the worst came to the worst, and Bonhoeffer the theologian had tried other ways to escape from his dilemma, that he took his stand and no longer ruled out that kind of resistance. Once tyranny threatened the lives of its neighbors in the name of those whom it ruled and thus besmirched their name, and once the means were at hand, Bonhoeffer felt that on moral grounds the hour for conspiracy had come.

After he had become connected with that "conspiracy" Bonhoeffer assumed that his church would no longer be able to use him once the facts came to light. He knew that the church was not yet in a position to support him in something for which he could not ask it to accept joint responsibility. And he knew why his Confessing church refused to place his name on the intercession lists: not only because it had to be cautious in a matter of some danger, nor simply because it did not yet know all the details of the conspirators' activity. It was also because it could not yet think along the lines on which Bonhoeffer was committing himself in response to the extraordinary demands of the situation.

This "borderline situation" led Bonhoeffer to abandon all outer and inner security. By entering this kind of conspiracy he renounced command, applause, and the backing of general opinion.

> He cannot even demonstrate its ethical validity when he must be most certain of it. He takes it on himself to be condemned before everything and

everybody. Indeed, however anxious the responsible person is for success, he must not turn even this success into a god who is with him. Only the true transcendent God knows whether, at the moment of action, that action has really been taken here in the name of life. And if the sacrifice is made and success is denied, there remains something equivocal about the best names. Bonhoeffer said in a sermon as early as 1932, without knowing how prophetic it was, that times would come again when martyrdom would be called for, "but this blood . . . will not be so innocent and dear as that of the first who testified. On our blood a great guilt would lie: that of the useless servant who is cast into the outer darkness."[311]

An Appraisal. It is possible, from different perspectives, to regard Bonhoeffer's participation in the German conspiratorial resistance as significant or as of only secondary importance.

In terms of his personal commitment, Bonhoeffer bore the burden of the conspiracy as few other figures in the political opposition. He gave himself as completely as any of them to their common fate. His profession explains why he was not with the conspiracy actively from as early as 1938, but only as a confidant. When he entered the political underground movement opportunistic motives were far removed from his range of vision. He entered into it without reservation, even sacrificing his professional reputation in the church and as a theologian.

Bonhoeffer's position in the resistance movement was of no great political importance; he did not overrate his place and his professional competence in that regard. On the contrary, in his book on ethics he tried to see what, in that dangerous game, depended on the ability to exercise a practiced and expert judgment on means, timing, and alliances. Political ambition was not one of his characteristics. Although he could not help seeing how practiced political expertise became a pretext for avoiding fundamental decisions, he unerringly made robust judgments in the political sphere, and he used them effectively. Only his journey to Sweden made Bonhoeffer politically important in the preparations for the coup. Even here it was evident that he neither could nor wanted to be merely a politician. He also knew quite well that his attempt to make contacts was only one among others that were often more expertly handled.

With regard to the planning for a future Germany and its constitutional forms, Bonhoeffer's share in the conspiracy was comparatively small, and we have no notes on it from his own hand. He instigated the Freiburg circle's work and influenced their choice of subjects and experts, but his personal involvement in their work was confined to theological and ethical cooperation. The position he had within the German resistance grew out of his background, his profession, and his personal guidance. He viewed this as an incentive to examine his church's traditions and its theology in depth, once he had time for such work again, because under the onslaught of National Socialism he had found church doctrine to be dangerously sterile. He often said that after he had finished his work in the conspiracy, he would like to return to his own profession, though with fresh insights.

In terms of his interpretation and intellectual grasp of the revolutionary act, Bonhoeffer certainly counted as one of the innermost circle. He immediately reflected on the dilemma of Oster's notifying the Dutch about the date of the German attack in the spring of 1940, which Bonhoeffer viewed as a pragmatic and powerful expression of the outrageous situation in which one could no longer love and save one's fatherland except through "treason." This was when he wrote his analysis of the breakdown of rationality, of the ethical rigorist, of the man of conscience, of duty and private virtue.[312] Two years later he wrote the essay "After Ten Years" for his family and companions, primarily Oster and Dohnanyi, as a Christmas present. In it he defended the location of their action, asserted the future fruitfulness of their enterprise, and soberly described the profound dangers of the path that was necessary:

> We have been silent witnesses of evil deeds; we have been drenched by many storms; we have learned the arts of equivocation and pretense; experience has made us suspicious of others and kept us from being truthful and open; intolerable conflicts have worn us down and even made us cynical. Are we still of any use?[313]

Bonhoeffer's statements in this essay about "conspiracy" were not apologies written after the event: on the contrary, it was written during one of the most promising phases of the resistance, in order to strengthen his friends in their course of action.[314]

When the numerous constitutional proposals of the resistance are forgotten—and they were soon overtaken by events—Bonhoeffer's analysis about a German conspiracy may still be interesting. In his capacity to express the spirit in which he and his friends were acting, he remains an effective witness to the resistance. But his merit here was that, as a Christian theologian of the resistance, he did not simply observe and analyze from an aloof and critical perspective, but shaped viable formulas in the midst of action.

He did not formulate the conspirators' common motivation as one more "faith in a single, all-conquering ideology . . . but [as] the common responsibility for Germany's shame, in which they knew themselves to be implicated, and for Germany's survival in the family of nations."[315] At Christmas 1942 Bonhoeffer wrote:

> The ultimate question for a responsible man to ask is not how he is to extricate himself heroically from the affair, but how the coming generation is to live. It is only from this question, with its responsibility towards history, that fruitful solutions can come, even if for the time being they are very humiliating.[316]

CHAPTER THIRTEEN

TEGEL: 1943–1944

The night of 5 April 1943 was cold in the reception cell in Tegel. Bonhoeffer could not bring himself to use the blankets of the wood bed; he could not stand their stench. Someone wept loudly in the next cell. The next morning dry bread was tossed through a crack in the door. The staff had been instructed not to speak to the new arrival. The warden called him a "scoundrel."[1]

Bonhoeffer was then taken to the solitary confinement ward, where those condemned to death were being held, bound hand and foot. A few days later he too was handcuffed when he was driven into town for his first interrogation at the Reich War Court (*Reichskriegsgericht*). As a member of the *Abwehr,* he came under the jurisdiction of a military court, but Colonel Roeder, who conducted the hearing, was always accompanied by officials from the Reich Central Security Office.

The old Tegel prison was one of the military interrogation prisons. Bonhoeffer was initially held on the third floor, but was later moved to cell 92 on the first floor, because of the increased risk of bombing raids.[2] He spent eighteen months in Tegel. On 8 October 1944 he was transferred to the detention center in the cellar of the Reich Central Security Office building on Prinz-Albrecht-Strasse.

Bonhoeffer's period in Tegel was filled by his stubborn but successful efforts to conceal the true facts. His family and friends helped him weave an intricate net of camouflage. Although the threads sometimes became tangled, the net held until after the catastrophe of 20 July 1944, when gravely incriminating material was found in an outpost of the Military Intelligence Office. The discovery of these documents in Zossen at the end of September 1944 ended Bonhoeffer's period of military confinement in Tegel.

Bonhoeffer's strategy during his interrogation by the War Court can only be understood as part of a greater whole. As chief defendant in the trial,

Hans von Dohnanyi was in far greater danger; through him his persecutors sought to strike at Canaris's entire *Abwehr* office. Several others were arrested as accomplices in the Dohnanyi case: Josef Müller and, initially, his wife Anni Müller and Christine von Dohnanyi. Thus Bonhoeffer's own trial depended on the status of Dohnanyi's; he impatiently hoped that it would be speeded up and was unhappy when there were delays. Bonhoeffer had to adapt his own behavior to whatever Dohnanyi did.

For this reason, the course of the Dohnanyi trial will be examined first, before looking at the case against Bonhoeffer, his period in Tegel, and his theological work there.

The Trial of Hans von Dohnanyi

Both Dohnanyi and Josef Müller were taken to the Wehrmacht prison at 64 Lehrter Strasse, which was for prisoners of officer rank.

Although the prison commandant, Lieutenant Colonel Maass, soon proved to be a true friend of Dohnanyi and his family, the strain on Dohnanyi was almost unbearable, especially in the first weeks. The entire fate of the resistance work outside the prison seemed to depend on him more than on anyone else, as did the fate of the *Abwehr* office and, of course, that of his family. On 12 April he learned that his wife had also been arrested; and, at first, no one was able to confer with Oster about the crucial "slips of paper." Dohnanyi saw his wife for the first time on 16 April, and on 19 April he saw Bonhoeffer. This was almost a relief; evidently they had not been caught contradicting each other.

During the resistance preparations the previous winter Dohnanyi had agreed to take as much personal responsibility as possible if any points arose that might incriminate the others. Being versed in military politics and legal matters, he could make the quickest and most expert decisions about which charges concerned *Abwehr* secrets, which only Canaris could acknowledge or withhold from investigation. Dohnanyi did everything he could to make the others who had been arrested seem as unimportant as possible. He even gave up the chance to write an Easter letter to his parents and children, instead writing a "personal" letter to Bonhoeffer in Tegel, calculating that Roeder would read it. On Good Friday, 23 April 1943, he wrote:

> My dear Dietrich, I don't know if I'll be allowed to send you this greeting, but I'll try. The bells are ringing outside for the service....
>
> You can't imagine how unhappy I am to be the reason that you, Christel, the children, and my parents should have to suffer like this, and that my

dear wife and you should have your freedom taken away. *Socios habuisse malorum* may be a comfort, but the *habere* is a terribly heavy burden. . . . If I knew that you all—and you personally—did not think badly of me, I'd feel so relieved. What wouldn't I give to know that you were all free again; what wouldn't I take on myself if you could be spared this affliction. It was wonderful to be able to see you. I've been able to speak to Christel also— but what can you say in front of other people. . . .

No one can know what it means not to be able to be with her in this time of trial. It certainly does not help in the matter. . . .

The Battlefronts. Although during Dohnanyi's trial the Wehrmacht's jurisdiction was formally respected, the real battle was between the office of the *Abwehr* on Tirpitzufer Allee and the Reich Central Security Office on Prinz-Albrecht-Strasse. Dohnanyi was both the key figure and the victim. The Reich Central Security Office remained discreetly in the background, but an observer kept it informed about the course of events, once Keitel had handed the affair over for investigation by the court.

The hearing was conducted by Dr. Manfred Roeder, a military judge from the Luftwaffe. He boasted of being Göring's frequent guest in Karinhall, and had won his spurs in 1942 with the death sentences against the Harnacks and Harro Schulze-Boysen in the *Rote Kapelle* trial.[3] Roeder had connections with the notorious S.S. leader Heinrich Müller. Rüdiger Schleicher, who had once been offered Roeder's job in the Reich War Court and declined it for reasons of conscience, recalled that Roeder had once told him, "I stand on the narrow bridge between the Gestapo and the War Court." Roeder sought and found support in the *Abwehr* itself, for there were naturally some resentful people in the legal department who had been angry when Canaris appointed Dohnanyi legal adviser over their heads. Thus Roeder had some success when he questioned members of the legal and financial departments of the *Abwehr*. This, of course, also intensified the countermeasures taken against him, which subsequently resulted in his being removed from the case. In the summer of 1943 Roeder had frequently questioned Canaris, who cleverly maintained the pretense of being anxious that the charges against Dohnanyi be thoroughly and quickly investigated.

A bitter struggle ensued between Roeder and Dohnanyi. Each of the two lawyers thought he perceived the true intentions of the other. As a Nazi, Roeder identified himself with the prosecution even during the interrogation phase. His aim from the beginning was to obtain a verdict of high treason against the state, and he treated the prisoner being held for interrogation as if he were already a criminal with no rights. He used various means to convey the potential extent of his power to Dohnanyi, and indicated that the case was arousing interest in the highest quarters. In fact, in the course of the investigation progress reports were given not only to Keitel, but to Heinrich Müller, Kaltenbrunner, Bormann, Himmler, and even Hitler himself. But the endurance and skill of his adversary made things difficult for Roeder and put the quick conclusion he had achieved in the *Rote Kapelle* trial ever further beyond his reach.

For Dohnanyi was not simply at the mercy of his accuser. Good friends in influential places sprang to his assistance, especially Canaris, who had a good grasp of the method of a forward defense. He provided cover for everything that Dohnanyi's friends did in order to harmonize the statements of the isolated prisoners. In the *Abwehr* Karl Ludwig Freiherr von Guttenberg, the editor of *Weisse Blätter,* was particularly active, as well as Emmi Bonhoeffer's brother Justus Delbrück; Dohnanyi had brought both of them into Canaris's department. Christine von Dohnanyi was released after four weeks through the intervention of various people, including her father. She continued to maintain complete contact with her husband, friends in the *Abwehr* office, and especially with Hans Oster, who had been dismissed on 5 April. Through these channels Dohnanyi and Canaris were able to send each other requests and suggestions about the conduct of the investigation.

Another important factor was the head of the Wehrmacht legal department, Dr. Lehmann, whom Keitel had instructed to place the whole affair in Roeder's hands. Lehmann was basically well disposed toward Dohnanyi; he successfully fought the suggestion that the prisoners should be dismissed from the Wehrmacht, which would have placed them at the mercy of the Gestapo. The tireless assistance of Dr. Karl Sack,[4] a judge of the general staff and chief of the army's legal department, was of crucial importance. Dohnanyi had come to appreciate Sack during the Fritsch crisis. He helped give the prisoners information wherever he could, and even spoke with Canaris after his dismissal in 1944. Sack found a way for Dr. Schulze zur Wiesche, a lawyer connected to the Confessing church, to visit Dohnanyi several times in his cell at Moabit and later in the prison hospital in Buch, in northeast Berlin. At that time Schulze zur Wiesche could not officially act for the defense since, as Dr. Sack told him, "it would soon emerge that he belonged to the same group as the accused."[5] Through fortunate coincidence Rüdiger Schleicher was able to frequent Sack's office without difficulty because he was a legal colleague and a member of the Luftwaffe legal department. In uniform he did not attract attention. Although running far greater risks as a civilian, Friedrich Justus Perels was also an intermediary for Sack's advice and warnings, which the family then encoded and passed on to the inmates of Moabit and Tegel in books and food parcels.

Despite their good intentions, Sack and his assistants sometimes pursued a different line than the prisoners, and the situation was assessed differently outside the prison. For example, after the first grave charges had been refuted, Dohnanyi and especially Bonhoeffer pressed for a rapid decision in their case. Dohnanyi placed his hopes in Canaris, whose position in 1943 was still solid, despite the dangerous information that the Reich Central Security Office had already acquired concerning the *Abwehr*. But Sack was afraid of the political volatility of the case; if the pace was forced, he worried, it might lead to an unfavorable decision by Hitler himself. He was satisfied as long as the case was not taken out of Roeder's hands. Sack's strategy was to keep the case out of the political arena—and he succeeded in this—and maneuver around Roeder, letting the case "run out of steam," as he put it, until the overthrow came. This strategy was dramatically validated when Josef Müller managed to detach his own trial from the others, and was acquitted at the beginning of March 1944. The preliminary work had been successful; the Gestapo, however, announced that it would put Müller in a concentration camp as soon as he was released.

With these kinds of helpers Dohnanyi and Bonhoeffer in their cells stayed informed about the progress of the coup preparations. This remained the case even after the breakup of Oster's resistance group in the *Abwehr* office, when a new center for the resistance had to be set up next door in Stauffenberg's and General Olbricht's offices. Until that point Bonhoeffer and Dohnanyi had few connections to Stauffenberg, who was a "newcomer." Stauffenberg, however, soon knew all about Dohnanyi and his case. Among other things, he procured the precious gasoline that enabled the tireless lawyer Schulze zur Wiesche to visit Dohnanyi in the prison hospital in Buch at the beginning of 1944.

Three Stages. The case against Dohnanyi went through three distinct stages. The first lasted until January 1944; during this period Roeder acted on behalf of the Reich War Court, with the Gestapo present, until he was forced to leave the case. The second stage ended on 20 July 1944; the plan during this time was to let the case run out of steam under Kutzner, who was the prosecutor for the Reich War Court. The third phase was dominated entirely by the Reich Central Security Office, represented by S.S. *Standartenführer* Walter Huppenkothen.

Roeder's Attack. Roeder treated the fateful slip of paper, seized at the time of Dohnanyi's arrest at the office on Tirpitzufer Allee, as proof of high treason against his country. Dohnanyi obstinately insisted that this document was part of the ordinary official *Abwehr* material. The nature of its contents, a code used in routine counterespionage, naturally had to be confirmed by Oster and Canaris. Roeder ordered that Dohnanyi's imprisonment be as unpleasant as possible; he refused to give him permission to write, read, or smoke, and threatened to "finish him off" and have him "tried summarily by the *Führer*" if he did not "talk."[6] When the secret connection with Oster was finally established and Oster was questioned by Roeder, he explained that the fateful "O" was his sign, and confirmed the official character of the document as an *Abwehr* coded card. After Canaris also refuted any suspicious interpretation and acknowledged the document as part of Dohnanyi's ordinary official work, the greatest danger was over. Only a few shortcomings in matters of official routine could be established—a ludicrous anticlimax in comparison with the initial sensational charges. But the mistrust and suspicion had not been alleviated.

Roeder began his second attack by investigating "Operation 7." With the help of the Reich Central Security Office he ordered Herr Ruge, one of his lawyers, to investigate Swiss bank accounts; Roeder found it hard to understand why these inquiries did not show that Dohnanyi had used that operation to line his own pockets. The slightest indiscretion by those in the know, even by those who were safe in Switzerland, could have produced serious complications. But no one slipped up, and the escapees in Switzerland kept as quiet as possible. Here again Canaris defended "Operation 7" as part of his department's work.

The refutation of the charges that Confessing pastors had been exempted from the military because Oster's and Dohnanyi's department had declared them indispensable for special duties was a long and wearisome task.[7] But these charges, too, gradually seemed more innocuous as it became clear that it was simply a concern that certain offices had been bypassed.

The fourth area of investigation concerned Bonhoeffer's official journeys. These were thought to show that Dohnanyi and Oster had infringed on the agreement between Canaris and Heydrich, the so-called Ten Commandments.[8] Here again, however, the responsibility was shifted to Canaris.

Roeder's persistent suspicion of Dohnanyi's official and private financial dealings lay behind all these attacks. He used documents selectively and imprecisely to isolate Dohnanyi morally. It was a great nervous strain on Dohnanyi to be forced to defend himself on this trivial level, for he was a very painstaking official. In light of the far greater danger that the political charges posed, however, it was a blessing when his enemies became bogged down in this detailed accounting for foreign currency, travel, taxes, and interest. This consumed a disproportionate amount of time without yielding any tangible results. This petty war within the jungle of war regulations concerning bookkeeping is only peripherally related to Bonhoeffer's story, and it moved into the background as the real charges became more important.

By the end of July 1943 the most dangerous phase of Roeder's attacks was over. It appeared that Dohnanyi's allies had managed to remove his case from the political danger zone into the realm of debatable questions of procedure. Meanwhile Dr. Sack had convinced Keitel that Roeder was less concerned with Dohnanyi's misdemeanors than with discrediting Keitel's subordinate, Admiral Canaris, and his department. Keitel told Dr. Lehmann to study the documents of the case and to report to him. As a result of this report, on 23 July 1943 Keitel ordered that the grave political charges be dropped and the case no longer be conducted as a matter of high treason. This was a considerable achievement, and it was still another victory for Canaris. Sack passed on the information to the prisoners that the remaining charges, concerning the military exemptions for pastors and the errors in matters of official routine, would not amount to very much.

Roeder's Removal. But this did not mean that the danger was entirely past, for Dohnanyi's accuser could still use matters of form and procedure to resurrect the political charges. Because of this Sack did everything possible to get rid of the dangerous Roeder and, therefore, to avoid a speedy conclusion of the case. Roeder could be removed either by complaints concerning the conduct of the case or by his being promoted to a higher post somewhere else. And, in fact, both things happened.

At the end of May 1943, Dohnanyi submitted a complaint about the conduct of the investigation to the War Court department chief, Dr. Alfred Schrag, who had been a fraternity colleague of Karl Bonhoeffer. Dohnanyi had to word it carefully, since it passed through Roeder's hands on its way through the official channels:

> On 19 April the investigating magistrate informed me that "the fate of my wife depended on what I said." . . . On 4 May he said that there could be no question of my being allowed to speak with her if I could not say anything more or different from what I had said previously. . . . I was put in an especially difficult position because, on 13 May, he confiscated the notes I had made for my defense during my confinement in order to refresh my memory. . . . This defense material has not been returned to me so far, and I haven't even been able to look at it in order to supplement the incomplete transcript. . . . In this connection I should like to mention that, according to something he said on the 9th of this month, it is doubtful that I shall

even be allowed to have a defense lawyer. . . . It is of great importance to me that what I say should be taken down in the form that I consider correct. This has not been the case with my statements since 13 May, when he refused to record in the transcript certain statements of mine that I considered important for my defense, and broke off the interrogation without ever continuing it again.

Soon afterward, Dohnanyi sent another letter to Schrag and Lehmann that did not go through the censors:

> . . . In accordance with the aim of the investigating magistrate to make the head of the department himself [Canaris], his chief of staff [Oster], and his closest colleague [Dohnanyi] appear politically unreliable, the charges have been presented without any attempt to discover the truth of the matter, without there being the least connection between what is said and the actual charges, and without any criminal consequences being established or being able to be established, so that their sole purpose is to destroy my character. . . . After the investigating magistrate failed to prove that there had been treasonable activities among [Canaris's] staff, which seemed to be an established fact for him before the inquiry had begun, he thought he could achieve his aim by the roundabout way of general political defamation. . . . In this interrogation he dealt once more with the document concerning "Operation 7," using a principle of selection that made it clear to me from the beginning that his attack was directed less against me than against the head of the department. . . . In connection with these cases the investigating magistrate seemed to accuse me—but in reality it was the head of the department—of lacking an impeccable political attitude and an "unhesitating readiness" to sacrifice for others. . . .

Complaints also came from other quarters. Dr. Duesterberg, a department chief in the high military command whom Canaris had frequently sent to the hearings in the War Court, made a verbal and then a written complaint that Roeder had tried to "pump" him during official meetings about the personal and political attitudes of *Abwehr* members. During a conference with Keitel, attended by *Abwehr* personnel including Canaris, Sack, Piekenbrock, Bentivegni, Klamroth, and Duesterberg, the majority agreed with a negative judgment concerning Roeder. In his complaint Duesterberg also mentioned that Roeder had called the troops serving the *Abwehr,* the "Brandenburg" division, a "bunch of shirkers." This reached the ears of their commander, General von Pfuhlstein. In his own written vindication Dohnanyi also stated that he had heard this expression from Roeder. Pfuhlstein had this confirmed to him when Dohnanyi was admitted to the Charité and could have special visitors. He went afterward to Roeder, who had been moved and promoted, and slapped him. As far as the case was concerned the Roeder era was over. In February 1944 Kutzner took over.

This brought a complete change in the manner of the investigation, but it did not diminish the threat to Dohnanyi. Keitel's prejudice against the Reich Central Security Office remained undiminished. This bias had led Dr. Langbehn to try to obtain a declaration from Himmler and Müller that the Reich Central Security Office had no further political interest in the case. Such a declaration would have encouraged Keitel to order that the whole affair be dropped. But Langbehn himself was arrested as he was preparing this step—a critical moment for Christine von Dohnanyi, who hastily had to destroy everything that might point to her connection with Langbehn.

The Charité. Eventually Keitel went so far that he withdrew the order that had eased the prison rules; this had been permitted because of Dohnanyi's illness.

Dohnanyi's health had been seriously affected by the constant strain. In the summer of 1943 he became severely ill. In June he developed an inflammation of the veins in both legs. The family attempted to bring in Dr. Sauerbruch, the leading German surgeon in Berlin, for consultation, but Roeder was able to prevent it at the time.

On the night of 23 November 1943 the heavy British bombing attacks began again, and the prison received its first direct hit. Dohnanyi's cell was struck by an incendiary bomb. He was found with disturbed speech and vision; he was suffering from a brain embolism. The next morning Sack got Dr. Lehmann—Roeder's telephone was out of order—to have Dohnanyi transferred on his own responsibility to Sauerbruch's clinic at the Charité hospital. Only two days later a furious Roeder confronted Sauerbruch at the Charité. Sauerbruch, however, declared that Dohnanyi's life was in danger due to the embolism, and refused to let him be moved. Unfortunately for Roeder, important military court documents had perished in the flames during the night raid. Roeder now gave orders that no one was to visit Dohnanyi aside from his wife and children. Nevertheless, Sauerbruch and his assistant Dr. Wohlgemuth permitted infringements of this order and concealed them.

Thus all of Dohnanyi's closest friends eventually made their way through the blackout to his bedside: Klaus Bonhoeffer and Rüdiger Schleicher, Perels, Delbrück, Guttenberg, and Otto John. Dohnanyi learned of the progress that had been made since October 1943 in the coup plans. Klaus Bonhoeffer and Otto John now belonged to the inner circle of conspirators and were working with Josef Wirmer and Jakob Kaiser. Using contacts that went through Spain, John provided Stauffenberg with information.

During those winter days new dates for the overthrow were set and then changed. Young officers like Axel von dem Bussche and a son of the Kleists of Schmenzin wanted to use an occasion when new uniforms were presented before Hitler to assassinate him. But the uniforms were burned in a bombing raid and the date for displaying them had to be changed. Still, after so many reversals, there was news that could cheer up Dohnanyi.

Several weeks after Roeder's first visit to Sauerbruch he sent some men with an ambulance to the Charité to collect Dohnanyi. Sauerbruch would not let them near his patient and ejected them from the clinic. But now Roeder convinced Keitel to ask Professor Max de Crinis to give an opinion on Dohnanyi's condition. De Crinis, Karl Bonhoeffer's successor at the university and now the director of the neurological clinic in the Charité, held a leadership position in the S.S. and was a close confidant of Schellenberg in the Reich Central Security Office. He provided the desired report. On 22 January 1944, while Sauerbruch was away, Roeder and a military doctor appeared in Dohnanyi's sickroom and removed him to the prison hospital in Buch. On 10 February 1944 de Crinis told the Reich Central Security Office:

> Group *Führer!* . . . As a result of my investigation von Dohnanyi was removed from the Charité Clinic and taken to the special hospital in Buch. . . . As you will see from my report, I have stated that Special Officer von Dohnanyi is fit to be tried and I estimate that he will be in eight to ten days. . . . Heil Hitler! Yours, de Crinis. Please inform District Chief Kaltenbrunner of this communication.

Playing Things Down. With this development the case looked less promising—despite the longed-for removal of Roeder, who was promoted to be a military judge with an air fleet in the Balkans. The Gestapo's interest did not seem to have diminished at all.

At the same time, there was more bad news from the circle of Dohnanyi's friends: Moltke and the Solf circle were arrested. Worst of all was Canaris's dismissal in February 1944, as the result of a totally unexpected event, a desertion from the *Abwehr* in Turkey. The Reich Central Security Office had achieved its aim; the entire *Abwehr* organization was placed under its jurisdiction.[9] Of even greater significance for Dohnanyi was the fact that Delbrück and Guttenberg had to leave the *Abwehr* network.

Despite this, Sack's strategy to let the case run out of steam was still successful. Not everything in the *Abwehr* changed overnight. Colonel Hansen, a coconspirator, continued to direct the military *Abwehr* as head of a department within the Reich Central Security Office until his involvement in the conspiracy became evident after the 20 July attempt.

Dohnanyi was acquainted with the new investigator, Kutzner, from his days at the Ministry of Justice and the Supreme Court in Leipzig. Kutzner handled the case without the political zeal of his predecessor. He, too, was under political pressure; still, he told Sack that nothing would come of Roeder's charges, either legally or practically. We may assume—as Christine von Dohnanyi believed—that Kutzner suspected the real situation; he was now working toward a trial with the political sting taken out of it. Christine von Dohnanyi was able to visit her husband regularly in Buch. Dr. Schulze zur Wiesche, who was very close to Perels, worked together with Dohnanyi in Buch on his written defense. Since Dohnanyi was not yet fit to be interrogated again, Josef Müller's trial was carried out as a separate case, concluding with the astonishing verdict of acquittal "because his innocence had been proved." Throughout, Müller maintained the position of "ignorance of who was responsible for what in the *Abwehr*" and successfully portrayed his assigned travels as counterespionage by the *Abwehr*. For a while Dohnanyi and Bonhoeffer regarded as a bluff Kaltenbrunner's threat to send Müller to a concentration camp if the verdict were confirmed. They urged that their own cases be concluded, since they believed that the situation at the state military court favored them. But Sack warned them against this. Then, in June 1944, Dohnanyi contracted a serious case of scarlet fever with diphtheria and peripheral paralysis. He had to be taken to the quarantined prison hospital in Potsdam. Kutzner could speak with him only through an insulated window.

Because the coup was expected daily, Sack was feverishly active. He obtained a postponement for the execution of Klaus Bonhoeffer's friend, Nikolaus von Halem, who had been condemned to death by the People's Court. At the beginning of July he got word to the sick Dohnanyi that Kutzner had finally asked Keitel to suspend the whole case. The suggestion was that Dohnanyi's trial should be postponed until the end of the war and that he should be interned in a sanatorium, thus remaining out of reach of the Gestapo. The strategy of "playing it down" was working. Then came 20 July 1944.

In the Hands of the Gestapo. On 21 July 1944 Dohnanyi's case fell entirely into the hands of the Gestapo. The defense ring in the legal department of the army was smashed, and Sack himself was among those condemned to death.

At 7:30 A.M. Criminal Commissioner Sonderegger, who had accompanied Roeder on 5 April 1943, called at the Bonhoeffer home on Marienburger Allee and inquired about Dohnanyi. The father referred him to his daughter Christine. Sonderegger also asked her about Oster, but she said she knew nothing about him. Dohnanyi's isolation in quarantine gave even the Gestapo difficulties. Karl Bonhoeffer was allowed to visit his son-in-law once again in his professional capacity as a doctor:

> I was able to see Hans last week. He is in a lamentable condition because of the appalling diphtherial paralysis which is, however, somewhat better in his face and throat, but still continues in his arms, legs and trunk and makes him almost incapable of moving. We may certainly expect that he will recover, but it is a terrible burden and test of patience for him and for Christel. Dietrich is in good health, and we hope to see him in the next few days. No doubt he suffers greatly from being isolated in these eventful times and finds it hard to concentrate on Dilthey, whom he is now studying for his *Ethics*.[10]

Only on 22 August did Sonderegger dare remove Dohnanyi from Potsdam in an ambulance and take him to the concentration camp of Sachsenhausen. For the first time, this stopped all contact between Dohnanyi and his wife for some time. On 5 October 1944 Huppenkothen entered the sickroom of the concentration camp and threw a document on Dohnanyi's bed, saying, "There! At last we've got the evidence against you we've been seeking for two years." Dohnanyi replied, "Oh, have you? Where did you find that?"[11] Huppenkothen had been assigned to examine the material that Sonderegger had found in Zossen on 20 or 22 September. In the document thrown onto Dohnanyi's bed there were photocopies of Dohnanyi's memorandum for the generals from the winter of 1939–1940, and a call to the German people he had written for Beck.

From this day on Dohnanyi made his sickness a weapon, the only one he had left. With superhuman energy he studied and practiced its symptoms in order to prolong them for as long as might be necessary. Perhaps in this way he would be able to prevent the destruction of those whose fate was linked to his until after the moment of the collapse of Nazi Germany. In this he almost succeeded.

The Investigation of Bonhoeffer

During his interrogations while awaiting trial Bonhoeffer did not have as much to conceal or take responsibility for as Dohnanyi. But much depended on how precisely Bonhoeffer held to the agreed rules of procedure. The slightest carelessness or discrepancy in his story could ruin everything; to have pursued his own course because of his profession or for reasons of private integrity would have been a genuine betrayal.

Thus Bonhoeffer accepted his situation, which had been decided and reflected on for a long time, and drew the consequences. His Lutheran tradition provided no guidance. "At first I wondered a good deal whether it was really for the cause of Christ that I was causing you all such grief; but I soon put that out of my head as a temptation . . . and accepted it cheerfully [that is, enduring his borderline situation], and have continued to do so until today."[12] The conspirators' battle was to be continued in prison under new conditions, but with the old skill and alertness.

Bonhoeffer had some fears about his physical and mental sensitivity in the face of possible torture. But it became clear that the new task brought with it the required strength. From the first day, he kept himself physically fit by doing exercises and eating whatever nourishing food his family and friends sent to his cell. At no stage in the long struggle did he give up his conviction that by his endurance he was sharing in a great cause: "The thing for which I should be condemned is so irreproachable that I may only be proud of it."[13]

Until 20 July 1944 Bonhoeffer calculated again and again that there were good reasons why his case should have a favorable outcome. Sometimes he even thought that his imprisonment would soon come to an end. There were both internal and external reasons for this. In a healthy sense of self-preservation, the natural instinct of a political prisoner is to continually set new dates for his release; hundreds of people in similar circumstances at the time did the same thing. But Bonhoeffer could base his optimism on the favorable course of the investigation, which naturally sometimes made him more impatient instead of more hopeful. Moreover, just like Dohnanyi, he was constantly informed about fresh preparations for the overthrow. Things went so far that his uncle, General von Hase, the city commandant of Berlin, ostentatiously visited his imprisoned nephew in Tegel. After this, Bonhoeffer wrote me on 30 June 1944: "I hope we shall be together again in the autumn!"[14]

Bonhoeffer's period at Tegel can be divided into three sections. The first, from April to July 1943, was taken up with the interrogation by Roeder and ended with the charge being filed. The second, from August 1943 to April 1944, was marked by his continually renewed hopes that there would be a trial; dates were fixed and then canceled. In the third, from April to September 1944, he accepted the strategy of "letting the case run out of steam."

In this period he concentrated once more on theology. After the discovery of the Zossen material, this period concluded with an escape plan and his eventual transfer to the Gestapo prison on Prinz-Albrecht-Strasse.

Fighting Chances. Bonhoeffer's basic hard struggle for his case came during the first of the three phases mentioned, between April and August 1943.

Under interrogation, what helped him in the first weeks of total isolation was holding to what the conspirators had carefully agreed upon: the strategy of pushing all responsibility for details onto those who gave the orders in the *Abwehr,* namely, Canaris, Oster, and Dohnanyi. In this way Bonhoeffer came through without involving himself in any serious contradictions.

Then began the prearranged passing of information from prison to prison through his family and friends. One way in which it was done was by making particular marks on the pages of the reading matter that Bonhoeffer, as a prisoner held for interrogation, was allowed to receive. For instance, Bonhoeffer asked for a volume by Karl Holl to be sent him from home. If the owner's name, "D. Bonhoeffer," was underlined in the book, that meant that it contained a message. The message was entered by putting a faint pencil mark under a letter every ten pages, starting from the back. The letters marked in this way formed, for instance, the sentence: "O. now officially acknowledges the Rome coding card," so that Bonhoeffer could now argue with confidence about the business of the slips of paper, if necessary. He replied in a similar way when he returned the book. Thus he once marked the message: "I'm not certain that the letter with Hans's corrections has been found, but think so." This referred to the issue of military exemption, especially Bonhoeffer's letter of complaint to the Gestapo of September 1940. The family sat for hours deciphering the messages, so that they could be taken to Dohnanyi, or Perels and Sack, or Delbrück and Canaris.

In Tegel prison the isolation to which Bonhoeffer was first condemned was eased after a short period. The fact that the prisoner was related to the city commandant of Berlin had become generally known, and the attitude of the wardens changed. Bonhoeffer's mother had asked her cousin to telephone Tegel. Suddenly, Bonhoeffer became a kind of star prisoner. The prison commandant, Captain Maetz, an official who always tried to do the right thing, gradually extended permission for his parents and his fiancée to visit him for the maximum period, if approved by the investigating magistrate, and also allowed him to receive vital packages. But above all, Bonhoeffer won the hearts of some of the guards, who ended up doing everything for him, carrying out the most dangerous assignments as go-betweens on his behalf. In June 1944, for example, it was possible for me to have a whole hour with him in the visitor's cell alone, when he had permission to receive a visitor, so that we were able to discuss many things unhindered. One of the wardens shut us in together. Roeder suspected that things were going on behind his back, even mentioning this to Commandant Maass at the prison on Lehrter Strasse, but he never found anything out. Even the Gestapo was not able to discover anything later. None of the kindly disposed guards ever betrayed anything, nor was one ever betrayed by the others.

After his initial severity Roeder behaved in a far more dignified way with Bonhoeffer than with his legal colleague Dohnanyi. Formally Bonhoeffer appeared to be far more cooperative than he actually was. He portrayed himself as a pastor unfamiliar with military and *Abwehr* matters:

> I am the last person to deny that I might have made mistakes in work so strange, so new and so complicated as that of the *Abwehr*. I often find it hard to follow the speed of your questions, probably because I am not used to them.[15]

Bonhoeffer used his inexperience as a weapon of defense. In contrast to the fears of many of those involved, he was not so ignorant that he made any disastrous mistakes. His triumphant remark in a letter to me on 30 November 1943 was justified: "Roeder was too anxious at first to finish me for good; but now he has to content himself with a most ridiculous charge, which will bring him little glory."[16]

During the period of interrogation Bonhoeffer used up a lot of paper in his cell writing drafts of letters to Roeder, in which he supplemented or corrected his statements after a hearing. Roeder had occasionally encouraged him to make these notes, and Bonhoeffer seized the opportunity to gain time and ponder how to build the edifice of his stories further. The notes that have been preserved give a fairly exact picture of what was at stake in this tiny corner of the resistance's fight, the way in which Bonhoeffer defended himself and concealed the real facts of the conspiracy, what he produced and what he suppressed. His fragmentary essay, "What Is Meant by 'Telling the Truth'?"[17] emerged during these months, and the notes reveal something of the true background of that study. Their confusing content mercilessly shows the consequences of the conspirators' struggle. The fact that Bonhoeffer wrote his essay in those weeks shows how much he was aware of his dilemma, and that he did not seek to pretend or hide anything from himself. He did something else. He could have destroyed his drafts, except for a few references to fact; instead he preserved them carefully and gave them to his parents to look after when he cleared his cell of its accumulated objects after 20 July.

The notes established the extent to which the investigation against Bonhoeffer paralleled that against Dohnanyi, covering the same four points: (1) his military exemption, as a means of escaping observation by the Gestapo, in order to be able to continue his church work; (2) "Operation 7," which was to save Charlotte Friedenthal, among others, who worked for the Confessing church; (3) the journeys, which were suspected to have been unrelated to Military Intelligence; and (4) the flagrant exemption from military service of officials of the Confessing church.[18] Each one of these points could approach what the investigation assumed from the beginning was "high treason and treason against the nation." But the investigation never uncovered the real facts of the conspiracy.

The Abwehr *Exemption.* The circumstances and the date of Bonhoeffer's exemption to serve in the *Abwehr* took up most of the interrogation. He was first accused of evading military service in September 1940, with the help of the *Abwehr,* and of seeking to circumvent the Gestapo ban on his public speaking and its requirement that he register with the police.

Bonhoeffer argued that the best way for him to escape the Gestapo, if further interference from it was to be expected, would have been regular enlistment in the military. He argued that the Gestapo's action was not directed against him alone, but was part of a routine injunction against six theologians, of whom he was one. Moreover, as he said,

> in order to avoid all further conflict, I withdrew into the Bavarian mountains in order to write a major scholarly work. I had informed the Gestapo, as was obligatory, and really had nothing more to fear from this quarter at all. . . . It was my brother-in-law who suggested to me that, with my church connections, I should enter the service of the *Abwehr.* Despite considerable inner scruples, I took advantage of his offer because it provided me with the war work that I had wanted ever since the beginning of hostilities, even making use of my ability as a theologian.[19]

With this explanation of a positive desire to serve, he countered the charge that he joined the *Abwehr* immediately after the Gestapo measures:

> This had meant a great inner release, since I saw it as a welcome opportunity to rehabilitate myself in the eyes of the state authorities, which I was anxious to do in view of the offensive and, to me, completely unjustified charge against me. The knowledge that I was being used by a military department was, therefore, to me of great importance personally. I made a great sacrifice for this chance of rehabilitation and for my work in the

service of the Reich, namely, by offering all my ecumenical connections for military use. I think that this idea of my rehabilitation played a role with my brother-in-law as well. He knows me well enough to realize that the political charge against me bore no relation to my own inner feelings and to know how much I suffered from it . . . Perhaps I may add that if I had really only wanted a dispensation in order to continue with church work, I could certainly have obtained this in Schlawe at the superintendent's request. . . .[20] But in January 1941, I received the dispensation, not for church work, but expressly for work in the *Abwehr* . . . How could it ever occur to me that there was any objection to my being made available for the *Abwehr,* since Admiral Canaris had desired and given the order for it, as was explicitly confirmed to me. When I asked sometimes whether the fact that I was regarded as persona non grata by the Gestapo could not cause difficulties, both for the *Abwehr* and for myself, I was told that these things had nothing to do with my military function and that the *Abwehr* worked with all kinds of people who were useful to it. This completely reassured me.[21]

Next to "all kinds of people" Bonhoeffer had first written "we work with enemies, Communists, Jews—why not with the Confessing church," but then crossed it out.

Roeder attacked from another quarter. It was not only to escape the Gestapo, but also to be able to continue with his church work; Roeder made the point that General Superintendent Dibelius had declared that he had been told this about Bonhoeffer. Bonhoeffer did not find this difficult to answer:

When meeting colleagues that I had largely avoided for this reason during the last years . . . I also found it difficult to talk about my present work. Insofar as they knew and asked about my ties to my brother-in-law, as General Superintendent Dibelius and Superintendent Diestel did, for example, I always told them—as I had arranged with my brother-in-law— that I was working for the Supreme Military Command in Munich and abroad on church assignments, as the Supreme Military Command was interested in church and ecumenical questions. Even Dibelius could not know that I was working for Military Intelligence, but could only deduce it; for, quite intentionally, I never told him. I also had to preserve the fiction that my work was primarily for the church, which—apart from security reasons—I did for the sake of the other pastors, to whose ears it might have come and done me harm. Hence I took care that my exemption was understood in this way in church circles. That it threw a rather strange light on me and on the military department concerned couldn't be helped. So Dibelius's evidence will also have been along these lines.[22]

As a matter of fact, Dibelius told me on 13 October 1961, "I was never interrogated by the War Court. What I said to Bonhoeffer about his exemption has never, I think, been divulged to anyone." Roeder's unscrupulous, unreal, and hence unintelligent way in trying to play off the so-called confessions of his victims against one another emerged from a note Dohnanyi made in this context for his defense, probably in August 1943:

> In one of my interrogations, Roeder said that Dietrich had "confessed" that he had been in constant touch with Dibelius, who had provided him with news of church politics and that he had passed these on to me. Since the latter statement is not true, the former isn't either. Alas, one of Roeder's many bluffs.

Bonhoeffer countered the charges concerning his exemption from military service, which arose as a result of statements made in autumn 1942 by Schmidhuber, the Munich consul, by calling his knowledge one-sided. He met Schmidhuber as a fellow prisoner in Tegel and was able to harmonize his own story with his. Bonhoeffer noted down the following for Roeder:

> I know . . . that he did not want Schmidhuber to know anything about the military assignments that I received directly from the Admiral. . . . I myself have certainly often expressed my joy at the opportunity they gave me to cultivate my ecumenical relations. It is no different from when a student or a chemist is sent abroad, for example, and is able to work where he finds it interesting and at the same time has particular military assignments to carry out.[23]

When it became clearer what the charges were going to be, probably around the end of June 1943, Bonhoeffer explicitly returned once more to the question of his exemption. In his statement he now appealed to the popular understanding of Romans 13 as expressing faith in authority, a view which, in fact, he pointedly opposed.

> As an argument it certainly may not have any cogency for you—but perhaps you will believe me personally, and it is with this hope that I say that it is very difficult for me to see how the earlier conflicts with the Gestapo, which, as I profoundly believe, emerged from a purely church position, led to my being held capable of such a grave offense against the obvious duties of a German toward his people and his Reich. I still cannot believe that this is the charge that is really leveled against me. In that case, would I have turned to an old officer's family, all of whose fathers and sons have been in the field since the beginning of the war, many of them winning the high-

est decorations and making the greatest sacrifice of life and limb, to find my future wife, who has herself lost both her father and her brother at the front? Would I have abandoned all the commitments that I had undertaken in America and returned to Germany before the outbreak of war, where I naturally would expect to be called up at once? Would I have volunteered as an army chaplain immediately after the war broke out? . . . If people want to know my idea of the Christian's duty of obedience toward authority, they should read my interpretations of Romans 13 in my book, *Discipleship*. The call to submit to the will and demands of authority for the sake of Christian conscience has probably seldom been expressed more strongly than there. This is my personal position on these questions. I cannot judge how much such personal arguments mean legally, but I cannot think they can be simply ignored.[24]

"Operation 7." The interrogations concerning the transport of fourteen Jews to Switzerland focused on the beginning of June 1943. Here Bonhoeffer had to be careful not to harm Dohnanyi's and Canaris's defense. He could rightly maintain that his part in the operation was only peripheral. He was responsible for including Charlotte Friedenthal in the group and also, by introducing Schmidhuber to Koechlin, for making it possible for the fourteen to travel to Switzerland. Thus he did not deny that he was concerned on behalf of someone who worked for the Confessing church and had asked Schmidhuber to help. "I shall not deny for a moment that in this whole case the charity and caring attitude of the church played an important part for me."[25]

There was a tough struggle between Roeder and Bonhoeffer concerning the exact moment at which Schmidhuber had been sent to Koechlin and at which Bonhoeffer had spoken to Friedenthal. The reason for this was that the accused members of the *Abwehr* were anxious that the date should be given as early as possible, that is, before the beginning of the deportation of the Jews from Berlin, so as to substantiate their claim that it was a genuine military operation and not a charitable work by the *Abwehr*. But Roeder sought to establish a later date so that he could prove that there had been collusion to camouflage what was going on: sabotage of the Jewish policy of the Nazis. In his oral interrogation Bonhoeffer had been led first to admit that the event took place on an indefinite date in spring of 1942. This is why he later corrected himself in writing to Roeder and stated definitely that he had sent Schmidhuber very soon after August 1941—and certainly before the deportation began.

"Operation 7" soon disappeared from the interrogation because Canaris explicitly covered it. Bonhoeffer could say to Roeder with a clear conscience:

> Fräulein Friedenthal . . . visited me once briefly and asked me if I thought
> that she could legitimately carry out the assignment which she presumed
> would be given her. At the time I said "yes." She spoke only of the fact of
> the assignment, not of its specific nature. I have never known what it
> was.[26]

He could say that quite honestly because the assignment had never had "a
specific nature."

The Journeys. In Bonhoeffer's notes made in Tegel in 1943 the foreign travels play a remarkably small part. Right up to September 1944 the investigation never came anywhere near the true facts.

Roeder was concerned primarily with why, how often, and how long
Bonhoeffer had stayed in Berlin between his assignments, a city from which
he had been banned by the Gestapo. Had he really been there in order to
resume church work? Bonhoeffer noted:

> I had to be in Berlin constantly for the following official reasons: 1. before
> and after every journey; 2. to make preparations for particular journeys
> which sometimes took a long time; 3. I was expressly told that I should be
> at the disposal of Admiral Canaris for special assignments, and so I was
> frequently asked for addresses, introductions and advice.[27]

Bonhoeffer described in detail to the investigating magistrate how the
long stay in Berlin from April to June 1941 was taken up with futile preparations for a trip to Sweden, because, among other things, the contacts with
Forell were unsuccessful. It was fortunate that Bonhoeffer was able to explain
a long stay in Berlin in the winter of 1941–1942 by saying he had pneumonia. In the autumn of 1942 Schmidhuber's arrest had forced the central
Abwehr office several times to make new plans:

> I myself repeatedly asked to be allowed to do some more traveling, as my
> military inactivity was becoming frustrating. I have already offered the
> personal reasons for my liking Berlin—that is, my books, which I needed
> for my work, and my elderly parents, whom I didn't want to leave more
> than necessary, especially in view of the air-raid warnings.[28]

The very full treatment in the hearing of Bonhoeffer's exemption from
military service was quite disproportionate to these meager findings concerning his foreign travel. It was only the problem of the exemption, and not
of the travel, that became the subject of Roeder's charges. This proves how

well Bonhoeffer and others managed to keep the conspiracy out of the danger zone. But above all it shows that the discovery during Dohnanyi's arrest of the note (with a new travel assignment for Bonhoeffer) signed with Beck's fateful "O" has been greatly overestimated in later accounts.

Niesel's Exemption. Bonhoeffer's attempts to use the *Abwehr* to free Confessing church officials for the service of the church took up far more of the hearing than his contacts abroad. Such church people were either brought directly into the *Abwehr,* as with Rott and myself, or through influencing other departments in the army high command to take them, as was the case with Wilhelm Niesel, Ernst Wolf, and Wilhelm Jannasch's son. After civil departments had been "combed through" to obtain recruits to replace the men lost at Stalingrad, and after the penalties for the evasion of military service became more severe, authorities were especially nervous on this score.

Among Roeder's finds during his 5 April search was a letter from Bonhoeffer to Dohnanyi, anxiously requesting help for Wilhelm Niesel, who was "threatened" with conscription. To Roeder the word "threatened" clearly supported the argument that Bonhoeffer had indulged in antimilitary activities. At the end of June 1943 Bonhoeffer wrote to Roeder:

> I must admit that (the word "threaten") taken by itself does make a very disagreeable impression. On the other hand, I should like to say the following: 1. If a man like Niesel had come under an officially recognized church authority, it would undoubtedly have declared him indispensable for purely church reasons. 2. Only a church whose faith has an inner strength can perform its grave service on behalf of its country during a war; but the church then needs some of its strong powers at home. . . . Whatever one thinks of the Confessing church, one thing can never be said without completely misunderstanding it, namely, that it ever regarded "conscription" as a "threat." The hundreds of young Confessing church pastors who volunteered and the large proportion of them who laid down their lives are sufficiently eloquent testimony to the contrary. Nor have I ever spoken to a single pastor of the Confessing church who did not joyfully embrace his enlistment as an inner liberation from the burden of political suspicion that rested upon the Confessing church, as a long-sought opportunity of proving his own position and readiness for self-sacrifice as a soldier. The fact that Pastor Niemöller volunteered for military service right at the beginning of the war had its effect on the Confessing church. . . . Because we can have a very clear conscience on this point, I thought that in a particularly urgent case such as Niesel's, I might and indeed had to preserve a pastor for the service of his church and his country, provided that this could be justified on military grounds. It was

not my job to know about the latter, which is why I consulted my brother-in-law. Many of my former pupils who have now been killed or are still on the front as soldiers have said that despite their joy in serving their country, they have only one anxiety, namely, that during this period the churches at home should not be left completely untended. . . . Two things influenced my action: I know that even religious people can have very different opinions about the church, but, particularly in wartime, no one should deny that the motivating force behind its conviction and its action is love of the German people and the desire to serve it during the war in the best possible way. Since the beginning of the war I have had several long discussions with Minister Gürtner, whom I knew personally, and asked that the church struggle be resolved and that the various sections of the Evangelical church should work together. I made suggestions to Dr. Gürtner on this subject, which he then discussed with Kerrl, the Minister for Church Affairs, who welcomed them with interest. In December 1940, during a walk together in Ettal which lasted several hours, Dr. Gürtner explicitly told me that he hoped to achieve this and discussed how he proposed doing so. His death one month later and the illness and death of Minister Kerrl have destroyed this hope. It was an attempt to establish peace within the church during the war, in order to make the maximum energy available for the war effort. Even this unsuccessful attempt means that I can believe I did everything possible to achieve the smoothest and greatest possible war effort on the part of the church.[29]

The side of the Confessing church that Bonhoeffer regarded as the most dubious had to serve here as his defense.

The Charges. The deeper suspicions of both Roeder and the Reich Central Security Office had not been entirely alleviated on any of the four counts: Bonhoeffer's military exemption, "Operation 7," Bonhoeffer's travels, or the military exemptions. The initial charges of high treason and treason against his country, however, could not be sustained. Only in autumn of 1944 did more substantial proof of this arise.

After Keitel's order not to proceed with the case on the basis of this suspicion, Roeder ended his interrogation of Bonhoeffer. On 30 July he told him that charges would now be filed and that Bonhoeffer should find someone to defend him. This was in marked contrast to Dohnanyi, whom Roeder threatened a few days later, saying that he would not permit him to choose his own defense lawyer. Bonhoeffer immediately wrote his parents two letters that were censored by Roeder:

30 July 1943. Dear Father and Mother, At our session today in the War Court Dr. Roeder gave me permission to write to you and to Rüdiger Goltz on the subject of my defense. Since I don't know Rüdiger's exact address in Bavaria, I wanted to ask you to contact him. I don't know whether he can do it himself because of the injury to his leg, which I hear has become worse. But he's sure to be able to recommend someone suitable. Dr. Roeder thought the defense lawyer would need one day on the documents, another for consulting with me, and another for the hearing, that is, three days in all. This is not a lot, but I imagine you too, Father, know many lawyers. And of course you know Dr. Sack[30] from the Lubbe case. But I wonder if such a "big gun" would really take on a case which must seem trivial to him. He's also supposed to be terribly expensive. I only wanted to remind you of this and can't judge it myself. I'm thinking in terms of a calm, experienced, older man who is not committed in the matter of church politics, someone who can be trusted as a lawyer and a person. I don't know anyone myself, but you'll find the right person. It would be nice if you could clarify this matter soon. By the way, I can write to you every four days now, which is wonderful for me. I think I'll alternate between you and Maria. Thank you for everything and please don't be worried. With love to you and all the family, your Dietrich.[31]

This was a carefully considered text. Bonhoeffer was making hints about his excellent connections to the investigating magistrate who read the letter. Von der Goltz, who had once defended Goebbels, was still regarded highly by Hitler. On the other hand, Bonhoeffer was telling his parents that none of the well-known Confessing church lawyers, such as Hans Holstein, should be brought in. In the letter of 3 August, which also passed through Roeder's hands, he indicated a certain disappointment:

As far as my request for a lawyer is concerned, I hope that you have not been worried, but are awaiting the course of events as calmly as I am. You really mustn't think that I am in any way depressed or worried. Of course it was a disappointment, as no doubt for you as well. But in some ways it is also a liberation to know that now the thing for which we have been waiting so long will be finally settled. I'm waiting daily for definite news. . . . If Rüdiger Goltz is not free on such short notice, it doesn't matter. Dr. Roeder explicitly said that it's something that any decent lawyer could do, and I'm happy as long as it's a competent, decent and warmhearted man, and a calm and dignified negotiator who will preserve the polished tone of the hearings, and you are the best judge of that. Personally, I think that it's best to say oneself what one has to say, but a lawyer is necessary for the legal matters, of which I know nothing. [He later added the following, which was meant sincerely.] . . . it would be good if the man took some time for me and wasn't too hasty. I think a lawyer ought to be like a doctor, who should never give the impression that he has too much to do.[32]

The charge against him now was that the exemptions of Bonhoeffer and Niesel had been an antimilitary act. All the other points were dropped; this is clear from Bonhoeffer's final letter to Roeder:

> Dear Herr Supreme War Court Counsel, You have allowed me to write you again, and I want to do so today for the last time before the trial. In the three days since you told me that I was going to be charged, I have taken your advice and tried to go over the whole affair in peace and quiet. I won't bother you with personal matters. I don't need to tell you what a charge against me of acting against the war effort means to me professionally and personally as far as my family is concerned; you know my professional and personal situation well enough. If the law demands that the charge should be made, then it must; I understand. Perhaps I didn't expect it because I was unfamiliar with the text of the law and also because I felt innocent of the charge and, having considered what you told me on Friday, still do. . . .[33]

A detailed justification followed in which Bonhoeffer stated how he viewed the two points of the charge—his own exemption and the attempt to help Niesel. Canaris knew and could answer for why he had been taken on by the *Abwehr,* and Dohnanyi would explain why they wanted to keep Niesel working for the church. In the meantime, Bonhoeffer's words about this had been conveyed to Dohnanyi.

Some weeks later Dr. Wergin, an excellent lawyer and a friend of Klaus Bonhoeffer, accepted the brief to defend Bonhoeffer. The War Court, now moved to Torgau, confirmed him as defense lawyer on 16 September 1943. After that Wergin was able to visit Bonhoeffer regularly in Tegel. Things seemed to be going well.

The Notes. The written notes that Bonhoeffer preserved from his bitter struggle to cover up and camouflage the conspiracy are important documents in giving a complete picture of his role in the conspiracy. To suppress them would be to falsify the true character of Bonhoeffer's solidarity with the conspirators. The political responsibility involved did not permit any "pious" exceptions. Exceptional times called for exceptional sacrifices.

Bonhoeffer did not for a moment refuse to sacrifice his integrity, but he did not do this easily. He thought it possible that his church, as the guardian of bourgeois morality and as an institution never before confronted by this kind of challenge, would hesitate to view him as one of its own. To do so would mean acquiring a new perspective. He wrote to me about this on 15 December 1943:

> Then[34] I should discuss with you whether you think that this trial, which has associated me with the *Abwehr* (I hardly think that has remained a secret), might prevent me from taking up my ministry again later on. At present you are the only person with whom I can discuss this question, and perhaps we shall be able to talk it over together if you are allowed to see me. Please think it over, and give me your candid opinion.[35]

This discussion took place. I myself was already too deeply involved in the reality of this situation, and did not argue against it. But I posed Bonhoeffer's question to his friend Hans Lokies, the head of the Gossner mission, and then gave Bonhoeffer the answer on 2 January 1944:

> He did not see any problem at the point when all the disguises are dropped, and as yet no one in authority or anywhere else has been able to deal seriously with this issue because of their ignorance. Nor did he think that there was a definite general mood against you, because the prestige that you enjoy as a theologian is too great and uncontested.[36]

But Bonhoeffer still knew what difficulties were in the way. He realized that the Old Prussian Council of Brethren could not place him on the intercessory prayer list. He was all the more delighted when he heard that the Breslau Confessing synod had remembered him by name in its prayers on 17 October 1943.[37]

He personally never doubted the course he had chosen and the opening of new insights. He calmly adopted 1 Peter 3:14 for himself: "But even if you do suffer for righteousness' sake, you will be blessed. Have no fear of them, nor be troubled."[38] And this serenity was combined with his words of Christmas 1942:

> Will our inward power of resistance be strong enough, and our honesty with ourselves remorseless enough, for us to find our way back to simplicity and straightforwardness?[39]

It was based on the fact that in his cell he was also able to write:

> "Cast me away! My guilt must bear the wrath of God;
> the righteous shall not perish with the sinner!"

They trembled. But with hands that knew no weakness
they cast the offender from their midst. The sea stood still.[40]

Second Phase: Dates for the Trial. Tensions eased after the charge was filed and
Roeder lost his acute interest in his victim. But the trial of Bonhoeffer's
patience was just beginning.

First he thought that after the last hearing in the War Court the trial
would be over by August. But nothing happened at all, because after the three
severe air raids on Hamburg Goebbels instigated a comprehensive evacuation plan for Berlin. Various courts were moved to Torgau, a small old town
on the river Elbe, sixty miles south of Berlin. This worried his family, for the
threat loomed for several days that Dohnanyi would be moved to Torgau as
well; this would have ended the vital communication between the prisoners
and those helping them. The department with oversight of the War Court
remained where it was, however; only Roeder himself disappeared for long
periods from Berlin.

A regular warrant was not issued against Bonhoeffer until 25 September
1943, when he was officially charged with subversion of the military forces.
This aroused his hopes again for an early trial date. Hassell's diary reveals the
interest of the members of the various resistance groups in the "Dohnanyi
case." In November 1943 Hassell wrote:

> A charge has now been brought against Dohnanyi. [Oster] has seen it and
> told me that there were a few slips on some points, but Goltz, who is to
> defend him, is reasonably optimistic. Politically, nothing seems to have
> crystallized despite the zealous efforts of the nasty prosecutor. [Oster] is
> now also accused because of two people he exempted. It is all part of an
> attack on Admiral Canaris's outfit because it makes the Party so
> uncomfortable.[41]

A possible trial date was set for 17 December 1943, but after Dohnanyi
fell ill this date was abandoned. The idea of proceeding with Bonhoeffer's
case separately was strongly attacked, because they didn't want to expose
Bonhoeffer alone to the imponderables of a trial that concerned *Abwehr*
matters.

Bonhoeffer was very unhappy about this decision and wrote on 18
December:

> As far as I could see, I should have been released on 17 December, but the
> jurists wanted to take the safe course, and now I shall probably be kept here
> for weeks if not months. The past weeks have been more of a strain than
> anything that has gone before that.[42]

Although Bonhoeffer thought that "on purely legal grounds there's basically no chance of a (negative) verdict,"[43] he was under no illusions about the fact that the Gestapo could intervene, with disagreeable consequences.

> I can (I hope) bear all things "in faith," even my condemnation, and even the other consequences that I fear (Ps. 18:29)[44] but to be anxiously looking ahead wears one down. Don't worry about me if something worse happens. Other Christians have already endured it.[45]

There were now hopes for a date in February 1944, after de Crinis declared Dohnanyi "capable of being tried" and Dohnanyi was taken to Buch, and after Josef Müller conducted his own case so well—without, however, succeeding in changing his own situation. Bonhoeffer again faced two possibilities:

> It looks as if something will be decided about me in a week's time. Hopefully. If it turns out that they send me in Martin's direction [Dachau, where Niemöller was], though I don't think that is likely, please put your mind at rest about it. I am really not at all worried as to what happens to me personally. So please don't you worry either.[46]

He was intensely disappointed by the new postponement, and very dissatisfied with his friends outside:

> About myself, I am sorry to have to tell you that I am not likely to be out of here before Easter. As long as Hans is ill, no changes can be taken in hand. I cannot help feeling that there has been a lot of messing about and fantasizing while the simplest things have been left undone. I'm sure that everyone concerned has meant well. . . . I am simply amazed that for the last six months nothing has actually been done, although people have obviously sacrificed a great deal of time and even sleep on my account with their deliberations and their discussions. The one thing that could have taken place automatically   namely that my case be settled before Christmas—has been prevented.[47]

The German title of *Letters and Papers from Prison*, *Widerstand und Ergebung* (resistance and surrender), was taken from this letter. It shows that these themes did not emerge from the grand context of one special day in the conspiracy, but from the agonizing disagreements among his friends concerning the best date for his trial.

Third Phase: Playing It Down. In April 1944 Sack sent final word to the cell in Tegel that Bonhoeffer should no longer count on any change soon through a trial date. This precipitated Bonhoeffer's most important creative period in Tegel. He now decisively began doing theological work.[48] Only now, on 4–5 May, did Bonhoeffer meet Kutzner, the new leader of the investigation. This calmed him, however, more than it aroused new tension:

> Just lately I have been in the city [in the War Court] again a few times; the result has been quite satisfactory. But since the question of the date is still unresolved, I am really losing interest in my case; I often quite forget it for weeks on end.[49]

Excitement was now coming from a quite different quarter: from the preparations for the coup, of which he could only be a passive observer. His expectations rose even more after his uncle, General von Hase, visited the guardroom in Tegel.[50] A week later Bonhoeffer wrote:

> Who knows—it may be that [letter writing] won't have to be too often now, and that we shall see each other sooner than we expect. . . . Very soon now we shall have to think a great deal about our journey together in the summer of 1940, and my last sermons.[51]

This was a hint about the impending coup in the East Prussian general headquarters. Finally, on 16 July, he spoke even more directly. His reference to his brother Klaus meant simply that the conspiracy had reached its goal:

> I am glad that Klaus is in such good spirits; he was so depressed for some time. I think all his worries will soon be over; I very much hope so for his own and the entire family's sake.[52]

The Escape Plan. After the debacle of 20 July 1944 the only church newspaper still permitted to publish wrote:

> The frightful day. While our brave armies, courageous unto death, are struggling manfully to protect their country and to achieve final victory, a handful of infamous officers, driven by their own ambition, ventured on a frightful crime and made an attempt to murder the *Führer*. The *Führer* was saved and thus unspeakable disaster averted from our people. For this we give thanks to God with all our hearts, and pray with all our church congregations for God's assistance [*sic!*] and help in the grave tasks that the *Führer* must perform in these most difficult times.[53]

Thousands in the church read this. For many it was not merely an editorial comment, but expressed their own opinion.

On 21 July Bonhoeffer was certain that his fate had been sealed. In the sick bay of the prison he heard the foreign news broadcasts; from his family he learned that Sonderegger was going after Dohnanyi or, rather, his quarantine station. A rumor that Oster had committed suicide reached Bonhoeffer, and he soon heard that Canaris had been arrested on 23 July. But nothing happened to him for weeks. He continued writing his theological work.

At the end of August a new danger threatened. On 18 August Hans John was arrested. As Rüdiger Schleicher's legal assistant, John had been sent on several journeys within Germany on behalf of the conspiracy. His brother Otto John had been able to escape to Spain in time. On 22 August Dohnanyi was taken to the Sachsenhausen concentration camp. "Renate will have written to you that Hans has meanwhile gone into the hospital in Brother [Kurt] Scharf's parish [i.e., in Sachsenhausen]. I am so sorry for Christel and for him; but perhaps he will have the advantage of quicker treatment. Please don't ever get anxious or worried about me, but don't forget to pray for me."[54] For safety Christine von Dohnanyi asked the people who were writing Bonhoeffer to stop this secret correspondence, smuggled via some of the guards. Bonhoeffer himself did not follow this advice for another month.

After the family's general situation rapidly deteriorated because of the discovery of the Zossen files, Bonhoeffer seriously began to consider a plan for escape; previously this had been only a vague idea. His most loyal guard, Corporal Knobloch, a worker from the north of Berlin, agreed to "disappear" with him. Other members of the conspiracy tried the same thing; only a few, such as Jakob Kaiser, succeeded in getting away. Knobloch wanted to go out the gate with Bonhoeffer while on duty and then disappear with him; the family obtained a mechanic's uniform for Dietrich. On Sunday, 24 September, Rüdiger and Ursula Schleicher drove to Berlin-Niederschönhausen with their daughter Renate Bethge and handed Knobloch a packet with the clothing, as well as money and food coupons, so that they could be left for the escapees in a summer garden house. Everything seemed ready for an escape in the first days of October. But the following Saturday put an end to this plan.

When Klaus Bonhoeffer returned home from work on 30 September he saw a suspicious car standing before his garden gate in Eichkamp. He immediately turned around and went to Marienburger Allee, to his sister Ursula Schleicher. One event followed another. That same day General von Hase's wife was released from prison. Her husband had been hanged. She was branded and had nowhere to stay; her own relatives refused to take her in. Ursula Schleicher offered her refuge. At almost this very moment Dietrich's emissary, the guard from Tegel, arrived to discuss details of the escape, false passports, and possible contacts with the chaplain to the Swedish Embassy. There was no time for this; they asked the guard to inform Dietrich of the new turn of events—the impending arrest of Klaus—and to come again soon.

A terrible night followed. Ursula Schleicher and her brother Klaus—his wife Emmi happened to be with her evacuated children in Schleswig-Holstein—struggled to find the solution: flight, suicide, or arrest. The next day, Sunday, 1 October, the Gestapo car appeared at the Marienburger Allee home at the same time church services began. Klaus was taken out of the same house as Dietrich had been eighteen months before, but now under far more ominous circumstances.

On Monday, 2 October the Tegel guard stood before the door again. He said that Dietrich had abandoned the escape plan, to avoid making things more difficult for his brother and exposing his parents and fiancée to additional danger. Two days later, on 4 October, Rüdiger Schleicher was arrested in his office. On 5 October the Gestapo also arrested Friedrich Justus Perels. The same day Dietrich wrote his poem on Jonah.[55]

On Sunday, 8 October Dietrich Bonhoeffer was taken from Tegel to the underground prison of the Reich Central Security Office on Prinz-Albrecht-Strasse. His fellow sufferer, Josef Müller, had been there since 27 September. This was the beginning of a period of totally new investigations.

This discussion of Bonhoeffer's period in Tegel, up to its end with his military arrest, has dealt with only one aspect of it. But Tegel also opened up for Bonhoeffer new areas of experience in life and in his theology. These areas were reflected in the published letters from prison that made him so well known.

The Cell in Tegel

Since his youth Bonhoeffer had been familiar with Tegel, the northwestern suburb of Berlin, because of its beautiful park with Schinkel's little mansion for the Humboldt brethren. Although an attractive area, it was bordered on the south by the Borsig locomotive factories—a target of Allied air attacks—and by a rambling old prison. Here Bonhoeffer lived for a year and a half in a room seven feet by ten with a wooden bed, a bench along the wall, a stool and a bucket, a wooden door with an observation hole to look in from the outside, and a garret window above his head on the other side.

We have more writings by Bonhoeffer from the eighteen months in this cell than we have from any other period of his life; they include notes, letters, scholarly and literary writings. They contain evidence of suffering and anger, but never of self-pity or any scruples about what he was doing:

> Driven and hunted by men,
> They make us helpless and condemn;
> Bearing the burdens of our abusers,
> It is we who are the accusers. . . .[56]

This was the attitude he showed all his visitors. When I once told Frau von Kleist-Retzow of the visit I was allowed to make to Bonhoeffer in June 1944, she replied, "How moving it must have been for you." I mentioned this in a letter to Bonhoeffer, adding: "of course it was 'moving,' but emotion was not our first concern, because we went cheerfully, focused and as quickly as possible in medias res. This is because you have no self-pity and do not, so to speak, look for any recognition of your 'role.'"

Nevertheless, this aesthetically inclined son of an upper-class family did have to wrestle with certain things in his situation, especially at the beginning of his unaccustomed new life. There was much that he did not speak of.

To Justify or Accept Responsibility. About life in prison and the strain of interrogations Bonhoeffer said, "I regard my being kept here . . . as being involved in Germany's fate, as I was resolved to be. I don't look back on the past and accept the present reproachfully."[57] There is surprisingly little mention in Bonhoeffer's papers from prison about why all this had to happen and how it happened. We have mentioned his reflections on his actions in his essay "What Is Meant by 'Telling the Truth'?" His literary writings also discuss the subject. Everything else that we have can be properly understood only in the context of the conspiracy and its consequences. All of it, however, is already the result of a considerable transformation.

Bonhoeffer had good reason to be cautious in giving an account—whether through a formal ethical treatise or in an apologia—of why he continued with the conspiracy during his imprisonment for interrogation. He ran the risk of providing his enemies with welcome material, and this prohibited any written treatment of the matter; but for him to apologize for his actions while he was still involved in them would have been inconsistent with Bonhoeffer's character.

Moreover, why should he justify himself when there was no competent forum he could address? The representatives of the church could not serve as such a forum. They were too unfamiliar with the events and the scope of the extermination of the Jews to be capable of grasping the necessity of the conspirators' involvement. Even the voices of those on the Councils of Brethren were almost silent. The professors of theology and ethics devoted little intellectual consideration to this crisis that confronted all ethics and which would one day lead to the emergence of new principles. The officials, soldiers, or the German public itself could not constitute such a forum, since they had long been complicit, either actively or silently, in the regime's outrages against justice.

Even abroad, there were very few in the ecumenical movement or among the neutral or allied nations who could have constituted a forum where Bonhoeffer would have viewed self-justification as appropriate. In part they were blind to the areas in which they were also complicit, such as in the policy against Jewish refugees. Bonhoeffer knew quite a bit about this. Otherwise, they had not yet experienced that division between loyalty to their government and loyalty to their country, as had the members of the German resistance; thus, those abroad were not in a position to judge.

Bonhoeffer did not set about defending his own actions—but he did want to take responsibility for them. He would have accepted the charge that what he had done was not a "good response" to the challenges of the times, but a very tardy one. His desire to give an account of his extraordinary behavior and enable it to be interpreted properly is evident, among other things, in the fact that he preserved all his notes. He viewed justification, however, as something that only God could do; for Bonhoeffer the responsible position was not to take this justification into his own hands, before, during, and after his actions.

Thus in Tegel he spoke only seldom or indirectly about his actions. The deepest reason was that the nature of his actions required that these occur without explanation and without approval. This occasionally became almost intolerable for him. In a fragment of a drama, written in 1943, his protagonist said:

> Let us learn to do what is just without words for a while. . . . He who knows himself close to death is decisive, but he is also silent. Without words, yes, not understood and alone if need be, he does what is necessary and just, he makes his sacrifice. . . .
>
> What kind of great words are these? Why am I pussyfooting? Why don't I simply say what I mean and know? Or if I don't want to do that, why

don't I keep altogether silent? How hard it is to do what is necessary and what is just completely without words, without being understood.[58]

Shock of the Arrest. The circumstances that accompanied this "wordless action"—namely, life in his cell—were more difficult for Bonhoeffer to cope with at the beginning than he wanted to admit. There was the meager food, the dirt, the thugs who had the keys, and the humiliation of the handcuffs, but he came to accept these things. His separation from his friends and family was more difficult to endure. He felt much more powerfully that he had become the victim of time, which dragged on with no fixed points to look forward to. He noted that his predecessor in the cell had relieved the pressure of his long suffering by scratching on the wall: "In a hundred years it'll all be over."[59]

The first thing he did was establish a strict daily routine from which he did not depart: physical exercise, his long-accustomed meditation, and, after his Bible was returned to him on the third day, memorizing and reading the Scriptures. He then proceeded to observe, as if in a psychological analysis, the break with his past that this arrest constituted and the way in which he experienced time, which had become an enemy. As soon as he was given pencil and paper he began to collect notes for an extended work. There was little writing material to begin with, and he had to use the most wretched scraps of paper.

Among these was a sheet from a writing pad on which, in the guardroom on 8 May 1943, his father had written down the exact contents of a food parcel he had brought to the prison for his son. In his father's hand, it is a long list including tobacco, matches, a tin of pork fat, malt extract, and pumpernickel. This scrap became welcome writing paper for Bonhoeffer. Between the names of the foodstuffs he noted ideas and half sentences that give moving testimony to the content of his meditations and analyses of those first weeks, ideas that later emerged in a more integrated fashion in many of the more organized writings of the weeks that followed. Thus we find on this scrap of paper:

> Separation from people, from work, the past, the future, from honor, from God. The various inner attitudes toward the past … forgetting … caesura—experiences—Fulfilled, unfulfilled, according to history—Self-deception, idealization; concerning the past and concerning the present. A sober view of things instead of illusions—The disappearance of memories, "self-pity" [he uses the English word]; for the one who has overcome: humor. Passing, killing time. Smoking and the emptiness of time.[60] Remembering the possible, although non-concrete. The significance of illusion.[61]

The back of the note includes, among other things:

> Recognize the past, fulfillment, thanks, penitence—the feeling of time—
> not only what is recognized is present? . . . Waiting—but, for example, fac-
> ing death quite calmly—the farmer's time, but no sense of "time" itself—
> the experience of time as the experience of separation, engaged couple,
> before God—the past. Why "In a hundred years all over" and not: until a
> short time ago everything was all right. No possession that outlasts time,
> no task.—Flight from the experience of time in dreams, the shock of awak-
> ening. In dreams, the past means the future, dreams are timeless.—Tooth
> of time, that is, gnawing time—also healing time, like the healing of a
> wound.[62]

It is understandable that the first study he conceived in his Tegel cell
became a piece on the "sense of time." He worked on it until June 1943.[63]
Unfortunately, it has been lost and only a few notes, such as those above,
have been preserved. This was his means of withstanding the terrible pressure of the first weeks. He obviously managed to avoid a constant anxious
preoccupation with his case, which would have exhausted his reserves.

As he tried to cope with the new situation the threat to his inner equilibrium came from two directions. He became uncertain about whether to
fight for his life or kill himself. He overcame this temptation more quickly
than the second one of worrying about how he was to deal with his past and
with his yearning for it.

We know little of his thoughts about escaping his situation through suicide. His words in December 1943 about the "grim impressions" that "often
pursue me into the night" and were difficult to overcome, "despite everything that I have written so far,"[64] are not necessarily connected to the temptation of suicide. But his first notes contain a statement that was never
repeated: "Suicide, not from a sense of guilt, but because I am basically
already dead, draw the line, sum up the balance."[65] There were undoubtedly some shocks at the beginning that led him to consider taking his life.
Undoubtedly, too, one of the first considerations of a man involved in political resistance and arrested in the midst of a conspiracy is to kill himself, and
thus to serve the cause by not becoming a traitor in a moment of weakness.
Bonhoeffer had sometimes spoken about whether he could withstand physical torture.

Thoughts of suicide occurred to him in two forms: in the form of concern for those continuing the struggle and because of his temptation to *tristitia*. He was able to shake his concerns off as soon as it seemed reasonable
that he could successfully divert his interrogators and manage to hold out.

The quickness with which he overcame his tendency toward depression almost surprised him—but here he was helped by the very necessity of focusing as much as possible on the strategy of the interrogation. His surprising success was evident in an early letter to his parents on 15 May 1943, on the occasion of my marriage to Renate Schleicher, where he wrote of the temptation that suddenly, for inexplicable reasons, affects one's "peace and composure . . . to rob one of what is most vital."[66] Unlike the earlier days of persistent melancholy in Finkenwalde, he assured me at the very beginning of his first letter from Tegel, in November 1943, that in the first weeks he had "been preserved from any serious spiritual trial" arising from his earlier *accidie* and *tristitia*, which often lay in wait for him, "with all its menacing consequences."[67] His fighting spirit won the upper hand. Bonhoeffer persisted in thinking "that the duty has been laid on me to hold out in this borderline situation with all its problems."[68]

The brief stage of desperate depression was followed by one of reflection about being cut off from his own life. He wrote of this experience in letters and studies, submitting the world from which he came to intense literary scrutiny and dealing with this theme lyrically also. To him, everything—his fiancée, family, and friends, even his ethical thinking—was part of the "past," up to the beginning of the great theological letters of 1944. But the blessing of being able to reflect rationally on this subject was threatened time and again:

> A few times in my life I have come to know what homesickness means. There is nothing more painful, and during these months in prison I have sometimes been terribly homesick.[69]

This was the other side of the remarkable attachment the Bonhoeffers had to their family, and there was a refusal to give this up in favor of a modern objectivity. He was not ashamed of his homesickness. Out of his abandonment to this suffering he wrote some impressive letters on the theme of "longing."[70]

The first attempt to express his situation in verse (in the early summer of 1944) came after his fiancée had been allowed to see him. After she left he saw his life moving inexorably away from him. He called the poem "The Past" ("*Vergangenheit*").[71] It is the most passionate of all his poems. He sent me the draft because he thought I was in a similar situation because of my separation from my wife due to the war:

> This dialogue with the past, the attempt to hold on to it and recover it, and above all, the fear of losing it, is the almost daily accompaniment of my

life here; and sometimes, especially after brief visits, which are always followed by long partings, it becomes a theme with variations. To take leave
of others, and to live on past memories, whether it was yesterday or last
year (they soon melt into one), is my ever-recurring duty. . . . In this
attempt of mine the crucial part is the last few lines. I am inclined to think
they are too brief. . . .[72]

The final verses expressed how he thought he could legitimately recapture his past life: in the Christian exercise of repentance and thanksgiving.
Even if he seldom managed to do this, in any case he transformed his own
experience into a helpful guide for those whose painful isolation threatened
to affect their capacity for living in the present and render them "incapable
of loving their neighbor."[73]

But there was one thing he refused to do, even when matters sometimes
became very bad for him: to let himself be thought of as a martyr. He
rebuked correspondents or visitors who spoke as if he were, or gave an
emphatically harmless interpretation of events:

These things must not be dramatized. I doubt very much whether I am
"suffering" any more than you or most people are suffering today. Of
course, a great deal here is horrible, but where isn't it? Perhaps we've made
too much of this question of suffering, and been too solemn about it. . . .
No, suffering must be something quite different, and have a quite different
dimension, from what I have so far experienced.[74]

The more serious things became, the less he spoke about them. Self-pity was
not tolerated in the family. After his first visit his father wrote to his son—
the censor read it too:

It was a great relief for us to be able to speak to you recently and to see with
our own eyes that you are, by and large, physically fit, and are withstanding the evil trial imposed upon you with a calm mind and the confidence
of a clear conscience.[75]

On 17 November, Bonhoeffer wrote to his mother:

You, dear Mother, wrote recently that you were "proud" that your children
were behaving so "decently" in such a terrible situation. In fact we have all
learned that from you both, especially when, at times of serious illness in
the family, you became so completely calm and did not show anything. So
it's probably something we inherited.

The Engagement. The wider family circle learned of Bonhoeffer's engagement at the very moment when the gates of Tegel prison separated the couple. With the sense of humor common to the family, Bonhoeffer described the grotesque situation of receiving congratulatory letters in his cell. But it was difficult that his fiancée now had to introduce herself to the family on her own—under circumstances in which people's minds were on entirely other matters than an engagement party.

How would the young girl from a landed estate in the Neumark fit into the family of a Berlin professor? When his parents visited the estate in Pätzig Bonhoeffer was relieved and delighted to receive his father's letter:

> Yesterday Frau von Wedemeyer read us her husband's memoirs of his father. . . . They interested me because, despite the quite different interests, the basic attitude to life and upbringing was nearly the same as that in our Swabian families.[76]

For the secretly engaged couple, the few weeks before the arrest seemed all too brief and affected by other matters. Now Maria von Wedemeyer, unfamiliar with the background of the political conspiracy and, at least at the beginning, with no knowledge of all the personal connections to government departments and Berlin acquaintances, had to leave plans and other considerations up to her in-laws and their friends, whom she hardly knew. She was not even able to be the first to make use of a permit to visit Dietrich in prison. Only four weeks after his parents' visit was she able to meet with Dietrich. After this visit on 24 June 1943 he wrote:

> I have just come back from seeing Maria—an indescribable surprise and joy! I had learned of it only a minute before. It's still like a dream—it is really an almost incomprehensible situation—how we shall think back to it later! What one can say at such a moment is so irrelevant, but that is not the main thing. It was so brave of her to come; I never dared to ask it of her, for it is much harder for her than it is for me. I know what I'm doing, but for her everything is unimaginable, bewildering, terrible. What a prospect, when this terrible nightmare is over![77]

At that point Bonhoeffer had not yet been able to organize his illegal lines of communication, so he could send greetings to his fiancée only in the letter to his parents that was allowed every ten days.

But Bonhoeffer's mother and Maria von Wedemeyer understood each other. Both of them possessed remarkable energy and inventiveness in discovering and utilizing even the smallest possibility of contact via the prison staff. They did not spare the members of the military court, nor the useful military officials in responsible posts. Without any qualms they put pressure on more hesitant people until they "functioned." Despite his concern for the difficulties of the girl's situation, Bonhoeffer was grateful that people were caring about him:

> When pastors were arrested, I sometimes used to think that it must be easiest for those of them who were unmarried. But I did not know then what the warmth that radiates from the love of a wife and family can mean in the cold air of imprisonment, and how in just such times of separation the feeling of belonging together through thick and thin actually grows stronger.[78]

Only at the conclusion of the interrogations did Roeder allow Bonhoeffer to write his fiancée directly. She received her first letter on 30 July 1943. But Bonhoeffer soon hesitated again:

> Dear parents, This letter is now going to you again instead of to Maria, as originally planned. I don't know whether it is right to send letters to her with my present address on the envelope. All that sort of thing gets talked about in the village, and there could be someone there who knows what Tegel, Seidelstrasse 39, means, and I would rather that Maria were spared that. Besides, at the moment she is not even at home, and I want to be all the more careful not to put her in a position which I cannot look after from here. She already has enough to put up with. So I'm waiting until I hear from her what she thinks about it all.[79]

As he awaited the dates for his trial that winter, he ventured to think about the wedding and their future arrangements. On 18 November 1943 he wrote me:

> My marriage plans: If I'm free and I'm not called up for at least a few months, I'll get married. If I have only two to three weeks before I am called up, I'll wait until the end of the war. What an engagement we're having![80]

He was looking forward to the way they would celebrate a wedding in Pätzig, although he knew very little about the Berneuchen customs: the nuptial mass in the morning, the wedding at midday, and the blessing for the journey in the evening—and all this in the beautifully painted village church of Pätzig. On 12 February 1944 he asked his fiancée:

Have you got your trousseau together yet? Where shall we get a radio? Would it be possible for me to exchange my big Bechstein for a baby grand? . . . If you should ever come across a harpsichord, grab it with both hands![81]

After his hopes for one of the dates had been dashed, he wrote in a different tone:

We have been engaged now for nearly a year and have never been alone together for one hour! Isn't it absurd . . . we have to talk and write about things that are not the most important ones for either of us; once a month we sit beside each other, like good children at school, and are then torn apart. We know practically nothing about each other, have no common experiences yet, even for these months we are going through separately. Maria thinks I am a model of virtue, an exemplary Christian and, to satisfy her, I have to write letters like an early martyr, and her image of me becomes more and more false. Isn't that an impossible situation for her? And yet she goes through everything with a marvelous naturalness.[82]

At the end of May 1944, when he wrote the poem "The Past," he heard "Solveig's Song" by Greig on the radio in the prison sick bay, and said he had been moved by this "triumph over the hostility of space, i.e., separation, and over the hostility of time, i.e., the past."[83]

I could not, for example, even bear tonight to imagine myself actually sitting with Maria in the garden by the water at your place, and our talking to each other into the night, etc. etc. That is mere self-torture that physically hurts. So I take flight in thinking, in writing letters, in my joy at your happiness and forbid myself—in self-defense—my own desire.[84]

After 20 July 1944 Bonhoeffer wanted his fiancée to avoid Berlin so that she would not be drawn into the complications or come to the attention of the Gestapo. On 3 August he wrote to me:

Maria will go to the Red Cross again, I think. . . . It is impossible to know where we shall meet again. Sometimes I think I have placed too great a burden on her. But who could have expected what has happened? And if I had been able to manage this case, the situation would have been quite different long ago. But you must not think that I feel bitter about this. I sometimes surprise myself by how "controlled"—or should I say "blunted"?— I am.[85]

But now more than ever Maria intended to come to Berlin. To avoid being called up for military duty she registered as an office assistant for Bonhoeffer's father, as was permitted because it was a medical office.

Unexpectedly the customary communication with Tegel continued to work for another two months. Then came the agonizing waiting for the escape and the possibility that Dietrich might have to disappear for an indefinite period. But 8 October brought a new situation. The two were never able to see each other again, and their written correspondence ceased almost entirely. From his imprisonment in the cellar at Prinz-Albrecht-Strasse he must have longed for Tegel, as far as his engagement was concerned.

The strain of life in Tegel did not destroy Bonhoeffer's positive attitude toward the needs of the times and the place. "We can have abundant life, even though many wishes remain unfulfilled."[86] He energetically sought out the tasks he fulfilled with joy, inside and outside the prison walls:

> The great thing is to stick to what one still has and can do—there is still plenty left.[87] But isn't it characteristic of a man, in contrast to an immature person, that his center of gravity is always where he actually is, and that the longing for the fulfillment of his wishes cannot prevent him from being his complete self, wherever he happens to be? . . . the more he has to overcome in order to live fully in the present, the more he will have the respect and confidence of his fellows.[88]

Thus with his newly discovered and self-imposed tasks he established a daily program that even found him pressed for time: "Unfortunately I hardly ever entirely complete my day's work."[89] His daily work consisted, with varying degrees of priorities, of his preparations for the interrogations and the trial, of a growing correspondence, of literary and theological projects, of an impressive row of books to be read, and finally of requests for chats and help that frequently came to him from his fellow prisoners and his wardens.

Correspondence. Letters became Bonhoeffer's elixir of life in Tegel. He lived for them and through them. Through them he exercised a compelling influence. For them he gradually set up a whole secret communication system.

The letters to his fiancée still exist. They run from the end of July 1943 to December 1944, and were delivered partly through the prison censors and partly in secret, via kindly disposed guards. They have been published as *Love Letters from Cell 92: The Correspondence between Dietrich Bonhoeffer and*

Maria von Wedemeyer. Then there are the letters to his parents, written from April 1943 till January 1945, which went through the censors. Finally there are Bonhoeffer's letters to me, about two hundred densely written pages, from November 1943 to August 1944; all of these were smuggled out. When my own arrest was imminent in October 1944 I quickly burned a final set of letters written in September 1944, since I had to assume that my ties to Bonhoeffer would be of interest.[90]

At first Bonhoeffer's only connection with the outside world was the one-page letter he was allowed to write to his parents every ten days. The length of time they took to arrive was subject to the varying bureaucratic conditions that affected Roeder, the censor. If he was away, as in August and September 1943, a letter might sit for weeks, and answers to questions could take a month or longer. This was one of the reasons why Bonhoeffer used illegal messengers as soon as he was able to. In his correspondence with me the delivery time soon grew longer again since, after January 1944, I could be reached only via the slow field post in Italy, with the exception of a holiday in the early summer of 1944.

When he wrote to his parents Bonhoeffer did something that he never did with other letters and rarely with his other writing: he made careful drafts, so that they were of the right length and content. Some of these drafts have been preserved[91] and help us to establish rough dates for the material covered in the interrogations, because he used these papers for the notes on the interrogation he was writing for Roeder. Of course such a precious letter home could not omit any request or question, but he did not want it to reveal any uncontrolled emotion that might disturb his family if it could not be immediately interpreted. Each of these letters presented him with the task of being the person he was in his cell, and yet of helping everyone else involved in their perspective on the situation. He could not deceive himself and others concerning the state of affairs, and yet he had to assure them that he was equal to the strain and was even using it as an area of new experiences for the future.

There is a difference in the way Bonhoeffer wrote to his parents and to friends. The letters to his parents show great intuition about their state of mind and are controlled; the others are much more frank. In accordance with Bonhoeffer's upbringing, emotions were indicated only in the manner of asking about the wishes and affairs of the other person. One's own needs seemed to be transposed into advice for others. And when things became particularly difficult one conveyed more than a hint of consciousness that one was passing with other people through a series of not only private but of exemplary experiences.

The difference in the letters is evident where Bonhoeffer expressed his impatience with the delay in getting a trial date. He hinted it only once with his parents,[92] whereas he wrote his friend several times to say what he thought of the "manipulation" of his family and how it was threatening his peace of mind for his work.[93] He knew only too well what an obstacle the sensitive imagination of his family could be:

> One all too easily takes a conversation, a fancy, a hope for an action. . . .[94] I wonder whether my excessive scrupulousness, about which you often used to shake your head in amusement (I'm thinking of our travels), is not a negative side of bourgeois existence—simply part of our lack of faith, a part that remains hidden in times of security, but comes out in times of insecurity in the form of "dread" (I don't mean "cowardice," which is something different: "dread" can show itself in recklessness as well as in cowardice), dread of straightforward, simple actions, dread of having to make necessary decisions. I've often wondered here where we are to draw the line between necessary resistance to "fate," and equally necessary submission.[95]

Actually Bonhoeffer caused his family anxiety only with this occasional impatience, which the limited perspective of his prison cell encouraged. One day, it too, vanished. He was able to write a year later about this, something that had greatly upset him at first. Out of natural self-defense, he had not only changed but, as he wrote, "today I can take a calmer view of other people, their predicaments and needs, and so I am better able to help them."[96]

Literary Attempts. It is impossible to imagine Bonhoeffer doing anything other than using his enforced leisure for new creative ends. The most beneficial self-protection for him was to objectify his experience of imprisonment through writing. Most of what he wrote in 1943 in Tegel concerned the explanation or systematization of the phenomenon that has already been mentioned: he saw his own world continually retreating from him. At first he remained entirely objective, in his study on time that has been lost. But then he found the courage to reflect on his world in a much more personal way. Around Pentecost, at the end of May, he began writing a play and started a novel soon after. He said later what joy these experiments had given him. The play failed because of his characters' overly reflective speeches, so he began again with the story of a contemporary middle-class family that he had "had in mind for a long time."[97] The novel fragment describes the encounter between a doctor's family from the big city and a family from a country estate, clearly reflecting the experiences of his own family and his own experiences in England and Pomerania. This fragment soon turns into long soliloquies more suitable for a chapter on ethics than a story,[98] but the account is shaped by actual specific experiences that the Bonhoeffer family lived through. His experience of all this, and what this experience meant for him when he was separated from it, also became part of the sermons he wrote in his cell on the celebration of Eberhard Bethge's wedding and the baptism of his son.[99]

In these literary attempts he was preoccupied by the clash between the honorable and the vulgar, as in his study from that same period, "What Is Meant by 'Telling the Truth'?"[100] This essay dealt with the lies of the truthful person and the truth of the liar, with the living element of honesty and loyalty in the world that had been seduced by power, small and great. Bonhoeffer was very concerned with the real embodiment of Germany, the real nature of its brilliant and its disastrous qualities, such as the immaturity in handling power and the apparent acquiescence in allowing its good name to be sullied. He reflected on the privilege, dearly paid for, of being one of the responsible bearers of this country's tradition.

In the drama fragment he makes the chief figure, Christoph, write a note showing what made him angry when he considered Germany;[101] the novel fragment also breaks off with questions about Germany.[102] Whereas Bonhoeffer used to write down his essays in their final form from condensed notes, not complete drafts, two full drafts have been preserved of that section of Christoph's notes, obviously central for Bonhoeffer, which declared that "the soiled words, freedom, fraternity, and even the word 'Germany,'" now had to be honored through silence and the simple doing of what had to be done,[103] in order to become respected again.

It was not until 1944 that he treated his personal theme of "the past" more subjectively and yet more universally than ever before, in the poem for his fiancée.[104] But this theme was then followed by another that carried him through the worst weeks of the year 1944. The new theme pointed entirely toward the future, and his own "borderline" situation was extended to provide an exemplary vision of future Christianity. Until then he had limited this theme to Germany because the focus of his own life had become more confined, but now he looked once more at the role of Christianity in the world.

How are we to judge Bonhoeffer's attempts at poetry? They are efforts to overcome his isolation. In this situation he had begun to write poetry for the first time since his youth. The venture fascinated him for months on end. The thoughts in these pieces are important, but they are so densely packed that they burst the forms of poem, novel, and drama. Poems such as "Sorrow and Joy," "Christians and Pagans," "The Friend," and "Stations on the Road to Freedom," will probably live on because they convey the particular situation in an original statement and in an appropriate form.[105] "Powers of Good" ("*Von guten Mächten*")[106] has already passed into the schoolbooks. But the attempted drama and the fragment of a novel emerge as ponderous. Adalbert Stifter's style, which Bonhoeffer so loved, was an obstacle for him, and the topic dominates Bonhoeffer so that he does not grant either the reader or himself any relief from it.

Letters and essays are the literary form, apart from his theological style, in which Bonhoeffer speaks directly and convinces. Summer evenings over the prison walls, Karl Barth's cigar, memories of Berlin concert halls, the rhythm of the church year or the surprise at holding a knife and fork in his hands again, the privileges of mothers-in-law, Berlin beer, the anger at shabby cowardice—all this, unintentionally, makes fascinating reading. It is serious, has touches of humor, and conveys the joy in earthly things that surprised the friends of the earlier Bonhoeffer, the theologian; they wrongly imagined him to be a fierce and radical teacher of eschatology. Instead, he praised "a beauty that is neither classical nor demonic, but simply earthly, though it has its own proper place. For myself, I must say that this is the only kind of beauty that really appeals to me."[107]

Studies and Readings. As the interrogations moved into the background he extended his daily work program with the intensive reading of theological works and, even more, of philosophy, history, and literature. This enabled him to forget all about his surroundings and the danger he was in; he was disturbed only when there was a hitch in the supply of books by his family, or if people failed to track down a particular work that he wanted. He felt "as if I had been given a term at a university with a series of good lectures. Of course, any creative output of my own has suffered badly."[108]

The list of books we know he read is impressive. The real list was probably even longer. He got his books from three sources. His parents provided him with most of them, and by no means all of them were used for coded messages. The prison library was also available to him, which, even after Goebbels's order purging all German libraries of the "filth" of the twenties, still had many surprises from the Prussian era to offer. He later exchanged books with other prisoners or received an occasional book from the prison chaplains, such as Karl Kindt's *Klopstock* from Pastor Dannenbaum. Existing sources make it possible to make a chronological list of his readings.[109]

1. There were not too many theological works. Unlike nineteenth-century literature, they do not seem to have offered him any particular comfort or guidance in his situation. He read some things from the prison library that he would normally never have come across, such as the three-volume treat-

ment of Christian social work, *History of Christian Acts of Love* (*Geschichte der christlichen Liebestätigkeit*), written in 1896 by the Hannover Lutheran pastor Gerhard Uhlhorn, which he read in May and June 1943. He enjoyed the travel letters from Palestine published in 1901 by Hermann Freiherr von Soden, the father of the Marburg professor Hans von Soden. Above all he delighted in the early church fathers, whom he tracked down in the Tegel library. They seemed more "contemporary" to him than the reformers, since they had done their thinking during a nonprivileged period for the church. Their ethical conflicts in a non-Christian environment seemed incomparably more exciting than the problems of the Augsburg national synod of 1530.

Bonhoeffer later asked to be allowed to see Barth's *Church Dogmatics,* volume II/2. He had received and read the page proofs of *The Doctrine of God,* Part 2, dealing with "God's election" and "the command of God." Thus, he knew of Barth's doctrine of election, but not of his doctrine of creation and his special ethics. Unfortunately, there is no record of Bonhoeffer's reaction to Barth's doctrine of election. In general we can probably say that Barth's account of the positive kerygmatic value of this controversial teaching, developed through a critique of Luther and Calvin, was close to Bonhoeffer's treatment in his seminar of the article on election in the Lutheran *Formula of Concord.* Bonhoeffer had taught that the significance of this dangerous doctrine should be sought in its proclamation of certainty, not in its threats.

Bonhoeffer's theological work in Tegel was done without the aid of theological classics and compendia, which he used less than most theologians in Germany, even when he had easier access to them. He had his Luther Bible, a Greek New Testament, and a concordance, but no commentary and no dictionary. With these tools he read, as he always had, book after book of Scripture, asking questions and meditating. The new questions that emerged in 1944 came less from theological publications than from his experiences with the War Court, among his fellow prisoners, and in reading secular literature.

2. The list of the philosophical, historical, and aesthetic books is more impressive than the theological. But it also reveals a certain limitation, especially in the literary selection. Bonhoeffer's reading during these last two years of his life was shaped by the isolation that National Socialism had brought to Germany. The library in Tegel had undoubtedly been restricted by Goebbels's measures to the classics of the previous century and the latest approved lists. But Bonhoeffer could hardly have filled this gap from other sources. It was unthinkable, for instance, that his family could have brought books by Thomas Mann, Franz Werfel, or more modern foreign authors to his cell, even though they still had sources where they could obtain them.

Thus Bonhoeffer shared the general fate of the Germans in being excluded from the mainstream of literary development in the world.

Bonhoeffer, however, was not greatly concerned about this lack. These literary restrictions coincided with his own inclinations. He wanted to become better acquainted with particular aspects of nineteenth-century literature and to rehabilitate the tradition of his forefathers, from Keller to Harnack, from Pestalozzi to Dilthey, over against more modern existentialist tendencies. For example, he conceived the idea of selecting something from Jeremias Gotthelf. These writers opened his cell to that familiar world from which he had been shut out; this is why they have such a dominant place on his Tegel reading list.

On the other hand, he did not greatly care for many contemporary authors, such as Ernst Wiechert and Werner Bergengruen, who were generally highly regarded in Germany. Even before his arrest he had little desire to read them. He wrote to his fiancée the reasons for this from his cell. In a letter to me of 28 November 1943 he used strong language in his description of "Rilke, Bergengruen, Binding, Wiechert, the latter three of which I regard as not up to our level, and the first as downright unhealthy":

> Unfortunately, Maria's generation has simply grown up with very bad contemporary literature, and they find it much more difficult to approach earlier writing than we do. The more we have known of the really good things, the more insipid the thin lemonade of later literature becomes, sometimes almost to the point of making us sick. Do you know a work of literature written in the last, say, fifteen years that you think has any lasting quality? I don't. It is partly idle chatter, partly propaganda, partly self-pitying sentimentality, but there is no insight, no ideas, no clarity, no substance and almost always the language is bad and constrained. On this subject I am quite consciously a *laudator temporis acti*.[110]

He asked his fiancée what she was reading, giving her friendly guidance:

> Can't you get hold of Rilke's *The Notebooks of Malte Laurids Brigge* from somewhere? I've been reading nothing but scholarly works of late, relaxing just occasionally with your Scheffel. Are you reading Fontane?[111]

> I'm delighted that you're reading Schütz![112] But forgive me for chuckling a little, because I've seldom inveighed any book as fiercely in recent times—though solely and exclusively in the company of theologians! But I think that it's only a danger to theologians—why, it would take too long to explain—and not to you. However, I'd welcome it if you took a strong dose of Kierkegaard (*Fear and Trembling, Practice in Christianity, Sickness unto*

Death) as an antidote. Have you by any chance read Jeremias Gotthelf's *Berner Geist*? It's time you read that too. I wonder if you would care for *Don Quixote*, which I love so much. Or *Wilhelm Meister*? That would be far more important to me than Fontane, who can wait awhile. Do you know Stifter's *From My Great-Grandfather's Portfolio* (*Aus der Mappe meines Urgrossvaters*)?[113]

The delightful discovery in Tegel was the nineteenth-century poet and novelist Adalbert Stifter. Bonhoeffer shared the experience of the other imprisoned 20 July conspirators, whose oppressive prison life was heartened by nothing as much as by Stifter's style, which seemed almost unreadable during the normal run of everyday life. In particular, Bonhoeffer's brother-in-law Rüdiger Schleicher felt this. Stifter's power and scope, his dwelling on things taken for granted such as a walk through the garden, had a uniquely transforming and restorative effect in prison:

> The intimate life of his characters—of course it is old-fashioned of him to describe only likeable people—is very pleasant in this atmosphere here, and makes one think of the things that really matter in life.[114]

It was one of Bonhoeffer's great moments in Tegel when, after his family at home had hunted for it for a long time without success, he unexpectedly came upon Stifter's *Witiko* in the prison library:

> For me it is one of the finest books I know. The purity of its style and character-drawing gives one a quite rare and peculiar feeling of happiness.[115]

It was naturally not only the literary quality of the book that fascinated him, but its theme, which placed his own life within the most universal context of the wide sweep of history, in a surprisingly comforting and purifying way. He discovered for himself what Hermann Bahr had already noted in *Witiko* in 1922:

> This old book seems to have waited just for us, to have been written especially for us . . . only now do we comprehend . . . the aim, of depicting "the terrible majesty of the moral law, which destroys . . . the great criminals and bends their violent schemes like straws, in such a powerful and brilliant way that people, seeing the terror of it . . . submit in trembling and wonder to the power that forbids evil. . . ."
>
> . . . then Witiko starts doing injustice for the sake of good and helps to bring out of this a new justice. . . . Where there has been a lasting victory for revolution it has always been the victory of legitimacy, the victory of illegal justice over a law that had become unjust. . . .

> New justice must always first expiate its defects through profound suf-
> fering; it must first be purified through fire, with the wrongdoing burned
> away. Only then, through penance, will justice finally emerge from good
> injustice.[116]

Bonhoeffer's preference for nineteenth-century literature was the result
of an inner disposition. He had an aversion to an unclear style, and he disliked rapt self-reflection and strained extravagance. He was averse to penetrating into hidden areas. He enjoyed the indication of internal events, in all
their nuances, through external actions:

> In my reading I'm now concentrating entirely on the nineteenth century.
> During these months I've read Gotthelf, Stifter, Immermann, Fontane and
> Keller with new admiration. A period in which people could write such
> clear and simple German must have had quite a healthy core. They treat the
> most delicate matters without sentimentality, the most serious without
> flippancy, and they express their convictions without pathos; there is no
> exaggerated simplifying or complicating of language or subject matter; in
> short, it's all very much to my liking, and seems to me very sound. But it
> must have meant plenty of hard work at expressing themselves in good
> German, and therefore plenty of opportunity for quiet.[117]

Thus he was able to affirm this fruit of his own personal isolation and that
of his country.

Naturally the degree to which the philosophical questions of the nineteenth century had remained unexplored did not escape him. And he regret-
fully accepted his limited knowledge of the sciences and technology that
emerged in the same century.[118]

Prison Life. Over time Tegel had given Bonhoeffer a mobility that one does
not expect from the prisons of the Third Reich and that the majority of
Hitler's victims did not enjoy. This was due partly to the nature of a military
prison, but partly also to Bonhoeffer's way of dealing with his guards.

Even in the military interrogation prison of Tegel—nicknamed "WUG"
—a noticeable attempt was made to carry out the severe punitive code of
Hitler's military forces. Still, next to these innovations the long-established
military code still existed. Certain rights of a prisoner held for interrogation
could be preserved if these were energetically and skillfully pursued.

Among the older staff at Tegel Bonhoeffer got to know a number of
guards who were strongly opposed to the regime. Others proved willing
and helpful when their "political" prisoners or their highly placed relations

showed them kindnesses or gave them gifts. Bonhoeffer's energetic protests against the customary rough behavior of the wardens were successful and they desisted. The staff consisted of privates and corporals who had spent years in the service, hard-boiled men unfit for fighting on the front.

To these men Bonhoeffer appeared to be an extraordinarily interesting prisoner: a pastor, admitted under the greatest secrecy, who turned out to be the nephew of the city commandant and was soon being taken for walks by Captain Maetz, the Tegel commandant. Thus this prisoner gradually became an influential inmate of the house. When the severe air raids in the winter of 1943–1944 upset the order of the prison many people discovered that being close to Bonhoeffer gave them a welcome feeling of safety, especially since Bonhoeffer never asked for more than could be reasonably expected of them. Many were glad he was there.

On 26 November 1943 the first severe night raid struck Borsig; the prison also received several hits. Bonhoeffer clearly proved himself during this ordeal by his particular prudence. For this reason the captain encouraged him to make a report concerning new protective measures. After the summer raids on Hamburg there had already been special drills for the self-protection of the prison; by the late summer of 1943 Bonhoeffer had been regularly brought from his cell during these drills for practices and when there were alarms. He was appointed the medical orderly for his section. Maetz had learned about Bonhoeffer's medical talent and liked to speak with him about improving air-raid precautions. As early as 3 July 1943 Bonhoeffer wrote to his parents concerning suggestions, both foolish and useful, for their air-raid shelter in the Marienburger Allee home: "I've spoken to the captain here about it."[119] Bonhoeffer used the contacts he developed in every way for the benefit of both the wardens and his fellow prisoners, in order to improve conditions or stem corruption. He gained deep insight into the persecutions, toadying, and favoritism that emanate from the front office and the kitchen staff in such a place.

His experience of the corruption there so haunted him that he wrote—probably in the summer of 1943—a little story ("Farewell, Comrade") in which he described this side of military life: a young, seriously wounded guard cannot preserve himself among his comrades because he does not join in the brutal treatment of the prisoners and the self-enrichment of those in the guardroom. Every feature of the sketch revealed exact knowledge of the customs of a "WUG."[120]

The Guards. The humanity of a few guards is to be thanked for the preservation of so much material from Bonhoeffer's period in Tegel. One day one of them brought him notepaper from the guardroom for his work. Many of them tried to rotate their duties so that they were assigned to the section of the corridor where Bonhoeffer's cell was. He was so good to have a conversation with, and one always got some sound advice in dealing with one's own little troubles. Sometimes they took up too much of his working time. Several, including a sergeant major, asked to be photographed with this prisoner in the courtyard. On 4 February 1944 a warden placed a birthday bouquet of early spring flowers from the prison greenhouse in his cell. Another offered to ask his country relations to send food parcels to Bonhoeffer's relatives. When the sirens howled and the bomber squadrons appeared to be flying directly over Tegel those in that section of the prison got as close as possible to Bonhoeffer, who seemed to remain so calm. A corporal who had to take Bonhoeffer back from the section to his cell asked him surreptitiously to pray for a quiet night.[121] One night when their own quarters were damaged by the explosions nearby they came to him "for a bit of comfort."[122] One guard who had to lock him in again after his exercise in the yard spontaneously asked for his pardon.

A firm and trusting relationship developed with some of the wardens. When I married Bonhoeffer's niece in the middle of May 1943 he was able to send his written wedding speech,[123] greetings, and present to us via one of the guards, a Corporal Linke. The same thing happened when his godson was baptized.[124] It occasionally happened, of course, that Bonhoeffer was cheated of money or gifts by someone he had asked to do something for him, but this was very seldom. Linke was the same guard who locked me in for an entire hour with Bonhoeffer in the visitor's cell and left us to talk alone. Corporal Holzendorf, among others, did the same sort of thing for Maria von Wedemeyer and the family. Bonhoeffer believed that some of these friendships would be lifelong and was deeply upset when one of those closest to him, Herr Engel, was killed in an air raid.[125] And finally it was Corporal Knobloch—he has disappeared—who acted as go-between for a whole year in the illegal correspondence between Bonhoeffer and myself. It was with this trustworthy man that Bonhoeffer prepared his escape plan.

Such wardens found plenty of pretexts to take Bonhoeffer to the "private section," the sick bay of the prison, even when there was no drill or alarm to make his presence necessary. There was a radio so that the air-raid warnings could be heard, and Bonhoeffer was able to listen, with other music lovers, to the *Missa Solemnis* or Pfitzner's *Palestrina*.[126] Except for the angelic choir he did not much enjoy the latter, much to the disappointment of a Pfitzner enthusiast. In this room he began to play chess with other prisoners and wardens, so that he once more occupied his mind with the theory of chess, as he had in his youth. On one of these occasions he returned to his old love of graphology and soon offered a number of clients analyses of their professional future.

> I am enjoying it very much; I am now working through Ludwig Klages's book. But I am not going to try it on my friends and relatives; there are enough people here who are interested in it. But I am convinced of the thing's reliability.[127]

Among the papers from Bonhoeffer's cell are a few notes with his analyses of handwriting.

Fellow Prisoners. At first Bonhoeffer was pursued, even in his dreams, by thoughts of those prisoners who were awaiting death to the left and right of his cell without his being able to reach them. In time, however, he was able to establish relationships with some of those condemned to death and, even more so, with prisoners held for interrogation. He tried to do something for them or to bring some pleasure into their lives.

The first opportunity for this was offered by a fellow prisoner who was sent to clean Bonhoeffer's cell in the early weeks. Bonhoeffer learned the details of events in the prison from him, and when a package arrived he shared its contents with him. In the early summer of 1943 Bonhoeffer initially refused the offer to take a cooler cell on the second floor because of the heat, since then another prisoner would have had to move into his cell.[128] Later, prisoners working somewhere together told one another when Bonhoeffer could be found in the sick bay, and then tried to arrange things so that they had something to do there, because "it is so nice to have a chat with me," as Bonhoeffer wrote.[129] Through these conversations Bonhoeffer learned of young prisoners accused of having left their company without leave, of antiwar activities or sabotage, and who were left in this situation without expert advice or even money for a defense lawyer. He then tried, for example, to get the relatives of those accused to visit his father during his consulting hours, on the chance that they could obtain a psychiatric report which would be useful in the trial of the person concerned. Or he asked his own defense lawyer, Dr. Wergin, his brother Klaus's friend, to take on the case. He even made money available from his or his parents' account to get the necessary legal help for some young man. Bonhoeffer actually managed to save several prisoners at Tegel from the worst, including an Italian named Lanfredi, who had been condemned to death at his first hearing, as Professor Latmiral attested in a letter of 2 April 1946. He could help others on their last journey only with his prayers:

> I hear outside a hasty, muffled tread,
> Near my cell it suddenly stops dead.
> I go all cold and hot,
> I know, oh, I know what . . .
> I go with you, brother, to that place
> And hear your last words, face to face:
> "Brother, when I cease to be,
> Pray for me!"[130]

In order to alleviate the lot of his fellow prisoners wherever he could, he used his privileged status with the captain and wrote a "Report on Prison Life"[131] in the hope that it would reach his uncle, the city commandant, who would set things in order. From his ample personal experience he described the degrading punishments, food, and living conditions of men held for interrogation, men who were generally intended to return to the front as combatants. For this report he got wardens he could trust to check the weight of the food rations and compare it with what was set in the regulations. He worked out his own system of punishments.

In the other report, after the severe raid on the Borsig factory, he mercilessly exposed the inadequate protection and preventative measures in the prison, suggesting that in view of the shortage of materials there should be far more shelters for protection against shrapnel, and that the prisoners' cells should be unlocked during raids. From the sick-bay shelter, he had heard too clearly the screams of those locked in, and seen how help for the wounded came far too late. Here his mother's heritage proved itself; she was always able to respond swiftly and creatively when disaster paralyzed those around her.

Although he was so ready to help, he was capable of making exceptions. A district Nazi Party leader who had been sent to Tegel for some transgression and had completely fallen apart attached himself to Bonhoeffer, who was in a position to obtain the odd favor for him. But when this man made an anti-Semitic remark Bonhoeffer immediately cut off "the few benefits" he had enjoyed and shunned him contemptuously.[132]

At Christmas 1943 he wrote prayers for the prisoners.[133] These came from his own prayer, his daily use of the Psalter and the chorales. He left out nothing, either in the trinitarian address or in the biblical language. The prison chaplains, Hans Dannenbaum and Harald Poelchau, had obtained illegal entry to Bonhoeffer's cell and distributed the prayers among the cells.

The prisoners included a number of educated men, including foreigners. Bonhoeffer became friendly with Dick Jones, probably an English officer, and exchanged books with him. In this way he obtained Hugh Walpole's thick volume of *The Herriers Chronicle* in the summer of 1944. The book already contained notes written by English prisoners of war in "Stalag LB 2," from where Jones had probably brought it to Tegel. In the early part of October 1944, fearing the worst, Bonhoeffer sent it home while he was again clearing his cell of illegal objects. His bookmark, a piece of the *Völkischer Beobachter* from the end of September 1944, was placed at page 1308 of the book. The novel tracing the story of a family through the centuries had clearly given him welcome distraction at the end.

Bonhoeffer became close to some Italian officers who were arrested in Germany after the Badoglio putsch for carrying "technical secrets" and had been brought to Tegel on 11 November 1943. He was especially attached to Professor Gaetano Latmiral and his friend Curcio. After the war Latmiral described his relationship with Bonhoeffer during the Tegel period:

> Only a minority of the guards were fanatics or ill-disposed. Most of them were decent or even good. I think that Dietrich's long stay among them had an influence. . . . He had received small concessions, for example, he was often allowed to go down to the sick bay, where he met many friends, or he was able to visit prisoners who sought his spiritual help. . . . When we took our walk together, half an hour or longer every day, we spoke of political, religious and scientific problems. He lent me the Weizsäcker book. . . . He explained to me the meaning of many passages in the Gospel and told me that he was writing a poem on the death of Moses, when Moses climbed Mount Nebo and God showed him, before he died, the land that would one day belong to his people, but that he would never enter. He loved this theme. . . .[134] He also spoke of the tragic fate of the German people, whose qualities and shortcomings he knew. He told me that it was very difficult for him to desire its defeat, but that it was necessary. He said he had little hope that a German government could save Germany from the worst consequences of defeat by sensibly capitulating. The Nazis had a fanatically tragic will to involve everyone in the catastrophe. He observed that to him Wagner's music was an expression of this barbarous pagan psychology. He stated that as a pastor it was his duty not just to comfort the victims of the man who drove down a busy street like a maniac, but to try to stop him.[135] The leading German families had partly expiated their guilt by trying to remove Hitler, though far too late. He said that he was not sure that he would see the end, for he feared that he would then be taken to a concentration camp where he would be killed along with other political prisoners. In that case he hoped that he would be able to accept death without fear, in the belief that it was in a just cause. . . . He was always so interesting and good-humored. He was the best and the most gifted man I have ever met.[136]

The Church in Prison. The Council of Brethren of the Confessing church in Berlin, of course, was unable to offer Bonhoeffer any help. It had to be careful not to become too involved with a man who was connected with "purely" political operations. But men such as Niesel, Asmussen, Böhm, Lokies, and others kept themselves informed of what was happening, either via Perels or myself. And undoubtedly the members of the Breslau synod thought the same as these men when they included Bonhoeffer's name in their intercessions, since they no longer maintained the strict distinction between church confession and political action as before.

At first things were as Bonhoeffer wrote in his first illegal letter to me: "I have not even been allowed to have a clergyman to see me here."[137] But after the situation eased following the hearings he received frequent visits from two pastors of the Berlin church. Pastor Hans Dannenbaum of the Berlin city mission, because he was a garrison pastor with the armed forces, had permission to visit the military prison. He used this as soon as he dared, despite the special ban in Bonhoeffer's case. After 1945 Dannenbaum described Bonhoeffer's cell as "an almost cozy retreat." Bonhoeffer, he said, even "liked to play the host in his cell," but accepted it gratefully when Dannenbaum concluded his visits with a reading from the Bible and prayer of intercession, just as he himself had done earlier and expected his Finkenwalde seminarians to do when they made pastoral visits.

The second clergyman to visit him was Pastor Dr. Harald Poelchau, a regular prison chaplain in the civil service, and thus in charge only of the civil part of the Tegel complex. But because of his precise knowledge of the place and the staff he increasingly ventured to visit Bonhoeffer's cell illegally after the end of 1943. Like Dannenbaum, he realized what an "assistant chaplain" they unexpectedly had in the prison.

Bonhoeffer himself held to the daily routine of Bible reading, prayer, and meditation. He was now glad that he knew so many of Paul Gerhardt's hymns by heart. The isolated man's need for certainty through a sign led him to cross himself, according to Luther's instruction. But in this environment he carefully observed the distinction between calling upon God and speaking this name before other people. The seriousness of the one ruled out the careless use of the name in the other.

After the spring of 1943 there had been no further religious services for Bonhoeffer. Once he said that he hardly missed them and was rather surprised.[138] Was this connected with the fact that such a "public" function could not be more than a solemn distraction for his fellow prisoners, with whom he lived at such close quarters? Therefore the open spiritual word had to wait for its appropriate time, and the "liturgical" had to remain in the realm of the "arcane," as Bonhoeffer called it in his theological letters.

Who knows whether Bonhoeffer would have tried to organize services if he had had the responsibility and the freedom to do so? He lived the life of hundreds around him and shared their anxieties, privations, and little joys. Spiritual contacts sprang up naturally. Special functions probably would have hindered rather than helped these contacts. Bonhoeffer was sometimes surprised at how he reacted to this situation without, however, seeking to make something formal out of it. But occasionally he was overcome by longing for the services he had once had in Finkenwalde amid the ordinands. This longing now belonged to the theme of the "past" with which he wrestled.

However restricted life in the Tegel cell was, it appeared in an almost rosy light in retrospect, compared with what people were enduring elsewhere. During this period Bonhoeffer did not have to go hungry, and when after an air raid the cold November air came through the smashed cell window, he did not have to freeze:

> A box of canned food and the travelling fur have just been handed to me. I asked to be taken down straightaway and hoped that I would still catch a glimpse of you.... Many, many thanks.... It's really wonderful how you always think of everything straightaway and also translate it into action.[139]

The influenza, rheumatism, and stomach troubles that beset him in August and December of 1943 and February 1944 were immediately fought with all the necessary medicines. Bonhoeffer had a lawyer for his case who visited him. And amid the general danger of life around him he wrote well-ordered wills. Above all, he had imposed on himself a precise daily routine, "so that sometimes, comically enough, I even feel that I have 'no time' here for this or that less important matter!"[140] And then there was the most important thing for him, his extensive correspondence.

Yet Bonhoeffer could not ignore what was happening outside: the progress of the conspiracy for another Germany, the pointless loss of life on the front, which included so many brethren from Finkenwalde, and the fate of the Jews. This remained a hidden but real burden behind everything that made life at Tegel bearable. Concerning this no more could be said than this: "As I see it, I am here for some purpose, and I only hope I may fulfill it."[141]

The New Theology

"The nonreligious interpretation of biblical terms in a world come of age" was Bonhoeffer's designation for a task that is only beginning to be understood, and which has been both welcomed and attacked since the appearance of his selected letters from prison in 1951–1952. In 1960 the *Encyclopedia Britannica,* in its article on Bonhoeffer, categorically rejected a description of him as nonreligious as "nonsense." Since Bishop Robinson's *Honest to God,* however, it has become common currency even among Anglicans in the debate concerning the future of Christianity and the church. Even the archbishop of Canterbury has preached and written on "nonreligious Christianity."[142] In the debate in Germany the argument arose about whether the origins of the phrase lay in the theology of Barth or of Bultmann and were more characteristic of one than the other. Others, in contrast, relegated it to the sphere of atheistic ideas.

The phrase was first used by Bonhoeffer during the final year of his life, when a new impulse moved him to reexamine his theology. This new approach gave him the optimistic sense of a breakthrough, a complete contrast to the situation in which he found himself at that time. He was clearly delighted to be making a new start on theological work. At the same time, he guessed that the task might be beyond his capacities and, as was always the case, called for an intense personal involvement:

> But even if we are prevented from clarifying our minds by talking things over, we can still pray, and it is only in the spirit of prayer that any such work can be begun and carried through.[143]

Thus it can be ruled out that Bonhoeffer's new attempt at a theology of God's solidarity with the world was intended to proclaim a simplistic intellectual open-endedness. On the contrary, he commended himself to the Holy Spirit precisely at the point where he set about taking the "*etsi deus non daretur*" seriously. The autonomy of "the world come of age" of which he now began to speak is not to be understood as the freedom of a Titan, but a freedom born of humility. The inevitable theological consequence—as inevitable as it was difficult—was Bonhoeffer's attempt to preserve a place in his new thinking for the "arcane discipline."

In the following discussion we shall consider first the conditions and questions that underscored Bonhoeffer's fresh theological start in Tegel. We shall then attempt to examine, under the heading of his main question "Who is Christ for us today?" the three key phrases "world come of age," "nonreligious interpretation," and "arcane discipline." These can also be illuminated by examining his friends' and pupils' surprised reaction to his letters. Hence we shall consider, in three successive sections, the inspiration, the key words, and the reception of the theological letters.

The New Impulse. April 1944 was clearly a milestone in Bonhoeffer's life in prison. We can see this from the change in his reading, his new manner of working, and the different tone of his letters. This change proved so long-lasting that even the shock about the failure of the attempt of 20 July 1944 did not interrupt it. His new work carried him through those weeks almost without any adverse effect.

The first letter of any length on the new theme was written on 30 April. As we have seen, there had been a preliminary decision concerning whether a date should be sought for the trial or not. Josef Müller's attempt in March to get off with an acquittal had failed; Dohnanyi's health offered no prospect for a hearing. Sack had told Bonhoeffer that he "had better not, for the time being, expect any change in my present position."[144]

Thus the time was passed in waiting constantly for new dates, which was especially detrimental to any ongoing work. The acceptance of a calm period was easier, and brought an increase of energy: "After a rather long unproductive period, I feel in better form for work now that spring is coming."[145] The introduction of the letter containing the first formulation of the new theme, written on 30 April, was as positive as could be:

> You've no need to worry about me at all, as I am getting on uncommonly well—you would be surprised if you came to see me. People here keep on telling me (as you can see, I feel very flattered by it) that I'm "radiating so much peace around me," and that I am "always so cheerful." ... You would be surprised, and perhaps even worried, by my theological thoughts and the conclusions that they lead to.[146]

There was now a remarkable change in Bonhoeffer's choice of reading material. Stifter, Gotthelf, Fontane, C. F. Meyer, and Gottfried Keller had confirmed and corrected his evolving ideas in the summer and winter of 1943. Now he asked for books by Dilthey, C. F. von Weizsäcker, and Ortega y Gasset, for Harnack's *History of the Prussian Academy* and W. F. Otto's *The Homeric Gods*. He was strongly drawn to source books of this kind and could become very inpatient: "Unfortunately the one thing I cannot do is to get hold of the right books."[147]

Bonhoeffer's literary work from his first year in Tegel (1943), such as the drama and novel fragments, was largely variations on the subject of "the past." In 1944 Bonhoeffer complained that these writings had become bogged down and that he could no longer concentrate on them.[148] This remained the case, although the theme of "the past" was expressed in poems in the summer of 1944 (especially in "The Past" and "Death of Moses"). The Allied invasion on 6 June revived many private wishes, just as 20 July destroyed great hopes, but the new theme remained dominant: "It is as you say: knowing is the most thrilling thing in the world, and that is why I am finding the work so fascinating," he wrote on 10 August 1944.[149] I needed only to make the slightest inquiry concerning the development of his new theme in my letters from Italy for him to reply immediately at length with further elaborations. Despite the interruption of air raids, he was generally able to continue where he had broken off.

The various writings of his first year in Tegel, which had attempted to return to the spirit of the nineteenth century, prepared the way for the return to long-forgotten theological themes of the period. Contrary to his attitude in the thirties, he was now concerned with the connecting link with the questions and fruits of this period: "It would be so useful to draw up a good genealogy here."[150] He said this in a letter of 9 March 1944, when he first took up again the idea of "the worldliness" of "anticlerical secularism," which was "Christian," not just "emancipated"—the theme at which he had stopped in *Ethics*.[151]

After his active "acceptance of guilt" in joining the conspiracy Bonhoeffer became possessed by a new passion for theology. Even before they ended, his political duties had liberated him for a new theological beginning, opening the lonely man's eyes for the conditions and possible form of Christian belief in the future. He already had begun to overcome the process that he had not yet endured to its bitter end.

Preparation. The specific roots of Bonhoeffer's new theology go back to particular ideas from his early period that he in part had retained and in part given new accents. Some of his own experiences had given them a new impulse. He felt that here he had to "break through the knots."

1. Theologically the way toward a "nonreligious interpretation" had clearly been prepared in Bonhoeffer's early Christology. Ebeling has noted correctly that this "interpretation" is first and last a christological one.[152] Our primary interest is in the fact that there is a certain continuity here. This is also true of the elements of his ecclesiology, even though the latter caused him great difficulty.

2. Even during his work on *Ethics* his theological perspective changed from that of *Discipleship*. Although his early Christology had to lead Bonhoeffer eventually to *Discipleship*, the exclusive claim of Christ he asserted there ran some risk of being narrow; thus, the one-sided cry of "the world for Christ" had to be counterbalanced by "Christ for the world." But this

altered the view of the world and of Christ. The Gospel's universal relevance and its limitedness in practice were incompatible. Ethics could no longer let itself be confined to a "Christian" sphere, capitulating to the secularism of western civilization. Even in the first chapters of *Ethics,* therefore, Bonhoeffer is speaking a new language, in that there is a new rationality—as, for example, in the section on the relevance of success.[153]

3. Biographically the primary forces driving Bonhoeffer forward were his experiences with the Confessing church and the political conspiracy.

We have already spoken of the distance that had grown between Bonhoeffer and his church, because the church was no longer clearly addressing the scandalous present situation, instead confining its proclamation purely to its own realm. Bonhoeffer naturally regarded it as an important task that this church should preserve the great Christian concepts in a period marked by the failure to grasp them. But he could not resign himself to the weakness and irrelevance of these venerable articles to the realities of the day. "The Confessing Church has now largely forgotten all about the Barthian approach, and has lapsed from positivism into conservative restoration." The great articles remain "undeveloped and remote, because they are not interpreted."[154]

His return from America and its consequences—what we have called the process of becoming a "man for his times"—played a very important part in this new development. To a degree that went far beyond mere friendly contacts, the conspiracy had brought together a group of people prepared to take responsibility; many of them came from sectors that had nothing to do with the church. With these people, whatever remnant still existed of sentimental piety could not be revived; very few could be brought back into the old "halls of religion." So far Bonhoeffer had thought through the ethics of the conspiracy for his friends, but the moment had to come when he sought to grasp the faith of the church in general in its relationship to this secular world—a world that his own family history had made him close to. What did the universal Christ and his name mean where people truly lived and bore responsibility for others? This question increased Bonhoeffer's desire for a new encounter with contemporary philosophical and scientific literature all the more.

4. It is surprising how little Bonhoeffer wrestled with the theological literature of his times as he approached the verge of his new conception.

It had been years since Bonhoeffer had paid attention to Gogarten's influence. Only after the war did Gogarten's attempt to elucidate the positive contribution of faith to this process of secularization come to light. Despite his visit to America in 1939, all Bonhoeffer knew of Tillich was what had been published before the Nazi period. It was this he had in mind when he argued for or against Tillich.[155]

Bonhoeffer had not forgotten Bultmann, but had responded to his commentary on St. John and essay on demythologizing; yet even Bultmann did not receive the attention that might have been expected. It is unlikely that Bonhoeffer realized at the time how much unrest Bultmann's essay would generate throughout the world over the years. Nevertheless, in his second theological letter[156] he related his new attempted formulations to Bultmann's demythologizing, at the same time differentiating his own perspective by saying, surprisingly, that Bultmann "did not go far enough."[157] On leave in 1944, after I had spoken to Friedrich Justus Perels about the discussion of Bultmann within the Council of Brethren, I wrote to Tegel:

> When I was telling Justus in passing that evening that you were preoccupied with the problem of Bultmann, he immediately said that he thought that it had been settled and that Bultmann was a man who would have to be 'excommunicated.' He might be a philosopher, but not a theological teacher. It's remarkable that the problem does not trouble him.[158]

Bonhoeffer replied at once that he viewed Bultmann as an ally against Barth's "defined limits," but again distinguished his own perspective from Bultmann's.[159] Bultmann is named three times in the prison letters. Bonhoeffer quotes him each time rather casually in connection with something that he wants to say himself, showing both that he is close to him and that he knows their views do not entirely coincide. He thought that he had absorbed certain elements of Bultmann in his new approach, while he did not find that Bultmann's essay expressed his own opinions. Bonhoeffer's thought has a different foundation, and hence a different terminology. He also meant something different from Bultmann by "interpretation." Despite all the sympathy he expressed for his views, Bonhoeffer regarded himself as different from Bultmann.

In 1944 Bonhoeffer might have said, with respect to his motives, that he had reached back more to his own early theological period than to his contemporaries. He set about his work in Tegel without being able to use any modern theological library, depending almost entirely on memory. The stimulus for his new writing did not proceed from the desire to contradict what he might have felt on reading Bultmann and Barth. Positions on these contemporary figures emerged incidentally, as it were, in the course of his own reflections on what he was immediately facing. Bonhoeffer regarded both the direction and the radical nature of his thinking as something quite new and shocking within the Confessing church. And, at that time, they were.

The Problem of the Caesura. Some of Bonhoeffer's remarks in 1943 were conservative in spirit. Faced with the air raids and the destruction they caused, he spoke again of a new beginning on a "Christian basis":

> The fact that the horrors of war are now coming home to us with such force will no doubt, if we survive, provide us with the necessary basis for making it possible to reconstruct the life of the nations, both spiritually and materially, on Christian principles.[160]

This was the language of *Ethics*; by the summer of 1944 this tone had vanished. Now we read:

> It will be the task of our generation, not to "seek great things," but to save and preserve our souls out of the chaos, and to realize that this is the only thing we can carry as a "prize" from the burning building.... We shall have to keep our lives rather than shape them, to hope rather than plan, to hold out rather than march forward.... It will not be difficult for us to renounce our privileges, recognizing the justice of history....[161]

> With respect to the "basis of Christianity" we are "being thrown back to the beginnings of comprehension."[162]

In *Ethics* Bonhoeffer had said that "what is 'Christian' consists of that fact that a person may and should live as a person before God."[163] This appears almost conventional compared with the statement of 1944: "Before God and with God we live without God."[164]

Such observations later raised the question as to where the essential change in Bonhoeffer's development occurred. Many placed the change before *Ethics*, others (for example, R. Gregor Smith, Hanfried Müller, J. A. T. Robinson, and H. J. Schultz) between *Ethics* and the 1944 letters from prison. They saw the real progress as having been made after the new start of April 1944, and described what had gone before more or less as a preparatory phase, if not indeed an orthodoxy that to some extent followed the "wrong tracks."[165] Others, including Karl Barth, also viewed April 1944 as a major turning point; but for them the worthwhile reading was what had gone before, mainly *Discipleship*, while they considered the theology of *Letters and Papers from Prison* immature and not worth passing on.

It is not altogether easy to decide the question of where the turning point came, if only because so many elements of continuity with the past can be traced even in *Discipleship*. *Discipleship* and *Letters and Papers from Prison* both end in a remarkably similar way, with the motif of *imitatio*. Moreover, many ideas of 1944 can be found already in *Ethics* and in the letters of 1943, such as the love of the richness of the Old Testament and the warning against too direct an approach to the New Testament,[166] the rejection of religious blackmail in acute distress,[167] or the attempt to give a "nonreligious interpretation" of Easter.[168]

Yet there is much evidence that there was a decisive new beginning in April 1944. This naturally does not mean that this division into periods makes what had gone before unimportant. On the contrary, it is part of the origin of the new. The building blocks are there and are being used. But the old arrangement of these building blocks has been altered, and there is clearly an extension of the theme that is tantamount to a change in theme. Bonhoeffer himself thought he was pursuing a completely new path. In the collapse of the "Christian West" he was seized by a belief in a changed face of Christianity that would be viable. The manner of his theology had made his most recent political steps possible, and these steps now influenced the new manner of his theology.

Bonhoeffer's Own View. The theological statements in Bonhoeffer's 1944 letters are often interpreted negatively, by ascribing them to the particular circumstances of imprisonment, which had certainly shattered his inner equilibrium. We do, in fact, have written evidence of this, but this comes from the first year in Tegel, whereas at the point of this new theological departure the shock of this situation could no longer adversely affect the calm of his thinking. The first theological letter of 30 April 1944, as we saw, opened with the double assurance of how well he was again, but also of what anxiety his new ideas and their consequences might cause me.[169]

Bonhoeffer certainly felt he had to undertake an unavoidable task that might overturn much traditional thinking. "As a 'modern' theologian who is still aware of the debt that he owes to liberal theology, I feel obliged to tackle these questions."[170]

When the first two great theological letters, of 30 April and 5 May,[171] reached the Italian front after a long journey through the post, I asked in return: "Would you, I wonder, allow these sections to be given to people like Albrecht Schönherr, Winfried Maechler and Dieter Zimmermann?"[172] Bonhoeffer's reply of 8 July was very reserved, although these men were not distant figures, but familiar comrades from Finkenwalde. "If you want of your own accord to send Albrecht Schönherr and others extracts from my letters, you can, of course, do so. *I* would not do it myself as yet, because you are the only person with whom I venture to think aloud, as it were, in the hope of clarifying my thoughts." The question of the significance of his ideas pursued him, however, and at the end of this long letter he added:

> Incidentally, it would be very nice if you didn't throw away my theological letters, but sent them from time to time to Renate, as they must surely be a burden for you there. I might like to read them again later for my work, perhaps. One can write some things in a more natural and lively way in a letter than in a book, and in letters I often have better ideas than when I'm writing for myself. But it's not important![173]

This passage, which contains an important judgment about himself, gave the authority years later to publish what had been preserved in the form of letters only, and thus to ensure that his writing was passed on.

Finally Bonhoeffer said again how much he regarded himself as being involved in a reshaping of theology; this was when he emerged from the stage of correspondence into that of actually writing the draft of a manuscript. It is in the last letter to me that has been preserved, that of 23 August 1944:

> I'm now working on the chapter "A Stocktaking of Christianity." ... Sometimes I'm quite shocked at what I say, especially in the first part, which is mainly critical; and so I am looking forward to getting to the more constructive part. But the whole thing has been so little discussed that it often sounds too clumsy. In any case, it can't be printed yet.[174]

Bonhoeffer's Work Style and Its Consequences. The volume *Letters and Papers from Prison* that has been compiled from Bonhoeffer's prison letters is nothing like the book he would have published on his new subject. We do not even possess any headings for the book he planned, only a few pages with a sketch under the formal heading "Outline for a Book" and three suggested chapter headings: (1) A Stocktaking of Christianity. (2) What Essentially Is Christian Faith? (3) Conclusions.[175] The posthumous *Letters and Papers from Prison* contains a letter in which he gave a rendition, both before and after this sketch, of an initial stage of his thinking.

The period of work that we know about comprises only four months. First came three months of discussion in letters, followed by one month's work on the outline, with the beginning of work on the actual writing of the manuscript. Of the latter, in which Bonhoeffer probably made considerable progress, we do not possess a single page.

Bonhoeffer began the theological dialogue through correspondence at the end of April. In one week he was able to write several letters solely to "tell what is constantly on my mind."[176] He frequently moved from correspondence to conception, a transition which was expressed also by his change from Latin script to his almost unreadable Gothic handwriting.[177]

In August he began to write the work, side by side with the letters. In this second stage he sent me that "Outline for a Book," in order to preserve the sketch along with other documents from the cell. In August and September Bonhoeffer hardly worked on anything but his future book. There were interruptions because of the bad news from his family, the escape plan, and finally his being taken to the Reich Central Security Office. During these weeks he had removed everything from his cell that he thought unnecessary but worth preserving—but not the manuscript of the work he was writing. We may safely assume that he took it with him to the cellar in the prison on Prinz-Albrecht-Strasse so that he could continue writing it.

Aside from the four months of theological letters between the end of April and the end of August 1944, there was another month of theological writing, in those letters that had not yet been sent off for safekeeping but had to be destroyed.[178]

Despite his initial complaints that he missed discussing this work, he did occasionally find people to whom he was able to speak at least a little about the things on his mind. Before anyone else learned of it the prison chaplains, Poelchau and Dannenbaum, heard about what was being written in Bonhoeffer's cell. Even years later Gaetano Latmiral could recall the ideas Bonhoeffer told him about during the prisoners' exercise periods in the prison yard.

Given the nature of these available sources, the inevitable question— often repeated since—was whether these were not fragments of early immature ideas (conceived, moreover, under the probable shock of imprisonment) and thus not to be taken seriously, or whether they present a recognizable vision whose influence is correctly growing. It seems to me that what we have is not the mature fruit of a new branch in Bonhoeffer's work, but it is also more than a vague, random attempt. Ultimately only the content of the brief fragments and their reception can decide this.

But some observations concerning Bonhoeffer's style of work confirm the validity of these statements during the first stage. With Bonhoeffer's earlier books there was generally a period of three or four years between his first ideas and the completion of the manuscript. For example, as early as 1932 he presented the first formulations of the ideas of *Discipleship* in seminars, Bible study groups, and sermons, and these already contained some of the key words. In 1935 and 1936 the book reached its final form, which had retained these very words. In the case of *Ethics* Bonhoeffer developed the core of his christological concept of reality in 1940, and began in 1942 for the last time to write the chapters. Here he made more changes than was the case in *Discipleship*, although still holding fast to a certain fundamental conception.

In general, therefore, Bonhoeffer's basic ideas set the stage very early for what was to come, and they fairly consistently retained the form in which they were first expressed. Given his manner of working we may well imagine that the 1944 sketches were preserved in their final form, having remained constant from the first stage of the letters in April to the second stage, in the outline made in August. His initial visions were always very clear-cut. Later he would further substantiate his basic theses, but without smoothing away their sharp edges. For Bonhoeffer something was always far more ready to be published when it presented a challenge that was supported by argument than when all possible objections to it had been painstakingly answered.

Bonhoeffer's life also offers examples of his tackling themes alongside a major work in order to relinquish them quickly to the experts—as was the case, for example, with his Christocentric interpretations of the Old Testament.[179] This subsidiary character cannot be ascribed to the work of 1944, however, because this is contradicted by Bonhoeffer's own words.

What we have here is undoubtedly the essential basic ideas of Bonhoeffer. His new starting point was quite clearly defined. Further work on it would inevitably have considered the consequences and given examples. But the basic ideas can be recognized in the letters where Bonhoeffer speaks in a carefree and abbreviated way, as one does with a dialogue partner with whom one shares common ideas and theological presuppositions.

The New Formula. After April 1944 Bonhoeffer's new theme was not simply the "nonreligious interpretation of biblical terms in a world come of age." As we said at the beginning, this key phrase is part of an explicitly stated larger theme, which Bonhoeffer expressed many times in the form of a question or central idea.[180]

The Main Question. With Bonhoeffer's fourfold declaration of his real purpose he places his ideas concerning nonreligious interpretation in the perspective within which he wishes them to be seen.

1. The theme is stated on 30 April, before Bonhoeffer begins his new discussions: "What bothers me incessantly is the question ... who Christ really

is for us today."[181] The chief question, then, is not *what* parts of the creed are still acceptable today, but who *he* is for us today. Bonhoeffer does not consider from a distance how much of tradition can be retained but, as in *Act and Being* and his Christology, inquires into the person of Christ and the way in which he encounters and defines us today.[182]

2. In the same letter, from the same standpoint, Bonhoeffer restates his question in a more differentiated manner while discussing the world come of age:

> If our final judgement must be that the Western form of Christianity, too, was only a preliminary stage to a complete absence of religion, what kind of situation emerges for us, for the church? How can Christ become the Lord of the religionless as well? . . . How do we speak of God—without religion, i.e., without the temporally conditioned presuppositions of metaphysics, inwardness and so on? How do we speak (or perhaps we cannot now even "speak" as we used to) in a "worldly" way about "God"? In what way are we "religionless—secular" Christians, in what way are we the *ecclesia,* those who are called forth, not regarding ourselves from a religious point of view as specially favored, but rather as belonging wholly to the world? In that case Christ is no longer an object of religion, but something quite different, really the Lord of the world. But what does that mean?[183]

Thus Bonhoeffer inquired into the way in which Christ is Lord, not into a method whereby we should present Christ today. With this kind of inquiry he renewed what he had said as early as 1932, namely, that it is not a question of how we ought to proclaim the Gospel today but, in view of the historical development of the western world, of who is its content. Given the presupposition of the presence of Christ, Bonhoeffer sought to understand his presence today.

3. On 8 June he expressed the theme in its most succinct form: "Christ and the world that has come of age."[184] Here Bonhoeffer criticizes the liberals, but also Heim and Althaus, for ultimately dispensing—albeit for different reasons—with Christ's antecedent and comprehensive claim to lordship. But that was the last thing Bonhoeffer wanted to attempt now.

4. Soon afterward, on 30 June, he presented another variation on the theme: "Let me just summarize briefly what I am concerned about: the claims of Jesus Christ on a world that has come of age."[185] Christ was, is, and will be the Lord. This lordship of Christ that Bonhoeffer is concerned with in all four formulations of his theme is saved by him from clericalization and hierarchical tendencies because this Lord exercises his lordship

always and solely through powerlessness, service, and the cross. But this lordship is undoubted. Bonhoeffer is not defending a lost lordship and certainly not any lost positions. Indeed, he wants to give up "positions" in order that he can learn to understand anew how the suffering and powerless Christ becomes the defining, liberating, and creative center of this world.

Having clearly and repeatedly stated the fundamental character of his inquiry into the presence of Christ, Bonhoeffer is able to define his task in another quite different and seemingly contradictory way. In reality, however, he is liberated by this fixed center, so that he has to defend the world against "the last of the knights":[186] "I therefore want to start from the premise . . . that we should frankly recognize that the world, and people, have come of age, that we should not run man down in his worldliness, but confront him at his strongest point with God."[187] This goal of acknowledging humanity's coming of age so fascinated later readers that many forgot that Bonhoeffer had framed his call to maturity within the theme of the presence of Christ, and even here, this call to maturity was not an isolated one. His phrase here is: "confront him with God." This passage in the letter also speaks about the majesty of the Word of God: "it reigns."[188] On one of my letters to him, with its anxious questions, Bonhoeffer jotted down notes for his reply, one of which is "Aristocratic Christianity."[189]

If this is the character of the subject Bonhoeffer was dealing with in Tegel, then his elaborations on this theme, from the very beginning, never entered the sphere of apologetics. The question of what can be demanded of a believer today is not the most important thing. There can be genuine doubt about the capability of the church or a generation to proclaim Christ, but no halfhearted doubt that faith will find what it is seeking. Within this main theme Bonhoeffer's analysis of time, which appeared more frequently now than in previous years, never acquired the pessimistic nuances so characteristic of Heim and Gogarten. Bonhoeffer could threaten, especially the church and its lack of faith, but he never prophesied dark despair. The dedication of oneself to Jesus of Nazareth and his presence is in no way diminished or done away with, as difficult as it might be to spell out. The "interpretation" Bonhoeffer sets in motion cannot remain within the sphere of contemplative, intellectual questions of understanding, in which things are explored without any regard for what such investigation might yield. His quest is part of a journey, as it were, from past engagement to new engagement. Bonhoeffer's theme entails setting out in order to discover the presence of Christ in the world of today: it is not a discovery of the modern world, nor a discovery of Christ from this modern world, but discovering *him* in this world. Bonhoeffer asks the simplest of questions, from which it is impossible to emerge unchanged: "Who are *you?*" and that is why he also mentions prayer at the very beginning of his essay.[190]

Hence this question governs Bonhoeffer's dialogue and must preserve, in the correct relation and proportion, the explosive formulas of the world come of age, nonreligious interpretation, and arcane discipline. Without the overriding theme of this question these concepts would fall apart and become stunted or superficial. As isolated intellectual phenomena, they have little to do with Bonhoeffer's thought; but within the christological perspective of his central theme they achieve their full and independent justification. The question "Who are *you* today?" involves two things. The first was Bonhoeffer's concern for arriving at the full christological answer in continuity with the past; the second was his concern that, in losing the freshness of past answers, the matter at hand was the adventure of a new christological answer.

The material of the prison letters can now be arranged, commented on, and interrelated in a way that parallels the three chapters in his "Outline for a Book":[191] (A) the world come of age (chapter 1: Stocktaking); (B) nonreligious interpretation (chapter 2: Worldly Faith); and (C) arcane discipline (chapter 3: Consequences for the Form of the Church).

(A) *The World Come of Age.* The judgment of a world come of age occupied much space in the letters. This complex of ideas aroused the greatest surprise and found the strongest echo among its first readers because of its refreshing analyses.

Bonhoeffer seems to be referring to a particular historical development, a stage to which our eyes must one day be opened if we want to remain in the present. He speaks of "a world *grown* of age" or of a "world *coming* of age,"[192] and more rarely of the "world come of age."[193] This avoids the misunderstanding that this development is a moral evolution, in the sense that the world has "grown better." The actual process is a growing up, with the concomitant responsibilities from which there is now no retreat. Even in a world again enslaved, this coming of age remains an ideal by which the world measures its condition and of which it dreams. Even the modern tyrant must portray his tyranny to his victims as a true liberation and granting of independence.

The concept of "coming of age" does not appear immediately in Bonhoeffer's theological letters, not until 8 June.[194] Until then he uses the concept of "autonomy" when describing the evolution of the various realms of life toward self-responsibility. On 8 June, however, he speaks of freeing ourselves from the "guardianship of 'God.'"[195] "God" here is in parentheses! Almost as soon as the phrase "coming of age" appears it dominates the scene. In using the phrase Bonhoeffer is thinking of Kant's formula: "The Enlightenment is the emergence of humanity from self-imposed immaturity. Immaturity is the incapacity to use one's own intelligence without the guidance of another person."[196] For a century this definition had been a great burden on the church; that is why Richard Rothe bravely transformed faith in the last century into ethics, defining the process of Christian evolution as a transformation of Christianity into the continually growing ethical autonomy of our coming of age. But Bonhoeffer now took Kant's irrevocable description of maturity as an essential element of his *theologia crucis*.

Bonhoeffer was not the first theologian who welcomed, instead of condemning, the evolution of secularization into a coming of age. If Bonhoeffer had been able to examine the material more thoroughly, he would have seen that the religious socialist Leonhard Ragaz and Paul Tillich had made similar breakthroughs earlier. The others, however, had been concerned with turning away from the Christology of the Reformation, whereas Bonhoeffer proclaimed this coming of age in the name of the crucified and risen Christ, and saw it as a necessary part of his Christology. For him it was the crucified Christ who enabled, judged, and renewed "true worldliness," "genuine this-worldliness," and "coming of age." This gave the category of "coming of age" a theological quality.

Theological Judgment. In connection with a critique of Bultmann, Bonhoeffer noted that he sought to "think theologically."[197] In Bonhoeffer the recognition of the world's coming of age is neither philosophy nor phenomenology, but the knowledge of God, that is, "theology." It is a knowledge that seeks to follow God where God has already preceded us. That is why Bonhoeffer's statement about the world come of age is first and last a theological statement. This is also truc of his statement about "unconscious Christianity."[198]

A theological statement is not a statistical operation, but preserves a proclamation of God about a portion of history. It has its moment in time, in which it is expressed in a committed and committing way. As a "theological statement" it possesses critical protesting and liberating elements. Bonhoeffer realized that it was high time to declare that the world had come of age, for the sake of God; he was unwilling to let Hitler dictate the image of that world. In this he was concerned not only with the knowledge of the world's maturity, but with unequivocally proclaiming that maturity. In this theological statement, seeing and recognizing are inseparably bound up with the judgment itself: namely, the acknowledgment of the world's maturity.

The objection that Bonhoeffer or the church is only restating what the world had already done on its own long ago misses the heart of the problem. It is quite legitimate for the church's blessing to be extended to a fait accompli. It always blesses "after the event," in order to express God's faithful love and involvement in a particular past piece of the history of individuals or communities. A curse or a blessing is always pronounced over something that has come into being, thereby determining its future progress. In the case of the "world come of age," not only had the church not blessed the autonomously evolving world, it had condemned it and declared it "godless." But if there is no declaration that it has come of age, then the world itself must pronounce it.

It was only at this point in his theological development that Bonhoeffer came upon this idea, but he then gave it an almost polemically important place in his discussions. It is true that he had long since stopped using the word "secularization," so commonly used by the church, to describe the modern development of the world.[199] Even before this Bonhoeffer seldom used it; he disliked its condemnatory tone. This was not how he wanted to characterize his issue. Thus he used the word that emphasized the positive element in the relationship between Christ and the modern world.

> Thus the world's coming of age is no longer an occasion for polemics and apologetics, but is now really better understood than it understands itself, namely on the basis of the gospel and in the light of Christ.[200]

Because Bonhoeffer never stopped thinking dialectically, his statements about the world's coming of age have two levels and do not merely level out into a positivism. The Gospel of the *theologia crucis* tolerates the world come of age and even accepts that such a world may deny the Gospel—and this in fact helps it find its own position and its essence. The unity and paradox of the *theologia crucis* and the world come of age found its most succinct expression in the now famous passage of 16 July 1944, when he wrote:

> ... that we have to live in the world *etsi deus non daretur*. And this is just what we do recognize—before God! God himself compels us to recognize it. So our coming of age leads us to a true recognition of our situation before God. God would have us know that we must live as people who manage our lives without him. The God who is with us is the God who forsakes us (Mark 15:34). The God who lets us live in the world without the working hypothesis of God is the God before whom we stand continually. Before God and with God we live without God. God lets himself be pushed out of the world on to the cross. He is weak and powerless in the

world, and that is precisely the way, the only way, in which he is with us and helps us.[201]

Within this possibility, of exploring the knowledge of the theology of the cross and the world's having come of age from both sides, Bonhoeffer is even able to venture stating the reverse: that recognizing the world's coming of age can help us to better understand the Gospel:

> To that extent we may say that the development towards the world's com-ing of age outlined above, which has done away with a false conception of God, opens up a way of seeing the God of the Bible, who wins power and space in the world by his weakness.[202]

Or, more daring still: "The world that has come of age is more godless, and perhaps for that very reason closer to God, than the world before its coming of age."[203] Bonhoeffer was far too alert a theologian not to know that every new piece of knowledge could become isolated and that the world's freedom to come of age could succumb to positivistic misuse. That is why he wrote on 21 July 1944—when it seemed very likely that he would not have the chance to communicate his ideas much longer:

> I don't mean the shallow and banal this-worldliness of the enlightened, the busy, the comfortable or the lascivious, but the profound this-worldliness, characterized by discipline and the constant knowledge of death and resurrection.[204]

But he was able to affirm so resolutely the world's coming of age precisely because it was so clearly related to the gospel of the cross. In fact, it was this new affirmation that initially preoccupied him more than anything else and caused him to reexamine his way of thinking. Now, with a different accent than he had used four years previously in the chapter "Inheritance and Decay" in *Ethics*, he presented the path of liberation of the western spirit, law, philosophy, and secular life. The pleasure he took in continually testing this was clear. Now modern "secularization," or preferably "worldliness," was viewed as a necessary and specific part of the Christian heritage, and Chris-tianity no longer denounced it. Secularization was no longer an evil falling away, but the free responsibility of Christianity; the secularizers were no longer powerful seducers, but the protagonists and midwives of humanity. The issue is recognizing a development that eventually will make the church guilty if it continues to demonize worldliness, instead of helping human beings realize their true humanity. For suddenly it becomes clear that humanity and the world's coming of age are inescapably interconnected.

Now a liberating movement begins to spread, in which the Christian listens to Feuerbach and Nietzsche—with a good conscience—and allows them their share in humanity's progress, as when they warn the church against becoming an apothecary that ministers to heavenly needs and leaves the world to its own devices. In contrast, the church's *theologia crucis* may serve the legacy of the Enlightenment as a protection against its own tendency toward the unrealistic. It corrects humankind's unquenchable urge to glorify, deify, or demonize its progress. It also moves in the other direction, perhaps even more necessary today: it protects the Enlightenment's proponents from the unfortunate tendency, born of a pessimistic resignation and skeptical agnosticism, toward sterile fragmentation of the individual and his or her work.

The effect of Bonhoeffer's remarks about coming of age was intensified because he made these astonishing statements at a time when he himself had become the helpless victim of the violence of disenfranchised leadership structures. Like Boethius, the philosopher of late antiquity imprisoned for high treason, Bonhoeffer strongly relativized what lay closest to him. At the time it seemed that we had never heard things expressed quite like this before: that the lordship of Christ corresponds to worldliness, and discipleship to a partaking in this world; that the natural, the profane, the rational, and the humane had its place, not against, but with this Christ.

(B) *Nonreligious Interpretation.* It is now a characteristic of the world come of age that the era of "religion" has passed. Bonhoeffer referred to the end of religion even before he spoke of the world coming of age. First he defined religion as "metaphysics and inwardness,"[205] but then it seems to be chiefly its guardianship that is done away with.

Hence the presence of Christ must be experienced in this "nonreligious interpretation." Bonhoeffer often approached this task, but without carrying it through to its conclusion.[206] Here he sensed the greatest objective difficulties. On 3 June I asked him about Bultmann; about the Protestant abandonment of any special sphere of their own; about the role of the liturgical and prophetic spheres, and the significance of tradition in this "interpretation."[207] His answer was as follows:

> You now ask so many important questions on the subjects that have been occupying me lately, that I should be happy if I could answer them myself. But it is all very much in the early stages: and, as usual, I am being led on more by an instinctive feeling for questions that will arise later than by any conclusions that I have already reached about them.[208]

But he was quite certain that the tasks of the future lay in this direction, that is, that the Gospel should be freed from its traditional trammels, understood and passed on: that it should, in other words, continue to live on in a "nonreligious" way.

In the course of his discussions Bonhoeffer varied the term used; he also spoke of a "worldly interpretation," "worldly reinterpretation,"[209] or "the new, nonreligious language."[210] For the most part he speaks of religionless "interpretation," once using the phrase "religionless Christianity," and at another point "being a religionless Christian" or "living without religion." It is worth noting that in German-speaking countries the only discussion of this has been about the expression "nonreligious interpretation," whereas in the English-speaking world the key phrase has been "religionless Christianity." In fact, there are two different issues involved: in the one case the problem of preaching, and in the other the problems of prayer and the institutional church. But Bonhoeffer is speaking about both of these.

He did not find the expression "nonreligious interpretation" as "enigmatic" as Barth did.[211] At any rate, Bonhoeffer was so sure of what he was saying that he had no reservations about giving his book the working title of "Nonreligious Interpretation in a World Come of Age," and devoted the work he proposed writing to this programmatic aim.

"Religion." How did Bonhoeffer understand "religion" and what could he have meant by "nonreligious interpretation"?

On closer examination, his use of the term "religion" has aroused many questions. But in Tegel Bonhoeffer never intended for a moment to write a historical or systematic monograph on the phenomenon of religion, as he had done at far greater length in *Act and Being,* for example. He hardly would have let himself be drawn into an argument as to whether he had completely clarified the term "religion." He would have admitted that what he was talking about, as an independent phenomenon detached from its relation to Christology, was not clearly defined and would look different if considered from other angles. The fact that he was not entirely unaware of this is proved by the books he read, which included Orelli's *General History of Religion* and Simmel's *Religion.* More recently he had also acquired G. van der Leeuw's *Phenomenology of Religion* and *Man and Religion,* as well as the comprehensive history of religion by Chantepie de la Saussaye.

Although he was always quick to dismiss the phenomenon of religion, within the framework of his overall theme of Christ's presence in a world come of age he assumed that some things now belonged to the past. He called these, according to his own tradition, "religion." They not only obscured one's view of the present world and Christ, but distorted it. The diametrically opposite distinction between faith and religion was among his fundamental experiences as a student. All of his sermons in Barcelona indicated what he had learned from Karl Barth and what he had seen in the Bible, through Barth's eyes, of opposition to religion. This view of faith and religion had become common among a large number of theologians in the Confessing church. In prison Bonhoeffer once again explicitly praised Barth's achievement: "Barth was the first theologian to begin the criticism of religion, and that remains his really great merit."[212] What was meant here by "religion" was that human activity which seeks to reach the beyond, to postulate a divinity, to invoke help and protection, in short: religion as self-justification.

Bonhoeffer emphasized that Barth was the first person "to have begun thinking" along the lines of a religionless Christianity, although he "did not carry it to completion,"[213] nor had he given any "concrete guidance . . . in the nonreligious interpretation of theological concepts."[214] When he spoke of Barth beginning but not thinking through, Bonhoeffer could have been thinking of Barth's very early essays (noted by Benkt-Erik Benktson), in which some of Barth's formulations bear an extraordinary resemblance to many of Bonhoeffer's concepts in 1944.

Bonhoeffer's treatment of the term "religion" differs, however, from that of Barth. Barth regarded religion as an unavoidable characteristic of the believer—just as Bonhoeffer had done in his early period, in *Act and Being*. But now the phenomenon of religion did not appear to Bonhoeffer to be an eternal concomitant human characteristic, but a transitory historical one, and therefore perhaps a unique "Western"[215] phenomenon that would not return. Here Bonhoeffer certainly went beyond Barth, but he had not sufficiently considered how disturbing all this was, so the statements that exist reveal a clear weak point.

The Characteristics of Bonhoeffer's Concept of Religion. Despite the fragmentary nature of his remarks, they do have characteristics that clearly reveal the contours of what Bonhoeffer describes in his letters as religion. Bonhoeffer himself gave an incidental definition of two of these qualities that explicitly remind us of earlier material: the metaphysical and the individualistic elements. The totality of his thought and action suggest other characteristics as well: the privileged character of religion, its partiality, its concept of the *deus ex machina*, its tendency to keep people subordinate, and its dispensable nature.

We may ask whether such characteristics must necessarily be features of "religion." Bonhoeffer considered them to be actually present, and believed that religion, with these characteristics, had become a western phenomenon, thus limiting the challenge and the nature of Jesus to a very specific direction. But this direction leads us into dead ends and should be abandoned. Dwelling here on the terminological objections could prevent us from seeing Bonhoeffer's real aim.

Metaphysics.

> ... to "interpret in a religious sense"? I think it means to speak on the one hand metaphysically, and on the other individualistically[216] ... the temporally conditioned presuppositions of metaphysics. ...[217] God ... in the conceptual forms of the absolute, metaphysical, infinite ...[218]

These were Bonhoeffer's own references to religion as a metaphysically determined entity. He was not thinking in terms of "immanence-transcendence," in order to eliminate transcendence in favor of immanence. On the contrary, he was particularly concerned here with regaining a genuine transcendence, in contrast to a metaphysics that had lost its value, as an "extended world" and a necessary prerequisite for any faith.[219]

Even as a student in Ritschl's Berlin, Bonhoeffer had seen the imprisonment of biblical faith in western philosophical metaphysics. Barth's theology had impressed this upon him even more. It appeared to Bonhoeffer that, in the long history of its metaphysical construction, the once overwhelming transcendence of faith has been reduced to something painfully remote. Supranatural and mythological formulations obscure the Gospel's direct immediacy, and the exotic nature of the context in which it is presented has nothing to do with the message itself. Instead of this, however, the metaphysically organized Christian religion provided the world with the kind of transcendence it longed for. God became necessary as the superstructure of being, and religious longing found its goal in a heavenly domain. Thus metaphysics seduces the Christian religion into thinking statically in terms of two spheres, and forces it to give its redemptive nature a one-sided emphasis.

Perhaps Bonhoeffer's use of the concept "metaphysics" needs some slight corrections by Tillich.[220] Still, Bonhoeffer's nonreligious interpretation is close to Tillich and Bultmann in what it rejects with the "metaphysical" misunderstanding of religion of the Gospel of Jesus. Just as Tillich wants to get rid of the "supranatural" and Bultmann the "mythological," Bonhoeffer, for the sake of God, wants to get rid of the "religious" trappings, the objectification of God that is conditioned by a particular age. Bonhoeffer is anxious to break up the traditional structure of dogmas and their concepts to discuss "theism" in order to begin a new dialogue with the "atheists."[221] Yet already, right next to Bonhoeffer's epistemologically orientated inquiry are other elements, voluntaristic and related to existence, which also play a strong part. Let us recall his early interest in "ethical transcendence":

> It is not with the beyond that we are concerned, but with this world as created and preserved, subjected to laws, reconciled, and restored. What is above this world is, in the Gospel, intended to exist *for* this world.[222]

According to the relevant sections in *Sanctorum Communio* and *Act and Being*, there is a close connection between the metaphysical and the subsequent individualistic element, because—as Bonhoeffer never tired of showing—in the epistemological transcendence of the metaphysical everything is ultimately "drawn" into the subject, which ultimately remains alone. Thus, in the letters as well, he always speaks of both together.

Individualism.

> To "interpret in a religious sense" means to speak . . . on the other hand individualistically.[223] The era of religion was actually an era of inwardness and conscience;[224] the temporally conditioned presuppositions of . . . inwardness;[225] the attempt to keep God's place secure at least in the sphere of the "personal," the "inner" and the "private";[226] Pietism as a last attempt to maintain evangelical Christianity as a religion. . . .[227]

These are the indications of religion understood as an individualistic entity.

As early as *Sanctorum Communio* Bonhoeffer had expounded the social dimension of all Christian concepts. Of course he always spoke very directly of the individual acceptance of faith; but he never lost sight of the social, anti-individualistic direction of faith and the kingdom of righteousness. He never became so rigorous that he rejected intense personal declarations of faith, such as those in the hymns of Paul Gerhardt; but he was uncomfortable with the tendency to direct one's gaze to the private human sphere and cultivate the "salvation of one's own soul" at the cost of the world and the *familia Dei*. This sensitivity grew so strong that he never thought of leading those who had "come of age" back into the confinement of this kind of individualistic inwardness.

Viewed in terms of the metaphysical objectification of God, nonreligious interpretation and existential interpretation may have seemed to be the same thing, but this does not appear to be the case with this second characteristic. The interest of the existential interpretation lies clearly with the individual, which encourages a sterility toward the kinds of questions that transcend the individual. Because of this it has been noted that there is a connection between Bultmann's theology and the pietistic world that Bonhoeffer termed "religious." Bonhoeffer suspected the same kind of connection when he extended his dislike of a pietistic or dogmatic pastoral care, which dwelled on the intimate sphere of human life or on the "inwardness" of human existence, to existential philosophy as well. He probably would have asked whether the modern existential interpretation was not subject to his verdict that the "secrets known to a man's valet" were "the hunting-ground of modern pastoral workers,"[228] and hence were part of the sphere of "religious interpretation" where "in those secret human places ... God is to have his domain."[229]

Partiality. We can now add a few important characteristics to these definitions of "religion" quoted by Bonhoeffer himself: characteristics that emerge from Bonhoeffer's life and theological convictions, or are clearly stated in the paraphrased form of the letters, thus giving an even more exact image of "nonreligious interpretation."

In his youth Bonhoeffer had been disturbed by Friedrich Naumann's question about the extent to which the Christian religion had become a separate area among the other areas of life, a mere section of the whole. God is assigned a more or less respectable sphere within the totality of life. This can be said of his teacher Reinhold Seeberg's subtle view of a "religious a priori," which is given its own domain alongside other a priori elements of life. The same thing is true of the quasi-religious areas that can be discussed in sociological or psychological terms. It could also be true of remnants of the past, relics of various kinds that can still be life-giving or that come into the province of culture. In the unstoppable process of secularization these areas that are still religiously alive are removed, one by one, from the number of relevant areas. Thus the Christian god also seems condemned to preside over only those areas of life that remain, as yet, unexplored. Bonhoeffer never tired of describing this fate of the Christian religion of being "continually in retreat."[230] "The religious act is always something partial; 'faith' is something whole, involving the whole of one's life."[231]

The fatal part of this process is that religion directs its entire interest toward its boundaries, keeping watch over them through its institutions. "The decisive factor: the church on the defensive. No taking risks for others."[232]

Deus ex Machina. Bonhoeffer most vividly described the common religious conception of God as a *deus ex machina* in the first verse of his poem "Christians and Pagans."[233] All religion depends on this concept. There must be a supreme being ("omnipotence, omniscience, omnipresence")[234] so that we can be rescued from dangers, have our mysteries solved, and hear our questions answered. This makes the Christian religion a spiritual pharmacy. The preacher points out to his listeners their need of help in order, then, to dispense to them the necessary remedies.

Bonhoeffer's concern here is to show that it is precisely religiosity, and even pietism, that can dangerously conceal humanity's real godlessness. Christ must not be made the "answer," the "solution," or the "medicine." Religion depends on the power of God, but "the Bible directs us to God's powerlessness and suffering."[235]

This idea, in turn, makes religion an escape from real life and from mature responsibility for it. It accustoms us to artificial satisfactions. Perhaps we ought to mention in this connection what Bonhoeffer says about "longing": that God is not there to fill the gaps. He stated this with particular clarity in the letter of Christmas Eve 1943.[236]

Privilege. The idea behind this characteristic of religion was named only once in the letters: "those who are privileged."[237] In fact, however, it played an ever-present role and was almost the most important idea of all.[238] Bonhoeffer's life consisted of a constant fight to overcome the dangerously privileged character of the Christian religion: in his decision to take up theology, his move from teaching to pastoral work, and then to "becoming a man for his own times" in the conspiracy against Hitler.

Throughout its history the Christian religion has been continually perverted into a form of privilege.[239] It did not prevent itself from being understood in various ways as a gift to especially favored people. This happened in every conceivable area of individual and social life and thought: materially, financially, legally, and as a gift, either physical or psychic, innate or acquired. Faith becomes a possession that is either deserved or undeserved. It appears as something thrust upon people, unrelated to anything else and propagated in terms of a restorative "positivism of revelation."[240] Its practice becomes the conventionally shaped luxury of those in certain social classes who have the time to afford it or are compelled by their circumstances to do so. Religion, in fact, had become the strongest guarantor of the assurance and continuation of the existing order, power structure, and ways of thought.

Here Bonhoeffer's remarks on religion as "law," as the condition of salvation—to which one must belong—are pertinent.[241] Religion has become essentially a way of distinguishing people. A victim of its divisive privileged character, it has fostered manifold acts of violence throughout history: Christians against non-Christians, theists against atheists, or whites against people of color.

Guardianship. Closely connected with this privileged character of religion is the role that it plays as the "guardian" of people who are regarded, at least in this respect, as not having come of age. This characteristic must be stressed because the Christian institutions—as well as the monarchical, patriarchal character of the Christian religion's categories of thinking—seem so ineradicable and solid, and also because these two things are essentially linked in Bonhoeffer. They interpret one another: "the nonreligious interpretation" "in a world come of age," or vice versa, "religious interpretation in a world that is treated as if it were not of age."

"Religious interpretation" is an exegesis of the Gospel of Christ's powerlessness that establishes priests (as the givers of life) or theologians (as the custodians of truth) as the guardians and the rulers of the church's people, creating and perpetuating a situation of dependence. Nothing will be as difficult as overcoming the monarchical and patriarchal structures of hierarchies, theologies, and, indeed, dogmas; coming of age contains an element that is alarmingly unreassuring.

Thus Bonhoeffer is able to speak of "orthodoxy" as the "attempt to rescue the church as an institution for salvation"[242] and of "false religious obligations and inhibitions."[243] On the other hand, he can also urge us to accept responsibility for others and make possible the mature cooperation and partnership of the world. "The church must share in the worldly problems of social human life, not dominating, but helping and serving."[244] And perhaps one reason for Bonhoeffer's personal influence was his mysterious capacity to help people on their way to maturity.

Dispensability. One characteristic of Bonhoeffer's concept of religion expressed in the letters from prison, namely, that religion is passing away, has already been mentioned. It should be considered once more, although Bonhoeffer never clarified the relation of Barth's systematic concept of religion to this historical one. Can faith ever escape becoming a religion, whether western, eastern, or African? But precisely in order to make faith possible, Bonhoeffer explains "religion" in its "Western form" as something we can do without and as a relic of past ages.[245] His judgment here is so certain because he regards the age of Jesus as something different from the age of religion.

Bonhoeffer regards the characteristics of religion we have mentioned as failing to recognize not just the presence, but the person of Jesus. The essential concern is always Jesus and the way in which he is present to us: (1) Jesus does not call for any acceptance of preliminary systems of thought and behavior; (2) he is anti-individualist, unprotected, and, in a totally vulnerable fashion, the man for others; (3) he does not pray as if prayer were a partial payment on the installment plan, but with his life; (4) he turns away from the temptation of the *deus ex machina*; (5) he turns away from the privileged classes and sits together with the outcasts; and (6) he liberates us to find our own responsible answer to life through his own powerlessness, which shames and utterly convinces us.

Bonhoeffer finds that Christians corroborate his analysis every day, since their Christian activity has, in fact, become a separate Sunday-like area within the whole of their lives. Pestalozzi expressed what had happened to religion in the language of his day, in an individualistic, but still valid way—as Hammelsbeck pointed out:

> I swung back and forth between feelings that drew me to religion and judgements that drew me away from it, the dead path of my era. I felt the essence of religion grow cold within me, without ever actually making a decision against religion. . . .
>
> In the unspeakable misery I underwent, the strength of the few isolated religious feelings of my younger years disappeared. . . .
>
> I do not believe, not because I regard non-belief as truth, but because the sum of my impressions of life has largely removed the blessing of faith from my innermost self. . . . Thus I am a long way from the fulfillment of myself and do not know the heights that I suspect that perfect truth is able to ascend.[246]

After the 20 July attempt in 1944 Adam von Trott urgently described the situation to his wife shortly before his execution: "Can our childlike Christian faith . . . grow and impress itself upon the entire weight and intensity of our problems today?" "Childlike Christian faith" was exactly the same as Bonhoeffer's "religion"; its "growth" corresponded to Bonhoeffer's search for the totality of faith in relation to mature responsibility in our contemporary involvement with the world, and Trott's word "impress" resembles Bonhoeffer's comprehensive understanding of "interpretation." Just before his death Trott was asking Bonhoeffer's question—half in hope, half in doubt.

In summary: if "religion" has a tendency to the "partial," we can speak of "nonpartial" interpretation instead of "nonreligious." Or, when Bonhoeffer says "worldly," we can speak of the "totality of interpretation, with all its relevance and claims." Here we see the reason for Bonhoeffer's love of Stifter's novel *Witiko*: "The 'religious act' is always something partial, 'faith' is something whole, involving the whole of one's life. Jesus does not summon to a new religion, but to life ... Young Witiko ... set out into the world 'to do the whole thing.'"[247] The "whole thing" is other people, the revelation of one's own godlessness, the acceptance of the common guilt, and the sharing of God's powerlessness in the world. In the fullest sense, Bonhoeffer's nonreligious interpretation is christological interpretation.

More Than a Program of Interpretation. Bonhoeffer's "nonreligious interpretation" offers solid and dependable criteria for the church's preaching and the living body of the congregation. Can it be used as a program of interpretation, with the interpretative tools of the study and practiced as a variation on "existential interpretation"? Gerhard Krause suggests so when, commenting on our attempts to present Bonhoeffer's ideas so far, he warns with some justification against viewing Bonhoeffer as so far removed from Bultmann.[248] Is Bonhoeffer's concept an interpretation without the supranatural dogmatic structure, such as J. A. T. Robinson contends in drawing the parallels with Tillich? Yes and no.

We have already suggested that Bultmann, Tillich, and Bonhoeffer resemble one another in certain respects. All three were able to say: "We are once again being driven right back to the beginnings of our understanding."[249] Bonhoeffer is very much concerned with the hermeneutical question and had realized its urgency even earlier. But he reacts differently: he confronts the church more. Moreover, it must be significant that each of these three men who formulated their views totally independent of one another arrived, on the basis of his different approach, to a different terminology for what he wanted to say. Bultmann did this on the basis of his philological work of translation and his pondering of its philosophical presuppositions; Tillich worked out of his philosophical interest in a reconciliatory universalism. And Bonhoeffer?

Ebeling has warned us against making Bonhoeffer the defender of a new "form" as against a new language.[250] There is no doubt that Bonhoeffer was passionately concerned with the contemporary relevance of the kerygma, with the way in which the Gospel can be expressed. Yet he strongly emphasized the area where philosophical, conceptual, and translation questions are transcended. His two chapters "A Stocktaking of Christianity" and "What Is Christian Faith" are followed by a third: "Consequences."[251] These "consequences" raise questions that are wholly concerned with the "form" of Christianity and cannot be ignored. Hence Bonhoeffer's nonreligious interpretation is more an ethical than a hermeneutical category, and also a direct call to repentance directed at the church and its present form—for the sake of the kerygma, the language.

The starting point of his thinking is characteristically linked with his interest in an "arcane discipline," in the constant relationship between the interpreter and the Lord whose power lies in his very powerlessness. This approach has remained a somewhat singular one in theological discussion, but it immediately raises the problem of Christian identity as soon as we begin to see the extent of our identification with the world. If nonreligious interpretation means identification, then arcane discipline guarantees identity.

Bonhoeffer's "program of interpretation" is familiar with the advice to the church to practice particular forms of silence,[252] for "it is not abstract argument, but example, that gives its word emphasis and power."[253] Thus honest intellectual effort is combined with ethical decisions. Bonhoeffer also discusses questions of understanding and method, but always arrives very soon at "conclusions" that are vulnerable, damaging, and readily open to criticism—as, for example, his conclusion about the giving away of the church's possessions. It is difficult to argue about what he says, for he soon reaches points that must be either accepted as prophetic or rejected. For Bonhoeffer questions of method that postpone the act of "interpretation," in the false expectation that they can be solved intellectually, cause our present encounter with the past and future Jesus Christ to disappear from view and lead us into false dependencies:

> We have thought it possible to ensure all the possibilities of any action in advance through thinking about them so that they happen automatically ... your thinking will be confined to what you take responsibility for in action.[254]

(C) *Arcane Discipline.* Everything presses now toward those passages in which Bonhoeffer speaks of the mystery of a "participation in the suffering of God on this earth,"[255] within which a "new fusion" occurs that will one day make available "the reconciling and redemptive language" in which "the world will be changed and renewed."[256] Bonhoeffer uses the term "arcane discipline" to describe this central mystery, addressing the "worshiping" side of this "participation," in both the greater and the more limited sense. In the general discussion of Bonhoeffer's ideas this arcane discipline has been considered the least; there has been the greatest uncertainty and also the greatest one-sidedness on this issue. Yet here the validity of the main theme is again immediately obvious, namely, the actual relationship to Christ as present, which can never be separated from the question: Who is Christ for us today? This is where we have statements about silence and invisibility, about the way in which the just man prays and acts, and about the difference between the ultimate and the penultimate.[257]

The actual phrase occurs only twice in the prison letters,[258] but it does occur in the very first account of his new theological work. Bonhoeffer was undoubtedly aware of the possibilities of a one-sided approach, once the inner balance of things was lost. Moreover, the question of arcane discipline was not as peripheral for him as the infrequency of the phrase might suggest. His whole personality led him to put a protective screen around the central events of life, and it was predictable that he would be interested in the early Christian practice of excluding the uninitiated, the unbaptized catechumens, from the second part of the liturgy in which the communion was celebrated and the Nicene Creed sung. This was the origin of the "arcane discipline." As students in Finkenwalde, we were surprised when Bonhoeffer sought to revive this piece of early church history of which we had never taken any notice.[259]

While Bonhoeffer developed his ideas on the nonreligious interpretation of Christianity in a world come of age, he never considered abandoning his connection with the traditional words and customs of the church. In the same letter in which he mentions the difference between himself and the *homo religiosus,* and also the problematical aspects of his *Discipleship*—this was in the isolation of 21 July 1944—he said:

> These theological thoughts are, in fact, always occupying my mind; but there are times when I am just content to live the life of faith without worrying about its problems. At those times I simply take pleasure in the day's devotions—in particular those of yesterday and today,[260] and I am always glad to go back to Paul Gerhardt's beautiful hymns.[261]

There is no doubt that Bonhoeffer regarded an arcane discipline as the indispensable counterpoint of nonreligious interpretation. Much to his own annoyance, he was not yet able to resolve this problem in a theologically satisfactory way. When he developed his new perspective he immediately raised the question of what was going to happen to the worship service, although not in the spirit of dismantling or even getting rid of it. On the contrary, he was concerned to preserve—as he explicitly states—a "genuine worship."[262] This means that he has no intention of simply including the religionless world within the church or making the church and the world the same thing. Bonhoeffer would be completely misunderstood if the realization of his worldly interpretation were conceived to mean that there would no longer be any community gathered for worship, and that word, sacrament, and the community could be simply replaced by *caritas*. In his nonreligious interpretation the church's self-sacrifice that Bonhoeffer was thinking of, both for the church and for himself, cannot be equated at all with the loss of its identity. On the contrary, this is precisely what is to be re-won.

For Bonhoeffer the discipline of prayer, meditation, worship, and coming together (in "genuine worship") is as essential—though, of course, reformable—as daily food and drink. But it is also as much an "arcane" affair as are the central events of life, which are not suitable for a missionary demonstration. The degree to which those who interpret Christianity in a nonreligious way are preserved, moved, and "spiritually nourished"—and the center from which this occurs—cannot be propagated or demonstrated externally, especially when circumstances have evolved that have destroyed the intelligible relation between the names of these life events and the world of those events around us.

Hence the church will not simply jettison such great names and concepts as "creation," "fall," "reconciliation," "the last things," "penance," and "resurrection," but continue to live in them. But if it can no longer relate them to the world come of age in such a way that their essence and life become eloquent and effective within this present world,[263] then the church should remain silent until there is again a call for them and the precious content of its words once more becomes compelling. Bonhoeffer's desire for an "arcane tact" and possible silence is more than can be reasonably asked, of course, from a "church of the word" that is continually speaking. But this is what he means: wherever propaganda is made for the Gospel, there the relationship between God's word and God's world is not evident. It cannot be established artificially. The invention of new words achieves nothing. This relationship is something Pentecostal. Banging on the recruiting drum destroys any Pentecostal beginnings. To force something on people is to abandon any hope of its really making a mark on them.

That is why Bonhoeffer seeks to reestablish an arcane discipline "whereby the *mysteries* of the Christian faith are sheltered against desecration."[264] These "mysteries" are creative events of the Holy Spirit, but they become "religious" objects, a "positivism of revelation," if they are offered without reason, forced on people and given away cheaply. Bonhoeffer also speaks of the church's obligation to choose both the time and the persons it is addressing, by taking account of "degrees of significance."[265] It can also be argued, from the other side, that arcane discipline protects the world just as much from violation by religion. Thus the arcane discipline acquires the important function of protecting the nonreligious interpretation of Christianity from relapsing into religion.

The Problems of Boundaries. But does this not abandon the ground that has been won? Does not the arcane discipline reconjure up the boundaries that were finally supposed to have been removed? No one can deny that *arcanum* ("mystery") separates, and that *disciplina* distinguishes.

Bonhoeffer firmly stressed the impossibility of thinking in two spheres. He said that this was a static concept that established a law[266] because "there is no real possibility of being a Christian outside the reality of the world and ... there is no real worldly existence outside the reality of Jesus Christ. There is no place to which the Christian can withdraw from the world, be this outwardly or in the realm of the inner life."[267] This means that to understand arcane discipline as a "place of retreat" would be to deny everything Bonhoeffer intended. And yet this issue must be worldliness—the one reality—as the reality of Christ, and the Christian existence within this world reality. Jörg Martin Meier expresses this unity in Bonhoeffer very well, by saying that by worldliness Bonhoeffer testifies to Christ as the real one, and by arcane discipline as the present one. Worldliness and arcane discipline "are correlated attitudes of the Christian resulting from the presence of the real one."[268]

Now there is probably no way of constructing a safeguard against a new boundary, unless the safeguard would come from the real and present Christ himself, who is our sole concern in dealing with the *arcanum*. But it proceeds from him in such a way that no new privilege and no place of retreat can be set up with impunity. In the *arcanum* Christ takes everyone who really encounters him by the shoulder, turning them around to face their fellow human beings and the world. There is no other safeguard against the assertion of two static realms and the law of a boundary that confers privilege.

Thus the paradox remains that there is a "boundary" of the arcane, so that barriers of privilege ultimately should be removed, and that the "barrier" of the arcane in fact distracts us from having a false interest in the barrier between the church and the world.

> If one wishes to speak, then, of the space or sphere of the church, one must bear in mind that the confines of this space are at every moment being overrun and broken down by the testimony of the church to Jesus Christ. And this means that all false (sic!) thinking in terms of spheres must be excluded, since it is deleterious to the proper understanding of the church. ...

Whoever sets eyes on the body of Jesus Christ in faith can never again speak of the world as though it were lost, as though it were separated from Christ; he can never again with clerical arrogance set himself apart from the world.[269]

But precisely because this is the case, it must be perceived in the sphere of the arcane. We enter the "sphere" of the arcane in order that there should be an end to spatial divisions. In other words, the "ultimate" is praised with the initiates gathered together, so that in the "penultimate" stage there can be a share in godlessness. Christ prays a cultic psalm and dies a profane death. Hammelsbeck has put it like this:

Our bond with Christ is arcane, in that, as chosen and privileged ones, we do not make this a matter of privilege and a special religious life. It is part of this *arcanum* that I support preaching, baptism and the Eucharist, that I worship, confess and give praise within the congregation.[270]

This means that worldliness and nonreligious interpretation in the world come of age must remain connected with the arcane discipline, and vice versa. If they do not mutually correct each other they become meaningless and banal. Arcane discipline without worldliness is a ghetto, and worldliness without arcane discipline is nothing more than a boulevard. In isolation, arcane discipline becomes liturgical monasticism and nonreligious interpretation an intellectual game. Although Bonhoeffer remained unsatisfied with his own formulations on this subject, he never considered the dissolution of one in favor of the other.

We might imagine it as follows: the life events of faith, praise, thanksgiving, and the fellowship of the communion table occur in the *arcanum*, and these are not interpreted outwardly. Christ, the center of this arcane discipline, continually sends out the "initiated" to participate in the life of the world by promising to encounter and question them there. They stand shoulder to shoulder with those in their sphere of work and "exist for others."[271] Thus they are awaiting the day when they also will "interpret," not by throwing a religious veil over what already exists, but by creating new life. They can make the sacrifice of being silent and incognito because they trust the Holy Spirit, who knows and brings on the time of the proclamation.

In the case of Bonhoeffer's nonreligious interpretation, grace has remained "costly." Perhaps it costs even more than had been realized at the time of *Discipleship*.

An Answer to the Main Question. Almost every time that Bonhoeffer set about outlining the theological and rational part of the nonreligious interpretation of scriptural concepts, he was interrupted by bombing raids. What he wrote down later on the subject has been lost. Thus we are left behind in new territory, without his map to guide us. Or has he perhaps shown us part of the way after all?

Let us first recall that by listing the structural elements of religious language Bonhoeffer established fairly decisive criteria for preaching. As the proclamation of Jesus in our world, preaching should not try to fill in the gaps, confine itself to individualism, serve as a spiritual salon, or speak of God as the *deus ex machina*. It must seek knowledge of the world and let the "children of the world" help to bring it about. It can describe the religious and ideological veils more courageously and clearly. It accepts limitations where it has lost its power over a group of people through its own failures and the retention of privileges. It will not be able to separate the preached word from the life of the preacher, because this very life speaks more loudly than any words. Only the life of "participation in the powerlessness of God in the world"[272] will speak a word of renewal. That is why the congregation must beware of preaching that can be imagined as taking place anywhere, under any circumstances, by anyone to anyone and at any time. As nonreligious interpretation, proclamation is far more than an objective process of translation.

But in the letters from prison there are some sections that can stand as instances of a nonreligious interpretation, although they cannot be simply copied out as such: the letters on the gap that is kept open;[273] the words of 27 March about Easter;[274] the letter on the Old Testament;[275] the interpretation of blessing;[276] the interpretation of messianic suffering;[277] the poem "Christians and Pagans,"[278] with its switch from the religious to the nonreligious Christian attitude; and finally the title of Christ as "the man for others."[279]

A comparison of Bonhoeffer's last sermons and interpretations with his earlier ones does not reveal any special differences that offer evidence of the new "method." The exegesis of the first three commandments in June–July 1944,[280] like the Pentecost services of 1944 on the texts for the day,[281] speak a language that is no different from before. This merely confirms how little Bonhoeffer viewed his task as suddenly finding other words. If this were what it was about, Barth's caricature would indeed have been correct:

A little "non-religious" language from the street, the newspaper, literature, and, if one is ambitious, from the philosopher may thus, for the sake of

communication, occasionally indeed be in order. . . . A little of the language
of Canaan, a little revelation positivism, can also be a good thing . . . and
will often . . . be still better understood even by the oddest strangers.[282]

But if we examine the exegeses and sermons to see to what extent those
seven elements of Bonhoeffer's view of religion we have mentioned are
avoided—to see what kind of life is the basis of the preaching, and to what
degree the crucified Christ is interpreted in his being turned toward the
world—we arrive at a more convincing conclusion. We see that being turned
toward the world and renouncing "religious" language had influenced Bonhoeffer's way of preaching even earlier.

But these observations still remain on the surface of Bonhoeffer's thinking. The main thing is not the Sunday morning sermons, but how Bonhoeffer interpreted his own life through this final theological draft. Perhaps
without even claiming it for himself in this way, he saw this as the relin-
quishment of a special Christian life and as the acceptance, once and for all,
of an incognito existence that could not be reversed—just as, independently of him but in that same year (1944), in another milieu and another language, Simone Weil and Henri Perrin did so in an equally exemplary way for
the Christianity of the future. Thus the essential issue is how Bonhoeffer's life
in the resistance movement and his nonreligious interpretation mutually
interpret each other.

With this theology of his final months Bonhoeffer—consciously or
unconsciously—prevented his career of solidarity (with the members of the
political resistance), which began as a "borderline case," from remaining
such; he thereby prevented an easy dismissal of this solidarity. Suddenly this
"borderline case" is made visible and validly interpreted as an example of
being Christian today, both in its task and in its destiny. This theology and
this life were a breakthrough, in which the nature of this exceptional path
revealed itself as the future normality: "being for others" as sharing in the
suffering of Jesus. Thus Bonhoeffer, as we have already said, added a new title
to the old ones of Jesus, one that is both intelligible and at the same time profound: "The man for others." For Bonhoeffer this is a strictly theological
statement that reveals truth that both shames and heartens us. It is a statement about existence, whose relation to reality is obvious. It contains an ethical impulse, prevents both the religious flight from the world and clerical
domination, and finally praises Jesus with words that are soaked in experience. This christological title of honor, "the man for others," is confession,
hymn, prayer, and interpretation.

An Unfinished Ecclesiology. It is a disturbing thing for the church that, at the end of his theological activity, Bonhoeffer did not give a completed ecclesiology that we could hold on to, but left this, of all things, entirely open. The theologians of the church feel the lack of this, and canon lawyers immediately pick up on the suggestions that are impossible for a *Volkskirche*. This difficulty is not only due to the fact that Bonhoeffer did not write more than a tiny fragment on the subject, he himself saw that it would be an arduous undertaking to give a theological account of the nature of the church, its liturgy and communal life, on the basis of his new ideas. He viewed his suggestions on "arcane discipline" and its "consequences" only as pointing in a certain direction.

Nevertheless, he had a fairly clear idea that the church should get rid of many things after the catastrophe of 1945 and find new constructions. He was probably too optimistic about the possibilities for a truly new beginning in 1945. He hoped for a new financial basis, and new forms of training, ministry, and confession. He hardly assumed that the *Volkskirche* that had become so discredited during the Nazi era could simply survive, and so he made all kinds of "frivolous" suggestions.[283] He did not imagine that the financial and organizational structures would emerge little changed; that the ministry would have to revise its structure in only one part of Germany; that it would prove so difficult to effect change in matters of training and confession; that his question of the "model" could become so much less important than that of terminology. On the basis of the renewal he had experienced—forced, to be sure—he hoped:

> It is important to me to say simply and clearly things that we so often like to shirk. Whether I shall succeed is another matter, especially if I cannot discuss it with you. I hope it may be of some help for the church's future.[284]

But Bonhoeffer failed not only in terms of practical ecclesiology, that is, with regard to the structure of the church after 1945, but also in his theological treatise on the doctrine of the church, with which he began his theological career so passionately and which ended with unsettled questions. At the end Bonhoeffer arrived at a stage that was highly critical of the church. His ecclesiology seemed entirely absorbed within the *theologia crucis*. Once his thinking had begun ecclesiologically; then this ecclesiology yielded to Christology, but during the period of *Discipleship* and the church struggle it once more aroused quite distinct connotations. Now he entered a phase where it was once again being called into question by Christology, but it would be wrong to conclude from this situation that Bonhoeffer was not interested in ecclesiology. For him everything depended on the *theologia crucis*, but the only form in which he knew this was in its urging us toward the concrete fellowship of those who share Christ's sufferings in the world.

It is impossible for us to complete the fragment. This is perhaps also a reflection of the situation, in that there can be no systematically complete conclusion in the movement between Christology and ecclesiology. In fact, everything was left very open at the end. In one of my last letters to Bonhoeffer, on 30 September 1944, 1 thanked him for the poem "The Death of Moses." At the end of these verses come the lines:

> To punish sin and to forgiveness you are moved,
> God, this people I have loved.
> That I bore its shame and sacrifices
> And saw its salvation—that suffices.[285]

By "its shame" he did not mean Christ and by "this people" he did not mean the church, but Germany.

In his last letter to me that has been preserved, on 23 August 1944, Bonhoeffer wrote:

> So you are taking the trouble to copy out extracts of my very transitory thoughts. I'm sure you'll consider everything that has to be considered if you pass them on to someone else, won't you? . . . By the way, you can imagine how delighted I am that you are busying yourself with them. How essential it would be to me now to be able to discuss and clarify all these problems. It will be one of the great days of my life when we are able to do that.

Of the true theologian Luther says: "*Vivendo, immo moriendo et damnando fit theologus, non intelligendo, legendo aut speculando*" ("It is not understanding, reading and speculation that make the theologian, but to live, no, more to die and be damned").[286]

Reactions. These letters appeared in the winter of 1951–1952, only after much hesitation and doubt about whether and how to publish these incomplete meditations. There was great surprise.

Until then, the image of Bonhoeffer was so influenced by *Discipleship* and his apparently radical orthodoxy in the struggle of the Confessing church that no one had expected that he, of all people, would again take up vehemently liberal questions. Even to his Finkenwaldians Bonhoeffer appeared in an unexpected light. Gerhard Ebeling was the first to react, and he described the posthumous work as having "practically the quality of a breviary":

> I should like to state explicitly that I am especially interested in the theological perspectives. Not, indeed, because I find them strange, but because they are a surprisingly major confirmation to me that I am a pupil of Bonhoeffer, precisely in those matters in which I have developed beyond the theological level of the Finkenwalde period and which have guided me toward a path which I only now know was his also.[287]

The second echo came from Helmut Thielicke:

> [*Letters and Papers from Prison*] has . . . completely filled my last week, accompanying me with an intensity and influencing my life in a way that nothing has for years. . . .[288]

Others were shocked. Karl Barth warned against this late Bonhoeffer. Replying to P. W. Herrenbrück's question about what he thought of Bonhoeffer's ideas altogether and, in particular, of the attacks on him, Barth said that the lonely prisoner might possibly have "peeped around some corner" and seen something that was true, but that it was too "enigmatic" and that it was better to stick to the early Bonhoeffer.[289]

Their surprise led people to bring out again the early works of Bonhoeffer that previously had not received much attention, and to discover with astonishment that there was a broad continuity between the Berlin beginnings and the Tegel period. Formulations and theological suggestions in *Letters and Papers from Prison* that people found shocking proved to be not as new as had been thought; they could be found, even in the same wording, in *Sanctorum Communio* or *Act and Being*, as well as in various other writings. The Christology was already there in *Act and Being* as Lutheran kenotic Christology (the whole fullness precisely in the total condescension, Philippians 2), and had been the real stimulus for his critique of Barth at the time. Bonhoeffer had preserved this Christology for fifteen years, constantly making it more profound, in order to ground the present power of Christ even more clearly in the weakness of the human suffering of Jesus. The phrase "being for others" had occurred already in *Act and Being* and in the Christology lecture. The concept of faith as being drawn into the vicarious being of Christ had been included in *Discipleship,* only now, instead of the judging element, the world-preserving one emerges much more encouragingly. The change of direction, from the metaphysical elements of Christology to its place at the "center of life," as well as the reference to Christ who refuses to be relegated to the psychological or moral boundaries of life, but is at the center and the "strongest places" of man—we had read all this before in *Creation and Fall*. The antimetaphysical transference of transcendence to one's neighbor, which seemed especially surprising to most people, could be found, in almost exactly the same form, as social transcendence, in *Sanctorum Communio*: "Whoever happens to be one's neighbor and reachable is the transcendent."[290] As early as 1932 Bonhoeffer severely criticized religious "otherworldliness." During his Berlin period he had dealt at length with the religious a priori as a key concept of his teacher Reinhold Seeberg.

The continuity seemed to go a surprisingly long way. But despite the same terminology and individual ideas, Bonhoeffer in 1944 was not merely saying the same thing he had said in 1932. The passionate theologian of 1932 had handled these terminological tools with the capacities of a young critical intellect. The theologian of 1944 used them with the capacities of an experience full to the brim. In 1932 Bonhoeffer was attacking the existing structures of the church and of thinking; in 1944 he felt that he was helping to liberate them for a new future.

But, with few exceptions, Bonhoeffer's voice was not widely welcomed among academic theologians. In 1964 William Hamilton declared that despite Bonhoeffer's general prestige and influence,

> Bonhoeffer has not been used very much by the professor, which is why there is such an astonishingly short list of books and articles on him, and an even shorter list of good books and articles.[291]

When *Letters and Papers from Prison* appeared in Germany the second round of the excited Bultmann debate was in full swing, and Gogarten's voice was making itself heard. Tillich, who had disappeared from the German scene, had reappeared; and Barth's doctrine of creation, ethics, and anthropology had revealed the new breadth of the old master. The questions of liberal theology had reemerged powerfully in 1952 after the testing period of dialectical theology and the period of a new confessional awareness. In this situation Bonhoeffer's cursory notes came too late for the academic discussion. All they could do was constitute secondary weapons for an armory that was already equipped with fixed types. When one was tired of Barth one could go to Bonhoeffer's "positivism of revelation" for ammunition. A defender of the existential interpretation felt confirmed by Bonhoeffer's "nonreligious interpretation" and was little interested in his eventual distinctions. If one despaired of the church one could discover "the world come of age" and see the opportunity of atheism in the name of Bonhoeffer's *theologia crucis*. Some of Bonhoeffer's pupils, educated in the spirit of Barth, sought to preserve Bonhoeffer from the Marburg influence (the Bultmann school).

In other words, the time was not favorable for Bonhoeffer's fragments to speak in their own right. They had their greatest effect wherever there was experimentation in small groups, wherever new parish structures and forms of political solidarity were being tried out, wherever the bastions of the *Volkskirche* and of social privilege were abandoned, and where questions of atheism and cooperation with non-Christians were accepted as part of the humanization of life together. Here Bonhoeffer has proven to be someone who encourages people to sail quickly out of harbors that have silted up.

The first wave of sporadic serious writing on his work[292] was followed by a second more comprehensive one. People initially thought either that Bonhoeffer could be very quickly categorized, or else that there was nothing that could really be learned from him. The use of Bonhoeffer's ideas by John A. T. Robinson,[293] if eclectically chosen for his own purposes (though all the more influential on that account), unleashed a new search for the specific nature of Bonhoeffer's contribution beyond the continental borders of Europe, in the English-speaking world, and beyond denominational barriers as well, among Roman Catholics.[294]

Bonhoeffer regarded the cause of Christ with optimism and serenity. Addressing my anxiety about scattered and possibly lost papers for his *Ethics* he wrote: ". . . even if you had forgotten it, it would probably emerge again indirectly somehow. Besides, my ideas were still incomplete."[295]

CHAPTER FOURTEEN

IN THE CUSTODY OF THE STATE: 1944–1945

Bonhoeffer's transfer from the Military Interrogation Prison to the guarded cellar at the Reich Central Security Office on 8 October 1944 fundamentally altered the conditions of his existence. Now his imprisonment became typical of Gestapo imprisonment during the Third Reich.

In Tegel the interrogations into Bonhoeffer's activities had been confined to more or less marginal aspects; now the most important activities became the subject of direct investigation. In Tegel he had not yet abandoned all hope for the cause; on the contrary, the trial itself seemed to have become part of the fight for Hitler's overthrow that was being conducted outside the prison. This hope had enabled Bonhoeffer to hold out in his relative isolation. He had known that those outside—his family, Perels, the indefatigable Dr. Sack, and his fellow conspirators—were all working for the cause. His particular task was to divert the attention of the enemy from their activities. As a result his sense of powerlessness had been limited. Almost to his last day in Tegel the tenuous connection he had been able to maintain with his friends had acted as a lifeline.

But now there was little point in maintaining the old masquerade before the enemy, since there was no one left working to bring about a political change. Sack and Perels, Canaris and Oster, Klaus Bonhoeffer and Rüdiger Schleicher had themselves been arrested, put into solitary confinement, and were being subjected to grueling interrogations.

Nevertheless, occasional periods still offered a ray of hope or the possibility of some friendly human contact. In the winter of 1944–1945 some of the commissars who were interrogating Bonhoeffer became so concerned at the seriousness of Germany's situation that even they were not above consulting him personally. At times both Bonhoeffer and Dohnanyi seem to have believed they could still outwit the forces bent on their destruction.

October 1944 and February 1945 were bad months for the Bonhoeffer family. In October the means of communication that had been built up between the prisoners in their cells, or between them and the parental home, were disrupted. There had been three further arrests, so that five members of the family were now in the Gestapo's hands. Hans von Dohnanyi was in the concentration camp in Sachsenhausen, Dietrich Bonhoeffer was in the prison on Prinz-Albrecht-Strasse, and Klaus Bonhoeffer, Rüdiger Schleicher, and I were in the wing of the prison at Number 3 Lehrter Strasse, which the Gestapo had taken over. The only advantage was that all of us were still imprisoned in Berlin or its suburbs. The families could still do something, even if it was just to send the packages received by the guards on our behalf.

Then in February 1945 Klaus Bonhoeffer and Rüdiger Schleicher were sentenced to death, and Dietrich was secretly moved from Berlin. It was months before his friends and family learned where he had been taken and what had finally happened to him.

The last six months of Bonhoeffer's life can be divided into three different stages. He spent the first four months in the cellar of the prison on Prinz-Albrecht-Strasse where he was interrogated repeatedly. During the next seven weeks he lived in a bunker in the concentration camp at Buchenwald. After this he spent seven days as part of a prison transport traveling through southern Germany. The end came in the concentration camp in Flossenbürg.

Prinz-Albrecht-Strasse

Concern in England. In October of 1944 the first article appeared on the other side of the English Channel that had the courage to inform the British public that the people who had been involved in the 20 July plot were not just another military clique intent on removing Hitler for their own selfish ends. The author of this article was Gerhard Leibholz; he portrayed the assassination attempt in positive terms by referring to the list of conspirators who had been executed:

> It is obvious that such a conspiracy had to be built up carefully and must have been prepared for many years. . . . In fact, it can be revealed today that the existence of a vast opposition movement, under the leadership of Beck, Goerdeler and Leuschner, had been known in this country for some time.

There is even evidence available that the execution of the plot was planned before the cumulative effect of military defeats had added its weight to the decision of the plotters to overthrow the present regime. . . . The loss of their battle will certainly not ease the task the Allies will have to perform later on in Germany.[1]

Leibholz was well acquainted with the names and the earlier history of the conspiracy, both from Bonhoeffer's visits in 1939 and from the reports given by Bishop Bell in 1942. He dared not reveal all he knew, however, and was forced to confine his remarks to whatever had been publicized about the trial through the garbled German radio accounts or in the neutral press. So far in these accounts Leibholz had not mentioned his own relatives in Berlin. Even the little he said in support of the conspirators, however, seemed to be too much for the British public. Churchill had given the cue for this reaction on 2 August, when he spoke in the House of Commons of the "conspiracy of militarists, simply a case of the highest personalities in the German Reich murdering one another."[2] When Leibholz, with Bell's help, tried to publish a word against this statement in one of the big daily newspapers, both *The Times* and the *Manchester Guardian* refused to print it. "I agree with you in the miserable playing-down of the significance of the Hitler plot," Bell wrote to Leibholz in the middle of September. Finally *The New English Weekly,* whose editors included T. S. Eliot, had the courage to publish Leibholz's article.[3] It appeared on 19 October, and immediately provoked a negative response from one of its readers: "Sir, I regret that you should have thought fit to find space for the article." The only positive response came from an immigrant. Months elapsed before the true facts of the case were publicly acknowledged.

Immediately after Churchill's speech in the House of Commons Bell had written to Leibholz expressing his great concern for the conspirators. Not everything he said was realistic, but it was all a sign of an ecumenical spirit. On 3 August he wrote to Leibholz in Oxford:

I heard Churchill yesterday—it was all "battle," and its reference to ideology and "internal disease" most depressing. I get more and more worried about the official attitude. I have written to Eden reminding him of the information I gave him two years ago from Stockholm and that the attempt of July 20 was made in far worse circumstances than ever possible in 1942 after the same two men were leaders Beck and Goerdeler—the same plan and organization, etc.: if only he had acted then! I have asked him at least to do what is possible to help those who can escape to escape;

for I suppose we have ways and means of assisting prisoners of war to escape. And I then also asked him to say a word encouraging those in Germany who are seeking to destroy the regime.

Two days later Bell wrote another letter, describing exactly what he had done. It reflected his characteristic tenacity in pursuing a goal he had set for himself:

> I had drafted a letter to Cranborne [leader of the House of Lords] setting out a series of considerations for "political warfare"; but on the publication of Goerdeler's name as the prime mover and actor by Himmler I decided to write direct to Eden pointing out how closely the information I brought from Stockholm in 1942 fitted in with the facts of 20 July 1944, reminding him of other names besides Beck and Goerdeler and including Witzleben (before of course the new denunciation option in today's press). I asked Eden whether he could not 1. take steps to help escape any other leaders of the Revolt not yet killed—by such steps (formidable as the task is) as might be taken to help our prisoners of war escape; and 2. even at this late hour make a strong public appeal over the heads of Hitler and Himmler to anti-Nazis in Germany and give them hope of a life of security for a Germany which has overthrown the Nazis. By the same post I wrote to Cranborne telling him what I had done and why.
>
> I had already written to Eden last week asking him whether he would care to do anything (via Stockholm e.g.) to help the clergy in Germany now in still greater peril, through the areas opened up in the summer of 1942. I have had no reply to this letter. . . . I heard Churchill . . . but he is living in a world of battles only, and seeing time with the mind of a child with regard to deep policy—for Home Affairs as well as the far graver matters of Europe. And disaster gets nearer and nearer. One feels so powerless. . . .
>
> I cannot tell you how deeply I share your and your wife's anxieties for Dietrich. May God spare him for the survival of the Church and Germany and the world. . . . I am writing to Winant to remind him of what I brought from Stockholm in 1942.[4]

Bell and the Leibholz family were astonished when weeks passed without any of the Bonhoeffers being named in the press reports. They tried to obtain information via Geneva. On 14 November Bell wrote to Leibholz:

> [Visser 't Hooft] has no reason to think [Bonhoeffer] has come to any harm, and believes him to be safe, so far as he knows. The fact that he had been in prison for so long before 20th July was very much to his advantage, for he could not well be incriminated.

Bonhoeffer was certainly no longer "safe" at this time, as Visser 't Hooft imagined him to be, but there were certain delays which undoubtedly afforded him some respite. It is true that, at the beginning, Bonhoeffer's involvement in the conspiracy was kept secret for a long time. Later on, as we shall see, his sentence was delayed because he became a subject of special interest to his interrogators. Even toward the end, the conclusion of his case was postponed once more by the chaos of the war.

New Inquiries. The discovery of the Zossen files, which made the situation so much worse for the resistance group, was the source of the first delay in the proceedings against Bonhoeffer. According to the information given by Huppenkothen during his trial in the 1950s, the Zossen file contained the following, among other items:

> Notes of plans for a coup d'état, written in 1938, partly in Oster's handwriting;
> A record of the results of discussions with the British government via the Vatican;
> A summary of the situation after the campaign in Poland, written by General Beck;
> A plan drawn up by General Oster for carrying out a coup d'état;
> Excerpts from the diary of Admiral Canaris, containing notes concerning the affairs of the resistance movement, also remarks about journeys to the front lines addressed to various commanders, for the purpose of winning their support for a revolution;
> Correspondence concerning the aforementioned activities of Bonhoeffer, and similar matters.[5]

These discoveries by the criminal investigator Sonderegger considerably increased the Reich Central Security Office's knowledge of the early history of the conspiracy. Its activities were now known to date back to 1938, to have extended as far as the Vatican and England, and to have involved a wide circle of people (on 20 July Hitler had simply spoken of "a tiny clique . . . of stupid officers"). When Hitler received this additional information he rescinded his original command for the prompt "liquidation" of the conspirators and ordered an extensive investigation of their activities.[6] Contrary to previous policy, the executions of some of those involved, who had already been condemned to death by the People's Court, were postponed for weeks or even months.

Since 20 July several information groups of the Reich Central Security Office had been at work for two months preparing dossiers for the trials to be held in the People's Court under Freisler. The results of these investigations, summarized in the "Kaltenbrunner Reports," reached Hitler at regular intervals via Martin Bormann. After the discovery of the Zossen files, however, an additional group was formed under the command of S.S. section leader Walter Huppenkothen, with special instructions to go through its contents and use them as the basis for further investigations. According to Huppenkothen's own statement during the trials against him later, he was given the task of producing his own report independently of the Kaltenbrunner Reports.[7] This document, drawn up especially for the *Führer*, consisted of about 160 pages, with a two-volume appendix that included photocopies and original documents. Its contents are said to have been treated as highly confidential, and to have existed in only three copies: one for Hitler, one for Himmler, and one for Kaltenbrunner and S.S. group leader Müller. It was a summary of the incriminating evidence collected against Canaris, Oster, Dohnanyi, Sack, Josef Müller, and Dietrich Bonhoeffer. Huppenkothen later maintained that all copies were destroyed; certainly none was ever found.

This special treatment would explain the surprisingly brief mention the otherwise extensive Kaltenbrunner Report gives the cases against Dohnanyi and Dietrich Bonhoeffer, compared with the relatively large amount of material devoted to the cases against Klaus Bonhoeffer and Rüdiger Schleicher,[8] both of whom had become involved in the coup plans only after the arrests of Dietrich Bonhoeffer and Hans von Dohnanyi. While Schleicher and particularly Klaus already had their own private connections to resistance groups, their role became more significant only after the dissolution of Oster's office and the need to restructure the resistance. From then on some of the meetings of the members of the Goerdeler and Stauffenberg circles were held in Klaus Bonhoeffer's or Rüdiger Schleicher's apartment. The future of Lufthansa, where Klaus was an official, was discussed at these meetings, and plans were made that he or Schleicher would take over certain offices if the coup were successful. The discovery of these activities was the reason that both were mentioned in the Kaltenbrunner Reports, which, incidentally, were extraordinarily inaccurate on some points. Klaus Bonhoeffer, Rüdiger Schleicher, and I (my interrogation focused almost exclusively on my role as Schleicher's son-in-law) were victims of the Günther and Baumer interrogation group in the Reich Central Security Office. This group was dissolved as early as December; it was said that Günther and Baumer had joined the fighting forces. On the basis of their preliminary investigations (in which they used torture) the public prosecutor of the

People's Court drew up an indictment against Klaus Bonhoeffer and Rüdiger Schleicher on 20 December.

In contrast, the cases of Dietrich Bonhoeffer and Dohnanyi never reached the People's Court. Dietrich Bonhoeffer only received passing mention in the Kaltenbrunner Reports, and even this was accompanied by factual inaccuracies.[9] The Kaltenbrunner Reports had ceased altogether by the Christmas of 1944, but Huppenkothen's information group continued to work energetically.

Thus it was that Dietrich Bonhoeffer's case received separate treatment. Of course, this was also due to the fact that it became part of the Reich Central Security Office investigation of the 20 July events rather late. The contents of the Kaltenbrunner Reports suggest that Hitler attached little importance to it, but in fact the reverse was true. As a result, Bonhoeffer and his closest friends were spared longer than some of the other conspirators. For those same reasons, however, he became the subject of a meeting held on 5 April 1945, in which Hitler made his final decision to execute them.

Huppenkothen. For Bonhoeffer the period of renewed interrogations lasted from October 1944 to January 1945. Huppenkothen and Sonderegger directed the investigation and, as we shall see, they used it to pursue their own interests within the Reich Central Security Office.

Walter Huppenkothen, a talented lawyer from the Rhineland, had begun his career in the Gestapo in 1935. Since 1941 he had been in charge of counterespionage (Group E) in Branch IV of the Reich Central Security Office ("Investigation and Combating of Enemy Activities"). In spring 1944, when Canaris's office was incorporated into the Reich Central Security Office, Branch IV was reorganized. While retaining his previous posts, Huppenkothen was also put in charge of the newly created department 3 of group A, which now included the area of responsibility concerned with military counterespionage, formerly under Canaris.

After 20 July Huppenkothen had been put in charge of an interrogation group within the general commission that had been set up to investigate the organization of the conspiracy. Huppenkothen's specific task was to shed light on the unproven but suspected connections of Canaris, Oster, and Dohnanyi to the coup preparations. He was to be assisted by Sonderegger, who with Roeder had first arrested Dohnanyi and Bonhoeffer, had attended the court martial where Roeder had produced his evidence, and finally had discovered the Zossen files on 20 September.

Huppenkothen was therefore the right man for this special commission. He naturally found himself in the position of having to play different roles at the same time. On the one hand, he had to pursue the charges of high treason against his victims; on the other hand, for his own group A 3 he had to investigate their connections to the resistance group in Military Intelligence, which the Reich Central Security Office had not known about. The secret service, now finally concentrated in the Reich Central Security Office, was to become even more powerful. This was one of the main reasons no one intended to hand such important figures as Dohnanyi and Bonhoeffer over to the People's Court. Despite the appalling interrogations they were subjected to, the victims could hope that the pronouncement of their sentences might be delayed until events overtook them.

In his biography of Canaris Abshagen described Huppenkothen as a man who was able to give "the impression of being an educated official of the governmental service or police force."[10] It is true that he never became openly aggressive. After threats of torture, which he left to others to carry out when things got that far, he was quite capable of offering his prisoners a cigarette and encouraging them to discuss matters, the clarification of which would be advantageous to both sides. Although he held every means of power, he usually pretended to sympathize with his prisoners. Sonderegger, on the other hand, was of humble origins. "It pleases him if one treats him as a gentleman, and he is not altogether without a heart; but he's crafty."[11] He did in fact help to ease conditions for Bonhoeffer and Dohnanyi in small ways.

The Interrogations. Klaus Bonhoeffer was tortured, and the notorious Commissar Stawitsky's treatment of Dohnanyi was infamous. It seems almost certain, however, that Dietrich Bonhoeffer was never subjected to torture, although his sufferings were great enough without this. Schlabrendorff reports that on the occasion when he encountered Bonhoeffer in the cellar of the Reich Central Security Office Bonhoeffer described the interrogations as "frankly repulsive." He added that at first he had been threatened with torture, and told that the fate of his fiancée, his parents, and the rest of his family depended upon his readiness to confess. But afterward there had been a change of tone. It is possible that Bonhoeffer's own personality may have had a salutary effect on his examiners. Captain Payne Best, who later encountered Bonhoeffer in Buchenwald, was impressed by his composure:

> He had always been afraid that he would not be strong enough to stand such a test but now he knew there was nothing in life of which one need ever be afraid.

Bonhoeffer realized quite early that, aside from his own case, the authorities were interested in what they could learn from him about the others. He exploited this situation to get some room to maneuver. In Bonhoeffer's last letter of 17 January 1945, where he wrote of his part in a "sacrifice for the nation," and which Sonderegger read and forwarded, he wrote:

> If there is anything you need to know perhaps you would phone Herr Commissar Sonderegger. . . . Herr Commissar Sonderegger would now and then accept [books] for me, if Maria were to bring them along. . . . Please also leave some writing paper with the Herr Commissar.[12]

So far only a very sketchy reconstruction of the contents and course of these interrogations has been possible. Huppenkothen maintained that he destroyed all the records in his possession before the arrival of the American army. The recollections of those who were involved in some way are often vague or colored by their own view of the situation, and the reports contradict each other in many respects. Only one official document concerning the case has so far been found (though this is admittedly a very important one). We must nonetheless try to gain some idea of the contents and course of the interrogations from these sources of unequal value. The best way of doing this is to discuss them in chronological order. We possess nothing from Bonhoeffer's own hand which could help in this matter, unless the two letters written after Christmas 1944 confirm our suppositions as to the stage the interrogations had reached by that time.

1. Fabian von Schlabrendorff, who had already been sent to the prison on Prinz-Albrecht-Strasse by the end of August 1944, was probably the first of the friends who was still alive to meet Bonhoeffer there. At this time, of course, he still knew very little in detail about Bonhoeffer's activities in the resistance group and even less about the defensive arguments and subterfuges Bonhoeffer had employed at Tegel to disguise the real facts of the situation from the enemy. During that period Schlabrendorff had been at the front, and had only occasionally come home to visit Berlin. In 1945 he wrote a report for Bonhoeffer's family that probably reflects the stage the interrogations reached between October and December 1944. It was a surprisingly optimistic description of the situation:

> He repeatedly told me the Gestapo had no clue to his real activities. He had been able to trivialize his acquaintance with Goerdeler. His connection with Perels . . . was not of sufficient importance to serve as an indictment. And as for his foreign travels and meetings with English church dignitaries, the Gestapo did not grasp their purpose and point. If the investigations were to carry on at the present pace, years might pass till they reached their conclusions. He was full of hope . . . he also thought he had represented his relation to his brother-in-law . . . von Dohnanyi in a plausible way to his interlocutors, so that this was not a grave charge against him.[13]

At the end of 1944 Schlabrendorff thought it possible that he himself might be released. In the event that this happened, Bonhoeffer asked him to visit his father and encourage him to seek a personal interview with Himmler.[14] Up to this time, therefore, he seems to have envisaged the possibility of still getting off without legal proceedings being taken against him. We shall see later what grounds existed for such a hope.

2. In November 1944 my own interrogations in the branch of the Central Security Office located on Kurfürstenstrasse brought me dangerously close to Bonhoeffer's case. Strange as it may seem, Commissar Baumer had concerned himself throughout my examination almost exclusively with my connections to Rüdiger Schleicher, but one afternoon he laid a thick typewritten file in front of me and showed me Bonhoeffer's signature on the last page. He said the file contained Bonhoeffer's confessions, and read several passages from it to me. I recognized parts of the Freiburg discussion of 1942 that dealt with the possibilities of contact between German and English churches in the event of a long armistice being arranged. None of this information was unfamiliar to me. I later learned that Günther and Baumer placed the same file before Perels and Walter Bauer during similar interrogations. I denied all knowledge of the contents of this file. I knew that Bonhoeffer had been able to hide the fact of our close association in the past, and I assumed that he would not, in any case, have made such a detailed confession. I also knew from my own interrogations that seven copies of the record were made and signed. I therefore came to the conclusion that the Gestapo had compiled the whole file from pieces of evidence obtained in various ways, and that Bonhoeffer's signature had then been added to it. Baumer soon returned to the topic of my frequent presence in the Schleicher household, which could be explained convincingly enough by my engagement and marriage to Rüdiger Schleicher's daughter. He never again raised the question of my relations with Dietrich Bonhoeffer.

This incident showed quite clearly, however, that by October or November 1944 the Central Security Office was well enough informed about the sphere and extent of Bonhoeffer's activities to give serious cause for alarm. Now they could not only interpret the information extracted during the interrogations in Tegel much more accurately; they had also uncovered some facts that were quite new to them. And yet the optimism reported by Schlabrendorff was not wholly unfounded.

3. Jørgen Glenthoj discovered and published the only document found so far which deals directly with the interrogations by the Central Security Office.[15] On 4 January 1945 Kaltenbrunner wrote a letter to the Ger-

man Foreign Ministry that was also presented to Ribbentrop. It consisted entirely of information obtained from Bonhoeffer during the interrogations concerning his meetings with Bishop Bell and the conditions in England.

There was no mention at all of treasonable activities on Bonhoeffer's part. The letter suggested that Bonhoeffer had succeeded in giving the impression that his visits abroad were made "in the national interest"—it was no longer possible to hide the fact that they had taken place. He also seems to have tried to make his presentation of the facts fit in with what he had said at the earlier interrogations conducted by Roeder, and above all, to make himself and his knowledge an object of continued interest to the Central Security Office. In the letter Kaltenbrunner wrote:

> The Protestant minister Dietrich Bonhoeffer, formerly pastor of the German Evangelical Congregation in London, who was arrested in connection with the conspiracy of 20.7.1944, went to Sweden and had meetings with Lord Bishop Bell of Chichester during May and June 1942 by order of the former Admiral Canaris. Bonhoeffer has given the following information concerning the nature of his discussions with Bell:
>
> Lord Bishop Bell, the most respected and best known of the Lord Bishops of the Church of England, and influential in the ecumenical movement, is considered to be a man who favors mutual understanding and the peaceful settlement of differences, as well as being an outspoken friend of the Germans. For this reason, and because of his attitude toward the conduct of the war, he had not become successor to Archbishop Lang of Canterbury as had been expected. He is said to have visited Germany often and to have been on familiar terms with Rudolf Hess. At the beginning he evidently tried to come to an understanding with the German Evangelical Church under [Reich Bishop] Müller but then turned his attention to the Confessing church and established connections with Niemöller, Dibelius and Koch.
>
> The purpose of Bishop Bell's visit to Sweden was, according to Bonhoeffer, to inquire into the relations between Sweden and the Soviet Union and study the movements in the Scandinavian churches. Bell explained that he had spoken at length with Eden before leaving England, and had asked him what he should do if peace feelers were extended from any particular direction in Sweden. Eden had told him quite bluntly that there was no question of England discussing peace terms before it had won the war. In this matter Eden was totally in agreement with Churchill.
>
> The attitude of Sir Stafford Cripps to these problems was quite different from that of Eden. It was quite wrong to say that Sir Stafford was a Bol-

shevik; he was more of a Christian Socialist. Sir Stafford evidently spoke with great concern about the power of Russia, which almost everyone in England underestimated. He had good relations with sources of information in Moscow and feared that no other power, not even England, would be in a position to stop the Russians from advancing as far as the Brandenburg Gate. He thought the consequences of a Russian victory were unforeseeable, as far as England was concerned. Bell had explained that church circles in England were more in agreement with this view of the situation than with Eden's.

When Lord Bishop Bell was asked whether the U.S.A. might intend to destroy England or absorb it into the federation, he replied that this was totally out of the question. America needed a strong bulwark in Europe, and England without its empire would not be strong. Bell did not wish to get into a discussion of a union between the U.S.A. and England.

During the course of the interview Bell had commented on the visit which Lord Beaverbrook had evidently recently made to Switzerland. Beaverbrook had held meetings with German industrialists and had discussed with them the possibilities of negotiating peace terms, with a view to forming a common front between the Western powers and Germany against Russia.[16]

The interrogations concerning these contacts with England took place around Christmastime at the latest. If Kaltenbrunner's letter can be taken as reliable evidence of Bonhoeffer's account of his activities in Sweden, then it is clear that Bonhoeffer had found a way to tell the truth without its harming anybody. He had also managed to give it a particular emphasis that would make it plausible to the people in the Central Security Office, if they had given any consideration to what would happen if the war ended or if there were a shift in the alliances between East and West. Aside from this Bonhoeffer had said enough about Beaverbrook to make further inquiries desirable if not imperative; this in itself could slow down the interrogations and be a means of gaining time. Above all this explains why Bonhoeffer believed, according to Schlabrendorff, that the Gestapo "hadn't caught on to the really essential matters." The visit to Sweden was clearly presented as being in the service of Military Intelligence, "by order of the former Admiral Canaris," and not at Beck's order. It is true that Bonhoeffer afterward admitted having played a part in the admiral's political information service, and that this contravened the "Ten Commandments." But the real nature of his journey—establishing connections between the conspirators and the English government in preparation for a coup—remained undiscovered, although Bonhoeffer had gone so far as to mention that it was concerned with "peace feelers," but naturally in a different context. The real reason for

Bonhoeffer's Swedish journey appears to have remained undiscovered to the very end.

In the early part of 1945 the Reich Central Security Office made serious efforts to discover what opinions the conspirators and their associates held about the outcome of the war, and to work out their possible role in bringing about a shift of alliances abroad. I myself was a witness to the fact that in the Lehrter Strasse prison, Albrecht Haushofer suddenly received every possible kind of concession in the way of books, food, and tobacco, to persuade him to write down his views of the political situation for Himmler and make the necessary suggestions for a solution. Dohnanyi was similarly encouraged to "describe what would have been the follow-up to the conspiracy of 20 July, as he saw it,"[17] and to assess the prospects for Germany's future. Nothing is directly known of any such approach to Bonhoeffer, but the whole tenor of the Kaltenbrunner letter is in accordance with these attitudes that were held for a while.

In a letter smuggled out on 25 February 1945, Dohnanyi told his wife that the commandant at the prison had "a soft spot for his prisoners and is fishing for an anchor for the future . . . the only solution is to gain time . . . and there are other siren songs as well."

4. In the earlier days of February, just after Dohnanyi had been moved from Sachsenhausen to the Central Security Office and before Bonhoeffer has disappeared from Berlin, the two brothers-in-law were able to see each other secretly and have a brief conversation. Bonhoeffer took advantage of the confusion caused by an air-raid alarm to get into Dohnanyi's cell for a few moments.[18] On this occasion Bonhoeffer told Dohnanyi that he had confessed to having played a part in Canaris's political information service, and Dohnanyi passed this information on to his wife when she saw him for the last time at the beginning of April in the state hospital. During the journey from Weiden to Buchenwald on 3–4 April Josef Müller reported having heard the same thing from Bonhoeffer: that he had stopped denying that his military exemption was connected to Canaris's political intelligence service.

5. In the later Huppenkothen trials S.S. judge Dr. Thorbeck gave a summary opinion concerning his interrogation of Bonhoeffer which he, as presiding judge of the court-martial, held in Flossenbürg on the night of 8 April. Thorbeck said that on that night Bonhoeffer had not attempted to deny "anything." Thorbeck's knowledge of the actual facts of the case, however, could only have been superficial.

The last smuggled letter written by Dohnanyi on 8 March 1945 contradicts the impression that the Gestapo officials were still on the wrong track with their questions. Part of the letter reads:

They've discovered everything, absolutely everything. I cannot think who
has betrayed us . . . and when all is said and done I don't care . . . P., by the
way, seems to have handled things badly when he was asked about Dietrich, and as a result Dietrich in his turn quoted me as his source—a
vicious circle of statements, which the Gestapo cleverly play off against
each of us to their own advantage. I don't think there is very much more
I can do to help.

6. In contrast to the view expressed in Dohnanyi's statement that they
knew "everything," Huppenkothen's interrogation officials in the Central
Security Office seem to have been far from satisfied with the results of their
investigations, according to Huppenkothen's own detailed account at his
trial in 1955. The reason for this was due partly to the difficulty in cooperating with other departments through the network of a complex organization and partly to the disruption caused by the increasing number of air
raids.

Sometimes the anxiety of those in the Central Security Office to obtain
more information about the organization of the resistance group and its
channels of communication seemed to overcome their desire to pass a hasty
sentence on their prisoners and be done with them. In Bonhoeffer's case, for
instance, new investigations were made into the ecumenical church connections. Although group B in department IV of the Central Security Office,
which dealt with the "churches and the Freemasons," had for years kept
careful watch over all church connections with the outside world, including
the activities of the Church Foreign Office, it was now deemed necessary to
examine the Confessing church channels which until then had existed secretly under the protection of Admiral Canaris, and which might be of use
again under changed circumstances. It is probable that Huppenkothen
sought information from other departments, in an attempt to check the reliability of Bonhoeffer's statements about his Swiss and English connections.
If this was so, then further official documents concerning Bonhoeffer's interrogations in the Central Security Office may well one day come to light in
the records preserved in the Ministry for Religious Affairs or even in the Foreign Office, if all the Central Security Office's own files on this complex
matter have indeed been destroyed.

Huppenkothen testified that such investigations were indeed made, both
in Germany and abroad, but that their progress was slowed and in some
cases made impossible after the end of 1944, as a result of the Allied air bom-
bardments.[19] In January 1945 things seem to have become somewhat easier for Bonhoeffer, on account of these difficulties and the interest his case

aroused in the Central Security Office. This is confirmed by the two letters he was able to write home during this period.[20]

To summarize, it can be said: (1) Subsequent discoveries and the statements of third parties showed that the facts of the case known to the Central Security Office from the Tegel period also included a knowledge of the Freiburg discussions, the meeting in Sigtuna, and the memoranda. (2) Friends who were implicated in the proceedings or who had implicated others were now in the custody of the Central Security Office. These included, besides his brothers and brothers-in-law, the Freiburg professors von Dietze, Lampe, and Ritter, as well as Walter Bauer, Hans John, and Friedrich Justus Perels. The last three were occasionally subjected to severe tortures, so that Dr. Bauer, for instance, who was in the cell next to mine, pleaded with me to get him some poison from Bonhoeffer's father if ever the chance arose, because he did not think he could endure the torture much longer. Bonhoeffer was no longer able to get in touch with any of them so that they could agree on what story to tell their interrogators. (3) Bonhoeffer had not yet given up trying to save the situation. When he was unable to deny facts he gave them a slanted meaning or introduced other facts that obscured or complicated the issue. For, as he said, "the only fight which is lost is that which we give up."[21]

Life in the Cellar. Bonhoeffer's period in the cellar of the Reich Central Security Office was spent first in cell 19 and then in cell 25. Schlabrendorff was in a neighboring cell. The cells were narrower than those in Tegel, being barely five feet wide by eight feet long. They contained nothing more than a table, a stool, and a bed that could be folded up during the day. At the beginning of February 1945 the heating system stopped working. Surprisingly enough, however, most of the prisoners suffered less on this account than might have been expected.

For breakfast and supper there was a mug of imitation coffee and two slices of bread and jam, and at midday there was some soup. Even though food parcels were no longer accepted so frequently by the guards, it appears that Bonhoeffer actually did receive what Maria von Wedermeyer or his parents or sisters brought to him every Wednesday. Payne Best's description of Bonhoeffer, whom he got to know toward the end of February in Buchenwald, has the ring of truth about it; "[He did] not look in the least like a man who had spent months in prison and who went in fear of his life."[22]

There was a washroom and lavatory at the end of the corridor, with a cold-water shower that the prisoners welcomed, despite the winter, because it gave them the opportunity for whispered conversations. Exercise in the prison yard, a common feature of life in most prisons, did not exist at Prinz-Albrecht-Strasse. But during the frequent air raids the prisoners were taken to a concrete air-raid shelter in the yard. This was the so-called Himmler Bunker. On these occasions it was not always possible to enforce the strict discipline that was normally the rule, and as a result the prisoners were often able to establish some kind of contact with one another. Schlabrendorff has described what happened in the air-raid shelter during the night of 3 February 1945, when Berlin suffered its worst air raid:

> Tightly squeezed together we were standing in our air-raid shelter when a bomb hit it with an enormous explosion. For a second it seemed as if the shelter were bursting and the ceiling crashing down on top of us. It rocked like a ship tossing in the storm, but it held. At that moment Dietrich Bonhoeffer showed his mettle. He remained quite calm, he did not move a muscle . . . as if nothing had happened.[23]

The behavior of the guards, who were now all S.S. men, toward their once high-ranking prisoners varied from downright sadism to the most formal politeness. Many of them complained about the conditions in general without necessarily being agents provocateurs. It frequently happened that the prisoners had no choice but to humble themselves before some brute in order to avoid brutal treatment. It is said of Bonhoeffer that even under these conditions he was able to command respect from the guards, "so that to my surprise, within a short time, he had won over his warders, who were not always kindly disposed."[24] Without the least embarrassment he would make modest requests, or inquire at the right moment about the personal circumstances or worries of his guards. He never demanded the impossible of them, since he could see that they too were in a nervous state. In a smuggled note of 25 February Dohnanyi wrote to his wife: "I have seen Dietrich; he looks cheerful. . . . Runge has a soft spot for Maria. . . . He thought Dietrich was a 'decent fellow.'"

The most encouraging aspect of the period Bonhoeffer spent at Prinz-Albrecht-Strasse was the chance it gave him to meet friends he had not seen for a long time. There was Schlabrendorff, who was in the neighboring cell, and whom Dietrich had not seen since he had become engaged to his cousin, Maria von Wedemeyer. Then there was Josef Müller, as well as Canaris and Oster, both of whom had thought they were in a far worse plight. There was also Goerdeler who, until his execution on 2 February, was only a few cells away from Bonhoeffer; later in Regensburg Bonhoeffer was able to give a report to Goerdeler's family. There was also Hans Böhm, the pastor and ecumenical officer of the Confessing church, who had been arrested for helping Gisevius and Nebe to escape. Finally, but only for a few days, there was Hans von Dohnanyi. Many of them enjoyed with Bonhoeffer the contents of the food parcels that were sent to him, and occasionally a strong smell of tobacco smoke emanated from one of the cells.[25]

Communication with his family in the Marienburger Allee home had been almost completely disrupted. Occasionally Sonderegger passed on a greeting or a message when he handed over the weekly parcel on Wednesdays, or allowed a note to accompany it. Bonhoeffer's parents received only two more letters from him, one written in haste for his mother's birthday on 28 December 1944[26]—the poem "Powers of Good" ("*Von guten Mächten*") was sent to her through Maria, who received it in a letter of 19 December 1944.[27] The other was written on 17 January 1945,[28] during the time when the Central Security Office was becoming interested in his knowledge of England. Bonhoeffer's parents never again obtained a permit to visit him.

Maria von Wedemeyer was in Berlin most of the time during these months. "It is a very great comfort for me to know that Maria is with you," Bonhoeffer wrote in the letter to his parents on 28 December 1944. The last letter which Maria herself received from her fiancée was dated 19 December 1944. On one occasion she succeeded in getting a personal interview with Huppenkothen, but she failed to obtain permission to visit Dietrich. The officers of the Central Security Office never made any serious attempt to extort information from her.

Theological Work. We assumed in an earlier chapter that Bonhoeffer continued to work on his "Nonreligious Interpretation of Biblical Concepts in a World Come of Age" and brought it considerably nearer to completion. Admittedly there is no actual proof to support this, and his brief letters make no direct reference to his work. The new series of interrogations to which he was now subjected may have slowed him down. Yet there are various indications that he continued to write.

We know that he worked on his manuscript up to the very last moment of his time in Tegel and that this already covered many sheets of paper. We also know that it was among the belongings he took with him to Prinz-Albrecht-Strasse. During his time at the Central Security Office he was in possession of writing materials—paper and a pencil—and in his last letter of 17 January he again asked for more paper to be sent to him along with the weekly food parcel. Schlabrendorff confirms that, unlike himself, Bonhoeffer was able to write in his cell and had the means to do so. There were other prominent prisoners of the Central Security Office who also wrote whole memoranda. Many of them were handcuffed, tightly at night but loosely during the day. This was not the case with Bonhoeffer.

We also know that while in the Central Security Office he received and read quite a number of books. In his letter of 17 January he complained that he had received no books with the weekly parcel, but that the matter could be rectified by speaking to Sonderegger. He then asked for a whole series of new works—Pestalozzi, Natorp, Plutarch. The volume of Plutarch, which Bonhoeffer did actually receive along with the works of other authors just before he was moved from Berlin, accompanied him as far as Schönberg and even found its way back to his family later. Dr. Hermann Pünder reported in the summer of 1945 that he had exchanged books with Bonhoeffer in Buchenwald. He gave him the biography of Julian the Apostate by the Geneva historian Bidez and received in return Kurt Leese's *Protestantism in Modern Times.*

Kurt Leese's book had appeared in 1941. At that time in the Confessing church Leese was viewed as a theological outsider. Bonhoeffer was now naturally very interested in a man who had attempted to understand and come to terms with the work of the previous generation of theologians, with Ritschl and Troeltsch, and the more recent intellectual history, including humanism and scientific discoveries. In Buchenwald Bonhoeffer shared a cell with General von Rabenau, who also had a doctorate in theology, and was able to have long conversations with him over a period of many weeks.

In addition, we know of Bonhoeffer's determination to keep strictly to the work schedule he had drawn up for himself in order to combat the strain of difficult days and weeks of interrogations. It is hardly conceivable, then, that during the entire four months he spent at Prinz-Albrecht-Strasse he was not engaged in some kind of theological work. He may possibly have chosen some other subject than that of the nonreligious interpretation, but if he did we know nothing about it.

Somewhere during the final stages of his journey a sheaf of manuscript notes must have been left behind with the rest of his belongings. But who would have been interested in preserving the illegible jottings of a prisoner, either while he was in transit or when the camp at Flossenbürg was being dismantled? Even those friends of his who managed to escape with their lives had other more pressing matters on their minds when the end came.

The last theological and developed witness from Bonhoeffer's hand is his poem "Powers of Good."[29] It is a prayer, similar in spirit to "Christians and Pagans,"[30] but without the didactic tone of the latter. The poem was meant for his mother and his fiancée.

Grim February. In the first days of February 1945 so many tragic things happened to the family that the demands placed on everyone, both at home and away from it, were almost too great to bear. One event overtook another: the destruction of Pätzig, Hans von Dohnanyi's removal to the cellar of the Reich Central Security Office and his infection with disease, the death sentence passed on Rüdiger Schleicher and Klaus Bonhoeffer by the People's Court, and the unexplained disappearance of Dietrich Bonhoeffer from Berlin.

1. At the end of January Maria von Wedemeyer returned home to Pätzig, on the other side of the Oder River. The Russian front was moving closer. Maria's mother wrote to Frau Bonhoeffer on 30 January 1945:

> Dear Frau Bonhoeffer, I've had to be very hard on you, so please forgive me. Despite twelve degrees of frost and an icy east wind, I've sent Maria with my three other children, Frau Döpke and her own two children, Fräulein Rath, who has a high temperature, and Frau Dimel, who's very delicate, their destination being a village in the neighborhood of Celle, where Herr Döpke has relatives. I need her help very badly now. It's really far too much for her. She has a Polish driver and the three best plough horses. Join me in praying that she proves equal to her difficult task. They should be there in two weeks, if all goes well, but the snow and wind have been very severe since then. I was strongly advised against Berlin. We are profoundly grateful to you for your offer to take the children. Herr Döpke wanted to get his family to his parents in the west at all costs. I couldn't let them leave in two wagons because there were not enough of the necessary spare parts and we would have needed another driver. We couldn't have afforded it.
>
> Perhaps we shall soon receive the order for a general evacuation to the west. We're secretly making advance preparations. I hope to be able to help save lives and prevent panic from setting in. Once she has seen the children settled in, Maria will try to make her way back to you, but it will take a considerable time.
>
> May God be merciful and protect you and yours, and spare you a long ordeal. It rests with Him whether we meet again in this life or the next. Either way, we can look forward to that time with great joy.
>
> Please accept my thanks for all the maternal and paternal love you bestow, and have bestowed, upon my child. Yours, Ruth Wedemeyer.[31]

Two days after this letter Pätzig was destroyed by artillery fire.[32]

Maria von Wedemeyer's trek across the Oder and Elbe was successful. When she reached Berlin two weeks later she found everything changed. Unable to get exact information from the Reich Central Security Office, she set out toward the south with a case of warm clothing to find Dietrich. She reached Dachau and eventually Flossenbürg, going the last four and a half miles on foot, carrying her case, only to be turned away at both places without any information.[33] She finally returned to Berlin amid the general disintegration—it was now March—hoping that people were better informed there, but no one knew anything. The officials at Prinz-Albrecht-Strasse would give no information.

2. At the end of January Huppenkothen's special group made a new attempt to speed up the inquiry which was dragging on. Dohnanyi, the key figure, was brought from Sachsenhausen to the Reich Central Security Office on 1 February. His illness was now disregarded. "So far they've left me almost entirely alone."[34] Now a brutal commissar named Stawitzky took over. He abandoned Dohnanyi to his presumed helplessness; for example, he never had him taken to the washroom or the lavatory. But Dohnanyi held out until Stawitzky was replaced after three weeks by Sonderegger. A doctor being held as a political prisoner in the cells on Lehrter Strasse was ordered to look after him. Dohnanyi was able to smuggle out a long note to his wife in the laundry parcel. He said:

> Three days ago a doctor . . . who is also a prisoner here, Dr. Eugen Ense . . . was asked to look after me. Until three days ago I was in the hands of a man who was simply a brute. He thought he could break my spirit by leaving me entirely uncared for. That went on for three weeks. I really began to stink. That helped. Now Sonderegger and Ense have come. Ense can visit me as he pleases—my cell door is open—and the worst is past. It was actually very funny, and I often laughed at how I looked. . . .
>
> I am using my illness as a weapon. It is helpful that people think I'm sicker than I am. . . . In fact I feel quite well and am well fed, thanks to you. At night I secretly teach myself to walk again. It's going quite well. I must become independent. During the day I'm the helpless invalid. . . .
>
> The only thing to do is gain time. I must make sure that I'm unfit to be questioned. The best thing would be for me to get a solid attack of dysentery. A culture must be available for medical purposes in the Koch Institute. If you wrap up some food in a red cloth and put an ink mark on the glass, then I'll know that it contains a decent infection that'll get me into the hospital. . . .
>
> They want to finish things off now by force, and that must be prevented. . . .
>
> Think about providing me with some infectious germs. Perhaps Zutt can prepare some such food for you. It mustn't be too long in coming, because I might be moved from Berlin. Wrap up the infected food in a red cloth. . . . If the whole thing's impossible, put a green paper around some-

thing. If I go into the hospital, the only possibility is a state hospital. . . . It would help with Huppenkothen if some doctor (father . . . ?) were to make a stupid inquiry about whether nursing and treatment, invalid transport, massage, and injections, were possible here. But don't you intervene! . . . And avoid a commissar named Stawitzky!

On 8 March the exchange of parcels brought the next note:

You can scarcely imagine the excitement when I saw a glass covered with red in the case. And then the book and the thermos flask. At last, at last a few lines from you—after over six months—a present. . . . The questioning continues, and it is clear what I can expect unless a miracle happens. The misery around me is so great that I would throw away what little life I have if you were not there. . . .

That is why I'm not frightened of any infectious illness. I know very well that I would lie down with the feeling that this would not only save my life, but that of many others whose situation is bound up with mine, certainly Dietrich's. Naturally I put the diphtheria culture in my mouth immediately and chewed thoroughly, but for practical reasons it wasn't possible to do it until half past seven at night. . . . And it seemed to me that the cotton wool had become quite dry. Now I'm eating the sweets as quickly as possible, I've heard that diphtheria bacilli are not very volatile, but can't stand dryness, needing moisture to keep alive. Incubation period is three to eight days. I'm afraid I may be immune and won't get anything. But it would always be possible to have a repeat.

I must get out of here into a hospital so that I can't be interrogated any longer. Fainting fits, heart attacks make no impression, and if I go to a hospital without a new illness it could even be dangerous, because they could cure me quickly. Sonderegger said today: "It is in your own interest for the hearing to come to an end soon. The Reichsführer [Himmler] does not want to keep you here. He wants you to get well." Shall I translate that? "Himmler wants to finish the hearing as quickly as possible. During the period while the charges are being prepared you are to go to a hospital, perhaps in central Germany or Bavaria (i.e., Buchenwald or Dachau), depending on the war situation—there we'll soon get you fit to be tried. In the state you're in we can hardly put you in front of a court, but in three or four weeks we'll have you ready." This is their game, and I'd so like to ruin it for them! Believe me—so far my view of things has been correct, unfortunately—there is no other solution than a serious new illness. Have no fear for me. I'll get over it, but even if I don't, much would be gained for the others and nothing lost for myself, for I have nothing more to lose. . . . I heard today from Sonderegger that Eberhard has also been arrested. . . . Incidentally, he's not been linked with me in any way. Sonderegger just asked how it happened that he had lived with us. . . .

> We must act as long as we can. The war or the S.S. can spoil things for us at any time, and I'm afraid of being moved from Berlin. I want to stay here in Berlin at all costs, as close as possible to you. As long as that is the case I am not at their mercy. It all comes back to the one solution: a new illness. It's terribly hard for your parents. I want so much to help. Can I do so in any other way?

The concerted effort succeeded. The medical inquiries from Karl Bonhoeffer and Professor Zutt at the Reich Security Central Office resulted in Dr. Tietz, the head of the neurological division of the state hospital, being consulted. About two weeks after Dohnanyi had written this note Dr. Tietze ordered him moved to the prison division on Scharnhorststrasse. Christine von Dohnanyi was allowed to have another secret meeting with her husband.

3. On the afternoon of 2 February, in the People's Court, not far from the Potsdamer Platz, Freisler handed down the death sentence to Klaus Bonhoeffer, Rüdiger Schleicher, Friedrich Justus Perels, and Hans John. That evening they were moved from the cells of prison wing B in Lehrter Strasse—I could see their cells from my own, which was opposite—to wing D, where a corridor was reserved for those condemned to death.

The next morning, early on Saturday, Ursula Schleicher and her daughter Dorothee set out to see the Reich high attorney, E. Lautz, about the death sentence. At the same time her husband's brother, Dr. Rolf Schleicher, went into town to appeal for mercy, Schleicher, a senior staff doctor in Stuttgart, had come to Berlin for the end of his brother's trial. When he arrived at the Potsdamer Platz underground station no one was allowed to go up on the street. The heaviest Allied daylight attack on the center of Berlin was just beginning. For two hours squadron after squadron flew over Berlin in the bright blue winter sky, transforming the area east of the zoo into a wilderness of smoke and ash. All services were cut off.

After the attack Rolf Schleicher walked to the People's Court nearby; it was on fire. His doctor's uniform was noticed, and he was called into the courtyard. He had to attend to some important person who had run across the courtyard and been hit by a piece of shrapnel. All Rolf Schleicher could do was establish that the man was dead. It was Roland Freisler, whose final death sentences the day before had been passed on Rolf's brother Rüdiger, Klaus Bonhoeffer, Perels, and Hans John. Rolf Schleicher refused to write a death certificate until he had been taken to Otto Thierack, the Minister of Justice. Thierack was quite shocked by the strange coincidence and promised that the execution would be delayed, and that the verdict would be reconsidered after a plea for mercy had been submitted. Hours later Rolf Schleicher was able to return to Marienburger Allee. He entered the room announcing: "The scoundrel is dead!"

Meanwhile Ursula Schleicher and her daughter had been unable to achieve anything. They went on foot to Lehrter Strasse and found that the prison had remained unharmed. She was able to see her husband only a few days later. Prisoners condemned to death were supposed to wear handcuffs all the time, but the guards at Lehrter Strasse occasionally dared to ignore this rule. They observed that, after the sentence was passed, these men were much calmer than during the period in which they were still being tried.

4. On the same 3 February Bonhoeffer's parents, accompanied by their daughter-in-law, Emmi Bonhoeffer, had left early to deliver a birthday parcel to Dietrich at Prinz-Albrecht-Strasse. In addition to the usual food there were books and a letter where his father wrote: "The memory of so many lovely things that you have experienced, and the hope for a speedy end to your time of trial, will help you to get through your birthday."[35] He intended this time to insist on the spot for permission to see his son.

After changing trains twice they reached the Anhalter underground station, but they too could not leave it because of the air-raid alarm. When the three of them were eventually able to leave the suffocating atmosphere of the station it was impossible to get through the ruins to the Reich Central Security Office. No one was admitted to the building, which had been badly hit. Full of anxiety, they turned back and started to walk home until they were able to get a train further out. Emmi Bonhoeffer went to Lehrter Strasse to inquire about her husband. They all arrived home covered with soot and ash. Only the next day did they learn that nothing had happened to the prisoners, despite the direct hit on the basement of the Reich Central Security Office.

His parents tried again to get into the Central Security Office on Wednesday, 7 February, the customary day to drop off parcels. This time their parcel, which also contained the Plutarch volume, was accepted, but they were not allowed to see their son. The accompanying letter read:

> 7.2.1945. Dear Dietrich, Your birthday letter for the 4th, which we wanted to bring on Saturday, did not reach you because of the raid. We were in the Anhalter underground station during the raid, and it wasn't particularly pleasant. Apart from looking like chimney sweeps afterward nothing happened to us. But later, when we tried to get to you, we were very anxious, as we weren't allowed to go in because of unexploded bombs.
>
> The next day we learned that nothing had happened to the prisoners. I hope that is true. . . . Maria is taking her brothers and sisters west. . . .

Unfortunately I had no luck at the library.[36] Pestalozzi is lent out only for the reading room. Natorp was checked out. Karl Friedrich has chosen the Plutarch for your birthday. I hope that this letter reaches you. We are looking forward to being allowed to see you soon. There are many things to be sorted out at our age, things that have to be discussed with one's children. I'm typing this so that it can be more easily read. Our hearty greetings, Your Father.[37]

This was the last message Dietrich Bonhoeffer received from his family.

On the afternoon of 7 February Bonhoeffer was taken from Berlin to an unknown destination. Only on 14 February, the next day they took a package, did Maria von Wedemeyer and his parents discover there was no longer anyone at Prinz-Albrecht-Strasse to receive their gifts.

Maria's grandmother, Frau von Kleist-Retzow, also celebrated her birthday on 4 February in the remote village of Klein-Krössin. Although frail, she had lost none of her energy and judgment. But she was preparing for the Russian invasion; she intended to stay. In the autumn of 1945 Maria's mother managed again to reach Klein-Krössin by a long trek on foot through what had now become Polish territory. Dietrich Bonhoeffer's old patroness was dying, but she lived long enough to learn what had happened. A few hours later she died.

On 2 February Bishop Bell wrote from Chichester to Dietrich's twin sister in Oxford on the occasion of their shared birthday:

My dear Mrs. Leibholz, I cannot help thinking very much of Dietrich and you in these days of momentous happenings in Germany. And I take the opportunity of our common birthday to express once again with all the sincerity I possess my affection for and deep trust in Dietrich, as well as my ardent hopes and prayers for his deliverance. I can judge how anxious you must be as the war in all its violence approaches Berlin. Would God that the whole Hitler castle might be brought down in ruin, even now, and so the means granted for the surrender of the German forces and the saving of that true German soul which is yet so precious a care to those silent, suppressed and persecuted multitudes of true patriots like Dietrich, for the gradual if costly rebuilding of the nation. We must pray that God may bring the war to an end, with the breaking of Hitler's spell, and save Europe from even more pitiless destruction. And may the lives of those most needed, as we humans see it, for recovery and illumination be saved. And may God of His mercy guide the three Allied Leaders to seek a common policy as may give hope for unity and charity in Europe, and space and freedom for the European family of nations to breathe again the spirit of the Christian tradition and faith.

We are now at the climax—God grant wisdom, mercy and peace. With love to you all, and especially words of love to Dietrich. Yours affectionately, George Chichester.

Emergency Quarters. The raid on 3 February had lasting consequences. Bonhoeffer was never again brought before Huppenkothen's group of investigators, although—as Dohnanyi's removal on 1 February clearly showed—a new approach was being taken toward the affairs of the "Zossen men."

In 1955 Huppenkothen related how much the Reich Central Security Office had been affected by the 3 February Allied raids. Many offices had to be set up in emergency escape quarters in remote areas of the Reich, creating unimaginable difficulties in communication. Sachsenhausen was cleared because the fighting was moving closer. The "house prison" at Prinz-Albrecht-Strasse could be used only to a very limited extent. Only those prisoners whose trial was about to come up were to remain there; everyone else had to be housed elsewhere. In his book *The Venlo Incident* Payne Best, who had been imprisoned for several days in the Reich Central Security Office after the Sachsenhausen prisoners were moved south, gives a savagely humorous account of the indescribable apprehension at Prinz-Albrecht-Strasse during those February days.

At midday on 7 February twenty prisoners were summoned to be removed elsewhere. Twelve men had to stand and wait with their baggage next to a prison van that had, at the most, eight seats; among them were the former governor of Belgium and northern France, General von Falkenhausen; Gottfried Count Bismarck, Werner von Alvensleben and Dr. Josef Müller; Dr. Hermann Pünder, who was later in the cell next to Bonhoeffer; the Navy corvette captain Franz Liedig, who worked for Military Intelligence and had been involved as early as 1938 in the putsch plans; Ludwig Gehre, a colleague of Oster and friend of Otto John; and Dietrich Bonhoeffer. Canaris, Oster, military judge Sack, General Thomas, Major General Halder, Dr. Hjalmar Schacht, Oster's colleague Dr. Theodor Strünck, and the former Austrian chancellor von Schuschnigg were in front of a second van. As later became clear, the first van was bound for the Thuringian concentration camp, Buchenwald, and the second for the Flossenbürg camp in the Upper Palatinate.

It is hard to ascertain the principle behind the selection of these two groups. Were they chosen according to the prominence of their members, or was there already a possibility that some of them might be useful in prisoner exchanges with the Allies? Was the decisive factor the importance of the still unrevealed information possessed by the prisoners? There was no criterion, however, that applied to all the members of the two groups.

The prisoners could not fail to sense the general confusion; this raised their hopes, and the sudden encounter with old friends gladdened their hearts. But when they were loaded into the vans, Josef Müller and Dietrich Bonhoeffer were handcuffed. Dietrich protested but to no avail. Josef Müller says that he then exhorted him: "Let us go calmly to the gallows as Christians." Only in Buchenwald were the handcuffs removed.

Buchenwald

We have an excellent chronicler of the period in Buchenwald. Payne Best, the British secret service officer captured in 1939 at Venlo, has given a vivid and graphic account of the situation in this camp in his book *The Venlo Incident*.[38] He arrived in Buchenwald on 24 February with the English officer Hugh Falconer, a Russian air force officer named Kokorin who was a nephew of Molotov, and General von Rabenau.

The Location. The air-raid shelter cells in Buchenwald set aside for the prominent prisoners were damp, cold, and without daylight. They lay outside the actual area of the camp beneath houses that had been built originally for camp officials; after the air raids they had again been converted into command headquarters and barracks. The basement cells were at first intended for S.S. members who had committed criminal offenses. In August 1944 the Allies had bombed buildings outside the camp; it was reported that on this occasion Communist leader Ernst Thälmann, Interior Minister Rudolf Breitscheid, and Princess Mafalda of Hesse had been killed. After that, whenever there was an air-raid alarm the sentries went quickly to trenches some distance away, and the prisoners were locked in their cells until it was over. It was said that there was also munition stored in the cellars.

Two walls divided the wide central corridor of the cellar lengthwise into three parallel corridors with gaps in them. First on the left was the washroom. Then came the cells: next to the damp washroom was Cell 1, with Bonhoeffer and von Rabenau, who joined him after a fortnight; Cell 2, with Dr. Pünder and Liedig; Cell 3, with Dr. Heberlein, the former ambassador to Spain, and his wife; Cell 4, with von Alvensleben and von Petersdorff; Cell 5, a more comfortable cell, with von Falkenhausen; Cell 6, with Hugh Falconer; Cell 7, with Wassili Kokorin; Cell 8, with Josef Müller and Captain Gehre. The larger cells were on the right: the guards' room was opposite No. 8; then Cell 9, with a Fräulein Heidl; Cell 10, with Dr. Sigmund Rascher; Cell 11, with Payne Best; Cell 12, with Dr. Hoepner, a brother of the executed general. Payne Best's cell, Cell 11, was directly opposite Bonhoeffer's, but not directly visible because of the dividing wall.

The camp commandant himself assigned the cells on the night of 7–8 February. The subordinate guards then inflicted various petty sufferings. The food consisted of a soup at midday and some bread, fat, and marmalade in the evening. According to the instructions of the Reich Central Security Office, the prisoners were to be kept in a condition in which they could be interrogated. Since the fighting was coming closer and closer to the camp, and refugees were flooding into Thuringia from east and west, obtaining supplies became a serious problem.

There were no walks in the fresh air because there was no way of ensuring proper surveillance outside the camp area. Instead the prisoners managed to get permission to use the central corridor of the cellar, divided into three, for their "walks." It was too arduous a task for the sentries to take each of the seventeen prisoners separately under guard around the corridors, so they all took their exercise at the same time. In this way the prisoners made one another's acquaintance. Best tells us that there were even little black market deals with tobacco, undertaken by workers who had access to these things for the prominent prisoners in the camp.[39] Best apparently managed to brighten the mood among the prisoners in the cells, and Bonhoeffer helped him: "He was cheerful, ready to respond to a joke."[40]

Companions in Suffering. Bonhoeffer became friendly with the man in the next cell, Dr. Hermann Pünder, a Catholic politician from the Rhineland who survived the Third Reich. As we have already heard, they exchanged books,[41] and their conversations were about culture, politics, and future relations between Catholics and Protestants.

After a good two weeks Friedrich von Rabenau arrived to join Bonhoeffer in his cell. In a somewhat critical comparison with the other people in the cellar Falconer said: "I think they were the only pair of prisoners sharing a cell who got on really well together and enjoyed each other's company."[42] General von Rabenau had not commanded troops, but had been the head of the military archives. He was the author of the lengthy biography of military leader Hans von Seeckt that had appeared in 1940.[43] Bonhoeffer owned a copy and undoubtedly knew which passages had made it possible for the book to be printed.

Von Rabenau had been an early intermediary between Beck's resistance group and some of the leading generals who tried in 1940 to influence Brauchitsch. In March 1941 Hassell and Goerdeler discussed with von Rabenau whether Brauchitsch could be approached again. Before 20 July Goerdeler regularly sent von Rabenau as a trusted emissary to the individual generals.[44] Retired from active service in 1942, the old general had completed a degree at the theological faculty of Berlin University and added the licentiate to his honorary doctorate. The Reich Central Security Office had tracked down von Rabenau as a friend of Goerdeler's; like Bonhoeffer, he was executed in Flossenbürg.

The life and milieu of Friedrich von Rabenau, general and theologian, did not have much in common with Bonhoeffer's, yet the five weeks they spent together seem to have been stimulating for both. According to Pünder, von Rabenau was still writing his memoirs in Buchenwald. He cannot recall whether Bonhoeffer was also writing, but did remember that Bonhoeffer and von Rabenau had "enthusiastic doctrinal discussions that I was sometimes able to listen to with great interest."[45] Payne Best even gave the theologian a chess set, so that Bonhoeffer could again follow his old passion.

Von Rabenau had arrived from Berlin with Payne Best. At the first opportunity in the washroom, he introduced Best to his friend Bonhoeffer. Bonhoeffer was happy to have the chance to speak English again. This Englishman knew nothing of Bonhoeffer's past, background, or significance. Among his later descriptions of his fellow prisoners—some spiteful, some humorous—Best gave the following account of Bonhoeffer's first impression on him:

> Bonhoeffer was all humility and sweetness; he always seemed to diffuse an atmosphere of happiness, of joy in every smallest event in life, and of deep gratitude for the mere fact that he was alive. There was something dog-like in the look of fidelity in his eyes and his gladness if you showed that you liked him. He was one of the very few men I have ever met to whom his God was real and ever close to him.

In a personal letter to the Bonhoeffer family he later wrote:

> In fact my feeling was far stronger than these words imply. He was, without exception, the finest and most lovable man I have ever met.

Best spoke of how most of the prisoners complained:

> . . . with the exception of Falkenhausen and Bonhoeffer . . . Bonhoeffer was different; just quite calm and normal, seemingly perfectly at his ease. . . . his soul really shone in the dark desperation of our prison . . . [we were] in complete agreement that our warders and guards needed pity far more than we and that it was absurd to blame them for their actions.[46]

Hopes for Liberation. As Easter Sunday dawned on 1 April 1945 the thunder of American cannons from the Werra could be heard in the basement. Who could now imagine that there would be a resumption of the interrogations and a session of the People's Court? Escape plans were considered once more, though without practical results. A sentry named Sippach gave orders that the prisoners should be ready to leave at a moment's notice. One guard told the prisoners that they would be going on foot. Did that mean execution in the woods? Another knew there was a truck available.

In Berlin Bonhoeffer's parents had tried again to trace him via the prison on Prinz-Albrecht-Strasse. They wrote to him:

> Since you left Berlin we have heard nothing of you, and presumably you have heard nothing from us. . . . We would like to send you the laundry and those little things we were able to send in the past, but so far there has been no way of doing so. I hope that Christel will discover something today at Prinz-Albrecht-Strasse. . . . Permission to write elderly people like us should be granted more frequently. Your Father.
>
> My thoughts are with you day and night, worrying about how you are getting on. I hope you are able to do some work and reading and are managing to stay reasonably healthy. God help you and us through this difficult period. Your old mother. We are staying in Berlin whatever happens.[47]

The letter was returned. Nothing more was accepted at the Prinz-Albrecht-Strasse prison, and no one would give any information.

Flossenbürg

What we know of the final week of Bonhoeffer's life comes from Payne Best's detailed account, which continues as far as Schönberg (3–8 April 1945). There are also the accounts of survivors, including Hermann Pünder, Josef Müller, Frau Goerdeler, and Fabian von Schlabrendorff. Finally, we have the details from the trials of Huppenkothen and Dr. Thorbeck, held in southern Germany from 1951 to 1955.

The Move to Schönberg. The move from Buchenwald was probably ordered in Berlin. Otherwise, the camp commanders would have carried out the general orders to kill special prisoners in the event of an enemy approach, and not make a truck available for them in the midst of a disastrous transport and food situation. In fact, instructions were apparently given to take some of the prisoners to Flossenbürg and others further south.

Later in the evening of Tuesday, 3 April 1945, a huge closed truck rolled out of Buchenwald into the night. It used wood for fuel, and there was a great pile of it in the back of the truck for the generator. Behind the wood the special prisoners had to make do, with whatever possessions they were still carrying, in a space intended for eight people at the most. The vehicle never went faster than twenty miles an hour, and stopped every hour. The air filters had to be cleaned, the generator filled, and the motor stoked every fifteen minutes. Each time the air in the stoking area became intolerable. There was no light and nothing to eat or drink. But as the stack of wood grew smaller the prisoners could take turns going to the back door, two by two and get some fresh air from the opening. Bonhoeffer, who sat next to Payne Best, found the remnants of his stock of tobacco and divided it among them. He "insisted on contributing it to the common good . . . he was a good and saintly man."[48] In the gray dawn someone saw a village; they were traveling southeast. The prisoners on the truck guessed that they were going to Flossenbürg; for them it was an ominous name. Yet the guards produced unexpected food and they had breakfast.

Around noon on Wednesday they reached Weiden. Now they would find out whether or not they were to turn left into the valley toward Flossenbürg. The truck stopped. There was some conversation outside: "Drive on, we can't take you . . . too full!" And the truck set off again—straight ahead, to the south. So it was not going to the extermination camp? But a few miles further two police motorcyclists signaled to it to stop. Müller and Liedig were called out and their things pulled from the pile of luggage at the back. Bonhoeffer leaned back so as not to be seen. The unfortunate Gehre jumped out after them; he had shared a cell with Müller and wanted to stay with him.

Were orders given and then changed again in the general chaos? Were three men from the truck to be sent to Flossenbürg? The final events in Flossenbürg suggest that Bonhoeffer was supposed to be the third, but he now seemed to have been replaced by Gehre. Or had the whole transport, in fact, been intended for Flossenbürg, and only here had it been decided, given the general situation, that the transport leader himself should find a new place to take all but a few selected people?

Finally the truck moved on. Now that Flossenbürg lay behind them, the guards became more friendly. They let the prisoners get out at a farmer's house. They were allowed to go to a pump in the yard, and a peasant woman brought a jug of milk and rye bread. It was a bright afternoon in the beautiful Nab valley.

The van drove into Regensburg at dusk. Every lodging seemed full. At last a door opened, and the men were ordered to go into the prison attached to the courthouse. They objected to the guards' brusque tone. "Aristocrats again!" said one of the guards. "Get up with the others on the second floor!" The relatives of Goerdeler, Stauffenberg, Halder, Hammerstein, and Hassell, old and young, were being held in the upstairs corridors. The new arrivals had to go five into a single cell, but they were able to choose their cellmates. Von Rabenau, Pünder, von Falkenhausen, and Hoepner shared Bonhoeffer's cell. The kitchens were closed, but the prisoners made so much noise that an intimidated guard found some vegetable soup and distributed it with some bread.

On Thursday morning the doors were opened so the prisoners could wash. There were great reunions in the corridors, introductions and exchanges of information. Best relates that the scene was more like a great reception than a morning in prison. The guards tried helplessly to get the men back into their cells. At last food was brought to the cells, and eventually the "cases" were again sitting behind locked doors. Bonhoeffer spent most of his time at the little opening in the cell door and told the various relatives what he knew of his fellow prisoners in Prinz-Albrecht-Strasse. He was able to tell Frau Goerdeler about the last weeks of her husband's life. Bonhoeffer may well have thought that he had now escaped the worst danger. An air-raid alarm interrupted their conversations. The railroad switchyard outside lay in ruins, but they were all safe in the basement. When they were allowed upstairs again the scene from that morning repeated itself.

As evening approached things grew quieter; exhaustion overcame them. One of the Buchenwald guards reappeared and, in the rainy night, took the men down to the wood-burning truck. They set off in a good mood and traveled along the Danube. After a few miles the van skidded and stopped. As an expert, Hugh Falconer confirmed that the steering was broken; nothing could be repaired there on the road. They asked passersby to order a replacement van from the Regensburg police. Despite their pistols, the guards were uncomfortable among the burned-out cars beside the road. The rain drummed on the roof.

At last, in the morning light of 6 April, the guards let their prisoners out to stretch their legs and warm themselves. Toward midday a bus appeared from Regensburg with all its windows intact. The prisoners' possessions were loaded onto it; Bonhoeffer still had some books with him. The Buchenwald guard, who had become quite humane, had to stay behind with the wreck; ten new men with automatic pistols took over the transport. But it was still a pleasure to drive through the lovely valley in the more comfortable bus, up from the Danube, past the monastery of Metten, into the Bavarian woods that Adalbert Stifter had written about. The driver told some village girls who wanted a lift that the party in the elegant bus was a film group making a propaganda film. The guards fetched a capful of eggs from a farmer's house, but only for their own consumption.

By early afternoon they had arrived in Schönberg, twenty-five miles north of Passau. They began to unload outside a school where family members of some of the resistance leaders were already imprisoned. The "special prisoners" were taken to a classroom on the first floor; from its windows on three sides they could see the green mountain valley. There were proper beds with colored blankets; the door was locked, but it was bright and warm. Bonhoeffer sat for a long time at the open window sunning himself, chatting with Pünder and learning Russian with Kokorin. His bed was next to Kokorin's.

> He did a great deal to keep some of the weaker brethren from depression and anxiety. He spent a good deal of time with Wasily Wasiliew Kokorin, Molotov's nephew, who was a delightful young man although an atheist. I think your brother divided his time with him between instilling the foundations of Christianity and learning Russian.[49]

The atmosphere was lively; they laughed and wrote their names over the beds. Only the food problem was not solved. When they complained what they were told was certainly true: that the area was overflowing with refugees, and no vehicle, let alone gasoline, could be found to be requisitioned. Later, of course, there was enough gasoline and vehicles for other purposes. Finally the other prisoners, who had more freedom, made contact with some compassionate villagers. A great dish with steaming potatoes for the hungry prisoners appeared, and the next day there was potato salad.

Saturday was a quiet, beautiful day. It began with Payne Best taking an electric razor out of his luggage; each of the men was able to shave with the precious instrument, which was connected to an outlet in the classroom. The large room even made it possible for them to exercise a little. Everyone assumed that there would be no more trials, given the general confusion in the country.

Meanwhile, however, the apparatus of the Reich Central Security Office continued to function with unexpected efficiency. It was even able to correct mistakes that had already been made.

The Death Sentence. At a noon meeting with Hitler on 5 April the decisions were apparently made. Among other matters, they included the order that Bonhoeffer and Dohnanyi were not to survive.[50] That afternoon the Reich Security Department ordered the measures that were carried out in the days that followed.

On Thursday, 5 April 1945, Kaltenbrunner issued the appropriate instructions. He was certainly advised by Group Leader Müller, and Hitler's approval at least was obtained. It is possible that Hitler gave the orders. Whether Himmler was involved is doubtful.[51]

On the evening of 5 April Dr. Tietze received a message at the state hospital that Dohnanyi was to be "transferred" the next morning to Sachsenhausen. Tietze quickly summoned Christine von Dohnanyi so that she could see her husband once more, but it was not possible overnight to arrange an escape plan. Tietze sedated Dohnanyi heavily to make him incapable of being tried. Sonderegger collected him very early on 6 April. Dr. Tietze immediately wrote down the events that followed:

> Sonderegger stood in front of the hospital waiting for a car that was to come from Prinz-Albrecht-Strasse. I wanted to go to Dohnanyi, but Sonderegger wouldn't let me and engaged me in a conversation that went more or less as follows:
> T: Do you want to start the trial now?
> S: The matter is settled.
> T: Does that mean the end of Dohnanyi?
> S: It's his own fault. He has worked against the *Führer* and had every opportunity. How could he work against the *Führer*, who gave him such a well-paid job? Dohnanyi's behavior was ungrateful.
> T: Do you want to kill him?
> S: (Evasive answer . . . then): We know that he was the mastermind behind the 20 July plot.
> T: Where are you taking him?
> S: I don't know yet.
> T: Do you already have the charges against him and will there still be a trial?
> S: We already have all the evidence against him, we don't need anything else.
> T: Does that mean death?
> S: (Shrugged his shoulders).

That same morning Huppenkothen also went to Sachsenhausen. Together with the commandant of the concentration camp he held a hasty court-martial in which they condemned Dohnanyi, who was lying half-conscious on a stretcher, to death.

In the meantime the Reich Central Security Office ordered the director of the prison, Governor Gogalla, to travel to Flossenbürg on Saturday, 7 April, and from there to Schönberg and Dachau. Gogalla was given several "secret state papers" that he had to deliver in Flossenbürg, Schönberg, and Dachau; these papers apparently contained instructions about who was to be killed and who was to be moved further south. By coincidence Payne Best later discovered the original of one of these "secret state papers" in Dachau. It was submitted to the court during Huppenkothen's trial and contained the orders to move certain important prisoners and treat them courteously, as well as orders for the "liquidation" of Georg Elser, the man who attempted to assassinate Hitler in Bürgerbräu in 1939, and who was imprisoned in Dachau.[52] The secret state paper with orders concerning Bonhoeffer has not been found; it was probably destroyed according to instructions.

On Saturday, 7 April Huppenkothen and his wife were in Gogalla's convoy of cars traveling south and carrying gasoline, a large number of cases, and important documents that supposedly included Canaris's diary. Huppenkothen arrived in Flossenbürg that day and immediately began to set up a summary court-martial. Dr. Otto Thorbeck, an S.S. judge, had been summoned from Nuremberg on the evening of 5 April. Traveling by freight train as far as Weiden, he arrived Sunday morning and bicycled the remaining twelve miles to Flossenbürg. Everything was ready to try Canaris, Oster, Sack, Strünck, Gehre, and Bonhoeffer. But the list of people in the camp did not tally. Where was Bonhoeffer? That Saturday night inmates in many of the cells were asked whether they were not Bonhoeffer, sent over from Buchenwald. Schlabrendorff was shouted at twice: "'But you are Bonhoeffer!'"[53] The same thing happened to Josef Müller and Liedig.

Bonhoeffer was not there. He must have remained with the transport going south, but it was not too late to rectify the error that had been made on the night of 3–4 April in Weiden. The Reich Central Security Office still had enough cars and gas to send a transport commando at least a hundred miles through the hilly countryside to Schönberg and back.

The End. In the school in Schönberg they celebrated the Sunday after Easter. According to accounts from Pünder, Best, and Falconer, Pünder asked Bonhoeffer to hold a morning service. But Bonhoeffer had no desire to do this; the majority of his comrades were Catholic, and there was young Kokorin. Bonhoeffer had given him his Berlin address in return for Kokorin's Moscow one, but he didn't want to ambush him with a church service. But then Kokorin himself said he was in favor of it, and so Bonhoeffer, by general request, held the service. He read the texts for Quasimodo Sunday, said the prayers, and explained the text of the day to his comrades: "With his wounds we are healed" (Isaiah 53:5) and "Blessed be the God and Father of our Lord Jesus Christ! By his great mercy we have been born anew to a living hope through the resurrection of Jesus Christ from the dead" (1 Peter 1:3). He spoke about the thoughts and decisions this captivity had produced in everyone. After this service the other prisoners wanted to smuggle Bonhoeffer over to their room so that he could hold a service there also. But it was not long before the door was opened and two civilians called out: "Prisoner Bonhoeffer, get ready and come with us!"

He could still get his things together. He wrote his name and address in large letters with a blunt pencil in the front, back, and middle of his Plutarch volume, leaving the book behind to reveal a trail in the subsequent chaos. One of Goerdeler's sons took the book and gave it to Bonhoeffer's family years later, as the last existing evidence of his life. It was the same book that he had requested on 17 January and had received in the Reich Central Security Office on 7 February.

He asked Payne Best to remember him to the bishop of Chichester if he should ever reach his home. "This is the end—for me the beginning of life" were his last words recorded by Best.[54] He quickly ran down the stairs and received a farewell greeting from Frau Goerdeler.

The journey this Sunday must have lasted until late evening. The summary court, with Thorbeck presiding, Huppenkothen as prosecutor, and the camp commandant Kögl as assistant, maintained that it convened for a long time. It interrogated each prisoner individually and confronted them with one another: Canaris and Oster, Sack, Strünck and Gehre, and finally Dietrich Bonhoeffer as well. After midnight Canaris returned to his cell after an absence of some time and signaled, with a series of knocks to a Danish colonel named Lunding in the next cell, that it was all up with him.[55]

Before dawn the first transport of those who were joining the mysterious caravan into the Alps left Flossenbürg: Schacht, Halder, von Bonin, the Schuschnigg family, General Thomas. Gogalla was in charge of this transport. On the way the van stopped in Schönberg and took on Falkenhausen, Kokorin, Best, and Falconer, among others. In Dachau Martin Niemöller also became part of this select group.

In Flossenbürg, however, the executions took place in the gray dawn that Monday. The camp doctor saw Bonhoeffer without knowing at the time who he was. Ten years later he wrote:

> On the morning of that day between five and six o'clock the prisoners, including Admiral Canaris, General Oster . . . and state attorney Dr. Sack were taken from their cells and the verdicts of the court martial read out to them. Through the half-open door in one room of the huts I saw Pastor Bonhoeffer, before taking off his prison garb, kneeling on the floor

praying fervently to his God. I was most deeply moved by the way this unusually lovable man prayed, so devout and so certain that God heard his prayer. At the place of execution, he again said a short prayer and then climbed the steps to the gallows, brave and composed. His death ensued after a few seconds. In the almost fifty years that I worked as a doctor, I have hardly ever seen a man die so entirely submissive to the will of God.[56]

Prince Philip of Hesse, who had been imprisoned for years in Flossenbürg, took two books out of a pile of effects in the guardroom on that Monday morning. In one of them, Kantorowicz's *Friedrich II von Hohenstaufen*, he discovered Wilhelm Canaris's name. Bonhoeffer's name was in the other, a volume of Goethe illustrated with etchings. The books were taken from him. All the remaining possessions, like the corpses, were burned.[57]

The Bitter End

All communication with Hans von Dohnanyi had ended after his wife's nocturnal visit to the police hospital on 5 April. According to Sonderegger— and there is no reason to doubt him here—Dohnanyi was executed in Sachsenhausen on the same day as Bonhoeffer, 9 April.

In Berlin the family's efforts to save the lives of Rüdiger Schleicher and Klaus Bonhoeffer continued throughout March and April. Rüdiger Schleicher's former boss, Dr. Brandenburg, who directed the air division in the Ministry of Public Transport before 1933, made a plea for mercy and gave a fine portrait of Schleicher:

His frankness and his love of truth in every situation were clearly unbounded. He seemed truly incapable of seeing the intrigue and dirty side of life. Despite this his work was always successful. The fruits of his efforts . . . were always won with honorable means; I used to call him jokingly "our Parsifal." Lies and deception were quite foreign to his nature. His fearlessness and trust in others stemmed from the same source: his rocklike conviction, which permeated his whole being, of the reality and truth of "justice." The word had for him the gravest religious content. Perhaps the key to another quality lies here. He constantly worried about whether his own ideas really were in tune with justice, whether someone was suffering an injustice, whether the inner meaning of an idea had been really expressed or presented in an entirely truthful way. . . . Not that the certainty of his work would have suffered from this! But he sometimes surprised us by suddenly speaking against his own point of view. In a sense, his inner thoughts were in a constant state of argument.

During the period of interrogations and confrontations such a person must have suffered almost beyond the limits of endurance. After the death sentence was handed down, however, he radiated an irresistible serenity, cheering up his fellow prisoners with friendly glances during his exercise in the prison yard. He did not say one word about himself in his last letters. When his wife came to see him she would not accept his farewell letters; she did not want to show him that the fight to obtain a pardon might have to be abandoned. Hence these letters have been lost.

Klaus Bonhoeffer feared a resumption of the trial almost more than he feared waiting for the execution of his sentence. On a piece of paper, written before the announcement of the death sentence, he wrote:

> I am not afraid of being hanged, but I don't want to see those faces again . . . so much depravity. . . . I'd rather die than see those faces again. I have seen the Devil, and I can't forget it.

When Karl-Friedrich Bonhoeffer visited his brother after the sentencing in the visitors' cell at Lehrter Strasse, Klaus told him he had the St. Matthew Passion beside him on his folding table. Karl-Friedrich commented that it was nice that he could hear the music in his imagination as he read the score. Klaus answered, "Yes, but the words also! The words!" The farewell letters that he wrote to his parents, wife, and children, have been preserved. In one he wrote:

> I hardly dare to utter the hope that the family might miraculously emerge quite unscathed from the great disaster. For a long time it has swept over people like a natural catastrophe, and nature is wasteful. But I think that the storm will soon pass over our house. There will be an end to the persecutions, and it will seem to the survivors that they have been dreaming. . . .
>
> I don't merely want to live, but to do the most I can with my life. Since this must now happen through my death, I have made friends with it also. On this ride between death and the Devil, death is a noble companion. The Devil adapts himself to the times and has even worn the cavalier's sword. This is how the Enlightenment idealized him. The Middle Ages, which spoke of his bad smell, knew him better.
>
> In any case, it is a much clearer obligation to die than to live in confused times, which is why those who are destined to die were always called fortunate.[58]

After a sudden decision by S.S. group leader Müller, an execution detachment from the Reich Central Security Office collected sixteen prisoners from the Gestapo section of the prison in Lehrter Strasse on the night of 22

April, on the pretext that they were being transferred somewhere else in order to be released. After a hundred yards the S.S. men shot the group on the Ulap grounds near Lehrter station. Among those who died were Klaus Bonhoeffer, Rüdiger Schleicher, Hans John, Friedrich Justus Perels, and Albrecht Haushofer.

One of the group, H. Kosney, was able to escape. It was through him that on 31 May the family conclusively learned what had happened to Klaus and Rüdiger. They are buried with Friedrich Justus Perels, Hans John, and many other unknown victims in a bomb crater in the cemetery in Dorotheen-stadt.[59] Their families and those who survived the prisons held a memorial service for them on 11 June 1945.

Josef Müller and Fabian von Schlabrendorff had long before been removed from Flossenbürg; they had escaped with other survivors over the Alps to Italy and into American custody. There they also encountered Martin Niemöller. Since all ties to Berlin had been broken, it was they who sent the news of Dietrich Bonhoeffer's fate to Visser 't Hooft in Geneva, who in turn conveyed it to Bishop Bell and Dietrich's sister's family in Oxford. Freudenberg telegraphed Julius Rieger on 30 May from Geneva:

> Just received sad news that Dietrich Bonhoeffer and his Klaus have been murdered in Concentration Camp Clossburg near Neustadt about 15 April short time before liberation region by American army—Stop—Please inform family Leibholz and his friends—Stop—We are united in deep sorrow and fellowship—Freudenberg.[60]

At the end of the war Maria von Wedemeyer was searching for Bonhoeffer in western Germany; the incredible news reached her in June. His parents were the last to know what had happened, when Hans-Bernd Gisevius came to Berlin in July and the memorial service for Bonhoeffer was broadcast from London by the BBC.

Bishop Bell, Franz Hildebrandt, and Julius Rieger held his memorial service on 27 July 1945 in Holy Trinity Church, Kingsway, London.[61] The announcement of this public memorial service for a German, and the BBC's broadcast of it, was an unusual event in those months. The reports of the appalling discoveries in the Bergen-Belsen concentration camp had reached the British public only after the hostilities had ended; this had considerably reduced the public's willingness to render differentiated judgments about the vanquished country.

The church was packed to the doors with English people and German emigrants, theologians and laypeople, including Bonhoeffer's twin sister and her family. In his sermon the bishop described what Bonhoeffer had meant for ecumenism, from the first moment of his martyrdom:

> His death is a death for Germany—indeed for Europe too . . . his death, like his life, marks a fact of the deepest value in the witness of the Confessional [sic] Church. As one of a noble company of martyrs of differing traditions, he represents both the resistance of the believing soul, in the name of God, to the assault of evil, and also the moral and political revolt of the human conscience against injustice and cruelty. He and his fellows are indeed built upon the foundation of the Apostles and the Prophets. And it was this passion for justice that brought him, and so many others . . . into such close partnership with other resisters, who, though outside the Church, shared the same humanitarian and liberal ideals. . . .
>
> For him and Klaus . . . there is the resurrection from the dead; for Germany redemption and resurrection, if God pleases to lead the nation through men animated by his spirit, holy and humble and brave like him; for the Church, not only in that Germany which he loved, but the Church Universal which was greater to him than nations, the hope of a new life.[62]

Bonhoeffer's own church in Berlin-Brandenburg was a long way from this attitude when, during those weeks, it made a strict distinction between Christian martyrdom and political resistance. In an announcement from the pulpits on the first anniversary of the 20 July attempt, it presented Paul Schneider as "a martyr in the full sense of the word" and did not mention Bonhoeffer's name. Indeed, the church announced that it could never approve the conspiracy of 20 July 1944, "whatever the intention behind it might have been. But among those who were forced to suffer there were innumerable people who had never wanted such a conspiracy."[63]

A pastor in Bielefeld, Westphalia, took a similar view. He appealed to the Bonhoeffer family to protest against the naming of streets after Paul Schneider and Dietrich Bonhoeffer next to streets named for other resistance members, "because we don't want the names of our colleagues, who were killed for their faith, lumped together with political martyrs." Karl Bonhoeffer replied:

> My son certainly would not have wanted streets to be named after him. On the other hand, I am sure that it would not have been his desire to distance himself from those murdered for political reasons, with whom he had lived for years in prison and concentration camps. I therefore would rather decline from protesting against the decision of the town council, all the more so since the choice of the two ministers seems to indicate that the council has made its selection irrespective of the men's political attitudes.[64]

During those summer months the last surviving brother, Karl-Friedrich Bonhoeffer, tried to reestablish his physics institute in Leipzig. The Americans were about to hand over Leipzig to the Russians. Cut off from all news, he thought he possibly might not survive the coming weeks. Thus he wrote the story of the last months for his children, who had been evacuated to the Harz Mountains:

> I want to tell you about all this. Why? Because my thoughts are now there, there in the ruins from which no news reaches us, where three months ago I visited Uncle Klaus in prison after he had been condemned to death. Those Berlin prisons! How little I knew about them a few years ago, and with what different eyes I've come to see them since. The Charlottenburg interrogation prison where Aunt Christel was held for a time, the Tegel military interrogation prison, where Uncle Dietrich was for eighteen months, the military prison at Moabit where Uncle Hans was, the S.S. prison in Prinz-Albrecht-Strasse, where Uncle Dietrich was kept behind bars in the basement for six months, and the prison in Lehrter Strasse where Uncle Klaus was tortured and Uncle Rüdiger suffered, and where they were held for two months after their death sentences.
>
> I waited in front of the heavy iron gates of all these prisons when I was in Berlin "on business" during the last years. I took Aunt Ursel and Christel, Aunt Emmi and Maria there; they often went every day, taking things or collecting them. They often went in vain, often they were insulted by contemptible officials, but sometimes they also found a friendly guard who was a human being and delivered greetings, accepted something outside the prescribed hours or gave food to the prisoners despite the ban.
>
> Ah, the taking of food! It wasn't altogether easy in those last years, and Aunt Ursel in particular couldn't do enough. She became as thin as a skeleton. Those were tragic scenes when Uncle Rüdiger sent out the food again with the message that he had enough. Who believed him? Aunt Ursel sent it in again and it came back again. Uncle Klaus was different! He always ate everything sent to him. It was not so bad for Uncle Dietrich while he was in Tegel. He got on well there with the prison staff, and the prison commandant was a humane man. It wasn't too bad for Uncle Hans either, to begin with. His prison commandant was almost like a friend to him. But then he became ill and was taken to the Charité Surgical Clinic under Sauerbruch, where I saw him for the last time. After he was taken to prison again he got scarlet fever and diphtheria, and was in bed for nearly six months with post-diphtheria paralysis, ending up at the Oranienburg concentration camp and the state hospital of Berlin.
>
> And now! The last time I was in Berlin was at the end of March. I had to go back shortly before grandfather's seventy-seventh birthday. Uncle Klaus and Uncle Rüdiger were still alive; via the doctor Uncle Hans gave us

news that did not seem entirely hopeless. There was no trace of Uncle Dietrich, who had been removed from Berlin by the S.S. at the beginning of February. It was probably on 8 April, shortly before I left Friedrichs-brunn to come to you, that I telephoned from Leipzig for the last time to speak to your grandparents. At that time everything was just the same. That is now more than two months ago. What are all the things that must have happened before Berlin was occupied by the Russians? Someone who came from there said that 4,000 political prisoners had been killed first. And what happened during the occupation, and afterward? Are they all still alive? Did grandfather and grandmother survive those difficult days? Both were already on the verge of exhaustion. In the last years grandmother had many attacks of weakness, with loss of memory, a consequence of the overwork, excitement and malnutrition of recent years. They had no prop-er help in the house. Uncle Dietrich spoke at some length to someone on 5 April, near Passau [probably the day he was in Regensburg]. From there he was supposed to have been taken to the Flossenbürg concentration camp near Weiden.

Why isn't he here yet? . . .[65]

After the family had learned everything Karl Bonhoeffer wrote to a col-league, Professor Paul Jossmann, who had emigrated to Boston:

I hear you know that we have suffered greatly and lost two sons and two sons-in-law through the Gestapo. As you can imagine, this has taken its toll on us old folk. For years, we endured the tension, the anxiety about those arrested and those who were not yet arrested but in danger. But since we all agreed about the necessity of action, and my sons were also fully aware of what they could expect if the plot miscarried, and had resolved if nec-essary to lay down their lives, we are sad, but also proud of their straight and narrow attitude. We have fine memories of both sons from prison . . . that move both of us and their friends greatly.

APPENDIX 1

THE ZOSSEN FILES

Notes by Christine von Dohnanyi, 1945–1946

Editor's note: After the defeat of Nazi Germany Christine von Dohnanyi made three statements concerning the Zossen files. It was the discovery of these files, of course, that had provided the Reich Central Security office with the evidence that led to the intensified interrogations and, eventually, the executions of the Bonhoeffer family members and several other resistance members. In the early postwar period Christine von Dohnanyi was shaken by the suspicions of some people that, by not destroying the files, either she or her husband had unwittingly enabled the Nazi security police to uncover the rest of the conspiracy. She felt it imperative to record her recollections about the files.

The first statement is undated. The second was a reply to inaccurate information that German General Georg Thomas gave to Allied authorities in his report of 20 July 1945. The third was written to give the U.S. officers at the Nuremberg trials more complete information about the conspiracy.

I. (Undated). [My husband], during his period of employment as a minister in the Ministry of Justice, had prepared a document. At that time, word of almost every scandal in the Party or its organizations reached the Justice Minister personally. These were passed on, without exception, to my husband—usually with an order from Hitler that the proceedings be dismissed. Under the title "Chronicle," my husband had made a complete list of all these cases, and thus had a detailed record of the Party leaders' criminal actions. The murders and attempted murders in the concentration camps, the atrocities in these camps that had become known, the regional governors' customary currency marketeering, the unpleasant corruption in the Hitler

Youth and among S.A. leaders—there was hardly any offense that wasn't list-ed in this Chronicle. He had compiled this Chronicle together with a card index, which made it possible to find the offenses of individual leading Party figures and the files about these offenses. These notes were disguised by including several especially prominent "criminal" cases in monasteries, etc., so as to cover up their true purpose. Over the years, my husband had added to this material and completed it. There were speeches by Hitler, reports on the treatment of prisoners of war, films of the atrocities in Poland, reports on the background of "Bloody Sunday" in Bromberg, Goebbels's instruc-tions for the pogroms against the Jews, and more such material. My husband was convinced that, in certain cases, these reports could be supplemented with information learned from other departments. He told me that these documents had to be enough to open the eyes of anyone who willing to see the truth about Hitler and his regime.

II. (Response to General Thomas, July 1945). I would like to add a few remarks on the question about the location of the documents hidden by my husband, because much has been said erroneously about this. In par-ticular, General Thomas's account has given me reason to do this.[1] The fact is that the only knowledgeable report about these documents can come from me, since I conveyed the negotiations between my husband and Beck about these documents while my husband was in prison. I have already reported these details to various Allied officials. My own reflections and the last information I received from my husband have led me to conclude that the entire documents were not taken to or near Colonel Schrader's hunt-ing lodge in the Lüneberg Heath, as we had been promised, but only that some of them were hidden there.[2] Because of this, some of them fell into the Gestapo's hands. This conclusion is also supported by the statements of Colonel Schrader's chauffeur, Mr. Kerstenhahn. I gather that not all the documents fell into Gestapo possession since my husband, as he told me, was charged in October 1944 on the basis of his memorandum to the gen-erals, the appeal to the German people that he had written, and other things from this material (in copied form, as he told me), but not with the Chronicle and the material from 1933–1938, which without any doubt would have especially angered the Gestapo. In their interrogations of the different men, the Gestapo gave various contradictory information about where they had found it. Needless to say, the files were never buried on our property, nor would I ever have arrived at the idea of handing over these files, which would have incriminated my husband very seriously, to the Gestapo.

I assume that when the possibilities of communication have finally improved, I will be able to shed more light on this affair and perhaps even find another portion of the documents. From the Gestapo side, the division leader Huppenkothen, who personally confronted my husband with copies of these documents in the concentration camp, could offer the most useful statement, or criminal commissar Sonderegger, who was the official in charge of the proceedings; his fate is unknown to me. Huppenkothen is in an Allied prison.

III. (Written for U.S. officers during the Nuremberg trials: probably 1946). In the spring of 1942, my husband was warned by the lawyer Dr. Langbehn and Mr. Gehre that he was being watched by the Gestapo. His mail and telephone were under surveillance, as was he. According to Langbehn, this had been ordered by Heydrich or Bormann; in Gehre's opinion, this was at the wish of a man named Sommer, and had been initiated by [Rudolf] Hess's ministry.

After that, my husband avoided going out to Zossen, where the safe with the documents stood. As far as I can recall, Oster drove out with Guttenberg or Delbrück. In any case, my husband's safe at the high military command was "cleaned out" and the important documents that were to be safeguarded until after the end of the war were taken there. As far as I can recall, the safe (according to my husband's description) stood in a particularly deep cellar and, at the time when Zossen was still the headquarters, had been given to my husband by Colonel Groscurth for the dangerous documents.

In the period during and after the arrest of my husband on 4 April 1943, the following events took place: several days before my husband's arrest, Ministerial director Lehmann got word to him through Canaris that there was no question of his arrest in the coming days because of the Fromm crisis and a few other events that had suddenly arisen. Due to these crises, the Gestapo and war courts had other strong interests. This proved to be incorrect. My husband was arrested the day after Canaris had given him this message.

So my husband still had the key to the Zossen safe; it was lying in his safe at the high military command. As a disguise, he always had this key tied to a folder in which there were various notes with descriptions for clearly official files, in addition to different codes for secret official papers; these included the coded index of the contents of the Zossen safe. Roeder and Sonderegger, the arresting officers, searched my husband's safe in his presence for banned political documents and threw the folder with the key back into the safe, assuming it was solely an official object. My husband saw this. After my husband had been led away, Oster immediately took the key.

I was arrested at the same time as my husband and was released on 30 April 1943, since they believed our statement that I knew nothing. After that, I was able to contact my husband through the prison commander, Lieutenant Colonel Maass. Sack, who had already contacted him during my imprisonment, had recommended Maass to us as being absolutely trustworthy.

The first question that Maass conveyed to me from my husband was whether everything concerning the files was in order. I was to contact Oster immediately and tell him that the documents had to be destroyed. The Gestapo was looking for them. (Here I must add: under the pressure of interrogation, a member of the Military Intelligence had testified that at one point in Rome he had been told to convey the message from the Vatican to my husband: "Documents have been destroyed." During our interrogations, my husband and I were repeatedly questioned about the documents.)

Delbrück carried the message to Oster that he and Guttenberg were the only ones from Military Intelligence who had regular contact with my husband (through me). Oster sent word to my husband that his mind could be completely at ease. He had the matter in hand. Schrader had already been notified. The matter "was in order." (Here I must add that the possibility that Schrader would take the documents to the Lüneberg Heath in an emergency had been discussed earlier.)

Around August or September, my husband asked me again what had happened. At that point I asked Delbrück to question Oster. If I remember correctly, Oster was not in Berlin at the time, and so Perels took things over, sending Sack to ask Beck.

Beck responded that the documents could not be destroyed; they were historically important. As far as I can recall, Beck at the time was ill or convalescing, and my husband had the impression that perhaps at that point he couldn't see the matter clearly. In any case he told me: "I don't give a damn about history, tell him: this will cost heads!" I then asked Perels to go to Sack a second time and insist on their destruction.

Perels reported to me: Beck asked me to tell your husband that the material could not be destroyed, especially the things from 1939 to 1940. We must be able to prove to the world later that we did not act only once all was lost, but already at the point when the world still believed in our victory. (He then mentioned a second document that I have forgotten.) I personally conveyed this to my husband when I was allowed to speak to him in September or October.

My husband replied: "This has always been Beck's argument; and a case can indeed be made for it. He should do what he thinks right, but for God's sake he should see to it that nothing happens. I owe that to the people over there (he meant the Vatican and England)."

I conveyed this to Perels verbatim.

In the winter of 1943, while my husband lay in the Charité, these considerations were repeated with Perels, Delbrück, and, as far as I recall, with [Otto] John. My husband worried constantly that something careless could happen when they were being moved. He told Delbrück at the time: "Every note in those things is a death sentence; just watch out in moving them. I don't even know how you will manage it with this pile of things." (By that time Delbrück was no longer in the *Abwehr*).

The situation worsened after Canaris's demotion. In February 1944, my husband asked again about Perels: "What has happened?" Perels's reply at that point was almost agitated: my husband had been told repeatedly that he could relax; the files were secure. I didn't ask any further, because I assumed that they didn't want to tell me, as a woman, where the files really were. After 20 July 1944 and the report of Schrader's death, my husband asked again from the infirmary in Potsdam, where at that point he lay in the quarantine ward: "he wanted now to know where his files were."

Perels told me: "six meters underground, at Schrader's hunting lodge in the Lüneberg Heath."

In the aftermath of the 20 July attempt, the Gestapo prohibited me from entering the infirmary in Potsdam. My husband sent me a message via his nurse: I was to take over his "books" (this was our name for the Zossen files) when no one else was there to care for them. A few days later my husband was taken to the Sachsenhausen concentration camp.

At the beginning of November, I received a letter from my husband in the concentration camp, with the following encoded text: "A weakling must have admitted everything, we must win time."

Then three secret messages came from the prison on Prinz-Albrecht-Strasse. In one of them stood: "I don't know who the traitor is. Ultimately, it doesn't matter to me, but they have everything."

I secretly spoke with my husband two more times in Berlin, in Dr. Tietze's office in the police hospital. He [Dohnanyi] told me the following:

On 5 October 1944, Huppenkothen appeared in the Sachsenhausen concentration camp and threw onto his bed the photocopies of his 1939 memorandum to the generals, which along with Dr. Müller's Vatican report had been given to the generals to move them to act. Huppenkothen also showed him the appeal to the German people that he [Dohnanyi] had drafted for Beck and the X-report (as far as I recall), with the words: "Here we have what we have been seeking for two years." My husband told me that he simply gathered the things and asked, apparently very calmly: "So, you have it? Where did you get them?" Huppenkothen replied: "They were found in Zossen." When my husband didn't believe this (given the numerous assurances of his comrades, he had no reason to), Huppenkothen (or Sonderegger) named the officer who had betrayed the hiding place. Huppenkothen then told my husband that there was no point in denying that he was the author, that the matter was too clear. Under the circumstances, my husband then didn't deny it.

They wanted to put every kind of pressure on him to name who had been a member of the conspiracy in 1939–1940. They let him lie there in the cellar at Prinz-Albrecht-Strasse, with no kind of help, sick with diphtheria, which had serious consequences. (The criminal councillor Stawitzky was responsible for this.) If he would testify, they promised to release him for hospitalization and he could have contact with the family. They told him that everything was out in the open now. He wouldn't be incriminating anyone if he testified. The *Führer* only wanted his impressions, "how he viewed the things that had led to 20 July." To his last day, he refused and took refuge in his illness. He was taken back to Sachsenhausen on 5 April 1945 and did not return.

My conjecture about the final fate of the documents is that Schrader really did take some of the documents to the Lüneberg Heath. The testimony of his chauffeur, Mr. Kerstenhahn, supports this. According to Kerstenhahn, there was no second journey, because an officer refused to give him fuel. This is also supported by the fact that several people (e.g., von Etzdorf, delegate Schmidt, Kordt), whose involvement in my husband's circles would clearly have emerged from some of the documents, were not arrested. Moreover, I am convinced that they would have accused my husband of certain documents that would have particularly outraged the Gestapo, such as the chronicle of Nazi crimes and swindles that my husband had compiled with Gürtner's permission in the Justice Ministry. The same holds true for the files about the Fritsch proceedings. My husband told me that Huppenkothen did not confront him with these things. In the haste of our final conversation, I did not have time to ask anything more.

I have described things here as I experienced them. I have omitted nothing but the name of the officer whom the Gestapo told my husband was the traitor. I will not give this name, because my husband asked me to tell no one of the Gestapo's suspicions; he himself did not wish to believe it.

Today, it is my conviction that Oster took these documents that were more or less my husband's personal possessions to a secure place, just as he had promised my husband; but that, in compliance with Beck's order, those files related to the plans from 1939–1940 remained readily accessible in Zossen.

This would explain Oster's behavior toward my husband, which is otherwise inexplicable. It would explain why von Etzdorf, Schmidt, and Kordt were not arrested, and would essentially substantiate Huppenkothen's testimony.

This would mean, of course, that a crucial and interesting portion of the documents are still hidden in the Lüneberg Heath and could be searched for.

BONHOEFFER'S READINGS IN PRISON

Editor's note: Where English translations of the works cited exist only the English titles are given. Otherwise, German titles are followed by the English translation of the title in parentheses. Where the date is unknown, it is not given.

Theology

G. Uhlhorn	*Die christliche Liebestätigkeit* (Christian Charity)— May/June 1943
H. von Soden	*Reisebrief aus Palästina 1901* (Letter from Palestine 1901)—June 1943
K. Holl	—June 1943
?	*Über den Aberglauben* (Superstition)
Tertullian	November 1943
Cyprian	November 1943
Early church fathers	November 1943
E. C. Hoskyns, F.N. Davey	*The Riddle of the New Testament*
O. Schilling	*Lehrbuch der Moraltheologie* (Textbook of Moral Theology)—June 1943
T. à Kempis	*The Imitation of Christ*—November/December 1943
K. Barth	*Church Dogmatics,* Volume II/2—January 1944
K. Leese	*Der Protestantismus im Wandel der neueren Zeit* 1941 (Protestantism through the Ages)— March 1945

Philosophy, Science, Art

I. Kant	*Anthropology*—May 1943
M. Heidegger	*Phänomenologie des Zeitbewusstseins* (Phenomenology of the Concept of Time)—June 1943
P. de Kruif	*Microbe Hunters*—August 1943
R. Benz	*Die deutsche Musik* (German Music)—October 1943
N. Hartmann	*Systematische Philosophie* (Systematic Philosophy)—October 1943
J. Ortegy y Gasset	*The Roman Empire*—October 1943
W. Dilthey	*Poetry and Experience*—January/February 1944
W. Dilthey	*Von deutscher Dichtung und Musik* (German Poetry and Music)—January/February 1944
J. Ortega y Gasset	*History As a System*—May 1944
J. Ortega y Gasset	*Wom Wesen geschichtlicher Krisen* (The Essence of Historical Crises)—May 1944
C. F. von Weiszäcker	*Zum Weltbild der Physik* (The Worldview of Physics)—May 1944
W. Dilthey	*Weltanschauung und Analyse des Menschen seit Renaissance und Reformation* (Worldview and Analysis of Humans since the Renaissance and Reformation)—May/June 1944
L. Klages	*Handschrift und Charakter* (Handwriting and Character)
?	*Der Magdeburger Dom* (The Magdeburg Cathedral)
H. Rothe	*Daumier und die Justiz* (Daumier and Justice)
W. F. Otto	*The Homeric Gods*—June 1944
P. Natorp	*Sozialpädagogik* (Social Pedagogy)—January 1945

History

K. von Hase	*Ideal und Irrtümer 1872* (Ideals and Illusions)—June 1943
G. Ritter	*Weltwirkung der Reformation* (The Reformation's Effect upon the World)—June/July 1943
E. von Naso	*Moltke: Mensch und Feldherr* (Moltke: Man and Commander)—July 1943
H. Delbrück	*Weltgeschichte* (World History)—August/October 1943

?	*Geschichte der Prostitution* (A History of Prostitution)
W. Schur	*Das Zeitalter des Marius und Sulla* (The Age of Marius and Sulla)—September/October 1943
A. von Harnack	*Geschichte der preußischen Akademie* (History of the Prussian Academy)—February 1944
K. Kindt	*Klopstock*—March 1944
H. Pfeffer	*Das britische Empire und die USA* (The British Empire and the United States of America)—May 1944
Plutarch	*Lives of Illustrious Men*—March/April 1945

Literature

J. Gotthelf	*Wealth and Welfare*—April 1943
J. Gotthelf	*Berner Geist*—May 1943
J. Paul	?—May 1943
A. Stifter	*The Forest Path*—May/June 1943
J. Gotthelf	*Jakobs Wanderungen durch die Schweiz* (Jacob's Travels through Switzerland)—May/June 1943
?	*Häuser über dem Rhein* (Houses above the Rhine)—June 1943
R. M. Rilke	?—June 1943
F. Reuter	*Seven Years of My Life*—June 1943
F. Reuter	*Seed-Time and Harvest, or During My Apprenticeship*—June 1943
P. Calderón	*Dramen* (Dramas)—June 1943
T. Fontane	*Jenny Treibel*—June/July 1943
G. Keller	*Der grüne Heinrich* (Green Heinrich)—June/July 1943
A. Stifter	*Indian Summer*—July 1943
J. Gotthelf	*Uli der Knecht* (Uli the Farm Servant)—July 1943
F. Reuter	*Kein Hüsung*—July 1943
K. L. Immermann	?—July 1943
C. F. Meyer	*Jürg Jenatsch*—July 1943
T. Fontane	*A Suitable Match*—August 1943
T. Fontane	*The Stechlin*—August 1943
?	*Buch für Sanitätswesen* (Book for Medical Orderlies)—August 1943
W. Hauff	*Fairy Tales of Wilhelm Hauff*—August 1943
W. Hauff	*Lichtenstein*

?	*Schachtheorie* (Chess Theory)
T. Storm	?—August/September 1943
W. Raabe	*Der Hungerpastor*—September/October 1943
J. W. Goethe	*Wilhelm Meister*
J. Paul	*Der Siebenkäs*—October 1943
J. Paul	*Flegeljahre* (Years of My Youth)—October 1943
?	*Englische Grammatik* (English Grammar)—October 1943
?	*Scotland Yard*
A. Stifter	*Selected Works*—October/November 1943
A. Stifter	*Witiko*—November 1943
W. D. Rasch	*Lesebuch der Erzähler* (Storybook) November 1943
J. W. Goethe	*Reynard the Fox*—November 1943
W. von Scholz	*Die Ballade* (Ballads) November 1943
F. Reck-Malleczewen	*Briefe der Liebe aus acht Jahrhunderen* (Eight Centuries of Love Letters)—November 1943
W. H. Riehl	*Geschichten aus alter Zeit, Novellen* (Tales from Ancient Times)—December 1943
R. Schneider	*Sonette*
H. Walpole	*The Herriers Chronicle*—January/September 1944
C. Dickens	?
J. V. von Scheffel	?
Euripedes	?—June 1944
F. Dostoevsky	*The House of the Dead*—July 1944
G. von Bülow	*Briefe* (Letters)—August 1944
?	*Mariages* (Marriages), [novel]
J. H. Pestalozzi	*Leonard and Gertrude*—January 1945
J. H. Pestalozzi	*Abendstunde eines Einsiedlers* (Evening of an Emigrant)—January 1945
J. W. Goethe	?—March/April 1945

NOTES

Editor's note: Where several English translations exist only the most recent is cited, and the corresponding pages in the recently published German series *Dietrich Bonhoeffer Werke* (DBW) are bracketed. In the English translations of these volumes, *Dietrich Bonhoeffer Works* (DBWE), each page also cites the corresponding page in the German editions. For that reason, page numbers in the German volumes are given here to enable readers to find those passages in the English *Dietrich Bonhoeffer Works* as those volumes appear.

The earlier German anthology of Bonhoeffer's work, *Gesammelte Schriften* (GS), is cited only where a work has not been included in *Dietrich Bonhoeffer Werke*, or where *Gesammelte Schriften* contains a complete version that has only been excerpted elsewhere.

No publishing information is included for citations of works (principally letters) that remain unpublished or in private collections.

Unless otherwise noted, all translations of Bonhoeffer's work are from those works listed in Abbreviations.

Foreword

1. See "Dietrich Bonhoeffer and the Jews," 43–96 in William J. Peck, ed., *Ethical Responsibility: Bonhoeffer's Legacy to the Churches* (Lewiston, N.Y.: Edwin Mellen, 1981); "Nichts scheint mir in Ordnung," 30–40 in *Ethik in Ernstfall: Dietrich Bonhoeffers Stellung zu den Juden und ihre Aktualität,* Wolfgang Huber and Ilse Tödt, eds. (Munich: Christian Kaiser, 1982); and "Beiträge zur Erneuerung des Verhältnisses von Christen und Juden," Part I of his *Erste Gebot und Zeitgeschichte* (Munich: Christian Kaiser, 1991).

2. LLC.

3. V. Barnett, *For the Soul of the People: Protestant Protest against Hitler* (New York: Oxford University Press, 1992). See also her *Bystanders: Conscience and Complicity in the Holocaust* (Westport, Conn.: Greenwood Press, 1999).

Chapter 1. Childhood and Youth: 1906–1923

1. See J. Kalckreuth, *Wesen und Werk meines Vaters: Lebensbild des Malers Graf Leopold von Kalckreuth* (1968).

2. Letter to E. Bethge, 25.3.1944, LPP, 239 [see DBW 8: 367].

3. Letter, 28.12.1916.

4. Karl August von Hase, *Annalen meines Lebens* (1891), 5.

5. LPP, 209 [see DBW 8: 319].

6. "Address to Students, 1881," in Karl Alfred von Hase, *Unsre Hauschronik: Geschichte der Familie Hase in vier Jahrhunderten* (1898), 227.

7. K. Bonhoeffer, *Lebenserinnerungen* (photocopies made for the family, 1946–1948), 51f.

8. DBW 7: 91–92.

9. G. Wunder, *Ratsherrn der Reichsstadt Hall 1487–1803*, vol. 40 (Württembergisch-Franken, 1962), 127.

10. K. Bonhoeffer, *Lebenserinnerungen*, 7.

11. Karl August von Hase, *Ideal und Irrtümer*, 7th ed. (1917), 211.

12. K. Bonhoeffer, *Lebenserinnerungen*, 13.

13. Ibid., 35.

14. Ibid., 16.

15. Ibid., 38.

16. See R. Gaupp, in *Deutsche Zeitschrift für Nervenheilkunde*, vol. 161, 3.

17. DBW 7: 113–17.

18. S. Leibholz, "Childhood and Home," IKDB, 22–23.

19. K. Bonhoeffer, *Lebenserinnerungen*, 85.

20. Letter, 22.1.1944, LLC, 91–92.

21. Communication to author from Susanne Dress.

22. FFP, 43–47 [see DBW 7: 63–71].

23. "Grundfragen einer christlichen Ethik," DBW 10: 324.

24. NRS, 191–92 [see DBW 12: 244–45].

25. Cf. TF, 423–24, 427 [see DBW 13: 272–73; DBW 14: 303].

26. Cf. G. Sterz, "Karl Bonhoeffer 1868–1948," in *Grosse Nervenärzte*, vol. 1, ed. K. Kolle (1956), 17–26.

27. E. Jones, *Sigmund Freud: Life and Work*, vol. 2 (London: 1958), 279. A more recent and differentiated portrait of the relationship between Karl Bonhoeffer and Freud is in Clifford Green, "Two Bonhoeffers on Psychoanalysis," in *A Bonhoeffer Legacy*, ed. A. J. Klassen (Grand Rapids, Mich.: Eerdmans, 1981), 58–75.

28. Cf. R. Gaupp, *Deutsche Zeitschrift für Nervenheilkunde*, 5–6.

29. K. Bonhoeffer, *Lebenserinnerungen*, 94.

30. LPP, 211 [see DBW 8: 322].

31. K. Bonhoeffer, *Lebenserinnerungen*, 98.

32. S. Leibholz, "Childhood and Home," IKDB, 30.

33. K. Bonhoeffer, *Lebenserinnerungen*, 104.

34. TF, 201–3, excerpt [see DBW 11: 398–408; DBW 14: 764–70].

35. Letter, 15.7.1918, DBW 9: 13–14.

36. See W. Kranz, *Die Kultur der Griechen* (1943).

37. K. Bonhoeffer, *Lebenserinnerungen*, 105.

38. Letter, 11.1.1919, DBW 9: 19.

39. DBW 9: 20.

40. Letter, 20.5.1919, DBW 9: 21–22.

41. Letter to his grandmother, 19.8.1919, DBW 9: 23.

42. Communication to author from W. Dreier, 2.6.1965.

43. "Grundfragen einer christlichen Ethik," DBW 10: 325.

44. NRS, 76–77 [see DBW 10: 576–77].

45. NRS, 195ff. [see DBW 12: 242–60].

46. Letter, 7.7.1922, DBW 9: 44.

47. Communication to author from Peter H. Olden, 1946.

48. The confirmation was on 15 March 1921. Pastor Priebe wrote the confirmation verse (Romans 1:16) in Greek on Bonhoeffer's certificate. See DBW 9: 31.

49. Letter, 2.2.1934, DBW 13: 90.

50. S. Leibholz, "Childhood and Home," 23ff.

51. When he was invited in 1939 to give the Croall lectures in Edinburgh, he planned to speak on death. Cf. DBW 15: 261.

52. DBW 11: 373–74.

53. LPP, 129 [see DBW 8:187].

54. DBW 11: 369–72.

55. Letter, 1.11.1920, DBW 9: 30.

56. Communication to author from Maria Brendel, née Weigert, 12.12.1965.

57. F. Naumann, Letter 19 in *Briefe über Religion*, 7th ed. (1917), 61.

58. For an account of Dehn's work in Moabit, see G. Dehn, *Die alte Zeit, die vorigen Jahre* (1962).

59. DBW 9: 201–18.

60. Ibid., 218. See F. Naumann, *Werke,* vol. 1 (1964), 587: "Emotions remain, while the concepts change" ("Die Gefühle bleiben, während die Begriffe wechseln").

61. Evaluation, 1.2.1923, DBW 9: 218, n. 154.

Chapter 2. Student Years: 1923–1927

1. Letter, 22.10.1928.

2. DBW 9: 53, 60.

3. K. Bonhoeffer, *Lebenserinnerungen*, 31.

4. Letter, May 1923, DBW 9: 50–51.

5. Letter to author from R. Held, 15.3.1965.

6. LPP, 245 [see DBW 8: 376].

7. W. Dreier, 2.6.1965.

8. H. U. Esche, 23.3.1965.

9. Reinhardt was the Prussian minister of war in 1919, later associated with Reich military minister Noske; as head of the military command he helped put down the Kapp putsch. See F. L. Carsten, *Reichswehr und Politik 1918–1933*, 2d ed. (1965), esp. 62–66.

10. DBW 9: 66–67.

11. DBW 9: 69.

12. DBW 9: 73.

13. As compared to Hitler's abortive putsch in Munich on 9.11.1923.

14. Letter to his parents, 1.12.1923, DBW 9: 73.

15. See K. Kupisch, *Studenten entdecken die Bibel* (1964), 117.

16. Letter to his great-aunt H. Countess Yorck, 3.11.1923, DBW 9: 64.

17. Letter to his parents, May 1923, DBW 9: 51.

18. In his Göttingen thesis on Schlatter, H. Vogt compares Schlatter's *Dogmatik*, 41f., with Bonhoeffer's *Ethics*, 155f., and concludes that Schlatter's belief that "denial of the reality of the world means the loss of nature, the self, and God" corresponds with Bonhoeffer's contention that the destruction of the natural means the destruction of life. See DBW 6: 169.

19. W. Trillhaas, *Zeitschrift für Theologie und Kirche,* vol. 52 (1955), 285–87, 292–93, and *Religion in Geschichte und Gegenwart*, 3d ed., vol. 4 (Tübingen: J. C. B. Mohr, 1960), 1328.

20. LPP, 74 [see DBW 8: 111].

21. Cf. NRS, 347ff. [see DBW 12: 213–31].

22. Letter to his parents, 16.8.1923, DBW 9: 58. He had already read the speeches as a student.

23. F. D. E. Schleiermacher, *Reden über die Religion*, ed. G. C. B. Pünjer (1879), 68.

24. Letter to his parents, May 1923, DBW 9: 51.

25. Letter to his parents, 3.11.1923, DBW 9: 63.

26. DBW 9: 77.

27. DBW 9: 81.

28. DBW 9: 81.

29. LPP, 238 [see DBW 8: 365].

30. DBW 9: 83–84.

31. DBW 9: 89.

32. LPP, 194, 212 [see DBW 8: 293, 323].

33. Letter to his parents from Tripoli, 9.5.1924, DBW 9: 123–24.

34. DBW 9: 100.

35. Letter to his parents, 19.4.1924, DBW 9: 115–16. According to the diary the priest's name was Platte-Platenius.

36. DBW 9: 88.

37. DBW 8: 335.

38. DBW 9: 89.

39. DBW 9: 89–90.

40. DBW 9: 103.

41. DBW 9: 111.

42. DBW 9: 110.

43. DBW 9: 94.

44. Letter to his parents, 19.4.1924, DBW 9: 115.

45. DBW 9: 109–10.

46. LPP, 218 [see DBW 8: 334–35].

47. Letter to his parents, 21.5.1924, DBW 9: 129.

48. Letter to his parents, 27.5.1924, DBW 9: 134.

49. Ibid.

50. DBW 10: 486.

51. Letter from D. Albers to D. Bonhoeffer, 14.4.1929, DBW 10: 142.

52. Communication to author from W. Dreier, 2.6.1965.

53. DBW 9: 583–84.

54. SC (DBWE 1), 236, n. 31; 271, n. 430.

55. A. von Zahn-Harnack, *Adolf Harnack*, 1st ed. (1936), 496f.

56. Letter, 29.7.1946.

57. Communication to author from E. Fink, 30.5.1964.

58. DBW 9: 410–30.

59. NRS, 28–29 [see DBW 10: 157–58].

60. DBW 9: 477. See also his address at Harnack's memorial service, DBW 10: 346–49.

61. Communication to author from H. Goes, 29.7.1946.

62. AB (DBWE 2), 46, 58, 80, 89, 137.

63. NRS, 61–62 [see DBW 10: 370].

64. In his essay "Luther's Kreuzesmeditation und die Christuspredigt der Kirche" H. M. Müller notes Holl's emphasis on Luther's notion of *conformitas* [see *Kerygma und Dogma*, vol. 15, no. 1 (1969), 35–49]. "Conformation (*Gleichförmigkeit*) to Christ" became a key phrase for Bonhoeffer.

65. LPP, 30, 50 [see DBW 8: 92, 179].

66. Hans Ehrenberg, *Östliches Christentum*, vols. 1 and 2 (1923–1925).

67. Ibid., vol. 2, 246ff.

68. Ibid., vol. 1, 333–34.

69. See his lecture "The Nature of the Church" (1932), excerpted in TF, 82–87 [see DBW 11: 239–303].

70. Communication to author from E. Fink, 30.5.1964.

71. It can be shown that he had also thoroughly studied large portions of J. Ficker's edition of Luther's *Lectures on Romans*, 3d ed. (1925).

72. In his dissertation "Adolf von Harnack als Lehrer Dietrich Bonhoeffers" (Humboldt University, Berlin 1969) C. J. Kaltenborn traces such elements much more strongly to Harnack's influence.

73. Cf. L. Richter, "Reinhold Seeberg's Beitrag zu theologischen Gegenwartsfragen," in *Zeichen der Zeit* (1959), 133–37; G. Koch, "Reinhold Seeberg und die Bekennende Kirche," in *Kirche in der Zeit* (1959), 208–11.

74. R. Seeberg, *Christliche Dogmatik*, vol. 1 (1924), 103.

75. R. Seeberg, *Lehrbuch der Dogmengeschichte*, vol. 4, 3d ed. (1917), 340.

76. Letter from Barcelona, 20.7.1928, DBW 10: 82.

77. Letter from R. Widmann, 25.2.1926, DBW 9: 159.

78. Letter to his parents, 9.8.1924, DBW 9: 141.

79. Ibid.

80. Letters from W. Dreier, 8.9.1924 and 18.11.1924, and the letter from Hans Christoph von Hase, February 1925.

81. F. Gogarten, *Die religiöse Entscheidung* (1921).

82. Reprinted in James M. Robinson, ed., *The Beginnings of Dialectic Theology* (1968), 163–87.

83. A. von Zahn-Harnack, *Adolf Harnack*, 530–31.

84. Ibid., 536.

85. Letter from A. von Harnack to Bonhoeffer, 22.12.1929, DBW 10: 160.

86. LPP, 229 [see DBW 8: 352].

87. M. Strauch, *Die Theologie Karl Barths* (1924).

88. Ibid.

89. AB (DBWE 2), 90–91.

90. Communication to author from R. Widmann, 28.9.1965.

91. DBW 9: 160–61.

92. LPP, 280 [see DBW 8:404]. B.-E. Benktson, "Christus und die mündiggewordene Walt: Eine Studie zur Theologie Dietrich Bonhoeffers," *Svensk teologisk Kvartalskrift*, vol. 40, no. 2 (1964).

93. Pages cited are from K. Barth, *Des Wort Gottes und die Theologie* (Munich, 1929).

94. LPP, 126 [see DBW 8: 184].

95. DBW 9: 270, n. 278.

96. In *Enders-Kawerau*, vols. 12–18 [see DBW 9: 271–305].

97. DBW 9: 323, n. 98.

98. DBW 9: 305–6.

99. DBW 9: 322.

100. DBW 9: 307.

101. DBW 9: 317.

102. DBW 9: 312–13.

103. DBW 9: 320.

104. R. Seeberg, "Zur Frage nach dem Sinn und Recht einer pneumatischen Schriftauslegung," *Zeitschrift für Systematische Theologie*, vol. 4 (1926), 3–59. Also R. Seeberg, "Zum Problem der pneumatischen Exegese" *Sellin-Festschrift* (1927), 127–37.

105. DBW 9: 154.

106. DBW 9: 154–55.

107. Letter, 31.8.1925, DBW 9: 155.

108. The reference is to the four-volume *Soziologie* and *Die Einleitung in das Studium der Soziologie* by H. Spencer.

109. DBW 9: 156–57.

110. Thus D. Böhler wrote the author on 2 July 1964: "At the time of *Sanctorum Communio* Bonhoeffer had absorbed the bourgeois Hegelian renaissance but hardly Hegel himself."

111. SC (DBWE 1), 221.

112. Ibid., 228.

113. K. Barth, "Wünschbarkeit und Möglichkeit eines allegemeinen reformierten Glaubensbekenntnisses," *Theology and Church,* 112ff.

114. Letter from R. Widmann to D. Bonhoeffer, 17.11.1925, DBW 9: 158.

115. P. Althaus, *Communio Sanctorum* (1929).

116. Letter, 13.10.1930.

117. G. W. F. Hegel, *Sämtliche Werke,* vol. 14, part III, ed. G. Lasson (1923), 198.

118. E. Grisebach, *Die Grenzen des Erziehers und seine Verantwortung* (1924).

119. See the very characteristic criticism of Barth in SC (DBWE 1), 169–70, n. 28.

120. Cf. *Lutherische Monatshefte* (June 1965), 264.

121. K. Barth, *Church Dogmatics* IV/2 (1960), 641.

122. DBW 9: 452–73.

123. NRS, 32 [see DBW 9: 477].

124. DBW 9: 441–52.

125. *Zeitschrift für neutestamentliche Wissenschaft* (ZNTW), vol. 24 (1925), 116–17 [see DBW 9: 441–42].

126. DBW 9: 452.

127. DBW 9: 444.

128. AB (DBWE 2), 99.

129. DBW 9: 355–410.

130. See H. Pfeifer, "Das Kirchenverständnis Dietrich Bonhoeffers: Ein Beitrag zur theologischen Prinzipienlehre" (dissertation, Heidelberg, 1964), 67ff. [see DBW 9: 408].

131. Only an incomplete rough draft remains; see DBW 9: 325–35.

132. DBW 9: 336–37.

133. DBW 9: 439–40.

134. M. Honecker, *Kirche als Gestalt und Ereignis: Die sichtbare Gestalt der Kirche als dogmatisches Problem* (1963), 156.

135. F. H. R. von Frank, *Theologie der Concordienformal* (1858).

136. DBW 9: 521–24, 532.

137. DBW 9: 532, n. 63.

138. Paper, June 1926, DBW 9: 517–532.

139. DBW 9: 586.

140. DBW 10: 46.

141. DBW 9: 186–87.

142. K. Barth, "The Righteousness of God," in *The Word of God and the Word of Man* (1916), 14 [see DBW 9: 487].

143. Sermon, May 1926, DBW 9: 514.

144. DBW 9: 546.

145. DBW 9: 546, n. 74.

146. DBW 9: 605.

147. DBW 9: 607–8.

148. DBW 9: 185–86.

149. Letter, 13.3.1928.

150. Letter from R. Widmann, 13.3.1926, DBW 9: 162.

151. Ibid., 162–63.

152. Communication to author from R. Widmann, 28.9.1965.

153. DBW 9: 164.

154. Ibid.

155. DBW 10: 20–21.

156. Excerpts from letters to Bonhoeffer, 1929–1931.

157. DBW 10: 21.

158. NRS, 32f. [see DBW 9: 476–79].

159. DBW 9: 477.

160. DBW 9: 478–79.

Chapter 3. Assistant Pastor in Barcelona: 1928

1. DBW 10: 20.

2. DBW 10: 25.

3. DBW 10: 19.

4. Letter to H. Rössler, 7.8.1928, DBW 10: 90.

5. Geneva had not yet become the ecumenical center it was later. The offices and secretariats of organizations like the International Social Science Institute (where Hans Schönfeld worked after 1928), the World Student Alliance, the YMCA, and the YWCA moved there to be closer to the headquarters of the League of Nations. The office of *Life and Work*, however, was only beginning to consider a secretariat in Geneva, and the World Alliance for Promoting International Friendship through the Churches established its office there only three years later.

6. Letter to his parents, 22.2.1929, DBW 10: 132–33.

7. DBW 10: 19.

8. DBW 10: 20.

9. DBW 10: 22.

10. Letter from Klaus Bonhoeffer to his grandmother, 16.4.1928.

11. DBW 10: 25.

12. DBW 10: 23.

13. Letter to his parents, 17.5.1928, DBW 10: 58.

14. Letter to R. Seeberg, 20.7.1928, DBW 10: 84.

15. Cf. E, 69f., 189 [see DBW 6: 35, 66–67]; fragment of novel in FFP, 125, 197 [see DBW 7: 183]; and LPP, 125, 217 [see DBW 8: 24–25, 333].

16. Letter to his parents, 8.6.1928, DBW 10: 62.

17. Letter to R. Seeberg, 20.7.1928, DBW 10: 83.

18. Letter to his parents, 17.5.1928, DBW 10: 57–58.

19. Letter to R. Seeberg, 20.7.1928, DBW 10: 82–84.

20. Letter from S. Leibholz, 12.4.1928.

21. Letter to his parents, 11.4.1928, DBW 10: 48.

22. DBW 8: 129.

23. Letter from Klaus Bonhoeffer to the Schleichers, 16.5.1928.

24. Letter, 11.7.1928, DBW 10: 74.

25. Letter, 13.7.1928.

26. Letter from Klaus Bonhoeffer to Dietrich, n.d.

27. Communication to author from H. U. Esche, 25.3.1965.

28. DBW 10: 27.

29. DBW 10: 136.

30. DBW 10: 86.

31. DBW 10: 137.

32. Letter to his grandmother, 23.2.1928, DBW 10: 36.

33. Ibid.

34. Letter to his parents, 20.2.1928, DBW 10: 32–33.

35. Letter to R. Seeberg, 20.7.1928, DBW 10: 82.

36. DBW 10: 23–32.

37. Letter to his parents, 20.2.1928, DBW 10: 34.

38. Letter, 6.3.1928, DBW 10: 38.

39. Letter, 13.3.1928, DBW 10: 40.

40. DBW 10: 72.

41. Letter to K.-F. Bonhoeffer, 7.7.1928, DBW 10: 70–72.

42. Letter, 14.8.1928, DBW 10: 96. The book was K. Bonhoeffer, *Beiträge zur Kenntnis des grossstädtischen Vagabundentums* (1900).

43. DBW 10: 26.

44. Letter to his grandmother, 5.6.1928, DBW 10: 60.

45. DBW 10: 24–25.

46. DBW 10: 27.

47. DBW 10: 122.

48. Letter to his parents, 10.12.1928, DBW 10: 115.

49. Letter to Superintendent M. Diestel, 18.6.1928, DBW 10: 65.

50. Letter to his parents, 27.11.1928, DBW 10: 112.

51. Ibid.

52. Letter to H. Rössler, 7.8.1928, DBW 10: 91–92.

53. Cf. DBW 10: 499–521.

54. *The Confessions of St. Augustine,* trans. F. J. Sheed, (Kansas City: 1970), 5–7 [see DBW 10: 456, 535].

55. DBW 10: 457, 459.

56. Sermon on 1 Cor. 12:9, 9.9.1928, DBW 10: 505–11.

57. DBW 10: 457.

58. Sermon on Matt. 28:20, 15.4.1928, DBW 10: 470, 473.

59. Sermon on Rev. 3:20, 1 Advent 1928, DBW 10: 533.

60. DBW 10: 513–16.

61. DBW 10: 500, 501–2.

62. Letter to his parents, 30.7.1928, DBW 10: 88.

63. DBW 10: 285.

64. See DBW 10: 287–302.

65. DBW 10: 302.

66. DBW 10: 117.

67. DBW 10: 302–3.

68. DBW 10: 307.

69. DBW 10: 310–14.

70. DBW 10: 315.

71. DBW 10: 316.

72. DBW 10: 319.

73. DBW 10: 319–20.

74. LPP, 362 [see DBW 8: 537].

75. DBW 10: 321.

76. Letter to his parents, 6.2.1929, DBW 10: 131.

77. "What Is a Christian Ethic?" NRS, 39, 41 [see DBW 10: 331, 327].

78. DBW 10: 323.

79. DBW 10: 326.

80. NRS, 41, 39 [see DBW 10: 329, 330].

81. DBW 10: 338–40.

82. DBW 10: 338.

83. DBW 10: 337.

84. But see SC (DBWE 1), 118.

85. F. Naumann, Letter 19, in *Briefe über Religion,* 61ff., 75 [see DBW 10: 340]: ". . . as soon as we say we recognize only the principle of love we shall never be able to take any action in the face of God and the world that creates the impression of hardness. But such action is necessary if we are to live."

86. See E. Bizer, "Der Fall Dehn," in *Festschrift für Günther Dehn,* ed. W. Schneemelcher (1957), 239–61.

87. NRS, 48 [see DBW 10: 345].

88. Ibid.

89. Letter to his parents, 6.2.1929, DBW 10: 131.

90. Letter, 18.12.1928, DBW 10: 118.

91. Letter, 20.7.1928, DBW 10: 84.

92. Letter, 10.10.1928, DBW 10: 102–3.

93. Letter, 19.10.1928, DBW 10: 106.

94. Letter to R. Seeberg, 20.7.1928, DBW 10: 85.

95. Letter, 7.8.1928, DBW 10: 92.

96. DBW 10: 105.

97. Letter to his parents, 6.2.1929, DBW 10: 129.

Chapter 4. Assistant Lecturer in Berlin: 1929–1930

1. K. Bonhoeffer, *Lebenserinnerungen*, 114.

2. E. Peterson, *Theologische Traktate* (1951), 301.

3. "Karl Barth zum Kirchenkampf," *Theologische Existenz Heute*, no. 49 (neue Folge, 1956), 91.

4. Letter to H. Rössler, 25.12.1932, DBW 12: 41.

5. Letter to H. Rössler, 23.2.1930, DBW 10: 169–70.

6. DBW 14: 112–13.

7. Letter, 19.6.1931.

8. SC (DBWE 1), 134.

9. On the word order *Communio Sanctorum*, cf. SC (DBWE 1), 122, n. 1.

10. SC (DBWE 1), 166, n. 26; 242, n. 111; 257, n. 129.

11. *Theologische Literaturzeitung* (ThLZ) (1931), col. 590f.

12. *Reformierte Kirchenzeitung* (March 1931), 4.

13. *Protestantenblatt*, vol. 64, no. 45, cols. 717–18.

14. *Zwischen den Zeiten,* vol. 11 (1933), 56.

15. Letter to K.-F. Bonhoeffer, 7.7.1928, DBW 10: 72.

16. AB (DBWE 2), 157–61.

17. *Christliche Welt* (1929), 525.

18. H. Stephan, *Die evangelische Theologie: Ihr jetziger Stand und Aufgabe systematische Theologie,* Heft 3 (1928).

19. *Christliche Welt* (1929), 528.

20. AB (DBWE 2), 77–78, n. 89; 96–97, n. 24.

21. Ibid., 90.

22. The only reference is AB (DBWE 2), 154.

23. The twenty-second edition of R. Otto's *The Idea of the Holy* was published in 1929. It had been translated into all the principal languages.

24. See, for example, B. H. Knittermeyer's review, *Zwischen den Zeiten*, vol. 11 (1933), 179ff.

25. AB (DBWE 2), 90–91.

26. LPP, 382 [see DBW 8: 559].

27. AB (DBWE 2), 95.

28. NRS, 69 [see DBW 10: 378].

29. Letter, 6.3.1931.

30. DBW 11: 63.

31. ThLZ (1933), col. 188ff.

32. W. Frei, in ThLZ, no. 5 (1957).

33. H. Müller, *Von der Kirche zur Welt* (1961), 152.

34. Letter to his grandmother, 18.8.1930, DBW 10: 194.

35. Hans-Christoph von Hase, *Die Gegenwart Christi in der Kirche* (Gütersloh, 1934).

36. W. Dress, *Die Theologie Gersons: Eine Untersuchung zur Verbindung von Nominalismus und Mystik im Spätmittelalter* (Gütersloh, 1931).

37. E. Zinn, *Die Theologie des Friedrich Christoph Oetinger* (dissertation, Gütersloh, 1932).

38. F. Hildebrandt, EST. *Das lutherische Prinzip*, in *Studien zur systematischen Theologie*, Heft 7 (dissertation, Göttingen, 1931).

39. A. von Zahn-Harnack, *Adolf Harnack*, 436. Quotation from letter, 18.12.1929, in NRS, 28 [see DBW 10: 158].

40. See letter from A. Harnack to Bonhoeffer, 22.12.1929, DBW 10: 160.

41. NRS, 30 [see DBW 10: 347–48].

42. Letter, 19.6.1930, DBW 10: 180–81.

43. LPP, 129 [see DBW 8: 187].

44. G. Bernanos, *Under the Sun of Satan* (1950), 226.

45. Ibid., 292.

46. G. Bernanos, *Der Abtrünnige* (1929; reprint in German under the title *Der Betrug*, 1963), 51f.

47. Letter, 18.10.1930, DBW 10: 201.

48. DBW 10: 185–86.

49. Otto Dibelius's book, *Das Jahrhundert der Kirche,* appeared in 1927 with a violet cover. The title of Barth's rebuttal was an allusion to Cicero's oracle "Quosque tandem" ("how long, pray tell . . .") against Cataline; Barth was expressing his disgust and impatience with Dibelius's book.

50. *Christliche Welt* (1929), 809.

51. Letter to high government counsel O. Morsbach at the Academic Exchange Service, 11.1.1930, DBW 10: 164–65.

52. Letter, 3.2.1930.

53. *The U.S. and the War*, political addresses by Elihu Root, comp. and ed. R. Bacon and J. B. Scott (1918).

54. TF, 189–90 [see DBW 10: 385].

55. *Christliche Welt* (1929), 858.

Chapter 5. America: 1930–1931

1. Letter to his grandmother, 6.9.1930, from aboard the *Columbus,* DBW 10: 197.

2. Letter from Christine von Dohnanyi, November 1930.

3. Letter, 21.12.1930.

4. Letter, January 1931.

5. Letter, 23.2.1931, DBW 10: 245.

6. See his subsequent lecture, 4.2.1932, Berlin, DBW 11: 220.

7. Letter to S. Leibholz, 21.2.1931, DBW 10: 227.

8. The number of Nazi party delegates in the Reichstag increased from 14 to 107.

9. Letter, 20.3.1931.

10. Letter, 7.4.1931.

11. TF, 187–93 [see DBW 10: 381–88, in English].

12. Letter to S. Leibholz, 7.11.1930, DBW 10: 206–7.

13. Invitation issued by the Memorial Methodist Church, 6.11.1930.

14. Letter to his grandmother, 12.4.1931, DBW 10: 251.

15. DBW 10: 392.

16. WF, 235–36, 242 [see DBW 15: 231, 239].

17. Cf. TF, 10 [see DBW 10: 274].

18. DBW 12: 204–5; DBW 15: 231, 452–53.

19. Letter, 24.1.1931.

20. DBW 10: 222.

21. *Christliche Welt* (1931), 43.

22. DBW 10: 586–87, 584.

23. Deut. 32:48-52 [see DBW 10: 582–87].

24. Communication to author from J. Lasserre.

25. LPP, 369 [see DBW 8: 541].

26. TF, 187–95 [see DBW 10: 381–88, in English].

27. TF, 192 [see DBW 10: 581, in English].

28. J. Lasserre, *War and the Gospel* (London: James Clarke Ltd., 1962), 34.

29. P. Lehmann, in 13 March 1960 BBC program with E. Bethge, R. Niebuhr, F. Hildebrandt, H. L. Henriod, W. A. Visser 't Hooft, et al. (BBC archive reference: LP26507-8).

30. Ibid.

31. NRS, 86ff. [see DBW 10: 262–80].

32. NRS, 86 [see DBW 10: 263].

33. WF, 233f. [see DBW 15: 228–29].

34. NRS, 89–91 [see DBW 10: 265–68].

35. Letter to D. Bonhoeffer from W. Lutgert, 18.2.1931, DBW 10: 236.

36. *Union Seminary Quarterly Review*, vol. 12, no. 2 (1957), 3ff.

37. "Thus the proposition 'The revelation of God is executed not in the realm of ideas but in the realm of reality' [see DBW 10: 436] or the idea that the concept of substance is inappropriate to Christian thought [see DBW 10: 440–41] is attributed to Barth, although Barth's paper 'Fate and Idea in Theology' [in *The Way of Theology in Karl Barth*, ed. H. Martin Rumscheidt (Alliance Park, Pa.: Pickwick Publications, 1986), 25–62] shows that this absolute antithesis between idea and reality is not what Barth means. It is also striking that Bonhoeffer does not shrink from putting into Barth's mouth the concept of 'boundary' that he had developed himself. In the sentence: 'Barth could say: *reflecte fortiter, sed crede fortius*' [NRS, 372 (see DBW 10: 448)], for instance, Bonhoeffer is quoting himself [see AB, 135]!" H. Pfeifer, *Das Kirchenverständnis Dietrich Bonhoeffers: Ein Beitrag zur theologischen Prinzipienlehre* (dissertation, Heidelberg, 1964), 79.

38. NRS, 362 [see DBW 10: 435].

39. DBW 10: 423–33.

40. NRS, 114ff. [see DBW 10: 455–60].

41. NRS, 88 [see DBW 10: 264].

42. DBW 10: 643.

43. DBW 10, 429, n. 38. See also DBW 10: 423, n. 1: Lyman.

44. Handwritten annotation by R. Niebuhr on "The religious experience of grace and the ethical life," DBW 10: 423, n. 5.

45. See the letters to H. Rössler, 18.10.1931 and 25.12.1932, DBW 11: 32–34; DBW 12: 38–41.

46. DBW 10: 252.

47. DBW 10: 268–69.

48. NRS, 86–87 [see DBW 10: 262–80, esp. 268–71].

49. DBW 10: 391.

50. DBW 10: 393. See also DBW 6: 145.

51. E, 127 [see DBW 10: 394].

52. According to Shaw's postscript, during the First World War the anti-German League secured the closing of that small German church, obviously with the agreement of the Anglican bishops, who regarded it as unseemly that God should be worshiped in German. "As far as I have observed, the only people who gasped were the Freethinkers." Cf. G. B. Shaw, *Androcles and the Lion* (Harmondsworth, England: Penguin, 1957), 156ff.

53. According to a letter to R. Niebuhr, 6.2.1933; cf. DBW 10: 391.

54. DBW 10: 395–97.

55. DBW 10: 278.

56. DBW 10: 203–13, esp. 210.

57. Letters, 19.11.1930 and 21.1.1931, DBW 10: 226–28.

58. E, 351 [see DBW 6: 357].

59. DBW 10: 401.

60. Letter from Karl Bonhoeffer, 20.3.1931.

61. DBW 10: 402.

62. DBW 10: 406.

63. Ibid.

64. DBW 10: 404. Because of this, the slogan advocated among the German universities was that every respectable German student should study for several semesters in East Prussia.

65. DBW 10: 405.

66. R. Niebuhr, *Union Seminary Quarterly Review*, vol. 1, no. 3 (1946), 3.

67. Letter, 25.12.1932, DBW 12: 41.

68. P. Lehmann, BBC talk, 13.3.1960.

69. Letter to H. Rössler, 18.10.1931, DBW 11: 33.

70. Letter, 3.11.1930.

71. Letter from his mother, 20.1.1931.

72. Letter from his father, 12.1.1931.

73. Letter from Rüdiger Schleicher, 1.1.1931.

74. NRS, 72–73 [see DBW 10: 238].

75. DBW 10: 222.

76. DBW 10: 244.

77. At the end of 1928 Günther Dehn was violently attacked in the right-wing press because of a speech he made in Magdeburg about Christ and war. Now he was again denounced as a "pacifist and slanderer of our dead heroes." The church authorities failed to defend him and many professors refused to support him. Cf. E. Bizer, "Der Fall Dehn," *Festschrift für Günther Dehn* (1957), 231f.

78. *Zwischen den Zeiten*, no. 2 (1931).

79. Letter, 23.2.1931, DBW 10: 244.

80. He was referring to *Sanctorum Communio*.

81. DBW 10: 253.

Chapter 6. Lecturer and Pastor: 1931–1932

1. Letter to E. Sutz, 8.10.1931, TF, 383–84 [see DBW 11: 28].

2. Letter to H. Rössler, 18.10.1931, DBW 11: 33.

3. NRS, 37 [see DBW 10: 90].

4. NRS, 123 [see DBW 11: 28].

5. See the documentation of notes taken in Bonhoeffer's lecture courses and seminars, DBW 11, Part II: 3, 4, 9, 10; DBW 12, Part II: 1, 2, 12.

6. Letter to his father, 28.3.1932, DBW 11: 78.

7. Postcard, 15.7.1931, NRS, 119 [see DBW 11: 17].

8. It was an evening with Benedictines from the monastery in Maria Laach.

9. Letter, 14.7.1931, DBW 11: 15.

10. Related by Winfried Maechler. In *Act and Being* Bonhoeffer quotes the passage from Luther: "For such blasphemies shall once sound more pleasant in God's ear than even the Hallelujahs or any other hymn of praise because they have been forced out by the devil against the will of the people." AB (DBWE 2), 160, n. 31. He referred to it again in 1932 in his lecture "Das Wesen der Kirche," DBW 11: 293, n. 377. See also E, 110 [see DBW 6: 115].

11. TF, 383 [see DBW 11: 19].

12. Ibid.

13. TF, 382 [see DBW 11: 18–19].

14. *Zwischen den Zeiten*, no. 3 (1932), 189ff.

15. See the observation in *Zwischen den Zeiten*, no. 4 (1932), 351, footnote: "the defamation of the idea of 'Führer' practiced by more than one representative of dialectical theology.... It is the shepherd's duty to lead, if only to the pasture which God makes grow."

16. DBW 11: 88.

17. Cf. E. Bizer, "Der Fall Dehn," *Festschrift für Günther Dehn* (1957), 239ff.

18. Letter to his father, 28.3.1932, DBW 11: 78.

19. Letter, 4.2.1933, DBW 12: 48–49. Cf. the further correspondence between Barth and Bonhoeffer, 14. and 18.4.1933, DBW 12: 56–57, 60–61, also 57–59.

20. See SC (DBWE 1), 106, 123ff.; AB (DBWE 2), 83, 90ff., 93f., 123ff., 153ff.

21. NRS, 64 [see DBW 10: 373].

22. DBW 12: 48–49.

23. NRS, 357 [see DBW 12: 228]. The entire review is included in NRS, 347–59 [see DBW 12: 213–31]. This makes his 1944 observation about "positivism of revelation" as an object of thought, so to speak, more intelligible.

24. Theologische Literaturzeitung (1932), 563ff. [see DBW 12: 203].

25. Cf. K. Barth, Church Dogmatics III/1 (1960), 195.

26. K. Barth, Church Dogmatics IV/2, 533ff., 641.

27. DBW 11: 17.

28. K. Barth, Anselm: Fides quaerens Intellectum (Richmond, Va.: John Knox Press, 1960).

29. K. Barth, Church Dogmatics I/1, trans. G. W. Bromiley (1960), viii.

30. NRS, 140 [see DBW 11: 51].

31. According to J. Kanitz's lecture notes, DBW 11: 211, 203.

32. WF, 121 [see DBW 14: 252].

33. Letter to E. Sutz, 24.7.1931, in TF, 383 [see DBW 11: 20].

34. AB (DBWE 2), 84.

35. Letter to E. Sutz, 24.7.1931, TF, 383 [see DBW 11: 20].

36. Letter to E. Sutz, August 1932, DBW 11: 100.

37. Letter to H. Rössler, 25.12.1932, DBW 12: 41.

38. Letter to H. Rössler, 25.12.1932, DBW 12: 39.

39. DBW 12: 39.

40. Letter to E. Sutz, 17.5.1932, DBW 11: 89.

41. DBW 11: 416–23.

42. DBW 11: 89.

43. NRS, 237 [see DBW 13: 15].

44. Cf. NRS, 160ff. [see DBW 11: 330]; SC (DBWE 1), 278.

45. DBW 11: 212–13.

46. TF, 387–88 [see DBW 12: 37].

47. LPP, 369 [see DBW 8: 542].

48. Letter to E. Sutz, 28.4.1934, TF, 411–12 [see DBW 13: 128–29].

49. DBW 11: 19.

50. LPP, 145 [see DBW 8: 209].

51. NRS, 141–49 [see DBW 11: 228–37].

52. NRS, 141 [see DBW 11: 228].

53. NRS, 142 [see DBW 11: 229].

54. DBW 11: 229; J. Glenthøj, "Dietrich Bonhoeffer und die Ökumene," MW 2: 128.

55. DBW 11: 229–33, 235.

56. DBW 10: 338.

57. NRS, 145 [see DBW 11: 232].

58. DBW 14: 795, n. 54.

59. DBW 14: 795.

60. DBW 14: 796.

61. DBW 14: 814.

62. Ibid.

63. *Monatsschrift für Pastoraltheologie*, nos. 5/6 (1932), col. 167–72. Because of the publication date the catechism has been erroneously connected with the confirmation instruction Bonhoeffer gave in Wedding; cf. *Zeichen der Zeit*, no. 6 (1957), 213–18, and MW 2: 128.

64. *Junge Kirche* (1933), 122.

65. *Christliche Welt* (1930), 947.

66. DBW 11: 129.

67. Letter, 29.5.1931, DBW 10: 259–60. The *Deutschkirchler* and *Stahlhelm* were nationalist groups.

68. The statement's description of the "situation" was that the Allies had openly broken the promises made to Germany at the time of its surrender in 1918. Germany had been robbed of space in which to live and breathe and was being depleted by payments falsely depicted as reparations. The Allied disarmament obligation undertaken in the peace treaty had been flagrantly broken.

69. For the full text of this article see *Christliche Welt* (1931), 605.

70. *Christliche Welt* (1931), 1034.

71. *Kirchliches Jahrbuch* (1931), 480, 483.

72. See *Die Eiche*, no. 3 (1931), 218.

73. Ibid., 337.

74. NRS, 119–20 [see DBW 11: 17].

75. Letter to E. Sutz, 24.7.1931, NRS, 122 [see DBW 11: 21–22].

76. Letter, 29.5.1931, DBW 10: 259.

77. F. Siegmund-Schultze, in *Die Eiche* (1931), 481.

78. Ibid.

79. *Christliche Welt* (1931), 975, 982.

80. *Die Eiche* (1931), 457.

81. *Foi et Vie*, no. 30, 611, in *Die Eiche* (1932), 268.

82. *Die Eiche* (1931), 453.

83. DBW 11: 127–28.

84. *Die Eiche* (1931), 449.

85. DBW 11: 314, n. 5, in English.

86. Cf. letter from H. Schönfeld to A. Runestam, 6.2.1932, MW 5: 52.

87. Letter, 22.4.1944, LPP, 275f. [see DBW 8: 397].

88. R. H. Bainton, *Here I Stand* (1950), 62.

89. DBW 12: 416.

90. Communication to author from J. Kanitz, 1955.

91. NRS, 149 [see DBW 11: 63].

92. Letter from Finkenwalde, 27.1.1936, DBW 14: 112–14.

93. DBW 13: 272–73.

94. DBW 14: 146–48.

95. DBW 11: 369–74.

96. Letter to E. Sutz, 25.12.1931, TF, 384 [see DBW 11: 50].

97. *Christliche Welt* (1930), 1162.

98. This also provides a clue to the date, since in July 1932 Papen announced that his government would stop participating in the Geneva negotiations. See *Die Eiche*, no. 4 (1932), 305ff., where Siegmund-Schulze expressed his disapproval that Germany had now assumed the role of saboteur, at a time when France had maneuvered itself into a position of relative isolation.

98. Cf. his letter to K. Barth, 24.10.1933, TF, 391 [see DBW 13: 13].

100. NRS, 181 [see DBW 11: 325, 326–27].

101. Editor's translation, NRS, 170–71 [see DBW 11: 341].

102. PTB, 24–27. Also excerpted in TF, 89–92 [see DBW 12: 264–78].

103. Letter, 25.12.1931, TF, 384 [see DBW 11: 50].

104. Letter to E. Sutz, 27.10.1932, DBW 11: 117.

105. According to a 6 January 1969 communication from Prof. J. Narzynski in Warsaw, none of Bonhoeffer's papers can be found in Altdamm (Dabie) or Finkenwalde.

106. DBW 11: 239–303.

107. DBW 11: 303–13.

108. DBW 12: 153–78.

109. Ibid., 178–99.

110. DBW 12: 279–348.

111. DBW 11: 139–213.

112. DBW 11: 214–15.

113. Letter to E. Sutz, 26.2.1932, NRS, 149 [see DBW 11: 63].

114. See TF, 83ff. [see DBW 11: 239–303].

115. SC (DBWE 1), 247–49.

116. Letter, 17.5.1932, DBW 11: 88.

117. DBW 12: 39.

118. NRS, 161 [see DBW 11: 331].

119. DBW 11: 89.

120. DBW 11: 294.

121. DBW 11: 271.

122. PTB, 27–47, and NRS, 153–57 [see DBW 12: 264–78, 235–39].

123. DBW 11: 303–13.

124. NRS, 157ff. [see DBW 11: 327–49, 350–57].

125. DBW 11: 416–23.

126. See esp. DBW 12: 39.

127. AB (DBWE 2), 32, 153.

128. DBW 15: 499–503, 516.

129. CF (DBWE 3), 22–23. For other references to Bonhoeffer's method see CF (DBWE 3), 53, 82–83, 85, 88.

130. According to U. Köhler's notes; cf. CF (DBWE 3), 22–23, n. 9.

131. CF (DBWE 3), 21–22.

132. Letter, 17.1.1934, DBW 13: 79.

133. *Theologische Blätter*, no. 4 (1934), 110–12.

134. Eugen Gerstenmaier, for instance, in his 1938 book *Die Kirche und die Schöpfung*, does not mention Bonhoeffer's book, although one of his chapters is titled "Creation and Sin" and another is devoted to the problem of "Act and Being" and is titled as such.

135. K. Barth, *Church Dogmatics* III/1, 194–95.

136. DBW 12: 153–78.

137. DBW 12: 178.

138. DBW 12: 178–79.

139. E. Brunner, *God and Man* (1936), 136ff.

140. See DBW 12: 187.

141. DBW 12: 279–348.

142. K. Heim, *Glaube und Denken*. See NRS, 347–59 [see DBW 12: 213–31].

143. Order dated 11.11.1931, DBW 11: 39.

144. Letter to H. Rössler, 18.10.1931, DBW 11: 33.

145. Letter to E. Sutz, 8.10.1931, NRS, 124 [see DBW 11: 29].

146. Order dated 12.6.1931. Cf. DBW 11: 23.

147. *Christliche Welt* (1932), 669.

148. Letter, 10.7.1931, DBW 11: 14.

149. DBW 11: 394–96, 396–98, 414–16; DBW 12: 431–33.

150. DBW 11: 224–25.

151. *Die Technische Hochschule*, no. 99 (1932), 200f. [see DBW 11: 226–27].

152. Editor's translation, NRS, 140, and TF, 384 [see DBW 11: 50].

153. Letter to E. Sutz, 25.12.1931, TF, 384 [see DBW 11: 50].

154. IKDB, 58, 65–66.

155. Letter to E. Sutz, 26.2.1932, TF, 385 [see DBW 11: 64].

156. Editor's translation, TF, 385–86 [see DBW 11: 64].

157. Ibid.

158. Ibid., [see DBW 11: 65].

159. DBW 11: 414.

160. See DBW 15: 482.

161. Letter, 28.3.1932, DBW 11: 77.

162. TF, 385 [see DBW 11: 64].

163. Letter to E. Sutz, 17.5.1932, DBW 11: 90.

164. R. Rother, "A Confirmation Class in Wedding," IKDB, 57ff.

165. DBW 11: 112–13.

166. Letter to A. Schnurmann, 23.11.1932, DBW 12: 26–27.

167. DBW 12: 31.

168. DBW 12: 45.

169. TF, 217–18 [see DBW 12: 439–47].

170. Letter to K.-F. Bonhoeffer, 12.1.1933, DBW 12: 45–46.

171. Minutes, St. Bartholomaeus church council meeting, 2.2.1933 and 28.2.1933.

172. Letter, 24.10.1933, TF, 391 [see DBW 13: 12–13].

173. FFP, 13–47 [see DBW 7: 51–57].

174. *Christliche Welt* (1931), 694, 740.

175. *Christliche Welt* (1932), 142, 1103.

176. See MW V: 80–81.

177. Letter to E. Sutz, 17.5.1932, DBW 11: 90.

178. Letter to E. Sutz, 27.10.1932, DBW 11: 118.

179. Letter to E. Sutz, 17.5.1932, DBW 11: 89–90.

180. DBW 12: 28.

181. DBW 10: 221, 265.

182. Sermon on Matt. 8:23, 15.1.1933, DBW 12: 443.

183. Letter, 29.5.1932, DBW 11: 427.

184. Sermon, 29.5.1932, DBW 11: 426–35.

185. DBW 11: 100, 102, 63.

186. On 12.6.1932 and 19.6.1932, DBW 11: 435–43, 444–53.

187. TF, 196 [see DBW 11: 380–81]. Similar references in letter to E. Sutz, 8.10.1931, TF, 383–84 [see DBW 11: 28].

188. DBW 11: 400.

189. DBW 11: 440–41.

190. DBW 11: 446.

191. DBW 11: 456–57.

192. Bonhoeffer's text was Revelations 2:4ff.

193. DBW 12: 423–25.

194. DBW 12: 429–30.

195. See, for example, DBW 11: 423–26, 463–66.

196. *Die Eiche* (1931), 99, 230.

197. Letter, 28.10.1931, DBW 11: 36.

198. Letter, 14.2.1932, DBW 11: 60.

199. *Christliche Welt* (1932), 142; *Die Eiche* (1932), 253f.

200. DBW 11: 314, n. 5, in English.

201. F. A. Iremonger, *William Temple* (1948), 403.

202. NRS, 173ff. [see DBW 11: 317–27].

203. DBW 12: 22.

204. Letter to Bonhoeffer, 11.11.1932, DBW 12: 23.

205. See DBW 12: 43.

206. DBW 12: 260–63.

207. DBW 12: 261, 262.

208. Further details are in MW V: 60–62, 63–64 [see DBW 12: 46].

209. DBW 12: 210.

210. Letter to Bonhoeffer from Bishop Jensen of the Moravian Brethren, 6.10.1933, DBW 12: 148, and n. 2.

211. DBW 11: 314–16.

212. DBW 11: 316.

213. DBW 11: 88.

214. DBW 11: 358.

215. DBW 11: 359.

216. DBW 12: 432.

217. Adolf Mádr, a Czechoslovakian pastor, has researched this conference and the events leading up to it in detail: "Die Tschechoslowakische Kirche und die regionale Jugendfriedenskonferenz des Weltbundes in Ciernohorské Kúpele vom 20–30.7.1932 in der Tschechoslowakei mit der Teilnahme Dietrich Bonhoeffers," manuscript and documentation, Brno 1964–1965. The Czechs were strongly oriented toward liberal theology and the social gospel; the appearance of a German who agreed with them had a significant impact. Added to that was his clear warning at the time against National Socialism and (as some participants attested) his insistence that he had to leave the conference early because of the German elections. Bonhoeffer's impact on this conference was stronger and had a longer legacy than he realized at the time. Mádr's work establishes that this encounter continued to influence the development of Czech theology and its subsequent political resistance. See also *Zeichen der Zeit*, no. 3 (1967), 106ff.

218. DBW 11: 344–47.

219. DBW 11: 327.

220. Letter to E. Sutz, August 1932, DBW 11: 99–100.

221. NRS, 159 [see DBW 11: 329].

222. NRS, 171f. [see DBW 11: 342].

223. Editor's translation, NRS, 168 [see DBW 11: 338].

224. NRS, 172 [see DBW 11: 343].

225. *Die Eiche*, no. 4 (1932), 308–9.

226. DBW 11: 359–60.

227. Letter, 7.5.1932.

228. According to F. Siegmund-Schultze in *Die Eiche* 1932, 13ff., 183, 304ff.

229. F. A. Iremonger, *William Temple*, 376.

230. According to J. Richter in *Die Eiche* (1932), 326.

231. Letter, August 1932, DBW 11: 101.

232. Letter, 6.8.1932, DBW 11:99.

233. *Yorkshire Post*, 27.9.1932. Cf. DBW 11: 360, n. 15; 360–61, n. 23.

234. DBW 11: 416–23.

235. DBW 11: 362, 365–66.

236. NRS, 182–89, excerpt in TF, 103–4 [see DBW 11: 350–57].

237. Editor's translation, TF, 103 [see DBW 11: 352].

238. NRS, 185 [see DBW 11: 353].

239. DBW 11:357.

240. See the reports in *Die Eiche* (1933), 99ff.

241. Report from the World Alliance (1932–1933), 5.

242. PTB, 34 [see DBW 12: 269].

243. PTB, 36 [see DBW 12: 270].

244. Editor's translation, speech at Ciernohorské Kúpele; see TF, 98 [see DBW 11: 332].

Chapter 7. Berlin: 1933

1. *Christliche Welt* (1933), 45. See also *Reformierte Kirchenzeitung*, vol. 82, no. 49 (4 December 1933), 386.

2. On 26.2.1933, DBW 12: 448–49.

3. Karl Bonhoeffer, *Lebenserinnerungen*.

4. Letter to E. Sutz, 14.4.1933, TF, 410 [see DBW 12: 59].

5. Letter to K. Barth, 24.10.1933, TF, 391 [see DBW 13: 13].

6. Letter to E. Sutz, 14.4.1933, DBW 12: 59.

7. DBW 12: 240.

8. See the essays by H. E. Tödt and E.-A. Scharffenorth in IBF 4: 139–83, 184–234.

9. NRS, 199 [see DBW 12: 254].

10. Editor's translation, NRS, 202, 204 [see DBW 12: 257, 259–60].

11. DBW 12:47.

12. NRS, 190–204 [see DBW 12: 242–60]; also delivered at the technical university, 23.2.1933, cf. DBW 12: 52.

13. *News Letter* (March 1933), 10.

14. *Christliche Welt* (1933), 240.

15. *Völkischer Beobachter* 36/37 (5 June 1933).

16. DBW 12: 453, 454.

17. Werner Hofer, *Der Nationalsozialismus: Dokumente 1933–1945* (1957), 53.

18. DBW 12: 59.

19. The main proceedings against Marinus van de Lubbe did not begin until 21 November 1933; he was executed on 10 January 1934.

20. *Monatsschrift für Psychiatrie und Neurologie*, vol. 89 (1934), 185–213.

21. Karl Bonhoeffer, *Lebenserinnerungen*, 115.

22. G. Bracher, W. Sauer, and G. Schulz, eds., *Die nationalsozialistische Machtergreifung*, 2d ed. (1962), 82.

23. *Christliche Welt* (1933), 239.

24. Cf. Kurt Scharf, "Dr. Dibelius im Kampf der Bekennenden Kirche," in *Die Stunde der Kirche* (1950), 35.

25. G. van Norden, *Kirche in der Krise 1933* (1963), 175.

26. W. Hofer, *Der Nationalsozialismus*, 56.

27. It appeared under this euphemistic title in the official Nazi law bulletin, *Reichsgesetzblatt*, vol. 1, no. 175 (7 April 1933).

28. W. Hofer, *Der Nationalsozialismus*, 283f.

29. Cf. the account in the *Reichsanzeiger*, 82 (6 April 1933).

30. W. Hofer, *Der Nationalsozialismus*, 57.

31. G. van Norden, *Kirche in der Krise 1933*, 45.

32. E, 189 [see DBW 6: 36].

33. H. Müller, *Katholische Kirche und Nationalsozialismus* (Munich: Nymphen-
berger Verlags-Handlung, 1963).

34. *Christliche Welt* (1933), 413.

35. TF, 410 [see DBW 12: 57–58].

36. DBW 12: 60–61.

37. Letter to E. Sutz, 14.4.1933, TF, 410 [see DBW 12: 58]. H. E. Tödt, in a differentiated and convincing way, qualifes this assessment; see IBF 4: 139–83; IBF 5:
85–117.

38. E. Stoltenhoff's letter to Menn, reprinted in G. van Norden, *Kirche in der Krise
1933*, 60.

39. "Die Kirche vor der Judenfrage," NRS, 221–29 [see DBW 12: 349–58].

40. NRS, 227–29 [see DBW 12: 355–58].

41. NRS, 229 [see DBW 12: 358].

42. NRS, 222–27 [see DBW 12: 350–55].

43. NRS, 222 [see DBW 12: 350].

44. Prov. 31:8.

45. NRS, 222 [see DBW 12: 350].

46. NRS, 223 [see DBW 12: 350–51].

47. Concerning the review of A. de Quervain's book, "Das Gesetz des Staates," see
the lecture "Jüngste Theologie" (1932/1933), DBW 12: 169.

48. NRS, 223, 224 [see DBW 12: 351–52].

49. "Neuer Anfang," *Christliche Welt* (1933), 377f.

50. NRS, 225 [see DBW 12: 353].

51. NRS, 226 [see DBW 12: 354].

52. NRS, 225 [see DBW 12: 353].

53. NRS, 223 [see DBW 12: 351].

54. NRS, 226 [see DBW 12: 354].

55. Letter to E. Sutz, 14.4.1933, TF, 410 [see DBW 12: 57].

56. DBW 13: 34–35.

57. Letter, 14.4.1933, TF, 388 [see DBW 12: 56].

58. Letter, 18.4.1933, DBW 12: 60.

59. Cf. WF, 243–44 [see DBW 13: 75, 267, in English; DBW 15: 188, in English].

60. Minutes, Novi Sad meeting, 4, 5.

61. N.d., DBW 12: 55.

62. Annual Report, Life and Work (September 1933), 45.

63. Annual Report, The World Alliance (1932–1933), 20–21, 33.

64. K. Bonhoeffer, *Lebenserinnerungen*, 118.

65. Ibid., 115.

66. *Christliche Welt* (1933), 476.

67. DBW 12: 66–67.

68. DBW 12: 462, 463. See also TF, 209–12.

69. Annual Report, The World Alliance (1933/1934), 21.

70. DBW 12: 59, n. 10, makes clear that Bonhoeffer was not in Basel.

71. *Gotthardbriefe* (27 May 1933), 80.

72. Cf. DBW 12: 78–80.

73. DBW 12: 78, n. 3.

74. DBW 13: 37.

75. DBW 12: 78–79.

76. DBW 12: 79. According to Otto Dudzus, the student was Ernst Tillich.

77. DBW 12: 85. The comments enclosed in brackets are from the notes of the Hungarian student Ferene Lehel [see IKDB, 68ff.].

78. *Junge Kirche*, no. 2 (30 June 1933), 22–23. See DBW 12: 85, n. 20.

79. Postcard, 26.6.1933, DBW 12: 91.

80. Letter, 27.6.1933.

81. From G. van Norden, *Kirche in der Krise 1933*, 74.

82. Cf. DBW 12: 94–96.

83. Pamphlet, 4.7.1933, DBW 12: 92–94.

84. See G. Niemöller, *Die erste Bekenntnissynode der Deutschen Evangelischen Kirche zu Barmen* (1959), 42.

85. Letter to E. Sutz, 17.7.1933, TF, 410–11 [see DBW 12: 98].

86. Ibid. [see DBW 12: 97–98].

87. G. van Norden, *Kirche in der Krise 1933*, 82.

88. *Junge Kirche* (1933), 43, 59.

89. W. Niemöller, *Die Evangelische Kirche im Dritten Reich* (1956), 87.

90. *Deutsches Volkstum* (1933), 918ff.

91. See, for example, GS 2: 59–61 (by F. Hildebrandt).

92. *Junge Kirche* (1933), 60.

93. See DBW 12: 100.

94. DBW 12: 99–100.

95. Letter, 28.10.1933, DBW 13: 16.

96. Letter, 6.11.1933, DBW 13: 22.

97. J. Beckmann, ed., *Kirchliches Jahrbuch 1933–1944* (1948), 22.

98. TF, 213–16 [see DBW 12: 465–70].

99. *Gotthardbriefe*, 95.

100. *Junge Kirche* (1933), 80ff.

101. Cf. *Kirchliches Jahrbuch 1930*, 492–93.

102. DBW 12: 105–6.

103. Letter, 21.7.1933, DBW 12: 103, in English.

104. Cf. DBW 12: 101.

105. Letter to E. Sutz, 17.7.1933, TF, 411 [see DBW 12: 98].

106. Letter, 21.7.1933, DBW 12: 103–4, in English.

107. Communication to author from H. Sasse, 28.9.1956.

108. Letter to F. W. Singer, 19.7.1933, DBW 12: 102.

109. Letter, 21.8.1933, DBW 12: 119.

110. Letter, 20.8.1933, DBW 12: 117.

111. "Riederauer Thesen zur Volksmission," in the series "Bekennende Kirche," no. 1, ed. Christian Stoll (1933).

112. *Junge Kirche* (1933), 44ff.

113. Ibid., 99–101.

114. NRS, 141–49 [see DBW 11: 228–37].

115. *Junge Kirche* (1933), 122.

116. TF, 419 [see DBW 12: 117–18].

117. Letter to K. Barth, 24.10.1933, TF, 391–92 [see DBW 13: 14].

118. On 28.11.1933, from a copy by J. Rieger.

119. Cf. DBW 12: 362, n. 1.

120. From notes taken by J. Rieger, DBW 13: 39.

121. Letter to M. Niemöller, 5.12.1933.

122. *Das Bekenntnis der Väter und die Bekennende Gemeinde* (Christian Kaiser, Munich). The subtitle reads: "Submitted for Consideration by a Group of Evangelical Theologians and Published in Their Name by Martin Niemöller" [cf. DBW 12: 503–7].

123. TF, 391f. [see DBW 13: 14].

124. Letter, 20.8.1933, DBW 12: 118.

125. *Christliche Welt* (1933), 840.

126. An early form of this pamphlet is probably printed in C. S. Macfarland's "Appeal to the Ministers of the Old Prussian Union" in *The New Church and the New Germany* [a book on church and state in Germany in 1933], 68–71. J. Glenthøj has discovered that during the last days of July Bonhoeffer probably dictated this passage to Jürgen Winterhager, so that the latter could translate it for Macfarland. See Glenthøj's account and documentation in MW 5: 103–4.

127. In his dissertation, "Christologie als Modell der Gesellschaft," J. Schwarz established that statements from Bonhoeffer's *Sanctorum Communio* have been polemically and at times literally repeated in this pamphlet.

128. DBW 12: 408–15.

129. Letter, 13.9.1933.

130. Letter to F. Siegmund-Schultze, 6.11.1933, DBW 13: 22.

131. DBW 12: 412.

132. DBW 12: 414.

133. Ibid.

134. *Junge Kirche* (1933), 273. The Erlangen Gutachten was signed 25 September 1933.

135. Ibid., 269f.

136. Ibid., 270.

137. DBW 12: 413, 414.

138. *Christliche Welt* (1933), 912.

139. *Die Deutsche Evangelische Kirche und die Judenfrage,* 36.

140. Niemöller's parish calendar contains the following entry: "6.9 11 A.M. J.B. [Young Reformation movement] and Gospel and Church [group] at hostel: Discussion Knak-Bonhoeffer. Stählin, etc. 8 P.M. Bonhoeffer and lots of students, Röhricht, Hildebrandt, 2:15 A.M. to bed."

141. Cf. his letter to J. Richter, 13.9.1933.

142. DBW 12: 122.

143. DBW 12: 128–30.

144. Letter, 9.9.1933, TF, 389–90 [see DBW 12: 124].

145. NRS, 232–33 [see DBW 12: 126–27].

146. DBW 12: 123.

147. Text provided by W. Niemöller, 23.3.1958.

148. See the early draft, 24.9.1933, by Bonhoeffer and Hildebrandt, DBW 12: 135–36.

149. DBW 12: 141–44.

150. TF, 389 [see DBW 12: 124].

151. Minutes, Novi Sad meeting, 2, 15, 37ff.; see *Die Eiche* (1933), 368ff.

152. Minutes (duplicated), Sofia, 8.

153. Communication to author from H. L. Henriod, 29.3.1958.

154. Letter, 6.11.1933, DBW 13: 23.

155. DBW 13: 23.

156. Minutes (duplicated), Sofia, 12f.

157. Letter from J. Richter to F. Siegmund-Schultze, 6.11.1933, DBW 13: 23; see MW 5: 341–44.

158. Letter, 25.9.1933.

159. Letter, 28.10.1933, DBW 13: 16.

160. *Die Eiche* (1933), 372–81.

161. DBW 13: 23.

162. DBW 13: 23–24.

163. Letter, 6.11.1933, DBW 13: 22.

164. Zentralarchiv, Berlin: Archive Deutsche Evangelische Kirche, Kirchenkanzlei III, 474, 30.11.1933.

165. Expert opinions, cf. *Die Evangelische Kirche in Deutschland und die Judenfrage* (Geneva, 1945), 46ff.

166. *Evangelium im Dritten Reich,* 41; W. Niemöller, *Kampf und Zeugnis* (1948), 64; the class of the preachers' seminary in Saxony had suddenly been transformed into an S.A. unit. Cf. Gertrud Staewen's report in W. Niemöller, *Wort und Tat im Kirchenkampf* (1969), 67f.

167. DBW 13: 39.

168. Communication to author from F. Hildebrandt.

169. Ibid.

170. Letter to F. Siegmund-Schultze, 6.11.1933, DBW 13: 22.

171. TF, 393 [see DBW 12: 145–46, 147].

172. Cf. DBW 12: 145, n. 29.

173. DBW 12: 416–19.

174. DBW 12: 418.

175. *Bonhoeffer Gedenkheft*, ed. E. Bethge (1947), 26.

176. DBW 12: 508–9.

177. Besides the undated manuscript in Bonhoeffer's writing, there are notes taken by W.-D. Zimmermann, probably in the summer or autumn of 1933, and notes by J. Rieger, London, where Bonhoeffer gave a lecture in April 1934 on "Church and Youth" for the German YMCA.

178. Communication to author from J. Rieger, 9.12.1960.

179. Letter, 24.10.1933.

Chapter 8. London: 1933–1935

1. Letter, 24.10.1933, TF, 391 [see DBW 13: 13–14].

2. TF, 289–392 [see DBW 12: 124–28; DBW 13: 11–15, 31–34].

3. NRS, 238–39 [see DBW 13: 31, 33]. In September 1933 Bonhoeffer, under very new circumstances, linked his own fate with that of Jonah (LPP, 398–99 [see DBW 8: 606]).

4. Letter, 22.12.1933, DBW 13:55.

5. Letter to E. Sutz, 28.4.1934, TF, 411 [see DBW 13: 128].

6. Letter to K.-F. Bonhoeffer, January 1934, DBW 13:75.

7. DBW 13: 167.

8. NRS, 243 [see DBW 15: 188, in English].

9. Letter to K.-F. Bonhoeffer, January 1934, DBW 13: 75. See also the letter to R. Niebuhr, 13.7.1934, concerning the novelist A. T. Wegner, DBW 13: 169–71.

10. See TF, 217–48 [see DBW 13: 313–43, 347–56, 359–63, 365–418].

11. Letter to E. Sutz, 28.4.1934, DBW 13: 129.

12. See DBW 13: 344–46 on Luke 9:57-62 and the three followers of Jesus, and CD, 59ff. [see DBW 4: 48–50].

13. TF, 223 [see DBW 13: 332].

14. DBW 13: 407, in English.

15. DBW 13: 405, in English.

16. DBW 13: 378–404.

17. Letter to G. Leibholz, 23.11.1933, DBW 13: 35

18. See J. Rieger, *Dietrich Bonhoeffer in England* (1966).

19. DBW 12: 508–9, and n. 1.

20. TF, 416 [see DBW 13: 44–45].

21. TF, 417 [see DBW 13: 47]. See also *Junge Kirche* (1934), 25, and M. Niemöller's reply to this protest: "in times that were already difficult enough, you made my life even more difficult!" DBW 13: 59.

22. DBW 13: 48.

23. Letter to M. Niemöller, 15.12.1933, DBW 13: 49.

24. Letter to his grandmother, 21.12.1933, DBW 13: 52.

25. DBW 13: 58.

26. From the minutes of the clergy meetings, in St. George's parish files, London.

27. From J. Rieger's notes on Bonhoeffer's lecture in Bradford, DBW 13: 41.

28. For complete text see DBW 13: 41–43.

29. From a handwritten note by Bonhoeffer. Cf. DBW 13: 42, n. 39.

30. DBW 13:44.

31. Heckel means the new "Spiritual Ministry" without Hossenfelder, but including H. Lauerer, A. Beyer, A. Weber, and F. Werner, and also Ludwig Müller's forced resignation as honorary patron of the German Christians.

32. DBW 13: 50.

33. From the files of St. George's Church and parish association, London.

34. DBW 13: 49–50.

35. DBW 13: 70.

36. DBW 13: 71.

37. DBW 13: 73.

38. Letter, 2.1.1934, DBW 13: 64.

39. Regarding these events, see esp. J. Glenthøj, *Hindenburg, Göring und die evangelischen Kirchenführer: Arbeiten zur Geschichte des Kirchenkampfes*, vol. 15, 45ff.

40. Letter, 17.1.1934, NRS, 263 [see DBW 13: 79].

41. DBW 13: 77.

42. TF, 397 [see DBW 13: 81, in English].

43. Letter, 23.10.1933, GS 1: 183.

44. See the excellent documentation—for all these events—by J. Glenthøj: *Dansk Theologisk Tidsskrift*, vol. 26, no. 4, 224ff., and *Arbeiten zur Geschichte des Kirchenkampfes*, vol. 15 (1958), 70ff.

45. Letter to F. Wehrhan, 17.1.1934, DBW 13: 78.

46. Letter to F. Wehrhan, 19.1.1934, DBW 13: 84.

47. See W. Niemöller's works on the dramatic chancellery reception, *Hitler und die evangelischen Kirchenführer: Zum 25. Januar 1934* (1959), and "Epilog zum Kanzlerempfang," in *Evangelische Theologie* (1960), 107–24; also the works by J. Glenthøj cited above and Heckel's report on 8.2.1934, DBW 13: 99.

48. J. Beckmann, ed., *Kirchliches Jahrbuch 1933–1944*, 39 [see DBW 13: 85].

49. Zentralarchiv, Berlin: Archive Deutsche Evangelische Kirche, Kirchenkanzlei III, 334/34. 31.1.1934 [see DBW 13: 85].

50. Letter to T. de Félice, n.d., DBW 13: 65.

51. Letter to T. de Félice, n.d., DBW 13: 84.

52. DBW 13: 348, 351.

53. From the files of the Association of Congregations, signed Bruno Schröder, London. Cf. DBW 13: 95–96.

54. DBW 13: 97.

55. From the files of St. George's Church, London. See DBW 13: 97–104.

56. DBW 13: 99.

57. Letter, 12.12.1933.

58. *Junge Kirche* (1934), 346.

59. J. Beckmann, ed., *Kirchliches Jahrbuch 1933–1944*, 39 [see DBW 13: 85].

60. Ibid., 105–6.

61. Ibid., 103.

62. Letter from B. Schröder to T. Heckel, 9.2.1934, DBW 13: 106–7; letter from T. Heckel to B. Schröder, 15.2.1934.

63. DBW 13: 136–37.

64. DBW 13: 149.

65. Letter to K.-F. Bonhoeffer, January 1934, DBW 13: 75.

66. Namely, Bishop A. C. Headlam, who played a leading role in Faith and Order. He repeatedly offered his help to the German Christians and later to Heckel, received J. von Ribbentrop, and wrote letters to *The Times* in favor of the new Germany. He utterly repudiated the Confessing church.

67. Pastor Dr. J. Rieger of St. George's Church prohibited it.

68. Letter, 6.11.1933, DBW 13: 24.

69. G. K. A. Bell, *A Brief Sketch of the Church of England* (1928).

70. Ecumenical Archives, Geneva.

71. Letter, 15.11.1933.

72. Letter to F. Siegmund-Schultze, 6.11.1933, DBW 13: 23.

73. See H. von Koenigswald, *Birger Forell* (1952), 97ff.

74. Letter, 11.9.1934, TF, 412 [see DBW 13: 205].

75. TF, 395 [see DBW 13: 28–29, in English].

76. NRS, 255 [see DBW 13: 29, in English].

77. TF, 395f. [see DBW 13: 36, in English].

78. DBW 16: 468.

79. CD, 11.

80. DBW 14: 100–101.

81. DBW 13: 69–70.

82. Letter, 4.1.1934, NRS, 257 [see DBW 13: 68].

83. DBW 13: 66.

84. Koechlin drafted an initial form of this article; see *G. Bell—A. Koechlin, Briefwechsel 1933–1954*, ed. A. Lindt (1969), 102–3, 107–8.

85. See DBW 13: 75, and n. 4.

86. TF, 397 [see DBW 13: 82].

87. See the minutes of the Council meeting, Fanö, 63–65.

88. Cf. DBW 13: 93, n. 8.

89. Letter, 5.2.1934, DBW 13: 93.

90. TF, 397 [see DBW 13: 109, in English].

91. The delegation was to be invited to Paris, April 1934. Cf. DBW 13: 114.

92. From J. Rieger's diary, 27.2.1934. Cf. DBW 13: 111–12.

93. Zentralarchiv, Berlin: Archive Deutsche Evangelische Kirche, Kirchliches Aussenamt K III, 637 II, 27.2.1934.

94. Letter to E. Sutz, 28.4.1934, DBW 13: 127.

95. NRS, 264–65. See DBW 13: 115–17.

96. DBW 13: 117.

97. DBW 13: 118.

98. Letter, 28.4.1934, DBW 13: 127–28.

99. TF, 395 [see DBW 13: 28, in English].

100. Invitation from H. Schönfeld to Bonhoeffer, 17.1.1934, "as a well-informed representative from the World Alliance." See DBW 13: 80–81, cf. 119.

101. Note on Bonhoeffer's telegram, Ecumenical Archives, Geneva. Communication to author from A. Boyens. See DBW 13: 119, and n. 1.

102. NRS, 268–69 [see DBW 13: 114–15, in English].

103. DBW 13: 120–21.

104. TF, 395 [see DBW 13: 28, in English].

105. TF, 397 [see DBW 13: 81–82].

106. Letter, 14.3.1934, in English, TF, 400 [see DBW 13: 112].

107. TF, 400 [see DBW 13: 122, in English].

108. DBW 13: 123, and n. 10.

109. H. Hermelink, *Kirche im Kampf* (1950), 87; see DBW 13: 126, n. 4.

110. DBW 13: 132, in English.

111. TF, 403 [see DBW 13: 134].

112. DBW 13: 137.

113. DBW 13: 138, in English.

114. Letter, 15.3.1934, in English, TF, 403 [see DBW 13: 141].

115. The Barmen Theological Declaration (6 theses; 1934). Reprinted in full in *Church and Society*, vol. 85, no. 6 (July/August 1995), 124–25.

116. Cf. DBW 13: 203.

117. *Junge Kirche* (1934), 673.

118. Letter, 28.4.1934, TF, 411 [see DBW 13: 128]. In a letter to R. Niebuhr, 13 July 1934 [see DBW 13: 170], Bonhoeffer expressed astonishment that no pastors had been shot during the Röhm putsch.

119. DBW 13: 365.

120. DBW 13: 370–71.

121. DBW 13: 372.

122. DBW 13: 205.

123. Letters to T. de Félice, 17.6.1934 and 12.8.1934, DBW 13: 152, cf. 182.

124. Letter to T. de Félice, 4.7.1934, DBW 13: 161.

125. Letter to T. de Félice, 12.8.1934, DBW 13: 182.

126. Letter to T. de Félice, 4.7.1934, DBW 13: 161–62.

127. Letter to T. de Félice, DBW 13: 182.

128. Letter to T. de Félice, DBW 13: 181.

129. Letter, 14.6.1934, DBW 13: 151.

130. NRS, 279–82 [see DBW 13: 163–65, in English].

131. Letter to Henriod, 12.7.1934, TF, 406 [see DBW 13: 167].

132. NRS, 282–83 [see DBW 13: 166–67, in English].

133. NRS, 276 [see DBW 13: 158–59, in English].

134. NRS, 284–328. Cf. DBW 13: 168, n. 5, in English.

135. NRS, 285–86. Cf. DBW 13: 178, n. 4, in English.

136. TF, 406–7 [see DBW 13: 178].

137. R. Rouse and S. C. Neill, *A History of the Ecumenical Movement 1917–1954* (London, 1954), 583.

138. W. Stapel, "Die politisierende ökumenische Weltkonferenz in Fanö," *Deutsches Volkstum*, no. 2 (September 1934).

139. Letter, 8.8.1934, TF, 406 [see DBW 13: 179].

140. TF, 406–7 [see DBW 13: 179].

141. NRS, 288 [see DBW 13: 186].

142. Letter to his grandmother, 19.8.1934, DBW 13: 187.

143. Minutes, meeting of the Council, Fanö (1934), 37.

144. DBW 13: 203.

145. Minutes, meeting of the Council, Fanö (1934), 50–52. See W. Birnbaum, "Kirchenkampf—Fanö Anno 34: Kritische Anmerkungen zu Marc Boegners Memoiren," *Welt und Wort*, vol. 26, no. 8 (August 1971), 404–11.

146. Minutes, meeting of the Council, Fanö (1934), 51–52.

147. Ibid., 51.

148. Ibid., 52f.

149. Ibid., 75.

150. Ibid., 60. Cf. DBW 13: 200, n. 8.

151. *The Times*, 7 September 1934.

152. *Junge Kirche* (1934), 704–5.

153. *Junge Kirche* (1934), 705, 750.

154. For example, W. Niemöller, *Kampf und Zeugnis* (1948), 254ff.

155. NRS, 294–95 [see DBW 13: 201–2, 202–3, in English].

156. TF, 141 [see DBW 14: 381].

157. DBW 13: 295–97 [English translation in GS 1: 444–46].

158. Letter, 10.8.1934, DBW 13: 184, n. 3.

159. Letter, 13.8.1934, NRS, 288 [see DBW 13: 184].

160. DBW 13: 181.

161. Minutes, meeting of the Council, Fanö (1934), 31.

162. Letter, 12.12.1933, FA 120/33, Ecumenical Archives, Geneva, "General Church Struggle 1933."

163. Minutes, meeting of the Council, Fanö (1934), 39.

164. *World Alliance Handbook* (1935), 46.

165. G. F. Allen, in *The Church in Action*, no. 6 (Oxford), 2.

166. TF, 227–29 [see DBW 13: 298–301; 302–5, in English; 298, n. 1].

167. The manuscript of this sermon no longer exists.

168. NRS, 343–44 [see DBW 12: 316; DBW 14: 398–99]. See also Bonhoeffer's lecture course "Das Wesen der Kirche" (1932), DBW 11: 286–87, on the concept of "council."

169. TF, 228 [see DBW 13: 301].

170. TF, 228 [see DBW 13: 300].

171. TF, 228 [see DBW 13: 299–300].

172. O. Dudzus, "Stopping the Wheel," IKDB, 90.

173. R. Rouse and S. C. Neill, *History of the Ecumenical Movement*, 583.

174. As related by W. Maechler, "Vom Pazifisten zum Widerstandskampfer: Bonhoeffers Kampf für die Entrechteten," MW 1: 92.

175. NRS, 292–94.

176. DBW 13: 196, n. 19.

177. Minutes, meeting of the Council, Fanö (1934), 39. Cf. DBW 13: 197.

178. Cf. Memorandum to T. de Félice 29.1.1935, DBW 13: 278–79.

179. DBW 13: 278.

180. Minutes, meeting of the Council, Fanö (1934); see DBW 13: 200–201.

181. DBW 13: 200.

182. Related by J. Lasserre, 17.12.1965. For more on Bruay see MW 5: 237 [see DBW 13: 202, 208].

183. Hildebrandt and Bell met on 15 October 1934; see A. Lindt, *Briefwechsel* (1969), 157–58.

184. Letter, 24.10.1934, in English, NRS, 277–78 [see DBW 13: 211].

185. The date of the plebiscite was 13 January 1935.

186. J. Beckmann, ed., *Kirchliches Jahrbuch 1933–1944*, 77.

187. St. Paul's, Sydenham, St. Mary's, St. George's, the Hamburg Church (all in London); Hull, Liverpool, South Shields, Newcastle. There are forty-four signatures, twenty-four of them from Bonhoeffer's and Rieger's parishes; see DBW 13: 220, cf. 215.

188. Letter, 17.11.1934, DBW 13: 236.

189. DBW 13: 220–21.

190. DBW 13: 222–23.

191. DBW 13: 241–43.

192. For full text see DBW 13: 223–24.

193. DBW 13: 224, 225.

194. Ibid., 225.

195. MW 5: 152; cf. DBW 13: 247, and n. 10.

196. DBW 13: 231–34. For the vigorous argument in the correspondence between Bonhoeffer and Rössler that followed, see DBW 13: 237–41, 253–56.

197. DBW 14: 43.

198. DBW 13: 234.

199. DBW 13: 246–49.

200. Cf. A. Freudenberg, "Visits to Geneva," IKDB, 166 [see DBW 13: 250–53].

201. DBW 14: 43.

202. Letter, 27.11.1934, DBW 13: 245.

203. DBW 13: 245–46.

204. *Gesetzblatt*, no. 70 (German Evangelical Church, 1934).

205. DBW 13: 257–58, 258–61.

206. This is in the letter to Baron Schroeder, president of the Association of Congregations, DBW 13: 257–58.

207. DBW 13: 259.

208. DBW 13: 261.

209. DBW 13: 230, 258.

210. Letter, 21.1.1935, DBW 13: 273–74.

211. DBW 13: 262–63.

212. Cf. DBW 13: 262, n. 1.

213. The complete minutes are in DBW 13: 263–65.

214. DBW 13: 265.

215. On sections II and V see also G. Niemöller, "Die deutschen evangelischen Gemeinden in London und der Kirchenkampf," *Evangelische Theologie,* vol. 3 (1959), 131–46.

216. DBW 13: 75.

217. TF, 412 [see DBW 13: 129].

218. TF, 420 [see DBW 13: 145–46].

219. WF, 119 [see DBW 14: 249].

220. TF, 229 [see DBW 13: 301].

221. ". . . expect a letter and invitation from him [Gandhi]," he said in a letter to R. Niebuhr, 13.7.1934, DBW 13: 171.

222. J. Rieger, "Contacts with London," IKDB, 95.

223. Letter, 22.10.1934, in English, NRS, 295–96 [see DBW 13: 210].

224. Letter, invitation from Mahatma Gandhi to Bonhoeffer, 1.11.1934, in *Collected Works of Mahatma Gandhi*, vol. 59 (1969), 273; see DBW 13: 213–14.

225. Letter to K.-F. Bonhoeffer, January 1934, DBW 13: 75.

226. DBW 13: 137.

227. Letter to J. Winterhager, May 1934, DBW 13: 148.

228. Letter to his grandmother, 22.5.1934, TF, 419–20 [see DBW 13: 145].

229. DBW 13: 150.

230. Communication to author from F. Hildebrandt [see DBW 13: 150, and n. 4].

231. Letter, 19.8.1934, DBW 13: 187.

232. TF, 412 [see DBW 13: 204–5].

233. DBW 13: 209, in English.

234. J. Rieger, "Contacts with London," IKDB, 9/f.

235. A postcard written, but not sent, to "Ernst," probably Ernst Cromwell, DBW 13: 285.

236. DBW 13: 278–79.

237. See DBW 14: 267–70.

238. DBW 13: 267–69.

239. A. Lindt, *Briefwechsel*, 185.

240. *Junge Kirche* (1935), 559–62.

241. Letter from D. Bonhoeffer to G. Bell, 7.1.1935, DBW 13: 268, in English.

242. Letter from F. Hildebrandt to Koch, 12.1.1935, DBW 13: 270–71.

243. According to J. Rieger's diary, DBW 13: 212–13.

244. GS 2: 198, in English. See also A. Lindt, *Briefwechsel*, 215.

245. DBW 13: 206.

246. K. Barth, "Die Kirche Jesu Christi," *Theologische Existenz Heute,* no. 5 (1933), 7f.

247. Letter, 15.5.1934, DBW 13:141, in English.

248. Letter, 12.7.1934, NRS, 277 [see DBW 13:168, in English].

Chapter 9. Preachers' Seminary: 1935

1. DBW 14: 97–98.

2. W. Rott, "Something Always Occurred to Him," IKDB, 132.

3. In his endeavor to give the work of the seminary an ecumenical orientation, Bonhoeffer arranged contacts for a visiting delegation from the Swedish church to make profitable use of this interval (cf. MW 5: 157–58). This plan was realized in a different form and under different circumstances in March 1936.

4. DBW 14: 45–46.

5. General military conscription had been introduced on 16 March 1935.

6. B. Riemer to E. Bethge, 27.8.1935.

7. See DBW 14: 166.

8. See *Dying We Live: The Final Messages and Records of the Resistance* (New York: Pantheon Books, 1956), 203ff.

9. DBW 13: 250.

10. From a duplicated copy in the possession of the author.

11. DBW 14: 79.

12. DBW 14: 369–77. See also G. Krause, "Bruderschaft und Kirche 1934–1936 in Pommern," in G. Sprondel, ed., *Zeugnis und Dienst: Beiträge zu Theologie und Kirche in Geschichte und Gegenwart. Günther Besch zum 70. Geburtstag* (1974), 101.

13. DBW 14: 878–904.

14. Letter, 30.8.1935, DBW 14: 74.

15. DBW 14: 75.

16. DBW 14: 851–60.

17. W. Niemöller's diary on the meeting in Dahlem, in W. Niemöller, *Aus dem Leben eines Bekenntnispfarrers* (1961), 145.

18. DBW 14: 66–68.

19. NRS, 297–98 [see DBW 14: 65].

20. *Wort der 3. pommerschen Bekenntnissynode an unsere jungen Theologen.* Landeskirchlichen Archiv der Evangelischen Kirche Westfalens, Bielefeld, Nachlass Wilhelm Niemöller (5, 1).

21. See the confirmation address, TF, 294ff. [see DBW 14: 476–81, 482].

22. H. von Petersdorff, *Kleist-Retzow: Ein Lebensbild* (1907).

23. NRS, 308–25, excerpted in TF, 149–52 [see DBW 14: 399–421].

24. WF, 57–61 [see DBW 14: 945–50].

25. H. Asmussen, *Ordnung des Gottesdienstes* (1936).

26. Bonhoeffer did not himself put this remark in writing. See H. Traub, "Two Recollections," IKDB, 156.

27. BWP, 168–75 [see DBW 14: 495–99; DBW 5: 38–53].

28. BWP, 142ff. [see DBW 14: 510–13].

29. DBW 11: 427.

30. DBW 14: 324, 325, n. 25. Cf. DBW 14: 489–90, n. 39.

31. BWP, 140ff; also NRS, 308, 315f. [see DBW 14: 399–400, 408–11, 483–85].

32. DBW 14: 481.

33. DBW 14: 482.

34. BWP, 127–28 [see DBW 14: 502–7].

35. Cf. DBW 14: 507, n. 105.

36. DBW 14: 487, 325, 490, 491.

37. Cf. DBW 14: 307–16.

38. DBW 14: 316–21.

39. DBW 14: 307–9.

40. NRS, 326ff. [see DBW 14: 378–99].

41. WF, 75ff. [see DBW 14: 655–80].

42. Karl Barth also used this pair of concepts in 1934; cf. "Gottes Wille und unsere Wünsche," in *Theologische Existenz Heute,* no. 7 (1934), 16–30.

43. DBW 14: 310–16.

44. See K. Barth, *Church Dogmatics* I/1, 103–4.

45. DBW 14: 314–15.

46. DBW 14: 315, n. 54.

47. DBW 14: 293; DBW 16: 71.

48. Cf. DBW 14: 321, n. 31.

49. DBW 14: 321.

50. WF, 118 [see DBW 14: 238]. The reference is to M. Schneckenburger, *Vergleichende Darstellung des lutherischen und reformierten Lehrbegriffs* (1855).

51. DBW 14: 98.

52. DBW 4: 29.

53. CD, 48–56 [see DBW 4: 33–43].

54. Regarding the first lecture see CD, 63 [see DBW 4: 52]. On the rich young man see CD, 70–71 [see DBW 4: 59–65].

55. See CD, 64–68 [see DBW 4: 53–57, 57–59].

56. CD [Cf. DBW 4: 191, n. 28].

57. "I'm currently working on a manuscript that deals with the question of the Sermon on the Mount, etc.," he wrote to R. Niebuhr on 13 July 1934, DBW 13: 171.

58. See K. Barth, *Church Dogmatics* IV/2, 533.

59. NRS, 42ff. [see DBW 14: 422–34].

60. Cf. DBW 4: 12, foreword.

61. This was Bonhoeffer's inscription in the copy given to E. Bethge.

62. DBW 15: 15.

63. DBW 15: 21.

64. Letter, 3.1.1938, DBW 15: 22–23.

65. WF, 199; TF, 443 [see DBW 14: 146–50, 81–83].

66. DBW 16: 102.

67. Letter, 19.9.1936, WF, 116; TF, 430 [see DBW 14: 235–36].

68. Letter, 14.10.1936, WF, 119–21 [see DBW 14: 250, 252].

69. K. Barth, *Church Dogmatics* IV/2, 533.

70. "Our Way according to the Testimony of Scripture" (1938), WF, 178 [see DBW 15: 414].

71. CD, 63 [see DBW 4: 52].

72. CD, 278 [see DBW 4: 275].

73. CD, 65 [see DBW 4: 54].

74. LPP, 123 [see DBW 8: 179].

75. CD, 242 [see DBW 4: 233].

76. CD, 186 [see DBW 4: 181].

77. CD, 393 [see DBW 4: 303].

78. DBW 15: 371–406.

79. CD, 62ff. [see DBW 4: 53–56].

80. Cf. DBW 6: 137–62.

81. Second Sunday in Advent 1943, LPP, 157 [see DBW 8: 226].

82. H. Müller, *Von der Kirche zur Welt* (1961), 20, 38, 197ff.

83. LPP, 369 [see DBW 8: 542].

84. NRS, 45 [see DBW 10: 332].

85. DBW 12: 233–34.

86. In Barcelona, TF, 381 [see DBW 10: 91–92]; also AB (DBWE 2), 157–61.

87. CF (DBWE 3), 88–91, 113, 135, 140 [see DBW 3: 82–86, 105, 127, 130].

88. AB (DBWE 2), 94.

89. Cf. DBW 11: 285; DBW 12: 234.

90. DBW 13: 344–46.

91. DBW 13: 129.

92. In his dissertation, "Christus als Vorbild und Versöhner: Eine kritische Studie zum Problem des Verhältnisses von Gesetz und Evangelium im Werke Sören Kierkegaards" (Humboldt University, Berlin 1968), Traugott Vogel explored traces of Kierkegaard in Bonhoeffer's *Cost of Discipleship*. He discovered Kierkegaardian formulations that are not present in the edition of Kierkegaard (Schrempf) that Bonhoeffer had used earlier. He concluded that Bonhoeffer might have read them in the von Kütemeyer edition of Kierkegaard's journal writings, "Der Einzelne und die Kirche: Über Luther und dem Protestantismus" (1934). This volume is part of Bonhoeffer's library, and the terminology that Vogel detected is, in fact, underlined by Bonhoeffer: for example, the statement about the necessary situations for belief (Kütemeyer, 152, 159), Luther's talk of grace after twenty years of fasting and self-mortification (153), and the concept of "results" (182).

93. Winter 1932–1933, PTB, 40ff. [see DBW 12: 237–76]; see also "Die Kirche vor der Judenfrage" (April 1933), NRS, 223–24 [see DBW 12: 351–53].

94. Especially characteristic is "Dein Reich Komme" ("Thy Kingdom Come"), PTB, 27ff. [see DBW 12: 264–78].

95. DBW 14: 257.

96. LPP, 369 [see DBW 8: 542].

97. Letter from Professor Baumgärtel, GS 4: 339.

98. WF, 30 [see DBW 14: 76].

99. DBW 10: 378–80.

100. On 14 September 1933 (!), W. Stählin had urged Bonhoeffer to attend a meeting in Marburg of the Berneucher, to consider "plans for a cloistered community" ("disciplined community life," "physical work," "a ritualistic life with the practice of meditation"). At that time however, it sounded to Bonhoeffer like too much emphasis on a working community and too little on the Sermon on the Mount. Stählin wrote: "To reach an agreement with you on working together personally with young people would be much more important for me than this church politics." See DBW 12: 131–32.

101. Letter, May 1934, DBW 13: 148.

102. Letter, 14.1.1935, DBW 13: 272–73.

103. DBW 13: 129.

104. TF, 412 [see DBW 13: 204].

105. DBW 13: 178–79.

106. See A. Lindt, *Briefwechsel,* 162; DBW 14: 39.

107. WF, 57 [see DBW 14: 945–50].

108. DBW 5: 69–73.

109. Letter to K. Barth, 19.9.1936, TF, 431 [see DBW 14: 237–38].

110. Application, 17.11.1935, TF, 262f. [see DBW 14: 910–11].

111. WF, 29ff. [see DBW 14: 75–80].

112. DBW 14: 76.

113. Letter to W. Staemmler, 27.6.1936, DBW 14: 175.

114. Cf. DBW 14: 80.

115. Application to the Old Prussian Council of Brethren, WF, 33 [see DBW 14: 80].

116. WF, 31 [see DBW 14: 77].

117. DBW 5: 13–102.

118. WF, 57ff. [see DBW 14: 945–50].

119. "Der Morgen," DBW 14: 871–75.

120. BWP, 134ff. [see DBW 14: 480–81].

121. Cf. DBW 14: 516.

122. DBW 14: 516–17.

123. Letter to E. Sutz, 11.9.1934, TF, 412 [see DBW 13: 205].

124. Letter to E. Sutz, 24.10.1936, TF, 413f. [see DBW 14: 256].

125. Letter to E. Bethge 31.7.1936, DBW 14: 210.

126. DBW 14: 111, 112.

127. Letter, 25.1.1936, DBW 14: 106–7, 221.

128. TP, 71, 74f., 89, 105 [see DBW 16: 73–74, 76, 102, 128, 198].

129. Cf. DBW 14: 39.

130. Statement, 27.6.1935, DBW 14: 47–49.

131. Minutes, first meeting of the ecumenical council of the Provisional Church Administration, 27. 6.1935, MW 5: 243.

132. GS 1: 227; cf. MW 5: 242–43.

133. Letter to church president Karl Koch, 4.6.1935, DBW 14: 41–44.

134. DBW 14: 41.

135. Minutes, first meeting of the ecumenical council of the Provisional Church Administration, 27. 6.1935, MW 5: 243.

136. MW 5: 243–44.

137. NRS, 326 [see DBW 14: 378–99].

138. See GS 2: 199, in English.

139. DBW 14: 42.

140. DBW 14: 66–68.

141. Minutes, meeting of the executive committee, Chamby, 18–22.8.1935, 45.

142. The written instructions to issue the invitation came from Bell to Henriod, 24 June 1935; cf. DBW 14: 46.

143. DBW 13: 278–79.

144. H. L. Henriod, *The Joint Ecumenical Youth Commission: How and Why It Came to Be* (Geneva, 1936), 8.

145. Ibid.

146. Minutes, Chamby meeting, 53, 72.

147. Letter from Espy to Bonhoeffer, 13.4.1936. Cf. letter from Espy to Bonhoeffer, 7.5.1936, DBW 14: 153–55.

148. Information supplied by A. Boyens on the basis of the Life and Work archives, Geneva, 23.12.1965.

149. Letter from Schönfeld to Gerstenmaier, 2.6.1936, DBW 14: 164–65.

150. Minutes, Chamby meeting, 45, 48.

151. Ibid., 56.

152. Ibid.

153. DBW 14: 51, n. 1.

154. Letter, 22.6.1935, DBW 14: 52, n. 5.

155. NRS, 137–38 [see DBW 11: 328].

156. Letter from Hodgson to Bonhoeffer, 9.7.1935, DBW 14: 52, in English.

157. DBW 14: 53–56, in English.

158. DBW 14: 55.

159. DBW 14: 56.

160. DBW 14: 56–57.

161. DBW 14: 59.

162. Ibid.

163. DBW 14: 60, in English.

164. NRS, 326–44, excerpted in TF, 140–48 [see DBW 14: 378–99].

165. TF, 140 [see DBW 14: 378–79].

166. Ibid.

167. DBW 14: 379.

168. DBW 14: 381.

169. DBW 14: 382.

170. DBW 14: 383.

171. Ibid.

172. DBW 14: 384.

173. DBW 14: 385 [see TF, 143–44].

174. DBW 14: 387 [see NRS, 333].

175. DBW 14: 388 [see NRS, 334].

176. DBW 14: 389 [see NRS, 334].

177. DBW 14: 393.

178. DBW 14: 396. [see NRS, 341].

179. Ibid.

180. DBW 14: 397 [see NRS, 342; TF, 147].

181. DBW 14: 398.

182. DBW 14: 399 [see NRS, 344; TF, 147–48].

183. Armin Boyens further points out that W. A. Visser 't Hooft, in a paper written for the Oxford conference ("Die Kirche als ökumenische Gemeinschaft" in *Die Kirche und ihr Dienst in der Welt* [1937], 79–96), "plainly draws on the questions raised by Bonhoeffer" even though his understandable reluctance to make mention of German writers in the Confessing church precluded any personal reference to Bonhoeffer. But at the time even Visser 't Hooft's "thoughts on the 'Church in the Churches' attracted no attention." They were not taken up until 1948 in Amsterdam, where Visser 't Hooft cited only three theologians who had been important for his ecclesiological position: Karl Barth, Dietrich Bonhoeffer, and William Temple [letter from A. Boyens to E. Bethge, 7.7.1966].

184. CD, 173ff. [see DBW 4: 167–75].

185. See W. Niemöller, *Kampf und Zeugnis der Bekennenden Kirche* (1948), 289.

186. Ibid., 455–56.

187. See W. Niesel, *Um Verkündigung und Ordnung der Kirche*, 20.

188. DBW 14: 875 77.

189. DBW 14: 88.

Chapter 10. Finkenwalde: 1936–1937

1. TF, 166 [see DBW 14: 676].

2. See W. Niemöller, *Kampf und Zeugnis*, 303f.; G. Niemöller, *Die erste. Bekenntnissynode der Deutschen Evangelischen Kirche zu Barmen*, vol. 1 (1959), 233ff.

3. DBW 14: 101–2.

4. H. Brunotte, "Antwort auf den 'Osnabrücker Aufruf' vom 10.12.35," in G. Niemöller, *Die erste Bekenntnissynode,* 206.

5. DBW 14: 103–4.

6. Letter, 29.2.1936, from the Provincial Council of Brethren of Saxony to its candidates for the ministry.

7. Cf. DBW 14: 105, n. 1.

8. Based on Bonhoeffer's handwritten notes entitled "From Barmen to Oeynhausen," cf. DBW 14: 597–601.

9. DBW 14: 106–12.

10. DBW 14: 107–8, 110–11.

11. DBW 14: 108.

12. DBW 14: 930–31.

13. DBW 14: 937.

14. DBW 14: 930–45.

15. J. Beckmann, ed., *Kirchliches Jahrbuch 1933–1944,* 107–8.

16. Letter from E. Bethge to G. Vibrans, 21.1.1936.

17. Cf. DBW 14: 108.

18. DBW 14: 109–10.

19. WF, 127 [see DBW 14: 263].

20. DBW 14: 655–80.

21. Letter to Lic. G. Koch, 8.12.1935; see W. Niemöller, *Die Evangelische Kirche im Dritten Reich,* 181.

22. Finkenwalde newsletter, 22.7.1936, DBW 14: 200.

23. A. Schönherr, Finkenwalde newsletter, 15.1.1936, GS 2: 464.

24. Cf. DBW 14: 104–5.

25. DBW 14: 920–25.

26. TF, 270 [see DBW 14: 924].

27. LPP, 129, 39 [see DBW 8: 187].

28. DBW 14: 115–16.

29. DBW 14: 118.

30. WF, 40 [see DBW 14: 124].

31. DBW 14: 118–20, 132.

32. DBW 14: 132–33.

33. *Junge Kirche,* vol. 4, no. 9 (1936), 420–26.

34. DBW 14: 121.

35. DBW 14: 125.

36. DBW 14: 142–43.

37. DBW 14:167.

38. Cf. DBW 14: 125.

39. MW 5: 185.

40. DBW 14: 126.

41. *Junge Kirche,* vol. 9 (1936), 420.

42. Cf. DBW 14: 155–56.

43. DBW 14: 159–60.

44. Newsletter, 22.5.1936.

45. MW 5: 196.

46. DBW 14: 290.

47. WF, 54; GS 2: 474.

48. Minutes, meeting of the World Alliance management committee, Chamby (1936), 46.

49. DBW 14: 103.

50. Cf. DBW 14: 214.

51. DBW 14: 213–14.

52. DBW 14: 248.

53. DBW 14: 930–45; 655–80.

54. DBW 14: 954–69; 786–819.

55. DBW 14: 829–43.

56. Cf. DBW 14: 292–93.

57. DBW 15: 371–406.

58. Cf. DBW 14: 314.

59. DBW 14: 102.

60. WF, 39 [see DBW 14: 122].

61. WF, 40 [see DBW 14: 124–25].

62. DBW 14: 659–60.

63. DBW 14: 109–10.

64. WF, 93 [see DBW 14: 676].

65. Ibid.

66. DBW 14: 676–77, n. 45.

67. Letter, 17.8.1936.

68. That is, to the Council of Brethren; letter from Bonhoeffer to E. Bethge, 11.7.1936, DBW 14: 187.

69. Letter to the members of Finkenwalde, 22.7.1936, DBW 14: 201.

70. TF, 143 [see DBW 14: 383].

71. Letter, 19.9.1936, WF, 118 [see DBW 14: 238].

72. W. Elert spoke of "Bonhoeffer's blasphemous words in which he makes our Lord God responsible for human action . . . with this [he] has left the church of the Reformation." In K. D. Schmidt, *Dokumente des Kirchenkampfes II*, Dokument 306, 885.

73. Letter, 24.10.1936, TF, 414 [see DBW 14: 257].

74. DBW 14: 679.

75. See letter to G. Vibrans, DBW 14: 191–93.

76. H. Sasse "Wider das Schwärmertum," in *Allgemeine Evangelische Lutherische Kirchenzeitung*, vol. 69, no. 33 (1936), col. 780.

77. Related by H. Gollwitzer in a letter to E. Wolf, 21.8.1936.

78. Here follow some sentences from Bonhoeffer's essay that describe the Confessing church as the true church in Germany.

79. In the preceding text it had been argued that even Bavaria, for example, held this view.

80. "Kirche oder Gruppe? Ein Briefwechsel v. Rat der Evangelischen Bekenntnissynode im Rheinland" (1936), 19, 23–27. Peter Brunner, who drew up this position, says of his authorship (20.6.1965): "Section I (pp. 22–mid 27) may be from me—with the exception of a very slight revision and a few insertions. The same is true of Section IV (p. 30f.), except for the conclusion beginning on the middle of p. 31. In sections II and III (pp. 27–30) I suspect a greater expansion of my draft. Here I find it difficult to pick out the parts that were most likely to have derived from my formulations. . . . Where necessary, I could prove with certainty that I represented the factual theological contents after pp. 23ff. in the Rhinish Council. I can also recall that I wrote what was on mid-page 25 ("Before we continue . . .").

81. DBW 14: 700–701.

82. WF, 86f. [see DBW 14: 668].

83. *Evangelische Theologie* (October 1936), 398–405. WF, 97–106 [see DBW 14: 691–700]. For Gollwitzer's article see DBW 14: 680–91.

84. Letter, 10.2.1937.

85. WF, 110 [see DBW 14: 696].

86. DBW 14: 924.

87. A. Schönherr in the Finkenwalde newsletter; cf. DBW 14: 31.

88. DBW 14: 708–9.

89. Ibid., 930–35.

90. *Junge Kirche* (1936), 64–69, 157–61, 197–203; see DBW 14: 878–904.

91. DBW 14: 904, n. 97.

92. Ibid., 185–86.

93. F. Baumgärtel, *Die Kirche ist Eine—die alttestamentliche jüdische Kirche und die Kirche Jesu Christi? Eine Verwahrung gegen die Preisgabe des Alten Testaments* (1936).

94. *Das Evangelische Westfalen* (September 1936), 142.

95. See GS 4: 336–43.

96. Letter from Baumgärtel to Baumann, GS 2: 339.

97. On this matter see the instructive dissertation by Martin Kuske available in English: *The Old Testament As the Book of Christ: An Appraisal of Bonhoeffer's Interpretation* (Philadelphia: Westminster Press, 1976).

98. Proclamation in the Finkenwalde newsletter, 22.7.1936, DBW 14: 204.

99. DBW 14: 195–96.

100. GS 2: 466.

101. From the Finkenwalde newsletter, 22.7.1936, DBW 14: 195–96.

102. Baumann to Baumgärtel, 26.10.1936, GS 4: 242.

103. For text and further details see W. Niemöller, *Die Bekennende Kirche sagt Hitler die Wahrheit* (1954). Also J. Beckmann, ed., *Kirchliches Jahrbuch 1948*, 130ff.

104. Forty-ninth Occasional Letter, exclusively for members of Confessing congregations (Rhineland Evangelical Confessing synod, 2 March 1936), 23.

105. W. Niemöller, *Die Bekennende Kirche sagt Hitler die Wahrheit,* 45.

106. From the Finkenwalde newsletter, 22.7.1936, DBW 14: 200.

107. Letter, 28.7.1936, DBW 14: 207.

108. Cf. the session of the Reich Council of Brethren, 29.10.1936; W. Niemöller, *Die Bekennende Kirche sagt Hitler die Wahrheit,* 48.

109. In October 1933 he succeeded F. Hildebrandt in his pastorate in Klein-Machnower.

110. Letter, 18.11.1935, DBW 14: 100.

111. DBW 14: 189.

112. Communication to author from Werner Koch, 12.7.1948.

113. WF, 74. Cf. DBW 14: 217.

114. Letter to E. Bethge, 6.8.1936, DBW 14: 216; also Bishop Bell's letter to *The Times,* 4.8.1936.

115. Letter to E. Bethge, 23.7.1936, DBW 14: 204; cf. 193–94.

116. The date of announcement was still uncertain.

117. Letter, 6.8.1936, WF, 74 [see DBW 14: 215].

118. Cf. DBW 14: 229, n. 6.

119. Communication to author from A. Boyens, 30.8.1965.

120. See Finkenwalde newsletter, 22.9.1936.

121. WF, 72 [see DBW 14: 189–90].

122. Letter to E. Bethge, 23.7.1936, DBW 14: 205.

123. *Christliche Welt,* no. 16 (1936). See WF, 73 [see DBW 14: 720, n. 37].

124. WF, 73–74, excerpt [see DBW 14: 216–17].

125. See the notes taken while Bonhoeffer repeated this lecture at Finkenwalde, DBW 14: 714–20.

126. DBW 14: 720, n. 37.

127. Cf. DBW 14: 77.

128. Cf. DBW 14: 1068–70, appendix.

129. WF, 161, 162 [see DBW 14: 199, 201–3].

130. Newsletter, 24.6.1936, DBW 14: 169.

131. GS 2: 503.

132. TF, 457–58 [sec DBW 16: 321, 373].

133. WF, 66 [see DBW 14: 166, n. 3; 183–84; 199].

134. Cf. DBW 14: 175–79.

135. Cf. DBW 14: 218–19.

136. Cf. DBW 14: 264, 270.

137. DBW 14: 265.

138. Letter, 9.12.1938, DBW 15: 89–90.

139. DBW 14: 212.

140. L. Müller, *Deutsche Gottesworte* (1936), 9, 17.

141. BWP, 165 [see DBW 14: 514].

142. BWP, 165–68 [see DBW 14: 513–17].

143. WF, 62 [see DBW 14: 76].

144. BWP, 166–67 [see DBW 14: 515–16].

145. DBW 14: 514.

146. Cf. DBW 14: 171–73.

147. He means, for example, Bible reading during home visits.

148. WF, 62 [see DBW 14: 195].

149. LPP, 279 [see DBW 8: 405].

150. Letter from O. Dudzus to Bonhoeffer, 11.1.1939, DBW 15: 106.

151. Cf. DBW 14: 203–4.

152. DBW 14: 161.

153. Letter to H. L. Henriod, 16.6.1936; EZA Berlin (previously Kirchliche Hochschule Berlin, Kirchenkampfarchiv, file no. 260, 49).

154. The English original in the archives in Geneva says "ecclesiastical authority"; characteristically, at the time it was translated for the Provisional Church Administration in Berlin as "spiritual authority."

155. From a copy of the translation of Henriod's letter from the files of the Provisional Administration.

156. Information supplied by A. Boyens from the archives of Life and Work, Geneva, 30.8.1965.

157. Letter from Bishop Bell to Bishop Eidem, 8.9.1936.

158. See minutes, Chamby meeting, 2, 4.

159. For months church president Koch had tried to cooperate with the committees in Westphalia, but this was now over; cf. DBW 14: 217, 222.

160. Letter to M. Niemöller, 12.8.1936, DBW 14: 224–25.

161. Letter from Bishop Bell to Bishop Eidem, 8.9.1936.

162. MW 2: 171.

163. Minutes, Chamby meeting, 67.

164. From Zoellner's speech on 25.8.1936; see MW 5: 252–53.

165. Minutes, Chamby meeting, 69.

166. Letter, 19.9.1936, DBW 14: 239–40.

167. WF, 115ff. [see DBW 14: 234–39].

168. Zentralarchiv, Berlin: Archive Deutsche Evangelische Kirche, Kirchliches Aussenamt 4942/36, 28.9.1936.

169. Cf. DBW 14: 232.

170. Letter from H. Schönfeld, 12.12.1933.

171. In addition to the "scholarly works" mentioned by Heckel in his report, there were also Gerstenmaier's own theological studies. Before beginning work in Heckel's office—incidentally, at a time when hostility between Heckel and Bonhoeffer was at its height—Gerstenmaier completed his doctorate under Brunstäd with his work "Creation and Revelation: A Systematic Investigation of a Theology of the First Article," in which he examined such questions as creation and people [*Volk*] in accordance with his teacher's decidedly anti-Barthian ideas. He incorporated parts of this dissertation in an extensive book, *Die Kirche und die Schöpfung*, which was completed in November 1937 and published by Furche-Verlag in 1938. In it he cites with approval passages from Althaus like "The self-contained we-consciousness

of a people [*Volk*] is not the product of the sum of a number of individuals but is an underived primal creation" [dissertation, 65, n. 1, quoted in *Die Kirche und die Schöpfung*, 78, n. 1). He then expounds upon these ideas: "[The] disturbance of structure to which the makeup of a community succumbs in history . . . does not mean the differences in essence among peoples and races, or the individual characteristics of the respective communal aspects, but their confusion and mixture—the negative intersection between them, which leads to degeneracy. We must not only address the confusion of blood and race as structural disturbance, but also its historical and state-related nature that prevents the shared unfolding of a unified sense of community and shared individuality [*Volksindividualität*], by entirely or partly submitting the power of one of their creaturely/historical characteristics to a threatening foreign state." He adds: "We may consider, for example, the plight of German racial groups [*Volksgruppen*] under a foreign policy, struggling for their existence— for their inherited creation" [dissertation, 67, or in *Die Kirche und die Schöpfung*, 89]. Later we read: "Wherever there is a struggle for those things created by God, for their existence the church must bless the weapons and join in the struggle" and, as a corollary, the observation: "This holds true particularly with regard to the politicoracial attempts at reintegration that are concerned with the reestablishment of true community. . . ." [*Die Kirche und die Schöpfung*, 269f.]. Gerstenmaier's foreword to the book contains information on his sources and sponsors: "The broad perspective, in which the present struggle on the part of the communal structure of people and church for the very basis of their existence is offered, has provided the author with cosmopolitan impressions of the struggle abroad by German ethnic groups of foreign nationality and by the German Protestant diaspora. Not least, this perspective has provided impressions derived from research work in the ecumenical movement as well as from church affairs abroad." After thanking his Rostock teacher he also thanks "no less the Director of the Foreign Office of the German Evangelical Church, Bishop Dr. Theodor Heckel, whose ideas and sharing of the most valuable impressions contributed very fundamentally to the development of this work."

172. WF, 147ff. [see DBW 14: 280–82].

173. Cf. Minutes, Chamby meeting, 68–69.

174. Provisional Administration report II D, 3, 3803/36, 13.11.1936.

175. The conference was at La Borcarderie from 8 to 15 September 1936 on "Christian Youth and the Way to Peace."

176. DBW 14: 239.

177. GS 1: 271–72, in English.

178. Ibid., 272, in English.

179. WF, 134. Cf. DBW 14: 271.

180. WF, 135–37. Cf. DBW 14: 275–76, in English.

181. WF, 134 [see DBW 14: 271].

182. This letter dated 24 March 1937 from Bonhoeffer to Henriod was found by A. Boyens in the Geneva archives; it is reproduced in full in DBW 14: 277–80.

183. Letter from C. von Dietze, 19.4.1969.

184. DBW 14: 283, in English.

185. From the "Bericht über das III. Ökumenische Seminar vom 28. Juli bis 14. August 1936 in Genf," written by "Herr Dozent Lic. Meinhold from Kiel" to the Reich Ministry of Education (copied from the files of the Ministry for Religious Affairs, no. 2931, IX 06).

186. Copied in the DEK archives in Hannover, file C-I-IV, with the entry number of the Reich Ministry of Education, registered in the files of the Ministry for Religious Affairs together with the above-mentioned paper by Lic. Meinhold.

187. Ibid., G I 20043/37.

188. Even after 1945 Menn and Schönfeld never mentioned the Confessing church in their articles about the relationship of the German Evangelical Church and the ecumenical movement. (Menn in *Kirchliches Jahrbuch* [1950]; Schönfeld in *Ordnung Gottes und Unordnung der Welt* [1948].)

189. GS 2: 505.

190. Letter to *The Times*, 27.3.1937, in English. Cf. DBW 14: 276, n. 2.

191. WF, 129ff. [see DBW 14: 267–70].

192. GS 2: 514.

193. TF, 436 [see DBW 14: 260].

194. *Zeitschrift für Elektrochemie,* vol. 62, 223.

195. He had already helped out on 4 July and remained after Hildebrandt emigrated.

196. As in the Finkenwalde newsletter.

197. Letter to Ruth Roberta Stahlberg, n.d., DBW 16: 25.

198. J. Zutt in *Der Nervenarzt*, vol. 20, no. 6 (1949), 242f.

199. DBW 14: 779.

200. DBW 14: 783.

201. Ibid.

202. Notes by J. Mickley. Candidates gave reports on Gogarten and Asmussen. Cf. DBW 14: 778, n. 1.

203. TF, 436 [see DBW 14: 261].

204. Cf. DBW 14: 845–49; 845, n. 49; 847, n. 60.

205. G. Ebeling, *Evangelische Evangelienauslegung: Eine Untersuchung zu Luthers Hermeneutik* (1942).

206. Letter, 24.10.1936, DBW 14: 257.

207. WF, 149ff. [see DBW 14: 829–43, 844].

208. WF, 160 [see DBW 14: 843].

209. H. Sasse, *Was heisst lutherisch?* (1936).

210. Quotations from Bonhoeffer's notes on Sasse's book.

211. WF, 118 [see DBW 14: 238].

212. Finkenwalde newsletter, 24.6.1937, DBW 14: 293.

213. DBW 16: 15–16, 17–18, 25–27, 35. Bonhoeffer's remarks are in DBW 15: 548–53.

214. Letter, 22.7.1936, WF, 64 [see DBW 14: 197].

215. TP, 71–72 [see DBW 16: 71].

216. Letter, 4.9.1936, GS 2: 503.

217. DBW 14: 222, 217.

218. W. Niemöller, *Kampf und Zeugnis der Bekennenden Kirche* (1948), 353.

219. Letter, 10.8.1936, DBW 14: 221–22.

220. Report of the Council of Brethren at the general assembly, enclosure to letter, 17.10.1936.

221. DBW 14: 700–713.

222. See G. Niemöller, *Die erste Bekenntnissynode der Deutschen Evangelischen Kirche zu Barmen*, vol. 1 (1959), 236.

223. W. Niesel, *Um Verkündigung und Ordnung der Kirche*, 23, 27.

224. DBW 14: 170–71; thus the three eastern seminaries protested against the silent transition to the church committees.

225. E. Bethge in the Finkenwalde newsletter; cf. DBW 14: 263.

226. W. Niemöller, *Kampf und Zeugnis der Bekennenden Kirche*, 380.

227. J. Beckmann, ed., *Kirchliches Jahrbuch 1933–1944*, 162.

228. Cf. E. Klügel, *Die lutherische Landeskirche Hannovers und ihr Bischof 1933–1945*, 503, appendix E: "Acts of coercion by state and party . . . towards pastors of the regional church of Hanover."

229. Communication to author from E. Rose.

230. DBW 16: 185.

231. TF, 471 [see DBW 15: 225–26].

232. Newsletter, 24.6.1937, DBW 14: 291–92.

233. DBW 14: 301.

234. See W. Niesel, *Um Verkündigung und Ordnung der Kirche*, 51–57.

235. DBW 15: 14.

236. W. Rott, "Something Always Occurred to Him," IKDB, 135.

237. W. Niemöller, *Die Evangelische Kirche im Dritten Reich*, 343 [see DBW 14: 298].

238. DBW 14: 299.

Chapter 11. The Collective Pastorates: 1938–1940

1. Letter, 1.10.1938.

2. Letter to J. Rieger, 4.10.1937, DBW 14: 300.

3. E. Bethge, 19.1.1940.

4. Letter to his parents, 29.1.1940, DBW 15: 289.

5. Letter to his parents, 14.2.1940, DBW 15: 291–92.

6. Letter to his parents, 27.2.1940, DBW 15: 293–94.

7. Letter to his parents, 6.3.1940, DBW 15: 295–96.

8. Letter from G. Lehne to Bonhoeffer, 2.2.1939, DBW 15: 129–30.

9. DBW 15: 48.

10. DBW 15: 72.

11. Letter to E. Sutz, 19.9.1938, DBW 15: 72.

12. Letter to P. Lehmann, 14.12.1938, DBW 15: 91.

13. Letter to J. Rieger, December 1938, DBW 15: 94.

14. H.-W. Jensen, "Life Together," IKDB, 152.

15. Letter, 29.11.1937, TF, 427 [see DBW 14: 303].

16. DBW 15: 33–34.

17. O. Dudzus, "Arresting the Wheel," IKDB, 82.

18. W. Niemöller, *Kampf und Zeugnis*, 437.

19. WF, 163 [see DBW 15: 38].

20. See J. Beckmann, ed., *Kirchliches Jahrbuch 1933–1944*, 237ff.

21. Ibid., 262.

22. DBW 15: 63.

23. See "Karl Barth zum Kirchenkampf," *Theologische Existenz Heute*, 79–83.

24. DBW 15: 50–57.

25. DBW 15: 56.

26. DBW 15: 56–57.

27. In its treatment of the loyalty oath issue.

28. DBW 15: 64, 66–67.

29. DBW 15: 69–70.

30. See G. Niemöller, *Die erste Bekennissynode der Deutschen Evangelischen Kirche zu Barmen*, vol. 1 (1959), 247–54.

31. Text according to J. Beckmann, ed., *Kirchliches Jahrbuch 1933–1944*, 265.

32. 20.10.1938; ibid., 265f.

33. Theophil Wurm, *Erinnerungen aus meinem Leben*, 2d ed. (1953), 147f.

34. G. Maltusch, "When the Synagogues Burned," IKDB, 150.

35. DBW 15: 81–84.

36. It is more probable that Bonhoeffer said so in 1935. See E. Bethge, "Das Erbe des Getöteten," IBF 3: 195–96.

37. W. Krause, in a letter from O. Kistner, January 1939, DBW 15: 123.

38. Letter from H. Hofmann, 3.2.1939, DBW 15: 134–35.

39. Letter from O. Kistner, January 1939, DBW 15: 122.

40. Letter from G. Krause, 18.2.1939, DBW 15: 151.

41. Newsletter about patience, 20.11.1938, TF, 443 [see DBW 15: 81–82].

42. Letter, 28.1.1939, TF, 427 [see DBW 15: 116–17].

43. Letter to the young brethren in Pomerania, TF, 437–42 [see DBW 15: 23–32, esp. 27].

44. *Gesetzblatt der Deutschen Evangelischen Kirche*, no. 3 (1938).

45. The Epiphany synod of 1939 therefore addressed a special message to the Westphalians; see W. Niesel, *Um Verkündigung und Ordnung der Kirche* (1949), 72–73.

46. Newsletter, 23.8.1938, DBW 15: 59.

47. Letter from F. Onnasch, 3.9.1938.

48. "Our Way according to the Testimony of Scripture," TF, 168ff. [see DBW 15: 407–31].

49. WF, 176–77 [see DBW 15: 411–12].

50. TF, 171 [see DBW 15: 419].

51. WF, 193 [see DBW 15: 430].

52. W. Niesel, *Um Verkündigung und Ordnung der Kirche*, 71.

53. Newsletter, 14.2.1939, DBW 15: 146–47.

54. DBW 15: 170–71.

55. This, for example, was what the Magdeburg consistory demanded of E. Bethge on 13 March 1939.

56. Letter from E. Bethge to the consistory of the province of Saxony, 17.3.1939.

57. Newsletter from W. Staemmler, 2.5.1939.

58. "Our Way according to the Testimony of Scripture," TF, 168ff. [see DBW 15: 407–31].

59. Letter from R. Lynker, 3.2.1939, DBW 15: 137.

60. DBW 15: 143.

61. Newsletter from W. de Boor and G. Sass, 13.2.1939, DBW 15: 138–45, esp. 144–45.

62. DBW 15: 430, n. 108.

63. Letter, 18.2.1939, DBW 15: 150–54.

64. Letter from F. Onnasch, 24 and 28.1.1939.

65. Letter, 16.2.1939.

66. Minutes, by A. Ohnesorge, 19–20.2.1939.

67. Ibid.

68. Letter from F. Onnasch, 1.3.1939.

69. Minutes, by A. Ohnesorge, 19–20.2.1939.

70. DBW 15: 499–535.

71. DBW 15: 530.

72. H. Traub, "Two Recollections," IKDB, 157.

73. Cf. DBW 16: 506–35.

74. This referred to "Church and State," and the letter to Hromádka.

75. *Christianity and Crisis*, vol. 5, no. 2 (1945), 6.

76. See Christine von Dohnanyi's notes on the Zossen files, in appendix 1 of this volume. See also H. O. Deutsch, *Verschwörung gegen den Krieg* (1969), 309–24.

77. Letter from Gross-Schlönwitz, 29.6.1938, DBW 15: 41.

78. See the "Hossbach-Protokoll," in W. Hofer, *Der Nationalsozialismus: Dokumente 1933–1945* (1957), 193–96.

79. Related by Christine von Dohnanyi, 1945.

80. Letter, 23.1.1939, DBW 15: 115.

81. Related by Christine von Dohnanyi, 1945.

82. W. Schellenberg, *Memoiren* (1956), 40–41.

83. H. Krausnick, in *Die Vollmacht des Gewissens* (1956), 315.

84. Parish minutes, St. George's Church, 72f.

85. H. Krausnick, *Die Vollmacht des Gewissens*, 365.

86. Paul von Hase's predecessor as city commandant was General Seifert; Witzleben's successor as commanding general of the Third Army Corps was a General Kurt Haase. Scholars, including Wheeler-Bennett, have often confused the two.

87. Communication to author from K. H. Reimer.

88. G. Reitlinger, *Die Endlösung* (1956), 9.

89. DBW 15: 62 and 63.

90. See the report by Marianne, eleven years of age at the time, in S. Leibholz-Bonhoeffer, *The Bonhoeffers: Portrait of a Family* (Chicago, 1994), 113–16.

91. Letter, 10.11.1938, DBW 15: 77–78.

92. DBW 15: 124.

93. See E. Bethge, "Gegen den Strom der Zeit," from a correspondence between Lord Bishop of Chichester G. K. A. Bell and G. Leibholz during the war years, in *Die moderne Demokratie und ihr Recht: Festschrift für G. Leibholz*, ed. K. D. Bracher, C. Dawson, W. Geiger, and R. Smend (1966), 3ff.

94. Letter from E. Bethge, 21.8.1938.

95. Cf. DBW 15: 115.

96. DBW 15: 165–69.

97. Letter, n.d., "Saturday" from "Köslin," DBW 15: 169–70.

98. DBW 15: 72.

99. DBW 15: 90.

100. Letter from London, 25.3.1939, TF, 468 [see DBW 15: 160, in English].

101. Letter from R. Niebuhr to H. S. Leiper, DBW 15: 165, in English.

102. Letter, 15.6.1939, TF, 477 [see DBW 15: 187–88, in English].

103. LPP, 174, 272 [see DBW 8: 253, 391].

104. Letter, 25.3.1939, DBW 15: 158–61. Cf. TF, 467–68; GS 1: 400.

105. Letter, 13.4.1939, WF, 210 [see DBW 15: 164].

106. J. Rieger, "Contacts with London," IKDB, 100.

107. DBW 15: 157–58, 161–63.

108. TF, 468 [see DBW 15: 159].

109. WF, 208 [see DBW 15: 162, in English].

110. The letter is in the Ecumenical Archives, Geneva.

111. WF, 205 [see DBW 15: 159, in English].

112. Letter, 31.3.1939, MW 5: 258.

113. Letter, 1.4.1939, MW 5: 258–59.

114. Letter, 3.4.1939, MW 5: 259.

115. J. Beckmann, ed., *Kirchliches Jahrbuch*, 293ff.

116. A manifesto to the Christian churches, in the Ecumenical Archives, Geneva.

117. Letter to Bishop Bell, 25.3.1939, TF, 467 [see DBW 15: 158–59, in English].

118. W. A. Visser 't Hooft, *Zeugnis eines Boten* (1945), 6f.

119. R. Rouse and S. Neill, *A History of the Ecumenical Movement*, 707.

120. DBW 15: 165.

121. J. Beckmann, ed., *Kirchliches Jahrbuch*, 297.

122. *Junge Kirche*, no. 8 (1939), 309.

123. WF, 212f. [see DBW 15: 175–76].

124. J. Beckmann, ed., *Kirchliches Jahrbuch*, 300f.

125. Letter to E. Bethge, 4. and 6.6.1939, from London, WF, 213–14 [see DBW 15: 179, 182]. He was thinking of having Bethge come over later.

126. WF, 216 [see DBW 15: 217–19].

127. WF, 214–17, 227–42, 246–47 [see DBW 15: 217–40].

128. DBW 15: 173.

129. Letter, 31.5.1939, DBW 15: 178.

130. TF, 478 [see DBW 15: 189].

131. WF, 211–12 [see DBW 15: 167, in English].

132. WF, 227 [see DBW 15: 220].

133. TF, 469 [see DBW 15: 222–23].

134. TF, 477–79 [see DBW 15: 188–89, 192–93].

135. TF, 470 [see DBW 15: 224].

136. TF, 471 [see DBW 15: 227].

137. TF, 472 [see DBW 15: 228–29].

138. TF, 472–73 [see DBW 15: 229–30].

139. Letter, 22.6.1939. DBW 15: 194.

140. Bethge's italics, TF, 473 [see DBW 15: 230–31].

141. TF, 479 [see DBW 15: 210, in English].

142. DBW 15: 232.

143. TF, 474 [see DBW 15: 234].

144. TF, 575–76 [see DBW 15: 235–37].

145. DBW 15: 211.

146. TF, 476 [see DBW 15: 239].

147. TF, 476 [see DBW 15: 236].

148. WF, 225 [see DBW 15: 204–5].

149. DBW 15: 209.

150. Consisting of R. Niebuhr and P. Lehmann, DBW 15: 169.

151. DBW 15: 213, in English.

152. DBW 15: 211, in English.

153. WF, 246–47 [see DBW 15: 139–240].

154. TF, 477 [see DBW 15: 240].

155. During this period Bonhoeffer also spoke with the English writer W. H. Auden, who wrote the poem "Friday's Child" about Bonhoeffer, as Auden told Christoph von Dohnanyi.

156. TF, 470 [see DBW 15: 224].

157. TF, 470–71 [see DBW 15: 225].

158. NRS, 92–118 [see DBW 15: 431–60].

159. NRS, 101ff. [see DBW 15: 441–45].

160. NRS, 102 [see DBW 15: 441–42].

161. CD, 186, 215 [see DBW 4: 181, 206].

162. NRS, 102–3 [see DBW 15: 442–43].

163. NRS, 104–5 [see DBW 15: 444–45].

164. NRS, 117 [see DBW 15: 459].

165. NRS, 93 [see DBW 15: 433].

166. TF, 477, excerpt of DBW 15: 240.

167. Letter, 22.7.1939, WF, 248f. [see DBW 15: 253].

168. WF, 250 [see DBW 15: 260–61, in English].

169. W.-D. Zimmermann, in *Begegnungen mit Dietrich Bonhoeffer* (Munich, 1964), 6.

170. TF, 447 [see DBW 15: 271].

171. J. Wach, *Das Problem des Todes in der Philosophie unserer Zeit* (1934); F. Dehn, *Das Gespräch vom Tode* (1938); G. Barbarin, *Der Tod als Freund* (1937) (from the French, purchased by Bonhoeffer in 1939; see the quote from Montaigne on p. 46).

172. K. Bonhoeffer, *Lebenserinnerungen*, 120.

173. TF, 446 [see DBW 15: 270].

174. See *Vollmacht des Gewissens* (European Publications, 1956), 377.

175. W. Niemöller, *Die Evangelische Kirche im Dritten Reich*, 391.

176. *Daily Telegraph*, 3.11.1939.

177. Letter, 6.9.1939, DBW 15: 262.

178. DBW 15: 262, 264, 264–65.

179. Letter from Sigurdshof, 27.2.1940, DBW 15: 293.

180. DBW 15: 23.

181. *Meditating on the Word,* ed. and trans. David McI. Gracie (Cambridge, Mass.: Cowley Publications, 1986), 103–45 [see DBW 15: 499–535].

182. J. Beckmann and F. Linz, *Meine Worte werden nicht vergehen* (1940), 42–46; G. Eichholz, *Herr tue meine Lippen auf* (1941), 120ff., 124ff., 141ff., 145ff. [see DBW 15: 492–98, 554–77].

183. Bonhoeffer always offered short outlines for the candidates in his homiletics seminar.

184. Letter, 20.5.1940, DBW 16: 34.

185. Letter, 14.9.1940, DBW 16: 61.

186. Letter, 17.2.1941, DBW 16: 151.

187. Bonhoeffer's essays for the supplement are in DBW 15: 537–53 and DBW 16: 471–74, 475–81, 490–93. The correspondence with Baumann is in DBW 16: 15–16, 17–18, 25–27, 35.

188. See R. Rouse and S. Neill, *A History of the Ecumenical Movement*, 708f.; A. Johnson, *Eivind Berggrav* (1960), 110–14.

189. Cf. F. von Schlabrendorff, *Eugen Gerstenmaier im Dritten Reich* (1965), 26.

190. See G. Ritter, *Karl Goerdeler* (1954), 252.

191. General Church Institute in Sigtuna, to be set up by Dr. Nils Ehrenström, intended to "proceed in close association with German Protestantism."

192. Dr. Gerstenmaier, representative of the Church Foreign Affairs Office of the German Evangelical Church, report to the Department of Political Culture and Information of the Foreign Office on the journey from 27 September to 2 October 1939, 8. Cf. also the account in F. von Schlabrendorff's *Eugen Gerstenmaier im Dritten Reich*, 26.

193. Regarding the conspiracy in the winter of 1939–1940, see H. O. Deutsch's detailed study, *Verschwörung gegen den Krieg* (1969), particularly concerning the "X-Bericht" (X-report) and Groscurth's diaries.

194. L. Poijakov and J. Wulf, *Das Dritte Reich und seine Diener* (1956), 517.

195. On those proceedings see *Vollmacht des Gewissens*, 408ff.

196. Letter, 15.1.1940, DBW 15: 287.

197. H. O. Deutsch offers more exact details about the "X-Bericht" (X-report) in *Verschwörung gegen den Krieg*, 309–24.

198. U. von Hassell, *Vom anderen Deutschland* (1946), 124.

199. *Vollmacht des Gewissens*, 473.

200. Report by Christine von Dohnanyi; see *Vollmacht des Gewissens*, 487.

201. See F. Bauer, "*Oster und das Widerstandsrecht*" in *Politische Studien*, no. 154, 188–94.

202. E, 67 [see DBW 6: 62].

203. LPP, 16f. [see DBW 8: 38].

204. H.-W. Jensen, "Life Together," IKDB, 154.

205. CD, 113 [see DBW 4: 108].

206. LPP, 128–29 [see DBW 8: 188].

207. LPP, 275 [see DBW 8: 397].

208. TP, 89 [see DBW 16: 128].

Chapter 12. Travels: 1940–1943

1. LPP, 162 [see DBW 8: 236].

2. TP, 63, excerpt of DBW 16: 46.

3. W. Niesel, "From Keelson to Principal of a Seminary," IKDB, 147.

4. Communication to author from W. Rott, 14.2.1966.

5. Diary of Anna Ohnesorge, director of studies, at that time a member of the Pomeranian Council of Brethren for Catechetical Questions.

6. E, 77ff. [see DBW 6: 75, 77].

7. LPP, 161 [see DBW 8: 234].

8. Letter, 26.8.1940, DBW 16: 60.

9. Order of the Reich Interior Ministry, 24.7.1940.

10. Decree, 12.7.1940; cf. J. Beckmann, ed., *Kirchliches Jahrbuch 1933–1944*, 460.

11. Cf. DBW 16: 166–67.

12. See W. Niemöller, *Die Evangelische Kirche im Dritten Reich*, 369f.

13. See J. Beckmann, ed., *Kirchliches Jahrbuch*, 412ff.

14. T. Wurm, *Erinnerungen aus meinem Leben* (Stuttgart, 1953), 157.

15. TP, 95 [see DBW 16: 151, 153].

16. J. Beckmann, ed., *Kirchliches Jahrbuch*, 350.

17. Letter to H.-W. Jensen, 14.5.1941, DBW 16: 180.

18. W. Niemöller, *Die Evangelische Kirche im Dritten Reich*, 247f.

19. DBW 16: 228, 233.

20. TP, 82 [see DBW 16: 89].

21. Letter to his parents, 22.12.1940, DBW 16: 100.

22. W. Niesel, *Kirche unter dem Wort*, 1978, 214, n. 9, explains that a church (the *Hofkirche*) in Breslau had practically claimed his exemption from military service.

23. Letter to E. Bethge, 1.12.1940, TP, 81 [see DBW 16: 85].

24. J. Beckmann, ed., *Kirchliches Jahrbuch*, 466f.

25. Cf. DBW 16: 118.

26. Newsletter, 14.2.1941.

27. Ibid.

28. Letter, 5.10.1941.

29. Letter from H. Doebert, 13.1.1942.

30. Letter, 15.8.1941, TP, 126 [see DBW 16: 195].

31. Letter from J. Mickley, 9.1.1942.

32. TP, 187 [see DBW 16: 252–53].

33. TP, 187–88 [see DBW 16: 253].

34. Ibid.

35. TP, 188 [see DBW 16: 253–54].

36. According to information from H. Rössler, approximately sixty Confessing theologians who were under his jurisdiction in the Rhineland and were in the Wehrmacht were legalized in 1942–1943.

37. TP, 95 [see DBW 16: 153].

38. No notes of these lectures remain.

39. Letter from E. Bethge to a friend; n.d.

40. Letter to E. Bethge, 26.8.1940 [see DBW 16: 60].

41. Among the documents found after the war in the central state police office in Düsseldorf was a copy of the decree sent by the Reich Central Security Office in Berlin with that reference number to all German state police offices, dated 22 August 1940: "Due to his subversive activity, I issue against Pastor Dietrich Bonhoeffer of Schlawe, Pomerania, a prohibition against speaking in public anywhere within the Reich territory. By order, signed Roth." Attached is a "statement" by the Düsseldorf Gestapo dated 20 September 1940: "I request that any necessary action be taken in respect of the undermentioned persons . . . 1. Bonhoeffer, Dietrich . . . is forbidden to speak in public in the Reich. Report if B. moves there or otherwise comes to notice. Any public appearance is to be prevented." Similar provisions are laid down against seven other Confessing pastors, including Gollwitzer, Linz, Kreck, and Super-intendent Onnasch of Köslin. Bonhoeffer very soon found out in Ettal how effective such Gestapo circulars were: "There was an inquiry about me here, about what I was

doing here and why I was over there [in the Benedictine monastery] so often." Letter to E. Bethge, 10.12.1940, TP, 83 [see DBW 16: 92].

42. DBW 16: 61–62.

43. Letter to his parents, 8.10.1940, cf. also DBW 16: 66.

44. Letter, 16.11.1940, TP, 70 [see DBW 16: 72].

45. Letter, 16.11.1940, TP, 70 [see DBW 16: 70].

46. Cf. DBW 16: 413, n. 22.

47. G. von Rad, "Meetings in Early and Late Years," IKDB, 178.

48. Letter to H.-W. Jensen, 26.12.1940, DBW 16: 102.

49. Newsletter, March 1942, DBW 16: 241–42.

50. Newsletter, May 1940, TP, 58ff. [see DBW 16: 29–32].

51. Letter from F. E. Schröter, 29.9.1940.

52. Letter from E. Klapproth, 5.2.1942.

53. Letter from E. Sander, 4.2.1942, DBW 16 :238–39.

54. Letter from E. Pfisterer, 25.10.1941.

55. DBW 16: 243–44; see also the letter to the widow, DBW 16: 245–46.

56. DBW 16: 224.

57. Letter to E. Bethge, 24.8.1941, TP, 103 [see DBW 16: 196–97].

58. Letter to Bonhoeffer, 12.12.1941, DBW 16: 234.

59. Letter to H.-W. Schleicher, 10.10.1942, TP, 139f. [see DBW 16: 363–64].

60. Letter, 9.10.1940, TP, 67 [see DBW 16: 65].

61. DBW 16: 563–87.

62. This appeared in summer 1943 in *Theologische Studien*, no. 14 of the Protestant publishing house Zollikon. See also F. Schröter, in *Beiträge zur Evangelischen Theologie*, vol. 2 of *Kirche und Amt: Zur Frage von Taufe und Ordination, Amt und Sakrament*, ed. E. Wolf (1939).

63. TP, 163 [see DBW 16: 586].

64. Cf. DBW 16: 582. For the complete text see TP, 143–44 [see DBW 16: 563–87].

65. See SC (DBWE 1), 166; also AB (DBWE 2), 159–60.

66. SC (DBWE 1), 167.

67. CD, 44 [see DBW 4: 30]; WF, 152ff. [see DBW 14: 834–35].

68. CD, 65–66, 231–35 [see DBW 4: 81, 221–26].

69. CD, 255–56 [see DBW 4: 250–51].

70. LPP, 237 [see DBW 8: 364].

71. J. Beckmann, ed., *Kirchliches Jahrbuch*, 383–88.

72. DBW 16: 228–33.

73. E, 299–315 [see DBW 16: 600–619].

74. See W. Niesel, *Um Verkündigung und Ordnung der Kirche*, 105–10.

75. Ibid., 110.

76. E, 310 [see DBW 16: 613].

77. E, 310 [see DBW 16: 614].

78. E, 311–12 [see DBW 16: 614–15, 556–57].

79. E, 313 [see DBW 16: 617].

80. Cf. DBW 16: 617, n. 113.

81. Letter, 11.5.1934, DBW 13: 139–40.

82. Letter, 14.2.1941, TP, 93 [see DBW 16: 145].

83. R. Bultmann, *Offenbarung und Heilsgeschehen*, vol. 7 (1941), 27–69.

84. "Mitteilungen an die Mitglieder," no. 1 (1941), 6–10 (duplicated).

85. Letter, 24.3.1942, DBW 16: 248.

86. "Protokoll der fünften Tagung am 17.6.1942" (duplicated).

87. Ibid.

88. Letter, 25.7.1942, DBW 16: 344–45.

89. See G. Krause, "Dietrich Bonhoeffer und Rudolf Bultmann," in *Zeit und Geschichte: Dankesgabe an Rudolf Bultmann zum 80. Geburtstag*, ed. E. Dinkler (1964), 457ff. Unfortunately, Krause does not explain here what else Bonhoeffer's interpretation might signify.

90. TF, 412 [see DBW 13: 204].

91. DBW 16: 248.

92. DBW 15: 112–14.

93. DBW 15: 114.

94. Reichwein was executed after the failure of the 20 July 1944 plot.

95. O. Hammelsbeck, "In Discussion with Bonhoeffer," IKDB, 181.

96. In the circles that included Anna von Gierke, Gertrud Bäumer, Elly Heuss-Knapp, and Eduard Spranger.

97. A draft is among Bonhoeffer's papers.

98. Nothing of this has been kept.

99. O. Hammelsbeck, *Vita: Pädagogische Autobiographie* (1959), 42 (duplicated).

100. Ibid., 45.

101. DBW 16: 381.

102. O. Dilschneider, *Die evangelische Tat* (1940). For Bonhoeffer's response, see DBW 16: 550–62. Here J. Moltmann could be asked whether, in his critique [MW 3: 52] that Bonhoeffer had concentrated one-sidedly on the personal phenomena and disregarded the objective, he paid enough attention to Bonhoeffer's discussion with Dilschneider.

103. LPP, 163 [see DBW 8: 237].

104. H. Bürkle, *Die Frage nach dem 'kosmischen Christus' als Beispiel einer ökumenisch orientierten Theologie in Kerygma und Dogma* (1965), 195.

105. For the sequence and dating of the fragments see DBW 6: 470, 16–17.

106. Cf. E, 60 [see DBW 6: 347].

107. E, 110 [see DBW 6: 126–33].

108. E, 109–10 [see DBW 6: 124].

109. LPP, 157, 168f., 280f., 326, 341 [see DBW 8: 226, 244, 406, 477–78, 509].

110. E, 131 [see DBW 6: 149].

111. E, 132 [see DBW 6: 151].

112. Letter to E. Bethge, 10.12.1940, TP, 83 [see DBW 16: 92].

113. E, 149 [see DBW 6: 171].

114. E, 150 [see DBW 6: 173].

115. E, 213 [see DBW 6: 247].

116. E, 225–26 [see DBW 6: 261].

117. E, 265 [see DBW 6: 372].

118. E, 293 [see DBW 6: 406].

119. E, 292 [see DBW 6: 404].

120. Ibid.

121. Cf. D. Bonhoeffer, *Zettelnotizen,* supplementary volume to DBW 6.

122. LPP, 14 [see DBW 8: 34].

123. Letter to E. Bethge, 25.6.1942, TP, 137–38 [see DBW 16: 325].

124. GS 1: 397f., in English.

125. For example, H. Fraenkel and R. Manvell, *Der 20. Juli* (1964), 65, and T. Prittie, *Germans against Hitler* (1964), 137.

126. TP, 112 [see DBW 16: 538].

127. DBW 16: 103.

128. On Ettal in general see TP, 69–95 [see DBW 16: 67–156]; on criticism of Asmussen's *Una sancta-Praktiken,* TP, 71 [see DBW 16: 70]; on Gürtner's burial, TP, 90 [see DBW 16: 139]; on the problems of confessing one's sins, TP, 92 [see DBW 16: 139]; and on reading from his books in the monastery, DBW 16: 102.

129. TP, 91 [see DBW 16: 135].

130. J. Glenthøj, "Bonhoeffer und die Ökumene," MW 2: 198. According to Barth's official calendar, Bonhoeffer visited him on 4 March 1941 (evening), as well as on the 6th and 7th (in the morning, and on the 6th with Gisevius). Bonhoeffer obviously traveled via Zurich-Basel-Geneva.

131. Letter, 15.2.1941, DBW 16: 157.

132. Letter, 25.2.1941, DBW 16: 158–59.

133. G. Ritter, *Carl Goerdeler und die deutsche Widerstandsbewegung* (1954), 252, 316.

134. See A. Freudenberg, "Visits to Geneva," IKDB, 167.

135. For W. A. Visser 't Hooft's evaluation of the visit see A. Boyens, *Kirchenkampf und Ökumene 1939–1945,* 171ff., 202. Boyens attaches high importance to this visit, particularly on the basis of N. Ehrenström's notes in his calendar [see DBW 16: 159–61]. According to these notes, Bonhoeffer met Visser 't Hooft, Freudenberg, and Ehrenström on 8 March 1941, and also on 10 March 1941 (where they discussed "the work among Jewish refugees"), later joined by Guillon. On 11 March 1941 Bonhoeffer also met Henriod. On 12 March 1941 "notes for a memo on Christian peace aims" were discussed with Bonhoeffer; on 13 March 1941 there was a debate on "church and world" with Bonhoeffer; and, on 15 March 1941, there was "a theological colloquium on the ethical proclamation and action of the church, internationally and vis à vis the world, its legitimacy, and its forms. Visser 't Hooft, Freudenberg, d'Espine, Courvoisier, Leehardt, Senarclens, Nils Ehrenström, and some others, around Bonhoeffer."

136. Letter, 19.3.1941, DBW 16: 163.

137. From a copy given to the author by W. A. Visser 't Hooft [see DBW 16: 166–67].

138. TP, 99–101 [see DBW 16: 170–71].

139. TP, 99 [see DBW 16: 178].

140. DBW 16: 181].

141. *Letters of Herbert Hensley Henson* (London, 1951), 130.

142. U. von Hassell, *Vom anderen Deutschland: Aus den nachgelassenen Tagebüchern 1938–1944* (1946), 202, entry dated 4 May 1941. See also H. Graml, "Die deutsche Militäropposition vom Sommer 1940 bis zum Frühjahr 1943," in "Aus Politik und Zeitgeschichte," supplement to the weekly paper *Das Parlament*, 16 July 1958, 361.

143. Moltke helped write this document; see K. H. Abshagen, *Canaris, Patriot und Weltbürger* (1959), 307.

144. On H. von Tresckow's reactions see H. Graml, "Die deutsche Militäropposition," 362.

145. U. von Hassell, *Vom anderen Deutschland,* 214.

146. Ibid., 212.

147. LPP, 15 [see DBW 8: 36].

148. Ibid.

149. W. A. Visser 't Hooft, *Memoirs* (London, 1973), 152–53. Ehrenström's calendar notes [see DBW 16: 202] on 3 September 1941: Bonhoeffer in Geneva. "Amazing news: the opposition plans to get rid of Hitler and the Nazi regime are getting increasingly crystallized" (A. Boyens, *Kirchenkampf und Ökumene,* 174). On 5 September 1941: "Bonhoeffer . . . while here, he has again written memos to be forwarded by Visser 't Hooft to Bell, Paton etc. . . ." (Visser 't Hooft was in France from 13 to 28 September 1941; see A. Boyens, *Kirchenkampf und Ökumene,* 105).

150. Letter, 25.9.1941, in English, DBW 16:211.

151. *Germany, the West and the Possibility of a New International Order* (report on behalf of the study department of the Universal Council for Life and Work, Winter 1939–1940); "Christianity, Politics, and Power," in *Christian News-Letter Books* (London, 1942), with a preface by L. Hodgson; "Germany between West and East," in *The Fortnightly* (October 1942), under the pseudonym S. H. Gerhard; "Ideology in the Post-War Policy of Russia and the Western Powers," in *The Hibbert Journal* (January 1944); "The Opposition Movement in Germany," in *The New English Weekly* (19 October 1944), 5f. Cf. now G. Leibholz, *Politics and Law* (1965), 91–132, 154–73, 174ff., 182ff., 210ff.

152. Letter, 25.9.1941, DBW 16: 210.

153. G. Bell, *Christianity and World Order* (London, 1940), 83.

154. Ibid., 84.

155. Ibid., 85.

156. Ibid., 87.

157. Ibid., 105f.

158. Letter from G. Bell to G. Leibholz, 27.8.1941.

159. G. Bell, *Christianity and World Order*, 88–101.

160. Ibid., 92.

161. G. Ritter, *Carl Goerdeler*, 318.

162. G. Bell, *The Church and Humanity 1939–1946* (London, 1946), 50, 56.

163. TP, 108ff. [see DBW 16: 536–41, in English].

164. W. Paton, *The Church and the New Order* (London: S.C.M. Press, 1941), 75.

165. Ibid., 85.

166. Ibid., 179.

167. TP, 110–11 [see DBW 16: 543–44, in English].

168. DBW 16: 541.

169. TP, 107–8 [see DBW 16: 548, in English].

170. Bethge's italics, DBW 16: 203.

171. Ibid.

172. Letter, 6.1.1942.

173. Letter, 30.10.1941, in English.

174. Letter from H. P. van Dusen to W. A. Visser 't Hooft, 27.11.1941. Van Dusen also received the memorandum [cf. DBW 16: 203], and forwarded it to John Foster Dulles.

175. See MW 2: 185.

176. DBW 16: 547.

177. O. Salomon, "The Guest," IKDB, 170ff. Cf. DBW 16: 209.

178. DBW 16: 206–7.

179. Ibid., 206–7, 207–8.

180. Freudenberg, "Visits to Geneva," IKDB, 169.

181. W. A. Visser 't Hooft, *Zeugnis eines Boten*, 7.

182. Letter, 25.9.1951, DBW 16: 210.

183. Letter to E. Bethge, 26.8.1941, TP, 105 [see DBW 16: 198].

184. Letter, 19.9.1941, DBW 16: 204.

185. DBW 16: 216. The two reports are on pp. 212–14 and 214–17.

186. See H. G. Adler, *Theresienstadt 1941–1945: Das Antlitz einer Zwangsgemeinschaft* (1955), 18–19, and letter to E. Bethge, 3.7.1956.

187. Report by Dr. Arnold, 1946.

188. DBW 16: 217–18.

189. DBW 16: 220. Copied from the archives of the World Council of Churches, Geneva. The letter is dated Berlin, October 1941.

190. U. von Hassell, *Vom anderen Deutschland*, 228, 231, 238, 248.

191. Ibid., 235.

192. Ibid., 246.

193. Letter from W. Krause, 21.12.1941.

194. He wrote in September 1941 from Zurich; DBW 16: 204–5.

195. Letter to the Leibholz family, 17.4.1942, DBW 16: 262–63.

196. For exact dates see Freya von Moltke, *Helmuth James von Moltke 1907–1945: Anwalt der Zukunft* (1975), 182ff.

197. Langbehn had connections to the S.S. For a time he was in the resistance's list of cabinet members, probably as minister of justice.

198. A. Johnson, *Eivind Berggrav, Mann der Spannung* (1960), 138.

199. Letter, 29.1.1957.

200. Bonhoeffer's pocket notebook of 1942 has only a few entries. For the Norwegian journey they are:

> "April, Friday 10th. 10:35 depart St. [Stettin Station in Berlin]—Sassnitz Hotel Viktoria.
> Saturday 11th. 4 o'clock ferry to Trelleborg. Night at Malmö.
> Sunday 12th. dep. 8 A.M. arr. Oslo 12 A.M.
> Monday 13th. Oslo.
> Tuesday 14th. Oslo.
> Wednesday 15th. Oslo.
> Thursday 16th. Day to Stockholm.
> Friday 17th. Stockh. Evening to Malmö. Plane.
> Saturday 18th. Plane 10 min. to Cop[enhagen]. 4 o'clock to B[erlin]."

201. DBW 16: 262–63.

202. DBW 16: 259–61.

203. Reported by G. Bell to G. Leibholz, 20 June 1942, DBW 16: 324.

204. E. Gerstenmaier, "Graf Moltke und die Kreisauer," in *Christ und Welt*, 21 March 1957.

205. See the Barth-Bonhoeffer correspondence of May 1942, DBW 226–72, 277–78.

206. Letter to the Leibholz family, from Zurich, 13.5.1942, DBW 16: 266.

207. H. Rothfels, in *Vierteljahreshefte für Zeitgeschichte* (October 1957), 388–97; GS 1: 410.

208. Communication to author from W. A. Visser 't Hooft, 30.5.1961.

209. According to J. Glenthøj, Schönfeld left Geneva on 18 May; MW 5: 267.

210. Letter, from Zurich, 23.4.1942, DBW 16: 267–77.

211. In fact, the bishop could not fly back to London until 9 June [see DBW 16: 299].

212. Account by Christine Dohnanyi, 1945.

213. DBW 16: 299–300.

214. Cf. the difference in wording: 1945 "to the best of my belief" (GS 1: 393); 1957 "he had known nothing of Schönfeld's visit" (GS 1: 404).

215. DBW 16: 313–14.

216. Ibid., 315–20.

217. Ibid., 343, 345–48.

218. GS 1: 390–98.

219. See also DBW 16: 321–23, 327–37.

220. Jørgen Glenthøj's introduction to his important publication of the Kaltenbrunner document of 4 January 1945 about Bonhoeffer's interrogation by the Reich Central Security Office [see DBW 16: 461–63] disagrees with my theory [see *Evangelische Theologie*, no. 9 (1966), 463f.]. I still think that he has at least misread what I wrote, and that his discovery does not provide as comprehensive a picture of

the events in Sigtuna as Bell's notes. A comparable picture would have to come from someone who was actually involved in Sigtuna, not secondhand.

The Kaltenbrunner document originated at the turn of the year 1944–1945, and not from May/June 1942. Bell's reports try to describe the real meaning of the occurrence itself from the point of view of a participant in the events, as far as he can possibly throw light on the truth. What Kaltenbrunner wrote, however, is primarily the indirect report of the Reich Central Security Office with a definite political purpose, on statements of someone involved in Sigtuna [i.e., Bonhoeffer]. These statements were made as a cover; he certainly does *not* reveal the true content of the Sigtuna talks. The document is invaluable, because it gives us a glimpse of the circumstances, methods, and possibilities of Bonhoeffer's interrogations in the winter of 1944–1945. It portrays how Bonhoeffer, on *Canaris*'s behalf, explored the British conditions. But Bonhoeffer came to Sigtuna with an assignment from *Beck*, not Canaris. According to this document Bonhoeffer did not even hint at this. This corresponds with what we know of Bonhoeffer's interrogations from other sources that Glenthøj disregards. Glenthøj also neglected to place the interrogation report in the context of the struggle between the Reich Central Security Office and the *Abwehr* over political or military intelligence, within which Bonhoeffer's statements in the 1943 interrogations, and apparently again in the winter of 1944–1945, were important and relieving for the *Abwehr*, diverting attention from Beck as the one who had commissioned him.

Unfortunately, Glenthøj now connects these many interrelated facts with a theory about the Zossen files that only further obscures the facts (which have not been cleared up) about the Zossen safe and the discovery by criminal commissar Sonderegger. This tends to falsify the Zossen files' purpose and nature. (The Zossen documents, their origin, and fate are discussed elsewhere in this book, particularly in the notes by Christine von Dohnanyi, appendix 1.) Glenthøj assumes that Bonhoeffer's official report on Sigtuna to Canaris was found at Zossen. It was neither necessary for the Reich Central Security Office to find this, since it would have had an official copy from the confiscated *Abwehr* files, nor was it possible, since the Zossen safe was not there for those kinds of reports. If any report about the journey had been found, it would have been to *Beck*, but that is unlikely. Glenthøj offers no proof or evidence that makes such a discovery likely. If he is basing this on the Huppenkothen trial (during the 1950s) and the taped testimony from those proceedings (told to me orally), then precise verification would be needed of the actual words used. During the trial there was indeed reference to the discovery of Bonhoeffer's notes in Zossen, but it was never said that this concerned a Sigtuna report, let alone the official one (which was a cover-up) to Canaris. The written verdict against Huppenkothen in 1955, which mentions discoveries in Zossen, does not mention any such material. Christine von Dohnanyi, who is particularly well informed about the contents of the Zossen files, has never mentioned a Sigtuna report by Bonhoeffer in connection with them.

Only under a mistaken view of the nature of the Zossen documents (Glenthøj says summarily and misleadingly: "The Zossen documents consisted of material from Canaris's office," 465) is it possible to suppose that the Sigtuna report to Canaris was in Zossen. The official, and of course "secret," reports of Bonhoeffer's journeys for the *Abwehr* to Sweden, Norway, and Switzerland were naturally prepared for Canaris as files for the Tirpitzufer office, and there was every reason to suppose that they were there. I myself, after a journey to Switzerland in 1943, provided an "official" report of that kind for the Canaris files, so that it would be available there in case someone checked. During Bonhoeffer's interrogations by Roeder in the summer of 1943, the Sigtuna journey had already been treated as an *Abwehr* matter for which Canaris was responsible; it was only risky because the *Abwehr* had exceeded its competence according to the Prague agreement, but this had been concealed by Canaris.

The Zossen safe was never a place for keeping official secret reports to Canaris; if it had been, reports on many similar journeys would or should have been kept there. It was the place for material that did not fall within Dohnanyi and Oster's official *Abwehr* responsibilities, preserved under orders from Beck, to be used later as arguments to prove the legitimacy of a revolt or coup after it would have happened. This was probably with Canaris's knowledge and passive consent; parts of his diary, which was not an official document, were kept there! The X-report of Josef Müller's 1939–1940 negotiations in Rome, for example, was kept there; it contained responsible promises and conditions given by the Allies in case of a putsch. The 1942 Sigtuna trip, however, was a first feeler put out by the conspirators, which was doomed from the beginning to fail. It produced nothing that could have been kept in the Zossen safe, and, as far as we can ascertain from primary and secondary sources, Bonhoeffer in the winter of 1944–1945 was not interrogated about Beck's Sigtuna errand, nor had he been previously by Roeder. If Sigtuna had led to encouraging results, there might have been enough reason to place relevant documents in the safe. If the safe was to be used for documentary evidence of contacts that had just been begun, why did it contain nothing about the "enemy" contacts (often far more important) that had been made through Trott, Moltke, Goerdeler, Hassell, and others? Dohnanyi and Oster certainly did not use that highly political and dangerous hiding place as a depository for unnecessary things. Glenthøj's reconstruction, however, supports the impression that that was exactly what they did; his assumption is therefore "unfortunate." Without this assumption, however, Glenthøj's discovery and other clarifications are important and have wider significance; for that reason they should be relieved of his erroneous Sigtuna thesis.

221. Letter, 20.6.1942, DBW 16: 324.

222. Cf. DBW 16: 290.

223. Ibid.

224. H. Rothfels, "Zwei aussenpolitische Memoranden," in *Vierteljahreshefte für Zeitgeschichte* (October 1957), 388.

225. Ibid., 389.

226. Cf. G. Ritter, *Carl Goerdeler*, 322.

227. Ibid., 322, 515; H. Rothfels, "Zwei aussenpolitische Memoranden," 388.

228. DBW 16: 320, 345.

229. DBW 16: 300–303.

230. DBW 16: 537, 544.

231. Asked by a newspaper about Vansittartism, Bell, after consulting Leibholz, defined it as follows: "A disease which causes those who suffer from it to identify Nazism with Germany, and to see in Nazism a specific German phenomenon, which could never flourish on any other soil. The gravity of the disease varies in different individuals. Those who suffer from it in its extreme form regard all Germans as butcher-birds just as the Nazis regard all Jews as sub-man" [*Illustrated* (London, 11 October 1943), 17]. Vansittart himself answered the same question: "The essence of Vansittartism is that the real enemy is German militarism, of which Nazism is the last and worst manifestation. Militarism is nationwide in Germany. It is, therefore, nonsense to say that we have the end of it when we have rid ourselves of Hitler. We have to rid Germany of the system which brought both wars. No one has yet suggested that Nazism or Fascism bred the last war" [ibid., 16].

232. Letter to G. Leibholz, 1.6.1942, DBW 16: 306, in English.

233. DBW 16: 305.

234. DBW 16: 341.

235. DBW 16: 313, 319, and n. 12.

236. DBW 16: 313–14, 327.

237. DBW 16: 329.

238. DBW 16: 343, in English [see TP, 181].

239. G. Ritter, *Carl Goerdeler*, 321.

240. Cf. DBW 16: 376–77, n. 2.

241. H. Rothfels, *Die deutsche Opposition gegen Hitler: Eine Würdigung* (1949), 166–67.

242. DBW 16: 343, n. 1.

243. DBW 16: 346.

244. *Christian News Letter*, 24.6.1942.

245. G. Bell, *The Church and Humanity*, 74, 76; italics are the author's.

246. Ibid., 84.

247. H. Fraenkel, *The Other Germany* (London, 1942); cf. DBW 16: 379.

248. DBW 16: 378.

249. Letter to S. Leibholz, 4.12.1942.

250. Letter from G. Bell to G. Leibholz, 11.12.1942.

251. G. Bell, *The Church and Humanity*, 95–109; see also DBW 16: 378, n. 6.

252. Reprinted in G. Bell, *The Church and Humanity*, 95–109.

253. DBW 16: 378, n. 6.

254. Letter from G. Bell to G. Leibholz, 16.3.1943.

255. TP, 185–86 [see DBW 16: 353; 343, n. 1, in English].

256. Letter to G. Leibholz, 14.10.1942.

257. Letter from G. Bell to H. Johansson, 3.12.1942, DBW 16: 376–80.

258. Letter, 12.1.1943.

259. See also U. von Hassell, *Vom anderen Deutschland,* 308.

260. There follows the reference to the aforementioned BBC broadcast; letter intended for Bonhoeffer, 3.11.1942, DBW 16: 375–76.

261. Letter, 7.4.1943.

262. LPP, 164 [see DBW 8: 238].

263. Letter, 9.7.1942, DBW 16: 339.

264. TP, 185f. [see DBW 16: 353, in English].

265. Letter sent from Vitznau, 30.8.1942.

266. G. Ritter, *Carl Goerdeler,* 295.

267. DBW 16: 589–95, 596–600.

268. DBW 16: 587–89.

269. *Lutherische Informationsblatt,* vol. 1, no. 17, 284f.

270. W. Paton, *The Church and the New Order,* 76.

271. Ibid., 179.

272. G. Bell, *Christianity and World Order,* 107.

273. P. Althaus, *Luther in der deutschen Kirche der Gegenwart* (1940), 24f.

274. TP, 108–9 [see DBW 16: 537].

275. In a sermon on 20 July 1960 Otto Dibelius said that Bonhoeffer did in fact tell him of his ecumenical meetings, but did not disclose the conspiracy to him until the beginning of 1943—to Dibelius's dismay: "I underestimated then the depth of conscience that existed in those circles."

276. Letter from C. von Dietze, 23.4.1969.

277. DBW 16: 466–67.

278. Letter from C. von Dietze, 23.4.1969.

279. "Staat und Kirche," DBW 16: 506–35.

280. E, 327, 259 [see DBW 6: 354–64].

281. On the documents concerning the Kreisau group's sessions see T. Steltzer, *Sechzig Jahre Zeitgenosse* (1966), 307ff., 317ff.

282. DBW 16: 359–60.

283. U. von Hassell, *Vom anderen Deutschland,* 292.

284. See C. Petry, *Studenten aufs Schafott: Die Weisse Rose und ihr Schicksal* (1968). Dr. Falk Harnack's recollection (on pp. 77f. and 87f.) that at the end of 1942 he contacted and spoke with Dietrich and Klaus Bonhoeffer, at the request of the Munich students, and even arranged a personal meeting for the end of February 1943 with Hans Scholl, needs to be pursued.

285. Letter, 27.11.1942, DBW 16: 371.

286. DBW 16: 199.

287. Ibid., 372.

288. F. von Schlabrendorff, *Offziere gegen Hitler* (1946), 69ff.; E. Zeller, *Geist der Freiheit* (1952), 139ff.

289. LPP, 145 [see DBW 8: 209].

290. DBW 16: 385–86.

291. Ibid., 390.

292. LPP, 98.

293. Letter from E. Bethge to R. Schleicher, 10.2.1943, DBW 16: 384.

294. This recollection does not correspond to the account in K. H. Abshagen, *Canaris, Patriot und Weltbürger*, 351. But it agrees with what Christine von Dohnanyi wrote down as early as 1945.

295. See H. B. Giservius, *To the Bitter End* (New York: Da Capo Press, 1998). See also R. Abshagen, *Canaris*, 358f.; G. Ritter, *Carl Goerdeler*, 346; G. Buchheit, *Der deutsche Geheimdienst* (1966), 419f.

296. From "After Ten Years," LPP, 15f. [see DBW 8: 35–36].

297. DBW 16: 350–51.

298. Letter, 25.6.1942, DBW 16: 325–26.

299. DBW 16: 370.

300. Letter to E. Bethge, who was in a similar situation regarding young Renate Schleicher, having encountered opposition created by her parents' anxiety, 28.11.1942, DBW 16: 371.

301. DBW 16: 372.

302. Letter to his parents, 4.6.1943, DBW 8: 90–91.

303. LPP, 174 [see DBW 8: 253].

304. LPP, 129 [see DBW 8: 188].

305. K. D. Bracher, *Die deutsche Diktatur*, 498, estimates that in connection with 20 July 1944 "around 5,000 people were put to death because of Civil Court sentences, not counting sentences by War Courts."

306. See "20 Juli 1944. Ein Drama des Gewissens und der Geschichte," in *Dokumente und Berichte* (1960), 3d ed., 214ff.; A. Leber, ed., *Das Gewissein steht auf* (1954), 187f.; T. Prittie, *Germans against Hitler* (1964), 127.

307. E. Bethge, "Adam von Trott und der Deutsche Widerstand," in *Vierteljahreshefte für Zeitgeschichte*, vol. 11, no. 3 (1963), 213–23.

308. Asmussen reports that in 1942 he did not join freely, but was pulled into it, *Lutherische Informationsblatt*, vol. 1, no. 17, 284f.

309. J. Courvoisier, "Theological Existence," IKDB, 174f.; also O. Hammelsbeck, "In Discussion with Bonhoeffer," IKDB, 179.

310. E. Bethge, "Adam von Trott und der Deutsche Widerstand," 219–20.

311. Ibid., 222.

312. DBW 6: 64–66.

313. LPP, 16 [see DBW 8: 38].

314. See Bonhoeffer's discussion about the function of optimism, LPP, 15 [see DBW 8: 36].

315. Bethge, "Adam von Trott und der Deutsche Widerstand," 219.

316. LPP, 7 [see DBW 8: 25].

Chapter 13. Tegel 1943–1944

1. LPP, 248 [see DBW 8: 380–81].

2. LPP, 106 [see DBW 8: 153].

3. "Rote Kapelle" was the Gestapo's term for a Communist resistance group led by Harro Schulze-Boysen and Arvid and Mildred Harnack. The group was uncovered in autumn of 1942; during the trials that followed seventy-five of its members were condemned to death (cf. A. Leber, ed., *Das Gewissen entscheidet*, 111).

4. See H. Bösch, *Heeresrichter Dr. Karl Sack im Widerstand* (1967).

5. Communication to author from Dr. Schulze zur Wiesche, 2.6.1966. Schulze zur Wiesche came from the Rhineland, and was at the time a high commissary in the Administration for Army Equipment.

6. According to an entry in Dohnanyi's diary, 5.5.1943.

7. The Berlin *Abwehr* office issued an order on 22 June 1943 (Amt Ausland/ Abwehr ZO No. 467/6, secret) to all affiliated *Abwehr* offices to reexamine rigorously all cases of exemption from military service.

8. Mentioned in the previous chapter, the agreement between Canaris's *Abwehr* office and Heydrich's Reich Central Security Office, delineating the jurisdiction of each office.

9. This created a grotesque situation in which even *Abwehr* soldiers from the Confessing church (such as Pastor Willi Rott) automatically became members of the Reich Central Security Office. Because of this, at the end of the war Rott disappeared for months without a trace in "automatic imprisonment" in the U. S. camp for civil internees in Moosburg.

10. Letter to E. Bethge, 30.7.1944, DBW 8: 552–53.

11. As he reported to his wife in their secret correspondence. Cf. Christine von Dohnanyi's report on the Zossen files in appendix 1.

12. LPP, 129 [see DBW 8: 187–88].

13. LPP, 131 [see DBW 8: 190].

14. LPP, 342 [see DBW 8: 505].

15. DBW 16: 401–2.

16. DBW 8: 216.

17. E, 358ff. [see DBW 16: 619–29].

18. DBW 16: 401–3, 405–23.

19. DBW 16: 410, 411.

20. He is referring to the exemptions granted to pastors in this church district, which came about due to the good relations between Superintendent Block and Major von Kleist in Schlawe; DBW 16: 412.

21. DBW 16: 411–13.

22. DBW 16: 413–14.

23. DBW 16: 414.

24. DBW 16: 416–17.

25. The notes concerning "Operation 7" were written around 10 to 12 June 1943; see DBW 16: 407.

26. DBW 16: 401.

27. DBW 16: 414.

28. DBW 16: 415, 416.

29. DBW 16: 417–20.

30. Not Dr. Karl Sack.

31. DBW 8: 120–21.

32. DBW 8: 125–27.

33. DBW 16: 420–21.

34. "Then" meaning when I could have a long conversation with him in person.

35. LPP, 162 [see DBW 8: 235–36].

36. DBW 8: 268.

37. DBW 8: 199.

38. LPP, 129 [see DBW 8: 188].

39. LPP, 178 [see DBW 8: 38].

40. LPP, 399 [see DBW 8: 606].

41. U. von Hassell, *Vom andern Deutschland*, 333.

42. LPP, 166f. [see DBW 8: 241–42].

43. LPP, 136 [see DBW 8: 198].

44. "Yea, by thee I can crush a troop; and by my God I can leap over a wall."

45. Letter, 22.12.1943, LPP, 173 [see DBW 8: 252].

46. Letter, 14.2.1944, LPP, 213 [see DBW 8: 325].

47. Letter, 21.2.1944, LPP, 216f., 215f. [see DBW 8: 330–31].

48. LPP, 272 [see DBW 8: 391].

49. Letter, 7.5.1944, LPP, 289 [see DBW 8: 240].

50. LPP, 340, 342 [see DBW 8: 503, 505]. Alexander von Hase says that his father was largely responsible for the successful postponement of the trial and for keeping it in the Army justice system, since he served as executive president of the *Reichskriegsgericht* for about ten months, substituting for the ailing General Bastian. During that period Bonhoeffer's parents frequently visited von Hase in the headquarters. Communication to author, 9.1.69.

51. LPP, 344, 346f. [see DBW 8: 509, 512].

52. LPP, 358 [see DBW 8: 528].

53. *Pfarramt und Theologie*, no. 7/8, 35.

54. Letter, 23.8.1944, LPP, 393 [see DBW 8: 575–76].

55. LPP, 398 [see DBW 8: 606].

56. DBW 8: 520.

57. LPP, 174 [see DBW 8: 253–54].

58. FFP, 34 [see DBW 7: 49–50].

59. DBW 8: 62, 70.

60. See the reference in LPP, 50 [see DBW 8: 92], to "Kant's interpretation of 'smoking' as a means of entertaining oneself."

61. DBW 8: 60–61.

62. DBW 8: 61–63.

63. LPP, 39, 50, 54, 129 [see DBW 8: 70, 92, 101, 188].

64. LPP, 162 [see DBW 8: 235].

65. DBW 8: 64.

66. LPP, 39 [see DBW 8: 70].

67. LPP, 128f. [see DBW 8: 187].

68. Ibid.

69. Letter, 18.12.1943, LPP, 167 [see DBW 8: 243].

70. LPP, 167–69, 176f., 233f., 271f. [see DBW 8: 243–45, 255–56, 358–59, 389–90].

71. LPP, 320ff. [see DBW 8: 468–71].

72. Letter, 5.6.1944, LPP, 319 [see DBW 8: 466–67].

73. LPP, 233f. [see DBW 8: 359].

74. Letter, 9.3.1944, DBW 8: 356–57.

75. Letter, 25.5.1943, DBW 8: 83.

76. Letter, 27.3.1944, DBW 8: 372.

77. DBW 8: 106–7.

78. LPP, 70 [see DBW 8: 105].

79. Letter, 7.8.1943, LPP, 89 [see DBW 8: 128].

80. DBW 8: 192.

81. LLC, 180–81.

82. Letter to E. Bethge, 15.12.1943, DBW 8: 236.

83. LPP, 313 [see DBW 8: 457].

84. DBW 8: 456.

85. DBW 8: 554–55.

86. LPP, 234 [see DBW 8: 359].

87. LPP, 39 [see DBW 8: 69–70].

88. LPP, 233 [see DBW 8: 358].

89. Letter, 22.10.1943, LPP, 121 [see DBW 8: 175].

90. Cf. DBW 8: 610, n. 5; 3, n. 25.

91. Cf. DBW 8: 3, n. 12.

92. LPP, 215 [see DBW 8: 330].

93. LPP, 173f., 217 [see DBW 8: 251–52, 332–33].

94. He is thinking here of his brother Klaus.

95. Letter, 21.2.1944, LPP, 217 [see DBW 8: 332–33].

96. LPP, 276 [see DBW 8: 398].

97. LPP, 129f. [see DBW 8: 189].

98. See DBW 7; FFP.

99. LPP, 41ff., 294ff. [see DBW 8: 73–80, 428–36].

100. DBW 16: 619–29.

101. FFP, 33f. [see DBW 7: 49].

102. FFP, 126f. [see DBW 7: 185–86].

103. FFP, 34 [see DBW 7: 49].

104. DBW 8: 468–71.

105. DBW 8: 493–94, 515–16, 585–89, 570–72.

106. DBW 8: 607–8.

107. LPP, 239 [see DBW 8: 367].

108. Letter to his parents, 22.10.1943, LPP, 121 [see DBW 8: 175–76].

109. See appendix 2, "Bonhoeffer's Readings in Prison," at the end of this volume.

110. DBW 8: 214.

111. Letter, 15.2.1944. LLC, 182f.

112. P. Schütz, *Warum ich noch Christ bin* (1938); *Das Evangelium, dem Menschen unserer Zeit dargestellt* (1940).

113. Letter, 18.2.1944, LLC, 185f.

114. LPP, 50 [see DBW 8: 92–93].

115. LPP, 125 [see DBW 8: 182].

116. In his essay "Stifter," reprinted in *Der goldene Schnitt* (1960), 199, 214.

117. Letter, 25.7.1943, LPP, 78 [see DBW 8: 117].

118. LPP, 308, 311 [see DBW 8: 212, 449].

119. DBW 8: 110.

120. DBW 7: 193–204.

121. LPP, 157 [see DBW 8: 227].

122. LPP, 203 [see DBW 8: 310].

123. LPP, 41ff. [see DBW 8: 73–80].

124. LPP, 294f. [see DBW 8: 425–36].

125. S. Dress, "Meetings in Tegel," IKDB, 215ff.

126. LPP, 276f., 288 [see DBW 8: 600, 399].

127. DBW 8: 376.

128. LPP, 87, 106 [see DBW 8: 125, 153].

129. LPP, 172 [see DBW 8: 249].

130. From "Night Voices in Tegel," LPP, 355 [see DBW 8: 523].

131. LPP, 248ff., 134, 171 [see DBW 8: 217–18, 380–86].

132. LPP, 157f., 172, 194f., 204f. [see DBW 8: 227, 249, 294, 312].

133. LPP, 139ff. [see DBW 8: 204–8].

134. TF, 518ff. [see DBW 8: 590–98].

135. See DBW 12: 353, and O. Dudzus, "Stopping the Wheel," IKDB.

136. Letters from G. Latmiral to G. Leibholz, 6.3.1946 and 2.4.1946.

137. LPP, 128 [see DBW 8: 186].

138. LPP, 164 [see DBW 8: 238].

139. Letter to E. Bethge, 29.11.1943, LPP, 149 [see DBW 8: 215].

140. LPP, 119 [see DBW 8: 173].

141. LPP, 289 [see DBW 8: 421].

142. A. M. Ramsay, *Sacred and Secular* (London 1965), chapter 4.

143. Letter, 3.8.1944, LPP, 379 [see DBW 8: 555].

144. Letter, 11.4.1944, LPP, 272 [see DBW 8: 391].

145. Letter, 22.4.1944, LPP, 277 [see DBW 8: 399].

146. LPP, 279 [see DBW 8: 402].

147. LPP, 204 [see DBW 8: 312].

148. DBW 8: 512.

149. LPP, 384 [see DBW 8: 563].

150. LPP, 230 [see DBW 8: 353].

151. DBW 8: 353; DBW 6: 404–5.

152. MW 2: 19ff.

153. E, 76ff. [see DBW 6: 76–78].

154. LPP, 328 [see DBW 8: 481].

155. LPP, 327 [see DBW 8: 480]. Bonhoeffer's critique of Tillich is confirmed in H. Cox's *The Secular City* (1965), 79–84.

156. Letter, 5.5.1944, LPP, 285 [see DBW 8: 414].

157. Ibid.

158. Letter, 3.6.1944, LPP, 317 [see DBW 8: 463].

159. Letter, 8.6.1944, LPP, 328 [see DBW 8: 482].

160. Letter, 27.11.1943, LPP, 146 [see DBW 8: 211].

161. DBW 8: 433, 434.

162. Letter, 21.5.1944, LPP, 279ff. [see DBW 8: 433–35, also 211].

163. E, 292 [see DBW 6: 404].

164. LPP, 360 [see DBW 8: 534].

165. H. Müller, *Von der Kirche zur Welt*, 20.

166. Letter, 5.12.1943, LPP, 157 [see DBW 8: 226].

167. LPP, 199 [see DBW 8: 301].

168. LPP, 240 [see DBW 8: 368–69].

169. See LPP, 279f. [see DBW 8: 402].

170. Letter, 3.8.1944, LPP, 378 [see DBW 8: 555].

171. LPP, 278ff., 285ff. [see DBW 8: 401–8, 413–16].

172. DBW 8: 497–98.

173. DBW 8: 513.

174. LPP, 393 [see DBW 8: 576].

175. LPP, 380–83 [see DBW 8: 556–61].

176. DBW 8: 402.

177. LPP, 287 [see DBW 8: 416].

178. DBW 8: 3, n. 25.

179. See M. Kuske, *Das Alte Testament als Buch von Christus*, 33, n. 2.

180. See Bonhoeffer's own classification in LPP, 344 [see DBW 8: 509]: "... a few thoughts to our theme. The biblical side of the matter ... the nonreligious interpretation of biblical concepts ..."

181. LPP, 279 [see DBW 8: 402].

182. AB (DBWE 2), 126–27. See also DBW 12: 282–89.

183. LPP, 280 [see DBW 8: 404–5].

184. LPP, 327 [see DBW 8: 479].

185. LPP, 342 [see DBW 8: 504]. The American theologian T. Altizer (*The Gospel of Christian Atheism* [Philadelphia, 1966]) could not put it like this, but at most speaks of a "claim on Christ by a world become secular."

186. DBW 8: 403.

187. LPP, 346 [see DBW 8: 511].

188. DBW 8: 512.

189. Letter, 3.6.1944, DBW 8: 461–64.

190. DBW 8: 555. For the contrast betwen the questions as to who and to what see DBW 12: 282, 289; cf. DBW 8: 558: "Who is God?"—not "What is God?"

191. LPP, 380ff. [see DBW 8: 556–61].

192. LPP, 326, 341, 342, 360, 380 [see DBW 8: 477, 503, 504, 533, 557].

193. LPP, 327 [see DBW 8: 537].

194. DBW 8: 511.

195. LPP, 326 [see DBW 8: 477].

196. The introductory statement of Immanuel Kant's *What Is Enlightenment?* (1784). In two dissertations—Ernst Feil, *Christus und die mündig gewordene Welt* (Münster, 1970), and Christian Gremmels, *Die mündige Welt: Sozialethische Erwägungen zur Planung* (Marburg, 1970)—a convincing case is made that the concept "being of age" (*Mündigkeit*) emerged from Bonhoeffer's reading of Dilthey from January to May 1944 [see appendix 2], among other things. Thus it emerged less from an immediately Kantian enlightenment than from Dilthey's philosophy of life, which Bonhoeffer admittedly takes almost literally and weaves into his theological reflections.

197. LPP, 185 [see DBW 8: 414].

198. LPP, 373 [see DBW 8: 545]. The term comes from R. Rothe; cf. Rothe, "Zur Orientierung über die gegenwärtige Aufgabe der deutsch-evangelischen Kirche 1862," in *Gesammelte Vorträge und Abhandlungen* (1886), 36.

199. The last time he used it was in an early section of *Ethics*, 97 [see DBW 6: 103].

200. LPP, 329 [see DBW 8: 482].

201. LPP, 360f. [see DBW 8: 533–34].

202. LPP, 361 [see DBW 8: 534–35].

203. LPP, 362 [see DBW 8: 537].

204. LPP, 369 [see DBW 8: 541].

205. DBW 6: 105.

206. LPP, 279ff., 285ff., 294ff., 344ff., 361ff. [see DBW 8: 414, 481, 529, 546].

207. DBW 8: 463–64.

208. LPP, 325 [see DBW 8: 476].

209. LPP, 286 [see DBW 8: 535, 416].

210. LPP, 300 [see DBW 8: 436].

211. MW 1: 121. In R. G. Smith, ed., *World Come of Age* (Philadelphia: Fortress Press, 1967), 90.

212. LPP, 286 [see DBW 8: 415].

213. LPP, 280 [see DBW 8: 404].

214. LPP, 328 [see DBW 8: 481].

215. LPP, 280 [see DBW 8: 404].

216. LPP, 285f. [see DBW 8: 414].

217. LPP, 280 [see DBW 8: 405].

218. LPP, 381 [see DBW 8: 559].

219. LPP, 381f. [see DBW 8: 558].

220. See P. Tillich, "The Question of Reality as a Whole," in *Systematic Theology*, vol. 1 (1968), 21.

221. See D. Ugrinovic, "Das nichtreligiöse Christentum Dietrich Bonhoeffers und seiner Fortsetzer," in *Monatszeitschrift der Akademie der Wissenschaften der USSR, Voprosy Filozofii*, no. 2 (1968), 94–102.

222. LPP, 286 [see DBW 8: 415]; see also DBW 1: 31.

223. LPP, 285f. [see DBW 8: 414].

224. LPP, 279 [see DBW 8: 402].

225. LPP, 280 [see DBW 8: 405].

226. LPP, 344 [see DBW 8: 509].

227. LPP, 381 [see DBW 8: 557].

228. LPP, 344 [see DBW 8: 509].

229. LPP, 345 [see DBW 8: 510–11].

230. LPP, 311 [see DBW 8: 454].

231. LPP, 362 [see DBW 8: 537].

232. LPP, 381 [see DBW 8: 558].

233. LPP, 348f. [see DBW 8: 515].

234. LPP, 381 [see DBW 8: 558].

235. LPP, 361 [see DBW 8: 534].

236. LPP, 176ff., but also 167ff. [see DBW 8: 255, 243–45].

237. LPP, 280–81 [see DBW 8: 405].

238. LPP, 299 [see DBW 8: 434].

239. See also the 1932 lecture, "Das Wesen der Kirche," DBW 11: 245–51, excerpted in TF, 85.

240. LPP, 280, 286, 328, 329 [see DBW 8: 404, 415, 481–82].

241. LPP, 281, 299 [see DBW 8: 406, 482].

242. LPP, 381 [see DBW 8: 557].

243. LPP, 361 [see DBW 8: 535].

244. LPP, 382f. [see DBW 8: 560].

245. DBW 8: 404.

246. J. H. Pestalozzi, *Letter to Nikolovius* (1793).

247. LPP, 200, 362 [see DBW 8: 537, 303].

248. G. Krause, *Dietrich Bonhoeffer und Rudolf Bultmann*, 439ff.

249. LPP, 299 [see DBW 8: 435].

250. G. Ebeling, MW 2: 34f.

251. DBW 8: 560.

252. LPP, 299f. Cf. DBW 8: 435.

253. LPP, 383 [see DBW 8: 561].

254. LPP, 298 [see DBW 8: 433].

255. Cf. DBW 8: 537.

256. LPP, 300 [see DBW 8: 436].

257. Letters, 30.4.1944 and 5.5.1944, DBW 8: 405–6; the baptismal address, DBW 8: 435: the poem "Christians and Pagans," DBW 8: 515–16; also DBW 16: 23, 668. Gisela Meuss has traced the element of arcane discipline throughout Bonhoeffer's work: "Arkandisziplin und Weltlichkeit bei Dietrich Bonhoeffer," MW 3: 68–115. In addition, there is the model of his own prayer discipline and his own uninterpreted actions.

258. LPP, 281, 286 [see DBW 8: 405, 415]. The word "secret" is used.

259. DBW 14: 526, 549–51, 553. See also the arcane element of "confession" (which may not be used propagandistically) in his 1932 lecture course "Das Wesen der Kirche," DBW 11: 285: "The first confession before the world is an action that initially interprets itself."

260. "Some boast of chariots, and some of horses. . . . The Lord is my shepherd. . . ."

261. LPP, 369 [see DBW 8: 541].

262. LPP, 328 [see DBW 8: 481].

263. See also R. Prenter, "Dietrich Bonhoeffer and Karl Barth's Positivism of Revelation," in R. G. Smith, ed., World Come of Age, 98, 102.

264. LPP, 286 [see DBW 8: 415].

265. DBW 8: 415.

266. E, 193ff. [see DBW 6: 46].

267. E, 198 [see DBW 6: 47].

268. J. M. Meier, "Weltlichkeit und Arkandisziplin bei Dietrich Bonhoeffer," in Theologische Existenz Heute, no. 136 (1966), 79.

269. E, 200, 203 [see DBW 6: 50, 53].

270. O. Hammelsbeck, "Zu Bonhoeffers Gedanken über die mündig gewordene Welt," MW 1: 55–56.

271. Cf. DBW 8: 558. E. Lange has convincingly described this issue within the framework of a duality of an ecclesia/diaspora phase of the congregation in his "Der Pfarrer in der Gemeinde heute," Monatsschrift für Pastoraltheologie, no. 6 (1966), 199–229.

272. LPP, 362 [see DBW 8: 537].

273. DBW 8: 255.

274. LPP, 240 [see DBW 8: 368–69].

275. LPP, 336 [see DBW 8: 499–501].

276. LPP, 374 [see DBW 8: 548–49].

277. LPP, 362, 391 [see DBW 8: 536].

278. LPP, 348f. [see DBW 8: 515–16].

279. LPP, 382 [see DBW 8: 559].

280. PTB, 50ff. [see DBW 16: 658–72].

281. DBW 16: 651–58.

282. K. Barth, *The Humanity of God* (Richmond, Va.: John Knox Press, 1960), 59.

283. LPP, 382f. Cf. DBW 8: 560–61.

284. LPP, 383 [see DBW 8: 561].

285. TF, 518ff. [see DBW 8: 598].

286. *Martin Luther*, Weimarer Ausgabe, vol. 5, 163, 28, Operationes in psalmos, 1518/1521.

287. Letter, 30.9.1951.

288. Letter, 11.10.1951.

289. MW 1: 121f. In R. G. Smith, ed., *World Come of Age*, 90.

290. Compare DBW 8: 558 [see LPP 282] with SC (DBWE 1), 31–33.

291. "Bonhoeffer, Christology and Ethic United," in *Christianity and Crisis*, vol. 24, no. 17 (1964), 195.

292. R. G. Smith, *The New Man* (London, 1956); G. Ebeling, "The Nonreligious Interpretation of Biblical Concepts," in *Word and Faith*, 98–161; J. D. Godsey, *The Theology of Dietrich Bonhoeffer* (1960); H. Müller, *Von der Kirche zur Welt* (1960); M. Marty, *The Place of Bonhoeffer* (London, 1963).

293. J. A. T. Robinson, *Honest to God* (1963).

294. G. Krause, "Dietrich Bonhoeffer und Rudolf Bultmann," in *Zeit und Geschichte: Dankesgabe an Rudolf Bultmann zum 80. Geburtstag* (1964), 439–60; H. Ott, *Reality and Faith: The Theological Legacy of Dietrich Bonhoeffer* (1966); J. A. Phillips, *The Form of Christ in the World, a Study of Bonhoeffer's Christology* (London, 1967); E. Feil, *The Theology of Dietrich Bonhoeffer*; T. R. Peters, "Gebot und Verheissung: Die Ethik in der theologischen Entwicklung Dietrich Bonhoeffers" (thesis, Walberberg, 1969).

295. Letter, 18.12.1943, LPP, 129 [see DBW 8: 188].

Chapter 14. In the Custody of the State: 1944–1945

1. *The New English Weekly*, vol. 26, no. 1, 6.

2. G. Bell, *The Church and Humanity*, 174.

3. G. Leibholz, *Politics and Law* (Leyden, 1965), 210f.

4. Letter, 5.8.1944.

5. Verdict in the trial of W. Huppenkothen, 15.10.1955, 1 KS 21/50 (Landgericht Munich), AK Schw, 4/55 (Landgericht Augsburg). Huppenkothen's statements agree in part with Christine von Dohnanyi's recollections concerning parts of the documents. See her statement about the Zossen files in appendix 1.

6. Ibid., statement by W. Huppenkothen, 18.

7. Ibid., 41.

8. *Spiegelbild einer Verschwörung: Die Kaltenbrunner-Berichte an Bormann und Hitler über das Attentat vom 20. Juli 1944*, ed. K. H. Peter (1961).

9. For instance, they speak of more than one journey taken with Moltke. But see J. Glenthøj's thesis in "Dietrich Bonhoeffer vor Kaltenbrunner," *Evangelische Theologie,* no. 9 (1966), 480ff., and my discussion of its underlying assumption in note 220, chapter 12.

10. K. H. Abshagen, *Canaris, Patriot und Weltbürger* (1959), 378.

11. H. von Dohnanyi in a smuggled note, 25.2.1945.

12. DBW 8: 610–11.

13. F. von Schlabrendorff, "In Prison with Dietrich Bonhoeffer," IKDB, 228.

14. Ibid., 188.

15. J. Glenthøj, "Bonhoeffer vor Kaltenbrunner," in *Evangelische Theologie,* no. 9 (1966), 462–99, cf. 853ff. [see DBW 16: 461–63].

16. DBW 16: 461–63.

17. According to Christine von Dohnanyi.

18. Reported by Christine von Dohnanyi and J. Müller, as well as from F. von Schlabrendorff, "In Prison with Dietrich Bonhoeffer," IKDB, 228f.

19. Verdict in the trial of W. Huppenkothen, 19.

20. LPP, 399, 401 [see DBW 8: 609, 610–11].

21. F. von Schlabrendorff, "In Prison with Dietrich Bonhoeffer," IKDB, 228.

22. Letter from P. Best to S. Leibholz, 2.3.1951.

23. F. von Schlabrendorff, "In Prison with Dietrich Bonhoeffer," IKDB, 229f.

24. Ibid., 218.

25. Ibid., 229.

26. LPP, 399 [see DBW 8: 609].

27. LLC, 268–70.

28. LPP, 399, 401 [see DBW 8: 610–11].

29. LPP, 400f. [see DBW 8: 607–8].

30. DBW 8: 515–16.

31. LLC, 275–76.

32. Part of Bonhoeffer's library was stored there also, including the Erlangen Luther edition and the rosewood cupboard from Minna Herzlieb [see DBW 8: 319].

33. Cf. DBW 8: 614–15.

34. H. von Dohnanyi, in a smuggled note, 25.2.1945.

35. DBW 8: 613.

36. DBW 8: 611.

37. DBW 8: 613–14.

38. P. Best, *The Venlo Incident,* 171ff.

39. Ibid., 178ff.

40. Letter from P. Best to S. Leibholz, 2.3.1951.

41. Payne Best's remark that the prisoners had nothing besides their clothing is probably not quite true.

42. Letter from H. Falconer to S. Leibholz, 1.10.1945.

43. General F. von Rabenau, *Seeckt, Aus seinem Leben 1918–1936* (1940).

44. G. Ritter, *Carl Goerdeler,* 383.

45. H. Pünder in an address on the opening of the Dietrich Bonhoeffer school in Pulheim near Cologne, 19.9.1960.

46. Letter from P. Best to S. Leibholz, 2.3.1951.

47. DBW 8: 615–16.

48. P. Best, *The Venlo Incident*, 180.

49. Letter from H. Falconer to S. Leibholz, 1.10.1945.

50. In *Geist der Freiheit* E. Zeller says: "It was only in the last month of the war, when Canaris's entire diary was discovered, that an enraged Hitler had the entire circle of people who had not yet been tried condemned by a hastily formed S.S. field court and executed on 9 April (Canaris, Oster, Dohnanyi, Bonhoeffer, Gehre, Strünck, Sack)" [466]. The source for this seems to be criminal commissar Sonderegger's statement in the W. Huppenkothen trial. This is rather thin evidence; the actual sequence of events was probably more complicated. G. Ritter writes: "The immediate reason for the execution of all the conspirators still alive in Flossenbürg was (according to Sonderegger) the discovery of Canaris's complete diary in April 1945, which aroused Hitler's special anger" [*Carl Goerdeler*, 546]. G. Buchheit writes: "Only at the beginning of 1945 did General Buhle, who happened to be quartered in Zossen, find the diaries I–V and six books of 'travel reports' in a metal cupboard and give them to the chief officer guarding the *Führer*, S.S. District Leader Rattenhuber. The latter gave them to Kaltenbrunner on 6 April. After Rattenhuber returned to Munich from a Russian prisoner-of-war camp, he called on Dr. Josef Müller, whom he had known before, and told him that Kaltenbrunner had ordered the immediate "execution of the conspirators on Hitler's orders" [*Der deutsche Geheimdienst, Geschichte der militarischen Abwehr* (1966), 445].

51. According to W. Huppenkothen. Cf. verdict in the trial of W. Huppenkothen, 21.

52. Ibid., 23f.

53. F. von Schlabrendorff, "In Prison with Dietrich Bonhoeffer," IKDB, 230.

54. In P. Best, *The Venlo Incident*, 200, we read: "We bade him goodbye. He drew me aside. 'This is the end,' he said, 'for me the beginning of life,' and then he gave me a message to give, if I could, to the Bishop of Chichester, a friend to all evangelical pastors in Germany." Bishop Bell has given a more complete account of these last words. According to the notes he made immediately in 1945 when Best told him, they were: "Tell him (he said) that for me this is the end but also the beginning. With him I believe in the principle of our Universal Christian brotherhood which rises above all national interests, and that our victory is certain—tell him too that I have never forgotten his words at our last meeting" [cf. DBW 16: 468]. This more detailed version was recorded earlier than the one in Payne Best's book. Best was not sufficiently aware of the shared history of Bell and Bonhoeffer to attach much importance to the second part of his message when writing his book. But Bell particularly cherished this reminder of their conversations together in Sweden in 1942, and so he put it down in his notes in 1945.

There is, incidentally, a passage in the letters from Tegel prison that closely resembles Bonhoeffer's last words. When, on 21 August 1944, he spoke of immersing oneself in the life, words, actions, sufferings, and death of Jesus, he continued: "it is certain that our joy is hidden in suffering, and our life in death," LPP, 391 [see DBW 8: 573].

55. Testimony by H.-M. Lunding in the W. Huppenkothen trial; see *Urteil* (1955), 50f.

56. H. Fischer-Hüllstrung, "A Report from Flossenbürg," IKDB, 232.

57. According to research by R. von Plessen and communications from A. von Falkenhausen and R. Goerdeler, it is probable that General von Rabenau, like Bonhoeffer, was transported from Schönberg to Flossenbürg on 8 April and executed there on 9 April.

58. Dietrich and Klaus Bonhoeffer, *Auf dem Wege zur Freiheit: Gedichte und Briefe aus der Haft* (1946).

59. Cf. the report in the *Frankfurter Allgemeine Zeitung*, 18 July 1962, 11.

60. Cf. J. Rieger, "Contacts with London," IKDB, 103.

61. Cf. *Bonhoeffer Gedenkheft* (1946).

62. Ibid., 9.

63. Duplicated copy of the announcement, in the author's possession.

64. Letter, 11.2.1948.

65. DBW 8: 619–21.

Appendix 1. The Zossen Files

1. Account of his imprisonment and interrogation given by General Georg Thomas, 20.7.1945. According to this, Huppenkothen told Thomas that Oster and Dohnanyi had "admitted all their actions."

2. Schrader was the director of one of the *Abwehr* departments in the Armed Forces High Command (OKW) and committed suicide on 28 July 1944. In a letter dated 11 August 1967 H. Fraenkel told this author that he had learned a different version from Schrader's son: "There wasn't any hunting lodge on the heath; the papers (including Canaris's diary) were hidden in Gross-Denkte (near Brunswick) with a brother-in-law of Frau Schrader. Frau Schrader burned them shortly after Schrader's suicide, so as not to endanger those who had not yet been arrested."

CHRONOLOGY

1906	4 February, Dietrich Bonhoeffer born in Breslau
1912	Father appointed to Berlin University; family moves to Berlin
1923	Theological studies in Tübingen
1924	Further theological studies in Berlin
1927	Qualifies for licentiate under R. Seeberg with *Sanctorum Communio*
1928	17 January, first theological examination; 15 February, assistant pastor in Barcelona
1929	Assistant to W. Lütgert in Berlin (until 1930)
1930	18 July, qualifies as university teacher with *Act and Being*; 5 September, leaves for New York to study at Union Theological Seminary
1931	In July first meeting with Karl Barth in Bonn; after 1 August, lecturer at the theological faculty in Berlin; 1–5 September, attends World Alliance Conference in Cambridge where he is appointed youth secretary; 15 November, ordination; winter 1931–1932, lecture course "The History of Systematic Theology in the Twentieth Century" and seminar "The Concept of Philosophy and Protestant Theology"; from November (until March 1932), in charge of a confirmation class in Berlin-Wedding
1932	In the summer term, lecture course "The Nature of the Church" and seminar "Is There a Christian Ethic?"; buys a hut in Biesenthal; July and August, attends ecumenical meetings in Ciernohorské, Kúpele, Geneva, and Gland; winter term, lecture courses "Creation and Sin" (published in 1933 as *Creation and Fall*) and "Recent Theology," and seminar on "Problems of a Theological Anthropology"
1933	1 March, radio talk "The *Führer* Principle"; April, article "The Church and the Jewish Question"; summer term, lecture course "Christology"; August, pamphlet "The Aryan Clause in the Church"; September, preliminary work with Niemöller on Pastors' Emergency League pledge; 17 October, begins London pastorate
1934	22–30 August, ecumenical conference in Fanö; 28 August, becomes co-opted member of Universal Christian Council for Life and Work; 4–8 September, with Jean Lasserre in Bruay; 5 November, London parishes repudiate the Reich church government

1935   March, visits Anglican communities; 15 April, farewell visit to Bishop Bell in Chichester; 26 April, preachers' seminary opens in Zingst (by the Baltic); 24 June, seminary moves to Finkenwalde; July, article "The Confessing Church and the Ecumenical Movement"; 6 September, establishment of a brothers' house proposed to Provisional Church Administration

1936   February, last Berlin faculty lecture "Discipleship"; 29 February–10 March, preachers' seminary visits Denmark and Sweden; 22 April, lecture in Finkenwalde "On the Question of the Church Community"; 5 August, authorization to teach at university withdrawn; 20 August, Life and Work meeting in Chamby

1937   February, last participation in an ecumenical conference in London; 1 July, Niemöller arrested; end of September, preachers' seminary closed by police; November, twenty-seven former Finkenwalde seminarians arrested, *Discipleship* published; 5 December, beginning of collective pastorates in Köslin and Gross-Schlönwitz (later Sigurdshof)

1938   11 January, expulsion from Berlin; February, first contacts with Sack, Oster, Canaris, and Beck; 20 June, meeting of former Finkenwaldians in Zingst, Bible study "Temptation"; September, *Life Together* written in Göttingen; 26 October, lecture "Our Way according to the Testimony of Scripture"

1939   10 March, journey to London for talks with Bishop Bell, Visser 't Hooft, Niebuhr, and Leibholz; 2 June, leaves for United States; 20 June, letter of refusal to Leiper; 27 July, back in Berlin

1940   15 March, end of term in Köslin and Sigurdshof; two days later Gestapo orders closure; June and July, visitations in East Prussia; 14 July, dissolution of study conference in Blöstau; August, talks with Oster and Dohnanyi on military exemption and work for the *Abwehr* office; 4 September, forbidden to speak in public and required to report regularly to the police; September and October, work on *Ethics* at Klein-Krössin; 30 October, assigned to *Abwehr* office in Munich; from 17 November, visits to the Benedictine abbey in Ettal

1941   24 February–24 March, first journey to Switzerland; 27 March, forbidden to print or publish; 29 August–26 September, second journey to Switzerland, together with Visser 't Hooft writes to W. Paton on *The Church and the New Order*; October, first deportations of Jews from Berlin, "Operation 7"

1942   10–18 April, journey with Moltke to Norway and Stockholm; May, third journey to Switzerland; 30 May–2 June, flies to Stockholm to meet Bishop Bell

1943   17 January, engagement to Maria von Wedemeyer; 13 March and 21 March, attempted assassinations of Hitler; 5 April, house search and arrest, sent to Tegel prison; at the same time, Hans von Dohnanyi and Müller arrested with their wives; 29 April, arrest warrant drawn up, charged with "subversion of the armed forces"

1944   January, chief interrogator Roeder dismissed; February, Canaris dismissed and the *Abwehr* incorporated into the Reich Central Security office; 6 March, first big daylight air raid on Tegel; 30 April, first theological letter; May, charge indefinitely postponed; 20 July, von Stauffenberg's attempt on Hitler's life; 22 September, Gestapo commissar Sonderegger discovers files in the *Abwehr* bunker in Zossen; early October, escape plan; 5 October, plan abandoned because of fear of reprisals following arrests of Klaus Bonhoeffer, Schleicher, and Perels; 8 October, taken to the Gestapo prison in the cellar at Prinz-Albrecht-Strasse

1945   7 February, sent to Buchenwald concentration camp; 3 April, removed from Buchenwald to Regensburg; 5 April, execution ordered at Hitler's midday conference; 6 April, moved to Schönberg; 8 April, moved to Flossenbürg; during the night, summary court-martial; 9 April, executed together with Oster, Sack, Canaris, Strünck, and Gehre; Hans von Dohnanyi killed in Sachsenhausen; 23 April, Klaus Bonhoeffer, Schleicher, and Perels killed in Berlin

INDEX